The

PRACTICAL
TANYA

Also by Chaim Miller

The Kol Menachem Chumash – Gutnick Edition

The Kol Menachem Chumash (Hebrew) – Leviev Edition

Rambam: Principles of Faith – Slager Edition

The Kol Menachem Haggadah – Slager Edition

The Kol Menachem Megillah – Slager Edition

The Five Books of Moses, Lifestyle Books – Slager Edition

Prayers for Friday Night, Lifestyle Books – Slager Edition

The Kol Menachem Tehillim – Schottenstein Edition

Turning Judaism Outward: A Biography of Rabbi Menachem Mendel Schneerson

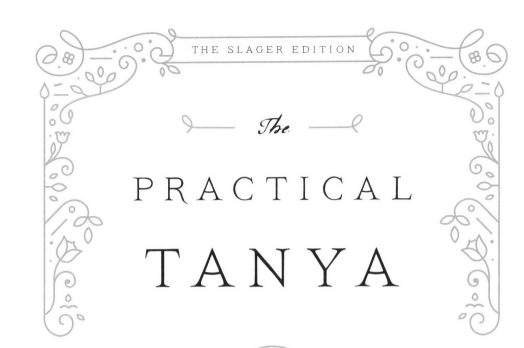

THE SLAGER EDITION

The

PRACTICAL

TANYA

PART ONE

THE BOOK FOR INBETWEENERS

RABBI

SHNEUR

ZALMAN of LIADI

ADAPTED BY

CHAIM MILLER

GUTNICK LIBRARY
OF JEWISH CLASSICS

ISBN-13: 978-1-934152-37-9 | ISBN-10: 1-934152-37-4

© Copyright 2016 by Chaim Miller

Published and distributed by: Kol Menachem 827 Montgomery Street, Brooklyn, NY 11213.

1-888-580-1900 | 1-718-951-6328 | 1-718-953-3346 (Fax)

www.kolmenachem.com | orders@kolmenachem.com

Contact the author at: chaimmiller@gmail.com | rabbichaimmiller.com

First Edition — 2016; Second Edition — 2017.

Praise for *The Practical Tanya*

"An astonishing accomplishment... and suitable for anyone... even those who do not read in Hebrew and are not familiar with esoteric texts."

—Rabbi Moshe Wolfson, *Mashgiach Ruchani Yeshivas Torah Ve-Da'as.*

"It is wonderful that this sacred text has now been clarified in a way that anyone can benefit from it."

—Rabbi Gavriel Zinner, author *Nitei Gavriel,* Rav of Congregation *Nitei Gavriel.*

"An important contribution... makes the flow of the *Tanya* very clear for all who study.

—Rabbi Yehuda Leib Schapiro, *Yeshiva Gedola* Rabbinical College of Greater Miami.

"With a masterful command of the English language, Rabbi Miller has managed to open up the *Tanya* to the wider public... not an easy task!"

—Rabbi Nochum Kaplan, Director, *Merkos* Office of Education.

"A lucid and scholarly translation... will undoubtedly assist multitudes."

—Rabbi Moshe Bogomilsky, *halachic* authority, author of *Vedibarta Bam* series.

"Brings the warmth, genius, and inspiration of the *Tanya* to life.... This work will certainly help inspire souls."

—Rabbi Zev Reichman, Director, Mechina Program, Yeshiva University.

"Rabbi Chaim Miller has made it accessible to everyone.... This book will awaken, inspire, and challenge you."

—Daniel Matt, translator of *The Zohar: Pritzker Edition.*

"Quite simply the best version in the English language."

—Rabbi Dov Greenberg, Chabad of Stanford University.

"A wonderful work which makes the *Tanya* accessible and understandable to a whole new generation of spiritual explorers... beautifully written."

—Rabbi Mark Wildes, Director, *Manhattan Jewish Experience.*

"A new classic.... Practical and relevant in the fast-moving, rapidly-changing technological era in which we live."

—Rabbi Mendel Lew, Stanmore & Canons Park Synagogue, U.K.

"Rabbi Chaim Miller's crisp, lucid and contemporary translation promises... concrete strategies for personal spiritual growth."

—Henry Abramson, Dean, Touro College, Brooklyn.

TRANSLATOR'S INTRODUCTION

THE TANYA'S AUTHOR — RABBI SHNEUR ZALMAN OF LIADI

Rabbi Shneur Zalman Baruchovitch[1] was born in 1745 in the small town of Liozna (Liozno), Belarus, to Rivkah and Baruch, a descendant of Rabbi Yehudah Loew (Maharal) of Prague (d. 1609). At the age of fifteen he moved to the neighboring city of Vitebsk and married Sterna Segal, the daughter of a local businessman. He showed exceptional intellectual talents[2] and, at around the age of twenty, was attracted to Chasidism.[3] For a number of years, he attended the court of Rabbi Dov Ber Friedman ("the Maggid," 1704–1772 of Mezritch/Mezhirichi, Ukraine),[4] accepting him as spiritual men-

---

1. The life of Rabbi Shneur Zalman is discussed in several biographical works: Chaim Meir Heilman, *Beis Rebbi: Toldos Admor Ha-Zaken Ba'al Ha-Tanya* (Berditchev, 1802); Mordechai Teitelbaum, *Ha-Rav Mi-Liadi Umifleget Chabad,* 2 vols. (Warsaw, 1909/10–1912/13); Nissan Mindel, *Rabbi Schneur Zalman of Liadi, A Biography* (Brooklyn: Kehos, 1969, fifth printing 2002); Rabbi Avraham Chanoch Glitzenstein, *Sefer Ha-Toldos Rabbi Shneur Zalman Mi-Liadi,* 4 vols. (Kfar Chabad: Kehos, 1986); Naftali Loewenthal, *Communicating the Infinite: The Emergence of the Habad School* (Chicago University Press, 1990), chapters 2-3; Rabbi Shalom Avzton, *The Alter Rebbe, Rabbi Schneur Zalman of Liadi* (Brooklyn, 2005); Rabbi Shalom Ber Levin, *Toldos Chabad Be-Russia Ha-Tzaris* (Brooklyn: Kehos, 2010), chapters 1-34; Rabbi Avraham Vaisfiche (trans.), *Events in the Life of Rabbi Schneur Zalman of Liadi from the Diary of Rabbi Yosef Yitzchak of Lubavitch* (Brooklyn: Kehos, 2014); *Toldos Rabenu* in Rabbi Moshe Yehudah Kroll *et. al, Sefer Likutei Amarim Tanya* (Bnei Brak: Pe'er Mikdashim, 2014), pp. 29-81. For a critical, academic biography see: Immanuel Etkes, *Ba'al Ha-Tanya: Rabbi Shneur Zalman of Liady and the Origins of Habad Hasidism* (Brandeis University Press, 2015). Etkes reconstructs a historical narrative based on available documents and is dismissive of Chabad internal traditions.

2. "At the age of eighteen, he completed the study of the *Talmud* with its major commentaries" (Introduction of Rabbi Shneur Zalman's sons to *Shulchan Aruch Ha-Rav*, Shklov, 1814; Kehos 2001 edition, p. 8). Apparently, for the next fifteen years he reviewed the entire *Talmud* at least once a year since, "we heard from his holy mouth that while he was residing in the community of Mogilev on the Dnieper river [in 1777], he reviewed the *Talmud* for the sixteenth time" (*ibid.* p. 10 and note 22).

3. *Ibid.* See also written testimony of Rabbi Shneur Zalman in Rabbi Shalom Ber Levin (ed.), *Igros Kodesh Admor Ha-Zaken* (Brooklyn: Kehos, 2012), p. 221.

4. The foremost Chasidic leader after the death of the *Ba'al Shem Tov* in 1760.

tor and master. The Maggid, at the time, was in the last few years of his life, and Rabbi Shneur Zalman was one of his youngest disciples. Nevertheless, Rabbi Shneur Zalman, "was extremely precious, to no limits, in the eyes of our master [the Maggid], who would praise him greatly, all the time."[5]

Rabbi Shneur Zalman was only twenty-six when the Maggid assigned him the mammoth task of completely re-codifying the *Shulchan Aruch* (Code of Jewish Law), incorporating all the major commentaries that had appeared since the book's publication, two centuries earlier.[6] While this would become Rabbi Shneur Zalman's life-long task, a significant portion of the work was completed already in 1772-3.[7]

The Maggid also assigned his own son, Rabbi Avraham, to be a personal tutor to Rabbi Shneur Zalman in Chasidic thought. This would prove to be a significant influence, as Rabbi Shneur Zalman later wrote that "my Chasidic teachings are sayings uttered by the holy mouth of our great Rabbi [the Maggid] o.b.m, *and his son, o.b.m.,* of Mezritch" (emphasis added).[8]

Rabbi Shneur Zalman's outstanding mastery of the Talmudic literature positioned him, even at an early age, in an important role of defending attacks on the Chasidic movement from Rabbinic authorities, which escalated sharply in this period and continued for the next thirty years. The Chasidism of the *Ba'al Shem Tov* and the Magid had originated in Podolia, in South-East Poland, a region which was ripe with Sabbatianism, Frankism

5.   1805 Letter of Rabbi Levi Yitzchak of Berdichev in Levin, *Igros Kodesh,* p. 508.

6.   For a list of commentaries incorporated by Rabbi Shneur Zalman in his *Shulchan Aruch* see Kehos 2001 edition, p. 9n15.

7.   Levin, *Toldos Chabad* chapters 15-19. The *Shulchan Aruch Ha-Rav,* as the work later became known, was published posthumously by Rabbi Shneur Zalman's sons in 1814-16. The work is incomplete since the author's original manuscript was destroyed in the 1810 fire in Liadi, and a complete copy had not been made. Small sections of the work were published in the author's lifetime on Torah Study (1794) and Blessings on Pleasurable Acts (1800). In one responsum, Rabbi Shneur Zalman refers directly to his consultation with the Maggid in matters of Jewish law: "This legal analysis (*pilpul*)... is from the summer of 1772 when I was in the home of our great Rabbi and master, the famous Gaon, Rabbi Dov Ber, in the Jewish community of Rovno, and he gave his sacred approval to me in this matter" (Rabbi Shalom Ber Levin (ed.) *Responsa of Rabbi Shneur Zalman* (Brooklyn: Kehos, 2007), p. 40). See also Rabbi Menachem Mendel Schneerson (Rabbi Shalom Ber Levin ed.), *Igros Kodesh*, vol. 19, p. 400.

8.   See below pp. xiv, xviii. According to a tradition noted by Heilman, Rabbi Shneur Zalman once commented that all the other disciples of the Maggid had received wisdom through the "filter" of teacher-to-student. Rabbi Shneur Zalman's association with Rabbi Avraham, on the other hand, enabled him to receive "unfiltered" wisdom from the Maggid, in the fashion of father-to-son. Since Rabbi Shneur Zalman received more, he eventually disclosed more (*Beis Rebbi,* p. 22, note 1; see also ibid. p. 88, note 1).

and other heterodoxies. It is understandable, then, that when Chasidism began to spread to the established Jewish centers four hundred miles to the north, it was strongly resisted by the mainstream Rabbinic establishment.

In the spring of 1772 an outright "war" was proclaimed on Chasidim, when Rabbi Eliyahu of Vilna (1720-97, the "Vilna Gaon"), the most revered scholar in Europe at the time, proclaimed that "it was a duty to repel them and pursue them and reduce them and drive them from the land."[9] The result was, as Rabbi Shneur Zalman later recalled in a private letter, "he permitted our blood to be spilled like water in 1772."[10]

A few months earlier, an attempt had been made to avert this crisis by a senior member of the Maggid's court, Rabbi Menachem Mendel of Vitebsk (1730-1788), who payed a visit to the Vilna Gaon to appease him. The fact that Rabbi Shneur Zalman, at the age of twenty-seven, was chosen to accompany Rabbi Menachem Mendel for this visit, shows us what an exemplary Torah scholar he had become. The Gaon, however, had already formed his opinion and refused to greet them.[11] In the same year, Rabbi Shneur Zalman participated in a debate with the Rabbis of Shklov, one of the most important communities in Belarus, which also did not end well for the Chasidim.[12]

As Rabbi Shneur Zalman's role as a public figure grew (after his senior colleagues' emigration to the Land of Israel in 1777),[13] Rabbi Shneur Zalman stood at the front during the struggle with those who opposed Chasidism (Misnagdim). His constituency of Belarus was an area where the conflict was at its strongest, and he also had many followers in Lithuania, including Vilna. He defended the Chasidim in a renewed "war" against them in 1787, responding to the Misnagdim, while cautioning Chasidim to exercise restraint.[14] In 1797, the Gaon renewed his ban on Chasidism, and Rabbi Shneur Zalman again advised his followers how to respond.[15]

9.   *Zemir Aritsim Ve-Charvos Tzurim* (Aleksnitz, 1772), article six.

10. Levin, *Igros Kodesh,* p. 239.

11. *Ibid.* p. 182; *Zemir Aritsim, ibid.* See Levin, *Toldos Chabad,* pp. 17-18.

12. Levin, *Igros Kodesh* p. 345; *Toldos Chabad,* p. 18.

13. See below, p. xiv.

14. See Levin, *Igros Kodesh,* pp. 16-29; *ibid.,* editor's introduction p. 50-52. This policy of restraint followed the approach the Maggid had taken in 1772.

15. *Ibid.,* p. 194-7. For an extensive chronicle of the early conflict between Chasidim and their opponents see: Mordechai Wilensky, *Chasidim u-Misnagdim,* 2 vols., (Jerusalem: 2nd rev. ed. 1990).

After the Gaon's passing the same year, the conflict escalated to an un-precedented degree, with the Misnagdim seeking the help of the government authorities to have Rabbi Shneur Zalman arrested in 1798 and again, in 1801.[16] After his second release, he transferred his court from Liozna, where he had taught Chasidism from around 1783,[17] to the nearby town of Liadi.

During the Napoleonic wars, Shneur Zalman feared that if Russia were conquered by the French, and Jews would be emancipated, the integrity of the traditional Jewish community would be undermined. Therefore he sup-ported the Russian regime, prayed for its success and even conducted es-pionage for the Russian army. With the invasion of the French in 1812, Rabbi Shneur Zalman and his family fled. After wandering hundreds of miles in the bitter Russian winter for four months, Rabbi Shneur Zalman fell ill and passed away, at the age of sixty-eight. He was buried in Haditz in Poltava.[18]

Rabbi Shneur Zalman and Sterna had three sons and three daughters. His oldest son Rabbi Dov Ber (1773-1827), established a Chasidic court in Lubavitch (Lyubavichy) which became the home of the Chabad-Lubavitch dynasty for the next hundred years. Rabbi Shneur Zalman's writings include the *Shulchan Aruch Ha-Rav,* a new edition of *Siddur Nusach Ha-Arizal,*[19] the *Tanya,* a commentary on the *Zohar,*[20] and Chasidic discourses he de-livered from 1793-1812.[21]

---

16. See Levin, *Toldos Chabad,* chapter 13. The date of his first release, 19th *Kislev* (on the Lunar Calendar), is celebrated to this day as a watershed moment in the Chabad movement. The first imprisonment is documented extensively in Rabbi Yehoshua Mondshine, *Ha-Ma'asar Ha-Rishon* (Moscow: Knizhniki, 2012). See also Rabbi A. C. Glitzenstein, (Rabbi Jacob Immanuel Schochet trans.), *The Arrest And Liberation of Rabbi Shneur Zalman Of Liadi* (Brooklyn: Kehos, 1964). For the socio-political context of Rabbi Shneur Zalman's struggles with his opponents see David E. Fishman, *Russia's First Modern Jews: The Jews of Shklov* (New York and London: New York University Press, 1995), pp. 1-21.

17. See below p. xv.

18. These events are chronicled in detail in Rabbi Yehoshua Mondshine, *Ha-Ma'asar Ha-Acharon* (Moscow: Knizhniki, 2012).

19. Published by the author in 1803. See Rabbi Gedalia Oberlader and Nachum Greenwald (eds.), *Ha-Siddur* (Monsey: Heichal Menachem, 2003).

20. Published by Rabbi Shneur Zalman's son, Rabbi Dov Ber, in Kapust 1816. Revised edition published by Kehos (Brooklyn, 2015).

21. These discourses were delivered orally in Yiddish and were transcribed in Hebrew by students and members of his family. Selections from this material were initially published as *Torah Or* (Kapust, 1837) and *Likutei Torah* (Zhitomir, 1848). The complete set of discourses has been published as *Ma'amarei Admor Ha-Zaken* (Kehos: Brooklyn, 1958-2015), 27 volumes. See Levin, *Toldos Chabad* chapters 26-8.

THE COMPOSITION OF THE TANYA

Before the *Tanya* was sent to print in 1796, manuscripts had been circulating widely for at least three years. A number of these early editions have survived, and were published by *Kehos* in 1981 as *Likutei Amarim First Versions, Based on Earliest Manuscripts.*[22]

The earliest *Tanya* manuscript in our possession dates back to 1792/3.[23] Rabbi Shneur Zalman's discourses from the fall of 1792 onwards also make explicit reference to the *Tanya*.[24] Unfortunately, discourses prior to this date have not surfaced, and we therefore have no documentary evidence of how the *Tanya's* teachings were formulated and disseminated before this period.[25]

In the "Author's Introduction"[26] — which is, in fact, a pastoral letter written in 1795 — Rabbi Shneur Zalman indicated that the *Tanya* was a collection of the advice he had offered to his disciples in private counseling sessions.[27] According to internal Chabad tradition, these private communications took place throughout the 1780s,[28] and during 1790-94, Rabbi Shneur Zalman delivered the material publicly in his sermons.[29] Evidently, the *Tanya* was a work in progress for many years.[30]

---

22. The nine manuscripts in the Chabad-Lubavitch library are described on pp. 583-5 of the work. A further manuscript is found in Leningrad, MS 177a. For an overview of the "First Versions" see discussion of Rabbi David Olidort in *Be-Ohr Ha-Chasidus* (Brooklyn: Heichal Menachem, 1997), issue 35, pp. 11-13.

23. MS 750, Chabad-Lubavitch Library, New York.

24. See *Ma'amarei Admor Ha-Zaken,* Short Discourses (Brooklyn: Kehos, 1981), p. 190.

25. Levin, *Toldos Chabad,* p. 69. Rabbi Levin has conjectured that *Tanya* manuscripts first started to circulate in the summer of 1792.

26. Below, pp. 12-26.

27. See below, p. 23. This is indicated by the name of the book *Likutei Amarim* ("An anthology of teachings"). The term *amarim* suggests orally delivered teachings which the author had collected into book form. See Rabbi Yosef Yitzchak Schneersohn, *Likutei Diburim* (Brooklyn: Kehos, 1957), p. 70b.

28. Rabbi Yosef Yitzchak Schneersohn, (Rabbi Shalom Ber Levin ed.), *Igros Kodesh,* volume 4, (Brooklyn, Kehos, 1983), p. 274. An earlier letter (*ibid.* p. 28), dates the counseling sessions to 1779-81.

29. *Idem., Sefer Ha-Sichos* 5703, (Brooklyn: Kehos, 1965), p. 23. See p. 59 *ibid.,* that an earlier version of the *Tanya* was included by Rabbi Shneur Zalman in his discourses as early as 1782. This coincides with Rabbi Shneur Zalman's first public appointment to a formal leadership role in the same year (see p. xiv).

30. One internal tradition indicates that Rabbi Shneur Zalman first began to formulate the book's contents just a few years after the Maggid's passing in 1772: "Our Rebbe spent twenty years composing the *Tanya*... until 1795" (*Igros Kodesh, ibid.,* p. 264). Another

To help contextualize this tradition concerning the *Tanya's* early development, let us briefly review what we know about Rabbi Shneur Zalman's gradual ascent to communal leadership during this period.

After being present at the Maggid's passing in Annapoli at the end of 1772, Rabbi Shneur Zalman stayed on for a few months to continue studying with the Maggid's son, Rabbi Avraham.[31] Rabbi Shneur Zalman then returned home to Vitebsk, where he had been living since his marriage in 1760. During this period Rabbi Shneur Zalman was a disciple/colleague of Rabbi Menachem Mendel of Vitebsk (now in Horodok/Gorodok), one of the older students of the Maggid who had become the leading Chasidic Rabbi in Belarus. Since Vitebsk and Horodok were only twenty miles apart, Rabbi Shneur Zalman was able to make several visits to Rabbi Menachem Mendel until he emigrated to the Land of Israel in the summer of 1777.[32]

Rabbi Menachem Mendel's plan was to continue leading the Chasidim in Belarus from a distance via correspondence, along with his junior colleague, Rabbi Avraham of Kalisk, who had joined the large group that emigrated to the Land of Israel. After a while, however, many Chasidim grew dissatisfied with this arrangement, and began to seek alternative leadership from other Chasidic Rebbes in neighboring regions. As a result, in 1782, Rabbis Menachem Mendel and Avraham deemed it necessary to appoint three local mentors in White Russia, not as a substitute for their own authority, but as a "second tier" of leadership. These mentors were: Rabbi Yisrael of Polotsk, Rabbi Yissachar Ber of Lubavitch,[33] and Rabbi Shneur Zalman.[34] This is the first documented indication we have of any formal leadership position by Rabbi Shneur Zalman after the passing of the Maggid, a decade earlier. It was also around this time, in 1783, that Rabbi Shneur Zalman resettled in

---

tradition describes the *Tanya* as the culmination of forty years of study and inner work on the part of the author (Rabbi Yosef Yitzchak Schneersohn, *Sefer Ha-Ma'amarim 5708*, p. 177).

31. Heilman, *Beis Rebbi,* chapter 4. Rabbi Avraham passed away shortly afterwards in 1776.

32   According to Michael Radkinson (*Toldos Amudei Chabad* (Koenigsberg, 1876), p. 34), Rabbi Shneur Zalman made four visits to Rabbi Menachem Mendel before he emigrated. See also Levin, *Toldos Chabad,* chapter 8. The reasons for the emigration remain unclear.

33. Rabbis Yisrael of Polotsk and Yissachar Ber of Lubavitch were both disciples of the Maggid who had attached themselves to Rabbi Menachem Mendel of Vitebsk after the Maggid's passing. They were considerably older than Rabbi Shneur Zalman; Rabbi Yissachar Ber had, in fact, been Rabbi Shneur Zalman's childhood teacher. Rabbi Yisrael of Polotsk joined the emigration to Israel in 1777, but subsequently returned to White Russia.

34. For the above see Levin, *Igros Kodesh,* p. 485; Ya'akov Barnai, *Igros Chasidim Me-Eretz Yisrael* (Jerusalem: Yad Yitzchak Ben Zvi, 1980), pp. 86, 92-93, 96.

his childhood home of Liozna, where he would remain and gradually build his Chasidic following for the next two decades.[35] (For two years prior to that, he lived in Horodok, presumably offering some informal leadership to the Chasidic community established there by Rabbi Menachem Mendel in 1773-7).[36]

The tripartite leadership established in 1782 did not continue for too long, as in 1785-6 Rabbis Menachem Mendel and Avraham of Kalisk impressed upon Rabbi Shneur Zalman to accept the spiritual leadership of the Chasidim of Belarus solely upon himself, (still as a "second tier" but with much greater authority).[37] Rabbi Shneur Zalman's leadership appears to have been fully consolidated around 1789, at which point we find no further documents suggestive of local opposition to his leadership.[38]

Rabbi Menachem Mendel of Vitebsk passed away in 1788, and the Chasidic community in Israel continued to be led by Rabbi Avraham of Kalisk. However, while Rabbi Shneur Zalman had accepted Rabbi Menachem Mendel as his senior authority, he did not show the same deference towards Rabbi Avraham of Kalisk. This became very clear later when Rabbi Avraham publicly criticized the *Tanya,* eventually maneuvering a complete organizational split with Rabbi Shneur Zalman.

If we place all these details alongside the oral traditions we have regarding the early formulation of the *Tanya,* the following picture emerges. Immediately after the passing of the Maggid, Rabbi Shneur Zalman continued to incubate his master's teachings through close consultation with the Maggid's son and with Rabbi Menachem Mendel of Vitebsk. Rabbi Shneur Zalman's public role emerged gradually, from informal leadership in 1781 (in Horodok), formal/joint leadership in 1782, and sole leadership which was consolidated between 1786-8. It was throughout this period in the 1780s that Rabbi Shneur Zalman delivered the *Tanya's* teachings to his disciples, honing them during private counseling sessions. After the passing of Rabbi Menachem Mendel in 1788 and the neutralization of all internal opposition to his appointment (by 1789), Rabbi Shneur Zalman's leadership was fully autonomous. It was *at this point* that he started to deliver the *Tanya* public-

---

35. See Levin, *Igros Kodesh Admor Ha-Zaken* p. 219; *idem., Toldos Chabad,* p. 32. After his second arrest in 1802, he relocated to Liadi.

36. *Ibid.,* p. 29.

37. Barnai, *Igros,* pp. 132, 146-9. Rabbi Yisrael of Polotsk had passed away in 1782 (or 1784). Rabbi Yissachar Ber of Lubavitch accepted the leadership of Rabbi Shneur Zalman (*Beis Rebbe,* p. 15b), and passed away in 1794.

38. For controversy in 1788 surrounding Rabbi Shneur Zalman's appointment, see Barnai, *Igros,* pp. 174-5, 181-3 and Levin, *Igros,* pp. 39-43.

ly, in his discourses. Soon afterwards, the distribution of *Tanya* manuscripts began, no later than the summer of 1792.[39]

The distribution of the manuscripts was prompted, at least in part, by the success of Rabbi Shneur Zalman's leadership—he could no longer handle the flow of visitors flocking to see him. Some time before 1793 he issued the "Liozna Regulations," severely curtailing the extent to which his disciples could visit him for a private meeting.[40] This, together, with the dissemination of the *Tanya* manuscripts, represented an attempt to broaden the influence of his leadership while reducing the demands on him personally. After an initial meeting with Rabbi Shneur Zalman, a disciple could be guided in worship through the assistance of the *Tanya,* as taught by a large number of local mentors in each community.[41] The approach proved wildly successful, and Rabbi Shneur Zalman's following grew in large numbers to eventually become the largest Chasidic group in Eastern Europe at the time.[42] After the split with Rabbi Avraham of Kalsik, in 1805/6, Rabbi Shneur Zalman's movement came to be known as Chabad Chasidism, due to its emphasis on the mind in worship.[43] The *Tanya*, however, transcended many of the organizational and geographic boundaries of the Chasidic movement, and its study became widespread in circles well beyond Chabad.[44] As the most thorough and accessible practical guide to emanate from the Maggid's school, the *Tanya* eventually came to be known as the "Bible" (*Torah Shebiksav*) of Chasidic thought.[45]

39. For a review of other Chasidic books that were printed in a similar period to the *Tanya,* see Loewenthal, pp. 45*ff.*

40. See Levin, *Toldos Chabad,* chapter 12.

41. See below, p. 24.

42. See Rabbi Yehoshua Mondshine, *Meeting of the Alter Rebbe with Rabbi Nachman of Bratslav* [Hebrew], in *Mayanosecha* (Jerusalem, 2014), issue 39, p. 11.

43. See p. xxi. CHaBaD being an acronym for *chochmah, binah* and *da'as,* the intellectual powers of the soul, see below pp. 55*ff.*

44. For comments by a vast range of Jewish thinkers about the *Tanya,* see Rabbi Avraham Shmuel Bukiet, *Nezer Ha-Tanya,* volume 2 (Kfar Chabad, 2007), pp. 357-433. For the spiritual benefits of *Tanya* study see Rabbi Moshe Nisilevitch, *Tanya Kadisha Ve-Kocho Ha-Eloki* (Kiryat Malachi 2004).

45. Rabbi Yosef Yitzchak Schneersohn, *Igros Kodesh,* volume 4, p. 264. The term *Torah Shebiksav* (Written Torah) here has a number of implications: 1) The *universal appeal* and accessibility of the *Tanya*; 2) that it is a *primary source* for the Chasidus of the Besht and Maggid; 3) its *authoritativeness,* as a work penned by a Chasidic Rebbe, in contrast to most Chasidic works which were noted down by students; 4) that it was written with *extreme precision* and attentiveness to small textual nuances. See Rabbi Menachem Mendel Schneerson, *Likutei Sichos,* volume 20 (Brooklyn: Kehos, 1982), pp. 183-4; *idem., Toras Menachem, Hisva'aduyos* 5721, vol. 1, (Brooklyn: Lahak, 2005), pp. 149-150; idem., *Sichos Kodesh* 5741, volume 2 (Brooklyn, 1986), p. 30. On the precision

ORIGINS OF THE TANYA'S TEACHINGS

It is not an easy task to trace the system of thought on which the *Tanya* was based, since Chasidic wisdom was transmitted only orally from the movement's inception until 1780.[46] Some important preliminary work has been done in this field by Rabbi Nachum Greenwald, who has traced close parallels to ideas in the *Tanya* in other recorded teachings of the Maggid of Mezritch and *Ba'al Shem Tov*[47]; but we still lack a clear picture of how the *Tanya* was assembled from the sources available to Rabbi Shneur Zalman, and to what extent the author added his own enhancements and elaborations.[48]

An important, first hand account by Rabbi Shneur Zalman of the Kabbalistic works that informed him is found in the testimony he provided to the Russian authorities during his 1798 arrest and imprisonment. He states that while Kabbalistic wisdom "is written in books, nevertheless, a person must begin his study by one Rav, and he can then subsequently study from the books. That is what happened with me: When I was approximately twenty years old... I traveled to Mezritch and I began to study Kabbalah there with Rabbi Ber o.b.m., and since then I study by myself from many respectable

of the text, see sources compiled in: Rabbi Michael Golomb (ed.), *Sha'arei Limud Ha-Chasidus* (Brooklyn: Va'ad Le-Hafatzas Sichos, 1998), pp. 86-92.

46. The first Chasidic book, *Toldos Ya'akov Yosef,* was printed in 1780, probably forty years or more after the *Ba'al Shem Tov* began teaching Chasidism. The following decades, however, witnessed a revolution in Chasidic publishing and by 1815, sixty-eight Chasidic books had been printed. According to one account, the *Ba'al Shem Tov* sharply opposed the recording of his teachings on paper (Ben Amos and Mintz (trans.), *In Praise of the Ba'al Shem Tov,* (Bloomington, 1970), p. 179). The Maggid, on the other hand, is said to have encouraged the publication of his own teachings (see introduction of Rabbi Shlomo of Łuck to *Maggid Devarav Le-Ya'akov* (revised edition, Brooklyn: Kehos, 1972), p. 3a).

47. See Greenwald, *Transformation,* in note 74. For selections from the thought of early Chasidism in English see Rabbi Norman Lamm, *The Religious Thought of Hasidism: Text and Commentary* (New Jersey: Ktav, 1999).

48. According to one account that has reached us: "Once a Chasid found Rabbi Shneur Zalman studying the *Tanya*. He asked him, 'Do you really study the *Tanya* [which you, yourself wrote]?' Rabbi Shneur Zalman replied, 'I find (perceive?) more original ideas here than in Mezritch' (Rabbi Menachem Mendel Schneerson, *Igros Kodesh* vol. 3, p. 19). While this anecdote clearly points to the presence of some original content in the *Tanya*, nevertheless, from Rabbi Shneur Zalman's stated response, it seems that this fact came as a surprise to his disciple. Apparently, the perception of *Tanya* as containing "more original ideas than in Mezritch" was *not* the common perception. In fact, the tone of Rabbi Shneur Zalman's response suggests, perhaps, that *even he* was surprised at the "original ideas" in the text, and that these were insights he only "found" or "perceived" at a later date "between the lines," after writing the book.

books of the Kabbalah, both earlier and later works, according to my own understanding."[49]

Rabbi Shneur Zalman then mentions a number of works by name from which he had drawn, after being initiated in Kabbalistic study by the Maggid: *Sha'arei Orah* by Rabbi Yosef Gikatilla (1248-1305), *Pardes Rimonim* by Rabbi Moshe Cordovero (1522–1570), *Shefa Tal* by Rabbi Shabbetai Sheftel Horowitz (c. 1561-1619), *Etz Chaim* by Rabbi Chaim Vital (1542-1620), as well as the *Zohar*.[50]

After the passing of the Maggid in 1772, we know that Rabbi Shneur Zalman continued as a student of the Maggid's son, Rabbi Avraham until 1776, when he died at the young age of 36. Rabbi Shneur Zalman was also extremely close with his senior colleague at the Maggid's court, Rabbi Menachem Mendel of Vitebsk/Horodok.[51] Even after Rabbi Menachem Mendel emigrated to the Land of Israel in 1777, he sustained an extensive scholarly correspondence with Rabbi Shneur Zalman and the Chasidic community in Belarus,[52] which is mentioned explicitly in the "Author's Introduction" as a source which informed the *Tanya*.

The vast majority of the *Tanya*, however, is undoubtedly based on oral teaching which the author heard in Mezritch. As Rabbi Shneur Zalman wrote in a letter to his colleague, Rabbi Avraham of Kalisk, "I did not ask for your approval for my Chasidic teachings, since they are sayings uttered by the holy mouth of our great Rabbi [the Maggid] o.b.m, and his son, o.b.m., of Mezritch."[53]

---

49. Levin, *Igros Kodesh Admor Ha-Zaken*, p. 221.

50. *Ibid.* Interestingly, there is no mention of Rabbi Isaiah Horowitz's *Shnei Luchos Ha-Bris* (17th Century) or the writings of Rabbi Yehudah Loew (Maharal) of Prague (d. 1609), which, according to an internal tradition of Chabad Chasidim, served as sources for the *Tanya* (see Rabbi Menachem Mendel Schneerson, *Igros Kodesh* vol. 17, p. 92; idem., *Sichos Kodesh* 5730, vol. 2, pp. 495-6; ibid. 5741, p. 830). Presumably these two works, which are of a more ethical nature, were familiar to Rabbi Shneur Zalman before his formal Kabbalistic study with the Maggid.

Nissan Mindel observes in his introduction to the *Tanya*: "The *Zohar* is mentioned in the *Tanya* (part I) forty-nine times; Luria, ten times; Vital and his works, twenty-nine times; Maimonides (Code) five times; Nachmanides, once." Mindel also suggests Bachya ben Asher's Commentary on the Bible as a source for the *Tanya*.

51. Rabbi Menachem Mendel's teachings are collected in *Pri Ha'aretz* (Kapust, 1814), *Pri Etz* (Zhitomir, 1874), and *Likutei Amarim* (Lvov, 1911). See also below pp. 72, 232. See also Loewenthal, p. 4, that Rabbi Menachem Mendel encouraged scholastic, Kabbalistic study.

52. Below, p. 22. The correspondence appears in Barnai, *Igros Chasidim*; Rabbi Avraham Surasky, *Yesod Ha-Ma'alah* (Bnei Brak, 2000), volume 2.

53. 1805 letter to Rabbi Avraham of Kalisk in *Igros Admor Ha-Zaken*, p. 340. See also

From the conflict which erupted between Rabbi Avraham of Kalisk and Rabbi Shneur Zalman after the publication of the *Tanya*, we can glean some insight into how Rabbi Shneur Zalman might have received his teaching from the Maggid. One of Rabbi Avraham's key criticisms was, "I do not approve... that you have taken the words of our holy Rabbi of Mezritch, which are the words of our holy Rabbi the *Ba'al Shem Tov*, and mixed them together with the holy words of Rabbi Yitzchak Luria."[54]

Rabbi Avraham perceived the "mixing" of Chasidic wisdom and Kabbalah in the *Tanya* as Rabbi Shneur Zalman's own innovation. Rabbi Shneur Zalman, however, insisted that this synthesis originated from the Maggid, "they are teachings uttered by the holy mouth of our great Rabbi." In another letter, Rabbi Shneur Zalman makes the point more emphatically "I came but to explain the words of the Ba'al Shem Tov, of blessed memory, and of his disciples, according to the Kabbalah of Rabbi Yitzchak Luria, of blessed memory... as I heard from my masters."[55]

Could Rabbi Avraham and Rabbi Shneur Zalman have argued over a simple fact, whether or not the Maggid had taught the Lurianic underpinnings of the *Ba'al Shem Tov's* thought?

One possibility is that the Maggid taught his various disciples according to their abilities and interests. Sensing that certain students were more interested in the integration of Chasidus with Lurianic Kabbalah, the Maggid developed this theme to a greater extent with them.[56] If this is the case, the emphasis on Kabbalah in Rabbi Shneur Zalman's writings may simply represent a more advanced type of teaching he had received from the Maggid (and his son).[57]

However, what seems more likely is that Rabbi Avraham *was* aware of (at least some of) the Kabbalistic content in the Maggid's teaching, but he viewed it as a communication aimed exclusively at the elite group who were

below pp. 57-8 for a further citation from this letter. It is important to note that Rabbi Avraham's polemic with Rabbi Shneur Zalman was complicated by other organizational and financial matters. See Loewenthal, *Communicating,* pp. 77-85.

54. Barnai, *Igros* p. 239.

55. *Tanya, Igeres Ha-Kodesh*, section 25; Levin, *Igros Kodesh,* p. 156. Rabbi Levin dates the letter to around 1795.

56. See, for example, the questions in Kabbalah posed to the Maggid by Rabbi Levi Yitzchak of Berditchev, and the answers he received. *Kedushas Levi* (Jersualem 1978), addendum.

57. See above note 8. See also Rabbi Nachum Greenwald, *The Development of Chabad Chasidus from the Torah of the Maggid of Mezritch* [Hebrew], in *Heichal Ha-Besht,* issue 7, (Rabbi Ya'akov Leib Altein *et. al.,* eds., Brooklyn 2004), pp. 45*ff.* For the development of the Maggid's teachings through his son, see also Loewenthal, p. 248n73.

privy to hear it at the Maggid's table; it was not something to be shared with the masses. This seems to be the thrust of Rabbi Avraham's stated objection to Rabbi Shneur Zalman over the *Tanya's* contents, "Too much oil may, G-d forbid, cause the light to be extinguished.... In their approach to almost all their Chasidim, our teachers took great care with their words, speaking only ethical teachings (*musar*), striving to bring them faith in the Sages."[58]

Rabbi Avraham's argument was: If Rabbi Shneur Zalman had heard Kabbalistic teaching from the Maggid, he should have realized that it was not something to be publicized, just as the Maggid himself had been highly selective with whom he shared this wisdom. Instead of muting this element of the Maggid's teachings, Rabbi Shneur Zalman had amplified it in the *Tanya*, citing ideas from Lurianic Kabbalah extensively.

At the core of the dispute was the question: How is Chasidus to be adapted for mass consumption? Rabbi Shneur Zalman was of the opinion that at least a modified version of the advanced concepts and techniques he had learned in Mezritch could be made available for the public.[59] This was not mere conjecture, as the *Tanya* represented practical wisdom which Rabbi Shneur Zalman had shared with his disciples personally (see below, p. 21). He was not concerned that "too much oil may cause the light to be extinguished," because he had tested, with a wide range of students, exactly how much "oil" was a suitable amount. The "Book of the Inbetweeners" represented as much of the Maggid's wisdom that ordinary people could reasonably implement in their worship, if they would try hard and seek clarification from their mentors, where necessary.

The ideological tension between Rabbis Avraham of Kalisk and Shneur Zalman appears to have echoed a similar difference of emphasis in the prior generation of Chasidic masters, between the Maggid of Mezritch and Rabbi Pinchas of Koretz (1728-1790). Rabbi Pinchas was a close colleague/disciple of the *Ba'al Shem Tov,* but he did not embrace the subsequent leadership of the Maggid. A notable issue dividing them was the question whether the teachings of the *Ba'al Shem Tov* should be taught within the framework of Lurianic Kabbalah. The Maggid is said to have expounded on Kabbalah even in public and he emphasized the knowledge necessary to achieve higher states of mind, whereas Rabbi Pinchas advised not to seek

---

58. Barnai, *Igros,* p. 240. For more on the disagreement see Loewenthal, pp. 51-54, 77-90; Etkes, pp. 209-258; Nehemia Polen, *Charismatic Leader, Charismatic Book: Rabbi Schneur Zalman's Tanya and His Leadership,* in Suzanne Last Stone, (ed.), *Rabbinic and Lay Communal Authority* (New York: Yeshiva University Press, 2006), pp. 60-61; Rabbi Nachum Greenwald (ed.) *Harav* (2015), p. 430n129.

59. As we will see in the "Author's Introduction" (p. 24), Rabbi Shneur Zalman advised that a mentorship program be established alongside the dissemination of the book.

lofty rungs of insight, but to worship G-d with simple faith.[60] If this description is accurate, Rabbi Shneur Zalman's propensity to integrate Chasidic teachings with Lurianic Kabbalah is in direct continuum with his master, and is more the Maggid's innovation than Rabbi Shneur Zalman's.[61]

In any case, subsequent to the publication of the *Tanya*, and Rabbi Avraham's criticism of it, the more scholarly, speculative approach to Chasidism taught by Rabbi Shneur Zalman came to be known as the "Chabad school."[62] We find the term first used by Rabbi Shneur Zalman in an 1805 letter, over a decade after the *Tanya's* initial circulation, though, apparently, it was not a term coined by the author of *Tanya* himself.[63]

PRINTINGS OF THE TANYA

Details of the early printings of the *Tanya* from 1796-1814 will be discussed below (p. 1-11). According to Chabad sources, the *Tanya* was an immediate success, and forty-thousand copies were printed in the first three years.[64] By 1815 it had been reprinted eleven times, making it the most frequently printed Chasidic book of the period. The *Tanya* continued to enjoy regular reprinting over the next century, and prior to the authoritative Vilna edition of *Tanya* in 1900, there were twenty-nine separate printings of the work, all of which have been carefully documented by Rabbi Yehoshua Mondshine.[65]

The Vilna printing has become a "standard edition" of the *Tanya*, since its text was carefully corrected against earlier editions and manuscripts by

60. See sources cited in Rabbi Abraham J. Heschel, *The Circle of The Ba'al Shem Tov: Studies in Hasidism* (Chicago University Press, 1985), pp. 19-22; Israel Zinberg (Bernard Martin trans.), *A History of Jewish Literature,* vol. 9, (New York: Ktav, 1976), p. 100.

61. Rabbi Shneur Zalman emphasized his direct continuity with the Maggid's thought by stressing, on the title page (below pp. 1-2), that the *Tanya* was merely wisdom "anthologized" from his teacher. An internal Chabad tradition describes how Rabbi Shneur Zalman naturally shied away from leadership, and was only convinced to speak in public when his wife assured him, "They are only coming here to hear what you merited to learn from your teacher" (see *Toras Menachem* 5743, vol. 2, p. 1072).

62. The Kabbalistic/scholastic content of Rabbi Shneur Zalman's public discourses was considerably enriched after his release from imprisonment by the Russian authorities in 1798. According to Chasidic tradition, Rabbi Shneur Zalman saw his release as a sign that his approach to teaching Chasidus had been ratified in heaven, and he subsequently pursued the path more vigorously. See Greenwald, *Harav,* pp. 387-431.

63. See Levin, *Toldos Chabad,* chapters 9, 14.

64. Mindel, *Rabbi Schneur Zalman,* p. 122.

65. Rabbi Yehoshua Mondshine, *Torath Habad: Bibliographies of Habad Hasiduth Books,* volume 1 (Brooklyn: Kehos, 1981). Rabbi Mondshine provides details of the Tanya's censorship.

Rabbi Asher Grossman of Nikolayev (d. 1920), under the supervision of the Fifth Lubavitcher Rebbe, Rabbi Shalom Dov Ber Schneersohn. The initial printing was only four or five thousand copies, but the text has served as the source for all subsequent printings of the *Tanya*.[66]

After Rabbi Grossman's passing, many further corrections that he had made were discovered in his notes, which formed the basis for the extensive erratum published by the Seventh Lubavitcher Rebbe in 1953.[67] Initially the Rebbe was reluctant to make any changes to the text itself, which was photo-reproduced from the earlier edition, but in subsequent years changes to the text were gradually introduced.[68]

In 1978 the Rebbe initiated a campaign to print the *Tanya* in every country that had a Jewish presence.[69] Later, during Chanukah of 1983 he made a "personal plea" to print the *Tanya* in every city that had even a minimal Jewish presence.[70] Within three weeks, over eighty editions had been printed. The campaign prompted a large, ongoing response from his followers and by 2008 a remarkable 5300 editions of the *Tanya* had been printed in different locations![71] The Rebbe also encouraged the translation

---

66. The *Practical Tanya* is not intended to replace the classic Vilna edition (which since 1953, has been published by Kehos), but is offered as a study-guide to complement the classic edition, similar to the works of Rabbis Steinsalz, Altein, Green and Ginsberg.

67. The erratum (*luach ha-tikun*) was appended to the 1953 reprint of the Vilna edition. The Rebbe added an extensive index to the *Tanya* which he had prepared. The 1953 edition also included as an appendix for the first time a list of the *Tanya* readings (*moreh shiur*) for the daily study of *Chitas* (*Chumash, Tehillim* and *Tanya*), which had been instituted by the Sixth Lubavitcher Rebbe in 1942 (see Rabbi Yosef Yitzchak Schneersohn, *Igros Kodesh*, vol. 7, p. 30). The readings were divided by the Sixth Rebbe himself. For other guidance from the Chabad Rebbes on the study of *Tanya* see: Bukiet, *Nezer Ha-Tanya*, pp. 179-226; Golomb, *Sha'arei Limud*, pp. 27-8.

68. For the above see: Rabbi Yehoshua Mondshine, *One Hundred Years Since the Printing of Tanya, Tomchei Temimim, 1900-2000* [Hebrew], in *Kfar Chabad*, issue 880 (2000); Levin, *Toldos Chabad*, chapter 25. The Rebbe was initially very concerned that the 1943 Tel Aviv edition of the *Tanya* had been re-typeset and not photo-reproduced from the Vilna edition, but when he checked the text and saw that it was accurate, he gave the project his blessing (Mondshine ibid.).

69. *Sichos Kodesh* 5738, volume 3, pp. 302-5; 316-7. All *Tanyas* were to be reproduced from the Vilna edition. Initially these efforts were not coordinated, resulting in different source texts being used, some of which were outdated. This prompted the Rebbe to establish a central office for the printing campaign, which was managed by Rabbi Shalom Jacobson, under the aegis of Kehos. See *Likutei Sichos* vol. 26, p. 319.

70. *Toras Menachem, Hisva'aduyos* 5744, vol. 2, p. 724. See also ibid, pp. 811-6, 834-5, 853; *Likutei Sichos* ibid. pp. 320-7. For other directives of the Rebbe see: Bukiet, *Nezer Ha-Tanya*, volume 2, pp. 267-281.

71. See introduction to *Mivtza Hadfasas Sefer Ha-Tanya* (Kfar Chabad: Agudas Chasidei Chabad, 2008). The pamphlet also lists all editions that had been printed in Israel at the

of *Tanya* into different languages,[72] and editions have appeared in Yiddish (1956), English (1962), Italian (1967), Spanish (1969), French (1975), Arabic (1976), Russian (1976), Portuguese (1981), German (1985), Hungarian (2001) and in Braille (1991-2).

COMMENTARIES ON THE TANYA

a.) Commentary in discourses of the Chabad Rebbeim

Rabbi Shneur Zalman's successors, the Rebbes of Chabad, did not offer a formal, systematic commentary on the *Tanya*.[73] Their preferred mode of teaching was the *ma'amar* (Chasidic discourse), an oral presentation which differed considerably from the *Tanya*, both in style and content.[74]

Surprisingly, direct references to the *Tanya* in the discourses are relatively sparse. From the nearly two hundred volumes of discourses which have been published by Kehos,[75] comments on the first book of *Tanya* fill only two volumes.[76] This material is complex, and is, generally speaking, not

time of publication. *Tanyas* have been printed in such unusual locations as: The jail cell in which Rabbi Shneur Zalman was imprisoned, Kennedy Airport, Yasser Arafat's office and Mount Everest!

72. *Likutei Sichos* vol. 22, p. 186; vol. 24, p. 10; *Sichos Kodesh* 5728, p. 298.

73. With the exception of the *reshimos* of the Seventh Rebbe, Menachem Mendel Schneerson, as we shall see below, section 'e.' Some written notes of the third Lubavitcher Rebbe, Rabbi Menachem Mendel Schneersohn (*Tzemach Tzedek*) on *Tanya* have appeared in *Kitzurim Ve-Ha'aros Be-Sefer Ha-Tanya* (Brooklyn, Kehos 1948). A few notes of *Tzemach Tzedek* are found in *Likutei Hagahos Le-Sefer Ha-Tanya* (Brooklyn: Kehos, 1974).

74. For the differences in approach between *Tanya* and the discourses in the works of Rabbi Shneur Zalman, see: Rabbi Nachum Greenwald, *The Transformation Of The Besht's Teachings, And Those Of His Students, From Oral To Written Form* [Hebrew], in *Heichal Ha-Besht* issue 9, (Rabbi Ya'akov Leib Altein *et. al.,* eds., Brooklyn 2004), p. 40*ff.*

75. A partial list includes: Rabbi Shneur Zalman, *Ma'amarei Admor Ha-Zaken*, 27 volumes; Rabbi Dovber Shneuri ("Mitteler Rebbe," 1773-1827), *Ma'amarei Admor Ha-Emtzoie,* 18 volumes; Rabbi Menachem Mendel Schneersohn (*Tzemach Tzedek,* 1789-1866), 41 volumes; Rabbi Shmuel Schneersohn ("Rebbe Maharash," 1834-1882), *Likutei Torah, Toras Shmuel,* 19 volumes; Rabbi Shalom Dovber Schneersohn ("Rebbe Rashab," 1860-1920), *Sefer Ha-Ma'amarim,* 26 volumes; Rabbi Yosef Yitzchak Schneersohn ("Rebbe Rayatz," 1880-1950), *Sefer Ha-Ma'amarim,* 21 volumes; Rabbi Menachem Mendel Schneerson (1902-1994), *Sefer Ha-Ma'amarim,* 31 volumes.

76. Rabbi Aharon Chitrik ed., *Likutei Amarim Tanya Be-Tziruf Ma'arei Mekomos, Likut Perushim, Shinui Nuscha'os* (Brooklyn: Kehos 1992), 2 vols. An expanded treatment by Kehos (*Likutei Amarim Tanya im Likut Peirushim Me-Raboseinu Nesi'einu*), incorporating texts published subsequent to Rabbi Chitrik's anthology, began to appear in 2014. As of this writing, pamphlets have appeared on chapters 2-7 and 19. Many additional

aimed at clarifying the literal meaning of the text, but rather, elaborating on Chabad theosophy.

b.) Early Commentaries

Very little commentary on the *Tanya* was formally penned or published before the second half of the twentieth century.[77] This was probably due to both the large cost of printing, and the general conservatism which prevailed in the Chasidic community, which discouraged the publication of original Torah thoughts.[78]

c.) The Tomchei Temimim School

The establishment of the Lubavitch Yeshivah (*Tomchei Temimim*) in 1897, led to a traditional school of *Tanya* interpretation associated with the Yeshivah's teachers and its students. The most significant figure in this movement was Rabbi Shmuel Grunem Esterman (1860-1921). From the Yeshivah's beginnings, Reb Grunem taught in various branches of the organization, and in 1905 he was formally appointed *mashpia* (spiritual mentor and teacher of Chasidus) in the central Yeshivah in Lubavitch.

Notes from Reb Grunem's in-depth *Tanya* classes in the Yeshivah survived, and have circulated in type-written copies for decades.[79] They have recently been published in a number of editions.[80]

Reb Grunem also influenced a generation of students, a number of whom became notable teachers of *Tanya* in the interwar years and early post-World War Two period. Notes or classes have been published from the following students of the Lubavitcher Yeshivah in Russia: Rabbi Shmuel

discourses elaborate on themes discussed in the *Tanya*, without directly referencing the work.

77. Exceptions are: Rabbi Aaron Horowitz of Starosselje (1766-1828), *Sha'arei Avodah* (Shklov, 1821); Rabbi Avraham Tzvi Brodna, *Kuntres Likutei Biurim Be-Sefer Ha-Tanya* (Jerusalem, 1922). We also have a significant Kabbalistic commentary on the *Tanya* penned as marginal notes by the Seventh Lubavitcher Rebbe's father, Rabbi Levi Yitzchak Schneerson (1878-1944), *Likutei Levi Yitzchak, Ha'aros al Sefer Ha-Tanya* (Brooklyn: Kehos, 1970). A nineteenth century *Tanya* commentary which has recently been published from manuscript is: Rabbi Ya'akov Kadaner, *Biur Tanya* (Brooklyn: Kehos, 2012).

78. See comments of the Seventh Rebbe when attempting to reverse this trend, in *Sefer Ha-Sichos* 5748, vol. 1, (Brooklyn: Kehos, 1989), p. 249. See note 114.

79. Printed in Brooklyn (1957, 1960), Montreal (1958), Kfar Chabad (1967, 1979). Parts of the commentary were also included in Rabbi Aharon Chitrik's, anthology (see note 76).

80. Chaim Luria (ed.), *Kisvei Ha-Rashag Esterman* (Israel, 2015); *Biur al Ha-Tanya me-ha-Mashpia Shmuel Grunem Esterman z'l* (Brooklyn: Kehos, 2016).

Levitin (1883-1974),[81] Rabbi Avraham Eliyahu Plotkin (1889-1949),[82] Rabbi Alter Simchovitch (1890-1939),[83] Rabbi Chaim Shaul Brook (1894-1965),[84] Rabbi Shlomo Chaim Kesselman (1894-1971),[85] Rabbi Nissan Nemenov (1904-1984),[86] Rabbi Alexander Sender Yudasin (d. 1982),[87] and Rabbi Yehoshua Korf (1905-2007).[88]

None of these works, however, provided a full, running commentary on the *Tanya*, clarifying the text line-by-line. Rather, they offered elucidation of difficult points and offered in-depth analysis based on Chasidic discourses. They were, to draw a parallel to *Talmud* commentary, the *Tosfos* and not the *Rashi*.

d.) Running Commentaries

The first complete, running commentary to the *Tanya*, accessible even to the beginner, was *Lessons in Tanya* by Rabbi Yosef Wineberg (1917-2012). Rabbi Wineberg was born in Poland to a family of Trisker Chasidim and studied in the Lubavitcher Yeshivah in Warsaw/Otwosk for several years, until its destruction at the outbreak of World War Two. (The center of the Lubavitch movement had relocated to Warsaw in 1934, after the Sixth Rebbe, Rabbi Yosef Yitzchak Schneerson, was forced to leave Russia in 1927). From 1960, Rabbi Wineberg began to broadcast regular *Tanya* classes in Yiddish over the WEVD radio network in New York, based on the lessons he had heard in the Lubavitcher Yeshivah in Poland, delivered by Rabbi Baruch Friedman *hy'd*. Rabbi Wineberg's broadcasts were acclaimed for their clarity and he eventually completed the five books of *Tanya* over the course of twenty-two years. They were published in book form, initially in

81. Notes from his *Tanya* classes penned by one of his students, appear in Rabbi Avraham Weingarten, *Nitzotzei Ohr* (Brooklyn, 2007), pp. 38-93.

82. Rabbi Shmuel Plotkin (ed.), *Biur Le-Tanya* (Brooklyn, 2015).

83. Rabbi Alter Simchovitch (Rabbi Yitzchak Wilhelm ed.), *Kuntres Tziyunim L'Tanya* (Brooklyn: Kehos, 2014).

84. Recorded by his students in Uri ben Shahar (ed.), *Sefer Zikaron Le-Ha-rav Ha-Ga'on Ha-Chasid, Reb Chaim Shaul Brook a'h* (Rishon Letziyon, 1971).

85. From the notes of his students, published in Rabbi Avraham Wolf (ed.), *Biurey Reb Shlomo Chaim* (Kfar Chabad: Kehos, 2011).

86. Recorded by his student, Rabbi Shalom Dovber Shanowitz (ed.), *Biurey Ha-Rav Nissan al Ha-Tanya* (Brooklyn, 1996).

87. Written and published by the author as *Ha-Lekach Ve-Ha-Libuv* (Kfar Chabad, 1968), 2 volumes.

88. Rabbi Yehoshua Korf, *Likutei Biurim Be-Sefer Ha-Tanya* (Brooklyn, 1968-1980), 2 vols. In addition to insights from Reb Grunem, Rabbi Korf also included material from Rabbis Plotkin, Brook and Nemenov. Of all the above works, Rabbi Korf's is the most thorough and probably the most influential.

Yiddish as *Shiurim Be-Sefer Ha-Tanya* in 1980,[89] and were later translated into English, as *Lessons in Tanya.*[90]

Rabbi Wineberg's classes were considerably enhanced by the encouragement and editorial collaboration of the Seventh Lubavitcher Rebbe, Rabbi Menachem Mendel Schneerson. The Rebbe rigorously edited all of Rabbi Wineberg's transcripts before they were broadcast, correcting and extensively annotating the text. In hundreds of concise, penetrating analyses, the Rebbe contributed greatly to the understanding of many points in the *Tanya*, and his overall editorial supervision lent authority to the work.[91] In addition to personally encouraging Rabbi Wineberg in his efforts, the Rebbe also praised the *Tanya* broadcasts publicly on several occasions in his sermons.[92]

A recurring theme in the Rebbe's annotations was his deference to the oral tradition of *Tanya* interpretation as it had been taught in the Lubavitcher Yeshivah system in Russia. Since Rabbi Wineberg had the "luxury" of the Rebbe reviewing his work, he was more than content for his esteemed editor to be final arbiter of any unclear passages. The Rebbe, however, would regularly respond to Rabbi Wineberg, "Clarify how this was learned in *Tomchei Temimim,*" i.e., in the Lubavitcher Yeshivah. The Rebbe himself had not studied in the Yeshivah, and humbly prioritized any available traditional interpretation over his own analysis.[93]

---

89. *Shiurim Be-Sefer Ha-Tanya* (Brooklyn: Kehos 1980), on chapters 1-34. A volume on the entire *Sefer Shel Beinonim* appeared in 1982, on *Sha'ar Ha-Yichud Ve-Ha-Emunah* and *Igeres Ha-Kodesh* in 1984; and on *Igeres Ha-Kodesh* and *Kuntres Acharon* in 1986.

90 Rabbis Levy Wineberg and Shalom B. Wineberg (trans.), *Lessons in Tanya* (Brooklyn: Kehos, 1987-1993), 5 volumes.

91. Even before the publication of *Shiurim Be-Sefer Ha-Tanya,* many of these annotations had been collected by Rabbi Yehoshua Mondshine and included in Rabbi Yehoshua Korf's, *Likutei Biurim Be-Sefer Ha-Tanya*. From there, they were also reproduced in Rabbi Aharon Chitrik's anthology. Recently, scans of the Rebbe's handwritten edits of the entire series have been made available online at http://www.hagaos.com/ (accessed June 2016).

92. For a list of citations, see Rabbi Michoel Seligson, *Sefer Ha-Maftechos Le-Sichos Kodesh* 5695-5752 (Brooklyn, 2011), p. 991 (entry "Radio").

    Another series of beginners' *Tanya* classes over the radio were delivered in Israel, beginning shortly before Rabbi Wineberg's broadcasts, by Rabbi Nachum Goldshmidt (1905-1976). Rabbi Goldshmidt was a childhood friend of the Rebbe, and had learned in the Lubavitcher Yeshivah in Rostov from 1923. He was a gifted teacher of Chasidic thought, and after emigrating to Israel in 1935, devoted much energy to this cause. His radio *Tanya* classes (on the first fifteen chapters of *Likutei Amarim*) were published posthumously from his notes, in *Biurey Ranag al Ha-Tanya* (Bnei Brak, 1977).

93. The Rebbe was familiar with the printed notes from Rabbi Shmuel Grunem's classes, which he references regularly in his *reshimos* on *Tanya* (see below). But he was

A further significant development in the elucidation of *Tanya* was a masterful oral presentation by Rabbi Yoel Kahn. Rabbi Kahn was born in Russia in 1930, and emigrated with his family to Israel at the age of six. He studied in the Chabad *Yeshivas Achei Temimim* in Tel Aviv, where he learned from Chasidic mentor Rabbi Chaim Shaul Brook, and Talmudic scholar Rabbi Dovid Povarsky (who later led the Ponevezh Yeshiva).

Rabbi Kahn served for over forty years as the chief scholar responsible for memorizing[94] the Seventh Rebbe's highly complex talks as they were delivered, so that they could be later transcribed. He edited and annotated many of the Rebbe's sermons/discourses for publication, and he also compiled the Chabad Encyclopedia.[95] He has been a mentor and teacher to generations of Chasidim and is considered a uniquely authoritative exponent of Chabad thought.

Rabbi Kahn's in-depth, running commentary on the *Tanya* was formally recorded in 566 segments of approximately 20-30 minutes each. (The total run time is 219 hours!) Rabbi Kahn's delivery (in Yiddish) is energetic and renders subtle concepts with exceptional clarity. He draws extensively from the *Tomchei Temimim* school and from the Rebbe's comments (in Rabbi Korf's *Likutei Biurim*), to which he adds his own insights and analogies. The result is a blend of traditional and scholastic interpretation, which is both comprehensive and lucid.[96]

> conscious that students in the Yeshivah may recall various interpretations that had not been written down. For the decision of the Rebbe's father not to send his son to the Lubavitcher Yeshivah, see Rabbi Chaim Miller, *Turning Judaism Outward* (Brooklyn: Kol Menachem, 2014), pp. 4-5 and notes 10-11. In his handwritten edits, the Rebbe would often write "Clarify how this was explained in *Tomchei Temimim*" (see for example his comments on chapter 38, p. 10 and 14 at http://www.hagaos.com/). Responding to one of Rabbi Wineberg's requests for clarification in 1963, the Rebbe wrote: "Are there not members of the community here, especially elders and Rabbis, who learned *Tanya* in *Tomchei Temimim*, or from the elders in their generation? If you can find a few such people, at least, clarify this matter with them" (*Teshurah*, Spritzer-Rosenfeld, 5767, p. 11).

94 Jewish law forbids the use of recording devices on the Sabbath and Festivals when most of these sermons were delivered.

95 *Sefer Ha-Arachim — Chabad*, 7 vols. (Brooklyn: Kehot, 1970-2009).

96. I mention Rabbi Kahn's treatment in particular, due to its exceptional clarity and reliability, but there are many other talented teachers of *Tanya* in our generation who have recorded and disseminated their oral classes. Among those available on the internet today include classes of (in Hebrew): Rabbis Chaim Shalom Deitsch, Zalman Gopin, Mendel Vechter, Yechezkel Sofer and Mordechai Elon; and in English: Rabbis Yosef Yitzchak Jacobson, Manis Friedman, Shneur Zalman Gafne, Yehoshua Gordon z'l, Moshe Weinberger, Ben-Tzion Krasnianski and Ronnie Fine. Two written commentaries to the *Tanya* which aim to offer a basic understanding are: Rabbi Avraham Alashvili, *Tanya Mevuar* (Nachlas Har Chabad: Nachlas Sefer, 1998), and Rabbi Shlomo Yitzchak Frank, *Tanya Le-Am* (Acre, Israel: 2010), 2 volumes.

While many of Rabbi Kahn's interpretations are his own original thoughts, his treatment has become authoritative and popular. Years before the rise of the internet, his lectures on *Tanya* enjoyed wide dissemination through the "Chasidus over the Telephone" network, and recently they have been adapted into written form.[97]

e.) Reshimos

After the Rebbe's passing in 1994, a project was initiated to publish the contents of his private notebooks (*reshimos*). Among the six hundred pages of *reshimos*, forty pages contained a near complete work entitled, "sources, notes and short comments on the Book for Inbetweeners." The notes had been composed in three drafts, the first dating back to the 1930s with later, expanded versions following, perhaps as late as the 1960s, when further sources had became available. In his introduction to the 1953 *Kehos* reprint of the *Tanya*, the Rebbe announced that the publication of a "complete *Tanya*" with annotations was "forthcoming," but for reasons that remain unclear, the work did not materialize in his lifetime.

In their current published form, the *reshimos* on *Tanya* are presented alongside the text of the *Tanya,* with elucidation and annotation from the editors. A parallel commentary, entitled *likutei perushim,* collects other previously published comments from the Rebbe on *Tanya,* including his annotations on *Lessons in Tanya,* as well as insights scattered in sermons and correspondence. (The references in this book do not distinguish between the *reshimos* and *likutei perushim,* and refer to them both simply as *Notes on Tanya*).[98]

f.) Recent Multi-volume Works

The most recent phase of commentaries on *Tanya* has been a series of multi-volume works (in Hebrew) based on the above material, and offering further clarification. These works are Rabbi Yekusiel Green's *Tanya im Maskil Le-Eitan* (20 volumes),[99] Rabbi Levi Yitzchak Ginsberg's *Peninei*

97   Rabbi Moshe Link (ed.), *Likutei Amarim Tanya im Biurim u-Peninim,* (Israel: Machon Ma'or She-be-Torah, 2013), 2 volumes. Additional volumes have appeared on the other sections of *Tanya.*

98.   After gradually appearing in pamphlet form from 1995 onwards, the *Notes on Tanya* were eventually published in book form in 2014.

99.   Rabbi Yekusiel Green, *Tanya im Maskil Le-Eitan* (Kfar Chabad, 1982-2014). Seven volumes are devoted to *Likutei Amarim.* A further four volumes explain *Sha'ar Ha-Yichud Ve-Ha-Emunah,* one volume on *Igeres Ha-Teshuvah* and five volumes on *Igeres Ha-Kodesh/Kuntres Acharon.* Additional volumes analyze various themes in the *Tanya.* Rabbi Green's work was first to gather all extant *Tanya* commentaries into one place and is helpful as an encyclopedic resource. It is, however, surpassed in clarity by the works of Rabbis Ginsberg and Altein.

Ha-Tanya (11 volumes),[100] and Rabbi Ya'akov Leib Altein's *Tanya im Perush Chasidus Mevu'eres* (4 of 7 projected volumes have been published).[101]

f.) Other works

In recent years, a number of commentaries have been published on the *Tanya* which are not predominantly based on the above material, and are largely written for (and by) non-Chabad audiences. These include Rabbi Adin Steinsalz's *Biur Tanya,*[102] Rabbi Yoram Abergel's *Betzur Yarum*,[103] Rabbi Moshe Wolfson's *Likutei Oros* and the *Tanya* lectures of his son-in-law, Rabbi Mordechai Silver,[104] Rabbi Yitzchak Meir Morgenstern's *Biurim Be-Sefer Ha-Tanya,*[105] and Moshe Hallamish's *Nesiv Le-Tanya*.[106]

g.) Sources of the Tanya

A number of works have sought to trace the numerous sources cited by the *Tanya*. Rabbi Jacob Immanuel Schochet was the first to make available

---

100. Rabbi Levi Yitzchak Ginsberg, *Peninei Ha-Tanya* (Kfar Chabad: Ufaratzta 1993-2016). 11 volumes covering the entire *Likutei Amarim* and one volume on *Igeres Ha-Teshuvah*. *Peninei Ha-Tanya* is an extremely readable, exhaustive treatment of the *Tanya*, based primarily on the commentary of Rabbi Yoel Kahn. The author digresses frequently to elaborate on various themes as they are explained in Chabad discourses and the work is aimed at those that have studied in Chabad Yeshivos (and are not offended by the author's messianist beliefs, which are reiterated throughout the book).

101. Rabbis Ya'akov Leib Altein *et. al*, *Likutei Amarim Tanya im Perush Chasidus Mevu'eres* (Brooklyn: Heichal Menachem, 2008-2016), 4 volumes covering chapters 1-29. Rabbi Altein's work is the most rigorous *Tanya* commentary to date, and is pitched primarily to those that have studied in Yeshivos (both non-Chabad and Chabad).

102. Rabbi Adin Even-Israel/Steinsalz, *Biur Tanya* (Jerusalem: Sifrei Milsa, 1997), 8 volumes, is based on a series of orally delivered classes by the author, adapted for publication in Hebrew by Meir Hanegbi. Part of the commentary has appeared in English in Rabbi Yaakov Tauber and Yaacov David Shulman (trans.), *Opening the Tanya* (San Francisco: Jossey-Bass, 2003), on chapters 1-12; *Learning from the Tanya* (2005), on chapters 13-26; and *Understanding the Tanya* (2007), on chapters 27-37. Rabbi Steinsaltz does draw from some of the texts mentioned above, but the commentary is largely his own thoughts and elaborations. Aimed at a general audience unfamiliar with Chasidic literature, the work has enjoyed a considerable degree of popularity.

103. Rabbi Yoram Abergel, *Betzur Yarum* (Netivot, Israel: Kol Rina, 1997-2013), 7 volumes (2 volumes on *Igeres Ha-Teshuvah* and five volumes on *Likutei Amarim* chapters 1-29). Rabbi Abergel was a leading Sefardic Rabbi in Israel until his untimely passing in 2015, at the age of 58.

104 Rabbi Moshe Wolfson, *Likutei Oros* (Brooklyn 2009), on chapters 1-7; Rabbi Silver's lectures have been adapted in: Rabbi Zev Reichman, *Path to the Tree of Life* (Judaica Press, 2014-16), 2 volumes, on chapters 1-19.

105. On chapters 1-24, printed in *Yam Ha-Chochmah* 5769, (Jerusalem, 2009), pp. 455-565,

106 Moshe Hallamish, *Nesiv Le-Tanya: Biurim Be-Ha'aros Le-Sefer Shel Beinonim* (Jerusalem 2005), offers extensive annotations and insights into all 53 chapters.

an extensive list of sources,[107] and the subsequent publication of the Lubav-ticher Rebbe's *reshimos,* added to this field considerably. Drawing on these two works, further source lists were presented by Rabbi Avraham Alashvili in *Tanya Mevuar,*[108] Rabbi Ya'akov Leib Altein in *Chasidus Mevu'eres and* Moshe Hallamish in *Nesiv Le-Tanya.* A recent annotated *Tanya,* building on all these resources, and adding further cross-references to published works of Rabbi Shneur Zalman (and other classical texts), has been pub-lished by *Pe'er Mikdashim.*[109]

THE "PRACTICAL TANYA"

While many excellent summaries of the *Tanya* have been written to con-vey its message, without the reader having to decipher the complex He-brew original,[110] somehow, the *Tanya's* "magic" only seems to work if you study the text itself. Therefore, while I have preferred in the past to adapt Chasidic works rather than to translate them, I have opted in this case for a direct translation with commentary.

---

107. Rabbi Jacob Immanuel Schochet, *Ma'arei Mekomos Ba-Sefer Ha-Tanya* (Brooklyn: Kehos 1987).

108. See note 96.

109. Rabbi Moshe Yehudah Kroll *et. al, Sefer Likutei Amarim Tanya* (Bnei Brak: Pe'er Mikdashim, 2014).

110. Summaries of each chapter were first prepared by the Third Lubavitcher Rebbe, *Tzemach Tzedek* (see note 73). For a list of works summarizing the *Tanya* see Mondshine, *Torath Habad,* pp. 200-206. Helpful summaries are also found in the *Tanya* commentaries of Rabbis Green, Ginsberg and Altein (see notes 99-101). For recent, book-length chapter summaries see: Rabbi Adin Steinsaltz (Yehuda Hanegbi trans.), *The Long Shorter Way: Discourses on Chassidic Thought* (New Jersey: Jason Aronson, 1988; reprinted by Maggid Books, Jerusalem, 2014); Rabbi Shmuel Weinfeld, *Simanei Ha-Amarim,* (Jerusalem: Eshkol, 1990); Shulamis Shmida, *Tanya Ohr Ayn Sof* (Israel, 2008); Robert Kremnizer, *Sparks of Tanya: A Simplified Guide To Knowing, Understanding and Applying Chabad Philosophy* (Brooklyn: Kehos, 2014), 2 vols.; Rabbi Nadav Cohen (Zalman Nelson trans.), *G.P.S. For The Soul: A Clear, Easy to Understand Exploration of the Tanya's Essential Concepts* (Kfar Chabad: Chish, 2014). Audio chapter summaries are available from Rabbi Manis Friedman. For general themes of the *Tanya* see: Nissan Mindel, *Rabbi Schneur Zalman of Liadi, volume 2, The Philosophy of Chabad* (Brooklyn: Kehos, 1973; revised edition, 2007); Roman A. Foxbrunner, *Habad: The Hasidism of R. Shneur Zalman of Lyady* (Tuscaloosa: University of Alabama Press, 1992); Rabbi Tuvia Blau, *Ner Limshichi: Iyunim ve-Ha'aros Be-Tanya Kadisha* (Jerusalem: Chazak, 2014; third edition); Yechiel Harari, *The Psychology and Biography of Rabbi Shneur Zalman of Liadi* [Hebrew] (Tel Aviv: Yediot Aharonot, Sifre Chemed, 2015). Since the structure and content of the *Tanya* has been amply reviewed in these works, I will not delve into the matter here.

This has posed a number of challenges. First, the Hebrew text of the *Tanya* is extremely hard to translate since, besides its propensity for long, run-on sentences, the language is dense and esoteric. A direct, word-for-word translation without any elucidation or commentary would therefore be virtually incomprehensible to the uninitiated reader. I have attempted to solve these problems in this edition by adding extensive interpolations and comments in a lighter typeface, offset from the actual translation, which appears in bold.

In the published *Tanya* commentaries that are available, there is a tendency to elaborate upon the slightest of details, in an attempt to unearth the enormous insight buried within the text. While this material is often fascinating, I have tried to avoid this type of exegesis out of the concern that *Tanya* study should not become a totally cerebral exercise. Ultimately, the *Tanya* is a guide to "worshiping G-d with the heart and the mind,"[111] and I have tried to capture this emphasis in the commentary. When translating terms and explaining the text, my concern has always been: What does this mean for us readers, practically speaking, as we struggle to experience G-d and worship Him?

I have endeavored to render the *Tanya* clear and understood, without unnecessary embellishment. If a passage is self-explanatory with a plain translation, I leave it at that. On the other hand, an esoteric phrase or complex citation might require a whole page of commentary to be understood. My concerns are always: 1.) translate, 2.) clarify and 3.) render practical, as briefly and as clearly as possible. It is due to this emphasis that I have named this work the *Practical Tanya*.[112]

Another important theme in the commentary is the *flow of argument* in the text. In many instances, it is not immediately clear why the author introduces certain ideas or citations. Other passages seem, at first glance, repetitive. Making extensive use of the published *Tanya* commentaries, I have tried to discern the meticulous inner structure of the text, pointing out how each phrase continues from the previous one, and what unstated questions the author might implicitly be answering. In a similar vein, I have also tried to indicate how each chapter follows from the previous one, and

---

111. Handwritten note of the Lubavitcher Rebbe, reproduced in *Teshurah,* Block-Wenger 2016, p. 90.

112. The *Tanya* is, of course, inherently practical without my commentary, as it was based on actual advice that the author offered to his disciples. Also, by using this title I do not wish to imply that all the other excellent commentaries on the *Tanya* are impractical. I simply aim to highlight that my primary concern has been to render the text as a clear, practical guide — not to detract in any way from the important endeavor of plumbing the depths of the text and demonstrating the wisdom in its smallest nuances.

which clusters of chapters seem to be addressing a single theme. I have also subdivided each chapter into sections, each with their own heading, to make study easier and the *Tanya's* structure more apparent.

To understand and elucidate the text I have relied primarily on three commentaries: The Lubavitcher Rebbe's *Notes on Tanya*, Rabbi Yoel Kahn's lectures and Rabbi Yehoshua Korf's *Likutei Biurim*.[113] Since these works have been drawn upon extensively, in almost every line of this book, I have not cited them each time. I have, of course, adapted their ideas into my own words, and, where necessary, added my own elaborations to bring out the practical relevance of the text.[114]

The *Tanya* makes hundreds of citations from Scripture, *Talmud, Midrash, Zohar,* texts of Lurianic Kabbalah and other classic works, all of which are sourced in my translation. As is common in Rabbinic works from this period, citations are also made for linguistic/stylistic purposes. For example, a scriptural verse may be employed, not to offer an original insight or proof, but simply to add a certain richness to the text. Sometimes the citation will be altered to fit the syntax of the *Tanya*, with a change of tense, wording or other slight modifications.[115] In all these cases I have presented such phrases as actual citations, noting their source in parentheses, so that the reader gets a sense of how the *Tanya* text has been woven together. It also makes clear to the English reader why the *Tanya* sometimes makes use of seemingly extravagant or "flowery" wording, because it is, in fact, borrowing from Scripture or another classic work.[116]

---

113. Discussed above, pp. xxv-xxviii. The works of Ginsberg and Altein, which are based on these three sources, have also been helpful in clarifying certain passages.

114. A statement attributed to the Fourth Lubavitcher Rebbe, Rabbi Shmuel Schneersohn, sanctioned students to offer commentaries on the *Tanya*, even if the student could not be certain of their authenticity, provided that the insights were of practical relevance in worship (Rabbi Shalom Dov Ber Schneersohn, *Igros Kodesh*, vol. 2, p. 720; Rabbi Yosef Yitzchak Schneersohn, *Sefer Ha-Sichos* 5702, p. 83). The Seventh Lubavitcher Rebbe greatly encouraged his disciples to think and write creatively in both Talmudic and Chasidic teachings. See sources in Golomb, *Sha'arei Limud*, p. 33-5.

115. The precise use of citations and their "modification" from original sources, receives much scholarly attention in the Rebbe's *reshimos*.

116. Regrettably, I have not always been able to include a translation of the words *yisborach* (blessed) or *baruch hu* (blessed is He), which appear frequently in the *Tanya* after G-d's name. In English, the term interrupts the flow to a greater extent than in Hebrew, and in a long, run-on sentence I have sometimes felt it necessary to omit it. I have also not rendered all the parentheses from the Hebrew text into the English translation, and, on occasion, I have added parentheses to the translation to make longer sentences more comprehensible.

In addition to direct citations, I have also added references to unidentified sources from which the *Tanya* seems to have drawn some of its themes and ideas. Many of these have already been noted in existing works mentioned above, and, in the limited time available to me for further research, I was able to identify quite a few additional sources.

The Hebrew text of the *Tanya* appears twice in this book. On the top of the page is the text of the classic Vilna edition, with which most existing students of the *Tanya* are already familiar; and below, the corrected, vocalized (*menukad*) Hebrew text appears, blended with the translation and commentary.[117]

In preparing the translation I have aimed to be as literal as possible, out of respect for the precision and sanctity of the original text. But good translation is always a judicious balance between precision and flow, and in a text as difficult as the *Tanya*, an entirely literal translation would often be unreadable. One significant modification I have made consistently is to switch the third person references ("he will come to realize") to the second person ("you will come to realize.") This, I believe, better captures in English the practical orientation of the text.

A PERSONAL NOTE

The *Tanya* has had an enormously positive influence on my life, and I hope that you, too, will benefit greatly from its wisdom. My first encounter with the book was in the summer of 1992, when I was a twenty year-old college student attending the *Ivy League Torah Study Program* in upstate New York. We only managed to study a few chapters that summer, but I was intrigued and purchased a set of *Lessons In Tanya* before returning to Leeds University, in England. That year, I studied the whole book, and even drew diagrams to summarize every chapter.

The *Tanya* opened a world of insight for me that I did not believe existed within Judaism. I had grown up with some traditional observance, and had attended Kenton United Synagogue, but I had found no real intellectual or spiritual stimulation in these activities. Being Jewish was important to me in a cultural sense—I mixed in the social circles of North-West London, and I was committed to marrying Jewish—but for my first twenty years I had

---

117. There has been an aversion to printing the *Tanya* text with vowels (*nekudos*), due to a Chasidic tradition which discouraged it (see Rabbi Yosef Yitzchak Schneersohn, *Igros Kodesh,* vol. 4, p. 267). In recent years, however, a number of vocalized editions have appeared, and, out of deference to the tradition, they are always printed as an accompaniment to the non-vocalized text.

seen no indication that Judaism offered real insight into higher living. For me, being Jewish was just an ethnicity, and sometimes a challenging one.

The *Tanya* changed all this. In these pages, I discovered that Judaism was intellectually sophisticated, not only in the Maimonidean sense of abstract philosophy, but as a deep psychology. The *Tanya* was extremely relatable; it offered a "guide to the soul" which resonated as real and applicable. And its sublime, esoteric terminology added a transcendent dimension so that the *Tanya's* wisdom was directed simultaneously at the body, mind, emotions and spirit. Somehow, all these psychospiritual tools had been seamlessly integrated with traditional Judaism, the Biblical and Rabbinic laws with which I was (to some extent) familiar. As I absorbed more of the *Tanya's* wisdom, I experienced an inner transformation.

When Rabbi Yeremi and Shoshana Angyalfi, the Chabad representatives in Leeds, invited me for the first time to stay for Shabbos in the spring of 1993, they were shocked to discover that a student in the university, who showed no outward signs of being a Chasid, was familiar with the entire *Tanya!*

Providence works in strange ways. Five years later, I married the Angyalfi's oldest daughter, Chani. Countless times, my father-in-law would encourage me, "You must translate the *Tanya!*" but I was always deterred by the enormity of the project.

Now that the first part has been completed, I feel that a circle has been closed. I hope this work will repay my "debt," in some small measure, to this special and sacred book.

Amid the elation of having translated and explained all fifty-three chapters of the *Tanya*, I am reminded of the Rebbe's words to "the participants in the publication of the small edition of the Bilingual *Tanya*," in 1981.

"I take exception, however, to the comment, 'the project is now completed—not to imply, G-d forbid, that the publication part of it is in any way incomplete. But this part is only a prelude to the essential part of the project, namely, to disseminate this sacred book and its central message.... This task—to see to it that the book and its message reach every Jew, man and woman... is only in its beginning."[118]

---

118. Letter dated 21st *Iyar* 1981, reproduced in *Teshurah* Ohana-Gorman.

ACKNOWLEDGMENTS

First and foremost I extend my gratitude to David and Lara Slager whose outstanding generosity has made this book possible, as well as most of my other works throughout the last decade. The Slager family have set an example to the Jewish community, both in their personal lives and with their outstanding philanthropic efforts towards an impressive array of causes across the globe. I wish David, Lara, and their precious children Hannah and Sara Malka, all the abundant blessings that they deserve.

I extend my heartfelt wishes to Rabbi Meyer Gutnick, co-founder and director of Kol Menachem publishing, who had the courage to invest in an unknown author, and since then has been an unfailing source of material support and moral encouragement for my work. Motivated by a great love for the Rebbe, and recognizing the urgency of spreading his Torah teachings, Rabbi Gutnick has chosen to invest his own natural talent at "getting things done" into a very worthy cause. In the merit of this, and all his many other impressive philanthropic efforts, may G-d bless him, together with his dear wife Shaindy, and all their wonderful children and grandchildren, with *chasidishe nachas* and only revealed and open goodness.

I am grateful to my father-in-law, Rabbi Yeremi Angyalfi for scrutinizing the entire text and offering many helpful corrections and comments; and to Rabbi Yisroel Dovid Klein, for critically reading the entire manuscript and checking many of the sources. I extend my thanks to Rabbi Shmuel Rabin for carefully checking the Hebrew texts. The beautiful cover of this book was designed by the exceptionally talented Yossi Belkin. I am also grateful to Adam Greiss, my teacher at the School of Visual Arts, for astute critique of the typographic design.

For assistance with proofreading I thank: Yehudis Homnick and Natalie Ling.

To my parents, Trevor and Denise Miller, for their love, for investing in my education and for supporting me in becoming a rabbi, even if they would have preferred I had become a doctor.

And finally, to my greatest support, my wife Chani, and to my wonderful children: Leah, Mendel, Mushka, Levi, Esther Miriam, Ariella and Menucha, my greatest pride and joy.

Chaim Miller

16th *Tammuz*[119] 5776

---

119. The day on which the Torah was first translated, into Greek. See *Likutei Sichos* vol. 24, pp. 1-11.

ספר לקוטי אמרים חלק ראשון

AUTHOR'S TITLE PAGE

The "title page" of the *Tanya* was written by the author to formally name his work and offer a brief "mission statement" of the book's purpose.

סֵפֶר לִקּוּטֵי אֲמָרִים — **A book** entitled *"An Anthology of Teachings"* (*Likutei Amarim*).

The *Tanya* is not an "anthology" in the sense of a "cut-and-paste" selection from other works; it's more of a *synthesis* of various teachings that the author had received, both written and oral, which had then been enlarged upon by the author and adapted for practical implementation in daily life (see below, pp. 2, 23).

The collected sermons of Rabbi Dov Ber of Mezritch (d. 1772), Rabbi Shneur Zalman's teacher, were published in 1781 with the same title, *Likutei Amarim,* and it is surely no coincidence that the *Tanya* (first published in 1796), was given the same name. While Rabbi Shneur Zalman undoubtedly put much of his own creative input into the pages of the *Tanya,* he chose to emphasize the direct continuity of his work with Rabbi Dov Ber's ideas by giving it the same name as his master's work.

Despite the author's choice of title, this book came to be generally known by the public as *"Tanya,"* the Hebrew word with which the book begins. (This name had been in common use before the *Tanya* was printed, when it had circulated in manuscript form). Already in the second printing of the work in 1799, the title *Tanya* formally appears, and has since become a permanent fixture.

חֵלֶק רִאשׁוֹן — **Part One.**

The first printed edition of the *Tanya* contained two parts. Part One, *The Book of the Inbetweeners* (*Sefer Shel Beinoinim*), is a psychologically orientated guide to worship. Part Two, *Gateway to Oneness and Faith* (*Sha'ar Ha-Yichud ve-ha-Emunah*) focuses on the esoteric philosophy which forms the foundation of Chasidic thought.

(Though we cannot be certain, it appears that Rabbi Shneur Zalman had originally composed *Gateway to Oneness and Faith* as Part One of the book, but later made the decision to place the more practical *Book of the Inbetweeners* at the beginning of his published work.)

The second printing of the *Tanya*, in 1799, included a third section, entitled *Letter on Repentance, (Iggeres Ha-Teshuvah)*, which had already been in broad circulation in manuscript form since the summer of 1792. A later printing, published posthumously by the author's sons in 1814, included a fourth part, *Sacred Letter, (Igeres Ha-Kodesh)* containing various scholarly letters written by the author; and a fifth part, *Final Tract, (Kuntres Acharon)*, containing material which the author had composed at the same time the original *Tanya* was being written.

הַנִּקְרָא בְּשֵׁם סֵפֶר שֶׁל בֵּינוֹנִים

מְלוּקָט מִפִּי סְפָרִים וּמִפִּי סוֹפְרִים קְדוֹשֵׁי עֶלְיוֹן נ"ע מְיוּסָד עַל
פָּסוּק כִּי קָרוֹב אֵלֶיךָ הַדָּבָר מְאֹד בְּפִיךָ וּבִלְבָבְךָ לַעֲשׂוֹתוֹ. לְבַאֵר

הַנִּקְרָא בְּשֵׁם — Part One of the *Tanya* **is called by the name,** סֵפֶר שֶׁל בֵּינוֹנִים — *"The Book of the Inbetweeners" (Sefer Shel Beinoinim).*

The *Tanya* will teach you to set *reasonable goals* in your relationship with G-d. You're probably not one of the holiest people who has ever lived, nor are you irredeemably wicked. Like most people, your spiritual flame probably fluctuates from one day to the next, and you are often torn by the question of whether to be good or to be selfish. It is for such "normal" people that this book was written. And that's why it was called by the author *"The Book of the Inbetweeners."*

(The term "inbetweener" (*beinoni*), does, in fact, have a precise definition, which we will discover in chapters 12-14).

וּמִפִּי סוֹפְרִים — **Anthologized from** various published **texts,** קְדוֹשֵׁי מְלוּקָט מִפֵּי סְפָרִים עֶלְיוֹן נִשְׁמָתָם עֵדֶן — **and from** the unpublished wisdom of various **teachers of exceptional holiness, whose souls are in heaven.**

The author is intentionally vague about his sources, but that is not surprising when we consider that the original printing of the *Tanya* did not even bear the author's name.

The "published texts" which the *Tanya* quotes most extensively (besides the basic canon of Scripture, *Talmud* and *Midrash*), are: the *Zohar* and Rabbi Chaim Vital's *Etz Chaim* and *Pri Etz Chaim*. Maimonides is mentioned occasionally, as is Rabbi Moshe Cordovero's *Pardes*. An internal Chabad tradition points to Rabbi Isaiah Horowitz's *Shnei Luchos Ha-Bris* (17th century) and the writings of Rabbi Yehudah Loew (Maharal) of Prague (d. 1609) as sources for the *Tanya*.

"Teachers of exceptional holiness, whose souls are in heaven" certainly refers to Rabbi Dov Ber of Mezritch (d. 1772), Rabbi Shneur Zalman's teacher, and Rabbi Dov Ber's teacher Rabbi Yisrael *Ba'al Shem Tov* (1698-1760) from whom the Chasidic movement originated. We should also include Rabbi Dov Ber's son, Avraham "the angel" (1739-1776), who was a personal teacher of Rabbi Shneur Zalman, and Rabbi Menachem Mendel of Vitebsk (d. 1788) who was a colleague and in many ways a teacher of Rabbi Shneur Zalman.

מְיוּסָד עַל פָּסוּק כִּי קָרוֹב אֵלֶיךָ הַדָּבָר מְאֹד בְּפִיךָ וּבִלְבָבְךָ לַעֲשׂוֹתוֹ — **Part One** of this book is **based on the verse,** *"For this (body of) commandment(s) which I am commanding you this day, is not beyond you, nor is it far away....* **Rather, the thing is very much within reach for you, in your mouth and in your heart, so that you can do it"** (*Deuteronomy* 30:14).

This is a practically orientated work. It's going to explain how the worship of G-d that is demanded from you is *"very much within reach for you."*

הֵיטֵב אֵיךְ הוּא קָרוֹב מְאֹד בְּדֶרֶךְ אֲרוּכָה וּקְצָרָה בעזה"י.

2B הַסְכָּמַת הָרַב הֶחָסִיד הַמְפוּרְסָם אִישׁ אֱלֹהִי קָדוֹשׁ יֵאָמֶר לוֹ מוֹהר"ר מְשׁוּלָם זוּסִיל מֵאַנִיפָּאלִי:

The *Tanya* will not directly comment on this verse until chapter 17. Up to that point, the book will be teaching you core knowledge that you need to discern about what is "within reach" and what isn't. You're going to learn the "anatomy" and "physiology" of your soul and gain a profound understanding of the soul/body conflict.

לְבָאֵר הֵיטֵב אֵיךְ הוּא קָרוֹב מְאֹד — **To clarify well how** authentic worship **is** *"very much within reach,"* בְּדֶרֶךְ אֲרוּכָה וּקְצָרָה — **in a** *"long-but-short way'"* (*Talmud, Eruvin* 53b), בְּעֶזְרַת ה' יִתְבָּרֵךְ — **with the help of G-d, may He be blessed.**

The *Tanya's* reference here is to a story in the *Talmud*: *"Rabbi Yehoshua said: Once I was walking along the path, and I saw a child sitting at a crossroads. I asked him: 'Which path will lead me to the city?' He said: 'One path is short-but-long, and one path is long-but-short.' I took the short-but-long one. Once I arrived at the city, I found the passageway blocked off by meandering gardens and orchards. I turned back and said to the child: 'My son! Didn't you describe this path as short?' He replied: 'Didn't I also say it was long!'"*

A "short-but-long" path is one that makes you feel as if you're making quick progress, but fails to get you to the final destination. A "long-but-short" path takes more time and effort to follow, but it gets you where you want to go.

The *Tanya* is your "long-but-short" path to worshiping G-d. It's not a "quick fix" and there's no instant magic. You're going to have to do some real spiritual work. But if you're willing to do that, you can begin to worship G-d authentically and be on the path to fulfilling your mission in life.

RABBINIC APPROBATIONS

APPROBATION FROM RABBI ZUSYA OF ANNAPOL

Before publishing the *Tanya*, Rabbi Shneur Zalman sent a manuscript of the work to two senior colleagues for their approval and blessing to print the book. As is customary in Rabbinic works, these approbations were printed at the beginning of the book.

הַסְכָּמַת הָרַב הֶחָסִיד הַמְפוּרְסָם — **Approbation from the renowned Rav and Chasid,** אִישׁ אֱלֹהִי קָדוֹשׁ יֵאָמֶר לוֹ — **a G-dly man, who** *"shall be called holy"* (*Isaiah* 4:3), מוֹרֵנוּ וְרַבֵּנוּ הָרַב — **our guide, Rav and teacher,** רַבִּי מְשׁוּלָם זוּסִיל מֵאַנִיפָּאלִי — **Rabbi Meshullam Zusil** Lipman (1718-1800) **of Annapol** (Hannopil, Ukraine).

הנה בראותי את הכתבים של הרב האי גאון איש אלקים
קדוש וטהור אספקלריא המאירה וטוב אשר עשה ואשר
הפליא ה' חסדו ונתן בלבו הטהור לעשות את כל אלה להראות
עם ה' דרכיו הק'. ורצונו היה שלא להעלות את הכתבים ההם
לבית הדפוס מחמת שאין דרכו בכך. רק מחמת התפשטות
הקונטרסים ההם בקרב כל ישראל בהעתקות רבות מידי
סופרים משונים ומחמת ריבוי העתקות שונות רבו הט"ס
במאד. והוכרח להביא הקונטרסים ההם לבית הדפוס.

Rabbi Zusil (Zusya) of Annapol was an outstanding disciple of Rabbi Dov Ber, the Maggid of Mezrich. A rich tradition of Chasidic storytelling depicts Rabbi Zusya as a modest and kind man who was extremely sincere and authentic. The few of his teachings that have survived show that, contrary to popular legend, he was a scholar. Some of his teachings and those of his sons were collected in *Menoras Zahav* (1902).

הִנֵּה בְּרָאוֹתִי אֶת הַכְּתָבִים שֶׁל הָרַב — **Now I have seen the writings of the Rav,** author of the *Tanya,* הָאי גָאוֹן אִישׁ אֱלֹקים קָדוֹשׁ וְטָהוֹר — this genius, *"man of G-d"* (1 *Samuel* 2:27), **holy and pure,** אַסְפַּקְלַרְיָא הַמְּאִירָה — a visionary that perceives through *"clear glass"* (*Talmud, Yevamos* 49b), וְטוֹב אֲשֶׁר עָשָׂה — **and I have seen the good** work **that he has done,** וַאֲשֶׁר הִפְלִיא ה' חַסְדּוֹ — that G-d *"has performed His wondrous kindness"* (*Psalms* 31:22), וְנָתַן בְּלִבּוֹ הַטָּהוֹר לַעֲשׂוֹת אֶת כָּל אֵלֶּה — and **has inspired** the author's **heart to do all this** work, לְהַרְאוֹת עִם ה' דְּרָכָיו הַקְּדוֹשִׁים — **to show G-d's people His holy ways.**

וּרְצוֹנוֹ הָיָה שֶׁלֹּא לְהַעֲלוֹת אֶת הַכְּתָבִים הָהֵם לְבֵית הַדְּפוּס — The author's original **in**tention was **not to submit these writings for publication,** מֵחֲמַת שֶׁאֵין דַּרְכּוֹ בְּכָךְ — **because that's not his way,** as we see from the fact that he had not submitted his *Shulchan Aruch,* (Code of Jewish Law) penned decades earlier, for publication.

רַק מֵחֲמַת הִתְפַּשְׁטוּת הַקּוּנְטְרֵסִים הָהֵם בְּקֶרֶב כָּל יִשְׂרָאֵל — **But since those** handwritten **pamphlets** containing the *Tanya* **have** already **been disseminated among all Israel,** בְּהַעְתָּקוֹת רַבּוֹת מִידֵי סוֹפְרִים מְשׁוּנִּים — **copied many times by different scribes,** וּמֵחֲמַת רִבּוּי הַעְתָּקוֹת שׁוֹנוֹת רַבּוּ הַטָּעִיּוֹת סוֹפְרִים בִּמְאֹד — **and as a result of the numerous copies, very many scribal errors have resulted,** וְהוּכְרַח לְהָבִיא הַקּוּנְטְרֵסִים הָהֵם לְבֵית הַדְּפוּס — **it has been necessary to submit those pamphlets for publication.**

Even at the end of the eighteenth century, when the *Tanya* was first published, printing Jewish esoteric wisdom was still considered "dangerous" by many. (The fear of misinterpretation, that big ideas would be corrupted by small minds, has always been associated with writings that are influenced by the Kabbalah.) Here, Rabbi Zusya is possibly suggesting that, in this particular case, any concerns that we might have about publishing the *Tanya* need to be disregarded for a very practical reason. Prior to its publication in 1796, the *Tanya* had already been circulated

וְהֵעִיר ה' אֶת רוּחַ הַשּׁוּתָּפִים ה"ה הָרַבָּנִי הַמּוּפְלָג הַוָּתִיק
מוֹהֵר"ר שָׁלוֹם שַׁכְנָא בְּמוֹהֵר"ר נֹחַ וְה"ה הָרַבָּנִי הַמּוּפְלָג
הַוָּתִיק מוֹהֵר"ר מָרְדְּכַי בְּמוֹהֵר"ר שְׁמוּאֵל הַלֵּוִי לְהָבִיא
הַקוּנְטְרֵסִים הָהֵם לְבֵית הַדְּפוּס בִּסְלַאוִויטָא וּלְפָעֳלָא טָבָא

quite broadly in manuscript form, probably since the summer of 1792, resulting in "many scribal errors" which had corrupted the text available to the public. When publishing an unavailable work, one might have to consider the relative merits of disclosing subtle wisdom to a large audience; but, in this case, Rabbi Zusya intimated, a corrupted text was already in circulation, and printing was now necessary to fix the problem.

Rabbi Zusya's approbation does not aim to overtly challenge the prevailing, conservative approach to publishing Kabbalistic works. It simply argues that, in this particular case, such an approach would be counterproductive.

(What Rabbi Zusya does not mention is that some of the "scribal errors" had been introduced by bogus scribes in order to discredit the Chasidic movement.)

וְהֵעִיר ה' אֶת רוּחַ הַשּׁוּתָּפִים — **And G-d has inspired** two publishing **partners,** הֵרֵי הוּא — the first being the outstanding, distinguished Rabbi, הָרַבָּנִי הַמּוּפְלָג הַוָּתִיק — מוֹרֵנוּ **— our guide and teacher,** וְרֵבֵּנוּ — הָרַב רַבִּי שָׁלוֹם שַׁכְנָא **— Ha-Rav, Reb Shalom Shachna,** בֶּן מוֹרֵנוּ הָרַב וְרֵבֵּנוּ רַבִּי נֹחַ **— son of our guide, Rav and teacher, Reb Noach** Altschuler, וַהֲרֵי הוּא הָרַבָּנִי הַמּוּפְלָג הַוָּתִיק **— and the second being an outstanding, distinguished Rabbi,** מוֹרֵנוּ הָרַב וְרֵבֵּנוּ רַבִּי מָרְדְּכַי **— our guide, Rav and teacher, Reb Mordechai,** בֶּן מוֹרֵנוּ הָרַב וְרֵבֵּנוּ רַבִּי שְׁמוּאֵל הַלֵּוִי **— son of our guide, Rav and teacher, Reb Shmuel, the Levite,** Horowitz, לְהָבִיא הַקוּנְטְרֵסִים הָהֵם לְבֵית — הַדְּפוּס בִּסְלַאוִויטָא **— to bring these pamphlets to be published in Slavita,** Ukraine.

וּלְפָעֳלָא טָבָא אָמַרְתִּי יִישַׁר חֵילָא **— And for this fine act, I congratulate them.**

The two individuals responsible for first publishing the *Tanya* were Rabbi Shalom Shachna Altschuler (d. 1807) and Rabbi Mordechai Horowitz.

Rabbi Shalom Shachna was the son-in-law of Rabbi Shneur Zalman and father of the third Chabad Rebbe, Rabbi Menachem Mendel, (also known as *Tzemach Tzedek*). Rabbi Noach Altschuler, Shalom Shachna's father, was a wealthy businessman and disciple of Rabbi Menachem Mendel of Vitebsk. He was possibly a descendant of Rabbis David and Yechiel Altschuler (18th century), authors of an important commentary on *Tanach, Metzudos David/Metzudos Tziyon*. Rabbi Noach's wife, Ruchama Friedman, was a sister of the Maggid, Rabbi Dov Ber of Mezritch. Rabbi Noach died when Shalom Shachna was a young child, and Rabbi Shneur Zalman took the boy into his house and brought him up.

Rabbi Mordechai Horowitz was a publisher from the town of Shklov, who was later active in bringing Jewish books to print in various locations from 1806-1826, including Rabbi Shneur Zalman's *Siddur* (in 1816) and *Shulchan Aruch* (in 1814 and 1826), as well as later printings of the *Tanya* (1806 and 1814).

אמרתי יישר חילא אך עלו בלבם מגור מסביב מן הדפוסים
אשר רבו שדרכן להזיק ולקלקל המאושרים אי לזאת גמרנו
בלבינו ליתן הסכמה לבל ירים איש את ידו ואת רגלו לגרום
להמדפיסים הנ"ל שום היזק חס ושלום בהשגת גבול בשום
אופן. ואסור לשום אדם לדפוס הספר הנ"ל בלתי ידיעת
המדפיסים הנ"ל עד משך חמש שנים רצופים מיום דלמטה
ושומע לדברי אלה יבא עליו ברכת טוב הכ"ד הדורש זאת
לכבוד התורה היום יום ג' שנכפל בו כי טוב פ' תבא שנת

Rabbis Altschuler and Horowitz probably made use of the famous publishing house in Slavita owned by Rabbi Moshe Shapira, (son of famed Chasidic leader and close disciple of the Ba'al Shem Tov, Rabbi Pinchas of Korets); but, we cannot be sure they did not use a different press in the same town, since none of the books published in Slavita during 1791-98 make reference to a particular printing press. It is also not clear that Rabbi Moshe's press was even open in 1796, when the publication of the *Tanya* began. Rabbi Zusya's approbation also seems to imply that Rabbis Altschuler and Horowitz were the actual publishers, bearing financial responsibility for the project, and not mere agents acting on behalf of the author to bring the work to a previously established publisher (see Rabbi Shalom Ber Levin, *Toldos Chabad Be-Russia Ha-Tzaris* (Brooklyn: Kehos, 2010), chapter 24).

אַךְ עָלוּ בְּלִבָּם מָגוֹר מִסָּבִיב — **The** publishers **were, however, gripped by** *"terror on every side"* (*Jeremiah* 20:3), מִן הַדְּפוֹסִים אֲשֶׁר רַבּוּ שֶׁדַּרְכָּן לְהַזִּיק וּלְקַלְקֵל הַמְאוּשָּׁרִים — **due to the growing number of** untrustworthy **publishers who cause damage and ruin to the reliable ones.**

Due to the competition among Jewish presses, a Rabbinic approbation also served to protect the publisher's rights so that they could recoup their investment. Rabbi Zusya now issues a ruling that no other printer is authorized to reproduce the *Tanya* for the next five years.

אִי לָזֹאת גָּמַרְנוּ בְּלִבֵּנוּ לִיתֵּן הַסְכָּמָה — **This being the case, we have resolved to give an approbation** to this work, לְבַל יָרִים אֶת יָדוֹ וְאֶת רַגְלוֹ — **so that** *"no man shall raise hand or foot"* (*Genesis* 41:44), לִגְרוֹם לְהַמַּדְפִּיסִים הַנִּזְכָּרִים לְעֵיל שׁוּם הֶיזֵק — to cause, **G-d forbid, any damages to the above-mentioned publishers,** חַס וְשָׁלוֹם — **infringing their copyright in any fashion,** בְּהַשָּׂגַת גְּבוּל בְּשׁוּם אוֹפֶן — וְאָסוּר לְשׁוּם אָדָם לִדְפֹּס הַסֵּפֶר הַנִּזְכָּר לְעֵיל בִּלְתִּי יְדִיעַת הַמַּדְפִּיסִים הַנִּזְכָּרִים לְעֵיל — **and it is forbidden for any person to print this book without the knowledge of the above-mentioned publishers,** עַד מֶשֶׁךְ חָמֵשׁ שָׁנִים רְצוּפִים מִיּוֹם דִּלְמַטָּה — **for a total of five years from the date below.**

וְשׁוֹמֵעַ לִדְבָרַי אֵלֶּה יָבֹא עָלָיו בְּרְכַּת טוֹב — **And he who listens to these words of mine will receive a blessing of goodness.**

הֲלֹא כֹּה דִּבְרֵי הַדּוֹרֵשׁ זֹאת לִכְבוֹד הַתּוֹרָה — **These are the words of one who demands this for the Torah's honor,** הַיּוֹם יוֹם ג' שֶׁנִּכְפַּל בּוֹ כִּי טוֹב פָּרָשָׁה תָּבֹא — **today, Tuesday,**

פְּדוּתֵינוּ לפ״ק. הַקָּטָן מְשׁוּלָם זוּסִיל מַאנִיפָּאלִי.

הַסְכָּמַת הָרַב הֶחָסִיד הַמְפוּרְסָם אִישׁ אֱלֹהִי קָדוֹשׁ יֵאָמֶר לוֹ
מֹהוֹר״ר יְהוּדָא לֵיב הַכֹּהֵן:

חָכְמַת אָדָם תָּאִיר פְּנֵי הָאָרֶץ בִּרְאוֹתִי יְדֵי קֹדֶשׁ הַמְחַבֵּר הָרַב
הַגָּאוֹן אִישׁ אֱלֹקִים קָדוֹשׁ וְטָהוֹר חָסִיד וְעָנָיו אֲשֶׁר מִכְּבָר נִגְלָה
מִסְתָּרָיו יוֹשֵׁב בְּשֶׁבֶת תַּחְכְּמֹנִי אֵצֶל אֲדוֹנֵינוּ מוֹרֵינוּ וְרַבֵּינוּ
גָּאוֹן עוֹלָם וְדָלָה מַיִם מִבְּאֵר מַיִם חַיִּים וְכָעֵת יִשְׂמַח יִשְׂרָאֵל

the day when *"it was good"* (*Genesis* 1:10, 12) **was said twice, of the Torah portion** *Tavo,* שְׁנָת פְּדוּתֵינ"וּ לִפְרָט קָטָן — **year 556 of the** sixth **millennium (1796).**

From the date of this approbation, the printing process took around three months until the book was published on the 20th *Kislev* 5557 (1796).

הַקָּטָן מְשׁוּלָם זוּסִיל מַאֲנִיפָּאלִי — Rabbi **Meshullam Zusil, "the small one," of Annapol** (Hannopil, Ukraine).

APPROBATION FROM RABBI YEHUDA LEIB OF ANNAPOL

The *Tanya's* second approbation, in its first printing, was from Rabbi Yehuda Leib *ha-kohen* of Annapol (d. 1806), originally a disciple of the Vilna Gaon, who later became a close student of the Maggid of Mezritch. He was the author of *Ohr Ha-Ganuz* (Lemberg, 1866).

Why did Rabbi Shneur Zalman ask these two Rabbis in particular for their approbation? Possibly because they, together with Rabbi Shneur Zalman, had been present at the Maggid's passing in Annapol, and continued to study together there for a period of time afterwards (see Chaim Meir Heilman, *Beis Rebbi* (Berdichev, 1902), chapter 4. The Maggid's son, Rabbi Avraham, had also been present, but he had passed away in 1776.) Practically speaking, Annapol, where both Rabbis lived, was close to Slavita where the printing took place (see Levin, *ibid.*).

הַסְכָּמַת הָרַב הֶחָסִיד הַמְּפוּרְסָם — **Approbation from the celebrated Rabbi and Chasid,** אִישׁ אֱלֹהִי קָדוֹשׁ יֵאָמֶר לוֹ — **a G-dly man, who** *"shall be called holy"* (*Isaiah* 4:3),** מוֹרֵנוּ וְרַבֵּנוּ הָרַב — **our guide, Rav and teacher,** רַבִּי יְהוּדָא לֵיב הַכֹּהֵן — Rabbi **Yehuda Leib,** *ha-kohen.*

חָכְמַת אָדָם תָּאִיר פְּנֵי הָאָרֶץ — *"A man's wisdom lights up the face"* (see *Ecclesiastes* 8:1) **of the earth,** בִּרְאוֹתִי יְדֵי קֹדֶשׁ הַמְחַבֵּר — **upon seeing the sacred work of the author's hands,** הָרַב הַגָּאוֹן אִישׁ אֱלֹקִים קָדוֹשׁ וְטָהוֹר — **the Rav, genius,** *"man of G-d"* (1 *Samuel* 2:27), **holy and pure,** חָסִיד וְעָנָיו — **pious and humble man,** אֲשֶׁר מִכְּבָר **whose hidden** greatness **has long been disclosed,** נִגְלָה מִסְתָּרָיו — **whose hidden** greatness **has long been disclosed,** יוֹשֵׁב בְּשֶׁבֶת תַּחְכְּמֹנִי אֵצֶל אֲדוֹנֵינוּ מוֹרֵינוּ וְרַבֵּינוּ גָּאוֹן עוֹלָם — **who** *"sat in the seat of wisdom"* (2 *Samuel* 23:8), **with our master, guide and teacher, the genius of the world, the**

בהגלות דברי קדשו המחובר להביא לבית הדפוס ללמד לעם
ה' דרכי קדש כאשר כל אחד יחזה בפנימיות דבריו והמפורסם
אין צריך ראיה רק מחשש קלקול הדבר שלא יגרום היזק
למדפיסים באתי ליתן תוקף ואזהרה לבל ירים איש את ידו
ורגלו לדפוס עד משך חמש שנים מיום דלמטה ושומע לדברי
אלה יבוא עליו ברכת טוב הכ"ד המדבר זאת לכבוד התורה
היום יום ג' פרשה תבא תקנ"ו לפ"ק. יהודא ליב הכהן.

Maggid of Mezritch, וְדָלָה מַיִם מִבְּאֵר מַיִם חַיִּים — and was his student, **drawing wa-ter from the "well of living water"** (*Genesis* 26:19).

וְכָעֵת יִשְׂמַח יִשְׂרָאֵל בְּהִגָּלוֹת דִּבְרֵי קָדְשׁוֹ — **And now "Israel will rejoice"** (*Psalms* 14:7), **with the public release of his holy words,** הַמְחוּבָּר לְהָבִיא לְבֵית הַדְּפוּס לְלַמֵּד לְעַם ה', דַּרְכֵי קֹדֶשׁ — **which have been compiled for publication, to guide G-d's people in the paths of holiness,** כַּאֲשֶׁר כָּל אֶחָד יֶחֱזֶה בִּפְנִימִיּוּת דְּבָרָיו — **as any person can see by looking at the inner content of his words.**

"Israel will rejoice" refers to the Jewish people, the *Tanya's* intended audience. But it is also an allusion to Israel *Ba'al Shem Tov,* whose teachings form the founda-tion of the *Tanya* (see *Likutei Sichos* vol. 2, p. 307).

וְהַמְפוּרְסָם אֵין צָרִיךְ רְאָיָה — **That which is public knowledge needs no** further **proof,** רַק מֵחֲשַׁשׁ קִלְקוּל הַדָּבָר שֶׁלֹּא יִגְרוֹם הֶיזֵק לַמַּדְפִּיסִים — **only out of concern for po-tential loss, so that no damages are inflicted on the publishers,** בָּאתִי לִיתֵּן תּוֹקֶף לְבַל יָרִים אִישׁ אֶת יָדוֹ וְרַגְלוֹ לִדְפוֹס וְאַזְהָרָה — **I hereby reinforce the legal warning,** — **that "no man shall raise his hand or his foot"** (*Genesis* 41:44) **to print** this book, עַד מֶשֶׁךְ חָמֵשׁ שָׁנִים מִיּוֹם דִּלְמַטָּה — **until five years from the date below.**

וְשׁוֹמֵעַ לִדְבָרַי אֵלֶּה יָבוֹא עָלָיו בְּרְכַּת טוֹב — **And he who listens to these words of mine will receive a blessing of goodness.**

הֲלֹא כֹּה דִּבְרֵי הַמְדַבֵּר זֹאת לִכְבוֹד הַתּוֹרָה — **These are the words of one who states this for the Torah's honor,** הַיּוֹם יוֹם ג' פְּרָשָׁה תָּבֹא תקנ"ו לִפְרָט קָטָן — **this Tuesday of the Torah portion** *Tavo,* **year 556 of the** sixth **millennium (1796).**

יְהוּדָא לֵיב הַכֹּהֵן — Rabbi **Yehuda Leib,** *ha-kohen.*

STATEMENT FROM THE AUTHOR'S SONS

20TH KISLEV LEAP

The *Tanya* was reprinted in seven different editions during Rabbi Shneur Zalman's lifetime, all without the author's name. Only in the 1814 Shklov edition, published after Rabbi Shneur Zalman's passing in 1812, did the author's name appear for the first time.

הסכמת הרבנים שי' בני הגאון המחבר ז"ל נ"ע.

היות שהוסכם אצלינו ליתן רשות והרמנא להעלות על מכבש
הדפוס לזכרון לבנ"י כתוב דברי יושר ואמת דברי אלקים חיים
של א"א מו"ר ז"ל כתובים בכתב ידו הקדושה בעצמו ולשונו
הקדוש שכל דבריו כגחלי אש בוערות ילהיבו הלבבות לקרבן
לאביהן שבשמים. ובשם אגרת הקדש נקראו שרובם היו אגרת
שלוח מאת כ"ק להורות לעם ה' הדרך ילכו בה והמעשה אשר
יעשון ומחמת שבכמה מקומות הציב לו ציונים בס' לקוטי

Another new feature in the 1814 Shklov edition was the inclusion of letters and writings of Rabbi Shneur Zalman that had some connection with the book's themes, (added as parts four and five of the *Tanya;* see above, p. 1). In order to formally authorize the inclusion of this material in the book, Rabbi Shneur Zalman's sons wrote the following statement of approval.

This statement was clearly different in character to the two Rabbinic approbations that appeared in the first edition, which represented the encouragement of Rabbi Shneur Zalman's senior colleagues to publish the book, based on the quality of its contents. In the following statement, Rabbi Shneur Zalman's sons were obviously not vouching for the quality of their father's work, but merely giving their formal consent to include additional materials in the *Tanya.*

הַסְכָּמַת הָרַבָּנִים שֶׁיִּחְיוּ בְּנֵי הַגָּאוֹן הַמְחַבֵּר זִכְרוֹנוֹ לִבְרָכָה נִשְׁמָתוֹ עֵדֶן — **Statement of approval from the Rabbis, may they be well, sons of the distinguished author, of blessed memory, whose soul is in heaven.**

הֱיוֹת שֶׁהוּסְכַּם אֶצְלֵינוּ לִיתֵּן רְשׁוּת וְהַרְמָנָא — **It has hereby been agreed upon by us to grant permission and authorization,** לְהַעֲלוֹת עַל מַכְבֵּשׁ הַדְּפוּס לְזִכָּרוֹן לִבְנֵי יִשְׂרָאֵל — **to submit for publication,** *"as a remembrance for sons of Israel"* (*Exodus* 39:7), כָּתוּב דִּבְרֵי יוֹשֶׁר וֶאֱמֶת — *"written upright words of truth"* (*Ecclesiastes* 12:10), דִּבְרֵי אֱלֹקִים חַיִּים — *"words of the living G-d"* (*Talmud, Eruvin* 13b), שֶׁל אֲדוֹנֵנוּ אָבִינוּ מוֹרֵנוּ וְרַבֵּנוּ זִכְרוֹנוֹ לִבְרָכָה — **of our master, our father, our guide, and our teacher, of blessed memory,** כְּתוּבִים בִּכְתָב יָדוֹ הַקְּדוֹשָׁה בְּעַצְמוֹ וּלְשׁוֹנוֹ הַקָּדוֹשׁ — **written in person, by his own sacred hand, in his own sacred words,** שֶׁכָּל דְּבָרָיו כְּגַחֲלֵי אֵשׁ בּוֹעֲרוֹת יַלְהִיבוּ הַלְבָבוֹת לְקָרְבָן לַאֲבִיהֶן שֶׁבַּשָּׁמַיִם — **whose every word** *"is like burning coals of fire"* (*Ezekiel* 1:13), **igniting their hearts to bring them closer to their Father in heaven.**

וּבְשֵׁם אִגֶּרֶת הַקֹּדֶשׁ נִקְרְאוּ — **These works have been added as an addendum to the *Tanya*, entitled *Sacred Letter* (*Igeres Ha-Kodesh*),** שֶׁרוּבָּם הָיוּ אִגֶּרֶת שָׁלוּחַ מֵאֵת — **most of which were pastoral letters sent by his holy eminence,** כְּבוֹד קְדֻשָּׁתוֹ — **our father,** לְהוֹרוֹת לְעַם ה' הַדֶּרֶךְ יֵלְכוּ בָהּ וְהַמַּעֲשֶׂה אֲשֶׁר יַעֲשׂוּן — **to guide G-d's people in** *"the path to follow and the things that they must do"* (*Exodus* 18:20).

אמרים שלו וד"ת עניים במקום אחד ועשירים במ"א ומה גם
בשביל דבר שנתחדש בו קונטרס אחרון על איזה פרקים אשר
כתב בעת חיברו הס' לק"א פלפול ועיון עמוק על מאמרי זהר
וע"ח ופע"ח שנראים כסותרים זא"ז וברוח מבינתו מישבם כל
דיבור על אופניו שכתב בלק"א ראו ראינו שראוי ונכון לחברם
עם ספר לקוטי אמרים ואגה"ת של כ"ק א"א מו"ר ז"ל. אי
לזאת באנו להטיל גודא רבה וגזרת נח"ש דרבנן דלית לה
אסוותא שלא ירים איש את ידו להדפיס כתבניתם או זה בלא
זה משך חמשה שנים מיום דלמטה ברם דא צריך לאודועי

וּמֵחֲמַת שֶׁבְּכַמָּה מְקוֹמוֹת הַצִּיב לוֹ צִיּוּנִים בְּסֵפֶר לְקוּטֵי אֲמָרִים שֶׁלּוֹ — **And** this text is also relevant as an addendum to the *Tanya* because **in many places he makes refer-ence to his book,** *Likutei Amarim,* the book of *Tanya,* וְדִבְרֵי תוֹרָה עֲנִיִּים בְּמָקוֹם אֶחָד וַעֲשִׁירִים בְּמָקוֹם אַחֵר — and *"the Torah speaks sparsely in one place, and richly in another"* (*Jerusalem Talmud, Rosh Ha-Shanah* 3:5) the author clarifies "more richly" in these letters some points which he had dealt with more "sparsely" in the *Tanya.*

וּמָה גַּם בְּשְׁבִיל דָּבָר שֶׁנִּתְחַדֵּשׁ בּוֹ — **And also** the addendum serves another purpose, **for fresh material that has been added,** קוּנְטְרֵס אַחֲרוֹן עַל אֵיזֶה פְּרָקִים — entitled *Final Tract* **(***Kuntres Acharon***), expanding** on some chapters in *Likutei Amarim,* אֲשֶׁר כָּתַב בְּעֵת חִיבְּרוֹ הַסֵּפֶר לְקוּטֵי אֲמָרִים — **which he wrote at the same time he was composing the book,** *Likutei Amarim,* פִּלְפּוּל וְעִיּוּן עָמוֹק עַל מַאֲמְרֵי זֹהַר וְעֵץ חַיִּים — offering **a profound and penetrating** וּפְרִי עֵץ חַיִּים שֶׁנִּרְאִים כְּסוֹתְרִים זֶה אֶת זֶה **analysis of various statements in the** *Zohar, Etz Chaim* **and** *Pri Etz Chaim,* **that seem to contradict each other,** וּבְרוּחַ מְבִינָתוֹ מִיַשְׁבָם כָּל דִּיבּוּר עַל אוֹפָנָיו — **and with his insightful mind, he resolves each** *"word in its own right way"* (*Proverbs* 25:11), שֶׁכָּתַב בְּלְקוּטֵי אֲמָרִים — following the system of thought **that he had presented in** *Likutei Amarim.*

רָאוֹ רָאִינוּ — *"We have clearly seen"* (*Genesis* 26:28), שֶׁרָאוּי וְנָכוֹן לְחַבְּרָם עִם **"We have clearly seen"** (Genesis 26:28), סֵפֶר לְקוּטֵי אֲמָרִים וְאִגֶּרֶת הַתְּשׁוּבָה — that it is appropriate and fitting that *Igeres Ha-Kodesh* and *Kuntres Acharon* **be appended to the book** *Likutei Amarim/Igeres Ha-Teshuvah,* שֶׁל כְּבוֹד קְדֻשַּׁת אֲדוֹנֵנוּ אָבִינוּ מוֹרֵנוּ וְרַבֵּנוּ זִכְרוֹנוֹ לִבְרָכָה — **of his holy eminence, our master, our father, our guide and our teacher, of blessed memory.**

אִי לְזֹאת בָּאנוּ לְהָטִיל גּוּדָא רַבָּה וּגְזֵרַת נִדּוּי חֵרֶם שַׁמְתָּא דְּרַבָּנָן דְּלֵית לָהּ אַסְוָותָא — **This** being the case, we hereby place a prohibition and decree, a non-repealable **Rabbinic ban, censure and excommunication,** שֶׁלֹּא יָרִים אִישׁ אֶת יָדוֹ לְהַדְפִּיס **that** *"no man shall raise his hand"* (*Genesis* 41:44), **to print** the book in כְּתַבְנִיתָם **this form** with the new addendum, אוֹ זֶה בְּלֹא זֶה — **or one without the other,** מֶשֶׁךְ חֲמִשָּׁה שָׁנִים מִיּוֹם דְּלְמַטָּה — **for five years from the date below.**

בְּרַם כְּגוֹן דָּא צָרִיךְ לְאוֹדוּעֵי — **But the following must be made known,** שֶׁבַּעֲוֹנוֹתֵינוּ הָרַבִּים סָפוּ תַמּוּ כְּתְבֵי יָדוֹ הַקְּדוֹשָׁה בְּעַצְמוֹ — that as a result of our many sins, many of

שבעו"ה ספו תמו כתבי ידו הקדושה בעצמו אשר היו בדקדוק
גדול לא חסר ולא יתר אות א' ולא נשאר כ"א זה המעט מהרבה
אשר נלקטו אחד לאחד מהעתקות המפוזרים אצל התלמידים
ואם המצא תמצא איזה טעות שגיאות מי יבין ימצא הטעות
דמוכח מטעות סופר והכוונה תהיה ברורה:

נאום דוב בער בא"א מו"ר הגאון החסיד קדוש ישראל מרנא
ורבנא שניאור זלמן ז"ל נבג"מ.

ונאום חיים אברהם בא"א מו"ר הגאון החסיד מרנא ורבנא
שניאור זלמן זצ"ל נבג"מ.

ונאום משה בא"א מו"ר הגאון החסיד שניאור זלמן ז"ל
נבג"מ.

אֲשֶׁר הָיוּ בְּדִקְדּוּק גָּדוֹל the manuscripts written by his own sacred hand are missing, לֹא חָסֵר וְלֹא יָתֵר אוֹת אַחַת — manuscripts that he wrote **with extreme precision, with** not *"one missing or extra letter"* (*Tur, Orach Chaim,* chapter 36), וְלֹא נִשְׁאַר כִּי אִם זֶה הַמְעַט מֵהַרְבֵּה — and all that remains are those few copies **of the many** original manuscripts, אֲשֶׁר נִלְקְטוּ אֶחָד לְאֶחָד מֵהַעְתָּקוֹת הַמְפוּזָרִים אֵצֶל הַתַּלְמִידִים — which have been painstakingly gathered from copies dispersed among the students.

וְאִם הִמָּצֵא תִמָּצֵא אֵיזֶה טָעוּת — And *"if there indeed should be found"* (*Exodus* 22:3) any error, שְׁגִיאוֹת מִי יָבִין — *"Who can discern errors?"* (*Psalms* 19:13), יִמָּצֵא הַטָּעוּת דְּמוּכָח מִטָּעוּת סוֹפֵר וְהַכַּוָּנָה תִּהְיֶה בְּרוּרָה — an unmistakable error can be taken as a scribe's mistake, but the meaning should be self-evident.

הַיּוֹם יוֹם ה' כ"ב אִיָּיר תקע"ד לִפְרָט קָטָן — Dated this Thursday, 22nd *Iyar*, 5574 (1814).

נְאוּם דּוֹב בֶּער — Declared by Dov Ber, בֶּן אֲדוֹנִי אָבִי מוֹרִי וְרַבִּי — son of my master, father, guide and teacher, הַגָּאוֹן הֶחָסִיד קְדוֹשׁ יִשְׂרָאֵל — the genius and Chasid, holy one of Israel, כְּבוֹד מָרָנָא וְרַבָּנָא שְׁנֵיאוֹר זַלְמָן — his honor, our master and our teacher Shneur Zalman, זִכְרוֹנוֹ לִבְרָכָה נִשְׁמָתוֹ בְּגִנְזֵי מְרוֹמִים — of blessed memory, whose soul rests in the hidden treasure-houses of heaven.

וּנְאוּם חַיִּים אַבְרָהָם — And declared by Chaim Avraham, בֶּן אֲדוֹנִי אָבִי מוֹרִי וְרַבִּי — son of my master, father, guide and teacher, הַגָּאוֹן הֶחָסִיד מָרָנָא וְרַבָּנָא שְׁנֵיאוֹר זַלְמָן — the genius and Chasid, our master and our teacher Shneur Zalman, זֵכֶר צַדִּיק לִבְרָכָה — may the memory of the righteous be a blessing, נִשְׁמָתוֹ בְּגִנְזֵי מְרוֹמִים — whose soul rests in the hidden treasure-houses of heaven.

וּנְאוּם מֹשֶׁה — And declared by Moshe, בֶּן אֲדוֹנִי אָבִי מוֹרִי וְרַבִּי — son of my master, father, guide and teacher, הַגָּאוֹן הֶחָסִיד מָרָנָא שְׁנֵיאוֹר זַלְמָן — the genius and Chasid, our master Shneur Zalman, זִכְרוֹנוֹ לִבְרָכָה נִשְׁמָתוֹ בְּגִנְזֵי מְרוֹמִים — of blessed memory, whose soul rests in the hidden treasure-houses of heaven.

הקדמת המלקט

והיא אגרת השלוחה לכללות אנשי שלומינו יצ"ו:

AUTHOR'S INTRODUCTION

SECTION ONE: CAN A BOOK BE YOUR PERSONAL MENTOR?

20TH KISLEV REGULAR | 21ST KISLEV LEAP

הַקְדָּמַת הַמְלַקֵּט — **Author's Introduction** to Part One, "*The Book of the Inbetweeners.*"

The distribution of the *Tanya*, first in manuscript and then in printed form, was intended to reduce the overwhelming flow of visitors to the author, Rabbi Shneur Zalman. Pressure had mounted on him to such an extent that in an emotionally charged pastoral letter penned to his followers in 1793, Rabbi Shneur Zalman wrote of *"the great bitterness with which my life is literally embittered"* from a seemingly endless stream of visitors who shared their sorrows with him. He lamented that, *"I am too weary to bear the mental distraction and lost worship resulting from my thinking over these matters deeply, in order to give a proper response"* (*Igros Kodesh Admor Ha-Zakein* (Brooklyn 2012), p. 113).

Stressing the gravity of the situation, Rabbi Shneur Zalman disclosed that, on occasion, these pressures had led him to contemplate abandoning his position entirely: *"And how many times do I truly despise my life at this level! Many times, I have decided in my heart to remove my dwelling from this country"* (*ibid.* p. 114).

In an attempt to alleviate these problems, Rabbi Shneur Zalman strictly limited the frequency with which his followers were permitted to visit him, and he distributed the *Tanya* as a kind of "replacement" for the personal meeting. In these pages, he distilled and compiled the spiritual advice which he had been offering visitors for many years.

Understandably, Rabbi Shneur Zalman's followers preferred the intimacy of an actual encounter with their spiritual master, and there was some resistance to replacing meetings with a written text. Was it even possible for a text to offer *personalized* advice for people's problems? In the "Author's Introduction" Rabbi Shneur Zalman addresses these concerns.

וְהִיא אִגֶּרֶת הַשְּׁלוּחָה לִכְלָלוּת אַנְשֵׁי שְׁלוֹמֵינוּ — The "Author's Introduction" **is**, in fact, **a pastoral letter that was sent** in 1795 **to the whole of our community,** יְבָרְכֶם צוּרֵנוּ וְיִשְׁמְרֵם — **may** G-d, **our Rock, bless them and protect them.**

As we have seen, Rabbi Shneur Zalman had distributed the *Tanya* in handwritten manuscript form as early as the summer of 1792. The following pastoral letter was penned to his followers in 1795, after the manuscripts had been widely distributed, to clarify how a written text might act as a replacement for a personal meeting.

אֲלֵיכֶם אִישִׁים אֶקְרָא שִׁמְעוּ אֵלַי רוֹדְפֵי צֶדֶק מְבַקְשֵׁי ה' וְיִשְׁמַע
אֲלֵיכֶם אֱלֹקִים לְמִגָּדוֹל וְעַד קָטָן כָּל אנ"ש דִּמְדִינָתֵינוּ
וּסְמוּכוֹת שֶׁלָּהּ אִישׁ עַל מְקוֹמוֹ יָבֹא לְשָׁלוֹם וְחַיִּים עַד הָעוֹלָם
נס"וּ אכי"ר:

הִנֵּה מוֹדַעַת זֹאת כִּי מַרְגְּלָא בְּפוּמֵי דְאֱינָשֵׁי בְּכָל אנ"ש לֵאמֹר כִּי
אֵינָהּ דּוֹמָה שְׁמִיעַת דִּבְרֵי מוּסָר לִרְאָיָּה וּקְרִיאָה בַּסְּפָרִים
שֶׁהַקּוֹרֵא קוֹרֵא לְפִי דַּרְכּוֹ וְדַעְתּוֹ וּלְפִי הַשָּׂגַת וּתְפִיסַת שִׂכְלוֹ

When the *Tanya* was submitted for publication a year later, the author chose to include this letter as an introduction to the work. (There were, however, some modifications for the printed edition, as we shall see below.)

שִׁמְעוּ אֵלַי רוֹדְפֵי צֶדֶק — *"To you, O men, I call"* (*Proverbs* 8:4), אֲלֵיכֶם אִישִׁים אֶקְרָא — *"Listen to me, you who pursue righteousness and who seek G-d"* מְבַקְשֵׁי ה' — *"And G-d will listen to you"* (*Judges* 9:7), וְיִשְׁמַע אֲלֵיכֶם אֱלֹקִים — (*Isaiah* 51:1), *"from the greatest to the smallest"* (*Esther* 1:5), כָּל אַנְשֵׁי שְׁלוֹמֵנוּ — לְמִגָּדוֹל וְעַד קָטָן — all members of our community, in our land and its en-דִּמְדִינָתֵינוּ וּסְמוּכוֹת שֶׁלָּהּ — virons, אִישׁ עַל מְקוֹמוֹ יָבֹא לְשָׁלוֹם — each of whom *"shall go to their place in peace"* (see *Exodus* 18:23), וְחַיִּים עַד הָעוֹלָם — with *"the blessing of everlasting life"* (*Psalms* 133:3), נֶצַח סֶלָה וָעֶד — *"forever and ever, selah"* (*Liturgy,* Blessings before *Shema*), אָמֵן כֵּן יְהִי רָצוֹן — Amen, may it be G-d's will.

After this formal introduction, typical at the opening of a pastoral letter, Rabbi Shneur Zalman turns immediately to the community's concern: Can a spiritual manual replace a personal meeting?

כִּי מַרְגְּלָא בְּפוּמֵי דְאֱינָשֵׁי הִנֵּה מוֹדַעַת זֹאת — Now, *"this thing is known"* (*Isaiah* 12:5), בְּכָל אַנְשֵׁי שְׁלוֹמֵנוּ לֵאמֹר — that throughout our community, it's common for people to say, כִּי אֵינָהּ דּוֹמָה שְׁמִיעַת דִּבְרֵי מוּסָר לִרְאָיָּה וּקְרִיאָה בַּסְּפָרִים — that you can't compare hearing spiritual guidance from a living teacher, in flesh and blood **to seeing and reading it in books.**

Before stating his view that a book *can* sometimes be an effective source for personal spiritual mentorship, Rabbi Shneur Zalman will first spend some time validating the community's concern that it cannot.

שֶׁהַקּוֹרֵא קוֹרֵא לְפִי דַּרְכּוֹ וְדַעְתּוֹ — The reason why, generally speaking, a book cannot provide personal, spiritual guidance is because **the reader** of a book inevitably **reads subjectively, through** the lens of **his own understanding,** וּלְפִי הַשָּׂגַת וּתְפִיסַת שִׂכְלוֹ בַּאֲשֶׁר הוּא שָׁם — and according to the ability and grasp of his mind, *"at the place where he is found"* (*Genesis* 21:17), and that subjectivity or limited comprehension might prevent him from absorbing the author's intended message.

Another concern is that, besides plain misinterpretation, the reader's own spiritual standing might be so low that he is incapable of applying the teachings found in a spiritual manual to his life situation.

באשר הוא שם ואם שכלו ודעתו מבולבלים ובחשיכה יתהלכו
בעבודת ה' בקושי יכול לראות את האור כי טוב הגנוז
בספרים אף כי מתוק האור לעינים ומרפא לנפש ובר מן דין
הנה ספרי היראה הבנויים ע"פ שכל אנושי בודאי אינן שוין
לכל נפש כי אין כל השכלים והדעות שוות ואין שכל אדם
זה מתפעל ומתעורר ממה שמתפעל שכל חבירו וכמו שארז"ל
גבי ברכת חכם הרזים על ששים ריבוא מישראל שאין

וְאָם שְׂכְלוֹ וְדַעְתּוֹ מְבוּלְבָּלִים — **And if** the reader's **mind and opinions are confused,** וּבַחֲשֵׁיכָה יִתְהַלְכוּ בַּעֲבוֹדַת ה' — **and, when it comes to worship of G-d,** *"he wanders about in darkness"* (*Psalms* 82:5), בְּקוֹשִׁי יָכוֹל לִרְאוֹת אֶת הָאוֹר כִּי טוֹב הַגָּנוּז בַּסְּפָרִים — **then only with difficulty will he** *"see the light that's good"* (see *Genesis* 1:4), **that's hidden in the sacred books,** אַף כִּי מָתוֹק הָאוֹר לָעֵינַיִם וּמַרְפֵּא לַנָּפֶשׁ — **even though** the content of these sacred book is *"sweet light to the eyes"* (*Ecclesiastes* 11:7), **and healing for the soul.**

Even a well-crafted spiritual manual won't be helpful to a person who's not in a fit state to appreciate its message. The book may be *"sweet light to the eyes,"* but if you are *"wandering in the darkness"* you will miss its inspirational message.

But even for those readers who *are* sufficiently competent to make use of a spiritual self-help manual, another more theoretical concern needs to be addressed. Is it really possible to write a one-size-fits-all spiritual manual for general consumption?

וּבַר מִן דֵּין הִנֵּה סִפְרֵי הַיִרְאָה הַבְּנוּיִים עַל פִּי שֵׂכֶל אֱנוֹשִׁי — **And besides this concern, when texts of religious inspiration are based on human reasoning** by a single author, בְּוַדַּאי אֵינָן שָׁוִין לְכָל נֶפֶשׁ כִּי אֵין כָּל הַשְׂכָלִים וְהַדֵּעוֹת שָׁווֹת — **they certainly won't have a universal appeal, because the minds and attitudes** of readers **aren't alike,** וְאֵין שֵׂכֶל אָדָם זֶה מִתְפָּעֵל וּמִתְעוֹרֵר מִמַּה שֶׁמִּתְפָּעֵל וּמִתְעוֹרֵר שֵׂכֶל חֲבֵירוֹ — **and what inspires or stimulates one mind won't inspire or stimulate another.**

At a personal meeting, the mentor can tailor his advice to the particular *"mind and attitude"* of a student. But how could a book reliably address the vast spectrum of individual needs present in a large readership?

To strengthen this question, the *Tanya* cites sources which prove that *"the minds and opinions (of readers) aren't alike."*

וּכְמוֹ שֶׁאָמְרוּ רַבּוֹתֵינוּ זִכְרוֹנָם לִבְרָכָה גַּבֵּי בְּרְכַּת חֲכַם הָרָזִים עַל שְׁשִׁים רִיבּוֹא מִיּשְׂרָאֵל — **As our Sages of blessed memory taught in connection with the blessing** that Jewish law instructs us to **recite upon seeing** a large crowd of **six hundred thousand of Israel,** *"Blessed is He who is wise in knowing secrets,"* meaning that G-d alone knows the hidden thoughts of all these different people, שֶׁאֵין דֵּעוֹתֵיהֶם דּוֹמוֹת זוֹ — *"since their attitudes are not the same,* just as their faces are not the same" (*Talmud, Brachos* 58a).

The *Talmud* clearly validates the notion that: 1) A vast intellectual diversity is pres-

דעותיהם דומות זו לזו וכו' וכמ"ש הרמב"ן ז"ל במלחמות שם
בפירוש הספרי גבי יהושע שנאמר בו איש אשר רוח בו שיכול
להלוך נגד רוחו של כל אחד ואחד וכו'. אלא אפילו בספרי

ent in a large group; 2) G-d alone (and not a book founded on human intellect) can penetrate the minds and hearts of such a diversified group.

וּכְמוֹ שֶׁכָּתַב הָרַמְבַּ"ן זִכְרוֹנוֹ לִבְרָכָה בְּמִלְחָמוֹת שָׁם — **And, as Nachmanides, of blessed memory, wrote in his commentary,** *Milchamos Hashem, ibid.,* where he offered further insight into this matter.

In his commentary, Nachmanides refers to a passage in a subsequent discussion in the *Talmud* (on the next page, 58b):

"Rav Pappa and Rav Huna, son of Rabbi Joshua, were going along the way, when they met Rav Chanina, son of Rav Ika... He said to them, 'Seeing you is like seeing six hundred thousand of Israel, so I will recite... "Blessed is He Who is wise in knowing secrets.""

Why did Rav Chanina consider seeing other Jewish sages *"like seeing six hundred thousand of Israel"?*

בְּפֵירוּשׁ הַסִּפְרִי גַּבֵּי יְהוֹשֻׁעַ — Nachmanides explains this by citing and **explaining** *Sifri's* **comment about Joshua,** שֶׁנֶּאֱמַר בּוֹ אִישׁ אֲשֶׁר רוּחַ בּוֹ — **who was described by** Scripture as *"a man who has spirit within him"* (*Numbers* 27:18).

Clearly, *every* living person *"has spirit within him,"* so in praising Joshua as *"a man who has spirit within him,"* what particular quality was Scripture referring to?

שֶׁיָּכוֹל לַהֲלוֹךְ נֶגֶד רוּחוֹ שֶׁל כָּל אֶחָד וְאֶחָד וְכוּ' — *Sifri* answers that the verse refers to a rare talent, *i.e.,* that Joshua *"could accommodate himself to the spirit of each individual"* (*Sifri, Numbers,* section 140), and this was due to the spirit of G-d within him (Nachmanides).

According to Nachmanides, Rav Chanina considered seeing Rav Pappa and Rav Huna *"like seeing six hundred thousand of Israel"* because Rav Chanina deemed these Sages as able to *"accommodate the spirit of each individual."* They could intuit the emotional needs and intellectual biases of any person, offering advice accordingly.

Obviously, this is something possible only in person, not in a book.

SECTION TWO: WHY A SPIRITUAL MENTOR IS NECESSARY

The above discussion, which pointed to the limits of a book in providing personalized guidance, related to "texts of religious inspiration based on *human reasoning.*"

But what if a book limited itself entirely to the *received wisdom* of Torah texts? Wouldn't teachings received through Divine inspiration transcend the human limitation of having a particular audience?

הֵירָאֶה אֲשֶׁר יְסוֹדוֹתָם בְּהַרְרֵי קוֹדֶשׁ מִדְרְשֵׁי חֲזַ"ל אֲשֶׁר רוּחַ ה'
דִּבֶּר בָּם וּמִלָּתוֹ עַל לְשׁוֹנָם וְאוֹרַיְתָא וְקוּדְשָׁא בְּרִיךְ הוּא כּוֹלָא חַד וְכָל
שִׁשִּׁים רִבּוֹא כְּלָלוּת יִשְׂרָאֵל וּפְרָטֵיהֶם עַד נִיצוֹץ קַל שֶׁבַּקַּלִּים
וּפְחוּתֵי הָעֵרֶךְ שֶׁבְּעַמֵּינוּ בְּנֵי יִשְׂרָאֵל כּוּלְּהוּ מִתְקַשְׁרָאן בְּאוֹרַיְתָא
וְאוֹרַיְתָא הִיא הַמְּקַשֶּׁרֶת אוֹתָן לְהַקָּבָּ"ה כַּנּוֹדָע בַּזֹהַ"ק הֲרֵי זֶה

אֶלָּא אֲפִילוּ בְּסִפְרֵי הַיִּרְאָה אֲשֶׁר יְסוֹדוֹתָם בְּהַרְרֵי קוֹדֶשׁ — **But even with texts of religious inspiration** that *"have their foundations in the holy peaks"* (see *Psalms* 87:1), מִדְרְשֵׁי חֲכָמֵינוּ זִכְרוֹנָם לִבְרָכָה — *i.e.,* they are based on **the teachings of our Sages of blessed memory,** אֲשֶׁר רוּחַ ה' דִּבֶּר בָּם וּמִלָּתוֹ עַל לְשׁוֹנָם — **to whom higher insight was revealed** since *"the spirit of G-d spoke through them; His word was on their tongue"* (see 2 *Samuel* 23:2; *Talmud, Sanhedrin* 99a), וְאוֹרַיְתָא וְקוּדְשָׁא בְּרִיךְ הוּא כּוֹלָא חַד — **and** *"the Torah* (of the Sages) *and G-d are totally one"* (see *Zohar* 1, 24a; 2, 60a; see pp. 71, 262), so you might have thought these texts could speak to every person regardless of background, nevertheless, even these Divinely inspired texts do not seem to rule out the need for personal mentorship, as we shall see.

Before addressing the pitfalls, the *Tanya* will first dwell upon the deep relevancy of Torah texts to our souls, from a Kabbalistic perspective.

וְכָל שִׁשִּׁים רִבּוֹא נִשְׁמוֹת כְּלָלוּת יִשְׂרָאֵל וּפְרָטֵיהֶם וּפְרָטֵי פְּרָטֵיהֶם — **And all six hundred thousand soul-roots in Israel, their divisions and subdivisions** into millions of souls throughout history, are deeply bound with the Torah.

The census of Jews in the Sinai Desert totaled around six hundred thousand individuals (*Numbers* 1:46). According to the Kabbalah, this hints to a mystical reality that G-d formed six hundred thousand basic "soul units" within Israel, and each individual soul is a "spark" or "subdivision" from one of these core six hundred thousand units (see Rabbi Chaim Vital, *Sha'ar Ha-Gilgulim,* chapter 17).

The *Tanya* dismisses the notion that the Torah is connected only with the *general energy* of the Jewish souls, and not to each individual soul "spark" *in particular.* If the Torah were only connected to the souls in general, we would understand why some particular souls might struggle to implement certain Torah ideas. But, if *"all the six hundred thousand soul-roots in Israel, their divisions and subdivisions"* are deeply bound with the Torah, surely all its teachings should speak directly to every single one of our souls? If this is the case, why can't a spiritual manual be written, based on Torah teachings, that would have a universal appeal?

עַד נִיצוֹץ קַל שֶׁבַּקַּלִּים וּפְחוּתֵי הָעֵרֶךְ שֶׁבְּעַמֵּינוּ בְּנֵי יִשְׂרָאֵל — **This** intimate bond between the souls of Israel and the Torah is true **down to the** soul-spark within the **most irreverent and ignoble of our people, the children of Israel,** כּוּלְּהוּ מִתְקַשְׁרָאן בְּאוֹרַיְתָא — **they are all deeply connected to the Torah,** וְאוֹרַיְתָא הִיא הַמְּקַשֶּׁרֶת אוֹתָן — **and the Torah connects them deeply with** G-d, **the Blessed Holy One,** לְהַקָּדוֹשׁ בָּרוּךְ הוּא — כַּנּוֹדָע בַּזֹהַר הַקָּדוֹשׁ — **as we know from the sacred** *Zohar* (3, 73b).

The *Zohar* (ibid.) teaches, *"Three levels are tied with one another, the Blessed

דרך כללות לכללות ישראל ואף שניתנה התורה לידרש בכלל
ופרט ופרטי פרטות לכל נפש פרטית מישראל המושרשת בה

Holy One, the Torah and Israel." We all, without exception, have a deep soul connection with the Torah, whatever our current spiritual standing may be.

If this is the case, shouldn't "inspirational texts" based on Torah teachings speak
to us all personally and intimately?

The *Tanya* will now demonstrate a pitfall in this logic.

הֲרֵי זֶה דֶּרֶךְ כְּלָלוּת לִכְלָלוּת יִשְׂרָאֵל — **But this** connection of all souls to G-d, via the
Torah, **is only** a connection to the Torah's *general principles* of spiritual guidance
aimed at **the Jewish people** *as a whole.*

The Torah, as it has been transmitted to us, doesn't articulate an individualized
path of spiritual guidance for every person's unique temperament. To be sure, every Torah teaching contains incredible wisdom relevant to us all; but, the Torah's
personalized message of spiritual guidance *for each soul* is not explicitly stated —
that message needs to be "teased out" from the texts, on an individual basis.

(We are not speaking here of the Torah's legal (*halachic*) directives, which are
binding on all Israel and have been clarified in precise detail. "Torah" in the context
of this discussion refers to the spiritual guidance implicit in the wisdom of Scripture,
Talmud and *Midrash* (as well as Kabbalistic works), that relates to our inner lives and
personal struggles.)

And that's why even "inspirational texts based on Torah teachings" require mentorship from a teacher who knows you personally. The teachings need to be applied by an expert to your unique set of intellectual and emotional needs.

SECTION THREE: WHY YOU CAN'T DO IT ON YOUR OWN

Still you might ask: Why can't I take "inspirational texts based on Torah teachings"
and interpret their special message to me *on my own*? Why is a mentor necessary?

The *Tanya* will answer that, in principle, such an approach makes a lot of sense,
but practically speaking, it's unlikely to work.

וְאַף שֶׁנִּיתְנָה הַתּוֹרָה לִידָּרֵשׁ בִּכְלָל וּפְרָט וּפְרָטֵי פְּרָטוּת — **And even though the Torah
was given** not as a closed text, but one that was intended **to be expounded by
general rules** that lead to **specific applications, in extreme detail** — which means
that the Torah's personal message to your soul could, in principle, be "teased out"
from the texts by you — nevertheless, as we shall see, there is no fool-proof method
of doing this.

The Torah is an "open canon." As individuals in each successive generation offer
novel interpretations of the classical texts, those new interpretations are also hal-
lowed as "Torah" (provided that they are consistent with existing Torah principles).

הרי אין כל אדם זוכה להיות מכיר מקומו הפרטי שבתורה:
והנה אף בהלכות איסור והיתר הנגלות לנו ולבנינו מצאנו ראינו
מחלוקת תנאים ואמוראים מן הקצה אל הקצה ממש ואלו

The Torah is constantly expanding in content, with progressively more clarification and insight.

How could all these new interpretations be considered as genuine Torah? The Sages explained: *"Every new insight that a veteran scholar was destined to introduce was already given to Moshe at Sinai"* (see *Talmud, Megilah* 19b). What they meant was, "You might think that this is your original insight, but your soul is, in fact, echoing a pre-existing Torah energy which has never been precisely articulated."

לְכָל נֶפֶשׁ פְּרָטִית מִיִּשְׂרָאֵל הַמוּשְׁרֶשֶׁת בָּה — And, according to the Kabbalah, the reason why **each individual soul in Israel** is able to "expound" and "tease out" original Torah readings is because each soul actually **has its roots in** the Torah energy of its own future reading.

The energy of the "new" Torah reading that you introduced for the first time actually predated you, in the Torah's fountain of energy disclosed at Mount Sinai. The reason why you were empowered to creatively suggest this fresh reading is because your soul is "rooted" in a particular "nugget" of Torah energy, corresponding to that reading.

Based on this reasoning, it would seem that you are *uniquely positioned* to expound the Torah's personalized message to your own life. While that message was not stated explicitly in the existing texts, your soul is actually empowered to "tease out" that message more than anyone else who has ever lived! Armed with Torah texts to interpret, you ought to be the best guide possible to your own inner life.

While in theory all this may be true, the *Tanya* now laments the sobering reality that it probably won't happen.

הֲרֵי אֵין כָּל אָדָם זוֹכֶה לִהְיוֹת מַכִּיר מְקוֹמוֹ הַפְּרָטִי שֶׁבַּתּוֹרָה — **Nevertheless, not every person merits to identify his own unique "location" in the Torah** and "tease out" the Torah's personalized message to him or her.

In an ideal world you would easily recognize the Torah's personalized message to you; it's certainly within the capabilities of your soul. But even if you had all the textual skills and background knowledge necessary, the notion of being your own mentor is fraught with difficulty. On a practical level, the *Tanya* warns us that it is simply unlikely to be effective.

To further illustrate the complexities of Torah interpretation, the *Tanya* will bring an example from the case of Jewish legal texts.

וְהִנֵּה אַף בְּהִלְכוֹת אִיסּוּר וְהֵיתֵּר — **Now, even in the case of the legal discussions concerning what is permissible and forbidden,** the discussion of universally binding, practical activities, הַנִּגְלוֹת לָנוּ וּלְבָנֵינוּ — matters which do not concern the complex

ואלו דברי אלהים חיים לשון רבים על שם מקור החיים

לנשמות ישראל הנחלקות דרך כלל לשלשה קוין ימין ושמאל

4A   ואמצע שהם חסד וגבורה וכו' ונשמות ששרשן ממדת חסד

and subjective inner life of man, but rather, external and objective acts that are **"re-vealed to us and our children"** (*Deuteronomy* 29:28), מְצָאנוּ רָאִינוּ מַחֲלוֹקֶת תַּנָּאִים, וְאָמוֹרָאִים מִן הַקָּצֶה אֶל הַקָּצֶה מַמָּשׁ — even in this case, **"we have found, we have seen"** (*Lamentations* 2:16), **that the earlier and later Sages expressed differences of opinion, literally from one extreme to another.**

If a state of confusion exists even in matters of the external/objective (law), then how can you possibly expect to have clarity when trying to derive inner/subjective lessons of spiritual guidance?

Before continuing to make this point, the *Tanya* first notes that the difference of opinion among the Sages was not a matter of intellectual bias, but resulted from the spiritual temperament ingrained in their souls.

וְאֵלוּ וָאֵלוּ דִּבְרֵי אֱלֹהִים חַיִּים — **And** we are taught that even contradictory views expressed by the Talmudic sages are true and authentic, **"both of them are words of the living G-d (Elokim chaim)"** (*Talmud*, *Eruvin* 13b).

How could contradictory positions both be true? This issue has been discussed at length in Jewish traditional texts (for a discussion and analysis of various approaches see: Rabbi Chaim Miller, *Rambam: Principles of Faith, Principles 8-9* (2007), pp. 107-142). Here the *Tanya* will offer an answer based on Kabbalah.

לְשׁוֹן רַבִּים עַל שֵׁם מְקוֹר הַחַיִּים לְנַשְׁמוֹת יִשְׂרָאֵל — Note that in this citation from the *Talmud*, the words *Elokim* ("G-d") and *chaim* ("living") **are stated in the plural, to suggest** that the diversity of opinions among the Sages stems from plurality of different energies in the "fountain" of Divine emanation, in **the living source of the souls of Israel.**

The Kabbalists understood that Rabbinic controversy is rooted in the very structure of revelation, as Rabbi Shlomo Luria (16th century) explains:

"The Kabbalists explained that the basis for this is that all the souls were present at Sinai and received [the Torah] by means of the forty-nine spiritual 'channels'.... Each one perceived the Torah through his own channel and in accordance with his own intellectual capacity.... Therefore, being that all the words of the Sages are true, they are said to be 'words of the living G-d,' even when they contradict one another" (*Maharshal*, author's introduction to *Yam Shel Shlomo, Bava Kama*).

The *Tanya* now clarifies that the many different "channels" through which the Torah was received by the Sages' souls, can be divided into three general "paths."

הַנֶּחְלָקוֹת דֶּרֶךְ כְּלָל לִשְׁלֹשָׁה קַוִּין יָמִין וּשְׂמֹאל וְאֶמְצַע שֶׁהֵם חֶסֶד וּגְבוּרָה וְכוּ' — This spiritual source is **split**, generally speaking, **into three paths: 1) "right," 2)"left" and 3) "center," representing** 1) **generosity (chesed)**, 2) **discipline (gevurah)**, and 3) their

הנהגתן גם כן להטות כלפי חסד להקל כו' כנודע וכ"ש וק"ו
בהנסתרות לה' אלהינו דאינון דחילו ורחימו דבמוחא ולבא דכל
חד וחד לפום שיעורא דיליה לפום מה דמשער בליביה כמ"ש
בזה"ק על פסוק נודע בשערים בעלה וגו':

אך ביודעיי ומכיריי קאמינא הם כל אחד ואחד מאנ"ש
שבמדינותינו וסמוכות שלה אשר היה הדבור של חיבה

וּנְשָׁמוֹת שֶׁשָּׁרְשָׁן מִמִּדַּת חֶסֶד הַנְהָגָתָן גַּם כֵּן לְהַטּוֹת כְּלַפֵּי harmonization, respectively, חֶסֶד לְהָקֵל כו' — **where the souls rooted in the attribute of** *chesed* **subliminally tended to be lenient in their legal decisions, being inclined toward generosity, and the souls rooted in** *gevurah***, subliminally tended to be more strict,** כַּנּוֹדָע — **as is known** from the *Zohar* (3, 245a).

וְכָל שֶׁכֵּן וְקַל וָחֹמֶר בְּהַנִּסְתָּרוֹת לַה' אֱלֹהֵינוּ — So, **if there are inherent complexities in interpreting practical, legal texts, then, how much more so will there be far greater complexities in** the interpretation of *"the hidden things, that are for G-d, our G-d"* (*Deuteronomy* ibid.), דְּאִינּוּן דְּחִילוּ וּרְחִימוּ דְּבְמוֹחָא וְלִבָּא — **namely,** a person's inner world of **reverence and love** of G-d, **in the brain and heart** (see *Zohar* 3, 123b), דְּכָל חַד וְחַד לְפוּם שִׁיעוּרָא דִילֵיהּ — *"each individual according to his own capabilities,"* לְפוּם מַה דְּמְשַׁעַר בְּלִבֵּיהּ כְּמוֹ שֶׁכָּתוּב בַּזֹּהַר הַקָּדוֹשׁ — *"according to the scope of his heart etc.,"* **as stated in the holy** *Zohar* (1:103a), עַל פָּסוּק נוֹדָע בַּשְׁעָרִים בַּעְלָהּ וְגו' — **in its commentary on the verse,** *"Her husband is known in the gates"* (*Proverbs* 31:23; cited in chapter 44, p. 564).

In conclusion: It would be unwise for a person to attempt to "tease out" personalized Torah guidance for his or her own inner life, due to the immense difficulties and complexities that the task imposes.

SECTION FOUR: THE AUTHOR'S REPSONSE

21ST KISLEV REGULAR | 22ND KISLEV LEAP

Rabbi Shneur Zalman has delivered a lengthy and scholarly validation of his community's concern that *"you can't compare hearing spiritual guidance (from a living teacher, in flesh and blood) to reading it in books."* A person's inner, spiritual life is too unique, it would seem, to be dealt with effectively in a book for general consumption.

Why, then, did the author write the *Tanya*? He seems to have proved unequivocally that a book can't fulfill the required task of spiritual counseling!

Rabbi Shneur Zalman responds:

אַךְ בְּיוֹדְעַיי וּמַכִּירַיי קָאָמִינָא — **But** *"I am speaking to those who know me and recognize me"* (see *Talmud, Megillah* 15a), הֵם כָּל אֶחָד וְאֶחָד מֵאַנְשֵׁי שְׁלוֹמֵנוּ — **to every single person in our community,** שֶׁבִּמְדִינָתֵינוּ וְסָמוּכוֹת שֶׁלָּהּ — **found in this country**

מצוי בינינו וגילו לפני כל תעלומות לבם ומוחם בעבודת ה'
התלויה בלב אליהם תטוף מלתי ולשוני עט סופר בקונטריסים

and its environs, בֵּינֵינוּ מָצוּי חִיבָּה שֶׁל הַדִּבּוּר הָיָה אֲשֶׁר — **since there have** already
been intimate conversations between us in private meetings, תַּעֲלוּמוֹת כָּל לְפָנַי וְגִילוּ
וּמוֹחָם לִבָּם — **and you have revealed to me everything in the depths of your hearts
and minds,** בַּלֵּב הַתְּלוּיָה ה' בַּעֲבוֹדַת — **connected with the worship of G-d, which depends on the heart,** מִלָּתִי תִּטּוֹף אֲלֵיהֶם — **to you** *"my speech streams"* (*Job* 29:22),
סוֹפֵר עֵט וּלְשׁוֹנִי — **and** *"my tongue is like the pen of a scribe"* (*Psalms* 45:2).

The advice of the *Tanya* was not written in a vacuum and did not result merely
from detached, theoretical speculation; it was the cumulation of advice delivered
by the author in practical counseling sessions with his disciples for over a decade.
Rabbi Shneur Zalman had witnessed the same issues arise repeatedly and, based
on the wisdom of his teachers and classical Jewish texts, he had developed a system that was effective for his audience. The format of a book might normally tend
to be aloof and impersonal, but when a book is written by someone you know and
is based on discussions that have already taken place, the communication gap is
significantly bridged.

The *Tanya* was written for disciples whom Rabbi Shneur Zalman knew intimately; they had already *"revealed to me everything in the depths of their hearts and
minds."* That is why the author could confidently offer them advice in written form
that would be acutely relevant to their inner struggles.

However, after it was first published in 1796, the *Tanya* rapidly outgrew its initial core audience. Of the sixty-eight Chasidic books that were published from the
movement's beginnings until the end of 1815, the *Tanya* was reprinted the most
(eleven times). Today, over two hundred years after its initial publication, the *Tanya*
is studied by tens of thousands across the globe — readers who live very different
lives than the *Tanya's* 19th century audiences. It appears that the author achieved
the very feat which he argued could not be done: to write a one-size-fits-all spiritual
manual for a very broad readership, regardless of time and place! In fact, the *Tanya*
has enjoyed such universal appeal that it has been coined the "Bible" (*Torah Shebiksav*) of Chasidic thought.

How has the *Tanya* appealed so strongly to those who do not "know and recognize" the author, a relationship which this introduction stresses as so important?

What we can sense from all of the above discussion is that Rabbi Shneur Zalman
was acutely aware of the detached nature of a book, and he strove to overcome
it. He understood that the personal views of a single author ("texts based on human reasoning") would have limited appeal; even the received wisdom of classical
Jewish texts needed a very practical articulation to shift the hearts and minds of
ordinary people. Over the course of decades of personal counseling, he incubated
the ideas which would eventually become the *Tanya*, carefully testing their effec-
tiveness. In these "intimate conversations" with both scholars and working people
of average learning, Rabbi Shneur Zalman developed a deep understanding of hu-

אֵלוּ הַנִּקְרָאִים בְּשֵׁם לִקּוּטֵי אֲמָרִים מְלוּקָּטִים מִפִּי סְפָרִים וּמִפִּי
סוֹפְרִים קְדוֹשֵׁי עֶלְיוֹן נִשְׁמָתָם עֵדֶן הַמְפוּרְסָמִים אֶצְלֵינוּ וְקָצָת
מֵהֶם נִרְמָזִין לְחַכִּימִין בְּאִגְּרוֹת הַקֹּדֶשׁ מֵרַבּוֹתֵינוּ שֶׁבְּאֶרֶץ הַקֹּדֶשׁ
תִּבָּנֶה וְתִכּוֹנֵן. וְקָצָתָם שָׁמַעְתִּי מִפִּיהֶם הַקָּדוֹשׁ בִּהְיוֹתָם פֹּה עִמָּנוּ

man nature, of people who wanted to be good, but were all too often swayed by their inner demons. This enabled him to construct an effective and powerful bridge between the esoteric, Chasidic wisdom he had received from his masters and the harsh realities of everyday life.

While he lived a long time ago, in a place far away, through reading this book you will develop your own "intimate conversation" with the author. Perhaps, like so many whose lives have been transformed by the *Tanya*, you will come to "know and recognize" Rabbi Shneur Zalman as a personal mentor of your own.

בְּקוּנְטְרֵיסִים אֵלּוּ הַנִּקְרָאִים בְּשֵׁם לִקּוּטֵי אֲמָרִים — I speak to you **in these pamphlets which have been called by the name,** *An Anthology of Teachings* (*Likutei Amarim*).

Recall that this "Author's Introduction," is, in fact, a letter circulated to the Chasidic community prior to the publication of the *Tanya* as a printed book. At that time, the text had been made available to the community in manuscript form, in a series of pamphlets.

The fact that the *Tanya* is essentially a collection of pamphlets explains why it lacks an overarching, formal structure. But that also means that you don't necessarily have to read the book in order. You can pick a section which relates to the spiritual struggle that concerns you at any given moment, since, in any case, that piece might have appeared as a separate "pamphlet" in its own right.

In the "Author's Title Page," Rabbi Shneur Zalman already made a vague reference to the sources on which the *Tanya* was based. He returns to the subject here, in slightly more detail.

מְלוּקָּטִים מִפִּי סְפָרִים — **This book** **anthologized from** various **texts,** וּמִפִּי סוֹפְרִים קְדוֹשֵׁי עֶלְיוֹן נִשְׁמָתָם עֵדֶן — **and from** various **teachers of exceptional holiness, whose souls are in heaven,** הַמְפוּרְסָמִים אֶצְלֵינוּ — **who are well known to us.**

The *Tanya* was originally published without the name of the author, which explains why Rabbi Shneur Zalman is intentionally vague about his sources (see p. 2). He suffices to say that his teachers are "well known to us."

וְקָצָת מֵהֶם נִרְמָזִין לְחַכִּימִין — **And a few of these** teachings are *"alluded to, for the wise"* (*Midrash Proverbs* 22:8), בְּאִגְּרוֹת הַקֹּדֶשׁ מֵרַבּוֹתֵינוּ שֶׁבְּאֶרֶץ הַקֹּדֶשׁ — **in the sacred letters from our Rabbis in the Holy Land,** תִּבָּנֶה וְתִכּוֹנֵן בִּמְהֵרָה בְּיָמֵינוּ אָמֵן — *"may it stand built"* (*Numbers* 21:27), **speedily in our days, Amen.**

וְקָצָתָם שָׁמַעְתִּי מִפִּיהֶם הַקָּדוֹשׁ — **And a few of** the teachings **I heard from their holy mouths,** בִּהְיוֹתָם פֹּה עִמָּנוּ — **while they were here with us,** before departing for the holy land.

וכולם הן תשובות על שאלות רבות אשר שואלין בעצה כל
אנ"ש דמדינתינו תמיד כל אחד לפי ערכו לשית עצות בנפשם
בעבודת ה' להיות כי אין הזמן גרמא עוד להשיב לכל אחד
ואחד על שאלתו בפרטות וגם השכחה מצויה על כן רשמתי
כל התשובות על כל השאלות למשמרת לאות להיות לכל אחד
וא' לזכרון בין עיניו ולא ידחוק עוד ליכנס לדבר עמי ביחידות

The author refers here to the teachings of his senior colleagues, Rabbi Menachem Mendel of Vitebsk (1730?-1788) and Rabbi Avraham Katz of Kalisk (1741-1810) who had emigrated to the Land of Israel in 1777. Despite this, they continued to lead the Chasidic community in Belarus from a distance, through extensive written correspondence. (This line was omitted by Rabbi Shneur Zalman in the 1806 Shklov edition of the *Tanya*, after he had already split with Rabbi Avraham, see pp. xix-xx).

Rabbi Shneur Zalman now reiterates how the *Tanya* was formulated as a result of personal meetings with his disciples, and that it is now being distributed in written form to alleviate the over-burdensome stream of visitors requesting counsel.

וְכוּלָם הֵן תְּשׁוּבוֹת עַל שְׁאֵלוֹת רַבּוֹת אֲשֶׁר שׁוֹאֲלִין בְּעֵצָה כָּל אַנְשֵׁי שְׁלוֹמֵנוּ דִּמְדִינָתֵינוּ תָּמִיד — **And all** the teachings collected here **are** based on **responses** offered by me **to the many requests for advice posed constantly by all the members of our community in this country,** כָּל אֶחָד לְפִי עֶרְכּוֹ — **each one at his own level,** לָשִׁית עֵצוֹת בְּנַפְשָׁם בַּעֲבוֹדַת ה' — *"to seek advice for their souls" (Psalms* 13:3), **in the worship of G-d,** לִהְיוֹת כִּי אֵין הַזְּמַן גְּרָמָא עוֹד לְהָשִׁיב לְכָל אֶחָד וְאֶחָד עַל שְׁאֵלָתוֹ בִּפְרָטוּת **for time** no longer permits me to answer each person's inquiry individually.

As we shall soon see, the *Tanya* is *not* fashioned as a question and answer book. The author does not share with us the issues that had been posed to him by his community, and many chapters of the *Tanya* appear more theoretically than practically orientated. But here in the "Author's Introduction," the author wishes to make clear that, despite superficial appearances, the content of this book is based on "tried and tested" advice offered to real people.

Another simple reason that prompted the *Tanya* to be written, was to make a permanent record of Rabbi Shneur Zalman's advice for later reference.

וְגַם הַשְּׁכְחָה מְצוּיָה — **And also,** *"forgetfulness is abound" (Eichah Rabah* 5:1), and visitors to Rabbi Shneur Zalman may have had trouble recalling later on what they had been advised in a personal meeting.

עַל כֵּן רָשַׁמְתִּי כָּל הַתְּשׁוּבוֹת עַל כָּל הַשְּׁאֵלוֹת — **Therefore, I have noted down all the responses** originally delivered by myself orally **to all the requests for advice** posed by members of the community, לְמִשְׁמֶרֶת לְאוֹת — *"as a safekeeping, as a sign"* (*Numbers* 17:25), לִהְיוֹת לְכָל אֶחָד וְאֶחָד לְזִכָּרוֹן בֵּין עֵינָיו — **so that every individual** will have *"a remembrance between his eyes"* (see *Exodus* 13:9), of the information, after he returns home.

כי בהן ימצא מרגוע לנפשו ועצה נכונה לכל דבר הקשה עליו
בעבודת ה' ונכון יהיה לבו בטוח בה' גומר בעדינו: ומי
שדעתו קצרה להבין דבר עצה מתוך קונטריסים אלו יפרש
שיחתו לפני הגדולים שבעירו והם יבוננוהו ואליהם בקשתי
שלא לשום יד לפה להתנהג בענוה ושפלות של שקר ח"ו
וכנודע עונש המר על מונע בר וגודל השכר ממאמר רז"ל
ע"פ מאיר עיני שניהם ה' כי יאיר ה' פניו אליהם אור פני

The author makes a personal plea to his followers to accept the *Tanya* as a substitute for private meetings.

וְלֹא יִדְחוֹק עוֹד לִיכָּנֵס לְדַבֵּר עִמִּי בִּיחִידוּת — **And** I trust **you will no longer press to come and speak with me privately,** כִּי בָּהֶן יִמְצָא מַרְגּוֹעַ לְנַפְשׁוֹ וְעֵצָה נְכוֹנָה — **for** **in these** responses recorded here, **you will find inner peace and good advice,** לְכָל דָּבָר הַקָּשֶׁה עָלָיו בַּעֲבוֹדַת ה' — **in everything that troubles you in the worship of G-d,** וְנָכוֹן יִהְיֶה לִבּוֹ בָּטוּחַ בַּה' גּוֹמֵר בַּעֲדֵינוּ — **and "*your heart (will be) firm, trusting in G-d*"** (*Psalms* 112:7), **who completes** everything **for us.**

The *Tanya* is not, by any means, a simple work. To decipher its original Hebrew requires a reasonable background in Rabbinic texts, and some familiarity with Kabbalistic ideas. Rabbi Shneur Zalman is conscious that the book's relatively advanced pitch might render it inaccessible to many in his community, and he now stresses the crucial role of local support and mentorship.

וּמִי שֶׁדַּעְתּוֹ קְצָרָה לְהָבִין דְּבַר עֵצָה מִתּוֹךְ קוּנְטְרֵיסִים אֵלּוּ — **And if your "*powers of comprehension are too weak*"** (*Rambam, Laws of Torah Study* 4:4), **to understand the** intended **practical advice from** reading **these pamphlets** yourself, יְפָרֵשׁ שִׂיחָתוֹ לִפְנֵי הַגְּדוֹלִים שֶׁבְּעִירוֹ וְהֵם יְבוֹנְנוּהוּ — **consult your local scholars, and "*they will instruct you*"** (see *Deuteronomy* 32:10).

Rabbi Shneur Zalman now requests the cooperation of the scholars themselves.

וַאֲלֵיהֶם בַּקָּשָׁתִי שֶׁלֹּא לָשׂוּם יָד לָפֶה — **And to those** scholars, **I urge you** to be forthcoming with advice, **do not to place "*a hand upon your mouth*"** (*Proverbs* 30:32), לְהִתְנַהֵג בַּעֲנָוָה וְשִׁפְלוּת שֶׁל שֶׁקֶר חַס וְשָׁלוֹם — **to, G-d forbid, act with false humility and modesty,** claiming that you do not know the answer when, in fact, you do.

וְכַנּוֹדָע עוֹנֶשׁ הַמַּר עַל מוֹנֵעַ בַּר — **The bitter punishment for "*one who withholds (spiritual) sustenance*"** (*ibid.* 11:26), **is well known** (from *Talmud, Sanhedrin* 91b), וְגוֹדֶל הַשָּׂכָר — **and,** conversely, **the great reward,** for sharing Torah wisdom is also well known, מִמַּאֲמַר רַבּוֹתֵינוּ זִכְרוֹנָם לִבְרָכָה עַל פָּסוּק מֵאִיר עֵינֵי שְׁנֵיהֶם ה' — **from our Sages' teaching** (*Talmud, Temurah* 16a) **on the verse** (*Proverbs* 29:13), that when one who is poor in wisdom is enlightened by one rich in wisdom, it is mutually beneficial, and "*G-d gives light to the eyes of both of them.*"

כִּי יָאִיר ה' פָּנָיו אֲלֵיהֶם — **For** when the scholar will assist a reader in understanding this book, "*G-d will shine His face upon (both of) you*" (see *Numbers* 6:25), אוֹר פְּנֵי מֶלֶךְ חַיִּים — "*the light of the King's face, which is life*" (*Proverbs* 16:15).

מלך חיים. ומחיה חיים יזכנו ויחיינו לימים אשר לא ילמדו
עוד איש את רעהו וגו' כי כולם ידעו אותי וגו' כי מלאה
הארץ דעה את ה' וגו' אכי"ר:

והנה אחר שנתפשטו הקונטריסים הנ"ל בקרב כל אנ"ש הנ"ל
בהעתקות רבות מידי סופרים שונים ומשונים הנה ע"י

4B

ריבוי ההעתקות שונות רבו כמו רבו הט"ס במאוד מאוד
ולזאת נדבה רוחם של אנשים אפרתים הנקובים הנ"ל מע"ל
לטורח בגופם ומאודם להביא את קונטריסים הנ"ל לבית הדפוס

The author concludes with a blessing.

וּמְחַיֶה חַיִּים יְזַכֵּנוּ וִיחַיֵּינוּ לַיָמִים אֲשֶׁר לֹא יְלַמְּדוּ עוֹד אִישׁ אֶת רֵעֵהוּ וְגוֹ' כִּי כוּלָם יֵדְעוּ אוֹתִי וְגוֹ' — And may the One-Who-Gives-Life grant you merit and sustain you until the days when, *"one man will no longer teach his friend and every man his brother, saying, 'Know G-d,' for they shall all know Me, from the least of them unto the greatest of them"* (Jeremiah 31:33), כִּי מָלְאָה הָאָרֶץ דֵעָה אֶת ה' וְגוֹ' — *"For the earth will be filled with the knowledge of G-d,* as the waters cover the sea" (Isaiah 11:9), אָמֵן כֵּן יְהִי רָצוֹן — Amen, may it be G-d's will.

SECTION FIVE: PRE-PUBLICATION NOTE

23RD KISLEV LEAP

Rabbi Shneur Zalman's pastoral letter of 1795 concluded here. In 1796, when submitting the *Tanya* to print, the author added the following lines.

וְהִנֵּה אַחַר שֶׁנִּתְפַּשְּׁטוּ הַקּוּנְטְרֵיסִים הַנִּזְכָּרִים לְעֵיל בְּקֶרֶב כָּל אַנְשֵׁי שְׁלוֹמֵנוּ הַנִּזְכָּרִים לְעֵיל — Now, after these pamphlets that we have mentioned spread throughout the entire community stated above, בְּהַעְתָּקוֹת רַבּוֹת מִידֵי סוֹפְרִים שׁוֹנִים וּמְשׁוּנִים — in multiple copies, through a variety of different copyists, הִנֵּה עַל יְדֵי רִיבּוּי הַהַעְתָּקוֹת שׁוֹנוֹת — what has happened is that through the numerous different copies, רַבּוּ כְּמוֹ רַבּוּ הַטָעֻיוֹת סוֹפְרִים בִּמְאֹד מְאֹד — the number of copyist errors *"has increased and increased"* (Zechariah 10:8), to a very great extent.

Many of these "errors" had, in fact, been intentionally introduced by copyists hired by opponents of the Chasidic movement to discredit the author. This became apparent over time from questions which Rabbi Shneur Zalman received about the *Tanya*'s alleged content and from corrupted copies that some of the author's followers were able to purchase.

וְלָזֹאת נָדְבָה רוּחָם שֶׁל אֲנָשִׁים אֶפְרָתִים הַנְּקוּבִים הַנִּזְכָּרִים לְעֵיל מֵעֵבֶר לַדַף — And this has prompted the generous spirit of those noble men mentioned overleaf (p. 5), Rabbi Shalom Shachna Altschuler and Rabbi Mordechai Horowitz, לִטְרוֹחַ בְּגוּפָם — to go to great personal וּמְאוֹדָם לְהָבִיא אֶת קוּנְטְרֵיסִים הַנִּזְכָּרִים לְעֵיל לְבֵית הַדְפוּס

מְנוּקִים מכל סיג וט"ס ומוגהים היטב ואמינא לפעלא טבא
יישר חילא ולהיות כי מקרא מלא דבר הכתוב ארור מסיג
גבול רעהו וארור בו קללה בו נידוי ח"ו וכו' ע"כ כיהודה
ועוד לקרא קאתינא למשדי גודא רבא על כל המדפיסים
שלא להדפיס קונטריסים הנ"ל לא על ידי עצמן ולא על ידי
גירא דילהון בלתי רשות הנקובים הנ"ל משך חמש שנים
מיום כלות הדפוס ולשומעים יונעם ותבא ברכת טוב כה
דברי המלקט ליקוטי אמרים הנ"ל:

and financial lengths, to publish the above-mentioned pamphlets, מְנוּקִים מִכָּל סִיג
וְטָעִיּוֹת סוֹפְרִים וּמוּגָּהִים הֵיטֵב — in an edition that is **completely untainted, free from
copyists' errors, and carefully proofread,** וְאָמִינָא לְפָעֲלָא טָבָא יִישַׁר חֵילָא — and *"I
say for the good deed, 'Well done!'"* (see *Exodus Rabah*, 20:10).

The "author's introduction" concludes with a copyright notice to protect the interests of the publishers.

וְלִהְיוֹת כִּי מִקְרָא מָלֵא דִּבֶּר הַכָּתוּב אָרוּר מַסִּיג גְּבוּל רֵעֵהוּ — **And since Scripture states
explicitly,** *"Cursed (arur) is anyone who moves their neighbor's boundary stone"*
(*Deuteronomy* 27:17), encroaching on his rights, וְאָרוּר בּוֹ קְלָלָה בּוֹ נִידּוּי חַס וְשָׁלוֹם וְכוּ׳
— **where** the term *arur* implies both curse and excommunication (*Talmud, Shevuos*
36a), **G-d forbid,** עַל כֵּן כִּיהוּדָה וְעוֹד לְקְרָא קָאתֵינָא — **therefore, I come** with the following statement in the spirit of the *Talmud's* comment, "(How can you cite the law
from) **Judah** *in addition* to **Scripture?**" (*Kidushin* 6a).

The *Talmud* objected to a legal precedent from the province of Judah being cited
to support an explicit Scriptural ruling. If it is stated in Scripture, no further proof is
necessary.

In a similar vein, Rabbi Shneur Zalman points out that, since the prohibition of
copyright infringement has already been stated scripturally (in the above citation),
the following comments really add nothing to the severity of the transgression.

לְמִשְׁדֵי גּוּדָא רַבָּא עַל כָּל הַמַּדְפִּיסִים — **I place a strict prohibition on all publishers,**
שֶׁלֹּא לְהַדְפִּיס קוּנְטְרֵיסִים הַנִּזְכָּרִים לְעֵיל — **against publishing the above-mentioned**
pamphlets of the *Tanya,* לֹא עַל יְדֵי עַצְמָן וְלֹא עַל יְדֵי גִּירָא דִילְהוֹן — **neither by themselves or through their agency,** בִּלְתִּי רְשׁוּת הַנְּקוּבִים הַנִּזְכָּרִים לְעֵיל — **without**
the permission of the above-named authorized publishers, מֶשֶׁךְ חָמֵשׁ שָׁנִים מִיּוֹם
כְּלוֹת הַדְּפוֹס — **for a period of five years from the day of publication** of this book,
וְלַשּׁוֹמְעִים יוּנְעַם וְתָבוֹא עֲלֵיהֶם בִּרְכַּת טוֹב — and **those who adhere** to this ruling, *"will
delight, and a blessing of goodness will come upon them"* (*Proverbs* 24:25).

כֹּה דִּבְרֵי הַמְלַקֵּט לִקוּטֵי אֲמָרִים הַנִּזְכָּרִים לְעֵיל — **These are the words of the author of**
Likutei Amarim, **mentioned above,** Rabbi Shneur Zalman.

פֶּרֶק א תַנְיָא   [בספּ"ג דנדה] מַשְׁבִּיעִים אוֹתוֹ   5A
תְּהִי צַדִיק וְאַל תְּהִי רָשָׁע וַאֲפִי' כָל

CHAPTER 1

AM I GOOD OR BAD?

SECTION 1: FIVE TYPES OF PEOPLE

22ND KISLEV REGULAR | 24TH KISLEV LEAP

In his "Author's Introduction," Rabbi Shneur Zalman revealed that the *Tanya* contains, *"responses offered by me to the many requests for advice posed constantly by all the members of our community in this country, each one at his own level, 'to seek advice for their souls' (Psalms 13:3), in the worship of G-d"* (p. 23).

While Rabbi Shneur Zalman did not record in the *Tanya* the "requests for advice" which were posed to him, from the "responses" offered throughout the book, we can deduce the types of questions he was probably asked.

If we were to reconstruct the "request for advice" the author addresses here at the opening of the book, it might read as follows: *"Rebbe, however hard I try to connect to G-d, I feel like a failure. I want to come close to G-d, but even when I succeed in religious practice, my inner demons still bother me. I have peak moments when I feel close to G-d, but they are not sustainable. What should I do? Will I ever succeed?"*

To address this concern, the *Tanya* will offer us a meticulously structured guide to the inner life. We will learn how consciousness is multilayered and is influenced by a variety of different spiritual and physical forces. We will discover how our emotions function, as well as how our minds deduce and process information. And we will address fundamental questions of identity: *Who am I? What do I want?*

After completing this initial discussion, we will have a powerful set of tools to manage self-awareness. We will know what we are capable of spiritually and what is beyond reach. We will be aware of our mental and emotional limitations, but we will continue to challenge them daily, implementing a realistic and effective method.

In classic Rabbinic style, the *Tanya* will frame this discussion of self-awareness with a series of questions on selected quotes from the *Talmud*. These questions will be posed here, at the outset of chapter one, and after delving into the inner workings of human consciousness, the answers will be revealed in chapters 13 and 14.

תַּנְיָא [בְּסוֹף פֶּרֶק ג' דְּנִדָּה] — **The Rabbis taught [at the end of chapter three] of** Tractate *Nidah* (30b) of the *Talmud*, מַשְׁבִּיעִים אוֹתוֹ תְּהִי צַדִּיק וְאַל תְּהִי רָשָׁע — **that before a**

הָעוֹלָם כּוּלּוֹ אוֹמְרִים לְךָ צַדִּיק אַתָּה הֱיֵה בְּעֵינֶיךָ כְּרָשָׁע
וְצָרִיךְ לְהָבִין דְּהָא תְּנַן [אָבוֹת פ״ב] וְאַל תְּהִי רָשָׁע בִּפְנֵי
עַצְמֶךָ וְגַם אִם יִהְיֶה בְּעֵינָיו כְּרָשָׁע יֵרַע לְבָבוֹ וְיִהְיֶה עָצֵב
וְלֹא יוּכַל לַעֲבוֹד ה׳ בְּשִׂמְחָה וּבְטוּב לֵבָב וְאִם לֹא יֵרַע לְבָבוֹ
כְּלָל מִזֶּה יָכוֹל לָבוֹא לִידֵי קַלּוּת חַ״ו. אַךְ הָעִנְיָן כִּי הִנֵּה
מָצִינוּ בַּגְּמָרָא ה׳ חֲלוּקוֹת. צַדִּיק וְטוֹב לוֹ צַדִּיק וְרַע לוֹ רָשָׁע

child is born, his or her soul **"is made to swear an oath, 'Be a righteous person (tzadik), and do not be a wicked person (rasha),'"** וַאֲפִילוּ כָּל הָעוֹלָם כּוּלּוֹ אוֹמְרִים — **"'and even if the entire world tells you, "You are righteous,"'"** לְךָ צַדִּיק אַתָּה — הֱיֵה בְּעֵינֶיךָ כְּרָשָׁע — **"'you should consider yourself like a wicked person.'"**

The *Talmud's* insistence that *"you should consider yourself like a wicked person,"* seems to contradict another lesson taught by the *Mishnah:*

דְּהָא תְּנַן [אָבוֹת פֶּרֶק ב׳] וְאַל תְּהִי רָשָׁע בִּפְנֵי — **Some clarification is needed,** וְצָרִיךְ לְהָבִין עַצְמֶךָ — **because doesn't the *Mishnah* say** [Tractate *Avos* chapter two, *Mishnah* 13] the precise opposite, *"Don't consider yourself to be a wicked person"*?

Practically speaking, there is an obvious reason why the advice of Tractate *Nidah,* that *"you should consider yourself like a wicked person,"* might be counterproductive.

וְגַם אִם יִהְיֶה בְּעֵינָיו כְּרָשָׁע יֵרַע לְבָבוֹ וְיִהְיֶה עָצֵב וְלֹא יוּכַל לַעֲבוֹד ה׳ בְּשִׂמְחָה וּבְטוּב לֵבָב — **And also, if you consider yourself like a wicked person,** as Tractate *Nidah* suggests, **you will become downhearted and depressed, and you won't be able to worship G-d joyfully and positively.**

וְאִם לֹא יֵרַע לְבָבוֹ כְּלָל מִזֶּה — **But if,** on the other hand, **you don't become sad** *at all* **from this** "wickedness" of yours, יָכוֹל לָבוֹא לִידֵי קַלּוּת חַס וְשָׁלוֹם — **you could come to be flippant** about your moral and religious responsibilities, **G-d forbid.** (This question will be fully answered much later in chapters 31 and 34).

To solve this problem, we need to first define the terms "righteous person" (*tzadik; pl. tzadikim*) and "wicked person" (*rasha; pl. resha'im*).

אַךְ הָעִנְיָן — **Now,** let's get to **the explanation** of these terms.

כִּי הִנֵּה מָצִינוּ בַּגְּמָרָא ה׳ חֲלוּקוֹת — **For in the *Talmud* we find five categories,** צַדִּיק וְטוֹב לוֹ — **"the *tzadik* who has it good"** in this world, צַדִּיק וְרַע לוֹ — **"the *tzadik* who has it bad"** in this world, רָשָׁע וְטוֹב לוֹ — **"the *rasha* who has it good"** in this world, רָשָׁע וְרַע לוֹ — **"the *rasha* who has it bad"** in this world (*Talmud, Brachos* 7a), וּבֵינוֹנִי — **and the "inbetweener"** (*beinoni*) **who is neither a *tzadik* nor a *rasha,*** but has elements of both (*ibid.* 61b).

The discussion in Tractate *Brachos* revolves around the classic theological question of why some righteous people suffer ("the *tzadik* who has it bad"), while some wicked people prosper ("the *rasha* who has it good"). But that issue is not the *Tanya's* concern here. What is of interest is the *Talmud's* translation of these terms.

וטוב לו רשע ורע לו ובינוני. ופירשו בגמרא צדיק וטוב לו
צדיק גמור צדיק ורע לו צדיק שאינו גמור וברעיא
מהימנא פ' משפטים פי' צדיק ורע לו שהרע שבו כפוף
לטוב וכו' ובגמרא ספ"ט דברכות צדיקים יצ"ט שופטן כו'

וּפֵירְשׁוּ בַּגְּמָרָא — And, after dismissing various possible interpretations, **the Talmud** finally **explains** (ibid. 7a) that the worldly fortune or misfortune of a tzadik is actually a reflection of his or her inner perfection, צַדִּיק וְטוֹב לוֹ צַדִּיק גָּמוּר — **"the tzadik who has it good"** in this world enjoys a fortunate life because he or she is **totally righteous**, צַדִּיק וְרַע לוֹ צַדִּיק שֶׁאֵינוֹ גָמוּר — **"the tzadik who has it bad"** in this world suffers misfortune because he or she is **not totally righteous.**

Taken at face value, the terms "tzadik who has it good" and "tzadik who has it bad" describe an *external reality* of worldly fortune or misfortune; but what piques the *Tanya's* interest here is the *Talmud's* translation of these terms as states of *inner reality.* (The "totally righteous" tzadik has clearly achieved a significantly greater degree of self-mastery than the "not totally righteous" tzadik.)

PRACTICAL LESSONS

For the majority of us—who are less than perfect, but not terribly wicked—the question of self-image is a challenging one. If we are willing to face the harsh reality of our imperfections, we may become depressed. If we try to ignore them, we could become indifferent.

In the *Zohar,* a primary text of the Kabbalah (Jewish esotericism), the inner state of the "tzadik who has it bad" is described further.

וּבְרַעְיָא מְהֵימְנָא פָּרָשַׁת מִשְׁפָּטִים פֵּירֵשׁ צַדִּיק וְרַע לוֹ — And in the section of the *Zohar* called **Raya Mehemna** (**"Faithful Shepherd"**), **on the Torah portion of** *Mishpatim* (*Zohar* 2, 117b), the term **"tzadik who has it bad"** is further **clarified** as an inner state, שֶׁהָרַע שֶׁבּוֹ כָּפוּף לַטּוֹב וְכוּ' — it means **that the bad within him is suppressed by the good, etc.**

According to the *Zohar,* the "bad" of the "tzadik who has (it) bad" refers to an *inner* defect in character (and not merely a bad life-situation of misfortune). However, that inner bad is overwhelmed and "suppressed" by the tzadik's overall good.

Having touched upon the meaning of tzadik and rasha (in both perfect and imperfect forms), we now turn to the beinoni ("inbetweener").

וּבַגְּמָרָא סוֹף פֶּרֶק ט' דִּבְרָכוֹת — And in the *Talmud,* at the **end of chapter nine of** Tractate **Brachos** (61b), it is written, צַדִּיקִים יֵצֶר טוֹב שׁוֹפְטָן כוּ' — *"In the case of tzadikim, the 'impulse to good' (yetzer tov) is their* internal *judge of what to do or not to do, etc.,"* רְשָׁעִים יֵצֶר הָרָע שׁוֹפְטָן — *"in the case of resha'im, the 'impulse to evil' (yetzer hara) is their* internal *judge of what to do or not to do, etc.,"* בֵּינוֹנִים זֶה וְזֶה שׁוֹפְטָן וְכוּ' — *"in the case of 'inbetweeners,' both* good and bad impulses *are their* internal *judges of what to do or not to do, etc."*

רשעים יצה"ר שופטן בינונים זה וזה שופטן וכו' אמר רבה
כגון אנא בינוני א"ל אביי לא שביק מר חיי לכל בריה
וכו' ולהבין כל זה באר היטב וגם להבין מה שאמר איוב
[ב"ב פ"א] רבש"ע בראת צדיקי' בראת רשעי' כו' והא
צדיק ורשע לא קאמר. וגם להבין מהות מדרגת הבינוני

This insight of the *Talmud* will remain, for the moment, unclear. That the righteous are guided by their 'impulse to good' and the wicked by their 'impulse to evil,' seems self-evident without the *Talmud's* words. That "inbetweeners" are guided by both good and bad impulses doesn't seem to tell us very much.

The confusion over the term "inbetweener" is highlighted by the subsequent discussion recorded in the *Talmud*, between two Sages.

אָמַר רַבָּה כְּגוֹן אֲנָא בֵּינוֹנִי — *"Rabah said, 'I, for example, am an inbetweener,'"*

אָמַר לֵיהּ אַבַּיֵי לָא שָׁבִיק מַר חַיֵּי לְכָל בְּרִיָה וְכו' — *"Abaye said back to him, 'Master, you are denying everybody life etc.,"* because if you, one of the most pious sages, are a mere "inbetweener," then there can be no righteous people at all!

Evidently, the distinction between "inbetweener" and *tzadik* is a subtle one. Even if Rabah was speaking out of humility, his self-definition as an "inbetweener" had to be plausible for a person of his demonstrable piety.

וּלְהָבִין כָּל זֶה בַּאֵר הֵיטֵב — We need a lot of clarification about all of this!

To summarize our unresolved questions so far: 1) If I fulfill my prenatal oath to always consider myself "like a *rasha*," how will I be able to maintain a positive and joyful attitude? 2) What is the *real* difference between the different categories of *tzadik, rasha* and *beinoni*? And, 3) What logic led Rabah to deem himself to be a *beinoni*?

One final *Talmudic* quote, about the issue of determinism.

וְגַם לְהָבִין מַה שֶׁאָמַר אִיוֹב [בָּבָא בַּתְרָא פֶּרֶק א'] — Also, we need to clarify what Job said (*Talmud*, **Bava Basra, chapter one,** 16a), רִבּוֹנוֹ שֶׁל עוֹלָם בָּרֵאתָ צַדִּיקִים בָּרֵאתָ רְשָׁעִים כו' — *"Master of the Universe! You have created righteous people and You have created wicked people, etc."*

וְהָא צַדִּיק וְרָשָׁע לֹא קָאֲמַר — This is problematic because when the "angel supervising conception" questions G-d about the fate of a future child, that angel **"doesn't mention** in his questions if the child will be **righteous or wicked"** (*Talmud, Nidah* 16b), since the matter will obviously be left to the individual's free choice.

How can Job assert that "G-d *created* righteous people" when it is up to the individual to decide whether he or she will be righteous or not? (This question will be answered below in chapter 14, p. 173 and chapter 27, p. 312).

שֶׁבּוּדַאי אֵינוֹ מֶחֱצָה זְכִיּוֹת וּמֶחֱצָה עֲווֹנוֹת שֶׁאִ"כ אֵיךְ טָעָה
רַבָּה בְּעַצְמוֹ לוֹמַר שֶׁהוּא בֵּינוֹנִי וְנוֹדַע דְּלֹא פָּסִיק פּוּמֵיהּ
מִגִּירְסָא עַד שֶׁאֲפִי' מַלְאַךְ הַמָּוֶת לֹא הָיָה יָכוֹל לִשְׁלוֹט בּוֹ
וְאֵיךְ הָיָה יָכוֹל לִטְעוֹת בְּמֶחֱצָה עֲווֹנוֹת ח"ו. וְעוֹד שֶׁהֲרֵי
בְּשָׁעָה שֶׁעוֹשֶׂה עֲווֹנוֹת נִקְרָא רָשָׁע גָּמוּר [וְאִם אַח"כ עָשָׂה
תְּשׁוּבָה נִקְרָא צַדִּיק גָּמוּר] וַאֲפִילוּ הָעוֹבֵר עַל אִיסּוּר קַל

SECTION TWO: WHAT IS A BEINONI?

We remain confused about the precise nature of the "inbetweener" (*beinoni*). The *Tanya* now probes the meaning of this term.

וְגַם לְהָבִין מַהוּת מַדְרֵגַת הַבֵּינוֹנִי — **We also need a real understanding of "inbetweener" status,** שֶׁבְּוַדַּאי אֵינוֹ מֶחֱצָה זְכִיּוֹת וּמֶחֱצָה עֲווֹנוֹת — **for it definitely can't be** understood as a person whose **proportion of merits to transgressions is equal,** שֶׁאִם כֵּן אֵיךְ טָעָה רַבָּה בְּעַצְמוֹ לוֹמַר שֶׁהוּא בֵּינוֹנִי — **because if that were the case, how could Rabah have mistaken himself for a *beinoni*,** when such a degree of error could not be attributed to humility?

Even in an attempt to portray himself as humble, no Rabbi would falsely claim, "I eat non-kosher food a few times a week." "Inbetweener" status can't possibly mean that a person's transgressions are equal to his *mitzvos*, because, Rabah would never make such a ludicrous claim about himself, even if he was acting modestly.

In fact, as the *Talmud* states elsewhere, Rabah's religious diligence was legendary.

וְנוֹדַע דְּלֹא פָּסִיק פּוּמֵיהּ מִגִּירְסָא עַד שֶׁאֲפִילוּ מַלְאַךְ הַמָּוֶת לֹא הָיָה יָכוֹל לִשְׁלוֹט בּוֹ — **For** Rabah **famously did not allow his mouth to stop studying, to the extent that even the "Angel of Death" could not overpower him,** since he was occupied with a *mitzvah* constantly (*Talmud*, *Bava Metzia* 86a), וְאֵיךְ הָיָה יָכוֹל לִטְעוֹת בְּמֶחֱצָה עֲווֹנוֹת חַס וְשָׁלוֹם — **so how could he have wrongly assessed** himself **to have transgressions in equal proportion** to his *mitzvos*, **G-d forbid?**

Having ruled out this simple understanding of an "inbetweener," we now question if the very notion of an intermediate status is possible.

וְעוֹד שֶׁהֲרֵי בְּשָׁעָה שֶׁעוֹשֶׂה עֲווֹנוֹת נִקְרָא רָשָׁע גָּמוּר — **Also,** as we shall soon see, **at the moment when a person transgresses, he is classified** by the Sages **as a total *rasha*,** [וְאִם אַחַר כָּךְ עָשָׂה תְּשׁוּבָה נִקְרָא צַדִּיק גָּמוּר] — **and if he subsequently repents he is classified as a total *tzadik*** (Rabbi Yitzchak of Vienna, *Ohr Zarua*, (Israel: Machon Yerushalayim, 2010), p. 105), so at what point could he be "inbetween"?

Perhaps the "inbetween" status means that the person upholds Biblical law, but neglects Rabbinic law? The *Tanya* now rules out this possibility.

וַאֲפִילוּ הָעוֹבֵר עַל אִיסּוּר קַל שֶׁל דִּבְרֵי סוֹפְרִים מִקְרֵי רָשָׁע — **And even a person who violates a minor Rabbinic precept is considered a *rasha*,** כִּדְאִיתָא בְּפֶרֶק ב' דִּיבָמוֹת

של דברי סופרים מקרי רשע כדאיתא בפ״ב דיבמות
ובפ״ק דנדה ואפילו מי שיש בידו למחות ולא מיחה נק׳
רשע [בפ״ו דשבועו׳] וכ״ש וק״ו במבטל איזו מ״ע שאפש׳
לו לקיימה כמו כל שאפשר לו לעסוק בתורה ואינו עוסק
שעליו דרשו רז״ל כי דבר ה׳ בזה וגו׳ הכרת תכרת וגו׳
ופשיטא דמקרי רשע טפי מעובר איסור דרבנן וא״כ ע״כ
הבינוני אין בו אפי׳ עון ביטול תורה ומש״ה טעה רבה

5B

וּבְפֶרֶק קַמָּא דְנִדָּה — **as stated in the** *Talmud*, **chapter two of** Tractate *Yevamos* (20a) **and the first chapter of** Tractate *Nidah* (12a).

Another possible approach to the "inbetween" status — which will now be ruled out — would be a person who does not transgress himself, but passively allows others to transgress.

וַאֲפִילוּ מִי שֶׁיֵּשׁ בְּיָדוֹ לִמְחוֹת וְלֹא מִיחָה נִקְרָא רָשָׁע ו׳ [בְּפֶרֶק ו׳ דִשְׁבוּעוֹת] — **And a person is termed a** *rasha* **even if he had the opportunity to reprimand someone else, but failed to do so** [*Talmud*, **chapter six of** *Sh'vu'os* (39b)].

Now, if a person is rendered a *rasha* through the lesser transgressions of: a) *passively* facilitating a Biblical violation, or b) violating a *Rabbinic* prohibition,

וְכָל שֶׁכֵּן וְקַל וָחוֹמֶר בִּמְבַטֵּל אֵיזוֹ מִצְוַת עֲשֵׂה שֶׁאֶפְשָׁר לוֹ לְקַיְּמָה — **then, all the more so,** would someone who a) *actively* neglects, b) a *Biblical* command that he could have observed, would definitely be classified as a *rasha*.

כְּמוֹ כָּל שֶׁאֶפְשָׁר לוֹ לַעֲסוֹק בַּתּוֹרָה וְאֵינוֹ עוֹסֵק — **Such as,** to cite a common example, **any person who had the opportunity to study Torah** (a Biblical command), **but failed to do so,** שֶׁעָלָיו דָרְשׁוּ רַבּוֹתֵינוּ זִכְרוֹנָם לִבְרָכָה כִּי דְבַר ה׳ בָּזָה וְגוֹ׳ הִכָּרֵת תִּכָּרֵת וְגוֹ׳ — **to whom the Sages applied the verse,** *"he has expressed contempt for the word of G-d... that soul will be cut off, etc.,"* (Numbers 15:31; *Talmud, Sanhedrin* 99a), וּפְשִׁיטָא דְמִקְרֵי רָשָׁע טְפֵי מֵעוֹבֵר אִיסוּר דְּרַבָּנָן — **obviously** this person who failed to observe a Biblical command **deserves the title 'rasha' more than one who violates a Rabbinic prohibition.**

וְאִם כֵּן עַל כָּרְחֲךָ הַבֵּינוֹנִי אֵין בּוֹ אֲפִילוּ עֲווֹן בִּיטּוּל תּוֹרָה — **So you are forced** to conclude **that the "inbetweener" is not even guilty of the** common **transgression of neglecting to study Torah** for a single moment.

These proofs lead us to the conclusion that a person who transgresses Jewish Law *in any way* must be termed a *rasha*.

For the onlooker, then, the *tzadik* and *beinoni* are indistinguishable; neither are guilty of any transgression whatsoever, Biblical or Rabbinic. The distinction between them must be an *internal* one.

בעצמו לומר שהוא בינוני*
והא דאמרי' בעלמא דמחצ'
על מחצה מקרי בינוני ורוב
זכיות מקרי צדיק הוא שם
המושאל לענין שכר ועונש

הגהה

(ומ"ש בזוהר ח"ג ד' רל"א כל
שממוטין עונותיו וכו' היא שאלת

וּמִשּׁוּם הָכֵי טָעָה רַבָּה בְּעַצְמוֹ לוֹמַר שֶׁהוּא בֵּינוֹנִי — **And that is why Rabah** was able to **make a mistake about himself and claim he was a *beinoni*.***

We still do not know Rabah's exact reasoning as to why he considered himself a *beinoni,* (the *Tanya* will clarify this later, in chapter 13). But what has now become clear is that Rabah made a *reasonable claim*, since the difference between a *tzadik* and a *beinoni* is not externally manifested to the observer. Even the fact that Rabah "*did not allow his mouth to stop studying*" was not conclusive since*, "the 'inbetweener' is not even guilty of the transgression of neglecting to study Torah.*"

23RD KISLEV REGULAR | 25TH KISLEV LEAP

The *Tanya* now addresses a clear and familiar reference to the "inbetweener" as one whose transgressions equal his *mitzvos.*

וְהָא דְּאָמְרִינָן בְּעָלְמָא דְמֶחֱצָה מְחֶצָה מִקְרֵי בֵּינוֹנִי וְרֹוב זְכִיּוֹת מִקְרֵי צַדִּיק — **And as for the common reference** in Rabbinic texts **to the *beinoni* as one with an equal proportion** of transgressions to merits, **and to the *tzadik* as one with a majority of merits** (see *Talmud, Rosh Hashanah* 16b; *Rashi ibid.*), which directly contradicts what we have demonstrated so far, that a *beinoni* does not transgress at all, הוּא שֵׁם

---

*הַגָּהָה — **NOTE.** This note, written by the author, discusses a statement in the *Zohar* which appears to contradict our conclusion here in the *Tanya*, (that neither the "inbetweener" nor *tzadik* are ever guilty of transgression).

וּמַה שֶּׁכָּתוּב בַּזֹּהַר חֵלֶק ג' דַּף רל"א שֶׁמְמוֹעֲטִין עֲוֹנוֹתָיו וְכוּ' — This conclusion, that a *tzadik* is never guilty of transgression, appears to contradict **what is written in the *Zohar* (part 3, page 231a),** that *"any (tzadik) who has few transgressions"* atones for them through suffering in this world, so he can fully merit the afterlife.

The *Tanya* will answer that, while such a statement does appear in the *Zohar*, it represents an *incorrect* presumption of one of the Sages, Rav Hamnuna.

הִיא שְׁאֵלַת רַב הַמְנוּנָא לְאֵלִיָּהוּ — But, actually, this citation doesn't represent the *final position* of the *Zohar* but is merely part of **a *question* posed by Rav Hamnuna,** which was answered and corrected by **Eliyahu.**

Rav Hamnuna asked Eliyahu: Doesn't the title "a *tzadik* who has it bad" refer to a man who suffers in this world to atone for his few transgressions, so that he can fully merit the afterlife?

לְפִי שֶׁנִּדּוֹן אַחַר רֻבּוֹ וּמִקְרֵי
צַדִּיק בְּדִינוֹ מֵאַחַר שֶׁזָּכָה
בַּדִּין אֲבָל לְעִנְיָן אֲמִיתַּת

רַב הַמְנוּנָא לְאֵלִיָּהוּ אֲבָל לְפִי תְּשׁוּבַת
אֵלִיָּהוּ שָׁם הַפֵּי' צַדִּיק וְרַע לוֹ הוּא
כְּמַ"שׁ בְּרַ"מ פָּרָשַׁת מִשְׁפָּטִים דִּלְעֵיל
וְשִׁבְעִים פָּנִים לַתּוֹרָה):

הַמּוּשְׁאָל לְעִנְיַן שָׂכָר וְעוֹנֶשׁ — **this represents a figurative,** imprecise **use of the terms** *tzadik* and *beinoni,* **for the purpose of illustrating** an entirely different discussion: the method by which G-d **rewards and punishes**.

לְפִי שֶׁנִּדּוֹן אַחַר רֻבּוֹ — **This is because a person is judged** by G-d **according to the majority** of his transgressions or merits, וּמִקְרֵי צַדִּיק בְּדִינוֹ מֵאַחַר שֶׁזָּכָה בַּדִּין — **and he is classified as "righteous"** not *as a person,* but *in his verdict,* **when he is acquitted in judgment** by G-d (*Rambam, Laws of Teshuvah,* 3:1,5).

The use of the terms *tzadik* and *beinoni* in the context of Divine reward and punishment is imprecise and irrelevant to our discussion of the real meaning of these terms, as a measure of character.

There is a major difference, the *Tanya* suggests, between being "righteous in verdict," and "a righteous person" (*tzadik*). When discussing whether a person will receive a Divinely allotted reward, the Sages will sometimes "appropriate" the term *tzadik* to describe the outcome of a heavenly verdict. One who is "righteous in verdict" for a reward, must have a majority of merits; the "*beinoni* in verdict" will have an equal ratio of merits to transgressions.

אֲבָל לְפִי תְּשׁוּבַת אֵלִיָּהוּ שָׁם פֵּירוּשׁ צַדִּיק וְרַע לוֹ הוּא — **But Eliyahu's answer** corrected Rav Hamnuna's view, explaining **that the meaning of "*tzadik* who has it bad"** is (not one who suffers for his *own* transgressions in this world, but) one who atones in this world for the transgressions *of others.*

כְּמוֹ שֶׁכָּתוּב בְּרַעְיָא מְהֵימְנָא פָּרָשָׁה מִשְׁפָּטִים דִּלְעֵיל — **So the** *conclusion* of this discussion in the *Zohar* (the view expressed by Eliyahu) **is consistent with the above citation from** *Raya Mehemna,* **portion of** *Mishpatim,* that "a *tzadik* who has it bad" doesn't actually transgress, and it is merely that "the bad within him is suppressed by the good."

This argument, however, seems to imply that Rav Hamnuna's suggestion was foolish. Surely Rav Hamnuna knew that *"the 'inbetweener' is not even guilty of the transgression of neglecting to study Torah,"* a fact which is clear from explicit teachings of our Sages cited here in chapter one?

וְשִׁבְעִים פָּנִים לַתּוֹרָה — Obviously Rav Hamnuna knew this, but he wondered whether there was another possible interpretation since, *"there are seventy facets to the Torah"* (*Numbers Rabah* 13:16).

In conclusion: The discussion in *Zohar* 3, 231a does not contradict the *Tanya's* conclusions here in chapter one.

שם התואר והמעלה של מעלת ומדרגות חלוקות
צדיקים ובינונים ארז"ל צדיקים יצ"ט שופטן שנא' ולבי
חלל בקרבי שאין לו יצה"ר כי הרגו בתענית אבל כל מי
שלא הגיע למדרגה זו אף שזכיותיו מרובים על עונותיו

However, as the *Tanya* has demonstrated, when these terms are used precisely, as descriptions of character, neither the *tzadik* nor *beinoni* are guilty of any transgression at all.

So if neither the *tzadik* nor the *beinoni* transgress, what distinguishes them? The *Tanya* returns to the only real definition that we have — the one from Tractate *Brachos,* cited above.

אֲבָל לְעִנְיַן אֲמִיתַּת שֵׁם הַתּוֹאַר וְהַמַּעֲלָה שֶׁל מַעֲלַת וּמַדְרֵגוֹת חֲלוּקוֹת צַדִּיקִים וּבֵינוֹנִים — **But when speaking of the** *true,* inner, **definitive quality that distinguishes the** character of *tzadikim* **from** *beinonim*," אָמְרוּ רַבּוֹתֵינוּ זִכְרוֹנָם לִבְרָכָה צַדִּיקִים יֵצֶר טוֹב שׁוֹפְטָן — **the Sages taught** (*Talmud*, *Brachos* 61b), "*In the case of tzadikim, their 'impulse to good' is their* (internal) *judge.*"

We encountered this teaching above and its precise meaning remained unclear. The *Tanya* will now cite the next line of the *Talmud*, which will enable us to define the *tzadik* and *beinoni* categorically.

שֶׁנֶּאֱמַר וְלִבִּי חָלָל בְּקִרְבִּי — The *Talmud* (*ibid.*) continues, "*As King David states in the verse, 'My heart is empty within me,'*" (*Psalms* 109:22), שֶׁאֵין לוֹ יֵצֶר הָרָע — an "empty heart" means **that** the *tzadik* **is devoid of an "impulse to evil"** (*Jerusalem Talmud, Sotah* 5:5; *Korban Ha-Eidah* ibid.).

"*In the case of tzadikim, their 'impulse to good' is their* (internal) *judge,*" means that it is their *only and exclusive* internal judge; the "impulse to evil" has been "emptied" and voided from *tzadikim* completely. And this is "*the true, definitive quality*" of their status.

How is it possible for a person to be devoid of an "impulse to evil"?

כִּי הֲרָגוֹ בְּתַעֲנִית — In the case of King David, this was **because he annihilated its** influence, subduing it **through fasting** (*Korban ha-Eidah* ibid.).

(Another text suggests that King David employed a different method, "*annihilating it through Torah study*" — *Zohar Chadash, Tikunim* 106d).

This level, where the "impulse to evil" has been annihilated, represents the *true* distinction between the *tzadik* and the *beinoni*. While neither of them actually transgress, the *beinoni* retains the impulse to do so, whereas the *tzadik* has annihilated that urge completely.

אֲבָל כָּל מִי שֶׁלֹּא הִגִּיעַ לְמַדְרֵגָה זוֹ — **But anyone who has not yet reached this level** of annihilating the "impulse to evil," אַף שֶׁזְּכִיּוֹתָיו מְרוּבִּים עַל עֲוֹנוֹתָיו — **even if his merits outweigh his transgressions,** which means that, *figuratively speaking,* he

אינו במעלת ומדרגת צדיק כלל ולכן ארז"ל במדרש
ראה הקב"ה בצדיקים שהם מועטים עמד ושתלן בכל
דור ודור וכו' וכמ"ש וצדיק יסוד עולם: אך ביאור הענין
על פי מ"ש הרח"ו ז"ל בשער הקדושה [ובע"ח שער נ '

would be described as "righteous" in verdict, as we learned above, אֵינוֹ בְּמַעֲלַת
וּמַדְרֵגַת צַדִּיק כְּלָל — in reality, as long as he has not annihilated his "impulse to evil,"
he's not at the level of *tzadik* at all.

The *tzadik*, who has annihilated his "impulse to evil" is consequently quite a rare
phenomenon.

וְלָכֵן אָמְרוּ רַבּוֹתֵינוּ זִכְרוֹנָם לִבְרָכָה בְּמִדְרָשׁ — **That's why our Sages taught in a**
midrash, רָאָה הַקָּדוֹשׁ בָּרוּךְ הוּא בְּצַדִּיקִים שֶׁהֵם מוּעָטִים עָמַד וּשְׁתָלָן בְּכָל דּוֹר וָדוֹר וְכוּ'
— ***"The Blessed Holy One saw that the tzadikim were few, so He carefully placed***
them in each generation" (*Talmud, Yoma* 38b).

If the *tzadik* was merely one whose "merits outweigh his transgressions," there
would certainly be more than a "few" of them. The *tzadik* would be a relatively
common phenomenon.

וּכְמוֹ שֶׁכָּתוּב וְצַדִּיק יְסוֹד עוֹלָם — **We also find a higher level of *tzadik* whose**
righteousness is unparalleled by any other in his generation, **as the verse states,**
"the tzadik is the foundation of the world" (*Proverbs* 10:25).

In conclusion: We have managed to define the status of the *beinoni* by a process
of elimination. He is neither a *rasha,* guilty of actual transgression, nor is he a *tzadik,*
who has succeeded in eliminating his "impulse to evil." The *beinoni* is perfect on the
outside, but still somewhat rotten on the inside.

At first glance this would seem irrelevant to most of us, who are far from perfect
even on the outside. But, as we shall see, the schism within the *beinoni* will provide
important insight into our inner struggle, and it will help us to discern the spiritual
goals which are achievable from those that are not.

SECTION THREE: THE DOCTRINE OF TWO SOULS

Here we are introduced to a central concept around which the *Tanya* is based, the
doctrine of "two souls."

אַךְ בֵּיאוּר הָעִנְיָן — **Now that it is clear we are speaking of an inner, psychological**
distinction that distinguishes the *beinoni* from the *tzadik*, **let us turn to an explanation**
of this matter from Kabbalistic sources, which illuminate the inner workings of man.

עַל פִּי מַה שֶׁכָּתַב הָרַב חַיִּים וִיטַאל זִכְרוֹנוֹ לִבְרָכָה בְּשַׁעֲרֵי הַקְּדוּשָׁה — **The following**
is **based on what Rabbi Chaim Vital, of blessed memory, writes in *Sha'arei***
Ha-Kedushah ("*Gates of Holiness,*" volume 1, sections 1-2), [וּבְעֵץ חַיִּים שַׁעַר נ' פֶּרֶק ב']
— **and in *Etz Chaim*, section 50, chapter 2.**

פ"ב] דלכל איש ישראל אחד צדיק ואחד רשע יש שתי
נשמות דכתיב ונשמות אני עשיתי שהן שתי נפשות

Rabbi Chaim ben Yosef Calabrezi Vital (1542-1620) was a major figure in the "Safed School" of Kabbalists that flourished in the middle part of the sixteenth century. He was the closest disciple of Rabbi Yitzchak Luria (*Arizal*, 1534-1572), the most inspired and influential thinker of modern Kabbalah. *Arizal* wrote very little, passing on at a young age, and it was Rabbi Chaim Vital who was largely responsible for committing the incredibly intricate and complex system of his master to writing. The most comprehensive Lurianic work penned by Rabbi Chaim Vital is *Etz Chaim* ("*Tree of Life*"), which took over twenty years to complete, though following the author's wishes, the book was not published in his lifetime. The final manuscript of *Etz Chaim* was edited and completed by Jerusalem Kabbalist, Rabbi Meir Poppers, in 1653 and published for the first time in 1782. Rabbi Poppers also collected the teachings of Rabbi Chaim Vital on prayer and its devotional meditations in another volume, *Pri Etz Chaim* ("*The Fruit of the Tree of Life*"). As we shall see, the *Tanya* quotes both *Etz Chaim* and *Pri Etz Chaim* extensively.

In addition to recording the teachings of his master, Rabbi Chaim Vital also penned some of his own compositions. The most influential of these was *Sha'arei Ha-Kedushah*, an introductory text to Kabbalistically inspired living, with a strong emphasis on ethical conduct. It was first published in 1734, though manuscripts had been circulating more than a century beforehand.

The remainder of chapter one of the *Tanya* closely mirrors the first two chapters of *Sha'arei Ha-Kedushah*.

דְּלְכָל אִישׁ יִשְׂרָאֵל אֶחָד צַדִּיק וְאֶחָד רָשָׁע יֵשׁ שְׁתֵּי נְשָׁמוֹת — In *Sha'arei Ha-Kedushah*, we learn **that every person in Israel, both** *tzadik* **and** *rasha*, **possesses** *two* **souls**, referred to in the *Tanya* as the Animal Soul, and the Divine Soul.

The confrontation between *two entire souls* presented here in the *Tanya*, sharpens the struggle depicted in Rabbinic literature of conflicting "impulses" or "inclinations" within a single psyche. In the *Tanya's* world-view, you really do have two different minds and two sets of conflicting feelings. This approach will prove helpful in validating your inner struggle and finding effective methods to tackle it.

(In stating that two souls are possessed by *"every person in Israel, both tzadik and rasha,"* the *Tanya* rejected the view of some earlier Kabbalists that only the *tzadik* has a Divine Soul—see Rabbi *Avraham Azulai* (c. 1570–1643), *Chesed Le-Avraham* 3:25).

The *Tanya* cites a scriptural source for the presence of two souls in a single person.

וּכְדִכְתִיב וּנְשָׁמוֹת אֲנִי עָשִׂיתִי — **As the verse states,** *"For this is what the high and exalted One says... the spirit that enwraps itself is from Me,* **and the souls which I have made"** (Isaiah 57:15-16; *Likutei Torah* of *Arizal* ibid.).

נפש אחת מצד הקליפה וסטרא אחרא והיא המתלבשת
בדם האדם להחיות הגוף וכדכתיב כי נפש הבשר בדם

The first half of this verse refers to "the spirit" in the singular, suggesting that we are speaking here of a single individual. The verse then concludes that G-d placed in that one person *"souls (plural) which I have made."*

שֶׁהֵן שְׁתֵּי נְפָשׁוֹת — **These are two** complete, independent **souls** in their own right, and not merely levels within a single soul.

In chapter two, we will be introduced to the second, Divine Soul. For the remainder of this chapter we will familiarize ourselves with the first, Animal Soul.

נֶפֶשׁ אַחַת מִצַּד הַקְּלִיפָּה — **One soul stems from the** egocentric forces known as *kelipah* (Sha'arei Ha-Kedushah ibid.).

Throughout the *Zohar*, and in all subsequent works of Kabbalah, the negative forces in the universe are referred to as *kelipah* (pl. *kelipos*), which literally means "peel" or "shell."

The *kelipos* are so-called because they distort our perception of reality, causing us to focus on the external and false, rather than the inner and the true, just as the worthless peel obscures the valuable fruit within.

Kelipah is the consciousness of "unmodified perception," taking the sensory world at face-value by looking exclusively at its "peel" while ignoring its "core." Therefore, it makes you think of yourself as independent from G-d. The resulting attitude is one of selfishness and an urge for sensory gratification.

וְסִטְרָא אָחֳרָא — These forces of *kelipah* are also known, in the *Zohar* and Kabbalsitic literature, as **the "other side"** (*sitra achra*), *i.e.,* that which is not holy.

While being careful not to depart from the monotheistic belief that G-d is the only real power, the *Zohar* tends to describe reality in dualistic terms. The universe, we are taught, is pervaded by two powers, *kedushah* (holiness; goodness) and its opposite, the "other side," both vying for influence. In its worldly manifestation, the "other side" of *kelipah* is a very real and powerful force, and its presence in your Animal Soul is responsible for much inner tension.

(We will elaborate more on the nature of *kelipah* and *sitra achra* in chapter 6, p. 83*ff*. In chapter 9, the *Tanya* will explain why the dualism implicit in the doctrine of the "other side" does not violate Judaism's monotheistic beliefs. See p. 121.)

וְהִיא הַמִּתְלַבֶּשֶׁת בְּדַם הָאָדָם לְהַחֲיוֹת הַגּוּף — The Animal Soul of *kelipah* is **embodied in your blood, energizing your body,** וּכְדִכְתִיב כִּי נֶפֶשׁ הַבָּשָׂר בַּדָּם הִיא — **as the verse states,** *"the soul of the flesh is in the blood"* (Leviticus 17:11).

The *Tanya* emphasizes that the evil and selfish inclinations of your Animal Soul are *embodied* within you. These desires do not arise from an external, metaphysical force or "demon" that incites you, whispering in your ear. Your carnal passions are

היא וממנה באות כל המדות רעות מארבע יסודות רעים

very much part of you. (Later on, this will represent another important element of the *Tanya's* validation of your struggles.)

The analogy of "peel" also offers us some insight into how the Animal Soul accesses the body, as *Sha'arei Ha-Kedushah* (ibid.) explains:

> *"The pure (Divine) Soul which is the 'fruit'... is invested within in the impure (Animal) Soul, which is called the 'peel (kelipah) of the fruit,' and both of them together are invested in... the body. Thus, the component parts of the holy (Divine) Soul are situated **within** the component parts of the impure (Animal) Soul, and the component parts of the impure (Animal) Soul are inside the component parts of the body"* (see below, p. 322).

PRACTICAL LESSONS

The Kabbalah teaches that we possess two souls. The first, Animal Soul energizes the body and disposes us to basic temperaments, usually negative. Its point of synergy with the body is the blood.

The spiritual energy of the Animal Soul is from *kelipah* (peel; husk), a cosmic force that allows us to perceive only the sensory (like a peel which conceals the fruit inside), and blinds us to the truth of things beyond their appearance.

The Animal Soul is the source of negative traits such as anger, lust, silliness, mockery, boasting, laziness and depression. But it can also motivate acts of kindness and compassion.

Only your Animal Soul has direct access to your body as a whole; it alone is "in the blood." (As we shall see in chapter 9 (p. 113), the Divine Soul's influence is limited to the emotions of the heart and thoughts of the brain).

וּמִמֶּנָּה בָּאוֹת כָּל הַמִּדוֹת — **From** the Animal Soul, which is invested directly into the body, **all the** bodily **temperaments arise.**

This is a reference to the classical model of "four temperaments." In this system, various natural temperaments or "humors" of the personality are understood to arise from the *body itself*, rather than from the mind *etc.* The "four temperaments": choleric, phlegmatic, sanguine and melancholic, closely parallel the classical subdivision of matter into four elemental forms: fire, water, air and earth.

In the Kabbalah, this idea is developed further and the four elements are depicted not only in physical, but also in *spiritual* phenomena. Just as the body is composed of four physical elements, the soul is understood to be composed of four spiritual elements: fire, water, air and earth.

Following these classical models, the *Tanya* will now explain that the four temperaments of the body actually flow from four spiritual "elements" present in the Animal Soul.

רָעוֹת מֵאַרְבָּעָה יְסוֹדוֹת רָעִים שֶׁבָּהּ — The **negative** temperaments **stem from the negative** side of the Animal Soul's **four** spiritual **elements.**

שבה דהיינו כעס וגאוה מיסוד האש שנגבה למעלה. ותאות התענוגים מיסוד המים כי המים מצמיחים כל מיני תענוג. והוללות וליצנות והתפארות ודברים בטלים

According to the Kabbalah, each of the four elements, both in their physical and spiritual forms, has a good and an evil side. As Rabbi Chaim Vital explains (*ibid.*):

"You should know that Adam's sin, eating from the Tree of Knowledge of good and evil, resulted in both his soul and body likewise becoming a mixture of good and evil... and this caused such a mixing to occur in all the (physical and spiritual) worlds. Now there is nothing which does not contain both good and evil."

Echoing Rabbi Chaim Vital's discussion, the *Tanya* now details the four elements of the Animal Soul alongside the bodily temperaments they give rise to. We will begin with the "negative side" of the elements, which is the strongest energy in the Animal Soul.

דְהַיְינוּ כַּעַס וְגַאֲוָה מִיסוֹד הָאֵשׁ — **Namely,** a) the "choleric" temperament of **anger and arrogance from the** negative side of **the element of fire** in the Animal Soul, שֶׁנִגְבָּה לְמַעְלָה — the overstated self-image of arrogance **reflecting** physical **fire's tendency to rise upwards.**

Rabbi Chaim Vital explains: *"It is the result of a person's arrogance that he becomes angry, seeing that people do not comply with his will. If he were humble, recognizing his shortcomings, he would not become angry at all. So arrogance and anger are, in fact, the same temperament."*

This negative temperament, *"has three derivatives: 1. Resentment in the heart, for without arrogance their would be no resentment in the heart. 2. Seeking power and honor, to show off to others. 3. Hatred for somebody because he is greater than you."*

וְתַאֲוַת הַתַּעֲנוּגִים מִיסוֹד הַמַּיִם — b) The "phlegmatic" temperament of seeking physical **gratification and pleasures, which stems from the** negative side of the **element of water,** in the Animal Soul, כִּי הַמַּיִם מַצְמִיחִים כָּל מִינֵי תַעֲנוּג — reflecting the physical reality *"that all pleasures are* ultimately **cultivated from water"** (*Sha'arei Ha-Kedushah*, ibid.).

The derivatives of this negative temperament *"are two: 1) Coveting: (desiring to) steal your friend's money, or his wife, and everything that he has, in order to indulge in them. 2) Jealousy, to be jealous of your wealthy friend etc.,"* (ibid.)

וְהוֹלְלוּת וְלֵיצָנוּת וְהִתְפָּאֲרוּת וּדְבָרִים בְּטֵלִים מִיסוֹד הָרוּחַ — c) The "sanguine" temperament arising **from** the negative side of **the element of air** in the Animal Soul: **silliness, mockery, boasting** of virtues you don't have, **and** other **worthless discussion,** that benefits neither body nor soul.

These traits are insubstantial, like air. Their attitude reflects airy "lightness" and a lack of responsibility.

מִיסוֹד הרוח. ועצלות ועצבות מיסוד העפר. וגם מדות 6A
טובות שבטבע כל ישראל בתולדותם כמו רחמנות וג"ח

וְעַצְלוּת וְעַצְבוּת מִיסוֹד הֶעָפָר — **and,** d) The "melancholic" temperament of **laziness and depression,** stemming **from the** negative side of the **element of earth** in the Animal Soul.

It is important to recall that we are speaking here of inherent, *bodily* temperaments (stemming from the Animal Soul which is *embodied* "in the blood"). These are natural propensities with which you were born and to which you will automatically "default" in the absence of enlightenment and spiritual work.

While our discussion of the negative side of the Animal Soul has been detailed, the *Tanya's* treatment of the positive side will be brief, (presumably because the energy of the Animal Soul is predominantly negative).

וְגַם מִדּוֹת טוֹבוֹת שֶׁבְּטֶבַע כָּל יִשְׂרָאֵל בְּתוֹלְדוֹתָם — **But also the positive temperaments, with which,** the *Talmud* testifies, **all Israel are naturally born,** כְּמוֹ רַחֲמָנוּת וּגְמִילוּת חֲסָדִים בָּאוֹת מִמֶּנָּה — **such as** *"compassion and generosity"* (*Talmud, Yevamos* 79a), **stem from** the Animal Soul.

Sha'arei Ha-Kedushah (ibid.) states that the "good side" of your Animal Soul's four elements mirrors their "bad side" precisely. In place of arrogance and anger, the good side of your Animal Soul's "fire"draws you to humility, leading you not to take things personally and get angry. Rather than seeking pleasure, the good side of "water" despises bodily excess. The good side of "air," instead of inspiring "worthless talk," leads you to be impeccable with your words. And the good side of

A CHASIDIC THOUGHT

I possess two sorts of consciousness, two ways of interpreting the meaning of reality. My Animal Soul conceives the world purely in terms of sensory perception, the visual and the empirical. Since my five senses cannot directly experience the spiritual or the Divine, my Animal Soul mistakenly views itself as possessing an independent existence from G-d and has a self-centered orientation.

My second, Divine Soul interprets the world through the more abstract lens of contemplation. It attempts to discern the truth of things beyond their deceptive appearance, believing that the direct experience of the senses is short-sighted. Its natural tendency is to be drawn to its source.

The task of my Divine Soul is to enlighten my Animal Soul about its erroneous perception and to teach it the truth beyond its limited sensory faculties.

באות ממנה כי בישראל נפש זו דקליפה היא מקליפ'
נוגה שיש בה ג"כ טוב והיא מסוד עץ הדעת טוב ורע:
משא"כ נפשות אומות עובדי גלולים הן משאר קליפות
טמאות שאין בהן טוב כלל כמ"ש בע"ח שער מ"ט פ"ג וכל

"earth" in the Animal Soul encourages you to be joyous, out of the conviction that every occurrence is orchestrated by G-d for the best.

As we have learned, the mixture of good and bad in the Animal Soul resulted from the Sin of the Tree of Knowledge, which *"caused such a mixing to occur in all the (physical and spiritual) worlds."* The *Tanya* now examines this point further.

כִּי בְּיִשְׂרָאֵל נֶפֶשׁ זוֹ דְקְלִיפָּה הִיא מִקְּלִיפַּת נוֹגַהּ שֶׁיֵּשׁ בָּהּ גַּם כֵּן טוֹב — **Because, in the case of Israelites, this** Animal **Soul of** *kelipah* **is from** a derivative called *kelipas nogah* **("bright** *kelipah***"), which contains some** easily accessible sparks of **good too,** וְהִיא מִסּוֹד עֵץ הַדַּעַת טוֹב וָרָע — this mixing of good sparks resulting **from the secret of the** Biblical **"Tree of Knowledge of Good and Evil"** (*Etz Chaim* 49:3).

The *Zohar* refers to four derivatives of *kelipah*, alluded to by the verse, *"(1) a stormy wind... (2) a great cloud, with (3) flashing fire, and (4) brightness (nogah)"* (*Ezekiel* 1:4). As we will soon see, the first three of these *kelipos* are completely negative and impure. But concerning the fourth derivative, "brightness," the *Zohar* explains, *"even though this side is nothing but the side of impurity, there is brightness around it and man does not have to drive it away... there is no need to treat it with disdain"* (*Zohar* 2, 203b. See also *ibid.* 227a-b).

The fourth *kelipah, nogah,* is predominantly a negative, egocentric energy like the other three *kelipos,* and *"is nothing but the side of impurity."* But, on the other hand, its "brightness" indicates a spark of holiness lying just below the surface, which could be redeemed under the right circumstances. (We will discuss this at length later on, in chapter 7).

Etz Chaim (*ibid.*) explains that this "brightness" resulted from the sin of the Tree of Knowledge, which *"primarily affected only kelipas nogah."*

And it is here that *Etz Chaim* introduces a national element into the discussion, stating that while *"the Animal Soul of Israel... is from nogah,"*

מַה שֶּׁאֵין כֵּן נַפְשׁוֹת אוּמּוֹת הָעוֹלָם — this is not the case with the souls of the evil **"nations of the world,"** הֵן מִשְּׁאָר קְלִיפּוֹת טְמֵאוֹת שֶׁאֵין בָּהֶן טוֹב כְּלָל כְּמוֹ שֶׁכָּתוּב בְּעֵץ חַיִּים שַׁעַר מ"ט פֶּרֶק ג' — **which, as stated in** *Etz Chaim,* **section 49, chapter 3, stem from** the three **other, impure** *kelipos* that *"are devoid of any (overt) good."**

---

*For the stress that this refers specifically to *"evil* nations" and to the lack of *"overt"* good" see comments of Rabbi Hillel Malisov of Paritch (1795-1864), a close disciple of Rabbi Shneur Zalman, in *Ma'amarei Admor Ha-Emtzoi, Kuntresim* (Brooklyn: Kehos, 1995), p. 144; Rabbi Menachem Mendel of Lubavitch, *Kitzurim Ve-Ha'aros Le-Sefer Likutei Amarim* (Brooklyn: Kehos, 1948), p. 3. See also below, author's note to chapter 6, pp. 90-91.

טיבו דעבדין האומות עובדי גלולים לגרמייהו עבדין
וכדאיתא בגמרא ע"פ וחסד לאומים חטאת שכל צדקה
וחסד שאומות עובדי גלולים עושין אינן אלא להתייהר כו':

Etz Chaim's distinction between the Animal Souls of Israelites and the "nations of the world" is alarming for contemporary readers, but it was normative in the *Zohar* and in the major texts of medieval and early-modern Kabbalah. It also echoed sentiments expressed by a number of teachings in the *Talmud* and *Midrash,* (although some *Talmudic* Rabbis did espouse a positive view of "the nations").

וְכָל טִיבוּ דְּעָבְדִין הָאֻמּוֹת לְגַרְמַיְיהוּ עָבְדִין — *Etz Chaim's* approach is supported by teachings of the *Zohar,* such as *"All good (that the nations do), they do for themselves"* (*Tikunei Zohar* 22a; see also *Zohar* 1, 47a, 131b), וְכַדְאִיתָא בַּגְּמָרָא עַל פָּסוּק וְחֶסֶד לְאֻמִּים חַטָּאת — and some teachings of the *Talmud,* such as its commentary on the verse, *"the kindness of the nations is sinful"* (*Proverbs* 14:34) שֶׁכָּל צְדָקָה וְחֶסֶד שֶׁאֻמּוֹת הָעוֹלָם עוֹשִׂין אֵינָן אֶלָּא לְהִתְיַיהֵר כוּ' — that, according to Rabban Gamliel, *"all the charity and kindness done by the nations (of the world) is 'sinful' to them since **they only do it to put on airs etc.,"*** (*Talmud, Bava Basra* 10b).

While this sharp national distinction does surface again, the thrust of the *Tanya* is not national but psychological. Therefore the question of how the modern reader might contextualize *Etz Chaim's* views—a point which has been explored extensively by scholars**—need not overly concern us here.

** For contemporary Chabad interpretations see: Rabbi Chaim Miller, *Turning Judaism Outward* (New York: Kol Menachem, 2014), pp. 336-7; Rabbi Adin Steinsaltz, *Opening the Tanya* (San Francisco: Jossey-Bass 2003), pp. 68-69; Rabbi Ya'akov Leib Altein *et al.* (eds.), *Chasidus Mevu'eres, Tanya,* vol. 1 (New York: Heichal Menachem, 2008), [Hebrew] p. 71, and notes 60-61; Rabbi Yitzchak Ginsburgh, *Kabbalah and Meditation for the Nations* (Kfar Chabad: Gal Einai, 2006). For academic discussions see: Elliot Wolfson, *Venturing Beyond: Law and Morality in Kabbalistic Mysticism* (Oxford University Press, 2006), pp. 5n15, 26-57, 73-128; idem., *Open Secret: Postmessianic Messianism and the Mystical Revision of Menahem Mendel Schneerson* (Columbia University Press, 2009), pp. 44, 152-3, 184-5, 224-264; Shaul Magid, *From Metaphysics to Midrash: Myth, History, and the Interpretation of Scripture in Lurianic Kabbala* (Indiana University Press, 2008), pp. 143-149, 295n41; Alan Brill, *Judaism and Other Religions: Models of Understanding* (Palgrave Macmillan, 2010), pp. 164-173; Jody Myers, *Kabbalah for the Gentiles: Diverse Souls and Universalism in Contemporary Kabbalah* in Boaz Huss (ed.), *Kabbalah and Contemporary Spiritual Revival* (Ben-Gurion University of the Negev Press, 2011), pp. 181-212; Moshe Hallamish, *The Attitude of the Kabbalists to Non-Jews* [Hebrew], in Hallamish and Kasher, *Filosophia Yisraelit* (Papyrus, 1983), pp. 49-71; Hanan Balk, *The Soul of a Jew and the Soul of a Non-Jew,* in *Hakira: The Flatbush Journal of Jewish Law and Thought,* vol. 16 (2013), p. 47-76. For the psychological as opposed to national thrust of the *Tanya,* see Jonathan Garb, *Yearnings of the Soul: Psychological Thought in Modern Kabbalah* (University of Chicago Press, 2015), p. 52. See also handwritten note of the Lubavitcher Rebbe, reproduced in *Teshurah, Block-Wenger* 2016, p. 49.

פרק ב ונפש   השנית בישראל היא חלק אלוה
ממעל ממש כמ"ש ויפח באפיו
נשמת חיים ואתה נפחת בי וכמ"ש בזוהר מאן דנפח

CHAPTER 2

THE PIECE OF G-D IN YOU

SECTION ONE: YOUR SECOND SOUL

24TH KISLEV REGULAR | 26TH KISLEV LEAP

In chapter one, the *Tanya* introduced us to Rabbi Chaim Vital's doctrine of two souls. We learned that the first, Animal Soul, is driven by an egocentric energy called *kelipah* and is largely responsible for bad temperaments. In this chapter, we will examine the second, Divine Soul.

וְנֶפֶשׁ הַשֵּׁנִית בְּיִשְׂרָאֵל — **The second soul in the Israelite,** the so-called Divine Soul, הִיא חֵלֶק אֱלוֹהַּ מִמַּעַל — **is** *"a piece of G-d above"* (*Job* 31:2), מַמָּשׁ — **literally.**

The description of the soul as "literally" Divine is striking, since Jewish teachings are usually careful to emphasize a sharp distinction between the Creator and His creations. Rabbi Chaim Vital explains: *"The soul's light arises and flows from the light of the ten sefiros (Divine powers) themselves, without any intermediary; which is why the verse states, 'You are children of G-d your G-d' (Deuteronomy 14:1); for (the soul) is like a child who is completely attached to his father, from whom his being flows"* (*Sha'arei Ha-Kedushah* 3:2).

The application of the verse *"a piece of G-d above"* to describe this attachment of the soul dates back to Safed Kabbalist Rabbi Moshe Cordovero (*Ramak*, 1522–1570; in *Pardes Rimonim* 31:3). Rabbi Elijah de Vidas (1518–1592), *Ramak's* student, used this phrase in his popular Kabbalistic work *Reishis Chochmah* (2:1), which appeared in print as early as 1578, and from there it became a standard reference in the Kabbalistic/ethical literature. (The emphasis "literally" is first found in Rabbi Shabbetai Sheftel Horowitz (c. 1561-1619), *Shefa Tal* (Hanau, 1612), introduction.)

כְּמוֹ שֶׁכָּתוּב וַיִּפַּח בְּאַפָּיו נִשְׁמַת חַיִּים — **The idea of a Divine Soul is suggested by the verse** describing man's creation, *"And (G-d) blew into his nostrils the breath of life"* (*Genesis* 2:7).

Nachmanides (*Ramban*, 1194–c. 1270), an early Spanish Kabbalist, was the first to explain this verse as evidence of a Divine Soul: *"This verse hints for us the virtue of the soul.... It states that '(G-d) breathed into his nostrils a soul of life,' to inform you that (the soul) is not derived from the elements... rather, it is the spirit of G-d"* (*Ramban*, commentary to *Genesis* 2:7).

מתוכיה נפח פי' מתוכיותו ומפנימיותו שתוכיות ופנימיות
החיות שבאדם מוציא בנפיחתו בכח: כך עד"מ נשמות
ישראל עלו במחשבה כדכתיב בני בכורי ישראל בנים
אתם לה' אלהיכם פי' כמו שהבן נמשך ממוח האב כך

וְאַתָּה נְפַחְתָּ בִּי — **And** the same idea is suggested by the phrase, *"The soul... **You breathed it into me"*** (Liturgy, Morning Prayers).

וּכְמוֹ שֶׁכָּתוּב בַּזֹהַר מַאן דְּנָפַח מִתּוֹכֵיהּ נָפַח — **And, as** the Sages of **the *Zohar* state,** that unlike speaking, which uses relatively little breath, *"One who blows, blows from his innards,"* פֵּירוּשׁ מִתּוֹכִיּוּתוֹ וּמִפְּנִימִיּוּתוֹ — **meaning from the innermost depths of his being,** שֶׁתּוֹכִיּוּת וּפְנִימִיּוּת הַחַיּוּת שֶׁבָּאָדָם מוֹצִיא בִּנְפִיחָתוֹ בְּכֹחַ — **for when a person blows forcibly, he exhales with a deep-rooted, inner energy.**

The Biblical metaphor of "blowing in" man's soul suggests that G-d has a deep, inward attachment with the soul, in distinction to the rest of creation, which arose through the more superficial "speech" of G-d, ("G-d *said*, let there be...").

(While the *Tanya* refers to this as a teaching of the "*Zohar*," it is not found in our *Zohar* text. It is, however, cited as a teaching "of the Sages" by Rabbi Naftali Hertz Bacharach in *Eimek Ha-Melech, "Valley of the King,"* (16:10), published in 1648).

PRACTICAL LESSONS

Your Divine Soul is a "piece of G-d," literally. G-d is more present in your soul than in any other part of the universe.

A further teaching which illustrates the intimate connection between the "second soul" and G-d, is the *Midrashic* idea of the Jewish people arising in G-d's "mind" prior to creation.

כָּךְ עַל דֶּרֶךְ מָשָׁל נִשְׁמוֹת יִשְׂרָאֵל עָלוּ בְּמַחֲשָׁבָה — **In the same vein,** the *Midrash* **depicts the Jewish souls as having** *"arisen in the mind of G-d"* (*Genesis Rabah* 1:4), before the creation of the world.

This intimate connection is also depicted scripturally as a parental relationship.

כְּדִכְתִיב בְּנִי בְכוֹרִי יִשְׂרָאֵל — **As the verse states,** *"Israel, My firstborn son"* (*Exodus* 4:22), בָּנִים אַתֶּם לַה' אֱלֹהֵיכֶם — *"You are children to G-d, your G-d"* (*Deuteronomy* 14:1).

What is the connection between the *Midrashic* idea of souls arising from the "mind" of G-d and the Biblical metaphor of souls as "children" of G-d?

To clarify this point, the *Tanya* now enters into a discussion which will be central to our chapter, concerning the spiritual origins of a child in his or her father.

פֵּירוּשׁ כְּמוֹ שֶׁהַבֵּן נִמְשָׁךְ מִמּוֹחַ הָאָב — **This means that just as** *"a child is 'derived' from the brain of the father"* (*Tikunei Zohar* 35a), כָּךְ כִּבְיָכוֹל נִשְׁמַת כָּל אִישׁ יִשְׂרָאֵל נִמְשָׁכָה מִמַּחֲשַׁבְתּוֹ וְחָכְמָתוֹ יִתְבָּרֵךְ — **likewise, each person in Israel is "derived"** from G-d's blessed thought and wisdom, so to speak (*Reishis Chochmah* 4:1).

כביכול נשמת כל איש ישראל נמשכה ממחשבתו
וחכמתו ית' דאיהו חכים ולא בחכמה ידיעא אלא הוא
וחכמתו א' וכמ"ש הרמב"ם*

הגהה

והודו לו חכמי הקבלה כמ"ש בפרדס

מהרמ"ק וגם לפי קבלת האר"י ז"ל

שהוא המדע והוא היודע
כו' ודבר זה אין ביכולת

From antiquity until the early modern period, it was believed that male seed was physically derived from the cerebral matter of the brain, passing down the spine, and exiting through a duct at the spine's base. While this was later shown to be anatomically incorrect, the Kabbalists accepted the brain/spine/seed pathway as spiritually valid. (In one of his discourses, Rabbi Shneur Zalman made clear that he understood the idea non-literally: *"It must be a spiritual power that emerges from the brain"*—*Torah Ohr* 16a.) Here the *Tanya* uses the brain/seed/child connection to illustrate how the "children of G-d" are connected with the "thought and wisdom" of G-d, their "father."

But this only demonstrates how the soul is connected with G-d's "wisdom." How are we to explain that every soul is a "piece" of G-d *Himself*?

To answer this question, the *Tanya* will now probe the unique quality of G-d's wisdom, how it differs from human wisdom.

דְּאִיהוּ חַכִּים וְלָא בְּחָכְמָה יְדִיעָא — Concerning G-d's wisdom, *Tikunei Zohar* states, *"He is wise, but not with wisdom as we know it"* (17b).

The way G-d knows something is fundamentally different to the way humans know things. A person and his knowledge remain two separate entities; information is something *acquired*.

אֶלָּא הוּא וְחָכְמָתוֹ אֶחָד — **But,** in the case of G-d, *"He and His wisdom are one,"* וּכְמוֹ שֶׁכָּתַב הָרַמְבַּ"ם — **as** *Rambam* **writes.***

שֶׁהוּא הַמַּדָּע וְהוּא הַיּוֹדֵעַ כו' — *Rambam* explains **that,** unlike humans, G-d is simultaneously the "power to know," the "knower" and the "known," וְדָבָר זֶה אֵין בִּיכוֹלֶת

---

*הַגָּהָה — **NOTE.** The *Tanya* cited *Rambam* to prove that "G-d and His wisdom are one." This is problematic since *Rambam* followed the school of Jewish Philosophy that was often at odds with Kabbalah (on which the *Tanya* is based).

וְהוֹדוּ לוֹ חַכְמֵי הַקַּבָּלָה — Nevertheless, in this instance, **the sages of the Kabbalah concurred with** *Rambam* that, *"He and His knowledge are one,"* כְּמוֹ שֶׁכָּתוּב בַּפַּרְדֵּס מֵהָרַמַ"ק — **as Rabbi Moshe Cordovero writes in** *Pardes* (4:4).

וְגַם לְפִי קַבָּלַת הָאַר"י זִכְרוֹנוֹ לִבְרָכָה יַצִּיבָא מִילְּתָא — **And even according to Lurianic Kabbalah,** which is the *Tanya's* primary source, *Rambam's* view **can be reconciled** as follows:

הָאָדָם לְהָבִינוֹ עַל בּוֹרְיוֹ כו' יְצִיבָא מִילְתָא בְּסוֹד הַתְלַבְּשׁוּת אוֹר אֵ"ס
כְּדִכְתִיב הַחֵקֶר אֱלוֹהַּ תִּמְצָא ב"ה עַל יְדֵי צִמְצוּמִים רַבִּים בְּכֵלִים
וּכְתִיב כִּי לֹא מַחְשְׁבוֹתַי דַחַב"ד דַּאֲצִילוּ' אַךְ לֹא לְמַעְלָה מֵהָאֲצִילוּ'

'הָאָדָם לְהָבִינוֹ עַל בּוֹרְיוֹ כו — *"but this concept defies coherent mortal comprehension,"* — כְּדִכְתִיב הַחֵקֶר אֱלוֹהַּ תִּמְצָא — as the verse states, *"Can you find G-d by searching?"* (*Job* 11:7), וּכְתִיב כִּי לֹא מַחְשְׁבוֹתַי מַחְשְׁבוֹתֵיכֶם וְגוֹ — and it is also written, *"For My thoughts are not your thoughts etc."* (*Isaiah* 55:8; paraphrased from *Mishneh Torah, Laws of Foundations of the Torah* 2:10; *Laws of Teshuvah* 5:5).

Rambam understood that G-d *is* His knowledge. The school of Kabbalah, on the other hand, described G-d as something much higher than knowledge — an abstract, "Infinite Light." (G-d's knowledge, the Kabbalists taught, is a mere *emanation* of that light).

We can reconcile the two views by arguing that, according to Lurianic Kabbalah, *Rambam's* view was correct, *in a certain context.*

בְּסוֹד הַתְלַבְּשׁוּת אוֹר אֵין סוֹף בָּרוּךְ הוּא עַל יְדֵי צִמְצוּמִים רַבִּים בְּכֵלִים — *Rambam's* view can be contextualized **through the secret doctrine of how the "Infinite Light"** of G-d **underwent multiple diminishments to** the point that it could **enter** finite **"vessels."**

Any description of the creation process must explain the paradox of how an infinite G-d gives rise to a finite world. Lurianic Kabbalah describes this transition as a process of infinite Divine "lights" entering and becoming enmeshed in (somewhat) finite, Divine "vessels." In this "secret doctrine," G-d's knowledge is perceived as a quality endowed by the "vessels," not the "lights."

Therefore, the *Tanya* suggests, *Rambam's* description of "G-d as knowledge" is true, from a Lurianic perspective, *of the vessels,*

דְּחָכְמָה בִּינָה וְדַעַת — of G-d's intellectual powers of *chochmah* (inquiry), *binah* (cognition) and *da'as* (recognition).

As we will discuss at length in the next chapter, G-d's intellect is understood by the Kabbalah to function through three distinct powers: inquiry, cognition and recognition.

דַּאֲצִילוּת — G-d's intellectual power functions **in the World of *Atzilus* ("Emanation"),** the world of Divine attributes.

We are speaking here of *G-d's* intellect, which functions in the highest of the spiritual worlds, *Atzilus.*

אַךְ לֹא לְמַעְלָה מֵהָאֲצִילוּת — **But** *Rambam's* assertion that G-d is synonymous with His knowledge is **not** correct **above** *Atzilus,* which is the realm of "Infinite Light" devoid of any definitive characteristics (such as intellect).

מחשבותיכם וגו' ואף שיש   וכמ"ש במ"א שא"ס ב"ה מרומם
רבבות מיני חלוקי מדרגות   ומתנשא רוממות אין קץ למעלה מעלה
בנשמו' גבוה על גבוה לאין   ממהות ובחי' חב"ד עד שמהות ובחי'
   6B   קץ כמו גודל מעלת נשמות האבות ומשה רבינו

יתברך כמ"ש כולם בחכמה עשית: חב"ד נחשבת כעשייה גופניית אצלו

In conclusion: The *Tanya* offers us two metaphors to illustrate the intimate union of the Divine Soul with G-d: a) It was "blown" from G-d's "innards"; b) It is derived from G-d's wisdom, which is totally one with Him.

SECTION TWO: ARE ALL SOULS EQUAL?

The notion that *every* Divine Soul is "a piece of G-d," seems to fly in the face of a commonly accepted view in works of the Kabbalah, that there is a hierarchy of souls—some exalted, others ordinary.

וְאַף שֶׁיֵּשׁ רְבָבוֹת מִינֵי חִלּוּקֵי מַדְרֵגוֹת בַּנְּשָׁמוֹת — **And even though there are tens of thousands of different levels of souls (neshamos),** גָּבוֹהַּ מֵעַל גָּבוֹהַּ לְאֵין קֵץ — *"one higher than the other"* (Ecclesiastes 5:7), **to no end,** this poses no contradiction to each soul being "a piece of G-d," as we shall see.

Before explaining why this is the case, the *Tanya* brings some examples of different soul levels.

כְּמוֹ גוֹדֶל מַעֲלַת נִשְׁמוֹת הָאָבוֹת וּמֹשֶׁה רַבֵּינוּ עֲלֵיהֶם הַשָּׁלוֹם — **Such as the superior quality of the souls of the Patriarchs and of Moshe (Moses) our teacher, peace**

וּכְמוֹ שֶׁכָּתוּב בְּמָקוֹם אַחֵר — **As is explained elsewhere** (*Tanya, Sha'ar Ha-Yichud Ve-Ha-Emunah,* chapter 9), שֶׁאֵין סוֹף בָּרוּךְ הוּא מְרוֹמָם וּמִתְנַשֵּׂא רוֹמְמוּת אֵין קֵץ — **that the Blessed Infinite** Light is **incomparably higher and more exalted than the energies of chochmah, binah and da'as** of the World of *Atzilus,* לְמַעְלָה מַעְלָה מִמַּהוּת וּבְחִינַת חָכְמָה בִּינָה וָדַעַת עַד שֶׁמַּהוּת וּבְחִינַת חָכְמָה בִּינָה וָדַעַת נֶחְשֶׁבֶת כַּעֲשִׂיָּה גוּפָנִיִּית אֶצְלוֹ יִתְבָּרֵךְ — **to the extent that,** from the perspective of the "Infinite Light," even **the energies of chochmah, binah and da'as of the World of Atzilus are considered by G-d** as remote **as physical action.**

When viewed from the perspective of infinitude, all finite things seem equally remote, (both "vessels" that produce Divine intellect and the physical world).

כְּמוֹ שֶׁכָּתוּב כּוּלָם בְּחָכְמָה עָשִׂיתָ — **As the verse** hints, when it **states,** *"You made them all with chochmah"* (Psalms 104:24), equating *"chochmah"* (Divine intellect) with "making" (*i.e.,* physical action).

In conclusion: The *Tanya* can confidently quote *Rambam's* teaching that *"G-d and His knowledge are one,"* even in a Kabbalistic discussion, since, from a certain perspective, *Rambam's* statement is true according to the Kabbalah.

ע״ה על נשמות דורותינו אלה דעקבי משיח׳ שהם
בחי׳ עקביים ממש לגבי המוח והראש וכן בכל דור
ודור יש ראשי אלפי ישראל שנשמותיהם הם בחי׳
ראש ומוח לגבי נשמות ההמון וע״ה וכן נפשות לגבי
נפשות כי כל נפש כלולה מנפש רוח ונשמה מכל
מקום שרש כל הנפש רוח ונשמה כולם מראש כל
המדריגות עד סוף כל דרגין המלובש בגוף עמי הארץ

עַל נִשְׁמוֹת דּוֹרוֹתֵינוּ אֵלֶּה דְּעִקְבֵּי מְשִׁיחָא — over the quality of the souls of these historically late **generations,** depicted by the *Talmud* as *"the footsteps of the Messiah"* (*Talmud, Sotah* 49b), שֶׁהֵם בְּחִינַת עִקְבַיִים מַמָּשׁ לְגַבֵּי הַמּוֹחַ וְהָרֹאשׁ — the term "foot" suggesting that **these** souls **literally have the** quality of **"feet" compared to the** souls of earlier generations, which had the quality of the **"brain" and "head."**

The difference in quality of souls extends, not only from one generation to another, but even *within* a single generation.

And — וְכֵן בְּכָל דּוֹר וָדוֹר יֵשׁ רָאשֵׁי אַלְפֵי יִשְׂרָאֵל שֶׁנִּשְׁמוֹתֵיהֶם הֵם בְּחִינַת רֹאשׁ וּמוֹחַ similarly, in every generation, there are leaders in Israel whose souls are like the "brain" and "head," לְגַבֵּי נִשְׁמוֹת הֶהָמוֹן וְעַמֵּי הָאָרֶץ — **compared to the souls of masses and ignorant people,** which are lower.

PRACTICAL LESSONS

Your Divine Soul is rooted in the very same place as the most righteous souls who have ever lived!

These differences in the quality are to be found not only when comparing the more sophisticated layer of the souls (*neshamos*) to each other, but even when comparing the most basic soul levels (*nefashos*).

וְכֵן נְפָשׁוֹת לְגַבֵּי נְפָשׁוֹת — **So too,** even when comparing *nefashos* of higher souls **with** *nefashos* of lower souls, there is a major difference between them in quality, even in this basic soul-layer, which you might imagine to be equal in all people.

The *Tanya* briefly reminds its readers of the three-layered structure of the soul, described in the *Zohar*.

כִּי כָּל נֶפֶשׁ כְּלוּלָה — **For,** as we know, **every soul contains** three layers, מִנֶּפֶשׁ — *nefesh,* body-intelligence, רוּחַ — *ruach,* emotional-intelligence, וּנְשָׁמָה — and *neshamah,* self-conscious intelligence (*Zohar* 3, 70b).

However, despite these vast differences, all souls do, in fact, share the same root.

מִכָּל מָקוֹם שֹׁרֶשׁ כָּל הַנֶּפֶשׁ רוּחַ וּנְשָׁמָה כּוּלָם — **Nevertheless, the root of every** *nefesh, ruach* **and** *neshamah,* מֵרֹאשׁ כָּל הַמַּדְרֵיגוֹת — **from the very highest level** of soul, עַד סוֹף כָּל דַּרְגִין הַמְלוּבָשׁ בְּגוּף עַמֵּי הָאָרֶץ וְקַל שֶׁבְּקַלִּים — **to the very lowest of** soul

וְקל שבקלים נמשך ממוח העליון שהיא חכמה עילאה
כביכול כמשל הבן הנמשך ממוח האב שאפי׳ צפרני
רגליו נתהוו מטפה זו ממש ע״י שהייתה תשעה חדשים
בבטן האם וירדה ממדרגה למדרגה להשתנות ולהתהוו׳
ממנה צפרנים ועם כל זה עודנה קשורה ומיוחדת ביחוד
נפלא ועצום במהותה ועצמותה הראשון שהיתה טפת
מוח האב וגם עכשיו בבן יניקת הצפרנים וחיותם נמשכת

ranks, found in simple folk and the most religiously irreverent people, נִמְשָׁךְ מִמּוֹחַ הָעֶלְיוֹן שֶׁהִיא חָכְמָה עִילָּאָה כְּבְיָכוֹל — all these souls, without exception, **flow from the** loftiest Divine energies, referred to **figuratively** in the Kabbalah as *Mo'ach Ila'ah,* **"Supernal Brain"** (*Etz Chaim* 13:3), **which is** also called **"Supernal Wisdom,"** *Chochmah Ila'ah,* (*Zohar* 1, 34a).

The *Tanya* has "democratized" the hierarchy of souls, arguing that each soul *in its root* is attached to G-d's "brain" and "wisdom."

But if all souls have the same exalted source, how are we to explain the huge differences in their abilities? To answer this question the *Tanya* draws again on the brain/seed/child metaphor we encountered earlier.

כְּמְשַׁל הַבֵּן הַנִּמְשָׁךְ מִמּוֹחַ הָאָב — **As in the** above **metaphor of a child,** born from seed which is **"derived" from the father's brain,** שֶׁאֲפִילוּ צִפָרְנֵי רַגְלָיו נִתְהַוּוּ מִטְפָּה זוֹ מַמָּשׁ — **where even the** child's **toenails are formed from the very same drop** of seed as the child's higher faculties, עַל יְדֵי שֶׁהָיְיתָה תִּשְׁעָה חֲדָשִׁים בְּבֶטֶן הָאֵם — **through a nine-month gestation in the mother's womb,** וְיָרְדָה מִמַּדְרֵגָה לְמַדְרֵגָה לְהִשְׁתַּנּוֹת וּלְהִתְהַוּוֹת מִמֶּנָּה צִפָרְנַיִם — **during which time, the seminal drop "derived" from the** father's brain, **is progressively downgraded and transformed to the point that** even the child's **nails are formed from it.**

While all parts of the child's body share the same seminal origin, some limbs and organs represent a more "downgraded" expression of their source than others: the same "drop" produces both the phenomenally complex brain as well as the simple nail. Through a similar spiritual "gestation," a single lofty spiritual source ("Supernal Wisdom") can give rise to the souls of both spiritual giants and "irreverent people."

וְעִם כָּל זֶה עוֹדֶנָּה קְשׁוּרָה וּמְיוּחֶדֶת בְּיִחוּד נִפְלָא וְעָצוּם בְּמַהוּתָהּ וְעַצְמוּתָהּ הָרִאשׁוֹן — **Nevertheless,** even in the nail, the drop has only changed in its *manifest form,* but in terms of *inner identity,* it **remains bound and unified, in a wondrous and powerful unity, with its original core essence,** שֶׁהָיְיתָה טִפַּת מוֹחַ הָאָב — **as it existed in the** seminal drop, rooted spiritually in **the father's brain.**

Even in the child's body itself, all organs are spiritually "nourished" by the brain:

וְגַם עַכְשָׁיו בַּבֵּן יְנִיקַת הַצִפָרְנַיִם וְחִיּוּתָם נִמְשֶׁכֶת מֵהַמּוֹחַ שֶׁבָּרֹאשׁ — **And even now, in** the child, the nails draw their spiritual **nourishment and energy from the brain in** the child's **head.** (We will see the significance of this point later on, in section three.)

מהמוח שבראש כדאיתא בגמ' [נדה שם] לובן שממנו
גידים ועצמות וצפרנים [וכמ"ש בע"ח שער החשמל
בסוד לבושים של אדם הראשון בגן עדן שהיו צפרנים
מבחי' מוח תבונה] וככה ממש כביכול בשרש כל הנפש
רוח ונשמה של כללות ישראל למעלה בירידתו ממדרגה
למדרגה על ידי השתלשלות העולמות אבי"ע מחכמתו
ית' כדכתיב כולם בחכמה עשית נתהוו ממנו נפש רוח

The *Tanya* now cites two sources for the relationship between the father's "drop" and the child's nails:

כְּדְאִיתָא בַּגְמָרָא [נִדָּה שָׁם] לוֹבֶן שֶׁמִּמֶּנּוּ גִידִים וְעֲצָמוֹת וְצִפָּרְנַיִם — As the *Talmud* states (*Nidah ibid.,* 31a), **"The white (seed of the father) from which tendons, bones and nails are formed,"** — [וְכְמוֹ שֶׁכָּתוּב בְּעֵץ חַיִּים שַׁעַר הַחַשְׁמַל — and as *Etz Chaim, Sha'ar ha-Chashmal* (41:1) states, בְּסוֹד לְבוּשִׁים שֶׁל אָדָם הָרִאשׁוֹן בְּגַן עֵדֶן — concerning the secret of Adam's clothes in the Garden of Eden, שֶׁהָיוּ צִפָּרְנַיִם — that were, according to the *Midrash*, attached to his body like **nails** (*Pirkei de-Rabbi Eliezer,* section 14), [מִבְּחִינַת מוֹחַ תְּבוּנָה] — these "nails" were spiritually **nourished from mental energy,** offering us another connection between nails and the brain.

Having depicted in detail how even the lowest parts of a child retain a profound connection to the seed—and thereby to the brain of the father—the *Tanya* will now clarify how this is mirrored spiritually, in terms of the soul.

וְכָכָה מַמָּשׁ כְּבִיכוֹל בְּשֹׁרֶשׁ כָּל הַנֶּפֶשׁ — Mirroring this precisely (although, figuratively), רוּחַ וּנְשָׁמָה שֶׁל כְּלָלוּת יִשְׂרָאֵל לְמַעְלָה — is the supernal root of the *nefesh, ruach* and *neshamah* of all Israel, בִּירִידָתוֹ מִמַּדְרֵגָה לְמַדְרֵגָה עַל יְדֵי הִשְׁתַּלְשְׁלוּת הָעוֹלָמוֹת אֲצִילוּת בְּרִיאָה יְצִירָה וַעֲשִׂיָּה מֵחָכְמָתוֹ יִתְבָּרֵךְ — as they descended, rung by rung, from G-d's **wisdom** (the "brain of the father"), **through the chain of** the four spiritual **worlds,** which are called *Atzilus* ("Emanation,") *Beriah* ("Creation,") *Yetzirah* ("Formation") and *Asiyah* ("Action"), כְּדִכְתִיב כּוּלָם בְּחָכְמָה עָשִׂיתָ — as the verse states, **"You made them all with wisdom"** (*Psalms* 104:24).

A CHASIDIC THOUGHT

Why do I feel such a "wondrous and powerful unity" with my own biological child? Because that child (all of that child!) came from my seed, which is an essential expression of who I am.

In the same sense, I am a "child" of G-d, since my soul is derived, in one way or another, from His "Supernal Wisdom," which is an essential expression of who He is.

 וְנִשְׁמָה שֶׁל עַמֵּי הָאָרֶץ וּפְחוּתֵי הָעֵרֶךְ וְעִם כָּל זֶה עוֹדֵינָה קְשׁוּרוֹת וּמְיוּחָדוֹת בְּיִחוּד נִפְלָא וְעָצוּם בְּמַהוּתָן וְעַצְמוּתָן הָרִאשׁוֹן שֶׁהִיא הַמְשָׁכַת חָכְמָה עִילָאָה כִּי יְנִיקַת וְחִיוּ' נֶפֶשׁ רוּחַ וְנִשְׁמָה שֶׁל עַמֵּי הָאָרֶץ הוּא מִנֶּפֶשׁ רוּחַ וְנִשְׁמָה שֶׁל הַצַּדִּיקִים וְהַחֲכָמִים רָאשֵׁי בְּנֵי יִשְׂרָאֵל שֶׁבְּדוֹרָם: וּבָזֶה יוּבַן מַאֲמַר רַזַ"ל עַל פָּסוּק וּלְדָבְקָה בוֹ וְשֶׁכָּל הַדָּבֵק בת"ח

7A

Later on, we will explore the system of four spiritual worlds in more detail. For now, it is sufficient to appreciate that they represent a gradual spiritual "downgrade," starting with G-d's "wisdom" and ending with reality as we know it. In our metaphor, this parallels the nine-month gestation in the womb, which "downgrades" the seed into limbs and organs, even the lowly nails.

נִתְהַווּ מִמֶּנּוּ נֶפֶשׁ רוּחַ וּנְשָׁמָה שֶׁל עַמֵּי הָאָרֶץ וּפְחוּתֵי הָעֵרֶךְ — The result of this spiritual "downgrade" through the four worlds is that **from** Supernal, Divine wisdom ("brain") the **nefesh, ruach** and **neshamah of simple folk and common people** (the "nails") **are formed,** וְעִם כָּל זֶה עוֹדֵינָה קְשׁוּרוֹת וּמְיוּחָדוֹת בְּיִחוּד נִפְלָא וְעָצוּם בְּמַהוּתָן וְעַצְמוּתָן הָרִאשׁוֹן — **but nevertheless,** like a biological child, those souls **still remain bound with a wondrous and awesome unity with their original, essential source,** שֶׁהִיא הַמְשָׁכַת חָכְמָה עִילָאָה — **which is a** direct **emanation of "Supernal Wisdom."**

In conclusion: All Divine Souls share the same exalted source and are equal at that level.

SECTION THREE: A LEADER'S SOUL

In Section Two, our emphasis was on the relationship between the souls and G-d. In Section Three, we will discuss how souls can influence *each other.*

Above, the *Tanya* stated, *"In the child, the nails draw their (spiritual) nourishment and energy from the brain in the (child's) head"* (p. 50). "The child" is symbolic of the collective souls of Israel, so the implication here is that lower souls of ordinary people ("the child's nails"), can be "spiritually nourished" by the souls of our leaders ("the child's head").

כִּי יְנִיקַת וְחַיּוּת נֶפֶשׁ רוּחַ וּנְשָׁמָה שֶׁל עַמֵּי הָאָרֶץ הוּא מִנֶּפֶשׁ רוּחַ וּנְשָׁמָה שֶׁל הַצַּדִּיקִים וְהַחֲכָמִים — **This is because the** *nefesh, ruach* **and** *neshamah* **of the simple folk are nurtured and energized from the** *nefesh, ruach* **and** *neshamah* **of the** *tzadikim* **(spiritual giants) and the scholars,** רָאשֵׁי בְּנֵי יִשְׂרָאֵל שֶׁבְּדוֹרָם — *"the heads of children of Israel"* (*Numbers* 13:3), **in their generation.**

This idea of a soul-connection between spiritual master and disciple became a central focus of the Chasidic movement, though, as the *Tanya* will now demonstrate, it is based on earlier sources.

מעלה עליו הכתוב כאלו נדבק בשכינה ממש כי ע"י
דביקה בתלמידי חכמים קשורות נפש רוח ונשמה של
עמי הארץ ומיוחדות במהותן הראשון ושרשם שבחכמה
עילאה שהוא ית' וחכמתו א' והוא המדע כו' [והפושעים
ומורדים בתלמידי חכמים יניקת נפש רוח ונשמה שלהם
מבחי' אחוריים של נפש רוח ונשמת ת"ח] ומ"ש בזהר

וּבְזֶה יוּבַן מַאֲמַר רַבּוֹתֵינוּ זִכְרוֹנָם לִבְרָכָה עַל פָּסוּק וּלְדָבְקָה בּוֹ — **And this explains a teaching of our Sages of blessed memory on the verse,** *"And attach yourself to Him"* (Deuteronomy 30:20), שֶׁכָּל הַדָּבֵק בְּתַלְמִידֵי חֲכָמִים מַעֲלֶה עָלָיו הַכָּתוּב כְּאִלּוּ נִדְבַּק בַּשְּׁכִינָה — **that anyone who attaches himself to scholars is considered by Scripture to have attached himself to the Divine Presence** (*Talmud Kesubos* 111b; *Rashi* to *Deuteronomy* 11:22), מַמָּשׁ — **literally.**

It seems strange, at first glance, that we might "attach" ourselves to the Divine Presence through connecting with human teachers. But, based on the above insight (the fundamental connection between all souls), we can understand this literally.

כִּי עַל יְדֵי דְּבִיקָה בְּתַלְמִידֵי חֲכָמִים — **Because by attaching themselves to scholars,** קְשׁוּרוֹת נֶפֶשׁ רוּחַ וּנְשָׁמָה שֶׁל עַמֵּי הָאָרֶץ וּמִיוּחָדוֹת בְּמַהוּתָן הָרִאשׁוֹן וְשָׁרְשָׁם שֶׁבְּחָכְמָה עִילָּאָה — **the** *nefesh, ruach* **and** *neshamah* **of the simple folk become** consciously **connected with their original source and root in the "Supernal Wisdom"** of G-d,

שֶׁהוּא יִתְבָּרֵךְ וְחָכְמָתוֹ אֶחָד וְהוּא הַמַּדָּע כו' — **and** once connected with "Supernal Wisdom" they are connected to G-d Himself, since *"He and His wisdom are one"* and *"He is the 'power to know'"* etc., (above, from *Rambam*).

PRACTICAL LESSONS

Your Divine Soul will be nourished through attachment to Jewish leaders who help you to discover your inner connectedness to G-d.

This concept of *"tzadikim and scholars"* as a soul-nexus can be understood through, *"the relationship of an electric powerhouse with a lamp that is connected to it by a wire. In order to light his lamp, one must find the right switch or push the correct button. The soul of every Jew is 'a part of' and is connected with G-d, but in order for one to enjoy the great benefits of it, the correct switch must be found or the proper button pushed"* (Rabbi Menachem Mendel Schneerson, *Yechidus,* March 7, 1960). Through "attachment" to the *tzadik*, the *Tanya* suggests, it becomes easier to find that "switch."

[וְהַפּוֹשְׁעִים וּמוֹרְדִים בְּתַלְמִידֵי חֲכָמִים — **And as for those who sin and rebel against the scholars,** יְנִיקַת נֶפֶשׁ רוּחַ וּנְשָׁמָה שֶׁלָּהֶם מִבְּחִינַת אֲחוֹרַיִים שֶׁל נֶפֶשׁ רוּחַ וְנִשְׁמַת תַּלְמִידֵי חֲכָמִים] — **their** *nefesh, ruach* **and** *neshamah* **are** still **nourished from the** *nefesh, ruach* **and** *neshamah* **of the scholars,** but indirectly so, **from "behind"**(*achorayim*) **so to speak.** (For more on the concept of *achorayim,* see p. 250).

ובזהר חדש שהעיקר תלוי שיקדש עצמו בשעת תשמיש
דווקא משא"כ בני עמי הארץ כו' היינו משום שאין לך
נפש רוח ונשמה שאין לה לבוש מנפש דעצמות
אביו ואמו וכל המצות שעושה הכל ע"י אותו הלבוש
כו' ואפי' השפע שנותנים לו מן השמים הכל ע"י
לבוש זה ואם יקדש את עצמו ימשיך לבוש קדוש
לנשמת בנו ואפילו היא נשמה גדולה צריכה לקידוש

SECTION FOUR: THE SOUL AT CONCEPTION

The *Zohar* teaches that, at the time of conception, parents ought to *"focus desire on attaching to the Blessed Holy One,"* thereby, *"drawing down holy souls from above"* (*Zohar* 3, 49b).

וּמַה שֶּׁכָּתוּב בַּזֹהַר וּבְזֹהַר חָדָשׁ — **As for what is written in the *Zohar* and *Zohar Chadash*** (11a), שֶׁהָעִיקָר תָּלוּי שֶׁיְּקַדֵּשׁ עַצְמוֹ בִּשְׁעַת תַּשְׁמִישׁ דַּוְוקָא, — **that the main determining factor** of the soul's quality **is sanctity during the actual sexual union,** מַה שֶּׁאֵין כֵּן בְּנֵי עַמֵּי הָאָרֶץ כו' — **which simple folk fail to do** *etc.*, which explains why their children are also "simple," possessing ordinary souls.

How does this square with our previous conclusion that all souls derive from the *same* lofty source ("Supernal Wisdom")?

The *Tanya* answers that the *Zohar* is not referring to the Divine Soul *itself*, but to its "garment" (*levush*), a kind of spiritual interface through which the Divine Soul communicates with the Animal Soul.

הַיְינוּ מִשּׁוּם שֶׁאֵין לְךָ נֶפֶשׁ רוּחַ וּנְשָׁמָה שֶׁאֵין לָהּ לְבוּשׁ מִנֶּפֶשׁ דְעַצְמוּת אָבִיו וְאִמּוֹ — **This is because every** *nefesh, ruach* and *neshamah*, without exception, possesses a "garment" derived essentially from his father's and mother's *nefesh*.

This "garment" has a very broad reach, influencing all the *mitzvos* that the soul performs, as well as the blessings that flow to it from above.

וְכָל הַמִּצְוֹת שֶׁעוֹשֶׂה הַכֹּל עַל יְדֵי אוֹתוֹ הַלְּבוּשׁ כו' — **And all the** *mitzvos* that the soul **does are** influenced **by that garment,** which protects the soul from the transgressions of prior incarnations, וַאֲפִילוּ הַשֶּׁפַע שֶׁנּוֹתְנִים לוֹ מִן הַשָּׁמַיִם הַכֹּל עַל יְדֵי לְבוּשׁ זֶה — **and even the blessings that flow to the person from heaven are all given through that "garment."**

It is the quality of this "garment," and not the soul itself, that depends on the sanctity of the parent's thoughts.

וְאִם יְקַדֵּשׁ אֶת עַצְמוֹ יַמְשִׁיךְ לְבוּשׁ קָדוֹשׁ לְנִשְׁמַת בְּנוֹ — **If the** parents **sanctify themselves** during conception, **they will draw down a holy "garment" for the soul of their child,** וַאֲפִילוּ הִיא נְשָׁמָה גְדוֹלָה צְרִיכָה לְקִדּוּשׁ אָבִיו כו' — **and even if it is a very lofty soul, it still needs the father's** and mother's **sacred intent** during conception, because the "garment" influences all the soul's worship, as well as the blessings it receives.

אביו כו' אבל הנשמה עצמה הנה לפעמים נשמת
אדם גבוה לאין קץ בא להיות בנו של אדם נבזה
ושפל כו' כמ"ש האר"י ז"ל כל זה בליקוטי תורה
פ' וירא ובטעמי מצות פ' בראשית:

פרק ג   וְהִנֵּה   כל בחי' ומדרגה משלש אלו נפש
רוח ונשמה כלולה מעשר בחי'
כנגד עשר ספירות עליונות שנשתלשלו מהן הנחלקות

אֲבָל הַנְּשָׁמָה עַצְמָהּ — **But as for the** Divine **Soul** *itself*, its quality is not influenced by the parent's thoughts, הִנֵּה לְפְעָמִים נְשָׁמַת אָדָם גָּבוֹהַּ לְאֵין קֵץ בָּא לִהְיוֹת בְּנוֹ שֶׁל אָדָם נִבְזֶה וְשָׁפָל כו' — **as we see that sometimes the soul of an inestimably great person, will enter the child of a disgraceful, lowly person,** such as Avraham who was born to Terach (*Genesis* 11:26).

כְּמוֹ שֶׁכָּתַב הָאֲרִ"י זִכְרוֹנוֹ לִבְרָכָה כָּל זֶה בְּלִיקּוּטֵי תוֹרָה פָּרָשַׁת וַיֵּרָא וּבְטַעֲמֵי מִצְוֹת פָּרָשַׁת בְּרֵאשִׁית —**All this** insight in Section Four **was stated by** *Arizal* **in** *Likutei Torah*, *Parshas Vayera* **and in** *Ta'amei ha-Mitzvos, Parshas Bereshis.*

In conclusion: Every one of us receives a Divine Soul from G-d, regardless of our parent's intentions at the time of conception.

CHAPTER 3

YOUR THREE BRAINS

SECTION ONE: THE ANATOMY OF YOUR SOUL

25TH KISLEV REGULAR | 27TH KISLEV LEAP

In chapter two you were introduced to your Divine Soul, which is literally, *"a piece of G-d above."* Your Divine Soul enables you to think about G-d and develop feelings for Him. In this chapter, we will delve more into the structure of your Divine Soul and learn how it processes ideas and generates feelings.

וְהִנֵּה כָּל בְּחִינָה וּמַדְרֵגָה מִשְּׁלֹשׁ אֵלּוּ נֶפֶשׁ רוּחַ וּנְשָׁמָה — **Now, each of these three facets/ levels** of your Divine Soul: *nefesh* (body-intelligence), *ruach* (emotional-intelligence) **and** *neshamah* (self-conscious intelligence), כְּלוּלָה מֵעֶשֶׂר בְּחִינוֹת כְּנֶגֶד עֶשֶׂר סְפִירוֹת עֶלְיוֹנוֹת שֶׁנִּשְׁתַּלְשְׁלוּ מֵהֶן — **contains ten powers, mirroring the ten heavenly** *sefiros* (Divine energies) **from which they originate.**

לשתים שהן שלש אמות ושבע כפולות פי' חכמה

In Kabbalah, G-d is described as an unknowable, Infinite Light, from which a mere glimmer reaches the rest of the universe. While the Infinite Light defies mortal imagination, Kabbalah does introduce various symbols to depict how the "glimmer" of light is transmuted on its journey to this world.

The core symbolism, which we find reflected at virtually every level, is a system of ten "energies" or "potencies," referred to by *Sefer Yetzirah* as *sefiros*, (sing. *sefirah*). The term has no single, definitive translation and implies a wide range of themes: heavenly spheres (*galgalim*), circles (*igulim*), lights (*oros*), mystical colors (*livnat ha-sappir*), numbers (*misparim*), primal utterances (*ma'amaros*), and character attributes (*midos*).

The soul, at all of its levels and facets, is ultimately a reflection of the *sefiros*. In the following section, the *Tanya* examines how different elements of the psyche are molded by the various *sefiros*.

הַנֶחְלָקוֹת לִשְׁתַּיִם — In *Sefer Yetzirah* (1:2), the influence of the ten *sefiros* at the time of creation **is split into two** groups, שֶׁהֵן שָׁלֹשׁ אִמּוֹת וְשֶׁבַע כְּפוּלוֹת — **which are *"the three 'mothers' and the seven 'doubles.'"***

Sefer Yetzirah discusses the mystical secret of how the world was created through the means of Hebrew letters, and it classifies the letters into various groups. The three "mothers" are the letters *alef, mem* and *shin*, the beginning, middle and penultimate letters of the Hebrew alphabet. They encompass the entire alphabet and symbolize the ultimate root of everything in G-d. (The last letter, *taf* was not used as it is a "double.")

The seven "doubles," are the letters *beis, gimel, daled, kaf, peh, reish* and *taf.* These letters have a "double" identity, since they can be pronounced "soft" or "hard," through the addition of a *dagesh* mark (the small dot in the middle of a letter. For example, the letter ב with a *dagesh*, is pronounced as a hard *beis*, whereas ב without a *dagesh,* is pronounced as a softer, *veis*).

This "double" identity of these letters is symbolic of the two ways G-d relates externally to His creations: draw close with kindness (be "soft"); or, push away with judgment (be "hard"). Before the world was created, this dilemma did not exist; but once there is a world, G-d is constantly faced with the decision: be soft, or be hard?

"Doubles" therefore represent the way G-d deals practically with the created world *outside* Him, so to speak. "Mothers" represent the *internal* "mind" of G-d (see Rabbi Shneur Zalman, *Ma'amarei Admor Ha-Zakein, Inyanim,* volume 1, (Brooklyn: Kehos, 2008), p. 98).

This distinction, between the "mothers" and "doubles," helps us understand that there are two types of *sefiros*.

פֵּירוּשׁ חָכְמָה בִּינָה וָדַעַת — **This means: *chochmah* (inquiry), *binah* (cognition) and**

בִּינָה וָדַעַת וְשִׁבְעַת יְמֵי הַבִּנְיָן חֶסֶד גְּבוּרָה תִּפְאֶרֶת
כוּ' וְכָךְ בְּנֶפֶשׁ הָאָדָם שֶׁנֶּחְלֶקֶת לִשְׁתַּיִם שֵׂכֶל וּמִדּוֹת.
הַשֵּׂכֶל כּוֹלֵל חָכְמָה בִּינָה וָדַעַת. וְהַמִּדּוֹת הֵן אַהֲבַת ה'
וּפַחְדּוֹ וְיִרְאָתוֹ וּלְפָאֲרוֹ כוּ' וְחַבַּ"ד נִקְרְאוּ אִמּוֹת וּמָקוֹר

da'as (recognition), the first three of the ten *sefiros*, correspond to the "mothers," the internal "mind" of G-d.

וְשִׁבְעַת יְמֵי הַבִּנְיָן — The last seven of the ten *sefiros* are alluded to by **the seven days of Creation,** because they are G-d's tools to deal with the external world, חֶסֶד גְּבוּרָה תִּפְאֶרֶת — these are the *sefiros* of **chesed** (giving), **gevurah** (restraint), כוּ' — and **tiferet** (harmony), which harmonizes *chesed* and *gevurah, etc.* (The remaining four *sefiros* continue along this theme).

וְכָךְ בְּנֶפֶשׁ הָאָדָם שֶׁנֶּחְלֶקֶת לִשְׁתַּיִם — **And** just as G-d has two types of *sefiros*, serving His inner "self" and the external world, **similarly, the human soul is divided in two,** שֵׂכֶל וּמִדּוֹת — **intellect** serving the "self," **and emotions,** to relate to others.

In fact, all ten Divine *sefiros* are mirrored in the human soul:

PRACTICAL LESSONS

Ultimately, I can control my emotions because what I feel is always an outcome of what I think.

הַשֵּׂכֶל כּוֹלֵל חָכְמָה בִּינָה וָדַעַת — **The** human **intellect,** like the Divine, **contains** *chochmah* (inquiry), *binah* (cognition) **and** *da'as* (recognition), וְהַמִּדּוֹת הֵן אַהֲבַת ה' וּפַחְדּוֹ וְיִרְאָתוֹ וּלְפָאֲרוֹ כוּ' — **and the emotions which are love of G-d, trepidation and reverence of Him, venerating Him,** *etc.*

You only want something after you understand *why* it is good. You only fear something after you first understand its danger. So, the *Tanya* now explains, the relationship between intellect and emotion is somewhat like a mother that gives birth to a child.

וְחָכְמָה בִּינָה וָדַעַת נִקְרְאוּ אִמּוֹת וּמָקוֹר לַמִּדּוֹת כִּי הַמִּדּוֹת הֵן תּוֹלְדוֹת חָכְמָה בִּינָה וָדַעַת — *Chochmah, binah* and *da'as* are called the "mothers" and source of the emotions, because emotions are the "children" of the intellect.

Most of *Tanya's* advice builds on this principle: If you think about G-d, you will come to feel and experience G-d. That is why the meditative process, to which we will be introduced in this chapter, is so important.

In a letter, written in 1805 defending the teachings of the *Tanya* to one of his critics, Rabbi Shneur Zalman revealed that this emphasis on meditative work was not his innovation.

"In order for there to be reverence of G-d, there must be deep contemplation and meditation, as stated in *Likutei Amarim*. Everyone in the regions of Volhyn

למדות כי המדות הן תולדות חב"ד: וביאור הענין כי
הנה השכל שבנפש המשכל' שהוא המשכיל כל דבר   7B
נקרא בשם חכמה כ"ח מ"ה וכשמוציא כחו אל הפועל
שמתבונן בשכלו להבין דבר לאשורו ולעמקו מתוך איזה
דבר חכמה המושכל בשכלו נקרא בינה והן הם אב ואם

and the Ukraine who has ever had a whiff of the teachings of the *Ba'al Shem Tov* and his disciples knows the explanation of the holy *Zohar's* teaching, that *binah* is the '*mother of the children*' (*Psalms* 113:9; *Zohar* 1, 219a; *Pardes Rimonim* 1:2). The 'children' are love and reverence (of G-d)... and they are 'born' through meditation and deep contemplation on the greatness of G-d, each person according to his ability. Just as it is impossible to give birth to a child without a mother, so too, it is impossible to revere G-d without meditative work" (Rabbi Shalom Ber Levin (ed.), *Igros Kodesh Admor Ha-Zaken,* (Brooklyn: Kehos, 2012), p. 342).

SECTION TWO: WHERE DO FEELINGS COME FROM?

כִּי הִנֵּה הַשֵּׂכֶל שֶׁבַּנֶּפֶשׁ הַמַּשְׂכֶּלֶת שֶׁהוּא הַמַּשְׂכִּיל — **Let's explore this idea,** כָּל דָּבָר — the Divine (rational) Soul's intellect, which is its power to understand all things, נִקְרָא בְּשֵׁם חָכְמָה כ"ח מָ"ה — **is called by the name** *chochmah,* **which is the fusion of two Hebrew words,** *ko'ach,* **"power," and** *mah,* **"what?"** (*Zohar* 3, 34a).

Chochmah is the "power (ability) to say, 'What is this?'"— an inquisitiveness and openness to the unknown.

Ko'ach also means "potential," suggesting that at the level of *chochmah,* an idea is raw and undeveloped. Its precise contours subsequently need to be drawn by *binah.*

וּכְשֶׁמּוֹצִיא כֹחוֹ אֶל הַפּוֹעַל — **When you bring the potential** in *chochmah* **to fruition,** שֶׁמִּתְבּוֹנֵן בְּשִׂכְלוֹ לְהָבִין דָּבָר לַאֲשׁוּרוֹ וּלְעָמְקוֹ — **through meditating in your mind, to clarify an idea in its full richness and depth,** מִתּוֹךְ אֵיזֶה דְּבַר חָכְמָה הַמוּשְׂכָּל בְּשִׂכְלוֹ — beginning with **the** raw *chochmah* **concept found in your mind,** נִקְרָא בִּינָה — **this** contemplative process **is called "***binah***"** (cognition).

A CHASIDIC THOUGHT

My natural, sensory consciousness sees a world devoid of G-d. But through thinking about G-d, my consciousness will yield a more intuitive awareness of the Divine Presence. I will then, at least momentarily, be more excited by what my mind sees than what my senses feel.

המולידות אהבת ה' ויראתו ופחדו כי השכל שבנפש
המשכלת כשמתבונן ומעמיק מאד בגדולת ה' איך
הוא ממלא כל עלמין וסובב כל עלמין וכולא קמיה
כלא חשיב נולדה ונתעוררה מדת יראת הרוממות במוחו
ומחשבתו לירא ולהתבושש מגדולתו ית' שאין לה
סוף ותכלית ופחד ה' בלבו ושוב יתלהב לבו באהבה

וְהֵן הֵם אָב וָאֵם הַמּוֹלִידוֹת אַהֲבַת ה' וְיִרְאָתוֹ וּפַחְדּוֹ — **These** mental processes of *chochmah* and *binah* **are the "father" and "mother" which "give birth" to love of G-d, as well as reverence and trepidation of Him.**

PRACTICAL LESSONS

It's not enough just to think positively. In order for my thoughts to have a real, lasting effect on my feelings, three precise mental processes are necessary: *chochmah* (inquiry), *binah* (cognition) and *da'as* (recognition).

For me to have real, lasting feelings for G-d, I need to use my *chochmah, binah* and *da'as* to internalize how:

a.) The universe is saturated with G-d.

b.) The universe is engulfed in G-d.

c.) Everything is utterly insignificant in His presence.

26TH KISLEV REGULAR | 28TH KISLEV LEAP

What should be the *content* of these meditations? In his *Shenei Luchos Ha-Bris*, Rabbi Isaiah Horowitz (c. 1565–1630) explains: *"When a person will contemplate briefly (G-d's) greatness and majesty, he will feel reverence and shame, since reverence arises from shame"* (*Shaloh, Be-Asarah Ma'amaros, Ma'amar* 3-4, section 99b).

The *Tanya* elaborates on this theme. (We will revisit these meditations in more detail in chapters 41-43).

כִּי הַשֵּׂכֶל שֶׁבַּנֶּפֶשׁ הַמַּשְׂכֶּלֶת כְּשֶׁמִּתְבּוֹנֵן וּמַעֲמִיק מְאֹד בִּגְדוּלַת ה' — **Because when the cognitive powers of your** Divine **(rational) Soul focus deeply on the greatness of G-d,** אֵיךְ הוּא מְמַלֵּא כָל עָלְמִין — **how, a.)** all existence is saturated with G-d, *"He fills all worlds"* (see *Zohar* 3, 225a), וְסוֹבֵב כָּל עָלְמִין — **and b.) how** all existence is engulfed in G-d, *"He transcends all worlds"* (*ibid*; see chapter 23, pp. 265-6), וְכוּלָּא קַמֵּיהּ כְּלָא חָשִׁיב — **c.) and how** existence is voided by G-d, *"in His presence, everything is considered zero"* (*ibid.* 1, 11b), נוֹלְדָה וְנִתְעוֹרְרָה מִדַּת יִרְאַת הָרוֹמְמוּת בְּמוֹחוֹ וּמַחֲשַׁבְתּוֹ — **then as a result of this contemplation, a sense of reverence of** G-d's **majesty (***yiras ha-romemus***), will be born in your thinking mind,** לִירֹא וּלְהִתְבּוֹשֵׁשׁ מִגְּדוּלָתוֹ יִתְבָּרֵךְ — **to revere** G-d **and to feel shame** in the presence of **His blessed greatness,** שֶׁאֵין לָהּ סוֹף וְתַכְלִית — **which is without end or limit.**

וּפַחַד ה' בְּלִבּוֹ — Following this intellectual experience of reverence "in your thinking mind," palpable emotion will follow, **the trepidation of G-d in your heart.**

עֹזָה כְרִשְׁפֵּי אֵשׁ בַּחֲשִׁיקָה וַחֲפִיצָה וּתְשׁוּקָה וְנֶפֶשׁ שׁוֹקֵקָה

לִגְדוּלַת אֵין סוֹף בָּ"ה וְהִיא כְּלוֹת הַנֶּפֶשׁ כְּדִכְתִיב נִכְסְפָה

After the mental and emotional reverence, love will follow.

וְשׁוּב יִתְלַהֵב לִבּוֹ בְּאַהֲבָה עַזָּה כְרִשְׁפֵּי אֵשׁ — **And after that, your heart will be ignited with a rapturous love, like** *"flaming fire"* (Song 8:6).

The experience of "revering G-d's majesty" and why it subsequently stimulates love of G-d, is described by Rabbi Dov Ber of Mezritch.

"*Yiras ha-romemus* (reverence of G-d's majesty) is not the same as *yiras ha-onesh* (fear of G-d's punishment). *Yiras ha-romemus* is the reverence of a king, where a profound sense of shame keeps you from approaching the king, due to his awesome greatness. And, as a result of that, you come to love the king more, since despite his greatness and awesomeness, he still takes care of all the country's citizens, providing for their needs.

"*Yiras ha-onesh* is not that way; such a fear would cause you to distance yourself from the king. But what real difference is there between fearing punishment from the king and fearing a bear or another wild animal? Out of your fear for the bear, you keep your distance from it, because you're scared for your life. *Yiras ha-onesh* of G-d is the same thing. It causes you to distance yourself from Him and you're scared to approach Him, for perhaps He will punish you" (Rabbi Dov Ber of Mezritch, *Ohr Torah, Psalms,* section 211).

The *Tanya* continues to describe the feelings of love for G-d that your meditation ought to generate.

בַּחֲשִׁיקָה וַחֲפִיצָה וּתְשׁוּקָה — **You should be aflame with** *"fervor (chashikah) and desire (chafitzah)"* (Genesis Rabah 80:7), **and longing (teshukah),** וְנֶפֶשׁ שׁוֹקֵקָה *"a craving soul"* (Psalms 107:9), **for the greatness of the Blessed Infinite Light**.

Midrash Rabah discerns three expressions of passion from the narrative in *Genesis 34: devikah* (attachment), *chashikah* (fervor), and *chafitzah* (desire).

Devikah is expressed when *"you perform a mitzvah, or refrain from a prohibition correctly, but without emotional arousal"* (Shaloh ibid., sections 119-123), which explains why the *Tanya* does not mention it here in a discussion of "flaming love."

At the level of *chashikah,* you are not lacking any inspiration and *"you have the energy of a lion to carry out anything decreed by the Blessed Holy One"* (ibid.).

Chafitzah represents an even more intense state where, unlike physical desires which subside when you are satisfied, your desire for G-d never diminishes. *"And upon completing a mitzvah which came your way... you are not satisfied by what you have done. On the contrary, now you have a stronger desire"* (ibid.).

וגם כלתה נפשי וגו' וכתיב צמאה נפשי לאלהים וגו'
וכתיב צמאה לך נפשי וגו' והצמאון הוא מיסוד האש
שבנפש האלהית וכמ"ש הטבעיים וכ"ה בע"ח שיסוד
האש הוא בלב ומקור המים והליחות מהמוח וכמ"ש
בע"ח שער נ' שהיא בחי' חכמה שנקרא מים שבנפש

וְהִיא כְּלוֹת הַנֶּפֶשׁ — This love is the "languishing of the soul" (*kelos ha-nefesh*) which we find in Scripture, 'וְגוֹ — as the verse states, *"My soul yearns, indeed, it languishes etc.,"* (*Psalms* 84:3), 'וְגוֹ וְכָסְפָה וְגַם כָּלְתָה נַפְשִׁי וְגוֹ — and another verse states, *"My soul thirsts for G-d, etc.,"* (*ibid.* 42:3), וּכְתִיב צָמְאָה — 'וְגוֹ לְךָ נַפְשִׁי וְגוֹ — and another verse states, *"My soul thirsts for You, etc.,"* (*ibid.* 63:2).

The experience of *kelos ha-nefesh* was described by Bachya ibn Pakuda (11th century), in his *Chovos Ha-Levavos,* "Duties of the Heart":

PRACTICAL LESSONS

I let my *chochmah* flow by being intellectually curious, imaginative and by looking at the bigger picture.

Next, I use my *binah* by being logical and detail orientated, carefully examining the raw concept from my *chochmah*.

"What is love of G-d? It is kelos ha-nefesh, the 'languishing of the soul'; the soul's shift toward the Creator, to attach itself to His supernal light. For the soul is pure and spiritual, and it tends towards spiritual things similar to itself. By nature, it removes itself from what is opposite to its nature, namely the physical body...."

"When the light of wisdom penetrates the soul, it reveals to her the disgrace of having turned to the body in love, and having been drawn after it in thought... she will desist from this... and will turn in her thoughts to seek ways of her salvation from the great trap she is ensnared in and by which she had been so greatly tempted. Then she will separate from the world and all of its pleasures, and will despise the body and its lusts" (*Chovos Ha-Levavos,* Love of G-d, chapter 1; see *Reishis Chochmah* 2:1).

The *Tanya* traces this passionate arousal to its source in the elemental matrix of the soul.

וְהַצִּמָּאוֹן הוּא מִיסוֹד הָאֵשׁ שֶׁבַּנֶּפֶשׁ הָאֱלֹהִית — **This thirsting,** as a natural result of meditation, **comes from the elemental fire of the Divine soul,** וּכְמוֹ שֶׁכָּתְבוּ הַטִּבְעִיִּים וְכֵן הוּא בְּעֵץ חַיִּים — **as the natural scientists write, and** *Etz Chaim* (5:5) **states similarly,** שֶׁיְּסוֹד הָאֵשׁ הוּא בַּלֵּב — **that the element of fire is in the heart,** stimulating emotion, וּמְקוֹר הַמַּיִם וְהַלֵּיחוֹת מֵהַמּוֹחַ — whereas the element of **water and moisture is rooted in the brain,** וּכְמוֹ שֶׁכָּתוּב בְּעֵץ חַיִּים שַׁעַר נ' שֶׁהִיא בְּחִינַת חָכְמָה שֶׁנִּקְרָא מַיִם שֶׁבַּנֶּפֶשׁ הָאֱלֹהִית — **as stated in** *Etz Chaim,* **section 50,** that *chochmah* is the elemental **water of the Divine Soul.**

האלהית ושאר המדות כולן הן ענפי היראה והאהבה
ותולדותיהן כמ"ש במקום אחר. והדעת הוא מלשון
והאדם ידע את חוה והוא לשון התקשרות והתחברות
שמקשר דעתו בקשר אמיץ וחזק מאוד ויתקע מחשבתו
בחוזק בגדולת אין סוף ב"ה ואינו מסיח דעתו כי אף מי
שהוא חכם ונבון בגדולת א"ס ב"ה הנה אם לא יקשר
דעתו ויתקע מחשבתו בחוזק ובהתמדה לא יוליד בנפשו

Having now described in detail how contemplation of the mind "gives birth" to the emotions of reverence and love, our discussion comes to a close, since:

וּשְׁאָר הַמִּדּוֹת כּוּלָן הֵן עַנְפֵי הַיִּרְאָה וְהָאַהֲבָה וְתוֹלְדוֹתֵיהֶן — all the other emotions are merely **branches and derivatives of reverence/fear and love**, כְּמוֹ שֶׁכָּתוּב בְּמָקוֹם אַחֵר — **as is explained elsewhere** (see *Tanya, Igeres Ha-Kodesh* section 15).

An emotion is your reaction to something outside of you. While you might experience a vast range of emotions, they essentially fall into two categories: You are either drawn to the thing (love) or repelled by it (fear).

SECTION THREE: HOW TO USE YOUR DA'AS

We have now explained the role of the first two *sefiros* (*chochmah* and *binah*), the fourth and fifth (*chesed* and *gevurah*, which give rise to love and reverence), and *sefiros* six to ten, which are derivatives of four and five. But the third *sefirah*, *da'as*, (recognition) still remains elusive.

וְהַדַּעַת הוּא מִלְשׁוֹן וְהָאָדָם יָדַע אֶת חַוָּה וְהוּא לְשׁוֹן הִתְקַשְׁרוּת וְהִתְחַבְּרוּת — **The term *da'as* implies "bonding" and "joining," as in, *"Adam knew (yoDa) Eve"* (Genesis 4:1), שֶׁמְּקַשֵּׁר דַּעְתּוֹ בְּקֶשֶׁר אַמִּיץ וְחָזָק מְאֹד — suggesting that, like physical bonding, *da'as* is a process **of focusing your mind with a very firm and strong bond**, וְיִתְקַע מַחֲשַׁבְתּוֹ בְּחוֹזֶק בִּגְדוּלַת אֵין סוֹף בָּרוּךְ הוּא — **an intense fixation of thought, on the greatness of the Blessed Infinite Light**, וְאֵינוֹ מַסִּיחַ דַּעְתּוֹ — **without losing concentration.**

Da'as does not add any new information which was not fathomed by *chochmah* and *binah*. Rather, it fosters an attachment to the existing idea, to render it "real" and relevant.

כִּי אַף מִי שֶׁהוּא חָכָם וְנָבוֹן בִּגְדוּלַת אֵין סוֹף בָּרוּךְ הוּא — **Because even if you appreciate the greatness of the Blessed Infinite Light with your *chochmah* and *binah*,** הִנֵּה אִם לֹא יְקַשֵּׁר דַּעְתּוֹ וְיִתְקַע מַחֲשַׁבְתּוֹ בְּחוֹזֶק וּבְהַתְמָדָה — **unless you bond your *da'as*, focusing your mind with**

PRACTICAL LESSONS

The crucial step, which generates feelings that are real and sustainable, is *da'as*. I use my *da'as* by personalizing an idea, sensing how it is relevant to me and my life experience.

יראה ואהבה אמיתית כי אם דמיונות שוא ועל כן הדעת
הוא קיום המדות וחיותן והוא כולל חסד וגבורה פי' אהבה
וענפיה ויראה וענפיה:

intensity and consistency, לֹא יוֹלִיד בְּנַפְשׁוֹ יִרְאָה וְאַהֲבָה אֲמִיתִּית — **you will not produce genuine love and reverence in your soul,** כִּי אִם דְּמְיוֹנוֹת שָׁוְא — **but only worthless delusions** of love and reverence, that you will not be able to sustain, because only *da'as* makes the concept of G-d personally relevant to you.

וְעַל כֵּן הַדַּעַת הוּא קִיּוּם הַמִּדּוֹת וְחִיּוּתָן — **Therefore, *da'as* ensures the sustainability of the emotions and their energy.**

וְהוּא כּוֹלֵל חֶסֶד וּגְבוּרָה — Since all the emotions ultimately depend on *da'as,* it **incorporates *chesed* and *gevurah*,** פֵּירוּשׁ אַהֲבָה וַעֲנָפֶיהָ וְיִרְאָה וַעֲנָפֶיהָ — *i.e.,* **love and its derivatives, reverence and its derivatives.**

   (We will discuss the practical application of *da'as* in chapter 9, p. 115-6; chapter 16, p. 190; and at length in chapter 42, pp. 529*ff.*).

(We will discuss the practical application of *da'as* in chapter 9, p. 115-6; chapter 16, p. 190; and at length in chapter 42, pp. 529*ff.*).

CHAPTER 4

YOUR INNER/OUTER SELVES

SECTION ONE: THE "CLOTHES" OF YOUR SOUL

27TH KISLEV REGULAR | 29TH KISLEV LEAP

Are your thoughts really you? Or are they just the chatter of the mind, detached from your true self, which runs much deeper?

   To provide a nuanced answer to this question, the *Tanya* will describe your thoughts as the "clothing" of your soul.

   The clothes you wear express your personality, and yet, at the same time, they are not actually you. On different days, you wear different outfits, all of which tell us something about you, but none of which fully encapsulates the enigma which lies within you. They are *tools of expression* which give us a glimpse into who you are, without ever revealing the whole picture.

   That is how you should relate to your thoughts. They are what your soul is "wearing" at any given moment. Your soul never bares herself; it always expresses — and hides — itself through a "garment" of thought.

   Up to this point, you probably looked at your thoughts as your inner world, and your spoken words and actions as your outer life. The *Tanya* will teach you here that

פרק ד

וְעוֹד יש לכל נפש אלהית שלשה לבושים שהם מחשבה דבור ומעשה של תרי"ג מצות התורה שכשהאדם מקיים במעשה כל מצות מעשיות ובדבור הוא עוסק בפירוש כל תרי"ג מצות והלכותיהן ובמחשבה הוא משיג כל מה שאפשר לו להשיג בפרד"ס התורה הרי כללות תרי"ג אברי נפשו מלובשים בתרי"ג מצות התורה ובפרטות בחי' חב"ד

even your thoughts are really your outer self, a mere set of tools that can be steered by your soul in any direction.

וְעוֹד יֵשׁ לְכָל נֶפֶשׁ אֱלֹהִית שְׁלֹשָׁה לְבוּשִׁים — **Furthermore, every Divine Soul possesses three "garments."**

As the *Tanya* has previously explained, you possess two souls. An Animal Soul, which is self-orientated, and a Divine Soul, which desires to follow G-d.

G-d's will was revealed to mankind at Sinai through the 613 *mitzvos* (commandments) of the Torah; so it follows that the "garments" of the Divine soul,

שֶׁהֵם מַחֲשָׁבָה דִבּוּר וּמַעֲשֶׂה שֶׁל תַּרְיַ"ג מִצְוֹת הַתּוֹרָה — **are** every **thought, spoken word or deed** devoted to the **613** *mitzvos* of the Torah.

The most fully awakened state of consciousness is when all your "garments" are devoted to G-d, and not to yourself.

שֶׁכְּשֶׁהָאָדָם מְקַיֵּם בְּמַעֲשֶׂה כָּל מִצְוֹת מַעֲשִׂיּוֹת — **Since, when you practically observe all the action-related** *mitzvos,* וּבְדִבּוּר הוּא עוֹסֵק בְּפֵירוּשׁ כָּל תַּרְיַ"ג מִצְוֹת וְהִלְכוֹתֵיהֶן, **and you use your speech to discuss the 613** *mitzvos* **and their laws,** וּבְמַחֲשָׁבָה הוּא — מַשִּׂיג כָּל מַה שֶׁאֶפְשָׁר לוֹ לְהַשִּׂיג בִּפְשָׁט רֶמֶז דְרוּשׁ וְסוֹד הַתּוֹרָה — **and you immerse your thought in whatever you can grasp from Torah** texts, which are analyzed through four different methods: *peshat* (literal), *remez* (allegorical), *derush* (homiletical), and *sod* (mystical), הֲרֵי כְּלָלוּת תַּרְיַ"ג אֶבְרֵי נַפְשׁוֹ מְלוּבָּשִׁים בְּתַרְיַ"ג מִצְוֹת הַתּוֹרָה — **then your whole Divine Soul** (including all her 613 sub-components), **is "dressed" through her "garments,"** of action, speech and thought, **in the 613** *mitzvos* **of the Torah.**

Your soul and the *mitzvos* are deeply compatible. Corresponding precisely to the 613 *mitzvos* are 613 "components" of your soul which become fully engaged through observing the *mitzvos* (Rabbi Chaim Vital, *Sha'arei Ha-Kedushah* 1:1).

30TH KISLEV LEAP

The *Tanya* describes in more detail, the total immersion of your soul, via her garments, into Torah.

וּבִפְרָטוּת בְּחִינוֹת חָכְמָה בִּינָה וָדַעַת שֶׁבְּנַפְשׁוֹ מְלוּבָּשׁוֹ בְּהַשָּׂגַת הַתּוֹרָה — **To be precise: your soul's** *chochmah, binah,* **and** *da'as* **are fully engaged, through the garment**

שבנפשו מלובשות בהשגת התורה שהוא משיג בפרד"ס
כפי יכולת השגתו ושרש נפשו למעלה. והמדות שהן
יראה ואהבה וענפיהן ותולדותיהן מלובשות בקיום
המצות במעשה ובדבור שהוא ת"ת שכנגד כולן כי
האהבה היא שרש כל רמ"ח מ"ע וממנה הן נמשכות
ובלעדה אין להן קיום אמיתי כי המקיימן באמת הוא

שֶׁהוּא מַשִּׂיג בִּפְשָׁט רֶמֶז דְּרוּשׁ וְסוֹד, of thought, **in grasping the Torah that you study,** כְּפִי יְכוֹלֶת הַשָּׂגָתוֹ וְשֹׁרֶשׁ נַפְשׁוֹ לְמַעְלָה — **which, exercising the full capacity of your intellect and your soul's spiritual root, you master in** *peshat, remez, derush,* **and** *sod.*

In this state, not only is your mind awakened, but your emotions too.

PRACTICAL LESSONS

Your thoughts are not you. They are the "clothing" or "garments" of your soul; part of your external life, just like your speech and action.

You can bind even these outer "garments" to G-d through observing the *mitzvos* and studying Torah, in the realms of thought, speech and action.

וְהַמִּדּוֹת שֶׁהֵן יִרְאָה וְאַהֲבָה וְעַנְפֵּיהֶן וְתוֹלְדוֹתֵיהֶן מְלוּבָּשׁוֹת בְּקִיּוּם הַמִּצְוֹת בְּמַעֲשֶׂה וּבְדִבּוּר — **And the emotional powers of your soul, namely reverence and love (along with all their derivatives) are** fully **engaged in observing the Torah through her "garments" of action and speech,** שֶׁהוּא תַּלְמוּד תּוֹרָה שֶׁכְּנֶגֶד כּוּלָן — **the** highest use of speech **being** verbalizing **the study of Torah which is** *"equal to all the commandments"* (*Mishnah, Peah* 1:1).

Why is practical observance of the *mitzvos* an expression of love?

כִּי הָאַהֲבָה הִיא שֹׁרֶשׁ כָּל רַמַ"ח מִצְוֹת עֲשֵׂה — **For love is the motivator behind all 248 commands of action** (*Zohar* 3, 122b), וּמִמֶּנָּה הֵן נִמְשָׁכוֹת וּבִלְעָדָה אֵין לָהֶן קִיּוּם אֲמִיתִי — **they all flow from** love, **and have no true basis without it.**

Of the 613 *mitzvos*, 248 are positive commands of action ("do's"), and 365 are prohibitions ("don'ts"), to refrain from a certain action. While it is possible to observe the precepts out of habit, for the sake of social acceptance or for some other ulterior motive, the 248 commands of action can only be observed authentically if they are motivated by love of G-d.

You might imagine that your love of G-d would take its fullest expression as a purely emotional experience. But, just as you would express your absolute love for another person with a physical embrace, the Kabbalah teaches that a person who truly loves G-d will also want to "embrace" Him too, so to speak.

כִּי הַמְקַיְּימָן בֶּאֱמֶת הוּא הָאוֹהֵב אֶת שֵׁם ה' וְחָפֵץ לְדָבְקָה בּוֹ בֶּאֱמֶת — **Because the person who observes** the 248 action-related commands **authentically,** is one who **loves**

האוהב את שם ה' וחפץ לדבקה בו באמת ואי אפשר
לדבקה בו באמת כי אם בקיום רמ"ח פקודין שהם
רמ"ח אברין דמלכא כביכול כמ"ש במקום אחר והיראה
היא שרש לשס"ה לא תעשה כי ירא למרוד במלך
מלכי המלכים הקב"ה. או יראה פנימית מזו שמתבושש

G-d's Name and desires to truly be attached to Him, וְאִי אֶפְשָׁר לְדַבְקָה בּוֹ בֶּאֱמֶת — **and it's impossible to truly attach yourself to G-d,** כִּי אִם בְּקִיּוּם רַמַ"ח פְּקוּדִין שֶׁהֵם רַמַ"ח אֶבְרִין דְּמַלְכָּא כְּבִיְכוֹל — **without observing the 248 commands, which are the 248 "organs of the King"** (*Tikunei Zohar* 74a), **so to speak,** כְּמוֹ שֶׁנִּתְבָּאֵר בְּמָקוֹם אַחֵר — **as is explained elsewhere** (below, chapter 23, p. 257).

Classically, *mitzvos* are perceived as instructions or "commandments" given by G-d to man. Observing them is an expression of obedience to a higher authority. But in the language of the *Zohar*, *mitzvos* are perceived as "organs" of G-d, something into which His actual being is projected. That is why Chasidic thought stresses that "*mitzvah*" is best translated as "connection," from the Aramaic root, *tzavsah* (Rabbi Shneur Zalman, *Short Discourses*, (Brooklyn: Kehos, 1981), p. 148).

A mitzvah is a connection ritual, a sacred technology which brings you into an intimate bond with G-d.

Of course, you are always connected to G-d. He created you; He keeps you alive. You see His wonders every day in nature in human kindness and in the small miracles of life. But a *mitzvah* is an intimate connection, rather like a hug or a kiss. When you connect intimately with someone, all your layers fall away, as essence meets essence.

When you do a *mitzvah* you "embrace" G-d and "kiss" Him, so to speak. The mystics even compared a *mitzvah* to the intimacy of a husband and wife (see chapter 46, p. 597). For a moment, you transcend all the trappings of your life, and are one with G-d. A *mitzvah* may be ritual and rules in form, but it is love in substance.

וְהַיִּרְאָה הִיא שֹׁרֶשׁ לְשַׁסַ"ה לֹא תַעֲשֶׂה — **Reverence, on the other hand, is the motivator behind** refraining from **the 365 prohibitions** of the Torah (*Zohar* 3, 122b).

PRACTICAL LESSONS

The 248 commands of action can only be performed authentically when motivated by love of G-d. The 365 prohibitions should be motivated by reverence.

While it is love that motivates you to do something for your beloved (to observe the 248 commands), it is the feeling of reverence that causes you to refrain from activities despised by Him (the 365 prohibitions of the Torah).

כִּי יָרֵא לִמְרוֹד בְּמֶלֶךְ מַלְכֵי הַמְּלָכִים הַקָּדוֹשׁ בָּרוּךְ הוּא — **Because you revere** Him, to the extent that you will not **rebel against the Supreme King of kings, the Blessed Holy One.**

מִגְדוּלָתוֹ לִמְרוֹת עֵינֵי כְבוֹדוֹ וְלַעֲשׂוֹת הָרַע בְּעֵינָיו כָּל
תּוֹעֲבַת ה' אֲשֶׁר שָׂנֵא שֶׁהֵם הַקְּלִיפּוֹת וְסִטְרָא אַחֲרָא אֲשֶׁר
יְנִיקָתָם מֵהָאָדָם הַתַּחְתּוֹן וַאֲחִיזָתָם בּוֹ הוּא בְּשַׁ"ה מִצְוֹת
לֹא תַעֲשֶׂה. וְהִנֵּה שְׁלֹשָׁה לְבוּשִׁים אֵלוּ מֵהַתּוֹרָה וּמִצְוֹתֶיהָ
אַף שֶׁנִּקְרָאִים לְבוּשִׁים לְנֶפֶשׁ רוּחַ וּנְשָׁמָה עִם כָּל זֶה

At this basic level, you do not appreciate *why* violating a prohibition will distance you from G-d. You are simply aware of the *result*, that it will be considered an act of disobedience against Him and that is undesirable to you.

אוֹ יִרְאָה פְּנִימִית מִזּוֹ — **Or it may be a deeper reverence than this,** where the very prohibited act *in itself* is painful to you, שֶׁמִּתְבּוֹשֵׁשׁ מִגְּדוּלָתוֹ לִמְרוֹת עֵינֵי כְבוֹדוֹ — **since you feel ashamed in the presence of** G-d's **greatness** *"to insult His honor"* (*Isaiah* 3:8), וְלַעֲשׂוֹת הָרַע בְּעֵינָיו כָּל תּוֹעֲבַת ה' אֲשֶׁר שָׂנֵא — **by doing what is** *"evil in His eyes... all those disgusting things which G-d hates"* (*Deuteronomy* 12:31).

At the level of "deeper reverence," you appreciate *why* G-d "hates" the Biblically prohibited activities,

הֵם הַקְּלִיפּוֹת וְסִטְרָא אַחֲרָא — because **they are** the energy of all the negative forces of the universe, **the** *kelipos* **and** *sitra achra,* אֲשֶׁר יְנִיקָתָם מֵהָאָדָם הַתַּחְתּוֹן — **which draw their life force from mortal man's** transgressions, וַאֲחִיזָתָם בּוֹ הוּא בְּשַׁ"ה מִצְוֹת לֹא תַעֲשֶׂה — **and their hold on him is through the 365 prohibitions.**

So you recoil from any of these 365 activities out of the awareness of how damaging they are to the universe.

SECTION TWO: "MERGING" WITH G-D

28TH KISLEV REGULAR | 1ST TEVES LEAP

Up to this point, chapter 4 has clarified the importance of the "outer self" (the "garments" of thought, speech and action) in completing the "inner self" of intellectual and emotional conviction. Merely to love G-d and fear him in the heart is not enough; you need to express those feelings too, by devoting your thoughts, your words and your actions to Him.

Still, the devotion of your "outer self" could easily be seen as the mere "icing on the cake." Doesn't inner devotion represent the most substantive connection to G-d and not the "garments"? Aren't they called "garments" for a reason, to indicate their secondary status to the core intellectual and emotional powers of the soul?

While this would be a reasonable assumption, the *Tanya* now rejects it.

וְהִנֵּה שְׁלֹשָׁה לְבוּשִׁים אֵלוּ מֵהַתּוֹרָה וּמִצְוֹתֶיהָ — **Now these three "garments," when devoted to the Torah and its commandments,** אַף שֶׁנִּקְרָאִים לְבוּשִׁים לְנֶפֶשׁ רוּחַ וּנְשָׁמָה — **although they are referred to as** mere **"garments"** of the core of the soul,

גבהה וגדלה מעלתם לאין קץ וסוף על מעלת נפש רוח
ונשמה עצמן כמ"ש בזהר דאורייתא וקב"ה כולא חד
פי' דאורייתא היא חכמתו ורצונו של הקב"ה והקב"ה
בכבודו ובעצמו כולא חד כי הוא היודע והוא המדע
וכו' כמ"ש לעיל בשם הרמב"ם. ואף דהקב"ה נקרא   8B

the nefesh, ruach and neshamah, עִם כָּל זֶה גְּבָהָה וְגָדְלָה מַעֲלָתָם לְאֵין קֵץ וְסוֹף עַל — **nevertheless, they are of an infinitely greater level and quality than the actual nefesh, ruach and neshamah.**

The *Tanya* has made a striking, seemingly bizarre, proposition that the "clothes" are more important than the "person," that the outer life of the soul is vastly more significant that its inner convictions. And "infinitely" so!

כְּמוֹ שֶׁכָּתוּב בַּזֹהַר — **As the Zohar teaches,** דְּאוֹרַיְיתָא וְקוּדְשָׁא בְּרִיךְ הוּא כּוּלָּא חַד that *"the Torah and G-d are totally one"* (see *Zohar* 1, 24a; 2, 60a), פֵּירוּשׁ דְּאוֹרַיְיתָא — הִיא חָכְמָתוֹ וּרְצוֹנוֹ שֶׁל הַקָּדוֹשׁ בָּרוּךְ הוּא וְהַקָּדוֹשׁ בָּרוּךְ הוּא בִּכְבוֹדוֹ וּבְעַצְמוֹ כּוּלָּא חַד **meaning that the Torah, which is the wisdom and will of G-d,** something that would seem to be a mere glimmer of the Divine essence, is, in fact, **completely one with G-d Himself, in all His glory.**

But if the Torah, and its *mitzvos*, are merely the "wisdom and will of G-d," and not His actual self, how could we say that He is truly one with them?

כִּי הוּא הַיּוֹדֵעַ וְהוּא הַמַּדָּע וְכוּ' — **Because He is** simultaneously **the knower, the power to know,** and the known, כְּמוֹ שֶׁנִּתְבָּאֵר לְעֵיל בְּשֵׁם הָרַמְבַּ"ם — **as explained above, citing *Rambam*** (p. 46).

A CHASIDIC THOUGHT

There is a vast difference between being "one" with G-d, as opposed to being "close" to Him. You might be extremely close to your best friend, your spouse or your child, but ultimately you are two distinct people with different interests. Your arm, on the other hand, is totally one with you. It never has to decide whether it wishes to go along with your decisions and it will never betray you.

Your soul is a "child" of G-d. It is also one of G-d's "lovers"—but it is not one with Him. A *mitzvah*, on the other hand, is a "limb" of G-d, it is part of Him, so to speak. So when your "garment" of thought, speech or action, does a *mitzvah*, that garment actually becomes one with G-d's very self, so to speak.

אֵין סוף וְלִגְדוּלָתוֹ אֵין חֵקֶר וְלֵית מַחֲשָׁבָה תְּפִיסָא בֵּיהּ
כְּלָל וְכֵן בִּרְצוֹנוֹ וְחָכְמָתוֹ כְּדִכְתִיב אֵין חֵקֶר לִתְבוּנָתוֹ
וּכְתִי' הַחֵקֶר אֱלוֹהַּ תִּמְצָא וּכְתִיב כִּי לֹא מַחְשְׁבוֹתַי
מַחְשְׁבוֹתֵיכֶם הִנֵּה עַל זֶה אָמְרוּ בִּמְקוֹם שֶׁאַתָּה מוֹצֵא
גְּדוּלָתוֹ שֶׁל הַקָּבָּ"ה שָׁם אַתָּה מוֹצֵא עֲנַוְתָנוּתוֹ וְצַמְצָם

While it is impossible for a human being to fully understand, G-d has invested Himself in the Torah to such an extent that He has become completely one with it.

Still, the assertion seems counterintuitive. The Torah is a set of very detailed laws, defining the time, place and precise contours of every single *mitvzah*. Failure to observe any of these minutiae will either compromise the act or disqualify it. How could all this be "totally one" with G-d, who transcends all limitation and is utterly infinite?

וְאַף דְּהַקָּדוֹשׁ בָּרוּךְ הוּא נִקְרָא אֵין סוֹף — **And while the Blessed Holy One is called** throughout the Kabbalah as *Ein Sof* (**"Without End"**), וְלִגְדוּלָתוֹ אֵין חֵקֶר **— and "His greatness can never be fathomed"** (*Psalms* 145:3), וְלֵית מַחֲשָׁבָה תְּפִיסָא בֵּיהּ כְּלָל, — and **"No thought can grasp Him at all"** (*Tikunei Zohar* 17a), וְכֵן בִּרְצוֹנוֹ וְחָכְמָתוֹ **— and similarly, His will and His wisdom are also** depicted as non-graspable, **as the verse states, "His understanding no one can fathom"** (*Isaiah* 40:28), וּכְתִיב הַחֵקֶר אֱלוֹהַּ תִּמְצָא **— and it is also written, "Can you, through searching, find G-d?"** (*Job* 11:7), וּכְתִיב כִּי לֹא מַחְשְׁבוֹתַי מַחְשְׁבוֹתֵיכֶם **— and it is written, "For My thoughts are not your thoughts"** (*Isaiah* 55:8), nevertheless, G-d's infinitude and utter oneness is, in fact, perfectly consistent with the limited and detailed laws of the Torah.

הִנֵּה עַל זֶה אָמְרוּ בִּמְקוֹם שֶׁאַתָּה מוֹצֵא גְּדוּלָתוֹ שֶׁל הַקָּדוֹשׁ בָּרוּךְ הוּא שָׁם אַתָּה מוֹצֵא עֲנַוְתָנוּתוֹ **— To** explain **this it has been taught, "In the same place that you find the greatness of G-d, there you find His humility"** (*Talmud, Megillah* 31a; *Yalkut Shimoni, Psalms* section 794).

At the literal level, the *Talmud* is merely noting how Scripture will sometimes place a verse that speaks of the greatness of G-d right next to another that speaks of His humility. But here, the *Tanya* interprets the *Talmud's* teaching in a metaphysical sense, as a musing on G-d's infinitude.

Usually we think of infinity as *limitless expansiveness*, the ability to extend in any direction without end. However, as Kabbalist Rabbi Meir ibn Gabbai observed, if you would say that G-d is *only* infinite and can never express Himself in a finite way, you would, ironically, be limiting Him. You would be saying there is one thing which G-d cannot, in fact, do!

To resolve this paradox, R' Meir Ibn Gabbai suggested that G-d has *both* the ability to express Himself infinitely and finitely, if He so wishes, *"otherwise you diminish His perfection"* (*Avodas Ha-Kodesh* 1:8).

הקב"ה רצונו וחכמתו בתרי"ג מצות התורה ובהלכותיהן
ובצרופי אותיות תנ"ך ודרשותיהן שבאגדות ומדרשי
חכמינו ז"ל בכדי שכל הנשמה או רוח ונפש שבגוף
האדם תוכל להשיגן בדעתה ולקיימן כל מה שאפשר
לקיים מהן במעשה דבור ומחשבה וע"י זה תתלבש
בכל עשר בחינותיה בשלשה לבושים אלו. ולכן
נמשלה התורה למים מה מים יורדים ממקום גבוה
למקום נמוך כך התורה ירדה ממקום כבודה שהיא

In this vein, the *Tanya* offers us a fresh reading of the *Talmud's* teaching: *"In the same place that you find the greatness of G-d"* — i.e., His ability to be infinite, *"there you find His humility"* — He can also express Himself in a finite way, through the finite garb of a precise *mitzvah* ritual; and that is His true greatness!

וְצִמְצֵם הַקָּדוֹשׁ בָּרוּךְ הוּא רְצוֹנוֹ וְחָכְמָתוֹ בְּתַרְיַ"ג מִצְוֹת הַתּוֹרָה וּבְהִלְכוֹתֵיהֶן — **And the Blessed Holy One has "compacted" His will and wisdom into the 613 commandments of the Torah, and their associated laws,** וּבְצֵרוּפֵי אוֹתִיּוֹת תּוֹרָה נְבִיאִים וּכְתוּבִים — **and into the texts of the Torah, Prophets and Writings (*Tanach*),** וּדְרָשׁוֹתֵיהֶן — as well as their commentaries in the שֶׁבַּאֲגָדוֹת וּמִדְרְשֵׁי חֲכָמֵינוּ זִכְרוֹנָם לִבְרָכָה — **as well as their commentaries in the** *Agados* and *Midrashim* (homilies) of the Sages, of blessed memory.

Just as a *mitzvah* represents the infinite will of G-d in a finite garb, the sacred texts and rituals of Judaism are a finite expression of the limitless wisdom of G-d.

Why did G-d perform this metaphysical wonder of expressing His infinite self in finite form?

בִּכְדֵי שֶׁכָּל הַנְּשָׁמָה אוֹ רוּחַ וָנֶפֶשׁ שֶׁבְּגוּף הָאָדָם — **This was in order that all the** *neshamah,* **or** *ruach* **and** *nefesh* **in your body,** תּוּכַל לְהַשִּׂיגָן בְּדַעְתָּהּ וּלְקַיְּמָן כָּל מַה — should be able to mentally grasp these *mitzvos* and sacred שֶׁאֶפְשָׁר לְקַיֵּם מֵהֶן — **texts and to observe them as best as possible,** בְּמַעֲשֶׂה דִבּוּר וּמַחֲשָׁבָה — **in action, speech and thought,** וְעַל יְדֵי זֶה תִּתְלַבֵּשׁ בְּכָל עֶשֶׂר בְּחִינוֹתֶיהָ בִּשְׁלֹשָׁה לְבוּשִׁים אֵלּוּ — **and thereby "dress" all the ten powers** of your soul (described in chapter 3) **in these three "garments"** of action, speech and thought, becoming totally one with G-d.

2ND TEVES LEAP

The *Tanya* now cites another *Talmudic* teaching which sheds further light on this idea, the fusion of an infinite will and wisdom with the finite vessels of Torah texts and rituals.

וְלָכֵן נִמְשְׁלָה הַתּוֹרָה לְמַיִם — **Therefore, the Torah has been compared** by the *Talmud* **to water,** מַה מַּיִם יוֹרְדִים מִמָּקוֹם גָּבוֹהַּ לְמָקוֹם נָמוּךְ — **for just as water has the tendency to flow from a higher level to a lower one** (*Talmud, Ta'anis* 7a), כָּךְ

רצונו וחכמתו יתברך ואורייתא וקודשא בריך הוא
כולא חד ולית מחשבה תפיסא ביה כלל. ומשם נסעה
וירדה בסתר המדרגות ממדרגה למדרגה בהשתלשלות
העולמות עד שנתלבשה בדברים גשמיים וענייני עולם
הזה שהן רוב מצות התורה ככולם והלכותיהן וצרופי
אותיות גשמיות בדיו על הספר עשרים וארבעה
ספרים שבתורה נביאים וכתובים כדי שתהא כל
מחשבה תפיסא בהן ואפי' בחי' דבור ומעשה שלמטה
ממדרגת מחשבה תפיסא בהן ומתלבשת בהן ומאחר

הַתּוֹרָה יָרְדָה מִמְּקוֹם כְּבוֹדָהּ שֶׁהִיא רְצוֹנוֹ וְחָכְמָתוֹ יִתְבָּרֵךְ — in a similar way, the Torah has descended from its sublime setting in G-d's blessed will and wisdom, וְאוֹרַיְיתָא — where *"the Torah and G-d are totally one"* (*Zohar* 1, 24a; 2, 60a), וְקוּדְשָׁא בְּרִיךְ הוּא כּוּלָּא חַד — and *"No thought can grasp Him at all"* (*Tikunei Zohar*, 17a), וְלֵית מַחֲשָׁבָה תְּפִיסָא בֵּיהּ כְּלָל — and from there, the Torah has journeyed downwards, through *"the hidden places in the steps"* (*Song* 2:14), וּמִשָּׁם נָסְעָה וְיָרְדָה בְּסֵתֶר הַמַּדְרֵגוֹת — unaffected by the step-by-step, downward spiral of spiritual worlds, not suffering any dilution or diminishment at all, מִמַּדְרֵגָה לְמַדְרֵגָה בְּהִשְׁתַּלְשְׁלוּת הָעוֹלָמוֹת — to the final point where G-d's will is "dressed" in physical objects and worldly concepts, עַד שֶׁנִּתְלַבְּשָׁה בִּדְבָרִים גַּשְׁמִיִּים וְעִנְיְינֵי עוֹלָם הַזֶּה — which is the context of virtually all the Torah's commandments and their laws, שֶׁהֵן רוֹב מִצְוֹת הַתּוֹרָה כְּכוּלָּם וְהִלְכוֹתֵיהֶן — as well as its sacred texts, written in physical form, ink on parchment, וּבְצֵרוּפֵי אוֹתִיּוֹת גַּשְׁמִיּוֹת בִּדְיוֹ עַל הַסֵּפֶר — in the twenty-four books of the *Tanach.* עֶשְׂרִים וְאַרְבָּעָה סְפָרִים שֶׁבַּתּוֹרָה נְבִיאִים וּכְתוּבִים

כְּדֵי שֶׁתְּהֵא כָּל מַחֲשָׁבָה תְּפִיסָא בָּהֶן — All this was in order that every mind should be able to grasp them, since even a simple person or a child can read the *Tanach,* וַאֲפִילוּ בְּחִינַת דִּבּוּר וּמַעֲשֶׂה שֶׁלְּמַטָּה מִמַּדְרֵגַת מַחֲשָׁבָה — and even the outer "garments" of speech and action, which are more superficial than thought, תְּפִיסָא בָּהֶן וּמִתְלַבֵּשֶׁת בָּהֶן — should be able to grasp them and "dress" in them.

29TH KISLEV REGULAR

וּמֵאַחַר שֶׁהַתּוֹרָה וּמִצְוֹתֶיהָ מַלְבִּישִׁים כָּל עֶשֶׂר בְּחִינוֹת הַנֶּפֶשׁ — And since the Torah and its *mitzvos* provide a complete set of "clothing" for all ten powers of your soul,

A CHASIDIC THOUGHT

The Torah was not merely given "from heaven"; it is a taste of heaven itself. The *mitzvos* provide Divine "clothing" into which every part of my consciousness and behavior can "dress" itself.

שהתורה ומצותיה מלבישים כל עשר בחי' הנפש וכל
תרי"ג אבריה מראשה ועד רגלה הרי כולה צרורה
בצרור החיים את ה' ממש ואור ה' ממש מקיפה
ומלבישה מראשה ועד רגלה כמ"ש צורי אחסה בו
וכתיב כצנה רצון תעטרנו שהוא רצונו וחכמתו יתברך 9A
המלובשים בתורתו ומצותיה. ולכן אמרו יפה שעה
אחת בתשובה ומעשים טובים בעולם הזה מכל חיי

וְכָל תַּרְיַ"ג אֲבָרֶיהָ מֵרֹאשָׁה וְעַד רַגְלָה — **and for all the** soul's **613 sub-components, from "head" to "foot,"** each of which find expression in a specific *mitzvah,* הֲרֵי כּוּלָהּ צְרוּרָה בְּצְרוֹר הַחַיִּים אֶת ה' — **it follows that** through dressing in all this "clothing," your soul **becomes completely** *"bound in the bundle of life with G-d"* (*I Samuel* 25:29), מַמָּשׁ — **literally.**

Having used the analogy of "clothing" to depict the *extent* to which the Torah attaches you to G-d, the *Tanya* now stresses the *quality* of that attachment.

וְאוֹר ה' מַמָּשׁ מַקִיפָה וּמַלְבִּישָׁה מֵרֹאשָׁה וְעַד רַגְלָה — **And it is the light of G-d, literally,** that engulfs your soul, **dressing her from head to foot.**

Torah and *mitzvos* offer: 1.) *immersion* of your being in Divine "garments"; 2.) attachment to the most *transcendent power* of the universe, "the light of G-d."

כְּמוֹ שֶׁכָּתוּב צוּרִי אֶחֱסֶה בּוֹ — **As the verse states,** *"He is my Rock, in whom I take refuge"* (*Psalms* 18:3), וּכְתִיב כַּצִנָּה רָצוֹן תַּעְטְרֶנּוּ — **and it is written,** *"as with a shield, the will* of G-d *surrounds him"* (*ibid.* 5:3), שֶׁהוּא רְצוֹנוֹ וְחָכְמָתוֹ יִתְבָּרֵךְ הַמְלוּבָּשִׁים בְּתוֹרָתוֹ וּמִצְוֹתָיה — **referring to His blessed will and wisdom "dressed" in His Torah and its commandments** (see Rabbi Menachem Mendel of Vitebsk, *Pri Ha'aretz, Parshas Vayeishev*).

SECTION THREE: RETHINKING THE AFTERLIFE

3RD TEVES LEAP

The *Tanya's* emphasis on the undiminished presence of G-d within a *mitzvah,* has broader repercussions about our understanding of the afterlife.

וְלָכֵן אָמְרוּ יָפָה שָׁעָה אַחַת בִּתְשׁוּבָה וּמַעֲשִׂים טוֹבִים בָּעוֹלָם הַזֶּה מִכָּל חַיֵּי עוֹלָם הַבָּא — **This explains why** the *Mishnah* **teaches:** *"Better is one hour of repentance and good deeds in this world than all the life of the world-that-is-coming"* (*Avos* 4:17).

At first glance, the *Mishnah's* assertion is difficult to comprehend. How could any experience in this world, where G-d's presence is veiled, be superior to the next world, where His glory will be revealed?

At the simple level, the *Mishnah* speaks of the advantage of having the *opportunity* to come closer to G-d. In this world, you can draw closer to G-d with "repentance

עוֹלָם הַבָּא כִּי עוֹלָם הַבָּא הוּא שֶׁנֶּהֱנִין מִזִּיו הַשְּׁכִינָה
שֶׁהוּא תַּעֲנוּג הַהַשָּׂגָה וְאִי אֶפְשָׁר לְשׁוּם נִבְרָא אֲפִי'
מֵהָעֶלְיוֹנִים לְהַשִּׂיג כִּי אִם אֵיזוֹ הֶאָרָה מֵאוֹר ה' וְלָכֵן
נִקְרָא בְּשֵׁם זִיו הַשְּׁכִינָה אֲבָל הקב"ה בִּכְבוֹדוֹ וּבְעַצְמוֹ
לֵית מַחֲשָׁבָה תְּפִיסָא בֵּיהּ כְּלָל כִּי אִם כַּאֲשֶׁר תְּפִיסָא

and good deeds." In the next world, your relationship with Him will be blissful, but static. There will be no room for growth (*Rashi*). While you might be *closer* to G-d in the next world, your relationship is *more meaningful* now.

That is the classic understanding. However, based on the insight of this chapter, the *Tanya* will now reinterpret the *Mishnah* according to a new paradigm, that *we really are closer* to G-d in this world than the next, literally.

First we need to examine how Judaism depicts the experience of the afterlife:

כִּי עוֹלָם הַבָּא הוּא שֶׁנֶּהֱנִין מִזִּיו הַשְּׁכִינָה — Because in the world-that-is-coming, "*we enjoy the radiance of the Divine Presence*" (*Talmud, Brachos* 17a), שֶׁהוּא תַּעֲנוּג הַהַשָּׂגָה — which refers to the pleasure of understanding G-d, that was not possible for the soul while contained in a body (*Rambam, Laws of Teshuvah* 8:2).

Being freed from the body allows the soul an unprecedented insight into the Divine, from which it derives tremendous pleasure. But ultimately, that experience has its limits since the soul is finite in its abilities.

וְאִי אֶפְשָׁר לְשׁוּם נִבְרָא אֲפִילוּ מֵהָעֶלְיוֹנִים לְהַשִּׂיג כִּי אִם אֵיזוֹ הֶאָרָה מֵאוֹר ה' — But it is impossible for any created entity, even a very lofty one, such as a disembodied soul, to grasp more than a glimmer of Divine light.

The soul cannot bridge the chasm between creation and Creator; it can appreciate only so much of G-d as its finite, cognitive powers permit. For even the Divine Soul, "*does not lose its separate identity completely, to be extinguished and literally absorbed in G-d's light and to merge completely (with G-d) in absolute unity. Rather, (the soul retains) its separate identity*" (p. 390).

וְלָכֵן נִקְרָא בְּשֵׁם זִיו הַשְּׁכִינָה — For this reason the *Talmud* is careful to refer to the experience of the next world as basking in the mere "radiance" of the Divine Presence and not the Divine Presence itself, which remains elusive, אֲבָל הַקָּדוֹשׁ בָּרוּךְ הוּא בִּכְבוֹדוֹ וּבְעַצְמוֹ — but with regard to G-d Himself, in His glory, לֵית מַחֲשָׁבָה תְּפִיסָא בֵּיהּ כְּלָל — "*No thought can grasp Him at all*" (*Tikunei Zohar* 17a), not even that of a disembodied soul in the next world.

By contrast, as we have elaborated at length, the experiencing of G-d as He is "dressed" in Torah and *mitzvos* in *this* world is one of total immersion in the Divine.

ומתלבשת בתורה ומצותיה אזי היא תפיסא בהן(*)
ומתלבשת בהקב"ה ממש דאורייתא וקב"ה כולא חד.
ואף שהתורה נתלבשה בדברים תחתונים גשמיים הרי זה
כמחבק את המלך ד"מ שאין הפרש במעלת התקרבותו
ודביקותו במלך בין מחבקו כשהוא לבוש לבוש אחד בין
שהוא לבוש כמה לבושים מאחר שגוף המלך בתוכם.

*) בכ"י ליתא תיבת בהן.

כִּי אִם כַּאֲשֶׁר תְּפִיסָא וּמִתְלַבֶּשֶׁת בַּתּוֹרָה וּמִצְוֹתֶיהָ — Except when you "grasp Him" and are "dressed in" the Torah and its mitzvos, אֲזַי הִיא תְּפִיסָא בָּהֶן וּמִתְלַבֶּשֶׁת בְּהַקָּדוֹשׁ בָּרוּךְ הוּא מַמָּשׁ — only then you literally "grasp," and are "dressed in" the Blessed Holy One, דְּאוֹרַיְיתָא וְקוּדְשָׁא בְּרִיךְ הוּא כּוּלָּא חַד — since "the Torah and G-d are totally one" (see Zohar 1, 24a; 2, 60a).

In contrast to the next world, where your soul will only appreciate a glimmer of G-d from a distance, in this world you can experience G-d Himself. That's because He is utterly one with the Torah and its mitzvos in which you immerse your Divine Soul and its "garments" of thought, speech and action.

Therefore the Sages taught, *"Better is one hour of repentance and good deeds in this world,"* when you are truly one with G-d, *"than all the life of the world-that-is-coming,"* when you'll be separate from Him, since the soul cannot perform mitzvos in the afterlife.

Reversing the traditional model, where G-d remains obscured in this world and is finally available in the afterlife, Chasidic thought radically reconsiders Divine "accessibility." G-d is fully present in the experience of Torah and mitzvos in this world, but only a distant presence in all the wondrous revelations of the afterlife.

While this may seem counterintuitive, it is really a logical conclusion of the *Zohar's* teaching that *"the Torah and G-d are totally one."*

וְאַף שֶׁהַתּוֹרָה נִתְלַבְּשָׁה בִּדְבָרִים תַּחְתּוֹנִים גַּשְׁמִיִּים — For although the Torah is immersed in mundane, physical things through which the mitzvos are observed, הֲרֵי זֶה כִּמְחַבֵּק אֶת הַמֶּלֶךְ דֶּרֶךְ מָשָׁל — this can be compared to hugging a human king, שֶׁאֵין הֶפְרֵשׁ בְּמַעֲלַת הִתְקָרְבוּתוֹ — where there is no difference in the level of closeness and bonding achieved by the embrace, וּדְבֵיקוּתוֹ בַּמֶּלֶךְ בֵּין מְחַבְּקוֹ כְּשֶׁהוּא לָבוּשׁ לְבוּשׁ אֶחָד בֵּין שֶׁהוּא לָבוּשׁ כַּמָּה לְבוּשִׁים — whether you hug him while he is dressed in one robe or dressed in several robes, מֵאַחַר שֶׁגּוּף הַמֶּלֶךְ בְּתוֹכָם — since the king himself is inside them.

PRACTICAL LESSONS

Even though the mitzvah is a this-worldly ritual, it's really like hugging a king while he is dressed in a robe. The robe doesn't get in the way of the hug.

You can't get closer to G-d than that, because through the embrace you are one with Him. Even the afterlife can't compete.

וְכֵן אִם הַמֶּלֶךְ מְחַבְּקוֹ בִּזְרוֹעוֹ גַּם שֶׁהִיא מְלוּבֶּשֶׁת תּוֹךְ
מַלְבּוּשָׁיו כמ"ש וִימִינוֹ תְּחַבְּקֵנִי שֶׁהִיא הַתּוֹרָה שֶׁנִּתְּנָה
מִימִין שֶׁהִיא בְּחִי' חֶסֶד וּמַיִם:

פרק ה וְלִתּוֹסֶפֶת בִּיאוּר בְּאֵר הֵיטֵב לְשׁוֹן תְּפִיסָא
שֶׁאָמַר אֵלִיָּהוּ לֵית מַחֲשָׁבָה

G-d's will and wisdom is "dressed" in the Torah and *mitzvos*; their worldly "garbing" does not detract from the quality of the "hug" you achieve through them. A hug is a hug, no matter how many layers of clothes are present.

וְכֵן אִם הַמֶּלֶךְ מְחַבְּקוֹ בִּזְרוֹעוֹ — **Also,** the same is true in the reverse, *i.e.,* **when the king** initiates the embrace, **offering a hug with his arm,** גַּם שֶׁהִיא מְלוּבֶּשֶׁת תּוֹךְ מַלְבּוּשָׁיו — **even though it is garbed in his robes,** it does not affect the quality of the connection.

With this we can understand why the Torah is compared to the "right arm" of G-d:

כְּמוֹ שֶׁכָּתוּב וִימִינוֹ תְּחַבְּקֵנִי — **As the verse states,** *"And His right hand embraces me"* (*Song* 2:6), שֶׁהִיא הַתּוֹרָה שֶׁנִּתְּנָה מִימִין — **meaning the Torah which was given by G-d's** *"right hand"* (*Deuteronomy* 33:2), שֶׁהִיא בְּחִינַת חֶסֶד — **which is symbolic of benevolence** (*Tikunei Zohar* 17a), *i.e.,* G-d's willingness to "dress" His infinite self in finite garments, for our benefit, וּמַיִם — **and water** (*Zohar* 3, 355a), alluding to the idea that G-d's presence was not diminished by the worldly garbing of the Torah and *mitzvos*, just as water remains the same after it flows from a higher place to a lower one (as explained above, pp. 70-71).

CHAPTER 5

TOTAL IMMERSION IN THE DIVINE

SECTION ONE: AN UNPARALLELED UNITY WITH G-D

30TH KISLEV REGULAR | 4TH TEVES LEAP

As we learned in chapter four, the greatest bonding experience with G-d is through Torah study and *mitzvah* observance. In this chapter, the *Tanya* will explore why, of these two activities, Torah study offers the more intense connection.

וְלִתּוֹסֶפֶת בֵּיאוּר בְּאֵר הֵיטֵב לְשׁוֹן תְּפִיסָא שֶׁאָמַר אֵלִיָּהוּ לֵית מַחֲשָׁבָה תְּפִיסָא בָּךְ כוּ' — **Let's clarify in more depth the term "grasp,"** in Elijah's statement, *"No thought can grasp You etc.,"* (*Tikunei Zohar* 17a).

תְּפִיסָא בָּךְ כו'. הִנֵּה כָּל שֵׂכֶל כְּשֶׁמַּשְׂכִּיל וּמַשִּׂיג בְּשִׂכְלוֹ אֵיזֶה מוּשְׂכָּל הֲרֵי הַשֵּׂכֶל תּוֹפֵס אֶת הַמּוּשְׂכָּל וּמַקִּיפוֹ בְּשִׂכְלוֹ וְהַמּוּשְׂכָּל נִתְפָּס וּמוּקָּף וּמְלוּבָּשׁ בְּתוֹךְ הַשֵּׂכֶל שֶׁהִשִּׂיגוֹ וְהִשְׂכִּילוֹ וְגַם הַשֵּׂכֶל מְלוּבָּשׁ בַּמּוּשְׂכָּל בְּשָׁעָה שֶׁמַּשִּׂיגוֹ וְתוֹפְסוֹ בְּשִׂכְלוֹ ד"מ

When you understand something, you "own it" and it becomes absorbed in your mind. This, the *Tanya* will suggest, is what the *Zohar* implies by the term "grasping."

הִנֵּה כָּל שֵׂכֶל כְּשֶׁמַּשְׂכִּיל וּמַשִּׂיג בְּשִׂכְלוֹ אֵיזֶה מוּשְׂכָּל — **Now, when your mind processes and masters an idea,** הֲרֵי הַשֵּׂכֶל תּוֹפֵס אֶת הַמּוּשְׂכָּל וּמַקִּיפוֹ בְּשִׂכְלוֹ — **your mind** initially **"grasps" the** basic point of the **idea, mentally engulfing it.**

When you understand something, your mind absorbs it and "engulfs" it, like a sponge soaking up a puddle of water.

At this early stage, however, you have only "engulfed" and absorbed the *basic point* of the idea. Now that you are intrigued, your mind desires to fully master the idea's inner logic and broader implications. Only after this analysis is complete can you fully grasp the idea.

וְהַמּוּשְׂכָּל נִתְפָּס וּמוּקָּף וּמְלוּבָּשׁ בְּתוֹךְ הַשֵּׂכֶל שֶׁהִשִּׂיגוֹ וְהִשְׂכִּילוֹ — And after it has been thoroughly analyzed by your mind, **the idea becomes** fully **grasped, engulfed and absorbed in your mind (that figured** the idea **out and mastered it).**

וְגַם — But there is **yet another** dimension to the experience of mentally "grasping," and this takes place *between* the time when you initially grasp the basic point of the idea and your final mastery of it, הַשֵּׂכֶל מְלוּבָּשׁ בַּמּוּשְׂכָּל בְּשָׁעָה שֶׁמַּשִּׂיגוֹ וְתוֹפְסוֹ בְּשִׂכְלוֹ — because **during** the interim **time when your mind is processing the** initial **idea,** attempting to fully **grasp it, then** the reverse is true: it is **your mind that is absorbed in the idea,** because it is captivated by it.

Until you have mastered the idea, it still captivates you, which means that *you are absorbed in the idea.* As soon as you have mastered it fully, it ceases to captivate you, since you have absorbed everything there is to know about the subject. At that point, *the idea is absorbed in you (Notes on Tanya).*

PRACTICAL LESSONS

As you *master* a Torah text, your soul absorbs its Divine light. The Torah nourishes your soul inside, like food.

As you become *captivated* by a Torah text, desiring to fully master it, your soul is absorbed in Divine light, dressing in it like a garment.

Now, when the idea studied is *from the Torah,* a text which is "one with G-d," then the resulting union with G-d is an extremely intimate one, where you are "absorbed" in G-d, while He is also "absorbed" in you, so to speak.

כשאדם מבין ומשיג איזו הלכה במשנה או בגמרא
לאשורה על בוריה הרי שכלו תופס ומקיף אותה וגם
שכלו מלובש בה באותה שעה. והנה הלכה זו היא
חכמתו ורצונו של הקב"ה שעלה ברצונו שכשיטעון
ראובן כך וכך דרך משל ושמעון כך וכך יהיה הפסק
ביניהם כך וכך ואף אם לא היה ולא יהיה הדבר הזה
לעולם לבא למשפט על טענות ותביעות אלו מכל מקום
מאחר שכך עלה ברצונו וחכמתו של הקב"ה שאם
יטעון זה כך וזה כך יהיה הפסק כך הרי כשאדם יודע
ומשיג בשכלו פסק זה כהלכה הערוכה במשנה או
גמרא או פוסקים הרי זה משיג ותופס ומקיף בשכלו

9B

כְּשֶׁאָדָם מֵבִין וּמַשִּׂיג אֵיזוֹ הֲלָכָה בְּמִשְׁנָה אוֹ בִּגְמָרָא — By way of illustration, דֶּרֶךְ מָשָׁל לַאֲשׁוּרָה עַל בּוּרְיָהּ — when you are in the process of analyzing and fully mastering a ruling of the *Mishnah* or *Gemara* (*Talmud*), הֲרֵי שִׂכְלוֹ תּוֹפֵס וּמַקִּיף אוֹתָהּ — your intellect progressively **grasps and "engulfs"** the ruling, absorbing all its details and ramifications, וְגַם שִׂכְלוֹ מְלוּבָּשׁ בָּהּ בְּאוֹתָהּ שָׁעָה — **and yet, at the same time, your mind is absorbed in it** and is captivated by it.

וְהִנֵּה הֲלָכָה זוֹ הִיא חָכְמָתוֹ וּרְצוֹנוֹ שֶׁל הַקָּדוֹשׁ בָּרוּךְ הוּא — **Now this ruling** of the *Talmud* **represents the wisdom and will of the Blessed Holy One,** שֶׁעָלָה בִּרְצוֹנוֹ שֶׁכְּשֶׁיִּטְעוֹן — **that it arose in His** רְאוּבֵן כָּךְ וְכָךְ דֶּרֶךְ מָשָׁל וְשִׁמְעוֹן כָּךְ וְכָךְ יִהְיֶה הַפֶּסֶק בֵּינֵיהֶם כָּךְ וְכָךְ — **will what the final ruling would be when, for example, Reuven will present a particular legal argument and Shimon a certain counter-argument** (see Rabbi Meir ibn Gabbai, *Avodas Ha-Kodesh* 3:23; Rabbi Chaim Miller, *Rambam: Thirteen Principles of Faith, Principles 8-9* (Brooklyn: Kol Menachem, 2007), p. 29-62; 143-160).

Absorbing this Divine "wisdom and will" into your mind, while at the same time being captivated (absorbed) by it, represents a very powerful union with G-d.

But what if you study a part of the Torah that has no practical relevance. Does that still represent the "wisdom and will of G-d"?

וְאַף אִם לֹא הָיָה וְלֹא יִהְיֶה הַדָּבָר הַזֶּה לְעוֹלָם — **And even if this scenario never came to pass and never will,** לָבֹא לְמִשְׁפָּט עַל טַעֲנוֹת וּתְבִיעוֹת אֵלוּ — and there will never be **actual litigation involving these particular legal arguments and claims,** מִכָּל מָקוֹם — **nevertheless, since it arose in** מֵאַחַר שֶׁכָּךְ עָלָה בִּרְצוֹנוֹ וְחָכְמָתוֹ שֶׁל הַקָּדוֹשׁ בָּרוּךְ הוּא — **the will and wisdom of the Blessed Holy One,** שֶׁאִם יִטְעוֹן זֶה כָּךְ וְזֶה כָּךְ יִהְיֶה הַפֶּסֶק כָּךְ — **what the final ruling would be if one person would present a certain legal argument and another person, a corresponding counter-argument,** הֲרֵי כְּשֶׁאָדָם יוֹדֵעַ — it follows that when you understand this ruling with your וּמַשִּׂיג בְּשִׂכְלוֹ פֶּסֶק זֶה — **mind,** כַּהֲלָכָה הָעֲרוּכָה בְּמִשְׁנָה אוֹ גְמָרָא אוֹ פוֹסְקִים — as the law is prescribed by

רצונו וחכמתו של הקב"ה דלית מחשבה תפיסא ביה
ולא ברצונו וחכמתו כי אם בהתלבשותם בהלכות
הערוכות לפנינו וגם שכלו מלובש בהם והוא יחוד
נפלא שאין יחוד כמוהו ולא כערכו נמצא כלל בגשמיות
להיות לאחדים ומיוחדים ממש מכל צד ופנה. וזאת

הֲרֵי זֶה מַשִּׂיג וְתוֹפֵס וּמַקִּיף בְּשִׂכְלוֹ רְצוֹנוֹ **the Mishnah, Gemara or later authorities,** וְחָכְמָתוֹ שֶׁל הַקָּדוֹשׁ בָּרוּךְ הוּא — **you thereby understand, grasp and engulf with your mind the wisdom and will of the Blessed Holy One.**

דְּלֵית מַחֲשָׁבָה תְּפִיסָא בֵּיהּ וְלֹא בִּרְצוֹנוֹ וְחָכְמָתוֹ — And as we have explained in the previous chapter, the *Zohar* states, **"no thought can grasp Him,"** **not His will nor His wisdom,** since no finite mortal can "grasp" something infinite, כִּי אִם בְּהִתְלַבְּשׁוּתָם בַּהֲלָכוֹת הָעֲרוּכוֹת לְפָנֵינוּ — **yet the exception** to this rule **is when** that Divine wisdom and will **is "dressed" in the final rulings of Jewish law, which have been codified for us.**

As we have learned in chapter four, G-d "compacted" His infinite wisdom and will into the finite garb of these Torah laws.

וְגַם — And, as we have seen, not only does your mind absorb these Divine laws through study, **but also** the reverse is true, שִׂכְלוֹ מְלוּבָּשׁ בָּהֶם — **your mind becomes absorbed *in* them,** as it is captivated by them.

What is it like for your mind to be "absorbed" and engulfed by the Divine and, at the same time, have the Divine totally absorbed within you?

וְהוּא יִחוּד נִפְלָא שֶׁאֵין יִחוּד כָּמוֹהוּ — **This is a phenomenal merging experience** of two beings, **there is no other merging experience like it,** וְלֹא כְּעֶרְכּוֹ נִמְצָא כְּלָל בְּגַשְׁמִיּוּת — **nothing remotely comparable exists in the physical world,** לִהְיוֹת לַאֲחָדִים וּמְיוּחָדִים מַמָּשׁ מִכָּל צַד וּפָנָה — **where you become completely one** with another entity **from every conceivable perspective** and yet retain your own existence.

Physically, it is impossible to engulf something else and, at the same time, be engulfed by it. Yet when you study the Torah, that is precisely what happens: you engulf (master) the Torah and it engulfs (captivates) you.

Is there a "phenomenal merging experience," too, when you study other forms of wisdom besides Torah? The mind would seem to operate the same way, regardless of what you study.

PRACTICAL LESSONS

The most intimate bond you can have with G-d is through studying His word, in the Written and Oral Torah.

This total immersion in Divine light, inside and out, can only be achieved through Torah study.

מַעֲלָה יְתֵרָה גְדוֹלָה וְנִפְלָאָה לְאֵין קֵץ אֲשֶׁר בְּמִצְוַת
יְדִיעַת הַתּוֹרָה וְהַשָּׂגָתָהּ עַל כָּל הַמִּצְוֹת מַעֲשִׂיּוֹת וַאֲפִי'
עַל מִצְוֹת הַתְּלוּיוֹת בְּדִבּוּר וַאֲפִי' עַל מִצְוַת תַּלְמוּד
תּוֹרָה שֶׁבְּדִבּוּר כִּי עַ"י כָּל הַמִּצְוֹת שֶׁבְּדִבּוּר וּמַעֲשֶׂה
הַקָּבָּ"ה מַלְבִּישׁ אֶת הַנֶּפֶשׁ וּמַקִּיפָה אוֹר ה' מֵרֹאשָׁה
וְעַד רַגְלָהּ. וּבִידִיעַת הַתּוֹרָה מִלְּבַד שֶׁהַשֵּׂכֶל מְלוּבָּשׁ
בְּחָכְמַת ה' הִנֵּה גַּם חָכְמַת ה' בְּקִרְבּוֹ מַה שֶּׁהַשֵּׂכֶל
מַשִּׂיג וְתוֹפֵס וּמַקִּיף בְּשִׂכְלוֹ מַה שֶּׁאֶפְשָׁר לוֹ לִתְפּוֹס

There is, however, a key distinction. When you study astronomy, for example, you do not become one with the planets themselves; your mind unites with *the concept* of the planets. There remains an inherent duality between the idea and its subject.

On the other hand, *"G-d looked into the Torah and created the world"* (*Zohar* 3, 161b); Torah is the blueprint of creation itself. When you study something in the Torah, that thing is a *direct product* of the idea as it exists in the Torah, and you therefore have a "phenomenal merging experience" (*Toras Menachem* vol. 18, pp. 313-4).

SECTION TWO: BEING AND NON-BEING

1ST TEVES REGULAR

וְזֹאת מַעֲלָה יְתֵרָה גְדוֹלָה וְנִפְלָאָה לְאֵין קֵץ — **This is the endlessly great and wonderful advantage,** אֲשֶׁר בְּמִצְוַת יְדִיעַת הַתּוֹרָה וְהַשָּׂגָתָהּ עַל כָּל הַמִּצְוֹת מַעֲשִׂיּוֹת — **possessed by the** *mitzvah* **of knowing and mastering the Torah over all the other** *mitzvos* **that involve action,** וַאֲפִילוּ עַל מִצְוֹת הַתְּלוּיוֹת בְּדִבּוּר — **even those** *mitzvos* **connected with speech,** since speaking is a type of action (see p. 412), וַאֲפִילוּ עַל מִצְוַת תַּלְמוּד תּוֹרָה שֶׁבְּדִבּוּר — in fact, "knowing and mastering" the Torah with your mind has an advantage **even over the** *mitzvah* **of verbalizing the Torah** which you **study** (see Rabbi Shneur Zalman, *Laws of Torah Study* 2:12).

Why is the *mitzvah* of knowing the Torah greater than any *mitzvah* of action?

כִּי עַל יְדֵי כָּל הַמִּצְוֹת שֶׁבְּדִבּוּר וּמַעֲשֶׂה — **Since with all of the** *mitzvos* **involving speech or action,** הַקָּדוֹשׁ בָּרוּךְ הוּא מַלְבִּישׁ אֶת הַנֶּפֶשׁ וּמַקִּיפָה אוֹר ה' — **there is a "one-way"** absorption of the person *into* the Divine, **as the soul is absorbed in G-d and surrounded by the light of G-d,** מֵרֹאשָׁה וְעַד רַגְלָהּ — **from "head" to "foot."**

וּבִידִיעַת הַתּוֹרָה מִלְּבַד שֶׁהַשֵּׂכֶל מְלוּבָּשׁ בְּחָכְמַת ה' — **But with** the *mitzvah* of **knowing the Torah, in addition to your mind being absorbed into Divine wisdom** and losing its identity, הִנֵּה גַּם חָכְמַת ה' בְּקִרְבּוֹ — **you also absorb the Divine wisdom into your** egoic mind, מַה שֶּׁהַשֵּׂכֶל מַשִּׂיג וְתוֹפֵס וּמַקִּיף בְּשִׂכְלוֹ מַה שֶּׁאֶפְשָׁר לוֹ לִתְפּוֹס וּלְהַשִּׂיג, מִידִיעַת הַתּוֹרָה — **as your mind masters, grasps and absorbs whatever Torah knowledge you are able to absorb and master.**

ולהשיג מידיעת התורה איש כפי שכלו וכח ידיעתו
והשגתו בפרד"ס. ולפי שבידיעת התורה התורה
מלובשת בנפש האדם ושכלו ומוקפת בתוכם לכן
נקראת בשם לחם ומזון הנפש כי כמו שהלחם הגשמי
זן את הגוף כשמכניסו בתוכו וקרבו ממש ונהפך שם
להיות דם ובשר כבשרו ואזי יחיה ויתקיים כך בידיעת

אִישׁ כְּפִי שִׂכְלוֹ וְכֹחַ יְדִיעָתוֹ — In fact, the capacity to fill "being" with Divine light **is limited in each case according to the person's mind and his cognitive powers,** וְהַשָּׂגָתוֹ בִּפְשָׁט רֶמֶז דְּרוּשׁ וְסוֹד — **and his grasp of** *peshat* (literal), *remez* (allegorical), *derush* (homiletical), and *sod* (mystical) methods of Torah interpretation.

וּלְפִי שֶׁבִּידִיעַת הַתּוֹרָה — **Still,** even though your capacity may be limited, filling your being with Divine light is particularly powerful, **because, with** the *mitzvah* of **knowing the Torah,** הַתּוֹרָה מְלוּבֶּשֶׁת בְּנֶפֶשׁ הָאָדָם וְשִׂכְלוֹ וּמוּקֶּפֶת בְּתוֹכָם — **the Torah is absorbed in your soul/mind and is engulfed by them.**

This inner absorption of Divine light is alluded to by the scriptural comparison of Torah to "bread" and "food."

לָכֵן נִקְרֵאת בְּשֵׁם לֶחֶם וּמְזוֹן הַנֶּפֶשׁ — **That is why** Torah **is called "bread" and "food" of the soul** (see *Proverbs* 25:21; *Zohar* 2,21b), כִּי כְּמוֹ שֶׁהַלֶּחֶם הַגַּשְׁמִי זָן אֶת הַגּוּף — **for just as physical bread nourishes your body only when it is actually absorbed inside you,** כְּשֶׁמַּכְנִיסוֹ בְּתוֹכוֹ וְקָרְבוֹ מַמָּשׁ וְנֶהְפָּךְ שָׁם לִהְיוֹת דָּם וּבָשָׂר כִּבְשָׂרוֹ וַאֲזַי — **and it only keeps you alive after it has been transformed into blood and *"flesh of your flesh"*** (see *Genesis* 2:23), יְחְיֶה וְיִתְקַיֵּים — כָּךְ בִּידִיעַת הַתּוֹרָה וְהַשָּׂגָתָה בְּנֶפֶשׁ

A CHASIDIC THOUGHT

When you do a *mitzvah*, you surrender your will to G-d's will. The experience of emptying your ego, at least for that moment, allows His Infinite Light to flood into the "empty space" you vacated. Your being is "drowned" in G-d.

But it is a "one way" process. Your ego had to remove itself to let Him in, which means that there is something lacking in terms of *merging* of your self with G-d. In a sense, you did not really become one with G-d; you simply got out of the way so He could occupy your space.

With Torah study, you not only *vacate* the ego, allowing the light of G-d in (as is the case with every *mitzvah*); but you also *fill* the ego with Divine wisdom.

10A התורה והשגתה בנפש האדם שלומדה היטב בעיון
שכלו עד שנתפסת בשכלו ומתאחדת עמו והיו לאחדים
נעשה מזון לנפש וחיים בקרבה מחיי החיים אין סוף ברוך
הוא המלובש בחכמתו ותורתו שבקרבה וז"ש ותורתך
בתוך מעי וכמ"ש בע"ח שער מ"ד פ"ג שלבושי הנשמות
בגן עדן הן המצות והתורה היא המזון לנשמות שעסקו
בעולם הזה בתורה לשמה וכמ"ש בזהר ויקהל דף
ר"י ולשמה היינו כדי לקשר נפשו לה' ע"י השגת

הָאָדָם שֶׁלּוֹמְדָהּ הֵיטֵב בְּעִיּוּן שִׂכְלוֹ — the same is true with your soul's knowledge and mastery of Torah, when you study it well, focusing the mind, עַד שֶׁנִּתְפֶּסֶת בְּשִׂכְלוֹ — to the point where the Torah is absorbed by your intellect, merging with it to become one, נַעֲשָׂה מָזוֹן לַנֶּפֶשׁ — then it provides nourishment for the soul, וְחַיִּים בְּקִרְבָה מֵחַיֵּי הַחַיִּים אֵין סוֹף בָּרוּךְ הוּא — and life for it, from the Giver of life, the Blessed Infinite Light, הַמְלוּבָּשׁ בְּחָכְמָתוֹ וְתוֹרָתוֹ שֶׁבְּקִרְבָהּ — which is "dressed" in His wisdom, in His Torah, now absorbed inside it.

The Torah is compared to "bread" and "food" since it fills your soul with Divine light, thereby nourishing and sustaining it.

וְזֶהוּ שֶׁכָּתוּב וְתוֹרָתְךָ בְּתוֹךְ מֵעָי — This is the meaning of the verse, *"Your Torah is in my innards"* (Psalms 40:9).

SECTION THREE: HOW TORAH STUDY AFFECTS THE AFTERLIFE

The comparison between Torah and "food" is also found in Kabbalistic sources.

וּכְמוֹ שֶׁכָּתוּב בְּעֵץ חַיִּים שַׁעַר מ"ד פֶּרֶק ג' — As stated in *Etz Chaim,* section 44 (in the 1782 Koritz edition; in current editions, section 43), chapter 3, שֶׁלְבוּשֵׁי הַנְּשָׁמוֹת בְּגַן עֵדֶן הֵן הַמִּצְוֹת — that the *mitzvos* performed during your life provide "garments" for your soul in the afterlife, וְהַתּוֹרָה הִיא הַמָּזוֹן לַנְּשָׁמוֹת שֶׁעָסְקוּ בָּעוֹלָם הַזֶּה בַּתּוֹרָה לִשְׁמָהּ — while the Torah which you studied authentically (*lishmah*) in this world will be "food" for your soul in the afterlife, וּכְמוֹ שֶׁכָּתוּב בַּזֹּהַר וַיַּקְהֵל דַּף ר"י — as stated in the *Zohar, Vayakhel,* 2, 210a.

In the afterlife, your soul will be exposed to intense Divine revelation. To remain comfortable in that environment, it needs to: a.) protect itself from receiving more revelation than it can handle; and b.) absorb whatever is safe and comfortable for it.

The *mitzvos* you performed during your lifetime provide "garments" for the soul, to protect it from too much revelation. The Torah you studied in this world enriches the soul's capacity to absorb revelation in the future.

וְלִשְׁמָהּ הַיְינוּ כְּדֵי לְקַשֵּׁר נַפְשׁוֹ לַה' עַל יְדֵי — The term *lishmah* in this case means, הַשָּׂגַת הַתּוֹרָה אִישׁ כְּפִי שִׂכְלוֹ — the intention to attach your soul to G-d through un-

התורה איש כפי שכלו כמ"ש בפרע"ח [והמזון היא
בחי' אור פנימי והלבושים בחי' מקיפים ולכן אמרו
רז"ל שתלמוד תורה שקול כנגד כל המצות לפי שהמצות
הן לבושים לבד והתורה היא מזון וגם לבוש לנפש
המשכלת שמתלבש בה בעיונה ולימודה וכל שכן
כשמוציא בפיו בדבור שהבל הדבור נעשה בחי' אור
מקיף כמ"ש בפרע"ח]:

derstanding the Torah, according to your mind's ability, כְּמוֹ שֶׁכָּתוּב בִּפְרִי עֵץ חַיִּים
— as written in *Pri Etz Chaim* (*Sha'ar Hanhagas Ha-Limud, s.v. mori*).

Learning Torah *lishmah* ("for its sake") usually means that you study it as a Divine command ("for G-d's sake"). Here, *lishmah* is interpreted to mean that you were conscious of the Torah's *spiritual effect*, "to attach your soul to G-d."

While *Etz Chaim* and the *Zohar* drew a distinction between *mitzvos* as "garments" and Torah as "food", the *Tanya* will argue now that Torah can act in *both* capacities, as "garment" and "food."

[וְהַמָּזוֹן הִיא בְּחִינַת אוֹר פְּנִימִי — The soul's **"food" refers to its ability to internalize Divine light,** וְהַלְּבוּשִׁים בְּחִינַת מַקִּיפִים — its **"garments"** refer to its sensitivity to **transcendent Divine lights** which cannot be internalized.

וְלָכֵן אָמְרוּ רַבּוֹתֵינוּ זִכְרוֹנָם לִבְרָכָה שֶׁתַּלְמוּד תּוֹרָה שָׁקוּל כְּנֶגֶד כָּל הַמִּצְוֹת — **Therefore our Sages, of blessed memory, said, *"The study of the Torah is equal to all the mitzvos"*** (*Mishnah, Pe'ah* 1:1), לְפִי שֶׁהַמִּצְוֹת הֵן לְבוּשִׁים לְבַד וְהַתּוֹרָה הִיא מָזוֹן וְגַם לְבוּשׁ — **because the *mitzvos* are just "garments," whereas the Torah is both "food" and "garment,"** לְנֶפֶשׁ הַמַּשְׂכֶּלֶת שֶׁמִּתְלַבֵּשׁ בָּהּ בְּעִיוּנָהּ וְלִימוּדָהּ — **for the rational** Divine **Soul, which is absorbed in analyzing and studying** the Torah.

As we have discussed, Torah empowers your soul to absorb the Divine, and to be absorbed in it. In that sense, Torah is both "food" (which is absorbed in the soul) and a "garment" (by which the soul is surrounded and absorbed).

וְכָל שֶׁכֵּן כְּשֶׁמּוֹצִיא בְּפִיו בְּדִבּוּר — **Torah's role as a garment is further enhanced when you articulate the words verbally,** שֶׁהֶבֶל הַדִּבּוּר נַעֲשֶׂה בְּחִינַת אוֹר מַקִּיף — **since the breath exhaled into the words elicits transcendent Divine lights,** כְּמוֹ שֶׁכָּתוּב בִּפְרִי עֵץ חַיִּים] — **as stated** in the beginning of *Pri Etz Chaim.*

While Torah is primarily an experience of knowledge, Jewish law requires words of Torah to be verbalized as they are studied. This, the Kabbalah suggests, also endows the experience with the quality of a "garment," of transcendent Divine light.

In conclusion: By studying Torah and performing *mitzvos* in this world, your soul becomes equipped to receive Divine revelation in the afterlife. It is Torah study, in particular, that does this most effectively, especially when you say the words of Torah out loud.

פרק ו **והנה** זה לעומת זה עשה אלהים כי כמו
שנפש האלהית כלולה מעשר
ספירות קדושות ומתלבשת בשלשה לבושים קדושים
כך הנפש דסטרא אחרא מקליפות נוגה המלובשת
בדם האדם כלולה מעשר כתרין דמסאבותא שהן

CHAPTER 6

YOUR DARKER SIDE

SECTION ONE: INSIDE YOUR ANIMAL SOUL

2ND TEVES REGULAR | 5TH TEVES LEAP

The previous four chapters have elaborated on the Divine Soul, its nature (chapter 2), its mental and emotional powers (chapter 3), and its "garments" of thought, speech and action (chapters 4-5). In this chapter we return to the Animal Soul, (discussed in chapter 1), which is the source of negative, self-centered consciousness.

וְהִנֵּה זֶה לְעֻמַּת זֶה עָשָׂה אֱלֹהִים — Now *"G-d has made one opposite the other"* (*Ecclesiastes* 7:14).

To empower us with free choice, G-d has set the positive and negative forces within the universe in perfect equilibrium. The positive and negative forces have not only the same amount of power, they also have the same "architecture."

כִּי כְּמוֹ שֶׁנֶּפֶשׁ הָאֱלֹהִית כְּלוּלָה מֵעֶשֶׂר סְפִירוֹת קְדוֹשׁוֹת — For just as the Divine Soul is comprised of ten holy *sefiros* or "energies," וּמִתְלַבֶּשֶׁת בִּשְׁלֹשָׁה לְבוּשִׁים קְדוֹשִׁים — and these ten energies are "dressed" in three holy "garments" of pious thought, speech and action, כָּךְ הַנֶּפֶשׁ דְּסִטְרָא אָחֳרָא — the Animal Soul, too, has a similar architecture of ten energies and three "garments" of its own, only the force which powers it comes from the negative power of *sitra achra*, "the other side" of self-serving, egoic energy.

מִקְּלִיפּוֹת נוֹגַה — Specifically, its power is from the force known as *kelipas nogah*, the "bright" *kelipah*, whose negativity is not irredeemable and can be realigned for the good (see chapter 1, p. 42).

הַמְלוּבֶּשֶׁת בְּדַם הָאָדָם — While the Animal Soul is spiritual and not confined to a particular place, its point of interaction with the body is **in your blood, where it is present,** *i.e.,* it is the source of your physical vitality (see above, p. 38).

כְּלוּלָה מֵעֶשֶׂר כְּתָרִין דִּמְסָאֲבוּתָא — The ten powers (*sefiros*) **within** the Animal Soul are referred to by the *Zohar* as ten *"crowns of impurity"* (*Zohar* 3, 41b).

שבע מדות רעות הבאות מארבע יסודות רעים הנ"ל
ושכל המולידן הנחלק לשלש שהן חכמה בינה ודעת
מקור המדות כי המדות הן לפי ערך השכל כי הקטן
חושק ואוהב דברים קטנים פחותי הערך לפי ששכלו

To sin or engage in destructive behavior, you need to *detach* your consciousness from your inner self, which yearns to be good and wholesome. That is why the negative forces are described as a "crown," which is *detached* from the head.

שֶׁהֵן שֶׁבַע מִדּוֹת רָעוֹת הַבָּאוֹת מֵאַרְבָּעָה יְסוֹדוֹת רָעִים — **These** powers of the Animal Soul consist of **seven negative emotional powers, emanating from the four negative elements,** הַנִּזְכָּרִים לְעֵיל — as mentioned above, that the four elements of fire, water, air and earth naturally give rise to four categories of negative behavior: anger, self-indulgence, shallowness, and laziness (chapter 1, pp. 40-41).

The Divine Soul shares the same architecture as the Animal Soul: three mental and seven emotional powers. However, the way in which the emotions and intellect function in the Animal Soul is different.

The Divine Soul's emotions will arise only *after reflection*. To love or revere an invisible G-d, consciousness needs to depart from the tangible to the realm of abstract thought, so as to perceive the universe in a broader context. You will never have any feelings for G-d unless you contemplate the meaning of reality first.

For the Animal Soul, on the other hand, its emotions are natural and elemental, requiring little or no thought at all. They are the lower states of consciousness into which you will naturally regress, unless you make a concerted effort otherwise.

![PRACTICAL LESSONS]

PRACTICAL LESSONS

Unless you make a concerted effort, your Animal Soul will direct you towards a superficial life of self-gratification.

While your Animal Soul does possess intelligence, that intelligence is largely self-serving, advising the ego which pleasures to seek.

וְשֵׂכֶל הַמּוֹלִידָן הַנֶּחְלָק לְשָׁלֹשׁ — **The intellect** of the Animal Soul, **which produces** negative emotions and behaviors, mirrors the Divine Soul and **is divided into three,** שֶׁהֵן חָכְמָה בִּינָה וָדַעַת — which are *chochmah* (inquiry), *binah* (cognition) and *da'as* (recognition), מְקוֹר הַמִּדּוֹת — the source of the emotions (see chapter 3).

While thoughtless, visceral emotion represents the core behavior of the Animal Soul, it is not devoid of intellect. For even a pleasure-seeking impulse is based on basic knowledge, *e.g.,* you know ice cream tastes good, and therefore, you want it.

כִּי הַמִּדּוֹת הֵן לְפִי עֶרֶךְ הַשֵּׂכֶל — **Because the emotions are relative to the intellect,** כִּי הַקָּטָן חוֹשֵׁק וְאוֹהֵב דְּבָרִים קְטַנִּים פְּחוּתֵי הָעֵרֶךְ — which is why a child desires and **loves small, trivial things,** לְפִי שֶׁשִּׂכְלוֹ קָטָן וְקָצָר לְהַשִּׂיג דְּבָרִים יְקָרִים יוֹתֵר מֵהֶם —

קָטָן וְקָצָר לְהַשִּׂיג דְּבָרִים יְקָרִים יוֹתֵר מֵהֶם. וְכֵן מִתְכַּעֵס
וּמִתְקַצֵּף מִדְּבָרִים קְטַנִּים וְכֵן בְּהִתְפָּאֲרוּת וּשְׁאָר מִדּוֹת
וָעֶשֶׂר בְּחִיִּ אֵלּוּ הַטֻּמְאוֹת כְּשֶׁאָדָם מְחַשֵּׁב בָּהֶן אוֹ
מְדַבֵּר אוֹ עוֹשֶׂה הֲרֵי מַחֲשַׁבְתּוֹ שֶׁבְּמוֹחוֹ וְדִבּוּרוֹ שֶׁבְּפִיו
וְכֹחַ הַמַּעֲשִׂיּי שֶׁבְּיָדָיו וּשְׁאָר אֵיבָרָיו נִקְרָאִים לְבוּשֵׁי
מְסָאֲבוּ לָעֶשֶׂר בְּחִיִּ אֵלּוּ הַטֻּמְאוֹת שֶׁמִּתְלַבְּשׁוֹת בָּהֶן
בִּשְׁעַת מַעֲשֶׂה אוֹ דִּבּוּר אוֹ מַחֲשָׁבָה וְהֵן הֵם כָּל

10B

since his intellect is too small and immature to appreciate anything more valuable, וְכֵן מִתְכַּעֵס וּמִתְקַצֵּף מִדְּבָרִים קְטַנִּים — **similarly, the child is angered and infuriated by small things,** וְכֵן בְּהִתְפָּאֲרוּת וּשְׁאָר מִדּוֹת — **and the same is true with showing off and other** negative **traits,** which are all relative to the child's intellectual depth.

SECTION TWO: THERE ARE NO SPIRITUALLY NEUTRAL ACTIONS

Having described the ten core faculties of the Animal Soul, its intellect and emotions, we now turn to its tools of expression: the "garments" of thought, speech and action. While the "garments" of the Divine Soul are a vehicle for all things sacred, the Animal Soul expresses an opposing energy through its "impure" garments. Your conscious activities of thought, speech and action might be pure or impure at any given moment, depending on which of your two souls is powering them.

וָעֶשֶׂר בְּחִינוֹת אֵלּוּ הַטֻּמְאוֹת כְּשֶׁאָדָם מְחַשֵּׁב בָּהֶן אוֹ מְדַבֵּר אוֹ עוֹשֶׂה — **Now, when you use these ten impure powers** of the Animal Soul **to think, speak or act,** הֲרֵי מַחֲשַׁבְתּוֹ — **then that thought in your** שֶׁבְּמוֹחוֹ וְדִבּוּרוֹ שֶׁבְּפִיו וְכֹחַ הַמַּעֲשִׂיּי שֶׁבְּיָדָיו וּשְׁאָר אֵיבָרָיו **brain, or that word in your mouth, or that power of action in your hands, or other limbs,** נִקְרָאִים לְבוּשֵׁי מְסָאֲבוּ לָעֶשֶׂר בְּחִינוֹת אֵלּוּ הַטֻּמְאוֹת שֶׁמִּתְלַבְּשׁוֹת בָּהֶן בִּשְׁעַת מַעֲשֶׂה אוֹ דִּבּוּר אוֹ מַחֲשָׁבָה — **are called the "impure garments" into which the ten impure powers** of the Animal Soul **are "dressed" at the moment of action, speech or thought.**

An important paradigm shift which emerges from the *Tanya's* doctrine of two souls is that *there is no such thing as a spiritually neutral activity.* In Jewish Law we find three categories of behavior: 1.) the religiously required, such as keeping the Sabbath and the giving of charity; 2.) the religiously forbidden, such as eating pig or stealing; and c.) ordinary acts which are neither religiously required nor forbidden, such as checking your email or buying clothes. According to the *Tanya*, however, it would be a mistake to conclude that this third category is spiritually neutral. Even an "ordinary" behavior will either promote G-d consciousness or ego-consciousness, depending on your attitude. There is no third option.

Unless you make an effort to carry out an "ordinary" act amid a higher awareness, the inertia of the Animal Soul will steer it to ego-consciousness.

הַמַּעֲשִׂים אֲשֶׁר נַעֲשִׂים תַּחַת הַשֶּׁמֶשׁ אֲשֶׁר הַכֹּל הֶבֶל
וּרְעוּת רוּחַ וּכמ"ש בַּזֹּהַר בְּשַׁלַּח שֶׁהֵן תְּבִירוּ דְרוּחָא
כוּ' וְכֵן כָּל הַדִּבּוּרִים וְכָל הַמַּחֲשָׁבוֹת אֲשֶׁר לֹא לַה' הֵמָּה
וְלִרְצוֹנוֹ וְלַעֲבוֹדָתוֹ שֶׁזֶּהוּ פֵּי' לְשׁוֹן סִטְרָא אָחֳרָא פֵּי' צַד
אַחֵר שֶׁאֵינוֹ צַד הַקְּדוּשָּׁה וְצַד הַקְּדוּשָּׁה אֵינוֹ אֶלָּא הַשְׁרָאָה
וְהַמְשָׁכָה מִקְּדוּשָּׁתוֹ שֶׁל הַקַּבָּ"ה וְאֵין הַקַּבָּ"ה שׁוֹרֶה
אֶלָּא עַל דָּבָר שֶׁבָּטֵל אֶצְלוֹ יִתְבָּ' בֵּין בְּפוֹעַל מַמָּשׁ

וְהֵן הֵם כָּל הַמַּעֲשִׂים אֲשֶׁר נַעֲשִׂים תַּחַת הַשֶּׁמֶשׁ אֲשֶׁר הַכֹּל הֶבֶל וּרְעוּת רוּחַ — **It is these** thoughts, words and actions of the Animal Soul **that constitute** *"all the things that are done under the sun,"* which *"are all empty and a strain to the spirit"* (*Ecclesiastes* 1:14), וּכְמוֹ שֶׁכָּתוּב בַּזֹּהַר שֶׁהֵן תְּבִירוּ דְרוּחָא כוּ' — **and the** *Zohar* **writes in** the Torah portion of *Beshalach*, they are *"destructive to the spirit"* (*Zohar* 2, 59a).

6TH TEVES LEAP

וְכֵן כָּל הַדִּבּוּרִים וְכָל הַמַּחֲשָׁבוֹת אֲשֶׁר לֹא לַה' הֵמָּה וְלִרְצוֹנוֹ וְלַעֲבוֹדָתוֹ — **This applies** not only to actions but **also to any** ostensibly "neutral" **spoken words or thoughts which,** while not religiously forbidden, **are not** consciously **directed towards G-d, to** fulfill **His will, or in His worship**.

These, too, are powered by the Animal Soul and serve to strengthen negative, egoic forces.

With this in mind, we can appreciate why the negative forces of the universe are referred to by the Kabbalah as the *sitra achra*.

שֶׁזֶּהוּ פֵּירוּשׁ לְשׁוֹן סִטְרָא אָחֳרָא פֵּירוּשׁ צַד אַחֵר שֶׁאֵינוֹ צַד הַקְּדוּשָּׁה — **Because this is the meaning of** *sitra achra,* **which translates as "the other side,"** *i.e.,* anything which is **not the holy side**.

The "other side" includes all religiously forbidden activity *and* any ordinary acts "not directed towards G-d's will or worship."

What, then, is the definition of the "holy side"?

וְצַד הַקְּדוּשָּׁה אֵינוֹ אֶלָּא הַשְׁרָאָה וְהַמְשָׁכָה מִקְּדוּשָּׁתוֹ שֶׁל הַקָּדוֹשׁ בָּרוּךְ הוּא — **And the holy side includes only** something into which **G-d's holiness can be drawn and be present,** וְאֵין הַקָּדוֹשׁ בָּרוּךְ הוּא שׁוֹרֶה אֶלָּא עַל דָּבָר שֶׁבָּטֵל אֶצְלוֹ יִתְבָּרֵךְ — **and G-d's presence will only rest on a thing which has surrendered (**batel**) its ego to Him.**

In the *Tanya's* world-view, an experience of *bitul*, surrendering the ego to G-d, is a fundamental prerequisite to real living. It represents the departure from a *personal*

PRACTICAL LESSONS

There are no spiritually neutral actions. Even ordinary, non-sacred activities will serve to bring either unity or fragmentation to the universe, depending on your attitude.

כְּמַלְאָכִים עֶלְיוֹנִים בֵּין בְּכֹחַ כְּכָל אִישׁ יִשְׂרָאֵל לְמַטָּה
שֶׁבְּכֹחוֹ לִהְיוֹת בָּטֵל מַמָּשׁ לְגַבֵּי הַקָּבָּ"ה בִּמְסִירַת נַפְשׁוֹ
עַל קְדוּשַׁת ה'. וְלָכֵן אָמְרוּ רַזַ"ל שֶׁאֲפִי' אֶחָד שֶׁיּוֹשֵׁב

consciousness that attributes separate existence to the self, to gradually embrace a *transpersonal* vision that sees all existence as embedded in a universe saturated with the Divine.

Any shift of the Animal Soul in this direction — whether it be a mere willingness to listen to a higher truth, a purely cerebral appreciation of G-d's presence, or a total realignment of being — could be termed as *bitul*. Once *bitul* has begun, the ego is punctured and Divine light can start to seep through the cracks. Intensifying the experience of *bitul*, which can occur at many different levels, requires a lifetime of spiritual work.

בֵּין בְּפוֹעַל מַמָּשׁ כְּמַלְאָכִים עֶלְיוֹנִים — *Bitul* opens an individual to G-d, **regardless of whether it is an active,** conscious *bitul,* **as is** always **the case with the supernal angels** who are constantly enraptured by G-d's presence, בֵּין בְּכֹחַ — **or** even if the *bitul* **lies dormant.**

The lowest level of *bitul* is subconscious. Merely possessing a Divine Soul means that you have the potential for *bitul* dormant in your being.

כְּכָל אִישׁ יִשְׂרָאֵל לְמַטָּה — **This is** always **true of every person in Israel, down here** in this world, שֶׁבְּכֹחוֹ לִהְיוֹת בָּטֵל מַמָּשׁ לְגַבֵּי הַקָּדוֹשׁ בָּרוּךְ הוּא — **who** by virtue of his or her Divine Soul **has the potential for complete surrender to G-d,** בִּמְסִירַת נַפְשׁוֹ עַל **has the potential for complete surrender to G-d,** קְדוּשַׁת הַשֵּׁם — **by giving his** or her **life in martyrdom for G-d.**

A CHASIDIC THOUGHT

In its unenlightened state, my Animal Soul can appreciate only tangible reality. It lacks the tools to modify that perception, to see itself as Divine and sense the pulsating Divine energy that lies beneath the world's veil. Therefore, it mistakenly sees its own existence as separate from G-d. In what appears to be an utterly fragmented world, it follows the path of self-preservation and self-interest.

My Divine Soul, on the other hand, sees right through the false exterior of things and intuits the fundamental interconnectedness of reality and its Divine energy.

My challenge is to lift myself from the superficial, fragmented consciousness of my Animal Soul to the more penetrating, unified perception of my Divine Soul.

וְעוֹסֵק בַּתּוֹרָה שְׁכִינָה שְׁרוּיָה כו' וְכָל בֵּי עֲשָׂרָה
שְׁכִינְתָּא שַׁרְיָא לְעוֹלָם אֲבָל כָּל מַה שֶׁאֵינוֹ בָּטֵל אֶצְלוֹ
יִת' אֶלָּא הוּא דָּבָר נִפְרָד בִּפְנֵי עַצְמוֹ אֵינוֹ מְקַבֵּל חַיּוּת
מִקְּדוּשָׁתוֹ שֶׁל הַקָּבָּ"ה מִבְּחִי' פְּנִימִית הַקְּדוּשָׁה וּמַהוּתָהּ
וְעַצְמוּתָהּ בִּכְבוֹדָהּ וּבְעַצְמָהּ אֶלָּא מִבְּחִי' אֲחוֹרַיִים

As the *Tanya* will later elaborate, the phenomenon of martyrdom by so many Jews throughout history, many of whom were not religiously observant, suggests a latent power within the Jewish psyche to disregard all self-interest for G-d's sake. To the *Tanya*, this is evidence of a Divine presence in our souls (see chapters 18-19).

Here the *Tanya* draws on this idea to prove that there is an ever-present source of *bitul* within us all. Even if you have not achieved the most basic level of conscious *bitul,* in a subconscious layer of your soul, *bitul* is present. This dormant *bitul* is sufficient to enable G-d's presence to enter.

וְלָכֵן אָמְרוּ רַבּוֹתֵינוּ זִכְרוֹנָם לִבְרָכָה שֶׁאֲפִילוּ אֶחָד שֶׁיּוֹשֵׁב וְעוֹסֵק בַּתּוֹרָה שְׁכִינָה שְׁרוּיָה כו' — **That is why our Sages have said,** *"Even when a single person sits and studies the Torah, the Divine Presence rests on him,"* (*Mishnah, Avos* 3:6), regardless of the person's spiritual standing, because every Jew has a dormant *bitul* which is conducive to the Divine Presence, וְכָל בֵּי עֲשָׂרָה שְׁכִינְתָּא שַׁרְיָא — **and furthermore,** *"On any group of ten, the Divine Presence rests"* (*Talmud, Sanhedrin* 39a), לְעוֹלָם — **always,** even when they are not studying Torah or performing a *mitzvah.*

SECTION THREE: HOW DOES EVIL EXIST?

3RD TEVES REGULAR

An entity which lacks *bitul* cannot be a vessel for G-d's holiness.

אֲבָל כָּל מַה שֶׁאֵינוֹ בָּטֵל אֶצְלוֹ יִתְבָּרֵךְ אֶלָּא הוּא דָּבָר נִפְרָד בִּפְנֵי עַצְמוֹ — **Anything, however, which has not surrendered its ego to G-d, and** perceives itself **a separate entity to itself,** אֵינוֹ מְקַבֵּל חַיּוּת מִקְּדוּשָׁתוֹ שֶׁל הַקָּדוֹשׁ בָּרוּךְ הוּא — **will not receive its life-energy from G-d's holiness.**

This leaves us with the question: Where *does* such an entity derive its spiritual energy and life force from, if not from G-d? Doesn't the monotheistic belief of Judaism teach that everything exists by virtue of G-d's sustenance alone?

To solve this problem, the *Tanya* offers us a Kabbalistic insight into how evil forces come to exist. In contrast to the holy and the pure, which emanate directly from G-d, the evil and impure are also sustained by G-d's light, but indirectly so. Evil can only exist because it is a distant offshoot of the good, a pale shadow of its holy source.

מִבְּחִינַת פְּנִימִית הַקְּדוּשָׁה וּמַהוּתָהּ וְעַצְמוּתָהּ בִּכְבוֹדָהּ וּבְעַצְמָהּ — An impure entity does not receive its life energy directly **from the splendorous, inner, essential core of holiness itself,** אֶלָּא מִבְּחִינַת אֲחוֹרַיִים — **but from its "behind"** (*Etz Chaim* 34:1, 37:2).

שיורדים ממדרגה למדרגה רבבות מדרגות בהשתלשלות
העולמות דרך עלה ועלול וצמצומים רבים עד שנתמעט
כל כך האור והחיות מיעוט אחר מיעוט עד שיכול
להתצמצם ולהתלבש בבחי' גלות תוך אותו דבר
הנפרד להחיותו ולקיימו מאין ליש שלא יחזור
להיות אין ואפס כבתחלה מקודם שנברא ולכן
נקרא עולם הזה ומלואו עולם הקליפות וסטרא אחרא

You would greet a friend with a warm smile, but when meeting somebody you don't like, it might be hard to look him in the face. You might want to turn your back on him. Similarly, G-d gives life force to the negative and the impure, but He does so from "behind," so to speak, since He despises evil (see chapter 22, p. 250).

שֶׁיּוֹרְדִים מִמַּדְרֵגָה לְמַדְרֵגָה רְבָבוֹת מַדְרֵגוֹת בְּהִשְׁתַּלְשְׁלוּת הָעוֹלָמוֹת — The life force of impure things **descends** from its initially holy source **step by step, tens of thousands of times, through the spiral of** spiritual **worlds,** דֶּרֶךְ עִלָּה וְעָלוּל וְצִמְצוּמִים רַבִּים — **and it is diminished many times through cause-and-effect** transitions, עַד שֶׁנִּתְמַעֵט **to the point where its** Divine **light and energy has been so repeatedly diluted,** כָּל כָּךְ הָאוֹר וְהַחַיּוּת מִיעוּט אַחַר מִיעוּט עַד שֶׁיָּכוֹל לְהִתְצַמְצֵם וּלְהִתְלַבֵּשׁ בִּבְחִינַת גָּלוּת **that it can be diminished, garbed and exiled into an au-**תּוֹךְ אוֹתוֹ דָּבָר הַנִּפְרָד **tonomous entity,** לְהַחֲיוֹתוֹ וּלְקַיְּימוֹ מֵאַיִן לְיֵשׁ **to energize and sustain that thing's existence from nothing-to-something,** שֶׁלֹּא יַחֲזוֹר לִהְיוֹת אַיִן וָאֶפֶס כְּבַתְּחִלָּה מִקוֹדֶם שֶׁנִּבְרָא **to prevent it from reverting to be** *"null and void"* (Isaiah 40:17), **which was its primordial state.**

The logic here follows a principle, which we will elaborate upon in the second book of *Tanya*, that creation is a *continuous process.* If G-d would not constantly energize the creation, it would revert to the nothingness from which it came. Here the problem concerns evil: If G-d is not present in evil, then how can its existence constantly renew? The *Tanya* answers that G-d's presence *is* to be found in evil, but in such a diminished form ("diminished, garbed and exiled"), that it exhibits no Divine properties.

PRACTICAL LESSONS

G-d's presence can only rest where there is *bitul*, surrender of the ego.

The power of *bitul* is already dormant in your soul. You just need to bring it to the surface.

7TH TEVES LEAP

וְלָכֵן נִקְרָא עוֹלָם הַזֶּה וּמְלוֹאוֹ עוֹלָם הַקְּלִיפוֹת וְסִטְרָא אָחֳרָא — **Therefore, this** physical **world, and its contents, is the world of** *kelipos* **and** *sitra achra.*

The natural disposition of physical beings is to sense their own autonomous existence and see the world as having inherent reality outside of G-d. The predominant energy of the world, then, is *kelipah* and *sitra achra.*

וְלָכֵן כָּל מַעֲשֵׂה עוֹה"ז קָשִׁים וְרָעִים וְהָרְשָׁעִים גּוֹבְרִים
בּוֹ כְּמ"שׁ בְּע"ח שַׁעַר מ"ב סוֹף פ"ד* אֶלָּא שֶׁהַקְּלִיפּוֹת
הֵן נֶחְלָקוֹת לִשְׁתֵּי מַדְרֵגוֹת
זוֹ לְמַטָּה מִזּוֹ הַמַּדְרֵגָה
הַתַּחְתּוֹנָה הִיא שָׁלֹשׁ קְלִיפּוֹ'
הַטְּמֵאוֹת וְרָעוֹת לְגַמְרֵי וְאֵין
בָּהֶם טוֹב כְּלָל וְנִקְרְאוּ
בְּמֶרְכֶּבֶת יְחֶזְקֵאל רוּחַ

11A

הגהה

עִם הֱיוֹת בְּתוֹכוּ עֶשֶׂר סְפִי'
דְּעֲשִׂיָּה דִקְדוּשָׁה וּכְמ"שׁ בְּע"ח שַׁעַר
מ"ג וּבְתוֹךְ עֶשֶׂר סְפִי' דְּעֲשִׂיָּה אֵלּוּ הֵן
עֶשֶׂר סְפִי' דִּיצִירָה וּבְתוֹכָן עֶשֶׂר סְפִי'
דִּבְרִיאָה וּבְתוֹכָן עֶשֶׂר סְפִי' דַּאֲצִילוּת
שֶׁבְּתוֹכָן אוֹר א"ס ב"ה וְנִמְצָא אוֹר

וְלָכֵן כָּל מַעֲשֵׂה עוֹלָם הַזֶּה קָשִׁים וְרָעִים וְהָרְשָׁעִים גּוֹבְרִים בּוֹ — And *"that is why all the affairs of this world are tough and evil, and wicked men prevail,"* כְּמוֹ שֶׁכָּתוּב בְּעֵץ חַיִּים שַׁעַר מ"ב סוֹף פֶּרֶק ד' — as stated in *Etz Chaim,* section 42, end of chapter 4* (see also below, chapter 24, p. 274).

SECTION FOUR: THE THREE IMPURE KELIPOS

The *Tanya* now begins a categorization of the different entities in the universe powered by the various *kelipos*. We will begin here with the three impure *kelipos* (and continue with *kelipas nogah* in the next chapter).

אֶלָּא שֶׁהַקְּלִיפּוֹת הֵן נֶחְלָקוֹת לִשְׁתֵּי מַדְרֵגוֹת זוֹ לְמַטָּה מִזּוֹ — However, the *kelipos* are divided into two levels, one lower than the other, הַמַּדְרֵגָה הַתַּחְתּוֹנָה הִיא שָׁלֹשׁ קְלִיפּוֹת — the lower level contains three completely הַטְּמֵאוֹת וְרָעוֹת לְגַמְרֵי וְאֵין בָּהֶם טוֹב כְּלָל — impure and evil *kelipos,* that contain no overt good at all, וְנִקְרְאוּ בְּמֶרְכֶּבֶת יְחֶזְקֵאל

---

*הַגָהה — **NOTE.** This note addresses the apparent dualism implied by the concept of *kelipah* and *sitra achrah*. If *"this world, and its contents, is the world of kelipos and sitra achra"* then where is G-d to be found? The note will argue that G-d's presence is, of course, found throughout this world, but in a veiled fashion.

עִם הֱיוֹת בְּתוֹכוּ עֶשֶׂר סְפִירוֹת דַּעֲשִׂיָּה דִקְדוּשָׁה — Even though this world is predominately from *kelipah* and *sitra achra,* holiness is still contained in it, from the ten *sefiros* of the lowest of the four spiritual worlds, *Asiyah* (Action), וּכְמוֹ שֶׁכָּתוּב בְּעֵץ חַיִּים שַׁעַר מ"ג — as stated in *Etz Chaim,* section 43, chapter 1, וּבְתוֹךְ עֶשֶׂר סְפִירוֹת דְּעֲשִׂיָּה אֵלּוּ הֵן עֶשֶׂר סְפִירוֹת דִּיצִירָה — and since, when speaking of holy energy, all worlds are interconnected, **within these ten *sefiros* of *Asiyah* are the ten *sefiros* of the next world *Yetzirah* (Formation),** וּבְתוֹכָן עֶשֶׂר סְפִירוֹת דִּבְרִיאָה — and in them the ten *sefiros* of the next world *Beriah* (Creation), וּבְתוֹכָן עֶשֶׂר סְפִירוֹת דַּאֲצִילוּת שֶׁבְּתוֹכָן — and in them the ten *sefiros* of the highest world *Atzilus,* אוֹר אֵין סוֹף בָּרוּךְ הוּא — (Emanation), in which the Blessed Infinite Light is found.

וְנִמְצָא אוֹר אֵין סוֹף בָּרוּךְ הוּא מָלֵא כָּל הָאָרֶץ הַלֵּזוּ הַתַּחְתּוֹנָה — It follows, then, that in

סְעָרָה וְעָנָן גָּדוֹל וְגוֹ' וּמֵהֶן
נִשְׁפָּעוֹת וְנִמְשָׁכוֹת נַפְשׁוֹת
כָּל אוּמוֹת עוֹבְדֵי גִלּוּלִים וְקִיּוּם
גוּפָם וְנַפְשׁוֹת כָּל בַּעֲלֵי חַיִּים
הַטְּמֵאִים וַאֲסוּרִים בַּאֲכִילָה

וְקִיּוּם גוּפָם וְקִיּוּם וְחַיּוּת כָּל מַאֲכָלוֹת אֲסוּרוֹת
מֵהַצּוֹמֵחַ כְּמוֹ עָרְלָה וְכִלְאֵי הַכֶּרֶם כוּ' וּכְמוֹ שֶׁכָּתוּב בַּעֵץ
שַׁעַר מ"ט פ"ו וְכֵן קִיּוּם וְחַיּוּת כָּל הַמַּעֲשֶׂה דִּבּוּר
וּמַחֲשָׁבָה שֶׁל כָּל שַׁסַ"ה לֹא תַעֲשֶׂה וְעַנְפֵיהֶן כְּמוֹ שֶׁ
שָׁם סוֹף פ"ה:

א"ס ב"ה מְלֹא כָל הָאָרֶץ הַלָּזוּ
הַתַּחְתּוֹנָה עַל יְדֵי הִתְלַבְּשׁוּתוֹ בַּעֲשֶׂר
סְפִי' דְּאַרְבַּע עוֹלָמוֹת אֲבִי"ע כְּמוֹ"שׁ
בַּעֵץ שַׁעַר מ"ז פ"ב וּבְסֵפֶר גִּלְגּוּלִים
פֶּרֶק כ':

וְעָנָן גָּדוֹל וְגוֹ' — רוּחַ סְעָרָה וְעָנָן גָּדוֹל וְגוֹ' — in Ezekiel's vision of a heavenly **chariot, they are called** *"stormy wind... a great cloud, with flashing fire"* (Ezekiel 1:4).

וּמֵהֶן נִשְׁפָּעוֹת וְנִמְשָׁכוֹת נַפְשׁוֹת כָּל אוּמוֹת הָעוֹלָם וְקִיּוּם גוּפָם — These three *kelipos:* a.) **metaphysically power the souls, and sustain the bodies, of all the** wicked **nations of the world,** וְנַפְשׁוֹת כָּל בַּעֲלֵי חַיִּים הַטְּמֵאִים וַאֲסוּרִים בַּאֲכִילָה וְקִיּוּם גוּפָם b.) produce **the souls, and sustain the bodies, of all the impure living creatures that we are prohibited to eat,** וְקִיּוּם וְחַיּוּת כָּל מַאֲכָלוֹת אֲסוּרוֹת מֵהַצּוֹמֵחַ — and, c.) are **the sustenance and life-force of all forbidden food in the vegetable kingdom,** כְּמוֹ עָרְלָה וְכִלְאֵי הַכֶּרֶם כוּ' — **such as** *orlah* ("restricted fruit" — *Leviticus* 19:23-25) **and** *kilai hakerem* (produce of mixed vegetable/vine seeds " — *Deuteronomy* 22:9), וּכְמוֹ שֶׁכָּתוּב בַּעֵץ חַיִּים שַׁעַר מ"ט פֶּרֶק ו' — **as stated in** *Etz Chaim,* **section 49, chapter 6.**

וְכֵן קִיּוּם וְחַיּוּת כָּל הַמַּעֲשֶׂה דִּבּוּר וּמַחֲשָׁבָה שֶׁל כָּל שַׁסַ"ה לֹא תַעֲשֶׂה וְעַנְפֵיהֶן — **And,** d.) the three *kelipos* **are also the sustenance and life force of every action, spoken word and thought prohibited by the 365 negative commands and their derivatives,** כְּמוֹ שֶׁכָּתוּב שָׁם סוֹף פֶּרֶק ה' — **as is explained,** in *Etz Chaim ibid.,* **end of chapter 5.**

This discussion will continue directly in the following chapter, where we will address *kelipas nogah,* which can more easily be redeemed for the good.

---

truth **the Blessed Infinite Light fills all of this lowly earth,** and there is no dualism even in the lowest realms (see chapters 48-49).

עַל יְדֵי הִתְלַבְּשׁוּתוֹ בַּעֲשֶׂר סְפִירוֹת דְּאַרְבַּע עוֹלָמוֹת אֲצִילוּת בְּרִיאָה יְצִירָה וַעֲשִׂיָּה — **But,** from our perspective, we do not see the Infinite Light **since it is "dressed" in the ten** *sefiros* **of the four worlds,** *Atzilus, Beriah, Yetzirah* **and** *Asiyah,* כְּמוֹ שֶׁכָּתוּב **as stated in** *Etz Chaim,* **section 47, chapter 2,** וּבְסֵפֶר בַּעֵץ חַיִּים שַׁעַר מ"ז פֶּרֶק ב' — גִּלְגּוּלִים פֶּרֶק כ' — **and in** *Sefer ha-Gilgulim,* **chapter 20.**

In conclusion: While we are unable to perceive it, the Blessed Infinite Light of G-d is present even in this world.

פרק ז אַך נפש החיונית הבהמית שבישראל
שמצד הקליפה המלובשת בדם
האדם כנ"ל ונפשות בהמות וחיות ועופות ודגים טהורים
ומותרים באכילה וקיום וחיות כל הדומם וכל הצומח
המותר באכילה וכן קיום וחיות כל המעשה דבור
ומחשבה בענייני עוה"ז שאין בהם צד איסור לא שרש
ולא ענף משס"ה מצות לא תעשה וענפיהן דאורייתא
ודרבנן רק שאינן לשם שמים אלא רצון הגוף וחפצו

CHAPTER 7

NEGATIVE ENERGY

SECTION ONE: KOSHER PLEASURES

4TH TEVES REGULAR | 8TH TEVES LEAP

At the end of chapter 6, we began to discuss *kelipah* (pl. *kelipos*), the negative forces of the universe which veil the presence of G-d and promote ego-consciousness. The *kelipos,* we learned, fall into two general categories: a.) three "completely impure" *kelipos,* whose dark energy cannot be redeemed; and, b.) a fourth "bright" *kelipah* (*kelipas nogah*), which tends to hide G-d's presence, but whose veil can be penetrated through focused intention.

אַךְ — **But**, in contrast to the things mentioned at the end of the previous chapter, which are derived from the completely impure *kelipos,* the following are derived from "bright" *kelipah*:

נֶפֶשׁ הַחִיּוּנִית הַבַּהֲמִית שֶׁבְּיִשְׂרָאֵל שֶׁמִּצַּד הַקְּלִיפָה — **a.) The energizing Animal Soul in Israel, from "bright"** *kelipah,* הַמְלוּבֶּשֶׁת בְּדַם הָאָדָם כַּנִּזְכָּר לְעֵיל — **which is embodied in your blood, as stated above** (chapter 1, p. 38).

וְנַפְשׁוֹת בְּהֵמוֹת וְחַיּוֹת וְעוֹפוֹת וְדָגִים טְהוֹרִים וּמוּתָּרִים בַּאֲכִילָה — **b.) The souls of kosher cattle, animals, birds and fish, which are permissible to eat,** וְקִיּוּם וְחַיּוּת כָּל הַדּוֹמֵם — "bright" *kelipah* being **the sustenance and life-force** וְכָל הַצּוֹמֵחַ הַמּוּתָּר בַּאֲכִילָה — **of everything that is permissible to eat from the mineral and vegetable worlds.**

וְכֵן קִיּוּם וְחַיּוּת כָּל הַמַּעֲשֶׂה דִּבּוּר וּמַחֲשָׁבָה בְּעִנְיְנֵי עוֹלָם הַזֶּה — **c.)** "Bright" *kelipah* is **also the sustenance and life-force of every worldly act, spoken word or thought,** שֶׁאֵין בָּהֶם צַד אִיסּוּר לֹא שֹׁרֶשׁ וְלֹא עָנָף — **that has no trace of religious prohibition** מִשֵּׁס"ה מִצְוֹת לֹא תַעֲשֶׂה וְעַנְפֵיהֶן דְּאוֹרַיְיתָא *"in neither root nor branch"* (Malachi 3:19), וּדְרַבָּנָן — **from the 365 prohibitions and their offshoots, Biblical and Rabbinic.**

ותאותו ואפי' הוא צורך הגוף וקיומו וחיותו ממש אלא
שכוונתו אינה לשם שמים כדי לעבוד את ה' בגופו לא
עדיפי מעשה דבור ומחשבות אלו מנפש החיונית
הבהמית בעצמה והכל כאשר לכל נשפע ונמשך
ממדרגה השנית שבקליפות וסטרא אחרא שהיא קליפה
רביעית הנקראת קליפת נוגה שבעולם הזה הנקרא

11B

Why is such an activity considered to be from *kelipah*, the dark energy of the universe, if it is not prohibited in any way by the Torah?

רַק שֶׁאֵינָן לְשֵׁם שָׁמַיִם — **Only** this activity **is not carried out** *"for the sake of Heaven"* (*Mishnah, Avos* 2:12), אֶלָּא רְצוֹן הַגּוּף וְחֶפְצוֹ וְתַאֲוָתוֹ — **rather,** it is motivated by the **body's will, its desire and lust.**

As we learned in chapter 6, an activity might serve either to enhance awareness of the Divine energy which saturates the universe or to reinforce ego. Even an ostensibly kosher activity will bolster the ego unless it is consciously aligned with G-d, since the physical desires of the body are naturally self-serving.

וַאֲפִילוּ הוּא צוֹרֶךְ הַגּוּף וְקִיּוּמוֹ וְחִיּוּתוֹ מַמָּשׁ — A "kosher" activity will strengthen *kelipah* **even if it is a real bodily need for continued living,** אֶלָּא שֶׁכַּוָּנָתוֹ אֵינָהּ לְשֵׁם שָׁמַיִם — **so long as your intention is not** *"for the sake of Heaven,"* כְּדֵי לַעֲבוֹד אֶת ה' בְּגוּפוֹ — namely, **to worship G-d** at a later point **using your body.**

Even if a kosher activity is devoid of pleasure-seeking intent and is carried out purely to maintain a healthy body, it will still strengthen *kelipah* so long as G-d has not entered your consciousness. While this conclusion may seem harsh, it is consistent with the *Tanya's* core principle: either an act is directed towards G-d, or it is not. There are no spiritually neutral activities.

לֹא עֲדִיפֵי מַעֲשֵׂה דִּבּוּר וּמַחֲשָׁבוֹת אֵלּוּ מִנֶּפֶשׁ הַחִיּוּנִית הַבַּהֲמִית בְּעַצְמָהּ — **All these** unawakened **acts, spoken words and thoughts are not superior to the Animal Soul's energy itself,** which is focused on the self.

Just as you can't lift yourself up by grabbing your own hair, no force in the universe can transcend its own source without outside assistance. If an act is motivated exclusively by the Animal Soul, which is powered by self-centered *kelipah*, it simply cannot awaken to G-d.

וְהַכֹּל כַּאֲשֶׁר לַכֹּל נִשְׁפָּע וְנִמְשָׁךְ — **And** *"it is the same for all"* (*Ecclesiastes* 9:2), מִמַּדְרֵגָה הַשֵּׁנִית שֶׁבְּקְלִיפּוֹת וְסִטְרָא אָחֳרָא — all kosher objects and activities, as well as the Animal Soul itself, **are powered metaphysically by the second,** higher **level within *kelipos* and *sitra achra*,** שֶׁהִיא קְלִיפָּה רְבִיעִית הַנִּקְרֵאת קְלִיפַּת נוֹגַהּ — **which is the fourth *kelipah*, referred to as the "bright *kelipah*"** (see p. 42), because, while predominantly self-centered, it does contain a little good, making it "bright."

An act powered by *kelipas nogah* could either promote ego consciousness, or it could bring you to awareness of G-d. These two possibilities are suggested by

עוֹלַם הַעֲשִׂיָּה רוּבוֹ כְּכוּלּוֹ רַע רַק מְעַט טוֹב מְעוֹרָב
בְּתוֹכָהּ [שֶׁמִּמֶּנָּה בָּאוֹת מִדּוֹת טוֹבוֹת שֶׁבַּנֶּפֶשׁ הַבַּהֲמִית
שֶׁבְּיִשְׂרָאֵל כְּמוֹ"שׁ לְעֵיל] וְהִיא בְּחִי׳ מְמוּצַּעַת בֵּין שָׁלֹשׁ
קְלִיפּוֹת הַטְּמֵאוֹת לְגַמְרֵי וּבֵין בְּחִי׳ וּמַדְרֵגַת הַקְּדוּשָׁה
וְלָכֵן פְּעָמִים שֶׁהִיא נִכְלֶלֶת בְּשָׁלֹשׁ קְלִיפּוֹת הַטְּמֵאוֹת
[כְּמוֹ"שׁ בְּעֵ"ח שַׁעַר מ"ט רֵישׁ פ"ד בְּשֵׁם הַזֹּהַר] וּפְעָמִים

its name: on one hand, it is a self-serving *kelipah* (lit. "peel"), which conceals G-d's presence; but, on the other hand, it is "bright," and does not eclipse G-d fully. Still it's classified as a *kelipah,* a negative force, since its pull towards ego-consciousness predominates. It is a thick veil which lets only a little light through.

שֶׁבְּעוֹלָם הַזֶּה הַנִּקְרָא עוֹלָם הָעֲשִׂיָּה רוּבּוֹ כְּכוּלּוֹ רָע — **In this** physical **world, the World of** *Asiyah* **("Action"), evil predominates,** רַק מְעַט טוֹב מְעוֹרָב בְּתוֹכָהּ — **and only a little good is mixed in it.**

As we have seen, "evil" in the context of our discussion means a blocking of G-d consciousness; "good" is the power to unpeel the world's veneer so as to disclose G-d's presence. The world's ability to do this is very weak.

[שֶׁמִּמֶּנָּה בָּאוֹת מִדּוֹת טוֹבוֹת שֶׁבַּנֶּפֶשׁ הַבַּהֲמִית שֶׁבְּיִשְׂרָאֵל] כְּמוֹ שֶׁנִּתְבָּאֵר לְעֵיל — This **"little good" is the source of the positive qualities in the Animal Soul of Israel, explained above** (see p. 41).

The *Tanya* explains the relationship between *kelipas nogah* and other *kelipos.*

וְהִיא בְּחִינָה מְמוּצַּעַת בֵּין שָׁלֹשׁ קְלִיפּוֹת הַטְּמֵאוֹת לְגַמְרֵי וּבֵין בְּחִינַת וּמַדְרֵגַת הַקְּדוּשָׁה — The **"bright"** *kelipah* **is an intermediate category between the three completely impure *kelipos* and the realm of holiness.**

In the *Tanya's* world-view, the closest thing to a spiritually neutral activity, is an experience which is unawakened but technically kosher. Right now, the act eclipses G-d and nourishes self-centered consciousness, so it is categorized as *kelipah.* But being a "radiant" *kelipah,* which is very thinly veiled, its energy is easily redeemable.

וְלָכֵן פְּעָמִים שֶׁהִיא נִכְלֶלֶת בְּשָׁלֹשׁ קְלִיפּוֹת הַטְּמֵאוֹת — **That is why sometimes** *kelipas nogah* **will be absorbed by the three impure *kelipos* and nourish self-centered consciousness,** [כְּמוֹ שֶׁכָּתוּב בְּעֵץ חַיִּים שַׁעַר מ"ט רֵישׁ פֶּרֶק ד' בְּשֵׁם הַזֹּהַר] — **as is stated in *Etz Chaim,* section 49, beginning of chapter 4, citing the *Zohar* (2, 144b, 216a),** וּפְעָמִים שֶׁהִיא נִכְלֶלֶת וְעוֹלָה בִּבְחִינַת וּמַדְרֵגַת הַקְּדוּשָׁה — **but sometimes it will be uplifted and absorbed in the realm of holiness.**

שֶׁהִיא נִכְלֶלֶת וְעוֹלָה בִּבְחִי' וּמַדְרֵגַת הַקְּדוּשָׁה דְּהַיְינוּ
כְּשֶׁהַטּוֹב הַמְעוֹרָב בָּהּ נִתְבָּרֵר מֵהָרַע וְגוֹבֵר וְעוֹלָה
וְנִכְלָל בִּקְדוּשָׁה כְּגוֹן דִּ"מ הָאוֹכֵל בָּשָׂר שָׁמֵינָא דְּתוֹרָא
וְשׁוֹתֶה יַיִן מְבוּשָׂם לְהַרְחִיב דַּעְתּוֹ לַה' וּלְתוֹרָתוֹ כְּדַאֲמַר
רָבָא חַמְרָא וְרֵיחָא כו' אוֹ בִּשְׁבִיל כְּדֵי לְקַיֵּים מִצְוַת עוֹנֶג
שַׁבָּת וְיו"ט אֲזַי נִתְבָּרֵר חַיּוּת הַבָּשָׂר וְהַיַּיִן שֶׁהָיָה נִשְׁפַּע
מִקְּלִיפַּת נוֹגַהּ וְעוֹלָה לַה' כְּעוֹלָה וּכְקָרְבָּן. וְכֵן הָאוֹמֵר
מִילְתָא דִּבְדִיחוּתָא לְפַקֵּחַ דַּעְתּוֹ וּלְשַׂמֵּחַ לִבּוֹ לַה'
וּלְתוֹרָתוֹ וַעֲבוֹדָתוֹ שֶׁצְּרִיכִים לִהְיוֹת בְּשִׂמְחָה וּכְמוֹ
שֶׁעָשָׂה רָבָא לְתַלְמִידָיו שֶׁאָמַר לִפְנֵיהֶם מִילְתָא
דִּבְדִיחוּתָא תְּחִלָּה וּבַדְחֵי רַבָּנָן. אַךְ מִי שֶׁהוּא בְּזוֹלְלֵי

However, for a *kelipas nogah* act or entity to be redeemed from its self-centeredness, a process of refinement must occur:

דְּהַיְינוּ כְּשֶׁהַטּוֹב הַמְעוֹרָב בָּהּ נִתְבָּרֵר מֵהָרַע וְגוֹבֵר וְעוֹלָה וְנִכְלָל בִּקְדוּשָׁה — **Namely, when the good mixed in it is extracted from the bad, empowering** the good **to be uplifted to holiness and absorbed by it.**

Metaphysically, this is what happens when you mentally align an ordinary, worldly (but kosher) act with a higher purpose. The mental awakening empowers the good trapped in the "bright" *kelipah*, to be extracted and redeemed.

כְּגוֹן דֶּרֶךְ מָשָׁל הָאוֹכֵל בָּשָׂר שָׁמֵינָא דְּתוֹרָא וְשׁוֹתֶה יַיִן מְבוּשָׂם לְהַרְחִיב דַּעְתּוֹ לַה' וּלְתוֹרָתוֹ — **For example, eating marbled meat and fragrant wine to broaden your mind for G-d and His Torah,** כְּדַאֲמַר רָבָא חַמְרָא וְרֵיחָא כו' — as Rava said, *"Wine and fragrance sharpen a person's mind,"* (Talmud, Yoma 76b), אוֹ בִּשְׁבִיל כְּדֵי לְקַיֵּים מִצְוַת — or if you enjoy food and drink **to fulfill the *mitzvah* of taking pleasure in the Sabbath and festivals** (ibid., Shabbos 119a), עוֹנֶג שַׁבָּת וְיוֹם טוֹב אֲזַי נִתְבָּרֵר חַיּוּת הַבָּשָׂר וְהַיַּיִן שֶׁהָיָה נִשְׁפַּע מִקְּלִיפַּת נוֹגַהּ — then the meat and wine's *kelipas nogah* energy is refined, וְעוֹלָה לַה' כְּעוֹלָה וּכְקָרְבָּן — and it ascends to G-d like a burnt offering and like a sacrifice.

וְכֵן הָאוֹמֵר מִילְתָא דִּבְדִיחוּתָא לְפַקֵּחַ דַּעְתּוֹ — **Another example is the use of humor to sharpen your mind,** וּלְשַׂמֵּחַ לִבּוֹ לַה' וּלְתוֹרָתוֹ וַעֲבוֹדָתוֹ — and to put you in a joyous mood for G-d, His Torah and His worship, שֶׁצְּרִיכִים לִהְיוֹת בְּשִׂמְחָה — which ought to be carried out joyously, וּכְמוֹ שֶׁעָשָׂה רָבָא לְתַלְמִידָיו שֶׁאָמַר לִפְנֵיהֶם מִילְתָא — as Rava did with his students, when he commenced דִּבְדִיחוּתָא תְּחִלָּה וּבַדְחֵי רַבָּנָן — with a humorous remark to them, *"and the students would become cheerful"* (ibid., Shabbos 30b).

Judaism doesn't require you to desist from worldly activities and pleasures. If they are kosher, the good within them can be elevated "like a sacrifice" to G-d, so long as they are performed with an awakened consciousness, aligned to a higher purpose.

בשר וסובאי יין למלאת תאות גופו ונפשו הבהמית
שהוא בחי' יסוד המים מארבע יסודות הרעים שבה
שממנו מדת התאוה הנה ע"י זה יורד חיות הבשר והיין
שבקרבו ונכלל לפי שעה ברע גמור שבשלש קליפות
הטמאות וגופו נעשה להן לבוש ומרכבה לפי שעה עד
אשר ישוב האדם ויחזור לעבודת ה' ולתורתו כי לפי
שהיה בשר היתר ויין כשר לכך יכולים לחזור ולעלות
עמו בשובו לעבודת ה' שזהו לשון היתר ומותר כלומר
שאינו קשור ואסור בידי החיצונים שלא יוכל לחזור

12A

5TH TEVES REGULAR | 9TH TEVES LEAP

אַךְ מִי שֶׁהוּא בְּזוֹלְלֵי בָשָׂר וְסוֹבְאֵי יַיִן — **On the other hand, if you are one who** *"gorges on meat and guzzles wine"* (*Proverbs* 23:20), לְמַלֹּאת תַּאֲוַת גוּפוֹ וְנַפְשׁוֹ הַבַּהֲמִית — purely **to satisfy the desires of your body and Animal Soul,** שֶׁהוּא בְּחִינַת יְסוֹד הַמַּיִם, מֵאַרְבָּעָה יְסוֹדוֹת הָרָעִים שֶׁבָּה שֶׁמִּמֶּנּוּ מִדַּת הַתַּאֲוָה — **which comes from elemental water (from the negative** side **of the four elements in your Animal Soul), which is pleasure seeking (see chapter 1,** p. 40), הִנֵּה עַל יְדֵי זֶה יוֹרֵד חַיּוּת הַבָּשָׂר וְהַיַּיִן שֶׁבְּקִרְבּוֹ וְנִכְלָל — **then,** לְפִי שָׁעָה בְּרַע גָּמוּר שֶׁבְּשָׁלֹשׁ קְלִיפּוֹת הַטְּמֵאוֹת — **the energy of that meat or wine inside you will be absorbed,** *temporarily,* **in the complete negativity of the three impure** *kelipos,* וְגוּפוֹ נַעֲשֶׂה לָהֶן לְבוּשׁ וּמֶרְכָּבָה — **as your body becomes a "garment" and vehicle for them.**

Unlike an act powered by the three completely negative *kelipos,* whose evil is not redeemable, a kosher act which was marred by a self-gratifying intention will only strengthen the negative forces *temporarily.*

לְפִי שָׁעָה עַד אֲשֶׁר יָשׁוּב הָאָדָם וְיַחֲזוֹר לַעֲבוֹדַת ה' וּלְתוֹרָתוֹ — **Temporarily, until you repent and return to the worship of G-d and to His Torah.**

The "repentance" here is not for sinful behavior, but for religiously permissible acts performed purely for self-gratification. Having remorse for this self-indulgence will instantly redeem the good energy that was trapped in these acts and objects.

כִּי לְפִי שֶׁהָיָה בְּשַׂר הֶיתֵּר וְיַיִן כָּשֵׁר — **For since the meat and wine were permissible and kosher,** לְכָךְ יְכוֹלִים לַחֲזוֹר וְלַעֲלוֹת עִמּוֹ בְּשׁוּבוֹ לַעֲבוֹדַת ה' — **they are able to return and ascend with you** to holiness when you realign yourself to worship G-d.

שֶׁזֶּהוּ לְשׁוֹן הֶיתֵּר וּמוּתָּר — **This is implied by the Hebrew term** *heter,* **"permissible,"**

PRACTICAL LESSONS

If you partake in a kosher activity but forget about G-d, the negative energies of the universe (*kelipos*) are made stronger.

But the mistake is easily corrected —and the energy redeemed—by realigning your intentions later on.

ולעלות לה' רק שהרשימו ממנו נשאר בגוף ועל כן
צריך הגוף לחיבוט הקבר כמ"ש לקמן מה שאין כן
במאכלות אסורות וביאות אסורות שהן משלש קליפות
הטמאות לגמרי הם אסורים וקשורים בידי החיצונים
לעולם ואין עולים משם עד כי יבא יומם ויבולע המות
לנצח כמ"ש ואת רוח הטומאה אעביר מן הארץ או עד

כְּלוֹמַר שֶׁאֵינוֹ קָשׁוּר וְאָסוּר בִּידֵי — or *mutar,* "permitted," which literally mean "untied," הַחִיצוֹנִים שֶׁלֹא יוּכַל לַחֲזוֹר וְלַעֲלוֹת לה' — meaning to say that a kosher act, even if performed with self-serving motives, **is not** permanently **"tied up" and bound by the negative forces preventing it from returning and ascending to G-d.** All that is needed for this to take place is an appropriate realignment of intention.

רַק שֶׁהָרְשִׁימוּ מִמֶּנּוּ נִשְׁאָר בַּגוּף — **Nevertheless,** even after such realignment, **a trace** of the negative forces **remains in the body,** וְעַל כֵּן צָרִיךְ הַגוּף לְחִיבּוּט הַקֶּבֶר כְּמוֹ שֶׁיִּתְבָּאֵר לְקַמָּן — **requiring the body to undergo** *chibut ha-kever* **(cleansing after death), as will be explained below,** chapter 8 (p. 106).

וְכֵן הַחַיּוּת שֶׁבְּטִפּוֹת זֶרַע שֶׁיָּצְאוּ מִמֶּנּוּ בְּתַאֲוָה בַּהֲמִית — The idea of a kosher act being absorbed temporarily by the negative forces **applies also to the energy in any drops of male seed emitted with carnal desire,** שֶׁלֹא קֵדֵשׁ עַצְמוֹ בִּשְׁעַת תַּשְׁמִישׁ עִם אִשְׁתּוֹ טְהוֹרָה — **when a person failed to have sacred intentions when he was intimate with his wife,** even though the act was permitted, because she was **ritually pure** (see above p. 54).

SECTION TWO: FORBIDDEN PLEASURES

מַה שֶׁאֵין כֵּן בְּמַאֲכָלוֹת אֲסוּרוֹת וּבִיאוֹת אֲסוּרוֹת — **This** temporary absorption into negative forces **is not the case, however, with forbidden foods and forbidden sexual relations,** שֶׁהֵן מִשָּׁלֹשׁ קְלִיפּוֹת הַטְמֵאוֹת לְגַמְרֵי — **whose energy is from the three completely impure** *kelipos,* הֵם אֲסוּרִים וּקְשׁוּרִים בִּידֵי הַחִיצוֹנִים לְעוֹלָם — their energy remains *permanently* **tied and bound by the negative forces,** וְאֵין עוֹלִים מִשָּׁם — **and will not ascend from there.**

Judaism rejects the notion of a fundamental dualism in the universe, so even the negative forces must one day be redeemed.

עַד כִּי יָבֹא יוֹמָם וִיבֻלַּע הַמָּוֶת לָנֶצַח — Until *"their day comes"* (see *Jeremiah* 50:27) and *"death will be swallowed up forever"* (see *Isaiah* 25:8), כְּמוֹ שֶׁכָּתוּב וְאֶת רוּחַ — הַטּוּמְאָה אַעֲבִיר מִן הָאָרֶץ — **as the verse states,** *"I will remove the spirit of impurity from the earth"* (*Zechariah* 13:2).

Even in an unredeemed world, it's still possible to extract the energy of a forbidden act from the *kelipos,* through repentance. But since the energy is deeply enmeshed in the *kelipos*, the level of repentance needs to be particularly profound.

שיעשה תשובה גדולה כל כך שזדונות נעשו לו כזכיות
ממש שהיא תשובה מאהבה מעומקא דלבא באהבה
רבה וחשיקה ונפש שוקקה לדבקה בו ית' וצמאה נפשו
לה' כארץ עיפה וציה להיות כי עד הנה היתה נפשו
בארץ ציה וצלמות היא הסטרא אחרא ורחוקה מאור

אוֹ עַד שֶׁיַּעֲשֶׂה תְּשׁוּבָה גְדוֹלָה כָּל כָּךְ שֶׁזְּדוֹנוֹת נַעֲשׂוּ לוֹ כִּזְכִיּוֹת — Or until the person carries out such a profound repentance that *"his intentional sins become like merits for him"* (*Talmud, Pesachim* 86b).

The repentance is so deep that it actually transforms the sin into a merit, *i.e.*, the trapped energy will be redeemed from the *kelipos*,

מַמָּשׁ — literally.

Some commentators prefer not to interpret this statement of the *Talmud* literally, but the *Tanya* asserts that it *is* possible to transform a sin to a merit.

How could that be the case? A sin is a violation of G‑d's will which, at best, might be pardoned by G‑d. How could it be considered something positive, a "merit"?

To answer this question the *Tanya* addresses the specific level of repentance that is required.

שֶׁהִיא תְּשׁוּבָה מֵאַהֲבָה — This is achieved through repentance *"out of love"* (*ibid.*).

According to the *Talmud*, a sin is merely pardoned if repentance is done "out of fear"; but, it will be transformed to a merit, if the repentance is done "out of love."

מֵעוּמְקָא דְלִבָּא בְּאַהֲבָה רַבָּה — Namely, a repentance from the depths of your heart, with "great love" (see chapter 43, pp. 556-7), וַחֲשִׁיקָה וְנֶפֶשׁ שׁוֹקֵקָה לְדָבְקָה בּוֹ יִתְבָּרֵךְ — and the fervor of *"a craving soul"* (*Psalms* 107:9), to attach yourself to G‑d, וְצָמְאָה נַפְשׁוֹ לַה' כְּאֶרֶץ עֲיֵפָה וְצִיָּה — and *"thirsting for G‑d like a parched desert soil"* (*ibid.* 143:6), לִהְיוֹת כִּי עַד הֵנָּה הָיְתָה נַפְשׁוֹ בְּאֶרֶץ צִיָּה וְצַלְמָוֶת — realizing that, until now, your soul had been *"in a barren wilderness, in the shadow of death"* (*Jeremiah* 2:6), הִיא הַסִּטְרָא אָחֳרָא — namely the *sitra achra*, וּרְחוֹקָה מֵאוֹר פְּנֵי ה' בְּתַכְלִית — as distant as anything could be from G‑d's inner light.

It is the feeling of utter spiritual emptiness, of having reached "rock bottom," that inspires you to make a profound personal shift. Awakening at this lowest point, the thirst for G‑d is of an altogether different intensity to what you would ordinarily feel, like a man on the verge of death thirsting for water in the desert.

PRACTICAL LESSONS

A non-kosher activity always strengthens the *kelipos*.

That energy is not easily redeemed. You would need to repent with a profound thirsting for G‑d.

But through very deep repentance, you can actually transform your prior sins into merits.

פְּנֵי ה' בְּתַכְלִית וּלֹזֹאת צְמָאָה נַפְשׁוֹ עֹז מִצִמָאוֹן
נַפְשׁוֹת הַצַּדִּיקִים כְּמַאֲמָרָם ז"ל בִּמְקוֹם שֶׁבַּעֲלֵי תְּשׁוּבָה
עוֹמְדִים כו' וְעַל תְּשׁוּבָה מֵאַהֲבָה רַבָּה זוֹ אָמְרוּ שֶׁזְּדוֹנוֹת
נַעֲשׂוּ לוֹ כִזְכֻיוֹת הוֹאִיל וְעַל יְדֵי זֶה בָּא לְאַהֲבָה רַבָּה זוֹ
אֲבָל תְּשׁוּבָה שֶׁלֹּא מֵאַהֲבָה זוֹ אַף שֶׁהִיא תְּשׁוּבָה
נְכוֹנָה וְה' יִסְלַח לוֹ מִכָּל מָקוֹם לֹא נַעֲשׂוּ לוֹ כִזְכֻיוֹת וְאֵין
עוֹלִים מֵהַקְּלִפָּה לְגַמְרֵי עַד עֵת קֵץ שֶׁיְּבֻלַע הַמָּוֶת

וְלֹזֹאת צְמָאָה נַפְשׁוֹ עֹז מִצִמָאוֹן בְּיֶתֶר נַפְשׁוֹת הַצַּדִּיקִים — **Therefore, precisely because you feel so very distant from G-d, your soul now thirsts** for G-d **even more than the souls of the righteous thirst** for Him.

It was your distance from G-d *brought about by your sins* that inspired you to change. That is why your sins are literally "transformed to merits."

כְּמַאֲמָרָם זִכְרוֹנָם לִבְרָכָה בִּמְקוֹם שֶׁבַּעֲלֵי תְּשׁוּבָה עוֹמְדִים כו' — **That is why** our Sages, **of blessed memory, said,** *"In the place where ba'alei teshuvah (penitents) stand, even the perfectly righteous cannot stand"* (*Talmud, Brachos* 34b).

וְעַל תְּשׁוּבָה מֵאַהֲבָה רַבָּה זוֹ אָמְרוּ שֶׁזְּדוֹנוֹת נַעֲשׂוּ לוֹ כִזְכֻיוֹת — **It is regarding this** level of **repentance with "great love" about which the** Sages taught, *"his intentional sins become like merits for him,"* הוֹאִיל וְעַל יְדֵי זֶה בָּא לְאַהֲבָה רַבָּה זוֹ — **since it is through** these sins **that he came to this "great love."**

אֲבָל תְּשׁוּבָה שֶׁלֹּא מֵאַהֲבָה זוֹ — **But through a repentance which is not motivated by this degree of love,** אַף שֶׁהִיא תְּשׁוּבָה נְכוֹנָה וַה' יִסְלַח לוֹ — **even if it is an acceptable repentance and G-d will pardon him,** מִכָּל מָקוֹם לֹא נַעֲשׂוּ לוֹ כִזְכֻיוֹת — **nevertheless,** sins **will not be transformed into merits,** וְאֵין עוֹלִים מֵהַקְּלִפָּה לְגַמְרֵי — **and meta-** physically speaking, this means that their energy **will not be completely released** from the negative forces of *kelipah,* עַד עֵת קֵץ שֶׁיְּבֻלַע הַמָּוֶת לָנֶצַח. — **until the future time, when** *"death will be swallowed up forever."*

Your level of repentance not only affects your relationship with G-d, it also influences the energy balance in the universe. If you repent, but not out of "great love," your relationship with G-d will be healed (*"and G-d will pardon him"*), but the power you transferred to the negative forces will still remain in their clutches.

A CHASIDIC THOUGHT

The desire to come close to G-d is most passionate in a person who feels distant. A person who has not sinned, never experiences the distance, and therefore lacks the intense recoil felt by the *ba'al teshuvah.*

לנצח. אך החיות שבטפות זרע שיצאו ממנו לבטלה
אף שירדה ונכללה בשלש קליפות הטמאות הרי זו עולה
משם בתשובה נכונה ובכוונה עצומה בקריאת שמע
שעל המטה כנודע מהאר"י ז"ל ומרומז בגמרא כל
הקורא קריאת שמע על מטתו כאלו אוחז חרב של
שתי פיות כו' להרוג גופות החיצונים שנעשו לבוש

SECTION THREE: THE SPECIAL POWER OF BEDTIME SHEMA

6TH TEVES REGULAR | 10TH TEVES LEAP

אַךְ הַחַיּוּת שֶׁבְּטִפּוֹת זֶרַע שֶׁיָּצְאוּ מִמֶּנּוּ לְבַטָּלָה — **However, the energy in the drops of semen that a person emitted wastefully** represent an exception to the above.

The *Tanya* has taught that: a.) permitted acts without the correct, higher intention, and, b.) forbidden acts, both strengthen the negative forces of *kelipah*. The distinction between the two is only in terms of how easily the error can be corrected. If the act was permitted, a simple realignment of intention is sufficient to release the energy in the negative forces. But if the act was forbidden, a very profound repentance ("out of love") is required.

An exception to this rule is the forbidden act of emitting semen wastefully. While this would seem, at first glance, to fall into the category of forbidden acts that require a major repentance, the *Tanya* now teaches that the correction of this act is comparatively easy.

אַף שֶׁיָּרְדָה וְנִכְלְלָה בְּשָׁלֹשׁ קְלִיפּוֹת הַטְּמֵאוֹת — **For even though** the energy of this wastefully emitted semen **has been downgraded and absorbed in the three impure *kelipos,*** as is the case with all forbidden activity, הֲרֵי זוֹ עוֹלָה מִשָּׁם בִּתְשׁוּבָה נְכוֹנָה וּבְכַוָּונָה עֲצוּמָה בִּקְרִיאַת שְׁמַע שֶׁעַל הַמִּטָּה — **nevertheless, it can ascend from there** relatively easily, *i.e.,* without repentance "out of love," but rather, **through an ordinary repentance along with intense concentration during the recital of the** *Shema* **at bedtime,** כַּנּוֹדָע מֵהָאֲר"י זִכְרוֹנוֹ לִבְרָכָה — **as is known from Rabbi Yitzchak Luria, of blessed memory** (*Pri Etz Chaim, Bedtime Shema,* chapter 5).

To redeem the energy trapped in the negative forces by wasted semen, it is not necessary to carry out an extraordinary repentance "out of love." It is sufficient to feel remorse, to resolve not to carry out the forbidden activity again, and then the trapped energy can be redeemed by concentrating intensely on the words of the Bedtime *Shema*, (while conscious of the words' power to destroy negative forces).

וּמְרוּמָז בַּגְּמָרָא כָּל הַקּוֹרֵא קְרִיאַת שְׁמַע עַל מִטָּתוֹ כְּאִלּוּ אוֹחֵז חֶרֶב שֶׁל שְׁתֵּי פִיּוֹת כו' — **This** unique spiritual power of the Bedtime *Shema* **is hinted to in the** *Talmud, "If one recites the Shema at bedtime it is as if he held a 'double-edged sword'"* (*Psalms* 149:5; *Brachos* 5a), לַהֲרוֹג גּוּפוֹת הַחִיצוֹנִים שֶׁנַּעֲשׂוּ לְבוּשׁ לַחַיּוּת שֶׁבְּטִפּוֹת — a "sword"

12B לְחִיוּת שֶׁבַּטִּפּוֹת וְעוֹלָה הַחִיּוּת מֵהֶם כַּיָּדוּעַ לְיוֹ"ח.
וְלָכֵן לֹא הוּזְכַּר עֲוֹן זֶרַע לְבַטָּלָה בַּתּוֹרָה בִּכְלַל בִּיאוֹת
אֲסוּרוֹת אַף שֶׁחָמוּר מֵהֶן וְגָדוֹל עֲוֹנוֹ בִּבְחִי' הַגְּדָלוֹת
וְרִבּוּי הַטּוּמְאָה וְהַקְּלִיפּוֹת שֶׁמּוֹלִיד וּמַרְבֶּה בִּמְאֹד מְאֹד
בְּהוֹצָאַת זֶרַע לְבַטָּלָה יוֹתֵר מִבִּיאוֹת אֲסוּרוֹת רַק

which **destroys the** destructive **agents of the negative forces which absorbed energy from the drops** of semen, וְעוֹלָה הַחִיּוּת מֵהֶם — **enabling the energy to rise out of them,** כַּיָּדוּעַ לְיוֹדְעֵי חָכְמָה נִסְתָּרָה — **as is known to the masters of hidden** Kabbalistic **wisdom** (*Pri Etz Chaim, ibid.*).

The notion that wasting semen is something more easily corrected than other prohibitions is also alluded to by Scripture itself.

וְלָכֵן לֹא הוּזְכַּר עֲוֹן זֶרַע לְבַטָּלָה בַּתּוֹרָה בִּכְלַל בִּיאוֹת אֲסוּרוֹת — **That is why the Torah does not mention the sin of wasting semen in its list of forbidden sexual activities.**

The Torah states that Er and Onan, who purposefully wasted their seed, were *"evil in the eyes of G-d"* (*Genesis* 38:10), from which the *Talmud* concludes that the act is prohibited Biblically (*Nidah* 13a-b). The Torah also prohibits the *indirect* waste of seed as a result of lewd thoughts with the verse, *"Guard yourself from every evil thing"* (*Deut.* 23:10), from which the *Talmud* concludes, *"do not dwell on sexual thoughts during the day and come to impurity at night"* (*Talmud, Kesubos* 46a).

However, in *Leviticus* chapters 18 and 20 where the Torah lists all the sexual sins, there is no mention of wasting semen. The *Tanya* suggests that the omission in *Leviticus* hints to the theme of our discussion, that the spiritual damage caused by this prohibition is different than the other sexual sins.

אַף שֶׁחָמוּר מֵהֶן — **Even though** wasting seed **is considered a worse sin** than the other sexual prohibitions.

The omission from *Leviticus* does not imply that wasting seed is less serious than the other transgressions. In fact, the *Code of Jewish Law* considers the wasting of seed *"more serious than any of the prohibitions of the Torah"* (*Shulchan Aruch, Even Ha-Ezer* 23:1). The *Tanya* now explains why, spiritually speaking, this is so.

וְגָדוֹל עֲוֹנוֹ בִּבְחִינַת הַגְּדָלוֹת וְרִבּוּי הַטּוּמְאָה וְהַקְּלִיפּוֹת שֶׁמּוֹלִיד וּמַרְבֶּה בִּמְאֹד מְאֹד בְּהוֹצָאַת זֶרַע לְבַטָּלָה — **"His sin is great"** (*Genesis* 4:13), **due to the enormity and extremely abundant quantity of impurity and** *kelipos* **which result from emitting semen wastefully,** יוֹתֵר מִבִּיאוֹת אֲסוּרוֹת — **even more than through forbidden relations.**

This sin, then, is something of a paradox. On one hand, it is the most spiritually damaging of all sins; but, on the other hand, its damage is much more easily rectifiable than the other sexual prohibitions.

רַק שֶׁבְּבִיאוֹת אֲסוּרוֹת מוֹסִיף כֹּחַ וְחִיּוּת בִּקְלִיפָה טְמֵאָה בְּיוֹתֵר — **But in the case of the forbidden relations** in *Leviticus*, those sins **give power and energy to a** *kelipah*

שבביאות אסורות מוסיף כח וחיות בקליפה טמאה
ביותר עד שאינו יכול להעלות משם החיות בתשובה*

הגה"ה

אא"כ יעשה תשובה

(מפני שנקלטה ביסוד דנוקבא
דקליפה המקבלת וקולטת החיות
מהקדושה משא"כ בזרע לבטלה שאין
שם בחי' נוקבא דקליפה רק שכחותיה)

מאהבה רבה כל כך עד
שזדונות נעשו לו כזכיות
ובזה יובן מאמר רז"ל

עַד שֶׁאֵינוֹ יָכוֹל לְהַעֲלוֹת מִשָּׁם הַחַיּוּת בִּתְשׁוּבָה — **that is so extremely impure,** — that an ordinary **repentance does not have the power to extract the energy from there.***

While wasting semen is more serious in terms of the *"enormity and extremely abundant quantity"* of the negative energy it brings about, forbidden relations are worse in the sense that they give power and energy to a *kelipah* that is more "extremely impure," *i.e.,* that it is going to a worse destination. This extreme impurity renders the *kelipah* less willing to release the energy it has absorbed and a far greater repentance is required. So while emitting semen in vain causes *more spiritual damage,* the other sexual prohibitions are *harder to rectify* due to the extreme potency of the *kelipah* that they empower.

אֶלָּא אִם כֵּן יַעֲשֶׂה תְּשׁוּבָה מֵאַהֲבָה רַבָּה כָּל כָּךְ עַד שֶׁזְּדוֹנוֹת נַעֲשׂוּ לוֹ כִּזְכֻיּוֹת — The extreme impurity (of the other sexual sins) will cling to the energy they have been given **unless the person repents with such "great love" that his *"intentional sins are transformed into merits,"*** as discussed above.

וּבָזֶה יוּבַן מַאֲמַר רַבּוֹתֵינוּ זִכְרוֹנָם לִבְרָכָה — **With this** in mind, **we can understand our Sages' teaching,** אֵיזֶהוּ מְעֻוָּת שֶׁלֹּא יוּכַל לְתַקֵּן — *"What is 'a deviance that can-*

---

*הַגָּהָ"ה — **NOTE.** The *Tanya* offers a Kabbalistic insight into why the sin of wasting semen is more easily rectified than other forbidden relations.

מִפְּנֵי שֶׁנִּקְלְטָה בִּיסוֹד דְּנוּקְבָא דְּקְלִיפָּה — **This is because** with a forbidden union which involves a female partner, **the energy** in the semen **is absorbed by the "female bonding" element of the *kelipah*,** הַמְקַבֶּלֶת וְקוֹלֶטֶת הַחַיּוּת מֵהַקְּדוּשָׁה — **which receives and absorbs the energy from** the powers of **holiness.**

The presence of a female partner in this sinful act is also mirrored in the metaphysical realm: the "female" forces of *kelipah* receive and contain the energy in the semen. Once contained and enmeshed in *kelipah*, it is much harder to redeem this energy at a later point, which is why an intense repentance "out of love" is required.

מַה שֶּׁאֵין כֵּן בְּזֶרַע לְבַטָלָה שֶׁאֵין שָׁם בְּחִינַת נוּקְבָא דְּקְלִיפָה — **This is not the case with emitting semen in vain, where the female aspect of *kelipah* is absent.**

The absence of a physical recipient is mirrored in the spiritual realm: the forces of *kelipah* are unable to properly absorb and retain the spilled energy.

איזהו מעוות שלא יוכל וחיילותיה מלבישים לחיות שבטפות
לתקון זה שבא על הערוה כידוע לי"ח:
והוליד ממזר שאז גם אם יעשה תשובה גדולה
כל כך אי אפשר לו להעלות החיות לקדושה
מאחר שכבר ירדה לעולם הזה ונתלבשה בגוף
בשר ודם:

not be fixed' (Ecclesiastes 1:15)?" — זֶה שֶׁבָּא עַל הָעֶרְוָה וְהוֹלִיד מַמְזֵר — "*A person who had forbidden relations and caused an illegitimate child to be born*" (*Talmud, Chagigah* 9a), שֶׁאָז גַּם אִם יַעֲשֶׂה תְּשׁוּבָה גְדוֹלָה כָּל כָּךְ — **for, in that case, even if** the sinner **undertakes such a great repentance** that his "intentional sins are transformed into merits," אִי אֶפְשָׁר לוֹ לְהַעֲלוֹת הַחַיּוּת לִקְדוּשָׁה — **he still cannot elevate the energy to holiness,** מֵאַחַר שֶׁכְּבָר יָרְדָה לְעוֹלָם הַזֶּה וְנִתְלַבְּשָׁה בְּגוּף בָּשָׂר וָדָם — **since** the energy **has already come down into this world and has been dressed in a body of flesh and blood.**

The case of an illegitimate child graphically illustrates that a sin has two independent elements: a.) its effect on the sinner's relationship with G-d; and, b.) its spiritual ramifications for the universe. Even when a person repents and is pardoned by G-d for a forbidden union, if a child has been born there are clearly broader issues beyond the sin itself. The person can repent for the sin, but the ramifications remain.

The *Tanya's* lesson here is that beyond the notion of personal good and evil, sinful behavior introduces a negative energy into the universe that really has a life of its own. As well as correcting our wrongdoings in life we also must seek to eliminate the negative forces that we have caused to be unleashed.

But if there is no female element to receive the energy, why is the act damaging?

רַק שֶׁכְּחוֹתֶיהָ וְחֵיְלוֹתֶיהָ מַלְבִּישִׁים לַחַיּוּת שֶׁבַּטִּפּוֹת — **Only** instead of the female *kelipah itself* absorbing the energy, **its powers and hosts** of destructive spirits **provide** a much weaker form of containment **to dress the energy of the** spilled **drops** of semen, כַּיָּדוּעַ לְיוֹדְעֵי חָכְמָה נִסְתָּרָה — as is **known to those familiar with the hidden** Kabbalistic **wisdom** (*Pri Etz Chaim, ibid.*).

The absence of a substantive spiritual "container" in the case of wasted seed explains why this act is so easily reversible and at the same time, so spiritually damaging. Since the energy has not been properly contained by the negative forces, it is relatively easy to reverse the process and reclaim the energy; but precisely because this negative force is not well contained, its influence can flow without inhibition and restraint.

פרק ח ועוד זאת במאכלות אסורות שלכך
נקראים בשם איסור מפני שאף
מי שאכל מאכל איסור בלא הודע לשם שמים לעבוד
ה' בכח אכילה ההיא וגם פעל ועשה כן וקרא והתפלל
בכח אכילה ההיא אין החיות שבה עולה ומתלבשת
בתיבות התורה והתפלה כמו ההיתר מפני איסורה
בידי הס"א משלש קליפות הטמאות ואפי' הוא איסור

CHAPTER 8

NEGATIVE ENERGY (II)

SECTION ONE: THE LIMITS OF GOOD INTENTION

7TH TEVES REGULAR | 11TH TEVES LEAP

In the previous chapter, we discussed the case of a kosher experience carried out with bad intentions. Now we will address the opposite case, of a *non-kosher* experience carried out with *good* intentions.

וְעוֹד זֹאת בְּמַאֲכָלוֹת אֲסוּרוֹת שֶׁלְּךָ נִקְרָאִים בְּשֵׁם אִיסוּר — **Furthermore, there is reason why non-kosher foods are called** *issur,* **("chained"),** מִפְּנֵי שֶׁאַף מִי שֶׁאָכַל מַאֲכַל אִיסוּר בְּלֹא הוֹדַע לְשֵׁם שָׁמַיִם — **because even if you inadvertently eat a forbidden food** *"for the sake of Heaven"* (*Mishnah, Avos* 2:12), לַעֲבוֹד ה' בְּכֹחַ אֲכִילָה הַהִיא **with the intention to use that food's energy to worship G-d,** וְגַם פָּעַל וְעָשָׂה כֵּן וְקָרָא — **and,** not only was that your initial plan, **you actually fulfilled your intention, using the food's energy to study** Torah **and pray,** וְהִתְפַּלֵּל בְּכֹחַ אֲכִילָה הַהִיא אֵין הַחַיּוּת — **nevertheless, unlike the case of kosher** food, the spiritual **power in it will not be uplifted to become "dressed" in the words of Torah and prayer,** שֶׁבָּהּ עוֹלָה וּמִתְלַבֶּשֶׁת בְּתֵיבוֹת הַתּוֹרָה וְהַתְּפִלָּה כְּמוֹ הַהֶיתֵּר מִפְּנֵי אִיסוּרָהּ בִּידֵי הַסִּטְרָא אַחֲרָא מְשָׁלֵשׁ — **because it is "chained" to the** negative forces of *sitra achra,* קְלִיפוֹת הַטְּמֵאוֹת — **from the three impure** *kelipos.*

The "impurity" of these three *kelipos* expresses itself in an unwillingness to release the energy of an act carried out in their domain. Even if the act was a *mitzvah,* the most spiritually positive force in the universe, the energy remains "chained" to the negative forces and cannot be released.

וַאֲפִילוּ הוּא אִיסוּר דְּרַבָּנָן — **This is the case even when the prohibition is Rabbinic.**

Here the *Tanya* makes a bold assertion that even the energy of food prohibited by Rabbinic Law is powered by the impure *kelipos* and cannot be released to G-d.

דרבנן שחמורים דברי סופרים יותר מדברי תורה כו'
ולכן גם היצר הרע וכח המתאוה לדברים האסורים
הוא שד משדין נוכראין שהוא יצר הרע של אומות עו"ג
שנפשותיהם משלש קליפות הטמאות משא"כ היצה"ר

13A

This seems counterintuitive since the *kelipos* were put in place *by G-d* to power His universe. If an object was Biblically permitted and then the Rabbis outlawed it, how could that object's energy change from its original, Divinely alloted *kelipas nogah* to the impure *kelipos*?

It was in response to this concern that the following line was written (*Notes on Tanya*):

שֶׁחֲמוּרִים דִּבְרֵי סוֹפְרִים יוֹתֵר מִדְּבָרֵי תּוֹרָה כו' — For *"the words of the Scribes are even more stringent than the words of the Torah"* (*Talmud, Eruvin* 21b).

While Rabbinic law is, legally speaking, secondary to Torah law, Judaism has an equal, if not greater, reverence for the enactments of the Rabbis. This reverence, the *Tanya* suggests, is indicative of a special spiritual power granted to the Rabbis ("Scribes"). If they decree an object forbidden, the spiritual energy of that object will actually change from *kelipas nogah* to the impure *kelipos* (*Notes on Tanya*).

PRACTICAL LESSONS

Even good intentions can't help to elevate an experience which the Torah or the Rabbis have forbidden.

Now we have established that both Biblically and Rabbinically forbidden activities are powered by the three impure *kelipos*, we need to explain why an Animal Soul from *kelipas nogah* is drawn to these impure *kelipah* activities, which are more corrupt than its own energy?

וְלָכֵן גַּם הַיֵּצֶר הָרָע וְכֹחַ הַמִּתְאַוֶּה לִדְבָרִים הָאֲסוּרִים — Therefore the *yetzer hara* ("impulse to evil") and desire for forbidden things does not originate from the Animal Soul of *kelipas nogah,* but from an external influence, namely, הוּא שֵׁד מִשֵּׁדִין נוּכְרָאִין — one of the "foreign demons" (*Zohar* 3, 253a), שֶׁהוּא יֵצֶר הָרָע שֶׁל אוּמוֹת הָעוֹלָם שֶׁנַּפְשׁוֹתֵיהֶם מִשְּׁלֹשׁ קְלִיפוֹת הַטְּמֵאוֹת — which has the energy of the *yetzer hara* of wicked nations of the world, whose souls are from the three impure *kelipos* (see p. 42).

Your temptation to sin comes from *external* negative energy, which the *Zohar* refers to as a "demon." Only an energy from the three impure *kelipos* (a "foreign demon"), could tempt you to a forbidden activity, which is powered by the three impure *kelipos*. Your Animal Soul from *kelipas nogah* is naturally drawn only to permitted, *kelipas nogah* activity.

מַה שֶּׁאֵין כֵּן הַיֵּצֶר הָרָע וְכֹחַ הַמִּתְאַוֶּה לִדְבָרִים הַמּוּתָּרִים לְמַלֹּאת תַּאֲוָתוֹ הוּא שֵׁד מִשֵּׁדִין יְהוּדָאִין — On the other hand, the *yetzer hara* and desire to satisfy yourself with

וכח המתאוה לדברים המותרים למלאת תאותו הוא
שד משדין יהודאין לפי שיכול לחזור לקדושה כדלעיל.
אך מ"מ קודם שחזר לקדושה הוא ס"א וקליפה וגם
אח"כ הרשימו ממנו נשאר דבוק בגוף כי להיות כי מכל
מאכל ומשקה נעשה תיכף דם ובשר מבשרו ולכן
צריך הגוף לחיבוט הקבר לנקותו ולטהרו מטומאתו

kosher pleasures comes from what the *Zohar* (*ibid.*) calls **one of "the Jewish de-mons,"** *i.e., kelipas nogah,* לְפִי שֶׁיָּכוֹל לַחֲזוֹר לִקְדוּשָׁה כְּדִלְעֵיל — **for** even though the pleasure seeking impulse can cause you to forget G-d, **it can** easily **revert to holiness, as explained above** with a realignment of intention (see chapter 7, pp. 96-7).

אַךְ מִכָּל מָקוֹם קוֹדֶם שֶׁחָזַר לִקְדוּשָׁה הוּא סִטְרָא אָחֳרָא וּקְלִיפָה — **Nevertheless, before it reverts to holiness,** even this "kosher" act is still negative, and so it is powered by *sitra achra* and *kelipah,* since it was not carried out for a higher purpose.

SECTION TWO: KELIPAH DETOXIFICATION

We have learned that when a kosher pleasure is enjoyed out of indulgence, its *kelipas nogah* energy is downgraded and "tied" to the *sitra achra* by the three impure *kelipos,* but only *"temporarily, until you repent and return to the worship of G-d and to His Torah"* (p. 96).

Are there any long-term repercussions for having received energy *temporarily* from the three impure *kelipos?*

וְגַם אַחַר כָּךְ הָרְשִׁימוּ מִמֶּנּוּ נִשְׁאָר דָּבוּק בַּגּוּף — **Also, even after** a *kelipas nogah* experience has reverted to holiness from the domain of the three impure *kelipos,* **a trace of it remains attached to the body,** לִהְיוֹת כִּי מִכָּל מַאֲכָל וּמַשְׁקֶה נַעֲשָׂה תֵּיכֶף דָּם וּבָשָׂר מִבְּשָׂרוֹ — **since all the food and drink become the body's flesh and blood right away,** and while consumed for self-gratification, its energy is still under the domain of the three impure *kelipos.*

וְלָכֵן צָרִיךְ הַגּוּף לְחִיבּוּט הַקֶּבֶר — **Therefore,** since the body was a temporary home for the three impure *kelipos,* **the body must undergo** *chibut ha-kever* **(cleansing af-ter death),** לְנַקּוֹתוֹ וּלְטַהֲרוֹ מִטּוּמְאָתוֹ שֶׁקִּיבֵּל בַּהֲנָאַת עוֹלָם הַזֶּה וְתַעֲנוּגָיו — **to cleanse** and purify it from its contamination from kosher, **worldly pleasures and indulgenc-es,** מְטוּמְאַת קְלִיפַּת נוֹגַהּ וְשֵׁדִין יְהוּדָאִין — **from the impurity of** *kelipas nogah* **and "Jewish demons."**

According to Jewish tradition, after a person is dead and buried, his soul is re-turned to the body and four angels come to the person to beat him until the *kelipah* has been broken and removed from the soul. This is called *chibut ha-kever,* literally, "beating within the grave," as described at length in Tractate *Chibut Ha-Kever* (in Rabbi Naftali Hertz Hertzog (ed.), *Yalkut Ha-Ro'im,* Warsaw, 1885).

שְׁקִיבֵּל בַּהֲנָאַת עוֹלָם הַזֶּה וְתַעֲנוּגָיו מְטוּמְאַת קְלִיפַּת
נוֹגַהּ וּשְׁדִין יְהוּדָאִין אא"כ מִי שֶׁלֹּא נֶהֱנָה מֵעוֹה"ז כָּל
יָמָיו כְּרַבֵּינוּ הַקָּדוֹשׁ. וְעַל דְּבָרִים בְּטֵלִים בְּהֶיתֵּר כְּגוֹן
ע"ה שֶׁאֵינוֹ יָכוֹל לִלְמוֹד צָרִיךְ לְטַהֵר נַפְשׁוֹ מִטּוּמְאָה
זוֹ דִּקְלִיפָּה זוֹ ע"י גִּלְגּוּלָה בְּכַף הַקֶּלַע כְּמ"שׁ בַּזֹהַר פ'

Those who live in the Land of Israel, or those who pass away on Friday are spared *chibut ha-Kever.* Others can avoid this by: *"loving justice, loving rebuke, loving acts of kindness, bringing guests to one's home and praying with concentration"* (*ibid.* ch. 3). Another suggestion is to spend four hours per day saying words of Torah and Psalms (Rabbi Menachem Mendel Schneerson, *Ha-Yom Yom,* 7th *Teves*).

אֶלָּא אִם כֵּן מִי שֶׁלֹּא נֶהֱנָה מֵעוֹלָם הַזֶּה כָּל יָמָיו — A person will have *chibut ha-kever* unless he derived no pleasure from this world his entire life, כְּרַבֵּינוּ הַקָּדוֹשׁ — like the case of **our holy Rabbi** Yehudah *Ha-Nasi,* author of the *Mishnah,* who said on his death bed that he had enjoyed no pleasure from this world (*Talmud, Kesubos* 104a).

PRACTICAL LESSONS

Even a kosher indulgence leaves a negative trace in the body, unless you have G-d in mind.

Rabbi Yehudah *Ha-Nasi* was a wealthy man, *"from whose table neither lettuce, nor radish nor cucumber was ever absent either in summer or winter"* (*Talmud, Avodah Zarah* 11a). The *Tanya* cites his example in particular to show that a life of piety does not preclude a person from eating and drinking well. What gives the *kelipos* power is exclusion of G-d from the picture, indulging purely for self-satisfaction. Yehudah *Ha-Nasi* is called "our" Rabbi because he shows us how it is not necessary to detach ourselves from the world in order to be pious — what is important is the intention (*Notes on Tanya*).

8TH TEVES REGULAR

The *Tanya* now turns to another activity which, while permitted by Jewish Law, is nevertheless spiritually damaging and requires cleansing after death.

וְעַל דְּבָרִים בְּטֵלִים בְּהֶיתֵּר — **As for "worthless discussion"** devoid of Torah content or purpose that is spoken **in a permissible manner,** כְּגוֹן עַם הָאָרֶץ שֶׁאֵינוֹ יָכוֹל לִלְמוֹד — **for example, by an uneducated person who is unable to study,** and therefore is exempt from the requirement to study Torah all the time, צָרִיךְ לְטַהֵר נַפְשׁוֹ מִטּוּמְאָה זוֹ דִּקְלִיפָּה זוֹ — even though the "uneducated person" did not sin, **he must undergo a cleansing of his soul, to purify it from contamination with this** *kelipah* of "worthless discussion" which was not dedicated to G-d, עַל יְדֵי גִּלְגּוּלָהּ בְּכַף הַקֶּלַע — **and** this is achieved **through** the soul **being flung in** *kaf ha-kela, "the hollow of a sling,"* (*I Samuel* 25:29), כְּמוֹ שֶׁכָּתוּב בַּזֹּהַר פָּרָשַׁת בְּשַׁלַּח דַּף נ"ט — **as is stated in the** *Zohar,* **portion of** *Beshalach,* **volume 2, page 59**a.

בשלח דף נ"ט. אבל לדיבורים אסורים כמו ליצנות
ולשון הרע וכיוצא בהם שהן משלש קליפות הטמאות
לגמרי אין כף הקלע [לבדו] מועיל לטהר ולהעביר
טומאתו מהנפש רק צריכה לירד לגיהנם. וכן מי
שאפשר לו לעסוק בתורה ועוסק בדברים בטלים אין
כף הקלע לבדו מועיל לנפשו למרקה ולזככה רק
עונשים חמורים שמענישים על ביטול תורה בפרטות
מלבד עונש הכללי לכל ביטול מ"ע מחמת עצלות
בגיהנם של שלג כמבואר במ"א וכן העוסק בחכמות

In *kaf ha-kela* the soul enters a world of imagination, thinking it is still alive in this world, and it is drawn into the same inappropriate thoughts to which it had become accustomed. As the soul is "flung" from thought to thought, it experiences pain, which is cleansing (Rabbi Shneur Zalman, *Likutei Torah, Bamidbar* 75c).

Kaf ha-kela, however, only cleanses the soul from *permitted* (*kelipas nogah*) activities that were spiritually damaging. It will not cleanse the soul from actual sins.

אֲבָל לִדְבּוּרִים אֲסוּרִים כְּמוֹ לֵיצָנוּת וְלָשׁוֹן הָרָע וְכַיּוֹצֵא בָּהֶם — But with "forbidden discussions," such as mockery and *lashon hara* (slander) *etc.,* שֶׁהֵן מִשָּׁלֹשׁ קְלִיפוֹת הַטְּמֵאוֹת לְגַמְרֵי — which are powered from the three completely impure *kelipos,* אֵין כַּף הַקֶּלַע [לְבַדּוֹ] מוֹעִיל לְטַהֵר וּלְהַעֲבִיר טוּמְאָתוֹ מֵהַנֶּפֶשׁ — *kaf ha-kela* [alone] is not sufficient to cleanse and detoxify the soul from its impurity, רַק צְרִיכָה לֵירֵד לְגֵיהִנֹּם — rather, the soul must go down to *gehinom* (purgatory).

וְכֵן מִי שֶׁאֶפְשָׁר לוֹ לַעֲסוֹק בַּתּוֹרָה וְעוֹסֵק בִּדְבָרִים בְּטֵלִים — The same is true for someone who was able to immerse himself in Torah study, but instead immersed himself in "worthless discussion" devoid of Torah content or purpose, אֵין כַּף הַקֶּלַע לְבַדּוֹ מוֹעִיל לְנַפְשׁוֹ לְמָרְקָהּ וּלְזַכְּכָהּ — in that case, *kaf ha-kela* alone cannot help his soul to be cleaned and purified, since his activity has been sinful (*i.e.,* from the three completely impure *kelipos*), רַק עוֹנְשִׁים חֲמוּרִים שֶׁמַּעֲנִישִׁים עַל בִּיטוּל תּוֹרָה בִּפְרָטוּת — and to be cleansed, that soul needs specific, severe punishments for the particular sin of neglecting the Torah, מִלְבַד עוֹנֶשׁ הַכְּלָלִי לְכָל בִּיטוּל מִצְוַת עֲשֵׂה מֵחֲמַת עַצְלוּת — and that is besides the general punishment administered for the idle neglect of any positive commandment, which also applies in this case of neglecting Torah study, בְּגֵיהִנֹּם שֶׁל שֶׁלֶג כְּמְבוֹאָר בְּמָקוֹם אַחֵר — in the "*gehinom* of snow," as is explained elsewhere (Rabbi Chaim Vital, *Likutei Torah,* portion of *Shemos*).

A person usually transgresses a prohibition out of warmth, *i.e.,* desire and lust, whereas neglecting a positive command is a symptom of coolness and indifference. Therefore, in the afterlife, prohibitions are cleansed by a hot "*gehinom* of fire," and neglected commandments by a cool "*gehinom* of snow."

אומות עובדי גלולים בכלל דברים בטלים יחשב לענין עון
ביטול תורה כמ"ש בהלכות תלמוד תורה ועוד זאת יתרה
טומאתה של חכמת האומות עובדי גלולים על טומאת
דברים בטלים שאינו מלביש ומטמא רק המדות מיסוד
הרוח הקדוש שבנפשו האלהית בטומאת קליפת נוגה
שבדברים בטלים הבאים מיסוד הרוח הרע שבקליפה
זו בנפשו הבהמית כדלעיל ולא בחי' חב"ד שבנפשו מאחר

13B

SECTION THREE: SECULAR WISDOM

וְכֵן הָעוֹסֵק בְּחָכְמוֹת אומות הָעוֹלָם בְּכְלַל דְּבָרִים בְּטֵלִים יֵחָשֵׁב לְעָנְיַן עָוֹן בִּיטוּל תּוֹרָה — **Similarly, studying** even permitted (non-heretical) forms of **secular wisdom is considered a sinful neglect of Torah study, tantamount** in Jewish Law to "**worthless discussion,**" כְּמוֹ שֶׁכָּתוּב בְּהִלְכוֹת תַּלְמוּד תּוֹרָה — **as stated in** Rabbi Shneur Zalman's *Laws of Torah Study* (Shklov, 1794), chapter 3, law 7, (from *Sifri* to *Deuteronomy* 6:7).

According to this ruling, if a person has a choice, at any given moment, whether to study Torah or secular wisdom and he chooses the latter, he is considered to have neglected the commandment to study Torah.

וְעוֹד זֹאת יְתֵרָה טומְאָתָהּ שֶׁל חָכְמַת הָאוּמוֹת עַל טומְאַת דְּבָרִים בְּטֵלִים — **Also,** from a Kabbalistic perspective, **secular wisdom is** *more* **contaminating** for the soul **than "worthless discussion,"** שֶׁאֵינוֹ מַלְבִּישׁ וּמְטַמֵּא רַק הַמִּדּוֹת — **since** "worthless discussion" **only influences and contaminates the** *emotional* **attributes of the Divine Soul,** whereas secular wisdom contaminates the Divine Soul's *intellectual* attributes.

An impure faculty of the Animal Soul will only contaminate its corresponding faculty in the Divine Soul. Since "empty words" do not require any significant intellect on the part of the Animal Soul, they do not contaminate the Divine Soul's intellect.

מִיסוֹד הָרוּחַ הַקָּדוֹשׁ שֶׁבְּנַפְשׁוֹ הָאֱלֹהִית — "**Worthless discussion**" contaminates only the emotional attributes of the Divine Soul that stem **from its sacred element of "wind,"** בְּטומְאַת קְלִיפַת נוֹגַהּ שֶׁבְּדְבָרִים בְּטֵלִים הַבָּאִים מִיסוֹד הָרוּחַ הָרַע שֶׁבַּקְלִיפָּה זוֹ בְּנַפְשׁוֹ הַבַּהֲמִית — which become contaminated **by the** *kelipas nogah* **impurity of "worthless discussion" from the negative** side of the **Animal Soul's element of air,** כְּדִלְעֵיל — **as noted above** (chapter 1, p. 40).

"Empty words" feel good precisely because of their empty content. The lack of alignment to any purpose is related to "air" which flows freely in any direction, without resistance. As we have learned, the Animal Soul is primarily an emotional creature, and its natural activity flows from its elemental disposition. "Empty words" stem from the desire to be carefree and unrestrained.

וְלֹא בְּחִינוֹת חָכְמָה בִּינָה וָדַעַת שֶׁבְּנַפְשׁוֹ — But "worthless discussions" **will not** contaminate the intellectual **faculties of** *chochmah, binah* **and** *da'as* **in your** Divine

שהם דברי שטות ובורות שגם השוטים וע"ה יכולים לדבר
כן. משא"כ בחכמת האומות עובדי גלולים הוא מלביש
ומטמא בחי' חב"ד שבנפשו האלהית בטומאת קליפת
נוגה שבחכמות אלו שנפלו שמה בשבירת הכלי' מבחי'

Soul, מֵאַחַר שֶׁהֵם דִּבְרֵי שְׁטוּת וּבוּרוּת — **because** "worthless discussions" **are words of nonsense and ignorance,** שֶׁגַּם הַשּׁוֹטִים וְעַמֵּי הָאָרֶץ יְכוֹלִים לְדַבֵּר כֵּן — the proof of this **being that even fools and the uneducated can speak that way.**

מַה שֶׁאֵין כֵּן בְּחָכְמַת הָאוּמּוֹת הוּא מַלְבִּישׁ וּמְטַמֵּא בְּחִינוֹת חָכְמָה בִּינָה וְדַעַת שֶׁבְּנַפְשׁוֹ הָאֱלֹהִית — **Secular wisdom, however,** *does* **influence and contaminate the** intellectual **faculties of** *chochmah, binah* **and** *da'as* **of your Divine Soul,** בְּטוּמְאַת קְלִיפַּת נוֹגַהּ שֶׁבְּחָכְמוֹת אֵלּוּ — **with the impurity of** *kelipas nogah* **in these forms of wisdom.**

We are not speaking here of idolatrous or heretical wisdom, but of general knowledge that has no anti-religious content. Why should mathematics or medicine, for example, be "contaminating" for the soul? To answer this question, the *Tanya* draws on a Kabbalistic teaching.

שֶׁנָּפְלוּ שָׁמָּה בִּשְׁבִירַת הַכֵּלִים — **Secular wisdom has fallen there,** to the realm of *kelipas nogah,* **through** *Sheviras Ha-Kelim* ("Shattering of the Vessels").

One of the secrets of creation revealed by the Kabbalah is the "Shattering of the Vessels." As Rabbi Chaim Vital explains:

"To fashion pottery, the potter first takes an unformed mass of clay and then places his hand inside the mass to form it. Likewise, the Supernal Emanator put His 'hand,' i.e., a ray of light, into the amorphous mass.... As this light began to enter the mass, vessels were formed... all ten sefiros. Since keser (crown) was the purest and clearest of all the vessels, it could bear the light within it, but chochmah and binah, though more translucent than those below, were not like keser. Not having enough capacity, their 'backs' broke, and they fell from their position.

"As the light descended further, six points appeared — six fragments of what had been one point of light. Thus the vessels shattered. Their spiritual essence — the light — ascended back to the mother's womb, while the shattered vessels fell to the world of creation" (Rabbi Chaim Vital, Likutim Chadashim, 17–23).

While sacred in origin, the "falling" of these shattered vessels gave rise to the *kelipos,* since the vessel fragments contained an overwhelming amount of "mass" (self-awareness) and only a tiny glimmer of "light" (G-d-awareness). Therefore, earthly, secular knowledge, which was a product of the shattered vessels of *chochmah* and *binah,* has a propensity towards self and ego, and tends to "contaminate" the mind away from G-d consciousness.

אֲחוֹרַיִים שֶׁל חָכְמָה דִקְדוּשָׁה כִּידוּעַ לְיוֹדְעֵי חֵן אֶלָּא אִם כֵּן עוֹשֶׂה אוֹתָן קַרְדּוֹם לַחְתּוֹךְ בָּהֶן דְּהַיְינוּ כְּדֵי לְהִתְפַּרְנֵס מֵהֶן בְּרֶיוַח לַעֲבוֹד ה' אוֹ שֶׁיּוֹדֵעַ לְהִשְׁתַּמֵּשׁ בָּהֶן לַעֲבוֹדַת ה' אוֹ לְתוֹרָתוֹ וְזֶהוּ טַעֲמוֹ שֶׁל הָרַמְבַּ"ם וְרַמְבַּ"ן זִכְרוֹנָם לִבְרָכָה וְסִיעָתָן שֶׁעָסְקוּ בָּהֶן:

מִבְּחִינַת אֲחוֹרַיִים שֶׁל חָכְמָה דִקְדוּשָׁה — But the "Shattering of the Vessels" affected only the "backs" of sacred *chochmah* and *binah*, כַּיָּדוּעַ לְיוֹדְעֵי חָכְמָה נִסְתָּרָה — as is known to those familiar with hidden Kabbalistic **wisdom.**

As the above citation makes clear, the "Shattering of the Vessels" affected different *sefiros* to varying degrees. While the vessels of the six emotional *sefiros* were shattered completely, the intellectual *sefiros* suffered a shattering only of their "backs" (their external bias).

Practically, we see this in the extent to which human emotions and intellect are self-serving. Emotions, when devoid of intellect, are always self-serving; their holiness has been completely shattered. Intellect, on the other hand is, at its core, positive and helpful and only becomes corrupt through bias (see Rabbi Shneur Zalman, *Ma'amarei Admor Ha-Zakein, Inyanim* vol. 1, p. 223).

The *Tanya* now cites an exception to the above rule, a scenario where secular study would not be considered "contaminating," even according to the Kabbalah.

אֶלָּא אִם כֵּן עוֹשֶׂה אוֹתָן קַרְדּוֹם לַחְתּוֹךְ בָּהֶן — Secular knowledge will "contaminate" a person **unless he uses it as *"a spade with which to dig"*** (*Mishnah, Avos* 4:5), דְּהַיְינוּ כְּדֵי לְהִתְפַּרְנֵס מֵהֶן בְּרֶיוַח לַעֲבוֹד ה' — namely: a.) **to earn a comfortable livelihood, so as** to be able **to worship G-d,** אוֹ שֶׁיּוֹדֵעַ לְהִשְׁתַּמֵּשׁ בָּהֶן לַעֲבוֹדַת ה' אוֹ לְתוֹרָתוֹ — or, b.) **if he knows how to utilize** secular wisdom **in the service of G-d or His Torah,** *e.g.,* to clarify a point of law, or to defend Judaism from critics.

As is the case with any *kelipas nogah* entity, its negative, self-serving inertia can be neutralized by the correct intention and alignment. If secular wisdom is studied with a Torah purpose, *e.g.,* to earn a livelihood, so as to be able to worship G-d, or to directly enhance Torah, it will not have a contaminating effect.

וְזֶהוּ טַעֲמוֹ שֶׁל הָרַמְבַּ"ם וְרַמְבַּ"ן זִכְרוֹנָם לִבְרָכָה וְסִיעָתָן שֶׁעָסְקוּ בָּהֶן — **This was the reasoning of Maimonides and Nachmanides, of blessed memory, and their adherents, who immersed themselves in** secular studies.*

---

*For a discussion of this statement, see: Rabbi Chaim Miller, *Turning Judaism Outward* (New York: Kol Menachem, 2014), pp. 62-4.

פרק ט **והנה** מקום משכן נפש הבהמית שמקליפת
נוגה בכל איש ישראל הוא בלב בחלל
שמאלי שהוא מלא דם וכתיב כי הדם הוא הנפש ולכן
כל התאות והתפארות וכעס ודומיהן הן בלב ומהלב
הן מתפשטות בכל הגוף וגם עולה למוח שבראש
לחשב ולהרהר בהן ולהתחכם בהן כמו שהדם מקורו
בלב ומהלב מתפשט לכל האברים וגם עולה להמוח

CHAPTER 9

THE WAR INSIDE YOU

SECTION ONE: WHERE ARE YOUR TWO SOULS?

9TH TEVES REGULAR | 12TH TEVES LEAP

In the previous chapters of *Tanya* we have been introduced to our two souls, Divine and Animal — their origins, their internal functioning and their "garments" of expression. Now we turn to the *point of interaction* of each soul with the body.

וְהִנֵּה מְקוֹם מִשְׁכַּן נָפֶשׁ הַבַּהֲמִית שֶׁמִּקְלִיפַת נוֹגַהּ בְּכָל אִישׁ יִשְׂרָאֵל — **The Animal Soul from *kelipas nogah* within every person in Israel**, while generally found "in the blood (chapter 1, p. 38), **has a location** in the body **where it** primarily **rests,** הוּא בַּלֵּב — **which is in the heart, in the left chamber that is filled with** energized **blood,** וּכְתִיב כִּי הַדָּם הוּא הַנֶּפֶשׁ — **as the verse states,** *"for the blood is the soul"* (*Deuteronomy* 12:23; see *Zohar* 2, 107b; *Etz Chaim* 50:4), וְלָכֵן כָּל הַתַּאֲוֹת וְהִתְפָּאֲרוּת וְכַעַס וְדוֹמֵיהֶן הֵן בַּלֵּב — **which is why all your desires, pride and anger etc., come from the heart.**

וּמֵהַלֵּב הֵן מִתְפַּשְׁטוֹת בְּכָל הַגּוּף — **And from the heart,** the Animal Soul **spreads throughout the whole body,** וְגַם עוֹלֶה לַמּוֹחַ שֶׁבָּרֹאשׁ — **and also goes up to the head, to the brain,** לַחֲשֹׁב וּלְהַרְהֵר בָּהֶן וּלְהִתְחַכֵּם בָּהֶן — **where those** feelings which emerged in the heart **are thought about, contemplated and schemed upon** by the Animal Soul, כְּמוֹ שֶׁהַדָּם מְקוֹרוֹ בַּלֵּב וּמֵהַלֵּב מִתְפַּשֵּׁט לְכָל הָאֵבָרִים וְגַם עוֹלֶה לְהַמּוֹחַ שֶׁבָּרֹאשׁ — **in fact, the Animal Soul flows to the brain just as the blood flows to all the limbs, rising to the head (the brain) too, from its source in the heart.**

The Animal Soul functions in an emotional space. Its intellect is used largely to rationalize its desires and to plan how to obtain them. That is why the Animal Soul has just *one* focal "resting place" in the body, in the heart-center.

שבראש. אך מקום משכן נפש האלהית הוא במוחין
שבראש ומשם מתפשטת לכל האברים וגם בלב בחלל
הימני שאין בו דם וכמ"ש לב חכם לימינו והיא אהבת
ה' כרשפי שלהבת מתלהבת בלב משכילים המבינים
ומתבוננים בדעתם אשר במוחם בדברים המעוררים
את האהבה. וכן שמחת לבב בתפארת ה' והדר גאונו

אַךְ מְקוֹם מִשְׁכַּן נֶפֶשׁ הָאֱלֹהִית הוּא בַּמּוֹחִין שֶׁבָּרֹאשׁ — **But the place where the Divine Soul** primarily **rests is in the brain, in the head,** וּמִשָּׁם מִתְפַּשֶּׁטֶת לְכָל הָאֵבָרִים — **from where it flows to all the organs,** וְגַם בַּלֵּב — **and** the Divine Soul **also** has a secondary resting place **in the heart.**

In the case of the Divine Soul, there is importance to both mind *and* heart. The Divine Soul's main energy is a mental one, which is why its primary resting place is in the cognitive center of the brain. But the purpose of the Divine Soul's presence in the body is to achieve mastery of the emotions, which is why it also has a secondary resting place in the heart (*Notes on Tanya*).

בְּחֲלָל הַיְמָנִי שָׁאֵין בּוֹ דָּם — The Divine Soul's resting place in the heart is **in its right chamber, which is devoid of** energized **blood,** וּכְמוֹ שֶׁכָּתוּב לֵב חָכָם לִימִינוֹ — **as the verse states,** *"The heart of the wise man is on his right"* (*Ecclesiastes* 10:2; see *Zohar ibid.; Etz Chaim ibid.*).

The blood on the right side lacks energy to fuel the animal passions of the body. It is, therefore, the place in the heart where higher emotions for sacred things arise.

וְהִיא אַהֲבַת ה' כְּרִשְׁפֵּי שַׁלְהֶבֶת מִתְלַהֶבֶת בְּלֵב מַשְׂכִּילִים — **This** nexus of the Divine Soul in your heart produces your **love for G-d that, like** *"flaming fire"* (*Song* 8:6), **flares up in your "discerning heart"** (*chochmah*), הַמְּבִינִים וּמִתְבּוֹנְנִים בְּדַעְתָּם אֲשֶׁר בְּמוֹחָם — **when you use your brain to analyze** (with *binah*) **and come to recognize** (with *da'as*), בִּדְבָרִים הַמְּעוֹרְרִים אֶת הָאַהֲבָה — **ideas which arouse love of** G-d.

This is the basic meditation practice which the *Tanya* has described in chapter 3 (sections 2-3). Examples of these meditations include contemplating: 1) How G-dly light and energy is found within all physical objects, even though you can't see it. 2) How far your life is from G-d and how close you would really like to be. 3) How the angels worship G-d with utter dedication and love. 4) How, in its source, the world is absorbed in G-d. 5) How G-d renews the creation with a fresh energy each morning. 6) How wondrous is the world which G-d created (see Rabbi Yoel Kahan (ed.), *Sefer Ha-Arachim Chabad,* vol. 1 (Brooklyn: Kehos, 1970), pp. 545-557).

We now touch upon a more advanced type of meditation practice which will result in the presence of G-d being felt more tangibly.

וְכֵן שִׂמְחַת לֵבָב בְּתִפְאֶרֶת ה' וַהֲדַר גָּאוֹנוֹ — **Also,** the Divine Soul can bring **a rejoicing of the heart in the glory of G-d and** *"the splendor of His majesty"* (*Isaiah* 2:19),

כַּאֲשֶׁר עֵינֵי הֶחָכָם אֲשֶׁר בְּרֹאשׁוֹ בְּמוֹחַ חָכְמָתוֹ וּבִינָתוֹ מִסְתַּכְּלִים בִּיקָרָא דְמַלְכָּא וְתִפְאֶרֶת גְּדוּלָתוֹ עַד אֵין חֵקֶר וְאֵין סוֹף וְתַכְלִית כְּמוֹ בָאָר בְּמָקוֹם אַחֵר וְכֵן שְׁאָר מִדּוֹת קְדוֹשׁוֹת שֶׁבַּלֵּב הֵן מֵחַבַּ"ד שֶׁבַּמּוֹחִין. אַךְ הִנֵּה כְּתִיב וּלְאֹם מִלְאֹם יֶאֱמָץ כִּי הַגּוּף נִקְרָא עִיר קְטַנָּה וּכְמוֹ שְׁנֵי מְלָכִים נִלְחָמִים עַל עִיר אַחַת שֶׁכָּל אֶחָד רוֹצֶה לְכָבְשָׁהּ וְלִמְלוֹךְ עָלֶיהָ דְּהַיְינוּ לְהַנְהִיג יוֹשְׁבֶיהָ כִּרְצוֹנוֹ

14A

כַּאֲשֶׁר עֵינֵי הֶחָכָם אֲשֶׁר בְּרֹאשׁוֹ — when *"the eyes of the wise man that are in his head"* (see *Ecclesiastes* 2:14), בְּמוֹחַ חָכְמָתוֹ וּבִינָתוֹ — using his mental powers of *chochmah* and *binah*, מִסְתַּכְּלִים בִּיקָרָא דְמַלְכָּא וְתִפְאֶרֶת גְּדוּלָתוֹ — *"gaze at the glory of the King"* (*Zohar* 1, 38a-b) and *"the beauty of His greatness"* (*Esther* 1:4), עַד אֵין חֵקֶר וְאֵין סוֹף וְתַכְלִית — which is **unfathomable, endless and limitless.**

This second method of meditation involves, what the *Zohar* refers to as "gazing" at G-d. This does not refer to a physical vision, but a mental one, using the "mind's eye" ("the eyes of the wise man, that are *in his head"*). The experience is compared to "sight" since, after lengthy meditation, you reach the point where G-dliness becomes tangible and real.

כְּמְבוֹאָר בְּמָקוֹם אַחֵר — **This is as explained elsewhere** (see Rabbi Shneur Zalman, *Torah Or,* 47c; *Likutei Torah, Behar* 40c; *Shir Ha-Shirim* 29c; See also Rabbi Shalom Dov Ber Schneersohn, *Tract on Prayer,* chapter 1).

וְכֵן שְׁאָר מִדּוֹת קְדוֹשׁוֹת שֶׁבַּלֵּב הֵן מֵחָכְמָה בִּינָה וְדַעַת שֶׁבַּמּוֹחִין — In addition to the above, **the other holy emotions of the heart also originate from** *chochmah, binah* **and** *da'as* **in the brain** (see chapter 3).

SECTION TWO: YOUR INNER STRUGGLE

10TH TEVES REGULAR | 13TH TEVES LEAP

Up to this point in the *Tanya,* we have discussed the two souls, Divine and Animal, separately; but this should not lead us to conclude that they work independently from each other.

אַךְ הִנֵּה כְּתִיב וּלְאֹם מִלְאֹם יֶאֱמָץ — **However, the verse states,** *"And one nation shall overpower the other nation"* (*Genesis* 25:23).

As we shall see, the task of each soul (each "nation" within you) is to overpower the other soul's influence over the body.

כִּי הַגּוּף נִקְרָא עִיר קְטַנָּה — **For the body is called a "small city"** (*Talmud, Nedarim* 32b), וּכְמוֹ שְׁנֵי מְלָכִים נִלְחָמִים עַל עִיר אַחַת שֶׁכָּל אֶחָד רוֹצֶה לְכָבְשָׁהּ וְלִמְלוֹךְ עָלֶיהָ — **and just as two kings will fight over a city, each one desiring to conquer it and rule over it,** דְּהַיְינוּ לְהַנְהִיג יוֹשְׁבֶיהָ כִּרְצוֹנוֹ וְשֶׁיִּהְיוּ סָרִים לְמִשְׁמַעְתּוֹ בְּכָל אֲשֶׁר יִגְזוֹר עֲלֵיהֶם

וְשֶׁיִּהְיוּ סָרִים לְמִשְׁמַעְתּוֹ בְּכָל אֲשֶׁר יִגְזוֹר עֲלֵיהֶם. כָּךְ
שְׁתֵּי הַנְּפָשׁוֹת הָאֱלֹהִית וְהַחִיּוּנִית הַבַּהֲמִית שֶׁמֵּהַקְּלִיפָּה
נִלְחָמוֹת זוֹ עִם זוֹ עַל הַגּוּף וְכָל אֵבָרָיו שֶׁהָאֱלֹהִית חֶפְצָה
וּרְצוֹנָהּ שֶׁתְּהֵא הִיא לְבַדָּהּ הַמּוֹשֶׁלֶת עָלָיו וּמַנְהִיגָתוֹ וְכָל
הָאֵבָרִים יִהְיוּ סָרִים לְמִשְׁמַעְתָּהּ וּבְטֵלִים אֶצְלָהּ לְגַמְרֵי
וּמֶרְכָּבָה אֵלֶיהָ וְיִהְיוּ לְבוּשׁ לְעֶשֶׂר בְּחִינוֹתֶיהָ וְג' לְבוּשֶׁיהָ
הַנִּזְכָּרִים לְעֵיל שֶׁיִּתְלַבְּשׁוּ כֻּלָּם בְּאֵבְרֵי הַגּוּף וְיִהְיֶה הַגּוּף כֻּלּוֹ
מָלֵא מֵהֶם לְבַדָּם וְלֹא יַעֲבוֹר זָר בְּתוֹכָם חַ"ו דְּהַיְינוּ תְּלַת
מוֹחִין שֶׁבָּרֹאשׁ יִהְיוּ מְמֻלָּאִים מֵחַב"ד שֶׁבַּנֶּפֶשׁ הָאֱלֹהִית
שֶׁהִיא חָכְמַת ה' וּבִינָתוֹ לְהִתְבּוֹנֵן בִּגְדוּלָתוֹ אֲשֶׁר עַד

— *i.e.*, each king desiring **to conduct its inhabitants according to his will, so that they obey his every whim, in everything that he decrees on them,** כָּךְ שְׁתֵּי הַנְּפָשׁוֹת — **so too,** הָאֱלֹהִית וְהַחִיּוּנִית הַבַּהֲמִית שֶׁמֵּהַקְּלִיפָּה נִלְחָמוֹת זוֹ עִם זוֹ עַל הַגּוּף וְכָל אֵבָרָיו **the two souls, the Divine and the energizing Animal Soul from *kelipah*, fight each other over** control of **the body and all its limbs.**

שֶׁהָאֱלֹהִית חֶפְצָה וּרְצוֹנָהּ שֶׁתְּהֵא הִיא לְבַדָּהּ הַמּוֹשֶׁלֶת עָלָיו וּמַנְהִיגָתוֹ — **Your Divine Soul's desire and will is for exclusive rule over you and your conduct,** וְכָל הָאֵבָרִים יִהְיוּ סָרִים לְמִשְׁמַעְתָּהּ וּבְטֵלִים אֶצְלָהּ לְגַמְרֵי וּמֶרְכָּבָה אֵלֶיהָ — **and that all your limbs should obey and surrender themselves completely to it, becoming its** exclusive **vehicle** of expression, וְיִהְיוּ לְבוּשׁ לְעֶשֶׂר בְּחִינוֹתֶיהָ וְג' לְבוּשֶׁיהָ הַנִּזְכָּרִים לְעֵיל — **and be a vehicle of expression for its ten** intellectual and emotional **powers, and three "garments" of** sacred thought, speech and action, **mentioned above.**

שֶׁיִּתְלַבְּשׁוּ כֻּלָּם בְּאֵבְרֵי הַגּוּף וְיִהְיֶה כֻּלּוֹ מָלֵא מֵהֶם לְבַדָּם — **The** Divine Soul desires for its powers and "garments" **to influence all parts of the body and be in complete control of the body,** וְלֹא יַעֲבוֹר זָר בְּתוֹכָם חַס וְשָׁלוֹם — **with nothing else interfering, G-d forbid,** דְּהַיְינוּ תְּלַת מוֹחִין שֶׁבָּרֹאשׁ יִהְיוּ מְמֻלָּאִים מֵחָכְמָה בִּינָה וָדַעַת שֶׁבַּנֶּפֶשׁ הָאֱלֹהִית — and since the mind ultimately controls everything, **this means that the three faculties of your brain,** dealing with *inquiry, cognition* and *recognition,* **should be influenced entirely by the *chochmah, binah* and *da'as* of your Divine Soul.**

שֶׁהִיא חָכְמַת ה' וּבִינָתוֹ — Practically **this means,** as we have discussed in chapter 3 (p. 57-63), a focus on **the intellectual *inquiry* of G-d and *cognition*** of those ideas,

PRACTICAL LESSONS

Your Divine Soul and Animal (pleasure-seeking) Soul are both competing for control over your body.

The way to ensure that the Divine Soul wins is by meditating about G-d, using the techniques described in the *Tanya,* so that your heart will become saturated with love for G-d.

אין חקר ואין סוף ולהוליד מהן על ידי הדעת היראה
במוחו ופחד ה' בלבו ואהבת ה' כאש בוערה בלבו
כרשפי שלהבת להיות נכספה וגם כלתה נפשו בחשיקה
וחפיצה לדבקה בו בא"ס ב"ה בכל לב ונפש ומאד
מעומקא דלבא שבחלל הימני שיהיה תוכו רצוף אהבה
מלא וגדוש עד שתתפשט גם לחלל השמאלי לאכפיא
לס"א יסוד המים הרעים שבה שהיא התאוה שמקליפת
נוגה לשנותה ולהפכה מתענוגי עולם הזה לאהבת ה'

הִתְבּוֹנֵן בִּגְדוּלָתוֹ אֲשֶׁר עַד אֵין חֵקֶר וְאֵין סוֹף — **by pondering His unfathomable and endless greatness,** וּלְהוֹלִיד מֵהֶן עַל יְדֵי הַדַּעַת הַיִּרְאָה בְּמוֹחוֹ וּפַחַד ה' בְּלִבּוֹ — **which,** through *recognition*, **will lead to reverence in your mind and trepidation of G-d in your heart,** וְאַהֲבַת ה' כְּאֵשׁ בּוֹעֵרָה בְּלִבּוֹ כְּרִשְׁפֵּי שַׁלְהֶבֶת — **and** from the mind to the heart, **a love of G-d like a fire burning in your heart, like *"flaming fire,"*** לִהְיוֹת נִכְסָפָה — so that your *"soul will yearn, indeed, languish"* וְגַם כָּלְתָה נַפְשׁוֹ בַּחֲשִׁיקָה וַחֲפִיצָה (Psalms 84:3), **with fervor and desire,** לְדָבְקָה בּוֹ בְּאֵין סוֹף בָּרוּךְ הוּא בְּכָל לֵב וָנֶפֶשׁ וּמְאֹד — **to attach yourself to the Blessed Infinite Light, with all your *"heart, soul and might"*** (Deuteronomy 6:5).

This general meditation has already been introduced to us in chapter 3 (see also chapter 16, p. 190; chapters 42, pp. 529ff.). Now we can understand the dynamic of this meditation in terms of the locations of the competing souls in our bodies.

מֵעוּמְקָא דְלִבָּא שֶׁבֶּחָלָל הַיְמָנִי — **This meditation is aimed at reverence and love ema**nating **from the depths of the heart, from its right chamber** where the Divine Soul's emotions emerge, שֶׁיִּהְיֶה תּוֹכוֹ רָצוּף אַהֲבָה מָלֵא וְגָדוּשׁ — **the experience should be** so intense **that the right chamber is *"inlaid with love"*** (Song 3:10), **filled to capacity and overflowing,** עַד שֶׁתִּתְפַּשֵּׁט גַּם לֶחָלָל הַשְּׂמָאלִי — **so that** the love **spills over into the left side** of the heart **too,** the center of the Animal Soul.

לְאַכְפְיָא לְסִטְרָא אָחֳרָא יְסוֹד הַמַּיִם הָרָעִים שֶׁבָּהּ שֶׁהִיא הַתַּאֲוָה שֶׁמִּקְּלִיפַּת נוֹגַהּ — **The ef**fect of this love will be **to subdue the *sitra achra* and its negative element of water,** the source of lust and **desire for kosher pleasures from *kelipas nogah*** (see p. 40).

SECTION THREE: HEALING YOUR DARKER SIDE

We should initially seek to *tame* our darker side, though in some cases it can be *healed* completely (see pp. 127-9). These two phases are known as *iskafya*, "subduing" negativity, and *is'haphcha*, "transforming" it completely.

לְשַׁנּוֹתָהּ וּלְהָפְכָהּ מִתַּעֲנוּגֵי עוֹלָם הַזֶּה לְאַהֲבַת ה' — The love from the right side ought to be so powerful that it not only **changes but** ultimately **transforms the left side from seeking worldly pleasures, to love G-d.**

כמ"ש בכל לבבך בשני יצריך והיינו שיעלה ויבא
ויגיע למדרגת אהבה רבה וחיבה יתרה ממדרגת
אהבה עזה כרשפי אש והיא הנקראת בכתוב אהבה
בתענוגים להתענג על ה' מעין עולם הבא והענג הוא

Throughout the *Tanya*, several experiences of love of G-d are described, each differing in character and intensity. The above thoughts are aimed at producing the experience known as "love like flaming fire." This is sufficient to tame the Animal Soul, but not to transform it. Full transformation requires a more intense experience of love, to which the *Tanya* will now turn.

כְּמוֹ שֶׁכָּתוּב בְּכָל לְבָבְךָ בִּשְׁנֵי יְצָרֶיךָ — **As it is written,** *"You shall love G-d with all your heart (levavcha)"* (*Deuteronomy* 6:5), the use of the term *levav* (לבב) rather than the contracted form *lev* (לב), suggests the presence of two elements of the heart, leading the Sages to teach that you should love G-d, *"with both your impulses"* (*Talmud, Brachos* 54a), both the *yetzer tov* (impulse to good) and *yetzer hara* (impulse to evil). This is a state where the *yetzer hara* has been *transformed* to the good.

The Animal Soul just wants whatever it deems to be good for itself. Physical pleasures, which are tangible and easily experienced, will naturally allure the Animal Soul; but it could also be drawn to higher pleasures, such as meditating on G-d and feeling His presence. This is the "transformation" of *yetzer hara* to *yetzer tov* to which the Sages refer.

וְהַיְינוּ שֶׁיַעֲלֶה וְיָבֹא וְיַגִּיעַ לְמַדְרֵגַת אַהֲבָה רַבָּה וְחִיבָּה יְתֵרָה מִמַּדְרֵגַת אַהֲבָה עַזָה כְּרִשְׁפֵּי אֵשׁ — **This happens when you elevate yourself and eventually reach the level of "great love"** (*ahavah rabah*), **which is a more powerful term of endearment than the level of "strong love like flaming fire."**

As we have seen, love like "flaming fire" represents a "yearning and languishing" of the soul, *i.e.,* a desire to come close to something distant. "Great love," on the other hand, is an experience of closeness to G-d where you actually feel and enjoy His presence as something close.

14TH TEVES LEAP

וְהִיא הַנִקְרֵאת בַּכָּתוּב אַהֲבָה בַּתַעֲנוּגִים — **In Scripture this** "great love" **is referred to as** *"pleasurable love"* (*Song* 7:7), לְהִתְעַנֵג עַל ה' — **which is to take pleasure in G-d.**

A CHASIDIC THOUGHT

I can tackle the negative indirectly by focusing on the positive. If my Divine Soul will generate enough love for G-d, it will *overflow* into the domain of the Animal Soul.

בְּמוֹחַ חָכְמָה וְשֵׂכֶל הַמִּתְעַנֵּג בְּהַשְׂכָּלַת ה' וִידִיעָתוֹ כְּפִי
הַשָּׂגַת שִׂכְלוֹ וְחָכְמָתוֹ וְהוּא בְּחִי' הַמַּיִם וְזֶרַע אוֹר זָרוּעַ
שֶׁבִּקְדוּשַׁת נֶפֶשׁ הָאֱלֹהִית הַמְהַפֶּכֶת לְטוֹב אֶת בְּחִי'   14B

A love of "flaming fire" represents the intense desire to connect to G-d, *who remains distant.* It expresses itself in *will,* a yearning to follow the ways of G-d. Even though you are still drawn to the pleasures of this world, your passion is for a higher, more beautiful way of Torah life.

A "pleasurable love," represents the joy of *already* being connected to G-d. In this sense it resembles the love you have for yourself. (When you love yourself, there is no tempestuous (fiery) yearning to be drawn to another person who is separate from you. You just take pleasure in yourself — Rabbi Shalom Dov Ber Schneersohn, *Sefer Ha-Ma'amarim* 5670, p. 40; see below, chapter 40, p. 489.)

At this level of "pleasurable love" for G-d, you have neutralized your desires for worldly pleasure and sin, and even your Animal Soul desires only G-d. Your love of G-d is what the love of physical pleasure is for most people: natural and organic.

מֵעֵין עוֹלָם הַבָּא — It is **a foretaste of the world-that-is-coming.**

"Pleasurable love" resembles the experience of the future world-that-is-coming, where an intimacy with G-d will be felt as part of ordinary life.

וְהָעֹנֶג הוּא בְּמוֹחַ חָכְמָה וְשֵׂכֶל הַמִּתְעַנֵּג בְּהַשְׂכָּלַת ה' וִידִיעָתוֹ — **This delight is experienced in the mental faculties of inquiry and intelligence, by the sheer pleasure of understanding G-d and knowing Him,** כְּפִי הַשָּׂגַת שִׂכְלוֹ וְחָכְמָתוֹ — **according to the limits of your intellectual grasp and vision.**

In contrast to "love like a flaming fire," which is experienced primarily in the heart, "pleasurable love" has a strong mental component. This is because:

וְהוּא בְּחִינַת הַמַּיִם — **It is from** the element of **water.**

The intense yearning and passion with "love like flaming fire" stems from the experience of a distant G-d. "Pleasurable love," on the other hand, while representing a more powerful love, is ironically less enthusiastic (like cold water), as the Beloved is more real and immediate.

"Pleasurable love," being derived from elemental water, is a greater force against physical desires, which are also from water (see above, p. 40).

וְזֶרַע אוֹר זָרוּעַ שֶׁבִּקְדוּשַׁת נֶפֶשׁ הָאֱלֹהִית — **And "seed," the *"sown light"** (Psalms 97:11), **is within the Divine Soul's holiness.**

Probing deeper into the psyche, the *Tanya* here draws on the Kabbalistic description of man's origins. Commenting on the five-fold mention of "light" on the first day of Creation and "water" on the second day, the *Zohar* notes: *"When a person comes to be, he is first seed, which is 'light,' for that seed is the 'light' of all the limbs of the body.... Afterwards, that seed, which is 'light,' spreads and becomes 'water.'"*

המים שבנפש הבהמית שמהם באו תאות תענוגי
עוה"ז מתחלה וכמ"ש בע"ח שער נ' פרק ג' בשם הזהר
שהרע נהפך להיות טוב גמור כמו יצר טוב ממש
בהסיר הבגדים הצואים ממנו שהם תענוגי עוה"ז שהוא
מלובש בהם וכן שאר כל המדות שבלב שהן ענפי

By the moisture of the water, it becomes further detailed and the form of the body expands into these waters, growing in all directions" (Zohar 2, 167a).

Since light (seed) precedes water in the order of creation, through accessing the higher power of light in the Divine Soul, you are capable of transforming the "water" of the Animal Soul for the good.

הַמְהַפֶּכֶת לְטוֹב אֶת בְּחִינַת הַמַּיִם שֶׁבַּנֶּפֶשׁ הַבַּהֲמִית שָׁמֶהֶם בָּאוּ תַּאֲוַת תַּעֲנוּגֵי עוֹלָם הַזֶּה מִתְּחִלָּה — The Divine Soul's "sown light" **transforms the source of all desires for pleasures of this world, the element of water in the Animal Soul, to good.**

PRACTICAL LESSONS

Your Animal Soul is not evil; it just has crude tastes. Through meditation and the study of Chasidic wisdom, you can teach your Animal Soul to appreciate sacred and spiritual things too.

If this art is perfected, it is possible to completely eliminate the lustful desires of the Animal Soul and transform them into spiritual yearnings. But that doesn't mean you've given up on the pleasures of life; you've replaced them with even greater pleasures.

וּכְמוֹ שֶׁכָּתוּב בְּעֵץ חַיִּים שַׁעַר נ' פֶּרֶק ג' בְּשֵׁם הַזֹּהַר — **As it is written in** *Etz Chaim,* **section 50, chapter 3, citing the** *Zohar* **(3, 277a),** שֶׁהָרַע נֶהֱפָּךְ לִהְיוֹת טוֹב גָּמוּר כְּמוֹ יֵצֶר טוֹב מַמָּשׁ — **that the** "impulse to **evil" can be transformed into pure good, to be on par with the "impulse to good" itself.**

The "impulse to evil" is not *irredeemably* evil; it is simply a force for desire. By training it to appreciate the greater pleasure of immersing in G-dly wisdom, it can be transformed to naturally desire only good.

בְּהָסִיר הַבְּגָדִים הַצּוֹאִים מִמֶּנּוּ — This is done **through** the impulse to evil **shedding its** *"soiled garments" (Zechari-ah 3:4),* שֶׁהֶם תַּעֲנוּגֵי עוֹלָם הַזֶּה שֶׁהוּא מְלוּבָּשׁ בָּהֶם — **which are the pleasures of this world, in which it is clothed.**

In a similar fashion to an addict who cannot embrace a new life until he has rid himself of self-destructive behavior patterns, the Animal Soul cannot be drawn to the more subtle pleasures of G-dly wisdom unless it first divests itself of its past habits of worldly pleasures. (For more on this topic see chapter 43.)

We now return to our discussion of the "war" of two souls over the body. Up to this point we have noted how the Divine Soul seeks to control the body, bringing the heart to both revere and love G-d. Now we turn to other experiences.

היראה והאהבה יהיו לה' לבדו וכל כח הדבור שבפה
והמחשבה שבמוח יהיו ממולאים מן לבושי המחשבה
והדבור של נפש האלהית לבדה שהן מחשבת ה'
ותורתו להיות שיחתו כל היום לא פסיק פומיה מגירסא
וכח המעשיי שבידי' ושאר רמ"ח אבריו יהיה במעשה
המצות לבד שהוא לבוש השלישי של נפש האלהית
אך נפש הבהמית שמהקליפה רצונה להפך ממש

וְכֵן שְׁאָר כָּל הַמִּדּוֹת שֶׁבַּלֵּב שֶׁהֵן עַנְפֵי הַיִּרְאָה וְהָאַהֲבָה יִהְיוּ לַה' לְבַדּוֹ — **So too,** the Divine Soul desires **that the other emotions in the heart, the derivatives of reverence and love, be devoted exclusively to G-d.**

As we have learned (above chapter 3, p. 63), all human emotions are essentially offshoots of either reverence/fear (distancing) or love (coming close). The Divine soul seeks to control all these feelings, as well as all conscious activity.

וְכָל כֹּחַ הַדִּבּוּר שֶׁבַּפֶּה וְהַמַּחֲשָׁבָה שֶׁבַּמּוֹחַ יִהְיוּ מְמוּלָּאִים מִן לְבוּשֵׁי הַמַּחֲשָׁבָה וְהַדִּבּוּר שֶׁל נֶפֶשׁ הָאֱלֹהִית לְבַדָּהּ — The Divine Soul also wishes to have full control of **all the words in your mouth and the thoughts in your head, so that they are "dressed" exclusively with the thought and speech of the Divine Soul,** שֶׁהֵן מַחֲשֶׁבֶת ה' וְתוֹרָתוֹ — **which are thoughts of G-d and His Torah,** לִהְיוֹת שִׂיחָתוֹ כָּל הַיּוֹם לָא פָסִיק פּוּמֵיהּ — **they should be the topics of your conversation all day, so that your** מִגִּירְסָא — **mouth never ceases from study.**

וְכֹחַ הַמַּעֲשִׂיִּי שֶׁבְּיָדָיו וּשְׁאָר רַמַ"ח אֲבָרָיו — Similarly, the Divine Soul also wishes to have full control of **every action of your hands, as well as the other anatomical parts** of your body, which total **248** in number (*Mishnah Oholos* 1:8), יִהְיֶה בְּמַעֲשֵׂה הַמִּצְוֹת לְבַד — שֶׁהוּא לְבוּשׁ הַשְּׁלִישִׁי שֶׁל נֶפֶשׁ הָאֱלֹהִית — **so that they only perform *mitzvos*, using the Divine Soul's third "garment" of action.**

In Rabbinic anatomy, the body is divided into 248 parts, delineated by bones of the skeleton and their surrounding flesh. (A person is born with 270 bones, and through ossification of cartilage, that number eventually falls to 206 in adulthood. The *Mishnah*'s count of 248 bones apparently refers to the skeleton of a sixteen or seventeen year-old. See Yehudah Leib Katzenelson, *Ha-Talmud Ve-Chochmas Ha-Refuah* (Berlin 1928), pp. 258*ff.*).

SECTION FOUR: WHAT YOUR ANIMAL SOUL WANTS

Having offered a detailed explanation of what the Divine Soul desires, the *Tanya* notes briefly the wishes of the Animal Soul, which are self-understood.

אַךְ נֶפֶשׁ הַבַּהֲמִית שֶׁמֵּהַקְּלִיפָּה רְצוֹנָהּ לְהֶפֶךְ מַמָּשׁ — **However the Animal Soul, which is from *kelipah*, wills the exact opposite.**

לטובת האדם שיתגבר עליה וינצחנה כמשל הזונה
שבזה"ק:

לְטוֹבַת הָאָדָם — But the Animal Soul, and its negative drive, is ultimately **for your good,** שֶׁיִּתְגַּבֵּר עָלֶיהָ וִינַצְּחֶנָּה — it exists only so **that you will** be challenged to **overcome it and be victorious over it.**

In reality, the Animal Soul is hoping that you *don't* listen to its voice. It exists to give you free choice, and to offer you the challenge of overcoming its urges so as to bring you closer to G-d. It has to do its Divinely-allotted job of tempting you to make that challenge real.

כְּמְשַׁל הַזוֹנָה שֶׁבַּזֹּהַר הַקָּדוֹשׁ — **As in the harlot analogy, related in the holy *Zohar*** (2, 163a).

PRACTICAL LESSONS

Your Animal Soul is a gift from G-d to help you grow. By refusing to listen to its voice, your soul matures immensely. The Animal Soul is just doing its Divinely alloted job, but deep down it hopes that you won't listen to it!

The *Zohar* teaches: *"Everything that the Blessed Holy One has made, above and below, is all intended to manifest His glory, and all is for His service.... How can an evil servant come... luring people to an evil path... causing them to disobey the will of their Master?"*

"But actually, he is doing the will of his Master! This may be compared to a king who had an only son, whom he loved very much. He commanded him, in love, not to approach an evil woman.... The son agreed lovingly to follow his father's will."

"At the king's home, outside, was a harlot, attractive in appearance and beautiful in form. Some days later, the king said, 'I want to test my son's devotion to me.' He called for the harlot and said to her, 'Go and seduce my son,' to see his son's devotion to him."

"That harlot, what could she do? She went after his son and began... seducing him with all kinds of enticements. If that son is worthy and obeys his father's command, he rebukes her, pays no heed to her, and casts her away from him. Then the father rejoices in his son and brings him into his palace, giving him gifts and presents and great honor."

"But who caused all this honor for that son? You must admit, it was that harlot! And that harlot, does she deserve praise for this or not? Surely she does, from every angle. First, because she carried out the king's command; and second, because she brought upon the son all this honor, all this goodness, all this love of the king toward him."

פרק י והנה כשהאדם מגביר נפשו האלהית
ונלחם כל כך עם הבהמית עד
שמגרש ומבער הרע שבה מחלל השמאלי כמ"ש

CHAPTER 10

THE "TZADIK"

11TH TEVES REGULAR | 15TH TEVES LEAP

So far, the *Tanya* has given us a "tour" of the psyche, describing the Animal Soul (in chapters 1, 6-8), the Divine Soul (in chapters 2-5) and their conflict (in chapter 9).

Now that we have some familiarity with the souls' architecture, the *Tanya* will begin to address a number of questions which remain unanswered from chapter 1. 1) What is the difference between a "complete *tzadik*" and an "incomplete *tzadik*"? (to be answered in this chapter). 2) What is the difference between a "complete *rasha*" and an "incomplete *rasha*"? (to be answered in chapter 11). 3) If a *beinoni* ("inbetweener") never transgresses, how is he different from a *tzadik*? (to be answered in chapter 12). 4) How is it possible for a *tzadik*, such as Rabah, to mistakenly conclude that he is a *beinoni*? (to be answered in chapter 13). 5) Why did Job say that G-d "created *tzadikim*," which seems to violate the notion of free choice? (to be answered in chapter 14). Finally, this will lead us to answer the *Tanya's* opening question: 6) Why was your soul made to swear an oath before you were born, *"Be a tzadik, and don't be a rasha, etc."*? (to be answered in chapter 14).

The solution to all these problems will hinge on the *Tanya's* two-layered description of the soul, which contains: i.) a "deep core" (of ten powers) that determines your attitudes and desires; and ii.) a more superficial layer of "three garments," that control what you contemplate, say and do.

SECTION ONE: THE INCOMPLETE TZADIK

We will begin with a definition of the "incomplete *tzadik*." In chapter 1, we concluded that every *tzadik* (complete or incomplete) *"is devoid of an 'impulse to evil.'"*

The obvious question here is: If a person's "impulse to evil" has *completely* gone, why would we call him *incomplete*?

וְהִנֵּה כְּשֶׁהָאָדָם מַגְבִּיר נַפְשׁוֹ הָאֱלֹהִית וְנִלְחָם כָּל כָּךְ עִם הַבַּהֲמִית — **Now when a person strengthens** the influence of **his Divine Soul and wages war against the Animal Soul,** עַד שֶׁמְּגָרֵשׁ וּמְבַעֵר הָרַע שֶׁבָּהּ מֵחָלַל הַשְּׂמָאלִי — **to the extent that he manages to expel and eliminate its evil from the left chamber** of his heart, he is now a *tzadik*.

וּבִעַרְתָּ הָרָע מִקִּרְבְּךָ וְאֵין הָרָע נֶהְפָּךְ לְטוֹב מַמָּשׁ נִקְרָא
צַדִּיק שֶׁאֵינוֹ גָמוּר וְצַדִּיק וְרַע לוֹ דְּהַיְינוּ שֶׁיֵּשׁ בּוֹ עֲדַיִין
מְעַט מִזְעֵר רַע בְּחָלָל הַשְּׂמָאלִי אֶלָּא שֶׁכָּפוּף וּבָטֵל לְטוֹב
מֵחֲמַת מִיעוּטוֹ וְלָכֵן נִדְמֶה לוֹ כִּי וַיְגָרְשֵׁהוּ וַיֵּלֶךְ לוֹ כּוּלּוֹ
לְגַמְרֵי אֲבָל בֶּאֱמֶת אֵלּוּ חָלַף וְהָלַךְ לוֹ לְגַמְרֵי כָּל הָרַע שֶׁבּוֹ

As we learned in chapter 9, the passions of the Animal Soul take initial expression in the left side of the heart, where energized blood is found that fuels its passions. This individual has achieved an impressive degree of self-mastery, to the extent that his Animal Soul no longer harbors any desire for self-gratification.

כְּמוֹ שֶׁכָּתוּב וּבִעַרְתָּ הָרָע מִקִּרְבְּךָ — **As the verse states,** *"And you shall eliminate the evil from your midst"* (*Deuteronomy* 13:6).

This verse speaks, at the literal level, of the commandment to eliminate a false prophet from the Jewish community. Here the *Tanya* reads the word *mi-kirbecha* ("from your midst") hyperliterally, "And you shall eliminate the evil *from within you,"* implying an ethical imperative to achieve self-mastery.

וְאֵין הָרָע נֶהְפָּךְ לְטוֹב מַמָּשׁ — **Yet,** if the individual has achieved an impressive degree of self-mastery, but **the evil has not been** *completely transformed* **to good,** נִקְרָא צַדִּיק שֶׁאֵינוֹ גָמוּר וְצַדִּיק וְרַע לוֹ — he **is classified as an "incomplete** *tzadik"* **or a "***tzadik* **who has (it) bad"** (*Talmud, Brachos* 7a).

In chapter 1, the *Tanya* cited the *Zohar's* definition, *"In the 'tzadik who has (it) bad'— the bad within him is suppressed by the good"* (p. 29). Now we will explore this idea in more depth.

דְּהַיְינוּ שֶׁיֵּשׁ בּוֹ עֲדַיִין מְעַט מִזְעֵר רַע בְּחָלָל הַשְּׂמָאלִי — **That is to say, there still remains** in the heart's **left chamber** of the "incomplete *tzadik"* **a minuscule amount of evil,** אֶלָּא שֶׁכָּפוּף וּבָטֵל לְטוֹב מֵחֲמַת מִיעוּטוֹ — **only, being such a small amount, it is "suppressed" and voided by the good.**

There seems to be no evidence of this small amount of residual evil. Consciously, this "incomplete *tzadik"* only loves G-d and spiritual pursuits. The physical world and its temptations have lost their allure for him. His evil has been "voided."

וְלָכֵן נִדְמֶה לוֹ כִּי וַיְגָרְשֵׁהוּ וַיֵּלֶךְ לוֹ — **And that's why he imagines that** *"he's driven it away and it's gone from him"* (*Psalms* 34:1), כּוּלּוֹ לְגַמְרֵי — **all of it, completely.**

אֲבָל בֶּאֱמֶת אֵלּוּ חָלַף וְהָלַךְ לוֹ לְגַמְרֵי כָּל הָרַע שֶׁבּוֹ — **But, in truth, if all his evil had entirely left and departed,** הָיָה נֶהְפָּךְ לְטוֹב — it wouldn't merely be *absent*, **it would have been** *converted to* a positive force, **to goodness,** מַמָּשׁ — **literally.**

The Animal Soul is part of you, and you cannot rid yourself of it. It is there, desiring all the time. You can influence *what* it desires, by directing your mind to either spiritual or physical pleasures, but you cannot stop it desiring.

היה נהפך לטוב ממש. וביאור הענין כי הנה צדיק גמור
שנהפך הרע שלו לטוב ולכן נקרא צדיק וטוב לו והוא
ע"י הסרת הבגדים הצואים לגמרי מהרע דהיינו למאוס
מאד בתענוגי עוה"ז להתענג בם בתענוגות בני אדם
למלאת תאות הגוף בלבד ולא לעבודת ה' מפני
היותם נמשכים ונשפעים מהקליפה וס"א וכל מה

15A

In an "incomplete *tzadik*," the conscious desire for physical pleasures has departed, and he appears to have completely transformed his Animal Soul for the good. But the departure of these desires is deceptive. In reality, his Animal Soul has not been *transformed* to the good; if that were the case, we would find a greater passion towards positive things and a more powerful rejection of the negative. There is still a residual indifference to evil.

וּבֵיאוּר הָעִנְיָן — Let's explore this idea.

כִּי הִנֵּה צַדִּיק גָּמוּר שֶׁנֶּהְפַּךְ הָרַע שֶׁלּוֹ לְטוֹב — Now with a "complete *tzadik*," whose evil has been *transformed* to good, וְלָכֵן נִקְרָא צַדִּיק וְטוֹב לוֹ — which is why he is referred to as "the *tzadik* who has (it) good", הוּא עַל יְדֵי — he's achieved this הֲסָרַת הַבְּגָדִים הַצּוֹאִים לִגַמְרֵי מֵהָרַע through *completely* removing his evil "soiled garments."

As we explained in the previous chapter, emotional detachment from worldly pleasures (the "soiled garments" of the Animal Soul) is a necessary step to transforming the Animal Soul.

דְּהַיְינוּ לִמְאוֹס מְאֹד בְּתַעֲנוּגֵי עוֹלָם הַזֶּה — That is to say, he is deeply repulsed by the pleasures of this world, לְהִתְעַנֵּג בָּם בְּתַעֲנוּגוֹת בְּנֵי אָדָם לְמַלְּאת תַּאֲוֹת הַגּוּף בִּלְבַד וְלֹא לַעֲבוֹדַת ה' — *i.e.,* the notion of enjoying mortal plea-sures purely to gratify the body, and not in the worship

PRACTICAL LESSONS

The hallmark of a complete transformation of the Animal Soul is: a.) to be utterly repulsed by evil, or even the notion of self-gratification; and b.) to love G-d even with the Animal Soul.

of G-d, מִפְּנֵי הֱיוֹתָם נִמְשָׁכִים וְנִשְׁפָּעִים מֵהַקְּלִיפָה וְסִטְרָא אָחֳרָא — he finds the notion repulsive **because** these pleasures **are derived from, and powered by,** *kelipah* **and** *sitra achra.*

As we have learned, there are no spiritually neutral activities. Your kosher pleasure will enhance consciousness of G-d if your intentions are to elevate the experience to a higher purpose; but, if carried out for the sake of indulgence alone, the act hides G-d and strengthens the forces of negativity (*kelipah*).

To the "complete *tzadik*," all forms of *kelipah* are utterly objectionable, even enjoying a kosher sandwich while temporarily forgetting about G-d.

וְכָל מַה שֶׁהוּא מֵהַסִּטְרָא אָחֳרָא הַצַּדִּיק גָּמוּר הוּא שׂוֹנְאוֹ בְּתַכְלִית הַשִּׂנְאָה — **And the** "complete *tzadik*" completely and utterly detests *anything* that is from the *sitra*

שהוא מהס"א הצדיק גמור הוא שונאו בתכלית השנאה
מחמת גודל אהבתו לה' וקדושתו באהבה רבה
בתענוגים וחיבה יתרה הנ"ל כי הם זה לעומת זה
כדכתיב תכלית שנאה שנאתים לאויבים היו לי חקרני
ודע לבבי וגו' וכפי ערך גודל האהבה לה' כך ערך גודל
השנאה לס"א והמיאוס ברע בתכלית כי המיאוס הוא

achra, וּקְדוּשָׁתוֹ 'לַה אַהֲבָתוֹ גּוֹדֶל מֵחֲמַת — due to his profound love for G-d and His holiness, לְעֵיל הַנִּזְכָּרִים וְחִיבָה בַּתַּעֲנוּגִים יְתֵרָה רַבָּה בְּאַהֲבָה — with an exceptional love that is "great" and "pleasurable," mentioned above (chapter 9, p. 117).

Why must the "complete *tzadik*," utterly detest *kelipah* and *sitra achra?*

זֶה לְעוּמַּת זֶה הֵם כִּי — Because *"G-d has made one opposite the other"* (Ecclesiastes 7:14; see chapter 6).

There is no spiritually neutral zone. If you love G-d, you will detest anything that opposes G-d, any act that is from *kelipah* and *sitra achra.*

'וְגוֹ לְבָבִי וְדַע חָקְרֵנִי לִי הָיוּ לְאוֹיְבִים שְׂנֵאתִים שִׂנְאָה תַכְלִית כְּדִכְתִיב — As the verse states, *"I utterly detest them; they have become my enemies; probe me, O G-d, and know my heart, etc.,"* (Psalms 139:22-23).

King David asked G-d to probe his heart: Do I utterly detest the enemies of G-d? Love of G-d and contempt for that which opposes G-d are inversely related.

בְּתַכְלִית בְּרַע וְהַמִּיאוּס אָחֳרָא לְסִטְרָא הַשִּׂנְאָה גּוֹדֶל עֵרֶךְ כָּךְ 'לַה הָאַהֲבָה גּוֹדֶל עֵרֶךְ וּכְפִי — The rule is: **Directly proportional to the level and magnitude of your love of G-d will be the intensity of your detest for the *sitra achra* and your sense of complete repulsion for evil.**

The *Tanya* uses two terms here, "detest" and "repulsion," to refer to two different experiences of emotionally rejecting evil. "Detesting" is the rejection of the *abstract* forces of *kelipah* and *sitra achra* which conceal G-d. "Repulsion" refers to the rejection of the *tangible* allure of physical pleasures.

הַשִּׂנְאָה כְּמוֹ מַמָּשׁ הָאַהֲבָה הֵפֶךְ הוּא הַמִּיאוּס כִּי — If a person has achieved a complete transformation of the Animal Soul then his loathing of, and repulsion for, evil will be as powerful as his love, **since "repulsion" is literally the opposite of love** of G-d, **as is "detesting."**

If you detest the idea of smoking because it is damaging to your health, you will inevitably be repulsed by somebody actually smoking; they go hand in hand.

16TH TEVES LEAP

The "incomplete *tzadik*" is *not* completely repulsed by physical indulgence, which tells us that there is something lacking in the way he detests evil.

הפך האהבה ממש כמו השנאה. וצדיק שאינו גמור
הוא שאינו שונא הס"א בתכלית השנאה ולכן אינו
מואס ג"כ ברע בתכלית וכל שאין השנאה והמיאוס
בתכלית ע"כ נשאר איזה שמץ אהבה ותענוג לשם
ולא הוסרו הבגדים הצואים לגמרי מכל וכל ולכן לא
נהפך לטוב ממש מאחר שיש לו איזה אחיזה עדיין
בבגדים הצואים אלא שהוא בטל במיעוטו וכלא חשיב
ולכן נקרא צדיק ורע כפוף ובטל לו. ועל כן גם אהבתו

וְצַדִּיק שֶׁאֵינוֹ גָּמוּר הוּא שֶׁאֵינוֹ שׂוֹנֵא הַסִּטְרָא אָחֳרָא בְּתַכְלִית הַשִּׂנְאָה — With the "incomplete *tzadik*," since he does not utterly detest the *sitra achra*, וְלָכֵן אֵינוֹ מוֹאֵס גַּם כֵּן בְּרַע בְּתַכְלִית — he is therefore not completely repulsed by evil either.

וְכָל שֶׁאֵין הַשִּׂנְאָה וְהַמִּיאוּס בְּתַכְלִית עַל כָּרְחָךְ נִשְׁאַר אֵיזֶה שֶׁמֶץ אַהֲבָה וְתַעֲנוּג לְשָׁם — And so long as the loathing and repulsion is not absolute, there must necessarily remain a trace of love of evil and pleasure in the *sitra achra*, וְלֹא הוּסְרוּ הַבְּגָדִים הַצּוֹאִים לְגַמְרֵי מִכֹּל וָכֹל — meaning that the "soiled garments," his attachments to physical pleasures, have not been completely and thoroughly discarded, וְלָכֵן לֹא נֶהְפַּךְ לְטוֹב מַמָּשׁ מֵאַחַר שֶׁיֵּשׁ לוֹ אֵיזֶה אֲחִיזָה עֲדַיִין בַּבְּגָדִים הַצּוֹאִים — which means that his Animal Soul has not been completely transformed to good, since it still has some attachment to "soiled garments."

Why, then, is the "incomplete *tzadik*" not drawn at all to physical indulgence?

אֶלָּא שֶׁהוּא בָּטֵל בְּמִיעוּטוֹ וּכְלָא חֲשִׁיב — Only, with the "incomplete *tzadik*" that residual attachment to gratification is devoid of influence and effectively absent, due to its insignificant presence, וְלָכֵן נִקְרָא צַדִּיק וְרַע—כָּפוּף וּבָטֵל—לוֹ — and that is why such a person is called a *tzadik* "whose evil is suppressed" by the good," and voided for him (as stated in chapter 1, from the *Zohar*).

וְעַל כֵּן גַּם אַהֲבָתוֹ לַה' אֵינָהּ בְּתַכְלִית — But it is also for this reason, the presence of residual evil, that his love of G-d lacks its full intensity, וְלָכֵן נִקְרָא צַדִּיק שֶׁאֵינוֹ גָּמוּר — which is why he is termed an "incomplete *tzadik*."

It seems incorrect to call "incomplete" someone who has totally neutralized his desire for physical pleasure. Practically speaking, this person *has* completely mastered his darker side, which no longer troubles him. The *Tanya* therefore explains that the term "incomplete" refers, not to his status as *tzadik*, but to the intensity of his love for G-d. He has enough love for G-d to achieve complete self-mastery, to be a *tzadik,* it's just that he could have more (*Notes on Tanya*).

PRACTICAL LESSONS

The rule is: the more you love G-d, the more you will be repulsed by evil. There is no neutral ground.

לה' אינו בתכלית ולכן נקרא צדיק שאינו גמור. והנה
מדרגה זו מתחלקת לרבבות מדרגות בענין בחי' מיעוט
הרע הנשאר מאחת מארבע יסודות הרעים ובענין
ביטולו במיעוטו בששים עד"מ או באלף ורבבה וכיוצא
עד"מ והן הם בחי' צדיקים הרבים שבכל הדורות
כדאיתא בגמ' דתמניסר אלפי צדיקי קיימי קמי' הקב"ה
אך על מעלת צדיק גמור הוא שאמר רשב"י ראיתי בני

12TH TEVES REGULAR

וְהִנֵּה מַדְרֵגָה זוֹ מִתְחַלֶּקֶת לְרִבְבוֹת מַדְרֵגוֹת בְּעִנְיַן בְּחִינַת מִיעוּט הָרַע הַנִּשְׁאָר — **Now this status** of the "incomplete *tzadik*," **is subdivided into tens of thousands of levels, depending on the precise nature,** both qualitatively and quantitatively, **of the minuscule evil that remains** in him.

מֵאֶחָד מֵאַרְבָּעָה יְסוֹדוֹת הָרָעִים — Qualitatively, it might be **from (the negative side of) any of the four elements** (see chapter 1, pp. 39-41), וּבְעִנְיַן בִּיטוּלוֹ בְּמִיעוּטוֹ — and quantitatively it may differ in the extent to which its influence **is voided by dilution,** בְּשִׁשִּׁים עַל דֶּרֶךְ מָשָׁל אוֹ בְּאֶלֶף וְרִבְבָה וְכַיּוֹצֵא עַל דֶּרֶךְ מָשָׁל — **such as, for example,** dilution **by sixty, or a thousand, or ten thousand** *etc.*

In Jewish Law, different prohibited substances vary in the dilution that is required to render their presence insignificant. Generally, a non-kosher substance mixed with a different kosher one, requires a sixty-times dilution of kosher to non-kosher (*Talmud, Chullin* 97b). Occasionally we find cases of a thousand times dilution (*Rambam, Commentary to Mishnah, Terumos* 10:8), and even a ten-thousand times dilution (*Mishnah, Zevachim* 8:1).

The *Tanya* cites this idea to illustrate how there can be a large variety of ways in which an entity is rendered void. Each "incomplete *tzadik*" will differ in the quantity and quality of their voided evil.

וְהֵן הֵם בְּחִינוֹת צַדִּיקִים הָרַבִּים שֶׁבְּכָל הַדּוֹרוֹת — The various levels of "incomplete *tzadik*" **account for the many** *tzadikim* **found throughout the generations,** כְּדְאִיתָא בַּגְּמָרָא דְּתַמְנֵיסַר אַלְפֵי צַדִּיקֵי קַיְימֵי קַמֵּיהּ הַקָּדוֹשׁ בָּרוּךְ הוּא — **as the** *Talmud* **states,** *"Eighteen thousand tzadikim stand before the Blessed Holy One"* (*Sukkah* 45b).

While self-mastery is extremely difficult, many throughout history have achieved the level of "incomplete *tzadik*."

SECTION TWO: THE COMPLETE TZADIK

אַךְ עַל מַעֲלַת צַדִּיק גָּמוּר הוּא שֶׁאָמַר רַבִּי שִׁמְעוֹן בֶּן יוֹחַאי — **However, it was about the level of "complete** *tzadik*," that Rabbi Shimon ben Yochai said, רָאִיתִי בְּנֵי עֲלִיָּה וְהֵם מוּעֲטִים כוּ' — *"I have seen 'elevated men,' and they are few, etc.,"* (*ibid.*).

עליה והם מועטים כו' שלכן נקראים בני עליה שמהפכין
הרע ומעלים אותו לקדושה כדאיתא בזוהר בהקדמה
שכשרצה רבי חייא לעלות להיכל ר"ש בן יוחאי שמע
קלא נפיק ואמר מאן מנכון די חשוכא מהפכן לנהורא
וטעמין מרירו למיתקא עד לא ייתון הכא וכו': ועוד
נקראים בני עליה מפני שגם עבודתם בבחי' ועשה טוב
בקיום התורה ומצותיה הוא לצורך גבוה ומעלה מעלה
עד רום המעלות ולא כדי לדבקה בו ית' בלבד לרוות
צמאון נפשם הצמאה לה' כמ"ש הוי כל צמא לכו למים

15B

שֶׁלָּכֵן נִקְרָאִים בְּנֵי עֲלִיָּה — Which is why "complete *tzadikim*" are referred to as "elevated men," שֶׁמְּהַפְּכִין הָרַע וּמַעֲלִים אוֹתוֹ לִקְדוּשָׁה — because they *transform the evil* urge of their Animal Soul and elevate it to holiness, teaching the Animal Soul to love G-d.

To demonstrate that Rabbi Shimon viewed the "elevated men" as an elite class of complete *tzadikim,* the *Tanya* cites an account from the *Zohar.*

כְּדְאִיתָא בַּזֹהַר בַּהַקְדָּמָה — As is written in the *Zohar's* introduction (1, 4a), שֶׁכְּשֶׁרָצָה רַבִּי חִיָּיא לַעֲלוֹת לְהֵיכַל רַבִּי שִׁמְעוֹן בֶּן יוֹחַאי — that when Rabbi Chiya wanted to ascend to the heavenly chamber of Rabbi Shimon ben Yochai, שָׁמַע קָלָא נָפִיק וְאָמַר מַאן — he מִנְּכוֹן דִּי חֲשׁוּכָא מְהַפְּכָן לִנְהוֹרָא וְטַעֲמִין מְרִירוּ לְמִיתְקָא עַד לָא יֵיתוּן הָכָא וְכוּ' heard *"a voice break out and say... 'Who among you has transformed darkness into light, and bitter flavors into sweet ones, before arriving here?'"*

Rabbi Shimon, who, by his own testimony, was one of the "elevated men" (*Sukkah* ibid.), required others who wished to enter his spiritual abode to be of the same stature, to have completely transformed the Animal Soul.

17TH TEVES LEAP

וְעוֹד נִקְרָאִים בְּנֵי עֲלִיָּה — There is a further reason why the term "elevated men" is applied to the "complete *tzadik,*" מִפְּנֵי שֶׁגַּם עֲבוֹדָתָם בִּבְחִינַת וַעֲשֵׂה טוֹב בְּקִיּוּם הַתּוֹרָה because, in addition to their transformation of negativity, וּמִצְוֹתֶיהָ הוּא לְצוֹרֶךְ גָּבוֹהַ even their positive activities of Torah and *mitzvah* observance are devoted exclusively to G-d, וּמַעֲלָה מַעֲלָה עַד רוּם הַמַּעֲלוֹת — higher and higher, to the greatest of heights, וְלֹא כְּדֵי לְדַבְקָה בּוֹ יִתְבָּרֵךְ בִּלְבָד — i.e., their worship is not carried out merely to attach *themselves* to G-d, לְרַוּוֹת צִמְאוֹן נַפְשָׁם הַצְּמֵאָה לַה' — to satisfy a *personal* thirsting of their souls, which naturally thirsts for G-d, כְּמוֹ שֶׁכָּתוּב הוֹי כָּל צָמֵא לְכוּ — as the verse states, *"Ho, all who are thirsty, go to the water"* (Isaiah 55:1), לַמַּיִם וּכְמוֹ שֶׁנִּתְבָּאֵר בְּמָקוֹם אַחֵר — as is explained elsewhere (chapter 41, pp. 510-16).

A second defining quality of the "complete *tzadik,*" which distinguishes him from the "incomplete *tzadik,*" is the unusually elevated quality of his worship. For most

וכמ"ש במ"א אלא כדפירשו בתיקונים איזהו חסיד
המתחסד עם קונו עם קן דיליה לייחדא קב"ה ושכינתי'
בתחתונים וכמ"ש ברעי' מהימנא פ' תצא כברא
דאשתדל בתר אבוי ואימיה דרחים לון יתיר מגרמיה
ונפשיה ורוחיה ונשמתי' כו' ומסר גרמיה למיתה למייהו

people, worship satisfies personal, spiritual inclinations, since the soul naturally thirsts for G-d. The "complete *tzadik*" surpasses even this limitation and worships G-d in a way that transcends personal needs.

אֶלָּא כְּדְפֵירְשׁוּ בַּתִּיקוּנִים אֵיזֶהוּ חָסִיד הַמִּתְחַסֵּד עִם קוֹנוֹ — **Rather** the worship of the "complete *tzadik*" **is clarified by the** *Tikunei Zohar* (1b), in its comment on the *Zohar's* teaching, *"Who is a pious one (chasid)? A person who acts kindly (mischased) with his Creator"* (*Zohar* 2, 114b).

The "complete *tzadik*" acts only for G-d. All his "kindness" is an act of worship and is not self-serving in any way.

PRACTICAL LESSONS

A complete *tzadik* worships *only for* G-d's sake, i.e., to manifest G-d's Heavenly presence in the world.

Throughout history, very few individuals have achieved this.

עִם קַן דִּילֵיהּ — In explaining this teaching of the *Zohar*, the *Tikunei Zohar* notes that the term used here for "his Creator" (*kono*) resembles the word "nest" (*kan*). The *Tikunei Zohar* explains that the "pious one" is one who acts kindly, **with "His nest...** *which is the Shechinah."*

G-d's "nest," so to speak, is the *Shechinah,* the Divine Presence on earth. The "complete *tzadik*" devotes his entire life, not for himself, but for the sake of the *Shechinah.*

לְיַיחֲדָא קוּדְשָׁא בְּרִיךְ הוּא וּשְׁכִינְתֵּיהּ בַּתַּחְתּוֹנִים — **To unite** the *Shechinah* **down in this world, with "the Blessed Holy One,"** G-d's Heavenly presence.

In Heaven, the glory of G-d's presence shines brightly, but here on earth it is eclipsed. The point of our good deeds and worship on earth is to make G-d's Heavenly presence manifest here too. The Kabbalists referred to this as "uniting the *Shechinah* with the Blessed Holy One" (see below chapter 41, p. 516). And it is to this goal that the "complete *tzadik*" devotes himself exclusively.

וּכְמוֹ שֶׁכָּתוּב בְּרַעְיָא מְהֵימְנָא פָּרָשַׁת תֵּצֵא — **As** this selfless intent **is expressed in the** *Zohar*, **in the section called** *Ra'aya Mehemna* **in the Torah portion of** *Teitzei* (*Zohar* 3, 281a), כְּבְרָא דְּאִשְׁתַּדֵּל בָּתַר אֲבוֹי וְאִימֵּיהּ דְּרָחִים לוֹן יַתִּיר מִגַּרְמֵיהּ וְנַפְשֵׁיהּ וְרוּחֵיהּ וְנִשְׁמָתֵיהּ כו' — *"Like a son who exerts himself for his father and mother, whom he loves more than himself,* more than his own **nefesh, ruach** and **neshamah,** and everything of his own he considers as worthless, existing only to carry out the will of his mother and father," וּמָסַר גַּרְמֵיהּ לְמִיתָה עֲלַייהוּ לְמִיפְרַק לוֹן כו' — *"and he is* **prepared to die for them, to redeem them** from captivity."

למיפרק לון כו' וכמ"ש במ"א. [ושניהם עולים בקנה
אחד כי ע"י הבירורים שמבררים מנוגה מעלים מיין
נוקבין ונעשי' יחודים עליונים להוריד מיין דכורין שהם

וּכְמוֹ שֶׁנִּתְבָּאֵר בְּמָקוֹם אַחֵר — **As is explained elsewhere** (see chapter 41, p. 505 and chapter 44, pp. 568-71).

SECTION THREE: THE COMPLETE TZADIK'S POWER

In this chapter we have learned two reasons why, in the *Talmud*, Rabbi Shimon referred to the "complete *tzadikim*" as "elevated men": a.) they have *elevated their Animal Souls* completely to the good; and b.) their utterly selfless, *elevated worship* causes G-d's Heavenly presence to be manifest in this world.

In this concluding, parenthetical note, the *Tanya* points to a deeper connection between these two interpretations.

[וּשְׁנֵיהֶם עוֹלִים בְּקָנֶה אֶחָד — **And both** dynamics of the "elevated men" **work in synergy.**

At the core of Judaism is the reciprocal relationship between humans and G-d. Humans make the effort to worship G-d, and G-d responds by showering His blessings and manifesting His presence accordingly. The Kabbalah refers to the spiritual energy generated by human effort as "elevating feminine waters" and the response from G-d as "drawing down masculine waters."

כִּי עַל יְדֵי הַבֵּירוּרִים שֶׁמְּבָרְרִים מִנּוֹגַהּ — **For by means of the process of refinement, through** the tremendous effort of the "complete *tzadikim*" **refining** and transforming their Animal Souls from *kelipas nogah,* מַעֲלִים מַיִּין נוּקְבִין — **"feminine waters," are elevated** (Rabbi Yitzchak Luria, *Zohar Ha-Rakia* (Lvov, 1785), p. 66b).

וְנַעֲשִׂים יְחוּדִים עֶלְיוֹנִים — The relationship between "elevating feminine waters" and "drawing down masculine waters" is one of cause and effect. The energy of the "feminine waters" **stimulates** Heavenly activity, known as **"supernal unions,"** opening fresh channels by which Heavenly energy can manifest down on earth, namely, לְהוֹרִיד מַיִּין דְּכוּרִין — **to cause "masculine waters" to be drawn down** (*ibid.*).

The efforts of the "elevated men" produce corresponding results. It is the spiritual energy generated by their *elevated Animal Souls* that actually empowers their *elevated worship* to produce its result, *i.e.,* to cause G-d's Heavenly presence to be manifest in this world. (This is the connection between the above two interpretations of "elevated men.")

How, exactly, are these "masculine waters," these Heavenly energies, manifest on earth?

שֶׁהֵם הֵם מֵימֵי הַחֲסָדִים שֶׁבְּכָל מִצְוָה וּמִצְוָה מֵרמַ"ח מִצְוֹת עֲשֵׂה — **These** energies **are nothing other than the "waters of kindness" within each of the 248 positive**

הם מימי החסדים שבכל מצוה ומצוה מרמ"ח מצות
עשה שכולן הן בחי' חסדים ומיין דכורין דהיינו המשכת
קדושת אלהותו יתברך מלמעלה למטה להתלבש
בתחתונים כמ"ש במ"א]:

mitzvos (see Rabbi Jacob Joseph of Polonne, *Toldos Ya'akov Yosef* (Jerusalem 2010), vol. 2, pp. 738-9).

A *mitzvah* is considered a "kindness" on the part of G-d since, through the *mitzvah,* Heavenly energy flows into the world. It is called *"'waters of kindness,' since water expels the kelipos, which can only ground themselves through judgment and gevurah"* (Rabbi Shmuel Vital, *Sha'ar Ha-Mitzvos, Parshas Eikev*). This is the phenomenon of "masculine waters" that we have explained.

שֶׁכּוּלָן הֵן בְּחִינַת חֲסָדִים וּמַיִּין דְּכוּרִין — **For all of** the *mitzvos* **are expressions of "kindness" and "masculine waters,"** דְּהַיְינוּ הַמְשָׁכַת קְדוּשַׁת אֱלֹהוּתוֹ יִתְבָּרֵךְ מִלְמַעְלָה לְמַטָּה — **in that they cause Heavenly, G-dly energy to be manifest below,** לְהִתְלַבֵּשׁ — **and to become "dressed" in the lowly substance** of this world. בַּתַּחְתּוֹנִים

כְּמוֹ שֶׁנִּתְבָּאֵר בְּמָקוֹם אַחֵר] — **as is explained elsewhere,** in chapters 23, 35 and 37.

This, however, leaves us with a question: If *mitzvah* observance causes "masculine waters" to be manifest on earth, why should this be unique to the "complete *tzadik*"? Surely it applies to any person who observes the *mitzvos*?

While it is true that any *mitzvah* produces this result, it is the "complete *tzadik*" to whom it really matters. Even if an ordinary person is aware of the spiritual result of his *mitzvah,* that Heavenly energies will be manifest on earth, it probably won't be overwhelmingly important to him. Only with the "complete *tzadik*," who observes a *mitzvah* for *no other reason* than to manifest G-d in the world, does this dynamic between masculine and feminine waters truly work in synergy.

CHAPTER 11

THE "RASHA"

SECTION ONE: THE INCOMPLETE RASHA

13TH TEVES REGULAR | 18TH TEVES LEAP

In chapter 1, we were introduced to five categories of human being: "the complete *tzadik*," "the incomplete *tzadik*," "the complete *rasha*," "the incomplete *rasha*," and the "inbetweener" (*beinoni*).

פרק יא וְזֶה לעומת זה רשע וטוב לו לעומת צדיק
ורע לו דהיינו שהטוב שבנפשו האלהי'
שבמוחו ובחלל הימני שבלבו כפוף ובטל לגבי הרע
מהקליפה שבחלל השמאלי וזה מתחלק גם כן לרבבות
מדרגות חלוקות בענין כמות ואיכות הביטול וכפיפת
הטוב לרע ח"ו יש מי שהכפיפה והביטול אצלו מעט
מזער ואף גם זאת אינו בתמידות ולא תדיר לפרקים
קרובים אלא לעתים רחוקים מתגבר הרע על הטוב

In the previous chapter, we took a closer look at the two different levels of *tzadik*, "incomplete" and "complete." Now we will examine their conceptual opposites, the "incomplete" and "complete" *rasha*. (In the next chapter, we will turn to the *beinoni*).

וְזֶה לְעוּמַּת זֶה — *"G-d has made **one opposite the other**"* (*Ecclesiastes* 7:14).

The forces of evil mirror the forces of good. This is true not only in the spiritual realm, but also in the way these forces express themselves in the personality.

רָשָׁע וְטוֹב לוֹ לְעוּמַּת צַדִּיק וְרַע לוֹ — The **"***rasha* **who has (it) good,"** the incomplete *rasha*, **is the conceptual opposite of the "***tzadik* **who has (it) bad,"** the incomplete *tzadik*.

As we have learned in the previous chapter, the "incomplete *tzadik*" (or "*tzadik* who has (it) bad"), is overwhelmingly good. The minuscule amount of evil that remains in him is effectively voided by the abundance of good.

Corresponding to him is the "*rasha* who has (it) good" (the incomplete *rasha*).

דְּהַיְינוּ שֶׁהַטּוֹב שֶׁבְּנַפְשׁוֹ הָאֱלֹהִית שֶׁבְּמוֹחוֹ וּבְחֲלַל הַיְמָנִי שֶׁבְּלִבּוֹ — **This means that** in the incomplete *rasha,* **the good in his Divine Soul, found both in his brain and the right chamber of his heart** (see chapter 9), כָּפוּף וּבָטֵל לְגַבֵּי הָרַע מֵהַקְּלִיפָּה שֶׁבְּחֲלַל הַשְּׂמָאלִי — **is,** at least to some extent, **suppressed and voided by the evil in the left chamber** of his heart, which comes **from *kelipah*.**

Just as the status of "incomplete *tzadik*" is subdivided into many sub-levels,

וְזֶה מִתְחַלֵּק גַּם כֵּן לְרִבְבוֹת מַדְרֵגוֹת חֲלוּקוֹת — **this status, too,** of "incomplete *rasha*" **is subdivided into many tens of thousands of different levels,** בְּעִנְיַן כַּמּוּת וְאֵיכוּת הַבִּיטּוּל וּכְפִיפַת הַטּוֹב לָרַע — **depending on the extent to which the good is suppressed and voided by the evil, quantitatively and qualitatively,** חַס וְשָׁלוֹם — **G-d forbid.**

יֵשׁ מִי שֶׁהַכְּפִיפָה וְהַבִּיטּוּל אֶצְלוֹ מְעַט מִזְעָר — **For example, at one extreme, there is the person whose good is suppressed and voided** by his evil **to a minuscule extent,** וְאַף גַּם זֹאת אֵינוֹ בִּתְמִידוּת וְלֹא תָּדִיר לִפְרָקִים קְרוֹבִים — **and even then, it might not be a permanent state or even a common one, at frequent intervals,** אֶלָּא לְעִתִּים **רְחוֹקִים** מִתְגַּבֵּר הָרַע עַל הַטּוֹב וְכוֹבֵשׁ אֶת הָעִיר קְטַנָּה הוּא הַגּוּף — **and only on rare oc-**

וְכוֹבֵשׁ אֶת הָעִיר קְטַנָּה הוּא הַגּוּף אַךְ לֹא כוּלוֹ אֶלָּא
מִקְצָתוֹ לְבַד שֶׁיִּהְיֶה סָר לְמִשְׁמַעְתּוֹ וְנַעֲשֶׂה לוֹ מֶרְכָּבָה
וּלְבוּשׁ לְהִתְלַבֵּשׁ בּוֹ א' מִשְּׁלֹשָׁה לְבוּשֶׁיהָ הַנַּ"ל דְּהַיְינוּ
אוֹ בְּמַעֲשֶׂה לְבַד לַעֲשׂוֹת עֲבֵירוֹת קַלּוֹת וְלֹא חֲמוּרוֹת
ח"ו אוֹ בְּדִיבּוּר לְבַד לְדַבֵּר אֲבַק לְשׁוֹן הָרַע וְלֵיצָנוּת
וְכַהַאי גַּוְונָא אוֹ בְּמַחֲשָׁבָה לְבַד הִרְהוּרֵי עֲבֵירָה הַקָּשִׁים
מֵעֲבֵירָה וְגַם אִם אֵינוֹ מְהַרְהֵר בַּעֲבֵירָה לַעֲשׂוֹתָהּ אֶלָּא

casions will the evil in him overwhelm the good, conquering his body, the "small city" (see chapter 9), אַךְ לֹא כוּלוֹ אֶלָּא מִקְצָתוֹ לְבַד — and even then his evil may not conquer all of his body, but only a part of it, שֶׁיִּהְיֶה סָר לְמִשְׁמַעְתּוֹ — which will obey the whim of his evil.

The "incomplete rasha," may be overcome by his evil only rarely and to a minimal extent. Nevertheless, at that moment,

וְנַעֲשֶׂה לוֹ מֶרְכָּבָה וּלְבוּשׁ לְהִתְלַבֵּשׁ בּוֹ אֶחָד מִשְּׁלֹשָׁה לְבוּשֶׁיהָ הַנִּזְכָּרִים לְעֵיל — he becomes a vehicle and "garment" for evil, which becomes "dressed" in one of his Animal Soul's three "garments" of thought, speech and action, mentioned above.

In chapter 1, the Tanya demonstrated that, technically speaking, a person is classified as "rasha" just by committing one minor sin, or even by violating a Rabbinic law (see p. 31). Here, as we speak of an "incomplete rasha" at the top end of the spectrum, who has very little evil, the Tanya gives some examples of minor infractions that he might perform.

דְּהַיְינוּ אוֹ בְּמַעֲשֶׂה לְבַד לַעֲשׂוֹת עֲבֵירוֹת קַלּוֹת — This might be: a.) in the realm of action alone, carrying out some minor transgressions, וְלֹא חֲמוּרוֹת חַס וְשָׁלוֹם — and not major ones, G-d forbid.

Since one transgression is sufficient to render a person a "rasha," it might be in the realm of action alone, leaving the other "garments" of speech and thought untarnished.

אוֹ בְּדִיבּוּר לְבַד לְדַבֵּר אֲבַק לְשׁוֹן הָרַע וְלֵיצָנוּת וְכַהַאי גַּוְונָא — Or, b.) in the realm of speech alone, speaking some borderline slander or borderline mockery, etc.

אוֹ בְּמַחֲשָׁבָה לְבַד הִרְהוּרֵי עֲבֵירָה הַקָּשִׁים מֵעֲבֵירָה — Or, c.) it may be in the realm of thought alone, "thoughts of (committing a) sexual sin, which is worse than sinning itself" (Talmud, Yoma 29a).

These thoughts are considered "worse than sin" since they contaminate a person's highest faculty, the mind (Rabbi Judah Loew (Maharal), Nesivos Olam, Nesiv ha-Perishus, chapter 2).

וְגַם אִם אֵינוֹ מְהַרְהֵר בַּעֲבֵירָה לַעֲשׂוֹתָהּ אֶלָּא בְּעִנְיַן זִיווּג זָכָר וּנְקֵיבָה בָּעוֹלָם — Or even when a person does not contemplate committing an actual sexual sin, but mere-

בענין זיווג זכר ונקיבה בעולם שעובר על אזהרת
התורה ונשמרת מכל דבר רע שלא יהרהר ביום כו'
או שהיא שעת הכושר לעסוק בתורה והוא מפנה לבו
לבטלה כדתנן באבות הניעור בלילה כו' ומפנה לבו כו'
שבאחת מכל אלה וכיוצא בהן נקרא רשע בעת ההיא
שהרע שבנפשו גובר בו ומתלבש בגופו ומחטיאו
ומטמאו ואח"כ גובר בו הטוב שבנפשו האלהי' ומתחרט

ly fantasizes **about the intercourse of male and female,** שֶׁעוֹבֵר עַל אַזְהָרַת הַתּוֹרָה
וְנִשְׁמַרְתָּ מִכָּל דָּבָר רָע — **for which he is guilty of violating a Torah prohibition,**
"Guard yourself from every evil thing" (Deuteronomy 23:10), שֶׁלֹּא יְהַרְהֵר בַּיּוֹם כוּ'
— which the *Talmud* interprets, *"Do not dwell on sexual thoughts during the day
etc.,"* (Kesubos 46a).

Another example of a transgression which is very hard to avoid, even for a pious
person, is failing to study Torah at every available moment.

אוֹ שֶׁהִיא שְׁעַת הַכּוֹשֶׁר לַעֲסוֹק בַּתּוֹרָה וְהוּא מְפַנֶּה לִבּוֹ לְבַטָּלָה
— **Or, d.) when a suitable time comes for Torah study,
and he** *"turns his heart to empty things"* (Mishnah,
Avos 3:4), כְּדִתְנָן בְּאָבוֹת הַנֵּיעוֹר בַּלַּיְלָה וְכוּ' וּמְפַנֶּה לִבּוֹ כוּ'
— **as the** *Mishnah states* in Avos (ibid.) *"One who stays
awake at night... and turns his heart to empty things
bears guilt for his soul."*

שֶׁבְּאַחַת מִכָּל אֵלֶּה וְכַיּוֹצֵא בָהֶן נִקְרָא רָשָׁע בָּעֵת הַהִיא — **In**
any of these instances, or those similar, the person is
immediately classified as a *"rasha."*

Why does even a minor transgression render the person a *rasha?*

שֶׁהָרַע שֶׁבְּנַפְשׁוֹ גּוֹבֵר בּוֹ — **Because the evil in his** Animal **Soul overwhelmed** the good in his Divine Soul,
וּמִתְלַבֵּשׁ בְּגוּפוֹ וּמַחֲטִיאוֹ וּמְטַמְּאוֹ — **and having won con-**
trol, the Animal Soul **"dressed"** itself in his body, causing it to sin and become defiled.

PRACTICAL LESSONS

Someone that sins
once a year, and
someone that sins
once a minute
have something
in common: their
evil has not been
eliminated and can
overcome them. They
are currently at war
with their darker side.

This defines the *rasha:* The Animal Soul is strong enough to overwhelm the
Divine Soul *even once,* gaining control over *even one part of the body,* regardless
of how small the transgression might be.

For the high-end "incomplete *rasha,*" who has only a minuscule amount of evil in
his Animal Soul, it will probably not take long before he regrets what he did.

וְאַחַר כָּךְ גּוֹבֵר בּוֹ הַטּוֹב שֶׁבְּנַפְשׁוֹ הָאֱלֹהִית — **Afterwards the good in his Divine Soul**
will overwhelm him, וּמִתְחָרֵט וּמְבַקֵּשׁ מְחִילָה וּסְלִיחָה מֵה' — **and he will regret** what

ומבקש מחילה וסליחה מה' וה' יסלח לו אם שב
בתשובה הראויה על פי עצת חכמינו ז"ל בשלשה
חלוקי כפרה שהיה ר' ישמעאל דורש כו' כמ"ש במ"א.
ויש מי שהרע גובר בו יותר ומתלבשי' בו כל שלשה

he did, **and request G-d's forgiveness and pardon, וַה' יִסְלַח לוֹ — and G-d will** defi-nitely **forgive him.**

How can the *Tanya* be confident that "G-d will definitely forgive him"? Because the Sages have identified the criteria for acceptable repentance. If these guidelines are followed, the person can be confident that G-d has forgiven him.

אִם שָׁב בִּתְשׁוּבָה הָרְאוּיָה עַל פִּי עֲצַת חֲכָמֵינוּ זִכְרוֹנָם לִבְרָכָה — **Provided that he has followed the guidelines of our Sages, of blessed memory, how to carry out a** min-imally **acceptable repentance.**

Why does the *Tanya* refer here to a "minimally acceptable" repentance?

We are speaking here of the "incomplete *rasha*" who still harbors some evil in his Animal Soul. If he would have carried out a more profound *teshuvah*, "out of love" (see p. 100), he would have transformed all of the evil in his Animal Soul to good. Instead, he does a "minimally acceptable" *teshuvah*, which is sufficient to erase the negative effects of his sins, but not enough to change *inside*.

That is why the "incomplete *rasha*" is a serial offender. He goes through repeated cycles of sin, remorse, *teshuvah* and then, later on, he sins again. Even after he has atoned, and has been forgiven by G-d, he is still *capable* of sin due to the residual evil in his Animal Soul. So even after *teshuvah*, in the *Tanya's* eyes, he remains an "incomplete *rasha*."

The *Tanya's* classification of *tzadik* and *rasha* looks at your *inside*, your propen-sity for evil based on what lurks in your Animal Soul. In the *Tanya's* eyes, even after you have done *teshuvah* for your sins, you are still a *rasha* so long as you have not uprooted the cause of those sins, the residual evil in your heart.

בִּשְׁלֹשָׁה חִלּוּקֵי כַפָּרָה שֶׁהָיָה רַבִּי יִשְׁמָעֵאל דּוֹרֵשׁ כו' — The criteria for a "minimally ac-ceptable" repentance are detailed in the **three levels of atonement, expounded by Rabbi Yishmael** (*Talmud, Yoma* 86a), כְּמוֹ שֶׁנִּתְבָּאֵר בְּמָקוֹם אַחֵר — **as will be ex-plained elsewhere** (see *Tanya, Igeres Ha-Teshuvah,* chapter 1).

SECTION TWO: THE WICKED — PLAGUED BY GUILT

Up until this point, we have been discussing a very mild "incomplete *rasha*" who sins minimally and occasionally. Now we turn to the other end of the spectrum, to a more severe offender.

וְיֵשׁ מִי שֶׁהָרַע גּוֹבֵר בּוֹ יוֹתֵר — **There is also the person whose evil overwhelms him more strongly,** וּמִתְלַבְּשִׁים בּוֹ כָּל שְׁלֹשָׁה לְבוּשִׁים שֶׁל הָרַע — **and** in contrast to the

לבושים של הרע ומחטיאו בעבירות חמורות יותר
ובעתים קרובים יותר אך בינתיים מתחרט ובאים לו
הרהורי תשובה מבחי׳ הטוב שבנפשו שמתגבר קצת
בינתיים אלא שאין לו התגברות כל כך לנצח את הרע
לפרוש מחטאיו לגמרי להיות מודה ועוזב ועל זה אמרו
רז"ל רשעים מלאים חרטות שהם רוב הרשעים שיש

mild *rasha,* who may just sin in one area of thought, speech or action, in this more severe case, **evil is "dressed" in all three "garments"** of thought, speech and action, וּמַחֲטִיאוֹ בַּעֲבֵירוֹת חֲמוּרוֹת יוֹתֵר וּבְעִתִּים קְרוֹבִים יוֹתֵר — **and** in contrast to the mild *rasha,* who occasionally commits minor sins, this more severe *rasha* is overwhelmed by his evil, **causing him to commit more serious sins, more frequently.**

Nevertheless, even with this *rasha,* the influence of his evil side is "incomplete," and the good within him will surface too.

וּבָאִים לוֹ מִתְחָרֵט בֵּינָתַיִם אַךְ — **But between** bouts of sin, **he will experience remorse,** הַרְהוּרֵי תְשׁוּבָה — **and thoughts of repentance will enter his mind,** מִבְּחִינַת הַטּוֹב — **from the good within his soul, which gathers a little strength in the period between** sins.

In this case, however, his good is extremely weak and cannot sway his evil.

אֶלָּא שֶׁאֵין לוֹ הִתְגַּבְּרוּת כָּל כָּךְ לְנַצֵּחַ אֶת הָרַע — **However,** the good **does not gain sufficient traction to *win over* the evil,** לִפְרוֹשׁ מֵחֲטָאָיו לְגַמְרֵי — **to lead him to completely desist from his sins** through *teshuvah,* לִהְיוֹת מוֹדֶה וְעוֹזֵב — **to be one who** *"confesses and abandons"* (*Proverbs* 28:13) his sins.

וְעַל זֶה אָמְרוּ רַבּוֹתֵינוּ זִכְרוֹנָם לִבְרָכָה רְשָׁעִים מְלֵאִים חֲרָטוֹת — **It was in reference to such a person that the Sages, of blessed memory, said,** *"The wicked are full of regrets"* (*Reishis Chochmah, Sha'ar Ha'Yirah,* chapter 3).

This refers to a severe case of the low-end "incomplete *rasha,*" who has enough good to contemplate repentance regularly, but not enough to actually repent.

שֶׁהֵם רוֹב הָרְשָׁעִים שֶׁיֵּשׁ בְּחִינַת טוֹב בְּנַפְשָׁם עֲדַיִן — **This accounts for most *resha'im,* who still harbor some good in their souls.**

Most people, even if they commit serious transgressions all the time, still harbor some influence from their Divine Souls, which manifests as thoughts of guilt.

PRACTICAL LESSONS

So long as you have not transformed your Animal Soul to good, you are likely to follow a cycle of sin, repentance and sin again. That doesn't mean that your repentance was insincere; it just wasn't deep enough to really change you.

It's possible, through many sins, to banish the Divine Soul's *influence,* but never its *presence.*

בחי' טוב בנפשם עדיין. אך מי שאינו מתחרט לעולם
ואין באים לו ההרהורי תשובה כלל נקרא רשע ורע לו
שהרע שבנפשו הוא לבדו נשאר בקרבו כי גבר כל כך
על הטוב עד שנסתלק מקרבו ועומד בבחי' מקיף עליו
מלמעלה ולכן ארז"ל כל בי עשרה שכינתא שריא:

פרק יב וְהַבֵּינוֹנִי הוא שלעולם אין הרע גובר

16B

There is an extreme case, however, where the *rasha* never entertains thoughts of repentance, since his evil has gained full dominance over him.

אַךְ מִי שֶׁאֵינוֹ מִתְחָרֵט לְעוֹלָם וְאֵין בָּאִים לוֹ הַהִרְהוּרֵי תְשׁוּבָה כְּלָל — **But a person who never feels remorse and does not have any thoughts of repentance at all,** נִקְרָא שֶׁהָרַע שֶׁבְּנַפְשׁוֹ הוּא לְבַדּוֹ — **is classified as a "***rasha* **who has (it) bad,"** רָשָׁע וְרַע לוֹ נִשְׁאָר בְּקִרְבּוֹ — in this case, **the evil in his** Animal **Soul is all that remains** as having influence **within him,** כִּי גָבַר כָּל כָּךְ עַל הַטּוֹב עַד שֶׁנִּסְתַּלֵּק מִקִּרְבּוֹ — **for** the evil **has so overwhelmed the good, that it has caused** the good **to depart from inside him,** and good now has no role in his inner life.

Of course, this does not mean that he has actually lost his Divine Soul. It is only that its *influence* has been banished.

וְעוֹמֵד בִּבְחִינַת מַקִּיף עָלָיו מִלְמַעְלָה — His good still **exists, hovering above** his body, but it does not penetrate him.

וְלָכֵן אָמְרוּ רַבּוֹתֵינוּ זִכְרוֹנָם לִבְרָכָה אַכָּל בֵּי עֲשָׂרָה שְׁכִינְתָּא שַׁרְיָא — **That is why the Sages, of blessed memory, said,** *"Over every ten, the Divine Presence rests"* (*Talmud, Sanhedrin* 39a), even if they are on the level of a "*rasha* who possesses only bad." Because when the Divine Soul's influence is banished, its presence still hovers and "rests" above the body.

CHAPTER 12

THE "INBETWEENER"

SECTION ONE: WHAT IS A BEINONI?

14TH TEVES REGULAR | 19TH TEVES LEAP

וְהַבֵּינוֹנִי — **And** now that we have clarified the different levels of *tzadikim* (who have succeeded at self-mastery), and *resha'im* (who are failing at self-mastery), we can turn our attention to the elusive intermediate category, **the** *beinoni* **("inbetweener").**

כל כך לכבוש את העיר קטנ'
להתלבש בגוף להחטיאו דהיינו ששלש' לבושי נפש
הבהמית שהם מחשבה דבור ומעשה שמצד הקליפ'
אין גוברים בו על נפש האלהית להתלבש בגוף במוח
ובפה ובשאר רמ"ח אברים להחטיאם ולטמאם ח"ו
רק שלשה לבושי נפש האלהית הם לבדם מתלבשים
בגוף שהם מחשבה דבור ומעשה של תרי"ג מצות
התורה ולא עבר עבירה מימיו ולא יעבור לעולם ולא
נקרא עליו שם רשע אפי' שעה אחת ורגע אחד כל ימיו

In chapter 1, we already demonstrated that the *beinoni*, like the *tzadik*, never actually commits a sin. (That is why Rabah, who was a *tzadik*, was able to misidentify himself as a *beinoni* — p. 33.)

הוּא שֶׁלְעוֹלָם אֵין הָרַע גּוֹבֵר כָּל כָּךְ לִכְבּוֹשׁ אֶת הָעִיר קְטַנָּה לְהִתְלַבֵּשׁ בַּגּוּף לְהַחֲטִיאוֹ — The *beinoni* is a person **whose evil *never* gains enough momentum to conquer "the small city," to influence the body to sin.**

דְּהַיְינוּ שֶׁשְּׁלשָׁה לְבוּשֵׁי נֶפֶשׁ הַבַּהֲמִית שֶׁהֵם מַחֲשָׁבָה דִּבּוּר וּמַעֲשֶׂה שֶׁמִּצַּד הַקְּלִיפָּה — **This means that the three "garments" of the Animal Soul, which are thought, speech and action of *kelipah*,** אֵין גּוֹבְרִים בּוֹ עַל נֶפֶשׁ הָאֱלֹהִית — **never overcome the Divine Soul within him,** לְהִתְלַבֵּשׁ בַּגּוּף בַּמּוֹחַ וּבַפֶּה וּבִשְׁאָר רַמַ"ח אֵבָרִים — **so as to become "dressed" in his body, brain, mouth or the other anatomical parts, which total 248** (*Mishnah, Oholos* 1:8; see p. 120), לְהַחֲטִיאָם וּלְטַמְּאָם — **causing them to sin and be defiled,** חַס וְשָׁלוֹם — **G-d forbid.**

רַק שְׁלשָׁה לְבוּשֵׁי נֶפֶשׁ הָאֱלֹהִית הֵם לְבַדָּם מִתְלַבְּשִׁים בַּגּוּף — **Only the three "garments" of the Divine Soul, they alone influence the body,** שֶׁהֵם מַחֲשָׁבָה דִּבּוּר וּמַעֲשֶׂה שֶׁל תַּרְיַ"ג — מִצְוֹת הַתּוֹרָה — **namely, the thought, speech and action of the Torah's 613 *mitzvos*.**

Externally, at the level of "garments," the *beinoni* is identical to the *tzadik*.

וְלֹא עָבַר עֲבֵירָה מִיָּמָיו — **And** once he has reached the level of *beinoni,* it is as if he **has never committed any transgression in his life,** because any trace of prior sins has been wiped away through repentance (*Notes on Tanya*).

וְלֹא יַעֲבוֹר לְעוֹלָם — **And,** at his current level, we can be reasonably assured that he **will never transgress in the future.**

וְלֹא נִקְרָא עָלָיו שֵׁם רָשָׁע אֲפִילוּ שָׁעָה אַחַת וְרֶגַע אֶחָד כָּל יָמָיו — **And** we can be confident that **even for a moment, a single second of his life, he will never** involve himself in an activity that would cause him to **be categorized as a *rasha*.**

For example, in chapter 1 we learned that even if a person himself does not sin, but could have prevented someone else from sinning and failed to do so, he is classified as a *rasha*. The *beinoni* avoids this type of activity too.

אַך מהות ועצמות נפש האלהית שהן עשר בחינותיה
לא להן לבדן המלוכה והממשלה בעיר קטנה כי אם

How, then, is a *beinoni* different from a *tzadik*? In chapters 3 to 8 we learned how the soul functions at two levels, through *powers* and *garments*. The soul's *powers* represent an inner layer of consciousness, your intellectual and emotional "operating system," which shapes the way you perceive reality and react to the outside world. The garments of thought, speech and action, represent your "interface" between the soul's powers and the outside world.

As far as the *garments* are concerned, the *beinoni* resembles the *tzadik;* both *beinoni* and *tzadik* have achieved a level of self-mastery where the garments will always be controlled exclusively by the Divine Soul. It is in the area of the soul's *powers* that the *beinoni* and *tzadik* differ significantly, as the *Tanya* will now elaborate.

אַךְ מַהוּת וְעַצְמוּת נֶפֶשׁ הָאֱלֹהִית שֶׁהֵן עֶשֶׂר בְּחִינוֹתֶיהָ — **However,** in the case of a *beinoni,* **the Divine Soul's deep core, which is its ten powers** of intellect and emotion, לֹא לָהֶן לְבַדָּן הַמְּלוּכָה וְהַמֶּמְשָׁלָה בָּעִיר קְטַנָּה — **are not the only forces** attempting to **direct and dominate the "small city."**

As we learned in chapter 9, the war between the Divine and Animal Souls initially acts itself out in the heart. The Divine Soul, whose influence emerges on the right side of the heart, wants its feelings for G-d to overflow into the left side of the heart, where the Animal Soul's emotions of self-gratification emerge. Each soul desires to saturate the heart completely.

In the case of a *tzadik*, the Divine Soul's goal has been achieved, and the Animal Soul has been silenced completely.

But with the *beinoni*, the conflict remains. At an emotional level, the *beinoni* is still torn between love of G-d and the desire for self-gratification, though he has achieved enough self-mastery not to allow these feelings to surface behaviorally in any way.

While externally the *tzadik* and *beinoni* appear identical, their inner life is likely to be quite different. The *tzadik* exists in a state of inner peace, his whole being singularly devoted to G-d. For him, worship is innate and natural. The *beinoni,* on the other hand, lives a life of inner tension, with his heart tugged by strong forces in opposing directions. For him, worship remains a strongly disciplined practice, to contain his inner negativity and selfish drives, preventing them from surfacing at any moment.

SECTION TWO: THE BEINONI WHO FEELS LIKE A TZADIK

There are times, however, when the *beinoni* does enjoy inner peace, and the urges of his Animal Soul are temporarily quietened.

בעתים מזומנים כמו בשעת קריאת שמע ותפלה שהיא
שעת מוחין דגדלות למעלה וגם למטה היא שעת
הכושר לכל אדם שאז מקשר חב"ד שלו לה' להעמיק

כִּי אִם בְּעִתִּים מְזוּמָּנִים כְּמוֹ בִּשְׁעַת קְרִיאַת שְׁמַע וּתְפִלָּה — Except on particular occasions, such as when performing the *mitzvah* of reading the *Shema* or when at prayer.

The focused meditations of the *Shema* and of prayer can temporarily generate such emotion from the Divine Soul, on the right side of the heart, that the *beinoni's* Animal Soul, on the left side, is totally overwhelmed.

שֶׁהִיא שְׁעַת מוֹחִין דְּגַדְלוּת לְמַעְלָה — Because this is a time of expanded consciousness (*mochin de-gadlus*) of the Supernal Mind.

According to the Kabbalah, your mind is influenced by the state of the Supernal Mind at any given moment: When the output signal Above is more intense, your soul can pick it up more easily, below in this world.

If the Supernal Mind is broad and flowing (*mochin de-gadlus*), you will find it easier to take principles that you believe into your heart. If the Supernal Mind is constricted (*mochin de-katnus*), your cognitive powers will still be functional, but you will find it harder to take good ideas and make them real and relevant to your life (using the faculty of *da'as*).

When the Temple stood, the Supernal Mind was in a state of permanent expansiveness. Currently, however, it fluctuates during the day: During the morning, a time of invigoration and renewal, it flows in a state of expansiveness; but in the afternoon it wanes, becoming constricted in the evening (*Sha'ar Ha-Kavanos, Sha'ar Krias Shema,* chapter 6; see Rabbi Dov Ber of Lubavitch, *Toras Chaim, Exodus,* p. 281b).

וְגַם לְמַטָּה הִיא שְׁעַת הַכּוֹשֶׁר לְכָל אָדָם שֶׁאָז מְקַשֵּׁר חָכְמָה בִּינָה וְדַעַת שֶׁלוֹ לַה' — When the Supernal Mind is in a state of expansiveness, it is also an opportune time below, for every person to connect his intellectual faculties *chochmah, binah* and *da'as* to G-d, לְהַעֲמִיק דַּעְתּוֹ בִּגְדוּלַת אֵין סוֹף בָּרוּךְ הוּא — and profoundly meditate

A CHASIDIC THOUGHT

My inner core is unrefined, leading me to have a mixture of urges towards personal gratification and towards G-d. But if I focus my mind on the *Shema* and on prayer, at a time when the Supernal Mind is in a state of "expansiveness," I will experience a temporary flooding of emotions for G-d. Then, my urge for self gratification will be temporarily silenced.

דַעְתּוֹ בִּגְדוּלַת א"ס ב"ה וּלְעוֹרֵר אֶת הָאַהֲבָה כְּרִשְׁפֵּי
אֵשׁ בֶּחָלָל הַיְמָנִי שֶׁבְּלִבּוֹ לְדָבְקָה בּוֹ בְּקִיּוּם הַתּוֹרָה
וּמִצְוֹתֶיהָ מֵאַהֲבָה שֶׁזֶּהוּ עִנְיָן הַמְבוֹאָר בִּקְרִיאַת שְׁמַע
דְּאוֹרַיְיתָא וּבִרְכוֹתֶיהָ שֶׁלְּפָנֶיהָ וּלְאַחֲרֶיהָ שֶׁהֵן מִדְּרַבָּנָן
הֵן הֲכָנָה לְקִיּוּם הַקְּרִיאַת שְׁמַע כְּמוֹ שֶׁנִּתְבָּאֵר בְּמָקוֹם
אַחֵר. וְאָז הָרַע שֶׁבֶּחָלָל הַשְּׂמָאלִי כָּפוּף וּבָטֵל לַטּוֹב הַמִּתְפַּשֵּׁט בֶּחָלָל הַיְמָנִי
מֵחָכְמָה בִּינָה וְדַעַת שֶׁבְּמוֹחַ הַמְקוּשָּׁרִים בִּגְדוּלַת א"ס ב"ה. אֲבָל

on the greatness of the Blessed Infinite Light, וּלְעוֹרֵר אֶת הָאַהֲבָה כְּרִשְׁפֵּי אֵשׁ בֶּחָלָל
הַיְמָנִי שֶׁבְּלִבּוֹ — **thereby arousing the** *"flaming fire"* (Song 8:6) **of love in the right
chamber of his heart** where the Divine Soul manifests emotionally (see chapter 9),
לְדָבְקָה בּוֹ בְּקִיּוּם הַתּוֹרָה וּמִצְוֹתֶיהָ מֵאַהֲבָה — **to attach** himself **to G-d, through the
fulfillment of the Torah and its commandments, out of love.**

שֶׁזֶּהוּ עִנְיָן הַמְבוֹאָר בִּקְרִיאַת שְׁמַע דְּאוֹרַיְיתָא — All of **this is included in the Biblical
commandment to read the *Shema*, as it has been clarified** in Rabbinic sources.

The three-fold process of: 1.) focused meditation on G-d, leading to 2.) emotional
arousal, and 3.) a renewed commitment to observe the commandments, is indicated by the commandment to recite the *Shema* every morning and evening. The text
itself indicates these three activities: 1.) *"Hear O Israel, G-d is our G-d, G-d is one"*
— focused meditation on G-d; 2.) *"And you shall love G-d, your G-d"* — emotional
arousal; 3.) *"Bind them as a sign on your hand... write them on the door-posts of
your house etc.,"* — observance of the commandments.

וּבִרְכוֹתֶיהָ שֶׁלְּפָנֶיהָ וּלְאַחֲרֶיהָ שֶׁהֵן מִדְּרַבָּנָן — **And** this meditative-emotional arousal
is also the goal **of the blessings which precede and follow** the *Shema,* **which are
required by Rabbinic law,** הֵן הֲכָנָה לְקִיּוּם הַקְּרִיאַת שְׁמַע — **since these blessings are
aimed at preparing you to fulfill the** Biblical commandment of **reading the *Shema***
with the proper mind-set, כְּמוֹ שֶׁנִּתְבָּאֵר בְּמָקוֹם אַחֵר — **as is explained elsewhere,** in
chapter 46, p. 590, and chapter 49, pp. 630-36.

וְאָז הָרַע שֶׁבֶּחָלָל הַשְּׂמָאלִי כָּפוּף וּבָטֵל לַטּוֹב הַמִּתְפַּשֵּׁט בֶּחָלָל הַיְמָנִי — **At that time, the
evil in the left chamber** of his heart, where the Animal Soul manifests itself, **is temporarily suppressed and voided by the good which has spread to the right chamber,**
מֵחָכְמָה בִּינָה וְדַעַת שֶׁבְּמוֹחַ הַמְקוּשָּׁרִים בִּגְדוּלַת אֵין סוֹף בָּרוּךְ הוּא — **by the *chochmah,*
binah and *da'as* in his brain, which are** at that time **focused on the greatness of
the Blessed Infinite Light** of G-d, and are now receiving outside assistance from the
"expanded consciousness" of the Supernal Mind.

SECTION THREE: THE SECRET OF THE BEINONI'S SELF MASTERY

During prayer the *beinoni* may be devoid of any urge towards self-gratification, so
he might come to the mistaken conclusion that he has reached the level of *tzadik*

אחר התפלה בהסתלקות המוחין דגדלות א״ס ב״ה הרי
הרע חוזר וניעור בחלל השמאלי ומתאוה תאוה לתאות
עוה״ז ותענוגיו. רק מפני שלא לו לבדו משפט המלוכה
והממשלה בעיר אינו יכול להוציא תאותו מכח אל
הפועל להתלבש באברי הגוף במעשה דבור ומחשבה
ממש להעמיק מחשבתו בתענוגי עוה״ז איך למלאת 17A

(who has completely eliminated the evil in his Animal Soul). This impression, however, will soon be shattered after the experience of prayer has ended and he loses
the assistance from "expanded consciousness."

אֲבָל אַחַר הַתְּפִלָּה בְּהִסְתַּלְקוּת הַמּוֹחִין דְּגַדְלוּת אֵין סוֹף בָּרוּךְ הוּא — **However, after
prayer, when the expanded consciousness of the** Supernal Mind of the **Blessed
Infinite Light** of G-d **departs,** the *beinoni* loses the external assistance in focusing
his mind and heart, הֲרֵי הָרַע חוֹזֵר וְנִיעוֹר בְּחָלָל הַשְּׂמָאלִי — **and consequently the evil
in the left chamber** of his heart **reemerges and awakens,** וּמִתְאַוֶּה תַּאֲוָה לְתַאֲוֹת עוֹלָם
הַזֶּה וְתַעֲנוּגָיו — **leading him to have a desire for the temptations of this world and
its pleasures.**

With the departure of his focused meditation, assisted by the outside energy of
"expanded consciousness," the *beinoni* returns to his normal, conflicted self, harboring urges for both self-gratification and devotion to G-d.

However, this does not mean to say that the *beinoni* loses his self-control and
actually follows any of these urges. As far as his "external self" is concerned, in
thought, speech and action, the *beinoni* has achieved total mastery.

15TH TEVES REGULAR | 21ST TEVES LEAP

רַק מִפְּנֵי שֶׁלֹּא לוֹ לְבַדּוֹ מִשְׁפַּט הַמְּלוּכָה וְהַמֶּמְשָׁלָה בָּעִיר — **Only, since this** evil in the
left side of the heart **is not the only ruling power prevailing over the "small city,"**
אֵינוֹ יָכוֹל לְהוֹצִיא תַּאֲוָתוֹ מִכֹּחַ אֶל הַפּוֹעַל — the evil **is unable to bring its desire to
fruition,** לְהִתְלַבֵּשׁ בְּאֶבְרֵי הַגּוּף בְּמַעֲשֶׂה דִּבּוּר — *i.e.,* **to influence the body's parts, in
action or speech,** וּמַחֲשָׁבָה מַמָּשׁ — **or in substantive thought.**

The fact that the *beinoni* can hold back from acting on his desires or speaking
about them makes sense, since we are all in direct control of what we do and say.
But if the *beinoni* has experienced the urge for self-gratification, it must have also
entered his thoughts, which are not in a person's full control. How, then, can the
Tanya claim that the *beinoni* is successful in withholding his desires even from his
thoughts?

The *Tanya* indicated the answer to this question by stressing that the *beinoni*
succeeds only in refraining from "*substantive* thought," namely,

לְהַעֲמִיק מַחֲשַׁבְתּוֹ בְּתַעֲנוּגֵי עוֹלָם הַזֶּה אֵיךְ לְמַלֹּאת תַּאֲוֹת לִבּוֹ — from allowing his
thoughts to dwell on the pleasures of this world, how to satisfy his heart's desire.

תאות לבו כי המוח שליט על הלב [כמ"ש בר"מ פ'
פינחס] בתולדתו וטבע יצירתו שכך נוצר האדם
בתולדתו שכל אדם יכול ברצונו שבמוחו להתאפק
ולמשול ברוח תאותו שבלבו שלא למלאת משאלות
לבו במעשה דבור ומחשבה ולהסיח דעתו לגמרי
מתאות לבו אל ההפך לגמרי ובפרט אל צד הקדושה

The *beinoni* cannot stop the urge for self-gratification from entering his mind. What he can do is to refrain from *intentionally dwelling* on such thoughts, *i.e.*, having "substantive thought," by diverting his mind to something else (as we will discuss further on, in chapter 28).

Still, the self-mastery of the *beinoni* is difficult to fully understand. If he harbors the desire for self-gratification in his soul, surely at some point his desires will eventually overcome him? How can we be assured that *on every occasion* he will not allow his mind to dwell on these urges, or to act on them in any way?

To answer this question, the *Tanya* cites a fundamental teaching of the *Zohar* about human nature.

כִּי הַמּוֹחַ שַׁלִּיט עַל הַלֵּב [כְּמוֹ שֶׁכָּתוּב בַּזֹּהַר פָּרָשַׁת פִּינְחָס] בְּתוֹלַדְתּוֹ וְטֶבַע יְצִירָתוֹ — Since, inherently, and in its natural capacity, *"the brain rules over the heart"* [as stated in the *Zohar*, portion of *Pinchas* 3, 224a], שֶׁכָּךְ נוֹצַר הָאָדָם בְּתוֹלַדְתּוֹ — for that is how a man is formed at birth.

שֶׁכָּל אָדָם יָכוֹל בִּרְצוֹנוֹ שֶׁבְּמוֹחוֹ לְהִתְאַפֵּק וְלִמְשׁוֹל בְּרוּחַ תַּאֲוָתוֹ שֶׁבְּלִבּוֹ — This means that any person can, with the will-power of his brain, restrain himself and take control of his heart's urges, שֶׁלֹּא לְמַלֹּאת מִשְׁאֲלוֹת לִבּוֹ בְּמַעֲשֶׂה דִּבּוּר וּמַחֲשָׁבָה — so as to prevent his heart's desires from being enacted, spoken or contemplated, וּלְהַסִּיחַ דַּעְתּוֹ לְגַמְרֵי מִתַּאֲוֹת לִבּוֹ אֶל הַהֵפֶךְ לְגַמְרֵי — to divert his attention away from his heart's urges entirely, to something completely different.

By stressing that the "brain rules over the heart" as a *natural function,* the *Tanya* takes our discussion temporarily away from the war between good and evil. Your ability to divert a certain negative thought, or to refrain from a particular destructive action, does not depend on your level of self-mastery or on tapping into the powers

---

A CHASIDIC THOUGHT

No special talent must be learned for me to be in total control of my thought, speech or action. Through will-power alone ("the brain"), I can give or withhold active expression to any of my feelings. That doesn't mean it's *easy* for me to be in control, but it's *possible*.

כדכתיב וראיתי שיש יתרון לחכמה מן הסכלות כיתרון
האור מן החושך פי' כמו שהאור יש לו יתרון ושליטה
וממשלה על החושך שמעט אור גשמי דוחה הרבה מן
החשך שנדחה ממנו מאליו וממילא כך נדחה ממילא
סכלות הרבה של הקליפה וס"א שבחלל השמאלי

of good in the universe; it is simply *a function of the human condition* — your brain is able to exert sufficient will-power to control your actions and substantive thoughts.

In addition to this physical power to control the human urge, there is a metaphysical advantage too.

וּבִפְרָט אֶל צַד הַקְּדוּשָׁה — **This is particularly true** when you are attempting to coerce your will **in the direction of holiness,** כְּדִכְתִיב וְרָאִיתִי שֶׁיֵּשׁ יִתְרוֹן לַחָכְמָה מִן הַסֵּכְלוּת כִּיתְרוֹן הָאוֹר מִן הַחוֹשֶׁךְ — **as the verse states,** *"And I saw that there is an advantage to wisdom over stupidity, like the advantage of light over darkness"* (Ecclesiastes 2:13), פֵּירוּשׁ כְּמוֹ שֶׁהָאוֹר יֵשׁ לוֹ יִתְרוֹן וּשְׁלִיטָה וּמֶמְשָׁלָה עַל הַחוֹשֶׁךְ — **meaning that just as light has the "advantage" of control and dominance over darkness,** שֶׁמְּעַט אוֹר גִּשְׁמִי דּוֹחֶה הַרְבֵּה מִן הַחֹשֶׁךְ — **in that, physically, a small amount of light will push away a lot of darkness,** שֶׁנִּדְחֶה מִמֶּנּוּ מֵאֵלָיו וּמִמֵּילָא — **which is displaced automatically and effortlessly,** כָּךְ נִדְחֶה מִמֵּילָא סְכְלוּת הַרְבֵּה שֶׁל הַקְּלִיפָּה וְסִטְרָא אָחֳרָא שֶׁבֶּחָלָל הַשְּׂמָאלִי — **in the same way, a lot of "stupidity" of *kelipah* and *sitra achra* in the left chamber** of the heart **will be automatically pushed away** by a small amount of "light" from the Divine Soul.

It goes without saying that wisdom is preferable to stupidity, and light is preferable to darkness. Ecclesiastes comes to teach us the *dynamic* through which wisdom dispels stupidity. When you light a small candle in a large, dark room, you can suddenly see throughout the entire room. The same is true with spiritual enlightenment: As soon as an insight into higher living resonates with you as true, years or even decades of prior confusion can be instantly resolved.

The Divine Soul's advantage over the Animal Soul is that "wisdom (the Divine Soul) dispels stupidity (the Animal Soul)," effortlessly, just as light dispels darkness.

However, this does not violate the principle, *"G-d has made one opposite the other"* (Ecclesiastes 7:14), that the forces of evil equally match the forces of good (so as to give you free choice). It's just that good and evil pull

PRACTICAL LESSONS

Your brain (will-power) naturally rules over your heart (emotions). You might not be able to control your urges, but with your will-power you can prevent the urges from ever affecting your behavior.

"A small amount of light will push away a lot of darkness." Evil's strength is that it is tangible; its weakness is that it is instantly dispelled by spiritual enlightenment.

[כמאמר רז"ל אלא אם כן נכנס בו רוח שטות וכו']
מפני החכמה שבנפש האלהית שבמוח אשר רצונה
למשול לבדה בעיר ולהתלבש בשלשה לבושיה הנ"ל
בכל הגוף כולו כנ"ל שהם מחשבה דבור ומעשה תרי"ג
מצות התורה כנ"ל ואעפ"כ אינו נקרא צדיק כלל מפני
שיתרון הזה אשר לאור נפש האלהית על החושך וסכלות

you in different, but ultimately equal, ways. Evil's special allure is that its temptation is tangible and worldly. But evil's great weakness is that its bubble can burst instantly with a little wisdom and enlightenment.

[כְּמַאֲמַר רַבּוֹתֵינוּ זִכְרוֹנָם לִבְרָכָה אֶלָּא אִם כֵּן נִכְנַס בּוֹ רוּחַ שְׁטוּת וְכוּ'] — **As our Sages,** of blessed memory, taught, *"A man will not commit a sin unless a delusional spirit enters him" etc.,* (Talmud, Sotah 3a), מִפְּנֵי הַחָכְמָה שֶׁבַּנֶּפֶשׁ הָאֱלֹהִית שֶׁבַּמּוֹחַ — and the delusion caused by the Animal Soul can be instantly dispelled **by the wisdom of the Divine Soul, found in the brain,** אֲשֶׁר רְצוֹנָהּ לִמְשׁוֹל לְבַדָּהּ בָּעִיר — **whose will is to have exclusive control of the** "small **city,"** וּלְהִתְלַבֵּשׁ בִּשְׁלֹשָׁה לְבוּשֶׁיהָ הַנִּזְכָּרִים — **and to express itself in the three "garments"** לְעֵיל בְּכָל הַגּוּף כּוּלוֹ כַּנִּזְכָּר לְעֵיל — **mentioned above, throughout the entire body, as mentioned above,** שֶׁהֵם מַחֲשָׁבָה — **namely, the thought, speech and** דִּבּוּר וּמַעֲשָׂה שֶׁל תַּרְיַ"ג מִצְוֹת הַתּוֹרָה כַּנִּזְכָּר לְעֵיל — **action of the 613** *mitzvos* **of the Torah, mentioned above.**

SECTION FOUR: THE DEEP CORE OF THE BEINONI

16TH TEVES REGULAR | 22ND TEVES LEAP

וְאַף עַל פִּי כֵן אֵינוֹ נִקְרָא צַדִּיק כְּלָל — **Nevertheless,** despite absolute mastery over thought, speech and action, this person **could not in any way be classified as a** *tzadik.* He is neither a "complete *tzadik,*" nor even an "incomplete *tzadik.*"

מִפְּנֵי שֶׁיִּתְרוֹן הַזֶּה אֲשֶׁר לְאוֹר נֶפֶשׁ הָאֱלֹהִית עַל הַחוֹשֶׁךְ וְסִכְלוּת שֶׁל הַקְּלִיפָה הַנִּדְחָה מִמֵּילָא — **Because this advantage of the Divine Soul's light, that it automatically dis-**

A CHASIDIC THOUGHT

My desire to sin arises from my Animal Soul's delusion that I am a separate fragment, dislocated from the energy of G-d that lies behind all creation. A "delusional spirit" may render me temporarily unaware of my connectedness with G-d and my intrinsic oneness with every other person. But just as light dispels darkness, a lie soon becomes self-evident once true reality begins to emerge.

של הקליפה הנדחה ממילא אינו אלא בשלשה לבושֵׁיּ
הנ״ל ולא במהותה ועצמותה על מהותה ועצמותה של
הקליפה כי מהותה ועצמותה של נפש הבהמית
שמהקליפה שבחלל השמאלי לא נדחה כלל ממקומו
בבינוני אחר התפלה שאין רשפי אש אהבת ה׳
בהתגלות לבו בחלל הימני כי אם תוכו רצוף אהבה

pels the darkness and foolishness of *kelipah* **in the Animal Soul,** אֵינוֹ אֶלָּא בִּשְׁלֹשָׁה
לְבוּשֶׁיהָ הַנִּזְכָּרִים לְעֵיל — **functions only** at the superficial layers of the soul, **in the
three "garments" mentioned above** of thought, speech and action, וְלֹא בְּמַהוּתָהּ
וְעַצְמוּתָהּ עַל מַהוּתָהּ וְעַצְמוּתָהּ שֶׁל הַקְּלִיפָּה — **but it does not** help **the deep core** of
the Divine Soul in its war **against the deep core** of the Animal Soul, which is **from**
kelipah.

Imagine that in a debate you utterly refute one of your opponent's arguments
with an intelligent comment, over which everyone is in agreement. To every foolish
argument he raises, you have an intelligent counter-argument.

You may win the debate, but you have only succeeded in *deflecting* his attacks. It
is unlikely that you have actually *convinced* your opponent that you are right.

The same is true of the *beinoni*. To every attack from his Animal Soul, the *beinoni*
has an effective counter-attack from the wisdom and "light" of his Divine Soul. But
that does not mean that his Animal Soul has been convinced by his Divine Soul.

כִּי מַהוּתָהּ וְעַצְמוּתָהּ שֶׁל נֶפֶשׁ הַבַּהֲמִית שֶׁמֵּהַקְּלִיפָּה שֶׁבֶּחָלָל הַשְּׂמָאלִי לֹא נִדְחָה כְּלָל
מִמְּקוֹמָה בַּבֵּינוֹנִי — **Because, in the** *beinoni*, **the Animal Soul's** emotional **deep core**
of *kelipah,* **in the heart's left chamber, has not been displaced at all.**

The primordial "Shattering of the Vessels," caused damage primarily to the universe's emotions (see p. 110). That is the inner reason why the *beinoni* is unable to
heal the deep core of his Animal Soul, which is emotional in nature. This cosmic flaw
will be healed only with the Messianic Era (see *Etz Chaim,* 9:6; below chapter 37), or
close to it (*Toras Menachem, Sefer Ha-Sichos* 5751, volume 2, pp. 532-3).

אַחַר הַתְּפִלָּה — And, as we have seen, this becomes evident **after prayer,** שֶׁאֵין רִשְׁפֵּי
אֵשׁ אַהֲבַת ה׳ בְּהִתְגַּלּוּת לִבּוֹ בֶּחָלָל הַיְמָנִי — **when his fiery, flaming love for G-d is no**
longer awakened in his heart, in the right chamber. Then, the dormant *kelipah* in
the left side, which was silenced during prayer, re-awakens.

This doesn't mean that the *beinoni's* Divine Soul doesn't shine at all after prayer
and that he doesn't love G-d all day. It's only that during prayer, the love is intense
enough to saturate all of his heart and completely quieten his Animal Soul; whereas,
during the rest of the day, the Divine Soul's voice, while present, is more muted.

כִּי אִם תּוֹכוֹ רָצוּף אַהֲבָה מְסוּתֶּרֶת — **After** prayer, during the rest of the day, the
beinoni's heart is *"inlaid inside with love"* (*Song* 3:10), **but only** a milder form of

מְסוּתֶּרֶת שֶׁהִיא אַהֲבָה הַטִּבְעִית שֶׁבַּנֶּפֶשׁ הָאֱלֹהִית

כמ"ש לְקַמָּן וַאֲזַי יָכוֹל לִהְיוֹת סִכְלוּת הַכְּסִיל הָרַע

בְּהִתְגַּלּוּ' לִבּוֹ בַּחֲלָל הַשְּׂמָאלִי לְהִתְאַוּוֹת תַּאֲוָה לְכָל עִנְיְינֵי

גַּשְׁמִיּוּת עוֹה"ז בֵּין בְּהֶיתֵּר בֵּין בְּאִיסוּר ח"ו כְּאִלּוּ לֹא

הִתְפַּלֵּל כְּלָל אֶלָּא שֶׁבְּדָבָר שֶׁבָּאִיסוּר אֵינוֹ עוֹלֶה בְּדַעְתּוֹ

לַעֲשׂוֹת הָאִיסוּר בְּפוֹעַל מַמָּשׁ ח"ו אֶלָּא הַהִרְהוּרֵי עֲבֵירָה

17B

שֶׁהִיא אַהֲבָה love, known as ***ahavah mesuteres*** (*"dormant love"* — *Proverbs* 27:5), הַטִּבְעִית שֶׁבַּנֶּפֶשׁ הָאֱלֹהִית — **which is the innate love of the Divine Soul** which everyone naturally experiences, כְּמוֹ שֶׁיִּתְבָּאֵר לְקַמָּן — **as will be explained later,** in chapters 18-19 and 44.

Every Divine Soul possesses a natural love for G-d. In some individuals this may be hidden, obscured by the selfish interests of the Animal Soul, but it is always present. That's why it's called "hidden love," to stress that everyone has it, even if it is not yet manifest (see chapter 19). But it is not *always* hidden; in fact with the *beinoni,* the so-called "hidden" love is actually revealed and conscious during the day.

Being an innate property of the soul, the "hidden love" is undeveloped and mild in comparison to the "flaming" love aroused by meditation and prayer.

וַאֲזַי יָכוֹל לִהְיוֹת סִכְלוּת הַכְּסִיל הָרַע בְּהִתְגַּלּוּת לִבּוֹ בַּחֲלָל הַשְּׂמָאלִי — **And then,** after prayer when the more intense love subsides, **it becomes possible for the stupidity of *"the fool"*** (*Ecclesiastes* 2:14), **the evil** of the Animal Soul (*Ecclesiastes Rabah* 4:13) **to be expressed in the left chamber of his heart,** לְהִתְאַוּוֹת תַּאֲוָה לְכָל עִנְיְינֵי גַּשְׁמִיּוּת עוֹלָם הַזֶּה — **to desire the temptations of everything in this physical world,** בֵּין בְּהֶיתֵּר בֵּין בְּאִיסוּר חַס וְשָׁלוֹם — **whether they be permitted or, G-d forbid, prohibited,** כְּאִלּוּ לֹא הִתְפַּלֵּל כְּלָל — now it is **as if he had not prayed at all.**

The *tzadik* is not tempted by the pleasures of this world as a pursuit in itself, since he finds the notion of unadulterated self-gratification disgusting. The *beinoni,* on the other hand, is still drawn to this type of activity.

SECTION FIVE: THE BEINONI'S MIND CONTROL

אֶלָּא שֶׁבְּדָבָר אִיסוּר — **Nevertheless, in a case of** his desire **for something forbidden,** אֵינוֹ עוֹלֶה בְּדַעְתּוֹ לַעֲשׂוֹת הָאִיסוּר בְּפוֹעַל מַמָּשׁ — **it does not cross his mind to actually violate the prohibition** or to fail to observe a positive command, חַס וְשָׁלוֹם — **G-d forbid.**

אֶלָּא הַהִרְהוּרֵי עֲבֵירָה הַקָּשִׁים מֵעֲבֵירָה — **Rather,** they remain as mere ***"thoughts of sin, which are worse than sinning itself"*** (*Talmud, Yoma* 29a; see chapter 11, p. 133).

The *beinoni* cannot stop thoughts of sin from popping into his mind, even though the notion of actually transgressing is far from him. And even when such thoughts do arise, he quickly pushes them out of his mind.

הקשים מעבירה יכולים לפעול לעלות למוחו ולבלבלו
מתורה ועבודה וכמארז"ל ג' עבירות אין אדם ניצול מהן
בכל יום הרהור עבירה ועיון תפלה כו' רק שלזה מועיל
הרשימו במוחין ויראת ה' ואהבתו המסותרת בחלל

יְכוֹלִים לִפְעוֹל לַעֲלוֹת לְמוֹחוֹ וּלְבַלְבְּלוֹ מִתּוֹרָה וַעֲבוֹדָה — These thoughts **can cross his mind leading to a distraction from Torah and worship,** וּכְמַאֲמַר רַבּוֹתֵינוּ זִכְרוֹנָם לִבְרָכָה ג' עֲבֵירוֹת אֵין אָדָם נִיצוֹל מֵהֶן בְּכָל יוֹם הִרְהוּר עֲבֵירָה וְעִיוּן תְּפִלָּה כו' — **as our Sages, of blessed memory, taught,** *"Each day, there are three sins from which a man cannot save himself: thoughts of sin,* failure to **concentrate during prayer** *etc.,"* (*Talmud, Bava Basra* 164b).

The *Tanya* does not cite the Talmud's third example of a sin committed daily by the average person, which is "borderline slander," since this is an activity of speech, a faculty over which the *beinoni* has indeed achieved full mastery. But sinful and distracting thoughts will still pop into his head, both during the day, and, sometimes, during prayer. (For while the *beinoni* does pray with fervor, arousing love for G-d, he will have momentary lapses too.)

17TH TEVES REGULAR | 23RD TEVES LEAP

How can the *beinoni* successfully deflect all of his negative urges? We know that it is *possible*, since "the brain rules over the heart." But the brain only overcomes the heart by sheer will-power (as we learned above, *"any person can, with the will-power of his brain, restrain himself and take control of his heart's urges"*). How does the *beinoni* muster enough will-power to control *every* urge of his heart?

רַק שֶׁלָּזֶה מוֹעִיל הָרְשִׁימוּ בַּמּוֹחִין — **Rather, for this purpose** of ensuring that the "mind rules over the heart" on every occasion, the *beinoni* **benefits from the residual effects** of meditative prayer **in his brain,** that linger after the prayers are completed.

The *beinoni* has lost the intense experience of meditative prayer which temporarily whitewashed all urges of self-gratification, and he has returned to his "default"

PRACTICAL LESSONS

When you recite the *Shema* **and pray, if you meditate to the point that you get excited about G-d, that energy will help you exert your will-power for the good during the rest of the day.**

state, where urges do rise from his heart to his mind. Nevertheless, there are some after-effects of prayer on the mind during the rest of the day. Urges continue to rise from the heart, "as if he had not prayed at all," but the residual effects of prayer on the brain do sharpen its abilities to successfully "rule over the heart."

וְיִרְאַת ה' וְאַהֲבָתוֹ הַמְסוּתֶּרֶת בְּחָלָל הַיְמָנִי — The residual effects of prayer are sufficient to stimulate his innate **reverence of G-d and love** of G-d, which remain **hidden in the right chamber** of his heart, לְהִתְגַּבֵּר וְלִשְׁלוֹט עַל הָרַע הַזֶּה הַמִּתְאַוֶּה תַּאֲוָה —

הימני להתגבר ולשלוט על הרע הזה המתאוה תאוה
שלא להיות לו שליטה וממשלה בעיר להוציא תאותו
מכח אל הפועל להתלבש באברי הגוף ואפי' במוח
לבדו להרהר ברע אין לו שליטה וממשלה להרהר ח"ו
ברצונו שבמוחו שיקבל ברצון ח"ו הרהור זה הרע
העולה מאליו מהלב למוח כנ"ל אלא מיד בעלייתו לשם
דוחהו בשתי ידים ומסיח דעתו מיד שנזכר שהוא
הרהור רע ואינו מקבלו ברצון אפי' להרהר בו ברצון

so that whenever the *beinoni* **feels a desire** for self-gratification, **he will be strong and triumph over this evil,** שֶׁלֹּא לִהְיוֹת לוֹ שְׁלִיטָה וּמֶמְשָׁלָה בָּעִיר — **preventing it from gaining control and dominance over** his body, the **"small** city" — לְהוֹצִיא תַּאֲוָתוֹ — **and from bringing its desire to fruition,** לְהִתְלַבֵּשׁ בְּאֶבְרֵי הַגּוּף — מִכֹּחַ אֶל הַפּוֹעַל **to influence the limbs of** his **body.**

PRACTICAL LESSONS

In addition to total control over your behavior, you also have a large degree of control over your thoughts. You cannot stop inappropriate thoughts from entering your mind, but as soon as you become aware of them, you can choose to divert your mind to different thoughts.

The residual effects of love and reverence of G-d during prayer help the *beinoni* later in the day, not only with his inner struggle against speaking or doing something inappropriate, but also in his particularly challenging war against sinful thoughts.

וַאֲפִילוּ בַּמּוֹחַ לְבַדּוֹ לְהַרְהֵר בְּרָע — **And** the residual effects of prayer help the *beinoni* not to sin **even in the mind alone, to have bad thoughts,** אֵין לוֹ שְׁלִיטָה וּמֶמְשָׁלָה לְהַרְהֵר חַס וְשָׁלוֹם בִּרְצוֹנוֹ שֶׁבְּמוֹחוֹ — **because evil in the** left side of the *beinoni's* heart **does not have the control nor dominance to overcome the will-power of his brain, to make him contemplate** such thoughts, **G-d forbid.**

As we have seen, the evil in the left side of the *beinoni's* heart is sufficient to cause "bad thoughts" to pop into the *beinoni's* head; but it is not powerful enough to overcome the willpower in the *beinoni's* mind, which chooses not to dwell upon such thoughts.

שֶׁיְּקַבֵּל בִּרְצוֹן חַס וְשָׁלוֹם הִרְהוּר זֶה הָרָע הָעוֹלֶה מֵאֵלָיו מֵהַלֵּב לַמּוֹחַ — It stops him **from willingly embracing this bad thought, G-d forbid, which has risen involuntarily from his heart to his brain,** כַּנִּזְכָּר לְעֵיל — **as mentioned above** (p. 142).

אֶלָּא מִיָּד בַּעֲלִיָּיתוֹ לְשָׁם דּוֹחֵהוּ בִּשְׁתֵּי יָדַיִם — **Rather, as soon as** the bad thought **reaches** his mind, **he dismisses it** vigorously **"with two hands,"** וּמַסִּיחַ דַּעְתּוֹ מִיָּד — **i.e., as soon as** he realizes that it is a bad thought, he שֶׁנִּזְכָּר שֶׁהוּא הִרְהוּר רָע — **averts his mind** from it, and thinks about something else, וְאֵינוֹ מְקַבְּלוֹ בְּרָצוֹן — **and he refuses to willingly embrace** the thought, אֲפִילוּ לְהַרְהֵר בּוֹ בְּרָצוֹן — **not even to**

וכ"ש להעלותו על הדעת לעשותו ח"ו או אפי' לדבר
בו כי המהרהר ברצון נק' רשע באותה שעה והבינוני
אינו רשע אפי' שעה אחת לעולם. וכן בדברים
שבין אדם לחבירו מיד שעולה לו מהלב למוח איזו
טינא ושנאה ח"ו או איזו קנאה או כעס או קפידא
ודומיהן אינו מקבלן כלל במוחו וברצונו ואדרבה המוח
שליט ומושל ברוח שבלבו לעשות ההפך ממש
להתנהג עם חבירו במדת חסד וחיבה יתרה מודעת לו
לסבול ממנו עד קצה האחרון ולא לכעוס ח"ו וגם שלא

fantasize about it deliberately, וְכָל שֶׁכֵּן לְהַעֲלוֹתוֹ עַל הַדַּעַת לַעֲשׂוֹתוֹ חַס וְשָׁלוֹם — and **certainly not to consider actually doing it, G-d forbid,** אוֹ אֲפִילוּ לְדַבֵּר בּוֹ — or even **to talk about it.**

כִּי הַמְהַרְהֵר בְּרָצוֹן נִקְרָא רָשָׁע בְּאוֹתָהּ שָׁעָה — **For someone who deliberately fantasizes is classified as a** *rasha* **at that moment,** וְהַבֵּינוֹנִי אֵינוֹ רָשָׁע אֲפִילוּ שָׁעָה אַחַת לְעוֹלָם — **and** as we have learned at the beginning of this chapter, **the** *beinoni* never allows himself to become a *rasha*, **even for a single moment.**

The *beinoni's* self-control extends over both his personal religiosity and his behavior towards others.

וְכֵן בִּדְבָרִים שֶׁבֵּין אָדָם לַחֲבֵירוֹ — **Also in human relationships** the *beinoni* exhibits **complete self-control,** מִיָּד שֶׁעוֹלֶה לוֹ מֵהַלֵּב לַמּוֹחַ אֵיזוֹ טִינָא וְשִׂנְאָה חַס וְשָׁלוֹם — **as soon as a thought of ill-will or hatred, G-d forbid, rises from his heart to his mind,** אוֹ אֵיזוֹ קִנְאָה אוֹ כַּעַס אוֹ קְפֵידָא וְדוֹמֵיהֶן — **or any** thoughts of **envy, anger, or resentment, etc.,** אֵינוֹ מְקַבְּלָן כְּלָל בְּמוֹחוֹ וּבִרְצוֹנוֹ — **he categorically refuses to embrace** those thoughts **in his mind or with his will.**

However, in this case, it is not sufficient for the *beinoni* to merely repress his negative *thought*. He also needs to *act* in a contrary fashion,

וְאַדְרַבָּה הַמּוֹחַ שַׁלִּיט וּמוֹשֵׁל בָּרוּחַ שֶׁבְּלִבּוֹ — **On the contrary, it is his mind that controls and dominates the inclination of his heart,** לַעֲשׂוֹת הַהֶפֶךְ מַמָּשׁ — **to do the exact opposite,** לְהִתְנַהֵג עִם חֲבֵירוֹ בְּמִדַּת חֶסֶד וְחִיבָּה יְתֵרָה מוּדַעַת לוֹ — **to act in a kind way towards the individual, showing him extra affection.**

Even if another person acts abominably, the self-mastery of the *beinoni* demands a positive, loving response, devoid of any anger or resentment.

But is there any limit to the degradation the *beinoni* is required to suffer, before seeking some retribution?

לִסְבּוֹל מִמֶּנּוּ עַד קָצֶה הָאַחֲרוֹן וְלֹא לִכְעוֹס חַס וְשָׁלוֹם — He should **tolerate** the antagonist **to extreme limits, without becoming angry, G-d forbid,** וְגַם שֶׁלֹּא לְשַׁלֵּם לוֹ כְּפָעֳלוֹ — **and also to refrain from repaying** the antagonist **his just deserts,** even for the

לשלם לו כפעלו ח"ו אלא אדרבה לגמול לחייבים
טובות כמ"ש בזהר ללמוד מיוסף עם אחיו:

sake of justice and not out of anger, for this would be violate the prohibition not to *"take revenge nor bear a grudge against the members of your people"* (*Leviticus* 19:18), חַס וְשָׁלוֹם — **G-d forbid.**

אֶלָּא אַדְרַבָּה לִגְמוֹל לְחַיָּיבִים טוֹבוֹת — **Rather, on the contrary,** *"repay the guilty with positive acts"* (liturgy, *Bircas Ha-Gomel*).

You are the worst judge if someone has wronged you, since personal bias is so strong. But if you could be genuinely assured that somebody had been unfair to you or caused you harm, wouldn't a measured response be appropriate?

PRACTICAL LESSONS

If someone is mean or hurtful to you, remember that this is only happening because G-d felt that it would be helpful for the evolution of your soul.

Never seek revenge against people that hurt you. Actually, you should be nice to them, because, despite their malicious intent, they have really helped you. Either they have caused you to learn an important lesson or they have done something that will benefit you later on.

If somebody wronged you, *that misfortune was meant to happen to you,* regardless of who perpetrated it. Your antagonist happened to "volunteer" for the job, but if he would not have done so, G-d would have found another willing agent to do His work. For reasons that you probably can't fathom, that perceived "misfortune" was a necessary experience for the evolution of your soul — as the Sages put it, *"Everything that G-d does is for the good"* (*Talmud, Brachos* 60b). So, ironically, you should be *grateful* to your antagonist for sending you an experience which was valuable to you. (Of course, that was not the antagonist's intention, but if someone really helps you, you ought to repay them for the real value of their actions and not their motives).

כְּמוֹ שֶׁכָּתוּב בַּזֹּהַר לִלְמוֹד מִיּוֹסֵף עִם אֶחָיו — **As stated in the** *Zohar* (1, 201a), **we should learn from Joseph and the way he treated his brothers.**

When Joseph revealed his identity to his brothers, he said, *"Don't be upset or angry with yourselves that you sold me to this place, for... G-d sent me ahead of you to ensure your survival in the land..."* (*Genesis* 45:4-8).

In most cases we can't fathom why misfortunes happen to us, and we are required to exercise our faith in Divine Providence. But from the case of Joseph and his brothers, we see an overt example how, even when our eyes perceive only human brutality, Providence is judiciously at work. The *Tanya* stresses that we ought "to learn from Joseph and his brothers" and act kindly towards all our antagonists in every situation, because this Biblical example is a model for all human interaction (*Notes on Tanya*).

18A

פרק יג ובזה יובן לשון מאמרז"ל בינונים זה וזה
שופטן [פי' יצר טוב ויצר הרע]
דכתיב כי יעמוד לימין אביון להושיע משופטי נפשו
ולא אמרו זה וזה מושלים ח"ו כי כשיש איזו שליטה
וממשלה ליצר הרע בעיר קטנה אפי' לפי שעה קלה
נקרא רשע באותה שעה אלא היצה"ר אינו רק עד"מ

CHAPTER 13

THE BEINONI'S COMPLEX LIFE

SECTION ONE: THE BEINONI'S DEFAULT LEVEL

18TH TEVES REGULAR | 24TH TEVES LEAP

וּבְזֶה יוּבַן לְשׁוֹן מַאֲמַר רַבּוֹתֵינוּ זִכְרוֹנָם לִבְרָכָה — **With this** insight into the nature of the *beinoni* from chapter 12, **we can understand the teaching of our Sages, of blessed memory,** cited in chapter 1, בֵּינוֹנִים זֶה וְזֶה שׁוֹפְטָן — *"in the case of 'inbetweeners,' both good and bad impulses are their internal judges of what to do or not to do, etc.,"* (*Talmud, Brachos* 61b), [פֵּירוּשׁ יֵצֶר טוֹב וְיֵצֶר הָרָע] — **meaning** that they are guided by the *yetzer tov* (impulse to good) and the *yetzer hara* (impulse to evil).

דִּכְתִיב כִּי יַעֲמוֹד לִימִין אֶבְיוֹן לְהוֹשִׁיעַ מִשּׁוֹפְטֵי נַפְשׁוֹ — The *Talmud* (*ibid.*) cites proof, *"For the verse states, 'He (G-d) stands at the right hand of the poor person, to save him from those that guide his soul'"* (*Psalms* 109:31).

In chapter 12 we discussed how the *beinoni*, while torn inside between his two impulses, never allows his *yetzer hara* to control his behavior for one moment. With this in mind, we can now appreciate the *Talmud's* precise choice of wording that the *beinoni* has two internal "judges," the *yetzer tov* and *yetzer hara*.

וְלֹא אָמְרוּ זֶה וְזֶה מוֹשְׁלִים — The *Talmud* **did not say** that the *beinoni* is **"ruled" by both** impulses, which would imply that the *yetzer hara* would actually have some real control over his behavior, חַס וְשָׁלוֹם — **G-d forbid,** but merely that the *yetzer hara* "judges" the *beinoni* internally, voicing its opinion. That opinion, however, is never listened to by the *beinoni* in practice.

כִּי כְּשֶׁיֵּשׁ אֵיזוֹ שְׁלִיטָה וּמֶמְשָׁלָה לַיֵּצֶר הָרָע בָּעִיר קְטַנָּה — **For** as we have seen in chapters 11-12, **whenever the *yetzer hara* has any control and dominance over** the body, **the "small city,"** אֲפִילוּ לְפִי שָׁעָה קַלָּה — **even for a short while,** נִקְרָא רָשָׁע בְּאוֹתָהּ שָׁעָה — the person **is classified as a *rasha* at that time** and not a *beinoni*.

אֶלָּא הַיֵּצֶר הָרָע אֵינוֹ רַק עַל דֶּרֶךְ מָשָׁל כְּמוֹ שׁוֹפֵט וְדַיָּין הָאוֹמֵר דַּעְתּוֹ בַּמִּשְׁפָּט — **Rather,** in the case of the *beinoni*, **the *yetzer hara* is merely like, for example, a single magis-**

כְּמוֹ שׁוֹפֵט וְדַיָּין הָאוֹמֵר דַּעְתּוֹ בְּמִשְׁפָּט וְאע"כ יָכוֹל
לִהְיוֹת שֶׁלֹּא יִהְיֶה פְּסַק הֲלָכָה כָּךְ לְמַעֲשֶׂה מִפְּנֵי שֶׁיֵּשׁ
עוֹד שׁוֹפֵט וְדַיָּין הַחוֹלֵק עָלָיו וְצָרִיךְ לְהַכְרִיעַ בֵּינֵיהֶם
וְהַהֲלָכָה כְּדִבְרֵי הַמַּכְרִיעַ כָּךְ הַיֵּצֶה"ר אוֹמֵר דַּעְתּוֹ בְּחָלָל
הַשְּׂמָאלִי שֶׁבַּלֵּב וּמֵהַלֵּב עוֹלֶה לַמּוֹחַ לְהַרְהֵר בּוֹ וּמִיָּד
חוֹלֵק עָלָיו הַשּׁוֹפֵט הַשֵּׁנִי שֶׁהוּא הַנֶּפֶשׁ הָאֱלֹהִית שֶׁבַּמּוֹחַ
הַמִּתְפַּשֵּׁט בְּחָלָל הַיְמִנִי שֶׁבַּלֵּב מְקוֹם מִשְׁכַּן הַיֵּצֶר טוֹב
וְהַהֲלָכָה כְּדִבְרֵי הַמַּכְרִיעַ הוּא הקב"ה הָעוֹזְרוֹ לְהַיֵּצֶר טוֹב
כְּמַאֲמַר רז"ל אִלְמָלֵא הקב"ה עוֹזְרוֹ אֵין יָכוֹל לוֹ וְהָעוֹזֵר

trate or judge on a panel, **who offers his legal opinion,** וְאַף עַל פִּי כֵן יָכוֹל לִהְיוֹת שֶׁלֹּא יִהְיֶה פְּסַק הֲלָכָה כָּךְ לְמַעֲשֶׂה — **which, however, might not become the final legal ruling,** מִפְּנֵי שֶׁיֵּשׁ עוֹד שׁוֹפֵט וְדַיָּין הַחוֹלֵק עָלָיו — **being that there is another magistrate or judge who offers a dissenting opinion,** וְצָרִיךְ לְהַכְרִיעַ בֵּינֵיהֶם — **and** a third judge is required **to resolve between them,** וְהַהֲלָכָה כְּדִבְרֵי הַמַּכְרִיעַ — and *"the law follows the words of the* third *reconciliatory view"* (Talmud, Shabbos 39b).

כָּךְ הַיֵּצֶר הָרָע אוֹמֵר דַּעְתּוֹ בְּחָלָל הַשְּׂמָאלִי שֶׁבַּלֵּב — **In a similar way, the** *yetzer hara* first **states its opinion,** to follow a certain path of self-gratification, **in the heart's left chamber,** וּמֵהַלֵּב עוֹלֶה לַמּוֹחַ לְהַרְהֵר בּוֹ — **and from the heart it rises to the brain, to be contemplated,** וּמִיָּד חוֹלֵק עָלָיו הַשּׁוֹפֵט הַשֵּׁנִי שֶׁהוּא הַנֶּפֶשׁ הָאֱלֹהִית שֶׁבַּמּוֹחַ — **and is immediately opposed by the second judge, which is the Divine Soul in the brain,** הַמִּתְפַּשֵּׁט בְּחָלָל הַיְמִנִי שֶׁבַּלֵּב מְקוֹם מִשְׁכַּן הַיֵּצֶר טוֹב — **which** then **spreads to the heart's right side, the place where the** *yetzer tov* **rests.**

As we learned in chapter 9, the Divine Soul has two main "locations" in the body: the brain and the heart's right side. After rejecting a self-gratifying thought in the mind, the Divine Soul in the heart's right side then rejects it emotionally, as something undesirable.

How is the dispute resolved?

וְהַהֲלָכָה כְּדִבְרֵי הַמַּכְרִיעַ — **And** *"the law follows the words of the* third *reconciliatory view,"* הוּא הַקָּדוֹשׁ בָּרוּךְ הוּא הָעוֹזְרוֹ לְהַיֵּצֶר טוֹב — this "third judge" being none other than G-d, **the Blessed Holy One, who comes** immediately **to assist the** *yetzer tov,* כְּמַאֲמַר רַבּוֹתֵינוּ זִכְרוֹנָם לִבְרָכָה אִלְמָלֵא הַקָּדוֹשׁ בָּרוּךְ הוּא עוֹזְרוֹ אֵין יָכוֹל לוֹ — **as** our **Sages, of blessed memory, taught,** *"If the Blessed Holy One did not assist him, he could not overcome* the yetzer hara" (Talmud, Kiddushin 30b).

This represents a new insight. In chapter 12 we were led to believe that the *beinoni* achieves self-mastery over his behavior purely through his own merits. Here we learn that he only succeeds in the battle through Divine assistance.

What is this Divine assistance? And why did the *beinoni* of chapter 12 not seem to need it?

היא ההארה שמאיר אור ה' על נפש האלהית להיות
לה יתרון ושליטה על סכלות הכסיל ויצה"ר כיתרון

וְהָעֵזֶר הִיא הַהָאָרָה שֶׁמֵּאִיר אוֹר ה' עַל נֶפֶשׁ הָאֱלֹהִית — This "assistance" is a glimmer of G-d's light shining upon the Divine Soul.

But why does the Divine Soul need "a glimmer of G-d's light"? Surely this soul itself is G-dly?

The notion of a "Divine Soul" is something of a paradox. On one hand, it is a "soul," an autonomous spiritual entity which animates a human. And yet, on the other hand, we say that it is Divine— *"literally a piece of G-d above"* (chapter 2, p. 44).

The Divine Soul, then, has a dual identity: It has the wrappings and functionality of a human soul; but, unlike most creations, it can easily reconnect with its Divine essence and inner G-dly flame.

The "assistance" which the *Tanya* speaks of here is the Divine Soul's ability to get in touch with its true self—to stop, for a moment, being bound by the limitations of a "soul," and to behave in accordance with its inner, totally Divine identity (*Toras Menachem, Hisva'aduyos* 5744, volume 3, (Brooklyn: Lahak, 1990) pp. 1846-8).

לִהְיוֹת לָהּ יִתְרוֹן וּשְׁלִיטָה עַל סַכְלוּת הַכְּסִיל וְיֵצֶר הָרָע — This "assistance" enables the Divine Soul to have an advantage over, and control of the stupidity of *"the fool"* (*Ecclesiastes* 2:14), the *yetzer hara,* כִּיתְרוֹן הָאוֹר מִן הַחוֹשֶׁךְ — *"like the advantage of light over darkness"* (*ibid.* 2:13), כַּנִּזְכָּר לְעֵיל — as mentioned above.

In chapter 12, the *beinoni* was able to have complete control over his *yetzer hara*, "Since, inherently, and in its natural capacity, 'the brain rules over the heart'... any person can, with the will-power of his brain, restrain himself and take control of his heart's urges" (p. 143).

Here, however, in chapter 13, there is no mention that *"in its natural capacity, 'the brain rules over the heart.'"* Instead we are taught that the *beinoni* can only control his urges with the help of Divine assistance. What has prompted this change?

The principle that "the brain rules over the heart" is only effective in a case where the will-power of the brain has a *single-minded devotion* to a certain course of action. Then, even if the heart desires otherwise, the brain will always prevail. But *if the brain itself is unsure*, it will simply not be focused enough to "rule over the heart."

In chapter 12, the brain's will-power was completely devoted to overcoming the *yetzer hara*, since the *beinoni* benefited from the "residual effects" of contem-

PRACTICAL LESSONS

When you have two voices arguing in your head, one good and the other evil, the only way you can be sure to win over your *yetzer hara* (impulse to evil) is with Divine assistance.

This Divine assistance is actually G-d's light shining through your soul.

האור מן החושך כנ"ל. אַך מאחר שהרע שבחלל
השמאלי בבינוני הוא בתקפו כתולדתו להתאות תאוה
לכל תענוגי עוה"ז ולא נתבטל במיעוט לגבי הטוב ולא
נדחה ממקומו כלל רק שאין לו שליטה וממשלה
להתפשט באברי הגוף מפני הקב"ה העומד לימין אביון
ועוזר ומאיר לנפש האלהית לכן נקרא כרשע כמארז"ל

plative prayer in his brain lingering long after the prayers were completed (pp. 148-9). This "residual effect" helped the *beinoni* to retain the focus necessary in his brain to "rule over the heart" and conquer the *yetzer hara* in every instance.

Our chapter, however, speaks of the *beinoni* in his default "unenlightened" state, devoid of the residual effects of contemplative prayer. Now, we are told that the *yetzer hara* "first states its opinion in the heart's left chamber *and from the heart it rises to the brain, to be contemplated*" (p. 153). Since this "unenlightened" *beinoni* lacks the residual effects of prayer in his brain, his *yetzer hara* is able to rise from his heart and speak its opinion even in his brain. Now the principle that "the brain rules over the heart" will not help him, because *his own brain is confused by two voices.* That's why the "unenlightened" *beinoni* needs Divine assistance (*Notes on Tanya*).

SECTION TWO: THE BEINONI'S FAILURE TO TRANSFORM

25TH TEVES LEAP

The above discussion, about the "default," unenlightened level of the *beinoni,* will now help us answer a question posed at the beginning of the *Tanya.*

The *Tanya* had questioned the oath, that, according to the *Talmud,* the soul is made to swear prenatally: *"Even if the entire world tells you, 'You are a tzadik,' you should consider yourself like a rasha."* This was problematic since it seemed to contradict the *Mishnah's* advice, *"Don't consider yourself to be a rasha."*

The *Tanya* will now offer an answer to this question through a close reading of the *Talmud's* words. The oath does not, in fact, state that you must consider yourself an actual *rasha,* but rather, *"you should consider yourself **like** a rasha"* (ke-rasha).

Who is "like a *rasha*"? This term, the *Tanya* will argue, refers to a *beinoni.*

אַך מֵאַחַר שֶׁהָרַע שֶׁבֶּחָלָל הַשְּׂמָאלִי בַּבֵּינוֹנִי הוּא בְּתָקְפּוֹ כְּתוֹלַדְתּוֹ — **But since the evil** of the Animal Soul **in the left chamber of the** *beinoni's* **heart retains its innate strength,** לְהִתְאַוּת תַּאֲוָה לְכָל תַּעֲנוּגֵי עוֹלָם הַזֶּה — **and it is still tempted to desire every worldly pleasure,** וְלֹא נִתְבַּטֵּל בְּמִיעוּט לְגַבֵּי הַטּוֹב — **and its evil was not voided by dilution from** an overwhelming amount of **good,** (the hallmark of a *tzadik,* see p. 127), וְלֹא נִדְחָה מִמְּקוֹמוֹ כְּלָל — **and even its voice was not displaced** permanently, **at all,** (only temporarily, during prayer and study, see pp. 146-7), רַק שֶׁאֵין לוֹ

אֲפִילוּ כָּל הָעוֹלָם כּוּלוֹ אוֹמְרִים לְךָ צַדִּיק אַתָּה הָיָה
בְּעֵינֶיךָ כְּרָשָׁע וְלֹא רָשָׁע מַמָּשׁ אֶלָּא שֶׁיַּחֲזִיק עַצְמוֹ
לְבֵינוֹנִי וְלֹא לְהַאֲמִין לְהָעוֹלָם שֶׁאוֹמְרִים שֶׁהָרַע שֶׁבּוֹ
נִתְבַּטֵּל לְגַבֵּי הַטּוֹב שֶׁזוֹ מַדְרֵגַת צַדִּיק אֶלָּא יִהְיֶה בְּעֵינָיו

שְׁלִיטָה וּמֶמְשָׁלָה לְהִתְפַּשֵּׁט בְּאֵבְרֵי הַגּוּף — **rather,** its evil remains in full force and it **just lacks the control and dominance to spread** its influence **over the body's parts,** מִפְּנֵי הַקָּדוֹשׁ בָּרוּךְ הוּא הָעוֹמֵד לִימִין אֶבְיוֹן וְעוֹזֵר וּמֵאִיר לְנֶפֶשׁ הָאֱלֹהִית — and even that is not due to its own merits, but **because the Blessed Holy One** *"stands at the right hand of the poor person,"* **and assists him by illuminating his Divine Soul.**

לָכֵן נִקְרָא כְּרָשָׁע — **Therefore,** since the *beinoni's* evil remains as strong as ever, **he is referred to** by the *Talmud* as *"like a (ke-) rasha."*

The *beinoni* is "like a *rasha*" because: a.) *"The evil in the left chamber of the beinoni's heart retains its innate strength,"* and has not been voided or displaced (which may result in negative thoughts popping into his head); b.) Even the *beinoni's* external mastery is essentially due to Divine assistance, without which he would revert to being a *rasha*.

So it turns out that the character of the *beinoni* is predominantly "like a *rasha*," both inside and out.

כְּמַאֲמַר רַבּוֹתֵינוּ זִכְרוֹנָם לִבְרָכָה אֲפִילוּ כָּל הָעוֹלָם כּוּלוֹ אוֹמְרִים לְךָ צַדִּיק אַתָּה הֱיֵה בְּעֵינֶיךָ כְּרָשָׁע — **This explains the teaching of our Sages, of blessed memory** cited in chapter 1, *"Even if the entire world tells you, 'You are a tzadik,' you should consider yourself like a rasha,"* וְלֹא רָשָׁע מַמָּשׁ — the Sages were not suggesting that after achieving external mastery over the "garments" of thought, speech and action, you ought to look at yourself **as an actual** *rasha*, since this is simply not true, and it violates the *Mishnah's* advice, *"Don't consider yourself to be a rasha,"* אֶלָּא שֶׁיַּחֲזִיק עַצְמוֹ לְבֵינוֹנִי — **rather,** what the Sages meant to say was, "If the entire world tells you, 'You are a *tzadik*,' **you should consider yourself to be** 'like' a *rasha*," i.e., **a** *beinoni*.

People perceive only external behavior, and not inner refinement, so they could not possibly know if you are a *tzadik* or not. Even *you* don't know whether you've refined your inner evil, because its failure to surface doesn't mean it's not there.

וְלֹא לְהַאֲמִין לְהָעוֹלָם שֶׁאוֹמְרִים — **Do not believe the world's opinion,** "You are a *tzadik*," שֶׁהָרַע שֶׁבּוֹ נִתְבַּטֵּל — as this would mean **that the evil in you has** לְגַבֵּי הַטּוֹב

PRACTICAL LESSONS

Even if you achieve an external and internal self-mastery, never sinning or even desiring to sin, you cannot be sure that you are a *tzadik*. You may just be a *beinoni* whose evil is dormant.

Your external behavior is in your complete control; even your negative thoughts can be replaced with good ones. But your deep emotional core is resistant to change.

כְּאִלּוּ מַהוּתוֹ וְעַצְמוּתוֹ שֶׁל הָרַע הוּא בְּתָקְפּוֹ וּבִגְבוּרָתוֹ בֶּחָלָל הַשְׂמָאלִי כְּתוֹלַדְתּוֹ וְלֹא חָלַף וְהָלַךְ מִמֶּנּוּ מְאוּמָה וְאַדְּרַבָּה נִתְחַזֵּק יוֹתֵר בְּהֶמְשֵׁךְ הַזְּמָן שֶׁנִּשְׁתַּמֵּשׁ בּוֹ הַרְבֵּה בַּאֲכִילָה וּשְׁתִיָּה וּשְׁאָר עִנְיְנֵי עוֹה"ז וְאַף מִי שֶׁבְּתוֹרַת

been voided by the good, and this is very unlikely to be true, שֶׁזּוֹ מַדְרֵגַת צַדִּיק **—** **since this is the level of a** *tzadik,* a rare phenomenon (see p. 127).

אֶלָּא יִהְיֶה בְּעֵינָיו כְּאִלּוּ מַהוּתוֹ וְעַצְמוּתוֹ שֶׁל הָרַע הוּא בְּתָקְפּוֹ וּבִגְבוּרָתוֹ בֶּחָלָל הַשְׂמָאלִי כְּתוֹלַדְתּוֹ **— Rather, in your eyes, you should look at yourself as if the deep core of evil remains with its *full* inborn strength in your** heart's **left chamber,** וְלֹא חָלַף וְהָלַךְ מִמֶּנּוּ מְאוּמָה **—and it has not budged or departed from you *whatsoever.***

If a *beinoni* would look at himself as a *tzadik,* he would imagine that his battle with evil is over, so he might "lower his guard" and "relax," to some extent. Therefore the Sages stressed that a *beinoni* is essentially "like a *rasha*," in whom the *yetzer hara* is as strong as ever in the heart. With such strong negative energy lurking below the surface, it would be a grave error for the *beinoni* to relax his vigil for even a moment.

וְאַדְּרַבָּה נִתְחַזֵּק יוֹתֵר בְּהֶמְשֵׁךְ הַזְּמָן **— On the contrary,** not only has your Animal Soul failed to weaken, but **with the passing of time it has actually become stronger,** שֶׁנִּשְׁתַּמֵּשׁ בּוֹ הַרְבֵּה **— because you have made extensive use of it,** בַּאֲכִילָה וּשְׁתִיָּה **—** וּשְׁאָר עִנְיְנֵי עוֹלָם הַזֶּה **— through eating, drinking and other worldly activities.**

The Animal Soul is like a muscle: the more you use it, the stronger it gets. Even if all its desires are kosher, the fact that it drives you to eat and enjoy other pleasures daily, gives it strength.

So, in all likelihood, the *beinoni's* impression that he is a *tzadik* (who has eliminated the evil from his heart) couldn't be further from the truth. Not only has he failed to eliminate his evil, but over time it has grown even stronger.

(We still haven't yet fully answered the *Tanya's* second question in chapter 1 on this topic, *"Also, if you consider yourself 'like a rasha' (i.e., a beinoni) you will become sad and depressed and you won't be able to worship G-d joyfully and positively"* (p. 28). The thought that, after all your inner work, you are still only a *beinoni* in whom *"the deep core of evil remains with its full inborn strength in your left chamber, and it has not budged nor departed from you whatsoever,"* could be depressing. The *Tanya* will discuss this concern later on, pp. 353-60, 386*ff*.)

SECTION THREE: THE TZADIK "LOOK-ALIKE"

19TH TEVES REGULAR

One obvious problem with the above conclusion—that someone who has achieved self-mastery should never look at himself as a *tzadik,* but as a *beinoni*—is that presumably the *person himself knows* what is happening inside him? The "whole

ה' חפצו ויהגה בה יומם ולילה לשמה אין זו הוכחה כלל
שנדחה הרע ממקומו אלא יכול להיות שמהותו ועצמותו
הוא בתקפו ובגבורתו במקומו בחלל השמאלי רק
שלבושיו שהם מחשבה דבור ומעשה של נפש
הבהמית אינן מתלבשים במוח והפה והידים ושאר
אברי הגוף מפני ה' שנתן שליטה וממשלה למוח על

world" may err, because they judge the person only by his outward behavior, and have no information about his deep core, but surely the person knows whether or not he has the urge for self-gratification? If he never experiences such urges, couldn't he presume that he is a *tzadik?*

Even the "enlightened" *beinoni*, whose urges are temporarily silenced through the residual effects of prayer, will eventually return to his "default" state when the residue wears off, and he will experience urges once again. Where do we find a *beinoni* who experiences no urge for self-gratification and might mistakenly deem himself to be a *tzadik?* The *Tanya* gives us an example.

וְאַף מִי שֶׁבְּתוֹרַת ה' חֶפְצוֹ וְיֶהְגֶּה בָּה יוֹמָם וָלַיְלָה — **Even a person for whom** *"G-d's Torah is his delight, and he studies it day and night"* (Psalms 1:2), לִשְׁמָהּ — **and he studies the Torah with sincere devotion "for G-d's sake,"** nevertheless, he should not consider himself a *tzadik.*

PRACTICAL LESSONS

During (and for a while after) prayer, or while studying Torah, your *yetzer hara* may be quiet. But it's just fallen asleep; it will wake up again.

Here we have a new slant to the *beinoni* experience. Just as the *beinoni* immersed in meditative prayer found himself temporarily devoid of urges, a Torah scholar who devotes himself to study may also find that this mental immersion drowns out his urges.

The significant difference here is that, unlike prayer which is usually contained within a limited time period, it is possible to study Torah at every waking hour, day and night. So you could have the phenomenon of a *beinoni,* whose deep core remains unrefined, but still never feels the urge for self-gratification due to his immersion in Torah study (*Notes on Tanya*).

אֵין זוֹ הוֹכָחָה כְּלָל שֶׁנִּדְחָה הָרַע מִמְּקוֹמוֹ — **The** lack of self-gratifying urges for the full-time scholar **is no proof whatsoever that the evil has been dislodged from its place** in his Animal Soul.

אֶלָּא יָכוֹל לִהְיוֹת שֶׁמַּהוּתוֹ וְעַצְמוּתוֹ הוּא בְּתָקְפּוֹ וּבִגְבוּרָתוֹ בִּמְקוֹמוֹ בֶּחָלָל הַשְּׂמָאלִי — **Rather, it's possible that the deep core** of his Animal Soul **remains lodged in the left chamber** of the heart, **in all its strength and power,** רַק שֶׁלְּבוּשָׁיו שֶׁהֵם מַחֲשָׁבָה — **only that** this person feels refined inwardly because **his Animal Soul's**

דִּבּוּר וּמַעֲשֶׂה שֶׁל נֶפֶשׁ הַבַּהֲמִית אֵינָן מִתְלַבְּשִׁים בַּמּוֹחַ וְהַפֶּה וְהַיָּדַיִם וּשְׁאָר אֶבְרֵי הַגּוּף — **and it is only** that this person feels refined inwardly because **his Animal Soul's**

הלב ולכן נפש האלהית שבמוח מושלת בעיר קטנה
אברי הגוף כולם שיהיו לבוש ומרכבה לשלש' לבושיה
שיתלבשו בהם שהם מחשבה דבור ומעשה של תרי"ג
מצות התורה אבל מהותה ועצמותה של נפש האלהית
אין לה שליטה וממשלה על מהותה ועצמותה של נפש
הבהמית בבינוני כי אם בשעה שאהבת ה' הוא

"garments," of potentially evil **thought, speech and action, have no influence over
his brain, mouth and hands and the other parts of the body,** מִפְּנֵי ה' שֶׁנָּתַן שְׁלִיטָה
וּמֶמְשָׁלָה לַמּוֹחַ עַל הַלֵּב — **because G-d has allowed** the will-power of **the brain to
have control and dominance over** the emotions of **the heart.**

As we have seen, the principle that "the mind rules over the heart," applies only
when the mind knows exactly what it wants. When a person *"studies day and night,"*
his constant focus on Torah may empower his mind to overcome his heart on every occasion; but, in his deep core, this *beinoni* hasn't really changed. He is just
managing to maintain enough mental focus to take advantage of a physiological
"highway" between the mind and heart, which is a special gift from G-d. Without this
"tweak" his Animal Soul, which remains strong, would sometimes seize hold of him.

וְלָכֵן נֶפֶשׁ הָאֱלֹהִית שֶׁבַּמּוֹחַ מוֹשֶׁלֶת בָּעִיר קְטַנָּה — **Therefore,** because this *beinoni* who
studies day and night is able to constantly take advantage of the principle that "the
mind rules over the heart," **the Divine Soul in his brain dominates the "small city,"**
שֶׁיִּהְיוּ לְבוּשׁ וּמֶרְכָּבָה לִשְׁלֹשָׁה לְבוּשֶׁיהָ — **all the parts of his body,** אֶבְרֵי הַגּוּף כּוּלָּם
שֶׁיִּתְלַבְּשׁוּ בָּהֶם — **so that they** all **become a "garment" and "vehicle" influenced**
exclusively by the Divine Soul's **three "garments,"** שֶׁהֵם מַחֲשָׁבָה דִּבּוּר וּמַעֲשֶׂה שֶׁל
תְּרָיַ"ג מִצְוֹת הַתּוֹרָה — **namely, thought, speech and action related to the 613 commandments of the Torah.**

SECTION FOUR: WHEN THE BEINONI SUCCEEDS (PARTIALLY) WITH HIS DEEP CORE

אֲבָל מַהוּתָהּ וְעַצְמוּתָהּ שֶׁל נֶפֶשׁ הָאֱלֹהִית אֵין לָהּ שְׁלִיטָה וּמֶמְשָׁלָה עַל מַהוּתָהּ וְעַצְמוּתָהּ שֶׁל
נֶפֶשׁ הַבַּהֲמִית בַּבֵּינוֹנִי — **However,** as we have seen, the *deep core* of the *beinoni's*
Divine Soul has no control, nor dominance, over the *deep core* of his Animal Soul.

This rule, however, has an exception. While the *beinoni* is defined by the lack of
refinement of his deep emotional core, that does not mean to say that he never succeeds *at all*. There are occasions when he is able to have some minimal mastery, at
least, over the Animal Soul's deep core.

כִּי אִם בְּשָׁעָה שֶׁאַהֲבַת ה' הוּא בְּהִתְגַּלּוּת לִבּוֹ — The *beinoni* has no control over the
deep core of his Animal Soul **except when his love for G-d is manifested openly in**

בהתגלות לבו בעתים מזומנים כמו בשעת התפלה
וכיוצא בה ואף גם זאת הפעם אינה רק שליטה וממשלה

his heart, בָּה וְכַיּוֹצֵא הַתְּפִלָּה בִּשְׁעַת כְּמוֹ מְזוּמָּנִים בְּעִתִּים — at specific times, such as during prayer *etc.*

The *Tanya* indicates that, on occasion, it *is* possible for the *beinoni's* love of G-d on the right side of his heart, to partially encroach upon his Animal Soul's deep emotional core, on his heart's left side. While the *beinoni's* daily struggle is centered around mastery of the more superficial "garments" of the Animal Soul (thought, speech and action), he is also able to wage war, to a limited extent, with the inner powers of his Animal Soul's deep core (*Notes on Tanya*).

To sum up, we have now witnessed the *beinoni* in four different settings.

1. Not immersed in Torah or prayer. He experiences urges from the Animal Soul, and only succeeds in deflecting them through G-d's "assistance" of extra light shining in his soul. The deep core of the Animal Soul is unaffected (pp. 154-5).

2. For a period after meditative prayer. He experiences urges from the Animal Soul, and only succeeds in deflecting them through the clarity of mind that remains after prayer. This enables him to make use of the principle "the brain rules over the heart." The deep core of the Animal Soul is unaffected (pp. 143, 148).

3. During devotional Torah study. It is possible that he will not experience urges from the Animal Soul at all. If he does, he can succeed in deflecting them through the clarity of mind which has come from his Torah study, enabling him to make use of the principle "the brain rules over the heart." The deep core of the Animal Soul is unaffected (pp. 158-59).

4. During focused meditative prayer. He may not experience urges from the Animal Soul. Even the deep core of the Animal Soul may partially be affected by his intense love of G-d (pp. 140-41).

PRACTICAL LESSONS

Focused meditation during prayer is the only thing that can actually begin to change the deep emotional core of your Animal Soul.

At this fourth level the *beinoni* does seem to resemble the *tzadik*. Why, then, did the *Tanya* insist that the *beinoni* is always "like a *rasha*"?

לְבָד וּמֶמְשָׁלָה שְׁלִיטָה רַק אֵינָה הַפַּעַם זֹאת גַּם וְאַף — **For even in this case,** where the deep core of the *beinoni's* Animal Soul is influenced during meditative prayer, that influence **is limited to a mere** coercive **control and dominance** over the Animal Soul's deep core.

Unlike the *tzadik*, the *beinoni* does not actually *change* the deep core of his Animal Soul. He merely succeeds in curbing its desires, temporarily.

לבד כדכתיב ולאום מלאום יאמץ כשזה קם זה נופל
וכשזה קם כו' שנפש האלהית מתאמצת ומתגברת על
נפש הבהמית במקור הגבורות שהיא בינה להתבונן
בגדולת ה' א"ס ב"ה ולהוליד אהבה עזה לה' כרשפי
אש בחלל הימני שבלבו ואז אתכפיא ס"א שבחלל

כְּדִכְתִיב וּלְאוֹם מִלְאוֹם יֶאֱמָץ — **As the verse states,** *"One nation shall overpower the other nation"* (*Genesis* 25:23), the word "overpower" suggesting coercion rather than transformation, כְּשֶׁזֶּה קָם זֶה נוֹפֵל וּכְשֶׁזֶּה קָם כו' — **as** *Rashi* comments, *"When one rises the other one falls, and when the other one rises,* the first one falls."

With the *beinoni,* the Divine Soul may "rise over" and influence the deep core of the Animal Soul, but after prayer, the situation is reversed again.

In the next few lines, the *Tanya* briefly describes this experience, how such an intense love is generated and why it ultimately fails to be a permanent change.

שֶׁנֶּפֶשׁ הָאֱלֹהִית מִתְאַמֶּצֶת וּמִתְגַּבֶּרֶת עַל נֶפֶשׁ הַבַּהֲמִית — **When the Divine Soul overpowers and gains strength over the Animal Soul** through meditative prayer, בִּמְקוֹר הַגְּבוּרוֹת שֶׁהִיא בִּינָה — it draws on **the source of** *gevuros* (power; discipline), **which is** the power of *binah* (cognition).

Here we are taught a Kabbalistic secret as to why, of all religious activities, focused meditation has the unique power to touch the deep core of the Animal Soul.

According to the Kabbalah, the ten *sefiros* (energies that power the universe in general, and the soul in particular — see pp. 19, 641-2), are mapped out in three vertical "columns." To the right are the *sefiros* associated with expansiveness, imagination, giving, and boundlessness; the left side's energy is one of restraint, discipline, precision and containment. (The middle column seeks to harmonize and integrate the two extremes.)

Of the two poles, the left is endowed with a more intense power (as we see from our own lives, the immense power of discipline and precision).

Prolonged prayer meditation involves primarily the faculty of *binah* (cognition), because it requires a precise focusing of the mind. Since *binah* is on the left side of the *sefirotic* tree, it is the key to unlocking *gevurah* (emotional power), which is also on the left side.

In simple terms: An idea becomes especially powerful and compelling when you grasp it fully, in all its glorious detail.

לְהִתְבּוֹנֵן בִּגְדוּלַת ה' אֵין סוֹף בָּרוּךְ הוּא — This meditation takes place **through focusing** your mind **on the greatness of G-d, the Blessed Infinite One (***Ein Sof***),** וּלְהוֹלִיד אַהֲבָה עַזָּה לַה' כְּרִשְׁפֵּי אֵשׁ בְּחָלָל הַיְמָנִי שֶׁבְּלִבּוֹ — **giving birth to a powerful love like** *"flaming fire"* (*Song* 8:6) **for G-d, in your heart's right chamber** where the Divine Soul manifests, וְאָז אִתְכַּפְיָא סִטְרָא אַחֲרָא שֶׁבֶּחָלָל הַשְּׂמָאלִי — **then the** *sitra achra* of the Animal Soul **in the left chamber is subdued.**

הַשְׂמָאלִי אֲבָל לֹא נִתְבַּטֵּל לְגַמְרֵי בַּבֵּינוֹנִי אֶלָּא בַּצַּדִּיק
שֶׁנֶּאֱמַר בּוֹ וְלִבִּי חָלָל בְּקִרְבִּי וְהוּא מוֹאֵס בָּרַע וְשׂוֹנְאוֹ
בְּתַכְלִית הַשִּׂנְאָה וְהַמִּיאוּס אוֹ שֶׁלֹּא בְּתַכְלִית הַשִּׂנְאָה
כַּנִּ"ל. אֲבָל בַּבֵּינוֹנִי הוּא דֶּ"מ כְּאָדָם שֶׁיָּשֵׁן שֶׁיָּכוֹל
לַחֲזוֹר וּלֵיעוֹר מִשְּׁנָתוֹ כָּךְ הָרַע בַּבֵּינוֹנִי הוּא כָּיָשֵׁן בְּחָלָל
הַשְּׂמָאלִי בִּשְׁעַת ק"ש וּתְפִלָּה שֶׁלִּבּוֹ בּוֹעֵר בְּאַהֲבַת ה'
וְאַחַ"כ יָכוֹל לִהְיוֹת חוֹזֵר וְנֵיעוֹר. וְלָכֵן הָיָה רַבָּה מַחֲזִיק
עַצְמוֹ כְּבֵינוֹנִי אַף דְּלֹא פָּסִיק פּוּמֵיהּ מִגִּירְסָא וּבְתוֹרַת ה'

19A

אֲבָל לֹא נִתְבַּטֵּל לְגַמְרֵי בַּבֵּינוֹנִי — But, with the *beinoni,* the negativity of the Animal Soul **is not completely eliminated,** אֶלָּא בַּצַּדִּיק — this happens **only with a** *tzadik,* שֶׁנֶּאֱמַר בּוֹ וְלִבִּי חָלָל בְּקִרְבִּי — **about whom the verse states,** *'my heart is empty within me'* (*Psalms* 109:22; see chapter 1, p. 35).

וְהוּא מוֹאֵס בָּרַע וְשׂוֹנְאוֹ — It is only the *tzadik* **who is repulsed by evil and detests it,** בְּתַכְלִית הַשִּׂנְאָה וְהַמִּיאוּס — **in the case of the complete** *tzadik,* **he finds it absolutely detestable and repulsive,** אוֹ שֶׁלֹּא בְּתַכְלִית הַשִּׂנְאָה — **or,** in the case of the incomplete *tzadik,* **he detests it, but not absolutely,** כַּנִּזְכָּר לְעֵיל — **as above** (pp. 126-7).

SECTION FIVE: WHY A TZADIK MIGHT MISIDENTIFY HIMSELF

אֲבָל בַּבֵּינוֹנִי הוּא דֶּרֶךְ מָשָׁל כְּאָדָם שֶׁיָּשֵׁן — **But with the** *beinoni,* the evil of his Animal Soul **is comparable to a person who is asleep,** שֶׁיָּכוֹל לַחֲזוֹר וּלֵיעוֹר מִשְּׁנָתוֹ — **who is able to reawaken from his sleep once again.**

כָּךְ הָרַע בַּבֵּינוֹנִי הוּא כָּיָשֵׁן בְּחָלָל הַשְּׂמָאלִי — **That is how the evil exists in the** *beinoni,* בִּשְׁעַת קְרִיאַת שְׁמַע וּתְפִלָּה שֶׁלִּבּוֹ בּוֹעֵר בְּאַהֲבַת ה' — **while his heart burns with love for G-d when reading the** *Shema* **and praying, it is as if the evil were asleep in his heart's left side,** וְאַחַר כָּךְ יָכוֹל לִהְיוֹת חוֹזֵר וְנֵיעוֹר — **afterwards it can wake up again.**

We now return to another of the questions posed in chapter 1. The Talmudic sage Rabah was quoted as saying, "I am a *beinoni*." We wondered how it was possible for Rabah, who was a *tzadik,* to mistakenly conceive of himself as a *beinoni.* Even if externally speaking, a *beinoni* is indistinguishable from a *tzadik,* surely Rabah *himself* must have been aware that his love of G-d (and revulsion of evil) was at the level of a *tzadik*?

But now we know that the evil in the Animal Soul of a *beinoni* can simply be "asleep" and dormant, it makes sense why Rabah could conceive of himself as a *beinoni.* He simply looked at himself as a *beinoni* whose Animal Soul had drifted into a deep sleep, but, in its deep core, remained undisplaced and unrefined.

וְלָכֵן הָיָה רַבָּה מַחֲזִיק עַצְמוֹ כְּבֵינוֹנִי — **And that is why Rabah looked at himself as a** *beinoni,* אַף דְּלֹא פָּסִיק פּוּמֵיהּ מִגִּירְסָא — **even though** he possessed both the ex-

חפצו יומם ולילה בחפיצה וחשיקה ותשוקה ונפש
שוקקה לה' באהבה רבה כבשעת ק"ש ותפלה ונדמה
בעיניו כבינוני המתפלל כל היום וכמאמר רז"ל הלואי

ternal and internal experience of a *tzadik*; externally, **he did not allow his mouth to stop studying,** וּבְתוֹרַת ה' חֶפְצוֹ יוֹמָם וָלָיְלָה — **and** internally *"G-d's Torah was his delight… day and night"* (*Psalms* 1:2), בַּחֲפִיצָה וַחֲשִׁיקָה וּתְשׁוּקָה וְנֶפֶשׁ שׁוֹקֵקָה לַה', בְּאַהֲבָה רַבָּה — and the delight he experienced during his study was passionate, like a *tzadik,* **with the desire, fervor and longing of** *"a craving soul"* (*Psalms* 107:9), **for G-d, with "great love,"** כְּבִשְׁעַת קְרִיאַת שְׁמַע וּתְפִלָּה — **at the level** that could normally be experienced by a *beinoni* **when reciting the *Shema* and during prayer.**

Unlike any *beinoni* we have encountered up until now, whose intense love for G-d always subsides after prayer, Rabah managed to maintain this "high" the whole day, through a deeply devotional Torah study.

Why was this not proof for him that he was a *tzadik?*

Rabah reasoned as follows: When a *beinoni* is at prayer, he feels the intense passion similar to a *tzadik*, but the deep core of his Animal Soul actually remains unrefined and "asleep." Perhaps then too, my devotional Torah study throughout the day, continues along the same lines — it makes me feel like I have the passion of a *tzadik*, but my deep core remains unrefined. It is merely the "high" of Torah study that is camouflaging my unrefined evil and keeping it "asleep."

וְנִדְמֶה בְּעֵינָיו כְּבֵינוֹנִי הַמִּתְפַּלֵּל כָּל הַיּוֹם — **Therefore** Rabah **considered himself like a *beinoni* who spends the entire day at prayer.**

Since Rabah's Torah study had the same emotional intensity as prayer, it was as if he prayed all day. And since, when at prayer, the *beinoni's* Animal Soul is "asleep," Rabah was not certain if he was a *tzadik,* or merely a *beinoni* whose Animal Soul was in a deep sleep. Since the two are indistinguishable, Rabah assumed, out of humility, that he was of the lesser standing.

The *Tanya* cites a source for the idea that a person might "spend all day at prayer."

וּכְמַאֲמַר רַבּוֹתֵינוּ זִכְרוֹנָם לִבְרָכָה הַלְוַאי שֶׁיִּתְפַּלֵּל אָדָם כָּל הַיּוֹם כּוּלּוֹ — **As our Sages, of blessed memory, taught** that while there are only three obligatory prayer services per day, a person has the option of praying as many times as he desires, and, *"If only a person would spend the whole day in prayer!"* (*Talmud, Brachos* 21a).

Even if a *beinoni* could not achieve the deeply devotional Torah study of Rabah, he could spend the whole day in prayer (and remain at level 4, above, constantly). His internal experience would then be indistinguishable from the *tzadik*, even though his deep core would remain largely unrefined.

That is why, *"Even if the entire world tells you, 'You are a tzadik,' you should consider yourself like a rasha,"* i.e., a *beinoni*. Because even if you never experience an urge for sin or self-gratification, you might just be like a *"beinoni* who prays all day" who is indistinguishable from a *tzadik.*

שיתפלל אדם כל היום כולו: והנה מדת אהבה זו
האמורה בבינונים בשעת התפלה ע"י התגברות הנפש
האלהית כו' הנה לגבי מדרגת הצדיקים עובדי ה' באמת
לאמיתו אין בחי' אהבה זו נקראת בשם עבודת אמת
כלל מאחר שחולפת ועוברת אחר התפלה וכתיב
שפת אמת תכון לעד ועד ארגיעה לשון שקר ואעפ"כ
לגבי מדרגת הבינונים נקראת עבודה תמה באמת

SECTION SIX: THE BEINONI'S AUTHENTIC WORSHIP

<u>20TH TEVES REGULAR</u>

In the following section, we will discuss the *beinoni's* inability to sustain passion for G-d after prayer. If the love is not sustainable, does that mean it is not genuine?

וְהִנֵּה מִדַּת אַהֲבָה זוֹ הָאֲמוּרָה בְּבֵינוֹנִים בִּשְׁעַת הַתְּפִלָּה — **Now the extent of the *beinoni's* love during prayer, of which we have spoken,** עַל יְדֵי הִתְגַּבְּרוּת הַנֶּפֶשׁ הָאֱלֹהִית כוּ' — **which comes through a strengthening of the Divine Soul** over the Animal Soul, *etc.,* הִנֵּה לְגַבֵּי מַדְרֵגַת הַצַּדִּיקִים עוֹבְדֵי ה' בֶּאֱמֶת לַאֲמִיתּוֹ — **when compared with the level of *tzadikim*, who worship G-d with absolute authenticity,** אֵין בְּחִינַת אַהֲבָה זוֹ נִקְרֵאת בְּשֵׁם עֲבוֹדַת אֱמֶת כְּלָל — **this type of love** of the *beinoni* **could not be classified as "genuine worship,"** מֵאַחַר שֶׁחוֹלֶפֶת וְעוֹבֶרֶת אַחַר הַתְּפִלָּה — **since it dissipates and goes away after prayer.**

If something is not sustainable, it is probably not a genuine property, but the result of an external influence.

וּכְתִיב שְׂפַת אֱמֶת תִּכּוֹן לָעַד וְעַד אַרְגִּיעָה לְשׁוֹן שָׁקֶר — **As the verse states,** *"Truthful lips endure forever, but a lying tongue lasts only a moment"* (Proverbs 12:19).

Since the *beinoni* only feels love for G-d part of the day (when he prays), how could this be considered genuine? If your spouse told you that s/he loves you on some occasions, but at other times, s/he loves someone else instead, you wouldn't consider that genuine love.

וְאַף עַל פִּי כֵן — **Nevertheless,** this is only when we contrast the love of a *beinoni* to that of a *tzadik*, לְגַבֵּי מַדְרֵגַת הַבֵּינוֹנִים — **but with regard to the level that *beinonim* are capable of achieving,** נִקְרֵאת עֲבוֹדָה תַמָּה בֶּאֱמֶת לַאֲמִיתּוֹ שֶׁלָּהֶם — **the *beinoni's* love during prayer which later passes,** *can* **be classified as "ideal worship," which is absolutely authentic** *for them,* אִישׁ אִישׁ כְּפִי מַדְרֵגָתוֹ בְּמַדְרֵגַת הַבֵּינוֹנִים — **each individual relative to his level,** among the different levels of *beinonim.*

Even among *beinonim,* the capacity for emotional arousal differs. The rule is: Genuine worship for you is when you do your best.

The *Tanya* now explains why the love experienced by a *beinoni* during prayer is genuine. In a sense, the love *is* sustainable, since a *beinoni* is able to consistently reproduce the experience *every time he prays.*

לאמיתו שלהם איש כפי מדרגתו במדרגת
הבינונים והריני קורא באהבתם שבתפלתם ג"כ שפת
אמת תכון לעד הואיל ובכח נפשם האלהית לחזור
ולעורר בחי' אהבה זו לעולם בהתגברותה בשעת
התפלה מדי יום ביום ע"י הכנה הראויה לכל נפש כפי
ערכה ומדרגת' כי הנה מדת אמת היא מדתו של יעקב

וַהֲרֵינִי קוֹרֵא בְּאַהֲבָתָם שֶׁבִּתְפִלָּתָם גַּם כֵּן שְׂפַת אֱמֶת תִּכּוֹן לָעַד — **And I also consider their love, during their prayers,** as not just *relatively* genuine, but *categorically* genuine, on the level of **"Truthful lips endure forever,"** הוֹאִיל וּבְכֹחַ נַפְשָׁם הָאֱלֹהִית לַחֲזוֹר — **since their Divine Soul does have the ability to repeatedly arouse this love always,** וּלְעוֹרֵר בְּחִינַת אַהֲבָה זוֹ לְעוֹלָם — when בְּהִתְגַּבְּרוּתָהּ בִּשְׁעַת הַתְּפִלָּה מִדֵּי יוֹם בְּיוֹם — the Divine Soul **gains dominance each day during prayer,** עַל יְדֵי הַכָנָה הָרְאוּיָה — **through preparing properly** beforehand, לְכָל נֶפֶשׁ כְּפִי עֶרְכָּהּ וּמַדְרֵגָתָהּ — **each individual according to his soul's type and level.**

According to this second argument, the *beinoni* is *always* loving G-d, either actually or in potential. Since he is capable of bringing his potential love to actual expression at any time through proper preparation and prayer, his love of G-d is genuine and constant (*Notes on Tanya*).

SECTION SEVEN: WHAT IS "TRUTH"?

Having proposed that the *beinoni's* love of G-d is "true" and genuine, despite its tendency to vacillate, the *Tanya* now muses upon the nature of truth.

כִּי הִנֵּה מִדַּת אֱמֶת הִיא מִדָּתוֹ שֶׁל יַעֲקֹב — **Now the trait of "truth" was Jacob's paradigm** (*Zohar* 1, 213b, citing *Micah* 7:20).

According to the Kabbalah, Biblical stories are not merely an historical/instructional narrative, they depict the emergence of fundamental spiritual energies. The Patriarchs, for example, were not merely individuals of significance, they each embodied a *paradigm*, a radically new way of living which influences us all.

Jacob, says the *Zohar*, embodied the paradigm of "truth." (Jacob's essential character was that of an *"honest man"* (*Genesis* 25:27), whose *"mouth was consistent with his heart... not attuned to dishonesty"* — *Rashi* ibid.). As the third of the Patriarchs, Jacob integrated the energies which had preceded him: Abraham's path of "benevolence" and Isaac's way of "restraint."

Abraham's benevolence of spirit is crucial for mankind, but if overdone, will lead to the support of unworthy causes and, on a personal level, it causes self-sanctioned immorality and addiction. Isaac's path of restraint resolves many of these issues, but also has the side-effects of rigidity, harshness and obsessive-compulsive behavior.

הַנִּקְרָא בְּרִיחַ הַתִּיכוֹן הַמַּבְרִיחַ מִן הַקָּצֶה אֶל הַקָּצֶה מְרוֹם
הַמַּעֲלוֹת וּמַדְרֵגוֹת עַד סוֹף כָּל דַּרְגִּין וּבְכָל מַעֲלָה וּמַדְרֵגָה
מַבְרִיחַ תּוֹךְ נְקוּדָה הָאֶמְצָעִית שֶׁהִיא נְקוּדַת וּבְחִי׳ מִדַּת
אֱמֶת שֶׁלָּהּ וּמִדַּת אֱמֶת הִיא נַחֲלָה בְּלִי מְצָרִים וְאֵין לָהּ
שִׁעוּר לְמַעְלָה עַד רוּם הַמַּעֲלוֹת וְכָל מַעֲלוֹת וּמַדְרֵגוֹת

Jacob's third paradigm aims to selectively apply "benevolence" and "restraint," so as to optimize their virtues and eliminate undesirable effects. This is the path of "truth," since, as we have seen, truth is synonymous with sustainability, and the elimination of undesirable effects makes a project sustainable.

(In the Biblical narrative, we see that Jacob's path was completely "sustainable," in that all his children continued his faith; in contrast, the paths of Abraham and Isaac were not continued by all of their sons.)

הַנִּקְרָא בְּרִיחַ הַתִּיכוֹן הַמַּבְרִיחַ מִן הַקָּצֶה אֶל הַקָּצֶה — In the *Zohar* (2, 175b), Jacob and the paradigm of "truth" are also **referred to as the *"central bar"*** (*Exodus* 26:28) supporting the Tabernacle, *"which reaches from one end to the other"* (*ibid.*).

In Kabbalah, the Tabernacle is perceived as a "grand map" of the cosmos and the psyche. The Tabernacle's "central bar" symbolizes Jacob's paradigm of truth, since it is the only structural thread running throughout the *entire* Tabernacle.

The hallmark of "truth," then, is its *all-pervasiveness,* expressed by its sustainability under all circumstances and in every context,

מְרוֹם הַמַּעֲלוֹת וּמַדְרֵגוֹת עַד סוֹף כָּל דַּרְגִּין — **from the highest of elevations and planes, to the lowest of all rungs.**

The great virtue of truth is "it just works," regardless of your physical or spiritual address.

וּבְכָל מַעֲלָה וּמַדְרֵגָה — **And at each elevation and level,** just as the "central bar" passed through the middle of the Tabernacle's wall, מַבְרִיחַ תּוֹךְ נְקוּדָה הָאֶמְצָעִית — truth **penetrates the "focal point"** of any world or idea, שֶׁהִיא נְקוּדַת וּבְחִינַת מִדַּת אֱמֶת שֶׁלָּהּ — **which is the pivotal point of its "truth paradigm."**

PRACTICAL LESSONS

Even if you are not in love with G-d all the time, if you do your best, your worship is absolutely genuine.

In simple terms, the *Tanya* is teaching us that truth is not a single standard, but something which is calibrated *in context.* Every place, idea, and experience has its own "truth," depending on its precise location in the universe's complex time-space continuum.

So when we said before that the *beinoni's* love was true "for him," we were not exercising poetic license. Truth, at least in its Kabbalistic understanding, means dif-

שלמטה הם כאין לגבי מעלות ומדרגות שלמעלה מהן

[כידוע לי"ח שבחי' ראש ומוחין של מדרגות תחתונות

הן למטה מבחי' עקביים ורגלי מדרגות עליונות מהן

וכמאמר רז"ל רגלי החיות כנגד כולן]:

19B

ferent things in different contexts; and for the *beinoni*, true worship is having palpable love for G-d, even if it is only during prayer.

וּמִדַּת אֱמֶת הִיא נַחֲלָה בְּלִי מְצָרִים — **And the paradigm of "truth"** is what the *Talmud*
refers to as Jacob's **"unlimited inheritance"** to us (*Talmud, Shabbos* 118a), וְאֵין לָהּ
שִׁיעוּר לְמַעֲלָה עַד רוּם הַמַּעֲלוֹת — **and it has no upper** metaphysical **limit, reaching
to the highest of elevations.**

Just as G-d promised Jacob, *"you will spread out to the west, to the east, to
the north and to the south"* (*Genesis* 28:14), in all directions without any limitation,
Jacob's paradigm of "truth," too, has no metaphysical limitations.

וְכָל מַעֲלוֹת וּמַדְרֵגוֹת שֶׁלְמַטָּה הֵם כְּאַיִן לְגַבֵּי מַעֲלוֹת וּמַדְרֵגוֹת שֶׁלְמַעְלָה מֵהֶן — **And all**
**the lower levels and rungs are of no significance when compared with the levels
and rungs above them.**

Since the world depends on G-d, and is not sustainable independently from Him,
the world is not "true" when compared with G-d. Your life also, which began a number of years ago and will eventually end, is transitory when compared with the
existence of the world.

So the "paradigm of truth" is relative. What is "true" (permanent) in one context
turns out to be temporary in another.

This adds some depth to the *Tanya's* discussion about the love of the *tzadik* and
the love of the *beinoni*. While the *beinoni's* love may be true for him (in his context),
for the *tzadik*, it would be considered "of no significance."

[כַּיָּדוּעַ לְיוֹדְעֵי חָכְמָה נִסְתָּרָה] שֶׁבְּחִינַת רֹאשׁ — **As is known to sages of esoteric wisdom,**
וּמוֹחִין שֶׁל מַדְרֵגוֹת תַּחְתּוֹנוֹת — **that something considered the "head" and "brain"**
of lower rungs, הֵן לְמַטָּה מִבְּחִינַת עֲקֵבַיִים וְרַגְלֵי מַדְרֵגוֹת עֶלְיוֹנוֹת מֵהֶן — **is actually**
inferior to something considered the "heels" and "feet" of higher rungs.

וּכְמַאֲמַר רַבּוֹתֵינוּ זִכְרוֹנָם לִבְרָכָה — **As our Sages of blessed memory taught,**
רַגְלֵי הַחַיּוֹת כְּנֶגֶד כּוּלָן] — *"the distance from the earth to the firmament is a journey*
of 500 years, and the thickness of the firmament is a journey of 500 years, and
likewise the distance between one firmament and the other; and above them (the
seven heavens) are the holy living creatures (chayos ha-kodesh); **and the feet of**
the living creatures are equal to all of them together" (*Talmud, Chagigah* 13a).

From this passage in the *Talmud*, we see the exponential divide between each
rung of the spiritual hierarchy. At each plane, everything below is insignificant.

פרק יד וְהִנֵּה מדת הבינוני היא מדת כל אדם
ואחריה כל אדם ימשוך שכל
אדם יכול להיות בינוני בכל עת ובכל שעה כי הבינוני
אינו מואס ברע שזהו דבר המסור ללב ולא כל העתים

CHAPTER 14

LIVING IN THE "NOW"

SECTION ONE: HOW TO BECOME A BEINONI, NOW

21ST TEVES REGULAR | 26TH TEVES LEAP

Up to this point in the *Tanya*, our discussion has been theoretical. We have explored the various categories of *rasha, beinoni* and *tzadik,* and their inner psyche, but the author has not made known what he expects of us.

Now, in the fourteenth chapter, we are finally advised what can reasonably be achieved by the ordinary person, and what is beyond reach.

וְהִנֵּה מִדַּת הַבֵּינוֹנִי הִיא מִדַּת כָּל אָדָם — **Now, the level of the** *beinoni* **is a standard attainable by every person,** וְאַחֲרֶיהָ כָּל אָדָם יִמְשׁוֹךְ — **and,** practically speaking, **every person ought to aim towards it.**

While the level of *beinoni*, who has achieved absolute self-mastery in his action, speech and thought, might seem to be something attainable by only a small elite, the *Tanya* sets it as the universal standard. Not only is it *theoretically* attainable by us all, it is something that, *practically speaking,* we should all be striving for.

How long does the *Tanya* expect this exhaustive task to take us? Might it require a lifetime of spiritual work?

שֶׁכָּל אָדָם יָכוֹל לִהְיוֹת בֵּינוֹנִי בְּכָל עֵת וּבְכָל שָׁעָה — In fact, **any person can become a** *beinoni* **at any moment, at any time.**

Not only does the *Tanya* deem the level of *beinoni* to be attainable by everyone, it is practically possible *now*. As a *beinoni* you do not need to refine your inner, selfish core, you merely need to *behave* appropriately; and every person can be in complete control of his or her behavior.

(And while the *Tanya* stated in chapter 12 that the *beinoni, "has never committed any transgression in his life,"* past sins can be instantly erased through *teshuvah* — Notes on Tanya).

שֶׁזֶּהוּ דְּבָר הַמָּסוּר — **For the** *beinoni* **is not repulsed by evil,** כִּי הַבֵּינוֹנִי אֵינוֹ מוֹאֵס בָּרַע וְלֹא כָּל הָעִתִּים לַלֵּב — **since that is a** *"matter of the heart"* (*Talmud, Kidushin* 32b),

שָׁווֹת אֶלָּא סוּר מֵרַע וַעֲשֵׂה טוֹב דְּהַיְינוּ בְּפוֹעַל מַמָּשׁ
בְּמַעֲשֶׂה דִבּוּר וּמַחֲשָׁבָה שֶׁבָּהֶם הַבְּחִירָה וְהַיְכוֹלֶת
וְהָרְשׁוּת נְתוּנָה לְכָל אָדָם לַעֲשׂוֹת וּלְדַבֵּר וְלַחֲשׁוֹב גַּם
מַה שֶּׁהוּא נֶגֶד תַּאֲוַת לִבּוֹ וְהִפְכָה מַמָּשׁ כִּי גַם בְּשָׁעָה
שֶׁהַלֵּב חוֹמֵד וּמִתְאַוֶּה אֵיזוֹ תַּאֲוָה גַּשְׁמִיִּית בְּהֶיתֵּר אוֹ
בְּאִיסוּר ח"ו יָכוֹל לְהִתְגַּבֵּר וּלְהָסִיחַ דַּעְתּוֹ מִמֶּנָּה לְגַמְרֵי
בְּאָמְרוֹ לְלִבּוֹ אֵינֶנִּי רוֹצֶה לִהְיוֹת רָשָׁע אֲפִי' שָׁעָה אַחַת
כִּי אֵינֶנִּי רוֹצֶה לִהְיוֹת מוּבְדָּל וְנִפְרָד ח"ו מֵה' אֶחָד בְּשׁוּם

שָׁווֹת — **and,** for most people, to be constantly repulsed is not possible as their emotions **are not the same all the time.**

As we have seen, the *beinoni* is not in control of his deep emotional core, and may be troubled by conflicting, selfish emotions. Sometimes, during moments of spiritual elation, he will find it easier to quash those urges, while at other times, when he is feeling low, it will be more difficult.

אֶלָּא סוּר מֵרַע וַעֲשֵׂה טוֹב — The *beinoni* is not required to have mastery of his emotions, **only to** have impeccable behavior, to *"turn away from evil and do good"* (Psalms 34:15), דְּהַיְינוּ בְּפוֹעַל מַמָּשׁ בְּמַעֲשֶׂה דִבּוּר וּמַחֲשָׁבָה — *i.e.,* **practically, in actual deed, speech and thought.**

שֶׁבָּהֶם הַבְּחִירָה וְהַיְכוֹלֶת וְהָרְשׁוּת נְתוּנָה לְכָל אָדָם — **For, in these areas, every person has the freedom of will, the capacity, and the autonomy,** לַעֲשׂוֹת וּלְדַבֵּר וְלַחֲשׁוֹב גַּם — **to act, speak and think contrary to his heart's desire,** מַה שֶּׁהוּא נֶגֶד תַּאֲוַת לִבּוֹ וְהִפְכָה מַמָּשׁ — **even to the opposite extreme.**

This is the basic doctrine of free-choice, which has been clarified by *Rambam* (*Laws of Teshuvah,* chapter 5). The *Tanya* now advises us how to apply it practically, on every occasion, so as to achieve the self-mastery of a *beinoni*.

כִּי גַם בְּשָׁעָה שֶׁהַלֵּב חוֹמֵד וּמִתְאַוֶּה אֵיזוֹ תַּאֲוָה גַּשְׁמִיִּית — **For even when your heart lusts and desires a certain physical pleasure,** בְּהֶיתֵּר אוֹ בְּאִיסוּר חַס וְשָׁלוֹם — regard-less of **whether it is permitted or, G-d forbid, prohibited** by Jewish law, יָכוֹל לְהִתְגַּבֵּר — **you can strengthen yourself** not to succumb and com-pletely divert your attention from it, וּלְהָסִיחַ דַּעְתּוֹ מִמֶּנָּה לְגַמְרֵי בְּאָמְרוֹ לְלִבּוֹ אֵינֶנִּי רוֹצֶה לִהְיוֹת רָשָׁע אֲפִילוּ שָׁעָה אַחַת — **by saying to yourself, "I don't want to be a *rasha,* even for a moment."**

The key to reaching the mastery of a *beinoni,* is being fully present in the mo-ment. Don't be concerned with how pious you might have been in the past, or what your "story" tells you about how good or bad a person you are. You simply have to be in the "here and now." At this moment, do you want to be with G-d, or discon-nected from Him? The choice is yours.

כִּי אֵינֶנִּי רוֹצֶה לִהְיוֹת מוּבְדָּל וְנִפְרָד חַס וְשָׁלוֹם מֵה' אֶחָד בְּשׁוּם אוֹפֶן — You simply say to yourself, **"For I don't want to be separated and disconnected in any way, from the One G-d, G-d forbid."**

אופן כדכתיב עונותיכם מבדילים וגו' רק אני רוצה
לדבקה בו נפשי רוחי ונשמתי בהתלבשן בשלשה
לבושיו ית' שהם מעשה דבור ומחשבה בה' ותורתו

Don't look upon your account of good deeds and transgressions as an overall "score" by which you will one day be judged; a score which might be adjusted later if you allow yourself some temporary indulgence. Focus exclusively on the present. A *mitzvah* (or any detail of *halachah*) is your key to being connected to G-d now; a sin, or any violation of *halachah*, will separate you from G-d, right now.

כְּדִכְתִיב עֲונוֹתֵיכֶם הָיוּ מַבְדִּילִים וְגוֹ' — **As the verse states,** *"Your sins were a separation between you and G-d"* (Isaiah 59:2).

People tend to calculate whether they are going to do a *mitzvah* or a sin based on their *self-perception*. If I am a good person, I want to maintain that image of myself by continuing to act virtuously. If I see myself as a bad person, or someone who has a history of sinful behavior, then another lapse might seem to be okay.

The paradigm of the *beinoni* teaches us that all this doesn't really matter. Deep down you really are a selfish person; the deep core of your emotions seeks gratification. You're not going to change that very easily.

But that's not so important, because you don't "reside" in that deep core. You inhabit your consciousness — your thought, speech and action — and the Torah is your "tool" to connect every conscious experience with G-d.

G-d doesn't really care that much what's happening in your deep core. If He did, He would have given you the power to change it — but He didn't. What He did do, is give you power over your conscious behavior through which you can choose to connect with Him at every moment.

Don't worry about the question, "Am I a good or bad person?" because the answer to that is very simple: Much of your deep core *is* bad. At that level, you are simply "in it for yourself." That's not going to change.

Ask yourself another question: Despite the fact that, deep down, I am bad, do I want my conscious self to be one with G-d right now?

PRACTICAL LESSONS

Your actions, speech and thoughts are under your complete control. Right now, you can achieve total self-mastery, if you so desire.

The key to this is focusing on the "now." Don't obsess over how bad you were in the past. Say: Right now I want to be connected to G-d.

רַק אֲנִי רוֹצֶה לְדָבְקָה בּוֹ נַפְשִׁי רוּחִי וְנִשְׁמָתִי — **Rather, I want to connect** my entire consciousness, **my *nefesh, ruach* and *neshamah*, with Him,** בְּהִתְלַבְּשָׁן בְּשְׁלֹשָׁה לְבוּשָׁיו יִתְבָּרֵךְ — and this is done practically **by "dressing" them in His blessed "garments"** — שֶׁהֵם מַעֲשֶׂה דִּבּוּר וּמַחֲשָׁבָה בַּה' וְתוֹרָתוֹ וּמִצְוֹתָיו — **which are the action, speech and thought of G-d, His Torah and His commandments.**

ומצותיו מאהבה מסותרת שבלבי לה' כמו בלב כללו'
ישראל שנקראו אוהבי שמך ואפי' קל שבקלים יכול
למסור נפשו על קדושת ה' ולא נופל אנכי ממנו
בודאי אלא אלא שנכנס בו רוח שטות ונדמה לו שבעביר'
זו עודנו ביהדותו ואין נשמתו מובדלת מאלהי ישראל
וגם שוכח אהבתו לה' המסותרת בלבו אבל אני אינני

מֵאַהֲבָה מְסוּתֶרֶת שֶׁבְּלִבִּי לַה' — I can choose to connect to G-d at any time **by virtue of the love of G-d that is** always **dormant in my heart,** כְּמוֹ בְּלֵב כְּלָלוּת יִשְׂרָאֵל שֶׁנִּקְרְאוּ אוֹהֲבֵי שְׁמֶךָ — **as it is in the heart of all Israel, who are called "lovers of Your Name"** (*Psalms* 5:12).

A second piece of advice that the *Tanya* offers us when battling the urge for self-gratification, is to compare ourselves to the most irreverent Jew.

וַאֲפִילוּ קַל שֶׁבְּקַלִּים יָכוֹל לִמְסוֹר נַפְשׁוֹ עַל קְדוּשַׁת הַשֵׁם — Say to yourself, **"Even the most irreverent Jew is capable of giving up his life** when faced with the ultimatum, "Convert or die!" **to sanctify G-d's name,** וְלֹא נוֹפֵל אָנֹכִי מִמֶּנּוּ בְּוַדַּאי — **and surely, I am not worse than him?"**

As we will discuss at length in chapter 18 (pp. 218-9), the *Tanya* reads much significance into the historical phenomenon of Jewish martyrdom. The fact that otherwise irreverent Jews chose death over conversion in so many instances is proof to the *Tanya* of a dormant urge in all Jews to put aside personal gratification for the sake of G-d.

But if even the irreverent Jew possess this urge, how is it possible for him to sin?

אֶלָּא שֶׁנִּכְנַס בּוֹ רוּחַ שְׁטוּת — **It is only that** *"a delusional spirit enters him"* (*Talmud*, *Sotah* 3a; see chapter 12, p. 145), וְנִדְמֶה לוֹ שֶׁבַּעֲבֵירָה זוֹ עוֹדֶנּוּ בְּיַהֲדוּתוֹ — **and** unlike the case of conversion, where the person is fully aware that he will become separated from G-d, **he imagines that, even with committing this sin he will still retain his Jewishness,** וְאֵין נִשְׁמָתוֹ מוּבְדֶּלֶת מֵאֱלֹהֵי יִשְׂרָאֵל — **and his soul will not become disconnected from the G-d of Israel.**

The truth is that we live in the present, and right now, any sin (or even an act of kosher self-gratification from which G-d-consciousness has been removed) *will* disconnect you from G-d. To think otherwise is "delusional."

וְגַם שׁוֹכֵחַ אַהֲבָתוֹ לַה' הַמְסוּתֶרֶת בְּלִבּוֹ — In addition to making a person lose touch with his reverence of G-d, the "delusional spirit" also makes him **unconscious of the dormant love of G-d in his heart.**

This state of mind is called "delusional" because its absurdity is easily exposed. You know that deep in your heart you long to come close to G-d and that any sin will disconnect you.

רוֹצֶה לִהְיוֹת שׁוֹטֶה כָּמוֹהוּ לִכְפּוֹר הָאֱמֶת. מַשָׁא"כ
בְּדָבָר הַמָּסוּר לַלֵּב דְּהַיְינוּ שֶׁיְּהֵא הָרָע מָאוּס מַמָּשׁ בְּלֵב
וְשָׂנוּי בְּתַכְלִית שִׂנְאָה אוֹ אֲפִי' שֶׁלֹּא בְּתַכְלִית שִׂנְאָה
הִנֵּה זֶה אִי אֶפְשָׁר שֶׁיִּהְיֶה בָּאֱמֶת לַאֲמִיתּוֹ אֶלָּא עַ"יְ גּוֹדֶל
וְתוֹקֶף הָאַהֲבָה לַה' בִּבְחִי' אַהֲבָה בַּתַּעֲנוּגִים לְהִתְעַנֵּג   20A

אֲבָל אֲנִי אֵינֶנִי רוֹצֶה לִהְיוֹת שׁוֹטֶה כָּמוֹהוּ לִכְפּוֹר הָאֱמֶת — So say to yourself, "That person may allow himself to be delusional, **but I don't want to be a fool like him, to deny what is** obviously **true!"**

SECTION TWO: WHY YOU (PROBABLY) WON'T BECOME A TZADIK

27TH TEVES LEAP

Having taught us that behavioral perfection (*beinoni*) is immediately attainable, the *Tanya* now explains why emotional mastery (*tzadik*) is, for most of us, beyond reach.

מַה שֶׁאֵין כֵּן בְּדָבָר הַמָּסוּר לַלֵּב — **This** capacity for instant change **is not so with "matters of the heart,"** in the deep core of your Animal Soul, דְּהַיְינוּ שֶׁיְּהֵא הָרָע מָאוּס — **namely, that evil** and self-gratification **should actually be despised in your heart,** מַמָּשׁ בְּלֵב וְשָׂנוּי בְּתַכְלִית שִׂנְאָה — either **detested utterly,** as is the case with a complete *tzadik,* אוֹ אֲפִילוּ שֶׁלֹּא בְּתַכְלִית שִׂנְאָה — **or detested, but not utterly,** as is the case with an incomplete *tzadik,* (see pp. 125-8).

הִנֵּה זֶה אִי אֶפְשָׁר שֶׁיִּהְיֶה בָּאֱמֶת לַאֲמִיתּוֹ — While you might be able to conjure up these emotions sometimes, they **cannot be achieved in a truly genuine** (i.e., consistent) **way,** אֶלָּא עַל יְדֵי גּוֹדֶל וְתוֹקֶף הָאַהֲבָה לַה' — **unless** you develop **an immense and powerful love of G-d.**

בִּבְחִינַת אַהֲבָה בַּתַּעֲנוּגִים — As we learned in chapter 9, this can only be achieved by the experience of *"pleasurable love"* (*Song* 7:7).

To reach the level of *tzadik* you must experience "pleasurable love,"

לְהִתְעַנֵּג עַל ה' מֵעֵין עוֹלָם הַבָּא — **which is to take pleasure in G-d** alone, **in a way that is a foretaste of the world-that-is-coming,** וְעַל זֶה אָמְרוּ רַבּוֹתֵינוּ זִכְרוֹנָם לִבְרָכָה — **as** the Sages of blessed memory said, עוֹלָמְךָ תִּרְאֶה בְּחַיֶּיךָ כו' — *"You shall see your* next **world in your lifetime etc.,"** (*Talmud, Brachos* 17a; see p. 118).

If a person's pleasure is in the worship of G-d alone, and he has no desire for self-gratification, he has really attained the level of the afterlife in this world.

כִּי זֶהוּ כְּעֵין קִבּוּל שָׂכָר — **But not every person merits this,** וְאֵין כָּל אָדָם זוֹכֶה לְזֶה — **because** it's not so much an achievement of human worship, **but a kind of reward received** from G-d (as we will see at the end of the chapter).

"Pleasurable love" is compared to the experience of the next world, not only due to its unusual intensity, but also to stress that most people are unable to reach it. If

עַל ה' מֵעֵין עוה"ב. וְעַל זֶה אָמְרוּ רז"ל עוֹלָמְךָ תִּרְאֶה
בְּחַיֶּיךָ כו' וְאֵין כָּל אָדָם זוֹכֶה לָזֶה כִּי זֶהוּ כְּעֵין קִבּוּל שָׂכָר
וּכְדִכְתִיב עֲבוֹדַת מַתָּנָה אֶתֵּן אֶת כְּהוּנַּתְכֶם וְגו' כמ"ש
בְּמ"א. וְלָכֵן אָמַר אִיּוֹב בָּרָאתָ צַדִּיקִים וכו' וּכְדְאִיתָא
בְּתִיקּוּנִים שֶׁיֵּשׁ בְּנִשְׁמוֹת יִשְׂרָאֵל כַּמָּה מִינֵי מַדְרֵגוֹת
וּבְחִי'. חֲסִידִים גִּבּוֹרִים הַמִּתְגַּבְּרִים עַל יִצְרָם מָארֵי
תוֹרָה נְבִיאִים כו' צַדִּיקִים כו' ע"ש:

you do get there, it's more of a reward from G-d for your efforts than something you achieved entirely through your own merits.

וּכְדִכְתִיב עֲבוֹדַת מַתָּנָה אֶתֵּן אֶת כְּהוּנַּתְכֶם וְגו' — **As the verse states,** *"I have given you the service of your priesthood as a gift, etc.,"* (*Numbers* 18:7), where "priesthood" is a metaphor for the love of G-d, כְּמוֹ שֶׁנִּתְבָּאֵר בְּמָקוֹם אַחֵר — **as is explained elsewhere** (see chapter 43; *Tanya, Igeres Ha-Kodesh* 6, 18).

This insight will enable us to answer our remaining question from chapter 1.

וְלָכֵן אָמַר אִיּוֹב בָּרָאתָ צַדִּיקִים כו' — **That is why Job said,** *"Master of the Universe! You have created tzadikim etc."*

In chapter 1, we asked: How could Job imply that G-d *creates* a person as righteous, when this is surely something left to an individual's free choice?

But now we understand that free choice only extends to our behavior (thought, speech and action), *i.e.,* whether or not we choose to become a *beinoni*. We do not have free choice over our deep core, whether we will consistently experience "pleasurable love" and become a *tzadik*. The ability to reach the level of *tzadik* is really a question of natural disposition, of how we were "created," as Job put it.

וּכְדְאִיתָא בְּתִיקּוּנִים שֶׁיֵּשׁ בְּנִשְׁמוֹת יִשְׂרָאֵל כַּמָּה מִינֵי מַדְרֵגוֹת וּבְחִינוֹת — **As it is taught** in the *Tikunei Zohar* (1b) that among the souls of Israel there are many levels and types, חֲסִידִים גִּבּוֹרִים הַמִּתְגַּבְּרִים עַל יִצְרָם מָארֵי תוֹרָה נְבִיאִים כו' צַדִּיקִים כו' — "*chasidim* (pious ones), *giborim* (strong ones)," who overpower their evil inclination, "*masters of the Torah, nevi'im* (prophets), *etc., tzadikim etc.,*" עַיֵּין שָׁם — **Look there** in the *Tikunei Zohar.*

A CHASIDIC THOUGHT

I definitely have a dormant love for G-d, which is found in my Divine Soul. I might also develop a palpable love for G-d during prayer or at peak moments. But my failure to *sustain* that intensity of love on a permanent basis shows that my Animal Soul's deep core remains unrefined.

וּבְזֶה   יובן כפל לשון השבועה תהי צדיק ואל תהי
רשע דלכאורה תמוה כי מאחר שמשביעים
אותו תהי צדיק למה צריכים להשביעו עוד שלא יהיה
רשע. אלא משום שאין כל אדם זוכה להיות צדיק
ואין לאדם משפט הבחירה בזה כל כך להתענג על ה'
באמת ושיהיה הרע מאוס ממש באמת ולכן משביעים
שנית אל תהי רשע עכ"פ שבזה משפט הבחירה

The *Tikunei Zohar* teaches that different souls are suited to varying styles of worship. Some souls were created with the power to become *tzadikim*; others weren't.

22ND TEVES REGULAR | 28TH TEVES LEAP

וּבְזֶה יוּבַן כֶּפֶל לְשׁוֹן הַשְּׁבוּעָה תְּהִי צַדִּיק וְאַל תְּהִי רָשָׁע — **This will also enable us to explain the repetition in the oath** which the soul swears before birth, *"Be a tzadik! And do not be a rasha!"* (above, chapter 1).

דְּלִכְאוֹרָה תָּמוּהַּ — **At first glance, this seems bizarre,** כִּי מֵאַחַר שֶׁמַּשְׁבִּיעִים אוֹתוֹ תְּהִי צַדִּיק — **because if the** soul **has already been made to swear an oath to** *"be a tzadik,"* לָמָּה צְרִיכִים לְהַשְׁבִּיעוֹ עוֹד שֶׁלֹּא יִהְיֶה רָשָׁע — **what is the point in making him swear a further oath,** *"don't be a rasha"?*

We did not pose this question in chapter 1, but now we can answer it.

אֶלָּא מִשּׁוּם שֶׁאֵין כָּל אָדָם זוֹכֶה לִהְיוֹת צַדִּיק — **Rather, since not everyone is privileged to become a** *tzadik,* it's not enough just to promise to "be a *tzadik*," a task in which the soul may never succeed, וְאֵין לְאָדָם מִשְׁפַּט הַבְּחִירָה בָּזֶה כָּל כָּךְ — **for a person does not have a significant degree of free choice,** לְהִתְעַנֵּג עַל ה' בֶּאֱמֶת — whether or not he will experience a steady "pleasurable love," for G-d, וְשֶׁיִּהְיֶה הָרַע מָאוּס מַמָּשׁ בֶּאֱמֶת — or **if he will, on a consistent basis, absolutely detest evil,** these two qualities being the hallmark of a *tzadik.*

וְלָכֵן מַשְׁבִּיעִים שֵׁנִית — **Therefore,** since the soul may not succeed with the first oath, **it is made to swear a second one,** אַל תְּהִי רָשָׁע עַל כָּל פָּנִים — **if** you try to become a *tzadik* and do not succeed, **at the very least,** *"Do not be a rasha!"* and actually sin; rather, make sure you remain a *beinoni,* שֶׁבָּזֶה מִשְׁפַּט הַבְּחִירָה וְהָרְשׁוּת נְתוּנָה לְכָל אָדָם — **because in this matter, every person** *does* **have the freedom of choice and autonomy,** לִמְשׁוֹל בְּרוּחַ תַּאֲוָתוֹ שֶׁבְּלִבּוֹ — **to overcome the desires which arise in his**

PRACTICAL LESSONS

You will probably never achieve self-mastery over your deep emotional core, which seeks self-gratification. Unless your soul was built for that, it's not really possible.

But that shouldn't stop you trying. Take time in your week to meditate on ideas that will help you to change your inner core, at least a little.

והרשות נתונה לכל אדם למשול ברוח תאותו שבלבו
ולכבוש יצרו שלא יהיה רשע אפי' שעה אחת כל ימיו
בין בבחי' סור מרע בין בבחי' ועשה טוב ואין טוב אלא
תורה דהיינו תלמוד תורה שכנגד כולן. אך אעפ"כ
צריך לקבוע לו עתים גם כן לשית עצות בנפשו להיות
מואס ברע כגון בעצת חכמינו ז"ל אשה חמת מלאה

שֶׁלֹּא יִהְיֶה רָשָׁע אֲפִילוּ שָׁעָה, **and to win over his impulse** to evil, וְלִכְבּוֹשׁ יִצְרוֹ **heart,** אַחַת כָּל יָמָיו — **so that he will not be a** *rasha* **even for one moment in his entire life.**

בֵּין בִּבְחִינַת סוּר מֵרַע — And this consistency is possible **both in the area of** *"turn away from evil"* (refraining from the negative), בֵּין בִּבְחִינַת וַעֲשֵׂה טוֹב — **and in the realm of** *"do good"* (positive behavior).

וְאֵין טוֹב אֶלָּא תוֹרָה — And *"'good' refers to nothing other than Torah"* (*Talmud, Brachos* 5a), דְּהַיְינוּ תַּלְמוּד תוֹרָה שֶׁכְּנֶגֶד כּוּלָן — namely, *"the study of the Torah which is equal to them all"* (*Mishnah, Pe'ah* 1:1).

As we have discussed at length in chapter 5, the most intimate bond you can have with G-d is through studying the Torah, and this is available at every spare moment for the *beinoni*.

SECTION THREE: DON'T GIVE UP ON BECOMING A TZADIK

The sobering "reality check" that you will probably never reach the level of *tzadik*, doesn't mean that you should stop trying. Before you were born, your soul swore an oath that it would always try to "be a *tzadik*," even if it would never get there.

This is not a case of "banging your head against the wall," trying to succeed in a task which is doomed from the start. Even if you can't achieve the emotions of a *tzadik* in their full depth and on a consistent basis, you can achieve them partially, on occasion, and such an experience will be immensely beneficial (as we shall see).

A *tzadik* takes pleasure in worshiping G-d like you would enjoy a plate of good food. And he is disgusted by the idea of self-gratification, just as you are disgusted by dirt and filth. The key, then, to fulfilling your oath, is to spend some time contemplating the emptiness of physical pleasure and the joy of worship.

אַךְ אַף עַל פִּי כֵן צָרִיךְ לִקְבּוֹעַ לוֹ עִתִּים גַּם כֵּן — **Nevertheless, you ought to designate at least some time,** לָשִׁית עֵצוֹת בְּנַפְשׁוֹ — to *"seek advice for your soul"* (*Psalms* 13:3), לִהְיוֹת מוֹאֵס בְּרָע — to **develop a disgust for evil.**

It is not expected of you to despise evil consistently, like a *tzadik*, but you should do regular emotional work towards that goal.

כְּגוֹן בַּעֲצַת חֲכָמֵינוּ זִכְרוֹנָם לִבְרָכָה אִשָּׁה חֵמֶת מְלֵאָה צוֹאָה כוּ' — **For example** to counter sexual temptation, **our Sages advised** that, at the moment an unwanted urge

צואה כו'. וכהאי גוונא. וכן כל מיני מטעמים ומעדנים נעשים כך חמת מלא כו'. וכן כל תענוגי עוה"ז החכם רואה הנולד מהן שסופן לרקוב ולהיות רמה ואשפה וההפך להתענג ולשמוח בה' ע"י התבוננות בגדולת א"ס

arises, to look at a **woman as *"a pouch full of feces, etc.,"*** (*Talmud, Shabbos* 152a), וּכְהַאי גַוְונָא — **and other similar ideas.**

The "mind game" which this teaching plays is to supplant an image that the man finds attractive with one which is naturally repulsive to him. Logically, there is no reason why a man should find a woman attractive — as *Rashi* comments on this passage, that male attraction to the female is an irrational, "Divine decree." Similarly, there is no logical reason why we should be particularly repulsed by feces, a mixture of water, cellulose and minerals. But that is human nature.

Male attraction can easily be "turned off" by something he finds unattractive. Playing on this weakness, the Sages suggested that when a man's sexual attraction is undesirably strong, he should imagine the woman's intestines full of the very same fecal substance that he finds naturally repulsive. Perhaps this change of perspective will burst the bubble of his excitement.

וְכֵן כָּל מִינֵי מַטְעַמִּים וּמַעֲדַנִּים נַעֲשִׂים כָּךְ חֵמֶת מָלֵא כוּ' — **So, too,** when tempted by food, he can imagine **how all delicious foods and delicacies end up as a *"pouch full* of feces."**

Thinking what a delicious delicacy is going to look like after it has been digested may remove you from the spell of its allure, and stop you from wanting to eat it. The psychology here is that delight and repulsion are so very opposite that as soon as something is associated with repulsive imagery, it will be hard for you to find it delightful again.

וְכֵן כָּל תַּעֲנוּגֵי עוֹלָם הַזֶּה — **The same** principle **applies for all pleasures of this world,** הֶחָכָם רוֹאֶה הַנּוֹלָד מֵהֶן — ***"the wise person... sees the future outcome of them"*** (*Talmud, Tamid* 32a), שֶׁסּוֹפָן לִרְקוֹב וְלִהְיוֹת רִמָּה וְאַשְׁפָּה — **that in the end they rot, becoming worm-infested refuse.**

We all *know* what will eventually become of our pleasures; the question is how powerfully we are able to *visualize* the fact at the moment of temptation. A wise person "sees" the outcome of his potential actions before he indulges and successfully avoids unwanted temptation.

Using these types of meditation, even those of us who will never become *tzadikim* can begin to chip away at the deep emotional core of our Animal Souls and tone down our desire for self-gratification a few notches. In that way, we fulfill the oath sworn by our souls before birth, at least to *try* to "be a *tzadik*."

וְהַהֶפֶךְ לְהִתְעַנֵּג וְלִשְׂמוֹחַ בַּה' — In addition to your attempts to "despise evil," you should also carry out meditations **in the opposite direction, to take pleasure and**

ב"ה כפי יכולתו אף שיודע בנפשו שלא יגיע למדרגה
זו באמת לאמיתו כי אם בדמיונות אעפ"כ הוא יעשה
את שלו לקיים את השבועה שמשביעים תהי צדיק
וה' יעשה הטוב בעיניו. ועוד שההרגל על כל דבר
שלטון ונעשה טבע שני. וכשירגיל למאס את הרע
יהיה נמאס קצת באמת וכשירגיל לשמח לשמח ה' ע"י

20B

עַל יְדֵי הִתְבּוֹנְנוּת בִּגְדֻלַּת אֵין סוֹף בָּרוּךְ הוּא — **by meditating on the greatness of the Blessed Infinite Light** of G-d, **joy in G-d,** **כְּפִי יְכוֹלְתּוֹ** — **to the best of your ability.**

To fulfill your oath to "be a *tzadik*," you need to try a.) to be disgusted by evil; and, b.) to take real pleasure and joy in the worship of G-d. Practically, you do this by meditating on the ideas that will produce these emotions.

PRACTICAL LESSONS

The key to teaching your inner core to "detest evil" is *mind-association*. In your mind, associate self-gratifying experiences with things that are naturally disgusting to you.

If you practice this regularly, the force of habit alone will begin to condition your inner core.

אַף שֶׁיּוֹדֵעַ בְּנַפְשׁוֹ שֶׁלֹּא יַגִּיעַ לְמַדְרֵגָה זוֹ בֶּאֱמֶת לַאֲמִתּוֹ — **Even though you know, deep down, that you will never reach this level** of pleasure and joy in the worship of G-d, **genuinely and consistently,** **אַף עַל פִּי כֵן** — **except as a fond hope,** **כִּי אִם בְּדִמְיוֹנוֹת** **הוּא יַעֲשֶׂה אֶת שֶׁלּוֹ לְקַיֵּם אֶת הַשְּׁבוּעָה שֶׁמַּשְׁבִּיעִים תְּהִי צַדִּיק** — **nevertheless, you must do your best to fulfill the oath you were made to swear** before birth, to, **"be a *tzadik*,"** **וה' יַעֲשֶׂה הַטּוֹב בְּעֵינָיו** — **and "G-d will do what is good in His eyes"** (*2 Samuel* 10:12).

You must do what you can to reach the elusive level of *tzadik*. Whether or not you succeed is up to G-d.

But even if you do not succeed in becoming a *tzadik*, these types of meditations will make the struggle of fighting the *yetzer hara* easier for you. Once you have at least tasted the higher states of emotional refinement — despising evil even a little bit, and taking pleasure in G-d, even a little bit — the entire composition of the Animal Soul is weakened. You begin to crack its foundations (Rabbi Shalom Dov Ber Schneersohn, *Kuntres Etz Ha-Chaim,* chapter 7).

וְעוֹד — **And also,** even if your ability to despise evil and take pleasure in G-d lacks permanence and authenticity, **שֶׁהַהֶרְגֵּל עַל כָּל דָּבָר שִׁלְטוֹן** — **ultimately, the reality is** that *"habit rules all"* (Rabbenu Yonah, *Gates of Repentance* 2:30), **וְנַעֲשֶׂה טֶבַע שֵׁנִי** — **and** habit *"becomes second nature"* (Rabbi Meir Aldabi, *Shevilei Emunah* 4:2), **וּכְשֶׁיַּרְגִּיל לְמָאֵס אֶת הָרַע** — **so if you will make it your habit** to carry out the meditations **to detest evil,** **יִהְיֶה נִמְאָס קְצָת בֶּאֱמֶת** — **then,** out of habit alone, you will begin to **detest it genuinely,** at least **a little.**

התבוננות בגדולת ה' הרי באתערותא דלתתא
אתערותא דלעילא וכולי האי ואולי יערה עליו רוח
ממרום ויזכה לבחי' רוח משרש איזה צדיק שתתעבר
בו לעבוד ה' בשמחה אמיתית כדכתיב שמחו צדיקים
בה' ותתקיים בו באמת השבועה שמשביעים
תהי צדיק:

Attaining some of the positive emotions of the *tzadik,* however, is more difficult, since the above tactics we used for negative emotions won't work. Taking pleasure in G-d is not easy for people who are preoccupied with the experiences of the five senses. For this, you will probably need special assistance from G-d.

וּכְשֶׁיַּרְגִּיל לְשַׂמֵּחַ נַפְשׁוֹ בַּה' — **And when you will make it your habit to rejoice with your soul in G-d, 'ה,** עַל יְדֵי הִתְבּוֹנְנוּת בִּגְדוּלַת ה' — **through meditating upon the greatness of G-d,** הֲרֵי בְּאִתְעָרוּתָא דִלְתַתָּא אִתְעָרוּתָא דִלְעֵילָא — **since** *"with an awakening from below, there is an awaking from Above"* (*Zohar* 2, 135b), וְכוּלֵי הַאי וְאוּלַי יְעָרֶה — **perhaps, with all this** effort, *"a ruach (spirit) will pour upon him from on High"* (see *Isaiah* 32:15).

Unlike the negative emotions of detesting evil which you can learn yourself, the positive emotion of a "pleasurable rejoicing" in G-d requires some additional "spirit" granted to you through the grace of heaven.

While this might come to you as a result of your sustained efforts, it is by no means guaranteed. (That is why the *Tanya* stated earlier, "a person does not have *a significant degree of free choice* whether he will experience a steady pleasurable love".)

What exact form does this "spirit from on High" take?

וְיִזְכֶּה לִבְחִינַת רוּחַ מִשֹּׁרֶשׁ אֵיזֶה צַדִּיק שֶׁתִּתְעַבֵּר בּוֹ — **And if this happens, you will merit that the spirit of the soul-root of a particular** *tzadik* **will be "impregnated" into you,** לַעֲבוֹד ה' בְּשִׂמְחָה אֲמִיתִּית — **enabling you to genuinely worship G-d with joy, 'ה בַּה'** — **as the verse states that only** *"tzadikim are joyous with G-d"* (*Psalms* 97:12).

Soul-impregnation (*ibur*) is a kind of reincarnation that takes place during your lifetime, where, by Divine decree, a spark of a departed soul joins yours. When *ibur*

A CHASIDIC THOUGHT

Consistency can be achieved, even without full depth of feeling, through habit alone. If "detesting evil" like a *tzadik* cannot become your first nature, at least it can become your second nature, through prolonged, disciplined practice.

occurs, you become impregnated with a second dimension of spirit, often from a departed *tzadik*. This enables you to acquire some of the departed *tzadik's* qualities (see Rabbi Immanuel Chai Ricchi (1688-1743), *Mishnas Chasidim, Maseches Ibur Ha-Neshamos,* chapters 2-3).

וְתִתְקַיֵּים בּוֹ בֶּאֱמֶת הַשְּׁבוּעָה שֶׁמַּשְׁבִּיעִים תְּהִי צַדִּיק — **And then you will have truly fulfilled the oath that you were made to swear** before birth, to **"be a tzadik."**

This poses no contradiction to Job's statement that G-d "created *tzadikim,*" which implies that if your soul was not given the ability to become a *tzadik*, you cannot achieve it. Because, in this case, the *beinoni* did not become a *tzadik* on his own; he required a little of *someone else's* soul to do the job. As far as his own soul was concerned, he did not have the capability of becoming a *tzadik,* as Job had taught (*Notes on Tanya*).

CONCLUSION OF CHAPTERS 1–14

The first fourteen chapters of *Tanya* stand out as a self-contained unit, because it is here that the author lays down the core elements of his world-view — principles on which the rest of the book is based. The series of questions posed in chapter 1 are finally answered in chapters 13 and 14, providing closure to the interim discussions.

Chapters 1–14 also represent Rabbi Shneur Zalman's response to a problem which was probably shared by most people seeking his advice. Put succinctly, the question was probably something like this: *"Rebbe, however hard I try to connect to G-d, I feel like a failure. I want to come close to G-d, but even when I succeed in religious practice, my inner demons still bother me. I have peak moments when I feel close to G-d, but they are not sustainable. What should I do? Will I ever succeed?"*

PRACTICAL LESSONS

Without help from above, you won't be able to really "take pleasure in G-d." But it is still something you should long for and meditate towards.

Perhaps, if your efforts are sincere, G-d will give you some extra help by implanting an extra soul-spark in you, and you will succeed.

In a nutshell, the *Tanya's* answer in chapters 1–14 is: You have both "conscious behavior" (thought, speech and action) as well as a "deep emotional core." The Torah and its *mitzvos* guide you in how to connect your conscious behavior to G-d in the most profound way possible, at every moment of your life. That's where your focus should be. Your deep core will probably never change and will continue to taunt you with selfish urges for the rest of your life. But that doesn't mean you've failed. Actually, the fact that you can't completely change your deep core means that it's not your mission in life. The purpose of your existence is to fulfill your soul's promise to: a.) connect your conscious behavior to G-d at every moment ("Don't be a *rasha*"); and, b.) to develop the strongest emotional connection to G-d that you can (try your best to "be a *tzadik*"). It will probably always be a struggle, but G-d has tremendous pleasure from your ongoing efforts.

פרק טו ובזה יובן מ"ש ושבתם וראיתם בין
צדיק לרשע בין עובד אלהים
לאשר לא עבדו שההפרש בין עובד אלהים לצדיק
הוא שעובד הוא לשון הוה שהוא באמצע העבודה
שהיא המלחמה עם היצה"ר להתגבר עליו ולגרשו
מהעיר קטנה שלא יתלבש באברי הגוף שהוא באמת
עבודה ועמל גדול להלחם בו תמיד והיינו הבינוני.

CHAPTER 15

THE BEST VERSION OF YOURSELF
SECTION ONE: AVOIDING ROTE WORSHIP

23RD TEVES REGULAR | 29TH TEVES LEAP

In chapter 13, we learned that the experience of *beinoni* can occur at many levels. There is the "default," uninspired, *beinoni;* the *beinoni* at study and prayer, *etc.*

This chapter will broaden the discussion to include various classes of *beinonim,* differing in the levels of *effort* they invest. We will learn that it is possible for some *beinonim* to maintain their status with very little effort, while others must struggle greatly. This will lead to a discussion about the importance of effort in worship.

וּבָזֶה יוּבַן מַה שֶׁכָּתוּב — **Based on this** definition, that a *beinoni* is a person who never transgresses, **we can explain the verse,** וְשַׁבְתֶּם וּרְאִיתֶם בֵּין צַדִּיק לְרָשָׁע בֵּין עוֹבֵד אֱלֹהִים לַאֲשֶׁר לֹא עֲבָדוֹ — *"And you will again see* the distinction **between the tzadik and the rasha, between one who serves G-d and one who does not serve Him"** (*Malachi* 3:18).

Isn't the *tzadik* and the *"one who worships G-d"* the same thing?

שֶׁהֶהֶפְרֵשׁ בֵּין עוֹבֵד אֱלֹהִים לְצַדִּיק הוּא — **The difference between** *"one who serves G-d"* **and a** *tzadik* **is,** שֶׁעוֹבֵד הוּא לְשׁוֹן הֹוֶה — that *"one who serves"* **is a verb in the present tense,** שֶׁהוּא בְּאֶמְצַע הָעֲבוֹדָה — the use of a verb suggesting that this person **is in the ongoing process of worship,** שֶׁהִיא הַמִּלְחָמָה עִם הַיֵּצֶר הָרָע — **namely, the war with the** *yetzer hara,* לְהִתְגַּבֵּר עָלָיו וּלְגָרְשׁוֹ מֵהָעִיר קְטַנָּה — **to overcome it and chase it away from** the body, the **"small city,"** שֶׁלֹּא יִתְלַבֵּשׁ בְּאֶבְרֵי הַגּוּף — meaning that the *yetzer hara* **should never influence** any of **the body's limbs.**

שֶׁהוּא בֶּאֱמֶת עֲבוֹדָה וְעָמָל גָּדוֹל — **This truly requires a tremendous struggle and effort,** לְהִלָּחֶם בּוֹ תָּמִיד — **to constantly fight with it.**

אֲבָל הַצַּדִּיק נִקְרָא עֶבֶד ה' בְּשֵׁם הַתֹּאַר כְּמוֹ שֵׁם חָכָם
אוֹ מֶלֶךְ שֶׁכְּבָר נַעֲשָׂה חָכָם אוֹ מֶלֶךְ כָּךְ זֶה כְּבָר עָבַד
וְגָמַר לְגַמְרֵי עֲבוֹדַת הַמִּלְחָמָה עִם הָרָע עַד כִּי וַיְגָרְשֵׁהוּ
וַיֵּלֶךְ לוֹ וְלִבּוֹ חָלָל בְּקִרְבּוֹ. וּבְבֵינוֹנִי יֵשׁ ג״כ שְׁתֵּי מַדְרֵגוֹת
עוֹבֵד אֱלֹהִים וַאֲשֶׁר לֹא עֲבָדוֹ וְאעפ״כ אֵינוֹ רָשָׁע כִּי לֹא
עָבַר מִיָּמָיו שׁוּם עֲבֵירָה קַלָּה וְגַם קִיֵּם כָּל הַמִּצְוֹת
שֶׁאֶפְשָׁר לוֹ לְקַיְּמָן וְתַלְמוּד תּוֹרָה כְּנֶגֶד כֻּלָּם וְלֹא פָּסִיק

וְהַיְינוּ הַבֵּינוֹנִי — **So** it turns out that the "one who serves G-d," who is in the midst of an *ongoing* struggle, **is actually the *beinoni*.**

אֲבָל הַצַּדִּיק נִקְרָא עֶבֶד ה' בְּשֵׁם הַתֹּאַר — But the *tzadik* is usually **referred to by a noun, "*a servant of G-d*"** (*Deuteronomy* 34:5), כְּמוֹ שֵׁם חָכָם אוֹ מֶלֶךְ — which is **a title, like "scholar" or "king,"** that he has already achieved, שֶׁכְּבָר נַעֲשָׂה חָכָם אוֹ מֶלֶךְ — indicating that the person **has *already* become a scholar or king,** כָּךְ זֶה כְּבָר עָבַד וְגָמַר לְגַמְרֵי עֲבוֹדַת הַמִּלְחָמָה עִם הָרָע — **here, too,** the use of a noun implies that **this** person **has already "served" and completely finished his labor of fighting with the evil** in him, עַד כִּי וַיְגָרְשֵׁהוּ וַיֵּלֶךְ לוֹ — **to the extent that** "*he's driven it away and it's gone from him*"** (*Psalms* 34:1), וְלִבּוֹ חָלָל בְּקִרְבּוֹ — **and** he is a *tzadik* whose "*heart is empty within him*"** (*Psalms* 109:22; see p. 35), *i.e.,* he has no *yetzer hara* on the left side of his heart.

1ST SHEVAT LEAP

Our verse, then, mentions three categories: *"(1) the tzadik and (2) the rasha"* and *"(3) one who serves G-d (the beinoni)."* But whom does the fourth statement, *"one who does not serve Him,"* represent? We seem to have already covered every category, *tzadik, rasha* and *beinoni.*

The *Tanya* will demonstrate that *"one who does not serve Him,"* represents another, inferior type of *beinoni,* who makes a negligible effort to maintain his status.

וּבְבֵינוֹנִי יֵשׁ גַּם כֵּן שְׁתֵּי מַדְרֵגוֹת — **With *beinonim* there are also two levels,** עוֹבֵד אֱלֹהִים וַאֲשֶׁר לֹא עֲבָדוֹ — *"one who serves G-d"* and *"one who does not serve Him."*

וְאַף עַל פִּי כֵן אֵינוֹ רָשָׁע — The *beinoni* "who does not serve G-d" **is nevertheless not a *rasha*,** כִּי לֹא עָבַר מִיָּמָיו שׁוּם עֲבֵירָה קַלָּה — **because he has never committed** even **a minor transgression in his life** that has not been atoned for, וְגַם קִיֵּם כָּל הַמִּצְוֹת שֶׁאֶפְשָׁר לוֹ לְקַיְּמָן — **and he has also observed every *mitzvah* that was possible for him to observe,** וְתַלְמוּד תּוֹרָה כְּנֶגֶד כֻּלָּם — including *"the study of the Torah, which is equal to them all"* (*Mishnah, Pe'ah* 1:1), וְלֹא פָּסִיק פּוּמֵיהּ מִגִּירְסָא — **and he does not allow his mouth to stop studying.**

At first glance, the notion seems absurd. How could someone be a *beinoni,* always distancing the *yetzer hara* from his thought, speech and action, and *not* be considered "serving G-d"?

פוּמֵיהּ מִגִּירְסָא אֶלָּא שֶׁאֵינוֹ עוֹשֶׂה שׁוּם מִלְחָמָה עִם הַיֵּצֶר

לְנַצְּחוֹ עַ"י אוֹר ה' הַמֵּאִיר עַל נֶפֶשׁ הָאֱלֹהִית שֶׁבַּמּוֹחַ

הַשַּׁלִּיט עַל הַלֵּב כַּנַ"ל מִפְּנֵי שֶׁאֵין יִצְרוֹ עוֹמֵד לְנֶגְדּוֹ כְּלָל   21A

לְבַטְּלוֹ מִתּוֹרָתוֹ וַעֲבוֹדָתוֹ וְאֵין צָרִיךְ לִלְחוֹם עִמּוֹ כְּלָל

כְּגוֹן שֶׁהוּא מַתְמִיד בְּלִמּוּדוֹ בְּטִבְעוֹ מִתּוֹלַדְתּוֹ עַל יְדֵי

תִּגְבּוֹרֶת הַמָּרָה שְׁחוֹרָה וְכֵן אֵין לוֹ מִלְחָמָה מִתַּאֲוַת

נָשִׁים מִפְּנֵי שֶׁהוּא מְצוֹנָן בְּטִבְעוֹ וְכֵן בִּשְׁאָר תַּעֲנוּגֵי עוֹה"ז

הוּא מְחוּסַּר הַרְגֵּשׁ הֲנָאָה בְּטִבְעוֹ וְלָכֵן אֵין צָרִיךְ לְהִתְבּוֹנֵן

אֶלָּא — **But** despite absolute mastery over thought, speech and action, this *beinoni* is classified as, "one who does *not* serve G-d," for a simple reason, שֶׁאֵינוֹ עוֹשֶׂה שׁוּם מִלְחָמָה עִם הַיֵּצֶר לְנַצְּחוֹ — **because he is not actively fighting his *yetzer hara* at all, to overcome it,** עַל יְדֵי אוֹר ה' הַמֵּאִיר עַל נֶפֶשׁ הָאֱלֹהִית שֶׁבַּמּוֹחַ הַשַּׁלִּיט עַל הַלֵּב *— i.e.,* he is not **making use of the G-dly light which shines on his Divine Soul, within his brain,** to empower himself **to rule over** the urges of **his heart,** כַּנִּזְכָּר לְעֵיל — **as de-scribed above** (chapter 13, p. 154).

This *beinoni* "does not serve G-d," because he is not actively "at war" with his *yetzer hara*. He does not bother to employ the techniques we discussed in chapter 13 to maintain control of his Animal Soul.

But if the *beinoni*, by definition, has not eliminated the deep core of his Animal Soul, how can he afford *not* to fight with it? Why does he not stumble in sin?

מִפְּנֵי שֶׁאֵין יִצְרוֹ עוֹמֵד לְנֶגְדּוֹ כְּלָל — **Because** in this case, **his *yetzer hara* doesn't challenge him at all,** לְבַטְּלוֹ מִתּוֹרָתוֹ וַעֲבוֹדָתוֹ — **to draw him away from his study or his worship,** וְאֵין צָרִיךְ לִלְחוֹם עִמּוֹ כְּלָל — **so he doesn't have to fight it at all.**

What would cause a *yetzer hara* to be benign like this? The causes could be:

כְּגוֹן שֶׁהוּא מַתְמִיד בְּלִמּוּדוֹ בְּטִבְעוֹ מִתּוֹלַדְתּוֹ — **For example, a person whose inherent nature is to study constantly,** עַל יְדֵי תִּגְבּוֹרֶת הַמָּרָה שְׁחוֹרָה — **due to an abundance of "black bile,"** which leads to an analytical and serious temperament (according to the ancient science of "Humoralism," mentioned in the *Zohar* 3, 227b).

וְכֵן אֵין לוֹ מִלְחָמָה מִתַּאֲוַת נָשִׁים — **As well as a person who does not have to wrestle with a** strong **desire for women,** מִפְּנֵי שֶׁהוּא מְצוֹנָן בְּטִבְעוֹ — **because he is passion-less by nature.**

וְכֵן בִּשְׁאָר תַּעֲנוּגֵי עוֹלָם הַזֶּה — **And likewise with other worldly pleasures,** הוּא מְחוּסַּר הַרְגֵּשׁ הֲנָאָה בְּטִבְעוֹ — **he naturally lacks a** strong **feeling of enjoyment.**

All *yetzer haras* are not the same and some put up a weak fight. While a minimal level of love and reverence of G-d is still necessary to stay on track, those emo-tions could come naturally, without the need for major spiritual work. Such a case is called "one who does not serve G-d."

כל כך בגדולת ה' להוליד מבינתו רוח דעת ויראת ה'
במוחו להשמר שלא לעבור על מצות ל"ת ואהבת ה'
בלבו לדבקה בו בקיום המצות ות"ת כנגד כולן אלא
די לו באהבה מסותרת אשר בלב כללות ישראל
שנקראו אוהבי שמו ולכן אינו נקרא עובד כלל כי
אהבה זו המסותרת אינה פעולתו ועבודתו כלל אלא היא
ירושתנו מאבותינו לכלל ישראל וכמ"ש לקמן. וכן

וְלָכֵן — **And therefore,** since his *yetzer hara* offers a negligible pull, אֵין צָרִיךְ לְהִתְבּוֹנֵן כָּל כָּךְ בִּגְדוּלַת ה' — **he doesn't need to meditate too much on the greatness of G-d,** לְהוֹלִיד מִבִּינָתוֹ רוּחַ דַּעַת — **for his faculty of cognition (***binah***) to produce a sense of recognition (***da'as***),** as we discussed in chapter 3 (pp. 62-3), וְיִרְאַת ה' בְּמוֹחוֹ לְהִשָּׁמֵר שֶׁלֹּא לַעֲבוֹר עַל מִצְוֹת לֹא תַעֲשֶׂה — and consequently, that *da'as* gives rise to **reverence of G-d in his mind** and trepidation in his heart, **so as to be careful not to transgress any of the prohibitions.** All this is largely unnecessary, since his *yetzer hara* is so weak.

וְאַהֲבַת ה' בְּלִבּוֹ לְדָבְקָה בּוֹ בְּקִיּוּם הַמִּצְוֹת — Neither does he need to meditate to stir up **love of G-d in his heart,** to inspire himself **to connect to** G-d **through observing the** positive **commandments,** וְתַלְמוּד תּוֹרָה כְּנֶגֶד כּוּלָן — including **"the study of the Torah which is equal to them all,"** since he finds it possible to observe Jewish Law without a concerted effort.

At the core of the *Tanya's* worldview, are two convictions: a.) that you possess an inherent love of G-d, which may be dormant, but is always present; b.) that, through meditation on the greatness of G-d and contemplative prayer, you can stir up a much more powerful love.

The dormant love, ('a'), takes relatively little effort to awaken. The love which you stir up yourself, ('b'), is a huge, ongoing struggle (for someone who is not a *tzadik*).

The *beinoni* who "does not serve G-d" receives this title because he relies on dormant love ('a').

אֶלָּא — **Rather,** the *yetzer hara* of this *beinoni* is so negligible, דִּי לוֹ בְּאַהֲבָה מְסוּתֶּרֶת אֲשֶׁר בְּלֵב כְּלָלוּת יִשְׂרָאֵל — **that all he needs** to avoid its allure **is the "dormant love" found in the heart of all Israel** (see pp. 211ff), שֶׁנִּקְרְאוּ אוֹהֲבֵי שְׁמוֹ — **who are called "lovers of His Name"** (*Psalms* 69:37).

וְלָכֵן אֵינוֹ נִקְרָא עוֹבֵד כְּלָל — **Therefore,** this *beinoni* **cannot in any way be called "one who serves,"** כִּי אַהֲבָה זוֹ הַמְסוּתֶּרֶת אֵינָהּ פְּעוּלָּתוֹ וַעֲבוֹדָתוֹ כְּלָל — **because the** existence of **this "dormant love"** in his soul **was not brought about by him, nor is it in any way his achievement,** אֶלָּא הִיא יְרוּשָׁתֵנוּ מֵאֲבוֹתֵינוּ לְכָלַל יִשְׂרָאֵל — **rather, it is** our spiritual **"inheritance" from our Patriarchs to the whole of Israel,** וּכְמוֹ שֶׁיִּתְבָּאֵר לְקַמָּן — **as will be discussed below,** in chapters 18 and 44.

אַף מִי שֶׁאֵינוֹ מַתְמִיד בְּלִמּוּדוֹ בְּטִבְעוֹ רַק שֶׁהִרְגִּיל עַצְמוֹ
לִלְמוֹד בְּהַתְמָדָה גְדוֹלָה וְנַעֲשָׂה הַהֶרְגֵּל לוֹ טֶבַע שֵׁנִי דַּי
לוֹ בְּאַהֲבָה מְסוּתֶּרֶת זוֹ אא״כ רוֹצֶה לִלְמוֹד יוֹתֵר מֵרְגִילוֹתוֹ

Making use of the inherent, "dormant love" does not count as real spiritual work, because it was not earned through any effort in the first place. Rather, it is a natural proclivity of the soul, which was "inherited" from the Patriarchs.

Our discussion so far of "one who does not serve G-d," has been centered around a *beinoni* whose *yetzer hara* never really troubled him. Now we turn to another case: the *beinoni* who *did* have a bothersome *yetzer hara,* but has regulated it through disciplined practice so that it no longer bothers him. Worshiping G-d has now become his "second nature."

וְכֵן אַף מִי שֶׁאֵינוֹ מַתְמִיד בְּלִמּוּדוֹ בְּטִבְעוֹ — **The same** classification of a *beinoni* "who does not serve G-d" **is also applicable to a person who doesn't have a natural disposition to study all the time,** רַק שֶׁהִרְגִּיל עַצְמוֹ לִלְמוֹד בְּהַתְמָדָה גְדוֹלָה — **but has nevertheless trained himself to study with extreme persistence,** וְנַעֲשָׂה הַהֶרְגֵּל לוֹ טֶבַע שֵׁנִי — **and it has become normal for him, a "second nature."**

Many observant Jews share this kind of experience, in one way or another. For example, if you have kept kosher for a long time, you might have reached the point where you are not seriously tempted to eat non-kosher food. But that's not because you have transformed your deep core and eliminated the *yetzer hara*; it's just that the discipline of keeping kosher has become "second nature" to you.

דַּי לוֹ בְּאַהֲבָה מְסוּתֶּרֶת זוֹ — **For him,** the *beinoni* by "second nature," **this "dormant love" is enough** to maintain his level, without any extra effort, אֶלָּא אִם כֵּן רוֹצֶה לִלְמוֹד יוֹתֵר מֵרְגִילוֹתוֹ — **unless he wants to study more than he is accustomed,** in which case he will have to invest effort, and become "one who serves G-d," as we shall see in the following section.

In conclusion: A person who has disciplined himself to the point that his *yetzer hara* no longer bothers him might easily confuse himself with a *tzadik*; but he is far from the level of *tzadik*. The deep core of his Animal Soul has not been transformed to love G-d and detest evil. His *yetzer hara* fails to trouble him merely because it has been tamed by years of disciplined worship. He hasn't really changed inside; if he had, he would experience a profound "pleasurable love" of G-d and detest evil.

The hallmark of the *beinoni* "who does not serve G-d" is *stagnation*. He doesn't sin; his thought, speech and action follow G-d's will, and he has no strong urge to

PRACTICAL LESSONS

Behaving perfectly (in thought, speech and action) doesn't necessarily mean that you are serving G-d.

The hallmark of service is *effort*. If you're not wrestling with your darker side, you are not serving G-d. Period.

וּבְזֶה יוּבַן מַ"שׁ בַּגְּמָרָא דְעוֹבֵד אֱלֹהִים הַיְינוּ מִי שֶׁשּׁוֹנֶה
פִּרְקוֹ מֵאָה פְּעָמִים וְאֶחָד וְלֹא עֲבָדוֹ הַיְינוּ מִי שֶׁשּׁוֹנֶה
פִּרְקוֹ מֵאָה פְּעָמִים לְבַד וְהַיְינוּ מִשׁוּם שֶׁבִּימֵיהֶם הָיָה
הָרְגִילוּת לִשְׁנוֹת כָּל פֶּרֶק מֵאָה פְּעָמִים כִּדְאִיתָא הָתָם
בַּגְּמָרָא מָשָׁל מִשּׁוּק שֶׁל חַמָּרִים שֶׁנִּשְׂכָּרִים לַעֲשֶׂר פַּרְסֵי
בְּזוּזָא וּלְאֶחָד עֲשֶׂר פַּרְסֵי בִּתְרֵי זוּזֵי מִפְּנֵי שֶׁהוּא יוֹתֵר

do otherwise. But there is no growth in his worship. His nature (or "second nature"), enables him to function at what, for most people, would be a very high level; and while that is generally a good thing, it has a disadvantage too: it holds him back from growing. That is why he is classified as "one who does not serve G-d," because "service" implies an active mode of worship, and he is basically passive.

SECTION TWO: WHY EFFORT MATTERS

24TH TEVES REGULAR | 2ND SHEVAT LEAP

וּבָזֶה יוּבַן מַה שֶּׁכָּתוּב בַּגְּמָרָא — Based on this, we can explain the *Talmud's* statement, דְּעוֹבֵד אֱלֹהִים הַיְינוּ מִי שֶׁשּׁוֹנֶה פִּרְקוֹ מֵאָה פְּעָמִים וְאֶחָד — that *"one who serves G-d,"* refers to a person who reviews his studies 101 times, וְלֹא עֲבָדוֹ הַיְינוּ מִי שֶׁשּׁוֹנֶה פִּרְקוֹ מֵאָה פְּעָמִים לְבַד — and *"one who does not serve Him,"* refers to a person who reviews his studies only 100 times (*Talmud, Chagigah* 9b).

As the *Talmud* itself asks, after reviewing a lesson 100 times, a single extra review would seem to be relatively insignificant. Why should this earn a student the venerable title of "one who serves G-d"?

וְהַיְינוּ מִשּׁוּם שֶׁבִּימֵיהֶם הָיָה הָרְגִילוּת לִשְׁנוֹת כָּל פֶּרֶק מֵאָה פְּעָמִים — Because in those days it was normal to review each lesson 100 times.

Your *level* of worship doesn't determine if you are serving G-d or not. What matters is if you are *extending* yourself beyond what is normal and comfortable to you. If it's normal to review your studies 100 times, then to do it 101 times is "service."

כִּדְאִיתָא הָתָם בַּגְּמָרָא מָשָׁל מִשּׁוּק שֶׁל חַמָּרִים — As the *Talmud* itself offers an analogy from the donkey-drivers' rental market, שֶׁנִּשְׂכָּרִים לַעֲשֶׂר פַּרְסֵי בְּזוּזָא — where the donkeys could be hired for ten Persian miles for one *zuz* (silver coin), וּלְאֶחָד עֲשֶׂר פַּרְסֵי בִּתְרֵי זוּזֵי — whereas for eleven Persian miles, just one mile more, they charged double, two *zuzim,* מִפְּנֵי שֶׁהוּא יוֹתֵר מֵרְגִילוּתָם — because that extra mile extended them beyond their norm.

What, exactly, is added here by the "analogy from the donkey rental market"? There seems to be no fresh insight here.

The key point here is that the donkey is *rented;* it never becomes yours. That resembles the relationship between you and your Animal Soul: It may have all sorts

מרגילותם. ולכן זאת הפעם המאה ואחת היתרה על
הרגילות שהורגל מנעוריו שקולה כנגד כולן ועולה על
גביהן ביתר שאת ויתר עז להיות נקרא עובד אלהים
מפני שכדי לשנות טבע הרגילות צריך לעורר את
האהבה לה' ע"י שמתבונן בגדולת ה' במוחו לשלוט
על הטבע שבחלל השמאלי המלא דם הנפש הבהמית
שמהקליפה שממנה הוא הטבע וזו היא עבודה תמה   21B

of urges that you cannot fully control and "own," but you can "hire" the Animal Soul to serve G-d.

And this addresses an underlying question we have in this chapter. If I never fully transform (and "own") my Animal Soul, can I really be considered as serving G-d? The answer offered here by the *Tanya* is: Yes! You can "rent" your Animal Soul in the service of G-d. And as long as you extend your "animal" beyond its natural comfort zone, it will be considered real service (*Notes on Tanya*).

וְלָכֵן זֹאת הַפַּעַם הַמֵּאָה וְאַחַת — **Therefore,** when the student revises his studies for this 101st time, הַיִּתְרָה עַל הָרְגִילוּת שֶׁהוּרְגַּל מִנְּעוּרָיו — **over and above the norms ingrained in him since childhood,** שְׁקוּלָה כְּנֶגֶד כּוּלָּן — that one time counts as much as all of the other 100 times put together, וְעוֹלָה עַל גַּבֵּיהֶן בְּיֶתֶר שְׂאֵת וְיֶתֶר עֹז — and surpasses them in significance, with *"more dignity and more power"* (Genesis 49:3), לִהְיוֹת נִקְרָא עוֹבֵד אֱלֹהִים — so that this person could be called "one who serves G-d."

As the *Ba'al Shem Tov* taught, that with the 101st revision, *"you draw the 'one' (alef) into your studies, namely, the Master (Alufo) of the World, and it becomes 'study for the sake of Heaven'"* (Rabbi Moshe Chaim Ephraim of Sudilkov, *Degel Machaneh Efra'im,* (Brooklyn 2010), p. 290).

מִפְּנֵי שֶׁכְּדֵי לְשַׁנּוֹת טֶבַע הָרְגִילוּת — **Because to change your habitual nature,** צָרִיךְ לְעוֹרֵר אֶת הָאַהֲבָה לַה' — **you have to awaken** within yourself **the love of G-d,** עַל יְדֵי שֶׁמִּתְבּוֹנֵן בִּגְדוּלַת ה' בְּמוֹחוֹ — **through mindful meditation on the greatness of G-d,** לִשְׁלוֹט עַל הַטֶּבַע שֶׁבֶּחָלָל הַשְּׂמָאלִי — **to have control over your natural disposition** which is centered in **your heart's left chamber,** הַמָּלֵא דַם הַנֶּפֶשׁ הַבַּהֲמִית שֶׁמֵּהַקְּלִיפָּה — **that is filled with the blood of the Animal Soul, which is from** *kelipah,* שֶׁמִּמֶּנָּה הוּא הַטֶּבַע — **and that** *kelipah* **is where the "nature" comes from.**

The *beinoni* "who does not serve G-d," may behave impeccably in every way, but that's because he has trained himself to do so. Since his Animal Soul doesn't incite him to violate G-d's will, he leaves it unchallenged.

But serving G-d requires wrestling with yourself to become a better person. That means an ongoing process of actively strengthening your Divine Soul over the existing hold of your Animal Soul. And for this, the *Tanya* recommends regular "mindful meditation on the greatness of G-d," to stir up real emotions.

לבינוני. או לעורר את האהבה המסותרת שבלבו
למשול על ידה על הטבע שבחלל השמאלי שזו נקרא
ג"כ עבודה להלחם עם הטבע והיצר ע"י שמעורר
האהבה המסותרת בלבו משא"כ כשאין לו מלחמה
כלל אין אהבה זו מצד עצמה נקראת עבודתו כלל:

וְזוֹ הִיא עֲבוֹדָה תַּמָּה לַבֵּינוֹנִי — **And this is "ideal worship" for a** *beinoni* (see above chapter 13, pp. 164-5; see also *Zohar* 2, 184a, cited below p. 311).

Being "the best version of yourself" is not just a matter of impeccable thought, speech and action; you must also wrestle constantly with your darker side to grow.

Unless you are one of the rare souls who was born to be a *tzadik*, then *struggle will be your perfection.*

PRACTICAL LESSONS

Doing more than you are accustomed to (in Torah and *mitzvos*) is always a form of service, since it inevitably requires effort.

"Ideal service" of G-d doesn't mean becoming a *tzadik*. It means struggling to be the best person you can be.

To do this you need to practice mindful meditation on the greatness of G-d, to generate real feelings for G-d (or at least to awaken the existing love of G-d in your soul).

אוֹ לְעוֹרֵר אֶת הָאַהֲבָה הַמְסוּתֶּרֶת שֶׁבְּלִבּוֹ — **Or,** if mindful meditation does not bear its fruit and produce a passionate love for G-d, at least struggle **to awaken the "dormant love" in your heart,** לִמְשׁוֹל עַל יָדָהּ עַל הַטֶּבַע שֶׁבֶּחָלָל הַשְּׂמָאלִי — **so as to dominate your natural disposition that is** centered **in the left chamber** of your heart.

שֶׁזּוֹ נִקְרָא גַּם כֵּן עֲבוֹדָה — **For this, too, counts as "service,"** לְהִלָּחֵם עִם הַטֶּבַע וְהַיֵּצֶר — since it requires you **to wrestle with** your **nature and inclination,** עַל יְדֵי שֶׁמְּעוֹרֵר הָאַהֲבָה הַמְסוּתֶּרֶת בְּלִבּוֹ — **through awakening** at least the **"dormant love" of the heart,** sufficient for you to change.

Above we argued that an awakening of the soul's "dormant love" does *not* count as "service," because it *"was not brought about by him, nor is it in any way his achievement, rather, it is our spiritual 'inheritance.'"* How can the *Tanya* argue now that awakening the "dormant love" *is* sufficient to be considered "service"?

Our earlier case was speaking of a *minimal* awakening of "dormant love," sufficient to maintain a *stagnant* level of observance. But here the "dormant love" is being used to break free from the hold of the Animal Soul and grow. This more substantial awakening definitely requires considerable effort and where there is effort, there is "service."

מַה שֶּׁאֵין כֵּן כְּשֶׁאֵין לוֹ מִלְחָמָה כְּלָל — **But that's not the case if you have no battle at all** with your Animal Soul, אֵין אַהֲבָה זוֹ מִצַּד עַצְמָהּ נִקְרֵאת עֲבוֹדָתוֹ כְּלָל — this natural "dormant" **love** of G-d, which did not require a significant effort to awaken, **does not in itself qualify as "service" at all.**

To sum up: In chapter 15, we have encountered four different types of *beinoni,* who differ in the level of effort they make to serve G-d. We have met the "effortless" *beinoni* who has no significant inner struggle, because he was born with a naturally observant personality. We were introduced to the "static" *beinoni*, who did struggle in the past to reach his current level of observance, but now it has become his "second nature." Both these *beinonim* "do not serve G-d" because they invest no substantive effort in their worship.

When discussing the *beinoni* who "does serve G-d," the *Tanya* distinguished between "incomplete" and "ideal" levels of effort. The "incomplete" *beinoni* does wrestle with his emotions, but he doesn't make enough effort to generate real feelings for G-d, relying too much on merely arousing the natural "dormant love" hidden in his soul.

The "ideal" *beinoni,* on the other hand, devotes a lot of effort to mindful meditation aimed at developing a strong emotional attachment to his Creator. He may never fully saturate his heart with feelings for G-d, like a *tzadik*, but he struggles to do his very best. And since he is incapable of becoming a *tzadik* through his own innate talents, these ongoing efforts represent "ideal service" for him — the best person he can be.

CHAPTER 16

WHEN MEDITATION FAILS

SECTION ONE: YOUR LIFE'S MISSION

25TH TEVES REGULAR | 3RD SHEVAT LEAP

In chapters 12–14, the *Tanya* has offered us a very detailed insight into the *beinoni*, which is presented as the realistic religious ideal for every person.

When it comes to practical observance, the *beinoni* is a great success; but he struggles to maintain a steady emotional attachment to G-d. His feelings fluctuate between utter rapture, when his prayers and meditations go well, to thoughts of selfish, animalistic behavior, which may bother him much of the time.

The *Tanya* reassures us that all this is quite normal. When it comes to practical observance (both "between man and G-d" and "between man and his fellow"), we should expect nothing less than total self-control; but the emotional ride is going to be a roller coaster. Most of us will spend our lives with conflicting urges: a longing to worship G-d alongside a desire to be selfish. When this range of feelings surfaces, it should not be cause for alarm.

The solution proposed by the *Tanya* is to focus on the positive and stir up as much love and reverence for G-d as is possible, to make as many "deposits" in our

פרק טז וזה כלל גדול בעבודת ה' לבינונים העיקר הוא למשול ולשלוט על הטבע שבחלל השמאלי ע"י אור ה' המאיר לנפש האלהית שבמוחו לשלוט על הלב כשמתבונן במוחו בגדולת

emotional "bank account" as we can. Since the Animal Soul, which can never really be changed, will always pull us towards selfishness, we need to ensure that there is a strong pull in the other direction, towards G-d. And the way to do that, in the *Tanya's* view, is through prolonged and regular mindful meditation.

וְזֶה כְּלָל גָּדוֹל בַּעֲבוֹדַת ה' לַבֵּינוֹנִים — **For** *beinonim,* and those who seek to become *beinonim,* **the worship of G-d has this** one **all-encompassing principle:**

הָעִיקָר הוּא לִמְשׁוֹל וְלִשְׁלוֹט עַל הַטֶּבַע שֶׁבֶּחָלָל הַשְּׂמָאלִי — **The main thing is to dominate and control the natural** tendencies of the Animal Soul, **in the** heart's **left chamber.**

The all-encompassing principle is: *You must wrestle with your nature and seek to control it.*

As we saw in chapter 15, it's possible to have impeccable religious behavior and not be at war with the Animal Soul (either due to decreased passions or persistent discipline). But that's not enough to worship G-d properly. Even if your Animal Soul has been "tamed" and "trained" to behave impeccably in a certain area, you need to break your nature, and do more.

You are not expected to *transform* your Animal Soul to be your friend in worship. You just need to "dominate and control" its nature so that you can worship G-d.

How is this achieved?

עַל יְדֵי אוֹר ה' הַמֵּאִיר לַנֶּפֶשׁ הָאֱלֹהִית שֶׁבַּמּוֹחַ — **Through the Divine light which shines upon your Divine Soul,** that rests **in the brain.**

As we learned in chapters 12–13, the *yetzer hara* (impulse to evil), might trouble the *beinoni* in one of two ways.

a.) If he has *complete mental focus* to follow G-d's will, when urges arise from the *yetzer hara* it is relatively easy to diffuse them since, "the brain rules over the heart" (chapter 12, p. 143).

b.) But sometimes, especially when the *beinoni* is uninspired, the *yetzer hara* can send him into a state of *mental confusion* and he is unsure whether or not he wishes to follow G-d's will. It is at this point, when the *beinoni's* inner flame is at its weakest, that his struggle is the greatest. But G-d always offers him "assistance" in the form of *"light which shines upon the Divine Soul, which rests in the brain"* (see above, chapter 13, p. 154). That is why the *beinoni* is always able to be in control of his behavior, even in his darkest moments.

וְלִשְׁלוֹט עַל הַלֵּב — **And to** use the mind **to rule over the heart.**

א"ס ב"ה להוליד מבינתו רוח דעת ויראת ה' במוחו
להיות סור מרע דאורייתא ודרבנן ואפילו איסור קל של
דבריהם ח"ו ואהבת ה' בלבו בחלל הימני בחשיקה
וחפיצה לדבקה בו בקיום המצות דאורייתא ודרבנן
ות"ת שכנגד כולן. ויתר על כן צריך לידע כלל גדול
בעבודה לבינונים שגם אם אין יד שכלו ורוח בינתו

While the *beinoni* can expect G-d's assistance in times of confusion, it is preferable for him not to rely on that. If he is able to retain sufficient mental focus and the awareness that he wishes to follow G-d's will, he can rely on the mind's natural tendency to "rule over the heart."

This mental focus, however, does not come without the necessary preparations of meditation and prayer.

כְּשֶׁמִּתְבּוֹנֵן בְּמוֹחוֹ בִּגְדוּלַּת אֵין סוֹף בָּרוּךְ הוּא — **This happens through mindful meditation on the greatness of** G-d's **Blessed Infinite Light,** לְהוֹלִיד מִבִּינָתוֹ רוּחַ דַּעַת וְיִרְאַת ה' בְּמוֹחוֹ — **so that your** powers of *binah* (cognition) give rise to *"a spirit of da'as (recognition) and reverence of G-d"* (*Isaiah* 11:2), **in your mind.**

As we learned in chapter 3, *da'as* does not add any new information which was not fathomed by *binah* (cognition). Rather, it fosters a mental attachment to the existing idea, making it "real" and relevant.

לְהִיוֹת סוּר מֵרָע — **That** "reverence" of G-d in *da'as* enables you to make the firm decision **to** *"turn away from evil"* (*Psalms* 34:14), דְּאוֹרַיְיתָא וּדְרַבָּנָן — to avoid anything prohibited **Biblically or Rabbinically,** וַאֲפִילוּ אִיסוּר קַל שֶׁל דִּבְרֵיהֶם — down to **even a minor Rabbinic prohibition,** חַס וְשָׁלוֹם — **G-d forbid.**

In addition to reverence—a fear of distancing yourself from G-d through transgression—your meditation should generate the positive feelings of love.

וְאַהֲבַת ה' בְּלִבּוֹ בְּחָלָל הַיְמָנִי — **And love of G-d** will be generated **in your heart, in its right chamber** where the Divine Soul rests, בַּחֲשִׁיקָה וַחֲפִיצָה לְדָבְקָה בּוֹ — **with fervor and desire to attach yourself to Him,** בְּקִיּוּם הַמִּצְוֹת — **through observing the Biblical and Rabbinic** *mitzvos,* דְּאוֹרַיְיתָא וּדְרַבָּנָן — וְתַלְמוּד תּוֹרָה שֶׁכְּנֶגֶד כּוּלָּן — **and** *"the study of the Torah, which is equal to them all"* (*Mishnah*, *Pe'ah* 1:1; for detailed meditations to arouse love and reverence, see below chapters 41-50. See also above, chapter 3, pp. 59-61 and chapter 9, pp. 115-7).

PRACTICAL LESSONS

Your task in life is simply: to wrestle with your un-G-dly urges, and seek to control them.

The best way to strengthen yourself in this task is to meditate on G-d's greatness until you develop real feelings for Him.

משגת להוליד אהבת ה' בהתגלו' לבו שיהיה לבו בוער
כרשפי אש וחפץ בחפיצה וחשיקה ותשוקה מורגשת
בלב לדבקה בו רק האהבה מסותרת במוחו ותעלומות
לבו* דהיינו שהלב מבין
ברוח חכמה ובי' שבמוחו
גדולת א"ס ב"ה דכולא

הגהה

(והסיבה לזה היא מפני היות

SECTION TWO: WHEN MEDITATION ISN'T WORKING

The above description of the *beinoni's* struggle in life is, more or less, a summary of what had been stated in the previous chapters.

וְיֶתֶר עַל כֵּן צָרִיךְ לֵידַע כְּלָל גָּדוֹל בַּעֲבוֹדָה לַבֵּינוֹנִים — **But there is an additional,** second **all-encompassing principle of worship for** *beinonim* **that you need to know.**

Central to the religious life of the *beinoni,* is the ability to generate real feelings for G-d through meditation. But what happens if you employ all the correct techniques, and despite all your efforts, strong feelings don't come?

שֶׁגַּם אִם אֵין יַד שִׂכְלוֹ וְרוּחַ בִּינָתוֹ מַשֶּׂגֶת לְהוֹלִיד אַהֲבַת ה' בְּהִתְגַּלּוּת לִבּוֹ — The "additional principle" tells you how to react **if, even** after doing all the appropriate meditations, **your intellectual capacity and cognitive focus prove insufficient to generate a love of G-d "tangibly in your heart"** (Proverbs 18:2), שֶׁיִּהְיֶה לִבּוֹ בּוֹעֵר כְּרִשְׁפֵּי אֵשׁ — that **your heart should burn like "flaming fire"** (Song 8:6), וְחָפֵץ בַּחֲפִיצָה וַחֲשִׁיקָה וּתְשׁוּקָה מוּרְגֶּשֶׁת בַּלֵּב לְדָבְקָה בּוֹ — **and desire intensely, with a** palpable **desire, craving and longing in your heart, to attach yourself to Him.**

You carry out all the meditations advised by the *Tanya* at length, trying your best to generate a palpable excitement for G-d, but it doesn't happen.

רַק הָאַהֲבָה מְסוּתֶּרֶת בְּמוֹחוֹ וְתַעֲלוּמוֹת לִבּוֹ — **Rather, the love remains "concealed"** and stuck **in your brain, and in your "hidden places in the heart"** (Psalms 44:22).* *i.e.,* your heart does feel it, but in a less excited, muted fashion.

It *makes sense* to you to worship G-d, but you just don't feel "hungry" for it.

דְּהַיְינוּ שֶׁהַלֵּב מֵבִין בְּרוּחַ חָכְמָה וּבִינָה שֶׁבְּמוֹחוֹ גְּדוּלַת אֵין סוֹף בָּרוּךְ הוּא — *I.e.,* your **mind's inquiry and cognition of** G-d's **infinite blessed greatness does register in your heart,** דְּכוּלָּא קַמֵּיהּ כְּלָא חֲשִׁיב מַמָּשׁ — and your heart recognizes that **"in His presence, everything is considered zero"** (Zohar 1, 11b).

---

*הַגָּהָה — **NOTE.** In this note, the *Tanya* explains that a failure to generate palpable emotions for G-d through meditation need not be the result of poor meditation technique. It may just be that your soul is not cut out for it.

וְהַסִּבָּה לָזֶה — **And the reason for this** failure to generate palpable emotions for G-d through meditation, even when the meditation is carried out correctly, הִיא מִפְּנֵי הֱיוֹת

קְמִיהּ כְּלָא חֲשִׁיב מַמָּשׁ
אֲשֶׁר עַל כֵּן יָאֲתָה לוֹ יִתְבָּ׳
שֶׁתִּכְלֶה אֵלָיו נֶפֶשׁ כָּל חַי
לִידָּבֵק וּלְהִכָּלֵל בְּאוֹרוֹ. וְגַם נַפְשׁוֹ וְרוּחוֹ אֲשֶׁר בְּקִרְבּוֹ
כָּךְ יָאֲתָה לָהֶן לִהְיוֹת כָּלוֹת אֵלָיו בַּחֲשִׁיקָה וַחֲפִיצָה

המוחין שלו ונר״ן שלו מבחי׳ עיבור
והעלם תוך התבונה ולא מבחי׳ לידה
והתגלות כידוע לי״ח:

The problem here is that your feeling is more like a "consent" and "approval" rather than actual excitement.

אֲשֶׁר עַל כֵּן יָאֲתָה לוֹ יִתְבָּרֵךְ שֶׁתִּכְלֶה אֵלָיו נֶפֶשׁ כָּל חַי — **Therefore** you feel **it's "ap-propriate" that every living thing should yearn for Him,** לִידָּבֵק וּלְהִכָּלֵל בְּאוֹרוֹ — **to connect with His light, and be absorbed in it.**

Feeling that something is "appropriate" is not a very strong emotion. You agree that "every living thing" stands in G-d's presence and should be drawn to Him, but you don't actually feel drawn yourself, in a powerful, emotive sense.

וְגַם נַפְשׁוֹ וְרוּחוֹ אֲשֶׁר בְּקִרְבּוֹ כָּךְ יָאֲתָה לָהֶן לִהְיוֹת כָּלוֹת אֵלָיו — **And** on a personal level, you feel that **it's "appropriate" that your** *nefesh* and *ruach* soul powers **within you ought to yearn for Him,** בַּחֲשִׁיקָה וַחֲפִיצָה לָצֵאת מִנַּרְתֵּקָן הוּא הַגּוּף לְדָבְקָה בּוֹ — **with fervor and desire to break out of their bodily containment, so as to be attached**

הַמּוֹחִין שֶׁלּוֹ וְנֶפֶשׁ רוּחַ וּנְשָׁמָה שֶׁלּוֹ — **is because** this person's *mochin* **"brain energy"** and his soul energies of *nefesh* (basic functioning), *ruach* (emotional powers) and *neshamah* (intellectual powers), do not empower him with the ability to do so.

What, exactly, is lacking in this person's brain and soul energies that prevent him from carrying out a successful meditation, resulting in tangible emotion?

מִבְּחִינַת עִיבּוּר — Because his brain and soul energies, in their source, **derive from** the World of Emotion as it exists in a state of *ibur* **("gestation").**

The Kabbalists compared the process of thought generating emotion to gesta-tion followed by birth. In the World of Emotion, there are both undeveloped ("ges-tational") emotions, and those that are fully mature ("born"). This person's soul is rooted in the "gestation" energy, which is why he has a difficult time in giving "birth" to real emotion.

וְהֶעְלֵם תּוֹךְ הַתְּבוּנָה — "Gestation" energy is from the emotionally **muted "discern-ment" process,** וְלֹא מִבְּחִינַת לֵידָה וְהִתְגַּלּוּת — **and not from the realm of** emotional **"birth" and disclosure.**

The reason why this person's meditations are not producing emotions might be because his soul is rooted in cerebral energy ("discernment"), where emotions are still "gestating" and have not yet been born.

כַּיָּדוּעַ לְיוֹדְעֵי חָכְמָה נִסְתָּרָה — **As is known to the Kabbalists** (see *Etz Chaim* 23, 1-2; *Sha'ar Ha-Pesukim, I Samuel* 2:19).

22A

לצאת מנרתקן הוא הגוף לדבקה בו רק שבע"כ חיות
הנה בתוך הגוף וצרורות בו כאלמנות חיות ולית
מחשבה דילהון תפיסא ביה כלל כי אם כאשר תפיסא
ומתלבשת בתורה ובמצותי' כמשל המחבק את המלך
הנ"ל. ואי לזאת יאתה להן לחבקו בכל לב ונפש ומאד
דהיינו קיום התרי"ג מצות במעשה ובדבור ובמחשבה
שהיא השגת וידיעת התורה כנ"ל הנה כשמעמיק

to Him unrestrainedly, רַק שֶׁבְּעַל כָּרְחָן חָיוֹת הֵנָּה בְּתוֹךְ הַגּוּף — and you understand that **they only reside in your body against their will,** וּצְרוּרוֹת בּוֹ כְּאַלְמְנוּת חַיּוּת — *"bound... in living widowhood"* (2 *Samuel* 20:3), like a woman who is unable to remarry because her husband left her without a divorce.

Again this is largely an intellectual experience, with a mere "agreement" of the heart. G-d's presence ought to be powerful and overwhelming; you just don't feel that way.

וְלֵית מַחֲשָׁבָה דִילְהוֹן תְּפִיסָא בֵּיהּ כְּלָל — **And** you agree with the idea discussed in chapter 4 that, **"No thought** (of your soul) **can grasp Him at all"** (*Tikunei Zohar* 17a), כִּי אִם כַּאֲשֶׁר תְּפִיסָא וּמִתְלַבֶּשֶׁת בַּתּוֹרָה וּמִצְוֹתֶיהָ — **except when you're "grasped by,"** and **"dressed in"** the Torah and its *mitzvos,* כְּמָשָׁל הַמְחַבֵּק אֶת הַמֶּלֶךְ הַנִּזְכָּר לְעֵיל — **as in the above illustration of hugging the king,** *"where there is no difference in the level of closeness and bonding achieved by the embrace, whether you hug him when he is dressed in one robe or dressed in several robes, since the king himself is inside them"* (p. 74).

וְאִי לָזֹאת יָאֲתָה לָהֶן לְחַבְּקוֹ בְּכָל לֵב וְנֶפֶשׁ וּמְאֹד — **Therefore,** you feel that **it's "appropriate"** for your *nefesh* and *ruach* to **"hug"** G-d **with all your heart, soul and being,** דְּהַיְינוּ קִיּוּם הַתַּרְיַ"ג מִצְוֹת בְּמַעֲשֶׂה וּבְדִבּוּר וּבְמַחֲשָׁבָה — namely, through **observing the 613** *mitzvos* **in action, speech and thought,** שֶׁהִיא הַשָּׂגַת וִידִיעַת הַתּוֹרָה — **"thought" referring,** in particular, **to understanding and knowledge of the Torah,** כַּנִּזְכָּר לְעֵיל — **as mentioned above,** (see chapters 4 and 5).

SECTION THREE: WHY MEDITATION NEVER FAILS

Is it enough to feel that worshiping G-d is "appropriate," without having any stronger emotions in your heart?

Scripture appears to indicate otherwise. The Torah states, *"You shall love G-d with all your heart"* (Deuteronomy 6:5), implying that you are *commanded* to experience the emotion of love for G-d *in your heart.*

However, this notion of legislating an emotion is difficult to comprehend. "And the Rav, the Maggid of Mezritch asked: Is love not an emotion of the heart? You cannot command a person to feel a certain way in his heart, because either he has the

בענין זה בתעלומות תבונות לבו ומוחו ופיו ולבו שוין
שמקיים כן בפיו כפי אשר נגמר בתבונת לבו ומוחו
דהיינו להיות בתורת ה' חפצו ויהגה בה יומם ולילה
בפיו וכן הידים ושאר אברים מקיימים המצות כפי מה
שנגמר בתבונת לבו ומוחו הרי תבונה זו מתלבשת

emotion or he hasn't. A command won't help" (Rabbi Yosef Yitzchak Schneersohn, *Sefer Ha-Ma'amarim,* (Kehos: Brooklyn, 1986), p. 116).

We have an oral tradition of the Maggid's answer to this question, as it was communicated by one of Rabbi Shneur Zalman's close disciples, Rabbi Yitzchak Eizik Epstein (1770-1857) of Homil (Gomel, Belarus).

"I heard directly from the late Rebbe [Shneur Zalman], the following words: 'This is what I received from the Rav, the Maggid of Mezritch, of blessed memory, and he had received it from the *Ba'al Shem Tov.* The command, *"You shall love [G-d]"* means you must focus your mind and recognize intellectually,' (in Yiddish, he said: *'men zol zich araiyn tohn,'*—'you should immerse yourself') in ideas that ought to arouse love. Whatever the result will be, that is not the focus of the command (*ikar ha-mitzvah*)" (Rabbi Yitzchak Eizik Epstein, *Ma'amar Shenei Ha-Me'oros* (Poltava, 1918), p. 60; cf. *Rambam, Foundations of the Torah* 2:1; *Sifri, Deut., piska* 33).

Following this tradition, the *Tanya's* second "all-encompassing principle" will teach us: You must try to love G-d through meditating on "ideas that ought to arouse love"; but the result of your meditation, whether or not you feel love of G-d palpably in your heart, is not under your control. If all you can manage is the muted feeling that it's "appropriate" to love G-d, that will be considered "ideal worship" for you.

הִנֵּה כְּשֶׁמַּעֲמִיק בְּעִנְיָן זֶה בְּתַעֲלוּמוֹת תְּבוּנוֹת לִבּוֹ וּמוֹחוֹ — **Now, when you will contemplate this idea deeply,** how worship is "appropriate," **with the "discernment"** of your *"hidden places in the heart"* (*Psalms* 44:22) **and your brain,** וּפִיו וְלִבּוֹ שָׁוֵין — **and** *"your mouth and heart are consistent"* (*Talmud, Pesachim* 63a), **i.e., your mouth carries out whatever was decided through the discernment of your heart and mind,** דְּהַיְינוּ לִהְיוֹת בְּתוֹרַת ה' — **namely that,** *"G-d's Torah is your delight and (with your mouth) you study it day and night"* (*Psalms* 1:2), חֶפְצוֹ וְיֶהְגֶּה בָּהּ יוֹמָם וָלַיְלָה בְּפִיו וְכֵן הַיָּדַיִם וּשְׁאָר אֵבָרִים — **and likewise, your hands and other limbs observe the commandments, following what was resolved through the "discernment" of your heart and mind,** מְקַיְּימִים הַמִּצְוֹת כְּפִי מַה שֶׁנִּגְמַר בִּתְבוּנַת לִבּוֹ וּמוֹחוֹ then, as we shall see, this is enough to render your worship as "ideal."

To explain why you can manage without palpable love and reverence of G-d, we first need to understand the role of these emotions.

The *Tikunei Zohar* compares the love and reverence of G-d which accompany a *mitzvah* to the wings of a bird. Just as a bird cannot fly without two wings, a *mitzvah*

בְּמַעֲשֶׂה דִבּוּר וּמַחֲשֶׁבֶת הַתּוֹרָה וּמִצְוֹתֶיהָ לִהְיוֹת לָהֶם
בְּחִי' מוֹחִין וְחַיּוּת וְגַדְפִּין לְפָרְחָא לְעֵילָא כְּאִלּוּ עָסַק בָּהֶם
בִּדְחִילוּ וּרְחִימוּ מַמָּשׁ אֲשֶׁר בְּהִתְגַּלּוּת לִבּוֹ [בַּחֲפִיצָה
וַחֲשִׁיקָה וּתְשׁוּקָה מוּרְגֶּשֶׁת בְּלִבּוֹ וְנַפְשׁוֹ הַצְּמֵאָה לה'
מִפְּנֵי רִשְׁפֵּי אֵשׁ אַהֲבָתוֹ שֶׁבְּלִבּוֹ כנ"ל] הוֹאִיל וּתְבוּנָה
זוֹ שֶׁבְּמוֹחוֹ וְתַעֲלוּמוֹת לִבּוֹ הִיא הַמְּבִיאָתוֹ לַעֲסוֹק בָּהֶם

cannot soar heavenward, and be fully accepted by G-d, unless it is propelled by the "wings" of love and reverence (see below chapters 38-40). In Lurianic Kabbalah, this process of invigorating a *mitzvah* is depicted as an infusion of *mochin* ("brain energy") and *chayus* ("vibrancy") into the act.

The *Tanya* will now argue that even if your meditation fails to generate a palpable feeling of love and reverence for G-d, and you only develop a more muted sense of emotional discernment and "approval," that's enough to endow your *mitzvos* with their necessary "wings" and "vibrancy."

הֲרֵי תְבוּנָה זוֹ מִתְלַבֶּשֶׁת בְּמַעֲשֶׂה דִבּוּר וּמַחֲשֶׁבֶת הַתּוֹרָה וּמִצְוֹתֶיהָ — **In this case, the discernment** of the heart which you did achieve, **becomes "dressed" in each act, spoken word and thought of the Torah and its *mitzvos*,** לִהְיוֹת לָהֶם בְּחִינַת מוֹחִין וְחַיּוּת וְגַדְפִּין לְפָרְחָא לְעֵילָא — **providing the** Torah and *mitzvos* **with the necessary *mochin* ("brain energy"),** *chayus* **("vibrancy") and "wings" with which to soar heavenward.**

כְּאִלּוּ עָסַק בָּהֶם בִּדְחִילוּ וּרְחִימוּ מַמָּשׁ אֲשֶׁר בְּהִתְגַּלּוּת לִבּוֹ — It's now **as if you had observed** these *mitzvos* **with real reverence and love, palpably in your heart,** since the effect is the same: your *mitzvos* successfully soar towards the heavens.

Remarkably, your partially failed meditation is highly effective. It is just as if you had succeeded.

[בַּחֲפִיצָה וַחֲשִׁיקָה וּתְשׁוּקָה מוּרְגֶּשֶׁת בְּלִבּוֹ וְנַפְשׁוֹ הַצְּמֵאָה לה' — It's just as if you observed the *mitzvos* **with a heart and soul that thirsts for G-d with desire, fervor and longing,** מִפְּנֵי רִשְׁפֵּי אֵשׁ אַהֲבָתוֹ שֶׁבְּלִבּוֹ — **resulting from a love in your heart like** *"flaming fire"* (Song 8:6), כַּנִּזְכָּר לְעֵיל] — **as mentioned above.**

SECTION FOUR: HOW G-D BOOSTS YOUR MITZVOS

The obvious question is: How could this mere "discernment" of the heart replace real love and reverence? How does this muted emotional experience provide "wings" that are powerful enough to propel your *mitzvos* heavenward? In order to answer this, the *Tanya* will first demonstrate how instrumental this "failed" meditation (which only produced "discernment") actually was.

הוֹאִיל וּתְבוּנָה זוֹ שֶׁבְּמוֹחוֹ וְתַעֲלוּמוֹת לִבּוֹ — **For since this "discernment" of your mind and your** *"hidden places in the heart,"* הִיא הַמְּבִיאָתוֹ לַעֲסוֹק בָּהֶם — **actual-**

ולולי שהיה מתבונן בתבונה זו לא היה עוסק בהם כלל
אלא בצרכי גופו לבד [וגם אם הוא מתמיד בלמודו
בטבעו אעפ"כ אוהב את גופו יותר בטבעו] וזה רמזו
רז"ל באמרם מחשבה טובה הקב"ה מצרפה למעשה
והוה ליה למימר מעלה עליו הכתוב כאלו עשאה.

ly brought you to observe the *mitzvos,* וְלוּלֵי שֶׁהָיָה מִתְבּוֹנֵן בִּתְבוּנָה זוֹ לֹא הָיָה עוֹסֵק בָּהֶם כְּלָל — and if you had not meditated about this "discernment," you would never had observed those *mitzvos,* אֶלָּא בְּצָרְכֵי גּוּפוֹ לְבָד — rather, you'd have been busy exclusively with your body's needs, therefore G-d accepts your meager offering of "discernment" in the place of real love and reverence, as we shall see.

[וְגַם אִם הוּא מַתְמִיד בְּלִמּוּדוֹ בְּטִבְעוֹ] — And even if your natural disposition is to study all the time (see previous chapter, p. 182), [אַף עַל פִּי כֵן אוֹהֵב אֶת גּוּפוֹ יוֹתֵר בְּטִבְעוֹ] — nevertheless, "discernment" is still a crucial motivator of your Torah observance, because, ultimately, your nature is to love your body more than to worship G-d.

26TH TEVES REGULAR

The *Tanya* will now explain that, since G-d is pleased with your efforts to generate "discernment," and He is aware of the personal limitations holding you back from successful meditation, He assists your *mitzvos* to develop the necessary "wings."

וְזֶה רְמְזוּ רַבּוֹתֵינוּ זִכְרוֹנָם לִבְרָכָה — It was to this that our Sages, of blessed memory, alluded, בְּאָמְרָם מַחֲשָׁבָה טוֹבָה הַקָּדוֹשׁ בָּרוּךְ הוּא מְצָרְפָה לְמַעֲשֶׂה — in saying that the Blessed Holy One *"attaches a good thought to the deed"* (*Talmud, Kiddushin* 40a).

The *Talmud* immediately clarifies that this refers to a case where, *"a person has given thought to doing a mitzvah but was prevented from doing it by circumstances beyond his control. Scripture then credits him as though he had done it."*

But if this is so, the assertion that G-d "attaches" a good thought to the deed seems out of place. There was, in fact, no deed to "attach" the thought to — as the *Tanya* now asks.

וַהֲוָה לֵיהּ לְמֵימַר מַעֲלֶה עָלָיו הַכָּתוּב כְּאִלּוּ עֲשָׂאָהּ — The *Talmud* should have said in the first instance, not that G-d "attaches" a good thought to the deed, since in reality

PRACTICAL LESSONS

If you try your best to meditate but can't get passionate about G-d, that's okay. It could just be that you don't have a passionate soul.

G-d will "join the thought to the deed" and bring the fruits of your meditation to invigorate your *mitzvos,* even if they lack passion. This will be "ideal worship" for you.

אֶלָּא הָעִנְיָן כִּי דְּחִילוּ וּרְחִימוּ שֶׁבְּהִתְגַּלּוּת לִבּוֹ הֵם
הַמִּתְלַבְּשִׁים בְּמַעֲשֵׂה הַמִּצְוֹת לְהַחֲיוֹתָם לְפָרְחָא לְעֵילָא
כִּי הַלֵּב הוּא גַּ"כ חוּמְרִי כִּשְׁאָר אֵבָרִים שֶׁהֵם כְּלֵי
הַמַּעֲשֶׂה אֶלָּא שֶׁהוּא פְּנִימִי וְחַיּוּת לָהֶם וְלָכֵן יָכוֹל
לְהִתְלַבֵּשׁ בָּהֶם לִהְיוֹת לָהֶם גַּדְפִין לְהַעֲלוֹתָם. אַךְ
הַדְּחִילוּ וּרְחִימוּ שֶׁבַּתְּבוּנוֹת מוֹחוֹ וְתַעֲלוּמוֹת לִבּוֹ הַנַּ"ל

22B

there was no deed, but that "**Scripture credits him as though he had done it,**" as the *Talmud* indeed clarifies later on.

There is, however, a deeper significance in G-d "attaching" a good thought to a deed. The *Talmud* was alluding to our second "all encompassing principle," that if a *mitzvah* lacks palpable love and reverence, and has only an intellectually "discerned" emotion, G-d will accept this in the place of real feeling.

אֶלָּא הָעִנְיָן — **Rather, the explanation** lies in understanding the difference between "palpable" and "discerned" emotion.

What is the reason why palpable love and reverence of G-d are able to act as "wings" to a *mitzvah*?

כִּי דְּחִילוּ וּרְחִימוּ שֶׁבְּהִתְגַּלּוּת לִבּוֹ — **Because when love and reverence are palpable in your heart,** הֵם הַמִּתְלַבְּשִׁים בְּמַעֲשֵׂה הַמִּצְוֹת לְהַחֲיוֹתָם לְפָרְחָא לְעֵילָא — **they become "dressed" in the *mitzvah* acts, energizing them to soar heavenward,** כִּי הַלֵּב הוּא גַּם כֵּן חוּמְרִי כִּשְׁאָר אֵבָרִים שֶׁהֵם כְּלֵי הַמַּעֲשֶׂה — **because the "gap" between the heart and the other organs is not so big since the heart is also sensuous like the other limbs, the tools of action.**

For one thing to "dress" into another, they both need to be similar and compatible. Even though the heart is a complex, emotional hub, and the external limbs of the body are relatively superficial "tools" of action, the feelings of the heart *can* be "dressed" in external action, because these body parts share something in common with the heart: they are physical and sensuous.

אֶלָּא שֶׁהוּא פְּנִימִי וְחַיּוּת לָהֶם — **And while the heart does transcend and surpass** the other limbs in its complexity and centrality, it is not totally removed from them; **rather,** the heart **is the internal energy of the** other limbs, pumping blood to them.

וְלָכֵן יָכוֹל לְהִתְלַבֵּשׁ בָּהֶם — **That is why its** emotions *can* **"dress" in** the external limbs, לִהְיוֹת לָהֶם גַּדְפִין לְהַעֲלוֹתָם — **providing "wings" of ascent for their** actions.

However, this relationship between the heart and the external limbs only works when emotions are tangible and palpable. Then, the "sensual" element of the emotions provides necessary common ground for a relationship with the physical limbs.

אַךְ הַדְּחִילוּ וּרְחִימוּ שֶׁבַּתְּבוּנוֹת מוֹחוֹ וְתַעֲלוּמוֹת לִבּוֹ הַנִּזְכָּרִים לְעֵיל — **But the reverence and love which are "discerned" by your brain and your "*hidden places in***

גבהו דרכיהם למעלה מעלה מבחי' המעשה ואי אפשר
להם להתלבש בבחי' מעשה המצות להיות להם בחי'
מוחין וחיות להעלותן לפרחא לעילא אם לא שהקב"ה
מצרפן ומחברן לבחי' המעשה והן נקראות בשם מחשבה
טובה כי אינן דחילו ורחימו ממש בהתגלות לבו כי אם

the heart," mentioned above, גָּבְהוּ דַרְכֵיהֶם לְמַעְלָה מַעְלָה מִבְּחִינַת הַמַּעֲשֶׂה — are very much loftier than, and removed from, the sphere of physical action, וְאִי אֶפְשָׁר לָהֶם לְהִתְלַבֵּשׁ בִּבְחִינַת מַעֲשֵׂה הַמִּצְוֹת — and they are unable to descend to become "dressed" in the level of mitzvah acts.

The "discernment" of the mind and the feeling of "appropriateness" in the heart, are too removed from the World of Action to directly energize a mitzvah deed.

לִהְיוֹת לָהֶם בְּחִינַת מוֹחִין וְחַיּוּת לְהַעֲלוֹתָן לְפָרְחָא לְעֵילָא — They are, of their own accord, too sublime to provide the mochin and chayus of mitzvah acts, to propel them heavenwards.

However, the second "all encompassing principle" states that, contrary to the laws of metaphysics, these feelings are enough to provide your mitzvos with wings. But that is only due to Divine intervention.

אִם לֹא שֶׁהַקָדוֹשׁ בָּרוּךְ הוּא מְצָרְפָן וּמְחַבְּרָן לִבְחִינַת הַמַּעֲשֶׂה — Your mitzvos would not naturally ascend heavenward if it were not for the Blessed Holy One "attaching" and joining the "discernment" of your mind and the feeling of "appropriateness" in your heart with the mitzvah deed.

One problem that remains is why the Talmud refers to the "discernment" of the heart as "a good thought." Really, we are speaking here of an emotion, albeit a muted one, so why does the Talmud call it a "thought"?

וְהֵן נִקְרָאוֹת בְּשֵׁם מַחֲשָׁבָה טוֹבָה — The reason why the Talmud refers to these feelings with the term "a good thought," כִּי אֵינָן דְּחִילוּ וּרְחִימוּ מַמָּשׁ בְּהִתְגַּלוּת לִבּוֹ — is because they are not an actual love and reverence felt tangibly in your heart, כִּי אִם בִּתְבוּנַת מוֹחוֹ וְתַעֲלוּמוֹת לִבּוֹ — but only the "discernment" of your mind and

---

A CHASIDIC THOUGHT

Since you sincerely tried to generate love and reverence of G-d through sustained efforts at meditation, G-d "compensates" for your poor results by "joining" to your mitzvah whatever feelings you did succeed in generating. Even though these feelings are inherently too weak and distant to energize a deed, G-d closes the gap.

הגהה

(וכמ"ש בזוהר וע"ח דתבונה
אותיות ב"ן וב"ת שהן דחילו
ורחימו ולפעמים התבונה יורדת
להיות מוחין בנוק' דזעיר אנפין שהן
אותיות התורה והמצות והמשכיל
יבין):

בתבונת מוחו ותעלומות
לבו כנ"ל* אך צירוף זה
מצרף הקב"ה כדי להעלות
מעשה המצות ועסק
התורה הנעשים על ידי
מחשבה טובה הנ"ל עד

your **"hidden places in the heart"** (Psalms 44:22), כַּנִּזְכָּר לְעֵיל — **as mentioned above.***

The *Talmud* used the term "thought," rather than "feeling," because what you feel in the depths of your heart is so detached, that it resembles thought more than feeling.

SECTION FIVE: HOW HIGH DO YOUR MITZVOS ASCEND?

We each possess a natural "dormant" love for G-d, which is "built into" the soul. As we have seen, the "dormant" love is not *generated* by meditation; it merely needs to be released by the appropriate triggers. "Discernment," on the other hand, is not something we are born with and has to be learned through careful meditation.

In the following passage, the *Tanya* explains how the effects of natural "dormant" love differ from "discernment."

אַךְ צֵירוּף זֶה מְצָרֵף הַקָּדוֹשׁ בָּרוּךְ הוּא — **But this "attachment" by the Blessed Holy One, which joins** the "discernment" generated by your meditation to your *mitzvos,* כְּדֵי לְהַעֲלוֹת מַעֲשֵׂה הַמִּצְוֹת וְעֵסֶק הַתּוֹרָה הַנַּעֲשִׂים עַל יְדֵי מַחֲשָׁבָה טוֹבָה הַנִּזְכָּר לְעֵיל —

---

*הַגָּהָה — **NOTE.** This note discusses the source of "discernment" energy in the spiritual worlds above and why it fails to create palpable emotion.

וּכְמוֹ שֶׁכָּתוּב בַּזוֹהַר וְעֵץ חַיִּים דִּתְבוּנָה אוֹתִיּוֹת בֵּ"ן וּבַ"ת — **As stated in the *Zohar*** (3, 290b) **and *Etz Chaim* (15:4) that** the Hebrew word for **"discernment"** (*tevunah*) **contains the letters** which spell both words **"son"** (*ben*) **and "daughter"** (*bas*), שֶׁהֵן דְּחִילוּ וּרְחִימוּ — these two "children" alluding to **reverence and love,** which are generated by the "discernment."

In an ideal scenario, the "discernment" will "give birth" to tangible feelings for G-d. But, as we have seen, this sometimes does not happen, and instead G-d "joins" the discernment directly to the *mitzvah* act. In its spiritual root, this is because:

וְלִפְעָמִים הַתְּבוּנָה יוֹרֶדֶת לִהְיוֹת מוֹחִין בְּנוּקְבָא דִּזְעֵיר אַנְפִּין — **Sometimes "discernment"** bypasses *Ze'ir Anpin,* (the energy of emotion), and **descends** directly to provide **brain energy for *Nukvah,*** (the energy of action), שֶׁהֵן אוֹתִיּוֹת הַתּוֹרָה וְהַמִּצְוֹת — namely, pronouncing **letters of the Torah and** observing *mitzvos.*

עולם הבריאה מקום עליית
התורה והמצות הנעשים ע"י דחילו ורחימו שכליים אשר
בהתגלו' לבו ממש אבל בלא"ה נמי עולים לעולם היציר'

in order to elevate the *mitzvah* acts and Torah study which were brought about by your "good thought," your "discernment," mentioned above, עַד עוֹלַם הַבְּרִיאָה — has the effect of propelling your Torah and *mitzvos* to the World of *Beriah* ("Creation"), the World of Intelligence.

We function in the lowest of four worlds, the World of *Asiyah* ("Action"). At the top of the hierarchy is the World of *Atzilus* ("Emanation"), a world of pure Divinity, containing G-d's direct emanations and attributes.

Between *Asiyah* and *Atzilus* are two intermediate spiritual worlds. Directly above us is the World of *Yetzirah* ("Formation"), which is the World of Emotion; and, above that is the World of *Beriah* ("Creation"), the World of Intelligence.

Any emotions which are generated through meditation are ultimately rooted in the mind. Therefore the *mitzvos* that they inspire are propelled to the higher World of Intelligence (*Beriah*). As we have seen, a sense of "discernment" lacks the potency to effectively propel a *mitzvah*; but once G-d "joins the thought to the deed," propelling it upward, the *mitzvah* will reach the World of Intelligence, since, ultimately, it was inspired by a mental process of meditation.

PRACTICAL LESSONS

A *mitzvah* inspired by meditation will always soar higher in the heavens than one that isn't.

מְקוֹם עֲלִיַּית הַתּוֹרָה וְהַמִּצְוֹת הַנַּעֲשִׂים עַל יְדֵי דְחִילוּ וּרְחִימוּ שִׂכְלִיִּים אֲשֶׁר בְּהִתְגַּלּוּת לִבּוֹ מַמָּשׁ — Because this World of Intelligence is the place to where Torah and *mitzvos* ascend when they are carried out through intellectually generated love and reverence which is real and tangible in your heart.

In one of his discourses, Rabbi Shneur Zalman illustrates this concept with the verse, *"the mother is crouched over the chicks"* (*Deuteronomy* 22:6). Sometimes *binah* and "discernment," which is the "mother" of all emotion, will *directly* crouch over the "chicks," the words of Torah and action.

וְהַמַּשְׂכִּיל יָבִין — **And the wise will understand** (see Rabbi Shneur Zalman, *Ma'amarei Admor Ha-Zakein, Inyanim* vol. 1 (Brooklyn: Kehos, 2008), p. 248).

In conclusion: The reason why your intellectual "discernment" will sometimes inspire action directly, (without the medium of palpable emotion), is because a similar pathway exists in the spiritual worlds.

ע"י דחילו ורחימו טבעיים המסותרים בלב כל ישראל
בתולדותם כמ"ש לקמן באריכות:

פרק יז ובזה יובן מ"ש כי קרוב אליך הדבר מאד
בפיך ובלבבך לעשותו דלכאורה

אֲבָל בְּלֹאו הֲכֵי נַמֵּי עוֹלִים לְעוֹלָם הַיְצִירָה — **But even without** any intellectually generated emotion whatsoever, either tangible or "discerned," your Torah and *mitzvos* can,
in any case, ascend to the World of *Yetzirah,* עַל יְדֵי דְחִילוּ וּרְחִימוּ טְבָעִיִּים הַמְסוּתָּרִים
בְּלֵב כָּל יִשְׂרָאֵל בְּתוֹלְדוֹתָם — **through** awakening **the natural "dormant" reverence
and love found from birth in the heart of all Israel,** which is much easier to arouse.

Your natural "dormant" emotions for G-d will propel a *mitzvah* to the World of
Emotion. What is added by the feelings you generate by meditation (either "dis-
cerned" or "tangible") is that your *mitzvos* will be propelled to the higher World of
Intelligence.

כְּמוֹ שֶׁיִּתְבָּאֵר לְקַמָּן בַּאֲרִיכוּת — **As will be explained later on, at length,** in chapters
38, 39 and 44.

CHAPTER 17

WHAT IS WITHIN REACH?
SECTION ONE: WHY YOUR PURPOSE IS WITHIN REACH

27TH TEVES REGULAR | 4TH SHEVAT LEAP

The *Tanya* has consistently stressed that the key to developing real emotions for G-d
is through meditating upon His greatness. In chapter 16, we learned that even a meditation which fails to generate palpable emotion and is only felt more subtly in the
"hidden places in the heart" (*Psalms* 44:22), is sufficient to inspire genuine worship.

With this in mind, we will now turn to an important citation on the Author's Title
Page of the *Tanya*, on which the entire book is based, which suggests that worshiping G-d is "within reach."

וּבְזֶה יוּבַן מַה שֶּׁכָּתוּב — **Based on the above we can explain the verse** cited on the
Author's Title Page of the *Tanya* (p. 2), כִּי קָרוֹב אֵלֶיךָ הַדָּבָר מְאֹד בְּפִיךָ וּבִלְבָבְךָ לַעֲשׂוֹתוֹ
— *"For this (body of) commandment(s) which I am commanding you this day, is not
beyond you, nor is it far away.... **Rather, the thing is very much within reach for
you, in your mouth and in your heart, so that you can do it"** (Deuteronomy 30:14).

הוא בלבבך נגד החוש שלנו [והתורה היא נצחית]
שאין קרוב מאד הדבר להפך לבו מתאוות עוה"ז
לאהבת ה' באמת וכמ"ש בגמרא אטו יראה מילתא
זוטרתי היא וכל שכן אהבה. וגם אמרו רז"ל דצדיקים

This verse, which is central to the *Tanya*, will be the focus of our following discussions (until chapter 25). First, we will address an obvious question that will trouble any reader.

דְּלִכְאוֹרָה הוּא בִּלְבָבְךְ נֶגֶד הַחוּשׁ שֶׁלָּנוּ — **For, at first glance,** to observe the commandments, **"in your heart," is contrary to the experience of our senses.**

Who could honestly say that his heart is not drawn to things outlawed by the Torah?

[וְהַתּוֹרָה הִיא נִצְחִית] — **And the** entire **Torah is eternally** relevant to us, (see *Rambam, Laws of Foundations of the Torah* 9:1; *Laws of Teshuvah* 3:8).

The *Tanya* dismisses the idea that the verse in Deuteronomy was pitched exclusively at a spiritually elevated generation of years gone by. "The Torah is eternal," so this verse must be applicable to us too.

שֶׁאֵין קָרוֹב מְאֹד הַדָּבָר — **For** it would seem that **"the thing"** of desiring to observe the *mitzvos* "in your heart" **is *not* "very much within reach,"** לְהַפֵּךְ לִבּוֹ מִתַּאֲוַות עוֹלָם הַזֶּה לְאַהֲבַת ה' בֶּאֱמֶת — since this would require you **to turn your heart away from the desires of this world, to genuine love of G-d** instead.

You can't fully love G-d "in your heart," and, at the same time, desire self-gratification from "the pleasures of this world." As *Sefer Ha-Chinnuch* (*mitzvah* 418) states: *"One who focuses his thoughts on physical matters and the futilities of the world, not for the sake of Heaven, but merely to enjoy them or to achieve illusory honor, not intending to assist and strengthen good and upstanding people, violates the positive commandment to love G-d."*

As the *Tanya* will now demonstrate, not only is this experience *"contrary to the experience of our senses,"* it also appears to be contrary to the *Talmud*.

וּכְמוֹ שֶׁכָּתוּב בַּגְּמָרָא אָטוּ יִרְאָה מִילְתָא זוּטַרְתִּי הִיא — **As it is written in the *Talmud*,** *"Is reverence of G-d really a small thing?"* (*Brachos* 33b).

The *Talmud* itself recognizes that to revere G-d is challenging for us.

וְכָל שֶׁכֵּן אַהֲבָה — **And** if reverence of G-d is no "small thing," then **how much more so, love** of G-d.

Loving G-d is more difficult because, as the *Tanya* has just stated, you must *"turn your heart away from desiring the pleasures of this world,"* which is not required for reverence and awe of G-d (Rabbi Yosef Yitzchak Schneersohn, *Sefer Ha-Ma'amarim 5680-81* (Kehos: Brooklyn, 1987), pp. 325-6; for the higher status of love over reverence, see *Rambam, Laws of Teshuvah* 10:1).

דוקא לבם ברשותם. אלא דלעשותו ר"ל האהבה
המביאה לידי עשיית המצות בלבד שהיא רעותא
דלבא שבתעלומות לב גם כי אינה בהתגלות לבו

The *Tanya* now cites another proof from the Sages that developing emotions for G-d is a challenging task.

וְגַם אָמְרוּ רַבּוֹתֵינוּ זִכְרוֹנָם לִבְרָכָה — **Our Rabbis, of blessed memory, also taught,** דְּצַדִּיקִים דַּוְקָא לִבָּם בִּרְשׁוּתָם — **that it is exclusively** *tzadikim* who are *"in control of their hearts"* (*Genesis Rabah* 34:10), and can summon emotions at will.

To be *"in control* of the heart," the level of a *tzadik*, is very different from the experience of the *beinoni*, whose "brain *rules over* the heart" (see p. 143).

The *tzadik* is in full control of his heart and sustains authentic feelings for G-d consistently. The *beinoni,* on the other hand, is torn by an uncontrollable mixture of emotions in his heart, and only manages consistency in his religious *behavior* by using his mind to overrule the desires of his heart.

Our verse in *Deuteronomy*, then, cannot be suggesting that consistent reverence and love of G-d is "very much within reach" for everyone, since this is something experienced only by the *tzadik*. So what *does* the verse mean?

אֶלָּא — **Rather,** the words *"in your heart"* and *"so that you can do it"* constitute one single phrase, *i.e.,* — דְּלַעֲשׂוֹתוֹ רוֹצֶה לוֹמַר הָאַהֲבָה הַמְּבִיאָה לִידֵי עֲשִׂיַּית הַמִּצְוֹת בִּלְבָד, the words *"that you can do it,"* **refer to** a minimal level of **love, just what is needed to bring about the practical observance of the** *mitzvos.*

Worship of G-d is "in your heart," but only sufficiently "that you can do it"; no more than that. The verse is not suggesting that a consistent emotional bond to G-d is possible "in your heart." Rather, it teaches that to conjure enough feelings for G-d *to practically observe His commandments* is "within reach" for you. Inside you may still be torn emotionally, but generating the minimal arousal necessary for disciplined control of your actions should be manageable.

According to this interpretation, *Deuteronomy* 30:14 supports the second "all-encompassing principle" of chapter 16. Even if *"your intellectual capacity and cognitive focus prove insufficient to generate a love of G-d tangibly in your heart"* (p. 191), that is still acceptable since, *"'(in your heart) so that you can do it,' refers to a (minimal level of) love, sufficient only to bring about the practical observance of the mitzvos."*

שֶׁהִיא רְעוּתָא דְלִבָּא שֶׁבְּתַעֲלוּמוֹת לֵב — **This** "minimal love" **being the** *"desire of the heart"* (*Zohar* 3, 289b) **which is** generated at least subtly, in the *"hidden places in the heart"* (*Psalms* 44:22), through meditation, גַּם כִּי אֵינָהּ בְּהִתְגַּלּוּת לִבּוֹ כְּרִשְׁפֵּי אֵשׁ — **even if it is not palpable in your heart, like** *"flaming fire"* (*Song* 8:6).

As we learned in the previous chapter, while meditation will not always bring you to have tangible emotions for G-d, it should lead you at least to have a subtle feeling for G-d in your *"hidden places in the heart."*

כרשפי אש ודבר זה קרוב מאד ונקל לכל אדם אשר 23A
יש לו מוח בקדקדו כי מוחו ברשותו ויכול להתבונן בו
ככל אשר יחפוץ וכשיתבונן בו בגדולת א"ס ב"ה
ממילא יוליד במוחו על כל פנים האהבה לה' לדבקה
בו בקיום מצותיו ותורתו וזה כל האדם כי היום לעשותם

וְדָבָר זֶה קָרוֹב מְאֹד וְנָקֵל לְכָל אָדָם אֲשֶׁר יֵשׁ לוֹ מוֹחַ בְּקָדְקֳדוֹ — And this is the thing which is *"very much within reach"* and easily accessible for anyone who has *"a brain in his head"* (see *Talmud, Yevamos* 9a), כִּי מוֹחוֹ בִּרְשׁוּתוֹ — because you can control what you think in **your brain,** וְיָכוֹל לְהִתְבּוֹנֵן בּוֹ כְּכָל אֲשֶׁר יַחְפּוֹץ — and using your brain, **you can think about whatever you want,** וּכְשֶׁיִּתְבּוֹנֵן בּוֹ בִּגְדוּלַת אֵין סוֹף בָּרוּךְ הוּא — and if you will think about the greatness of the Blessed Infinite One, מִמֵּילָא יוֹלִיד בְּמוֹחוֹ עַל כָּל פָּנִים הָאַהֲבָה לַה' — you will inevitably generate, at least in your mind, a love for G-d, לְדָבְקָה בּוֹ בְּקִיּוּם מִצְוֹתָיו וְתוֹרָתוֹ — sufficient to inspire you to **attach yourself to Him through the practical observance of the** *mitzvos* **and** studying **His Torah.**

You can't choose to have feelings for G-d, but you can choose to think about His awesomeness. Even if your thoughts don't succeed in generating a strong emotional connection with G-d, you will be able to generate at least enough motivation to obey His will, *i.e.,* to observe the commandments.

So while loving G-d *intensely* may not be "very much within reach," generating a minimal feeling for G-d, sufficient to observe the *mitzvos, is* within your control.

5TH SHEVAT LEAP

וְזֶה כָּל הָאָדָם — And *"the conclusion of the matter is... observe His commandments, for this is the whole purpose of man"* (Ecclesiastes 12:13; see *A Chasidic Thought*).

כִּי הַיּוֹם לַעֲשׂוֹתָם כְּתִיב — For the verse states regarding the *mitzvos, "Do them today"* (Deuteronomy 7:11), שֶׁהַיּוֹם הוּא עוֹלָם הַמַּעֲשֶׂה דַּוְקָא — meaning that "today," *i.e.,* in this lifetime, in **the physical world, the specific** emphasis is on practical *mitzvos,* וּלְמָחָר כוּ' — and it is only *"tomorrow (in the afterlife) you will receive*

A CHASIDIC THOUGHT

If the thought that I might only be able to achieve a minimal love of G-d (sufficient to observe the commandments) seems disillusioning, Scripture reassures me: *"This is the whole purpose of man."* Judaism considers my outward behavior to be of primary importance. If I can achieve mastery at least in that area, I can be confident that I have achieved my purpose in life.

כתיב שהיום הוא עולם המעשה דוקא ולמחר כו' כמ"ש
במ"א. והמוח שליט בטבעו ותולדתו על חלל השמאלי
שבלב ועל פיו ועל כל האברים שהם כלי המעשה
אם לא מי שהוא רשע באמת כמארז"ל שהרשעים
הם ברשות לבם ואין לבם ברשותם כלל וזה עונש על

the reward" (*Talmud, Eruvin* 22a), כְּמוֹ שֶׁנִּתְבָּאֵר בְּמָקוֹם אַחֵר — **as is explained else-where** (see chapters 35-37).

Both Scripture and the *Talmud* indicate that your main emphasis in this lifetime should be a full, practical observance of the commandments. That is an achievable goal and you should feel a sense of accomplishment in it. Only in the afterlife will you "experience" G-d fully, with an unconflicted emotional intensity.

וְהַמּוֹחַ שַׁלִּיט בְּטִבְעוֹ וְתוֹלַדְתּוֹ עַל חָלָל הַשְּׂמָאלִי שֶׁבַּלֵּב — Observing all the *mitzvos* is entirely within your capabilities since, as we have learned in chapter 12, **inherently and naturally "*the brain rules over (the left side of) the heart*"** (*Zohar* 3, 224a), וְעַל פִּיו וְעַל כָּל הָאֵבָרִים שֶׁהֵם כְּלֵי הַמַּעֲשֶׂה — **and** through this path, it also rules **over the mouth and over all the limbs, the instruments of action.**

SECTION TWO: LOSING SELF-CONTROL

28TH TEVES REGULAR

So far we have discussed the *tzadik* who "is in control of his heart," and the *beinoni* (and aspiring *beinoni*), whose "brain rules over the heart." The *Tanya* now turns to a third category, the "absolute *rasha*," who is totally ruled by his feelings.

אִם לֹא מִי שֶׁהוּא רָשָׁע בֶּאֱמֶת — Generating enough love to observe the *mitzvos* is "very much within reach" for every person, **unless he is a "real *rasha*."**

The "real *rasha*" is the "complete *rasha*" ("*rasha* who has (it) bad") in whom "*the evil in his (Animal) Soul is all that remains (as having influence) within him, for (the evil) has so overwhelmed the good, that it has caused (the good) to depart from inside him*" (chapter 11, p. 137).

(The term "real *rasha*" would perhaps apply also to an incomplete *rasha* who has enough good to contemplate repentance, but not enough to actually repent, as discussed in chapter 11, section 2 — *Notes on Tanya.*)

כְּמַאֲמַר רַבּוֹתֵינוּ זִכְרוֹנָם לִבְרָכָה — **As our Sages, of blessed memory, taught,** שֶׁהָרְשָׁעִים הֵם בִּרְשׁוּת לִבָּם — that "*resha'im are controlled by their hearts*" (*Genesis Rabah ibid.*), וְאֵין לִבָּם בִּרְשׁוּתָם כְּלָל — **and their hearts aren't in their control at all.**

Like an addict, the "real *rasha*" has relinquished self-control to the extent that he is now ruled by his passions. But if "*inherently and naturally the brain rules over the heart*" as we have learned, how is it possible for "real *resha'im*" to lose self-control?

גודל ועוצם עונם ולא דברה תורה במתים אלו שבחייהם
קרוים מתים כי באמת אי אפשר לרשעים להתחיל
לעבוד ה' בלי שיעשו תשובה על העבר תחלה לשבר
הקליפו' שהם מסך מבדיל ומחיצה של ברזל המפסקת
בינם לאביהם שבשמים ע"י שבירת לבו ומרירת נפשו

עַל גּוֹדֶל וְעוֹצֶם עֲוֹנָם — **And this** loss of self-control **is a penalty** from Heaven, וְזֶה עוֹנֶשׁ — **imposed due to the extent and magnitude of their sins** (see *Rambam, Shemonah Perakim*, chapter 8).

How can this be reconciled with our verse in *Deuteronomy*, which states that observing the *mitzvos* is "very much within reach" for us all?

וְלֹא דִבְּרָה תוֹרָה בְּמֵתִים אֵלוּ — **And** when **the Torah** stated that observing the commandments was within everyone's ability, it **was not referring to these** real *resha'im*, who are considered as **"dead" people,** שֶׁבְּחַיֵּיהֶם קְרוּיִם מֵתִים — as the *Talmud* teaches that the *resha'im* **"are called 'dead' in their lifetime"** (*Talmud, Brachos* 18b), since they have "deadened" themselves to the good in their souls.

The verse in *Deuteronomy* only addressed those who are alive. For "real *resha'im*," who are "dead," the verse does not apply.

SECTION THREE: THE SPIRITUAL POWER OF TESHUVAH

This does not mean to say, however, that "real *resha'im*" are irredeemable. In their *present state* they may have buried the spark of good within them; but there is always the possibility of transformation through repentance.

כִּי בֶּאֱמֶת אִי אֶפְשָׁר לָרְשָׁעִים לְהַתְחִיל לַעֲבוֹד ה' בְּלִי שֶׁיַּעֲשׂוּ תְשׁוּבָה עַל הֶעָבַר תְּחִלָּה — **Because, in truth,** real *resha'im* **can't begin to worship G-d** on a regular basis **without first repenting for the past,** לְשַׁבֵּר הַקְּלִיפּוֹת שֶׁהֵם מָסָךְ מַבְדִּיל וּמְחִיצָה שֶׁל — **in order to shatter the** *kelipos* **which have** בַּרְזֶל הַמַּפְסֶקֶת בֵּינָם לַאֲבִיהֶם שֶׁבַּשָּׁמַיִם — **formed a** permanent **"curtain of separation" and an** *"iron wall ... which interposes between them and their Father in Heaven"* (see *Talmud, Pesachim* 85b).

These *resha'im* are held hostage, so to speak, by the negative energy they have brought upon themselves, through their repeated selfish actions. In order to sensitize themselves to their souls again, they first need to overcome that "blockage" through a profound *teshuvah*.

עַל יְדֵי שְׁבִירַת לִבּוֹ וּמְרִירַת נַפְשׁוֹ עַל חֲטָאָיו — This is done **through feeling heartbroken and embittered in their souls, over their sins.**

Teshuvah involves a variety of different elements (verbal confession, resolve not to sin again etc.,) but, spiritually speaking, it is the deep feeling of remorse that breaks through the "blockage" of negative energy which has ensnared the person.

עַל חֲטָאָיו כְּמוֹ שֶׁכָּתוּב בַּזֹּהַר עַל פָּסוּק זִבְחֵי אֱלֹהִים רוּחַ נִשְׁבָּרָה
לֵב נִשְׁבָּר וְגוֹ' שֶׁעַ"יְ לֵב נִשְׁבָּר נִשְׁבְּרָה רוּחַ הַטּוּמְאָה
דְּסַ"א [עַ"שׁ פ' פִּינְחָס ד' ר"מ וּפ' וַיִּקְרָא ד' ח' וד' ה' וד' ה' עַ"א
וּבְפִי' הָרַמַ"ז שָׁם] וְהִיא בְּחִי' תְּשׁוּבָה תַּתָּאָה לְהַעֲלוֹת

PRACTICAL LESSONS

If you persist, meditating about G-d will generate enough conviction in your mind to observe the *mitzvos* practically. You just need to have "a brain in your head."

Your meditation might fail to generate intense feelings for G-d in your heart, but that won't detract from your main purpose in this world, which is to observe the *mitzvos*.

By sinning consistently you could ensnare yourself in an "impure spirit" that compromises your ability to make further moral choices.

But however much you might become locked in these negative behavior patterns, *teshuvah* (repentance) is always effective to break yourself out of it.

כְּמוֹ שֶׁכָּתוּב בַּזֹּהַר עַל פָּסוּק — As the *Zohar* states on the verse, זִבְחֵי אֱלֹהִים רוּחַ נִשְׁבָּרָה לֵב נִשְׁבָּר וְגוֹ' — "*A broken spirit is a sacrifice for G-d, a heart that is broken* and *contrite, You do not reject, O G-d*" (Psalms 51:19), שֶׁעַל — יְדֵי לֵב נִשְׁבָּר נִשְׁבְּרָה רוּחַ הַטּוּמְאָה דְּסִטְרָא אָחֲרָא — that the impure spirit of the *sitra achra* is shattered by a broken heart, [עַיֵּין שָׁם פָּרְשַׁת פִּינְחָס דַּף ר"מ וּפָרְשַׁת וַיִּקְרָא דַּף ח'] וְדַף ה' עַמּוּד א' וּבְפֵירוּשׁ הָרַב מֹשֶׁה זָכּוּתָא שָׁם] — see *Zohar* on *Parshas Pinchas*, p. 240a-b, and on *Parshas Vayikra*, p. 8a-b and p. 5a, and the commentary of Rabbi Moshe Zacuto *ibid.*.

The *Zohar* states: "*When a man contaminates himself with his sins, he draws upon himself an impure spirit, which imposes itself on him, ruling over his desires....*"

"*At the time when the Temple stood, a man would offer his sacrifice... and feel remorse, thereby breaking down that (impure) spirit... But if that (impure) spirit is not broken, then his sacrifice is worth nothing and is given to the dogs.... And this is why Scripture says that the proper sacrifices of G-d are a 'broken spirit,' for that impure spirit has to be broken so that it will not be in control*" (*Zohar* 3, 240a-b).

6TH SHEVAT LEAP

וְהִיא בְּחִינַת תְּשׁוּבָה תַּתָּאָה — This shattering of an "impure spirit" that restores a person's ability to control himself, represents the level of "lower *teshuvah*."

The term *teshuvah*, literally translated as "repentance," is derived from the Hebrew term *shav*, meaning "return." *Teshuvah is the "return" or restoration of the soul to its prior, healthy state.* Broadly speaking, this can occur at two levels. Initially, there must be a return of the soul to its level prior to sin. This is referred to by the Kabbalah as "lower *teshuvah*."

Subsequently, there can be a further "return" of the soul, towards the level it enjoyed before it was born into a body, when it was totally intimate with G-d. This is re-

ה' תתאה להקימה מנפילתה שנפלה אל החיצוני' שהוא
סוד גלות השכינה כמארז"ל גלו לאדום שכינה עמהם
דהיינו כשהאדם עושה מעשה אדום מוריד וממשיך

ferred to as "higher *teshuvah.*" (These two levels are discussed at length in the third section of *Tanya*, *Igeres Ha-Teshuvah,* chapter 4 and onwards).

In our case, "lower *teshuvah*" is sufficient to release the "real *rasha*" from the impure spirit which holds him back from exerting the necessary discipline for worship.

לְהַעֲלוֹת הֵ"א תַּתָּאָה — **To restore the lower letter** *hei* of the Tetragrammaton (*Zohar*, 3, 122a), spelled in Hebrew: *yud, hei, vav* and *hei.*

The Kabbalists taught that sins actually damage the spiritual realms, a process symbolized by a fragmentation of the Tetragrammaton. When "lower *teshuvah*" is performed, the final, "lower" letter *hei* of the Tetragrammaton is symbolically restored. "Higher *teshuvah,*" on the other hand, has the effect of restoring the first, "higher" letter *hei* (Rabbi Chaim Vital, *Sha'ar Tikunei Avonos*, chapter 1, in *Sha'ar Ha-Yichudim*, (Lemberg, 1855), p. 33a-b).

לַהֲקִימָה מִנְפִילָתָה שֶׁנָּפְלָה אֶל הַחִיצוֹנִים — "Lower *teshuvah*" has the power **to "elevate"** the final, "lower" letter *hei* **from its "fall" into the shallow forces** of *kelipah*, a "fall" brought about by sin.

When the final *hei* is fragmented and dislocated from G-d's name, the negative forces of the universe become parasites for its "free" energy. The excruciating emotions of *teshuvah* are necessary to extract the *hei* from its enmeshment in the "shallow forces" and restore it back to the Tetragrammaton.

שֶׁהוּא סוֹד גָּלוּת הַשְּׁכִינָה כְּמַאֲמַר רַבּוֹתֵינוּ — **This is the secret of the** *Shechinah's* **exile,** זִכְרוֹנָם לִבְרָכָה גָּלוּ לֶאֱדוֹם שְׁכִינָה עִמָּהֶם — **as in the saying of our Rabbis, of blessed memory,** *"When the Jewish people **were exiled to Edom, the Shechinah was with them"*** (*Talmud, Megillah* 29a).

The *Shechinah*, G-d's presence on earth, is principally linked with the Land of Israel and the site of the Temple in Jerusalem. But the *Talmud* teaches that when the Jewish people were banished from their land, the *Shechinah* joined them in exile.

Normally, this is understood to mean that G-d continues to be present with the Jewish people, wherever they are found. But the Kabbalists emphasized a different angle, the *secret* of the *Shechinah's* exile. They stressed how this process was "painful" for the *Shechinah* herself, so to speak. She would "prefer" to be in her land, and when forced to join the Jewish people in exile, she "suffers" the pain of banishment too (*Sha'ar Ha-Yichudim ibid.*).

To further explain this "secret," the *Tanya* now offers commentary on the *Talmud's* statement, "when they were exiled *to Edom.*" Literally, this is a geographical reference to the Roman exile, beginning approximately 63 B.C.E., and continuing to the present day; but the *Tanya* offers a mystical reading of the *Talmud's* statement.

לְשֵׁם בְּחִי׳ וְנִיצוֹץ אֱלֹהוּת הַמְּחַיֶּה אֶת נר״ן שֶׁלּוֹ
הַמְּלוּבָּשִׁים בּוֹ בְּנֶפֶשׁ הַבַּהֲמִית מֵהַקְּלִיפָּה שֶׁבְּלִבּוֹ
שֶׁבֶּחָלָל הַשְּׂמָאלִי הַמּוֹלֶכֶת בּוֹ בְּעוֹדוֹ רָשָׁע וּמוֹשֶׁלֶת
בָּעִיר קְטַנָּה שֶׁלּוֹ וְנר״ן כְּבוּשִׁי׳ בְּגוֹלָה אֶצְלָהּ וּכְשֶׁנִּשְׁבָּר
לִבּוֹ בְּקִרְבּוֹ וְנִשְׁבְּרָה רוּחַ הַטּוּמְאָה וְס״א וְיִתְפָּרְדוּ כו׳
הִיא קָמָה מִנְּפִילָתָהּ וְגַם נִצָּבָה כמ״ש במ״א:

23B

דְּהַיְינוּ כְּשֶׁאָדָם עוֹשֶׂה מַעֲשֵׂה אֱדוֹם — **Namely, when a person** sins, **practicing the behavior of "Edom,"** מוֹרִיד וּמַמְשִׁיךְ לְשָׁם בְּחִינַת וְנִיצוֹץ אֱלֹהוּת — **he draws down there,** into his impure act, **that G-dly component and "spark"** found within his soul, הַמְּחַיֶּה אֶת נֶפֶשׁ רוּחַ וּנְשָׁמָה שֶׁלּוֹ — **which endows his** soul powers of *nefesh, ruach* **and** *neshamah* **with life.**

PRACTICAL LESSONS

Even a basic *teshuvah* has the power to free you from the "impure spirit" brought about by sin.

Your sins cause the *Shechinah* (Divine Presence) within you to be "exiled," which is "painful" for her. Your *teshuvah* redeems the *Shechinah* from her "exile."

In this reading, the "exile of the *Shechinah*," occurs *within the sinner himself.* Through his sinful acts, he causes the spark of G-d (*Shechinah*) *in his soul* to become enmeshed in the negative forces of *kelipah*. This forced displacement to the impure realms is extremely "painful" for the *Shechinah*.

הַמְּלוּבָּשִׁים בּוֹ — **The powers of the Divine Soul "dressed" in him** at the moment of sin become "exiled," בַּנֶפֶשׁ הַבַּהֲמִית מֵהַקְּלִיפָּה שֶׁבְּחָלָל הַשְּׂמָאלִי — trapped **by the Animal Soul of the *kelipah*, in the heart's left chamber,** הַמּוֹלֶכֶת בּוֹ בְּעוֹדוֹ רָשָׁע — **which rules over him, so long as he remains a *rasha*,** וּמוֹשֶׁלֶת בָּעִיר קְטַנָּה — **controlling his "small city,"** his body, וְנֶפֶשׁ רוּחַ שֶׁלּוֹ — **controlling his "small city,"** his body, וּנְשָׁמָה כְּבוּשִׁים בַּגּוֹלָה אֶצְלָהּ — **and his *nefesh, ruach* and *neshamah* are thereby held captive by it.**

To be a serial sinner is effectively to hold the Divine Soul as a "helpless" captive inside his body and Animal Soul, as the body descends into the negative forces.

וּכְשֶׁנִּשְׁבָּר לִבּוֹ בְּקִרְבּוֹ — **But when** the person does *teshuvah*, **breaking his heart inside him,** וְנִשְׁבְּרָה רוּחַ הַטּוּמְאָה וְסִטְרָא אָחֲרָא — **causing the impure spirit of *sitra achra* to be shattered,** as we learned above from the *Zohar*, וְיִתְפָּרְדוּ כו׳ — **"then** *all evildoers* **will be scattered"** (*Psalms* 92:10), *i.e.,* the negative forces in which the *Shechinah* was enmeshed, will crumble.

הִיא קָמָה מִנְּפִילָתָהּ וְגַם נִצָּבָה — **Then,** when the Divine spark in the individual is redeemed, **She** (the *Shechinah*) **"rises upright"** from her fall, **"and keeps standing too"** (see *Genesis* 37:7), כְּמוֹ שֶׁנִּתְבָּאֵר בְּמָקוֹם אַחֵר — **as is explained elsewhere,** (in *Igeres Ha-Teshuvah*, chapters 6-7).

פרק יח ולתוספת ביאור באר היטב מלת מאד
שבפסוק כי קרוב אליך הדבר
מאד וגו' צריך לידע נאמנה כי אף מי שדעתו קצרה
בידיעת ה' ואין לו לב להבין בגדולת א"ס ב"ה להוליד
ממנה דחילו ורחימו אפי' במוחו ותבונתו לבד אעפ"כ

CHAPTER 18

DORMANT LOVE IN YOUR SOUL

SECTION ONE: WHEN MEDITATION COMPLETELY FAILS

29TH TEVES REGULAR | 7TH SHEVAT LEAP

In chapter 17, the *Tanya* explained that observing the commandments is "within reach" and "easily accessible" for *"anyone who has a brain in his head."* This is because *"you can think about whatever you want and if you will think about the greatness of the Blessed Infinite One, you will inevitably generate, at least in your mind, a love for G-d, (sufficient) to (inspire you to) attach yourself to Him through the practical observance of the mitzvos"* (p. 204).

But this merely explains why the goal is generally "within reach" and achievable. We have yet to clarify why it is *"very much* within reach."

מְלַת מְאֹד שֶׁבַּפָּסוּק **— To further understand, with clarity,** וּלְתוֹסֶפֶת בִּיאוּר בָּאֵר הֵיטֵב
כִּי קָרוֹב אֵלֶיךָ הַדָּבָר מְאֹד וְגוֹ' **— the word** *me'od* **("very much") in the verse** discussed in chapter 17, *"Rather, the thing is very much (me'od) within reach for you, in your mouth and in your heart, so that you can do it"* (Deuteronomy 30:14), צָרִיךְ לֵידַע
נֶאֱמָנָה **— you need to have a profound recognition** of the following idea.

Up to this point in the *Tanya*, our emphasis has been on coming close to G-d through mind-work. This path was depicted as "within reach" and "easily accessible" since, *"inherently and naturally the brain rules over the heart."*

In the following chapters, the *Tanya* will present us with another, *even easier* path to worship, which is *"very much"* within reach. In contrast to the previous path which required you to *acquire* an awareness of G-d with your mind, this new path will be based on a quality *already present* in your soul, that merely needs to be unveiled.

כִּי אַף מִי שֶׁדַּעְתּוֹ קְצָרָה בִּידִיעַת ה' **— For even if your mind is weak when it comes to the mental appreciation of G-d,** וְאֵין לוֹ לֵב לְהָבִין בִּגְדוּלַּת אֵין סוֹף בָּרוּךְ הוּא **— and an understanding of the Blessed Infinite One's greatness is beyond your heart's capacity,** לְהוֹלִיד מִמֶּנָּה דְּחִילוּ וּרְחִימוּ אֲפִילוּ בְּמוֹחוֹ וּתְבוּנָתוֹ לְבַד **— and you fail to**

קרוב אליו הדבר מאד לשמור ולעשות כל מצות
התורה ות״ת כנגד כולן בפיו ובלבבו ממש מעומקא
דלבא באמת לאמיתו בדחילו ורחימו שהיא אהבה
מסותרת שבלב כללות ישראל שהיא ירושה לנו

develop enough intellectual appreciation of G-d **even to generate a mere "discern-ment" of love and reverence in your mind** (as we discussed in chapter 16), אַף עַל פִּי כֵן קָרוֹב אֵלֶיךָ הַדָּבָר מְאֹד — **nevertheless,** despite the failure of your meditation efforts, it still remains true that *"the thing is very much within reach for you,"* לִשְׁמוֹר וְתַלְמוּד וְלַעֲשׂוֹת כָּל מִצְוֹת הַתּוֹרָה, — **to carefully observe all the** *mitzvos* **of the Torah,** תּוֹרָה כְּנֶגֶד כּוּלָן — **including** *"the study of the Torah, which is equal to them all"* (*Mishnah, Pe'ah* 1:1), בְּפִיו וּבִלְבָבוֹ מַמָּשׁ — *"in your mouth and in your heart,"* liter-ally, מֵעוּמְקָא דְלִבָּא בֶּאֱמֶת לַאֲמִיתוֹ בִּדְחִילוּ וּרְחִימוּ — **from the genuine depths of your heart, with reverence and love,** if you will follow the second approach, below.

In chapter 16 we learned that if your meditation fails to produce palpable emotion, and only gives rise to a vague "discernment" in your mind and in the "hidden places of your heart," that's okay. Since most people can presumably do at least that, we concluded in chapter 17 that observing the commandments is "within reach."

But what if your meditation fails completely? You just can't concentrate enough to generate a vague "discernment" of G-d's greatness or even muted feelings for G-d?

The *Tanya* reassures us of another approach to attain love and reverence for G-d, not through mindful meditation; and this is a path available literally to everyone. To "discern" G-d through meditation is "within reach," but this second approach will be easier and more universally applicable; it is *"very much* within reach."

(These two paths are alluded to in the author's title page as the "long way" and the "short way" (see p. 3). Contemplating G-d's greatness, which takes time and patience, is the "long way" depicted up to chapter 17. The second, easier approach described in chapters 18-25 is the "short way" — Rabbi Shlomo Chaim Kesselman, *Biurey Reb Shlomo Chaim* (Kfar Chabad: Kehos, 2011), p. 57).

שֶׁהִיא אַהֲבָה מְסוּתֶרֶת שֶׁבְּלֵב כְּלָלוּת יִשְׂרָאֵל — This second approach involves the **"dormant love"** (*Proverbs* 27:5), **found in the heart of all Israel.**

There is a dormant love of G-d *already present in your soul*; you merely need to awaken it. This is "very much within reach" because we are speaking about some-thing that you already have, an innate property of your psyche.

שֶׁהִיא יְרוּשָׁה לָנוּ מֵאֲבוֹתֵינוּ — **It is an "inheritance" to us from our Patriarchs,** (see Rabbi Tzvi Elimelech of Dinov, *Igra De-Pirka* (Bnei Brak, 1999), section 178, p. 99).

The *Tanya* describes "dormant love" as an "inheritance," to stress that it is not something that you have earned through your own merits. It is something which you were born with because you are a descendant of the Patriarchs.

מאבותינו רק שצריך להקדי' ולבאר תחלה באר היטב
שרש אהבה זו ועניינה ואיך היא ירושה לנו ואיך נכלל
בה גם דחילו. והענין כי האבות הן הן המרכבה ועל

While the *Tanya* refers to the Patriarchs in general as bequeathing us a "dormant love," it is Avraham in particular who is associated with the traits of love and kindness (*Notes on Tanya*). As *Sefer Bahir* explains:

"Avraham, Yitzchak and Ya'akov were each given a particular power, corresponding to their actions. Avraham performed acts of kindness: He prepared food for everyone in his area and for all wayfarers. He acted kindly and went out to greet them, as it is written (Genesis 18:2), 'and he ran to greet them'.... G-d therefore granted him the same measure and gave him the attribute of kindness" (*Sefer Bahir*, section 135; for Avraham's influence on future souls, see *ibid.*, section 58).

But how, exactly, do you "inherit" love? Why is it described as "dormant"? And how might you bring it to a conscious experience? For the remainder of this chapter, and in following chapters, the *Tanya* will address these issues.

רַק שֶׁצָּרִיךְ לְבָאֵר וּלְהַקְדִּים תְּחִלָּה בַּאֵר הֵיטֵב — **Only, we must first offer an introductory explanation to clarify** four issues pertaining to inherited, "dormant love":

שֹׁרֶשׁ אַהֲבָה זוֹ — a.) **The root of this love,** because if it doesn't flow from the mind to the heart, how does it come to you? (answered in section 3 of this chapter).

וְעִנְיָינָהּ — and, b.) **Its defining property,** how it differs from other forms of love, (to be explained below in chapter 19, section 1).

וְאֵיךְ הִיא יְרוּשָׁה לָנוּ — and c.) **how it is our "inheritance,"** how can an emotion be inherited? (answered in section 2 of this chapter).

וְאֵיךְ נִכְלָל בָּהּ גַּם דְּחִילוּ — and d.) **how it includes also** an inherited capacity for **reverence,** as well as love, since the worship of G-d requires both love and reverence (to be explained below in chapter 19, section 4; and chapter 25, section 1).

SECTION TWO: "INHERITING" EMOTION

8TH SHEVAT LEAP

וְהָעִנְיָין — **And the answer** to question 'c' is as follows:

כִּי הָאָבוֹת הֵן הֵן הַמֶּרְכָּבָה — The *Midrash* teaches that *"the Patriarchs were genuinely a 'chariot' to G-d"* (Genesis Rabah 47:6).

Ramban writes of the Patriarchs, *"Their thoughts were never detached from the Supernal Light even for one moment"* (Igeres Ha-Kodesh, chapter 5). Their dedication to G-d was comparable to a physical chariot that never deviates to the right or left of its own accord, and follows its driver with relentless precision.

כן זכו להמשיך נר"ן לבניהם אחריהם עד עולם מעשר
ספירות דקדושה שבארבע עולמות אבי"ע לכל אחד

וְעַל כֵּן זָכוּ לְהַמְשִׁיךְ נֶפֶשׁ רוּחַ וּנְשָׁמָה לִבְנֵיהֶם אַחֲרֵיהֶם עַד עוֹלָם מֵעֶשֶׂר סְפִירוֹת דְּקְדוּשָׁה
— As a result, they merited that their future descendants would forever be endowed with soul powers of *nefesh, ruach* and *neshamah* from one of **the ten holy sefiros.**

The Patriarchs' reward for their outstanding devotion to G-d was that their descendants' souls would be sourced in holy energy (one of the ten *sefiros*).

In one of his discourses, Rabbi Shneur Zalman clarifies this idea through the *Talmud's* comment on a verse in Daniel. "*I, Daniel, alone saw the (mystical) vision. The men that were with me did not see the vision; but a great trembling fell upon them, so that they fled to hide themselves*" (Daniel 10:7). The *Talmud* asks: "*And if these men did not see the vision, why did they flee, trembling?*" And the *Talmud* answers, "*Because even though they did not see the vision, their mazalos saw it*" (*Talmud, Megillah* 3a).

PRACTICAL LESSONS

If you're not cut out for meditation, you can still unveil the "dormant love" in your heart, using the method outlined in chapters 18-25.

Even the most irreverent and sinful Jews have "dormant love" in their souls, something that was "inherited" from the Patriarchs.

Rabbi Shneur Zalman translates the term "*mazalos*" to mean, "*the root of the soul which is not enmeshed in the body... but it flashes and shines into the chochmah of the Divine Soul, which **is** enmeshed in the body.*" The *mazal*, "*literally 'sees' that there is no way of deviating from G-d,*" and communicates this subliminally to the conscious mind.

As a "chariot" to G-d, the Patriarchs experienced a conscious awareness of the Divine. "*Therefore, they merited, too, that their future descendants would forever be endowed with lofty souls, which would have (at least a subconscious) experience of their mazalos seeing (the Divine).*"

The immediacy of G-d's presence which the Patriarchs experienced *consciously*, would be experienced by their descendants *subconsciously* (*Ma'amarei Admor Ha-Zaken al Parshiot Ha-Torah ve-ha-Moa'dim,* (Brooklyn: Kehos, 1981), p. 366).

שֶׁבְּאַרְבַּע עוֹלָמוֹת אֲצִילוּת בְּרִיאָה יְצִירָה וַעֲשִׂיָּה — However, this does not mean that all the souls of Israel are equal, since each soul might be associated with any one of the ten holy *sefiros* as they are found in any one **of the four** spiritual **worlds: *Atzilus* (Emanation), *Beriah* (Creation), *Yetzirah* (Formation) and *Asiyah* (Action).**

The Kabbalah teaches that in the spiritual realms, there is a hierarchy of "worlds" and a soul might emanate from any one of them. For example, "*there are people*"

וְאֶחָד כְּפִי מַדְרֵגָתוֹ וּכְפִי מַעֲשָׂיו וְעַל כָּל פָּנִים אֲפִי' לְקַל
שֶׁבַּקַּלִּים וּפוֹשְׁעֵי יִשְׂרָאֵל נִמְשָׁךְ בְּזִיוּוּגָם נֶפֶשׁ דְּנֶפֶשׁ
דְּמַלְכוּת דַּעֲשִׂיָּה שֶׁהִיא מַדְרֵגָה הַתַּחְתּוֹנָה שֶׁבִּקְדוּשַׁת
הָעֲשִׂיָּה וְאעפ"כ מֵאַחַר שֶׁהִיא מֵעֶשֶׂר סְפִירוֹת קְדוּשׁוֹת

whose nefesh is from malchus of Asiyah, and others who are from yesod of Asiyah" (Rabbi Shmuel Vital, *Sha'ar Ha-Gilgulim* (Jerusalem, 1903), p. 2a).

A higher soul, from a higher *sefirah* or world, will find it easier to be aware of G-d and meditate upon His greatness. A soul emanating from a lower "location" will find it more challenging.

The *Tanya* notes briefly that your soul-level can ascend throughout your life.

לְכָל אֶחָד וְאֶחָד כְּפִי מַדְרֵגָתוֹ וּכְפִי מַעֲשָׂיו — **Each individual** begins life, **according to his souls'** initial **level** in the *sefiros* within the four worlds, **and** then his soul can ascend the *sefiros* and the worlds during his life, **following his** good **behavior.***

As *Sha'ar Ha-Gilgulim* teaches: *"Every person must rectify the whole spectrum (of sefiros) in Asiyah before his soul can receive from Yetzirah, since Yetzirah is greater than all of Asiyah. Similarly, in order for his soul to receive from Beriah, a person needs to rectify every part of his soul from Yetzirah, after which his soul can receive from Beriah. It is insufficient for him to rectify only the particular place in which his soul-root is grounded"* (ibid.).

וְעַל כָּל פָּנִים — **And,** while we may not all have lofty souls, they are all **at least** from one of the ten holy *sefiros*, without exception, אֲפִילוּ לְקַל שֶׁבַּקַּלִּים וּפוֹשְׁעֵי יִשְׂרָאֵל נִמְשָׁךְ בְּזִיוּוּגָם נֶפֶשׁ דְּנֶפֶשׁ דְּמַלְכוּת דַּעֲשִׂיָּה — so **even the most irreverent and sinful Jews will cause a** holy **soul to be endowed** to their children **through their act of conception, at the very least from** the lowest soul-level, *nefesh of nefesh,* **from** the lowest of the ten holy *sefiros,* **malchus,** and **from** the lowest of the four Worlds, *Asiyah,* שֶׁהִיא מַדְרֵגָה הַתַּחְתּוֹנָה שֶׁבִּקְדוּשַׁת הָעֲשִׂיָּה — **this** *nefesh* of *nefesh* of *malchus* **being the lowest rung in the sacred** World of *Asiyah.*

In summary: While accepting the hierarchy of souls described in the Kabbalah, the *Tanya* has nevertheless "democratized" all souls in the sense that they are all rooted in pure Divine energy, the *"ten holy sefiros."*

However low a soul's root may be, its direct connection with G-d will not be severed. All of the Patriarchs' descendants merit a soul which, in one way or another, is rooted in one of the "ten holy *sefiros*." There are no exceptions.

This provides us with an answer to question 'c' above: How is it possible to inherit love? The answer is: It is not the emotion itself we inherit, but a soul which is *predisposed* to love G-d, due to its lofty source in the Divine *sefiros.*

---

* This line has been interpreted in a number of different ways. See comments of Rabbi Ya'akov Leib Altein in *Kovetz Oholei Torah,* issue 1012 (Brooklyn, 2011), pp. 47-51; issue 1014, pp. 48-49.

הִיא כְּלוּלָה מִכּוּלָן גַּם מֵחָכְמָה דַּעֲשִׂיָּה שֶׁבְּתוֹכָהּ מְלוּבֶּשֶׁת
חָכְמָה דְּמַלְכוּת דַּאֲצִילוּת שֶׁבְּתוֹכָהּ חָכְמָה דַּאֲצִילוּת
שֶׁבָּהּ מֵאִיר אוֹר אֵין סוֹף בָּרוּךְ הוּא מַמָּשׁ כְּדִכְתִיב ה' בְּחָכְמָה

SECTION THREE: THE ROOT OF "DORMANT LOVE"

Now we turn to question 'a': What is the root of this inherited love? By what mechanism does it come to us?

The answer will be based on the idea that a sacred system is characterized by *cohesiveness* and *interconnectedness*. Every component is profoundly connected with every other component.

וְאַף עַל פִּי כֵן מֵאַחַר שֶׁהִיא מֵעֶשֶׂר סְפִירוֹת קְדוֹשׁוֹת — Even if a person has a soul from the lowest of the *sefiros* and from the lowest of the worlds, **nevertheless since it is** ultimately rooted in **one of the ten holy *sefiros*,** הִיא כְּלוּלָה מִכּוּלָן — it contains an element of **all the other** *sefiros*, inside it.

As a cohesive, spiritual system, every *sefirah* "contains" within it a component of all the other *sefiros*. In this way, the *sefiros* find each other "relatable" — even if they represent opposing energies — since each *sefirah* can always connect with the element of the "other" within itself.

גַּם מֵחָכְמָה דַּעֲשִׂיָּה — Due to this fundamental interconnectedness, **even** the lowest *sefirah* of the lowest world, *malchus* of *Asiyah*, contains within it the highest *sefirah* of that world, ***chochmah* of *Asiyah*.**

The principle of interconnectedness provides a "bridge," not only between the *sefiros* within a specific world, but also across one spiritual world to another. In this case, *chochmah* of *Asiyah* (the highest *sefirah* of the lowest world), is connected with *chochmah* in all the other worlds, including the highest world, *Atzilus*.

שֶׁבְּתוֹכָהּ מְלוּבֶּשֶׁת חָכְמָה דְּמַלְכוּת דַּאֲצִילוּת — **And within** the highest *sefirah* of the lowest world, *chochmah* of *Asiyah*, we find the veiled presence of the highest world, first through ***chochmah* within *malchus* of *Atzilus*** (the highest *sefirah* as it is found within the lowest *sefirah* of the highest world), שֶׁבְּתוֹכָהּ חָכְמָה דַּאֲצִילוּת — in **which is found *chochmah* of *Atzilus*** (the highest *sefirah* of the highest world).

Each *sefirah*, then, is a "window" to a higher one which is "included" within it, as a veiled presence. This facilitates a connection from one end of a world to the other, and then it bridges the gap separating the worlds.

Once the highest *sefirah* of the highest world is "unveiled" there is a direct connection with G-d's infinite presence (see author's note to chapter 6, pp. 90-91).

שֶׁבָּהּ מֵאִיר אוֹר אֵין סוֹף בָּרוּךְ הוּא מַמָּשׁ — **And in** the highest *sefirah* (*chochmah*) of the highest world, **the Blessed Infinite Light shines, literally.**

כְּדִכְתִיב ה' בְּחָכְמָה יָסַד אָרֶץ — **As the verse states,** *"G-d founded the earth with chochmah"* (*Proverbs* 3:19).

יסד ארץ וכולם בחכמה עשית ונמצא כי אין סוף ב"ה
מלובש בבחי' חכמה שבנפש האדם יהיה מי שיהיה
מישראל ובבחי' החכמה שבה עם אור א"ס ב"ה המלובש
בה מתפשטת בכל בחי' הנפש כולה להחיותה מבחי'
ראשה עד בחי' רגלה כדכתיב החכמה תחיה בעליה
[ולפעמים ממשיכים פושעי ישראל נשמות גבוהות
מאד שהיו בעמקי הקליפות כמ"ש בספר גלגולים]:

24A

וְכוּלָּם בְּחָכְמָה עָשִׂיתָ — And *"You have made them all with chochmah"* (Psalms 104:24).

These verses imply that G-d's direct connection with the universe is through the vehicle of *chochmah*. Once G-d's light floods *chochmah,* it then spreads to all the other *sefiros,* and to the rest of the universe.

As we have learned, *chochmah* represents an inquisitiveness and openness to the unknown (above p. 58). That is why *chochmah* alone is capable of acting as a receptacle to the Infinite Light of G-d: anything other than absolute openness would serve as a *finite* "structure" that would be incompatible with an *infinite* light.

וְנִמְצָא כִּי אֵין סוֹף בָּרוּךְ הוּא מְלוּבָשׁ בִּבְחִינַת חָכְמָה שֶׁבְּנֶפֶשׁ הָאָדָם יְהְיֶה מִי שֶׁיִהְיֶה מִיִּשְׂרָאֵל — So it turns out that, regardless of what kind of Jew you may be, the Infinite Light of G-d is present in the *chochmah* component of your soul, וּבְחִינַת הַחָכְמָה שֶׁבָּהּ עִם אוֹר אֵין סוֹף בָּרוּךְ הוּא הַמְלוּבָשׁ בָּהּ מִתְפַּשֶׁטֶת בְּכָל בְּחִינוּת הַנֶּפֶשׁ כּוּלָּהּ — and that component of *chochmah,* together with the Blessed Infinite Light present in it, then dissipates throughout your entire soul, to every component within it, לְהַחֲיוֹתָהּ energizing your soul at מִבְּחִינַת רֹאשָׁהּ עַד בְּחִינַת רַגְלָהּ all its levels, **"from head to foot,"** כְּדִכְתִיב הַחָכְמָה תְּחַיֶּה בְעָלֶיהָ — as the verse states, *"Chochmah gives life to those who posses it"* (Ecclesiastes 7:12).

In a parenthetical comment, the *Tanya* observes:

[וְלִפְעָמִים מַמְשִׁיכִים פּוֹשְׁעֵי יִשְׂרָאֵל נְשָׁמוֹת גְּבוֹהוֹת מְאֹד — And sometimes even **sinful Jews** when conceiving their children **will draw down very lofty souls,** שֶׁהָיוּ בְּעִמְקֵי הַקְּלִיפּוֹת — which had been trapped **in the depths of the** *kelipos* that opposed these souls coming on earth, due to their holiness, [כְּמוֹ שֶׁכָּתוּב בְּסֵפֶר גִּלְגּוּלִים] — **as is stated in** *Sefer Ha-Gilgulim* (chapter 32).

In a cause-and-effect universe, it seems bizarre that very sinful people would have the purity of intention necessary to "draw down" lofty souls for their children. But, based on the above, the phenomenon makes more sense. Even the most "sin-

PRACTICAL LESSONS

All the components of your soul are profoundly interconnected, so it's not hard to tap into your faith.

הִנֵּה הַחָכְמָה הִיא מְקוֹר הַשֵּׂכֶל וְהַהֲבָנָה וְהִיא לְמַעְלָה
מֵהַבִּינָה שֶׁהוּא הֲבָנַת הַשֵּׂכֶל וְהַשָּׂגָתוֹ וְהַחָכְמָה הִיא
לְמַעְלָה מֵהַהֲבָנָה וְהַהַשָּׂגָה וְהִיא מְקוֹר לָהֶן וְזֶהוּ לְשׁוֹן
חָכְמָה כּ"ח מַ"ה שֶׁהוּא מַה שֶׁאֵינוֹ מוּשָׂג וּמוּבָן וְאֵינוֹ
נִתְפָּס בְּהַשָּׂגָה עֲדַיִן וְלָכֵן מִתְלַבֵּשׁ בָּה אוֹר א"ס ב"ה
דְּלֵית מַחֲשָׁבָה תְּפִיסָא בֵּיהּ כְּלָל וְלָכֵן כָּל יִשְׂרָאֵל אֲפִילוּ
הַנָּשִׁים וְעַמֵּי הָאָרֶץ הֵם מַאֲמִינִים בַּה' שֶׁהָאֱמוּנָה הִיא
לְמַעְלָה מִן הַדַּעַת וְהַהַשָּׂגָ' כִּי פֶּתִי יַאֲמִין לְכָל דָּבָר וְעָרוּם

ful" Jew has *chochmah* in his soul, in which the Blessed Infinite Light shines, and that is certainly a sufficiently "lofty" energy to elicit a "lofty soul" (*Notes* on *Tanya*).

SECTION FOUR: THE "WINDOW" TO YOUR SOUL

1ST SHEVAT REGULAR | 9TH SHEVAT LEAP

Above, we touched upon why *chochmah* in particular serves as a "window to the soul" for the Infinite Light of G-d. The *Tanya* will now elaborate on this idea.

הִנֵּה הַחָכְמָה הִיא מְקוֹר הַשֵּׂכֶל וְהַהֲבָנָה — **Now,** as we learned in chapter 3, *chochmah* **(inquiry) is the source of all intelligence and cognition,** וְהִיא לְמַעְלָה מֵהַבִּינָה שֶׁהוּא — *chochmah* **precedes** *binah,* **which is** the experience of cog-nitively grasping הֲבָנַת הַשֵּׂכֶל וְהַשָּׂגָתוֹ an idea previously intuited in a "raw" state by *chochmah,* וְהַחָכְמָה **so it's** *chochmah* **that precedes, and** הִיא לְמַעְלָה מֵהַהֲבָנָה וְהַהַשָּׂגָה וְהִיא מְקוֹר לָהֶן **is the source of, cognition and grasping.**

וְזֶהוּ לְשׁוֹן חָכְמָה כּ"ח מַ"ה — **This is also reflected in the** Hebrew **word "*chochmah,*"** — the fusion of two Hebrew words, *ko'ach* ("power") and *mah* ("what?") (*Zohar* 3, 34a); *chochmah* is the "power (ability) to say 'What is this?'" an inquisitiveness and openness, שֶׁהוּא מַה שֶׁאֵינוֹ מוּשָׂג וּמוּבָן וְאֵינוֹ נִתְפָּס בְּהַשָּׂגָה עֲדַיִן — **to that which is not yet grasped and understood, and still defies comprehension.**

וְלָכֵן מִתְלַבֵּשׁ בָּה אוֹר אֵין סוֹף בָּרוּךְ הוּא — **And that is why the Blessed Infinite Light** *can* **be expressed there** in *chochmah,* דְּלֵית מַחֲשָׁבָה תְּפִיסָא בֵּיהּ כְּלָל — **because "***no thought can grasp (the Infinite Light) at all***"** (*Tikunei Zohar* 17a), therefore it is best captured by the pre-cognitive, intuitive and "open" qualities of *chochmah.*

וְלָכֵן כָּל יִשְׂרָאֵל אֲפִילוּ הַנָּשִׁים וְעַמֵּי הָאָרֶץ הֵם מַאֲמִינִים בַּה' — **That is why all Jews, even women** (who, when the *Tanya* was written, did not receive any formal educa-tion) **and** other **uneducated people, believe in G-d,** שֶׁהָאֱמוּנָה הִיא לְמַעְלָה מִן הַדַּעַת וְהַהַשָּׂגָה — **since faith** is rooted in *chochmah,* a level of the soul shared by every-body, and **is beyond knowledge and cognition.**

כִּי פֶּתִי יַאֲמִין לְכָל דָּבָר וְעָרוּם יָבִין וְגוֹ' — **For** *"the simpleton believes everything, and the sensible one uses his understanding etc."* (*Proverbs* 14:15), וּלְגַבֵּי הַקָּדוֹשׁ בָּרוּךְ

יבין וגו' ולגבי הקב"ה שהוא למעלה מן השכל והדעת
ולית מחשבה תפיסא ביה כלל הכל כפתיים אצלו ית'
כדכתיב ואני בער ולא אדע בהמות הייתי עמך ואני
תמיד עמך וגו' כלומר שבזה שאני בער ובהמות אני
תמיד עמך ולכן אפי' קל שבקלים ופושעי ישראל
מוסרים נפשם על קדושת ה' על הרוב וסובלים עינוים
קשים שלא לכפור בה' אחד ואף אם הם בורים ועמי

הוּא שֶׁהוּא לְמַעְלָה מִן הַשֵּׂכֶל וְהַדַּעַת — and with regard to the Blessed Holy One, who transcends understanding and knowledge, וְלֵית מַחֲשָׁבָה תְּפִיסָא בֵּיהּ כְּלָל — and "no thought can grasp Him at all," הַכֹּל כְּפְתָיִים אֶצְלוֹ יִתְבָּרֵךְ — we are all like "simpletons" compared to Him.

Faith is a foolish path for something that could be grasped by the mind. But with the Infinite Light of G-d, which cannot be contained by the finite tools of cognition, the appropriate connection is through faith.

כְּדִכְתִיב וַאֲנִי בַעַר וְלֹא אֵדַע בְּהֵמוֹת הָיִיתִי עִמָּךְ וַאֲנִי תָמִיד עִמָּךְ וְגוֹ' — As the verse states, "I was a fool, without knowledge, I was an animal towards You. Yet I was always with You etc.," (Psalms 73:22-23), כְּלוֹמַר שֶׁבָּזֶה שֶׁאֲנִי בַּעַר וּבְהֵמוֹת אֲנִי תָמִיד עִמָּךְ — i.e., it is precisely because "I was a fool" and "an animal" using my faculty of faith, and not reason, that "I was always with You" and connected to You.

SECTION FIVE: AWAKENING "DORMANT LOVE"

As an indication of the "dormant love" for G-d which can awaken within all of us, the Tanya highlights the historical phenomenon of forced conversion.

וְלָכֵן אֲפִילוּ קַל שֶׁבְּקַלִּים וּפוֹשְׁעֵי יִשְׂרָאֵל — That is why even the most irreverent and sinful Jews, מוֹסְרִים נַפְשָׁם עַל קְדוּשַׁת הַשֵּׁם עַל הָרוֹב — will, in the majority of cases, agree to "sanctify G-d's Name" and give up their lives when faced with a threat such as "serve idols or die," וְסוֹבְלִים עִינוּיִם קָשִׁים שֶׁלֹּא לִכְפּוֹר בַּהּ' אֶחָד — and they will suffer harsh torture rather than denounce the One G-d.

The fact that when given an ultimatum, many "irreverent and sinful Jews" chose to give up their lives for Judaism, is startling and counter-intuitive. It is conceivable that an extremely devoted Jew might choose to do the ultimate act of worship, and die for G-d; but for "irreverent" Jews, who reject Judaism as their day-to-day guidance and value system, the notion of martyrdom is hard to fathom.

The Tanya offers this as evidence for the presence of "dormant love" and faith in the hearts and souls of all Jews, regardless of their level of piety and religious education; a faith that will tend to surface when faced with a very great challenge.

וְאַף אִם הֵם בּוּרִים וְעַמֵּי הָאָרֶץ וְאֵין יוֹדְעִים גְּדוּלַּת ה' — Many "irreverent" Jews will sacrifice their lives for G-d, even if they are morally uncultivated, uneducated in

הארץ ואין יודעים גדולת ה'. וגם במעט שיודעים אין
מתבונני' כלל ואין מוסרי' נפשם מחמת דעת והתבוננות
בה' כלל. אלא בלי שום דעת והתבוננות רק כאלו
הוא דבר שאי אפשר כלל לכפור בה' אחד בלי שום
טעם וטענה ומענה כלל והיינו משום שה' אחד מאיר
ומחיה כל הנפש ע"י התלבשותו בבחי' חכמה שבה
שהיא למעלה מן הדעת והשכל המושג ומובן:

Judaism, **and ignorant of G-d's greatness,** וְגַם בַּמְעַט שֶׁיּוֹדְעִים אֵין מִתְבּוֹנְנִים כְּלָל
and even to the little knowledge that they do possess, they give little thought,
וְאֵין מוֹסְרִים נַפְשָׁם מֵחֲמַת דַּעַת וְהִתְבּוֹנְנוּת בַּה' כְּלָל — **so they are not choosing to give
up their lives as a result of any mental appreciation or careful thinking about G-d.**

אֶלָּא בְּלִי שׁוּם דַּעַת וְהִתְבּוֹנְנוּת — **Rather,** they give up their lives **without any mental
appreciation or careful thinking,** רַק כְּאִלוּ הוּא דָּבָר שֶׁאִי אֶפְשָׁר כְּלָל לִכְפּוֹר בַּה' אֶחָד,
as if it was simply impossible to denounce the One G-d, בְּלִי שׁוּם טַעַם וְטַעֲנָה וּמַעֲנֶה
כְּלָל — **without any reasoning or rational argument whatsoever.**

וְהַיְינוּ מִשׁוּם שֶׁה' אֶחָד מֵאִיר וּמְחַיֶּה כָּל הַנֶּפֶשׁ — **And this is,** as we have explained, **because all of the soul is illuminated and energized by the One G-d,** עַל יְדֵי הִתְלַבְּשׁוּתוֹ
בִּבְחִינַת חָכְמָה שֶׁבָּה — **through** G-d's Infinite Light **being present in** the soul's component of *chochmah,* שֶׁהִיא לְמַעְלָה מִן הַדַּעַת וְהַשֵּׂכֶל הַמּוּשָׂג וּמוּבָן — **which transcends fathomable knowledge and cognitive intellect.**

In the majority of cases, when faced with a huge test of faith, "dormant love" will
automatically awaken. But how do we access "dormant love" in the normal everyday setting? The *Tanya* will answer this question in the following chapters.

CHAPTER 19

WHAT CHOCHMAH FEELS LIKE
SECTION ONE: THE DEFINING PROPERTY OF "DORMANT LOVE"

2ND SHEVAT REGULAR | 10TH SHEVAT LEAP

In chapter 18, we were introduced to the idea of a "dormant love" present in our
souls, as an "inheritance" from the Patriarchs. The *Tanya* posed four questions
about this love, seeking an explanation for: *"a.) the root of this love; and b.) its
defining property; c.) why it is our inheritance; d.) why it includes also an inherited
capacity for reverence"* (above, p. 219).

פרק יט ולתוספת ביאור צריך לבאר היטב מ"ש

נר ה' נשמת אדם פי' שישראל

הקרוים אדם נשמתם היא למשל כאור הנר שמתנענע

תמיד למעלה בטבעו מפני שאור האש חפץ בטבע   24B

ליפרד מהפתילה ולידבק בשרשו למעלה ביסוד האש

הכללי שתחת גלגל הירח כמ"ש בע"ח ואף שע"י זה

In the previous chapter, we were given an elaborate answer to question 'a' (the love is rooted in the soul's *chochmah*); and question 'c' (it is inherited from the Patriarchs, because of their utter dedication to G-d).

Chapter 19 will offer an explanation for questions 'b' and 'd.' First we turn to question 'b': What is the defining property of "dormant love"?

וּלְתוֹסֶפֶת בֵּיאוּר — **To elucidate further** the idea of "dormant" love, present in our souls, צָרִיךְ לְבָאֵר הֵיטֵב מַה שֶׁכָּתוּב נֵר ה' נִשְׁמַת אָדָם — we first **need to clarify the verse,** *"Adam's soul is G-d's candle"* (*Proverbs* 20:27).

פֵּירוּשׁ שֶׁיִשְׂרָאֵל הַקְּרוּיִם אָדָם נִשְׁמָתָם הִיא לְמָשָׁל כְּאוֹר הַנֵּר — **This means that the souls of Israel, which are referred to as "Adam"** (*Talmud, Yevamos* 61a), **are comparable to the flame of a candle,** שֶׁמִּתְנַעֲנֵעַ תָּמִיד לְמַעֲלָה בְּטִבְעוֹ, — **which, by nature, continually flickers upwards.**

The *Tanya* now offers an explanation why the flame of a candle tends to flicker, as if it is trying to rise upward and detach itself from the wick.

מִפְּנֵי שֶׁאוֹר הָאֵשׁ חָפֵץ בְּטֶבַע לִיפָּרֵד מֵהַפְּתִילָה — **Because a fire's flame is naturally inclined to detach itself from the wick,** וְלִידָבֵק בְּשָׁרְשׁוֹ לְמַעְלָה — **so as to connect with its root, above,** בִּיסוֹד הָאֵשׁ הַכְּלָלִי — **in the core element of fire,** שֶׁתַּחַת גַּלְגַּל הַיָרֵחַ — **which is below the moon's orbit.**

In the Classical Model, the universe is seen as divided into two parts: the "terrestrial" region, which includes the earth and everything surrounding it, up to the moon's orbit; and the "celestial" region, which accounts for everything beyond the moon's orbit.

Everything in the terrestrial realm, is composed of four elements, earth, fire, air, and water. Since "rest" is the natural state of all terrestrial matter, earth, air, and water tend to seek their natural place at rest in the center of the earth (unless stopped by an impenetrable surface, like the ground). But the natural resting place of elemental fire is above us in the higher part of the "terrestrial realm," beneath the moon's orbit.

This explains why a flame tends to flicker, as if it is trying to detach itself from the wick, because, by nature, it is drawn to its elemental root above the earth.

כְּמוֹ שֶׁכָּתוּב בְּעֵץ חַיִּים — **As stated in** *Etz Chaim* (see section 50, chapter 8).

יכבה ולא יאיר כלום למטה וגם למעלה בשרשו
יתבטל אורו במציאות בשרשו אעפ"כ הוא חפץ
בטבעו. כך נשמת האדם וכן בחי' רוח ונפש חפצה
וחשקה בטבעה ליפרד ולצאת מן הגוף ולידבק בשרשה
ומקורה בה' חיי החיים ב"ה הגם שתהיה אין ואפס
ותתבטל שם במציאות לגמרי ולא ישאר ממנה מאומה
ממהותה ועצמותה הראשון אעפ"כ זה רצונה וחפצה

The Classical Model was embraced by the Sages (see, for example, *Numbers Rabah* 14:12), and was employed extensively by the Jewish Medieval Philosophers. Here the *Tanya* notes that this model was also used by Lurianic Kabbalah.

וְאַף שֶׁעַל יְדֵי זֶה יִכְבֶּה וְלֹא יָאִיר כְּלוּם לְמַטָּה — **And even though** by leaving its wick, and uniting with its source, the flame **would be extinguished, and would cease to shine at all down here,** וְגַם לְמַעְלָה בְּשָׁרְשׁוֹ יִתְבַּטֵּל אוֹרוֹ בִּמְצִיאוּת בְּשָׁרְשׁוֹ — **and even above,** once reabsorbed **in its source** in the core element of fire, **the identity of the** flame's **light would dissolve in its source,** אַף עַל פִּי כֵן בְּכָךְ הוּא חָפֵץ בְּטִבְעוֹ — **nevertheless, this is what** the flame **is naturally inclined to do.**

The flame's tendency is to reunite with its higher source, even though this would result in the physical flame being extinguished. In fact, even the flame's spiritual identity would be erased, as it is reabsorbed in its source, in the element of fire.

PRACTICAL LESSONS

Your soul is naturally drawn to G-d, like a flickering flame that "yearns" to depart from its wick.

כָּךְ נִשְׁמַת הָאָדָם — **In the same way, a person's** higher soul power of *neshamah,* וְכֵן בְּחִינַת רוּחַ וָנֶפֶשׁ — **as well** as even the lower soul **powers of *ruach* and *nefesh,*** חֲפֵצָה וְחָשְׁקָה בְּטִבְעָהּ לִיפָּרֵד וְלָצֵאת מִן הַגּוּף — **naturally** yearn and desire to be separated from the body and to leave it, וְלִידָּבֵק בְּשָׁרְשָׁהּ וּמְקוֹרָהּ בַּה' חַיֵּי הַחַיִּים בָּרוּךְ הוּא — **so as to attach themselves with** the soul's **root and source in G-d, the Giver of life, may He be blessed.**

Intuiting its source in G-d to be a superior level of existence than bodily incarnation, the soul naturally desires it.

הֲגַם שֶׁתִּהְיֶה אַיִן וָאֶפֶס — **Even though** by departing from the body and being reabsorbed in its source the soul powers **would become "*null and void*"** (see *Isaiah* 40:17), וְתִתְבַּטֵּל שָׁם בִּמְצִיאוּת לְגַמְרֵי — and the soul **would completely lose its identity there,** וְלֹא יִשָּׁאֵר מִמֶּנָּה — מְאוּמָה מִמַּהוּתָהּ וְעַצְמוּתָהּ הָרִאשׁוֹן — **and nothing would remain of its original character and substance,** once absorbed in its source, אַף עַל פִּי כֵן זֶה רְצוֹנָהּ וְחֶפְצָהּ בְּטִבְעָהּ — **nevertheless, this** departure from the body toward its source **is its natural will and desire.**

בטבעה וטבע זה הוא שם המושאל לכל דבר שאינו
בבחי׳ טעם ודעת וגם כאן הכוונה שרצון וחפץ זה
בנפש אינו בבחי׳ טעם ודעת ושכל מושג ומובן אלא
למעלה מהדעת ושכל המושג והמובן והיא בחי׳ חכמה
שבנפש שבה אור א״ס ב״ה. וזהו כלל בכל סטרא

Just as the flame is inclined to leave its wick and be reabsorbed in its source, even though this would result in its identity being erased, the soul desires likewise.

וְטֶבַע זֶה הוּא שֵׁם הַמּוּשְׁאָל — The description of **this** tendency of the flame and the soul as a **"nature" is non-literal,** לְכָל דָּבָר שֶׁאֵינוֹ בִּבְחִינַת טַעַם וָדַעַת — **referring to anything which is not** the product of **reasoning and logic.**

The desire for your identity to be dissolved in its source is not a rational one. It is an experience to which you are drawn intuitively and "naturally."

וְגַם כָּאן הַכַּוָּונָה שֶׁרָצוֹן וְחֵפֶץ זֶה בַּנֶּפֶשׁ אֵינוֹ בִּבְחִינַת טַעַם וָדַעַת — **Here, too,** our reference to the soul's "natural" will and desire, **implies that the soul's will and desire is not** the product of **reasoning and logic,** וְשֵׂכֶל מוּשָּׂג וּמוּבָן — **a graspable and intelligible rationale,** אֶלָּא לְמַעְלָה מֵהַדַעַת וְשֵׂכֶל הַמּוּשָּׂג וְהַמּוּבָן — **rather, it transcends** logic and any graspable or intelligible rationale.

We now have an answer to question 'b,' posed in the previous chapter: What is the defining property of the soul's "dormant love"? It is an intrinsic, supra-rational desire of the soul to leave the body and be reunited with its source in G-d.

SECTION TWO: WHY YOUR LOVE COULD REMAIN DORMANT

If all souls are naturally drawn to G-d, why doesn't everyone believe in Him? In the following section, the *Tanya* will explain that certain conditions need to be met for the soul's properties to be available and manifest.

וְהִיא בְּחִינַת חָכְמָה שֶׁבַּנֶּפֶשׁ — As we learned in chapter 18, the root of **the soul's** supra-rational intuition and faith **is its component of** *chochmah,* שֶׁבָּהּ אוֹר אֵין סוֹף בָּרוּךְ הוּא — **in which the Blessed Infinite Light** of G-d **is found.**

The soul is drawn powerfully to its source in G-d because the soul has *chochmah* within it. *Chochmah* acts as a "window" allowing G-d's light into the soul, offering a direct, embodied experience of the infinite.

But once that light has come into your soul through its "window," if the light is to continue flowing through the rest of your psyche, you must make yourself a suitable receptacle for it.

3RD SHEVAT REGULAR

וְזֶהוּ כְּלָל בְּכָל סִטְרָא דִקְדוּשָׁה — **And the following is a fundamental principle with all the forces of holiness.**

דקדושה שאינו אלא מה שנמשך מחכמה שנק' קודש
העליון הבטל במציאות באור א"ס ב"ה המלובש בו
ואינו דבר בפני עצמו כנ"ל ולכן נקרא כ"ח מ"ה והוא
הפך ממש מבחי' הקליפה וס"א שממנה נפשות אומות
העולם דעבדין לגרמייהו ואמרין הב הב והלעיטני להיות
יש ודבר בפני עצמו כנ"ל הפך בחי' החכמה ולכן

To understand how to make yourself a "container" for the Blessed Infinite Light which enters your soul through its "window" of *chochmah*, we first need to learn a "fundamental principle."

שֶׁאֵינוֹ אֶלָּא מַה שֶּׁנִּמְשָׁךְ מֵחָכְמָה — The "fundamental principle" is: the forces of holiness **are exclusively derived from** *chochmah.*

Chochmah is not merely a route to holiness, it is *the* route to holiness. Everything in the universe that is sacred must flow from *chochmah.*

שֶׁנִּקְרָא קוֹדֶשׁ הָעֶלְיוֹן — As we find that *chochmah* itself is actually **referred to as "Supernal holiness"** in the *Zohar* (3, 297a), since it is the root of everything holy.

הַבָּטֵל בִּמְצִיאוּת בְּאוֹר אֵין סוֹף בָּרוּךְ הוּא הַמְלוּבָּשׁ בּוֹ — And, as we have explained, this is because *chochmah's* own **identity is voided by the Blessed Infinite Light present within it,** וְאֵינוֹ דָּבָר בִּפְנֵי עַצְמוֹ — **so that it** doesn't feel itself to be **an independent thing** from G-d, כַּנִּזְכָּר לְעֵיל — **as explained above** (p. 216).

וְלָכֵן נִקְרָא כ"ח מָ"ה — And, as we have explained, **this is why it is referred to as** *ko'ach* **("power")** *mah* **("what?"),** the "power (ability) to say 'What is this?'", an inquisitiveness and openness to the unknown. The tendency to openness comes when you "empty" the ego, because the ego is always sure of itself.

PRACTICAL LESSONS

The power of *chochmah* in your soul acts as a "window" to G-d's light, offering a direct, embodied experience of the infinite.

Having defined holiness as the voiding of identity and ego, and an openness to something higher than Self, it follows that the counter-force of holiness, *kelipah*, is defined by the reverse.

וְהוּא הֵפֶךְ מַמָּשׁ מִבְּחִינַת הַקְּלִיפָּה וְסִטְרָא אָחֳרָא — **This is the complete opposite of** *kelipah* **and** *sitra achra,* שֶׁמִּמֶּנָּה נַפְשׁוֹת אוּמוֹת הָעוֹלָם דְּעָבְדִין לְגַרְמַיְיהוּ — **which produce the souls of the nations of the world** *"who are self-serving"* (*Tikunei Zohar* 22a; see chapter 1, p. 43).

וְאַמְרִין הַב הַב — **The tendency of** *kelipah* **is to say** only, *"Give me, give me!"* (*Proverbs* 30:15), וְהַלְעִיטֵנִי — **as Esau said to Jacob,** *"feed me!"* (*Genesis* 25:30), never wanting to give back in return, לִהְיוֹת יֵשׁ וְדָבָר בִּפְנֵי עַצְמוֹ כַּנִּזְכָּר לְעֵיל — **and**

נקראים מתים כי החכמה תחיה וכתיב ימותו ולא
בחכמה. וכן הרשעים ופושעי ישראל קודם שבאו
לידי נסיון לקדש השם כי בחי' החכמה שבנפש
האלהית עם ניצוץ אלהות מאור א"ס ב"ה המלובש
בה הם בבחי' גלות בגופם בנפש הבהמית מצד

this self-serving mentality **is caused by** the feeling of **ego and separateness** from G-d, **as stated above,** הֵפֶךְ בְּחִינַת הַחָכְמָה — **the opposite of** *chochmah's* **character.**

וְלָכֵן נִקְרָאִים מֵתִים — **Therefore** the forces of *kelipah* **are referred to as "dead"** (*Zohar* 3, 275a), כִּי הַחָכְמָה תְּחַיֶה — **because "***chochmah* **gives life"** (*Ecclesiastes* 7:12), וּכְתִיב יָמוּתוּ וְלֹא בְחָכְמָה — **and the verse states,** *"they die, without chochmah"* (*Job* 4:21).

Life is a result of *interconnectedness*. You are only alive because your organs and limbs work together in a wondrous unity. If your arm, for example, would lose its blood supply and nervous connections to the rest of the body, it would die.

In a broader sense, something is only "alive" if it is connected with G-d. *Kelipah*, and all that it embodies, is an energy of ego, fragmentation and disconnectedness. Therefore it is compared to death.

וְכֵן הָרְשָׁעִים וּפוֹשְׁעֵי יִשְׂרָאֵל — **Similarly with** *resha'im* **and sinners of Israel,** קוֹדֶם שֶׁבָּאוּ לִידֵי נִסָּיוֹן לְקַדֵּשׁ הַשֵּׁם — **before** a scenario arises where their dormant love is activated, when **they are put to the test to sanctify G-d's name** ("Convert or die!"), כִּי בְּחִינַת הַחָכְמָה שֶׁבַּנֶּפֶשׁ הָאֱלֹהִית עִם נִיצוֹץ אֱלֹהוּת מֵאוֹר אֵין סוֹף בָּרוּךְ הוּא הַמְלוּבָּשׁ בָּה — until that point they lack faith, **since the component of** *chochmah* **within their Divine Souls, which houses a spark of G-dliness from the Blessed Infinite Light,** הֵם בִּבְחִינַת גָּלוּת בְּגוּפָם — **is in a state of "exile" in their bodies.**

While "the sinners of Israel" do have a spark of G-d shining through the *chochmah* in their souls, that does not necessarily mean that they will have faith in G-d or be drawn to His worship. The light may remain blocked and "exiled,"

שֶׁבְּחָלָל — **in the Animal Soul, which is from** *kelipah,* בַּנֶּפֶשׁ הַבַּהֲמִית מִצַּד הַקְּלִיפָּה — **in the heart's left chamber,** הַשְּׂמָאלִי שֶׁבַּלֵּב — and that הַמּוֹלֶכֶת וּמוֹשֶׁלֶת בְּגוּפָם — *kelipah* **rules and dominates the bodies** of *resha'im.*

![black bar divider]

A CHASIDIC THOUGHT

While the opposite of good is evil, the opposite of holiness is a more subtle destructive force: ego. Ego is the "opaque self," a misguided sense of self-importance that acts as a blockage to G-d's Infinite Light in your soul. If *chochmah* is the "window" to your soul that allows G-d's light in, then ego is a thick curtain which blocks that light from your psyche.

25A

הקליפה שבחלל השמאלי שבלב המולכת ומושלת
בגופם בסוד גלות השכינה כנ"ל. ולכן נקראת אהבה
זו בנפש האלהית שרצונה וחפצה לדבק בה' חיי החיים
ברוך הוא בשם אהבה מסותרת כי היא מסותרת
ומכוסה בלבוש שק דקליפה בפושעי ישראל וממנה
נכנס בהם רוח שטות לחטוא כמאמר רז"ל אין אדם
חוטא כו' אלא שגלות הזה לבחי' חכמה אינו אלא לבחי'
המתפשטת ממנה בנפש כולה להחיותה אבל שרש

The egoic nature of *kelipah* inspires a self-serving mentality. If it succeeds, that sense of unhealthy self-importance will detach the person from the *chochmah* in his soul, leaving the Divine "spark" within *chochmah* exiled and powerless within him.

כַּנִּזְכָּר לְעֵיל — בְּסוֹד גָּלוּת הַשְּׁכִינָה — **According to the secret of the *Shechinah's* exile,** — **as mentioned above.**

As we have explained, the "exile of the *Shechinah*" (Divine Presence) can be understood Kabbalistically as referring to the spark of G-d (in *chochmah*) trapped inside a sinful person (see chapter 17, p. 208-9).

With this in mind, we can now appreciate why the presence of *chochmah* in the soul can be responsible for a *dormant* love.

וְלָכֵן נִקְרֵאת אַהֲבָה זוֹ בַּנֶּפֶשׁ הָאֱלֹהִית שֶׁרְצוֹנָהּ וְחֶפְצָהּ לִדְּבֵק בַּה' חַיֵּי הַחַיִּים בָּרוּךְ הוּא בְּשֵׁם אַהֲבָה מְסוּתֶּרֶת — **That is why this** natural, inherited **love of the Divine soul, whose will and desire is to connect with G-d, the blessed Giver of life, is called "dormant love"** (lit. "hidden love"), כִּי הִיא מְסוּתֶּרֶת וּמְכוּסָּה בִּלְבוּשׁ שַׂק דְּקְלִיפָּה — **because it's hidden and covered by a *"sackcloth garment"*** (*Esther* 4:2) **of *kelipah,*** בְּפוֹשְׁעֵי יִשְׂרָאֵל — **in the case of "sinners of Israel."**

וּמִמֶּנָּה נִכְנָס בָּהֶם רוּחַ שְׁטוּת לַחֲטוֹא — **And it is from** this *kelipah* that a **"delusional spirit" enters** the *resha'im*, to incite them **to sin,** כְּמַאֲמַר רַבּוֹתֵינוּ זִכְרוֹנָם לִבְרָכָה אֵין — **as our Rabbis, of blessed memory, taught:** *"A man will not commit a sin* unless a delusional spirit enters him" (*Talmud, Sotah* 3a; see below, chapter 24, p. 275).

SECTION THREE: CHOCHMAH "AWAKENED"

4TH SHEVAT REGULAR

Having emphasized how the Divine "spark" in *chochmah* remains exiled and powerless in "the sinners of Israel," the *Tanya* now stresses that it is never extinguished.

אֶלָּא שֶׁגָּלוּת הַזֶּה לִבְחִינַת חָכְמָה — **However, this "exile" of the** soul's **component of *chochmah,*** אֵינוּ אֶלָּא לַבְּחִינָה הַמִּתְפַּשֶּׁטֶת מִמֶּנָּה בַּנֶּפֶשׁ כּוּלָהּ לְהַחֲיוֹתָהּ — **is only true**

וְעִיקָר שֶׁל בְּחִי׳ חכמה שֶׁבַּנֶּפֶשׁ הָאֱלֹהִית הוּא בְּמוֹחִין
וְאֵינָהּ מִתְלַבֶּשֶׁת בִּלְבוּשׁ שַׂק דְּקְלִיפָּה שֶׁבַּלֵּב בְּחָלָל
הַשְּׂמָאלִי בְּבְחִי׳ גָּלוּת מַמָּשׁ. רַק שֶׁהִיא בְּבְחִי׳ שֵׁינָה
בָּרְשָׁעִים וְאֵינָהּ פּוֹעֶלֶת פְּעוּלָּתָהּ בָּהֶם כָּל זְמַן שֶׁעֲסוּקִים
בְּדַעְתָּם וּבִינָתָם בְּתַאֲווֹת הָעוֹלָם. אַךְ כְּשֶׁבָּאִים לִידֵי

of *chochmah's* **energizing influence** on the rest of the soul, אֲבָל שֹׁרֶשׁ וְעִיקָר שֶׁל בְּחִינַת חָכְמָה שֶׁבַּנֶּפֶשׁ הָאֱלֹהִית הוּא בַּמּוֹחִין — **but the** *root and core* of the Divine Soul's component of *chochmah* remains untrapped in the brain, וְאֵינָהּ מִתְלַבֶּשֶׁת בִּלְבוּשׁ שַׂק דְּקְלִיפָּה שֶׁבַּלֵּב בְּחָלָל הַשְּׂמָאלִי בְּבְחִינַת גָּלוּת מַמָּשׁ — **and does not actually become exiled and enmeshed in the "sackcloth garment"** of *kelipah,* **in the heart's left chamber.**

The "exile" of an entity implies that it is a.) present in a certain location; and yet, b.) stripped of its power and forced into activities against its will.

The *Tanya* clarifies here that it is only *chochmah's* "energizing influence" that remains both present *and* powerless ("exiled") within the sinful part of the person, the left side of the heart. The "root and core" of *chochmah,* however, is located in a part of the body uncontaminated by *kelipah*, the seat of the Divine Soul in the brain. Therefore it would not be correct to say that the "root and core" of the *chochmah* is "exiled," since *it is not present in a location of kelipah.* It is merely "dislocated" from the rest of the person and unable to have any effect.

רַק שֶׁהִיא בְּבְחִינַת שֵׁינָה בָּרְשָׁעִים וְאֵינָהּ פּוֹעֶלֶת פְּעוּלָּתָהּ בָּהֶם — **Rather, with** *resha'im*, **it is** as if the *chochmah* were **"asleep," failing to have an effect on them.**

In its "home turf," the brain, *chochmah* remains in full force. It just doesn't have any significant effect beyond that, so it's effectively "asleep."

כָּל זְמַן שֶׁעֲסוּקִים בְּדַעְתָּם וּבִינָתָם בְּתַאֲווֹת הָעוֹלָם — *Chochmah* remains "asleep" in *resha'im*, **so long as their** *da'as* **and** *binah* **are preoccupied with worldly pleasures.**

As we learned in chapter 3, for an idea to give rise to an emotion, three mental processes are required: *chochmah* (inquiry) *binah* (cognition) and *da'as* (recognition). Even in the case of *resha'im,* the "root and core" of their *chochmah* remains pure and intact; but *choch-*

PRACTICAL LESSONS

Only *chochmah* can be a channel for holiness, because the other parts of the soul are too inherently self-serving.

Your *chochmah* never becomes extinguished. It may become "exiled" and powerless due to repeated sinning, but it's always there, waiting to be re-awakened.

Chochmah is awakened by a test of faith, such as, "Convert or die," which explains why so many otherwise non-observant Jews have chosen martyrdom for their faith.

נסיון בדבר אמונה שהיא למעלה מהדעת ונגעה עד
הנפש לבחי' חכמה שבה אזי היא ניעורה משנתה
ופועלת פעולתה בכח ה' המלובש בה. וכמ"ש ויקץ
כישן ה' לעמוד בנסיון באמונת ה' בלי שום טעם ודעת
ושכל מושג לו להתגבר על הקליפות ותאוות עוה"ז
בהיתר ובאיסור שהורגל בהם ולמאוס בהם ולבחור לו
ה' לחלקו ולגורלו למסור לו נפשו על קדושת שמו ואף

mah fails to influence the heart because *binah* and *da'as* have been contaminated with an obsession for physical gratification.

אַךְ כְּשֶׁבָּאִים לִידֵי נִסָּיוֹן בִּדְבַר אֱמוּנָה — **But, when** *resha'im* **are confronted with a test** of life and death **in a matter of faith,** שֶׁהִיא לְמַעְלָה מֵהַדַּעַת — **which transcends** any logical considerations of *da'as*, וְנָגְעָה עַד הַנֶּפֶשׁ לִבְחִינַת חָכְמָה שֶׁבָּהּ — that test **touches the soul directly, reaching its component of** *chochmah.*

In day-to-day life, the *kelipah*-contaminated powers of *binah* and *da'as* successfully offer all sorts of rationalizations to *resha'im* as to why they ought to indulge in sinful behavior, effectively blocking *chochmah* from doing its work. But when it comes to an overt test of faith, which is clearly not a rational decision applicable to *binah* or *da'as*, these cognitive powers are bypassed and the decision rips directly through to *chochmah.*

אֲזַי הִיא נִיעוֹרָה מִשְּׁנָתָהּ וּפוֹעֶלֶת פְּעוּלָּתָהּ — **Then** *chochmah* **awakens from its "sleep" and does its work** of arousing faith, בְּכֹחַ ה' הַמְלוּבָּשׁ בָּהּ — **using the power of G-d invested in it,** וּכְמוֹ שֶׁכָּתוּב וַיִּקַץ כְּיָשֵׁן ה' — **as the verse states,** *"Then G-d awoke, as one asleep,"* (Psalms 78:65), *i.e.,* the power of G-d within the soul was aroused.

לַעֲמוֹד בְּנִסָּיוֹן בֶּאֱמוּנַת ה' — **This enables the person to succeed in a test of faith in G-d,** בְּלִי שׁוּם טַעַם וָדַעַת וְשֵׂכֶל מוּשָּׂג לוֹ — **without using any of his reasoning, knowledge or fathomable intellect,** לְהִתְגַּבֵּר עַל הַקְּלִיפוֹת וְתַאֲווֹת עוֹלָם הַזֶּה בְּהֶיתֵּר — **to prevail over the** *kelipos* **and this-worldly temptations to which he had been accustomed, whether they be permitted or prohibited,** וּבְאִיסּוּר שֶׁהוּרְגַל בָּהֶם וְלִמְאוֹס בָּהֶם — **and even to despise them,** realizing now how they separate him from G-d.

In a radical break from life-long attachment to physical gratification, this person disregards all rational considerations and chooses to suffer the pain of death so as not to transgress G-d's will. His *chochmah* has suddenly "woken up" from its dormant state and provided him with a surge of faith.

וְלִבְחוֹר לוֹ ה' לְחֶלְקוֹ וּלְגוֹרָלוֹ — **The arousal of** *chochmah* **empowers him to choose** *"G-d as his portion and his lot"* (see Psalms 16:5), לִמְסוֹר לוֹ נַפְשׁוֹ עַל קְדוּשַׁת שְׁמוֹ — **to give up his life for** G-d, **to sanctify G-d's Name,** rather than transgress.

וְאַף כִּי הַקְּלִיפוֹת גָּבְרוּ עָלָיו כָּל יָמָיו — **For, even though the** *kelipos* **had prevailed over him all his life,** וְלֹא יָכוֹל לָהֶם — **and,** like an addict, **he had been powerless**

כי הקליפות גברו עליו כל ימיו ולא יכול להם כמארז"ל
שהרשעים הם ברשות לבם מ"מ כשבא לידי נסיון
בדבר אמונה בה' אחד שיסודתה בהררי קודש היא
בחי' חכמה שבנפש האלהית שבה מלובש אור א"ס
ב"ה הרי כל הקליפות בטלים ומבוטלים והיו כלא היו
ממש לפני ה' כדכתיב כל הגוים כאין נגדו וגו' וכתיב כי
הנה אויביך ה' כי הנה אויביך יאבדו יתפרדו וגו' וכתיב
כהמס דונג מפני אש יאבדו וגו' וכתיב הרים כדונג נמסו.
והנה אור ה' א"ס ב"ה המלובש בחכמה שבנפש גדול   25B

against them, כְּמַאֲמַר רַבּוֹתֵינוּ זִכְרוֹנָם לִבְרָכָה שֶׁהָרְשָׁעִים הֵם בִּרְשׁוּת לִבָּם — **as our Rabbis, of blessed memory, taught that** *"the resha'im are controlled by their hearts"* (*Genesis Rabah* 34:10; see p. 205), מִכָּל מָקוֹם כְּשֶׁבָּא לִידֵי נִסָּיוֹן בְּדָבָר אֱמוּנָה בַּה' אֶחָד — **nevertheless, when it comes to an** unambiguous **test of his faith in the One G-d,** שֶׁיְסוֹדָתָה בְּהַרְרֵי קוֹדֶשׁ — a faith which, even in *resha'im*, *"has its foundations on the holy peaks"* (*Psalms* 87:1), הִיא בְּחִינַת חָכְמָה שֶׁבַּנֶּפֶשׁ הָאֱלֹהִית שֶׁבָּה מְלוּבָּשׁ — **this referring to the Divine Soul's component of** *chochmah,* אוֹר אֵין סוֹף בָּרוּךְ הוּא — **in which the Blessed Infinite Light is present,** הֲרֵי כָּל הַקְּלִיפּוֹת בְּטֵלִים וּמְבוּטָלִים — **then,** as soon as his *chochmah* awakens, **all the** *kelipos* **are rendered null and void.**

Once *chochmah* and its Divine light flood through the other parts of the soul, all the *kelipos* are rendered instantaneously powerless. This is because *kelipah* can only function under the illusion of fragmentation, and as soon as *chochmah* brings to light the fundamental unity of the universe, all *kelipos* are paralyzed.

The *Tanya* now offers various scriptural citations suggestive of this idea.

וְהָיוּ כְּלֹא הָיוּ מַמָּשׁ לִפְנֵי ה' — **Then it is though they had never been, literally,** since the *kelipos* are voided **in the presence of G-d** that shines through *chochmah,* כְּדִכְתִיב כָּל הַגּוֹיִם כְּאַיִן נֶגְדּוֹ וְגוֹ' — **as the verse states,** *"All the* wicked *nations are like nothing before Him"* (*Isaiah* 40:17), וּכְתִיב כִּי הִנֵּה אוֹיְבֶיךָ ה' כִּי הִנֵּה אוֹיְבֶיךָ יֹאבֵדוּ, יִתְפָּרְדוּ וְגוֹ' — **and it is written,** *"For behold, Your enemies, O G-d, for behold, Your enemies will perish, all evildoers will be scattered"* (*Psalms* 92:10), וּכְתִיב כְּהִמֵּס דּוֹנַג — **and it is written,** *"as wax melts before fire, so will the wicked perish* before G-d" (*ibid.* 68:3), וּכְתִיב הָרִים כַּדּוֹנַג נָמַסּוּ — **and it is written,** *"Mountains melt like wax* before G-d" (*ibid.* 97:5).

The *Tanya* cites four verses indicating the elimination of the *kelipos*, corresponding to the four divisions of *kelipah* (see p. 42). The first three verses refer to the three "completely impure" *kelipos*, so they speak of a total destruction and "perishing." The fourth verse refers to *kelipas nogah,* a mixture of good and evil, and therefore does not mention complete destruction (*Notes on Tanya*).

וְהִנֵּה אוֹר ה' אֵין סוֹף בָּרוּךְ הוּא הַמְּלוּבָּשׁ בַּחָכְמָה שֶׁבַּנֶּפֶשׁ — **Now, the light of the Blessed**

וְעָצוּם כָּל כָּךְ לִגְרַשׁ וּלְדַחוֹת הַס"א וְהַקְּלִיפּוֹת שֶׁלֹּא
יוּכְלוּ יִגְּעוּ אֲפִי' בִּלְבוּשָׁיו שֶׁהֵם מַחֲשָׁבָה דִבּוּר וּמַעֲשֶׂה
שֶׁל אֱמוּנַת ה' אֶחָד דְהַיְינוּ לַעֲמֹד בְּנִסָּיוֹן לִמְסוֹר נַפְשׁוֹ
אֲפִי' שֶׁלֹּא לַעֲשׂוֹת רַק אֵיזֶה מַעֲשֶׂה לְבַד נֶגֶד אֱמוּנַת
ה' אֶחָד כְּגוֹן לְהִשְׁתַּחֲווֹת לַעֲבוֹדָה זָרָה אַף שֶׁאֵינוֹ מַאֲמִין
בָּהּ כְּלָל בְּלִבּוֹ וְכֵן שֶׁלֹּא לְדַבֵּר תּוֹעָה ח"ו עַל אַחְדוּת ה'
אַף שֶׁאֵין פִּיו וְלִבּוֹ שָׁוִין רַק לִבּוֹ שָׁלֵם בָּאֱמוּנַת ה' וְזֶה

Infinite One, present in the soul's chochmah, גָּדוֹל וְעָצוּם כֹּחוֹ כָּל כָּךְ — **has such great and awesome power,** לִגְרַשׁ וּלְדַחוֹת הַסִּטְרָא אָחֳרָא וְהַקְּלִיפּוֹת שֶׁלֹּא יוּכְלוּ יִגְּעוּ אֲפִילוּ בִּלְבוּשָׁיו — **that it will expel and drive away the sitra achra and the kelipos even from touching** the soul's "garments," שֶׁהֵם מַחֲשָׁבָה דִבּוּר וּמַעֲשֶׂה שֶׁל אֱמוּנַת ה' אֶחָד — **which are thought, speech and action associated with faith in the One G-d.**

As we learned earlier, the soul is multi-layered, consisting of both an intellectual/emotional *deep core*, as well as more superficial *garments* of thought, speech and action.

Up to this point, chapter 19 has demonstrated that when the soul's "dormant love" is awakened, it can dispel the *kelipos* which had "trapped" the deep core (the emotions), bringing a surge of faith to the heart. But what if the "test of faith" merely involved the garments? Surely, it would be possible for a person to retain absolute faith in G-d within his heart, and just go through with an action or verbal statement of idol worship *not really meaning it,* so as to save his life?

The *Tanya* teaches us now that when *chochmah* is awakened, it reaches not only the soul's deep core, but even its garments too. So the person will have enough faith to resist even an "empty" act of idol worship (carried out with the garments).

דְהַיְינוּ לַעֲמֹד בְּנִסָּיוֹן לִמְסוֹר נַפְשׁוֹ אֲפִילוּ שֶׁלֹּא לַעֲשׂוֹת רַק אֵיזֶה מַעֲשֶׂה לְבַד נֶגֶד אֱמוּנַת ה' אֶחָד — **That is to say,** an awakened *chochmah* will inspire a person **to give up his life even to save himself from doing a mere "empty" act that is contrary to faith in the One G-d,** כְּגוֹן לְהִשְׁתַּחֲווֹת לַעֲבוֹדָה זָרָה אַף שֶׁאֵינוֹ מַאֲמִין בָּהּ כְּלָל בְּלִבּוֹ — **such as bowing to an idol, even though in his heart he doesn't believe in it at all,** וְכֵן שֶׁלֹּא לְדַבֵּר תּוֹעָה חַס וְשָׁלוֹם עַל אַחְדוּת ה' — **and likewise** he will be willing to give up his life **to avoid verbally attesting to a mistruth about G-d's unity, G-d forbid,** אַף שֶׁאֵין רַק פִּיו וְלִבּוֹ שָׁוִין — **even though his mouth would not be consistent with his heart,** לִבּוֹ שָׁלֵם בָּאֱמוּנַת ה' — **his heart remaining completely faithful to G-d.**

For an act of worship to be real, action must be aligned to intention. If a person believes in G-d and merely carries out an "empty" act of idol worship to save his life, there is no deep betrayal here; but the act is nevertheless forbidden by Jewish law. Observers certainly will not know what is in the person's heart when he bows to the idol, and the act gives the *perception* of real idol worship. Not wanting to bring even this (false) perception into the world, the person chooses to die instead. That is the intensity of faith that an "awakened" *chochmah* can bring.

נקרא דחילו הנכלל ברחימו שהיא אהבה הטבעית
שבנפש האלהית שבכללות ישראל שחפצה ורצונה
בטבעה לידבק בשרשה ומקורה אור א"ס ב"ה שמפני
אהבה זו ורצון זה היא יראה ומפחדת בטבעה מנגוע
בקצה טומאת ע"ז ח"ו שהיא נגד אמונת ה' אחד אפילו
בלבושיה החיצונים שהם דבור או מעשה בלי אמונה
בלב כלל:

SECTION FOUR: WHEN LOVE "CONTAINS" REVERENCE

In this final passage of chapter 19, the *Tanya* addresses question 'd' posed in the previous chapter: How does the inherited, dormant love present in every Jew also include the capacity for reverence?

וְזֶה נִקְרָא דְחִילוּ הַנִּכְלָל בִּרְחִימוּ — **And this** willingness to die for G-d, as a result of an awakened *chochmah*, **is called "reverence that is contained in love."**

Just because you love G-d does not necessarily mean that you would be willing to die for Him. The decision to die rather than transgress a cardinal prohibition of the Torah is motivated by reverence, the thought that such a sin would disconnect you from G-d. The *Tanya* refers to this as "reverence that is contained in love": you love G-d so much (due to your awakened *chochmah*), that you cannot bear to do anything that would compromise your connection with Him.

שֶׁהִיא אַהֲבָה הַטִּבְעִית שֶׁבַּנֶּפֶשׁ הָאֱלֹהִית שֶׁבִּכְלָלוּת יִשְׂרָאֵל — **This love comes naturally to the Divine Soul, found in all Israel,** שֶׁחֲפֵצָה וּרְצוֹנָהּ בְּטִבְעָהּ לִידָּבֵק בְּשָׁרְשָׁהּ וּמְקוֹרָהּ — **since its innate desire and will is to be attached to its root and source,** אוֹר אֵין סוֹף בָּרוּךְ הוּא — **the Blessed Infinite Light,** שֶׁמִּפְּנֵי אַהֲבָה זוֹ וְרָצוֹן זֶה — **and as a result of this love and will,** הִיא יְרֵאָה וּמְפַחֶדֶת בְּטִבְעָהּ מִנְּגוֹעַ בְּקָצֶה טוּמְאַת עֲבוֹדָה זָרָה חַס וְשָׁלוֹם — **the soul has a natural aversion to, and trepidation of, even the slightest association with the impurity of idol worship, G-d forbid,** שֶׁהִיא נֶגֶד אֱמוּנַת ה' אֶחָד — **which is in conflict with the faith in One G-d.**

אֲפִילוּ בִּלְבוּשֶׁיהָ הַחִיצוֹנִים שֶׁהֵם דִּבּוּר אוֹ מַעֲשֶׂה בְּלִי אֱמוּנָה בַּלֵּב כְּלָל — **And, as we have seen, this is even where** the association with idol worship **only involves the soul's outer "garments" of speech or action, without any faith whatsoever in the heart.**

---

*It is unclear whether the *Tanya's* statement "this is called 'reverence that is contained in love,'" refers to the specific case discussed in the previous passage (giving up one's life rather than perform an "empty" act of worship), or to the general notion of giving up one's life for G-d, discussed in the chapter. The commentary here follows the latter interpretation, cited in the name of "many important *mashpi'im*" in *Kovetz Oholei Torah*, issue 811 (2001), pp. 28-30. See also Rabbi Dovber of Lubavitch, *Sha'arei Orah* (Kapust, 1722), introduction, p. 2a; Rabbi Menachem Mendel Schneerson, *Toras Menachem, Hisva'aduyos* (New York: Va'ad Hanachos Lahak, 1999), vol. 12, p. 26.

פֶּרֶק כ וְהִנֵּה מוֹדַעַת זֹאת לְכֹל כִּי מִצְוַת וְאַזְהָרַת
ע"ז שֶׁהֵם שְׁנֵי דִבְּרוֹת הָרִאשׁוֹנִים
אָנֹכִי וְלֹא יִהְיֶה לְךָ הֵם כְּלָלוּת כָּל הַתּוֹרָה כּוּלָהּ. כִּי דִבּוּר
אָנֹכִי כּוֹלֵל כָּל רַמַ"ח מִצְוֹת עֲשֵׂה. וְלֹא יִהְיֶה לְךָ כּוֹלֵל
כָּל שַׁסַ"ה מִצְוֹת ל"ת וְלָכֵן שְׁמָעֵנוּ אָנֹכִי וְלֹא יִהְיֶה לְךָ

CHAPTER 20

NONDUAL JUDAISM

SECTION ONE: THE FIRST TWO COMMANDMENTS

5TH SHEVAT REGULAR | 11TH SHEVAT LEAP

In chapter 18 the *Tanya* began to explain how worshiping G-d is "very much within reach," based on the idea that we have all inherited a love for G-d, built into our souls. In chapter 19, we learned that, while this love may remain dormant, it will surface even in the most sinful person when faced with a test of faith, "Convert or die!"

This, however, leaves us with the original question in chapter 18 unanswered. If our "dormant love" only surfaces with a test of faith, how does that make worship "very much within reach" in an everyday setting, when our lives are not threatened by a religious ultimatum?

The answer to this question will require us to take a "crash course" in higher consciousness. The *Tanya* will spend the next four chapters elaborating on what is sometimes referred to as the "nondual idea," that everyone and everything manifests G-d. Eventually, in chapter 25, we will return to answer the question remaining from chapter 18.

Our discussion will center on a teaching of the *Zohar*, which the *Tanya* now cites.

וְהִנֵּה מוֹדַעַת זֹאת לְכֹל — Now *"this thing is known"* (Isaiah 12:5), **to everybody,** כִּי מִצְוַת וְאַזְהָרַת עֲבוֹדָה זָרָה — **that the** *mitzvah* **to accept only One G-d and the** Biblical **prohibition against idolatry,** שֶׁהֵם שְׁנֵי דִבְּרוֹת הָרִאשׁוֹנִים — **which are the** **first two** of the Ten **Commandments,** אָנֹכִי וְלֹא יִהְיֶה לְךָ — *"I am G-d, your G-d"* **and** *"You shall not have* any other gods" (Exodus 20:2-3), הֵם כְּלָלוּת כָּל הַתּוֹרָה כּוּלָהּ — **are a comprehensive** statement **which** thematically **incorporates the whole Torah,** כִּי דִבּוּר אָנֹכִי כּוֹלֵל כָּל רַמַ"ח מִצְוֹת עֲשֵׂה — **since the commandment** *"I am G-d,"* **in-** **corporates all the 248 positive** *mitzvos,* וְלֹא יִהְיֶה לְךָ כּוֹלֵל כָּל שַׁסַ"ה מִצְוֹת לֹא תַעֲשֶׂה **— and the commandment** *"You shall not have* any other gods" **incorporates the** **365 prohibitions** (*Zohar* 2, 91a).

לבד מפי הגבורה כמארז"ל מפני שהם כללות התורה
כולה. ולבאר היטב ענין זה צריך להזכיר תחלה
בקצרה ענין ומהות אחדותו של הקב"ה שנקרא יחיד

All the *mitzvos* are, in essence, an affirmation of monotheism and a rejection of idolatry, the theme of the first two commandments. The 248 positive commands ("You shall's") are an affirmation of One G-d; and the 365 prohibitions ("You shall not's") are a repudiation of idolatry.

וְלָכֵן שָׁמַעְנוּ אָנֹכִי וְלֹא יִהְיֶה לְךָ לְבַד מִפִּי הַגְּבוּרָה — **And that is why we only heard** the first two commandments, *"I am G-d, your G-d"* and *"You shall not have any other gods,"* directly **from the mouth of G-d, כְּמַאֲמַר רַבּוֹתֵינוּ זִכְרוֹנָם לִבְרָכָה — as our Sages, of blessed memory, taught,** that G-d said just the first two of the Ten Commandments, and the remainder were transmitted by Moses (*Talmud, Makos* 24a), מִפְּנֵי שֶׁהֵם כְּלָלוֹת הַתּוֹרָה כּוּלָּה — **because** for G-d to say the rest of the commandments was unnecessary, **since** the first two **incorporate the whole Torah.**

The fact that G-d spoke just two commandments, sent a clear message that Judaism can be summed up in just two themes: accept one G-d; and do not accept idolatry. From this it follows that every *mitzvah* is, at its core, a rejection of idol-worship.

SECTION TWO: THE NONDUALITY OF G-D

צָרִיךְ לְהַזְכִּיר תְּחִלָּה — **In order to have clarity in this matter,** וּלְבָאֵר הֵיטֵב עִנְיָן זֶה בְּקִצְרָה עִנְיָן וּמַהוּת אַחְדוּתוֹ שֶׁל הַקָּדוֹשׁ בָּרוּךְ הוּא — **we first need to mention briefly,** over the next two chapters, **the concept and deep ideology of G-d's nonduality.**

One of the most striking contributions of the Kabbalah, which became a central idea in Chasidic thought, was a highly innovative reading of the monotheistic idea. The belief in "one G-d" is no longer perceived as the mere rejection of other deities or intermediaries, but a denial of *any existence* outside of G-d.

As Rabbi Moshe Cordovero explains: *"Before anything was emanated, there was only the Infinite One (Ein Sof), which was all that existed. And even after He brought into being everything which exists, there is nothing but Him, and you cannot find anything that exists apart from Him, G-d forbid. For nothing exists devoid of G-d's power, for if there were, He would be limited and subject to duality, G-d forbid. Rather, G-d is everything that exists, but everything that exists is not G-d... Nothing is devoid of His G-dliness: everything is within it.... There is nothing but it"* (Rabbi Moshe Cordovero, *Elimah Rabasi*, p. 24d–25a; for sources in early Chasidism see: Rabbi Ya'akov Yosef of Polonne, *Ben Poras Yosef* (Piotrków 1884), pp. 140, 168; *Keser Shem Tov* (Brooklyn: Kehos 2004), pp. 237-8; Rabbi Menachem Mendel of Vitebsk, *Pri Ha-Aretz,* (Kopust 1884), p. 21).

This idea is often referred to as the *nonduality* of G-d. To say that the created world is a separate "substance" from G-d, would imply a certain duality, that there

ומיוחד וכל מאמינים שהוא לבדו הוא כמו שהיה קודם
שנברא העולם ממש שהיה הוא לבדו וכמ"ש אתה
הוא עד שלא נברא העולם אתה הוא משנברא כו' פי'
הוא ממש בלי שום שינוי כדכתיב אני ה' לא שניתי כי
עוה"ז וכן כל העולמות העליונים אינן פועלים שום שינוי

26A

are two types of existence in the universe, the Divine and non-Divine. In the nondual vision, there is only one existence or "substance" — G-d. Everything else is simply "dissolved" or absorbed in that oneness.

This concept *"is one of the central aspects of man's purpose in life, to establish this truth and to spread it to the utmost extent of his influence. This is not merely an idea but a way of life which is expressed in daily life, and which permeates the whole inner being of a Chasid"* (Rabbi Menachem Mendel Schneerson, (Nissan Mindel ed.), *The Letter And the Spirit,* vol. 3 (Brooklyn 2016), p. 280).

Obviously, the nondual reality is an extremely subtle concept, and it is something to which the second book of *Tanya, Sha'ar ha-Yichud ve-ha-Emunah,* devotes much attention. For the remainder of this chapter and the next, we will only touch upon the concept briefly. First, the *Tanya* offers some scriptural and Rabbinic references that are suggestive of nonduality.

PRACTICAL LESSONS

Every *mitzvah* is, in essence, either an affirmation of the One G-d or a repudiation of idol-worship.

שֶׁנִּקְרָא יָחִיד וּמְיוּחָד — In the *Midrash,* G-d is referred to as *"the One and only one"* (*Deuteronomy Rabah,* 2:31), implying that He is the only existence, וְכָל מַאֲמִינִים שֶׁהוּא לְבַדּוֹ הוּא — and in the liturgy it is written, *"Everyone believes of Him that He is the only One"* (High Holiday Liturgy), כְּמוֹ שֶׁהָיָה קוֹדֶם שֶׁנִּבְרָא הָעוֹלָם מַמָּשׁ שֶׁהָיָה הוּא לְבַדּוֹ — which implies that He remains now **exactly the same as He was before the world was created, when He was alone** and there was no other entity in the universe, וּכְמוֹ

שֶׁאוֹמְרִים אַתָּה הוּא עַד שֶׁלֹא נִבְרָא הָעוֹלָם אַתָּה הוּא וּמִשֶּׁנִּבְרָא כו' — as we say, *"You were alone before the world was created; You are alone since the world has been created"* (Morning Liturgy), פֵּירוּשׁ הוּא מַמָּשׁ בְּלִי שׁוּם שִׁינוּי — which, in a nondual reading **means that He literally has not changed** and G-d remains the only existence in the universe, even after He created the world, כְּדִכְתִיב אֲנִי ה' לֹא שָׁנִיתִי — as the verse states, *"I, G-d, have not changed"* (*Malachi* 3:6).

Clearly, the world *does* exist. Even nondual Judaism does not maintain that what we see is an illusion. It simply sees the universe as subsumed *within* G-d, having no separate identity from Him. This means that G-d's sole existence prior to creation has not changed, since creation did not produce any new entity *outside* of G-d.

כִּי עוֹלָם הַזֶּה וְכֵן כָּל הָעוֹלָמוֹת הָעֶלְיוֹנִים אֵינָם פּוֹעֲלִים שׁוּם שִׁינוּי בְּאַחְדוּתוֹ יִתְבָּרֵךְ בְּהִבָּרְאָם מֵאַיִן לְיֵשׁ — Because **neither the creation of this world something-from-nothing,**

באחדותו ית' בהבראם מאין ליש שכמו שהיה הוא
לבדו הוא יחיד ומיוחד קודם הבראם כן הוא לבדו הוא
יחיד ומיוחד אחר שבראם משום דכולא קמיה כלא
חשיב וכאין ואפס ממש כי התהוות כל העולמו' עליונים
ותחתונים מאין ליש וחיותם וקיומם המקיימם שלא
יחזרו להיות אין ואפס כשהיה אינו אלא דבר ה' ורוח

nor the creation of **all the spiritual worlds, brought about any change in G-d's nonduality,** שֶׁכְּמוֹ שֶׁהָיָה הוּא לְבַדּוֹ הוּא יָחִיד וּמְיוּחָד קוֹדֶם הִבָּרְאָם — **for just as He was the only, singular and exclusive existence before** the physical and spiritual worlds **were created,** כֵּן הוּא לְבַדּוֹ הוּא יָחִיד וּמְיוּחָד אַחַר שֶׁבְּרָאָם — **so too, He remains the only, singular and exclusive existence, after He created them.**

But if the world does exist, how can we say that G-d is the "only, singular and exclusive existence"?

מִשׁוּם דְּכוּלָּא קַמֵּיהּ כְּלָא חֲשִׁיב — **Because,** *"in His presence, everything is considered zero"* (*Zohar* 1, 11b), וּכְאַיִן וָאֶפֶס מַמָּשׁ — **literally, as if it were** *"null and void"* (see *Isaiah* 40:17).

The world does exist, but *in G-d's presence* it has no independent identity and existence, since it is perceived as part of His existence.

12TH SHEVAT LEAP

כִּי הִתְהַוּוּת כָּל הָעוֹלָמוֹת עֶלְיוֹנִים וְתַחְתּוֹנִים מֵאַיִן לְיֵשׁ — **For the cause by which the upper and lower worlds have come into being, something-from-nothing,** וְחַיּוּתָם וְקִיוּמָם הַמְקַיְּימָם שֶׁלֹּא יַחְזְרוּ לִהְיוֹת אַיִן וָאֶפֶס כְּשֶׁהָיָה — **and through which they continue to be energized and sustained in existence, so that they don't revert to be** *"null and void,"* **as they were previously,** אֵינוֹ אֶלָּא דְּבַר ה' וְרוּחַ פִּיו יִתְבָּרֵךְ הַמְלוּבָּשׁ בָּהֶם — **is nothing other than** *"G-d's word... and the breath of His mouth"* (*Psalms* 33:6), **which is present in them.**

Integral to a nondual understanding of the universe is the notion that the creation of something-from-nothing is an *ongoing process*. G-d must continue to will all of existence into being, otherwise it would revert to primordial nothingness. Borrowing the Biblical metaphor of creation through Divine speech, "G-d's word" must continually be "spoken" to ensure the ongoing existence of every detail of the universe.

PRACTICAL LESSONS

In the Chasidic paradigm, believing in One G-d doesn't just mean you reject the notion of other gods. It means you appreciate that G-d is nondual, i.e., there is no independent existence outside G-d.

It's not true that the world doesn't exist at all; it just doesn't exist *outside* G-d. If you were G-d, you wouldn't see a separate world, you would just see yourself.

פיו ית' המלובש בהם. ולמשל כמו בנפש האדם
כשמדבר דבר אחד שדבור זה לבדו כלא ממש אפי'
לגבי כללות נפשו המדברת שהוא בחי' לבוש האמצעי
שלה שהוא כח הדבור שלה שיכול לדבר דבורי' לאין

Chabad discourses often illustrate this idea with the analogy of a stone thrown into the air. In order to continue its ascent and counteract the gravitational pull downwards, the stone requires a continual supply of kinetic energy, provided by the initial thrust of the hand. As soon as this energy is exhausted, the stone begins to fall. The *motion* of the rock is analogous to the *existence* of the world: If G-d's creative input were to cease, the world's existence would revert to its more "natural" state of nothingness.

The need for a constant sustaining force points to a crippling fragility which plagues the existence of all matter. The rock, in our analogy, never changes in substance or character; it has not become a new "species" of "flying rock"; rather, it is a rock that *happens* to be flying due to an *acquired* quality of kinetic motion. Ongoing creation teaches us that even when the world does enjoy existence, that existence is *an acquired property and not an inherent one.* In the same way that, even as it soars upwards, the stone's natural tendency is to fall downwards, the universe similarly tends towards self-annihilation and "re-absorption" back into its Divine source. The apparently static phenomenon of the world's independent existence is, in fact, dynamically sustained by a constant creative drive. (For the above see: Rabbi Yoel Kahn, *Shiurim Be-Toras Chabad,* (Kfar Chabad: 2006), pp. 152-5).

SECTION THREE: AN ANALOGY FOR NONDUALITY

6TH SHEVAT REGULAR

וּלְמָשָׁל כְּמוֹ בְּנֶפֶשׁ הָאָדָם — Let's draw an example from the human psyche.

The source of this "example," which is the *Tanya's* key illustration of the nondual idea in this chapter and the next, is from the *Ba'al Shem Tov (Ma'amarei Admor Ha-Zakein, Inyanim,* vol. 2 (Brooklyn: Kehos, 2015), p. 494; see *Keser Shem Tov* ibid.).

כְּשֶׁמְּדַבֵּר דְּבּוּר אֶחָד שֶׁדִּבּוּר זֶה לְבַדּוֹ כְּלָא מַמָּשׁ — When you say a word, that single word is utterly insignificant, אֲפִילוּ לְגַבֵּי כְּלָלוּת נַפְשׁוֹ הַמְדַבֶּרֶת — even in comparison to the lower "garment" of the soul, the general power of speech, שֶׁהוּא בְּחִינַת לְבוּשׁ הָאֶמְצָעִי שֶׁלָּהּ — which, of the soul's three garments, thought, speech and action, is its middle garment, שֶׁהוּא כֹּחַ הַדִּבּוּר שֶׁלָּהּ שֶׁיָּכוֹל לְדַבֵּר דְּבּוּרִים לְאֵין קֵץ וְתַכְלִית — a single word is insignificant compared to the soul's **power of speech** since that power of speech **can produce a never-ending, infinite stream of words.**

Of what significance is one word when compared with the power of speech, that can produce words *endlessly*?

קָץ וְתַכְלִית וכ"ש לְגַבֵּי בְחִי' לְבוּשׁ הַפְּנִימִי שֶׁלָהּ שֶׁהוּא
הַמַּחֲשָׁבָה שֶׁמִּמֶּנָּה נִמְשְׁכוּ הַדִּבּוּרִים וְהִיא חַיּוּתָם וא"צ
לוֹמַר לְגַבֵּי מַהוּת וְעַצְמוּת הַנֶּפֶשׁ שֶׁהֵן עֶשֶׂר בְּחִינוֹתֶיהָ
הַנ"ל חב"ד כו' שֶׁמֵּהֶן נִמְשְׁכוּ אוֹתִיּוֹת מַחֲשָׁבָה זוֹ
הַמְלוּבָּשׁוֹת בְּדִבּוּר זֶה כְּשֶׁמְּדַבֵּר כִּי הַמַּחֲשָׁבָה הִיא ג"כ
בְּחִי' אוֹתִיּוֹת כְּמוֹ הַדִּבּוּר רַק שֶׁהֵן רוּחָנִיּוֹת וְדַקּוֹת יוֹתֵר

וְכָל שֶׁכֵּן לְגַבֵּי בְּחִינַת לְבוּשׁ הַפְּנִימִי שֶׁלָהּ שֶׁהוּא הַמַּחֲשָׁבָה — **All the more so** is that one spoken word insignificant **in comparison to** higher levels of the psyche, such as the soul's **innermost "garment," thought,** שֶׁמִּמֶּנָּה נִמְשְׁכוּ הַדִּבּוּרִים וְהִיא חַיּוּתָם — **from** which the spoken **words are derived and powered.**

If one word is insignificant when compared with the power of speech, then certainly it is of no significance compared with the power of thought, which produces all the content that is later spoken.

וְאֵין צָרִיךְ לוֹמַר לְגַבֵּי מַהוּת וְעַצְמוּת הַנֶּפֶשׁ — **And it goes without saying** that a single spoken word is insignificant **in comparison with the soul's** prelinguistic **deep core,** שֶׁהֵן עֶשֶׂר בְּחִינוֹתֶיהָ הַנִּזְכָּרִים לְעֵיל — which consists of the ten powers mentioned **above,** in chapter 3, חָכְמָה בִּינָה וָדַעַת כו' — *chochmah, binah* and *da'as etc.,* שֶׁמֵּהֶן נִמְשְׁכוּ אוֹתִיּוֹת מַחֲשָׁבָה זוֹ — **since it is from these** powers of the deep core **that the letters constituting the thought are** ultimately **drawn,** הַמְלוּבָּשׁוֹת בְּדִבּוּר זֶה כְּשֶׁמְּדַבֵּר — **and are subsequently expressed in the spoken word.**

Even in a human being we see that words of speech are utterly insignificant when compared to the higher powers of speech and thought, and certainly to the person himself, in his deep core. Apparently, then, we can say the same of G-d's "speech," through which the world was created and is sustained in existence, that it is of no significance compared with G-d Himself.

This adds a further dimension to our nondual understanding of the universe. In the previous section, we argued that the world has no independent existence since it is utterly reliant on G-d for its continuous existence. Here the argument is taken a step further: even the Divine power that creates the world (G-d's "speech") is of no significance compared to G-d Himself!

SECTION FOUR: YOUR SOUL HAS NO WORDS

In section three, *Tanya* described the "deep core" of the soul as pre-linguistic. We will now clarify this point further, so as to gain a deeper understanding of the *Ba'al Shem Tov's* "analogy" of nonduality.

כִּי הַמַּחֲשָׁבָה הִיא גַם כֵּן בְּחִינַת אוֹתִיּוֹת כְּמוֹ הַדִּבּוּר — **For** in the "garment" of **thought there are also letters** and words, **like in** "the garment" of **speech,** רַק שֶׁהֵן רוּחָנִיּוֹת וְדַקּוֹת יוֹתֵר — **only** in thought, those letters are **more intangible and subtle.**

אבל עשר בחי' חב"ד כו' הן שרש ומקור המחשבה
ואין בהם בחי' אותיות עדיין קודם שמתלבשות בלבוש
המחשבה. למשל כשנופלת איזו אהבה וחמדה בלבו
של אדם קודם שעולה מהלב אל המוח לחשב ולהרהר
בה אין בה בחי' אותיות עדיין רק חפץ פשוט וחשיקה
בלב אל הדבר ההוא הנחמד אצלו וכ"ש קודם שנפלה
התאוה והחמדה בלבו לאותו דבר רק היתה בכח
חכמתו ושכלו וידיעתו שהיה נודע אצלו אותו דבר
שהוא נחמד ונעים וטוב ויפה להשיגו ולידבק בו כגון

13TH SHEVAT LEAP

אֲבָל עֶשֶׂר בְּחִינוֹת חָכְמָה בִּינָה וָדַעַת כוּ' — **But** this is not the case within the deep core, in **the ten powers of** *chochmah, binah* **and** *da'as etc.,* הֵן שֹׁרֶשׁ וּמְקוֹר הַמַּחֲשָׁבָה — **which are the root and source of thought,** וְאֵין בָּהֶם בְּחִינַת אוֹתִיוֹת עֲדַיִין — these ten powers reflect a psychic state **prior to the emergence of letters,** קוֹדֶם שֶׁמִּתְלַבְּשׁוֹת בִּלְבוּשׁ הַמַּחֲשָׁבָה — **before** an idea or feeling **takes expression in the garment of "thought."**

The ten powers of the deep core, which represent your intellectual and emotional energy, are the driving force behind what you think and say. But in the deep core, there are no actual letters or words; these only crystallize later in the "garments" of thought and speech.

PRACTICAL LESSONS

The voiding of the world's existence occurs on two different levels. The world has no independent existence because: 1.) It's dependent on a Divine Power (G-d's "speech") for its continued existence; and, 2.) That Divine Power itself is utterly insignificant compared to G-d Himself.

לְמָשָׁל כְּשֶׁנּוֹפֶלֶת אֵיזוֹ אַהֲבָה וְחֶמְדָּה בְּלִבּוֹ שֶׁל אָדָם — **For example, when a** feeling of **love or desire** initially **falls into your heart,** קוֹדֶם שֶׁעוֹלָה מֵהַלֵּב אֶל הַמּוֹחַ לַחֲשֵׁב וּלְהַרְהֵר בָּהּ — **before it rises from the heart to the brain, to be contemplated,** אֵין בָּהּ בְּחִינַת אוֹתִיוֹת עֲדַיִין — **it doesn't have any** tangible **component letters** or words **yet,** רַק חֵפֶץ פָּשׁוּט וַחֲשִׁיקָה בַּלֵּב אֶל הַדָּבָר הַהוּא הַנֶּחְמָד אֶצְלוֹ — **it's just** a plain desire and fervor of the heart for the thing that you crave.

וְכָל שֶׁכֵּן קוֹדֶם שֶׁנָּפְלָה הַתַּאֲוָה וְהַחֶמְדָּה בְּלִבּוֹ לְאוֹתוֹ דָבָר — **And certainly** there was no need for words or letters **prior to the desire and craving for that thing falling into your heart,** רַק הָיְתָה בְּכֹחַ חָכְמָתוֹ וְשִׂכְלוֹ וִידִיעָתוֹ — when **your recognition of the thing as something desirable was merely in your** *chochmah,* **your intellect and mind,** שֶׁהָיָה נוֹדָע אֶצְלוֹ אוֹתוֹ דָבָר שֶׁהוּא נֶחְמָד וְנָעִים וְטוֹב וְיָפֶה לְהַשִּׂיגוֹ וּלְדָבְּקָ בּוֹ — *i.e.,* **when you were aware that this thing**

ללמוד איזו חכמה או לאכול איזו מאכל ערב רק

לאחר שכבר נפלה החמדה והתאוה בלבו בכח חכמתו   26B

ושכלו וידיעתו ואח"כ חזרה ועלתה מהלב למוח לחשב

ולהרהר בה איך להוציא תאותו מכח אל הפועל להשיג

המאכל או למידת החכמה בפועל הרי בכאן נולדה

בחי' אותיות במוחו שהן אותיות כלשון עם ועם

המדברים והמהרהרים בהם כל ענייני העולם:

is pleasant and desirable, and that it's a good idea to acquire it and connect to it, כְּגוֹן לִלְמוֹד אֵיזוֹ חָכְמָה אוֹ לֶאֱכוֹל אֵיזֶה מַאֲכָל עָרֵב — whatever that "thing" might be, **such as learning a particular subject, or eating a particular delicacy.**

When you first know or feel that something is good, you haven't yet expressed that desire in words. You tasted some ice-cream, it felt good, so when you see more ice cream, you want it. All that can take place without words or sentences forming in your mind.

רַק לְאַחַר שֶׁכְּבָר נָפְלָה הַחֶמְדָּה וְהַתַּאֲוָה בְּלִבּוֹ בְּכֹחַ חָכְמָתוֹ וְשִׂכְלוֹ וִידִיעָתוֹ — **It's only after the yearning and craving already fell into your heart** that the thing is desirable, **fueled by** the recognition of **your _chochmah_, intellect and mind** וְאַחַר כָּךְ חָזְרָה וְעָלְתָה מֵהַלֵב לַמּוֹחַ לַחֲשֵׁב וּלְהַרְהֵר בָּהּ — **and** that desire **subsequently ascended from the heart to the brain, to be pondered and contemplated upon,** אֵיךְ לְהוֹצִיא תַּאֲוָתוֹ מִכֹּחַ לְהַשִּׂיג הַמַּאֲכָל אוֹ לְמִידַת הַחָכְמָה — **how to actually carry out your desire,** אֶל הַפּוֹעַל בְּפוֹעַל — _i.e,_ **how to actually get hold of that food, or acquire that knowledge,** הֲרֵי בְּכָאן נוֹלְדוּ בְּחִינוֹת אוֹתִיּוֹת בְּמוֹחוֹ — **it is only at this point that letters must be born in your mind.**

It's only once you see the ice-cream in the store window that you start to think to yourself: Do I have enough money to buy this ice cream? How do I get into the store?

שֶׁהֵן אוֹתִיּוֹת כִּלְשׁוֹן עַם וָעַם הַמְדַבְּרִים וְהַמְהַרְהֲרִים בָּהֶם כָּל עִנְיְינֵי הָעוֹלָם — **These** letters of thought being **"of each nation, in their language"** (see _Esther_ 1:22), **in which they speak and contemplate all worldly things,** unlike the feelings of the heart which has a universal "language" of unarticulated desire.

This analysis offers us an even deeper insight into the "non-existence" of the world as a separate entity from G-d. In section three, we argued on a _quantitative_ basis that words are of no value compared to the powers of speech and thought. The power of speech can produce an infinite number of words and the power of thought can produce an infinite number of ideas to talk about; so, quantitatively speaking, one spoken word is "null and void" compared to the powers that create speech and thought.

פרק כא וְהִנֵּה מדת הקב"ה שלא כמדת בשר ודם
שהאדם כשמדבר דבור הרי הבל
הדבור שבפיו הוא מורגש ונראה דבר בפני עצמו

In this passage we have added a *qualitative* dimension to the voiding of the world's existence, arguing that in the deep core, there are no letters or words. While one word may be infinitely insignificant to the powers of speech and thought, the comparison still makes sense. But how could you even begin to measure words in relation to the deep core, where there are no words?

G-d's "word," then, is both quantitatively and qualitatively "null and void" compared to G-d himself. And if that is the case, the universe, whose existence is sustained by G-d's "word" is certainly "null and void. We can therefore affirm that *"neither the creation of this world something-from-nothing, nor the creation of all the spiritual worlds, brought about any change in G-d's nonduality, and just as He was the only, singular and exclusive existence before the physical and spiritual worlds were created, so too, He remains the only, singular and exclusive existence, after He created them"* (above, section 2).

CHAPTER 21

NONDUAL JUDAISM (II)

SECTION ONE: HUMAN AND DIVINE SPEECH

7TH SHEVAT REGULAR | 14TH SHEVAT LEAP

In the previous chapter, we "drew an example from the human psyche" to illustrate G-d's nonduality. Just as a few words of speech, we argued, are of negligible worth compared to the soul that produces them, so too, G-d's "speech" (through which He created the world) is of no worth compared to G-d Himself.

The *Tanya* now questions the validity of this comparison, which will launch us into a deeper understanding of G-d's nonduality.

וְהִנֵּה מִדַּת הַקָּדוֹשׁ בָּרוּךְ הוּא שֶׁלֹּא כְּמִדַּת בָּשָׂר וָדָם — Now, *"The Blessed Holy One's attributes are unlike the attributes of a man of flesh and blood"* (Talmud, Brachos 5a).

שֶׁהָאָדָם כְּשֶׁמְּדַבֵּר דִּבּוּר — For when a human being is in the process of speaking, הֲרֵי הֶבֶל הַדִּבּוּר שֶׁבְּפִיו הוּא מוּרְגָּשׁ וְנִרְאֶה דָּבָר בִּפְנֵי עַצְמוֹ — the breath causing that speech, which is exhaled through his mouth, is a separate entity from the person, an entity which can itself be felt and perceived.

מובדל משרשו שהן עשר בחי' הנפש עצמה אבל
הקב"ה אין דבורו מובדל ממנו ית' ח"ו כי אין דבר חוץ
ממנו ולית אתר פנוי מיני' ולכן אין דבורו ית'
כדבורינו ח"ו [כמו שאין מחשבתו כמחשבתינו
כדכתיב כי לא מחשבותי מחשבותיכם וכתיב כן גבהו
דרכי מדרכיכם וגו'] ולא נקרא דבורו ית' בשם דבור
רק עד"מ כמו שדבור התחתון שבאדם הוא מגלה
לשומעים מה שהיה צפון ונעלם במחשבתו כך למעלה

מוּבְדָּל מִשָּׁרְשׁוֹ — The speech actually leaves the person, and is **separated from its source,** שֶׁהֵן עֶשֶׂר בְּחִינוֹת הַנֶּפֶשׁ עַצְמָהּ — which is, ultimately, the soul's deep core, **the ten faculties of the soul itself.**

While speech originates deep within the psyche, once spoken, it leaves the person and becomes a "thing" unto itself.

אֲבָל הַקָּדוֹשׁ בָּרוּךְ הוּא — **But** this is not the case **with the Blessed Holy One,** אֵין דִּבּוּרוֹ מוּבְדָּל מִמֶּנּוּ יִתְבָּרֵךְ — **His speech is not separated from Himself,** חַס וְשָׁלוֹם — **G-d forbid,** כִּי אֵין דָּבָר חוּץ מִמֶּנּוּ — since *"there is nothing outside of Him"* (*Rashbatz, Magen Avos* 2:9; Rabbi Azriel of Gerona, *Perush Eser Sefiros,* beginning), וְלֵית אֲתַר פָּנוּי מִינֵּיהּ — and *"there is no place empty of Him"* (*Tikunei Zohar* 91b).

Your speech leaves your body, but G-d's "speech" does not leave Him, since He is everywhere.

וְלָכֵן אֵין דִּבּוּרוֹ יִתְבָּרֵךְ כְּדִבּוּרֵינוּ — **Therefore His speech is** *not* **like our speech,** חַס וְשָׁלוֹם — **G-d forbid.**

[כְּמוֹ שֶׁאֵין מַחֲשַׁבְתוֹ כְּמַחֲשַׁבְתֵּינוּ — **Just like His thought is** obviously **not like our thought,** כְּדִכְתִיב כִּי לֹא מַחְשְׁבוֹתַי מַחְשְׁבוֹתֵיכֶם — as the verse states, *"For My thoughts are not like your thoughts"* (Isaiah 55:8)] וּכְתִיב כֵּן גָּבְהוּ דְרָכַי מִדַּרְכֵיכֶם וְגוֹ' — **and the verse states,** *"So are My ways higher than your ways, etc."* (ibid. 9).

Why, then, does the Torah refer to G-d's "speech" at all, if no comparison can be drawn to human speech? Apparently, while the two types of "speech" differ fundamentally, there is a certain similarity to be drawn.

As we have seen, human and Divine "speech" differ in that the latter never departs from its Speaker. But, as the *Tanya* will now explain, both types of speech do share a certain quality: they are both *acts of disclosure.*

וְלֹא נִקְרָא דִּבּוּרוֹ יִתְבָּרֵךְ בְּשֵׁם דִּבּוּר רַק עַל דֶּרֶךְ מָשָׁל — **The term "speech" is used only metaphorically in** Scripture in reference to **G-d's speech,** in the following sense:

כְּמוֹ שֶׁדִּבּוּר הַתַּחְתּוֹן שֶׁבָּאָדָם הוּא מְגַלֶּה לַשּׁוֹמְעִים מַה שֶׁהָיָה צָפוּן וְנֶעְלָם בְּמַחֲשַׁבְתּוֹ — **Just as through "lower,"** human **speech, a person discloses to his listeners what was hidden and concealed in his thoughts,** כָּךְ לְמַעְלָה בְּאֵין סוֹף בָּרוּךְ הוּא — **the**

בא"ס ב"ה יציאת האור והחיות ממנו ית' מההעלם אל
הגילוי לברוא עולמות ולהחיותם נק' בשם דבור והן
הן עשרה מאמרות שבהן נברא העולם וכן שאר כל
התורה נביאים וכתובים שהשיגו הנביאים במראה
נבואתם. והרי דבורו ומחשבתו כביכול מיוחדות עמו
בתכלית היחוד ד"מ כמו דבורו ומחשבתו של אדם
בעודן בכח חכמתו ושכלו או בתשוקה וחמדה שבלבו
קודם שעלתה מהלב למוח להרהר בה בבחי' אותיות

same is true Above, with the Blessed Infinite One, יְצִיאַת הָאוֹר וְהַחַיּוּת מִמֶּנּוּ יִתְבָּרֵךְ — when **light and energy emerges** מֵהֶהֶעְלֵם אֶל הַגִּלּוּי לִבְרוֹא עוֹלָמוֹת וּלְהַחֲיוֹתָם — when **light and energy emerges out of Him, from concealment to disclosure, to create worlds and energize them,** נִקְרֵאת בְּשֵׁם דְּבּוּר — **it is called** an act of Divine **"speech."**

The metaphor of G-d's "speech" is used to indicate a Divine disclosure or revelation. Just as human speech discloses thoughts which were previously hidden, Divine "speech" is a process by which Divine powers are made available to recipients.

וְהֵן הֵן עֲשָׂרָה מַאֲמָרוֹת שֶׁבָּהֶן נִבְרָא הָעוֹלָם — **And this is precisely the** metaphysical process signified by the ***"Ten verbal utterances through which the world was created"*** (see *Mishnah, Avos* 5:1).

Scripture's statement *"G-d said, 'Let dry land appear'"* (*Genesis* 1:9), for example, is a metaphor for the emergence of *"light and energy from Him, from concealment to disclosure, to create worlds and energize them."*

וְכֵן שְׁאָר כָּל הַתּוֹרָה נְבִיאִים וּכְתוּבִים — **So too, all the other** words in the sacred texts of *Torah*, *Nevi'im* (Prophets) and *Kesuvim* (Writings), שֶׁהִשִּׂיגוּ הַנְּבִיאִים בְּמַרְאֶה נְבוּאָתָם — **which the prophets perceived in their prophetic visions** also represent a disclosure from G-d to the lower worlds, since all of Scripture is G-d's "word."

15TH SHEVAT LEAP

וַהֲרֵי דְּבּוּרוֹ וּמַחֲשַׁבְתּוֹ כִּבְיָכוֹל מְיוּחָדוֹת עִמּוֹ בְּתַכְלִית הַיִּחוּד — **Yet,** while human and Divine "speech" both share the property of disclosure, **His so-called "speech" and "thought"** differ from the human variety in that they **are** always **totally united and one with Him,** unlike human speech which departs from a person.

How, then, are we to imagine "G-d's speech"? It doesn't appear to be anything like speech as we know it, which always departs from the speaker.

דֶּרֶךְ מָשָׁל כְּמוֹ דִּבּוּרוֹ וּמַחֲשַׁבְתּוֹ שֶׁל אָדָם בְּעוֹדָן בְּכֹחַ חָכְמָתוֹ וְשִׂכְלוֹ — G-d's speech is, **for example, like the** pre-linguistic source of **human speech and thought, as it exists in potential, in a person's** *chochmah* **and intellect,** אוֹ בִּתְשׁוּקָה וְחֶמְדָּה שֶׁבְּלִבּוֹ קוֹדֶם — **or in a desire and craving of the** שֶׁעָלְתָה מֵהַלֵּב לַמּוֹחַ לְהַרְהֵר בָּהּ בִּבְחִינַת אוֹתִיּוֹת **heart, before rising from the heart to the brain, to be pondered upon linguistically,**

שֶׁאָז הָיוּ אוֹתִיּוֹת הַמַּחֲשָׁבָה וְהַדִּבּוּר הַזֶּה הַנִּמְשָׁכוֹת
מֵחֶמְדָּה וּתְשׁוּקָה זוֹ בְּכֹחַ בַּלֵּב וּמְיֻחָדוֹת שָׁם בְּתַכְלִית
הַיִּחוּד בְּשָׁרְשָׁן שֶׁהֵן הַחָכְמָה וְשֵׂכֶל שֶׁבַּמֹּחַ וְחֶמְדָּה 27A
וּתְשׁוּקָה שֶׁבַּלֵּב. וְכָכָה מַמָּשׁ דֶּרֶךְ מָשָׁל מְיֻחָדוֹת דִּבּוּרוֹ
וּמַחֲשַׁבְתּוֹ שֶׁל הַקָּבָּ"ה בְּתַכְלִית הַיִּחוּד בְּמַהוּתוֹ וְעַצְמוּתוֹ
יִת' גַּם אַחַר שֶׁיָּצָא דִּבּוּרוֹ יִת' אֶל הַפֹּעַל בִּבְרִיאוֹת
הָעוֹלָמוֹת כְּמוֹ שֶׁהָיָה מְיֻחָד עִמּוֹ קֹדֶם בְּרִיאַת הָעוֹלָמוֹ'

שֶׁאָז הָיוּ אוֹתִיּוֹת הַמַּחֲשָׁבָה וְהַדִּבּוּר הַזֶּה הַנִּמְשָׁכוֹת מֵחֶמְדָּה וּתְשׁוּקָה זוֹ בְּכֹחַ בַּלֵּב — **since** at that pre-linguistic level, **the "letters" of the thought or spoken phrase which** will later **evolve from that longing or desire, were still in potential in the heart.**

Somewhat like Divine speech, which never leaves the Speaker, the *psychic precursor* of human thought and speech (a raw awareness in the mind or a yearning of the heart) remains totally united with a person.

וּמְיֻחָדוֹת שָׁם בְּתַכְלִית הַיִּחוּד בְּשָׁרְשָׁן — **And** since the psychic precursor of the letters of thought and speech have not yet taken the distinct form of language, remaining as a mere feeling or whim, **they are completely united there with their root,** שֶׁהֵן הַחָכְמָה וְשֵׂכֶל שֶׁבַּמֹּחַ — **namely, the** *chochmah* **and intellect of the brain,** וְחֶמְדָּה וּתְשׁוּקָה שֶׁבַּלֵּב — **or the longing and desire in the heart.**

A phrase or thought only emerges as a separate entity from you when it takes the form of language. As it exists as a whim of your heart, or a general awareness in your mind, it is still completely one with you. And that's a good analogy to depict G-d's speech, which always remains one with Him.

8TH SHEVAT REGULAR

וְכָכָה מַמָּשׁ דֶּרֶךְ מָשָׁל מְיֻחָדוֹת דִּבּוּרוֹ וּמַחֲשַׁבְתּוֹ שֶׁל הַקָּדוֹשׁ בָּרוּךְ הוּא בְּתַכְלִית הַיִּחוּד בְּמַהוּתוֹ וְעַצְמוּתוֹ יִתְבָּרֵךְ — **This is a precise analogy for how the Blessed Holy One's thought and speech remain totally one with His blessed essence and self,** גַּם אַחַר שֶׁיָּצָא דִּבּוּרוֹ יִתְבָּרֵךְ אֶל הַפֹּעַל בִּבְרִיאוֹת הָעוֹלָמוֹת — **even after His "speech" has emerged, actually creating worlds,** כְּמוֹ שֶׁהָיָה מְיֻחָד עִמּוֹ קֹדֶם בְּרִיאַת הָעוֹלָמוֹת — **retaining the same level of unity with Him as it did before the worlds were created,** וְאֵין שׁוּם שִׁינּוּי כְּלָל לְפָנָיו יִתְבָּרֵךְ — **to Him, there is absolutely no change at all.**

Human speech, in its pre-linguistic root within the soul's deep core, begins in a state of total unity with the person. It is only when the speech reaches the outer "garments" of thought and speech, to be disclosed to recipients, that it becomes a separate entity. By contrast, G-d's "speech" remains absolutely one with Him even *after* an act of Divine disclosure.

What does all the above add to our discussion of G-d's nonduality in chapter 20?

In chapter 20 we learned the *Ba'al Shem Tov's* "example" of a spoken word having no significance compared to its speaker (who can speak endlessly, *etc.*). From

וְאֵין שׁוּם שִׁינּוּי כְּלָל לְפָנָיו יִת׳ אֶלָּא אֶל הַבְּרוּאִים
הַמְקַבְּלִים חִיּוּתָם מִבְּחִי׳ דִּבּוּרוֹ יִת׳ בִּבְחִי׳ יְצִיאָתוֹ כְּבָר
אֶל הַפּוֹעֵל בִּבְרִיאַת הָעוֹלָמוֹת שֶׁמִּתְלַבֵּשׁ בָּהֶם

this we concluded that the "word" of G-d, which created and continues to sustain the universe, is of no significance compared to G-d Himself. And if the power which creates the universe (G-d's "word") is of no significance, then certainly we could say that of the universe too.

There is, however, a major difference between a thing which is *comparatively* of "no significance" and a thing which has no (independent) existence *at all.* One word may capture nothing "of significance" of your soul, but that word is still a reality. It's just that *compared to your soul,* the word is devoid of value.

So after chapter 20, we might have concluded that the "non-existence" of the world (as an autonomous entity outside of G-d) is relative and not absolute. *Relative to G-d,* His "word" and the universe it created, is of no significance; but His "word" is nevertheless a distinct phenomenon, and so, therefore, is the universe.

Chapter 21 corrects this misconception. Here we learn that G-d's "word" is not merely "of no significance" (relatively speaking); it *absolutely* has no independent existence, because *"His speech is not separated from Himself."* So we can now affirm absolutely that *"neither the creation of this world something-from-nothing, nor the creation of all the spiritual worlds, brought about any change in G-d's non-duality."*

SECTION TWO: THE "DIMINISHMENT"

All this leaves us with an obvious question: If our existence is not separate from G-d's, why does it seem separate?

To shed some light on this paradox, the *Tanya* teaches us the Kabbalistic concept of *tzimtzum* (pl. *tzimtzumim),* the "diminishment" of G-d's light.

הַמְקַבְּלִים חִיּוּתָם אֶלָּא אֶל הַבְּרוּאִים — It's only from the creations' perspective, מִבְּחִינַת דִּבּוּרוֹ יִתְבָּרֵךְ — who receive their life-force from G-d's speech, בִּבְחִינַת יְצִיאָתוֹ כְּבָר אֶל הַפּוֹעֵל בִּבְרִיאַת הָעוֹלָמוֹת — that a process of "emergence" has actually taken place with the creation of the worlds, שֶׁמִּתְלַבֵּשׁ בָּהֶם לְהַחֲיוֹתָם — as the disclosure of G-d's energy and light through His speech, becomes enmeshed in the creations, giving them life.

In truth, *"neither the creation of this world something-from-nothing, nor the creation of all the spiritual worlds, brought about any change in G-d's nonduality."* However, *"from the creations' perspective"* this is not the case. We feel that we are indeed here, and that represents a significant change *to us* from before creation.

How was "the creations' perspective" made possible? The answer can be found in the esoteric doctrine of *tzimtzum.*

להחיות ע"י השתלשלו' מעלה לעלול וירידת המדרגו'
בצמצומים רבים ושונים עד שיוכלו הברואים לקבל
חיותם והתהוותם ממנו ולא יתבטלו במציאות וכל
הצמצומים הם בחי' הסתר פנים להסתיר ולהעלים
האור והחיות הנמשך מדבורו ית' שלא יתגלה בבחי'

וִירִידַת הַמַּדְרֵגוֹת לְעָלוּל מֵעָלָה הִשְׁתַּלְשְׁלוּת יְדֵי עַל — This "creation's perspective" came about **by a rung-by-rung downgrading** of G-d's light **through the cause-and-effect chain** of spiritual worlds, וְשׁוֹנִים רַבִּים בְּצִמְצוּמִים — **through numerous, diverse diminishments (*tzimtzumim*)** of the light, חַיּוּתָם לְקַבֵּל הַבְּרוּאִים שֶׁיּוּכְלוּ עַד — **to the point where creations are able to receive their life-force and creative energy from** the diminished light, מִמֶּנּוּ וְהִתְהַוּוּתָם — **without their** separate consciousness and **identity being erased** (see *Keser Shem Tov*, par. 237).

The Kabbalah teaches that to make room for the world, G-d needed to "diminish" Himself, so to speak, to recoil inwards, providing a space where "otherness" could emerge. This was the act of *tzimtzum* ("diminishment").

You only have an independent mind because G-d's creative power is concealed by the *tzimtzum*. If, at any moment, He were to reverse His "diminishing act," space and time would implode because the distinctions which make finite existence possible would be erased.

That means your consciousness is, in a sense, a lie. Your separate mind can only exist because G-d has hidden His presence. Remove that veil, and you will become reabsorbed in His oneness.

(This is, of course, only the "default" status of your unenlightened consciousness before you start to internalize the nondual idea and make it your reality).

16TH SHEVAT LEAP

The *Tanya* elaborates further on how the "diminishments" took place and why they are effective.

פָּנִים הֶסְתֵּר בְּחִינַת הֵם הַצִּמְצוּמִים וְכָל — **And all these "diminishments" are what** the Torah refers to as the **"Hiding of G-d's face"** (see *Deuteronomy* 31:17-18), לְהַסְתִּיר — a process of **hiding and obscuring** יִתְבָּרֵךְ מִדִּבּוּרוֹ הַנִּמְשָׁךְ וְהַחַיּוּת הָאוֹר וּלְהַעֲלִים — **the light and life-energy which come from G-d's "speech,"** גִּילוּי בִּבְחִינַת יִתְגַּלֶּה שֶׁלֹּא — **so that it should not be overly disclosed in a way** לְקַבֵּל הַתַּחְתּוֹנִים יוּכְלוּ שֶׁלֹּא רַב — **that the lower** created **worlds could not contain it,** causing them to lose their sense of independent consciousness.

The metaphor of "speech" in the Torah's account of creation conveys the paradox of the *tzimtzum*. On one hand, the letters of language are vehicles of communication and disclosure; they convey ideas to another person. But on the other hand,

גילוי רב שלא יוכלו התחתונים לקבל ולכן ג"כ נדמה
להם אור וחיות הדבור של מקום ב"ה המלובש בהם
כאלו הוא דבר מובדל ממהותו ועצמותו ית' רק שנמשך
ממנו ית' כמו דבור של אדם מנפשו. אך לגבי הקב"ה
אין שום צמצום והסתר והעלם מסתיר ומעלים לפניו
וכחשכה כאורה כדכתיב גם חשך לא יחשיך ממך

due to the inherent limitation of language, these same words also confuse and conceal. Since words reveal an idea and betray it at the same time, they are an excellent analogy for the simultaneous disclosure and concealment of the *tzimtzum*.

וְלָכֵן גַּם כֵּן נִדְמָה לָהֶם אוֹר וְחִיּוּת הַדִּבּוּר שֶׁל מָקוֹם בָּרוּךְ הוּא הַמְלוּבָּשׁ בָּהֶם — That's why it appears to the creations, **that the light and life-force of G-d's speech that is enmeshed in them,** כְּאִלּוּ הוּא דָּבָר מוּבְדָּל מִמַּהוּתוֹ וְעַצְמוּתוֹ יִתְבָּרֵךְ — **is as if it were something separate from His blessed essence and core,** רַק שֶׁנִּמְשָׁךְ מִמֶּנּוּ יִתְבָּרֵךְ כְּמוֹ דִּבּוּר שֶׁל אָדָם מִנַּפְשׁוֹ — **and** it appears as if the light and life-force **had been drawn out of Him, like human speech** that has become separate **from the person.**

The *Tanya* continues to elaborate on G-d's perspective.

אַךְ לְגַבֵּי הַקָּדוֹשׁ בָּרוּךְ הוּא אֵין שׁוּם צִמְצוּם וְהֶסְתֵּר וְהֶעְלֵם מַסְתִּיר וּמַעֲלִים לְפָנָיו — **But,** from G-d's perspective, **there has been no diminishment, hiding, or concealment that would hide or conceal anything in His presence.**

If you write a paragraph, simplifying a complex theory into a few sentences for a lay audience, you will have certainly "diminished" the theory from its original depth and complexity for your readership. But when *you* read the paragraph, it conjures up in your mind the original theory in its full glory. So, for you, there is no real diminishment, even in the abridged idea.

The same is true of G-d's creation through diminishment. When we, the "lay audience" look at it, we see G-d's presence eclipsed to a great extent. But when He looks at it, He sees no diminishment at all. For Him, the *tzimtzum* hides nothing.

וְכַחֲשֵׁכָה כָּאוֹרָה — **And** to Him *"darkness is the same as light"* (Psalms 139:12) כְּדִכְתִיב גַּם חֹשֶׁךְ לֹא יַחֲשִׁיךְ מִמֶּךְ וְגוֹ' — **as the verse states,** *"Even the darkness does not obscure You"* (ibid.).

A CHASIDIC THOUGHT

The process of *tzimtzum*/creation introduced, not a separate *existence* from G-d, but another *perspective*. To our eyes, it appears that G-d has made a separate world and endowed us with a separate consciousness. But from His perspective "we" are merely something that "happens" within G-d.

וגו' משום שאין הצמצומים והלבושי' דבר נפרד ממנו
ית' ח"ו אלא כהדין קמצא דלבושי' מיניה וביה כמ"ש
כי ה' הוא האלהים וכמ"ש במ"א ולכן קמיה כולא
כלא חשיב ממש:

This idea is expressed by the verse, *"darkness is the same as light."* From G-d's perspective, the *tzimtzum* required to create the world hides nothing of His presence. What, for us, is "darkness" and the concealment of G-d, is for Him, "light" and transparent.

מִשּׁוּם שָׁאֵין הַצַּמְצוּמִים וְהַלְּבוּשִׁים דָּבָר נִפְרָד מִמֶּנּוּ יִתְבָּרֵךְ חַס וְשָׁלוֹם — **For all the diminishments and filters are not something apart from Him, G-d forbid,** אֶלָּא כְּהָדֵין קַמְצָא דְּלְבוּשֵׁיה מִינֵיה וּבֵיה — **rather** they are, *"Like the snail, whose garment (the shell that hides it) is part of its body"* (Genesis Rabah 21:5; Ben Poras Yosef ibid).

In a dualistic view of the universe, there is G-d and some other anti-G-dly force opposing Him, be it the Satan, evil or pain. In nondual Judaism, everything is G-d, which means that even what seems to us as anti-G-d (concealment) is actually G-d. *The mask is made from the same Divinity as the Divinity it conceals.*

כְּמוֹ שֶׁכָּתוּב כִּי ה' הוּא הָאֱלֹהִים — **As the verse states,** *"For G-d (Havayah), is G-d (Elokim)"* (Deuteronomy 4:39; Keser Shem Tov p. 48), וּכְמוֹ שֶׁנִּתְבָּאֵר בְּמָקוֹם אַחֵר — **as is explained elsewhere** (see *Tanya, Sha'ar ha-Yichud ve-ha-Emunah* chapter 6).

In the Torah, G-d has many names, and the Kabbalah teaches that they are suggestive of different attributes of G-d. *Havayah* (the Tetragrammaton), refers to G-d's power of disclosure and revelation. *Elokim* (lit. "the Judge"), suggests concealment and the withholding of Divine revelation.

You might think that the goal is to get past *Elokim* (the forces that hide G-d; *tzimtzum*) and to experience His presence, *Havayah*. But in the nondual paradigm, the ultimate achievement is to see how even *Elokim* (*tzimtzum*) is also G-d at work and to be grateful for it (see *Keser Shem Tov* p. 257).

וְלָכֵן קַמֵּיה כּוּלָא כְּלָא חָשִׁיב — **That is why,** *"in His presence, everything is considered like zero"* (Zohar 1, 11b), מַמָּשׁ — **literally.**

Just as the snail sees its shell as part of its own body, G-d perceives the *tzimtzumim,* those very "veils" which

PRACTICAL LESSONS

Tzimtzum (Elokim) is that aspect of the Divine which shields us from G-d and facilitates our separate consciousness.

Havayah (and Divine "speech") is that aspect of the Divine that reveals G-d's light and energy to us.

Ultimately, *"Havayah* is *Elokim."* Both the light and the veil are both G-d, which means G-d can be found in every place and experience.

separate us from Him, as part of Himself. From His perspective, there is no independent existence from Him at all.

So in the final analysis: Is the world's existence real, or not? The answer suggested by the doctrine of *tzimtzum* is paradoxical. 1.) On one hand, G-d hid His presence (diminished His light) to make the world possible, and in that sense the world is not real. It only exists due to our *false perception* of G-d's overwhelming presence being veiled and diminished.

2.) On the other hand, the hiding of G-d's presence was carried out by *G-d himself,* so it must be something real. As *Tzemach Tzedek* writes, *"G-d decided in His mind that He was going to diminish His light... so it's something which really did happen"* (*Derech Mitzvosecha,* p. 54a). That means that our "false" perception of G-d's hiddenness *really exists* and was created by G-d.

If we combine these two points together, the conclusion is that, *"in His presence, everything is considered like zero."* The independent world that we see is of "zero" validity, because it only arises from a false perception. But the world is not *actually* "zero" — it is only "*like* zero" — because the force which maintains our perspective, the *tzimtzum,* is real.

CHAPTER 22

DENYING THAT G-D IS WITHIN YOU

SECTION ONE: EVERY CREATION EXPRESSES G-D'S ENERGY

9TH SHEVAT REGULAR | 17TH SHEVAT LEAP

In chapter 20, we learned the *Zohar's* teaching that the first two of the Ten Commandments "incorporate the entire Torah." The First Commandment *"I am G-d,"* incorporates the 248 positive *mitzvos,* and the Second Commandment *"You shall not have any other gods"* incorporates the 365 prohibitions.

To fathom the profundity of the *Zohar's* teaching, the *Tanya* began a nondual reading of the first two Commandments. In chapters 20 and 21 we explored the deeper meaning of *"I am G-d,"* the First Commandment (that G-d is the only true existence). Here, in chapter 22, we will be given a nondual reading of the Second Commandment, the prohibition against idolatry.

Once again, the *Tanya* will illustrate the nondual idea through the metaphor of G-d's "speech," which has been its teaching tool in the previous two chapters.

פרק כב רק שהתורה דברה כלשון ב״א ונקרא
בתורה דבורו של מקו׳ ב״ה בשם
דבור ממש כדבורו של אדם לפי שבאמת כך הוא
דרך ירידת והמשכת החיות לתחתונים בצמצומים
רבים ועצומים מינים ממינים שונים להבראות מהם   27B

רַק שֶׁהַתּוֹרָה דִּבְּרָה כִּלְשׁוֹן בְּנֵי אָדָם — Only, **"The Torah speaks** of G-d **in human terms"** (*Talmud, Brachos* 31b).

When referring to G-d, the Torah speaks anthropomorphically, employing human actions and emotions, which are clearly metaphorical. On this basis, *Rambam* explains in his third *Principle of Faith*, *"We are to believe that this One [G-d] which we have mentioned is neither a body nor a corporeal force.... Wherever the holy Scriptures describe Him in corporeal terms — such as walking, standing, sitting and speaking etc., — it is always metaphorical"* (*Rambam, Commentary to the Mishnah, Sanhedrin,* chapter 10).

וְנִקְרָא בַּתּוֹרָה דִּבּוּרוֹ שֶׁל מָקוֹם בָּרוּךְ הוּא בְּשֵׁם דִּבּוּר מַמָּשׁ כְּדִבּוּרוֹ שֶׁל אָדָם — **The Torah refers to G-d's "speech"** as if it were **real speech, like the speech of a person,** לְפִי שֶׁבֶּאֱמֶת כָּךְ הוּא — **because** Divine "speech," while not physical, **really does** have a profound similarity to human speech.

The Kabbalists taught that anthropomorphic Scriptural references to G-d's "hand," G-d's "eyes," *etc.,* are symbols of a higher reality. Rabbi Meir Ibn Gabbai writes: *"While the physical references to G-d in Scripture are not to be taken literally, they do nevertheless represent an extremely profound truth, describing how G-d's light flows outward from Him and reaches the creations.... In fact, our physical features were created in the image of much higher qualities, that are totally non-physical and which man cannot understand. Our organs are thus a 'reminder' of the spiritual emanations above"* (*Avodas Ha-Kodesh,* part 3, chapter 26).

PRACTICAL LESSONS

Everything in the universe receives G-d's life-energy in a way that is "tailor made" for that thing.

In this understanding, G-d's "hands" and "eyes" *do* exist as supernal emanations. While they don't possess the limitations of our physical organs, there is nevertheless some similarity with their physical counterparts. The physical organ is a "sign" or "reminder" of the emanation it represents.

דֶּרֶךְ יְרִידַת וְהַמְשָׁכַת הַחַיּוּת לַתַּחְתּוֹנִים — Divine "speech" resembles human speech as an act of disclosure **through which life-energy is drawn downwards to the lower worlds,** בְּצִמְצוּמִים רַבִּים וַעֲצוּמִים — **through numerous, profound diminishments.**

As we learned in the previous chapter, G-d "diminished" Himself, so to speak, to make "space" for the world. From His perspective, of course, He remains exactly

בְרוּאִים רַבִּים מִינִים מִמִּינִים שׁוֹנִים וכ"כ גָּבְרוּ וְעָצְמוּ
הַצִּמְצוּמִים וְהֶסְתֵּר פָּנִים הָעֶלְיוֹנִים עַד שֶׁיּוּכְלוּ לְהִתְהַוּוֹת
וּלְהִבָּרְאוֹת גַּם דְּבָרִים טְמֵאִים וּקְלִיפּוֹת וס"א וּלְקַבֵּל
חִיּוּתָם וְקִיּוּמָם מִדְּבַר ה' וְרוּחַ פִּיו ית' בְּהֶסְתֵּר פָּנִים
וִירִידַת הַמַּדְרֵגוֹת וְלָכֵן נִקְרָא אֱלֹהִים אֲחֵרִים מִפְּנֵי

the same as He was before, and no real diminishment has taken place (just as when you simplify an idea for an audience, you do not lose your full grasp of the concept). But from the world's perspective the "diminishments" (*tzimtzumim*) are very real.

מִינִים מִמִּינִים שׁוֹנִים לְהִבָּרְאוֹת מֵהֶם בְּרוּאִים רַבִּים מִינִים מִמִּינִים שׁוֹנִים — And there are a variety of different *tzimtzumim,* so that a large variety of different creations can come into being.

While G-d's sustaining energy pulsates in every detail of the universe, the energy of a rock is very different to that of a plant or an animal. That is why many different types of "diminishments" (*tzimtzumim*) were required, so that the Divine energy in each entity should be a perfect fit for its recipient.

SECTION TWO: THE ROOT OF EVIL

The concept of G-d's "diminishment" also sheds light on the question how evil can come to be in a nondual universe.

וְכָל כָּךְ גָּבְרוּ וְעָצְמוּ הַצִּמְצוּמִים וְהֶסְתֵּר פָּנִים הָעֶלְיוֹנִים — And these diminishments and the *"hiding of G-d's face"* (see *Deuteronomy* 31:17-18), are so great and profound in scope, עַד שֶׁיּוּכְלוּ לְהִתְהַוּוֹת וּלְהִבָּרְאוֹת גַּם דְּבָרִים טְמֵאִים וּקְלִיפּוֹת וְסִטְרָא אָחֳרָא — that they are able to cause impure things, *kelipos* and *sitra achra* to come into being and be created.

וּלְקַבֵּל חַיּוּתָם וְקִיּוּמָם מִדְּבַר ה' וְרוּחַ פִּיו יִתְבָּרֵךְ — These great *tzimtzumim enable* such negative entities to receive their life-sustaining energy from *"G-d's word... and the breath of His mouth"* (see *Psalms* 33:6), בְּהֶסְתֵּר פָּנִים וִירִידַת הַמַּדְרֵגוֹת — through such a profound *"Hiding of G-d's face,"* and descent through countless rungs, so that even evil is able to absorb the energy.

If G-d's light were to shine undiminished, evil would not be able to exist. But through numerous *tzimtzumim* the light is diminished to such an extent that it barely resembles its original source. In this highly diluted state, evil can draw from the light, since it is not recognizable as Divine. G-d's "face" is hidden.

וְלָכֵן נִקְרָאִים אֱלֹהִים אֲחֵרִים — And that's why the term *"other gods (elokim acheirim)"* (*Exodus* 20:2), is used in reference to the *kelipos* (*Tikunei Zohar* 56a).

The Second Commandment instructs us not to worship "other gods" (*elokim acheirim*). The *Tikunei Zohar* borrows this phrase and applies it to the negative

שיניקתם וחיותם אינה מבחי' פנים אלא מבחי' אחוריים
דקדושה ופי' אחוריים כאדם הנותן דבר לשונאו שלא
ברצונו שמשליכו לו כלאחר כתפו כי מחזיר פניו ממנו
משנאתו אותו כך למעלה בחי' פנים הוא פנימית
הרצון העליון וחפצו האמיתי אשר חפץ ה' להשפיע

forces and *kelipos*, based on a word-play of the word *acheirim* ("other"). The root, *a-ch-r* can also mean "behind," as in the verse, *"You will see My behind (achorai), but My Face will not be seen"* (*Exodus* 33:23). Since the negative forces come into existence only when G-d's "face" is hidden through powerful diminishment, the forces are metaphorically associated with G-d's "behind."

מִפְּנֵי שֶׁיְּנִיקָתָם וְחַיּוּתָם אֵינָה מִבְּחִינַת פָּנִים אֶלָּא מִבְּחִינַת אֲחוֹרַיִים דְּקְדוּשָׁה — **For the** negative forces **suck their energy, not from** G-d's **"face," but from the "behind"** *(achorayim)* **of the holy** energy (see *Etz Chaim* 34:1, 37:2).

וּפֵירוּשׁ אֲחוֹרַיִים — **And the** simple **meaning of "behind" is,** כְּאָדָם הַנּוֹתֵן דָּבָר לְשׂוֹנְאוֹ שֶׁלֹּא בִּרְצוֹנוֹ — **like a person who, against his will, must give something to his enemy,** שֶׁמַּשְׁלִיכוֹ לוֹ כִּלְאַחַר כְּתֵפוֹ — **so he just throws it backwards to the enemy over his shoulder,** כִּי מַחֲזִיר פָּנָיו מִמֶּנּוּ מִשִּׂנְאָתוֹ אוֹתוֹ — **because he has turned his face away** from the enemy **out of hatred for him.**

If you have to give something to a person whom you simply can't stand, you might just throw the thing over your shoulder, behind your back.

כָּךְ לְמַעְלָה — **It works similarly above.**

בְּחִינַת פָּנִים הוּא פְּנִימִית הָרָצוֹן הָעֶלְיוֹן וְחֶפְצוֹ הָאֲמִיתִי — G-d's **"face"** symbolizes His inner, actual will (*ratzon ha-elyon*) and true desire, אֲשֶׁר חָפֵץ ה' לְהַשְׁפִּיעַ חַיּוּת לְכָל הַקָּרוֹב אֵלָיו מִסִּטְרָא דְּקְדוּשָׁה — namely, **that G-d desires to bestow life-energy from the realm of holiness to all those that are close to Him.**

Obviously, G-d doesn't have an actual face. When we say that something is bestowed from G-d's "face," it means that He genuinely desires to give life-energy to that entity because it's something good.

PRACTICAL LESSONS

G-d genuinely desires to give good things life-energy, and He bestows it to them willingly from His "face."

Bad things and negative forces are also sustained by G-d's life-energy, but He does not desire to give it to them (and He does so merely to give us free choice).

Basically, there are two reasons why you might desire something: either a.) because it's something you desire; or, b.) because it's a means to an end.

G-d only sustains the negative forces because they are "a means to an end." Their presence endows us with free choice and enables us to choose good and eliminate evil. But the negative forces themselves are something that G-d "detests."

חיות לכל הקרוב אליו מסטרא דקדושה אבל הס"א
והטומאה היא תועבת ה' אשר שנא ואינו משפיע לה
חיות מפנימית הרצון וחפצו האמיתי אשר חפץ בה ח"ו
כ"א כמאן דשדי בתר כתפוי לשונאו שלא ברצונו
רק כדי להעניש את הרשעים וליתן שכר טוב לצדיקי'
דאכפיין לס"א וזה נקרא בחי' אחוריים דרצון העליון
ב"ה. והנה רצון העליון בבחי' פנים הוא מקור החיים
המחיה את כל העולמות ולפי שאינו שורה כלל על
הס"א וגם בחי' אחוריים של רצון העליון אינו מלובש

אֲבָל הַסִּטְרָא אָחֲרָא וְהַטּוּמְאָה הִיא תּוֹעֲבַת ה' אֲשֶׁר שָׂנֵא — But *sitra achra* and impurity are *"an abomination to G-d which He detests"* (*Deuteronomy* 12:31), וְאֵינוֹ מַשְׁפִּיעַ לָהּ חַיּוּת מִפְּנִימִית הָרָצוֹן וְחֶפְצוֹ הָאֲמִיתִּי אֲשֶׁר חָפֵץ בָּהּ — so He doesn't give these negative forces life-energy from His inner will and from a place of **true desire that He delights in,** חַס וְשָׁלוֹם — G-d forbid, כִּי אִם כְּמַאן דְּשָׁדֵי בָּתַר כַּתְפּוֹי לְשׂוֹנְאוֹ — **rather** G-d sustains the negative forces **like a person who throws something *"over his shoulder"*** (see *Zohar* 3, 184a), **to his enemy,** שֶׁלֹּא בִּרְצוֹנוֹ — since giving this item to his enemy **is not his true will.**

Why does G-d sustain the negative forces, if they do not represent His true will?

רַק כְּדֵי לְהַעֲנִישׁ אֶת הָרְשָׁעִים וְלִיתֵּן שָׂכָר טוֹב לַצַּדִּיקִים — He does this only *"to punish the wicked... and to give a good reward to the righteous"* (see *Mishnah, Avos* 5:1), *i.e.* to make our decisions meaningful, since the consequences of our actions will be a result of our free choice, דְּאַכְפְּיָין לְסִטְרָא אָחֲרָא — and G-d derives pleasure from those **who suppress the *sitra achra.***

וְזֶה נִקְרָא בְּחִינַת אֲחוֹרַיִים דְּרָצוֹן הָעֶלְיוֹן בָּרוּךְ הוּא — **This** Divine source of life-energy for the negative forces **is called the "behind" of the Blessed Divine Will.**

SECTION THREE: THE NEGATIVE FORCES RESIST AND DENY G-D

10TH SHEVAT REGULAR

We have learned that the negative forces and *sitra achra* do not receive their energy from G-d's "face" but from his "behind." Now the *Tanya* will explain that the negative forces differ not only in the *source* of the energy ("behind" as opposed to "face"), but also in the way that they *receive* the energy.

וְהִנֵּה רָצוֹן הָעֶלְיוֹן בִּבְחִינַת פָּנִים הוּא מְקוֹר הַחַיִּים הַמְחַיֶּה אֶת כָּל הָעוֹלָמוֹת — **Now, G-d's** will, His "face," is the source of all life, it energizes all the worlds.

וּלְפִי שֶׁאֵינוֹ שׁוֹרֶה כְּלָל עַל הַסִּטְרָא אָחֲרָא — But since this energy of G-d's "face" does not rest at all on the *sitra achra,* וְגַם בְּחִינַת אֲחוֹרַיִים שֶׁל רָצוֹן הָעֶלְיוֹן אֵינוֹ מְלוּבָּשׁ

בתוכה ממש אלא מקיף עליה מלמעלה לכך היא מקום
המיתה והטומאה ה' ישמרנו כי מעט מזער אור וחיות
שיונקת ומקבלת לתוכה מבחי' אחוריים דקדושה
שלמעלה הוא בבחי' גלות ממש בתוכה בסוד גלות
השכינה הנ"ל ולכן נקרא בשם אלהים אחרים שהיא

בְּתוֹכָה מַמָּשׁ — and even the "behind" of G-d's will does not actually become enmeshed in the *sitra achra*, אֶלָּא מַקִּיף עָלֶיהָ מִלְמַעְלָה — but that "behind" energy merely encircles it from above, לְכָךְ הִיא מְקוֹם הַמִּיתָה וְהַטּוּמְאָה — therefore the *sitra achra* is a zone of death and impurity, ה' יִשְׁמְרֵנוּ — may G-d protect us.

Even the energy that the *sitra achra* receives (from G-d's "behind"), does not become properly absorbed by it. The *sitra achra's* life-energy is largely trapped and has split off. It has become anti-life (since "life" is really the presence of life-energy within something).

But if the *sitra achra* doesn't absorb *any* life-energy, how could it possibly exist?

כִּי מְעַט מִזְעַר אוֹר וְחַיּוּת שֶׁיּוֹנֶקֶת וּמְקַבֶּלֶת לְתוֹכָהּ מִבְּחִינַת אֲחוֹרַיִים דְּקְדוּשָׁה שֶׁלְמַעְלָה — Because the tiny glimmer of light and minuscule amount of life-energy that the *sitra achra* does suck from the "behind" of G-d's holiness and receive inwardly, הוּא בִּבְחִינַת גָּלוּת מַמָּשׁ בְּתוֹכָהּ — remains totally exiled within the *sitra achra*.

The *sitra achra* does manage to absorb a "minuscule" amount of life-energy, sufficient for its existence, but even that remains "exiled" and unconsciously present within it.

בְּסוֹד גָּלוּת הַשְּׁכִינָה הַנִּזְכָּר לְעֵיל — As in the secret of the *Shechinah's* exile, mentioned above (pp. 208, 225).

וְלָכֵן נִקְרָא בְּשֵׁם אֱלֹהִים אֲחֵרִים — And therefore we can offer a second reason why the *sitra achra* is referred to as *"other gods (elokim acheirim)."*

In the previous section, the *Tanya* associated the negative forces with *elokim acheirim* ("other gods") since *acheirim* is suggestive of *achorayim* ("behind"), the spiritual source of the negative forces' energy.

Now we will be offered another explanation, based not on the *source* of the negative forces' energy above, but the negative forces' resistance to *receiving* that energy below.

שֶׁהִיא עֲבוֹדָה זָרָה מַמָּשׁ — The *sitra achra* is referred to as *"other gods (elokim acheirim),"* since it really is idol-

PRACTICAL LESSONS

Bad things and negative forces are unconscious of the fact that G-d sustains them with life-energy.

That's because their arrogance and ego lead them to believe that they are independent of G-d.

So "idolatry," in the nondual sense, is to deny G-d's presence *inside you.*

28A

ע"ז ממש וכפירה באחדותו של ממ"ה הקב"ה כי מאחר
שאור וחיות דקדושה הוא בבחי' גלות בתוכה אינה
בטילה כלל לגבי קדושת הקב"ה ואדרבה מגביה עצמה
כנשר לומר אני ואפסי עוד וכמאמר יאור לי ואני
עשיתני ולכן אמרו רז"ל שגסות הרוח שקולה כע"ז
ממש כי עיקר ושרש ע"ז הוא מה שנחשב לדבר
בפני עצמו נפרד מקדושתו של מקום ולא כפירה בה'

וּכְפִירָה בְּאַחְדוּתוֹ שֶׁל מֶלֶךְ מַלְכֵי הַמְּלָכִים הַקָּדוֹשׁ בָּרוּךְ הוּא — and it denies the atrous, nonduality of G-d, the King of kings, the Blessed Holy One.

The *sitra achra* resists G-d's life energy. Even the energy that it does absorb, remains in exile, unrecognized by the *sitra achra* as the power of G-d. This is idolatry, the denial of G-d.

SECTION FOUR: THE PSYCHOLOGY OF IDOLATRY

Why does the *sitra achra* deny G-d? As mentioned earlier, the source of G-d-rejection comes from the ego and an unwillingness to surrender the self.

כִּי מֵאַחַר שֶׁאוֹר וְחַיוּת דִּקְדוּשָׁה הוּא בִּבְחִינַת גָּלוּת בְּתוֹכָהּ — For since the holy light and life-energy remain exiled unconsciously within the *sitra achra*, אֵינָהּ בְּטֵילָה כְּלָל לְגַבֵּי — the *sitra achra* doesn't surrender itself at all to G-d's קְדוּשַׁת הַקָּדוֹשׁ בָּרוּךְ הוּא — holiness (see chapter 19, p. 223).

וְאַדְּרַבָּה מַגְבִּיהַּ עַצְמָהּ כַּנֶּשֶׁר — And, on the contrary, rather than humbling and surrendering itself to G-d, the *sitra achra* inflates its ego, making itself *"as high as an eagle"* (Jeremiah 49:16), לוֹמַר אֲנִי וְאַפְסִי עוֹד — saying, *"There's me, and there's no-one else besides me"* (Isaiah 47:8), וְכַמַּאֲמָר יְאוֹר לִי וַאֲנִי עֲשִׂיתָנִי — as in Pharaoh's egotistical statement, *"The river is mine, and I have made myself"* (Ezekiel 29:3,9).

וְלָכֵן אָמְרוּ רַבּוֹתֵינוּ זִכְרוֹנָם לִבְרָכָה שֶׁגַּסוּת הָרוּחַ שְׁקוּלָה כַּעֲבוֹדָה זָרָה מַמָּשׁ — That's why our Sages of blessed memory said that an inflated ego is equivalent to actual idolatry (Talmud, Sotah 4b).

Non-surrender hardens your ego, giving you a strong sense of separateness, which is a denial of G-d's presence within you and every other existing thing.

כִּי עִיקַּר וְשֹׁרֶשׁ שֶׁל עֲבוֹדָה זָרָה — For the basis and root of idolatry, i.e., the initial error of perception which leads to an inflated ego, הוּא מַה שֶׁנֶּחְשָׁב לְדָבָר בִּפְנֵי עַצְמוֹ נִפְרָד — is the perception of being an independent entity, separate מִקְּדוּשָׁתוֹ שֶׁל מָקוֹם — from G-d's sacred presence.

וְלֹא כְּפִירָה בָּהּ לְגַמְרֵי — And this conviction, that G-d exists, but that you are independent from Him (the "basis and root of idolatry"), is not yet a complete denial

לגמרי כדאיתא בגמ' דקרו ליה אלהא דאלהיא אלא
שגם הם מחשבים עצמם ליש ודבר בפני עצמו ובזה
מפרידים את עצמם מקדושתו של מקום ב"ה מאחר
שאין בטלים לו ית' כי אין קדושה עליונה שורה אלא
על מה שבטל לו ית' כנ"ל ולכן נקראי' טורי דפרודא
בזה"ק והרי זו כפירה באחדותו האמיתית דכולא קמיה
כלא חשיב ובטל באמת לו ית' ולרצונו המחיה את
כולם ומהוה אותם מאין ליש תמיד:

of G-d, כְּדְאִיתָא בַּגְּמָרָא דְּקָרוּ לֵיהּ אֱלָהָא דֶּאֱלָהַיָּא — **as the** *Talmud* **states that, "they refer to Him as the G-d of gods"** (*Talmud, Menachos* 110a), *i.e.,* these individuals express a belief that G-d exists, but they maintain that He does not have a direct involvement with their world, (which, they perceive, is controlled by their gods).

אֶלָּא שֶׁגַּם הֵם מַחֲשִׁיבִים עַצְמָם לְיֵשׁ וְדָבָר בִּפְנֵי עַצְמוֹ — **But** even though these individuals do not deny G-d completely, **they also perceive themselves as autonomous entities and independent beings.** וּבָזֶה מַפְרִידִים אֶת עַצְמָם מִקְּדוּשָׁתוֹ שֶׁל מָקוֹם בָּרוּךְ הוּא מֵאַחֵר שֶׁאֵין בְּטֵלִים לוֹ יִתְבָּרֵךְ — **and in this way they separate themselves from G-d's holiness, since** their sense of utter independence causes them **not to surrender themselves to Him.**

The description of separation from G-d as "idol worship" is rooted in the teachings of the *Ba'al Shem Tov* on the verse, *"that you turn away and worship other gods"* (Deuteronomy 11:16). *"He interpreted this: 'that you turn away'—as soon as you turn your attention away from attaching to the Blessed Holy One; 'you will worship other gods'"—it is as if you have become an idolator'"* (*Degel Machaneh Efra'im, Parshas Kedoshim*).

כִּי אֵין קְדוּשָׁה עֶלְיוֹנָה שׁוֹרָה אֶלָּא עַל מַה שֶׁבָּטֵל לוֹ יִתְבָּרֵךְ כַּנִּזְכָּר לְעֵיל — **For, as we have mentioned above** (chapter 6, p. 86; chapter 19, p. 223), **"Supernal holiness"** (*Zohar* 3, 297a), **only rests on something which is surrendered to Him.**

וְלָכֵן נִקְרָאִים טוּרֵי דְּפַרוּדָא בַּזֹהַר הַקָּדוֹשׁ — **Therefore the negative forces are called in the holy** *Zohar,* **"divided mountain peaks"** (*Zohar* 1, 158a), since their perception is one of separateness and division.

וַהֲרֵי זוֹ כְּפִירָה בְּאַחְדוּתוֹ הָאֲמִיתִית — **And this** non-surrendered self-image **is a denial of** G-d's **real nonduality,** דְּכוּלָּא קַמֵּיה כְּלָא חֲשִׁיב — that, *"in His presence, everything is considered like zero"* (*Zohar* 1, 11b), וּבָטֵל בֶּאֱמֶת לוֹ יִתְבָּרֵךְ — and all existence is **genuinely voided** of any separate identity **before G-d, may He be blessed,** וְלִרְצוֹנוֹ הַמְחַיֶּה אֶת כּוּלָּם וּמְהַוֶּה אוֹתָם מֵאַיִן לְיֵשׁ תָּמִיד — and before His will, which sustains all things and brings them into existence constantly, something-from-nothing.

פרק כג ועם   כל הנ"ל יובן ויבואר היטב בתוספ'
ביאור מה שאמרו בזהר דאורייתא'
וקב"ה כולא חד ובתיקוני' פירשו דרמ"ח פיקודין אינון

CHAPTER 23

NONDUAL TORAH

SECTION ONE: CONNECTION THROUGH MITZVOS

11TH SHEVAT REGULAR | 18TH SHEVAT LEAP

In chapters 20-21 we were introduced to the nondual idea, how everything is absorbed within the all-consuming presence of G-d.

But this raises a difficulty as to how we are to perceive Torah and *mitzvos*. If even a table and chair, in their essence, are really nothing other than G-d, then what makes the *mitzvos* special and holy? By suggesting that "there is nothing outside G-d," the nondual idea seems to equate the holy with the profane, violating a distinction which rests at the heart of the Torah.

This chapter will address the problem by drawing on the wisdom of chapter 22. There we learned that while everything is, in its essence, G-d, such an elevated viewpoint is not easily within our reach. We function in a realm of separate consciousness, made possible by massive "diminishments" of G-d's light, and the "hiding of His face." While G-d's view of the universe sees everything as part of Him, from our perspective, separate entities are real.

The *Tanya* will argue in this chapter that Torah represents a unique bridging of the two perspectives, Divine and human. Torah study enables the nondual reality of G-d to become accessible even in this world of separate consciousness.

וְעִם כָּל הַנִּזְכָּר לְעֵיל — **Based on the above discussion** of the nondual idea, in chapters 21-22, יוּבַן וִיבוֹאַר הֵיטֵב בְּתוֹסֶפֶת בֵּיאוּר מַה שֶׁאָמְרוּ בַּזֹּהַר — **we can explain the** *Zohar's* **teaching and clarify it well, with additional insight,** beyond our discussion in chapters 4-5, דְּאוֹרַיְיתָא וְקוּדְשָׁא בְּרִיךְ הוּא כּוּלָא חַד — that *"the Torah and G-d are totally one"* (see *Zohar* 1, 24a; 2, 60a).

In chapters 4-5 we learned that both Torah and *mitzvos* provide a profound "merging experience" with G-d, because *"the Torah and G-d are totally one."* Our chapter will continue to explore this idea "with additional insight."

וּבַתִּיקוּנִים פֵּירְשׁוּ — **The** *Tikunei Zohar* **explains** the special connection with G-d that occurs through *mitzvah* observance with the statement, דְּרַמַ"ח פִּיקוּדִין אִינּוּן

רמ"ח אברין דמלכא לפי שהמצות הן פנימיות רצון
העליון וחפצו האמיתי המלובש בכל העולמו' העליוני'
ותחתוני' להחיותם כי כל חיותם ושפעם תלוי במעשה
המצות של התחתוני' כנודע. ונמצא שמעשה המצות
וקיומן הוא לבוש הפנימי לפנימית רצון העליון
שממעשה זה נמשך אור וחיות רצון העליון להתלבש

רַמָ"ח אֶבְרִין דְּמַלְכָּא — that "the 248 positive mitzvos are the 248 organs of the King" (Tikunei Zohar 74a; cited in chapter 4, p. 66).

לְפִי שֶׁהַמִּצְוֹת הֵן פְּנִימִיּוּת רָצוֹן הָעֶלְיוֹן וְחֶפְצוֹ הָאֲמִיתִּי — The implication of this teaching is that the mitzvos are the innermost will of the Divine, and His true desire.

The Tikunei Zohar describes mitzvos as "organs" of G-d's metaphorical "body," to emphasize that they are a pure and unadulterated expression of G-d Himself.

But obviously, the mitzvos represent G-d expressing Himself in worldly terms:

הַמְלוּבָּשׁ בְּכָל הָעוֹלָמוֹת הָעֶלְיוֹנִים וְתַחְתּוֹנִים לְהַחֲיוֹתָם — The mitzvos represent G-d's inner self as it is "dressed" in all the created worlds, upper and lower, to give them life-energy.

But that doesn't mean the purpose of the mitzvos is to give the worlds their life energy. In fact, it's the other way around: G-d wants mitzvos to be observed and therefore He created the worlds, to make that possible (see Genesis Rabah 1:6).

כִּי כָל חַיּוּתָם וְשִׁפְעָם תָּלוּי בְּמַעֲשֵׂה הַמִּצְוֹת שֶׁל הַתַּחְתּוֹנִים — For the life-energy and flow to all the worlds is contingent on mitzvah-observance in our lower world.

Since the whole point of the world is to facilitate Torah and mitzvos, the world's existence depends upon them. In fact, it is through Torah and mitzvos that life-energy flows to the world.

PRACTICAL LESSONS

The mitzvos are G-d's deepest, inner will. They are the very reason that the world is here.

כַּנּוֹדָע — As is known, from the Zohar: "Whoever connects to the Blessed Holy One and performs the mitzvos of the Torah, he upholds the existence of the worlds, so to speak, the upper world and the lower world" (Zohar 3, 122a).

וְנִמְצָא שֶׁמַּעֲשֵׂה הַמִּצְוֹת וְקִיּוּמָן — So it follows that the mitzvah-acts as they are stated in the Torah and their fulfillment when the mitzvos are actually observed, הוּא לְבוּשׁ הַפְּנִימִי לִפְנִימִית רָצוֹן הָעֶלְיוֹן — are deep vehicles of expression for G-d's inner will, שֶׁמִּמַּעֲשֶׂה זֶה נִמְשָׁךְ אוֹר וְחַיּוּת רָצוֹן הָעֶלְיוֹן לְהִתְלַבֵּשׁ בָּעוֹלָמוֹת — since each of these acts causes the light and life-energy from G-d's will to be "dressed" in the worlds.

בעולמות ולכן נקרא' אברי דמלכא ד"מ כמו שאברי
גוף האדם הם לבוש לנפשו ובטלים לגמרי אליה מכל
וכל כי מיד שעולה ברצונו של אדם לפשוט ידו או
רגלו הן נשמעות לרצונו תכף ומיד בלי שום צווי
ואמירה להן ובלי שום שהייה כלל אלא כרגע ממש
כשעלה ברצונו. כך ד"מ החיות של מעשה המצות
וקיומן הוא בטל לגמרי לגבי רצון העליון המלובש בו

28B

The world is merely G-d's "external will," a "means to an end" to facilitate *mitzvah* observance. The *mitzvos,* on the other hand, are G-d's inner will and true desire. That is why the world is sustained by *mitzvos* (as the *Zohar* teaches), because it is for the sake of the *mitzvos* that the world exists.

19TH SHEVAT LEAP

וְלָכֵן נִקְרָאִים אֵבְרֵי דְמַלְכָּא דֶּרֶךְ מָשָׁל — **That's why** the *mitzvos* **are referred to meta-phorically** by the *Tikunei Zohar* as *"organs of the King."*

כְּמוֹ שֶׁאֵבְרֵי גוּף הָאָדָם הֵם לְבוּשׁ לְנַפְשׁוֹ — **For just as the organs of your body are ve-hicles of expression for your soul,** וּבְטֵלִים לְגַמְרֵי אֵלֶיהָ מִכֹּל וָכֹל — **since** the organs **are completely surrendered to** your soul **with all their being;** so too, the *mitzvos* are absolute expressions of the Divine will.

When you will your leg to move, it moves. And (if you are healthy), your leg won't move on its own, unless you instruct it to. So your leg, as well as all your other organs, are a reliable and direct expression of your will.

The same is true of *mitzvos.* The *Zohar* did not describe the *mitzvos* as "organs" to imply that G-d has a physical body. The *Zohar's* point was that the *mitzvos* are pure and direct expressions of the Divine will, just as your organs are an absolute reflection of your soul.

The *Tanya* now elaborates in more detail.

כִּי מִיָּד שֶׁעוֹלֶה בִּרְצוֹנוֹ שֶׁל אָדָם לִפְשׁוֹט יָדוֹ אוֹ רַגְלוֹ הֵן נִשְׁמָעוֹת לִרְצוֹנוֹ תֵּכֶף וּמִיָּד — **For** when a person wants to stretch out his hand or foot, then those limbs **obey his will immediately and unhesitatingly,** בְּלִי שׁוּם צִוּוּי וַאֲמִירָה לָהֶן — **without him having to** consciously **instruct or direct** the limbs, וּבְלִי שׁוּם שֶׁהִיָּה כְּלָל — **and without any pause at all,** אֶלָּא כְּרֶגַע מַמָּשׁ כְּשֶׁעָלָה בִּרְצוֹנוֹ — **rather,** they react **instantaneously as soon as the will** for them to move **arises.**

כָּךְ דֶּרֶךְ מָשָׁל הַחַיּוּת שֶׁל מַעֲשֵׂה הַמִּצְוֹת וְקִיּוּמָן — In the same way a person's limbs are totally surrendered to his will, **the same is true, figuratively,** with G-d's relationship to **the life-energy** invested **in the *mitzvah*-acts and their fulfillment,** הוּא בָּטֵל לְגַמְרֵי — לְגַבֵּי רְצוֹן הָעֶלְיוֹן הַמְלוּבָּשׁ בּוֹ — that energy is **completely surrendered to the Divine**

וְנַעֲשֶׂה לו מַמָּשׁ כְּגוּף לִנְשָׁמָה. וְכֵן הַלְּבוּשׁ הַחִיצוֹן
שֶׁל נֶפֶשׁ הָאֱלֹהִית שֶׁבָּאָדָם הַמְקַיֵּם וְעוֹשֶׂה הַמִּצְוָה
שֶׁהוּא כֹּחַ וּבְחִי' הַמַּעֲשֶׂה שֶׁלָהּ הוּא מִתְלַבֵּשׁ בְּחַיּוּת
שֶׁל מַעֲשֶׂה הַמִּצְוָה וְנַעֲשֶׂה הַמִּצְוָה ג"כ כְּגוּף לִנְשָׁמָה לָרָצוֹן
הָעֶלְיוֹן וּבָטֵל אֵלָיו לְגַמְרֵי וְעַל כֵּן גַּם אֵבְרֵי גּוּף הָאָדָם
הַמְקַיְּמִים הַמִּצְוָה שֶׁכֹּחַ וּבְחִי' הַמַּעֲשֶׂה שֶׁל נֶפֶשׁ הָאֱלֹהִית
מְלוּבָּשׁ בָּהֶם בִּשְׁעַת מַעֲשֶׂה וְקִיּוּם הַמִּצְוָה הֵם נַעֲשׂוּ

will "dressed" in the *mitzvos,* וְנַעֲשֶׂה לו מַמָּשׁ כְּגוּף לִנְשָׁמָה — and their relationship is literally like a body to a soul.

The reference to "life-energy" here has a two-fold implication. a.) It refers to the energy that *the person* invests in performing the *mitzvah.* b.) It also refers to the life-energy of *the object* used to fulfill the *mitzvah* (*Notes on Tanya*).

20TH SHEVAT LEAP

וְכֵן הַלְּבוּשׁ הַחִיצוֹן שֶׁל נֶפֶשׁ הָאֱלֹהִית שֶׁבָּאָדָם הַמְקַיֵּם וְעוֹשֶׂה הַמִּצְוָה — And similarly, when you fulfill and observe a *mitzvah,* the outermost "garment" of your Divine soul, שֶׁהוּא כֹּחַ וּבְחִינַת הַמַּעֲשֶׂה שֶׁלָהּ — which is the Divine Soul's **power/component of action,** הוּא מִתְלַבֵּשׁ בְּחַיּוּת שֶׁל מַעֲשֶׂה הַמִּצְוָה — becomes **immersed in the energy of the** *mitzvah* act, וְנַעֲשֶׂה גַם כֵּן כְּגוּף לִנְשָׁמָה לָרָצוֹן הָעֶלְיוֹן — **and that** "garment" of action **is also utterly surrendered to the Divine Will, like a body** is surrendered **to its soul.**

As we learned in chapter four, the Divine Soul has three "garments" of thought, speech and action. The "garment" of action is also absorbed into the *mitzvah* act, and becomes one with G-d.

In summary: A *mitzvah* absorbs into the Divine Will, a.) the life-energy of the *mitzvah* object itself; b.) the life-energy used by the person to perform the *mitzvah;*

PRACTICAL LESSONS

When you observe a *mitzvah*: a.) Your soul's "garment" of action; b.) the limb of your body that you used; c.) The energy that you used; and d.) the energy of the object you used—all connect directly with G-d, like a chariot to its rider.

and, c.) the action "garment" of the Divine Soul. The *Tanya* will now add one more to this list: d.) The physical limb used to perform the *mitzvah.*

וְעַל כֵּן גַּם אֵבְרֵי גּוּף הָאָדָם הַמְקַיְּמִים הַמִּצְוָה — And therefore, **your bodily organs, too, when you observe the** *mitzvah,* are surrendered to the Divine will, שֶׁכֹּחַ וּבְחִינַת — since your Divine Soul's **component/power** הַמַּעֲשֶׂה שֶׁל נֶפֶשׁ הָאֱלֹהִית מְלוּבָּשׁ בָּהֶם — **of action is invested in those** bodily organs, בִּשְׁעַת מַעֲשֶׂה וְקִיּוּם הַמִּצְוָה — **at the moment when you perform and observe the** *mitzvah,* הֵם נַעֲשׂוּ מֶרְכָּבָה מַמָּשׁ לָרָצוֹן הָעֶלְיוֹן — **these** organs **become an actual "chariot" for the Divine Will.**

מרכבה ממש לרצון העליון כגון היד המחלקת צדקה
לעניים או עושה מצוה אחרת. ורגלים המהלכות לדבר
מצוה וכן הפה ולשון שמדברי' דברי תורה והמוח
שמהרהר בד"ת וי"ש ובגדולת ה' ב"ה. וזהו שארז"ל
האבות הן הן המרכבה שכל אבריהם כולם היו
קדושים ומובדלים מענייני עוה"ז ולא נעשו מרכבה
רק לרצון העליון לבדו כל ימיהם: אך המחשבה

כְּגוֹן הַיָּד הַמְחַלֶּקֶת צְדָקָה לַעֲנִיִּים — For example, the hand which distributes charity to the poor, אוֹ עוֹשָׂה מִצְוָה אַחֶרֶת — or performs another *mitzvah,* וְרַגְלַיִם הַמְהַלְּכוֹת לִדְבַר מִצְוָה — or the feet that walk for a *mitzvah* activity, וְכֵן הַפֶּה וְלָשׁוֹן שֶׁמְּדַבְּרִים — or, similarly, the mouth and tongue which speak words of Torah, דִּבְרֵי תוֹרָה — וְהַמּוֹחַ שֶׁמְּהַרְהֵר בְּדִבְרֵי תוֹרָה וְיִרְאַת שָׁמַיִם וּבִגְדוּלַּת ה' בָּרוּךְ הוּא — or the brain which contemplates words of Torah or the reverence of Heaven, or the greatness of the blessed G-d.

The *Tanya* illustrates this idea with a citation from the *Midrash.*

וְזֶהוּ שֶׁאָמְרוּ רַבּוֹתֵינוּ זִכְרוֹנָם לִבְרָכָה הָאָבוֹת הֵן הֵן הַמֶּרְכָּבָה — And this is the meaning of our Sages' teaching, that *"the Patriarchs were genuinely a 'chariot'* to G-d" (*Genesis Rabah* 47:6; see above, chapter 18, p. 212).

"Chariot" refers not only to a surrender of the mind to G-d, but also of the body.

שֶׁכָּל אֵבְרֵיהֶם כּוּלָם הָיוּ קְדוֹשִׁים וּמוּבְדָּלִים מֵעִנְיָינֵי עוֹלָם הַזֶּה — Since all the Patriarchs' organs were sacred and detached from this-worldly concerns, וְלֹא נַעֲשׂוּ מֶרְכָּבָה רַק לָרָצוֹן הָעֶלְיוֹן לְבַדּוֹ כָּל יְמֵיהֶם — and, throughout all their days, their organs only acted as a "chariot" for the Divine will alone.

The *Tanya* is careful to distinguish here between the level of "chariot" achieved by the Patriarchs and the "chariot" brought about by *mitzvah*-observance of ordinary people. When we observe a *mitzvah*: a.) only the *particular organ* we make use of becomes a "chariot," and; b.) we are not observing *mitzvos* without interruption. But for the Patriarchs: a.) "all their limbs" were sacred and detached from this-worldly concerns"; and this was, b.) "throughout *all their days*," i.e., continuously (*Notes on Tanya*).

SECTION TWO: CONNECTION THROUGH TORAH

12TH SHEVAT REGULAR | 21ST SHEVAT LEAP

In chapter 5 we learned that the connection with G-d achieved through studying Torah is even more profound than the connection through *mitzvah* observance. The *Tanya* now picks up on this theme again, and will explain why the Torah experience is something even greater than a "chariot" to G-d.

וההרהור בד"ת שבמוח וכח הדבור בד"ת שבפה
שהם לבושי' הפנימים של נפש האלהית וכ"ש נפש
האלהית עצמה המלובשת בהם כולם מיוחדים ממש
ביחוד גמור ברצון העליון ולא מרכבה לבד כי רצון
העליון הוא הוא הדבר הלכה עצמה שמהרהר ומדבר

אַךְ הַמַּחֲשָׁבָה וְהַהִרְהוּר בְּדִבְרֵי תוֹרָה שֶׁבַּמּוֹחַ — **But thinking and contemplating words of Torah in your brain,** וְכֹחַ הַדִּבּוּר בְּדִבְרֵי תוֹרָה שֶׁבַּפֶּה — **or using your power of speech for words of Torah in your mouth,** falls in a different, higher category than *mitzvos* performed with the rest of your body.

שֶׁהֵם לְבוּשִׁים הַפְּנִימִים שֶׁל נֶפֶשׁ הָאֱלֹהִית — Torah study engages deeper parts of you, including thought and speech **which are the inner "garments" of your Divine Soul,** וְכָל שֶׁכֵּן נֶפֶשׁ הָאֱלֹהִית עַצְמָהּ הַמְלוּבֶּשֶׁת בָּהֶם — **and certainly your Divine Soul itself, which is "dressed" in these** "garments."

כּוּלָּם מְיוּחָדִים מַמָּשׁ בְּיִחוּד גָּמוּר בָּרָצוֹן הָעֶלְיוֹן — These inner garments, and the soul itself, **all merge *literally*, in complete union with the Divine will,** וְלֹא מֶרְכָּבָה לְבַד — **and they are not merely a "chariot."**

Through Torah study, your soul and its garments *actually merge* with the Divine will; in contrast to *mitzvos*, through which you ultimately remain distinct from the Divine will, just as a chariot remains separate from its rider.

כִּי רָצוֹן הָעֶלְיוֹן הוּא הוּא הַדָּבָר הֲלָכָה עַצְמָהּ שֶׁמְהַרְהֵר וּמְדַבֵּר בָּהּ — **Because the point of law which you think or talk about *is* the Divine Will.**

The key difference between *mitzvah*-acts and Torah is that a *mitzvah*-act *expresses* the Divine will, whereas Torah *is* the Divine will.

For example, consider the commandment (Divine will) to take an *esrog* (citron) on the festival of *Succos*, along with three other species of plants. When you do that, the Divine will expresses itself through the citron.

But if there was no such *mitzvah*, there would still be citrons in the world. And if the citron is taken on Passover, it does not express the Divine will. Clearly, the citron exists as an autonomous entity, which *under certain conditions* expresses the Divine will.

Now compare that with the Divine will itself, as expressed in the Torah: You shall take an *esrog* on *Succos!* (see *Leviticus* 23:40). If G-d had never willed this, the idea itself would not exist. The Torah's instruction is not merely a vehicle (chariot) which expresses the Divine will; it *is* the Divine will itself. So when you study that will,

PRACTICAL LESSONS

Torah study merges your inner "garments" of speech and action, and your soul itself, with G-d in total unity (more than *mitzvah* observance).

בה שכל ההלכות הן פרטי המשכות פנימיות רצון
העליון עצמו שכך עלה ברצונו ית' שדבר זה מותר
או כשר או פטור או זכאי או להפך וכן כל צרופי
אותיות תנ"ך הן המשכת רצונו וחכמתו המיוחדו' בא"ס

you achieve a deeper union with G-d than you do by observing a *mitzvah*, which is merely an *expression* of the will (see *Biurey Reb Shlomo Chaim*).

שֶׁכָּל הַהֲלָכוֹת הֵן פְּרָטֵי הַמְשָׁכוֹת פְּנִימִיּוּת רְצוֹן הָעֶלְיוֹן עַצְמוֹ — **For all the laws** of the Torah **are channels through which the inner Divine will itself flows.**

שֶׁכָּךְ עָלָה בִּרְצוֹנוֹ יִתְבָּרֵךְ שֶׁדָּבָר זֶה מוּתָּר אוֹ כָּשֵׁר אוֹ פָּטוּר אוֹ זַכַּאי — **When you study** Torah, your mind absorbs the idea **that it arose in His Will, that a certain entity is permissible (*mutar*), kosher** to eat, **exempt (*patur*), innocent (*zakai*)** in judgment, אוֹ לְהֶפֶךְ — **or the reverse,** *i.e.,* forbidden, non-kosher, obligated or guilty.

The Kabbalists perceived no detail of Jewish law as arbitrary. Even minutiae of the law convey the Divine will.

וְכֵן כָּל צֵרוּפֵי אוֹתִיּוֹת תּוֹרָה נְבִיאִים וּכְתוּבִים — **And, so too, the entire combination of letters that constitutes Torah** (Pentateuch), *Nevi'im* (Prophets) and *Ketuvim* (Writings), הֵן הַמְשָׁכַת רְצוֹנוֹ וְחָכְמָתוֹ — **are** channels of flow for **G-d's will and wisdom.**

In Jewish law, a particular *action* is an expression ("flow") of the Divine Will. In a sacred text, the *letters* act as the channels of flow.

הַמְיוּחָדוֹת בְּאֵין סוֹף בָּרוּךְ הוּא בְּתַכְלִית הַיִּחוּד — And that text is **merged in total union with the Blessed Infinite One.**

G-d is boundless, defying any concept that might contain or grasp Him. It seems counterintuitive, then, that Torah texts, which convey precise ideas through the use of specific letter-shapes, could be an authentic expression of their formless source.

But that, the Kabbalah teaches, is the miracle of Torah. Its every letter is a "container" for the infinite; a vessel in the world-of-form for the formlessness of G-d.

A CHASIDIC THOUGHT

Usually, the laws of the Torah are perceived as the instructions of a Higher Authority whom we are bound to follow. But in the Kabbalistic paradigm, the laws are also perceived as "channels of flow" through which Divine light and energy reach us. Not only do we *obey* G-d's will through the law, we also *receive* that will, as it flows into the universe through observing a particular precept.

ב"ה בתכלית היחוד שהוא היודע והוא המדע כו' וז"ש
דאורייתא וקב"ה כולא חד ולא אברין דמלכא לחוד
כפיקודין. ומאחר שרצון העליון המיוחד בא"ס ב"ה
בתכלית היחוד הוא בגילוי לגמרי ולא בהסתר פנים
כלל וכלל בנפש האלהית ולבושיה הפנימים שהם
מחשבתה ודבורה באותה שעה שהאדם עוסק בדברי
תורה הרי גם הנפש ולבושיה אלו מיוחדים ממש בא"ס
ב"ה באותה שעה בתכלית היחוד כיחוד דבורו

29A

שֶׁהוּא הַיוֹדֵעַ וְהוּא הַמַדֵּעַ כו' — As *Rambam* writes, **that He is** simultaneously **the knower, the power to know** and the knowledge, (see above, chapter 2, p. 46), *i.e.,* that G-d ("the knower") is totally one with the texts of the Torah ("the knowledge").

וְזֶהוּ שֶׁכָּתוּב דְּאוֹרַיְיתָא וְקוּדְשָׁא בְּרִיךְ הוּא כּוּלָא חַד — **And this is the meaning of the statement** from the *Zohar,* with which we began this chapter: ***"The Torah and G-d are totally one."***

וְלֹא אֲבָרִין דְּמַלְכָּא לְחוּד כְּפִיקוּדִין — The statement "totally one" means to say that the laws and texts of the Torah **are not merely "organs of the King,"** like the observed *mitzvos,* an "organ" referring to a separate entity which is devoted to G-d, like a chariot.

Mitzvos, when they are practically observed, fail to merge you with G-d in the highest mode possible, because: a.) the *mitzvos* are merely the "organs" of the King, and b.) they are performed by your outer "garment" of action.

Torah, on the other hand, is: a.) "Totally one" with G-d; and, b.) studied with your inner "garments" of speech and thought.

Only Torah study represents a complete merging with the Divine.

22ND SHEVAT LEAP

וּמֵאַחַר שֶׁרָצוֹן הָעֶלְיוֹן הַמְיוּחָד בְּאֵין סוֹף בָּרוּךְ הוּא בְּתַכְלִית הַיִּחוּד הוּא בְּגִילּוּי לְגַמְרֵי וְלֹא בְּהֶסְתֵּר פָּנִים כְּלָל וּכְלָל בַּנֶּפֶשׁ הָאֱלֹהִית — Now since the Divine Will, that is merged in total union with the Blessed Infinite One, is fully disclosed in the Divine Soul without any *"hiding of G-d's face"* at all, וּלְבוּשֶׁיהָ הַפְּנִימִים שֶׁהֵם מַחֲשַׁבְתָּה וְדִבּוּרָהּ — at the moment when you are involved with a Torah text, which engages your Divine Soul's **inner "garments,"** its thought and speech, בְּאוֹתָהּ שָׁעָה שֶׁהָאָדָם עוֹסֵק בְּדִבְרֵי תּוֹרָה הֲרֵי גַם הַנֶּפֶשׁ וּלְבוּשֶׁיהָ אֵלּוּ מְיוּחָדִים מַמָּשׁ בְּאֵין סוֹף בָּרוּךְ הוּא בְּאוֹתָהּ שָׁעָה בְּתַכְלִית הַיִּחוּד — it follows that your soul and its garments, too, are totally merged with the Blessed Infinite One at that moment.

In chapter 5 we learned that Torah study represents, *"a phenomenal merging experience (of two beings). There is no other merging experience like it."* What,

ומחשבתו של הקב"ה במהותו ועצמותו כנ"ל כי אין

then, is added here, in chapter 23, by stating, *"that the soul and her garments (of speech and action), too, are totally merged with the Blessed Infinite One at that moment"* of study?

The key innovation here is that Torah represents a disclosure of the Divine Will *"without any 'hiding of G-d's face' at all."* The *Tanya* draws on the nondual paradigm, introduced in chapters 20-22, with which we were not yet familiar in chapter 5.

In a nondual understanding of the universe, our goal is not to bridge the gap separating G-d from the universe; rather, we try to come to the realization that *there was no gap in the first place* (chapters 20-21). Even though our senses perceive a universe separate from G-d, that is only real from the perspective of G-d's "diminishments" and the "hiding of His face." If we are able to transcend that limited vision, we can come to a higher level of consciousness, that there has been no diminishment at all (chapter 22).

Our chapter then adds that, even if we have not yet reached this higher consciousness through meditation, it is a reality which has been implanted into the Torah. *"The Torah and G-d are totally one,"* says the *Zohar*, because the Torah represents the pure wisdom and will of G-d, devoid of any diminishments; a place where there has been no "hiding of the face."

PRACTICAL LESSONS

In Torah there is no "hiding of G-d's face." It is pristine, primordial wisdom that speaks from a higher, nondual reality.

With this in mind we can appreciate the subtle yet significant shift in perception from chapter 5 to chapter 23. In chapter 5, G-d and man are two separate entities, that come together in, *"a phenomenal merging experience."* But in chapter 23, the human mind merges with the Torah, a level of consciousness where there has been no "hiding of the face," *where there never was a separate existence from G-d in the first place.*

כְּיִחוּד דְּבוּרוֹ וּמַחֲשַׁבְתּוֹ שֶׁל הַקָּדוֹשׁ בָּרוּךְ הוּא בְּמַהוּתוֹ וְעַצְמוּתוֹ כַּנִּזְכָּר לְעֵיל

— **As we mentioned above** (chapter 21), **that G-d's thought and speech are totally one with His blessed essence and self,** so when your thought and speech are merged with the Torah, your faculties achieve **that same level of union.**

In chapter 21 we learned: *"G-d's speech is, for example, like the pre-linguistic source of human thought and speech, as it exists in potential, in chochmah and intellect or in a desire and craving of the heart, before rising from the heart to the brain, to be pondered upon linguistically.... This is an extremely precise analogy for how the Blessed Holy One's thought and speech remain totally one with His Blessed essence and self, even after His 'speech' has emerged, creating worlds, retaining the same level of unity with Him as it did before the worlds were created."*

שום דבר נפרד כי אם בהסתר פנים כנ"ל ולא עוד אלא
שיחודם הוא ביתר שאת ויתר עז מיחוד אור א"ס ב"ה
בעולמות עליונים מאחר שרצון העליון הוא בגילוי
ממש בנפש ולבושיה העוסקים בתורה שהרי הוא הוא
התורה עצמה וכל העולמות העליונים מקבלים חיותם
מאור וחיות הנמשך מהתורה שהיא רצונו וחכמתו

This is also true, the *Tanya* argues here, with G-d's "speech" in the Torah. G-d's infinite (formless) essence, is one with the text (form) of the Torah, so when your thought and speech are engaged with Torah, at that moment they are *totally* merged with G-d.

כִּי אֵין שׁוּם דָּבָר נִפְרָד כִּי אִם בְּהֶסְתֵּר פָּנִים — **Because nothing becomes separate** from G-d, **unless there is** *"hiding of G-d's face,"* — כַּנִּזְכָּר לְעֵיל — **as mentioned above** (chapter 22, pp. 250-51).

The Torah was never separate from G-d, as it did not suffer from the "hiding of G-d's face." Therefore it does not need to be reunited with Him. When we study the Torah, we merge our thought and speech in that overtly nondual energy, and absorb it.

SECTION THREE: EARTHLY TORAH AND HEAVENLY TORAH

The highest of the spiritual worlds is characterized by a transparency to the Divine, and does not suffer from the "hiding of G-d's face." The *Tanya* now addresses the question: What contains a higher disclosure of G-d, the highest spiritual world, or the Torah as it is manifest here in the lowest world?

וְלֹא עוֹד אֶלָּא שֶׁיִּחוּדָם — **And furthermore the merging** of the Divine Soul, and its "garments" of speech and thought with G-d, הוּא בְּיֶתֶר שְׂאֵת וְיֶתֶר עֹז מִיְּחוּד אוֹר אֵין סוֹף בָּרוּךְ הוּא בְּעוֹלָמוֹת עֶלְיוֹנִים — **is with** *"more dignity and more power"* (*Genesis* 49:3) **than the merging of the Blessed Infinite Light with** even **the upper,** most spiritual and transparent of **worlds.**

If Torah and the spiritual worlds are both compatible with the Infinite Light, why should Torah represent a *greater* disclosure?

מֵאַחַר שֶׁרָצוֹן הָעֶלְיוֹן הוּא בְּגִלּוּי מַמָּשׁ בַּנֶּפֶשׁ וּלְבוּשֶׁיהָ הָעוֹסְקִים בַּתּוֹרָה — **Because, when the** Divine **Soul and its garments are immersed in Torah, the Divine Will is fully disclosed in them,** שֶׁהֲרֵי הוּא הוּא הַתּוֹרָה עַצְמָהּ — **since,** as we have explained above (p. 264), **the Torah itself** *is* **the Divine Will,** and that is what is absorbed in the person's mind.

וְכָל הָעוֹלָמוֹת הָעֶלְיוֹנִים מְקַבְּלִים חַיּוּתָם מֵאוֹר וְחַיּוּת הַנִּמְשָׁךְ מֵהַתּוֹרָה — **Whereas the upper worlds** only *receive* their life-energy from the light and life-energy that is *drawn out* from the Torah.

יתֹ׳ כדכתיב כולם בחכמה עשית וא״כ החכמה שהיא
התורה למעלה מכולם והיא היא רצונו יתֹ׳ הנק׳ סובב
כל עלמין שהיא בחי׳ מה שאינו יכול להתלבש בתוך
עלמין רק מחיה ומאיר למעלה בבחי׳ מקיף והיא היא

G-d used the energy of Torah to create the worlds, and the worlds only exist for the sake of the Torah (above p. 257). So the "light and energy" present in the worlds is secondary: it is "for the sake of" the Torah.

Even if the upper worlds are fully transparent to the energy that creates them, they only contain secondary energy, and not primary energy, the type that enters your mind when you study the Torah itself.

The *Tanya* now cites proof that Torah energy created the worlds.

שֶׁהִיא רְצוֹנוֹ וְחָכְמָתוֹ יִתְבָּרֵךְ — Since the Torah, which **is His will and *chochmah,*** was the energy through which the world was created, כְּדִכְתִיב כּוּלָּם בְּחָכְמָה עָשִׂיתָ — **as the verse states, "*You made them all with chochmah*"** (*Psalms* 104:24), וְאִם כֵּן הַחָכְמָה שֶׁהִיא הַתּוֹרָה לְמַעְלָה מִכּוּלָּם — **so it follows that** G-d's *chochmah* (**which is the Torah), is higher than** the worlds, since it caused them.

The *Tanya* now takes the argument a stage further, suggesting that to say that the Divine will is "higher than the worlds" is an understatement.

וְהִיא הִיא רְצוֹנוֹ יִתְבָּרֵךְ — **And** this *chochmah,* the Torah, **is, in fact, the will of G-d,** הַנִּקְרָא סוֹבֵב כָּל עָלְמִין — **which is called *sovev-kol-almin*** by the *Zohar* (3, 225a).

In the Kabbalah, the term *sovev-kol-almin* (lit. "encircles-all-worlds") is used to refer to a light and energy that is *incompatible* with the created worlds. The light of *sovev* is too intense to engage with the worlds and become enmeshed with them, so as to provide energy to them. Therefore, *sovev-kol-almin* light metaphorically "encircles" the world, meaning that it cannot occupy the same metaphysical space as the world, due to its fundamental incompatibility (see *Etz Chaim* 1:2; Rabbi Naftali Hertz Bacharach, *Eimek Ha-Melech* 13:29).

שֶׁהִיא בְּחִינַת מַה שֶׁאֵינוֹ יָכוֹל לְהִתְלַבֵּשׁ בְּתוֹךְ עָלְמִין — *Sovev-kol-almin* **refers to the type of** Divine light and energy **which is unable to become enmeshed with the worlds** due to the light's intensity, רַק מְחַיֶּה וּמֵאִיר לְמַעְלָה — **and only provides energy and light** to the worlds indirectly and distantly, **from above,** בִּבְחִינַת מַקִּיף — **in a disengaged fashion.**

Even though the *sovev* light is generally incompatible with the worlds, some of its energy nevertheless does seep through to them. In fact, this is no small matter as it is the *sovev* energy that ultimately powers the creation of the worlds (through various filters and other processes). But due to its uncontainable character, the *sovev* light cannot interact directly with the worlds and instead influences them from a distance—hence its name, "encircles-all-worlds."

המתלבשת בנפש ולבושיה בבחי' גילוי ממש
כשעוסקים בד"ת ואע"ג דאיהו לא חזי כו' [ומשו' הכי
יכול לסבול משום דלא חזי משא"כ בעליונים]. ובזה
יובן למה גדלה מאד מעלת העסק בתורה יותר מכל
המצות ואפי' מתפלה שהיא יחוד עולמות עליונים

וְהִיא הִיא הַמִּתְלַבֶּשֶׁת בַּנֶּפֶשׁ וּלְבוּשֶׁיהָ בִּבְחִינַת גִּילּוּי מַמָּשׁ — **Yet** this incompatible, *sovev* light **is precisely what *does* become absorbed by, and fully disclosed in, the** Divine **Soul and its garments** of thought and speech, כְּשֶׁעוֹסְקִים בְּדִבְרֵי תוֹרָה — **at the time of Torah study.**

That is the miracle of a Torah text. It offers full disclosure of a Divine light and energy so powerful that it cannot be contained by the world; and yet that light and energy *has* been contained and made available to us in the sacred letters of the Torah.

Why, then, do our souls simply not expire when we read a Torah text?

וְאַף עַל גַּב דְּאִיהוּ לָא חָזֵי כוּ' — **"And even though they did not see** the vision, their *mazalos saw it"* (*Talmud, Megillah* 3a; see above, chapter 18, p. 213).

G-d arranged the universe in such a fashion that you remain unaware of the great influx of light to your soul during Torah study. It is only sensed subconsciously by your *mazal,* your "higher self."

[וּמִשּׁוּם הָכֵי יָכוֹל לִסְבּוֹל מִשּׁוּם דְּלָא חָזֵי — **And it is precisely because you** *"don't see it,"* **that you're able to withstand it.** If you *were* conscious of receiving an incompatible and overwhelming light, you would not survive the experience.

מַה שֶּׁאֵין כֵּן בָּעֶלְיוֹנִים] — **which is not the case in the upper worlds.**

The upper worlds, which are fully conscious of what they receive, could never withstand the spiritual exposure that you enjoy when reading a Torah text.

SECTION FOUR: TORAH — THE GREATEST RELIGIOUS EXPERIENCE

13TH SHEVAT REGULAR

וּבָזֶה יוּבַן לָמָּה גְּדָלָה מְאֹד מַעֲלַת הָעֵסֶק בַּתּוֹרָה יוֹתֵר מִכָּל הַמִּצְוֹת — **The above helps us to understand** the many sources in Jewish law which indicate that **Torah study is more virtuous than all the other** *mitzvos* (see *Mishnah, Peah* 1:1; *Talmud, Kidushin* 40a; *Mo'ed Katan* 9b), וַאֲפִילוּ מִתְּפִלָּה — **even** transcending the *mitzvah* of **prayer,** שֶׁהִיא יִחוּד עוֹלָמוֹת עֶלְיוֹנִים — **whose** spiritual influence is great, as stressed in the Kabbalah, that prayer **causes the upper worlds to merge** with higher layers of emanation, flooding the universe with Divine light (see *Zohar* 2, 213b).

This is because only Torah is literally "one with G-d" without any "hiding of the face" at all, as we have learned in this chapter.

וְהָא דְמִי שָׁאֵין תּוֹרָתוֹ אוּמָנָתוֹ צָרִיךְ לְהַפְסִיק הַיְינוּ
מֵאַחַר דְמַפְסִיק וּמְבַטֵּל בְּלָא"ה]. וּמִזֶה יוּכַל הַמַּשְׂכִּיל
לְהַמְשִׁיךְ עָלָיו יִרְאָה גְדוֹלָה בְּעָסְקוֹ בַּתּוֹרָה כְּשֶׁיִתְבּוֹנֵן
אֵיךְ שֶׁנַפְשׁוֹ וּלְבוּשֶׁיהָ שֶׁבְּמוֹחוֹ וּבְפִיו הֵם מְיוּחָדִי' מַמָּשׁ
בְּתַכְלִית הַיְחוּד בִּרְצוֹן הָעֶלְיוֹן וְאוֹר א"ס ב"ה מַמָּשׁ
הַמִּתְגַּלֶה בָּהֶם מַה שֶׁכָּל הָעוֹלָמוֹת עֶלְיוֹנִים וְתַחְתּוֹנִים
כְּלָא חֲשִׁיבֵי קַמֵיהּ וְכַאֵין וָאֶפֶס מַמָּשׁ עַד שֶׁאֵינוֹ מִתְלַבֵּשׁ
בְּתוֹכָם מַמָּשׁ אֶלָּא סוֹבֵב כָּל עָלְמִין בִּבְחִי' מַקִּיף
לְהַחֲיוֹת' עִיקַר חִיוּתָם רַק אֵיזוֹ הָאָרָה מִתְלַבֶּשֶׁת בְּתוֹכָם

29B

וְהָא דְמִי שָׁאֵין תּוֹרָתוֹ אוּמָנוּתוֹ צָרִיךְ לְהַפְסִיק] — **And as for the fact** that this seems to contradict the *Talmud's* **ruling (regarding a part-time Torah scholar) that he must stop** studying Torah to pray (*Talmud, Shabbos* 11a), which suggests that prayer transcends Torah in importance, הַיְינוּ מֵאַחַר דְמַפְסִיק וּמְבַטֵּל בְּלָאו הָכֵי — **this is** not because prayer is greater than Torah, but **because** the part-time scholar legitimately **stops** his studies **in any case and spends time devoid** of Torah (see *Rashi* ibid.). If he is inevitably going to stop studying, he might as well arrange his break at the time of prayer.

23RD SHEVAT LEAP

The *Tanya* now reflects practically on how we ought to take the message of this chapter to heart.

![PRACTICAL LESSONS]

PRACTICAL LESSONS

Your conscious mind doesn't perceive G-d's light in the Torah, otherwise you would expire when studying it.

וּמִזֶה יוּכַל הַמַּשְׂכִּיל לְהַמְשִׁיךְ עָלָיו יִרְאָה גְדוֹלָה בְּעָסְקוֹ בַּתּוֹרָה — **If you are wise, you can make use of this idea to become inspired with a great sense of reverence as you study Torah,** כְּשֶׁיִתְבּוֹנֵן אֵיךְ שֶׁנַפְשׁוֹ וּלְבוּשֶׁיהָ שֶׁבְּמוֹחוֹ וּבְפִיו — **by contemplating how your soul and its garments,** which express themselves **in your brain and in your mouth,** הֵם מְיוּחָדִים מַמָּשׁ בְּתַכְלִית הַיְחוּד בִּרְצוֹן הָעֶלְיוֹן **have literally merged in total oneness with the Divine will,** וְאוֹר אֵין סוֹף בָּרוּךְ הוּא מַמָּשׁ הַמִּתְגַּלֶה בָּהֶם — **and with the Blessed Infinite Light, literally, which is disclosed** in your soul and its garments.

מַה שֶׁכָּל הָעוֹלָמוֹת עֶלְיוֹנִים וְתַחְתּוֹנִים כְּלָא חֲשִׁיבֵי קַמֵיהּ — Then contemplate **how all the worlds, upper and lower, *"are considered zero in His presence"*** (*Zohar* 1, 11b), וּכַאֵין וָאֶפֶס מַמָּשׁ עַד שֶׁאֵינוֹ — **and are literally, *"null and void"*** (see *Isaiah* 40:17), מִתְלַבֵּשׁ בְּתוֹכָם מַמָּשׁ — **to the extent that** the Divine will **does not become substantially enmeshed in them,** אֶלָּא סוֹבֵב כָּל עָלְמִין בִּבְחִינַת מַקִּיף — **but is merely** *sovev-kol-almin* **in a disengaged fashion,** לְהַחֲיוֹתָם עִיקַר חִיוּתָם — **so as to give them their main life-energy,** רַק אֵיזוֹ הָאָרָה מִתְלַבֶּשֶׁת בְּתוֹכָם — **and only a glimmer**

מַה שֶּׁיְּכוֹלִים לַסְבּוֹל שֶׁלֹּא יִתְבַּטְּלוּ בִּמְצִיאוּת לְגַמְרֵי. וְזֶהוּ שֶׁכָּתוּב וַיְצַוֵּנוּ ה' אֶת כָּל הַחֻקִּים הָאֵלֶּה לְיִרְאָה אֶת ה' וְגוֹ' [וְעַל יִרְאָה גְדוֹלָה זוֹ אָמְרוּ אִם אֵין חָכְמָה אֵין יִרְאָה וְהַתּוֹרָה נִקְרֵאת אִצְטְלָה תַּרְעָא לְדַרְתָּא כְּמוֹ שֶׁ בִּמְ"א] אֶלָּא דְּלָאו כָּל מוֹחָא סָבִיל דָּא יִרְאָה כְּזוֹ. אַךְ גַּם מָאן

of that light **actually becomes enmeshed in** those worlds, מַה שֶּׁיְּכוֹלִים לַסְבּוֹל שֶׁלֹּא יִתְבַּטְּלוּ בִּמְצִיאוּת לְגַמְרֵי — and that minimal glimmer represents **the maximum they can withstand, without their existence becoming completely obliterated.**

The above "meditation" is essentially a summary of this chapter. The *Tanya* now adds another point.

וְזֶהוּ שֶׁכָּתוּב וַיְצַוֵּנוּ ה' אֶת כָּל הַחֻקִּים הָאֵלֶּה לְיִרְאָה אֶת ה' וְגוֹ' — **And this will** help us to explain **the verse, *"And G-d commanded us** to perform all these laws, in order to revere G-d"* (*Deuteronomy* 6:24).

The verse seems to have cause-and-effect the wrong way around. Surely, we first revere G-d and *as a result of that,* we choose to "perform all these laws"?

Evidently, there are two levels of reverence: 1.) A *basic* reverence necessary to inspire you to observe the laws of the Torah; and, 2.) the verse in Deuteronomy speaks of a *higher* level of reverence which follows *after* observance.

And it is this higher level of reverence you can reach through the above meditation; the awesome sense that, having studied Torah, *"your soul and her garments... have literally merged in total oneness with the Divine will."*

[וְעַל יִרְאָה גְדוֹלָה זוֹ אָמְרוּ אִם אֵין חָכְמָה אֵין יִרְאָה — **Of this higher reverence** the Sages said, *"If there's no wisdom, there's no reverence"* (*Mishnah, Avos* 3:17).

Here we have another source for the notion of two levels of reverence (one which leads to the observance of the Torah and one which results from it). The *Mishnah* states both that, *"If there's no reverence, there's no wisdom (Torah),"* referring to a lower level of reverence that inspires you to observe the Torah; and, *"if there's no wisdom, there's no reverence,"* suggesting a higher level of reverence which comes after the above meditation.

וְהַתּוֹרָה נִקְרֵאת אִצְטְלָה תַּרְעָא לְדַרְתָּא — **And, compared to** this higher level of reverence, **the Torah is called a** mere *"gateway to the dwelling"* (*Talmud, Yoma* 72b), i.e., the Torah brings you to this higher reverence, like a gateway that brings you into a building (*Rashi ibid.*).

כְּמוֹ שֶׁנִּתְבָּאֵר בְּמָקוֹם אַחֵר] — **As is explained elsewhere,** (see *Keser Shem Tov*, section 316).

אֶלָּא דְּלָאו כָּל מוֹחָא סָבִיל דָּא יִרְאָה כְּזוֹ — **However,** since it requires focused meditation on sublime concepts, **this** higher level of **reverence** is something *"not every mind can hold"* (*Tikunei Zohar* 116a; see *Shenei Luchos Ha-Bris,* p. 30b).

דלא סביל מוחו כלל יראה זו לא מינה ולא מקצתה
מפני פחיתות ערך נפשו בשרשה ומקורה במדרגות
תחתונים דעשר ספירות דעשיה אין יראה זו מעכבת
בו למעשה כמ"ש לקמן:

פרק כד וזה לעומת זה הן שס"ה מצות לא תעשה
דאורייתא וכל איסורי דרבנן מאחר

But this higher level of reverence is by no means necessary for worship, so you should not be troubled if it eludes you.

אַךְ גַּם מַאן דְּלָא סָבִיל מוֹחוֹ כְּלָל יִרְאָה זוֹ — **But even if your mind cannot hold this** higher **reverence,** לֹא מִינָהּ וְלֹא מִקְצָתָהּ — *"neither a part of it, nor a fraction of it"* (*Talmud, Sotah* 5a), מִפְּנֵי פְּחִיתוּת עֵרֶךְ נַפְשׁוֹ בְּשָׁרְשָׁהּ וּמְקוֹרָהּ — it's probably **due to the poor standing of your soul's root and source,** בְּמַדְרֵגוֹת תַּחְתּוֹנוֹת דְּעֶשֶׂר סְפִירוֹת דַּעֲשִׂיָּה — **somewhere in the lower echelons of the ten** *sefiros* of the lowest of the worlds, **the World of** *Asiyah.*

אֵין יִרְאָה זוֹ מְעַכֶּבֶת בּוֹ לְמַעֲשֶׂה — The failure to reach **this** higher **reverence does not in any way invalidate your** Torah **observance,** כְּמוֹ שֶׁיִּתְבָּאֵר לְקַמָּן — **as will be explained below,** in chapter 41, p. 506.

CHAPTER 24

DON'T BE DELUSIONAL

SECTION ONE: WHY EVERY PROHIBITION IS LIKE IDOL WORSHIP

14TH SHEVAT REGULAR | 24TH SHEVAT LEAP

Following our discussion of the positive *mitzvos* in the previous chapter, we will now turn to the prohibitions, which, spiritually speaking, have the opposite effect of the positive commands.

וְזֶה לְעוּמַּת זֶה — And *"G-d has made* **one opposite the other"** (*Ecclesiastes* 7:14), הֵן שס"ה מִצְוֹת לֹא תַעֲשֶׂה דְּאוֹרַיְיתָא — namely, the **365** *mitzvos* **of the Torah which are prohibitions,** וְכָל אִיסּוּרֵי דְּרַבָּנָן — **as well as all the prohibitions of Rabbinic law.**

How are these the "mirror image," spiritually speaking, of the positive commands?

שֶׁהֵן נֶגֶד רְצוֹנוֹ וְחָכְמָתוֹ ית' וְהֶפְכָּם מַמָּשׁ הֵם נִפְרָדִים
מִיְחוּדוֹ וְאַחְדוּתוֹ ית' בְּתַכְלִית הַפֵּירוּד מַמָּשׁ כְּמוֹ הַסִּטְרָא אַחֲרָא
וְהַקְּלִיפָּה הַנִּקְרֵאת ע"ז וֵאלֹהִים אֲחֵרִים מֵחֲמַת הֶסְתֵּר פָּנִים
שֶׁל רָצוֹן הָעֶלְיוֹן כַּנִּזְכָּר לְעֵיל. וְכֵן ג' לְבוּשֵׁי הַנֶּפֶשׁ שֶׁמִּקְּלִיפַּת

מֵאַחַר שֶׁהֵן נֶגֶד רְצוֹנוֹ וְחָכְמָתוֹ יִתְבָּרֵךְ — **Because these** Biblical and Rabbinic prohibitions are acts which **are against** G-d's **will and wisdom,** וְהֶפְכָּם מַמָּשׁ — **and they are the very opposite of** what He wants.

The *Tanya* now frames the discussion in terms of the nondual idea, which we learned in the previous chapters.

הֵם נִפְרָדִים מִיְחוּדוֹ וְאַחְדוּתוֹ יִתְבָּרֵךְ — **They** are acts **which have splintered from** G-d's **nondual** reality of **oneness,** בְּתַכְלִית הַפֵּירוּד מַמָּשׁ — **in a literal, complete detachment.**

In chapter 23 we learned that Torah and *mitzvos* represents a worldly "packaging" of nondual reality. Whether you are conscious of it or not, when you study Torah and observe *mitzvos*, your soul, mind and body are in a "place" of nondual energy, a Divine light which never suffered from any "diminishment."

Here, in chapter 24, we learn that prohibitions represent the very opposite of *mitzvos*: they are acts which represent a complete rejection of the nondual reality, affirming instead separate consciousness and detached reality.

כְּמוֹ הַסִּטְרָא אַחֲרָא וְהַקְּלִיפָּה הַנִּקְרֵאת עֲבוֹדָה זָרָה וֵאלֹהִים אֲחֵרִים — In this sense, the prohibitions **are like the** *sitra achra* **and** *kelipah* **which are called idolatry and "other gods,"** מֵחֲמַת הֶסְתֵּר פָּנִים שֶׁל רָצוֹן הָעֶלְיוֹן — **since their** existence is a product of the *"hiding of G-d's face,"* an eclipse **of the Divine will,** כַּנִּזְכָּר לְעֵיל — **as mentioned above,** chapter 22.

In the nondual paradigm, rejecting "idolatry" doesn't only mean you deny the existence of any *deity* outside G-d; it means that you reject the notion of *anything* existing outside G-d (see chapter 22). A prohibition of the Torah and "idolatry" are essentially coming from the same world view. They affirm: separateness and detachment from G-d are real.

In chapter 23 we learned that when a person does a *mitzvah*, his soul, "garments," as well as his body become a "chariot" to the Divine will, and merge with the sublime energy of G-d's nondual oneness. Now the *Tanya* will teach us that when a person transgresses a prohibition, the reverse happens: his soul, "garments," and his body merge with the powers of separateness and *kelipah*.

PRACTICAL LESSONS

Any transgression, detaches you completely from G-d at that moment, just like idolatry.

נוגה שבישראל שהם מחשבה דבור ומעשה המלובשי׳
בסס״ה ל״ת דאורייתא ודרבנן וכן מהות הנפש עצמה
המלובשת בלבושיה כולם מיוחדים ממש בס״א וקליפ׳
זו הנק׳ ע״ז ולא עוד אלא שבטלים וטפלים אליה וגרועים
ופחותים ממנה מאד כי היא אינה מלובשת בגוף חומרי

וְכֵן ג׳ לְבוּשֵׁי הַנֶּפֶשׁ שֶׁמִּקְלִיפַּת נוֹגַהּ שֶׁבְּיִשְׂרָאֵל — **And similarly, the three "garments" of** the Animal **Soul (in Israel), which are from** *kelipas nogah* (see chapter 7, p. 92), שֶׁהֵם הַמְלוּבָּשִׁים — the "garments" of **thought, speech and action,** מַחֲשָׁבָה דְּבוּר וּמַעֲשֶׂה בְּסַס״ה ל״ת תַּעֲשֶׂה דְּאוֹרַיְיתָא וּדְרַבָּנָן — **which are engaged in** any of **the 365 Torah or Rabbinic prohibitions,** וְכֵן מַהוּת הַנֶּפֶשׁ עַצְמָהּ הַמְלוּבֶּשֶׁת בִּלְבוּשֶׁיהָ — **and the core of the** Animal **Soul itself, that is enmeshed in those garments,** כּוּלָּם מְיוּחָדִים מַמָּשׁ בְּסִטְרָא אָחֳרָא וּקְלִיפָּה זוֹ — **all literally merge with the** utterly impure *sitra achra* and *kelipah,* when that prohibition is transgressed.

As we learned in chapter 7, the Animal Soul is built from *kelipas nogah* ("radiant *kelipah*"), an energy which, while tending to self-preoccupation, is capable of awakening to G-d. But when a prohibition is carried out, the soul of *kelipas nogah* and its "garments" are dragged down into the realm of the three utterly impure *kelipos,* where separate consciousness and denial of G-d's presence are the only available reality.

הַנִּקְרָאת עֲבוֹדָה זָרָה — These utterly impure *kelipos,* **being called "idolatry"** due to their perception of complete detachment from G-d.

SECTION TWO: TO BE WORSE THAN KELIPAH

The *Tanya* will now make the bold assertion that, if you transgress a prohibition, you are *worse* than *kelipah* itself.

Ultimately, these impure forces were created by G-d for a reason (to give you free choice) and they're just doing their job. You, on the other hand, should know better than to be sucked into their false allure.

וְלֹא עוֹד אֶלָּא שֶׁבְּטֵלִים וּטְפֵלִים אֵלֶיהָ — **And what is more,** when you transgress a prohibition, your Animal Soul and its garments **are subordinated to** the impure *kelipah* **and become its accessory,** וּגְרוּעִים וּפְחוּתִים מִמֶּנָּה מְאֹד — **and** so they are really **much worse and lower than** the impure *kelipah* itself.

The *Tanya* now offers two explanations why through transgressing a prohibition, you are worse than *kelipah* itself.

כִּי הִיא אֵינָה מְלוּבֶּשֶׁת בְּגוּף חוּמְרִי — **Because** 1.) The force of *kelipah* **has no physical body,** and by transgressing you endow it with one, allowing yourself to become a vehicle of expression for *kelipah*.

ויודעת את רבונה ואינה מורדת בו לפעול פעולתה
במשלחת מלאכי רעים שלה שלא בשליחותו של
מקום ב"ה ח"ו וכמאמר בלעם לא אוכל לעבור את פי
ה' וגו' ואף שנקרא ע"ז הא קרו ליה אלהא דאלהיא   30A
ואינם יכולי' לעבור כלל על רצונו ית' כי יודעי' ומשיגים
שהוא חיותם וקיומם שיונקים מבחי' אחוריים דאחוריי'

And the second reason why you become worse than the *kelipah* is:

וְיוֹדַעַת אֶת רִבּוֹנָה וְאֵינָה מוֹרֶדֶת בּוֹ — **And** 2.) The *kelipah* **"knows its Master and doesn't rebel against Him."**

The *Tanya's* reference here mirrors the Sages' description of a deviant Jew, who *"knows his Master (G-d) and intentionally rebels against Him,"* (*Toras Kohanim, Leviticus* 26:14). *Kelipah,* on the other hand, *"knows its Master and doesn't* rebel against Him."

While *kelipah* energy is unconscious of G-d's presence, it is aware of G-d's ultimate existence and authority, and never disobeys Him. So, in this sense, the transgressor is worse than *kelipah* itself, since a transgression *is* an act of disobedience against G-d, violating His will.

The — לִפְעוֹל פְּעוּלָתָהּ בְּמִשְׁלַחַת מַלְאֲכֵי רָעִים שֶׁלָּהּ שֶׁלֹּא בִּשְׁלִיחוּתוֹ שֶׁל מָקוֹם בָּרוּךְ הוּא *kelipah* does not **do its job of** *"sending out negative agents"* (*Psalms* 78:49), **without being told to do so by G-d,** חַס וְשָׁלוֹם — **G-d forbid.**

וּכְמַאֲמַר בִּלְעָם לֹא אוּכַל לַעֲבוֹר אֶת פִּי ה' וְגוֹ' — **As Bila'am,** who acted as an agent of the impure forces, **said,** *"I cannot transgress the word of G-d etc."* (*Numbers* 22:18).

But if this is the case, how can *kelipah,* which obeys G-d, be termed "idolatry"? Surely, idolatry represents disobedience towards G-d?

וְאַף שֶׁנִּקְרָא עֲבוֹדָה זָרָה — **And even though** *kelipah* **is called "idolatry,"** that is only because *kelipah* denies the presence of G-d *within itself;* but it does not deny G-d as the distant cause of the universe, הָא קָרוּ לֵיהּ אֱלָהָא דֶאֱלָהַיָּא — and idolators recognize this fact, and, *"They call Him (G-d) the 'G-d of gods'"* (*Talmud, Menachos* 110a), as we shall see below.

וְאֵינָם יְכוֹלִים לַעֲבוֹר כְּלָל עַל רְצוֹנוֹ יִתְבָּרֵךְ — **But** the *kelipos* **are totally unable to transgress G-d's will,** כִּי יוֹדְעִים וּמַשִּׂיגִים שֶׁהוּא חַיּוּתָם וְקִיּוּמָם — **because they know and understand that He is their life-energy and sustenance.**

Drawing from our discussion in chapter 22 (pp. 249-50), the *Tanya* reminds us how exactly the *kelipos* receive their life-energy.

שֶׁיּוֹנְקִים מִבְּחִינַת אֲחוֹרַיִים דַּאֲחוֹרַיִים שֶׁל רָצוֹן הָעֶלְיוֹן בָּרוּךְ הוּא — **Since they suck their** life-force **from the most external part of the Divine will's "behind,"** הַמַּקִּיף עֲלֵיהֶם — **which encompasses them** in a disengaged fashion.

של רצון העליון ב"ה המקיף עליהם אלא שיניקתם
וחיותם שבתוכם היא בבחי' גלות בתוכם להחשיב
עצמן אלהות והרי זו כפירה באחדותו אבל מ"מ אינן
כופרים וכחשו בה' לגמרי ולומר לא הוא אלא דקרו ליה
אלהא דאלהיא דהיינו חיותם וקיומם הנמשך ויורד
עליהם מרצונו ית' ולכן אינן עוברין רצונו ית' לעולם.
וא"כ האדם העובר על רצונו ית' הוא גרוע ופחות הרבה
מאד מהס"א וקליפה הנקראת ע"ז ואלהים אחרים והוא

While the *kelipos'* relationship with G-d is a distant one (they draw only from G-d's "behind," and 'in a disengaged fashion' — see chapter 22 ibid.), ultimately, they know where their sustenance comes from.

אֶלָּא שֶׁיְּנִיקָתָם וְחִיּוּתָם שֶׁבְּתוֹכָם הִיא בִּבְחִינַת גָּלוּת בְּתוֹכָם לְהַחֲשִׁיב עַצְמָן אֱלֹהוּת — **And they only consider themselves as gods because** they are unconscious of **the life-energy sucked** *inside them,* **which remains in a state of exile,** וַהֲרֵי זוּ כְּפִירָה בְּאַחְדוּתוֹ — and this denial of the Divine energy within them **constitutes a denial of** G-d's nondual **oneness.**

אֲבָל מִכָּל מָקוֹם אֵינָן כּוֹפְרִים וְכִחֲשׁוּ בַּה' לְגַמְרֵי וְלוֹמַר לֹא הוּא — **But, nevertheless they do not deny or repudiate G-d completely, and** *"say that He is not"* (Jeremiah 5:12), אֶלָּא דְּקָרוּ לֵיה אֱלָהָא דֶּאֱלָהַיָּא — **rather,** *"They call Him (G-d) the 'G-d of gods,'"* דְּהַיְינוּ חִיּוּתָם וְקִיּוּמָם הַנִּמְשָׁךְ וְיוֹרֵד עֲלֵיהֶם מֵרְצוֹנוֹ יִתְבָּרֵךְ — **recognizing that their life-energy and sustenance is derived from His will, which flows down** to them, from a distance (see chapter 23, p. 252).

וְלָכֵן אֵינָן עוֹבְרִין רְצוֹנוֹ יִתְבָּרֵךְ לְעוֹלָם — **And that is why they never violate His Will.**

The *kelipos* only resemble idolatry in the sense that they deny the presence of G-d within themselves. They do not, however, deny the fact that G-d exists, which is why they will never disobey Him.

וְאִם כֵּן — **And if this is the case,** that the *kelipos* will never disobey G-d, הָאָדָם הָעוֹבֵר עַל רְצוֹנוֹ יִתְבָּרֵךְ הוּא גָּרוּעַ וּפָחוּת הַרְבֵּה מְאֹד מֵהַסִּטְרָא אָחֲרָא וּקְלִיפָּה — **it follows that the person who violates G-d's will, is worse and much lower than the** *sitra achra*

A CHASIDIC THOUGHT

A belief in monotheism affirms that nothing happens in the universe without being orchestrated by G-d. Though negative occurrences in the universe may be through *kelipah's* agency, *kelipah* has no independent power and always follows the direct command of G-d.

בתכלי' הפירוד מיחודו ואחדותו של הקב"ה יותר ממנה
וכאלו כופר באחדותו יותר ממנה ח"ו. וכמ"ש בע"ח
שער מ"ב סוף פ"ד שהרע שבעו"הז החומרי הוא שמרי
הקליפות הגסות כו' והוא תכלית הבירור וכו' ולכן כל
מעשה עו"הז קשים ורעים והרשעים גוברים בו וכו':

and *kelipah* which will not violate G-d's will, הַנִּקְרֵאת עֲבוֹדָה זָרָה וֵאלֹהִים אֲחֵרִים —
and is called "idolatry" and "other gods."

וְהוּא בְּתַכְלִית הַפֵּירוּד מִיחוּדוֹ וְאַחְדוּתוֹ שֶׁל הַקָּדוֹשׁ בָּרוּךְ הוּא יוֹתֵר מִמֶּנָה — So the
transgressor **is utterly disconnected from G-d's nondual oneness, more than** the
kelipah itself, וּכְאִלּוּ כּוֹפֵר בְּאַחְדוּתוֹ יוֹתֵר מִמֶּנָה — **as if he denied G-d's oneness more
than** the *kelipah,* חַס וְשָׁלוֹם — **G-d forbid.**

How are human beings in this world capable of something "much lower and
worse" than the *kelipos* themselves?

וּכְמוֹ שֶׁכָּתוּב בְּעֵץ חַיִּים שַׁעַר מ"ב סוֹף פֶּרֶק ד' שֶׁהָרַע שֶׁבָּעוֹלָם
הַזֶּה הַחוּמְרִי הוּא — **As stated in *Etz Chaim,* section 42,
end of chapter 4, that the evil in this physical world is,**
שִׁמְרֵי הַקְּלִיפּוֹת הַגַּסּוֹת כוּ' וְהוּא תַּכְלִית הַבֵּירוּר וְכוּ' — **"the
dregs of the coarse kelipos, left over *at the very end of
the refinement process etc."***

PRACTICAL LESSONS

Kelipah doesn't
disobey G-d. So,
if you do disobey
Him, you're more
distant from G-d
than evil itself.

Passing down the spiritual worlds, there is a "refinement process" where most of the good is retained
above, and the "dregs" are sent down to the next world.
Upon reaching this physical world, all that is left are
dregs.

Since the *kelipos* themselves are a spiritual force
rooted in a world above our own, they exist in a purer,
more truthful place and consequently, are incapable of disobeying G-d. This physical world, on the other hand, which consists of "dregs" left over after all the good
has been extracted by the upper worlds, is a place of greater Divine eclipse.

וְלָכֵן כָּל מַעֲשֵׂה עוֹלָם הַזֶּה קָשִׁים וְרָעִים וְהָרְשָׁעִים גּוֹבְרִים בּוֹ וְכוּ' — **And *"that is why all
the affairs of this world are tough and evil, and wicked men prevail etc.,"*** (*ibid.*).

SECTION THREE: HOW TO AVOID TRANSGRESSION

15TH SHEVAT REGULAR

For the remainder of this chapter (and in the following chapter), the *Tanya* returns
to a question posed in chapter 18 which has not been fully answered: How can the
Torah imply that worshiping G-d is *"very much"* within reach?

וְלָכֵן אָמְרוּ רַזַ"ל עַל פָּסוּק כִּי תִשְׂטֶה אִשְׁתּוֹ אֵין אָדָם עוֹבֵר עֲבֵירָה וְכוּ' דְאַפִּי' אִשָּׁה הַמְנָאֶפֶת שֶׁדַּעְתָּהּ קַלָּה הָיְתָה מוֹשֶׁלֶת בְּרוּחַ תַּאֲוָתָהּ לוּלֵי רוּחַ שְׁטוּת שֶׁבָּהּ הַמְכַסֶּה וּמַסְתִּיר וּמַעֲלִי' אֶת הָאַהֲבָה מְסוּתֶּרֶת שֶׁבְּנַפְשָׁהּ הָאֱלֹהִית לִדְבְּקָה בֶּאֱמוּנַת ה' וְיִחוּדוֹ וְאַחְדוּתוֹ וְלֹא לִיפָּרֵד

In chapters 18-19 the *Tanya* answered that worshiping G-d is "very much within reach," because: a.) We naturally have the power of *chochmah* in our souls; and b.) *chochmah* is a direct "window" to G-d that enables us to look beyond ourselves and our egos. *Chochmah,* we learned, surfaces at times of crisis, such as when faced with forced conversion. But, this left us with the question: How do I access my *chochmah* on a day-to-day basis?

To answer this question, the *Tanya* launched into a long discussion of the nondual idea. We learned that there are only two perceptions of reality: a.) "consciousness," that everything is an expression of G-d (chapters 20-21); and b.) "unconsciousness" of G-d's presence, due to a "hiding of G-d's face" (chapter 22). Finally we learned that positive *mitzvos* are an expression of the reality of "consciousness" (chapter 23), while transgressions are a result of "unconsciousness" (chapter 24).

By saying that worshiping G-d is "very much within reach," the *Tanya's* assertion is that "consciousness" is possible at any time, and "unconsciousness" can always be eliminated (through *chochmah*). To demonstrate that, the *Tanya* will have to show us how the same process by which *chochmah* is accessed during emergencies, such as forced conversions, can be reproduced at any time and any place.

וְלָכֵן אָמְרוּ רַבּוֹתֵינוּ זִכְרוֹנָם לִבְרָכָה עַל פָּסוּק כִּי תִשְׂטֶה אִשְׁתּוֹ — **And that is why,** commenting on the verse, **"If (a man's) wife will go astray (sisteh)"** with another man (*Numbers* 5:12), **our Sages taught,** אֵין אָדָם עוֹבֵר עֲבֵירָה וְכוּ' — **"A man will not commit a sin** unless a delusional spirit (ruach shtus) enters him" (*Talmud, Sotah* 3a).

The Sages' assertion that *every* sin is caused by "delusion" and deceptive rationalizations seems, at first glance, exaggerated. Surely some sins are simply the result of overwhelming passions which lead a person to consciously and willingly violate Torah law?

The *Tanya* now argues that this is not the case, and, in fact, every sin is the result of "delusion" and "unconsciousness."

דַּאֲפִילוּ אִשָּׁה הַמְנָאֶפֶת שֶׁדַּעְתָּהּ קַלָּה הָיְתָה מוֹשֶׁלֶת בְּרוּחַ תַּאֲוָתָהּ — **For even** someone at a low spiritual level, such as **a weak-minded adulteress, could have controlled her lustful urges,** לוּלֵי רוּחַ שְׁטוּת שֶׁבָּהּ — **were it not for the "delusional spirit" within her,** הַמְכַסֶּה וּמַסְתִּיר וּמַעֲלִים אֶת הָאַהֲבָה מְסוּתֶּרֶת שֶׁבְּנַפְשָׁהּ הָאֱלֹהִית — **that covers, hides and conceals the "dormant love" in her Divine Soul.**

לִדְבְּקָה בֶּאֱמוּנַת ה' וְיִחוּדוֹ וְאַחְדוּתוֹ — **If disclosed, that "dormant love" would enable her to connect with her natural faith in G-d, His nonduality and His oneness,**

ח"ו מאחדותו אפי' נוטלים את נפשה ממנה לעבוד ע"ז
ח"ו ואפי' בהשתחואה לבדה בלי שום אמונה בלב כלל
וכ"ש לכבוש היצר ותאות הניאוף שהם יסורים קלים
ממיתה ה' ישמרנו וההפרש שאצלה בין איסור ניאוף

וְלֹא לִיפָּרֵד חַס וְשָׁלוֹם מֵאַחְדוּתוֹ — **so as not to become detached from His oneness, G-d forbid.**

As we learned in chapter 18, the "dormant love," which often awakens when a person is confronted with a life-or-death test of faith, is extremely powerful. It can inspire a person to give up his or her life rather than transgress.

אֲפִילוּ נוֹטְלִים אֶת נַפְשָׁהּ מִמֶּנָּה לַעֲבוֹד עֲבוֹדָה זָרָה חַס וְשָׁלוֹם — If given a test of faith **to worship idols, G-d forbid,** this same adulteress would have, in all likelihood, re-sisted transgressing, **even at the cost of her life,** וַאֲפִילוּ בְּהִשְׁתַּחֲוָאָה לְבַדָּהּ בְּלִי שׁוּם אֱמוּנָה בַּלֵּב כְּלָל — she would have **even** given her life rather than **offer an** "empty" **bow** to an idol, **in which she didn't believe at all in her heart,** (see p. 229).

The *Tanya* marvels at the inconsistency here:

וְכָל שֶׁכֵּן לִכְבּוֹשׁ הַיֵּצֶר וְתַאֲוַת הַנִּיאוּף — **Certainly, then, she could overcome the temptation and desire for adultery,** שֶׁהֵם יִסּוּרִים קַלִים מִמִּיתָה — a sacrifice which is **easier than suffering death,** ה' יִשְׁמְרֵנוּ — **may G-d spare us!**

Passing over the opportunity for an adulterous union, which she is not prepared to do, is a far smaller sacrifice than death, which she probably *would* be willing to do if put to the test, like so many other Jews. Why is she unwilling to make a relatively small sacrifice of a one-time pleasure, and yet, in another situation, she would be willing to sacrifice all future pleasures?

Clearly, a "delusional spirit" is at work to inspire such an inconsistency!

The *Tanya's* argument here, that any transgression might be avoided by contem-plating one's willingness to die for G-d, follows a pas-sage in *Sefer Chasidim* by Rabbi Yehudah "*Ha-Chasid*" of Regensburg (1150-1217), a German pietist and mystic.

"When something comes your way which is against G-d's will... or your 'impulse to evil' pressures you to transgress—contemplate that if you were faced with forced conversion, you would undergo torture or death for G-d.... Now if you would choose death over life, then all the more so should you resist your 'impulse to evil,' for this comparatively small matter" (*Sefer Chasidim,* section 154).

The *Tanya* now suggests how the "impulse to evil" might attempt to counteract this argument.

PRACTICAL LESSONS

The "delusion" of your Animal Soul is the misguided thought that a transgression is not a complete detachment from G-d.

לאיסור השתחואה לע"ז הוא ג"כ רוח שטות דקליפה
המלבשת לנפש האלהית עד בחי' חכמה שבה ולא עד
בכלל מפני אור ה' המלובש בחכמה כנ"ל. אבל
באמת לאמיתו אפי' עבירה קלה הרי העוברה עובר
על רצון העליון ב"ה והוא בתכלית הפירוד מיחודו
ואחדותו ית' יותר מס"א וקליפה הנקרא' אלהים אחרי'
וע"ז ממש ויותר מכל הדברים הנשפעים ממנה בע"הז
שהם בהמות טמאות וחיות ועופות טמאים ושקצים

30B

וְהַהֶפְרֵשׁ שֶׁאֶצְלָהּ בֵּין אִיסוּר נִיאוּף לְאִיסוּר הִשְׁתַּחֲוָאָה לַעֲבוֹדָה זָרָה — **And the distinction she** presumably **makes** in her mind **between the prohibition of bowing to an idol and that of adultery,** arguing that the latter is a far less severe transgression and is therefore "tolerable," הוּא גַם כֵּן רוּחַ שְׁטוּת דִּקְלִיפָּה — this argument **is also from the "delusional spirit" of** *kelipah.*

As we have seen, *any* transgression of the Torah, Biblical or Rabbinic, represents a profound disconnection from G-d. It is true that some transgressions have more grave *consequences* than others, but when we speak of *violating the Divine will*, every transgression shares that quality equally. To think otherwise is delusional.

Why is the "delusional spirit" effective when it comes to adultery, but it fails when it comes to an ultimate test of faith, such as bowing to idols?

הַמַּלְבֶּשֶׁת לַנֶּפֶשׁ הָאֱלֹהִית עַד בְּחִינַת חָכְמָה שֶׁבָּהּ — Because the "delusional spirit" **can obscure the Divine Soul's influence** only **up to the level of** *chochmah,* וְלֹא עַד בְּכְלָל — that is, **up to but not including** *chochmah* (see pp. 225-6).

מִפְּנֵי אוֹר ה' הַמְלוּבָּשׁ בַּחָכְמָה — And the reason why the "delusional spirit" can't obscure *chochmah* is **because of the Divine light that is present in** *chochmah* which enables *chochmah* to see truth directly and reject all rationalizations, כַּנִּזְכָּר לְעֵיל — **as mentioned above** (p. 215).

אֲבָל בֶּאֱמֶת לַאֲמִיתוֹ — **But in actual reality,** the idea that adultery is a more "tolerable" transgression is an unfounded rationalization, אֲפִילוּ עֲבֵירָה קַלָּה הֲרֵי הָעוֹבְרָה — because **even with a minor transgression, the perpetrator violates the Divine will,** עוֹבֵר עַל רְצוֹן הָעֶלְיוֹן בָּרוּךְ הוּא — and וְהוּא בְּתַכְלִית הַפֵּירוּד מִיִּחוּדוֹ וְאַחְדוּתוֹ יִתְבָּרֵךְ — **and is thereby detached completely from G-d's nondual** reality **and oneness.**

יוֹתֵר מִסְּטְרָא אַחֲרָא וּקְלִיפָּה — In fact, as we have learned above (in section 2), the transgressor is **even more** detached from G-d **than** *sitra achra* **and the** *kelipah* itself, הַנִּקְרֵאת אֱלֹהִים אֲחֵרִים וַעֲבוֹדָה זָרָה מַמָּשׁ — forces so distant from G-d that they **are referred to as "other gods" and literal "idolatry."**

וְיוֹתֵר מִכָּל הַדְּבָרִים הַנִּשְׁפָּעִים מִמֶּנָּה בְּעוֹלָם הַזֶּה — The transgressor is also lower than **all those things in this world which are powered by** *kelipah,* שֶׁהֵם בְּהֵמוֹת טְמֵאוֹת

ורמשים וכמאמר יתוש קדמך פי' דאף יתוש שמכניס
ואינו מוציא שהיא קליפ' היותר תחתונה ורחוקה מבחי'
הקדושה המשפעת בתכלית הריחוק קודמת לאיש
החוטא בהשתלשלות וירידת החיות מרצון העליון ב"ה
וכ"ש שאר בעלי חיים הטמאים ואפי' חיות רעות
שכולם אינם משנים תפקידם ופקודתו ית' שמרה רוחם

וְחַיּוֹת וְעוֹפוֹת טְמֵאִים וּשְׁקָצִים וּרְמָשִׂים — **namely non-kosher cattle, wild animals, and non-kosher birds, insects and reptiles.**

וְכַמַּאֲמָר יַתּוּשׁ קְדָמָךְ — **As the saying goes, "The mosquito preceded you!"** (*Talmud, Sanhedrin* 38a; see *Etz Chaim* section 42, chapter 3).

The *Talmud* teaches that in the Biblical account of creation, man was formed last to endow him with a sense of humility. As soon as man becomes arrogant, he can be reminded: "The mosquito preceded you."

Based on the insight of this chapter, the *Tanya* offers a deeper insight into the *Talmud's* words.

פֵּירוּשׁ דְּאַף יַתּוּשׁ שֶׁמַּכְנִיס וְאֵינוֹ מוֹצִיא — **Meaning that even the mosquito, which** is the most "selfish" creature of the Animal Kingdom in that **"it has an orifice for ingesting but not for excreting"** (*Talmud, Gittin* 56b). שֶׁהִיא קְלִיפָּה הַיּוֹתֵר תַּחְתּוֹנָה — indicating **that it is** powered by **the very lowest** and most selfish *kelipah,* וּרְחוֹקָה מִבְּחִינַת הַקְּדוּשָׁה — **and is** therefore **distant from the powers of holiness,** הַמַּשְׁפַּעַת בְּתַכְלִית הָרִיחוּק — the hallmark of holiness being the *opposite* of selfishness, **the willingness to give,** even to those who are very far, קוֹדֶמֶת לָאִישׁ הַחוֹטֵא — nevertheless, even this utterly selfish mosquito spiritually **"precedes"** and surpasses **a person who transgresses.**

For, as we have seen (in section 2), a person who chooses to transgress and violate G-d's will is far worse than all the *kelipos* which do not disobey G-d.

בְּהִשְׁתַּלְשְׁלוּת וִירִידַת הַחַיּוּת מֵרְצוֹן הָעֶלְיוֹן בָּרוּךְ הוּא — The mosquito precedes the transgressor **in terms of how far down from the Divine will** it receives **its life-energy.**

G-d is less "interested" in sustaining the transgressor than the mosquito, and this expresses itself in the fact that the mosquito receives its life-energy from a higher level in the chain of emanation.

וְכָל שֶׁכֵּן שְׁאָר בַּעֲלֵי חַיִּים הַטְּמֵאִים — If the transgressor is lower than the mosquito, **then all the more so** is he lower **than the other non-kosher members of the Animal Kingdom,** וַאֲפִילוּ חַיּוֹת רָעוֹת — **even the ferocious animals,** which, spiritually speaking, are greater than the mosquito, since they exhibit kindness as well as selfishness, שֶׁכּוּלָם אֵינָם מְשַׁנִּים תַּפְקִידָם וּפְקוּדָתוֹ יִתְבָּרֵךְ שָׁמְרָה רוּחָם — **since none of** the animals **deviate from their Divinely allotted role,** **"and His providence watches over their spirit"** (see *Job* 10:12).

ואע"ג דאיהו לא חזי כו'. וכמ"ש ומוראכם וחתכם יהיה
על כל חית הארץ וכפי' רז"ל שאין חיה רעה מושלת
באדם אא"כ נדמה לה כבהמה. והצדיקים שאין צלם
אלהים מסתלק מעל פניהם כל חיות רעות אתכפיין
קמייהו כמ"ש בזהר גבי דניאל בגוב אריות. וא"כ
החוטא ועובר רצונו ית' אפי' בעבירה קלה בשעת
מעשה הוא בתכלית הריחוק מקדושה העליונה שהיא
יחודו ואחדותו ית' יותר מכל בעלי חיים הטמאי' ושקצי'
ורמשים המושפעים מס"א וקליפת ע"ז ומה שפיקוח

וְאַף עַל גַּב דְּאִיהוּ לָא חָזֵי כו' — And *"even though they did not see it etc.,"* (*Talmud, Megillah* 3a), even though the animals may not be conscious that G-d's providence guides their every move, nevertheless, their spirit is aware, וּכְמוֹ שֶׁכָּתוּב וּמוֹרַאֲכֶם — as the verse states, *"And the fear and dread of you will fall on all the wild animals of the earth"* (*Genesis* 9:2), וּכְפֵירוּשׁ רַבּוֹתֵינוּ זִכְרוֹנָם — and as our Sages, of blessed memory, explained *"No wild animal has any power over a person unless he* (has sinned and therefore) *appears to it like an animal"* (*Talmud, Shabbos* 151b).

וְהַצַּדִּיקִים שֶׁאֵין צֶלֶם אֱלֹהִים מִסְתַּלֵּק מֵעַל פְּנֵיהֶם כָּל חַיּוֹת רָעוֹת אִתְכַּפְיָין קַמַּיְיהוּ — And with *tzadikim,* from whose face the Divine image never departs, all wild animals are subdued in their presence, כְּמוֹ שֶׁכָּתוּב בַּזֹּהַר גַּבֵּי דָנִיֵּאל בְּגוֹב אֲרָיוֹת — as stated in the *Zohar* (1, 191a) concerning Daniel in the lions' den.

וְאִם כֵּן הַחוֹטֵא וְעוֹבֵר רְצוֹנוֹ יִתְבָּרֵךְ אֲפִילוּ בַּעֲבֵירָה קַלָּה — If so, then a person who sins, violating G-d's will through even a minor transgression, בִּשְׁעַת מַעֲשֶׂה הוּא בְּתַכְלִית — is utterly distanced from הָרִיחוּק מִקְּדוּשָׁה הָעֶלְיוֹנָה שֶׁהִיא יִחוּדוֹ וְאַחְדוּתוֹ יִתְבָּרֵךְ — G-d's holiness, *i.e.,* His nondual oneness, at the moment of the sin, יוֹתֵר מִכָּל בַּעֲלֵי — more than all the non-kosher animals, insects and חַיִּים הַטְּמֵאִים וּשְׁקָצִים וּרְמָשִׂים — which are powered by the הַמּוּשְׁפָּעִים מִסִּטְרָא אַחֲרָא וּקְלִיפַּת עֲבוֹדָה זָרָה — *sitra achra* and the *kelipah* of idolatry.

In summary: All transgressions are a violation of G-d's will and therefore a rejection of His nondual oneness. When faced with the temptation to commit any transgression, say to yourself: There is essentially no difference between doing this sin and worshiping idols. Both will disconnect me from G-d *unequivocally*. With this thought in mind it is "very much within reach" to refrain from transgression.

SECTION FOUR: PROOF THAT ALL TRANSGRESSIONS ARE EQUAL

16TH SHEVAT REGULAR

In the following section, the *Tanya* will challenge the notion that all transgressions are equal violations of G-d's will, from a point of Jewish Law.

נֶפֶשׁ דוחה שאר עבירות וגם יעבור ואל יהרג היינו כפי'
חז"ל אמרה תורה חלל עליו שבת אחת כדי שישמור
שבתות הרבה ולא משו' קלות העבירות וחומרן [תדע
שהרי שבת חמורה ושקולה כע"ז לענין שחיטת מומר
לדבר אחד בי"ד סי' ב' משא"כ במומר לגילוי עריות

וּמַה שֶּׁפִּיקוּחַ נֶפֶשׁ דּוֹחֶה שְׁאָר עֲבֵירוֹת — **As for the** Talmudic principle **that,** unlike idolatry, for which a person must allow himself to be killed rather than transgress, **with other transgressions** this is not the case **and saving one's life takes precedence** (*Talmud, Yoma* 82a), וְגַם יַעֲבוֹר וְאַל יֵהָרֵג — **and** we are told **"transgress and do not allow yourself to be killed"** (*Talmud, Sanhedrin* 74a).

In Jewish Law, some *mitzvos* require us to sacrifice our lives for them, while others do not. But, as we shall see, this does not contradict the *Tanya's* argument that all transgressions are equal violations of G-d's will.

הַיְינוּ כְּפֵירוּשׁ חֲכָמֵינוּ זִכְרוֹנָם לִבְרָכָה — The requirement to transgress rather than be killed, **is to be understood** not as a value judgment of which prohibitions are more important in G-d's eyes, but **according to the Sages' explanation,** אָמְרָה תּוֹרָה חַלֵּל עָלָיו שַׁבָּת אַחַת כְּדֵי שֶׁיִּשְׁמוֹר שַׁבָּתוֹת הַרְבֵּה — **"The Torah says: Violate one Sabbath for a sick person, in order that he will be able to observe many more Sabbaths"** (*Talmud, Shabbos* 151b).

The Torah's instruction to *"transgress and do not allow yourself to be killed"* in the case of some prohibitions does not prove that these precepts are less important. Rather, as the Sages taught, it is simply *in the Torah's long-term interest* that a person should live, so that he will be able to observe more *mitzvos*.

וְלֹא מִשּׁוּם קַלּוּת הָעֲבֵירוֹת וְחוּמְרָן — The requirement to *"transgress and do not allow yourself to be killed"* is simply a pragmatic approach aimed at maximizing *mitzvah* observance (by keeping the person alive), **and is not motivated by** a value system of **major and minor transgressions** that evaluates idolatry as more severe.

[תֵּדַע — **Proof for this** can be derived from the following contradiction between two points of Jewish Law, שֶׁהֲרֵי שַׁבָּת חֲמוּרָה וּשְׁקוּלָה כַּעֲבוֹדָה זָרָה — **Sabbath violation is equally severe to idolatry,** לְעִנְיַן שְׁחִיטַת מוּמָר לְדָבָר אֶחָד — **in terms of** whether Jewish Law allows us to trust **the ritual slaughter performed by** a person who generally observes Jewish law, but **in one particular area** he is lax, בְּיוֹרֶה דֵעָה סִימָן ב' — **as** stated in the *Code of Jewish Law, Yoreh De'ah,* **chapter 2,** law 5.

A person who conducts ritual slaughter needs to be pious, because if he fails to observe Jewish Law properly, or does not inform the public of his errors, the community will be fed non-kosher meat.

But what if a ritual slaughterer is generally Torah observant, but he is lax about one particular prohibition? Jewish Law states that we *do* trust his ritual slaughter, so long as the precept in which he's lax is not idol worship or Sabbath violation.

ואפי' הכי פיקוח נפש דוחה שבת ולא ג"ע אלא דגזירת

31A הכתוב הוא] אלא שלאחר מעשה החטא אם היא

It appears from this ruling that both idol worship and the Sabbath are considered equally severe in Jewish Law.

מַה שֶּׁאֵין כֵּן בְּמוּמָר לְגִילּוּי עֲרָיוֹת — **Which is not the case with a person who is lax with forbidden relations,** such as adultery, where (unlike idol-worship and Sabbath violation) the law states that we *can* still trust the ritual slaughterer, if he is lax in just this one precept.

Apparently, Sabbath violation is more severe in Jewish law than adultery.

The *Tanya* now cites another point of law, which seems to prove that the reverse is true.

וַאֲפִילוּ הָכֵי פִּיקוּחַ נֶפֶשׁ דּוֹחֶה שַׁבָּת וְלֹא גִילּוּי עֲרָיוֹת — **Nevertheless, danger to life overrides the Sabbath laws,** as we noted above, **but it does not** override **forbidden relations,** (*Talmud, Yoma* 82b).

The law states that if a person is threatened with his life to conduct an act of forbidden relations, he is to give up his life. This suggests that Sabbath violation is *less* severe than forbidden relations, since (as we have seen above) a person is *not* required to give up his life rather than transgress the Sabbath.

What are we to conclude? There seem to be contradictory proofs as to the relative importance of Sabbath violation and forbidden relations.

אֶלָּא דִּגְזֵירַת הַכָּתוּב הוּא] — **Rather** this supports our argument above (that all the transgressions are equally severe violation of G-d's will), since the contradictory priorities required by Jewish law in different circumstances are clearly (not a value judgment but) **a matter of** non-rational, **Scriptural decree.** (The *Tanya's* argument here follows Rabbi Yehudah Ha-Chasid, *Sefer Chasidim* (according to Parma Manuscript, Rabbi Yehudah Wistinsky ed., Berlin 1891) section 157).

SECTION FIVE: THE MOMENT OF TRANSGRESSION

Another apparent proof that all transgressions are *not* equal is the variety of punishments prescribed by the Torah. If one transgression is punished more harshly than another, doesn't that imply that it is a greater violation of G-d's will?

The *Tanya* will now clarify that this is not the case, by drawing an important distinction between the *moment* of transgression and its *consequences*.

At the moment of transgression, all sins detach you from G-d completely; but after the sin has been completed, the spiritual consequence—*i.e.,* the damage that is done to your soul—is different in each case. And that is why the punishments differ, since their purpose is to fix the spiritual damage caused by the sin.

אֶלָּא שֶׁלְּאַחַר מַעֲשֵׂה הַחֵטְא — **But after the act of transgression** has passed,

מֶעֲבֵירוֹת שֶׁאֵין בָּהֶן כָּרֵת וּמִיתָה בִּידֵי שָׁמַיִם שֶׁאֵין נַפְשׁוֹ הָאֱלֹהִית מֵתָה לְגַמְרֵי וְנִכְרֶתֶת מִשָּׁרְשָׁהּ בֵּאלֹהִים חַיִּים רַק שֶׁנִּפְגַּם קְצָת דְּבֵיקוּתָהּ וַאֲחִיזָתָהּ בְּשָׁרְשָׁהּ בַּחֵטְא זֶה* הֲרֵי גַם נַפְשׁוֹ הַחִיּוּנִי' הַבַּהֲמִית הַמְלוּבָּשׁ בְּגוּפוֹ וְכֵן גּוּפוֹ חוֹזְרִים וְעוֹלִים מֵהַס"א וּקְלִיפָּה זוֹ וּמִתְקָרְבִים לִקְדוּשַּׁת נֶפֶשׁ הָאֱלֹהִית הַמְלוּבֶּשֶׁת בָּהֶם הַמַּאֲמִינָה בַּה' אֶחָד וְגַם

הגהה

(וּלְפִי עֵרֶךְ וְחִלּוּקֵי בְּחִי' הַפְּגַם בְּנֶפֶשׁ וּבְשָׁרְשָׁהּ בָּעֶלְיוֹנִים כָּךְ הֵם חִלּוּקֵי בְּחִי' הַמֵּירוּק וְהָעוֹנֶשׁ בְּגֵיהִנָּם אוֹ בָּעוֹלָם"ז לְכָל עָוֹן וְחֵטְא עוֹנֶשׁ מְיוּחָד לְמָרֵק וּלְהַעֲבִיר הַלִּכְלוּךְ וְהַפְּגַם וְכֵן בְּחַיָּיבֵי מִיתָה וְכָרֵת אֵין פּוֹגְמִין כֻּלָּם בְּשָׁוֶה):

אִם הִיא מֵעֲבֵירוֹת שֶׁאֵין בָּהֶן כָּרֵת וּמִיתָה בִּידֵי שָׁמַיִם — if the act **belongs to the category of transgressions which are neither penalized by** *kares* **("cutting off" of the soul), nor a "heavenly orchestrated death,"** the person can return to be connected to G-d, as we shall see.

שֶׁאֵין נַפְשׁוֹ הָאֱלֹהִית מֵתָה לְגַמְרֵי וְנִכְרֶתֶת מִשָּׁרְשָׁהּ בֵּאלֹהִים חַיִּים — **For,** in that case, **his Divine Soul is not extinguished completely or detached from its source in the living G-d,** רַק שֶׁנִּפְגַּם קְצָת דְּבֵיקוּתָהּ וַאֲחִיזָתָהּ בְּשָׁרְשָׁהּ בַּחֵטְא זֶה — **rather,** the soul's **attachment and rootedness in G-d becomes compromised in** the area of **this particular sin*** (see *Tanya, Igeres Ha-Teshuvah* chapter 5).

הֲרֵי גַם נַפְשׁוֹ הַחִיּוּנִית הַבַּהֲמִית הַמְלוּבֶּשֶׁת בְּגוּפוֹ וְכֵן גּוּפוֹ — **So** after the act of transgression, **his body and the energizing Animal Soul enmeshed in his body,** חוֹזְרִים וְעוֹלִים מֵהַסִּטְרָא אָחֳרָא וּקְלִיפָּה זוֹ — **return and rise from the** *sitra achra* **and from this** *kelipah* contamination, וּמִתְקָרְבִים לִקְדוּשַׁת נֶפֶשׁ הָאֱלֹהִית הַמְלוּבֶּשֶׁת בָּהֶם — **and they come close** again **to the holiness of the Divine Soul which is enmeshed in them,** הַמַּאֲמִינָה בַּה' אֶחָד — **which believes in One G-d.**

---

*הַגָּהָה — **NOTE.** The point of a Torah "penalty" is not to punish, but to cleanse a soul from the blemish caused by the sin. Therefore the "penalty" in each case,

וּלְפִי עֵרֶךְ וְחִלּוּקֵי בְּחִינוֹת הַפְּגַם בַּנֶּפֶשׁ וּבְשָׁרְשָׁהּ בָּעֶלְיוֹנִים — **will correspond to various different ways a soul (and its root above) might become blemished.**

כָּךְ הֵם חִלּוּקֵי בְּחִינוֹת הַמֵּירוּק וְהָעוֹנֶשׁ בְּגֵיהִנָּם אוֹ בָּעוֹלָם הַזֶּה — This is the reason for **the various forms of cleansing and punishment in Purgatory** in the next world, or suffering **in this world** לְכָל עָוֹן וְחֵטְא עוֹנֶשׁ מְיוּחָד — **each sin and transgression** having its particular punishment as prescribed by the Torah, לְמָרֵק וּלְהַעֲבִיר הַלִּכְלוּךְ וְהַפְּגַם — **to cleanse and remove the** spiritual **stain and blemish** that it caused.

וְכֵן בְּחַיָּיבֵי מִיתָה וְכָרֵת — **So too with** transgressions **punishable by death or** *kares*, אֵין פּוֹגְמִין כֻּלָּם בְּשָׁוֶה — **even though their punishment appears to be the same, they are not all equal in terms of the blemish** they inflict on the soul.

בשעת החטא היתה באמנה אתו ית' רק שהיתה
בבחי' גלות ממש תוך נפש הבהמית מס"א המחטיאה
את הגוף ומורידתו עמה בעמקי שאול למטה תחת
טומאת הס"א וקליפת ע"ז ה' ישמרנו ואין לך גלות גדול
מזה מאיגרא רמה כו' וכמש"ל דשרש ומקור נפשו' כל
בית ישראל הוא מחכמה עילאה והוא ית' וחכמתו אחד
וכו' והוא כמשל האוחז בראשו של מלך ומורידו למטה
וטומן פניו בתוך בית הכסא מלא צואה שאין לך עלבון
גדול מזה אפי' עושה כן לפי שעה שהקליפות וס"א
נקראים קיא צואה כנודע:

Even though the sin was a complete detachment from G-d, it was a temporary one; a momentary exile of the Divine Soul.

וְגַם בִּשְׁעַת הַחֵטְא הָיְתָה בָּאֲמָנָה אִתּוֹ יִתְבָּרֵךְ — **And even while the sin was being committed,** the Divine Soul *"retained her loyalty to Him"* (*Esther* 2:20), to G-d, רַק שֶׁהָיְתָה בִּבְחִינַת גָּלוּת מַמָּשׁ תּוֹךְ נֶפֶשׁ הַבַּהֲמִית מִסִּטְרָא אָחֳרָא — **only, it was in a state of complete exile,** trapped and powerless **within the Animal Soul of** *sitra achra,* הַמַּחֲטִיאָה אֶת הַגּוּף וּמוֹרִידָתוֹ עִמָּהּ בְּעֶמְקֵי שְׁאוֹל — **which caused the body to sin and dragged it down together** *"to the depths of the grave"* (*Proverbs* 9:18), לְמַטָּה מַטָּה — **so far down that they were lower** תַּחַת טוּמְאַת הַסִּטְרָא אָחֳרָא וּקְלִיפַּת עֲבוֹדָה זָרָה — **than the impurity of the** *sitra achra* **and the** *kelipah* **of "idolatry,"** ה' יִשְׁמְרֵנוּ — **may G-d protect us!**

מֵאִיגְּרָא רָמָה כו' — וְאֵין לְךָ גָּלוּת גָּדוֹל מִזֶּה — **And there is no greater exile than this,** *"a plunge from a high roof to a deep pit"* (*Talmud, Chagigah* 5b).

The *Tanya* now clarifies why to take the exiled Divine Soul and drag it down to the depths of *kelipah*, represents such a drastic move.

דְּשֹׁרֶשׁ וּמְקוֹר — וּכְמוֹ שֶׁנִּתְבָּאֵר לְעֵיל וְכוּ' — **As was explained above** (in chapter 2), נַפְשׁוֹת כָּל בֵּית יִשְׂרָאֵל — **that the root and source of every soul in the house of Isra-el,** הוּא מֵחָכְמָה עִילָאָה וְהוּא יִתְבָּרֵךְ וְחָכְמָתוֹ אֶחָד — **is from the "Supernal** *chochmah*,**"** which is so intimately bound with G-d that **"He and His** *chochmah* **are one,"** וְהוּא — כְּמָשָׁל הָאוֹחֵז בְּרֹאשׁוֹ שֶׁל מֶלֶךְ וּמוֹרִידוֹ לְמַטָּה וְטוֹמֵן פָּנָיו בְּתוֹךְ בֵּית הַכִּסֵּא מָלֵא צוֹאָה — **and to take such a holy entity as the soul and drag it into a sin, is comparable to taking the king's head, dragging it down and dunking his face into a toilet full of excrement,** שֶׁאֵין לְךָ עֶלְבּוֹן גָּדוֹל מִזֶּה — **and there's no greater humiliation than that,** אֲפִילוּ עוֹשֶׂה כֵּן לְפִי שָׁעָה — **even if a person does it for just a moment.**

שֶׁהַקְּלִיפּוֹת וְסִטְרָא אָחֳרָא נִקְרָאוֹת קִיא צוֹאָה — **The analogy is a precise one since the** *kelipos* **and** *sitra achra* **are referred to as** *"vomit and excrement"* (*Isaiah* 28:8), כַּנּוֹדָע — **as is known** from the *Zohar* (2, 154b).

פרק כה וזהו שכתוב כי קרוב אליך הדבר מאד
וגו' שבכל עת ובכל שעה בידו של
אדם וברשותו הוא להעבי' רוח שטות והשכחה מקרבו
ולזכור ולעורר אהבתו לה' אחד המסותרת בודאי
בלבבו בלי שום ספק. וז"ש ובלבבך ונכלל בה גם

CHAPTER 25

REMEMBERING YOUR SOUL'S DEVOTION

SECTION ONE: AWAKING FROM A "DELUSIONAL SPIRIT"

17TH SHEVAT REGULAR | 25TH SHEVAT LEAP

From chapter 18 up to this point, we have been in the process of explaining why worship is *"very much* within reach." In this chapter we will conclude the discussion.

וְזֶהוּ שֶׁכָּתוּב כִּי קָרוֹב אֵלֶיךָ הַדָּבָר מְאֹד וְגוֹ' — **And this** discussion in chapters 18-24 will enable us to explain **the verse, "Rather, the thing is *very much within reach* for you, etc."** (Deuteronomy 30:14).

שֶׁבְּכָל עֵת וּבְכָל שָׁעָה בְּיָדוֹ שֶׁל אָדָם וּבִרְשׁוּתוֹ הוּא לְהַעֲבִיר רוּחַ שְׁטוּת וְהַשִּׁכְחָה מִקִּרְבּוֹ — Worship is *"very much* within reach" **since at all times and at any moment you have the power and ability to rid yourself of the "delusional spirit" and "unconsciousness" inside you,** וְלִזְכּוֹר וּלְעוֹרֵר אַהֲבָתוֹ לַה' אֶחָד — **by recalling and awakening your love of the One G-d,** הַמְסוּתֶּרֶת בְּוַדַּאי בְּלִבָּבוֹ בְּלִי שׁוּם סָפֵק — **which, without any doubt, is definitely "dormant" in your heart** (see *A Chasidic Thought*).

The method of chapters 1-17, on the other hand, which requires you to *"think about the greatness of the Blessed Infinite One"* (p. 204), can't be conjured up "at every moment" since it takes some work to get there, and you have to be in the right frame of mind.

וְזֶהוּ שֶׁכָּתוּב וּבִלְבָבְךָ — **And this is the meaning of the words:** *"Rather, the thing is very much within reach for you, in your mouth **and in your heart,** so that you can do it."*

It is "very much within reach" for you to get excited about G-d "in your heart" since all you have to do is crack through the falsehood of the "delusional spirit" and allow the love which is *already* in your heart to awaken.

דחילו דהיינו שלא ליפרד בשום אופן מיחודו ואחדותו

יתברך אפי' במסירת נפש ממש בלי שום טעם ושכל מושג

אלא בטבע אלהי וכ"ש בשבירת התאוות הקלה מיסורי

מיתה שקרוב אליו הדבר יותר לכבוש היצר הן בבחי'

31B

וְנִכְלָל בָּהּ גַּם דְּחִילוּ — And included in the love **is also reverence.**

Love of G-d can only inspire acts of love, *i.e.,* the positive *mitzvos.* But if worshiping G-d is "very much within reach" then it should also be straightforward to awaken reverence of G-d, to inspire you to refrain from all the prohibitions.

The *Tanya* reminds us here of the solution to this problem in chapter 19, that "love contains reverence" (see p. 230).

דְּהַיְינוּ שֶׁלֹּא לִיפָּרֵד בְּשׁוּם אוֹפֶן מִיְחוּדוֹ וְאַחְדוּתוֹ יִתְבָּרֵךְ — Namely, that you love G-d so much that **you don't want be separated in any way from His nondual oneness.**

Reverence is "included" in love since you dread losing the intimate connection with G-d that you already have.

אֲפִילוּ בִּמְסִירַת נֶפֶשׁ מַמָּשׁ — Even if this means **actually giving up your life, בְּלִי שׁוּם טַעַם וְשֵׂכֶל מוּשָׂג — without any** compelling **reason or graspable logic, אֶלָּא בְּטֶבַע אֱלֹהִי — but simply because of the Divine** Soul found **naturally** within you.

The *Tanya* now revisits the advice offered at the end of the previous chapter, about how to arouse your "dormant love" and resist the "delusional spirit."

וְכָל שֶׁכֵּן בִּשְׁבִירַת הַתַּאֲווֹת — And if the "dormant love" can inspire you to give up your life for G-d, **all the more so** can it inspire you **to break free from your desires, הַקַּלָּה מִיִּסּוּרֵי מִיתָה — something which is** clearly **easier than the torture of** a martyr's **death,** which your soul would be willing to undergo, if need be.

שֶׁקָּרוֹב אֵלָיו הַדָּבָר יוֹתֵר לִכְבּוֹשׁ הַיֵּצֶר — Surely, then, **it is more** *"within reach for you"* **to overcome your evil inclination** which involves a relatively small sacrifice of pleasure, than to give up your life.

To bow down to an idol, or to do something that would completely disconnect you from G-d, is unthinkable! But once you bring to mind the message of chap-

---

A CHASIDIC THOUGHT

My "dormant love" is very much within reach and accessible to me *"at all times and at every moment,"* because all I have to do is awaken from the "unconsciousness" of my "delusional spirit." As soon as I realize the lies my mind has been telling me, I can awaken and feel the natural affinity that my soul has for G-d; my intuitive awareness of His presence everywhere.

סור מרע אפי' מעבירה קלה של דברי סופרים שלא
לעבור על רצונו ית' מאחר שנפרד בה מיחודו ואחדותו
כמו בע"ז ממש בשעת מעשה והרי גם בע"ז יכול
לעשות תשובה אח"כ. ואף שהאומר אחטא ואשוב
אין מספיקין כו' היינו שאין מחזיקים ידו להיות לו שעת

ter 24, that *every* transgression is an utter rejection of G-d, you begin to see all prohibitions in the same light.

In a nondual universe there are only two possible states of being: Either you are aligned to the reality that "there is no place devoid of Him"; or you have splintered from that reality into a delusional bubble of separateness. There is no intermediate state. To commit any transgression is to drag your being into a state of separateness and unconsciousness.

הֵן בִּבְחִינַת סוּר מֵרַע — This awareness will enable you **both to *"turn away from evil"*** (*Psalms* 34:15) and avoid transgressing any prohibitions, אֲפִילוּ מֵעֲבֵירָה קַלָּה שֶׁל — **even a minor rabbinic prohibition,** דְּבְרֵי סוֹפְרִים — שֶׁלֹּא לַעֲבוֹר עַל רְצוֹנוֹ יִתְבָּרֵךְ **so as not to transgress G-d's will,** which, as we learned in the previous chapter, is expressed *equally* in all prohibitions, Biblical and Rabbinic, מֵאַחַר שֶׁנִּפְרָד בָּה מִיְּחוּדוֹ וְאַחְדּוּתוֹ כְּמוֹ בַּעֲבוֹדָה זָרָה מַמָּשׁ בִּשְׁעַת מַעֲשֶׂה — **since, at the moment** of transgression, **your are separated from G-d's nondual oneness as if you had literally worshiped idols,** as we discussed at length in the previous chapter.

One of the techniques of the "delusional spirit" is to convince you that a transgression is tolerable now, since you will only be separate from G-d momentarily. But if that were the case, you could worship idols too, since:

וַהֲרֵי גַם בַּעֲבוֹדָה זָרָה יָכוֹל לַעֲשׂוֹת תְּשׁוּבָה אַחַר כָּךְ — **Even in the case of idolatry, you can repent afterward.**

The emotional revulsion for idolatry as a complete renunciation of faith should be shared with all transgressions which, at the moment of the deed, represent an utter rejection of G-d. You wouldn't worship idols on the premise that you could repent afterwards, so you shouldn't carry out any other transgression on the basis that it only separates you from G-d temporarily.

PRACTICAL LESSONS

Any time you are tempted to sin, just say to yourself: I wouldn't worship idols, and this is really the same thing — a complete detachment from G-d.

26TH SHEVAT LEAP

[וְאַף שֶׁהָאוֹמֵר אֶחֱטָא וְאָשׁוּב אֵין מַסְפִּיקִין כו' — **And as for the fact that,** *"If a person says 'I will sin now and I will repent for it later on,' he will not be given the opportunity to repent"* (*Talmud, Yoma* 85b), which implies that "repenting afterward" is

הכושר לעשות תשובה אבל אם דחק השעה ועשה
תשובה אין לך דבר שעומד בפני התשובה. ואעפ"כ
כל איש ישראל מוכן ומזומן למסור נפשו על קדושת
ה' שלא להשתחוות לע"ז אפי' לפי שעה ולעשות
תשובה אח"כ והיינו מפני אור ה' המלובש בנפשם
כנ"ל שאינו בבחי' זמן ושעה כלל אלא למעלה מהזמן

never an option, for any transgression, הַיְינוּ שֶׁאֵין מַחֲזִיקִים יָדוֹ לִהְיוֹת לוֹ שְׁעַת הַכּוֹשֶׁר לַעֲשׂוֹת תְּשׁוּבָה — **this** doesn't mean that it's *impossible* to intentionally sin and then repent afterwards; rather it means that heaven **won't assist you** and **provide you with a suitable moment to repent,** אֲבָל אִם דְּחַק הַשָּׁעָה וְעָשָׂה תְּשׁוּבָה — **but if you** *"seize the moment"* (*Talmud, Brachos* 64a) **and repent,** אֵין לְךָ דָּבָר שֶׁעוֹמֵד בִּפְנֵי [הַתְּשׁוּבָה] — then, ***"Nothing stands in the way of repentance"*** (*Rambam, Laws of Repentance* 3:14 from *Jerusalem Talmud, Pe'ah* 1:1).

If "nothing stands in the way of repentance" then it is conceivable that a person would worship idols, when forced to do so, having in mind that he will repent later on. Yet the notion is intolerable.

וְאַף עַל פִּי כֵן כָּל אִישׁ יִשְׂרָאֵל מוּכָן וּמְזוּמָּן לִמְסוֹר נַפְשׁוֹ עַל קְדוּשַׁת הַשֵּׁם — Despite the fact that you could, in theory, worship idols and then repent later on, **nevertheless, every person in Israel would be ready and willing to give up his life to "sanctify G-d's name,"** שֶׁלֹּא לְהִשְׁתַּחֲווֹת לַעֲבוֹדָה זָרָה אֲפִילוּ לְפִי שָׁעָה — **rather than bow to idols** *even for a moment,* וְלַעֲשׂוֹת תְּשׁוּבָה אַחַר כָּךְ — **and then repent afterwards,** since the knowledge that he would be utterly separate from G-d for that moment is unthinkable.

וְהַיְינוּ מִפְּנֵי אוֹר ה' הַמְלוּבָּשׁ בְּנַפְשָׁם — **And this is a result of Divine light enmeshed in their souls** through the power of *chochmah,* כַּנִּזְכָּר לְעֵיל — **as mentioned above,** in chapters 18-19.

שֶׁאֵינוֹ בִּבְחִינַת זְמַן וְשָׁעָה כְּלָל — Due to this Divine light, the power of *chochmah* **is not influenced by the passage of time at all,** אֶלָּא לְמַעֲלָה מֵהַזְּמַן — **rather, it tran-scends time.**

"Transcending time" means that you have awakened to a deeper reality than what is usually perceived by the senses and the mind.

Everything in this world has a *form*: it is old or new; beautiful or ugly; colorful or dull. All forms have something in common: they change, and eventually, they dis-integrate. Living forms are born, and later they die. As we age, we lose our youth, health and vitality. Every form that is created is ultimately destroyed.

Time is simply an instrument we use when looking at the world of form to mea-sure change. To "transcend time" means to look at the universe using a different register than form; to look at the *formless essence* which is the core of everything.

ושליט ומושל עליו כנודע. והן בבחי' ועשה טוב

When you can focus your attention on the fact that an object, plant, or person *just is*, regardless of what form it may take, you have come closer to perceiving its Divine essence. As we have learned, everything at its core is within G-d, which means that everything and every person is really a small "beacon" of existence, expressing the all-encompassing presence of G-d.

Time obscures that perspective, as it encourages us to look at form and change. But if you can begin to look deeper than that, you will have a different set of concerns: Right now, am I connected to G-d? Am I conscious of Him and awakened to His presence? Can I sense His presence in every thing, animate or inanimate? This is the level of consciousness at which your *chochmah* operates.

PRACTICAL LESSONS

Your power of *chochmah*, through which G-d's light shines, helps you to lift your perception beyond the worldly and the temporal.

For your *chochmah,* the idea that you might choose to be disconnected from G-d now and fix the breach later with *teshuvah* makes no sense at all. Because, for *chochmah, there is only the "now."* Form, time and change are simply too superficial a lens through which to view the universe, a "delusion" stemming from lower states of mind where an obsession with the external, masks G-d's presence.

וְשַׁלִּיט וּמוֹשֵׁל עָלָיו — The Divine light in your *chochmah* **also controls and dominates** your perception of time, כַּנּוֹדָע — **as is known** (see *Tanya, Sha'ar Ha-Yichud Ve-Ha-Emunah,* chapter 7).

Using your *chochmah* doesn't mean that you have to forget about the world of form and drift into a detached state. If you remain anchored in your *chochmah* you can still function in the changing world of time, but you will not be controlled by it.

Rather than constantly living in the shadow of your past experience, anxious about what the future may hold, if you use your *chochmah* and live in the "now," you will be able to change your perspective of how important the past and future really is. If you can feel "I am with G-d now," and "I sense G-d within all things" then your personal history and future uncertainties will cease to concern you so much. As you deal with the day-to-day ordeals of living in time, attachment to your *chochmah* will help to "control and dominate" your perception of time so that it doesn't overwhelm you.

SECTION TWO: WORSHIP IS "VERY MUCH WITHIN REACH"

18TH SHEVAT REGULAR | 27TH SHEVAT LEAP

So far, we have discussed how accessing your "dormant love" and *chochmah* make it "very much within reach" to avoid transgression. Now we turn our attention to how this same method can help you observe the positive commands.

להתגבר כארי בגבורה ואומץ הלב נגד היצר המכביד
את גופו ומפיל עליו עצלה מבחי' יסוד העפר שבנפש
הבהמית מלהטריח גופו בזריזות בכל מיני טורח ועבוד'
משא בעבודת ה' שיש בה טורח ועמל כגון לעמול
בתורה בעיון ובפה לא פסיק פומיה מגירסא וכמארז"ל
לעולם ישים אדם עצמו על דברי תורה כשור לעול
וכחמור למשאוי וכן לתפלה בכונה בכל כחו ממש וכן
בעבודת ה' שהוא בדבר שבממון כמו עבודת הצדקה
וכיוצא באלו ממלחמות היצר ותחבולותיו לקרר נפש

וְהֵן בִּבְחִינַת וַעֲשֵׂה טוֹב — **And, so too,** your "dormant love," once awakened, will help you **in the area of** positive observance, **"do good"** (*Psalms* 34:15), **לְהִתְגַּבֵּר** — **to be "strong like a lion"** (*Mishnah, Avos* 5:20), **with** strength and determination of the heart, **כָּאֲרִי בִּגְבוּרָה וְאוֹמֶץ הַלֵּב** **נֶגֶד הַיֵּצֶר הַמַּכְבִּיד אֶת גּוּפוֹ וּמַפִּיל עָלָיו עַצְלָה** — **against the impulse to evil that causes your body to feel heavy and makes you lazy,** **מִבְּחִינַת יְסוֹד הֶעָפָר שֶׁבַּנֶּפֶשׁ הַבַּהֲמִית** — that laziness stemming **from the Animal Soul's element of earth** (see chapter 1, p. 41).

מִלְהַטְרִיחַ גּוּפוֹ בְּזִרִיזוּת בְּכָל מִינֵי טוֹרַח — Laziness holds you back **from pushing your body enthusiastically with the different forms of exertion necessary, וַעֲבוֹדַת מַשָּׂא** **בַּעֲבוֹדַת ה' שֶׁיֵּשׁ בָּהּ טוֹרַח וְעָמָל** — **in the "strainful work"** (*Numbers* 4:47) **of serving G-d, which requires exertion and drive.**

As we learned in chapter 15, genuine worship of G-d requires effort. Even if you are enthusiastic about worship, it is important that you challenge yourself to do more than is comfortable. The *Tanya* offers us a few examples.

כְּגוֹן לַעֲמוֹל בַּתּוֹרָה בְּעִיּוֹן — **For example, "being driven in Torah study"** (*Talmud, Sanhedrin* 99b), **in depth, וּבַפֶּה לָא פָּסִיק פּוּמֵיה מִגִּירְסָא** — **and verbalizing** the words, so that your **"mouth doesn't stop studying"** (*Talmud, Shabbos* 5b), **וּכְמַאֲמַר רַבּוֹתֵינוּ** as — **זִכְרוֹנָם לִבְרָכָה לְעוֹלָם יָשִׂים אָדָם עַצְמוֹ עַל דִּבְרֵי תוֹרָה כְּשׁוֹר לְעוֹל וְכַחֲמוֹר לְמַשָּׂאוֹי** our Sages, of blessed memory, said: **"A person should always place upon himself the work of studying the Torah as an ox accepts the yoke, and as a donkey, its burden"** (*Talmud, Avodah Zarah* 5b).

וְכֵן לִתְפִלָּה בְּכַוָּנָה בְּכָל כֹּחוֹ מַמָּשׁ — **Similarly, with mindful prayer, which should be with your full power** of attention, **literally, וְכֵן בַּעֲבוֹדַת ה' שֶׁהִיא בְּדָבָר שֶׁבְּמָמוֹן כְּמוֹ** **עֲבוֹדַת הַצְּדָקָה** — **and likewise when serving G-d in your financial matters, such as the worship through charity,** you ought to stretch yourself to the utmost of your ability.

28TH SHEVAT LEAP

וְכַיּוֹצֵא בְּאֵלּוּ מִמִּלְחֲמוֹת הַיֵּצֶר וְתַחְבּוּלוֹתָיו — **And, so too, in other areas of the war against the "impulse to evil" and its tactics, לְקָרֵר נֶפֶשׁ הָאָדָם שֶׁלֹּא לְהַפְקִיר מָמוֹנוֹ**

האדם שלא להפקיר ממונו ובריאות גופו שלעמוד נגדו
ולכבשו קרוב מאד אל האדם כששים אל לבו אל שלנצח
היצר בכל זה ויותר מזה ולעשות הפכו ממש קל
מאד מיסורי מיתה ה' ישמרנו ויסורי מיתה ה' ישמרנו   32A
היה מקבל באהבה וברצון שלא ליפרד מיחודו ואחדותו
ית' אפי' לפי שעה להשתחות לע"ז ח"ו וכ"ש שיש לו
לקבל באהבה וברצון כדי לדבקה בו לעולם ועד דהיינו
כשיעשה רצונו ית' בעבודה זו יתגלה בה פנימית רצון
העליון בבחי' פנים וגילוי רב ולא בהסתר כלל וכשאין
שום הסתר פנים ברצון העליון אזי אין דבר נפרד כלל

וּבְרִיאוּת גוּפוֹ — which dampens your soul, telling you not to squander your money on charity, and not to compromise your body's wellbeing by exerting yourself
in worship, שֶׁלַּעֲמוֹד נֶגְדּוֹ וּלְכַבְּשׁוֹ קָרוֹב מְאֹד אֶל הָאָדָם — to stand strong against
the "impulse to evil" and to overcome it, is "very much within reach" for you,
כְּשֶׁיָּשִׂים אֶל לִבּוֹ שֶׁלְּנַצֵּחַ הַיֵּצֶר בְּכָל זֶה וְיוֹתֵר מִזֶּה וְלַעֲשׂוֹת הֶפְכּוֹ מַמָּשׁ — when you take
to heart our above discussion that to succeed against your impulse to evil, and
furthermore, to do the complete opposite of what it wants, קַל מְאֹד מִיִּסּוּרֵי מִיתָה ה'
יִשְׁמְרֵנוּ — is clearly easier than the torture of a martyr's death, may G-d spare us!
וְיִסּוּרֵי מִיתָה ה' יִשְׁמְרֵנוּ הָיָה מְקַבֵּל בְּאַהֲבָה וּבְרָצוֹן שֶׁלֹּא לִיפָּרֵד מִיִּחוּדוֹ וְאַחְדּוּתוֹ יִתְבָּרֵךְ
אֲפִילוּ לְפִי שָׁעָה — and yet you would have accepted the torture of a martyr's death
(may G-d spare us!) lovingly and willingly, so as to not be separated from G-d's
nondual oneness, even for a moment, לְהִשְׁתַּחֲוֹת לַעֲבוֹדָה זָרָה — through bowing
to idolatry, חַס וְשָׁלוֹם — G-d forbid.

וְכָל שֶׁכֵּן שֶׁיֵּשׁ לוֹ לְקַבֵּל בְּאַהֲבָה וּבְרָצוֹן כְּדֵי לִדְבָקָה בּוֹ — All the more so, should you
lovingly and willingly accept the "inconvenience" of exertion, so as to be connect-
ed with G-d, לְעוֹלָם וָעֶד — and eternally so.

The *Tanya* reminds us how worship connects us with G-d.

דְּהַיְינוּ כְּשֶׁיַּעֲשֶׂה רְצוֹנוֹ יִתְבָּרֵךְ בַּעֲבוֹדָה זוֹ — Since, when you carry out G-d's will
through this worship, יִתְגַּלֶּה בָּהּ פְּנִימִית רָצוֹן הָעֶלְיוֹן — the innermost Divine will
is disclosed in your actions, בִּבְחִינַת פָּנִים וְגִילּוּי רַב וְלֹא בְּהֶסְתֵּר כְּלָל — in a way that
G-d's "face" shines and is abundantly disclosed without any concealment at all,
וּכְשֶׁאֵין שׁוּם הֶסְתֵּר פָּנִים בָּרָצוֹן הָעֶלְיוֹן — and when the Divine will shines without any
"hiding of G-d's face," אֲזֵי אֵין דָּבָר נִפְרָד כְּלָל וְכָל כְּלָל לִהְיוֹת יֵשׁ וְדָבָר בִּפְנֵי עַצְמוֹ — then in
this overtly nondual space nothing can be separate in any way from G-d, and feel
itself to be an isolated, independent identity.

As we learned in chapter 23, a *mitzvah* represents *nondual reality embodied in
an act*, since G-d's will for that act stems from His "innermost will" that precedes all
the "diminishments" which took place to create this world.

וכלל להיות יש ודבר בפני עצמו ולזאת תהיינה נפשו
האלהית והחיונית ולבושיהן כולן מיוחדות בתכלית
היחוד ברצון העליון ואור א"ס ב"ה כנ"ל. ויחוד זה
למעלה הוא נצחי לעולם ועד כי הוא ית' ורצונו למעלה
מהזמן וכן גילוי רצונו שבדבורו שהיא התורה הוא נצחי
וכמ"ש ודבר אלהינו יקום לעולם ודבריו חיים וקיימים
כו' ולא יחליף ולא ימיר דתו לעולמים כו'. אלא שלמטה

וְלָזֹאת תִּהְיֶינָה נַפְשׁוֹ הָאֱלֹהִית וְהַחִיּוּנִית וּלְבוּשֵׁיהֶן — **Therefore,** when you do a *mitzvah*, **your Divine Soul,** your **energizing** Animal **Soul and their "garments,"** כּוּלָן מְיוּחֲדוֹת **are all merged in total union** בְּתַכְלִית הַיִּחוּד בְּרָצוֹן הָעֶלְיוֹן וְאוֹר אֵין סוֹף בָּרוּךְ הוּא **with the Divine will and the Infinite Light of G-d,** כַּנִּזְכָּר לְעֵיל — **as mentioned above,** in chapter 23 (pp. 256-7).

SECTION THREE: A MITZVAH LASTS FOREVER

29TH SHEVAT LEAP

If a *mitzvah* merges you with the "Infinite Light of G-d" which is beyond this finite world, does the connection transcend time? Through one *mitzvah* are you connected with G-d forever?

The *Tanya's* answer will be: yes and no. In the upper world, the connection is eternal, but down here, it is not.

וְיִחוּד זֶה לְמַעְלָה הוּא נִצְחִי לְעוֹלָם וָעֶד — **And, above** in the upper world, **this "merging"** with the Infinite Light of G-d through a *mitzvah* **is eternal, forever,** כִּי הוּא יִתְבָּרֵךְ וּרְצוֹנוֹ לְמַעְלָה מֵהַזְּמַן — **because G-d and His will transcend time.**

At first glance, the eternal persistence of each *mitzvah* in the spiritual realms appears to continue only so long as a person does not sin. For are we not taught that *"a sin extinguishes a mitzvah"* (*Talmud, Sotah* 21a)?

In truth, however, it is only a.) the person's *reward* for performing the *mitzvah*, and b.) its *positive effects* on the soul that become "extinguished" by sin. But the *mitzvah* itself persists eternally (Rabbi Menachem Mendel Schneerson, *Toras Menachem, Hisva'aduyos*, vol. 21, (Brooklyn: *Va'ad Hanachos Be-Lahak* 2002), p. 88).

וְכֵן גִּילּוּי רְצוֹנוֹ שֶׁבְּדִבּוּרוֹ שֶׁהִיא הַתּוֹרָה הוּא נִצְחִי — **And, so too, the disclosure of His will in His speech, the Torah, is eternal,** וּכְמוֹ שֶׁכָּתוּב וּדְבַר אֱלֹהֵינוּ יָקוּם לְעוֹלָם — **as** the verse states, *"And the word of G-d will stand forever"* (*Isaiah* 40:8), וּדְבָרָיו חַיִּים וְקַיָּימִים כוּ' — *"And His words are living and enduring, etc.,"* (*Liturgy, Morning Prayer*), וְלֹא יַחֲלִיף וְלֹא יָמִיר דָּתוֹ לְעוֹלָמִים כוּ' — and *"He will never alter or change his law"* (*Liturgy, Yigdal*).

הוא תחת הזמן ובאותה שעה לבדה שעוסק בה בתור'
או במצוה כי אח"כ אם עוסק בדבר אחר נפרד מהיחוד
העליון למטה. והיינו כשעוסק בדברים בטלים לגמרי
שאין בהם צורך כלל לעבודת ה' ואעפ"כ כשחוזר ושב

The *mitzvos* express the *essential* will of G-d, a desire which cannot be fully explained or defined, and consequently, cannot change or be modified according to
circumstance. G-d's essential will, being an expression of His inner identity, cannot
change, any more than G-d Himself can change. This sentiment was echoed in the
Talmudic teaching that *Anochi* ("I"), the first word of the Ten Commandments, is an
acronym for *Ana Nafshi Kesavis Yahavis* ("With My soul I have written, have given"
—*Talmud*, *Shabbos* 105a, according to the text of *Ein Ya'akov*). With this statement
G-d declared that the *mitzvos* given at Sinai are not merely an external manifestation of Divinity, some sort of means to an end which could become outdated, but
a direct expression of His inner essence, G-d's very "soul," so to speak. There are
no veils here, no layers of emanation, just a direct expression of G-d Himself (Rabbi
Menachem Mendel Schneerson, *Likutei Sichos* vol. 19, p. 182*ff*).

19TH SHEVAT REGULAR

The *Tanya* now explores another perspective from which a *mitzvah* is *not* eternal.

אֶלָּא שֶׁלְּמַטָּה הוּא תַּחַת הַזְּמַן — **However, below** in this
world, when you observe a *mitzvah*, the merging with
G-d *is* **subject to time,** וּבְאוֹתָהּ שָׁעָה לְבַדָּהּ שֶׁעוֹסֵק בָּהּ,
בַּתּוֹרָה אוֹ בְּמִצְוָה — **and the merging takes place only at
the time you are involved with Torah** study or *mitzvah*
observance, כִּי אַחַר כָּךְ אִם עוֹסֵק בְּדָבָר אַחֵר נִפְרָד מֵהַיִּחוּד
הָעֶלְיוֹן לְמַטָּה — **because, when you do some other** non-
Torah **activity afterwards, your merging with the** Infinite
Light **above is interrupted below.**

In the upper world, your connection to G-d through a
mitzvah is eternal and can never be broken. But below
in this world, the connection ceases as soon as your Torah activity is interrupted.

[וְהַיְינוּ כְּשֶׁעוֹסֵק בִּדְבָרִים בְּטֵלִים לְגַמְרֵי] — **The meaning of**
interruption through "other activity" **is when you involve yourself in** *completely
empty* **activities,** [שֶׁאֵין בָּהֶם צוֹרֶךְ כְּלָל לַעֲבוֹדַת ה'] — **which are devoid of any role
whatsoever in the worship of G-d.**

Even if you are not studying Torah or observing a *mitzvah*, your merging with G-d
from your previous *mitzvah* will continue (even down here in this world), so long
as you do not do something that will interrupt it. A non-religious activity will not
interrupt the connection unless it is "devoid of any role whatsoever in the worship
of G-d."

PRACTICAL LESSONS

Any *mitzvah* that
you do connects you
with G-d forever, in
the upper worlds
(and down here
too, temporarily).

לַעֲבוֹדַת ה' אח"כ לתורה ולתפלה ומבקש מחילה מה'
על שהיה אפשר לו לעסוק אז בתורה ולא עסק ה' יסלח
לו כמארז"ל עבר על מצות עשה ושב לא זז משם עד
שמוחלין לו. ולזה תקנו ברכת סלח לנו שלש פעמים
בכל יום על עון ביטול תורה שאין אדם ניצול ממנו בכל
יום וכמו התמיד שהיה מכפר על מצות עשה. ואין
זה אחטא ואשוב אא"כ שבשעת החטא ממש הוא

Taking care of bodily needs, or doing necessary business "for the sake of Heaven," will *not* interrupt a previous connection.

וְאַף עַל פִּי כֵן כְּשֶׁחוֹזֵר וְשָׁב לַעֲבוֹדַת ה' אַחַר כָּךְ לְתוֹרָה וְלִתְפִלָּה — **Nevertheless,** even after your connection is broken, **when you repent** for this lapse **and return to your worship, in Torah and in prayer,** וּמְבַקֵּשׁ מְחִילָה מֵה' עַל שֶׁהָיָה אֶפְשָׁר לוֹ לַעֲסוֹק אָז בַּתּוֹרָה וְלֹא עָסַק — **asking forgiveness from G-d for the failure to study Torah when you had the opportunity to do so,** ה' יִסְלַח לוֹ — **G-d will forgive you,** and your state of "merging" with G-d's Infinite Light will resume.

כְּמַאֲמַר רַבּוֹתֵינוּ זִכְרוֹנָם לִבְרָכָה עָבַר עַל מִצְוַת עֲשֵׂה וְשָׁב לֹא זָז מִשָּׁם עַד שֶׁמּוֹחֲלִין לוֹ — As our Sages, of blessed memory, taught: *"If one neglected to perform a positive mitzvah, and then repented, he is forgiven on the spot"* (*Talmud, Yoma* 86a).

וְלָזֶה תִּקְּנוּ בְּרַכַּת סְלַח לָנוּ שָׁלֹשׁ פְּעָמִים בְּכָל יוֹם — **And it was for this reason, that** **the blessing of "Forgive us"** in the *Amidah* (standing prayer) **was instituted** by the Sages **to be recited three times every day,** עַל עֲוֹן בִּיטוּל תּוֹרָה — **for the sin of neglecting Torah study,** שֶׁאֵין אָדָם נִיצוֹל מִמֶּנּוּ בְּכָל יוֹם — **from which** virtually **no man escapes, even for a single day.**

As a result of lapsing in Torah study, a person's connection with G-d's Infinite Light, brought about by his earlier Torah and *mitzvos*, will be interrupted (in this world). The *Tanya* suggests that it was "for this reason" that the Sages introduced a requirement to repent three times a day, to resume the connection which is often lost.

וּכְמוֹ הַתָּמִיד שֶׁהָיָה מְכַפֵּר עַל מִצְוֹת עֲשֵׂה — **And this is similar to the daily burnt-offering** in the Holy Temple **which atoned for** the neglect of **the positive** *mitzvos* (*Talmud, Zevachim* 6a; *Toras Kohanim, Leviticus* 1:4).

Since the prayer services were modeled on Temple service (*Talmud, Brachos* 26b), a regular atonement for neglected Torah study was introduced into the prayers, following the precedent of a regular sacrifice to atone for neglected *mitzvos*.

Above, however, we learned that a person is not supposed to transgress on the basis that he will repent later on (p. 286). Doesn't the idea of a formalized, thrice-daily repentance seem to condone such activity?

וְאֵין זֶה אֶחֱטָא וְאָשׁוּב — **But this does not** fall under the warning against saying, *"I will sin now and repent later on,"* אֶלָּא אִם כֵּן שֶׁבִּשְׁעַת הַחֵטְא מַמָּשׁ הוּא סוֹמֵךְ עַל

סוֹמֵךְ עַל הַתְּשׁוּבָה וּלְכָךְ חוֹטֵא כְּמוֹ שֶׁנִּתְבָּאֵר בְּמָקוֹם אַחֵר: וּבָזֶה
יוּבַן לָמָּה צִוָּה מֹשֶׁה רַבֵּינוּ עָלָיו הַשָּׁלוֹם בְּמִשְׁנֵה תוֹרָה לַדּוֹר
שֶׁנִּכְנְסוּ לָאָרֶץ לִקְרוֹת ק"ש פְּעָמִים בְּכָל יוֹם לְקַבֵּל עָלָיו   32B
מַלְכוּת שָׁמַיִם בִּמְסִירַת נֶפֶשׁ וַהֲלֹא הִבְטִיחַ לָהֶם פַּחְדְּכֶם
וּמוֹרַאֲכֶם יִתֵּן ה' וְגוֹ' אֶלָּא מִשּׁוּם שֶׁקִּיּוּם הַתּוֹרָה וּמִצְוֹתֶיהָ
תָּלוּי בָּזֶה שֶׁיִּזְכּוֹר תָּמִיד עִנְיַן מְסִירַת נַפְשׁוֹ לַה' עַל יִחוּדוֹ

הַתְּשׁוּבָה וּלְכָךְ חוֹטֵא — **unless, at the actual moment of the sin, you rely on your later *teshuvah*, and that itself motivates your sin,** כְּמוֹ שֶׁנִּתְבָּאֵר בְּמָקוֹם אַחֵר — **as is explained elsewhere,** in *Tanya, Igeres Ha-Teshuvah,* chapter 11.

The daily neglect of Torah study by most people is not a calculated act, carried out on the basis that it can be fixed later. It's just nearly impossible to have the focus necessary to study at every moment. Therefore it does not fall under the warning against sinning on the basis of later repentance.

SECTION FOUR: WHY THE SHEMA APPEARS IN DEUTERONOMY

30TH SHEVAT LEAP

Based on the above, the *Tanya* will explain why the *mitzvah* of reciting the *Shema* twice daily was only given to the Jewish people forty years after Sinai, when the children of those who had received the Torah were about to enter the Land of Israel.

וּבָזֶה יוּבַן לָמָּה צִוָּה מֹשֶׁה רַבֵּינוּ עָלָיו הַשָּׁלוֹם בְּמִשְׁנֵה תוֹרָה לַדּוֹר שֶׁנִּכְנְסוּ לָאָרֶץ — **Now we will be able to appreciate why, in** *Deuteronomy* (6:7), **Moses our teacher (*peace unto him!*) commanded the** second **generation, that was** about **to enter the Land** of Israel, לִקְרוֹת קְרִיאַת שְׁמַע פַּעֲמַיִם בְּכָל יוֹם — **to recite the *Shema* twice daily,** לְקַבֵּל עָלָיו מַלְכוּת שָׁמַיִם בִּמְסִירַת נֶפֶשׁ — a *mitzvah* whose purpose is *"to accept G-d's sovereign authority upon yourself,"* (*Talmud, Brachos* 13a) to the point that you are **willing for martyrdom** (*ibid.* 54a; 61b).

Why was reading the *Shema* only necessary for the second generation of Israelites, who would leave the desert and enter the Land of Israel?

וַהֲלֹא הִבְטִיחַ לָהֶם פַּחְדְּכֶם וּמוֹרַאֲכֶם יִתֵּן ה' וְגוֹ' — **Wasn't** the generation that entered the Land **promised,** *"No man will stand before you.... G-d will cast the trepidation and dread of you upon all the land where you will tread"* (*Deuteronomy* 11:25)?

This second generation had been given a direct Divine assurance that they wouldn't be killed by their enemies. Why, then, was it necessary for them to prepare themselves to be "willing for martyrdom" by reading the *Shema*?

אֶלָּא — **Rather,** this second generation didn't receive the *mitzvah* of *Shema* due to an actual threat to their lives, but for another reason, מִשּׁוּם שֶׁקִּיּוּם הַתּוֹרָה וּמִצְוֹתֶיהָ — because, in general, **Torah** תָּלוּי בָּזֶה שֶׁיִּזְכּוֹר תָּמִיד עִנְיַן מְסִירַת נַפְשׁוֹ לַה' עַל יִחוּדוֹ

שיהיה קבוע בלבו תמיד ממש יומם ולילה לא ימיש
מזכרונו כי בזה יוכל לעמוד נגד יצרו לנצחו תמיד בכל
עת ובכל שעה כנ"ל:

and *mitzvah* observance depends on you constantly reminding yourself of your own **willingness for martyrdom, for G-d's oneness.**

As we have learned (in chapters 24-25), an important technique to render *mitzvah* observance "very much within reach" is to recall the willingness for martyrdom shared by all Jews when faced with forced conversion, and then to frame any transgression in the same light, as a complete detachment from G-d.

This helps us understand why the *Shema* was only given to the second generation of Jews, who entered the Land of Israel. Unlike their parents' desert-generation — whose physical needs were taken care of by G-d and who lived in social isolation from any culture that might influence them — the second generation would face formidable challenges of worldly and cultural engagement. In order to resist these temptations, they needed to recall constantly the "dormant love" in their souls, *i.e.,* their willingness for martyrdom, and how they did not want to become detached from G-d, even for a moment. So based on the *Tanya's* insight, we can appreciate that this *mitzvah* was actually introduced at the perfect moment, when Jews were about to encounter assimilatory forces for the first time and needed tools to combat them.

שֶׁיִּהְיֶה קָבוּעַ בְּלִבּוֹ תָּמִיד מַמָּשׁ יוֹמָם וָלַיְלָה לֹא יָמִישׁ מִזִּכְרוֹנוֹ — The willingness for martyrdom **needs to be inscribed in your heart always, literally day and night it should not pass from your consciousness,** כִּי בָּזֶה יוּכַל לַעֲמוֹד נֶגֶד יִצְרוֹ לְנַצְּחוֹ תָּמִיד — be-**cause through this you will be able to stand against your "impulse to evil,"** בְּכָל עֵת וּבְכָל שָׁעָה — **at all times and at any moment,** כַּנִּזְכָּר לְעֵיל — **as mentioned above** in this chapter.

CHAPTER 26

HANDLING NEGATIVE EMOTIONS
SECTION ONE: A BASIC PRINCIPLE IN LIFE

20TH SHEVAT REGULAR | 1ST ADAR I LEAP

Up to this point in the *Tanya*, our discussion has centered around techniques for developing feelings for G-d. The first seventeen chapters focused on using the mind to think about G-d, to generate feelings for Him. In chapters 18-25 we learned a method to get in touch with the "dormant love" found in our souls.

פרק כו ברם   כגון דא צריך לאודעי כלל גדול
כי כמו שנצחון לנצח דבר
גשמי כגון שני אנשים המתאבקים זה עם זה להפיל
זה את זה. הנה אם האחד הוא בעצלות וכבדות ינוצח
בקל ויפול גם אם הוא גבור יותר מחבירו ככה ממש
בנצחון היצר אי אפשר לנצחו בעצלות וכבדות
הנמשכות מעצבות וטמטום הלב כאבן כ"א בזריזות
הנמשכת משמחה ופתיחת הלב וטהרתו מכל נדנוד
דאגה ועצב בעולם. ומ"ש בכל עצב יהיה מותר פי'

Now that we have discovered how to *awaken* love for G-d, we need to learn how to *maintain* it. The greatest challenge, which the *Tanya* will address in the following chapters, is maintaining an upbeat attitude at all times, and not to allow anything to dampen our spirits.

בְּרַם כְּגוֹן דָא צָרִיךְ לְאוֹדְעֵי כְּלָל גָּדוֹל — **But the following must be made known as an all-encompassing principle,** something to bear in mind always.

כִּי כְּמוֹ שֶׁנִּצָחוֹן לְנַצֵּחַ דָּבָר גַּשְׁמִי — **That just as with a physical competition,** כְּגוֹן שְׁנֵי אֲנָשִׁים הַמִּתְאַבְּקִים זֶה — עִם זֶה לְהַפִּיל זֶה אֶת זֶה — **such as two men wrestling together, each one trying to pull the other down,** הִנֵּה — אִם הָאֶחָד הוּא בְּעַצְלוּת וְכַבֵדוּת יְנוּצַח בְּקַל וְיִפּוֹל — **if one of them is sluggish and lethargic, he will easily be defeated and pulled down,** גַּם אִם הוּא גִבּוֹר יוֹתֵר מֵחֲבֵירוֹ — **even if** the sluggish one is **stronger than his opponent,** כָּכָה מַמָּשׁ בְּנִצָחוֹן הַיֵּצֶר — **the same is true, literally, with the fight against your impulse to evil,** אִי אֶפְשָׁר לְנַצְחוֹ בְּעַצְלוּת וְכַבֵדוּת — **you simply can't defeat it with sluggishness and lethargy,** הַנִּמְשָׁכוֹת מֵעַצְבוּת וְטִמְטוּם הַלֵּב — כְּאֶבֶן — **that comes from depression and a stony, desensitized heart** (see *Talmud, Yoma* 39a; *Bachaye* to *Exodus* 23:19).

כִּי אִם בִּזְרִיזוּת הַנִּמְשֶׁכֶת מִשְׂמְחָה וּפְתִיחַת — You will succeed **only with enthusiasm,** הַלֵּב וְטָהֳרָתוֹ מִכָּל נִדְנוּד דְּאָגָה וָעֶצֶב — **which results from joy and a receptive heart,** בָּעוֹלָם — **free from any hint of worry and sadness in the world.**

Of course, this is easier said than done. Everybody seems to have at least "a hint of worry" and periods of sadness. Later in the chapter, the *Tanya* will offer us powerful tools to free ourselves of negative emotions, but for now it is important that we take the "all encompassing principle" to heart: *You cannot succeed in self-mastery unless you can maintain a positive, upbeat approach to life.*

PRACTICAL LESSONS

To win the war against the "impulse to evil" you need to avoid sadness and maintain a positive, upbeat mood.

שיהיה איזה יתרון ומעלה מזה הנה אדרבה מלשון זה
משמע שהעצב מצד עצמו אין בו מעלה רק שיגיע ויבא
ממנו איזה יתרון והיינו השמחה האמיתית בה' אלהיו
הבאה אחר העצב האמיתי לעתים מזומנים על עונותיו
במר נפשו ולב נשבר שע"י זה נשברה רוח הטומאה

SECTION TWO: WHEN NEGATIVE FEELINGS ARE PRODUCTIVE

Before we get to the practical tools, the *Tanya* first questions whether the "all encompassing principle" is, in fact, true. In Scripture we seem to find an explicit teaching that sadness is of value.

וּמַה שֶּׁכָּתוּב בְּכָל עֶצֶב יִהְיֶה מוֹתָר — **As for the verse, *"In every sadness there will be profit"* (*Proverbs* 14:23),** פֵּירוּשׁ שֶׁיִּהְיֶה אֵיזֶה יִתְרוֹן וּמַעֲלָה מִזֶּה — **implying that there is some virtue and advantage to** sadness — this poses no challenge at all to our "all encompassing principle" that sadness is always counterproductive.

הִנֵּה אַדְרַבָּה מִלָּשׁוֹן זֶה מַשְׁמַע שֶׁהָעֶצֶב מִצַּד עַצְמוֹ אֵין בּוֹ מַעֲלָה — **For, on the contrary, the phrasing of this text** in the future tense ("In every sadness there *will be* profit") **suggests that the sadness *itself* has no virtue** at the time when it's experienced, רַק שֶׁיַּגִּיעַ וְיָבֹא מִמֶּנּוּ אֵיזֶה יִתְרוֹן — **rather, some sort of advantage will be gained** from it *later on* ("there *will be* profit").

The *Tanya* now argues that the "sadness" of this verse, which leads to "profit" refers to *carefully scheduled sessions of introspection*. At other times, throughout most of your waking hours, sadness is to be avoided to the utmost.

וְהַיְינוּ הַשִּׂמְחָה הָאֲמִיתִית בַּה' אֱלֹהָיו — **Namely** the "profit" of this sadness refers to **the genuine joy of** feeling close to **G-d, your G-d,** הַבָּאָה אַחַר הָעֶצֶב הָאֲמִיתִי לְעִתִּים **that comes after justified sadness over** מְזוּמָּנִים עַל עֲוֹנוֹתָיו בְּמַר נַפְשׁוֹ וְלֵב נִשְׁבָּר — **your transgressions, with a bitter soul and broken heart,** experienced **at specific times** dedicated to introspection.

שֶׁעַל יְדֵי זֶה נִשְׁבְּרָה רוּחַ הַטּוּמְאָה וְסִטְרָא אַחֲרָא — **Through this** sadness and introspection **the "impure spirit" and *sitra achra* will be shattered,** וּמְחִיצָה שֶׁל בַּרְזֶל הַמַּפְסֶקֶת

A CHASIDIC THOUGHT

Sadness is acceptable, indeed desirable, if it is: a.) experienced only occasionally, during specially scheduled times of introspection, and not when I'm going about my day-to-day life; and, b.) if it's "justified sadness over my transgressions." If both these conditions are met, even though the sadness itself is something negative, it will have a positive result.

וס"א ומחיצה של ברזל המפסקת בינו לאביו שבשמים
כמ"ש בזהר ע"פ רוח נשברה לב נשבר וגו' ואזי יקוים
בו רישיה דקרא תשמיעני ששון ושמחה וגו' השיבה
לי ששון ישעך ורוח נדיבה וגו' וזהו טעם הפשוט לתיקון
האר"י ז"ל לומר מזמור זה אחר תיקון חצות קודם
הלימוד כדי ללמוד בשמחה אמיתית בה' הבאה אחר
העצב שיש לשמחה זו יתרון כיתרון האור הבא מן   33A

בֵּינוֹ לְאָבִיו שֶׁבַּשָּׁמַיִם — as well as the *"iron wall… which interposes between you and your Father in Heaven"* (*Talmud, Pesachim* 85b), כְּמוֹ שֶׁכָּתוּב בַּזֹּהַר עַל פָּסוּק רוּחַ '(3, 8 a-b; 240a-b) **states on the verse,** *"A broken spirit… a heart that is broken* and contrite, you do not reject, O G-d" (Psalms 51:19).

As we learned in chapter 17, your transgressions create a barrier of negative energy which separates you from G-d, an *"iron wall … which interposes between you and your Father in Heaven."* This negative energy barrier can be overcome by *"a broken spirit… a heart that is broken and contrite"* (see pp. 206-7). This is the "profit" that will arise after a carefully executed session of soul-searching and sadness.

וַאֲזַי יְקוּיַּם בּוֹ רֵישֵׁיה דְּקְרָא — **And then,** when you break the negative energy barrier, **the preceding verses will be realized for you,** תַּשְׁמִיעֵנִי שָׂשׂוֹן וְשִׂמְחָה וְגוֹ' הָשִׁיבָה לִי שָׂשׂוֹן יִשְׁעֶךָ וְרוּחַ נְדִיבָה וְגוֹ' — *"Let me hear tidings of joy and gladness…. Restore to me the joy of Your salvation;* sustain me with *a generous spirit"* (Psalms 51:10, 14).

The above discussion sheds light on a Kabbalistic custom.

וְזֶהוּ טַעַם הַפָּשׁוּט לְתִיקּוּן הָאֲרִ"י זִכְרוֹנוֹ לִבְרָכָה לוֹמַר מִזְמוֹר זֶה — **And this is the basic reason why Rabbi Yitzchak Luria introduced the practice of saying this Psalm 51,** אַחַר תִּיקּוּן חֲצוֹת — **after** *Tikun Chatzos* **(Midnight Prayer),** קוֹדֶם הַלִּימוּד — **before the study** which follows (*Pri Etz Chaim, Sha'ar Tikun Chatzos*), כְּדֵי לִלְמוֹד בְּשִׂמְחָה אֲמִיתִּית בַּה' הַבָּאָה אַחַר הָעֶצֶב — **so that the study should be with the true joy of** closeness to **G-d which comes after sadness.**

Tikun Chatzos is a service mourning the destruction of the Temple consisting of selected Psalms, *vidui* (confession) and *kinos* (dirges), to be recited at midnight by individuals or small groups, sitting on the ground. It was instituted in the sixteenth century C.E. in the Kabbalistic circles of Safed. (Nowadays, it is barely practiced).

The *Tanya* notes that Psalm 51 was appended to *Tikun Chatzos* to ensure that the sadness of the service would yield its "profit," and shift the worshiper to a mood of joy, amid the awareness that his "negative energy field" had been shattered.

שֶׁיֵּשׁ לְשִׂמְחָה זוֹ יִתְרוֹן — **For a joy such as this** which comes after a period of melancholy **is superior,** כִּיתְרוֹן הָאוֹר הַבָּא מִן הַחֹשֶׁךְ דְּוְקָא — precisely *"like the advantage of light over darkness"* (*Ecclesiastes* 2:13), כְּמוֹ שֶׁכָּתוּב בַּזֹּהַר עַל פָּסוּק וְרָאִיתִי שֶׁיֵּשׁ

הַחֹשֶׁךְ דַּוְקָא כמ"ש בַּזֹּהַר עַל פָּסוּק וְרָאִיתִי שֶׁיֵּשׁ יִתְרוֹן
לַחָכְמָה מִן הַסִּכְלוּת כִּיתְרוֹן הָאוֹר כו' ע"ש וד"ל וּמִקְרָא
מָלֵא דִבֶּר הַכָּתוּב תַּחַת אֲשֶׁר לֹא עָבַדְתָּ אֶת ה' אֱלֹהֶיךָ
בְּשִׂמְחָה וְגו' וְנוֹדַע לְכָל פִּי' הָאֲרִ"י ז"ל עַל פָּסוּק זֶה:

יִתְרוֹן לַחָכְמָה מִן הַסִּכְלוּת כִּיתְרוֹן הָאוֹר כו' — **as the Zohar** (3, 47b) **states on the verse,** *"And I saw that there is an advantage to wisdom over stupidity, like the advantage of light over darkness (min ha-choshech)."*

"The advantage of light *over* darkness," could also be read, "the advantage of light that comes *from* darkness." Your joy is more powerful when it is a product of some serious soul-searching and the feeling of pain over your mistakes and shortcomings.

וְדַי לַמֵּבִין עַיֵּין שָׁם — **Look up this citation** in the *Zohar,* **but this should** already **be enough for the wise.**

The *Zohar* (*ibid*) states: *"The advantage of light comes only through darkness. What establishes white? Black, for were it not for black, white would not be recognized. And because of black, white is lifted up and made precious. Rabbi Yitzchak said: An analogy would be sweet and bitter. For a person does not recognize sweetness until he tastes bitter. What causes it to be sweet? The bitterness."*

PRACTICAL LESSONS

Sadness over religious matters is only appropriate at specially scheduled sessions of introspection, such as before going to sleep.

The sadness of these sessions helps to restore joy by breaking the negative energy field which surrounded you as a result of your sins.

וּמִקְרָא מָלֵא דִבֶּר הַכָּתוּב — **And Scripture is explicit about** this fundamental importance of eliminating sadness, תַּחַת אֲשֶׁר לֹא עָבַדְתָּ אֶת ה' אֱלֹהֶיךָ בְּשִׂמְחָה וְגו' — *"because you did not serve G-d, your G-d, with joy and with gladness of heart, from an abundance of everything (merov-kol). Therefore, you will serve your enemies, whom G-d will send against you, amid hunger, thirst, nakedness and total destitution etc"* (Deuteronomy 28:47-48; see Rambam, Mishneh Torah, Laws of Lulav 8:15).

וְנוֹדַע לְכָל פֵּירוּשׁ הָאֲרִ"י זִכְרוֹנוֹ לִבְרָכָה עַל פָּסוּק זֶה — **And Arizal's commentary on this verse is well known** (cited in Shenei Luchos Ha-Bris 286a).

The literal meaning of *me-rov kol* is *"from an abundance of everything."* It is because you didn't serve G-d with joy when you had "an abundance of everything," therefore the negative consequences came.

But *Arizal* reads *me-rov kol* as *"more than an abundance of everything."* According to this translation, the verse states: It was because you didn't experience *more joy in your worship of G-d than you did in the abundance of everything else,* that negative consequences followed.

וְהִנֵּה עֵצָה הַיְעוּצָה לְטַהֵר לִבּוֹ מִכָּל עֶצֶב וְנִדְנוּד
דְאָגָה מִמִּילֵי דְעַלְמָא וַאֲפִי׳ בְּנֵי חַיֵי וּמְזוֹנֵי
מוֹדַעַת זֹאת לְכָל מַאֲמַר רַזַ״ל כְּשֵׁם שֶׁמְבָרֵךְ עַל הַטּוֹבָה
כוּ׳ וּפֵירְשׁוּ בַּגְמָ׳ לְקַבּוֹלֵי בְּשִׂמְחָה כְּמוֹ שִׂמְחַת הַטּוֹבָה
הַנִּגְלֵית וְנִרְאֵית כִּי גַם זוֹ לְטוֹבָה רַק שֶׁאֵינָה נִגְלֵית

SECTION THREE: HOW TO COPE WITH SUFFERING

21ST SHEVAT REGULAR

Now the *Tanya* will teach us a powerful tool to eliminate the negative emotions of sadness and worry. (This tool is for sadness and worry about general life-problems, such as issues of health and finance. In section four, we will deal with sadness prompted by religious matters.)

וְהִנֵּה עֵצָה הַיְעוּצָה לְטַהֵר לִבּוֹ מִכָּל עֶצֶב וְנִדְנוּד דְּאָגָה מִמִּילֵי דְעָלְמָא — **Now the following is a** *"prescribed plan"* (Isaiah 14:26) **to free yourself from any sadness or hint of worry about material things,** וַאֲפִילוּ בְּנֵי חַיֵּי וּמְזוֹנֵי — **even** in the highly emotive areas of *"children, health and livelihood"* (see *Talmud, Mo'ed Katan* 28a).

מוֹדַעַת זֹאת לְכָל מַאֲמַר רַבּוֹתֵינוּ זִכְרוֹנָם לִבְרָכָה — **Everyone knows the teaching of our Sages, of blessed memory,** כְּשֵׁם שֶׁמְבָרֵךְ עַל הַטּוֹבָה כוּ׳ — *"A person is obligated to bless (G-d) for misfortune, in the same way that he blesses G-d for the good"* (*Mishnah, Brachos* 54a).

וּפֵירְשׁוּ בַּגְמָרָא לְקַבּוֹלֵי בְּשִׂמְחָה — **And, according to the** *Talmud* **this means,** *"you should accept* misfortune *joyously"* (ibid. 60b), כְּמוֹ שִׂמְחַת הַטּוֹבָה הַנִּגְלֵית וְנִרְאֵית — **with the same joy you would have for good which is open and manifest.**

The *Tanya* takes for granted here that the reader believes in *Hashgacha Pratis* (Divine Providence): that everything is orchestrated by G-d, so it *must* be good.

While everything is good at some level, we do not always perceive it. The good may be either "open and manifest — something which we can appreciate as good in the here and now — or a good which, to mortal eyes, remains hidden.

The *Talmud* suggests that we should joyously accept an occurrence that we can't perceive as "open and manifest good" (i.e., "misfortune"), *as if* we had seen the value in it. Since G-d allowed it to happen, it must be for the good.

כִּי גַם זוֹ לְטוֹבָה — The reason being **because even** this apparently bad occurrence *"is for the good, too"* (*Talmud, Ta'anis* 21a), רַק שֶׁאֵינָה נִגְלֵית וְנִרְאֵית לְעֵינֵי בָשָׂר — **though this fact is not clear or discernible with our mortal eyes.**

The above represents normative, Rabbinic theology. Now the *Tanya* adds an additional insight, based on the Kabbalah.

ונראית לעיני בשר כי היא מעלמא דאתכסי' שלמעלה
מעלמא דאתגלייא שהוא ו״ה משם הוי״ה ב״ה ועלמא

כִּי הִיא מֵעָלְמָא דְּאִתְכַּסְיָא שֶׁלְמַעֲלָה מֵעָלְמָא דְּאִתְגַּלְיָיא — **Because** this apparent misfortune **stems from the "unmanifest world" which is** *above* **the "manifest world."**

The higher, "unmanifest world" (*Zohar* 1, 18a; 154b) contains a greater good, but
one which cannot be appreciated by us here in the "manifest world." You ought to
accept seemingly unfortunate occurrences joyously amid the awareness that, paradoxically, they are an expression of a *higher* source which was unable to express
itself in this world as something positive.

שֶׁהוּא ו״ה מִשֵּׁם הֲוָיָ״ה בָּרוּךְ הוּא — The "manifest world" is represented by the last
two letters **of the Tetragrammaton,** *vav–hei*, ו״ה הוּא י״ה וְעָלְמָא דְּאִתְכַּסְיָא — **and the**
"unmanifest world" is represented by the first two letters of the Tetragrammaton,
yud–hei (Rabbi Naftali Hertz Bacharach, *Eimek Ha-Melech* 11:6).

The four letters of G-d's name, the Tetragrammaton (*yud-hei-vav-hei*) are subdivided by Kabbalists into two groups, indicating that G-d can be experienced in two

A CHASIDIC THOUGHT

The "manifest world" is plagued by *polarity*. North
only exists because of South; light because of dark;
sweetness because of bitterness; and pleasure because of pain.

You might like the idea of a life which is totally devoid
of pain and only offers pleasure, but that's actually impossible because
in the "manifest world" the two experiences are interrelated. They are
two ends of the same pole: If there was no pain, there would be no
pleasure.

In the "unmanifest world," there is only reality—*essence*, or you might
simply call it being. It's just G-d Himself, before He manifested the dual-
ities that we are familiar with. When you shift your consciousness to be
aligned with the "unmanifest world," your priority is not whether you
are feeling pain or pleasure; what matters is that you are *experiencing*
G-d. Pain may be unpleasant, but ultimately, it is also an expression of
G-d.

The shift in consciousness necessary to align yourself with the "unmanifest world" would be impossible if you didn't have *chochmah* in your
soul. *Chochmah* gives you the ability to look beyond your immediate
experience and be totally open to something beyond. In this case, it
enables you to look beyond your personal preference for pleasure over
pain, and focus on the transpersonal reality of being connected with the
"unmanifest world." That's far more precious than anything the manifest world has to offer.

דאתכסיא הוא י"ה וז"ש אשרי הגבר אשר תיסרנו י"ה
וגו' ולכן ארז"ל כי השמחים ביסורים עליהם הכתוב
אומר ואוהביו כצאת השמש בגבורתו כי השמחה היא
מאהבתו קרבת ה' יותר מכל חיי העוה"ז כדכתיב כי
טוב חסדך מחיים וגו' וקרבת ה' היא ביתר שאת
ומעלה אין קץ בעלמא דאתכסיא כי שם חביון עוזו

ways. The last two letters, *vav-hei,* refer to G-d as He is experienced in the manifest world. (The *vav,* which is a vertical line, symbolizes the journey downwards from unmanifest to manifest; and the *hei,* which extends fully in both vertical and horizontal directions, represents the diverse polarization of the manifest world).

The first two letters, yud-hei, refer to G-d as He is unmanifest. This is expressed by the formless *yud,* which typographically is just a dot, devoid of any polarity.

וְזֶהוּ שֶׁכָּתוּב אַשְׁרֵי הַגֶּבֶר אֲשֶׁר תְּיַסְּרֶנּוּ יָ"ה וְגו' — **And this is the meaning of the verse,** *"Fortunate is the man whom You, O G-d, admonish" (Psalms* 94:12), where G-d's name in the verse is spelled *yud-hei,* signifying the unmanifest.

When you experience pleasure, it can be harder to connect to G-d because your own enjoyment draws you away from G-d-consciousness. Pain and "admonishment," on the other hand, force you to shift your consciousness towards the unmanifest, and to forget about yourself—a "fortunate" predicament.

וְלָכֵן אָמְרוּ רַבּוֹתֵינוּ זִכְרוֹנָם לִבְרָכָה — **Therefore, our Sages, of blessed memory, taught,** כִּי הַשְּׂמֵחִים בְּיִסּוּרִים עֲלֵיהֶם הַכָּתוּב אוֹמֵר וְאוֹהֲבָיו כְּצֵאת הַשֶּׁמֶשׁ בִּגְבוּרָתוֹ — **that** *"Those who love Him are like the sun going out in its strength" (Judges* 5:31), **refers to those who** *"happily accept suffering" (Talmud, Shabbos* 88b).

This verse in *Judges* cited by the *Talmud* is, at first glance, elusive. What does *"happily accept suffering"* have to do with *"the sun going out in its strength"?* And how is it connected with the experience of love (*"those who love Him"*)?

כִּי הַשִּׂמְחָה הִיא מֵאַהֲבָתוֹ קִרְבַת ה' יוֹתֵר מִכָּל חַיֵּי הָעוֹלָם הַזֶּה — **Because this happy** acceptance of suffering **comes from a love of closeness to G-d that surpasses anything in this world,** כְּדִכְתִיב כִּי טוֹב חַסְדְּךָ מֵחַיִּים וְגו' — **as the verse states,** *"for (experiencing)* **Your kindness is better than** *(worldly) life" (Psalms* 63:4).

וְקִרְבַת ה' הִיא בְּיֶתֶר שְׂאֵת וּמַעֲלָה לְאֵין קֵץ בְּעָלְמָא דְּאִתְכַּסְיָא — **And if closeness with G-d** is what matters to you, then it is to be found *"with more dignity" (Genesis* 49:3), **and to an immeasurably greater extent in the "unmanifest world."**

The unmanifest precedes the manifest and transcends it. If you want to be closer to G-d then you would prefer a connection with the unmanifest, even if it is painful.

כִּי שָׁם חֶבְיוֹן עוּזּוֹ — **For** in the unmanifest world, *"there His strength is hidden" (Habakkuk* 3:4; see *Sefer Ha-Bahir,* section 148), וְיוֹשֵׁב בְּסֵתֶר עֶלְיוֹן — **and He** *"sits in secrecy on high" (Psalms* 91:1), *i.e.,* His presence is more powerful.

ויושב בסתר עליון ועל כן זוכה לצאת השמש בגבורתו
לעתיד לבא שהיא יציאת חמה מנרתקה שהיא מכוסה
בו בעוה"ז ולעתיד תתגלה מכסויה דהיינו שאז יתגלה
עלמא דאתכסיא ויזרח ויאיר בגילוי רב ועצום לכל
החוסים בו בעוה"ז ומסתופפים בצלו צל החכמה שהוא

וְעַל כֵּן זוֹכֶה לְצֵאת הַשֶּׁמֶשׁ בִּגְבוּרָתוֹ לֶעָתִיד לָבֹא — **That is why** through happily accepting suffering **you will merit** to experience **in the future, "*the sun going out in its strength,*"** שֶׁהִיא יְצִיאַת חַמָּה מִנַּרְתֵּקָה — **which refers to the sun emerging from** its protective **"filter,"** שֶׁהִיא מְכוּסָה בּוֹ בָּעוֹלָם הַזֶּה — which **screens** the sun **in this world,** וְלֶעָתִיד תִּתְגַּלֶּה מִכְּסוּיָה — **whereas in the future,** the sun **will appear out of its "filter."**

As the *Talmud* states, *"In the world-that-is-coming, there will be no purgatory. Rather the Blessed Holy One will bring the sun out of its 'filter,' and through it the righteous will be healed and the wicked will be judged (punished)"* (*Talmud, Nedarim* 8b).

PRACTICAL LESSONS

Even misfortunes in financial, health or family matters will not make you sad when, understanding that they come from G-d, you do not resist them and accept them willingly.

Suffering, in fact, connects you to G-d more deeply, as it rips through directly to the "unmanifest world."

דְּהַיְינוּ שֶׁאָז יִתְגַּלֶּה עָלְמָא דְאִתְכַּסְיָא — **In other words,** the removal of the sun from its "filter" is a metaphor for **a disclosure of the "unmanifest world."**

This answers our earlier question, why the *Talmud* cites a verse about *"the sun going out in its strength"* in reference to those who happily accept suffering. *"The sun going out in its strength"* is a metaphor for the spiritual disclosure of the unmanifest world in the future. By aligning your consciousness *now* to the unmanifest world, through transcending your personal experience of suffering, you make yourself ready for the future time when G-d will unveil the (presently) unmanifest world for all mankind.

וְיִזְרַח וְיָאִיר בְּגִילּוּי רַב וְעָצוּם — The (presently) unmanifest **will then shine and illuminate profusely and intensely,** לְכָל הַחוֹסִים בּוֹ בָּעוֹלָם הַזֶּה — *"to all those who took refuge in (G-d)"* (*Psalms* 18:31) **in the current era,** who had previously aligned themselves with a consciousness of the unmanifest by "happily accepting suffering."

וּמִסְתּוֹפְפִים בְּצִלּוֹ — **And** this experience will be possible only for those who **retreat in His "shade"** (*ibid.* 91:1), now in the current era, *i.e.,* they find G-d in even the "darker" experiences of pain and suffering.

צֵל הַחָכְמָה — **The *"shadow of chochmah"*** (*Ecclesiastes* 7:12), finding G-d in the "shadow" of suffering is made possible by using your *chochmah* (as explained above), which allows you to connect with G-d's *chochmah,* in the "unmanifest world" (the *yud* of the Tetragrammaton).

בחי' צל ולא אורה וטובה נראית וד"ל: אך העצבות
ממילי דשמיא צריך לשית עצות בנפשו לפטר ממנה
אין צריך לומר בשעת עבודה שצריך לעבוד ה'
בשמחה ובטוב לבב אלא אפילו מי שהוא בעל עסקים
ודרך ארץ אם נופל לו עצב ודאגה ממילי דשמיא   33B
בשעת עסקיו בידוע שהוא תחבולת היצר כדי להפילו

שֶׁהוּא בְּחִינַת צֵל וְלֹא אוֹרָה וְטוֹבָה נִרְאֵית — **Referring to the** unmanifest **quality of "shade" as opposed to the** manifested **"light" of overt goodness.**

Thus the Ba'al Shem Tov once told an individual, *"Accept with love everything that comes upon you in this world, and then you will be able to have both this world and the world-that-is-coming"* (Rabbi Ya'akov Yosef of Polonne, *Ben Poras Yosef* (Piotrków 1884), p. 82b).

וְדַי לַמֵּבִין — **And this should** already **be enough for the intelligent** reader.

SECTION FOUR: DEPRESSION OVER SINS

22ND SHEVAT REGULAR

The above method (section 3), was aimed specifically "to free yourself from any sadness or hint of worry *about material things.*"

אַךְ הָעַצְבוּת מִמִּילֵי דִשְׁמַיָּא — **But regarding sadness over religious matters** such as transgressions you have committed, צָרִיךְ לָשִׁית עֵצוֹת בְּנַפְשׁוֹ לִיפָּטֵר מִמֶּנָּה — **you need to *"take counsel from your soul"* (see** *Psalms* 13:3**) to rid yourself of** sadness.

Negative feelings, such as sadness, can be neutralized in one of two ways. You must either: a.) accept things as they are; or, b.) try to change the situation and remove the thing that is making you sad.

When it comes to sadness caused by the material circumstances of your life, such as health and finances, we have learned that the correct approach is "a," to happily *accept* your life-situation. But with "sadness over religious matters," you need to follow path "b" and *change* the situation, "to rid yourself of sadness."

אֵין צָרִיךְ לוֹמַר בְּשָׁעַת עֲבוֹדָה — **Obviously** you can't do this **at the time of actual worship,** שֶׁצָּרִיךְ לַעֲבוֹד ה' בְּשִׂמְחָה וּבְטוּב לֵבָב — **since you must *"worship G-d,* your G-d, *with joy and with gladness of heart* (***Deuteronomy* 28:47).**

During worship you can't allow negative emotions to surface.

אֶלָּא אֲפִילוּ מִי שֶׁהוּא בַּעַל עֲסָקִים וְדֶרֶךְ אֶרֶץ — **But even if you are involved in business and *"worldly affairs"* (***Mishnah, Avos* 3:17**),** אִם נוֹפֵל לוֹ עֶצֶב וּדְאָגָה מִמִּילֵי דִשְׁמַיָּא בְּשָׁעַת עֲסָקָיו — **and a sad thought or concern about religious matters occurs to you while you're doing business,** which is not a time of worship and so, in theory, does not have to be carried out "with joy and with gladness of heart," בְּיָדוּעַ שֶׁהוּא

אח"כ בתאוות ח"ו כנודע שאל"כ מאין באה לו עצבות
אמיתית מחמת אהבת ה' או יראתו באמצע עסקיו.
והנה בין שנפלה לו העצבות בשעת עבודה בת"ת או
בתפלה ובין שנפלה לו שלא בשעת עבודה זאת ישים
אל לבו כי אין הזמן גרמא כעת לעצבות אמיתית אפי'
לדאגת עונות חמורים ח"ו. רק לזאת צריך קביעות
עתים ושעת הכושר בישוב הדעת להתבונן בגדול' ה'
אשר חטא לו כדי שע"י זה יהיה לבו נשבר באמת

תַּחְבּוּלַת הַיֵּצֶר — nevertheless, **this is definitely a tactic of the impulse** to evil, כְּדֵי לְהַפִּילוֹ אַחַר כָּךְ בְּתַאֲווֹת חַס וְשָׁלוֹם — to weaken you so that, **after** feeling sad, **you will succumb to your desires, G-d forbid,** כַּנּוֹדָע — as is known to everyone.

How can the *Tanya* be sure that this is the "impulse to evil" at work?

PRACTICAL LESSONS

A sad spiritual standing caused by your sins should not be "accepted" but eliminated (through scheduled sessions of introspection).

At all other times sad thoughts about your spiritual standing should be "postponed" until the time for an introspective session comes.

שֶׁאִם לֹא כֵן מֵאַיִן בָּאָה לוֹ עַצְבוּת אֲמִיתִּית מֵחֲמַת אֲהַבַת ה' אוֹ יִרְאָתוֹ בְּאֶמְצַע עֲסָקִיו — **Because if this weren't the case, from where would justified sadness (arising from love or reverence of G-d) come to you in the middle of your business activities?**

The *Tanya* offers a practical suggestion.

וְהִנֵּה בֵּין שֶׁנָּפְלָה לוֹ הָעַצְבוּת בִּשְׁעַת עֲבוֹדָה בְּתַלְמוּד תּוֹרָה אוֹ בִּתְפִלָּה וּבֵין שֶׁנָּפְלָה לוֹ שֶׁלֹּא בִּשְׁעַת עֲבוֹדָה — So, regard-less of whether sadness comes upon you during wor-ship (Torah study or prayer), or it comes to you when not at worship, זֹאת יָשִׂים אֶל לִבּוֹ — the following is what you should tell yourself, כִּי אֵין הַזְּמַן גְּרָמָא כָּעֵת לְעַצְבוּת אֲמִיתִּית — "Now is not a good time to have justified sadness, אֲפִילוּ לְדַאֲגַת עֲווֹנוֹת חֲמוּרִים חַס וְשָׁלוֹם — it's not even the right time to worry about serious transgres-sions, G-d forbid."

But if sadness is not appropriate during worship or during work, then when *is* the appropriate time to surface negative emotions over "religious matters," so as to rid yourself of them?

רַק לְזֹאת צָרִיךְ קְבִיעוּת עִתִּים — **Rather, this task** of genu-ine introspection **requires specially scheduled sessions,** לְהִתְבּוֹנֵן — **an appropriate moment with a settled mind,** וּשְׁעַת הַכּוֹשֶׁר בְּיִשּׁוּב הַדַּעַת בִּגְדוּלַת ה' אֲשֶׁר חָטָא לוֹ — **to reflect on the greatness of G-d, against whom you have sinned,** כְּדֵי שֶׁעַל יְדֵי זֶה יִהְיֶה לִבּוֹ נִשְׁבָּר בֶּאֱמֶת בִּמְרִירוּת אֲמִיתִּית — **so that your heart will be genuinely broken with real remorse.**

במרירות אמיתית וכמבואר עת זו במ"א ושם נתבאר
ג"כ כי מיד אחר שנשבר לבו בעתים קבועים ההם אזי
יסיר העצב מלבו לגמרי ויאמין אמונה שלימה כי ה'
העביר חטאתו ורב לסלוח וזו היא השמחה האמיתית
בה' הבאה אחר העצב כנ"ל:

פרק כז ואם   העצבות אינה מדאגת עונות אלא
מהרהורים רעים ותאוות רעות

וּכְמְבוֹאָר עֵת זוֹ בְּמָקוֹם אַחֵר — **And elsewhere, it is explained when this time should be** (see chapter 41 and *Igeres Ha-Teshuvah* chapters 7 and 10, that the best time is at night, before you go to bed).

כִּי מִיָּד אַחַר שֶׁנִּשְׁבַּר לִבּוֹ בְּעִתִּים, וְשָׁם נִתְבָּאֵר גַּם כֵּן — **And there it is also explained,** קְבוּעִים הָהֵם — **that, during these sessions, immediately after having feelings of brokenheartedness,** אֲזַי יָסִיר הָעֶצֶב מִלִּבּוֹ לְגַמְרֵי — **you should then** not dwell on the feeling but **completely wipe away any sadness from your heart,** וְיַאֲמִין אֱמוּנָה שְׁלֵימָה כִּי ה' הֶעֱבִיר חַטָּאתוֹ וְרַב לִסְלוֹחַ — **and believe with perfect faith that G-d has erased your sin and that He is very forgiving.**

וְזוֹ הִיא הַשִּׂמְחָה הָאֲמִיתִית בַּה' הַבָּאָה אַחַר הָעֶצֶב — **And this is the genuine joy of closeness to G-d which comes after sadness,** כַּנִּזְכָּר לְעֵיל — **as mentioned above.**

CHAPTER 27

YOU'RE WONDERFULLY IMPERFECT
SECTION ONE: DEALING WITH INAPPROPRIATE THOUGHTS

23RD SHEVAT REGULAR | 2ND ADAR I LEAP

Chapter 27 is the second of three chapters offering advice for sadness and depression. In the previous chapter we discussed how to deal with sadness that comes because you have *actually* sinned. In this chapter and the next, we will deal with sadness that comes because you *desire* to do all sorts of sins, making your worship feel like something of a failure. Even after years of devotional prayer and observance, you can't seem to uproot these desires.

וְאִם הָעַצְבוּת אֵינָה מִדְּאֲגַת עֲוֹנוֹת — **But if your sadness is not from concern about your sins,** אֶלָּא מֵהִרְהוּרִים רָעִים וְתַאֲווֹת רָעוֹת שֶׁנּוֹפְלוֹת בְּמַחֲשַׁבְתּוֹ — **but rather, from** the fact that **bad thoughts and inappropriate desires pop into your mind,** consider the following.

שְׁנוֹפְלוֹת בְּמַחֲשַׁבְתּוֹ. הִנֵּה אִם נוֹפְלוֹת לוֹ שֶׁלֹּא
בִּשְׁעַת הָעֲבוֹדָה אֶלָּא בְּעֵת עִסְקוֹ בַּעֲסָקָיו וְדֶרֶךְ אֶרֶץ
וּכְהַאי גַוְונָא אַדְּרַבָּה יֵשׁ לוֹ לִשְׂמוֹחַ בְּחֶלְקוֹ שֶׁאַף
שְׁנוֹפְלוֹת לוֹ בְּמַחֲשַׁבְתּוֹ הוּא מַסִּיחַ דַּעְתּוֹ מֵהֶן לְקַיֵּם
מַה שֶׁנֶּאֱמַר וְלֹא תָתוּרוּ אַחֲרֵי לְבַבְכֶם וְאַחֲרֵי עֵינֵיכֶם
אֲשֶׁר אַתֶּם זוֹנִים אַחֲרֵיהֶם. וְאֵין הַכָּתוּב מְדַבֵּר בְּצַדִּיקִי'
לְקָרְאָם זוֹנִים ח"וּ אֶלָּא בַּבֵּינוֹנִים כַּיּוֹצֵא בּוֹ שְׁנוֹפְלִים לוֹ

When you are trying to live life piously, negative thoughts and inappropriate desires can be unnerving. They might make you feel there is something wrong with you, or that you have failed to achieve a basic level of worship.

הִנֵּה — **Well,** it depends *when* these thoughts occur to you, אִם נוֹפְלוֹת לוֹ שֶׁלֹּא בִּשְׁעַת הָעֲבוֹדָה — **if they pop into your** mind, **not during worship,** אֶלָּא בְּעֵת עִסְקוֹ בַּעֲסָקָיו וְדֶרֶךְ אֶרֶץ וּכְהַאי גַוְונָא — **but rather, when you are involved in business and** *"worldly affairs"* (*Mishnah, Avos* 3:17), etc., אַדְּרַבָּה יֵשׁ לוֹ לִשְׂמוֹחַ בְּחֶלְקוֹ — then, rather than being a cause of sadness, **on the contrary, you should be** *"happy with your lot"* (*ibid.* 4:1).

The *Tanya* will now explain why, far from being saddened by these inappropriate thoughts, they should actually be a cause for joy.

שֶׁאַף שְׁנוֹפְלוֹת לוֹ בְּמַחֲשַׁבְתּוֹ — Since you can rejoice in the fact that **even though** these inappropriate thoughts **popped into your mind,** הוּא מַסִּיחַ דַּעְתּוֹ מֵהֶן — you nevertheless chose not to dwell on them, and **you chose to divert your attention away from them** to something else.

You cannot decide what pops into your head, but you can divert your thoughts to another topic. Whenever an inappropriate thought occurs to you, don't get depressed about the fact that it happened. That's totally normal and it's not under your control in any case. Focus on the need to dismiss it as soon as possible through diverting your attention to something appropriate.

And then, rather than being sad, you can rejoice, because you did a *mitzvah*: you resisted dwelling on a negative thought.

The *Tanya* now clarifies precisely which *mitzvah* you will be fulfilling.

לְקַיֵּם מַה שֶׁנֶּאֱמַר וְלֹא תָתוּרוּ אַחֲרֵי לְבַבְכֶם וְאַחֲרֵי עֵינֵיכֶם אֲשֶׁר אַתֶּם זוֹנִים אַחֲרֵיהֶם — By refusing to dwell on a negative thought **you fulfill the verse,** *"And you shall not follow after your heart and after your eyes, after which you stray"* (*Numbers* 15:39; see *Rambam, Sefer Ha-Mitzvos,* prohibition 47).

וְאֵין הַכָּתוּב מְדַבֵּר בְּצַדִּיקִים — **Now this verse can't be speaking to** *tzadikim,* who have transformed themselves never to have inappropriate thoughts, לְקָרְאָם זוֹנִים חַס וְשָׁלוֹם — this cannot be the case, as the verse would not refer to *tzadikim* as **"strayers,"** **G-d forbid.**

הרהורי ניאוף במחשבתו בין בהיתר כו' וכשמסיח
דעתו מקיים לאו זה ואמרו רז"ל ישב ולא עבר עבירה
נותנים לו שכר כאלו עשה מצוה ועל כן צריך לשמוח
בקיום הלאו כמו בקיום מצות עשה ממש ואדרבה
העצבות היא מגסות הרוח שאינו מכיר מקומו ועל כן

34A

The verse states, "And you shall not follow after your heart and after your eyes, *after which you stray*," addressing those individuals who are at least tempted to follow their inappropriate thoughts.

אֶלָּא בְּבֵינוֹנִים כַּיּוֹצֵא בּוֹ — **Rather** the verse is addressing those who are still tempted by the impulse to evil, **such as** *beinonim* **and** *resha'im,* שֶׁנּוֹפְלִים לוֹ הִרְהוּרֵי נִיאוּף בֵּין בְּהֶיתֵּר כו' בְּמַחֲשַׁבְתּוֹ — **who do have lustful thoughts popping into their minds,** **whether they be** thoughts of **permitted activities or** forbidden ones (see above chapter 11, p. 133 and chapter 7, pp. 92-3).

וּכְשֶׁמַּסִּיחַ דַּעְתּוֹ מְקַיֵּים לָאו זֶה — I.e., the verse is speaking of people who *are* plagued by such thoughts **but subsequently avert their attention from** these thoughts, **fulfilling this Biblical prohibition,** *"And you shall not follow etc."*

Technically, however, you didn't do a *mitzvah* by pushing away these negative thoughts; you just avoided transgressing a prohibition (*And you shall not follow etc.*"). Why, then, should this lead you to joy? It makes sense that through a positive *mitzvah,* which brings you closer to G-d, you would become joyous; but now you seem to be no closer than before. You just avoided becoming more distant.

יָשַׁב וְלֹא וְאָמְרוּ רַבּוֹתֵינוּ זִכְרוֹנָם לִבְרָכָה — **And our Sages, of blessed memory, taught,** עָבַר עֲבֵירָה נוֹתְנִים לוֹ שָׂכָר כְּאִלּוּ עָשָׂה מִצְוָה — *"One who stays put (in the face of temptation) and does not transgress, will be given the same reward as if he had (actively) performed a positive mitzvah"* (*Talmud, Kidushin* 39b).

וְעַל כֵּן צָרִיךְ לִשְׂמוֹחַ בְּקִיּוּם הַלָּאו — **Therefore** after diverting your attention from an inappropriate thought **you ought to rejoice at having obeyed this Biblical prohibition,** כְּמוֹ בְּקִיּוּם מִצְוַת עֲשֵׂה מַמָּשׁ — with the same level of joy **as if you had actually fulfilled a positive** *mitzvah.*

SECTION TWO: HOW YOUR EGO TRICKS YOU

3RD ADAR I LEAP

The reality is that by diverting your attention from an inappropriate thought you have done everything right and nothing wrong. Why, then, would you imagine this to be a source of sadness in the first place?

וְאַדְרַבָּה הָעַצְבוּת הִיא מִגַּסוּת הָרוּחַ — **On the contrary, sadness** from inappropriate thoughts **comes from** *"an inflated ego"* (see *Talmud, Sotah* 4b).

יֵרַע לבבו על שאינו במדרגת צדיק שלצדיקים בודאי
אין נופלים להם ההרהורי שטות כאלו כי אילו היה מכיר
מקומו שהוא רחוק מאד ממדרגת צדיק והלואי היה
בינוני ולא רשע כל ימיו אפי' שעה אחת הרי זאת היא
מדת הבינונים ועבודתם לכבוש היצר וההרהור העולה

Such a sadness is not, as it may first appear, the result of a holy urge to become a better person. It's a trick of the ego.

PRACTICAL LESSONS

Don't get upset if your mind is constantly distracted by inappropriate thoughts (when not at worship). Actually, you should be happy since this gives you the opportunity to do a *mitzvah* and divert your mind from these inappropriate thoughts by contemplating something else.

Getting upset about inappropriate thoughts is delusional. It's your evil inclination trying to get you depressed by setting an unreasonable goal. First worry about achieving mastery over your thought, speech and action, which you *can* do.

שֶׁאֵינוֹ מַכִּיר מְקוֹמוֹ — **That you don't** *"know your place"* (see *Mishnah, Avos* 6:6), and realize that you haven't yet transformed yourself to be rid of the impulse to evil, וְעַל כֵּן יֵרַע לְבָבוֹ עַל שֶׁאֵינוֹ בְּמַדְרֵגַת צַדִּיק — **and** your inflated ego **makes you feel depressed that you're not at the level of** *tzadik*, שֶׁלַצַּדִיקִים בְּוַדַּאי אֵין נוֹפְלִים לָהֶם הִרְהוּרֵי שְׁטוּת כָּאֵלּוּ — **and since** *tzadikim* **definitely don't have such foolish thoughts,** you get sad when you do have them.

כִּי אִילוּ הָיָה מַכִּיר מְקוֹמוֹ שֶׁהוּא רָחוֹק מְאֹד מִמַּדְרֵגַת צַדִּיק — All this is delusional thinking of the ego, **because if you would** *"know your place"* **you would realize that you are very far from the level of** *tzadik*, and the expectation of being free from inappropriate thoughts is totally unrealistic.

וְהַלְוַאי הָיָה בֵּינוֹנִי וְלֹא רָשָׁע כָּל יָמָיו אֲפִילוּ שָׁעָה אַחַת — **And** a more realistic expectation would be: **If only you would become a** *beinoni* **and not be a** *rasha* **for even one moment, the whole of your life!**

As we learned above, to reach the level of *beinoni* you don't need to rid yourself of the *temptation* to sin, but only from *actual* sin. This goal is attainable by every person, since we are given control over our actions and thoughts. To aim towards an even greater goal, of eliminating the urge to sin (*tzadik*) before reaching complete mastery over thought, speech and action (*beinoni*), is unrealistic and counterproductive. It is, in fact, nothing other than a trick of the ego trying to get you depressed, which will lower your "resistance" to sin.

הֲרֵי זֹאת הִיא מִדַּת הַבֵּינוֹנִים וַעֲבוֹדָתָם — **What** *beinonim* **are capable of in their worship,** לִכְבּוֹשׁ הַיֵּצֶר וְהַהִרְהוּר הָעוֹלֶה — **is to** always **get the better of the impulse to evil and** expel inappropriate **thoughts that rise from**

מהלב למוח ולהסיח דעתו לגמרי ממנו ולדחותו בשתי
ידים כנ"ל ובכל דחיה ודחיה שמדחהו ממחשבתו
אתכפיא ס"א לתתא ובאתערותא דלתתא אתערותא
דלעילא ואתכפיא ס"א דלעילא המגביה עצמה כנשר
לקיים מ"ש אם תגביה כנשר וגו' משם אורידך נאם

the emotional center in the **heart to the brain,** וּלְהָסִיחַ דַּעְתּוֹ לְגַמְרֵי מִמֶּנּוּ — **to divert the mind completely from them,** וְלִדְחוֹתוֹ בִּשְׁתֵּי יָדָיִם — **and to dismiss** each inappropriate thought vigorously **"with two hands,"** כַּנִּזְכָּר לְעֵיל — **as mentioned earlier,** (chapter 12, p. 149).

If you aim for this lower goal of *beinoni* now, which is realistic, you can succeed and feel happy about your achievement. If you aim to be a *tzadik*, expecting not to have inappropriate thoughts at all, you are setting yourself up for disappointment.

SECTION THREE: YOUR STRUGGLE IS SACRED

4TH ADAR I LEAP

Is the worship of *beinonim* really inferior to that of *tzadikim*? It might seem that a person tempted by sin is more distant from G-d than one who is not, but that misses an essential point: *G-d derives pleasure from our struggle to be close to Him.*

There is nothing to be disappointed about if you spend your whole life as a spiritual warrior, constantly battling with your darker side. Every time you win, it brings great pleasure on High in a unique way that no *tzadik* can achieve, as the *Tanya* will now elaborate.

וּבְכָל דְּחִיָּה וּדְחִיָּה שֶׁמְּדַחֵהוּ מִמַּחֲשַׁבְתּוֹ — **And with each and every dismissal** of an inappropriate thought **which you** succeed in **dismissing from your mind,** אִתְכַּפְיָא סִטְרָא אָחֳרָא לְתַתָּא — the negative forces of *sitra achra,* **below** in this world, **are subdued** (see citations from *Zohar,* below).

When the negative forces tempt you to sin but fail, those forces become weaker and are subdued. The *sitra achra* in your Animal Soul may not be eliminated completely as it is with the *tzadik*, but every time you resist a transgression, the negative forces inside you take a blow.

וּבְאִתְעֲרוּתָא דִּלְתַתָּא אִתְעֲרוּתָא דִּלְעֵילָא — And, *"with an awakening from below, there is an awaking from Above"* (Zohar 2, 135b), וְאִתְכַּפְיָא סִטְרָא אָחֳרָא דִּלְעֵילָא — with the weakening of the *sitra achra* down here, **the sitra achra is subdued above,** in the higher worlds.

The *Tanya* now shows where this idea is hinted at in Scripture.

הַמַּגְבִּיהַ עַצְמָהּ כַּנֶּשֶׁר — And as, we learned in chapter 22, the *sitra achra* has the energy of an inflated ego, which **makes itself *"as high as an eagle"*** (Jeremiah 49:16; see p. 253), לְקַיֵּם מַה שֶּׁנֶּאֱמַר אִם תַּגְבִּיהַ כַּנֶּשֶׁר וְגוֹ' מִשָּׁם אוֹרִידְךָ נְאֻם ה' — so by

ה' וכמו שהפליג בזהר פ' תרומה [דף קכח] בגודל נחת
רוח לפניו ית' כד אתכפיא ס"א לתתא דאסתלק יקרא
דקב"ה לעילא על כולא יתיר משבח' אחרא ואסתלקות'
דא יתיר מכולא וכו'. ולכן אל יפול לב אדם עליו ולא
ירע לבבו מאד גם אם יהיה כן כל ימיו במלחמה זו כי
אולי לכך נברא וזאת עבודתו לאכפיא לס"א תמיד.

subduing it, you **fulfill the verse, "'If you lift yourself high like an eagle... from there I will bring you down,' says G-d"** (*Ovadiah* 1:4).

וּכְמוֹ שֶׁהִפְלִיג בַּזֹּהַר פָּרָשַׁת תְּרוּמָה [דַּף קכ"ח] בְּגוֹדֶל נַחַת רוּחַ לְפָנָיו יִתְבָּרֵךְ כַּד אִתְכַּפְיָא סִטְרָא אָחֳרָא לְתַתָּא — **And as the *Zohar*, in *Parshas Terumah* page 128a, enthuses about the immense pleasure brought to G-d when the *sitra achra* is subdued here below,** דְּאִסְתַּלֵּק יְקָרָא דְּקוּדְשָׁא בְּרִיךְ הוּא לְעֵילָּא עַל כּוֹלָּא יַתִּיר מִשְּׁבָחָא אָחֳרָא וְאִסְתַּלְקוּתָא דָּא יַתִּיר מִכּוֹלָּא וְכוּ' — **"Then the glory of the Blessed Holy One is exalted more than by any other praise, and this ascent is greater than all! Why? Because he causes the sitra achra to be subdued, and elevates the glory of the Blessed Holy One."**

In another place, the *Zohar* clarifies further: "There is no light other than that which comes out of darkness. For when this sitra (achra) is subdued, the glory of the Blessed Holy One ascends, and He is exalted in glory. There is no worship of the Blessed Holy One which does not come from darkness; and no good except that which comes from evil. When a person follows an evil path and then leaves it, the Blessed Holy One ascends in His glory. Therefore, total perfection is when good and evil (first struggle) together, (and then) rise to the good afterward... This is ideal worship" (*Zohar* 2, 184a; see also *ibid.* 67b. For the *Tanya's* discussion of "ideal worship" see above chapter 13, pp. 164-5; chapter 15, p. 187).

SECTION FOUR: DESTINED TO STRUGGLE

24TH SHEVAT REGULAR

וְלָכֵן אַל יִפּוֹל לֵב אָדָם עָלָיו — **Therefore, "no person should be downhearted"** (1 *Samuel* 17:32), וְלֹא יֵרַע לְבָבוֹ מְאֹד — **nor should you be too sad,** גַּם אִם יִהְיֶה כֵּן כָּל יָמָיו בְּמִלְחָמָה זוֹ — **even if you spend all your days in this struggle,** כִּי אוּלַי לְכָךְ נִבְרָא — **for perhaps it was for this purpose that you were created,** וְזֹאת עֲבוֹדָתוֹ לְאַכְפִּיָא לְסִטְרָא אָחֳרָא תָּמִיד — **to constantly *subdue* the *sitra achra* through your worship,** never to succeed in *eliminating* it from you.

As we have seen from the *Zohar*, there is tremendous value in struggle. It makes sense that G-d would create many people with the inability to eliminate the evil within them and only the ability to subdue it, so that they can spend their life in the precious task of struggling in worship. That's nothing to be sad about.

ועל זה אמר איוב בראת רשעים ולא שיהיו רשעים
באמת ח"ו אלא שיגיע אליהם כמעשה הרשעים
במחשבתם והרהורם לבד והם יהיו נלחמים תמיד
להסיח דעתם מהם כדי לאכפי' לס"א ולא יוכלו לבטלה
מכל וכל כי זה נעשה ע"י צדיקים. ושני מיני נחת רוח

וְעַל זֶה אָמַר אִיּוֹב בָּרָאתָ רְשָׁעִים — **It is about this** idea of being born to struggle **that Job said,** *"You have created wicked people"* (*Talmud*, Bava Basra 16a).

In chapter 1, we questioned Job's statement, *"Master of the Universe! You have created righteous people and You have created wicked people,"* which seems to imply predestination, something that is at odds with Judaism's core belief in free choice.

In chapter 14 the *Tanya* clarified the first half of Job's statement (*"You have created righteous people"*), interpreting it to mean that G-d created a certain number of people with *the potential* to rise above the level of *beinoni* and become a *tzadik*. Now we will address the second half of Job's statement, (*"You have created wicked people"*).

וְלֹא שֶׁיִּהְיוּ רְשָׁעִים בֶּאֱמֶת חַס וְשָׁלוֹם — **This doesn't mean that** G-d predestined some people **to actually be wicked, G-d forbid,** because this would take away their free choice, אֶלָּא שֶׁיַּגִּיעַ אֲלֵיהֶם כְּמַעֲשֵׂה הָרְשָׁעִים בְּמַחֲשַׁבְתָּם וְהִרְהוּרָם לְבָד — **but rather,** *"it will befall them as though they acted wickedly"* (*Ecclesiastes* 8:14), in their **thoughts and fantasies alone,** וְהֵם יִהְיוּ נִלְחָמִים תָּמִיד לְהָסִיחַ דַּעְתָּם מֵהֶם כְּדֵי לְאַכְפְּיָא לְסִטְרָא אָחֳרָא — **and they will be in a constant struggle to divert their attention from** these thoughts and fantasies **so as to subdue the** *sitra achra*, וְלֹא יוּכְלוּ לְבַטְלָהּ מִכֹּל וָכֹל — **but they will not be able to rid themselves completely** of the *sitra achra*, כִּי זֶה נַעֲשֶׂה עַל יְדֵי צַדִּיקִים — **since this is the** exclusive **accomplishment of** *tzadikim*.

Job's statement, *"You have created wicked people,"* doesn't meant that G-d has predestined anyone to *be* wicked. It simply means that many of us will struggle with the evil within us all our lives, and will never succeed in completely eliminating it. We will always harbor the urge to be wicked.

5TH ADAR I LEAP

Job's statement, that some people are destined to struggle while others are not, leaves us without clarity. Does G-d desire struggle or not?

PRACTICAL LESSONS

G-d gets immense pleasure when the *sitra achra* (negative forces) are subdued. That's something you can do (by resisting transgression) but a *tzadik* can't (because he doesn't want to sin).

לְפָנָיו יִתְבָּרֵךְ לְמַעְלָה. א' מביטול הס"א לגמרי ואתהפכא
ממרירו למתקא ומחשוכא לנהורא ע"י הצדיקים.
והשנית כד אתכפיא הס"א בעודה בתקפה וגבורתה
ומגביה עצמה כנשר ומשם מורידה ה' באתערותא
דלתתא ע"י הבינונים. וז"ש הכתוב ועשה לי מטעמים
כאשר אהבתי מטעמים לשון רבים שני מיני נחת רוח

34B

וּשְׁנֵי מִינֵי נַחַת רוּחַ לְפָנָיו יִתְבָּרֵךְ לְמַעְלָה — **And there are two ways in which G-d derives pleasure on High.**

G-d creates some individuals who will struggle forever, and some who will not, since there are two different ways in which He derives pleasure from human activity.

אֶחָד מִבִּיטוּל הַסִּטְרָא אָחֲרָא לְגַמְרֵי — **The first is from** *eliminating* **the** *sitra achra* **completely,** וְאִתְהַפְּכָא מִמְּרִירוּ לְמִתְקָא וּמֵחֲשׁוֹכָא לִנְהוֹרָא — thereby *transforming* bitter to sweet and darkness to light (*Zohar* 1, 4a), עַל יְדֵי הַצַּדִּיקִים — a task achieved by the *tzadikim.*

וְהַשֵּׁנִית כַּד אִתְכַּפְיָא הַסִּטְרָא אָחֲרָא בְּעוֹדָהּ בְּתָקְפָּהּ וּגְבוּרָתָהּ — **And the second, when** **the** *sitra achra* **is** *subdued,* **while it retains its full strength and power,** וּמַגְבִּיהַ עַצְמָהּ כַּנֶּשֶׁר — **and the inflated ego continues to make itself "as high as an eagle,"** וּמִשָּׁם מוֹרִידָהּ ה' — **and "from there,"** at its peak of strength and power, **G-d brings** the *sitra achra* **down,** subduing it, בְּאִתְעָרוּתָא דִלְתַתָּא — and He does so as a direct result of "*an awakening from below" i.e.,* when we struggle with the evil within us and overcome it, עַל יְדֵי הַבֵּינוֹנִים — a task achieved **by** beinonim.

וְזֶהוּ שֶׁאָמַר הַכָּתוּב וַעֲשֵׂה לִי מַטְעַמִּים כַּאֲשֶׁר אָהַבְתִּי — **And this** notion that G-d derives pleasure in two different ways is hinted **in the verse, "And make me delicacies that I love"** (Genesis 27:4), מַטְעַמִּים לְשׁוֹן רַבִּים שְׁנֵי מִינֵי נַחַת רוּחַ — where the use of the term "delicacies" in the plural, suggests two different kinds of gratification.

While, at the literal level, this verse was a request from Isaac to Esau to prepare food for him, the *Tikunei Zohar* reads it as a request from G-d to the Jewish people.

A CHASIDIC THOUGHT

G-d derives pleasure from both the transformation (*is'hapcha*) of evil, and the subduing (*iskafya*) of evil. Both phenomena have their own virtues. *Transformation* is more powerful in that evil is disposed of and eliminated. *Subduing* evil is more powerful in that the forces of evil are humiliated and shown to be impotent, even at the peak of their powers.

והוא מאמר השכינה לבניה כללות ישראל כדפי'
בתיקונים. וכמו שבמטעמים גשמיים ד"מ יש שני
מיני מעדנים אחד ממאכלים ערבים ומתוקים. והשני
מדברים חריפים או חמוצי' רק שהם מתובלים ומתוקני'
היטב עד שנעשו מעדנים להשיב הנפש. וז"ש הכתו'
כל פעל ה' למענהו וגם רשע ליום רעה פי' שישוב
מרשעו ויעשה הרע שלו יום ואור למעלה כד אתכפיא

וְהוּא מַאֲמַר הַשְּׁכִינָה לְבָנֶיהָ כְּלָלוּת יִשְׂרָאֵל כִּדְפֵירְשׁוּ בַּתִּיקוּנִים — **And, as the *Tikunei Zohar* explains (51b), these are the words of the *Shechinah* (Divine Presence) to her children, the Jewish people.**

וּכְמוֹ שֶׁבְּמַטְעַמִּים גַּשְׁמִיִּים דֶּרֶךְ מָשָׁל יֵשׁ שְׁנֵי מִינֵי מַעֲדַנִּים — In this context the verse implies that **just as, for example, with physical delicacies, there are two different types of gourmet foods,** אֶחָד מִמַּאֲכָלִים עֲרֵבִים וּמְתוּקִים — **the first are foods that are** naturally **pleasant and sweet,** וְהַשֵּׁנִי מִדְּבָרִים חֲרִיפִים אוֹ חֲמוּצִים — **and the second are sharp or acidic foods** that, in their natural form are quite unpalatable, רַק שֶׁהֵם מְתוּבָּלִים וּמְתוּקָּנִים הֵיטֵב עַד שֶׁנַּעֲשׂוּ מַעֲדַנִּים לְהָשִׁיב הַנֶּפֶשׁ — **only they have been seasoned and prepared so well that they have now become soul-stirring gourmet items.**

Similarly, on High, G-d derives pleasure from the "sweet" worship of *tzadikim*, who have eliminated any traces of the "bitter" from their personalities. But He also enjoys those that still harbor "sharp or acidic" traits, and yet struggle with them until they are "seasoned and prepared well" for G-d.

וְזֶהוּ שֶׁאָמַר הַכָּתוּב כֹּל פָּעַל ה' לַמַּעֲנֵהוּ וְגַם רָשָׁע לְיוֹם רָעָה — **And this is** also indicated by the verse, **"G-d has made everything for His sake, even the wicked for an evil day,"** (*Proverbs* 16:4), פֵּירוּשׁ שֶׁיָּשׁוּב מֵרִשְׁעוֹ וְיַעֲשֶׂה הָרַע שֶׁלּוֹ יוֹם וְאוֹר לְמַעְלָה — **meaning that** the wicked person **ought to repent from his wickedness, and thereby turn his evil into "day" and illumination Above,** כַּד אִתְכַּפְיָא סִטְרָא אָחֳרָא וְאִסְתַּלֵּק יְקָרָא דְּקוּדְשָׁא בְּרִיךְ הוּא לְעֵילָא — **as when the *sitra achra* is subdued and glory of the Blessed Holy One ascends on High** (as we learned above, from the *Zohar*).

Everything, including evil, was created for the sake of G-d. While G-d detests evil and desires its elimination, He does derive pleasure and "illumination" when evil is merely subdued. And that is why evil exists, to glorify G-d through its suppression (and eventually elimination).

SECTION FIVE: DELAYING GRATIFICATION

25TH SHEVAT REGULAR | 6TH ADAR I LEAP

Up to this point we have discussed subduing the *sitra achra* through resisting sinful activity. But, as the *Tanya* has explained at length, even permitted pleasures derive

ס"א ואסתלק יקרא דקב"ה לעילא. ולא עוד אלא אפי'
בדברים המותרים לגמרי כל מה שהאדם זובח יצרו
אפי' שעה קלה ומתכוין לאכפיא לס"א שבחלל
השמאלי כגון שחפץ לאכול ומאחר סעודתו עד לאחר
שעה או פחות ועוסק בתורה באותה שעה. כדאיתא
בגמ' שעה רביעית מאכל כל אדם שעה ששית מאכל
ת"ח. והיו מרעיבים עצמם שתי שעות לכוונה זו אף
שגם אחר הסעודה היו לומדים כל היום. וכן אם

their energy from the *sitra achra* (albeit the less potent form of *kelipas nogah* — see chapter 7). So another way of subduing the *sitra achra* is by delaying (or resisting) gratification from permitted pleasures.

וְלֹא עוֹד אֶלָּא אֲפִילוּ בִּדְבָרִים הַמּוּתָּרִים לְגַמְרֵי — **And what is more,** the "glory" and illumination of subduing the *sitra achra* can be achieved, not only by resisting sinful activity, **but even by** resisting **things that are totally permissible** in Jewish Law, כָּל מַה שֶׁהָאָדָם זוֹבֵחַ יִצְרוֹ אֲפִילוּ שָׁעָה קַלָּה — **so long as you** *"slaughter your impulse to evil"* (*Talmud, Sanhedrin* 43b) and resist indulgence in a permitted pleasure, **even for a short while,** וּמִתְכַּוֵּין לְאַכְפְּיָא לְסִטְרָא אָחֳרָא שֶׁבֶּחָלָל הַשְׂמָאלִי — **and** during this time **you have the intention of subduing the** *sitra achra* **in the** heart's **left chamber.**

The *Tanya* offers a practical example:

כְּגוֹן שֶׁחָפֵץ לֶאֱכוֹל וּמְאַחֵר סְעוּדָתוֹ עַד לְאַחַר שָׁעָה אוֹ פָּחוֹת — **For example, when you want to eat, but you delay your meal for an hour, or less,** וְעוֹסֵק בַּתּוֹרָה בְּאוֹתָהּ שָׁעָה — **and during that time you study Torah.**

כִּדְאִיתָא בַּגְּמָרָא שָׁעָה רְבִיעִית מַאֲכַל כָּל אָדָם שָׁעָה שְׁשִׁית מַאֲכַל תַּלְמִידֵי חֲכָמִים — **As the** *Talmud* states: *"The fourth hour is the time when all men eat, but the sixth hour is the time when Torah scholars eat"* (*Talmud, Shabbos* 10a), וְהָיוּ מַרְעִיבִים עַצְמָם שְׁתֵּי שָׁעוֹת לְכַוּוֹנָה זוֹ — which implies that **they denied themselves food for two** additional **hours with this intention** of subduing the *sitra achra,* אַף שֶׁגַּם אַחַר הַסְּעוּדָה הָיוּ לוֹמְדִים כָּל הַיּוֹם — **for otherwise, what was the point of delaying eating, if in any case they studied for the entire day after the meal?**

Since the scholars were doing the *mitzvah* of studying Torah all day, they clearly did not delay their meal in order to study more. Apparently, they saw value in delaying gratification, amid the awareness that this helped to subdue the *sitra achra.*

After this example of refraining from a permitted *action*, we turn to examples of holding back from permitted *speech* and *thought*.

וְכֵן אִם בּוֹלֵם פִּיו מִלְּדַבֵּר דְּבָרִים שֶׁלִּבּוֹ מִתְאַוֶּה מְאֹד לְדַבְּרָם מֵעִנְיָינֵי הָעוֹלָם — **So, too, if you hold back your mouth from saying something** permitted **about worldly matters that your heart really wants to say,** it also suppresses the *sitra achra.*

בולם פיו מלדבר דברים שלבו מתאוה מאד לדברם
מענייני העולם וכן בהרהורי מחשבתו אפי' במעט
מזעיר דאתכפיא ס"א לתתא אסתלק יקרא דקב"ה
וקדושתו לעילא הרבה ומקדושה זו נמשכת קדושה
עליונה על האדם למטה לסייעו סיוע רב ועצום לעבודתו
ית'. וז"ש רז"ל אדם מקדש עצמו מעט מטה מקדשין

וְכֵן בְּהִרְהוּרֵי מַחֲשַׁבְתּוֹ אֲפִילוּ בְּמְעַט מִזְעֵיר — **And similarly,** if you hold back **from the** pleasurable **thoughts of your mind** concerning permitted, worldly matters, **even in the smallest measure,** דְּאִתְכַּפְיָא סִטְרָא אָחֳרָא לְתַתָּא — **then the** *sitra achra* **is subdued below.**

אִסְתַּלֵּק יְקָרָא דְּקוּדְשָׁא בְּרִיךְ הוּא וּקְדוּשָׁתוֹ לְעֵילָא הַרְבֵּה — As a result of subduing the *sitra achra* below, through delaying or resisting permitted pleasures, **the glory and holiness of the Blessed Holy One ascends abundantly on High.**

7TH ADAR I LEAP

The *Tanya* now suggests that by delaying or refraining from even permitted pleasures, the *beinoni's* positive worship is also enhanced in a unique way, not shared by the *tzadik.*

וּמִקְּדוּשָׁה זוֹ נִמְשֶׁכֶת קְדוּשָׁה עֶלְיוֹנָה עַל הָאָדָם לְמַטָּה — **And** as a result of G-d's holiness ascending on high from your delayed gratification, some **"supernal holiness" is drawn from this** abundant **source down to you below,** לְסַיְּיעוֹ סִיּוּעַ רַב וְעָצוּם **— to provide you with plentiful and powerful assistance in your** לַעֲבוֹדָתוֹ יִתְבָּרֵךְ **worship of G-d.**

The *beinoni* is granted some of G-d's "supernal holiness" as a result of delaying permitted pleasures and subduing the *sitra achra.* The result of this is that he is empowered with "plentiful and powerful assistance" in his worship, something that even the *tzadik* does not enjoy (because he doesn't subdue the *sitra achra*).

וְזֶהוּ שֶׁאָמְרוּ רַבּוֹתֵינוּ זִכְרוֹנָם לִבְרָכָה — **And this is how our Sages, of blessed memory explained** the verse, *"Sanctify yourselves and you will become holy"* (*Leviticus* 11:44), אָדָם מְקַדֵּשׁ עַצְמוֹ מְעַט לְמַטָּה מְקַדְּשִׁין אוֹתוֹ הַרְבֵּה מִלְמַעְלָה — *"When a person sanctifies himself to a small extent below, he will be sanctified a great deal from above"* (see *Talmud, Yoma* 39a).

The path of subduing the *sitra achra,* which is unique to *beinonim,* brings about not only special qualities on High, but also a special empowerment below. This is the meaning of the seemingly repetitive verse, *"Sanctify yourselves and you will become holy."* If you will make the effort to subdue the *sitra achra* by delayed gratification (*"Sanctify yourselves"*), you will be endowed with a special power from G-d's holiness to help you in your worship (*"and you will become holy"*).

אותו הרבה מלמעלה לבד מה שמקיים מצות עשה
של תורה והתקדשתם וכו' כשמקדש עצמו במותר לו
ופי' והתקדשתם שתעשו עצמכם קדושים כלומר אף
שבאמת אינו קדוש ומובדל מס"א כי היא בתקפה
ובגבורתה כתולדתה בחלל השמאלי רק שכובש יצרו
ומקדש עצמו. והייתם קדושים כלומר סופו להיות
קדוש ומובדל באמת מהס"א ע"י שמקדשים אותו
הרבה מלמעלה ומסייעים אותו לגרשה מלבו
מעט מעט:

35A

I.e, the two parts of the verse *"(a) Sanctify yourselves and (b) you will become holy"* imply that:

לְבַד מַה שֶּׁמְּקַיֵּים מִצְוַת עֲשֵׂה שֶׁל תּוֹרָה וְהִתְקַדִּשְׁתֶּם וְכוּ' — **Besides** (a) **fulfilling a positive commandment of the Torah,** *"Sanctify yourselves,"* כְּשֶׁמְּקַדֵּשׁ עַצְמוֹ בְּמוּתָּר לוֹ — **by** *"sanctifying yourself through* (refraining from even) *that which is permissible to you"* (see *Ramban* to *Leviticus* 19:2), you also benefit from the result (b) of "becoming holy" and receiving special powers from G-d.

Before we turn to (b), the *Tanya* first clarifies why the term *"Sanctify yourselves"* suggests that it refers specifically to a *beinoni.*

וּפֵירוּשׁ וְהִתְקַדִּשְׁתֶּם שֶׁתַּעֲשׂוּ עַצְמְכֶם קְדוֹשִׁים — **And the phrase** *"Sanctify yourselves"* clearly refers to *beinonim* and not to *tzadikim* since it **implies** that you ought to achieve something that you do not have already, as if to say, **"You must bring sanctity** *upon* **yourselves,"** כְּלוֹמַר אַף שֶׁבֶּאֱמֶת אֵינוֹ קָדוֹשׁ — **in other words, even though you are not actually holy,** וּמוּבְדָּל מִסִּטְרָא אָחֳרָא כִּי הִיא בְּתָקְפָּהּ וּבִגְבוּרָתָהּ כְּתוֹלַדְתָּהּ — **nor removed from the** *sitra achra,* **which** has not been dislodged בְּחָלָל הַשְּׂמָאלִי — **from your heart's left chamber** at all and **is as strong and powerful as when you were born,** רַק שֶׁכּוֹבֵשׁ יִצְרוֹ וּמְקַדֵּשׁ עַצְמוֹ — **and** rather than eliminate the **impulse** to evil, **you merely control** its influence and *"sanctify yourself through (refraining from even) that which is permissible to you"* —

Nevertheless, by doing that, the result will be:

וְהָיִיתֶם קְדוֹשִׁים *(b)* — *"You will become holy,"* כְּלוֹמַר סוֹפוֹ לִהְיוֹת קָדוֹשׁ וּמוּבְדָּל בֶּאֱמֶת מֵהַסִּטְרָא אָחֳרָא — *i.e.,* **ultimately, you will become holy and genuinely detached from the** *sitra achra* in many areas of your life, עַל יְדֵי שֶׁמְּקַדְּשִׁים אוֹתוֹ הַרְבֵּה מִלְמַעְלָה — **as a result of being** *"sanctified a great deal from above,"* as the *Talmud* states, וּמְסַיְּיעִים אוֹתוֹ לְגָרְשָׁהּ מִלִּבּוֹ מְעַט מְעַט — **you will be helped, little by little, to rid the** *sitra achra* **from your heart.**

Even if you never reach the level of *tzadik*, by delaying and resisting permitted pleasures, you weaken your ties with the *sitra achra* and it will have less of a pull on you. As a result, your impulse to evil will gradually tempt you less.

פרק כח וַאֲפִילוּ אם נופלים לו הרהורי תאוות
ושאר מחשבות זרות בשעת
העבודה בתורה או בתפלה בכוונה אל ישית לב אליהן
אלא יסיח דעתו מהן כרגע. וגם אל יהי שוטה לעסוק
בהעלאת המדות של המחשבה זרה כנודע כי לא

WHEN YOUR MIND WANDERS

SECTION ONE: INAPPROPRIATE THOUGHTS DURING PRAYER

26TH SHEVAT REGULAR | 8TH ADAR I LEAP

Chapter 28 is the last of three chapters that offer us tools to avoid sadness in a variety of settings. After discussing sadness caused by inappropriate *actions* in chapter 26, chapter 27 taught us how to deal with inappropriate *thoughts and desires,* so as not to allow them to dampen our spirits.

But so far we have learned only how to deal with inappropriate thoughts that occur in a general setting, such as business or leisure. It is more disturbing, however, when these thoughts plague us when we're trying to pray or study Torah. What do we do then?

וַאֲפִילוּ אִם נוֹפְלִים לוֹ הִרְהוּרֵי תַּאֲווֹת וּשְׁאָר מַחֲשָׁבוֹת זָרוֹת בִּשְׁעַת הָעֲבוֹדָה בַּתּוֹרָה אוֹ בִּתְפִלָּה בְּכַוָּונָה — **And even if while worshiping** G-d **in Torah** study **or devotional prayer, you begin to fantasize about** physical **indulgences, or have other inappropriate thoughts,** אַל יָשִׁית לֵב אֲלֵיהֶן — **don't turn your heart to them,** אֶלָּא יַסִּיחַ דַּעְתּוֹ מֵהֶן כְּרֶגַע — **rather, divert your attention away from them immediately.**

The simple and practical way to deal with inappropriate thoughts is to ignore them completely.

וְגַם אַל יְהִי שׁוֹטֶה לַעֲסוֹק בְּהַעֲלָאַת הַמִּדּוֹת שֶׁל הַמַּחֲשָׁבָה זָרָה — **And don't be a fool and try to "elevate" the emotional content of the inappropriate thought** back to its source, כַּנּוֹדָע — a practice **known** from the *Ba'al Shem Tov.*

The advice to divert your attention away from inappropriate thoughts "immediately," represents a retreat from early Chasidic teachings, which advised that such thoughts should be "elevated."

The *Ba'al Shem Tov* taught a method of elevating inappropriate thoughts and reuniting them with their source, based on the principle that every negative energy is ultimately rooted in a positive one, from which it has "fallen." By lifting the energy back to its source, the fallen energy is realigned with its positive root.

נֶאֶמְרוּ דְּבָרִים הָהֵם אֶלָּא לַצַּדִּיקִים שֶׁאֵין נוֹפְלִים לָהֶם
מַחֲשָׁבוֹת זָרוֹת שֶׁלָּהֶם כ״א מִשֶׁל אֲחֵרִים. אֲבָל מִי
שֶׁנוֹפֵל לוֹ מִשֶׁלוֹ מִבְּחִי׳ הָרַע שֶׁבְּלִבּוֹ בַּחֲלַל הַשְּׂמָאלִי
אֵיךְ יַעֲלֵהוּ לְמַעְלָה וְהוּא עַצְמוֹ מְקוּשָׁר לְמַטָּה: אַךְ
אעפ״כ אַל יִפּוֹל לִבּוֹ בְּקִרְבּוֹ לִהְיוֹת מִזֶּה עָצֵב נִבְזֶה

For example, a thought of desire or lust is a "fallen" energy of *chesed* (kindness); a thought of violence, a "fallen" form of *gevurah* (severity). Since these energies originated in G-d they ought to be returned to G-d (*Keser Shem Tov*, section 99, 112).

כִּי לֹא נֶאֶמְרוּ דְּבָרִים הָהֵם אֶלָּא לַצַּדִּיקִים — **For this advice was meant only for** *tzadikim*.

The *Tanya* warns its readership not to dabble in this practice. For most of us, dwelling on a lustful thought is likely to lead to more lustful thoughts. For *tzadikim*, who have rid themselves of the urge for self-gratification, this technique can be effective, but for the rest of us, it will be counterproductive.

This, however, leaves us with a question: If this technique was intended only for *tzadikim*, why are they having inappropriate thoughts at all? Didn't we learn that the *tzadik* has refined himself to the extent that he is no longer plagued by such thoughts?

שֶׁאֵין נוֹפְלִים לָהֶם מַחֲשָׁבוֹת זָרוֹת שֶׁלָּהֶם כִּי אִם מִשֶׁל אֲחֵרִים — **For when** these *tzadikim* **have inappropriate thoughts, they are not** the product of **their own** negative energy, **but from** the negative energy of **others.**

There is a fundamental interconnectedness of all souls, especially those who enjoy close relationships in this world. Therefore, it is possible that while a *tzadik* will not have inappropriate thoughts stemming from his own desires, he may be plagued by thoughts from the negative energy he has absorbed from his disciples, or others close to him. It is in *that* case, the *Ba'al Shem Tov's* method is applicable.

אֲבָל מִי שֶׁנוֹפֵל לוֹ מִשֶׁלוֹ מִבְּחִינַת הָרַע שֶׁבְּלִבּוֹ בַּחֲלַל הַשְּׂמָאלִי — **But when your own inappropriate thoughts, caused by the evil in your heart's left chamber, pop into your** mind, אֵיךְ יַעֲלֵהוּ לְמַעְלָה וְהוּא עַצְמוֹ מְקוּשָׁר לְמַטָּה — **how could you possibly lift them upwards, when you, yourself, are tied below?**

You can't free your inappropriate thoughts from the powers of *kelipah* so long as you remain "tied up" and enmeshed with *kelipah* yourself.

Elevating inappropriate thoughts, then, is not an option, and your only choice is to divert your attention from them immediately, before they entice you further.

SECTION TWO: A POSITIVE ATTITUDE

אַךְ אַף עַל פִּי כֵן אַל יִפּוֹל לִבּוֹ בְּקִרְבּוֹ — **But nevertheless, don't allow your mood to deteriorate** from inappropriate thoughts, לִהְיוֹת מִזֶּה עָצֵב נִבְזֶה בִּשְׁעַת הָעֲבוֹדָה שֶׁצָּרִיךְ

בשעת העבודה שצריך להיות בשמחה רבה אלא
אדרבה יתחזק יותר ויוסיף אומץ בכל כחו בכוונת
התפלה בחדוה ושמחה יתירה בשומו אל לבו כי נפילת
המחשבה זרה היא מהקליפה שבחלל השמאלי העושה
מלחמה בבינוני עם נפש אלהית שבו. ונודע דרך
הנלחמים וכן הנאבקים יחד כשאחד מתגבר אזי השני

לְהְיוֹת בְּשִׂמְחָה רַבָּה — and allow this to bring sadness and self-loathing upon you during worship, which needs to be carried out with an abundance of joy.

In chapter 26, we learned the "all-encompassing principle" that a positive mood needs to be maintained at all times, as the impulse to evil tends to be successful when you feel down. An "inappropriate thought" cannot be allowed to dampen your spirits, especially during worship.

אֶלָּא אַדְּרַבָּה יִתְחַזֵּק יוֹתֵר וְיוֹסִיף אוֹמֶץ בְּכָל כֹּחוֹ בְּכַוָּנַת הַתְּפִלָּה בְּחֶדְוָה וְשִׂמְחָה יְתֵירָה — Rather, on the contrary, an inappropriate thought should strengthen you and intensify all your powers of concentration in prayer, with more happiness and joy.

The *Tanya* offers a powerful insight how to remain joyous when an inappropriate thought occurs.

בְּשׂוּמוֹ אֶל לִבּוֹ כִּי נְפִילַת הַמַּחֲשָׁבָה זָרָה הִיא מֵהַקְּלִיפָּה שֶׁבֶּחָלָל הַשְּׂמָאלִי — When you take to heart that the inappropriate thought popped into your mind from the *kelipah* in your heart's left chamber, הָעוֹשָׂה מִלְחָמָה בְּבֵינוֹנִי עִם נֶפֶשׁ אֱלֹהִית שֶׁבּוֹ — which, in your case of the (aspiring or actual) *beinoni,* is in competition with your Divine Soul, וְנוֹדַע דֶּרֶךְ הַנִּלְחָמִים וְכֵן הַנֶּאֱבָקִים יַחַד — and everyone knows that in a fight or wrestling match, כְּשֶׁאֶחָד מִתְגַּבֵּר אֲזֵי הַשֵּׁנִי מִתְאַמֵּץ לְהִתְגַּבֵּר גַּם כֵּן בְּכָל מַאֲמַצֵּי כֹחוֹ — when one person is winning, the competitor tries to make a comeback with all his might.

A CHASIDIC THOUGHT

An inappropriate thought is a sign of your *success* in prayer, so it should spark joy. When your Animal Soul saw that it was losing the competition for your attention, it felt the need to fight back, and so it threw you the thought.

Instead of getting depressed that, however hard you try to concentrate, you cannot rid yourself of inappropriate thoughts, say to yourself: "Wow, I was praying with such devotion that my Animal Soul felt really threatened and tried to do something about it! I must be doing really well!"

מתאמץ להתגבר ג"כ בכל מאמצי כחו. ולכן כשנפש
האלהית מתאמצת ומתגברת להתפלל אזי גם הקליפה
מתגברת כנגדה לבלבלה ולהפילה במחשב' זרה שלה
ולא כטעות העולם שטועים להוכיח מנפילת המחשבה
זרה מכלל שאין תפלתם כלום שאילו התפלל כראוי
ונכון לא היו נופלים לו מחשבות זרות. והאמת היה
כדבריהם אם היתה נפש אחת לבדה היא המתפללת
והיא המחשבת ומהרהרת המחשבות זרות. אבל
באמת לאמיתו הן שתי נפשות הנלחמו' זו עם זו במוחו
של אדם כל אחת חפצה ורצונה למשול בו ולהיות
המוח ממולא ממנה לבדה. וכל הרהורי תורה ויראת
שמים מנפש האלהית וכל מילי דעלמא מנפש הבהמית

35B

וְלָכֵן כְּשֶׁנֶּפֶשׁ הָאֱלֹהִית מִתְאַמֶּצֶת וּמִתְגַּבֶּרֶת לְהִתְפַּלֵּל — **And therefore when your Divine Soul intensifies its energies to pray,** אֲזַי גַּם הַקְּלִיפָּה מִתְגַּבֶּרֶת כְּנֶגְדָּהּ — **the** *kelipah* **intensifies itself against** your Divine Soul, לְבַלְבְּלָהּ וּלְהַפִּילָהּ בְּמַחֲשָׁבָה זָרָה שֶׁלָּהּ — **to disorient** your Divine Soul, **and to derail it with an** inappropriate **thought.**

27TH SHEVAT REGULAR

וְלֹא כְּטָעוּת הָעוֹלָם — **The above analysis runs contrary to the popular misconception,** שֶׁטּוֹעִים לְהוֹכִיחַ מִנְּפִילַת הַמַּחֲשָׁבָה זָרָה מִכְּלָל שֶׁאֵין תְּפִלָּתָם כְּלוּם — **of those who mistakenly argue that their prayers are rendered worthless by inappropriate thoughts,** שֶׁאִילוּ הִתְפַּלֵּל כָּרָאוּי וְנָכוֹן לֹא הָיוּ נוֹפְלִים לוֹ מַחֲשָׁבוֹת זָרוֹת — arguing that if **they had prayed acceptably and properly, they would have been free from inappropriate thoughts.**

But doesn't the presence of these thoughts represent a failure at some level?

וְהָאֱמֶת הָיָה כְּדִבְרֵיהֶם אִם הָיְתָה נֶפֶשׁ אַחַת לְבַדָּהּ — **If we each had just one soul, then they would have been correct,** הִיא הַמִּתְפַּלֶּלֶת וְהִיא הַמְחַשֶּׁבֶת וּמְהַרְהֶרֶת הַמַּחֲשָׁבוֹת זָרוֹת — since if **the same** soul that prayed was also the one thinking inappropriate thoughts then, either it's praying properly or it isn't, and the presence of inappropriate thoughts indicates that it isn't.

אֲבָל בֶּאֱמֶת לַאֲמִיתוֹ הֵן שְׁתֵּי נְפָשׁוֹת הַנִּלְחָמוֹת זוֹ עִם זוֹ בְּמוֹחוֹ שֶׁל אָדָם — **But in actual fact, you have two souls competing with each other in your brain,** כָּל אַחַת חֲפֵצָה — **the desire and will of each one** וּרְצוֹנָהּ לִמְשׁוֹל בּוֹ וְלִהְיוֹת הַמּוֹחַ מְמוּלָּא מִמֶּנָּה לְבַדָּהּ — being to control you, to fill your mind exclusively with its influence.

וְכָל הִרְהוּרֵי תּוֹרָה וְיִרְאַת שָׁמַיִם מִנֶּפֶשׁ הָאֱלֹהִית — **So** the presence of inappropriate thoughts does not reflect negatively on the devotion of your Divine Soul since all **your thoughts of Torah and fear-of-Heaven come from your Divine soul,** וְכָל מִילֵּי

רק שהאלהית מלובשת בה. והוא כמשל אדם
המתפלל בכוונ' ועומד לנגדו עו"ג רשע ומשיח ומדבר
עמו כדי לבלבלו שזאת עצתו בודאי שלא להשיב לו
מטוב ועד רע ולעשות עצמו כחרש לא ישמע ולקיים
מה שכתו' אל תען כסיל באולתו פן תשוה לו גם אתה
כך אל ישיב מאומה ושום טענה ומענה נגד המחשבה

דְּעָלְמָא מִנֶּפֶשׁ הַבַּהֲמִית — whereas all thoughts of **worldly matters come from the Animal Soul.**

The two types of thought, appropriate or inappropriate, are like different voices in your head emanating from different places. If there was just one "you" then a failure to concentrate all the time in prayer might be disappointing; but since you actually have two selves, an intense competition means that some real devotion is emanating from the "higher you," and the "lower you" is fighting back.

But if your two souls have such different personalities, why do you feel like one person? Why don't you *literally* hear two voices in your head?

רַק שֶׁהָאֱלֹהִית מְלוּבֶּשֶׁת בָּה — **Only, the Divine Soul is "dressed" in** the Animal Soul.

The Divine Soul does not have direct access to the body, and acts via the medium of the Animal Soul, into which it must "dress" (see p. 39). Therefore, your consciousness is uniform and you do not sense the presence of two souls.

But, the *Tanya* teaches, your metaphysical constitution is fundamentally split between two energies, radically altering the significance of a lack of concentration in prayer.

וְהוּא כְּמָשָׁל אָדָם הַמִּתְפַּלֵּל בְּכַוָּונָה — The situation **is comparable to the case of a man praying with concentration,** וְעוֹמֵד לְנֶגְדּוֹ עָרֵל רָשָׁע וּמֵשִׁיחַ וּמְדַבֵּר עִמּוֹ כְּדֵי לְבַלְבְּלוֹ — **and a nasty heathen stands next to him and tries to distract him by talking and mouthing off at him.**

שֶׁזֹּאת עֲצָתוֹ בְּוַדַּאי שֶׁלֹּא לְהָשִׁיב לוֹ מְטוֹב וְעַד רָע — In this case, **the best thing to do is definitely not to respond to** the antagonist, *"neither positively nor negatively"* (Genesis 31:29), וְלַעֲשׂוֹת עַצְמוֹ כְּחֵרֵשׁ לֹא יִשְׁמַע — but to act *"like a deaf man who does not hear"* (Psalms 38:14), וּלְקַיֵּים מַה שֶׁכָּתוּב אַל תַּעַן כְּסִיל כְּאִוַּלְתּוֹ פֶּן תִּשְׁוֶה לוֹ גַם אַתָּה — to fulfill the verse, *"Do not answer a fool by his folly, lest you, too, become like him"* (Proverbs 26:4).

Some things don't deserve the dignity of a response. Your inappropriate thought is just the *kelipah* in your heart trying to tease and taunt you when you are doing a nice job at devotional prayer. It's just a mental hooligan that is best ignored.

כָּךְ אַל יָשִׁיב מְאוּמָה וְשׁוּם טַעֲנָה וּמַעֲנֶה נֶגֶד הַמַּחֲשָׁבָה זָרָה — So **don't react in any way to an inappropriate thought** during prayer, **with any** internal **counter-argument or**

זרה כי המתאבק עם מנוול מתנוול ג"כ רק יעשה עצמו
כלא יודע ולא שומע ההרהורי' שנפלו לו ויסירם מדעתו
ויוסיף אומץ בכח כוונתו ואם יקשה לו להסירם מדעתו
מפני שטורדים דעתו מאד בחזקה אזי ישפיל נפשו
לה' ויתחנן לו ית' במחשבתו לרחם עליו ברחמיו
המרובים כרחם אב על בנים הנמשכים ממוחו וככה
ירחם ה' על נפשו הנמשכת מאתו ית' להצילה ממים
הזדונים ולמענו יעשה כי חלק ה' ממש עמו:

**כִּי הַמִּתְאַבֵּק עִם מְנֻוָּל מִתְנַוֵּל גַם כֵּן — for in wrestling with a filthy person,
you become filthy too.**

If you would hang around disgusting and immoral people their influence would
eventually rub off on you. So don't "hang around" with your negative thoughts either; don't let them get "under your skin." If you entertain them for more than a
moment, they will start to corrupt you.

**רַק יַעֲשֶׂה עַצְמוֹ כְּלֹא יוֹדֵעַ וְלֹא שׁוֹמֵעַ הַהִרְהוּרִים שֶׁנָּפְלוּ לוֹ — Just act as if you were
unaware of the inappropriate thoughts that popped into** your head, **and you didn't
hear them, וִיסִירֵם מִדַּעְתּוֹ וְיוֹסִיף אֹמֶץ בְּכֹחַ כַּוָּנָתוֹ — wipe them from your mind, and
intensify your powers of concentration.**

SECTION THREE: WHEN ALL ELSE FAILS

Of course, that is easier said than done. What do you do if inappropriate thoughts
keep coming back, again and again?

וְאִם יְקָשֶׁה לוֹ לַהֲסִירָם מִדַּעְתּוֹ — But if you find it hard to wipe inappropriate thoughts
from your mind, **מִפְּנֵי שֶׁטּוֹרְדִים דַּעְתּוֹ מְאֹד בְּחָזְקָה — because they intrude on your
mind with great force, אֲזַי יַשְׁפִּיל נַפְשׁוֹ לַה' — then humble yourself before G-d,
וְיִתְחַנֵן לוֹ יִתְבָּרֵךְ בְּמַחֲשַׁבְתּוֹ — and implore Him in your mind.**

There is no need to interrupt your *words* of prayer. Just implore G-d *in your mind*.

**כְּרַחֵם אָב — Implore him to have pity on you, great pity, לְרַחֵם עָלָיו בְּרַחֲמָיו הַמְרוּבִּים
"like the pity of a father on his children"** (Psalms 103:13), **עַל בָּנִים
הַנִּמְשָׁכִים** — who are "derived" from his brain manifest in his seed (see chapter 2,
p. 45), **מִמּוֹחוֹ — וְכָכָה יְרַחֵם ה' עַל נַפְשׁוֹ הַנִּמְשֶׁכֶת מֵאִתּוֹ יִתְבָּרֵךְ — implore G-d to have the same
pity on your** Divine **Soul which is "derived" from Him** (ibid.), **לְהַצִּילָהּ מִמַּיִם הַזֵּדוֹנִים**
— to save your soul from the *"raging waters"* (Psalms 124:5) of your turbulent mind
which is constantly disturbed by the Animal Soul.

וּלְמַעֲנוֹ יַעֲשֶׂה כִּי חֵלֶק ה' מַמָּשׁ עַמּוֹ — Implore Him to do it not because of your merit,
but **for His own sake, for *"His people are (literally) part of G-d"*** (Deuteronomy 32:9).

פרק כט אך עוד אחת צריך לשית עצות בנפשו'
הבינונים אשר לפעמים ועתים
רבים יש להם טמטום הלב שנעשה כאבן ולא יכול
לפתוח לבו בשום אופן לעבודה שבלב זו תפלה.
וגם לפעמים לא יוכל להלחם עם היצר לקדש עצמו
במותר לו מפני כבדות שבלבו וזאת היא עצה היעוצה
בזהר הקדוש דאמר רב מתיבתא בגן עדן אעא דלא

CHAPTER 29

SPIRITUAL INSENSITIVITY

SECTION ONE: A TOUGH CONVERSATION YOU NEED TO HAVE WITH YOURSELF

28TH SHEVAT REGULAR | 9TH ADAR I LEAP

As the *Tanya* has explained at length, every person is capable of becoming a *beinoni*, achieving self-mastery in the areas of thought, speech and action. But what the *beinoni* cannot necessarily sustain is *enthusiasm* over what he is doing.

Enthusiasm is especially necessary in two areas: a.) prayer, which is the "service of the heart"; and b.) delaying gratification from permissible activities.

אַךְ עוֹד אַחַת צָרִיךְ לָשִׁית עֵצוֹת בְּנַפְשׁוֹת הַבֵּינוֹנִים — **However, there is one other key area in which** aspiring (or actual) *beinonim* need to *"take counsel from your souls"* (see *Psalms* 13:3), אֲשֶׁר לִפְעָמִים וְעִתִּים רַבִּים יֵשׁ לָהֶם טִמְטוּם הַלֵּב שֶׁנַּעֲשָׂה כָאֶבֶן, — **when periodically and frequently your heart is desensitized (timtum ha-lev) to spirituality, as if it were stone,** וְלֹא יָכוֹל לִפְתּוֹחַ לִבּוֹ בְּשׁוּם אוֹפֶן לַעֲבוֹדָה שֶׁבַּלֵּב זוֹ תְּפִלָּה — **and you can't find any way to emotionally connect with prayer, the** *"service of the heart"* (*Talmud, Ta'anis* 2a).

וְגַם לִפְעָמִים לֹא יוּכַל לְהִלָּחֵם עִם הַיֵּצֶר — **And also, you are sometimes unable to put up a fight against the evil inclination,** לְקַדֵּשׁ עַצְמוֹ בְּמוּתָּר לוֹ — *"to sanctify yourself through that which is permissible to you"* (see above p. 315), *i.e.,* to delay gratification and possibly abstain from permissible activities, מִפְּנֵי כְּבֵדוּת שֶׁבְּלִבּוֹ — **due to a sluggishness in your heart.**

וְזֹאת הִיא עֵצָה הַיְעוּצָה בַּזֹּהַר הַקָּדוֹשׁ — **In such a case, the following** *"prescribed plan"* (*Isaiah* 14:26), is cited in the holy *Zohar,* דְּאָמַר רַב מְתִיבְתָּא בְּגַן עֵדֶן — **what** *"the head of the heavenly Yeshivah said."*

סליק ביה נהורא מבטשין ליה כו'. גופא דלא סליק 36A
ביה נהורא דנשמתא מבטשין ליה כו' פי' נהורא
דנשמתא שאור הנשמה והשכל אינו מאיר כל כך
למשול על חומריות שבגוף. ואף שמבין ומתבונן
בשכלו בגדולת ה' אינו נתפס ונדבק במוחו כל כך
שיוכל למשול על חומריו' הלב מחמת חומריותן וגסותן
והסיבה היא גסות הקליפה שמגביה עצמה על אור
קדושת נפש האלהית ומסתרת ומחשיכה אורה. ולזאת
צריך לבטשה ולהשפילה לעפר דהיינו לקבוע עתים

אָעָא דְּלָא סָלִיק בֵּיהּ נְהוֹרָא מְבַטְּשִׁין לֵיהּ כו' — "If a wooden beam won't ignite and give out its light, crush it and it will ignite," גּוּפָא דְּלָא סָלִיק בֵּיהּ נְהוֹרָא דְנִשְׁמָתָא מְבַטְּשִׁין — "if a body won't give out the light of its soul, crush it, and the soul's light will come out" (Zohar 3, 168a).

פֵּירוּשׁ נְהוֹרָא דְנִשְׁמָתָא — The meaning of the Zohar's phrase "a body won't give out the light of its soul," שְׁאוֹר הַנְּשָׁמָה וְהַשֵּׂכֶל אֵינוֹ מֵאִיר כָּל כָּךְ לִמְשׁוֹל עַל חוּמְרִיּוֹת שֶׁבַּגּוּף — is that your soul and your intelligence won't shine their light sufficiently to curb your body's sensuous urges, וְאַף שֶׁמֵּבִין וּמִתְבּוֹנֵן בְּשִׂכְלוֹ בִּגְדוּלַת ה' — and though your mind does appreciate the greatness of G-d, and meditates on it, אֵינוֹ נִתְפָּס — your mind still fails to grasp וְנִדְבָּק בְּמוֹחוֹ כָּל כָּךְ שֶׁיּוּכַל לִמְשׁוֹל עַל חוּמְרִיּוּת הַלֵּב — and absorb G-d's greatness, to the extent that it could curb your heart's sensuous urges, מֵחֲמַת חוּמְרִיּוּתָן וְגַסּוּתָן — because of the sensuality and vulgarity of both your mind and heart.

10TH ADAR I LEAP

וְהַסִּיבָה הִיא גַסּוּת הַקְּלִיפָּה — Despite your efforts at meditation, you don't have a spiritual awakening due to the vulgarity of the kelipah in your mind and heart, שֶׁמַּגְבִּיהַּ עַצְמָהּ עַל אוֹר קְדוּשַׁת נֶפֶשׁ הָאֱלֹהִית — which exerts itself over the Divine Soul's holy light, וּמַסְתֶּרֶת וּמַחֲשִׁיכָה אוֹרָהּ — hiding and blocking its light from illuminating the rest of your soul.

As we learned in chapter 19, the chochmah in your Divine Soul is a permanent "window" to G-d which can never be obscured. But what kelipah can do is block chochmah's energizing influence on the rest of the soul (its "light"), so that the chochmah itself remains trapped and "exiled" (p. 226). The Zohar's advice teaches you how to cause that light, which is already present in your soul, to shine into your mind and heart.

וְלָזֹאת צָרִיךְ לְבַטְּשָׁהּ וּלְהַשְׁפִּילָהּ לֶעָפָר — That's why the Zohar advises that you ought to metaphorically "crush" the body and raze it to the ground, דְּהַיְינוּ לִקְבּוֹעַ עִתִּים — which means practically, that you ought to schedule ego-deflating לְהַשְׁפִּיל עַצְמוֹ

להשפיל עצמו להיות נבזה בעיניו נמאס ככתוב ולב
נשבר רוח נשברה היא הס"א שהיא היא האדם עצמו
בבינונים שנפש החיונית המחיה הגוף היא בתקפה
כתולדתה בלבו נמצא היא היא האדם עצמו. ועל
נפש האלהית שבו נאמר נשמה שנתת בי טהורה היא

sessions, לִהְיוֹת נִבְזֶה בְּעֵינָיו נִמְאָס כַּכָּתוּב — **so that your** body's sensuality and vulgarity **become, in the words of Scripture,** *"disgusting in your eyes, and repulsive"* (*Psalms* 15:4).

SECTION TWO: YOUR CORE IDENTITY

וְלֵב נִשְׁבָּר רוּחַ נִשְׁבָּרָה — **And** as we learned above the *Zohar's* insight on *Psalms* 51:19, that *"a heart that is broken"* leads to *"a broken spirit,"* i.e., *"a heart that is broken"* dismantles the negative energy field that surrounds you (*"a broken (negative) spirit"*), הִיא הַסִּטְרָא אָחֳרָא — and this negative energy **is the** *sitra achra.*

In chapter 17 (p. 206), and chapter 26 (p. 298) we learned that a "negative energy field" is brought about through sins, and is broken through remorse over them. But here the *Tanya* applies the idea, not to sinful behavior (which is, of course, absent in the *beinoni*), but to the *person himself,* who ought to "schedule ego-deflating sessions" to see himself as "disgusting" and "repulsive."

But where did this negative energy field come from, if not from sin? And why is the session of introspection directed at the person and not at his negative energy?

שֶׁהִיא הִיא הָאָדָם עַצְמוֹ בַּבֵּינוֹנִים — **Because, in the case of** *beinonim,* the negative energy of *sitra achra* **is** identified with **the actual person himself.**

People who sin acquire a negative energy field as a result of their behavior. But, in a less pronounced way, the *beinoni* has a pre-existing negative energy built into his system at birth.

שֶׁנֶּפֶשׁ הַחִיּוּנִית הַמְחַיָּה הַגּוּף — **Since the energizing** Animal **Soul, which gives life to the body,** הִיא בְּתָקְפָּהּ כְּתוֹלַדְתָּהּ בְּלִבּוֹ — remains in its innate strength, as it was at birth, in the *beinoni's* heart (see chapter 13, p. 155), נִמְצָא הִיא הִיא הָאָדָם עַצְמוֹ — so the negative energy field is not something acquired; it's an integral part of **the person, himself.**

By directing the "spirit breaking" power of remorse and introspection towards his actual self, the *beinoni* can shatter the inner negative energy field that is preventing his mind and heart from being enthusiastic about worship.

However, this leaves us with a further question. Have we not learned that a person has not one, but two "selves," Divine and an Animal? Why, then, does the *Tanya* associate the "self" here only with the animal side?

שנתת בי דייקא מכלל שהאדם עצמו איננו הנשמה
הטהורה כי אם בצדיקים שבהם הוא להפך שנשמה
הטהורה שהיא נפש האלהית הוא האדם וגופם נקרא
בשר אדם. וכמאמר הלל הזקן לתלמידיו כשהיה הולך
לאכול היה אומר שהוא הולך לגמול חסד עם העלובה
ועניה הוא גופו כי כמו זר נחשב אצלו ולכן אמר שהוא
גומל חסד עמו במה שמאכילו כי הוא עצמו אינו רק

נְשָׁמָה שֶׁנָּתַתָּ בִּי — **And regarding the Divine Soul we say,** וְעַל נֶפֶשׁ הָאֱלֹהִית שֶׁבּוֹ נֶאֱמַר — **"The (Divine) Soul which You placed in me, is pure"** (*Morning Liturgy*), טְהוֹרָה הִיא שֶׁנָּתַתָּ בִּי דַּיְיקָא — **the text is precise in stating** that the Divine Soul was placed **"in me,"** מִכְּלָל שֶׁהָאָדָם עַצְמוֹ אֵינֶנּוּ הַנְּשָׁמָה הַטְּהוֹרָה — **implying that you, yourself are not the pure Divine Soul,** since the Divine soul was placed *into* yourself.

While it is true that you have two souls, you only have one "self"—the "self" being whichever consciousness represents your core identity. *Beinonim* (and *rashaim*) still identify primarily with their bodies and Animal Souls, and they see the Divine Soul as an "influence" more than an identity.

And that's why the "ego-deflating sessions" for *beinonim* can be directed simply at the "self," since, by default, this will target the body and Animal Soul.

כִּי אִם בַּצַּדִּיקִים שֶׁבָּהֶם הוּא לְהֵפֶךְ — **Except in the case of** *tzadikim,* **for whom it is the other way around,** שֶׁנְּשָׁמָה הַטְּהוֹרָה שֶׁהִיא נֶפֶשׁ הָאֱלֹהִית הוּא הָאָדָם — **and the "pure soul,"** *i.e.,* **the Divine Soul, is the "self."**

וְגוּפָם נִקְרָא בְּשַׂר אָדָם — **With** *tzadikim,* **their bodies** no longer represent their core identity, and they relate to the body as mere **"human flesh"** (*Exodus* 30:32).

A *tzadik*'s body is just his "flesh," something that *belongs* to him. It does not constitute his core identity. The *tzadik*'s primary frame of reference is his Divine Soul.

11TH ADAR I LEAP

וּכְמַאֲמַר הִלֵּל הַזָּקֵן לְתַלְמִידָיו — **We see this in the language used by Hillel the Elder to his disciples,** כְּשֶׁהָיָה הוֹלֵךְ לֶאֱכוֹל הָיָה אוֹמֵר — **that when going to eat, he used to say,** שֶׁהוּא הוֹלֵךְ לִגְמוֹל חֶסֶד עִם הָעֲלוּבָה וַעֲנִיָּה — **that he was going to perform an act of kindness to a** *"poor, miserable creature"* (*Leviticus Rabah* 34:3), הוּא גוּפוֹ — **referring to his body,** כִּי כְּמוֹ זָר נֶחְשַׁב אֶצְלוֹ — **because it was** *"like a stranger to him"* (see *Hosea* 8:12) in the sense that it was not his core identity, וְלָכֵן אָמַר שֶׁהוּא — גּוֹמֵל חֶסֶד עִמּוֹ בְּמַה שֶּׁמַּאֲכִילוֹ — **and that's why he would say that in feeding it, he was doing an act of kindness toward** his body, כִּי הוּא עַצְמוֹ אֵינוֹ רַק נֶפֶשׁ הָאֱלֹהִית לְבָד — **because his "self" was identified exclusively with his Divine Soul.**

Above (chapter 28, p. 322), however, we learned that the Divine Soul cannot influence the body directly, but does so through the medium of the Animal Soul, into

נפש האלהית לבד כי היא לבדה מחיה גופו ובשרו
שהרע שהיה בנפש החיונית המלובשת בדמו ובשרו
נתהפך לטוב ונכלל בקדושת נפש האלהית ממש
בצדיקים. אבל בבינוני מאחר שמהותה ועצמותה של
נפש החיונית הבהמית שמס"א המלובשת בדמו
ובשרו לא נהפך לטוב הרי היא היא האדם עצמו וא"כ
הוא רחוק מה' בתכלית הריחוק שהרי כח המתאוה 36B
שבנפשו הבהמית יכול ג"כ להתאוות לדברי' האסורים
שהם נגד רצונו ית' אף שאינו מתאוה לעשותם בפועל

which it must "dress." How, then, is it possible for the *tzadik*, to identify *exclusively* with his Divine Soul?

כִּי הִיא לְבַדָּהּ מְחַיָּה גּוּפוֹ וּבְשָׂרוֹ — **Because,** in the case of the *tzadik*, **his body and flesh are energized by** the Divine Soul **alone,** שֶׁהָרַע שֶׁהָיָה בַּנֶּפֶשׁ הַחִיּוּנִית הַמְלוּבֶּשֶׁת בְּדָמוֹ וּבְשָׂרוֹ — **since the evil within his energizing** Animal **Soul, "dressed" in his flesh and blood, has been transformed to good,** וְנִכְלַל בִּקְדוּשַׁת נֶפֶשׁ הָאֱלֹהִית מַמָּשׁ בַּצַּדִּיקִים — **and, in the case of** *tzadikim,* the transformed Animal Soul **has been completely absorbed into the Divine Soul's holiness.**

The Animal Soul (in the blood and flesh) still remains the "access" point for the body, even in a *tzadik*. Nevertheless, the *tzadik's* Animal Soul ceases to have an identity of its own, since it has been utterly transformed to good. It has now become "absorbed" and incorporated into the structure of the Divine Soul.

29TH SHEVAT REGULAR

אֲבָל בַּבֵּינוֹנִי מֵאַחַר שֶׁמַּהוּתָהּ וְעַצְמוּתָהּ שֶׁל נֶפֶשׁ הַחִיּוּנִית — **But in the case of a** *beinoni*, הַבַּהֲמִית שֶׁמִּסִּטְרָא אָחֳרָא הַמְלוּבֶּשֶׁת בְּדָמוֹ וּבְשָׂרוֹ לֹא נֶהְפַּךְ לְטוֹב — **since his energiz-ing, Animal Soul, "dressed" in his flesh and blood, has a deep core of** *sitra achra* **which hasn't been transformed to good,** הֲרֵי הִיא הִיא הָאָדָם עַצְמוֹ — **that consti-tutes** the *beinoni's* **actual identity.**

12TH ADAR I LEAP

וְאִם כֵּן הוּא רָחוֹק מֵה' בְּתַכְלִית הָרִיחוּק — **And this being the case, his** "identity" **is as far from G-d as can be,** שֶׁהֲרֵי כֹּחַ הַמִּתְאַוֶּה שֶׁבְּנַפְשׁוֹ הַבַּהֲמִית יָכוֹל גַּם כֵּן לְהִתְאַוּוֹת — **for even though the** *beinoni* **has achieved total mastery over his external "garments,"** his Animal Soul's appetite **has not been** *fundamentally* transformed at its deep core and **he is fully capable of craving for things forbidden** by the Torah, שֶׁהֵם נֶגֶד רְצוֹנוֹ יִתְבָּרֵךְ — **that violate G-d's Will.**

On the practical, external level, the *beinoni* is very close to G-d, as he makes sure his "garments" are always aligned with G-d's will. But at the level of his Animal Soul's deep core, *his real identity,* he is "as far from G-d as can be."

מַמָּשׁ ח"ו רק שאינם מאוסים אצלו באמת כבצדיקים
כמש"ל [פ' יב]. ובזה הוא גרוע ומשוקץ ומתועב יותר
מבעלי חיים הטמאים ושקצים ורמשים כנ"ל וכמ"ש
ואנכי תולעת ולא איש וגו' [וגם כשמתגברת בו נפשו

אַף שֶׁאֵינוֹ מִתְאַוֶּה לַעֲשׂוֹתָם בְּפוֹעַל מַמָּשׁ חַס וְשָׁלוֹם — And even if he doesn't desire to actually do forbidden acts, **G-d forbid, רַק שֶׁאֵינָם מְאוּסִים אֶצְלוֹ בֶּאֱמֶת כְּבַצַּדִּיקִים —** rather, it's just that he doesn't find them utterly repulsive, like *tzadikim* do, then he is still "as far from G-d as can be," because his Animal Soul remains his core identity, and that soul is derived from *sitra achra.*

PRACTICAL LESSONS

If you find yourself emotionally desensitized to Judaism in general, and prayer in particular, you might need to have a tough conversation with yourself, to deflate your ego.

By "talking" critically to your body and Animal Soul, you can break its negative energy field, and resensitize yourself.

While you have two souls, your core identity is your Animal Soul. So if you are harsh on yourself, that energy will automatically be directed to the Animal Soul.

כְּמוֹ שֶׁנִּתְבָּאֵר לְעֵיל [פֶּרֶק י"ב] — As we explained above (chapter 12), that so long as you are not repulsed by evil, *sitra achra* still has a hold on your Animal Soul.

וּבָזֶה — In this respect, that his core personality is still drawn to acts that violate G-d's will, **הוּא גָרוּעַ וּמְשׁוּקָץ וּמְתוֹעָב יוֹתֵר מִבַּעֲלֵי חַיִּים הַטְּמֵאִים וּשְׁקָצִים וּרְמָשִׂים — he is inferior to non-kosher animals, more disgusting than insects, and more repulsive than reptiles, כַּנִּזְכָּר לְעֵיל — as mentioned above** in chapter 24.

In chapter 24 (p. 271) we learned that a man who sins is inferior to the *sitra achra* itself (as well as all the species powered by the *sitra achra*, such as non-kosher animals, insects and reptiles). This is because, ultimately, the *sitra achra* was created by G-d and does its allotted task, unlike man who *chooses* to violate the Divine will.

Here the *Tanya* takes the argument a stage further: It is not only sinful *activity* which makes a person lower than *kelipah*, but even the *desire* (coupled with the ability) to do so.

וּכְמוֹ שֶׁכָּתוּב וְאָנֹכִי תוֹלַעַת וְלֹא אִישׁ וְגוֹ' — As the verse states, *"I am a worm, and not a man,"* in my desired behavior, and therefore I am, *"the shame of humanity and the disgrace of a nation"* (Psalms 22:7).

But as we have learned, there is at least one time when the *beinoni* feels a passionate love for G-d, like the *tzadik,* and that is during intense prayer. Perhaps then, the *beinoni* could be considered close to G-d, as he temporarily identifies with his Divine Soul?

The *Tanya* dismisses this theory:

האלהית לעורר האהבה לה' בשעת התפלה אינה באמת
לאמיתו לגמרי מאחר שחולפת ועוברת אחר התפלה
כנ"ל ספי"ג] ובפרט כשיזכור טומאת נפשו בחטאת
נעורים והפגם שעשה בעליוני' ושם הוא למעלה מהזמן
וכאלו פגם ונטמא היום ח"ו ממש ואף שכבר עשה

[וְגַם כְּשֶׁמִּתְגַּבֶּרֶת בּוֹ נַפְשׁוֹ הָאֱלֹהִית לְעוֹרֵר הָאַהֲבָה לַה' בִּשְׁעַת הַתְּפִלָּה — **And even when** the *beinoni's* **Divine Soul gains strength during prayer, arousing a** passionate **love for G-d,** אֵינָהּ בֶּאֱמֶת לַאֲמִיתוֹ לְגַמְרֵי — while this love is considered authentic, **it is not** absolutely **authentic, in a perfect sense,** מֵאַחַר שֶׁחוֹלֶפֶת וְעוֹבֶרֶת אַחַר הַתְּפִלָּה — **since it dissipates and goes away after prayer,** [כַּנִּזְכָּר לְעֵיל סוֹף פֶּרֶק י"ג] — **as mentioned above, at the end of chapter 13,** p. 164-5.

The fact that the love dissipates, shows that it was not absolutely genuine to begin with, and did not represent an elimination of *kelipah* from the core personality of the *beinoni*.

SECTION THREE: UPGRADING TESHUVAH

13TH ADAR I LEAP

וּבִפְרָט כְּשֶׁיִּזְכּוֹר טוּמְאַת נַפְשׁוֹ בְּחַטַּאת נְעוּרִים — The above ego-deflating sessions will be **especially** powerful **when you recall how your soul is contaminated from the** *"sins of youth"* (see *Psalms* 25:7; referring to seminal emission, see p. 100).

For the *beinoni*, these "sins of youth" are something from the past, for which he has already repented. Nevertheless, the *Tanya* offers the *beinoni* two humbling thoughts.

וְהַפְּגַם שֶׁעָשָׂה בָּעֶלְיוֹנִים — Firstly, **the "damage" that was caused in the upper worlds** by the "sins of youth" still persists, וְשָׁם הוּא לְמַעְלָה מֵהַזְּמָן — **since there,** in the upper worlds, **time poses no limits,** וּכְאִלּוּ פָּגַם וְנִטְמָא הַיּוֹם חַס וְשָׁלוֹם מַמָּשׁ — **and,** in the absence of time to distinguish one day from the next, **it is as if you had actually defiled yourself and caused this "damage" today, G-d forbid.**

This argument would apply equally to any sin, but the *Tanya* stresses "sins of youth" in particular since, as we have learned, the spiritual "damage" caused by this activity is great (p. 101).

וְאַף שֶׁכְּבָר עָשָׂה תְּשׁוּבָה נְכוֹנָה — **And even though you have since repented acceptably** for this sin, nevertheless, as we shall see, there is still something lacking.

Teshuvah (repentance) is an experience on two different levels. On the practical side, it is the decision never to commit a particular sin again. On the emotional side, it is the feeling of remorse over what you have done.

תשובה נכונה הרי עיקר התשובה בלב והלב יש בו
בחי' ומדרגות רבות והכל לפי מה שהוא אדם ולפי הזמן
והמקום כידוע ליודעים ולכן עכשיו בשעה זו שרואה
בעצמו דלא סליק ביה נהורא דנשמתא מכלל שהיום
לא נתקבלה תשובתו ועונותיו מבדילים או שרוצים
להעלותו לתשובה עילאה יותר מעומקא דלבא יותר
ולכן אמר דוד וחטאתי נגדי תמיד. וגם מי שהוא נקי

As long as you make a sincere practical commitment not to sin again, then your *teshuvah* is "acceptable," and you are forgiven. But, as the *Tanya* will now explain, the emotional component of *teshuvah* is ongoing, and can take place on many different levels.

הֲרֵי עִיקַּר הַתְּשׁוּבָה בַּלֵּב — **The most important element of *teshuvah* is its emotional component,** וְהַלֵּב יֵשׁ בּוֹ בְּחִינוֹת וּמַדְרֵגוֹת רַבּוֹת — **and emotions can be experienced across a very wide range,** וְהַכֹּל לְפִי מַה שֶׁהוּא אָדָם — **all depending on the individual's circumstances,** וּלְפִי הַזְּמַן — כַּיָּדוּעַ לַיוֹדְעִים — **and on the time and place,** וְהַמָּקוֹם — **as intelligent people realize.**

PRACTICAL LESSONS

Remember your past sins, which, even if you have atoned for them, persist in a spiritual sense.

You constantly mature through life, and that needs to be reflected in your *teshuvah*. While the emotional component of your *teshuvah* might have been fitting when you repented, it is probably not sufficient now.

וְלָכֵן עַכְשָׁיו בְּשָׁעָה זוֹ — **Therefore, now, at this time** in your life, long after your *teshuvah,* שֶׁרוֹאֶה בְּעַצְמוֹ דְּלָא סָלִיק בֵּיה נְהוֹרָא דְּנִשְׁמְתָא — **when you see for yourself that** you are spiritually desensitized and your body *"won't give out the light of its soul,"* מִכְּלָל שֶׁהַיּוֹם לֹא נִתְקַבְּלָה תְּשׁוּבָתוֹ — **the implication is that** while your *teshuvah* may have been sufficient in the past, for your personal standing and circumstances ***today,*** the emotional component of **your** prior ***teshuvah*** is unacceptable, וַעֲוֹנוֹתָיו מַבְדִּילִים — **and** today, **your** prior **sins are separating you** from G-d, resulting in your spiritual desensitization.

אוֹ שֶׁרוֹצִים לְהַעֲלוֹתוֹ לִתְשׁוּבָה עִילָּאָה יוֹתֵר — **Or** another possibility is that while your past *teshuvah* still remains acceptable, G-d **wants to lift you to a higher level of *teshuvah*,** מֵעוּמְקָא דְּלִבָּא יוֹתֵר — by "upgrading" the emotional component so that it is **from deeper within the heart.**

וְלָכֵן אָמַר דָּוִד וְחַטָּאתִי נֶגְדִּי תָמִיד — **And that is why King David said, *"And my sin is always before me"*** (*Psalms* 51:5), since even the acceptable *teshuvah* of the past can always be upgraded.

מחטאות נעורים החמורים ישים אל לבו לקיים מאמר
זה"ק להיות ממארי דחושבנא דהיינו לעשו' חשבון עם
נפשו מכל המחשבות והדיבורים והמעשים שחלפו
ועברו מיום היותו עד היום הזה אם היו כולם מצד
הקדושה או מצד הטומאה ר"ל דהיינו כל המחשבות
והדיבורים והמעשים אשר לא לה' המה ולרצונו
ולעבודתו שזהו פי' לשון ס"א כנ"ל [בפ"ו] ומודעת זאת

SECTION FOUR: THE IMPACT OF "NEUTRAL" ACTIVITIES

30TH SHEVAT REGULAR | 14TH ADAR I LEAP

וְגַם מִי שֶׁהוּא נָקִי מֵחַטּאוֹת נְעוּרִים הַחֲמוּרִים — And even if you are clean from serious "sins of youth," — יָשִׂים אֶל לִבּוֹ לְקַיֵּם מַאֲמַר זֹהַר הַקָּדוֹשׁ — commit in your heart to fulfill the holy **Zohar's** teaching, לִהְיוֹת מִמָּארֵי דְחוּשְׁבָּנָא — to be *"an expert accountant"* (*Zohar* 3, 178a).

The *Zohar* (ibid) states that each night, before going to sleep, *"a person must take account of the actions he did that day, repent for them, and ask for compassion for them.... And people who do this are called 'expert accountants.'"*

דְּהַיְינוּ לַעֲשׂוֹת חֶשְׁבּוֹן עִם נַפְשׁוֹ מִכָּל הַמַּחֲשָׁבוֹת וְהַדִּבּוּרִים וְהַמַּעֲשִׂים — Namely, you should make a personal account of all the thoughts, spoken words and actions, שֶׁחָלְפוּ וְעָבְרוּ מִיּוֹם הֱיוֹתוֹ — that have transpired and come to pass from the day you were born until today, עַד הַיּוֹם הַזֶּה אִם הָיוּ כֻלָּם — and ask yourself: Were מִצַּד הַקְּדוּשָׁה אוֹ מִצַּד הַטּוּמְאָה — they all from a context of holiness? Or were some from an impure context? רַחֲמָנָא לִצְלָן — May G-d protect us!

דְּהַיְינוּ כָּל הַמַּחֲשָׁבוֹת וְהַדִּבּוּרִים וְהַמַּעֲשִׂים — The definition of an impure context **being** even **all those** ostensibly "neutral" **thoughts, spoken words and actions,** אֲשֶׁר לֹא לַה' הֵמָּה וְלִרְצוֹנוֹ וְלַעֲבוֹדָתוֹ — which, while not religiously forbidden, **were not** consciously **directed towards G-d, to** fulfill **His will or in His worship,** שֶׁזֶּהוּ פֵּירוּשׁ לְשׁוֹן סִטְרָא אָחֳרָא — **since this is the meaning of** *sitra achra,* "the other side," *i.e.* anything which is not the holy side, כַּנִּזְכָּר לְעֵיל [בְּפֶרֶק ו'] — **as we learned above (chapter 6,** p. 86).

Even if you are not guilty of major sins, did you have thoughts, spoken words or actions which were not consciously dedicated to G-d? If you did, these activities had the energy of *sitra achra,* just like an actual sin — a further humbling thought for an ego-deflating session.

PRACTICAL LESSONS

Also call to mind all your "neutral" thoughts, spoken words and actions, which, in fact, were not really neutral but actually strengthened the negative forces (since they weren't devoted to G-d).

כִּי כָּל עֵת שֶׁהָאָדָם מְחַשֵּׁב מַחֲשָׁבוֹת קְדוֹשׁוֹת נַעֲשֶׂה
מֶרְכָּבָה בָּעֵת זוֹ לְהַהֵיכָלוֹת הַקְּדוֹשָׁה שֶׁמֵּהֶן מוּשְׁפָּעוֹת
מַחֲשָׁבוֹת הַלָּלוּ וְכֵן לְהֵפֶךְ נַעֲשֶׂה מֶרְכָּבָה טְמֵאָה בָּעֵת
זוֹ לְהַהֵיכָלוֹת הַטּוּמְאָה שֶׁמֵּהֶן מוּשְׁפָּעוֹת כָּל מַחֲשָׁבוֹת
רָעוֹת וְכֵן בְּדִבּוּר וּמַעֲשֶׂה. עוֹד יָשִׂים אֶל לִבּוֹ רוֹב
חֲלוֹמוֹתָיו שֶׁהֵם הֶבֶל וּרְעוּת רוּחַ מִשּׁוּם שֶׁאֵין נַפְשׁוֹ
עוֹלָה לְמַעְלָה וְכמ"ש מִי יַעֲלֶה בְּהַר ה' נְקִי כַפַּיִם וְגו'

37A

וּמוּדַעַת זֹאת כִּי כָּל עֵת שֶׁהָאָדָם מְחַשֵּׁב — And **"this thing is known"** (Isaiah 12:5), **that at any moment you think holy thoughts,** מַחֲשָׁבוֹת קְדוֹשׁוֹת נַעֲשֶׂה מֶרְכָּבָה — **you become, at that time,** בָּעֵת זוֹ לְהַהֵיכָלוֹת הַקְּדוֹשָׁה שֶׁמֵּהֶן מוּשְׁפָּעוֹת מַחֲשָׁבוֹת הַלָּלוּ — a **"chariot" for the holy "chambers"** in heaven **from which the thought flowed,** וְכֵן לְהֵפֶךְ נַעֲשֶׂה מֶרְכָּבָה טְמֵאָה בָּעֵת זוֹ לְהַהֵיכָלוֹת הַטּוּמְאָה — **and conversely,** whenever you think impure thoughts, **you become at that time an impure "chariot" for the impure "chambers,"** שֶׁמֵּהֶן מוּשְׁפָּעוֹת כָּל מַחֲשָׁבוֹת רָעוֹת — **from which all bad thoughts flow.**

וְכֵן בְּדִבּוּר וּמַעֲשֶׂה — **And the same is true with** holy and impure **speech and action.**

As we learned above (chapter 23, p. 256), through your "garments" of thought, speech and action, you become a physical embodiment ("chariot") for the powers which you choose to follow at that moment. Contemplate that whenever you were not conscious of G-d, you became a vehicle and embodiment for the impure forces of *sitra achra.*

SECTION FIVE: THE MEANING OF YOUR DREAMS

15TH ADAR I LEAP

עוֹד יָשִׂים אֶל לִבּוֹ רוֹב חֲלוֹמוֹתָיו שֶׁהֵם הֶבֶל וּרְעוּת רוּחַ — As a **further** source of humbling thoughts, **take to heart that** the content of **your dreams, in the majority of cases, are** *"vacuous and a strain to the spirit"* (Ecclesiastes 1:14), מִשּׁוּם שֶׁאֵין נַפְשׁוֹ עוֹלָה לְמַעְלָה — **because your soul is unable to ascend to heaven.**

If your soul successfully reached the heavens when you were sleeping, your dreams would have a holy and pure content. Empty or negative dream content suggests that your soul was unable to ascend to heaven.

וּכְמוֹ שֶׁכָּתוּב מִי יַעֲלֶה בְּהַר ה' נְקִי כַפַּיִם וְגו' — As the verse states, *"Who shall go up on the mount of G-d, and who shall stand up in His holy place? The clean of hands and the pure of heart"* (Psalms 24:3-4).

Only the pure are admitted to heaven (*"the Mount of G-d"*), so the rejection of your soul from there (during sleep) suggests that you are not *"clean of hands"* and *"pure of heart."*

וְאִינּוּן סְטְרִין בִּישִׁין אַתְיָין וּמִתְדַּבְּקָן בֵּיהּ וּמוֹדְעִין לֵיהּ
בְּחֶלְמָא מִילִין דְּעָלְמָא וכו' וּלְזִמְנִין דְּחַיְיכָן בֵּיהּ וְאַחֲזִיאוּ
לֵיהּ מִילֵי שְׁקַר וְצַעֲרִין לֵיהּ בְּחֶלְמֵיהּ כו' כמ"ש בזהר
ויקרא [ד' כ"ה ע"א וע"ב] ע"ש בַּאֲרִיכוּת. וְהִנֵּה כָּל מַה
שֶּׁיַּאֲרִיךְ בְּעִנְיָינִים אֵלוּ בְּמַחֲשַׁבְתּוֹ וְגַם בְּעִיּוּנוֹ בִּסְפָרִים
לִהְיוֹת לִבּוֹ נִשְׁבָּר בְּקִרְבּוֹ וְנִבְזֶה בְּעֵינָיו נִמְאָס כְּכָתוּב
בְּתַכְלִית הַמִּיאוּס וּלְמָאֵס חַיָּיו מַמָּשׁ הֲרֵי בָזֶה מְמָאֵס
וּמְבַזֶּה הַסִּטְרָא אַחֲרָא וּמַשְׁפִּילָהּ לֶעָפָר וּמוֹרִידָהּ מִגְּדוּלָתָהּ וְגַסּוּת
רוּחָהּ וְגַבְהוּתָהּ שֶׁמַּגְבִּיהַּ אֶת עַצְמָהּ עַל אוֹר קְדוּשַׁת
נֶפֶשׁ הָאֱלֹהִית לְהַחֲשִׁיךְ אוֹרָהּ. וְגַם יְרֵעִים עָלֶיהָ בְּקוֹל

What can you expect to dream when your soul is not admitted to heaven?

וְאִינּוּן סְטְרִין בִּישִׁין אָתְיָין וּמִתְדַּבְּקָן בֵּיהּ וּמוֹדְעִין לֵיהּ בְּחֶלְמָא מִילִין דְּעָלְמָא וכו' — **And** when the soul fails to enter heaven during sleep, *"those evil aspects come and cling to him, informing him of worldly matters, some false and some true,"* וּלְזִמְנִין *"and sometimes they toy* — דְּחַיְיכָן בֵּיהּ וְאַחֲזִיאוּ לֵיהּ מִילֵי שְׁקַר וְצַעֲרִין לֵיהּ בְּחֶלְמֵיהּ כו' *with him, show him falsehoods, tormenting him in his dream, etc."*

כְּמוֹ שֶׁכָּתוּב בַּזֹּהַר וַיִּקְרָא [דַּף כ"ה עַמּוּד א' וְעַמּוּד ב'] עַיֵּין שָׁם בַּאֲרִיכוּת — **As stated in** the *Zohar,* Portion of *Vayikra* (3, **25a-b**); see there at length.

1ST ADAR REGULAR

וְהִנֵּה כָּל מַה שֶּׁיַּאֲרִיךְ בְּעִנְיָינִים אֵלוּ — **Now the more time you will spend on these ideas,** בְּמַחֲשַׁבְתּוֹ וְגַם בְּעִיּוּנוֹ בִּסְפָרִים — **both in personal reflection and through studying sacred books** on these topics, לִהְיוֹת לִבּוֹ נִשְׁבָּר בְּקִרְבּוֹ — **to render yourself heartbroken inside,** וְנִבְזֶה בְּעֵינָיו נִמְאָס כְּכָתוּב בְּתַכְלִית הַמִּיאוּס — **and, in the words of Scripture,** *"disgusting in your eyes, and repulsive"* (*Psalms* 15:4), **utterly repulsive,** הֲרֵי בָזֶה — **so that you are completely repulsed by your life,** וּלְמָאֵס חַיָּיו מַמָּשׁ **— you thereby repulse and degrade the** *sitra achra,* מְמָאֵס וּמְבַזֶּה הַסִּטְרָא אַחֲרָא **with which your "self" is identified,** וּמַשְׁפִּילָהּ לֶעָפָר **— and you cast it down to the ground,** וּמוֹרִידָהּ מִגְּדוּלָתָהּ וְגַסּוּת רוּחָהּ וְגַבְהוּתָהּ — **humiliating it from its grandiosity, its inflated ego and its arrogance.**

שֶׁמַּגְבִּיהַּ אֶת עַצְמָהּ עַל אוֹר קְדוּשַׁת נֶפֶשׁ הָאֱלֹהִית לְהַחֲשִׁיךְ אוֹרָהּ — And that is **what led it to exert itself over your Divine Soul's holy** power of *chochmah,* **and block its light,** causing you to become spiritually desensitized.

SECTION SIX: A SECOND TACTIC

וְגַם יְרֵעִים עָלֶיהָ בְּקוֹל רַעַשׁ וְרוֹגֶז לְהַשְׁפִּילָהּ — **And** in addition to being *repulsed* at your Animal Soul, **you should also** employ a further technique of encouraging your

רעש ורוגז להשפילה כמאמר רז"ל לעולם ירגיז אדם
יצ"ט על יצ"הר שנאמר רגזו וגו' דהיינו לרגוז על נפש
הבהמית שהיא יצרו הרע בקול רעש ורוגז במחשבתו
לומר לו אתה רע ורשע ומשוקץ ומתועב ומנוול וכו'
ככל השמות שקראו לו חכמינו ז"ל באמת עד מתי
תסתיר לפני אור א"ס ב"ה הממלא כל עלמין היה הוה
ויהיה בשוה גם במקום זה שאני עליו כמו שהיה
אור א"ס ב"ה לבדו קודם שנברא העולם בלי שום
שינוי כמ"ש אני ה' לא שניתי כי הוא למעלה מהזמן

Divine Soul to **become *enraged*** with your Animal Soul, with ***"a thunderous voice"*** (*Ezekiel* 3:12) **of anger** in your head, **to humble** the *sitra achra*.

כְּמַאֲמַר רַבּוֹתֵינוּ זִכְרוֹנָם לִבְרָכָה לְעוֹלָם יַרְגִּיז אָדָם יֵצֶר טוֹב עַל יֵצֶר הָרַע שֶׁנֶּאֱמַר רִגְזוּ וְגוֹ' — **As our Sages of blessed memory, taught: *"A person should always make his impulse to good angry at his impulse to evil, as the verse states, 'Get angry,* and** *don't sin'"* (*Psalms* 4:5; *Talmud, Brachos* 5a), דְּהַיְינוּ לִרְגוֹז עַל נֶפֶשׁ הַבַּהֲמִית שֶׁהִיא — **meaning to say, get angry with your Animal Soul, *i.e,* your impulse to evil,** יִצְרוֹ הָרַע בְּקוֹל רַעַשׁ וְרוֹגֶז בְּמַחֲשַׁבְתּוֹ — **with *"a thunderous voice"* of anger in your head,** לוֹמַר לוֹ אַתָּה רַע וְרָשָׁע וּמְשׁוּקָץ וּמְתוֹעָב וּמְנֻוָּל וְכוּ' — **and say to it: "You are bad, sinful, disgusting, repulsive, and wretched!"** *etc.,* כְּכָל הַשֵּׁמוֹת שֶׁקְּרָאוּ לוֹ חֲכָמֵינוּ זִכְרוֹנָם לִבְרָכָה בֶּאֱמֶת — **along with all the similar terms with which our Sages of blessed memory have rightfully used for** the impulse to evil (see *Talmud, Succah* 52a).

PRACTICAL LESSONS

Another technique is to "get angry" at your Animal Soul, for lying to you and hiding G-d's presence from you.

עַד מָתַי תַּסְתִּיר לִפְנֵי אֵין סוֹף בָּרוּךְ הוּא — **Say to your** Animal Soul: **"For how much longer will you hide before the Blessed Infinite Light?"**

The *Tanya* offers a brief meditation on the nature of G-d's Infinite Light.

הַמְמַלֵּא כָּל עָלְמִין — **An Infinite Light that floods all the worlds,** הָיָה הֹוֶה וְיִהְיֶה בְּשָׁוֶה — **and is devoid of any lim**itation, such that simultaneously ***"He was, He is, and He will be"*** (*Shulchan Aruch, Orach Chaim* 5:1), **all at once,** גַּם בְּמָקוֹם זֶה שֶׁאֲנִי עָלָיו — **and even in this very place where I stand,** the Infinite Light shines, כְּמוֹ שֶׁהָיָה אוֹר

אֵין סוֹף בָּרוּךְ הוּא לְבַדּוֹ קוֹדֶם שֶׁנִּבְרָא הָעוֹלָם — **and His Infinite Light remains alone, just as it was before the world was created** since there is no existence independent from this light (see chapter 20, p. 233), בְּלִי שׁוּם שִׁינוּי — **and since there is no** new, independent existence, the Infinite Light has experienced **no actual change,** כְּמוֹ שֶׁכָּתוּב אֲנִי ה' לֹא שָׁנִיתִי — **as the verse states, *"For I, G-d, have not changed"*** (*Malachi* 3:6), כִּי הוּא לְמַעְלָה מֵהַזְּמַן וְכוּ' — **since G-d transcends time,** *etc.*

וכו' ואתה מנוול וכו' מכחיש האמת הנראה לעינים
דכולא קמיה כלא ממש באמת בבחי' ראייה חושיית.
והנה על ידי זה יועיל לנפשו האלהית להאיר עיניה   37B
באמת יחוד אור אין סוף בראייה חושיית ולא בחי'
שמיעה והבנה לבדה כמ"ש במ"א שזהו שרש כל
העבודה והטעם לפי שבאמת אין שום ממשות כלל
בס"א שלכן נמשלה לחשך שאין בו שום ממשות
כלל וממילא נדחה מפני האור וכך הס"א אף שיש בה
חיות הרבה להחיות כל בעלי חיים הטמאים ונפשות

The "enraged" conversation with your Animal Soul continues:

וְאַתָּה מְנֻוָּל וְכוּ' מַכְחִישׁ הָאֱמֶת הַנִּרְאָה לָעֵינַיִם — **But you, wretched one,** *etc.,* **deny** this **self-evident truth,** דְּכוּלָּא קַמֵּיהּ כְּלָא מַמָּשׁ בֶּאֱמֶת — that *"in His presence, every-thing is considered zero"* (*Zohar* 1, 11b), בִּבְחִינַת רְאִיָּה חוּשִׁיִּית — which is as obvious as if it were **seen visibly.**

What are the results we can hope for when following all of the above advice?

יוֹעִיל לְנַפְשׁוֹ הָאֱלֹהִית לְהָאִיר עֵינֶיהָ בֶּאֱמֶת יִחוּד זֶה — **And through this,** וְהִנֵּה עַל יְדֵי זֶה אוֹר אֵין סוֹף — **you will help the "eyes" of your Divine Soul to be enlightened by the nondual reality of** G-d's **Infinite Light,** בִּרְאִיָּה חוּשִׁיִּית — **with** the clarity and certainty normally associated with actual **sensory vision,** וְלֹא בְחִינַת שְׁמִיעָה וַהֲבָנָה לְבַדָּהּ — **without** the uncertainty which inevitably comes **through using deduction and logic alone,** כְּמוֹ שֶׁנִּתְבָּאֵר בְּמָקוֹם אַחֵר — **as is explained elsewhere,** שֶׁזֶּהוּ שֹׁרֶשׁ כָּל הָעֲבוֹדָה — **that this is the root of all worship** (see chapter 36).

SECTION SEVEN: EGO-DEFLATION BRINGS YOU CLOSER TO G-D

2ND ADAR REGULAR

וְהַטַּעַם לְפִי שֶׁבֶּאֱמֶת אֵין שׁוּם מַמָּשׁוּת כְּלָל בְּסִטְרָא אָחֳרָא — **The reason why** these "conversations" with the Animal Soul are effective **is because, in reality, the** *sitra achra* **has no substance at all.**

The *sitra achra* can only conceal the truth, but it has no real power. Once its lie is exposed, its allure is neutralized.

שֶׁלָּכֵן נִמְשְׁלָה לַחשֶׁךְ — **And that is why** the *sitra achra* **is compared to darkness,** שֶׁאֵין בּוֹ שׁוּם מַמָּשׁוּת כְּלָל וּמִמֵּילָא נִדְחָה מִפְּנֵי הָאוֹר — since darkness **has no sub-stance at all, and will be effortlessly banished by light.**

וְכָךְ הַסִּטְרָא אָחֳרָא אַף שֶׁיֵּשׁ בָּהּ חִיּוּת הַרְבֵּה לְהַחֲיוֹת כָּל בַּעֲלֵי חַיִּים הַטְּמֵאִים — **And while** the *sitra achra* seems to have considerable "substance" since it **has a lot of energy with which it animates all the non-kosher animals,** וְנַפְשׁוֹת אֻמּוֹת הָעוֹלָם וְגַם נֶפֶשׁ

אומות עכו"ם וגם נפש הבהמית שבישראל כנ"ל מ"מ
הרי כל חיותה אינה מצד עצמה ח"ו אלא מצד הקדושה
כנ"ל ולכן היא בטלה לגמרי מפני הקדושה כביטול
החשך מפני האור הגשמי רק שלגבי קדושת נפש
האלהית שבאדם נתן לה הקב"ה רשות ויכולת להגביה
עצמה כנגדה כדי שהאדם יתעורר להתגבר עליה
להשפילה ע"י שפלות ונמיכת רוחו ונבזה בעיניו נמאס
ובאתערותא דלתתא אתערותא דלעילא לקיים מ"ש
משם אורידך נאם ה' דהיינו שמסירה מממשלתה
ויכלתה ומסלק ממנה הכח ורשות שנתן לה להגביה

הַבַּהֲמִית שֶׁבְּיִשְׂרָאֵל — as well as the Animal **Souls of the** wicked **"nations of the world" and the Animal Souls of Israel,** כַּנִּזְכָּר לְעֵיל — **as mentioned above** (chapters 6-7), מִכָּל מָקוֹם הֲרֵי כָל חַיּוּתָה אֵינָה מִצַּד עַצְמָהּ חַס וְשָׁלוֹם — **nevertheless,** despite this apparent abundance of "substance," in reality, **its energizing power is not autonomous, G-d forbid,** אֶלָּא מִצַּד הַקְּדוּשָׁה — **but rather, its** power **is derived** indirectly **from** the powers of **holiness,** כַּנִּזְכָּר לְעֵיל — **as mentioned above,** (chapters 6 and 22), וְלָכֵן הִיא בְּטֵלָה לְגַמְרֵי מִפְּנֵי הַקְּדוּשָׁה — **and that's why,** being inherently devoid of substance, the *sitra achra* **is eliminated completely by the presence of holiness,** כְּבִיטוּל הַחֹשֶׁךְ מִפְּנֵי הָאוֹר הַגַּשְׁמִי — **just as** physical **darkness is eliminated by physical light.**

But if the *sitra achra* is so devoid of substance and power, why is it so difficult to overcome in our daily lives?

רַק שֶׁלְּגַבֵּי קְדוּשַׁת נֶפֶשׁ הָאֱלֹהִית שֶׁבָּאָדָם — **Only in the case of your Divine Soul's holy** power of *chochmah*, נָתַן לָהּ הַקָּדוֹשׁ בָּרוּךְ הוּא רְשׁוּת וִיכוֹלֶת לְהַגְבִּיהַּ עַצְמָהּ כְּנֶגְדָּהּ — **G-d granted** special **permission to** the *sitra achra* of the Animal Soul **to have the ability to exert itself against** the Divine Soul, כְּדֵי שֶׁהָאָדָם יִתְעוֹרֵר לְהִתְגַּבֵּר עָלֶיהָ — **so that you will be inspired to overcome it,** לְהַשְׁפִּילָהּ עַל יְדֵי שִׁפְלוּת וּנְמִיכַת רוּחוֹ — **and bring down** the *sitra achra* of your Animal Soul **through** the above meditations **of self-debasement and ego-deflation,** וְנִבְזֶה בְּעֵינָיו נִמְאָס — becoming *"disgusting in your eyes, and repulsive"* (*Psalms* 15:4).

וּבְאִתְעָרוּתָא דִלְתַתָּא אִתְעָרוּתָא דִלְעֵילָא — **And** if you do this, G-d will help you, since *"with an awakening from below, there is an awaking from Above"* (*Zohar* 2, 135b), לְקַיֵּים מַה שֶּׁנֶּאֱמַר מִשָּׁם אוֹרִידְךָ נְאָם ה' — **to fulfill the verse** said of the *sitra achra,* "*'If you lift yourself high like an eagle... **from there I will bring you down,' says G-d"*** (*Ovadiah* 1:4; see chapter 27, p. 311).

How, exactly, will G-d bring the *sitra achra* down?

דְּהַיְינוּ שֶׁמְּסִירָה מִמֶּמְשַׁלְתָּהּ וִיכָלְתָּהּ — **Namely, He will take** the *sitra achra's* **power and ability away,** וּמְסַלֵּק מִמֶּנָּה הַכֹּחַ וּרְשׁוּת שֶׁנָּתַן לָהּ לְהַגְבִּיהַּ עַצְמָהּ נֶגֶד אוֹר קְדוּשַׁת נֶפֶשׁ

עצמה נגד אור קדושת נפש האלהית ואזי ממילא
בטילה ונדחית כביטול החשך מפני אור הגשמי. וכמו
שמצינו דבר זה מפורש בתורה גבי מרגלים שמתחלה
אמרו כי חזק הוא ממנו אל תקרי ממנו כו' שלא האמינו
ביכולת ה' ואח"כ חזרו ואמרו הננו ועלינו וגו' ומאין
חזרה ובאה להם האמונה ביכולת ה' הרי לא הראה
להם משרע"ה שום אות ומופת על זה בנתיים רק
שאמ' להם איך שקצף ה' עליהם ונשבע שלא להביאם
אל הארץ ומה הועיל זה להם אם לא היו מאמינים
ביכולת ה' ח"ו לכבוש ל"א מלכי' ומפני זה לא רצו כלל
38A   ליכנס לארץ אלא ודאי מפני שישראל עצמן הם

הָאֱלֹהִית — by stripping it of the ability and permission it was given to exert itself **over the Divine Soul's holy** power of *chochmah,* וַאֲזַי מִמֵּילָא בְּטֵילָה וְנִדְחֵית — **and,** stripped of this power, **it will be effortlessly banished and eliminated,** כְּבִיטוּל הַחֹשֶׁךְ מִפְּנֵי אוֹר הַגַּשְׁמִי — **just as** physical **darkness is eliminated by physical light.**

SECTION EIGHT: A STORY OF EGO DEFLATION

וּכְמוֹ שֶׁמָּצִינוּ דָּבָר זֶה מְפוֹרָשׁ בַּתּוֹרָה גַּבֵּי מְרַגְלִים — **And we find this idea clearly in the Torah, concerning the spies** sent to scout the Land of Cana'an, שֶׁמִּתְּחִלָּה אָמְרוּ כִּי חָזָק הוּא מִמֶּנּוּ — **who initially said, "We are unable to go up against this people, for they are stronger than us"** (Numbers 13:31), אַל תִּקְרֵי מִמֶּנּוּ כו' — and the *Talmud* expounds their inner intent, **"Do not read** 'stronger **than us, but rather, 'stronger than He, (than G-d)"** (Talmud, Sotah 35a), שֶׁלֹּא הֶאֱמִינוּ בִּיכוֹלֶת ה' — suggesting that **they didn't believe in G-d's power** to help them conquer the land.

וְאַחַר כָּךְ חָזְרוּ וְאָמְרוּ הִנֶּנּוּ וְעָלִינוּ וְגוֹ' — **But afterwards they retracted** their position, **and said, "We're ready to go up to the place G-d spoke about"** (Numbers 14:40).

וּמֵאַיִן חָזְרָה וּבָאָה לָהֶם הָאֱמוּנָה בִּיכוֹלֶת ה' — **So how did they regain their belief in G-d's power?**

הֲרֵי לֹא הֶרְאָה לָהֶם מֹשֶׁה רַבֵּינוּ עָלָיו הַשָּׁלוֹם — **Moses, of** blessed memory, **had not showed them any** miraculous **sign or wonder in the interim period,** רַק שֶׁאָמַר לָהֶם אֵיךְ שֶׁקָּצַף ה' עֲלֵיהֶם וְנִשְׁבַּע שֶׁלֹּא לַהֲבִיאָם אֶל הָאָרֶץ — **all** he said to them was that G-d had become angry with them and had sworn not to bring them to the Land (ibid. 29-30), וּמַה הוֹעִיל זֶה לָהֶם — **but of what persuasive power was this** Divine anger, אִם לֹא הָיוּ מַאֲמִינִים בִּיכוֹלֶת ה' חַס וְשָׁלוֹם לִכְבּוֹשׁ ל"א מְלָכִים — **if they didn't believe in G-d's power, Heaven forfend, to help them conquer the thirty-one kings** that occupied the land, וּמִפְּנֵי זֶה לֹא רָצוּ כְּלָל לִיכָּנֵס לָאָרֶץ — **this being the reason why they didn't want to go into the land in the first place?**

מאמינים בני מאמינים רק שהס"א המלובשת בגופם
הגביה עצמה על אור קדושת נפשם האלהית בגסות
רוחה וגבהות' בחוצפה בלי טעם ודעת ולכן מיד שקצף
ה' עליהם והרעים בקול רעש ורוגז עד מתי לעדה
הרעה הזאת וגו' במדבר הזה יפלו פגריכם וגו' אני ה'
דברתי אם לא זאת אעשה לכל העדה הרעה הזאת
וגו' וכששמעו דברים קשים אלו נכנע ונשבר לבם
בקרבם כדכתיב ויתאבלו העם מאד וממילא נפלה
הס"א מממשלתה וגבהותה וגסות רוחה וישראל עצמן

From where did they suddenly acquire a faith which, shortly beforehand, seemed to be completely lacking? Nothing positive had happened to inspire them.

אֶלָּא וַדַּאי מִפְּנֵי שֶׁיִּשְׂרָאֵל עַצְמָן הֵם מַאֲמִינִים בְּנֵי מַאֲמִינִים — **Rather, we can be certain that** they didn't need to *acquire* faith **since Jews are inherently "believers, the children of believers"** (*Talmud, Shabbos* 97a), רַק שֶׁהַסִּטְרָא אָחֳרָא הַמְלוּבֶּשֶׁת בְּגוּפָם — **rather, it is only that the** *sitra achra* **found in their bodies, exerted itself over their Divine Soul's holy light,** הִגְבִּיהַ עַצְמָהּ עַל אוֹר קְדוּשַׁת נַפְשָׁם הָאֱלֹהִית בְּגַסּוּת רוּחָהּ **as a result of the** *sitra achra's* **inflated ego, arro-** וְגַבְהוּתָהּ בְּחוּצְפָה בְּלִי טַעַם וָדַעַת **gance and irrational** *chutzpah.*

וְלָכֵן מִיָּד שֶׁקָּצַף ה' עֲלֵיהֶם — **And therefore, as soon as G-d became angry with them,** וְהִרְעִים בְּקוֹל רַעַשׁ וְרוֹגֶז — **and was enraged with "a thunderous voice"** (*Ezekiel* 3:12) **of anger,** עַד מָתַי לָעֵדָה הָרָעָה הַזֹּאת וְגוֹ' בַּמִּדְבָּר הַזֶּה יִפְּלוּ פִּגְרֵיכֶם וְגוֹ' אֲנִי ה' דִּבַּרְתִּי אִם **saying, "How much longer (must I bear) this evil congregation... your corpses will fall in this desert.... I, G-d, have spoken; I will do this to the entire evil congregation etc.,"** (*Numbers* 14:27, 29, 35), לֹא זֹאת אֶעֱשֶׂה לְכָל הָעֵדָה הָרָעָה הַזֹּאת וְגוֹ' וּכְשֶׁשָּׁמְעוּ דְּבָרִים קָשִׁים אֵלּוּ נִכְנַע וְנִשְׁבַּר לִבָּם **their hearts were humbled and broken inside** בְּקִרְבָּם **them hearing these harsh words,** כְּדִכְתִיב וַיִּתְאַבְּלוּ הָעָם **as the verse states, "and the people mourned** מְאֹד **greatly"** (*ibid.* 39), וּמֵמֵּילָא נָפְלָה הַסִּטְרָא אָחֳרָא מִמֶּמְשַׁלְתָּהּ וְגַבְהוּתָהּ וְגַסּוּת רוּחָהּ — **and as a result, the** *sitra achra* **fell from its power, its arrogance and its inflated ego.**

![PRACTICAL LESSONS]

PRACTICAL LESSONS

Remind yourself that you *already* have faith and an emotional connection with G-d. These techniques are merely to remove a superficial blockage.

The people didn't *acquire* faith through some inspirational event. Rather, *their inherent faith surfaced* due to a negative event (G-d's anger) which dismantled the *sitra achra* that was blocking their faith.

וְיִשְׂרָאֵל עַצְמָן הֵם מַאֲמִינִים — **And the Jewish people are inherently believers,** the *sitra achra* acted only as a superficial blockage to their faith.

הם מאמינים ומזה יכול ללמוד כל אדם שנופלים לו
במחשבתו ספיקות על אמונה כי הם דברי רוח הס"א
לבדה המגביה עצמה על נפשו אבל ישראל עצמן הם
מאמינים כו' וגם הס"א עצמה אין לה ספיקות כלל
באמונה רק שניתן לה רשות לבלבל האדם בדברי
שקר ומרמה להרבות שכרו כפיתויי הזונה לבן המלך
בשקר ומרמה ברשות המלך כמ"ש בזה"ק:

שֶׁנּוֹפְלִים לוֹ וּמִזֶּה יָכוֹל לִלְמוֹד כָּל אָדָם — **And from this we can all learn a lesson,** בְּמַחֲשַׁבְתּוֹ סְפֵיקוֹת עַל אֱמוּנָה — that when **doubtful thoughts about faith pop into your head,** כִּי הֵם דְּבָרִי רוּחַ הַסִּטְרָא אַחֲרָא לְבַדָּהּ — **remember that they are just words emanating from the** *sitra achra,* הַמַּגְבִּיהַ עַצְמָהּ עַל נַפְשׁוֹ — which has exerted itself **over your** Divine **Soul,** אֲבָל יִשְׂרָאֵל עַצְמָן הֵם מַאֲמִינִים כוּ' — but Jews are inherently *"believers, the children of believers" etc.*

וְגַם הַסִּטְרָא אַחֲרָא עַצְמָהּ אֵין לָהּ סְפֵיקוֹת כְּלָל בָּאֱמוּנָה — **And what is more,** remember that **the** *sitra achra* itself **is a servant of G-d and believes in G-d without any doubts at all,** רַק שֶׁנִּיתַּן לָהּ רְשׁוּת לְבַלְבֵּל הָאָדָם בְּדִבְרֵי שֶׁקֶר וּמִרְמָה — **and it has only been granted permission** by G-d **to confuse you with lies and deception,** לְהַרְבּוֹת שְׂכָרוֹ — **so that your reward** for resisting its allure **will be greater.**

כְּפִתּוּיֵי הַזוֹנָה לְבֶן הַמֶּלֶךְ בְּשֶׁקֶר וּמִרְמָה בִּרְשׁוּת הַמֶּלֶךְ — In this respect, the *sitra achra* **is like a harlot who, with the permission of the king, tries to seduce the king's son with lies and deception,** כְּמוֹ שֶׁכָּתוּב בַּזֹּהַר הַקָּדוֹשׁ — **as stated in the holy** *Zohar* (see end of chapter 9, p. 121).

CHAPTER 30

HOW NOT TO JUDGE OTHERS
SECTION ONE: WHY OTHERS SHOULD MAKE YOU FEEL HUMBLE

3RD ADAR REGULAR | 16TH ADAR I LEAP

This chapter (which did not appear in the original manuscript versions of the *Tanya* and was added by the author to the first print edition), offers an important lesson on remaining humble and not judging others.

פרק ל **עוד** זאת ישים אל לבו לקיים מאמר רז"ל
והוי שפל רוח בפני כל האדם. והוי
באמת לאמיתו בפני כל האדם ממש אפי' בפני קל
שבקלים. והיינו ע"פ מארז"ל אל תדין את חבירך עד
שתגיע למקומו. כי מקומו גורם לו לחטוא להיות
פרנסתו לילך בשוק כל היום ולהיות מיושבי קרנות
ועיניו רואות כל התאוות והעין רואה והלב חומד ויצרו
בוער כתנור בוערה מאופה כמ"ש בהושע הוא בוער
כאש להבה וגו'. משא"כ מי שהולך בשוק מעט ורוב
היום יושב בביתו וגם אם הולך כל היום בשוק יכול
להיות שאינו מחומם כ"כ בטבעו כי אין היצר שוה **38B**

עוֹד זֹאת יָשִׂים אֶל לִבּוֹ — Also, take the following to heart.

לְקַיֵּם מַאֲמַר רַבּוֹתֵינוּ זִכְרוֹנָם לִבְרָכָה — Try **to fulfill the teaching of our Sages, of blessed memory,** וֶהֱוֵי שְׁפַל רוּחַ בִּפְנֵי כָּל הָאָדָם — *"Be humble in spirit before everyone"* (*Mishnah, Avos* 4:10), וֶהֱוֵי בֶּאֱמֶת לַאֲמִיתּוֹ בִּפְנֵי כָּל הָאָדָם מַמָּשׁ — which implies that you shouldn't just *act* humbly, but you should **literally and genuinely** *feel* humble **before everyone,** אֲפִילוּ בִּפְנֵי קַל שֶׁבַּקַּלִּים — **even before the most** religiously **irreverent person,** Jew or non-Jew (*Notes on Tanya*).

וְהַיְינוּ עַל פִּי מַאֲמַר רַבּוֹתֵינוּ זִכְרוֹנָם לִבְרָכָה — **And** the key to doing **this is by following** another **teaching of our Sages, of blessed memory,** אַל תָּדִין אֶת חֲבֵירְךָ עַד שֶׁתַּגִּיעַ לִמְקוֹמוֹ — *"Don't judge another person until you have been in his circumstances"* (*Mishnah, Avos* 2:4).

כִּי מְקוֹמוֹ גּוֹרֵם לוֹ לַחֲטוֹא — **Because it's "his circumstances" that caused him to sin,** לִהְיוֹת פַּרְנָסָתוֹ לֵילֵךְ בַּשּׁוּק כָּל הַיּוֹם — **for example, it could be that his work requires him to be around the marketplace all day,** exposed to its negative influences and temptations, וְלִהְיוֹת מִיּוֹשְׁבֵי קְרָנוֹת — **and,** at any moment when he is not doing business, he inevitably becomes one of *"those who sit at street corners"* (*Talmud, Brachos* 28b), surrounded by gossip, וְעֵינָיו רוֹאוֹת כָּל הַתַּאֲווֹת — **and his eyes see every form of temptation,** וְהָעַיִן רוֹאָה וְהַלֵּב חוֹמֵד — **and** *"when the eye sees, the heart craves"* (*Rashi* to *Numbers* 15:39), וְיִצְרוֹ בּוֹעֵר כְּתַנּוּר בּוֹעֵרָה מֵאוֹפֶה כְּמוֹ שֶׁכָּתוּב — **and** the passions of his **"impulse to evil" are ignited,** *"like an oven heated by a baker,"* as written in *Hosea* (7:4), הוּא בוֹעֵר כְּאֵשׁ לֶהָבָה וְגוֹ' — *"It blazes like a flaming fire"* (ibid. 6), *etc.*

מַה שֶׁאֵין כֵּן מִי שֶׁהוֹלֵךְ בַּשּׁוּק מְעַט — **This is quite different from a person who spends little time around the marketplace,** וְרֹב הַיּוֹם יוֹשֵׁב בְּבֵיתוֹ — **and most of the day sitting at home,** וְגַם אִם הוֹלֵךְ כָּל הַיּוֹם בַּשּׁוּק יָכוֹל לִהְיוֹת שֶׁאֵינוֹ מְחוּמָּם כָּל כָּךְ בְּטִבְעוֹ — and it's different, too, **from a person who is around the marketplace all day, but,**

בכל נפש יש שיצרו כו' כמ"ש במ"א. והנה באמת
גם מי שהוא מחומם מאד בטבעו ופרנסתו היא להיות
מיושבי קרנות כל היום אין לו שום התנצלות על
חטאיו ומיקרי רשע גמור על אשר אין פחד אלהי' לנגד
עיניו. כי היה לו להתאפק ולמשול על רוח תאוותו
שבלבו מפני פחד ה' הרואה כל מעשיו כמש"ל כי
המוח שליט על הלב בתולדתו. והנה באמת שהיא

as can be the case, is not so easily aroused by his nature to seek pleasure, כִּי אֵין
יֵשׁ — **since the impulse** to evil **is not the same in all people,** יֵשׁ
שֶׁיִּצְרוֹ כוּ' — **some people have a** particularly strong **impulse** to evil, while others do
not, כְּמוֹ שֶׁנִּתְבָּאֵר בְּמָקוֹם אַחֵר — **as is explained elsewhere** (see chapter 15, p. 182).

17TH ADAR I LEAP

The *Tanya* is quick to clarify that this argument (of judging people favorably due to
their circumstances), doesn't *excuse* sinful behavior; it just helps you to understand
it and soften your judgment of it.

וְהִנֵּה בֶּאֱמֶת גַּם מִי שֶׁהוּא מְחוּמָּם מְאֹד בְּטִבְעוֹ — **Now, in truth, even a person who is**
very easily aroused to seek pleasure, וּפַרְנָסָתוֹ הִיא לִהְיוֹת מִיּוֹשְׁבֵי קְרָנוֹת כָּל הַיּוֹם
— **and his work does require him to** *"sit at street corners"* **all day,** exposed to all sorts
of temptation and negative influences, אֵין לוֹ שׁוּם הִתְנַצְּלוּת עַל חֲטָאָיו — **has no jus-**
tification for his sins, וּמִיקְרֵי רָשָׁע גָּמוּר — **and,** the moment he sins, **he is classified**
as a complete *rasha* (see p. 143), עַל אֲשֶׁר אֵין פַּחַד אֱלֹהִים לְנֶגֶד עֵינָיו — **since** *"there*
is no trepidation of G-d before his eyes" (*Psalms* 36:2).

While some situations may be more challenging than others, ultimately, we all
have free choice over our actions, and should never excuse our own sins.

כִּי הָיָה לוֹ לְהִתְאַפֵּק וְלִמְשׁוֹל עַל רוּחַ תַּאֲוָתוֹ שֶׁבְּלִבּוֹ — **For he should have restrained**
himself and taken control of his heart's pleasure-seeking urges, מִפְּנֵי פַּחַד ה' הָרוֹאֶה
כָּל מַעֲשָׂיו — **due to the** *"trepidation of G-d,"* who watches over all his actions, כְּמוֹ
כִּי הַמּוֹחַ שַׁלִּיט עַל — **as has been explained above** (chapters 12, 17), שֶׁנִּתְבָּאֵר לְעֵיל
הַלֵּב בְּתוֹלַדְתּוֹ — **since inherently** and naturally in every person, *"the brain rules*
over the heart" (see p. 143).

SECTION TWO: ARE YOU FIGHTING YOUR "IMPULSE TO EVIL"?

18TH ADAR I LEAP

וְהִנֵּה בֶּאֱמֶת שֶׁהִיא מִלְחָמָה גְדוֹלָה וַעֲצוּמָה לִשְׁבּוֹר הַיֵּצֶר הַבּוֹעֵר כְּאֵשׁ לֶהָבָה מִפְּנֵי פַּחַד ה'
— **Now, to beat the impulse to evil, which** *"blazes like a flaming fire,"* **through**
"trepidation of G-d," **really is an enormous and difficult struggle,** וּכְמוֹ נִסָּיוֹן מַמָּשׁ
— **it's like a real test** of faith.

מלחמה גדולה ועצומ' לשבור היצר הבוער כאש להבה
מפני פחד ה' וכמו נסיון ממש. והלכך צריך כל אדם
לפי מה שהוא מקומו ומדרגתו בעבודת ה' לשקול
ולבחון בעצמו אם הוא עובד ה' בערך ובחי' מלחמה
עצומה כזו ונסיון כזה בבחי' ועשה טוב כגון בעבודת
התפלה בכוונה לשפוך נפשו לפני ה' בכל כחו ממש
עד מיצוי הנפש ולהלחם עם גופו ונפש הבהמית שבו
המונעים הכוונה במלחמה עצומה ולבטשם ולכתתם
כעפר קודם התפלה שחרית וערבית מדי יום ביום וגם

PRACTICAL LESSONS

Always judge others favorably because you don't know their circumstances and the power of their impulse to evil.

You're not living up to G-d's expectations if you're not aggressively fighting your impulse to evil, to have more devotion and less distractions.

The real question is: How much is a person actively engaged in the struggle? External levels of observance tell us little or nothing about what is going on inside another person.

And this, the *Tanya* suggests, gives us insight in how to "be humble in spirit before everyone," since *you don't know a person's struggle*. What you do know for sure, is that *you* could be struggling more.

וְהִלְכָךְ צָרִיךְ כָּל אָדָם לְפִי מַה שֶׁהוּא מְקוֹמוֹ וּמַדְרֵגָתוֹ בַּעֲבוֹדַת ה' — **Therefore every person must take into account his** current **standing and level in the worship of G-d,** לִשְׁקוֹל וְלִבְחוֹן בְּעַצְמוֹ אִם הוּא עוֹבֵד ה' בְּעֵרֶךְ וּבְחִינַת מִלְחָמָה עֲצוּמָה כָּזוֹ וְנִסָּיוֹן כָּזֶה — **to weigh and evaluate for himself if he is really worshiping G-d at the same level as** those faced with **the enormous struggles and tests,** mentioned above, people who are exposed to unimaginable temptations.

בְּבְחִינַת וַעֲשֵׂה טוֹב — This is both in positive areas of *"do good"* (*Psalms* 34:15), כְּגוֹן בַּעֲבוֹדַת הַתְּפִלָּה בְּכַוָּונָה לִשְׁפּוֹךְ נַפְשׁוֹ לִפְנֵי ה' בְּכָל כֹּחוֹ מַמָּשׁ — such as struggling **to worship through devotional prayer, "pouring out your soul before G-d"** (I *Samuel* 1:15), **literally with all your energy,** עַד מִיצוּי הַנֶּפֶשׁ — as *Sifri* teaches on the verse, *"You shall love G-d ... with all your soul"* (*Deuteronomy* 6:5)— *"Until the last drop of life is wrung out of you."*

וּלְהִלָּחֵם עִם גּוּפוֹ וְנֶפֶשׁ הַבַּהֲמִית שֶׁבּוֹ הַמּוֹנְעִים הַכַּוָּונָה בְּמִלְחָמָה עֲצוּמָה — As well as **fighting vigorously against your body and its Animal Soul which dampen your devotion,** וּלְבַטְשָׁם וּלְכַתְּתָם כֶּעָפָר — **to crush and grind their** opposition **to dust,** קוֹדֶם הַתְּפִלָּה שַׁחֲרִית וְעַרְבִית מִדֵּי יוֹם בְּיוֹם — **every day** as a preparation **before the**

בְּשָׁעַת הַתְּפִלָּה לְיַיגֵּעַ עַצְמוֹ בִּיגִיעַת נֶפֶשׁ וִיגִיעַת בָּשָׂר
כמ"ש לקמן באריכות. וכל שלא הגיע לידי מדה זו
להלחם עם גופו מלחמה עצומה כזו עדיין לא הגיע
לבחי' וערך מלחמת היצר הבוער כאש להבה להיות
נכנע ונשבר מפני פחד ה'. וכן בענין ברכת המזון וכל
ברכת הנהנין והמצות בכונה ואצ"ל כונת המצות
לשמן. וכן בענין עסק לימוד התורה ללמוד הרבה
יותר מחפצו ורצונו לפי טבעו ורגילותו ע"י מלחמה

morning and evening prayers. (The afternoon service, which comes in the middle of the day, does not afford much time for preparation).

וְגַם בְּשָׁעַת הַתְּפִלָּה לְיַיגֵּעַ עַצְמוֹ — **And** in addition to this preparation before prayer, **also during prayer** you ought **to exert yourself,** בִּיגִיעַת נֶפֶשׁ וִיגִיעַת בָּשָׂר — **toiling with your body** to silence its urges, **and toiling with your soul** to become excited about spiritual things, כְּמוֹ שֶׁיִּתְבָּאֵר לְקַמָּן בַּאֲרִיכוּת — **as will be explained later at length** (chapter 42, p. 531).

It is the extent of this struggle that determines whether or not you are actively fighting your impulse to evil.

וְכָל שֶׁלֹּא הִגִּיעַ לִידֵי מִדָּה זוֹ לְהִלָּחֵם עִם גּוּפוֹ מִלְחָמָה עֲצוּמָה כָּזוֹ — **And any person who has not adopted this approach of fighting this difficult war against the body,** עֲדַיִין לֹא הִגִּיעַ לִבְחִינַת וְעֵרֶךְ מִלְחֶמֶת הַיֵּצֶר הַבּוֹעֵר כְּאֵשׁ לֶהָבָה — **could not yet be described as** "fighting his impulse to evil," which *"blazes like a flaming fire,"* לִהְיוֹת — נִכְנָע וְנִשְׁבָּר מִפְּנֵי פַּחַד ה' — he has not **caused** his impulse to evil to **be subdued and "broken"** through *"trepidation of G-d."*

A person might observe all the *mitzvos* meticulously, and pray in synagogue three times a day, and yet he has not even *begun* to fight his impulse to evil. The test of this is: Is he struggling greatly?

וְכֵן בְּעִנְיַן בִּרְכַּת הַמָּזוֹן וְכָל בִּרְכוֹת הַנֶּהֱנִין וְהַמִּצְוֹת בְּכַוָּנָה — **Similarly with concentration during** other acts of devotional worship such as the Biblical requirement of **Grace after Meals,** as well as all the Rabbinically required **blessings, both over pleasurable experiences and before** *mitzvos,* וְאֵין צָרִיךְ לוֹמַר כַּוָּנַת הַמִּצְוֹת לִשְׁמָן — **and, it goes without saying,** having authentic intentions when performing the *mitzvos,* there must be an ongoing struggle with the impulse to evil, for more intense devotion and less distraction.

וְכֵן בְּעִנְיַן עֵסֶק לִימוּד הַתּוֹרָה — **And similarly with commitment to Torah study,** לִלְמוֹד הַרְבֵּה יוֹתֵר מֵחֶפְצוֹ וּרְצוֹנוֹ — **you should study much more than you want or desire,** לְפִי טִבְעוֹ וּרְגִילוּתוֹ — **by nature or by nurture,** עַל יְדֵי מִלְחָמָה עֲצוּמָה עִם גּוּפוֹ — **through an intense struggle with your body.**

עֲצוּמָה עִם גוּפוֹ. כִּי הַלּוֹמֵד מְעַט יוֹתֵר מִטִּבְעוֹ ה"ז
מִלְחָמָה קְטַנָּה וְאֵין לָהּ עֵרֶךְ וְדִמְיוֹן עִם מִלְחֶמֶת הַיֵּצֶר
הַבּוֹעֵר כְּאֵשׁ דְּמִקְרֵי רָשָׁע גָּמוּר אִם אֵינוֹ מְנַצֵּחַ יִצְרוֹ
לִהְיוֹת נִכְנָע וְנִשְׁבָּר מִפְּנֵי ה'. וּמַה לִּי בְּחִי' סוּר מֵרַע
וּמַה לִי בְּחִי' וַעֲשֵׂה טוֹב הַכֹּל הִיא מִצְוֹת הַמֶּלֶךְ הַקָּדוֹשׁ
יָחִיד וּמְיוּחָד ב"ה. וְכֵן בִּשְׁאָר מִצְוֹת וּבִפְרָט בְּדָבָר
שֶׁבְּמָמוֹן כְּמוֹ עֲבוֹדַת הַצְּדָקָה וְכה"ג. וַאֲפִי' בִּבְחִי' סוּר

39A

כִּי הַלּוֹמֵד מְעַט יוֹתֵר מִטִּבְעוֹ הֲרֵי זוֹ מִלְחָמָה קְטַנָּה — Because to study a little bit more than your natural inclination requires just a minor battle, וְאֵין לָהּ עֵרֶךְ וְדִמְיוֹן עִם — which can't be compared in any way to really fighting מִלְחֶמֶת הַיֵּצֶר הַבּוֹעֵר כְּאֵשׁ your impulse to evil which *"blazes like a fire,"* דְּמִקְרֵי רָשָׁע גָּמוּר אִם אֵינוֹ מְנַצֵּחַ יִצְרוֹ — for if you don't champion over your impulse to evil, לִהְיוֹת נִכְנָע וְנִשְׁבָּר מִפְּנֵי ה' subduing it and breaking it before G-d, you are classified as a "complete *rasha*."

All these thoughts should help you to "be humble of spirit before everyone" not to "judge another person until you have shared his circumstances." Before you judge, ask yourself: Am I really so holy myself? Have I even *begun* to fight my impulse to evil?

SECTION THREE: THE IRRELIGIOUS PERSON

וּמַה לִּי בְּחִינַת סוּר מֵרַע וּמַה לִי בְּחִינַת וַעֲשֵׂה טוֹב — And is there really any difference between *"turning away from evil"* and *"doing good"*? הַכֹּל הִיא מִצְוֹת הַמֶּלֶךְ הַקָּדוֹשׁ — they are all the *mitzvos* of the Holy King, the single and יָחִיד וּמְיוּחָד בָּרוּךְ הוּא unique one, Blessed be He!

The "religiously irreverent person" fails in the area of "turning away from evil"; he violates the Torah's prohibitions. Whereas the ostensibly religious person, if he fails to seriously fight his impulse to evil during prayer and worship, fails in the area of "doing good."

So who is worse? We cannot say one is better than the other, since both are seriously failing.

וְכֵן בִּשְׁאָר מִצְוֹת — So, too, with the other commandments there needs to be an active struggle with the impulse to evil, וּבִפְרָט בְּדָבָר שֶׁבְּמָמוֹן — especially in financial matters involving money, כְּמוֹ עֲבוֹדַת הַצְּדָקָה וּכְהַאי גּוֹנָא — such as worship through *tzedakah* (charity), *etc.*

20TH ADAR I LEAP

וַאֲפִילוּ בִּבְחִינַת סוּר מֵרַע — Even in the area of *"turning away from evil"* (avoiding transgression) in which, superficially, the religious person seems to succeed,

מרע יכול כל איש משכיל למצוא בנפשו שאינו סר
לגמרי מהרע בכל מכל כל במקום שצריך למלחמה
עצומה כערך הנ"ל ואפי' פחות מערך הנ"ל כגון להפסיק
באמצע שיחה נאה או סיפור בגנות חבירו ואפי' גנאי
קטן וקל מאד אף שהוא אמת ואפי' כדי לנקות עצמו
כנודע מהא דאר"ש לאביו רבינו הקדוש לאו אנא
כתבי' אלא יהודא חייטא כתביה וא"ל כלך מלה"ר [ע"ש
בגמרא רפ"י דב"ב]. וכה"ג כמה מילי דשכיחי טובא
ובפרט בענין לקדש עצמו במותר לו שהוא מדאורייתׁ'

יָכוֹל כָּל אִישׁ מַשְׂכִּיל לִמְצוֹא בְּנַפְשׁוֹ שֶׁאֵינוֹ סָר לְגַמְרֵי מֵהָרַע בְּכָל מִכָּל כֹּל — **any intelligent person can find areas in his life where he does not "turn away from evil" completely,** *"in everything, through everything and with everything"* (*Liturgy*, Grace After Meals), בְּמָקוֹם שֶׁצָּרִיךְ לְמִלְחָמָה עֲצוּמָה כְּעֵרֶךְ הַנִּזְכָּר לְעֵיל — **in every instance where an intense struggle is called for, in the measure described above.**

וַאֲפִילוּ פָּחוֹת מֵעֵרֶךְ הַנִּזְכָּר לְעֵיל — **Or even** a struggle **less than what is described above,** כְּגוֹן לְהַפְסִיק בְּאֶמְצַע שִׂיחָה נָאָה — **such as stopping in the middle of an enjoyable** but pointless **discussion,** אוֹ סִיפּוּר בִּגְנוּת חֲבֵירוֹ — **or to cease telling a negative story about someone,** וַאֲפִילוּ גְּנַאי קָטָן וְקַל מְאֹד — **even if the negative content is slight and minuscule,** אַף שֶׁהוּא אֱמֶת — and **even though** the negative content **is true,** וַאֲפִילוּ כְּדֵי לְנַקּוֹת עַצְמוֹ — **and even when the purpose** is not to speak negatively about the other person but merely **to demonstrate your own innocence.**

כַּנּוֹדָע מֵהָא דְּאָמַר רַבִּי שִׁמְעוֹן לְאָבִיו רַבֵּינוּ הַקָּדוֹשׁ — **As we know from what Rabbi Shimon said to his father, our holy Rabbi** Yehudah *ha-Nasi,* to demonstrate his innocence, לָאו אֲנָא כַּתְבֵיהּ — Rabbi Shimon said, *"I did not write this,"* problematic divorce document, אֶלָּא יְהוּדָא חַיָּיטָא כַּתְבֵיהּ — *"Rather, Yehudah the tailor wrote it,"* וְאָמַר לוֹ כַּלֵּךְ מִלְּשׁוֹן הָרַע — and his father replied, *"Keep away from lashon hara (slander),"* [עַיֵּין שָׁם בַּגְּמָרָא רֵישׁ פֶּרֶק י' דְּבָבָא בַּתְרָא] — **look there, in** the *Talmud, Bava Basra,* **beginning of chapter 10, 164b.**

וּכְהַאי גַּוְנָא כַּמָּה מִילֵי דִּשְׁכִיחֵי טוּבָא — **And there are so many common examples of things like this** which you probably do all the time.

וּבִפְרָט בְּעִנְיַן לְקַדֵּשׁ עַצְמוֹ בְּמוּתָּר לוֹ — **And especially** you should feel humbled about your shortcomings in **the area of** *"sanctifying yourself through (refraining from even) that which is permissible to you"* (see above p. 315), שֶׁהוּא מִדְּאוֹרַיְיתָא כְּמוֹ שֶׁכָּתוּב קְדוֹשִׁים תִּהְיוּ וְגוֹ'

PRACTICAL LESSONS

The irreligious person is less culpable for his major sins than you are for not fighting your impulse to evil properly.

With this in mind you should become "humble in spirit before everyone."

כמ"ש קדושים תהיו וגו' והתקדשתם וגו'. וגם ד"ס
חמורים מד"ת וכו'. אלא שכל אלו וכיוצא בהן הן
מעוונות שהאדם דש בעקביו וגם נעשו כהיתר מחמת
שעבר ושנה וכו'. אבל באמת אם הוא יודע ספר
ומחזיק בתורת ה' וקרבת אלקי' יחפץ גדול עונו מנשוא
ואשמתו גדלה בכפלי כפליים במה שאינו נלחם
ומתגבר על יצרו בערך ובחי' מלחמה עצומה הנ"ל
מאשמת קל שבקלים מיושבי קרנות הרחוקים מה'
ותורתו ואין אשמתם גדולה כ"כ במה שאינם כובשים

וְהִתְקַדִּשְׁתֶּם וְגוֹ' — which is, in fact, a Biblical requirement based on the verses, *"You should be holy, because I, G-d your G-d, am holy"* (*Leviticus* 19:2), and *"You should sanctify yourselves and be holy, for I am G-d, your G-d"* (ibid. 20:7; see above chapter 27, pp. 316-7).

וְגַם דְּבְרֵי סוֹפְרִים חֲמוּרִים מִדִּבְרֵי תוֹרָה וְכוּ' — And you can also find areas of Rabbinic law in which you have been lax, and *"The words of the Scribes are even more stringent than the words of the Torah"* (*Talmud, Eruvin* 21b, *Sanhedrin* 88b).

אֶלָּא שֶׁכֵּל אֵלּוּ וְכַיּוֹצֵא בָּהֶן הֵן מֵעֲווֹנוֹת שֶׁהָאָדָם דָּשׁ בַּעֲקֵבָיו — Yet all these things, and others are *"the sins which a person tramples under his feet"* (ibid., *Avodah Zarah* 18a) and fails to take seriously, וְגַם נַעֲשׂוֹ כְּהֶיתֵּר מֵחֲמַת שֶׁעָבַר וְשָׁנָה וְכוּ' — and these sins are now regarded as "permissible," since they have been violated repeatedly, *etc.,* (ibid., *Yoma* 86b).

21ST ADAR I LEAP

וּמַחֲזִיק — אֲבָל בֶּאֱמֶת אִם הוּא יוֹדֵעַ סֵפֶר — But in truth, if you are learned in Jewish texts, בְּתוֹרַת ה' — and you *"hold fast to G-d's Torah"* (ibid., *Sanhedrin* 90b), וְקִרְבַת אֱלֹקִים יֶחְפָּץ — and you *"desire to be close to G-d"* (see *Isaiah* 58:2), גָּדוֹל עֲוֹנוֹ מִנְּשׂוֹא — then even these "minor" sins should make you feel that *"your sin is too great to bear"* (see *Genesis* 4:13).

וְאַשְׁמָתוֹ גָדְלָה בְּכִפְלֵי כְפְלַיִם — And your culpability is far greater, *"doubled and redoubled"* (*Midrash Sechel Tov, Exodus* chapter 12), בְּמֶה שֶׁאֵינוֹ נִלְחָם וּמִתְגַּבֵּר עַל יִצְרוֹ — בְּעֵרֶךְ וּבְחִינַת מִלְחָמָה עֲצוּמָה הַנִּזְכֶּרֶת לְעֵיל — in that you fail to battle and overcome your impulse to evil, at the level of intense struggle mentioned above.

מֵאַשְׁמַת קַל שֶׁבַּקַּלִים מִיּוֹשְׁבֵי קְרָנוֹת — In this sense your culpability is more than that of the "most religiously irreverent person" who *"sits at street corners,"* הָרְחוֹקִים — and is far from G-d and His Torah. מֵה' וְתוֹרָתוֹ

וְאֵין אַשְׁמָתָם גְדוֹלָה כָּל כָּךְ — Because with those distant from G-d, their culpability is not so great, בְּמֶה שֶׁאֵינָם כּוֹבְשִׁים יִצְרָם הַבּוֹעֵר כְּאֵשׁ לֶהָבָה — in their failure to

יצרם הבוער כאש להבה מפני פחד ה' המבין ומביט אל
כל מעשיהם כאשמת כל הקרב הקרב אל ה' ואל תורתו
ועבודתו וכמשארז"ל גבי אחר שידע בכבודי וכו' ולכן
ארז"ל על ע"ה שזדונות נעשו להם כשגגות:

פרק לא **והנה** אף אם כשיאריך הרבה להעמיק 39B
בעניני' הנ"ל כשעה ושתי' להיות

מִפְּנֵי פַּחַד ה' הַמֵּבִין — overcome the impulse to evil which *"blazes like a flaming fire,"*
וּמַבִּיט אֶל כָּל מַעֲשֵׂיהֶם — as a result of *"trepidation of G-d"* who watches over and
"discerns all of their deeds" (see *Psalms* 33:15), כְּאַשְׁמַת כָּל הַקָּרֵב הַקָּרֵב אֶל ה' וְאֶל
תּוֹרָתוֹ וַעֲבוֹדָתוֹ — their culpability does not approach that of *"someone who comes
near to G-d"* (see *Numbers* 17:28), **to His Torah and His service,** because from the
religious person, more is expected.

וּכְמוֹ שֶׁאָמְרוּ רַבּוֹתֵינוּ זִכְרוֹנָם לִבְרָכָה גַּבֵּי אַחֵר — **As our Rabbis, of blessed memory,
taught about** *Acher,* one of the greatest Talmudic sages who later deviated from
traditional Judaism, שֶׁיָּדַע בִּכְבוֹדִי וְכוּ' — that his culpability was greater, *"because
he had known My glory"* (*Talmud, Chagigah* 15a, according to text of *Ein Ya'akov*).
He had been close to G-d and therefore he should have known better.

וְלָכֵן אָמְרוּ רַבּוֹתֵינוּ זִכְרוֹנָם לִבְרָכָה עַל עַמֵּי הָאָרֶץ — **And that is why, our Sages, of
blessed memory, taught in reference to those uneducated** in Judaism, שֶׁזְּדוֹנוֹת
נַעֲשׂוּ לָהֶם כִּשְׁגָגוֹת — that since they're unaware of the severity of their actions, **their
*"deliberate sins are considered as inadvertent acts"*** (*Talmud, Bava Metzia* 33b).

CHAPTER 31

FROM DEPRESSION TO JOY

SECTION ONE: DISMANTLING NEGATIVITY FROM WITHIN

5TH ADAR REGULAR | 22ND ADAR I LEAP

In chapters 29-30, the *Tanya* taught us a series of humbling meditations aimed at
solving the problem of *timtum ha-lev* (spiritual insensitivity). This chapter continues
along the same theme. We also will learn how to come out of the negative state of
mind and use humbling thoughts to propel us to positive and joyous states of mind.

וְהִנֵּה אַף אִם כְּשֶׁיַּאֲרִיךְ הַרְבֵּה לְהַעֲמִיק בָּעִנְיָנִים הַנִּזְכָּרִים לְעֵיל כְּשָׁעָה וּשְׁתַּיִם — **Now even
if you spend an hour or two** or more **delving into the above concepts** in chapters

בנמיכת רוח ולב נשבר יבא לידי עצבות גדולה לא
יחוש ואף שעצבות היא מצד קליפת נוגה ולא מצד
הקדושה כי בצד הקדושה כתיב עוז וחדוה במקומו
ואין השכינה שורה אלא מתוך שמחה וכן לדבר הלכה
וכו' אלא שאם העצבות היא ממילי דשמיא היא מבחי'
טוב שבנוגה [ולכן כתב האר"י ז"ל שאפי' דאגת העונות
אינה ראויה כ"א בשעת הוידוי ולא בשעת התפלה
ות"ת שצ"ל בשמחה שמצד הקדושה דוקא] אעפ"כ

29-30, **at great length,** וְלֵב נִשְׁבָּר רוּחַ בִּנְמִיכַת לִהְיוֹת — **to achieve ego-deflation and a broken heart,** גְדוֹלָה עַצְבוּת לִידֵי יָבָא — and as a result, **you get really depressed,** יָחוּשׁ לֹא — **it's not a cause for concern** (so long as it passes quickly — see below, section two).

הַקְּדוּשָׁה מִצַד וְלֹא נוֹגַה קְלִיפַת מִצַד הִיא שֶׁעַצְבוּת וְאַף — **Because although depression stems from** *kelipas nogah* **and not from holy energy** (see chapter 1, p. 41), it can still be something positive, as we shall see.

Before explaining how depression can have a positive result, the *Tanya* first brings proof that it doesn't come from a holy energy.

בִּמְקוֹמוֹ וְחֶדְוָה עוֹז כְּתִיב הַקְּדוּשָׁה בְּצַד כִּי — **Since, in reference to holy energy, the verse states,** *"Strength and gladness are in His place"* (1 Chronicles 16:27), וְכוּ' הֲלָכָה לִדְבַר וְכֵן שִׂמְחָה מִתּוֹךְ אֶלָא שׁוֹרָה הַשְּׁכִינָה וְאֵין — and *"The Divine Presence will only rest where there is joy in observing a mitzvah... and the same is true with study of the law etc.,"* (*Talmud, Shabbos* 30b).

דִּשְׁמַיָא מִמִילֵי הִיא הָעַצְבוּת שֶׁאִם אֶלָא — **But if it's a depression over spiritual things,** שֶׁבְּנוֹגַה טוֹב מִבְּחִינַת הִיא — while it is still derived from *kelipas nogah*, **it comes from the good part of** *kelipas nogah*.

The fundamental difference between holy energy and *kelipah* energy is that *kelipah* is obsessed with "self," whereas holiness is willing to transcend "self." Depression over spiritual things is a *kelipah* energy since it is focused on the shortcomings of self; but it's from the "good part" of *kelipah*, since, if handled properly, it can lead to a positive outcome.

לִבְרָכָה זִכְרוֹנוֹ הָאֲרִ"י כָּתַב [וְלָכֵן] — **And that is why Rabbi Yitzchak Luria, of blessed memory, taught** (*Pri Etz Chaim, Sha'ar Olam Ha-Asiyah* chapter 1), דַאֲגַת שֶׁאֲפִילוּ — רְאוּיָה אֵינָה הָעֲווֹנוֹת — **that even worrying about your sins is inappropriate** in most cases, הַוִידוּי בִּשְׁעַת אִם כִּי — **except when you are formally confessing** your sins to repent, תוֹרָה וְתַלְמוּד הַתְּפִלָה בִּשְׁעַת וְלֹא — but concern over your sins **should be avoided during prayer and Torah study,** בְּשִׂמְחָה לִהְיוֹת שֶׁצָרִיךְ — **which need to be carried out with joy,** דַוְוקָא הַקְּדוּשָׁה שֶׁמִצַד — **which comes from an exclusively holy energy.**

הֲרֵי כָךְ הִיא הַמִדָּה לְאַכְפְּיָא לְס"א בְּמִינָהּ וְדוּגְמָתָהּ. כְּמַאֲמַרַ"ל מִינֵיהּ וּבֵיהּ אַבָּא לְשַׁדֵּי' בֵּיהּ נַרְגָּא וּפָגַע בּוֹ כַּיּוֹצֵא בוֹ. וְעַ"ז נֶאֱמַר בְּכָל עֶצֶב יִהְיֶה מוֹתָר וְהַיִּתְרוֹן הִיא הַשִּׂמְחָה הַבָּאָה אַחַר הָעֶצֶב כְּדִלְקַמָן. אַךְ בֶּאֱמֶת

If depression over your spiritual standing comes from *kelipah*, how could it be a positive thing?

אַף עַל פִּי כֵן — **Nevertheless,** despite this depression stemming from *kelipah,* הֲרֵי כָךְ הִיא הַמִדָּה לְאַכְפְּיָא לְסִטְרָא אָחֳרָא בְּמִינָהּ וְדוּגְמָתָהּ — **the way to subdue the** *sitra achra* **is, in fact, through** unleashing **an identical or similar** energy back on it.

כְּמַאֲמַר רַבּוֹתֵינוּ זִכְרוֹנָם לִבְרָכָה — **As our Sages of blessed memory said** about Ovadiah, the Edomite convert who predicted the downfall of Edom, מִינֵיהּ וּבֵיהּ אַבָּא לְשַׁדְיָא בֵּיהּ נַרְגָּא — *"From the forest itself comes the handle for* **the axe** *which chops down the forest"* (*Talmud, Sanhedrin* 39b).

וּפָגַע בּוֹ כַּיּוֹצֵא בוֹ — **And** similarly we find in the *Talmud* that when a dangerous snake was killed by a dangerous person, Rabbi Yehudah Ha-Nasi commented that the snake had *"met one of its own kind"* (ibid., *Shabbos* 121b).

These two *Talmudic* sources indicate that sometimes a force is best destroyed by its own kind. The downfall of Edom was predicted by an Edomite convert, and a dangerous snake was killed by a dangerous person.

Why did the *Tanya* need to bring *two* sources? Because above we learned that the way to subdue the *sitra achra* is "through unleashing an *identical or similar* energy back on it." The case of Ovadiah represents a "similar" energy: It's not the axe's handle but the blade that fells the tree. The handle provides support — a "similar" energy. The snake, on the other hand, "met one of *its own kind*," i.e., a dangerous person — an "identical" energy (*Notes on Tanya*).

וְעַל זֶה נֶאֱמַר בְּכָל עֶצֶב יִהְיֶה מוֹתָר — **And about this it was said,** *"In every sadness there will be profit"* (*Proverbs* 14:23; see p. 297), וְהַיִּתְרוֹן הִיא הַשִּׂמְחָה הַבָּאָה אַחַר הָעֶצֶב — the **"profit" being the joy that comes** *after* the sadness, כְּדִלְקַמָן — **as we shall see.**

PRACTICAL LESSONS

Sometimes negativity needs to be met with negativity. A short bout of depressive thoughts can knock you out of a bad state.

SECTION TWO: "DEPRESSION" AND "BITTERNESS"

אַךְ בֶּאֱמֶת — **In truth, however,** the depression brought on by the meditations in chapters 29-30, needs to quickly do its job of dismantling the *sitra achra* and then pass, otherwise the experience will be counterproductive (*Notes on Tanya*).

אֵין לֵב נשבר ומרירות הנפש על ריחוקה מאור פני ה'
והתלבשותה בס"א נקראים בשם עצבות כלל בלשון
הקודש כי עצבות היא שלבו מטומטם כאבן ואין חיות
בלבו אבל מרירות ולב נשבר אדרבה הרי יש חיות
בלבו להתפעל ולהתמרמר רק שהיא חיות מבחי'
גבורות קדושות והשמחה מבחי' חסדים כי הלב כלול

אֵין לֵב נִשְׁבָּר וּמְרִירוּת הַנֶּפֶשׁ עַל רִיחוּקָהּ מֵאוֹר פְּנֵי ה' וְהִתְלַבְּשׁוּתָהּ בְּסִטְרָא אָחֳרָא נִקְרָאִים בְּשֵׁם עֲצָבוּת כְּלָל בִּלְשׁוֹן הַקּוֹדֶשׁ — The most positive outcome of **a broken heart and bitter soul (caused by distance from the light of G-d's "face" and being enmeshed with the *sitra achra*), is not at all what we call *atzvus* (depression) in Hebrew.**

A certain despondency is an inevitable consequence of internalizing the negative thoughts of chapters 29-30; but if these meditations are done sincerely and correctly, *atzvus* (depression) will be transmuted to a more productive form of negativity, which the *Tanya* will refer to as *merirus* (bitterness).

כִּי עֲצָבוּת הִיא שֶׁלִבּוֹ מְטוּמְטָם כָּאֶבֶן וְאֵין חַיּוּת בְּלִבּוֹ — **Since *atzvus*** is not an emotion you want to harbor for too long, since in that mode, **your heart is desensitized like a stone, and it is a heart devoid of vitality.**

אֲבָל מְרִירוּת וְלֵב נִשְׁבָּר — **Rather,** you should aim to transmute the *atzvus* immediately to *merirus* (bitterness) and brokenheartedness, אַדְרַבָּה הֲרֵי יֵשׁ חַיּוּת בְּלִבּוֹ לְהִתְפַּעֵל וּלְהִתְמַרְמֵר — **which, on the contrary, energize the heart to be stirred and embittered.**

Merirus (bitterness) is energizing, inducing an urge to rectify the past and improve the future. While characterized by grief and sorrow, it is ultimately constructive, since it leads to optimism and self-improvement.

Atzvus (depression), on the other hand, is paralyzing. It's a destructive form of grief that leads to apathy and a numbing of feeling. Instead of stimulating growth, it results in despair and self-pity, fueling a vicious cycle of deterioration. That is why it must not be allowed to linger.

רַק שֶׁהִיא חַיּוּת מִבְּחִינַת גְּבוּרוֹת קְדוֹשׁוֹת — **Rather** the reason why *merirus* is constructive is because, unlike *atzvus* which stems from *kelipah, merirus* **is an energy from holy *gevuros* (harshness).**

In holy energy there is both *chesed* (generosity) and *gevurah* (harshness). If an energy is holy, but harsh, it will lead you to *merirus,* a constructive and useful negativity.

כִּי הַלֵּב כָּלוּל וְהַשִּׂמְחָה מִבְּחִינַת חֲסָדִים — **And joy is from** the holy energy of ***chesed,*** מִשְׁתֵּיהֶן — **for the heart contains both** *chesed* and *gevurah,* and both are pathways to G-d.

משתיהן. והנה לעתים צריך לעורר בחי' גבורות
הקדושות כדי להמתיק הדינים שהם בחי' נפש הבהמי'
ויצה"ר כששולט ח"ו על האדם כי אין הדינים נמתקין
אלא בשרשן ולכן ארז"ל לעולם ירגיז אדם יצ"הט והיינו
בכל עת שרואה בנפשו שצריך לכך אך שעת הכושר

וְהִנֵּה לְעִתִּים צָרִיךְ לְעוֹרֵר בְּחִינַת גְּבוּרוֹת הַקְּדוֹשׁוֹת — **And so,** even though we usually steer away from *gevurah*, due to its severity, **sometimes it's necessary to arouse the powers of holy *gevurah*,** כְּדֵי לְהַמְתִּיק הַדִּינִים — **to "make judgments sweet"** **(*le-hamtik ha-dinim*).**

Usually, we counteract negativity by being more positive. But if you reach a state of *timtum ha-lev* (spiritual desensitization), it means that negative energy has managed to get a hold on you and trap you. To break out of this "jail" you need to confront the negativity "head on," by employing the counter-force of holy *gevurah* (in the form of *merirus*).

Holy *gevurah* works, not by overpowering impure *gevurah,* but by "sweetening" it. At its root, impure *gevurah* is actually derived from the holy version, only its connection has been lost, rendering the *gevurah* impure and negative. But when holy *gevurah* shines strongly into its impure offshoot, the energies are reconnected and the negative becomes positive and "sweet" again.

Practically, that's what happens when you use *merirus* to counteract your *timtum ha-lev* and *atzvus*. The holy *gevurah* of *merirus* shines into the *kelipah* that brought about your *timtum ha-lev,* and "sweetens" it.

שֶׁהֵם בְּחִינַת נֶפֶשׁ הַבַּהֲמִית וְיֵצֶר הָרָע — These "judgments" and impure *gevurah* energies of *timtum ha-lev* and *atzvus* come from the Animal Soul and impulse to evil, כְּשֶׁשּׁוֹלֵט חַס וְשָׁלוֹם עַל הָאָדָם — when they are allowed to have a controlling influence on a person, G-d forbid, כִּי אֵין הַדִּינִים נִמְתָּקִין אֶלָּא בְּשָׁרְשָׁן — and the "judgments" can only be eliminated by "sweetening" them at their source, through holy *gevurah.*

וְלָכֵן אָמְרוּ רַבּוֹתֵינוּ זִכְרוֹנָם לִבְרָכָה לְעוֹלָם יַרְגִּיז אָדָם יֵצֶר הַטּוֹב — **Therefore our Sages,** **of blessed memory, taught,** *"A person should always make his impulse to good angry at his impulse to evil"* (*Talmud, Brachos* 5a; see above p. 335), arousing holy *gevurah* (anger) against its impure counterpart (the impulse to evil).

וְהַיְינוּ בְּכָל עֵת שֶׁרוֹאֶה בְּנַפְשׁוֹ שֶׁצָּרִיךְ לְכָךְ — **"Always" doesn't mean "all the time," rather, whenever you see that your soul needs it,** because it's trapped in negative energy.

שֶׁהִיא שָׁעָה הַמְיוּחֶדֶת וּרְאוּיָה לְכָךְ לְרוֹב בְּנֵי אָדָם הִיא בְּשָׁעָה שֶׁהוּא עָצֵב בְּלָא"ה מִמִּילֵי דְעָלְמָא אוֹ כָּךְ בְּלִי שׁוּם סִבָּה אֲזַי הִיא שְׁעַת הַכּוֹשֶׁר לְהַפֵּךְ הָעֶצֶב לִהְיוֹת מִמְּרִי דְחוּשְׁבָּנָא הַנַּ"ל וּלְקַיֵּם מַאֲמַרְזַ"ל לְעוֹלָם יַרְגִּיז וְכוּ' כַּנַּ"ל וּבָזֶה יִפָּטֵר מֵהָעֶצְבוּת שֶׁמִּמִילֵי דְעָלְמָא וְאַחַ"כ יָבֹא לִידֵי שִׂמְחָה אֲמִיתִית דְהַיְינוּ שֶׁזֹּאת יָשִׁיב אֶל לִבּוֹ לְנַחֲמוֹ בְּכִפְלַיִם אַחַר הַדְּבָרִי' וְהָאֱמֶת הָאֵלֶּה הַנַּ"ל לֵאמֹר לְלִבּוֹ אֱמֶת הוּא כֵן בְּלִי סָפֵק שֶׁאֲנִי רָחוֹק מְאֹד מֵה' בְּתַכְלִית וּמְשׁוּקַץ וּמְתוֹעָב כוּ' אַךְ כָּל זֶה הוּא אֲנִי לְבַדִי הוּא הַגּוּף

40A

שֶׁהִיא שָׁעָה — **However,** generally speaking, **an ideal time** to do this, הַמְיוּחֶדֶת וּרְאוּיָה לְכָךְ לְרוֹב בְּנֵי אָדָם — **which, for most people, is a particularly ap-propriate time,** הִיא בְּשָׁעָה שֶׁהוּא עָצֵב בְּלָאו הָכֵי — **is when you're depressed in any case,** מִמִּילֵי דְעָלְמָא אוֹ כָּךְ בְּלִי שׁוּם סִבָּה — either **due to your material circumstanc-es, or you're simply** depressed **without any** obvious **reason,** אֲזַי הִיא שְׁעַת הַכּוֹשֶׁר לְהַפֵּךְ הָעֶצֶב — **then it's an ideal time to transmute the depression** into something positive.

לִהְיוֹת מִמְּרֵי דְחוּשְׁבָּנָא הַנִּזְכָּר לְעֵיל — And, practically speaking, you do this **by be-coming "an expert accountant" mentioned above** (p. 332), *i.e.,* to have a session of serious introspection, וּלְקַיֵּם מַאֲמַר רַבּוֹתֵינוּ זִכְרוֹנָם לִבְרָכָה לְעוֹלָם יַרְגִּיז וְכוּ' כַּנִּזְכָּר לְעֵיל — **to carry out our Sages' advice, mentioned above,** *"A person should al-ways make his* impulse to good angry at his impulse to evil," וּבָזֶה יִפָּטֵר מֵהָעֶצְבוּת שֶׁמִּמִּילֵי דְעָלְמָא — **and in that way you will rid yourself of your depression over material circumstances.**

SECTION THREE: A MEDITATION FROM BITTERNESS TO JOY

6TH ADAR REGULAR

דְהַיְינוּ וְאַחַר כָּךְ יָבֹא לִידֵי שִׂמְחָה אֲמִיתִית — And afterwards you will come to true joy, שֶׁזֹּאת יָשִׁיב אֶל לִבּוֹ לְנַחֲמוֹ בְּכִפְלַיִם — **by reflecting upon the following** positive med-itation **in your heart, so as to give yourself a double measure of comfort,** אַחַר הַדְּבָרִים וְהָאֱמֶת הָאֵלֶּה הַנִּזְכָּרִים לְעֵיל — **in the wake of** your earlier meditation on the **true,** but negative **words mentioned above** (in chapters 29-30).

The following will give you "a double measure of comfort" since: 1.) Your depres-sion will now be gone; and, b.) You will reach levels of joy that would not have been possible without the depression.

אֱמֶת הוּא כֵן בְּלִי סָפֵק שֶׁאֲנִי רָחוֹק מְאֹד מֵה' בְּתַכְלִית — **Say to yourself,** לֵאמֹר לְלִבּוֹ וּמְשׁוּקַץ וּמְתוֹעָב כוּ' — "What I said in my earlier, depressing meditation **is definitely true, that I am very far from G-d, as far as can be, as well as repulsive and disgrace-**

עם נפש החיונית שבו אבל מ"מ יש בקרבי חלק ה'
ממש שישנו אפי' בקל שבקלים שהיא נפש האלהית
עם ניצוץ אלקות ממש המלובש בה להחיותה רק שהיא
בבחי' גלות וא"כ אדרבה כל מה שאני בתכלי' הריחוק
מה' והתיעוב ושיקוץ הרי נפש האלהית שבי בגלות
גדול יותר והרחמנות עליה גדולה מאד ולזה אשים כל
מגמתי וחפצי להוציאה ולהעלותה מגלות זה להשיבה
אל בית אביה כנעורי' קודם שנתלבשה בגופי שהיתה
נכללת באורו ית' ומיוחדת עמו בתכלית וגם עתה כן
תהא כלולה ומיוחדת בו ית' כשאשים כל מגמתי בתור'

but — "אַךְ כָּל זֶה הוּא אֲנִי לְבַדִּי הוּא הַגּוּף עִם נֶפֶשׁ הַחִיּוּנִית שֶׁבּוֹ ,(above p. 335), **"ful *etc.*,** this is true only with what I consciously identify as 'me,' namely, my body with its energizing Animal Soul" (see p. 338), אֲבָל מִכָּל מָקוֹם יֵשׁ בְּקִרְבִּי חֵלֶק ה' מַמָּשׁ שֶׁיֶּשְׁנוֹ — "Nevertheless, within me is, '*a piece of G-d,*' literally, (*Job* 31:2; above p. 44), found even in the most religiously irreverent person," שֶׁהִיא נֶפֶשׁ — אֲפִילוּ בְּקַל שֶׁבְּקַלִּים הָאֱלֹהִית עִם נִיצוֹץ אֱלֹקוּת מַמָּשׁ הַמְלוּבָּשׁ בָּהּ לְהַחֲיוֹתָהּ "which is a Divine Soul, con- taining an actual spark of G-dliness enmeshed in the soul to energize it," — רַק שֶׁהִיא בִּבְחִינַת גָּלוּת "only, this Divine Soul is in a state of exile," וְאִם כֵּן אַדְּרַבָּה — "and if this is the case then I ought not to be depressed, but on the contrary, energized," כָּל מַה שֶׁאֲנִי בְּתַכְלִית הָרִיחוּק — מַה' וְהַתִּיעוּב וְשִׁיקוּץ "because the further I am alien- ated from G-d, and the more repulsive and disgraceful I become," — הֲרֵי נֶפֶשׁ הָאֱלֹהִית שֶׁבִּי בְּגָלוּת גָּדוֹל יוֹתֵר "it means that the Divine Soul inside me is more deep- ly exiled," וְהָרַחֲמָנוּת עָלֶיהָ גְּדוֹלָה מְאֹד — "and the more greatly she is to be pitied."

וְלָזֶה אָשִׂים כָּל מְגַמָּתִי וְחֶפְצִי — "Therefore I will make it my singular mission and desire," לְהוֹצִיאָהּ וּלְהַעֲלוֹתָהּ מִגָּלוּת זֶה — "to get her out of this exile and bring her back up," לַהֲשִׁיבָהּ אֶל בֵּית אָבִיהָ כִּנְעוּרֶיהָ — "'*returning her to her Father's house, as in her youth*'" (see *Leviticus* 22:13), קוֹדֶם שֶׁנִּתְלַבְּשָׁה בְּגוּפִי — "before she was placed in my body," שֶׁהָיְתָה נִכְלֶלֶת בְּאוֹרוֹ יִתְבָּרֵךְ וּמְיוּחֶדֶת עִמּוֹ בְּתַכְלִית — "when she was absorbed in G-d's blessed light and completely united with Him," וְגַם עַתָּה כֵּן תְּהֵא כְּלוּלָה וּמְיוּחֶדֶת בּוֹ יִתְבָּרֵךְ — "now, too, she is going to be absorbed in, and united with, G-d," כְּשֶׁאָשִׂים כָּל מְגַמָּתִי בַּתּוֹרָה — "when I will make Torah and *mitzvos* my singular mission," וּמִצְוֹת לְהַלְבִּישׁ בָּהֶן

PRACTICAL LESSONS

The more "repulsive and disgraceful" you find your body and Animal Soul to be, the more you should have pity on your Divine Soul trapped there, and resolve to free your Divine Soul through Torah and mitzvos.

ומצות להלביש בהן כל עשר בחינותיה כנ"ל ובפרט
במצות תפלה לצעוק אל ה' בצר לה מגלותה בגופי
המשוקץ להוציאה ממסגר ולדבקה בו ית' וזו היא בחי'
תשובה ומעשים טובים שהן מעשים טובים שעושה
כדי להשיב חלק ה' למקורא ושרשא דכל עלמין.
וזאת תהיה עבודתו כל ימיו בשמחה רבה היא שמחת

כָּל עֶשֶׂר בְּחִינוֹתֶיהָ — "to make all the Divine Soul's **ten faculties immersed in** Torah
and *mitzvos*," — כַּנִזְכָּר לְעֵיל — **as mentioned above** (chapter 23).

וּבִפְרָט בְּמִצְוַת תְּפִלָּה — "**Especially when** I will devote myself **to the** *mitzvah* **of
prayer**," לִצְעוֹק אֶל ה' בַּצַּר לָהּ מִגָּלוּתָהּ בְּגוּפִי הַמְשׁוּקָץ — "'*to cry to G-d in distress*'
(see *Psalms* 107:6), **from** the Divine Soul's **exile in my repulsive body**," לְהוֹצִיאָה
מִמַּסְגֵּר וּלְדַבְקָה בּוֹ יִתְבָּרֵךְ — "**to free her from imprisonment, to be attached to G-d.**"

This meditation lifts you out of the depressing thoughts of chapters 29-30, and
recontextualizes them in a motivational and inspirational light. The humbling mes-
sages of chapters 29-30 may be true, but they are only half the story because the
more "repulsive and disgraceful" your body and Animal Soul may be, the more you
should have pity on your Divine Soul trapped there; and the more motivated you will
be to do everything within your power to redeem it.

SECTION FOUR: THE MEANING OF "TESHUVAH"

וְזוֹ הִיא בְּחִינַת תְּשׁוּבָה וּמַעֲשִׂים טוֹבִים — **And this** approach to worship **is characterized by** the saying, **"*teshuvah* (repentance) and good deeds"** (*Mishnah*, *Avos* 3:13).

Normally, "*teshuvah*" and "good deeds" are perceived as two different activities.
You try your best to do "good deeds," but when you fail and do a "bad deed," you
repair that shortcoming with *teshuvah*.

But in the above meditation (section three), *teshuvah* could be understood, not as
a correction for bad deeds, but as the goal of "good deeds":

שֶׁהֵן מַעֲשִׂים טוֹבִים שֶׁעוֹשֶׂה כְּדֵי לְהָשִׁיב חֵלֶק ה' לִמְקוֹרָא וְשָׁרְשָׁא דְּכָל עָלְמִין — **Since
these "good deeds" are done to** *return (le-hashiv)* **your Divine Soul** which is *"a
piece of G-d,"* **back to the source and root of all the worlds.**

Usually translated as "repentance," *teshuvah* can also mean the "return" of the
soul to its rightful place. If, every time you do a *mitzvah* ("good deed"), your intention is to redeem your Divine Soul from captivity in your body, and return it to G-d (as
above, section three), then your good deeds *are* a form of *teshuvah*.

7TH ADAR REGULAR

בְּשִׂמְחָה רַבָּה — וְזֹאת תִּהְיֶה עֲבוֹדָתוֹ כָּל יָמָיו — **And this ought to be your lifelong task,**
הִיא שִׂמְחַת הַנֶּפֶשׁ בְּצֵאתָהּ מֵהַגּוּף הַמְתוֹעָב — **done with great joy, the joy of the soul**

הנפש בצאתה מהגוף המתועב ושבה אל בית אביה
כנעוריה בשעת התורה והעבודה וכמארז"ל להיות כל
ימיו בתשובה ואין לך שמחה גדולה כצאת מהגלות
והשביה כמשל בן מלך שהיה בשביה וטוחן בבית
האסורים ומנוול באשפה ויצא לחפשי אל בית אביו   40B

on its release from a "disgraceful" body וְשָׁבָה אֶל בֵּית אָבִיהָ כִּנְעוּרֶיהָ — *"returning to her Father's house, as in her youth,"* בִּשְׁעַת הַתּוֹרָה וְהָעֲבוֹדָה — which happens during Torah study and worship.

וּכְמַאֲמַר רַבּוֹתֵינוּ זִכְרוֹנָם לִבְרָכָה לִהְיוֹת כָּל יָמָיו בִּתְשׁוּבָה — As our Sages, of blessed memory, taught, you should be, *"all your days in teshuvah"* (*Talmud, Shabbos* 153a).

At the literal level, the *Talmud* is referring to *"teshuvah"* as repentance for sins. Since you want to make sure that you repent before you die, and you don't know when you're going to die, the *Talmud* advises you to be *"all your days in teshuvah."*

But according to the *Tanya's* understanding of *teshuvah* here (the redemptive soul-returning property of every *mitzvah*), we can read the *Talmud* hyperliterally. Regardless of whether you are repenting or not, you can *literally* be "all your days in *teshuvah*," by observing *mitzvos* which "return" your soul to G-d.

PRACTICAL LESSONS

וְאֵין לְךָ שִׂמְחָה גְדוֹלָה כְּצֵאת מֵהַגָּלוּת וְהַשְׁבִיָּה — **And there is no greater joy than the release from exile/captivity.**

Now we can appreciate why the depressing meditations of chapter 29-30 lead to increased joy afterwards, in the spirit of the verse, *"In every sadness there will be profit"* (see p. 297). The more you come to realize (from your depressing introspections) how the body represents a tragic captivity for the soul, the more you will be joyous at the soul's release, every time you do a *mitzvah* or study Torah.

All worship through Torah and mitzvos, is really a kind of *teshuvah*, in the sense that it facilitates the return of the trapped Divine Soul back to G-d.

כְּמָשָׁל בֶּן מֶלֶךְ שֶׁהָיָה בְּשִׁבְיָה וְטוֹחֵן בְּבֵית הָאֲסוּרִים וּמְנֻוָּל בְּאַשְׁפָּה — **Like** the joy of a prince who was kept in captivity, doing debasing work, **grinding in prison, disheveled with dirt,** וְיָצָא לַחָפְשִׁי אֶל בֵּית אָבִיו הַמֶּלֶךְ — and then he goes free, back home to his father, the king.

When the prince lived at home, before he went to prison, he was joyous. But the joy of returning to the palace after imprisonment, is so much greater.

Similarly, the fact that your Divine Soul is held captive in your "repulsive and disgraceful" body should not be cause for sadness at all; because every time you release your soul, through a *mitzvah*, its joy is far greater than anything it experienced before entering your body.

המלך ואף שהגוף עומד בשיקוצו ותיעובו וכמ"ש
בזהר דנקרא משכא דחויא כי מהותה ועצמותה של
הנפש הבהמית לא נהפך לטוב ליכלל בקדושה מ"מ
תיקר נפשו בעיניו לשמוח בשמחתה יותר מהגוף
הנבזה שלא לערבב ולבלבל שמחת הנפש בעצבון
הגוף. והנה בחי' זו היא בחי' יציאת מצרים שנאמר
בה כי ברח העם דלכאור' הוא תמוה למה היתה כזאת
וכי אילו אמרו לפרעה לשלחם חפשי לעולם לא היה
מוכרח לשלחם אלא מפני שהרע שבנפשות ישראל
עדיין היה בתקפו בחלל השמאלי כי לא פסקה זוהמתם

וְאַף שֶׁהַגּוּף עוֹמֵד בְּשִׁיקּוּצוֹ וְתִיעוּבוֹ — And even though the body remains "repulsive and disgraceful," — וּכְמוֹ שֶׁכָּתוּב בַּזוֹהַר דְּנִקְרָא מַשְׁכָא דְחִוְיָא — as in the *Tikunei Zohar's* reference to the body as *"the serpent's skin"* (10b; 48b), כִּי מַהוּתָהּ וְעַצְמוּתָהּ שֶׁל — since, even in a *beinoni*, the Animal הַנֶּפֶשׁ הַבַּהֲמִית לֹא נֶהְפַּךְ לְטוֹב לִיכָּלֵל בִּקְדוּשָׁה Soul's deep core has not been transformed to good, which would enable it to be incorporated into holiness, מִכָּל מָקוֹם תִּיקַר נַפְשׁוֹ בְּעֵינָיו — nevertheless, focus instead on your Divine Soul and let it be precious in your eyes, לִשְׂמוֹחַ בְּשִׂמְחָתָהּ — be joyous in your ability to redeem her, יוֹתֵר מֵהַגּוּף הַנִּבְזֶה — and let that joy mean more to you than your concern over **the disgusting body,** שֶׁלֹא לְעַרְבֵּב וּלְבַלְבֵּל שִׂמְחַת הַנֶּפֶשׁ בְּעַצְבוֹן הַגּוּף — so that the joy of your soul will be your primary focus and you won't allow it to be compromised and confused by the sad state of the body.

SECTION FIVE: YOUR DAILY "EXODUS FROM EGYPT"

וְהִנֵּה בְּחִינָה זוֹ הִיא בְּחִינַת יְצִיאַת מִצְרַיִם — And this approach of redeeming the soul from its captivity, is a kind of spiritual **"Exodus from Egypt,"** as we shall see.

שֶׁנֶּאֱמַר בָּהּ כִּי בָרַח הָעָם — Concerning the Exodus, **Scripture states,** that after requesting from Pharaoh to be released for just three days, *"the people fled"* (*Exodus* 14:5), and escaped Egypt permanently.

דְּלִכְאוֹרָה הוּא תָּמוּהַּ לָמָה הָיְתָה כָזֹאת — Now, at first glance, it seems bizarre that things had to happen this way, וְכִי אִילוּ אָמְרוּ לְפַרְעֹה לְשַׁלְחָם חָפְשִׁי לְעוֹלָם לֹא הָיָה מוּכְרָח לְשַׁלְחָם — for after witnessing the Ten Plagues **wouldn't Pharaoh have been forced to let them go,** even if they had asked to go free forever?

אֶלָּא מִפְּנֵי שֶׁהָרַע שֶׁבְּנַפְשׁוֹת יִשְׂרָאֵל עֲדַיִין הָיָה בְּתָקְפּוֹ — Rather, this was not a restriction stemming from Pharaoh, but **due to the evil in the Israelites'** Animal **Souls which was still in its** full **power,** בְּחָלָל הַשְּׂמָאלִי — **in the left chamber** of their hearts, where the Animal Soul resides (see p. 112), and that evil made them unwilling to leave Egypt permanently.

עד מתן תורה רק מגמתם וחפצם היתה לצאת נפשם
האלהית מגלות הס״א היא טומאת מצרים ולדבקה בו
ית׳ וכדכתיב ה׳ עוזי ומעוזי ומנוסי ביום צרה וגו׳ משגבי
ומנוסי וגו׳ והוא מנוס לי וגו׳ ולכן לעתיד כשיעביר ה׳
רוח הטומאה מן הארץ כתיב ובמנוסה לא תלכון כי

The Jews did not ask to become completely free from the evil of Egypt *because they were still drawn to it.* They had some "Egypt" in their souls.

כִּי לֹא פָּסְקָה זוּהֲמָתָם עַד מַתַּן תּוֹרָה — **For it was not until the Torah was given** at Sinai that, **"their impurity departed"** (*Talmud, Shabbos* 146a), and their Animal Souls were fully free from the evil of Egypt.

Nevertheless, while their Animal Souls were not ready to leave Egypt, their Divine Souls definitely were.

רַק מְגַמָּתָם וְחֶפְצָם הָיְתָה לָצֵאת נַפְשָׁם הָאֱלֹהִית מִגָּלוּת הַסִּטְרָא אָחֳרָא הִיא טוּמְאַת מִצְרַיִם וּלְדָבְקָה בּוֹ יִתְבָּרֵךְ — **Yet** despite the inertia of their Animal Souls, **their focus and desire was to release their Divine Souls from exile in the *sitra achra,* the impurity of Egypt, and connect to G-d.**

It was this tension, between the Animal Soul and the Divine Soul, that resulted in them initially resisting, and subsequently fleeing from Egypt. Initially, they weren't prepared to ask Pharaoh to leave Egypt permanently since their Animal Souls were still drawn to evil and unwilling to leave. But once they had left temporarily, and Sinai was "in sight," the yearning of their Divine Souls to leave Egypt could no longer be held back, and they tore themselves away from the pull of their Animal Souls, to leave forever.

וּכְדִכְתִיב ה׳ עוּזִי וּמָעוּזִי וּמְנוּסִי בְּיוֹם צָרָה וְגוֹ׳ — **As the** following three **verses** suggest, that G-d helps a person escape from the pull of a difficult situation, **"G-d is my strength and my fortress and my escape in the day of affliction etc.,"** (*Jeremiah* 16:19) מִשְׂגַּבִּי וּמְנוּסִי וְגוֹ׳ — **"my high tower and my escape etc.,"** (2 *Samuel* 22:2) וְהוּא מָנוֹס לִי וְגוֹ׳ — **"and He is my escape, etc.,"** (*Psalms* 59:17).

This understanding of the Exodus bears much similarity to the plight of the *beinoni.* Like the Israelites, who could not rid themselves of their pull towards Egypt, the *beinoni* cannot rid himself of the Animal Soul's allure. But that does not stop the *beinoni* from devoting all his energies to liberating the Divine Soul, just as the Israelites fled with full force towards Sinai.

וְלָכֵן לֶעָתִיד כְּשֶׁיַּעֲבִיר ה׳ רוּחַ הַטּוּמְאָה מִן הָאָרֶץ — **Therefore** this stands in contrast to **the future era, when G-d will** *"remove the spirit of impurity from the earth"* (*Zechariah* 13:2) eliminating the *sitra achra* and avoiding the need to "flee" from it, כְּתִיב וּבִמְנוּסָה לֹא תֵלֵכוּן כִּי הוֹלֵךְ לִפְנֵיכֶם ה׳ וְגוֹ׳ — and about this future time **the verse** states, *"You will not go out in haste,* **nor go by flight, for G-d will go before you etc.,"** (*Isaiah* 52:12).

הוֹלֵךְ לִפְנֵיכֶם ה' וְגוֹ'. וְלִהְיוֹת בְּחִי' תְּשׁוּבָה זוֹ בְּיֶתֶר
שְׂאֵת וְיֶתֶר עֹז מֵעוּמְקָא דְּלִבָּא וְגַם שִׂמְחַת הַנֶּפֶשׁ תִּהְיֶה
בְּתוֹסֶפֶת אוֹרָה וְשִׂמְחָה כַּאֲשֶׁר יָשִׁיב אֶל לִבּוֹ דַּעַת
וּתְבוּנָה לְנַחֲמוֹ מֵעַצְבוֹנוֹ וִיגוֹנוֹ לֵאמֹר כַּנַּ"ל הֵן אֱמֶת כו'
אַךְ אֲנִי לֹא עָשִׂיתִי אֶת עַצְמִי. וְלָמָּה עָשָׂה ה' כָּזֹאת
לְהוֹרִיד חֵלֶק מְאוֹרוֹ יִת' הַמְמַלֵּא וְסוֹבֵב כָּל עָלְמִין וְכוּלָּא
קַמֵּיהּ כְּלָא חָשִׁיב וְהִלְבִּישׁוֹ בְּמַשְׁכָא דְּחִיָּא וְטִפָּה סְרוּחָה
אֵין זֶה כִּי אִם יְרִידָה זוֹ הִיא צוֹרֶךְ עֲלִיָּה לְהַעֲלוֹת לַה' כָּל
נֶפֶשׁ הַחִיּוּנִית הַבַּהֲמִית שֶׁמִּקְּלִיפַּת נֹגַהּ וְכָל לְבוּשֶׁיהָ

With the *sitra achra* of the Animal Soul neutralized, there will be no need to flee violently from it to escape its pull. Rather, we will move forward peacefully.

SECTION SIX: A SECOND UPLIFTING MEDITATION

8TH ADAR REGULAR

וְלִהְיוֹת בְּחִינַת תְּשׁוּבָה זוֹ בְּיֶתֶר שְׂאֵת וְיֶתֶר עֹז מֵעוּמְקָא דְּלִבָּא — **In order that this sense** of *mitzvos* as **teshuvah** mentioned above (section four), be with *"more dignity and more power"* (Genesis 49:3), from the depths of the heart, וְגַם שִׂמְחַת הַנֶּפֶשׁ תִּהְיֶה בְּתוֹסֶפֶת אוֹרָה וְשִׂמְחָה — and in order than your soul should rejoice with additional *"light and joy"* (Esther 8:16), consider the following.

כַּאֲשֶׁר יָשִׁיב אֶל לִבּוֹ דַּעַת וּתְבוּנָה — A deepening of this experience will happen **when you will** further *"reflect in your heart with knowledge and discernment"* (see Isaiah 44:19), לְנַחֲמוֹ מֵעַצְבוֹנוֹ וִיגוֹנוֹ — **to find comfort from your distress and sorrow** (brought on by the meditations of chapters 29-30), לֵאמֹר כַּנִּזְכָּר לְעֵיל הֵן אֱמֶת כו' — after **saying** to yourself, **the above** meditation (in section three), *"It's definitely true that I am very far from G-d, etc.,"* you should continue with the following, empowering meditation.

אַךְ אֲנִי לֹא עָשִׂיתִי אֶת עַצְמִי — **"However,** while I am very far from G-d, **I was not the one who created myself,"** וְלָמָּה עָשָׂה ה' כָּזֹאת — **"and why has G-d done such a thing,"** לְהוֹרִיד חֵלֶק מְאוֹרוֹ יִתְבָּרֵךְ — **"to downgrade a 'piece' of His Blessed light,"** הַמְמַלֵּא וְסוֹבֵב כָּל עָלְמִין וְכוּלָּא קַמֵּיהּ כְּלָא חָשִׁיב — **"which** *'fills all worlds'* (see Zohar 3, 225a), and *'transcends all worlds'* (ibid.), and *'in His presence, everything is considered zero'"* (ibid. 1, 11b), וְהִלְבִּישׁוֹ בְּמַשְׁכָא דְּחִיָּא וְטִפָּה סְרוּחָה — **"to place it in a** despicable body, **a 'serpent's skin,'** a body which came from *'a putrid (seminal) drop'"* (Mishnah, Avos 3:1)?

אֵין זֶה כִּי אִם יְרִידָה זוֹ הִיא צוֹרֶךְ עֲלִיָּה — **"There is no other explanation other than** this 'downgrade' must be for the purpose of an even greater 'upgrade,'" לְהַעֲלוֹת לַה' כָּל נֶפֶשׁ הַחִיּוּנִית הַבַּהֲמִית שֶׁמִּקְּלִיפַּת נֹגַהּ — **"namely, to bring up to G-d, the**

הן בחי' מחשבה דבור ומעשה שלה ע"י התלבשותן
במעשה דבור ומחשבת התורה [וכמ"ש לקמן ענין
העלאה זו באריכות איך שהיא תכלית בריאת העולם]
ואו"כ איפוא זאת אעשה וזאת תהיה כל מגמתי כל ימי
חלדי לכל בהן חיי רוחי ונפשי וכמ"ש אליך ה' נפשי
אשא דהיינו לקשר מחשבתי ודבורי במחשבתו
ודבורו ית' והן הן גופי הלכות הערוכו' לפנינו וכן מעשה
במעשה המצות שלכן נקראת התורה משיבת נפש פי'
למקורה ושרשה וע"ז נאמ' פקודי ה' ישרים משמחי לב:

41A

whole energizing Animal Soul, from *kelipas nogah,"* — וְכָל לְבוּשֶׁיהָ הֵן בְּחִינוֹת מַחֲשָׁבָה
דִּבּוּר וּמַעֲשֶׂה שֶׁלָּה — **"and its 'garments,' which are its thought, speech and action,"**
עַל יְדֵי הִתְלַבְּשׁוּתָן בְּמַעֲשֶׂה דִּבּוּר וּמַחֲשֶׁבֶת הַתּוֹרָה — **"through their immersion in the
action, speech and thought of the Torah."**

In our earlier meditation (section three), we focused only on the joy of redeeming
the Divine Soul from the body; the body itself remained "despicable" and unredeemed. In this meditation, a new element is added *that the body is redeemable
too.* This will lead to an even greater joy.

[וּכְמוֹ שֶׁיִּתְבָּאֵר לְקַמָּן עִנְיַן הָעֲלָאָה זוֹ בַּאֲרִיכוּת — **Later** (in chapters 35-37), **we will explain this "elevation"** of the body and Animal Soul **at length,** אֵיךְ שֶׁהִיא תַּכְלִית בְּרִיאַת
הָעוֹלָם] — **how this is the purpose for which the world was created.**

וְאִם כֵּן אֵיפוֹא זֹאת אֶעֱשֶׂה — **"'This being the case, I shall do the following'"** (see
Genesis 43:11), וְזֹאת תִּהְיֶה כָּל מְגַמָּתִי כָּל יְמֵי חֶלְדִּי — **"and this will be my singular
mission, all my days on this earth,"** לְכָל בָּהֶן חַיֵּי רוּחִי וְנַפְשִׁי — **"'to place in these
(mitzvos), the life of my spirit'** (Isaiah 38:16) **and of my soul,"** וּכְמוֹ שֶׁכָּתוּב אֵלֶיךָ ה'
נַפְשִׁי אֶשָּׂא — **"as the verse states, 'To You, O G-d, I lift up my soul'"** (Psalms 25:1),
דְּהַיְינוּ לְקַשֵּׁר מַחֲשַׁבְתִּי וְדִבּוּרִי בְּמַחֲשַׁבְתּוֹ וְדִבּוּרוֹ יִתְבָּרֵךְ — **"which means, to bind my
thought and speech with G-d's thought and speech,"** וְהֵן הֵן גּוּפֵי הֲלָכוֹת הָעֲרוּכוֹת
לְפָנֵינוּ — **"this being through** study of **the body of Jewish Law which has been
codified for us,"** וְכֵן מַעֲשֶׂה בְּמַעֲשֵׂה הַמִּצְוֹת — **"and also through** binding my **actions
to Him, through observing the mitzvos."**

שֶׁלָּכֵן נִקְרֵאת הַתּוֹרָה מְשִׁיבַת נָפֶשׁ — **This is why the Torah is described as** *"Restoring
the soul"* (ibid. 19:8), פֵּירוּשׁ לִמְקוֹרָהּ וְשָׁרְשָׁהּ — **meaning that** it returns and "restores"
the soul **to its source and root.**

וְעַל זֶה נֶאֱמַר פִּקּוּדֵי ה' יְשָׁרִים מְשַׂמְּחֵי לֵב — **And concerning this** elevation of not only
the Divine Soul but the Animal Soul too, **the verse states,** *"The precepts of G-d are
just, rejoicing the heart"* (ibid. 9).

פרק לב וְהִנֵּה ע"י קיום הדברי' הנ"ל להיות גופו
נבזה ונמאס בעיניו רק שמחתו
תהיה שמחת הנפש לבדה הרי זו דרך ישרה וקלה לבא
לידי קיום מצות ואהבת לרעך כמוך לכל נפש מישראל
למגדול ועד קטן. כי מאחר שגופו נמאס ומתועב אצלו
והנפש והרוח מי יודע גדולתן ומעלתן בשרשן ומקורן

CHAPTER 32

LOVE YOUR FELLOW AS YOURSELF
SECTION ONE: RELATIONSHIPS AND THE EGO

9TH ADAR REGULAR | 23RD ADAR I LEAP

The tools and meditations in chapters 29-31 will help you to loosen the ties of your ego and find joy in the spiritual, through adopting the outlook of your Divine Soul. In this chapter we will discuss how this ego-less attitude will affect the way that you look at other people.

וְהִנֵּה עַל יְדֵי קִיּוּם הַדְּבָרִים הַנִּזְכָּרִים לְעֵיל — **Now, when you'll put into practice the above ideas** (in the previous chapter), לִהְיוֹת גּוּפוֹ נִבְזֶה וְנִמְאָס בְּעֵינָיו — **so that your body becomes "disgusting in your eyes, and repulsive"** (Psalms 15:4), רַק שִׂמְחָתוֹ תִּהְיֶה שִׂמְחַת הַנֶּפֶשׁ לְבַדָּהּ — **and you find happiness in the joy of your** Divine Soul **alone,** הֲרֵי זוֹ דֶּרֶךְ יְשָׁרָה וְקַלָּה — **this** frame of mind will be **an easily accessible, "straightforward path"** (Mishnah Avos, 2:1), לָבֹא לִידֵי קִיּוּם מִצְוַת וְאָהַבְתָּ לְרֵעֲךָ כָּמוֹךְ — **to come to fulfill the** mitzvah, **"Love your fellow as yourself"** (Leviticus 19:18), לְכָל נֶפֶשׁ מִיִּשְׂרָאֵל — extending love **to every soul in Israel,** לְמִגָּדוֹל וְעַד קָטָן — **"from great to small"** (Esther 1:5).

As Maimonides rules: *"Every person is commanded to love each and every individual of Israel, as much as (he loves) his own self, as the verse states, 'Love your fellow as yourself.'"* (Mishneh Torah, Hilchos De'os 6:3).

24TH ADAR I LEAP

כִּי מֵאַחַר שֶׁגּוּפוֹ נִמְאָס וּמְתוֹעָב אֶצְלוֹ — **For when your body** which separates you from others, **becomes "repulsive" and "disgraceful" to you,** you will appreciate more the value of the Divine Soul, which unites us all.

וְהַנֶּפֶשׁ וְהָרוּחַ מִי יוֹדֵעַ גְּדוּלָתָן וּמַעֲלָתָן — **And, as for the soul and spirit, who knows their greatness and worth,** בְּשָׁרְשָׁן וּמְקוֹרָן בֵּאלֹקִים חַיִּים — **in their root and source in the living G-d?**

באלקי' חיים. בשגם שכולן מתאימות ואב א' לכולנה
ולכן נקראו כל ישראל אחים ממש מצד שורש נפשם
בה' אחד רק שהגופים מחולקי'. ולכן העושי' גופם עיקר
ונפשם טפלה אי אפשר להיות אהבה ואחוה אמיתית
ביניהם אלא התלויה בדבר לבדה. וז"ש הלל הזקן על
קיום מצוה זו זהו כל התורה כולה ואידך פירושא הוא

Even if you disregard the concerns of the body, there might be an obstacle in coming to "love your fellow as yourself" from the soul's perspective. For example, if someone is inferior to you spiritually, you may find it difficult to love them "as yourself."

Therefore the *Tanya* states here: Even if someone *appears* to be lower than you, spiritually speaking, *"as for the soul and spirit, who knows their greatness and worth?"* You ought to humble yourself before this person, for perhaps his or her soul is greater than yours?

בְּשֶׁגַם שֶׁכּוּלָן מַתְאִימוֹת — And ultimately, at the level of essence, all souls are equal being that *"all of them are alike"* (Song 4:2), וְאָב אֶחָד לְכוּלָנָה — and *"they all have one father"* (Malachi 2:10).

Ultimately, it doesn't matter who has the greater soul powers; at the level of soul-essence, *we are all one and the same.* On that level, your love for your fellow will be *unconditional.*

וְלָכֵן נִקְרְאוּ כָּל יִשְׂרָאֵל אַחִים מַמָּשׁ — And that's why all Israel are called *"brothers"* (Deuteronomy 22:2), literally, מִצַּד שׁוֹרֶשׁ נַפְשָׁם בַּה' אֶחָד — due to their single **source** of their souls in the One G-d.

רַק שֶׁהַגּוּפִים מְחוּלָקִים — It's only their bodies that separate them.

וְלָכֵן הָעוֹשִׂים גּוּפָם עִיקָר וְנַפְשָׁם טְפֵלָה — And therefore, for those who make their bodies primary and their souls secondary, אִי אֶפְשָׁר לִהְיוֹת אַהֲבָה וְאַחֲוָה אֲמִיתִית בֵּינֵיהֶם — it's impossible for them to have genuine love and brotherhood among them, אֶלָּא הַתְּלוּיָה בְּדָבָר לְבַדָּה — but only *"a conditional love"* (Mishnah, Avos 5:16).

SECTION TWO: LOVING YOUR FELLOW IS "THE WHOLE TORAH"

25TH ADAR I LEAP

וְזֶהוּ שֶׁאָמַר הִלֵּל הַזָּקֵן עַל קִיּוּם מִצְוָה זוֹ — And this will help us explain **Hillel the Elder's** comment about observing this *mitzvah* of loving "your fellow as yourself," זֶהוּ כָּל הַתּוֹרָה כּוּלָהּ וְאִידָךְ פֵּירוּשָׁא הוּא כו' — *"it's the whole Torah, all of it. The rest is commentary, etc.,"* (Talmud, Shabbos 31a).

Hillel's statement was not an exaggeration. The *mitzvah* of loving your fellow has a spiritual dynamic which mirrors the spiritual cause-and-effect system of the Torah.

כו'. כִּי יְסוֹד וְשׁוֹרֶשׁ כָּל הַתּוֹרָה הוּא לְהַגְבִּיהַּ וּלְהַעֲלוֹ'
הַנֶּפֶשׁ עַל הַגּוּף מַעֲלָה מַעֲלָה עַד עִיקָּרָא וְשָׁרְשָׁא דְכָל
עָלְמִין וְגַם לְהַמְשִׁיךְ אוֹר א"ס ב"ה בִּכְנֶסֶת יִשְׂרָאֵל כמ"ש
לְקַמָּן דְהַיְינוּ בִּמְקוֹר נִשְׁמוֹת כָּל יִשְׂרָאֵל לְמֶהֱוֵי אֶחָד

As we have seen, the *cause* which brings you to love your fellow is disregarding the mentality of the Animal Soul/body, and shifting to the higher consciousness of the Divine Soul. The *effect* is that you bond and connect with your fellow.

These two phases (of initially transcending the physical and then returning to connecting with it, amid a higher consciousness), represent the fundamental basis of the Torah's spiritual dynamic:

כִּי יְסוֹד וְשׁוֹרֶשׁ כָּל הַתּוֹרָה הוּא — **For the Torah's whole basis and root-principle is** twofold.

The Kabbalists describe this cycle as "*ratso* followed by *shov*," which literally means "running" towards transcendence, and subsequently "returning" to the sensory, worldly reality.

לְהַגְבִּיהַּ וּלְהַעֲלוֹת הַנֶּפֶשׁ עַל הַגּוּף — The Torah's first "root principle" is **to raise and elevate the soul's** importance **over the body,** מַעֲלָה מַעֲלָה עַד עִיקָּרָא וְשָׁרְשָׁא דְכָל עָלְמִין — lifting the soul **higher and higher, to** *"the root and source of all worlds"* (*Zohar* 1, 11b). *i.e, ratso.*

וְגַם לְהַמְשִׁיךְ אוֹר אֵין סוֹף בָּרוּךְ הוּא בִּכְנֶסֶת יִשְׂרָאֵל כְּמוֹ שֶׁיִּתְבָּאֵר לְקַמָּן — **And also, as will be explained below** (chapter 41, p. 511), the second "root-principle" of the Torah is **to draw down G-d's Infinite Light into** the spiritual space referred to by the *Zohar* as *Kneset Yisra'el,* דְהַיְינוּ בִּמְקוֹר נִשְׁמוֹת כָּל יִשְׂרָאֵל — **which is the source of the souls of all Israel.**

This second phase ("*shov*," or "returning") is the mirror image of the first, a reconnecting of the transcendent reality reached by *ratso*, and drawing it back down into a more worldly entity, in this case, our souls.

לְמֶהֱוֵי אֶחָד בְּאֶחָד דַּוְקָא — **So that** *"one will merge with one"* (*Zohar* 2, 135a), *i.e.,* the one G-d will merge with our souls; and this happens **specifically** when they are

---

A CHASIDIC THOUGHT

The concerns of my body and ego direct me towards a scarcity mentality of competition and jealousy. The best route to fully "Love my fellow as myself," is to find happiness in the joy of my Divine Soul alone.

באחד דוקא ולא כשיש פירוד ח"ו בנשמות דקב"ה לא
שריא באתר פגים וכמ"ש ברכנו אבינו כולנו כאחד
באור פניך וכמ"ש במ"א באריכות: ומ"ש בגמ' שמי
שרואה בחבירו שחטא מצוה לשנאותו וגם לומר לרבו

וְלֹא כְּשֶׁיֵּשׁ פֵּירוּד חַס וְשָׁלוֹם בַּנְּשָׁמוֹת — **but not** united down below, in this world, **when there is division among the souls, G-d forbid,** דְּקוּדְשָׁא בְּרִיךְ הוּא לָא שַׁרְיָא בְּאֲתַר פְּגִים — for *"the Blessed Holy One, won't dwell in a blemished place"* (*Zohar* 3, 90b), וּכְמוֹ שֶׁאוֹמְרִים בָּרְכֵנוּ אָבִינוּ כּוּלָנוּ כְּאֶחָד בְּאוֹר פָּנֶיךָ — **and as we say, "Bless all of us, our Father, as one, with the light of Your face"** (*Liturgy, Amidah*), וּכְמוֹ שֶׁנִּתְבָּאֵר בְּמָקוֹם אַחֵר בַּאֲרִיכוּת — **as has been explained at length elsewhere.**

In order for the second phase (*shov*) to be effective, for G-d's Infinite Light to gush into *Kneses Yisrael* (the source of our souls), we need to be united down here in the physical world. If we are not united down here, *Kneses Yisrael* will be fragmented and won't receive G-d's Infinite Light, since *"the Blessed Holy One, won't dwell in a blemished place."*

From this brief insight we see that the *mitzvah* of loving your fellow has a spiritual dynamic which is central to the whole Torah. With this in mind, when you observe this *mitzvah,* it will bring even more joy (*"joy of your soul"* — p. 357), knowing that you are doing something central to the Torah's vision.

SECTION THREE: DOES IT APPLY TO EVERYBODY?

10TH ADAR REGULAR | 26TH ADAR I LEAP

While the Torah warns in general against harboring hatred for another (*"Do not hate your brother in your heart"* — *Leviticus* 19:17), the Rabbis taught that it is obligatory to show contempt towards a sinful person.

וּמַה שֶּׁכָּתוּב בַּגְּמָרָא שֶׁמִּי שֶׁרוֹאֶה בַּחֲבֵירוֹ שֶׁחָטָא מִצְוָה לִשְׂנָאוֹתוֹ — **And as for the** *Talmud's* **teaching that if you witness your friend sinning,** *"It's a mitzvah to show contempt for him"* (*Talmud, Pesachim* 113b), וְגַם לוֹמַר לְרַבּוֹ שֶׁיִּשְׂנָאֵהוּ — **and you should also inform his teacher, so he can show contempt for him as well** (*ibid.*) — this ruling has a very limited application, as we shall see.

Sefer Charedim, a codification of the *mitzvos* by Rabbi Elazar Azkari (16th century), adds an important stipulation to the *Talmud's* position: "If you see a person commit a sin, *and you rebuke him respectfully but he does not cease,* it's a *mitzvah* to show him contempt" (*Sefer Charedim,* chapter 35).

This means that showing contempt to the sinner is a requirement only where: a.) the sinner has been rebuked, and b.) he fails to listen, and continues to sin.

This, in turn, imposes a further, significant limitation, since the requirement to rebuke a sinner is only applicable in a particular scenario. The Torah states, *"You*

41B שישנאהו. היינו בחבירו בתורה ומצות וכבר קיים בו מצות הוכח תוכיח את עמיתך עם שאתך בתורה ובמצות ואעפ"כ לא שב מחטאו כמ"ש בס' חרדים אבל מי שאינו חבירו ואינו מקורב אצלו הנה ע"ז אמר

must repeatedly rebuke your associate (amisecha)" (*Leviticus* 19:17), and *"your associate"* is interpreted to mean, *"One who is like you. If he is like you in obedience to mitzvos, you are to rebuke him (when he sins), but if he is not... you are not called upon to rebuke him"* (*Seder Eliyahu Rabah,* chapter 18).

So, as the *Tanya* will now clarify, the *Talmud's* view (that it is a requirement, a *mitzvah*, to show contempt to a sinner), only applies when three conditions are present: 1.) The sinner is a Torah observant person; 2.) You have rebuked him respectfully; and, 3.) He doesn't listen to you.

PRACTICAL LESSONS

If you make your Divine Soul the main joy in your life, you will find it easier to "love your fellow as yourself."

You ought to "love your fellow" *unconditionally.*

הַיְינוּ בַּחֲבֵירוֹ בְּתוֹרָה וּמִצְוֹת — **Because** the *Talmud's* ruling **applies** not to any person, but specifically **to your** "associate," i.e., your equal in full **Torah and** *mitzvah* observance, וּכְבָר קִיֵּים בּוֹ מִצְוַת הוֹכֵחַ תּוֹכִיחַ אֶת עֲמִיתֶךָ — and it also only applies to an "associate" **towards whom you have already fulfilled the** *mitzvah,* **"You must repeatedly rebuke your fellow"** (*Leviticus* 19:17).

עִם שֶׁאִתְּךָ בְּתוֹרָה וּבְמִצְוֹת — And this *mitzvah* of rebuking your fellow applies exclusively to **someone "who is like you"** in Torah and *mitzvos* (above, from *Seder Eliyahu Rabah*), וְאַף עַל פִּי כֵן לֹא שָׁב מֵחֶטְאוֹ — and **nevertheless,** despite your attempts to respectfully correct his behavior, the person **has not ceased practicing this sin.**

כְּמוֹ שֶׁכָּתוּב בְּסֵפֶר חֲרֵדִים — As stated in *Sefer Charedim* (cited above).

These criteria are required to establish the intentionality of the sin. If the person is not "like you" in Torah and *mitzvos, i.e.,* not educated and observant, then even his *"deliberate sins are considered as inadvertent acts"* (*Talmud, Bava Metzia* 33b). Even if he is "like you," you cannot be sure that his act was intentional until you have clearly rebuked him and he fails to listen. Only at that point, is there a Rabbinic obligation to show him contempt (*Notes on Tanya*).

27TH ADAR I LEAP

אֲבָל מִי שֶׁאֵינוֹ חֲבֵירוֹ — **But in the case of a person who is not your "associate,"** and lacks the real knowledge and education necessary for "intentional" sin, וְאֵינוֹ מְקוֹרָב אֶצְלוֹ — **and is not close to you** and is therefore unlikely to accept your rebuke, there is no room at all for contempt, only love, הִנֵּה עַל זֶה אָמַר הִלֵּל הַזָּקֵן — **in such a**

הלל הזקן הוי מתלמידיו של אהרן אוהב שלום וכו'
אוהב את הבריות ומקרבן לתורה. לומר שאף
הרחוקים מתורת ה' ועבודתו ולכן נקראי' בשם בריות
בעלמא צריך למשכן בחבלי עבותו' אהבה וכולי האי

case, Hillel the Elder taught, הֱוֵי מִתַּלְמִידָיו שֶׁל אַהֲרֹן אוֹהֵב שָׁלוֹם וְכוּ' אוֹהֵב אֶת הַבְּרִיּוֹת וּמְקָרְבָן לַתּוֹרָה — **"Be of the disciples of Aharon: love peace** and pursue peace, **love all creatures and bring them close to the Torah"** (Mishnah, Avos 1:12).

לוֹמַר שֶׁאַף הָרְחוֹקִים מִתּוֹרַת ה' וַעֲבוֹדָתוֹ — **Meaning that even those who are distant from G-d's Torah and His worship,** וְלָכֵן נִקְרָאִים בְּשֵׁם בְּרִיּוֹת בְּעָלְמָא — **which is why they are referred to** here as mere **"creatures,"** having no merits of their own beyond the fact that they were **"created"** by G-d, צָרִיךְ לְמָשְׁכָן בְּחַבְלֵי עֲבוֹתוֹת אַהֲבָה — nevertheless, **you must "draw them in with thick cords of love"** (see Hosea 11:4).

וְכוּלֵּי הַאי וְאוּלַי יוּכַל לְקָרְבָן לְתוֹרָה וַעֲבוֹדַת ה' — **And then perhaps, with all this effort you will be able to bring them closer to the Torah and worship of G-d.**

Above, the *Tanya* stressed that love for another ought to be unconditional, due to all souls' equal *"root and source in the living G-d."* Yet here, the text stresses that there is a goal in extending love to the non-observant: *"perhaps, with all this effort you will be able to bring them closer to the Torah and worship of G-d."*

Is there a *goal* to loving your fellow? Or is love to be extended *unconditionally*?

The answer is that both are true. Jewish identity is mulitlayered, so the *mitzvah* to "love your fellow," is likewise multilayered.

At the level of *essence,* a Jew is connected to G-d regardless of his or her level of observance. However, the *manifest reality*, in the world as G-d created it, is that a connection to G-d comes through Torah and *mitzvos.*

A CHASIDIC THOUGHT

If I make my body and Animal Soul the main thing in my life, everything will be interpreted through the lens of personal gain and a "Win-Lose" mentality. My Animal Soul sees itself as a helpless fragment in an alien universe, disconnected from its Divine source and from other souls; so it constantly seeks to enrich itself, with no real concern for another.

My Divine Soul, on the other hand, has the attitude of "Win-Win." It knows that everything which happens to me is shared in some way with others, because the universe is an *integrated system.* It's a mistake to see whatever happens as something purely personal, because that's not the actual reality.

וְאוּלַי יוּכַל לְקָרְבָן לְתוֹרָה וַעֲבוֹדַת ה' וְהֵן לֹא לֹא הִפְסִיד
שְׂכַר מִצְוַת אַהֲבַת רֵעִים וְגַם הַמְקוֹרָבִים אֵלָיו וְהוֹכִיחָם
וְלֹא שָׁבוּ מֵעֲווֹנוֹתֵיהֶם שֶׁמִּצְוָה לִשְׂנֹאוֹתָם מִצְוָה לְאַהֲבָם

Above, when the *Tanya* taught that love should be extended unconditionally due to every soul's equal *"root and source in the living G-d,"* we were speaking of love towards a Jew's essence. But here, in stressing that *"perhaps, with all this effort you will be able to bring them closer to the Torah and worship of G-d,"* the *Tanya* speaks of the manifest reality, where a Jew's connection to G-d must be through the Torah.

Practically speaking, we need to incorporate both attitudes: to love each Jew's essence, by virtue of their soul; but this must also lead to their *manifest* connection with G-d, through Torah observance (*Notes on Tanya*).

וְהֵן לֹא — **And if not,** if you didn't succeed in bringing the person "closer to Torah and worship of G-d," רֵעִים אַהֲבַת מִצְוַת שְׂכַר הִפְסִיד לֹא — **you still didn't lose the reward for** observing the *mitzvah* of **loving your fellow,** which is carried out unconditionally.

SECTION FOUR: HOW TO RELATE TO INTENTIONAL SINNERS

28TH ADAR I LEAP

אֵלָיו הַמְקוֹרָבִים וְגַם — **And in the** above **case of** sinning **individuals who are close to you** and on par with you in observance, מֵעֲווֹנוֹתֵיהֶם שָׁבוּ וְלֹא וְהוֹכִיחָם — **whom you have rebuked, but they have not stopped sinning,** לִשְׂנֹאוֹתָם שֶׁמִּצְוָה — **towards** whom, as we learned above, **it's a *mitzvah* to show contempt to them,** לְאַהֲבָם מִצְוָה גַם כֵּן — that doesn't mean you should *just* show contempt to them, since **there's also a *mitzvah* to love them too!***

---

*There is a dispute among Jewish legal authorities whether the *mitzvah* to *"love your fellow as yourself"* is at all applicable to a person who is sinful. Some argue that Scripture's use of the phrase "your fellow," excludes a sinful person from this *mitzvah* (*Smag*, positive commands 9; *Hagahos Maimoni* to *Hilchos De'os* 6:3; *Yereim* par. 224). Other authorities disagree, arguing that the *mitzvah* to "love your fellow as yourself" applies even to the sinful (Rabbi Meir Abulafia, *Yad Ramah*, *Sanhedrin* 52b; see Rabbi Moshe Schick, *Maharam Schick al Taryag Mitzvos, Mitzvah* 244; Rabbi Yeruchum Fishel Perlow, commentary to *Sefer ha-Mitzvos Rasag*, p, 143d).

According to this second opinion, the Biblical command to *"love your fellow as yourself"* applies to everyone (even towards those whom there is a Rabbinic requirement to show contempt—see previous section). So there could be a case where there would be two *mitvzos* dictating your attitude to the same person: one of love, and the other of contempt!

The *Tanya* adopts the second opinion, that the *mitzvah* to *"love your fellow as yourself"* applies even to those sinful individuals to whom the *mitzvah* of showing contempt is applicable (*Notes on Tanya*).

ג"כ ושתיהן הן אמת שנאה מצד הרע שבהם ואהבה
מצד בחי' הטוב הגנוז שבהם שהוא ניצוץ אלקות שבתוכם
המחיה נפשם האלקית וגם לעורר רחמים בלבו עליה
כי היא בבחי' גלות בתוך הרע מס"א הגובר עליה
ברשעי' והרחמנות מבטלת השנאה ומעוררת האהבה
כנודע ממ"ש ליעקב אשר פדה את אברהם [ולא אמר
דה"עה תכלית שנאה שנאתים וגו' אלא על המינים

How could you have two contradictory engagements with the same person?

שֶׁנְאָה מִצַּד הָרַע שֶׁבָּהֶם — contempt, be-cause of the evil in them, וּשְׁתֵּיהֶן הֵן אֱמֶת — Both emotions are valid, וְאַהֲבָה מִצַּד בְּחִינַת הַטּוֹב הַגָּנוּז שֶׁבָּהֶם — and love, because of the component of good which is hidden in them, שֶׁהוּא נִיצוֹץ אֱלֹקוּת שֶׁבְּתוֹכָם — which is the spark of G-d within them, הַמְחַיֶּה נַפְשָׁם הָאֱלֹקִית — that energizes their Divine Souls.

In addition to love and contempt, the *Tanya* now intro-duces a third emotion: *compassion*. Through compas-sion, the two contradictory emotions of love and con-tempt can be reconciled.

וְגַם לְעוֹרֵר רַחֲמִים בְּלִבּוֹ עָלֶיהָ — Also, you ought to arouse compassion in your heart for that person's Divine Soul, כִּי הִיא בִּבְחִינַת גָּלוּת בְּתוֹךְ הָרַע מִסִּטְרָא אָחֲרָא — because it is a Divine Soul exiled amid the evil of the *sitra achra,* הַגּוֹבֵר עָלֶיהָ בָּרְשָׁעִים — which, in the case of *resha'im*, overpowers the Divine Soul.

וְהָרַחֲמָנוּת מְבַטֶּלֶת הַשִּׂנְאָה וּמְעוֹרֶרֶת הָאַהֲבָה — And com-passion has the effect of neutralizing contempt and awakening love, כַּנּוֹדָע מִמַּה שֶׁכָּתוּב לְיַעֲקֹב אֲשֶׁר פָּדָה אֶת אַבְרָהָם — as is known from the verse, *"To Ya'akov who redeemed Avraham"* (Isaiah 29:22).

Ya'akov is symbolic of compassion and Avraham of love. In a situation of contempt, love (Avraham) can be restored and "redeemed" through compassion.

When you feel "sorry" for someone who has harmed you, it tends to take away any hatred you might have for them. Compassion ensures that, in most cases, con-tempt will be neutralized and love will triumph.

[וְלֹא אָמַר דָּוִד הַמֶּלֶךְ עָלָיו הַשָּׁלוֹם תַּכְלִית שִׂנְאָה שְׂנֵאתִים וְגוֹ' אֶלָּא עַל הַמִּינִים וְהָאֶפִּיקוֹרְסִים — But when King David, of blessed memory said, *"With utter hatred do I hate them"* (Psalms 139:22), he was referring only to the extreme case of highly educat-ed heretics and non-believers that pose a threat to traditional Judaism, שֶׁאֵין לָהֶם

PRACTICAL LESSONS

Even if you find some-thing contemptible in another person, it's still a *mitzvah* to love them. You love the good in them and detest the bad.

Compassion has the power to neutral-ize contempt and transform it to love.

וְהָאֶפִּיקוֹרְסִים שֶׁאֵין לָהֶם חֵלֶק בֵּאלֹהֵי יִשְׂרָאֵל כִּדְאִיתָא
בַּגְּמָרָא רֵישׁ פֶּרֶק ט"ז דְּשַׁבָּת:

פֶּרֶק לג   עוֹד   זֹאת תִּהְיֶה שִׂמְחַת הַנֶּפֶשׁ הָאֲמִיתִי'
וּבְפְרָט כְּשֶׁרוֹאֶה בְּנַפְשׁוֹ בְּעִתִּים
מְזֻמָּנִים שֶׁצָּרִיךְ לְזַכְּכָהּ וּלְהָאִירָהּ בְּשִׂמְחַת לֵב אֲזַי

חֵלֶק בֵּאלֹהֵי יִשְׂרָאֵל — **who** have shed any *manifest* connection to Judaism and so *"have no portion in the G-d of Israel"* (*Sanhedrin* 102b), כִּדְאִיתָא בַּגְּמָרָא רֵישׁ פֶּרֶק ט"ז [דְּשַׁבָּת — **as stated in the** *Talmud,* **Tractate** *Shabbos,* **beginning of chapter 16,** 116a.

The *Tanya* stresses that this "hatred" is something which "King David said," because it is not something you should be practicing. When expressing "righteous indignation" for another person's actions, even though you appear to be taking the moral high ground, how do you know that you are not acting out of an impure motive? You may also have erred in judgment about your friend's "heresy," which may in fact be nothing more than a benign short-sightedness.

If you act with contempt towards another person, and you are wrong in your judgment, then you have hurt someone unjustifiably. But if you behave lovingly towards everyone, you are definitely doing a *mitzvah*.

CHAPTER 33

FEELING G-D; FEELING JOY

SECTION ONE: FINDING JOY IN G-D'S CLOSENESS

11TH ADAR REGULAR | 29RD ADAR I LEAP

Chapter 31 taught us two uplifting meditations to find comfort and joy (following the deeply humbling meditations of chapters 29-30). But in chapter 31, the insights are limited to joy that comes through *mitzvah* observance.

Here, in chapter 33, we learn a further meditation to bring "*true* joy," i.e., a joy that is not dependent on any activity, time or place. It is a joy that flows from your essential being and the presence of G-d found in your soul, your body, and in everything.

עוֹד זֹאת תִּהְיֶה שִׂמְחַת הַנֶּפֶשׁ הָאֲמִיתִּית — **Another method to find true joy in your soul,** וּבְפְרָט כְּשֶׁרוֹאֶה בְּנַפְשׁוֹ בְּעִתִּים מְזֻמָּנִים שֶׁצָּרִיךְ לְזַכְּכָהּ — **particularly when, on those specific occasions** when your heart becomes desensitized (see chapter 29, p. 324), **you see that it is in need of some cleansing,** וּלְהָאִירָהּ בְּשִׂמְחַת לֵבָב — **and it** needs **the light of a joyous heart.**

יעמיק מחשבתו ויצייר בשכלו ובינתו ענין יחודו ית'
האמיתי איך הוא ממלא כל עלמין עליונים ותחתונים
ואפי' מלא כל הארץ הלזו הוא כבודו ית' וכולא קמיה
כלא חשיב ממש והוא לבדו הוא בעליונים ותחתונים
ממש כמו שהיה לבדו קודם ששת ימי בראשית וגם
במקום הזה שנברא בו עולם הזה השמים והארץ וכל
צבאם היה הוא לבדו ממלא המקום הזה וגם עתה כן
הוא לבדו בלי שום שינוי כלל מפני שכל הנבראים
בטלים אצלו במציאות ממש כביטול אותיות הדבור
והמחשבה במקורן ושרשן הוא מהות הנפש ועצמותה
שהן עשר בחינותיה חכמה בינה ודעת כו' שאין בהם

42A

אֲזַי יַעֲמִיק מַחֲשַׁבְתּוֹ — What you could do then, is probe deeply in your mind, וִיצַיֵּיר בְּשִׂכְלוֹ וּבִינָתוֹ — picturing mentally and cognitively, עִנְיַן יִחוּדוֹ יִתְבָּרֵךְ הָאֲמִיתִּי — the concept of G-d's genuine nonduality, which we discussed in chapters 20-21.

The *Tanya* now briefly recaps the main themes of chapter 20-21.

אֵיךְ הוּא מְמַלֵּא כָּל עָלְמִין עֶלְיוֹנִים וְתַחְתּוֹנִים — How *"He fills all worlds"* (see *Zohar* 3, 225a), **upper and lower,** וַאֲפִילוּ מְלֹא כָּל הָאָרֶץ הַלֵּזוּ הוּא כְּבוֹדוֹ יִתְבָּרֵךְ — **and even how this** lowly, physical **world is filled with His glory** (see *Isaiah* 6:3).

וְכוּלָּא קַמֵּיהּ כְּלָא חֲשִׁיב — And *"in His presence, everything is considered zero"* (*Zohar*. 1, 11b), מַמָּשׁ — **literally.**

וְהוּא לְבַדּוֹ הוּא בָּעֶלְיוֹנִים וְתַחְתּוֹנִים מַמָּשׁ — And *"All believe that **He is One alone"*** (*Liturgy, High Holidays*), **in the upper and lower worlds, literally,** כְּמוֹ שֶׁהָיָה לְבַדּוֹ — קוֹדֶם שֵׁשֶׁת יְמֵי בְּרֵאשִׁית — **just as He was** alone **before the six days of creation.**

וְגַם בַּמָּקוֹם הַזֶּה שֶׁנִּבְרָא בּוֹ עוֹלָם הַזֶּה — And even in this space where our world was created, הַשָּׁמַיִם וְהָאָרֶץ וְכָל צְבָאָם — *"The skies, the earth and all their numerous components"* (*Genesis* 2:1), הָיָה הוּא לְבַדּוֹ מְמַלֵּא הַמָּקוֹם הַזֶּה — just as He was originally **alone, filling this space,** וְגַם עַתָּה כֵּן הוּא לְבַדּוֹ בְּלִי שׁוּם שִׁינוּי כְּלָל — **now, too, He is also alone, without any change whatsoever,** מִפְּנֵי שֶׁכָּל הַנִּבְרָאִים בְּטֵלִים אֶצְלוֹ בִּמְצִיאוּת מַמָּשׁ — **because the** separate **identity of all the creations is literally voided in His presence.**

The *Tanya* now recaps the illustration we learned earlier about the source of language in the soul.

כְּבִיטּוּל אוֹתִיּוֹת הַדִּיבּוּר וְהַמַּחֲשָׁבָה בִּמְקוֹרָן וְשָׁרְשָׁן — The separate identity of the creations are literally voided in His presence **just like the** component **letters of speech and thought are voided in their** pre-linguistic **source,** הוּא מַהוּת הַנֶּפֶשׁ וְעַצְמוּתָהּ — **which is the deep core of the soul,** שֶׁהֵן עֶשֶׂר בְּחִינוֹתֶיהָ חָכְמָה בִּינָה וָדַעַת כוּ' — name-

בחי' אותיות עדיין קודם שמתלבשות בלבוש המחשבה
[כמ"ש בפ' כ' וכ"א באריכות ע"ש] וכמ"ש ג"כ במ"א
משל גשמי לזה מענין ביטול זיו ואור השמש במקורו
הוא גוף כדור השמש שברקיע שגם שם מאיר ומתפשט
ודאי זיוו ואורו וביתר שאת מהתפשטותו והארתו
בחלל העולם אלא ששם הוא בטל במציאות במקורו
וכאילו אינו במציאות כלל: וככה ממש דרך משל
הוא ביטול העולם ומלואו במציאות לגבי מקורו שהוא
אור א"ס ב"ה וכמש"ש באריכו'. והנה כשיעמיק בזה

שָׁאֵין בָּהֶם בְּחִינַת אוֹתִיּוֹת עֲדַיִין — ly the soul's **ten powers, chochmah, binah, da'as etc.,** קוֹדֶם שֶׁמִּתְלַבְּשׁוֹת בִּלְבוּשׁ הַמַּחֲשָׁבָה, — at which point, letters have not yet crystallized, — since this is **before expression takes place in the "garment" of thought.**

[כְּמוֹ שֶׁנִּתְבָּאֵר בִּפְרָקִים כ' וְכ"א בַּאֲרִיכוּת עַיֵּין שָׁם] — **As was explained at length in chapters 20-21; see there.**

In the second book of *Tanya, Sha'ar Ha-Yichud Ve-Ha-Emunah,* another analogy is used to illustrate the nondual idea. Briefly, the *Tanya* touches upon this second analogy here.

וּכְמוֹ שֶׁנִּתְבָּאֵר גַּם כֵּן בְּמָקוֹם אַחֵר מָשָׁל גַּשְׁמִי לָזֶה — **And as is explained elsewhere** (*Sha'ar Ha-Yichud Ve-Ha-Emunah* chapter 3), **a** different, **physical example,** מֵעִנְיַן בִּיטוּל זִיו וְאוֹר הַשֶּׁמֶשׁ בִּמְקוֹרוֹ — of how the separate identity of the **sun's light and rays is voided inside its source,** הוּא גּוּף כַּדוּר הַשֶּׁמֶשׁ שֶׁבָּרָקִיעַ — **that** source **is the sun's physical globe,** seen **in the sky.**

שֶׁגַּם שָׁם מֵאִיר וּמִתְפַּשֵּׁט וַדַּאי זִיוּוֹ וְאוֹרוֹ וּבְיֶתֶר שְׂאֵת מֵהִתְפַּשְׁטוּתוֹ וְהֶאָרָתוֹ בַּחֲלַל הָעוֹלָם — **For also there,** inside the sun, **that light and those rays definitely shine forth even more powerfully than they shine forth in this world's atmospheric space,** אֶלָּא שֶׁשָּׁם הוּא בָּטֵל בִּמְצִיאוּת בִּמְקוֹרוֹ — **but there, in their source,** despite their greater intensity, **their** separate **identity** as individual rays of light **is extinguished,** וּכְאִילוּ אֵינוֹ בִּמְצִיאוּת כְּלָל — **and it's as if they simply don't exist.**

וְכָכָה מַמָּשׁ דֶּרֶךְ מָשָׁל הוּא בִּיטוּל הָעוֹלָם וּמְלוֹאוֹ בִּמְצִיאוּת לְגַבֵּי מְקוֹרוֹ — **And that's a very precise analogy for how the** separate **identity of the world and its contents is voided in relation to its source,** שֶׁהוּא אוֹר אֵין סוֹף בָּרוּךְ הוּא — **which is the Blessed Infinite Light** of G-d, וּכְמוֹ שֶׁנִּתְבָּאֵר שָׁם בַּאֲרִיכוּת — **as is explained there** in *Sha'ar Ha-Yichud Ve-Ha-Emunah* **at length.**

Having recapped the basic contours of the nondual idea, the *Tanya* now explains why, on a personal level, contemplating this deeper view of reality can bring you joy.

וְהִנֵּה כְּשֶׁיַּעֲמִיק בָּזֶה הַרְבֵּה — **Now, when you will probe this** nondual idea **extensively,** יִשְׂמַח לִבּוֹ וְתָגֵל נַפְשׁוֹ אַף גִּילַת וְרַנֵּן — **your heart will gladdened, and your soul "will**

הרבה ישמח לבו ותגל נפשו אף גילת ורנן בכל לב
ונפש ומאד באמונה זו כי רבה היא כי היא קרבת אלהים
ממש וזה כל האדם ותכלית בריאתו ובריאות כל
העולמות עליונים ותחתוני' להיות לו דירה זו בתחתוני'
כמ"ש לקמן באריכות. והנה כמה גדולה שמחת
הדיוט ושפל אנשים בהתקרבותו למלך בשר ודם
המתאכסן ודר אתו עמו בביתו וק"ו לאין קץ לקרבת

rejoice even with joy and singing" (Isaiah 35:2), בְּכָל לֵב וָנֶפֶשׁ וּמְאֹד בָּאֱמוּנָה זו כִּי רַבָּה
הִיא — with, *"all your heart, soul and might"* (see Deuteronomy 6:5), in this faith,
"for it is great" (Esther 1:20), כִּי הִיא קִרְבַת אֱלֹהִים מַמָּשׁ — since it is, literally, *"close-ness to G-d"* (Psalms 73:28).

וְזֶה כָּל הָאָדָם וְתַכְלִית בְּרִיאָתו — *"And this is the whole purpose of man"* (Ecclesiastes
12:13), and the reason for which he was created, וּבְרִיאַת כָּל הָעוֹלָמוֹת עֶלְיוֹנִים
וְתַחְתּוֹנִים — and it's also the reason for the creation of all the worlds, upper and
lower, לְהְיוֹת לוֹ דִירָה זוֹ בַּתַחְתּוֹנִים — to have this *"home (for G-d) in the lower
worlds"* (Midrash Tanchuma, Naso par. 16).

A central theme of Chasidic thought, which will be
explored in the coming chapters, is the Midrashic idea
that G-d created the universe in order to have a *Dirah
ba-Tachtonim* ("home in the lower (physical) worlds").
Here in chapter 33, *Dirah ba-Tachtonim* is understood
to mean thinking about G-d in a nondual way. Whenever you are aware that *"the separate identity of all the
creations is literally voided in His presence"* then your
consciousness becomes a "home for G-d in the lower
worlds."

PRACTICAL LESSONS

When you think about how everything is dissolved in G-d's presence, you will feel the joy of being very close to G-d.

כְּמוֹ שֶׁיִתְבָּאֵר לְקַמָּן בָּאֲרִיכוּת — As the concept of *Dirah
ba-Tachtonim* will be explained later on, at length in
chapters 36-37 and 49.

Even thinking about G-d's nondual oneness makes
your mind into a "home for G-d." And that is an especially powerful source of joy
because: a.) It affects your inner world; and b.) It's available to you always, at any
time and in any place.

The *Tanya* now examines why the *Midrash* uses the term "home" for G-d to express an intimate union, and why this ought to be a source of joy.

וְהִנֵּה כַּמָּה גְדוֹלָה שִׂמְחַת הֶדְיוֹט וּשְׁפַל אֲנָשִׁים — Now imagine the immense joy of an
ordinary person, *"the most lowly of men"* (Daniel 4:14), בְּהִתְקָרְבוּתוֹ לְמֶלֶךְ בָּשָׂר וָדָם
הַמִּתְאַכְסֵן וְדָר אִתּוֹ עִמּוֹ בְּבֵיתוֹ — if a human king were to come close to him by lodg-
ing and permanently living with him in his humble little house!

ודירת ממ״ה הקב״ה וכדכתיב כי מי הוא זה אשר ערב
לבו לגשת אלי נאם ה': ועל זה תיקנו ליתן שבח
והודיה לשמו ית' בכל בקר ולומר אשרינו מה טוב
חלקנו וכו' ומה יפה ירושתנו כלומר כמו שהאדם שש
ושמח בירושה שנפלה לו הון עתק שלא עמל בו כן
ויותר לאין קץ יש לנו לשמוח על ירושתנו

42B

לְקָרְבַת — וְקַל וָחוֹמֶר לְאֵין קֵץ — **All the more so, to an immeasurably greater extent,**
וּדִירַת מֶלֶךְ מַלְכֵי הַמְּלָכִים הַקָּדוֹשׁ בָּרוּךְ הוּא — should you be happy at the thought of
G-d, **the blessed King of kings, making His intimate "home"** with you!

וּכְדִכְתִיב כִּי מִי הוּא זֶה אֲשֶׁר עָרַב לִבּוֹ לָגֶשֶׁת אֵלַי נְאָם ה' — **As the verse** asks rhetorically,
"'For who is the one that has devoted his heart (sufficiently) **to come close to Me?'
says G-d"** (Jeremiah 30:21).

The prophet laments that in the natural course of things, it's impossible to come
really close to G-d. But that's only *without* the gift of nondual wisdom. Through the
insight of Chasidic teachings, G-d will come so close to you that His "address" actually becomes yours!

12TH ADAR REGULAR

וְעַל זֶה תִּיקְנוּ לִיתֵּן שֶׁבַח וְהוֹדָיָה לִשְׁמוֹ יִתְבָּרֵךְ בְּכָל בֹּקֶר — **And that's why it was es-**
tablished that every morning we *"offer praise and thanksgiving to (G-d's) name,"*
וְלוֹמַר אַשְׁרֵינוּ מַה טוֹב חֶלְקֵנוּ וְכוּ' וּמַה יָּפָה יְרוּשָׁתֵנוּ — **when we say, "Happy are we!
How good is our portion!** How pleasant is our lot! **How beautiful our heritage!"**
(Liturgy, Morning Prayers).

כְּמוֹ שֶׁהָאָדָם שָׂשׂ וְשָׂמֵחַ בִּירוּשָׁה שֶׁנָּפְלָה לוֹ הוֹן עָתֵק שֶׁלֹּא — **In other words,** כְּלוֹמַר
עָמַל בּוֹ — just as a person would rejoice greatly if he were to inherit an immense
fortune for which he didn't do any work, כֵּן וְיוֹתֵר מִכֵּן לְאֵין קֵץ — so too, and im-

---

A CHASIDIC THOUGHT

You take to heart that you are literally engulfed in G-d. Everything around you, and within you, is nothing other than a Divine indwelling, a ripple on the ocean of the Divine. You are "swimming" in the wondrous reality of G-d; you're breathing G-d, seeing G-d and dissolving in His presence. His warm, loving embrace is gently enveloping you to the point that you merge with Him and "come home" to your sacred source.

Such thoughts of extreme "closeness to G-d," when contemplated deeply, are a great source of joy.

שהנחילנו אבותינו הוא יחוד ה' האמיתי אשר אפי'
בארץ מתחת אין עוד מלבדו וזו היא דירתו בתחתונים
וז"ש רז"ל תרי"ג מצות ניתנו לישראל בא חבקוק
והעמידן על אחת שנאמר וצדיק באמונתו יחיה כלומר
כאלו אינה רק מצוה אחת היא האמונה לבדה כי ע"י
האמונה לבדה יבא לקיום כל התרי"ג מצות דהיינו

measurably more so, יֵשׁ לָנוּ לִשְׂמוֹחַ עַל יְרוּשָׁתֵנוּ שֶׁהִנְחִילוּנוּ אֲבוֹתֵינוּ — **ought we to rejoice at the inheritance we have received from our ancestors,** הוּא יְחוּד ה' הָאֲמִיתִּי — **the truth of G-d's** nondual **unity,** אֲשֶׁר אֲפִילוּ בָּאָרֶץ מִתַּחַת אֵין עוֹד מִלְּבַדּוֹ — that **even "in the earth below"** (Deut. 4:39), **"There is no other besides Him"** (ibid. 35).

In addition to the joy of your awareness of G-d's presence in all things, you should also celebrate the fact that this secret came to you without you having earned it. If you had not learned about the nondual reality, G-d would have remained distant from you. So thank Him every day for your access to this wisdom, and your soul's ability to appreciate it. It's your sacred inheritance.

וְזוֹ הִיא דִירָתוֹ בַּתַּחְתּוֹנִים — **And that** awareness of, and devotion to, G-d's nondual reality *is* His **"home in the lower worlds."**

SECTION TWO: FAITH, JOY AND ACTION

Below, in chapters 36-37, we will learn that G-d's "home in the lower worlds" is made through *mitzvah* observance. Yet here, in chapter 33, the emphasis appears to be different: We are taught that G-d's "home" is made through conscious faith in the nondual reality.

So where is G-d's home to be found? In your faith, or in your *mitzvos*?

The *Tanya* now clarifies that the two are intrinsically connected, two sides of the same coin, so to speak.

וְזֶהוּ שֶׁאָמְרוּ רַבּוֹתֵינוּ זִכְרוֹנָם לִבְרָכָה — **And this explains the teaching of our Sages, of blessed memory,** תַּרְיַ"ג מִצְוֹת נִיתְּנוּ לְיִשְׂרָאֵל — **"Six hundred and thirteen mitzvos were given to Israel,"** בָּא חֲבַקּוּק וְהֶעֱמִידָן עַל אַחַת שֶׁנֶּאֱמַר וְצַדִּיק בֶּאֱמוּנָתוֹ יִחְיֶה — **"but Habakkuk came and hinged them on one, as the verse states, 'The tzadik will be enlivened by his faith'"** (Habakkuk 2:4; Talmud, Makos 23b-24a).

כְּלוֹמַר כְּאִלּוּ אֵינָם רַק מִצְוָה אַחַת — **In other words, it's as if there was just one mitzvah,** הִיא הָאֱמוּנָה לְבַדָּה — **namely, the** *mitzvah* **of faith** in G-d alone, כִּי עַל יְדֵי הָאֱמוּנָה לְבַדָּהּ יָבֹא לְקִיּוּם כָּל הַתַּרְיַ"ג מִצְוֹת — **because it's through faith alone that you come to observe all six hundred and thirteen** *mitzvos.*

When you're grounded in nondual faith, *mitzvah* observance flows naturally from it. The *mitzvos* are no longer perceived as a long list of "commands" issued to you

כשיהיה לבו שש ושמח באמונתו ביחוד ה' בתכלית
השמחה כאלו לא היתה עליו רק מצוה זו לבדה והיא
לבדה תכלית בריאתו ובריאת כל העולמות הרי בכח
וחיות נפשו בשמחה רבה זו תתעלה נפשו למעלה
מעלה על כל המונעים קיום כל התרי"ג מצות מבית
ומחוץ. וזהו שאמר באמונתו יחיה יחיה דייקא כתחיית
המתים דרך משל כך תחיה כך נפשו בשמחה רבה זו

from a higher authority. You feel G-d's presence powerfully and intimately, and that motivates you to connect to Him at every opportunity through *mitzvah* observance.

A crucial ingredient for this "flow" from faith to observance, is *joy*.

דְּהַיְינוּ כְּשֶׁיִהְיֶה לִבּוֹ שָׁשׂ וְשָׂמֵחַ בֶּאֱמוּנָתוֹ בְּיָחוּד ה' — **Meaning that when your heart will find happiness and joy in your faith in G-d's** nondual oneness, בְּתַכְלִית הַשִׂמְחָה — as much happiness as can be, כְּאִלּוּ לֹא הָיְתָה עָלָיו רַק מִצְוָה זוֹ לְבַדָּהּ — **as if you had just this one** *mitzvah* to observe, וְהִיא לְבַדָּהּ תַּכְלִית בְּרִיאָתוֹ וּבְרִיאַת כָּל הָעוֹלָמוֹת — **and this** one *mitzvah* **alone is the ultimate purpose for which you and all the worlds were created,** הֲרֵי בְּכֹחַ — **then through the strength and energy that your soul will derive from this great happiness,** וְחַיּוּת נַפְשׁוֹ בְּשִׂמְחָה רַבָּה זוֹ **תִּתְעַלֶּה נַפְשׁוֹ לְמַעְלָה מַעְלָה עַל כָּל הַמּוֹנְעִים קִיּוּם כָּל הַתַּרְיַ"ג מִצְוֹת מִבַּיִת וּמִחוּץ — your soul will be uplifted to overcome anything preventing you, internally or externally, from observing all the 613** *mitzvos*.

PRACTICAL LESSONS

G-d is "at home" in the universe when you contemplate his nondual presence.

The nondual secret is your precious inheritance. Own it and celebrate it.

There's a cycle: contemplating your nondual faith leads to joy, which then invigorates *mitzvah* observance.

A *mitzvah* is faith concretized in action. While faith remains inside your mind and heart, it's more luminous and intense; in the *mitzvah* act, your faith is more manifest and contagious. Whenever you are *feeling* your faith or *expressing* it in action, you're making a "home" for G-d.

וְזֶהוּ שֶׁאָמַר בֶּאֱמוּנָתוֹ יִחְיֶה — **And this explains the verse** cited by the *Talmud* as a source for this idea, **"The tzadik will be enlivened by his faith,"** יִחְיֶה דַּיְיקָא — **the precise** use of the term **"will be enlivened,"** points to the invigorating property of faith, כִּתְחִיַּית הַמֵּתִים דֶּרֶךְ מָשָׁל כָּךְ תִּחְיֶה נַפְשׁוֹ בְּשִׂמְחָה רַבָּה זוֹ — **through this joy, your soul will be invigorated like the** future **revival of the dead, so to speak.**

The *Talmud* itself doesn't specify joy as the crucial ingredient that leads from faith into action. But the *Talmud* does hint to the presence of *some* invigorating force with the words "The *tzadik* will be enlivened by his faith." And that force, the *Tanya* suggests, is joy; a feeling of aliveness that propels us into action.

וְהִיא שמחה כפולה ומכופלת כי מלבד שמחת
הנפש המשכלת בקרבת ה' ודירתו אתו עמו. עוד זאת
ישמח בכפליים בשמחת ה' וגודל נחת רוח לפניו ית'
באמונה זו דאתכפיא ס"א ממש ואתהפך חשוכא
לנהורא שהוא חשך הקליפות שבע"הז החומרי
המחשיכים ומכסים על אורו ית' עד עת קץ כמ"ש קץ
שם לחשך [דהיינו קץ הימין שיעביר רוח הטומאה מן

SECTION THREE: SHARING IN G-D'S JOY

Up to this point we have been discussing the joy that you feel as a result of your faith, the joy of feeling G-d's presence. In this section, we'll turn our attention to G-d's joy. The *Tanya* will suggest that by focusing on G-d's joy, you too, will become even more joyous.

וְהִיא שִׂמְחָה כְּפוּלָה וּמְכוּפֶּלֶת — **And it's a joy that is doubled and redoubled,** since, as we shall see, there are a total of four ideas that lead to joy.

כִּי מִלְבַד שִׂמְחַת הַנֶּפֶשׁ הַמַּשְׂכֶּלֶת בְּקִרְבַת ה' — **Because besides** your personal **joy in appreciating: 1) how,** generally speaking, **G-d is close,** וְדִירָתוֹ אִתּוֹ עִמּוֹ — **and** furthermore, 2) **how He is** actually **making His home with you,** there are two further ideas about G-d's joy.

13TH ADAR REGULAR

עוֹד זֹאת יִשְׂמַח בְּכִפְלַיִם — **And this will bring you a redoubled joy,** בְּשִׂמְחַת ה' וְגוֹדֶל נַחַת רוּחַ לְפָנָיו יִתְבָּרֵךְ בֶּאֱמוּנָה זוֹ דְּאִתְכַּפְיָא סִטְרָא אַחֲרָא מַמָּשׁ — namely, when you contemplate 3) **G-d's joy and the immense pleasure brought to Him through this faith, which actually subdues (iskafya) the *sitra achra*,** וְאִתְהַפֵּךְ חֲשׁוֹכָא לִנְהוֹרָא — **and** furthermore, 4) it eliminates the *sitra achra*, **transforming (is'hapcha) "darkness" to "light."**

As we have learned, *"there are two ways in which G-d derives pleasure on High. The first is from eliminating the sitra achra completely... and the second, when the sitra achra is subdued"* (chapter 27, p. 313). So in addition to feeling joy at how your faith has brought you personally closer to G-d, you can also feel joy at the immense pleasure you have elicited on High through subduing *and* eliminating the *sitra achra*.

The *Tanya* now clarifies what is meant (in point 4, above) by "darkness."

שֶׁהוּא חֹשֶׁךְ הַקְּלִיפּוֹת שֶׁבָּעוֹלָם הַזֶּה הַחוּמְרִי — **This "darkness" referring to the *kelipos* in this physical world,** הַמַּחֲשִׁיכִים וּמְכַסִּים עַל אוֹרוֹ יִתְבָּרֵךְ — **which dim and obscure the light of G-d,** עַד עֵת קֵץ כְּמוֹ שֶׁכָּתוּב קֵץ שָׂם לַחֹשֶׁךְ — **and will continue to do so until the time** comes for this "darkness" to **end, as the verse states, *"He sets an end to darkness"*** (*Job* 28:3), [דְּהַיְינוּ קֵץ הַיָּמִין] — **referring to the *"End of Days"*** (*Daniel*

הארץ ונגלה כבוד ה' וראו כל בשר יחדיו וכמ"ש לקמן]
ובפרט בארצות עו"ג שאוירם טמא ומלא קליפות וס"א
ואין שמחה לפניו ית' כאורה ושמחה ביתרון אור הבא
מן החשך דייקא. וז"ש ישמח ישראל בעושיו פי' שכל
מי שהוא מזרע ישראל יש לו לשמוח בשמחת ה' אשר
שש ושמח בדירתו בתחתוני' שהם בחי' עשיה גשמיית
ממש. וז"ש בעושיו לשון רבים שהוא עו"הז הגשמי

43A

שֶׁיַּעֲבִיר רוּחַ הַטּוּמְאָה מִן הָאָרֶץ (12:13), — when G-d, *"will remove the spirit of impurity from the earth"* (Zechariah 13:2), — וְנִגְלָה כְּבוֹד ה' וְרָאוּ כָל בָּשָׂר יַחְדָּיו — *"and the glory of G–d will be revealed and all flesh will see together* that G-d is speaking" (Isaiah 40:5), וּכְמוֹ שֶׁיִּתְבָּאֵר לְקַמָּן] — as will be explained below, chapters 36-37.

וּבִפְרָט בְּחוּץ לָאָרֶץ — And this transformation of "darkness" to "light" is **especially pronounced** outside the Land of Israel **in the Diaspora,** where the "darkness" is stronger, שֶׁאֲוִיר אֶרֶץ הָעַמִּים טָמֵא — **since the air-space of other nations** was decreed **impure** by the Sages (*Talmud, Shabbos* 15a-b), וּמָלֵא קְלִיפּוֹת וְסִטְרָא אָחֲרָא — **and is full of** *kelipos* **and** *sitra achra*.

PRACTICAL LESSONS

Think about how your faith and *mitzvah* observance brings G-d much pleasure and joy. Tune into that, and you will share some of G-d's unbounded joy.

וְאֵין שִׂמְחָה לְפָנָיו יִתְבָּרֵךְ כְּאוֹרָה וְשִׂמְחָה בְּיִתְרוֹן אוֹר הַבָּא מִן הַחֹשֶׁךְ דַּיְיקָא — **And there is no joy before G-d like the light and joy** of eliminating the *kelipos* **which, uniquely, has** *"the advantage of light (emerging) from darkness"* (*Ecclesiastes* 2:13).

The *Tanya* offers a scriptural hint to the idea that we can share some of G-d's joy.

וְזֶהוּ שֶׁכָּתוּב יִשְׂמַח יִשְׂרָאֵל בְּעוֹשָׂיו — **And this is** the meaning of the verse, *"Let Israel rejoice in his Maker (osav)"* (Psalms 149:2), פֵּירוּשׁ שֶׁכָּל מִי שֶׁהוּא מִזֶּרַע יִשְׂרָאֵל — **meaning that every one who is of the seed of Israel,** יֵשׁ לוֹ לִשְׂמוֹחַ בְּשִׂמְחַת ה' — **ought to be joyous over G-d's joy,** אֲשֶׁר שָׂשׂ וְשָׂמֵחַ בְּדִירָתוֹ בַּתַּחְתּוֹנִים — **since** G-d **rejoices greatly in making His home in the lowest of worlds,** שֶׁהֵם בְּחִינַת עֲשִׂיָּה גַשְׁמִיִּת מַמָּשׁ — **namely, in the real physical world (*asiyah*).**

In Hebrew, the word *osav* ("his Maker") has the same grammatical root as the word *asiyah*, ("action.") The verse suggests that it is physical action which makes a "home for G-d below," bringing a special joy to G-d. And this, in turn, ought to bring us joy.

וְזֶהוּ שֶׁכָּתוּב בְּעוֹשָׂיו לְשׁוֹן רַבִּים — **And this explains why *osav* is written in the plural,** (lit. "his makers"), שֶׁהוּא עוֹלָם הַזֶּה הַגַּשְׁמִי הַמָּלֵא קְלִיפּוֹת וְסִטְרָא אָחֲרָא — the plural

המלא קליפות וס"א שנק' רשות הרבים וטורי דפרודא
ואתהפכן לנהורא ונעשים רשות היחיד ליחודו ית'
באמונה זו:

פרק לד   והנה   מודעת זאת שהאבות הן הן
המרכבה שכל ימיהם לעולם

alluding to **this physical world** of apparent multiplicity, due to the fact that **it is filled
with *kelipos* and *sitra achra,*** which conceal the true unity of G-d with creation.

שֶׁנִּקְרָא רְשׁוּת הָרַבִּים — For this reason the zone of *kelipos* and *sitra achra* **is referred to** by the *Zohar* (3, 244a) as the **"public domain"** (***reshus ha-rabim***), literally
the "domain of the *many*," implying a force which conceals the *unity* of G-d.

וְטוּרֵי דְפְרוּדָא — **And** the zone of *kelipos* and *sitra achra* is also referred to by the
Zohar as ***"divided mountain peaks"*** (*Zohar* 1, 158a), since their perception is that of
separateness and division (see above, chapter 22, p. 254).

וְאִתְהַפְּכָן לִנְהוֹרָא וְנַעֲשִׂים רְשׁוּת הַיָּחִיד לְיִחוּדוֹ יִתְבָּרֵךְ בָּאֱמוּנָה זוֹ — **And through the
transformation of these** negative forces **to light, they are rendered into a "private
domain"** (literally "domain of the one"), **of this faith** in G-d's nondual oneness.

CHAPTER 34

YOU CAN BE A "TEMPLE" FOR G-D
SECTION ONE: A BRIEF HISTORY OF DIVINE REVELATION

14TH ADAR REGULAR | 30TH ADAR I LEAP

In chapter 33 we learned to meditate on the joy of our faith in G-d's nondual presence, making G-d "at home" here on earth.

But faith is experienced only in a certain elevated part of your mind and heart;
and it also fluctuates with time. How do you fill all of your consciousness and being
with G-d's nondual presence, all of the time? Chapter 34 will argue that Torah study,
particularly in the area of Jewish Law (*Halacha*), achieves this goal.

But to understand why that is the case, we must first trace the history of elevated
consciousness in Judaism, beginning with the Patriarchs, leading up to the event at
Sinai, and beyond.

שֶׁהָאָבוֹת הֵן הֵן הַמֶּרְכָּבָה, וְהִנֵּה מוּדַעַת זֹאת — **Now,** ***"This thing is known"*** (*Isaiah* 12:5),
— that ***"the Patriarchs were genuinely a 'chariot' to G-d"*** (*Genesis Rabah* 47:6; see
above, chapter 18, p. 212; chapter 23, p. 259), שֶׁכָּל יְמֵיהֶם לְעוֹלָם לֹא הִפְסִיקוּ אֲפִילוּ

לא הפסיקו אפי' שעה אחת מלקשר דעתם ונשמתם
לרבון העולמים בביטול הנ"ל ליחודו ית' ואחריהם כל
הנביאים כל אחד לפי מדרגת נשמתו והשגתו ומדרגת
משרע"ה היא העולה על כולנה שאמרו עליו שכינה
מדברת מתוך גרונו של משה ומעין זה זכו ישראל
במעמד הר סיני רק שלא יכלו לסבול כמאמר רז"ל
שעל כל דיבור פרחה נשמתן כו' שהוא ענין ביטול

שָׁעָה אַחַת מְלְקַשֵּׁר דַּעְתָּם וְנִשְׁמָתָם לְרִבּוֹן הָעוֹלָמִים — **that throughout all their days they did not interrupt, even for a moment, their mind and soul connection with the Master of the World,** בְּבִיטוּל הַנִּזְכָּר לְעֵיל לְיִחוּדוֹ יִתְבָּרֵךְ — **at the level of egoless** devotion **to G-d's** nondual **oneness, mentioned above** (in the previous chapter).

At its core, Judaism is the experience of Divine consciousness in the human mind. The Patriarchs achieved this consistently ("all their days"), which is why they are considered the founders of our faith.

וְאַחֲרֵיהֶם כָּל הַנְּבִיאִים — **And following** the elevated states of mind reached by the Patriarchs, were **all the prophets,** כָּל אֶחָד לְפִי מַדְרֵגַת נִשְׁמָתוֹ וְהַשָּׂגָתוֹ — **each one** reaching an elevated state of mind **corresponding to his soul's level and mental capacity.**

וּמַדְרֵגַת מֹשֶׁה רַבֵּינוּ עָלָיו הַשָּׁלוֹם הִיא הָעוֹלָה עַל כּוּלָּנָה — **And the level of Moshe, our teacher, of blessed memory, surpasses them all,** שֶׁאָמְרוּ עָלָיו שְׁכִינָה מְדַבֶּרֶת מִתּוֹךְ גְּרוֹנוֹ שֶׁל מֹשֶׁה — **so that they said of him,** *"The Shechinah (Divine Presence) speaks from the throat of Moshe"* (see *Zohar* 3, 232a), without any filter at all.

Moshe was able to render himself as a perfect, non-resistant channel, making no modification or stylistic change to the word of G-d that he received (see Rabbi Chaim Miller, *Rambam: Principles of Faith, Principles 6-7* (Brooklyn: Kol Menachem 2009) pp. 230-7).

The common experience of the Patriarchs, prophets and Moshe, which makes them all key figures in Judaism, was their heightened state of mind through the awareness of the Divine reality. But while the Patriarchs experienced this on a purely personal level, Moshe was able to share some of this elevated consciousness with others.

וּמֵעַין זֶה זָכוּ יִשְׂרָאֵל בְּמַעֲמַד הַר סִינַי — **And, standing at Mount Sinai, the Jewish people merited a glimmer of this** level of Mosaic prophecy.

But there is an inherent problem with "sharing" a higher state of mind. If you're not ready and prepared for it, you won't be able to cope with it. And that's why, at Sinai, the Jewish people couldn't contain the experience.

רַק שֶׁלֹּא יָכְלוּ לִסְבּוֹל — **But** the Israelites at Sinai **were unable to withstand it,** כְּמַאֲמַר רַבּוֹתֵינוּ זִכְרוֹנָם לִבְרָכָה שֶׁעַל כָּל דִּיבּוּר פָּרְחָה נִשְׁמָתָן כו' — **as our Sages of blessed**

במציאות הנ"ל לכן מיד אמר להם לעשות לו משכן
ובו קדשי הקדשים להשראת שכינתו שהוא גילוי
יחודו ית' כמ"ש לקמן ומשחרב ב"המק אין להקב"ה
בעולמו משכן ומכון לשבתו הוא יחודו ית' אלא ארבע
אמות של הלכה שהוא רצונו ית' וחכמתו המלובשים
בהלכות הערוכות לפנינו ולכן אחר שיעמיק האדם

memory taught, *"At every Divine utterance their souls flew away etc.,"* (*Talmud*, *Shabbos* 88b; *Exodus Rabah* 29:2), שֶׁהוּא עִנְיַן בִּיטוּל בְּמְצִיאוּת הַנִּזְכָּר לְעֵיל — this de-parture of the souls **being the complete extinguishing of individual identity, which was just described** in reference to Moshe.

The challenge then was: How do we make a glimmer of the experience of Moshe, and the elevated minds that preceded him (prophets and Patriarchs), available to the community of ordinary people?

לָכֵן מִיָּד אָמַר לָהֶם לַעֲשׂוֹת לוֹ מִשְׁכָּן — **Therefore,** since the Jewish people were unable to contain this level of reve-lation within their minds, **straight after** the event at Sinai, G-d **instructed them to make** another structure in which this revelation could be manifest, namely, **the Taberna-cle** (see Nachmanides to *Exodus* 35:1), וּבוֹ קָדְשֵׁי הַקֳּדָשִׁים לְהַשְׁרָאַת שְׁכִינָתוֹ — **inside which there would be a "Holy of Holies"** for the *Shechinah* **to rest,** שֶׁהוּא גִּילּוּי יְחוּדוֹ יִתְבָּרֵךְ — **namely, a revelation of G-d's** nondual **oneness on earth,** כְּמוֹ שֶׁיִּתְבָּאֵר לְקַמָּן — **as will be explained be-low** (chapter 53).

Since the people's minds couldn't contain the aware-ness of G-d's nondual presence, a physical structure was made instead to house that revelation.

PRACTICAL LESSONS

The destruction of the Temple didn't result in G-d's presence being banished from any earthly presence. Now it's available in our sacred texts, "the four cubits of Jewish Law."

1ST ADAR II LEAP

וּמִשֶּׁחָרַב בֵּית הַמִּקְדָּשׁ אֵין לְהַקָּדוֹשׁ בָּרוּךְ הוּא בְּעוֹלָמוֹ מִשְׁכָּן וּמָכוֹן לְשִׁבְתּוֹ הוּא יְחוּדוֹ יִתְבָּרֵךְ — **And since the Holy Temple was destroyed, the Blessed Holy One has had no dwelling place in His world for His oneness, no** *"firm place for His rest-ing"* (see *Exodus* 15:17), אֶלָּא אַרְבַּע אַמּוֹת שֶׁל הֲלָכָה — **other than** *"the four cubits of Jewish law (Halachah)"* (*Talmud, Brachos* 8a), שֶׁהוּא רְצוֹנוֹ יִתְבָּרֵךְ וְחָכְמָתוֹ הַמְלוּבָּשִׁים בַּהֲלָכוֹת הָעֲרוּכוֹת לְפָנֵינוּ — **since the laws** (*halachos*) **which have been codified for us, express G-d's** undiluted **will and wisdom** (see chapters 4-5).

The destruction of the Temple did not result in G-d's presence being banished from any earthly presence. Now it's available in "the four cubits of Jewish Law," in our sacred texts which delineate how *mitzvos* are to be observed.

מחשבתו בענין ביטול הנ"ל כפי יכלתו זאת ישיב אל
לבו כי מהיות קטן שכלי ושרש נשמתי מהכיל להיות
מרכבה ומשכן ליחודו ית' באמת לאמיתו מאחר דלית
מחשבה דילי תפיסא ומשגת בו ית' כלל וכלל שום
השגה בעולם ולא שמץ מנהו מהשגת האבו' והנביאים
אי לזאת אעשה לו משכן ומכון לשבתו הוא העסק
בת"ת כפי הפנאי שלי בקביעות עתים ביום ובלילה

While so much has changed throughout the Biblical Era, the Temple Era and the Rabbinic Era, it has always been possible to embrace the presence of G-d. In the Biblical Era, this was achieved through elevated, prophetic minds; in the Temple Era, through presence of the *Shechinah* in the Temple, and even in the Rabbinic Era, G-d's presence can be found in Jewish Law. The method has changed, but the core has remained the same.

SECTION TWO: HOW YOUR MIND CAN BECOME G-D'S TEMPLE

All this provides a lesson in your daily struggle to become aware of G-d's presence. Chapter 33 taught that a true "home" for G-d is made when your consciousness is filled with the nondual awareness of G-d's presence. But what do you do when your mind doesn't produce the desired effect?

The *Tanya* offers us a lesson from history: When the revelation at Sinai couldn't be contained, they built a Temple to contain it. So, if your mind can't contain the Divine, make yourself a "Temple." Immerse yourself in "the four cubits of Jewish Law!"

וְלָכֵן אַחַר שֶׁיַּעֲמִיק הָאָדָם מַחֲשַׁבְתּוֹ בְּעִנְיַן בִּיטוּל הַנִּזְכָּר לְעֵיל כְּפִי יְכָלְתּוֹ — **So, therefore, after you have probed with your mind, to the best of your ability, the above idea of extinguishing** your separate identity through awareness of G-d's nonduality (as we discussed in chapter 33), זֹאת יָשִׁיב אֶל לִבּוֹ — when your mind has reached its limit and you can't focus on it any more, **say the following to your heart.**

כִּי מֵהְיוֹת קָטָן שִׂכְלִי וְשֹׁרֶשׁ נִשְׁמָתִי מֵהָכִיל לִהְיוֹת מֶרְכָּבָה וּמִשְׁכָּן לְיִחוּדוֹ יִתְבָּרֵךְ בֶּאֱמֶת לַאֲמִיתוֹ — **"Being that my mind and soul-root are too inadequate to become a genuine and consistent 'chariot' or 'tabernacle' for G-d's** nondual **oneness,** מֵאַחַר דְּלֵית מַחֲשָׁבָה דִּילִי תְּפִיסָא וּמַשֶּׂגֶת בּוֹ יִתְבָּרֵךְ כְּלָל וּכְלָל שׁוּם הַשָּׂגָה בָּעוֹלָם — **"since my mind can't grasp or understand Him in any way at all, with any thought-system in the world,"** וְלֹא שֶׁמֶץ מִנְהוּ מֵהַשָּׂגַת הָאָבוֹת וְהַנְּבִיאִים — **"not even 'a tag end of'** (*Job* 4:12) **the grasp of the Patriarchs or the prophets,"** אִי לָזֹאת אֶעֱשֶׂה לוֹ מִשְׁכָּן — וּמָכוֹן לְשִׁבְתּוֹ הוּא הָעֵסֶק בְּתַלְמוּד תּוֹרָה — **"this being the case, I shall make** myself a 'chariot' for Him and a *'firm place for His resting'* in a different way, that *is* possible for me, **through immersion in Torah study"** כְּפִי הַפְּנַאי שֶׁלִּי בִּקְבִיעוּת עִתִּים בַּיּוֹם — וּבַלַּיְלָה — **"scheduling fixed times** for study, **day and night, according to the time available to me."**

כְּדַת הַנִּיתְנָה לְכָל אֶחָד וְאֶחָד בְּהִלְכוֹת תַּלְמוּד תּוֹרָה 43B
וּכְמַאֲמַר רַזַ"ל אֲפִילוּ פֶּרֶק אֶחָד שַׁחֲרִית כוּ' וּבְזֶה יְשַׂמַּח
לִבּוֹ וְיָגִיל וְיִתֵּן הוֹדָאָה עַל חֶלְקוֹ בְּשִׂמְחָה וּבְטוּב לֵבָב עַל
שֶׁזָּכָה לִהְיוֹת אוּשְׁפִּיזְכָן לִגְבוּרָה פְּעָמִים בְּכָל יוֹם כְּפִי
הָעֵת וְהַפְּנָאי שֶׁלּוֹ כְּמִסַת יָדוֹ אֲשֶׁר הִרְחִיב ה' לוֹ: וְאִם
יַרְחִיב ה' לוֹ עוֹד אֲזַי טְהוֹר יָדַיִם יוֹסִיף אוֹמֶץ וּמַחֲשָׁבָה

No matter how much you struggle to appreciate G-d's nondual oneness, you can always make yourself a "Temple" to the Divine presence through the study of sacred texts. In fact, even if you are not a Torah scholar, and have limited time and ability to study, this path is still open to you.

כְּדַת הַנִּיתְנָה לְכָל אֶחָד וְאֶחָד בְּהִלְכוֹת תַּלְמוּד תּוֹרָה — So long as you follow *"the de-cree that was issued"* (Esther 3:15) **to each and every person in the** *Laws of To-rah Study* (Shulchan Aruch, Yoreh Deah, chapter 246), concerning how much each person ought to study, וּכְמַאֲמַר רַבּוֹתֵינוּ זִכְרוֹנָם לִבְרָכָה אֲפִילוּ פֶּרֶק אֶחָד שַׁחֲרִית כוּ' — **and in accordance with the teaching of our Sages of blessed memory,** that if time and/or ability are lacking, then **it's enough, "***even if a person has repeated only a single chapter in the morning* **and only a single chapter in the evening"** (Talmud, Menachos 99b).

וּבְזֶה יְשַׂמַּח הוֹדָאָה עַל חֶלְקוֹ בְּשִׂמְחָה — **And this should cheer your heart,** וְיָגִיל וְיִתֵּן לִבּוֹ וּבְטוּב לֵבָב — **and cause you to rejoice, giving thanks for your lot** in life, **"with joy and with gladness of heart** (Deuteronomy 28:47), עַל שֶׁזָּכָה לִהְיוֹת אוּשְׁפִּיזְכָן לִגְבוּרָה פְּעָמִים בְּכָל יוֹם — **for meriting,** when you study "a single chapter" **twice a day, to be** *"a host for the Almighty"* (Talmud, Yoma 12a), like the Holy Temple, כְּפִי הָעֵת וְהַפְּנָאי שֶׁלּוֹ — **according to the limits of your available time,** כְּמִסַת יָדוֹ אֲשֶׁר הִרְחִיב ה' לוֹ — **and according to the opportunities lavished upon you by G-d.**

SECTION THREE: HOW TO BE A "TEMPLE" FOR G-D ALL DAY

15TH ADAR REGULAR | 2ND ADAR II LEAP

וְאִם יַרְחִיב ה' לוֹ עוֹד — **And** you should make a firm decision now that **if G-d will lavish upon you** the time and ability to study Torah in the future, אֲזַי טְהוֹר יָדַיִם יוֹסִיף אוֹמֶץ — then *"the clean of hands will increase in strength"* (Job 17:9), and you will study Torah as much as you possibly can.

But right now, when you *can't* study for more than a limited time each day, how do you make yourself a "Temple" for G-d the rest of the day?

First the *Tanya* answers:

וּמַחֲשָׁבָה טוֹבָה כוּ' — **And the Blessed Holy One** *"attaches* **a good thought** *to the deed"* (Talmud, Kiddushin 40a; see above chapter 16, p. 196).

טובה כו' וגם שאר היום כולו שעוסק במשא ומתן
יהיה מכון לשבתו ית' בנתינת הצדקה שיתן מיגיעו
שהיא ממדותיו של הקב"ה מה הוא רחום וכו' וכמ"ש
בתיקונים חסד דרועא ימינא ואף שאינו נותן אלא חומש

If you decide now that you will study Torah all day whenever you will have the opportunity in the future, that's enough for G-d to *"attach a good thought to the (planned) deed"* and consider it as if you did actually study all day.

But you're still lacking a tangible expression of your "Temple." So the *Tanya* now offers a second suggestion, how to maintain your personal "Temple" status *in actual deed.* (*Notes on Tanya*).

וְגַם שְׁאָר הַיּוֹם כּוּלוֹ שֶׁעוֹסֵק בְּמַשָּׂא וּמַתָּן — **And even the rest of the entire day when you will be occupied with business,** unable to study Torah, יִהְיֶה מָכוֹן לְשִׁבְתּוֹ יִתְבָּרֵךְ — **you can be a** *"firm place for His resting"* **for G-d,** בִּנְתִינַת הַצְּדָקָה שֶׁיִּתֵּן מִיגִיעוֹ — **through giving charity, which is given from your hard-earned income.**

Of all the practical *mitzvos*, why does charity render you the closest to a "Temple" for G-d?

שֶׁהִיא מִמְּדוֹתָיו שֶׁל הַקָּדוֹשׁ בָּרוּךְ הוּא — **Since** charity **is one of the character traits of G-d,** מַה הוּא רַחוּם וְכוּ' — *"Just as He is merciful* and kind, so you must be merciful and kind"* (*Jerusalem Talmud, Pe'ah* 1:1), וּכְמוֹ שֶׁכָּתוּב בַּתִּיקוּנִים חֶסֶד דְּרוֹעָא יְמִינָא — **and as stated in the** *Tikunei Zohar* (17a), *"Chesed (generosity) is the 'right hand' of G-d."*

Ultimately, it is Torah, and not *mitzvos*, that makes you a "Temple" for the Divine, (as we learned above, "the Blessed Holy One has had *no* dwelling place in His world for His nondual oneness... *other than* the four cubits of Jewish law"). But if we were to choose one *mitzvah* as a very close approximation, it would be charity, because in giving charity you are emulating one of the attributes of G-d.

Even charity, though, is not something you can do totally, with all your income. So how could this even be an approximate replacement for all day-Torah study (which renders you a constant "Temple" for the Divine)?

A CHASIDIC THOUGHT

While it may not feel the same, Torah study resembles the experience of the Divine in the Holy Temple. In the Temple, G-d was "contained," so to speak, in the Holy of Holies. In Torah study, G-d's will is "contained" in the final legal rulings, which represent His undiluted will.

הֲרֵי הַחוּמָשׁ מַעֲלֶה עִמּוֹ כָּל הָאַרְבַּע יָדוֹת לַה' לִהְיוֹת
מָכוֹן לְשִׁבְתּוֹ יִת' כַּנּוֹדָע מַאֲמַר רַזַ"ל שֶׁמִּצְוַת צְדָקָה
שְׁקוּלָה כְּנֶגֶד כָּל הַקָּרְבָּנוֹת וּבַקָּרְבָּנוֹת הָיָה כָּל הַחַי עוֹלֶה
לַה' עַ"י בְּהֵמָה אַחַת וְכָל הַצּוֹמֵחַ עַ"י עִשָּׂרוֹן סֹלֶת אֶחָד
בָּלוּל בַּשֶּׁמֶן כוּ' וּמִלְּבַד זֶה הֲרֵי בִּשְׁעַת הַתּוֹרָה וְהַתְּפִלָּה

וְאַף שֶׁאֵינוֹ נוֹתֵן אֶלָּא חוֹמֶשׁ — **And even though you only give one-fifth** of your income to charity, (the preferred amount in Jewish law—*Shulchan Aruch, Yoreh Deah,* 249:1), הֲרֵי הַחוּמָשׁ מַעֲלֶה עִמּוֹ כָּל הָאַרְבַּע יָדוֹת לַה', — **nevertheless, this fifth elevates the other four parts with it to G-d,** לִהְיוֹת מָכוֹן לְשִׁבְתּוֹ יִתְבָּרֵךְ — **so that they** all become *"a firm place for His resting"* for G-d.

You can't give all your money to charity, because then you wouldn't be able to live. The Sages mandate that you give at least one-tenth of your net income to charity, and that you should preferably give one-fifth. Here the *Tanya* suggests that by giving one-fifth, the other four-fifths are elevated, rendering all your money (and all your business endeav- ors carried out to earn that money) a kind of "Temple" for G-d.

But what's the logic here? How do the four-fifths of your income *that you keep for yourself* attain the spiritu- al level of charity?

The *Tanya* offers two explanations:

כַּנּוֹדָע מַאֲמַר רַבּוֹתֵינוּ זִכְרוֹנָם לִבְרָכָה — **One illustration of** the logic here is **from the well-known statement of our Sages of blessed memory,** שֶׁמִּצְוַת צְדָקָה שְׁקוּלָה כְּנֶגֶד כָּל הַקָּרְבָּנוֹת — **that the** *mitzvah* **of charity is equivalent to all the sacrifices** (*Talmud, Sukkah,* 49b), וּבַקָּרְבָּנוֹת הָיָה — **and in the case of the sacrifices,** the *Zohar* (3, 240b) teaches **that one single animal** offered as the *Korban Tamid* (Daily Offer- ing), **caused the entire Animal Kingdom to be elevated to G-d,** וְכָל הַצּוֹמֵחַ עַל יְדֵי עִשָּׂרוֹן סֹלֶת אֶחָד בָּלוּל בַּשֶּׁמֶן כוּ', — **and the entire Plant Kingdom** was elevated **through,** *"One-tenth (of an eifah) of fine flour mixed with oil"* (*Leviticus* 14:21).

PRACTICAL LESSONS

Resolve in your heart that if you will have the opportunity to study all day you will do so, and G-d will consider it as if you actually did.

Also by giving to charity you elevate yourself to be like a "Temple" to G-d.

There is, however, a problem with this logic. One single animal did not *literally* "cause the entire Animal Kingdom to be elevated to G-d." All the animals in the world did not suddenly attain the sacred status of sacrifices when one sacrifice was offered. (What the *Tanya* means to say is that all animals became *very slightly* easier to elevate in the future). Due to this problem, the *Tanya* now offers a sec- ond explanation for the elevation dynamic (*Toras Menachem, Hisva'aduyos,* vol. 36 (Brooklyn: Lahak, 2007), pp. 246-7).

עולה לה' כל מה שאכל ושתה ונהנה מארבע הידות
לבריאות גופו כמ"ש לקמן. והנה בכל פרטי מיני
שמחות הנפש הנ"ל אין מהן מניעה להיות נבזה בעיניו
נמאס ולב נשבר ורוח נמוכה בשעת השמחה ממש
מאחר כי היותו נבזה בעיניו וכו' הוא מצד הגוף ונפש
הבהמית והיותו בשמחה הוא מצד נפש האלהית וניצוץ

וּמִלְּבַד זֶה — **And besides this** first explanation, 'הֲרֵי בִּשְׁעַת הַתּוֹרָה וְהַתְּפִלָּה עוֹלֶה לַה — **when you study Torah and** כָּל מַה שֶׁאָכַל וְשָׁתָה וְנֶהֱנָה מֵאַרְבַּע הַיָּדוֹת לִבְרִיאוּת גוּפוֹ **pray, you elevate to G-d everything that you ate, drank and benefited from, for the sake of your body's health, from the** remaining **four-fifths,** which were not elevated directly through the one-fifth of your income given to charity, כְּמוֹ שֶׁיִּתְבָּאֵר לְקַמָּן — **as will be explained later on,** in chapter 37, pp. 414*ff.*

In this second explanation, a good degree of your income which you keep for yourself is *actually* elevated to G-d, because the food and drink that your metabolism burns when praying and studying Torah is really elevated to holiness.

SECTION FOUR: INTEGRATING NEGATIVE/POSITIVE EMOTIONS

3RD ADAR II LEAP

A long section of the *Tanya* dealing with emotional "maintenance," which began in chapter 26 now draws to a close. In chapters 26-28 we learned various methods to deal with depression, arising from both material and spiritual concerns. In chapters 29-30, we learned a number of meditations to humble the spirit so as to overcome emotional insensitivity to spirituality (*timtum ha-lev*). And in chapters 31, and 33-34 we have learned a number of meditations to lead us to joy.

PRACTICAL LESSONS

It's possible to harbor negative and positive emotions at the same time; the negative being a reflection of your Animal Soul and the positive, your G-dly soul.

The *Tanya* concludes by stressing that the negative and positive emotions we have explored are not mutually exclusive, and it is possible to integrate both into your heart at the same time.

וְהִנֵּה בְּכָל פְּרָטֵי מִינֵי שִׂמְחוֹת הַנֶּפֶשׁ הַנִּזְכָּרִים לְעֵיל — **Now** with all the above detailed meditations that bring **joy to the soul,** אֵין מֵהֶן מְנִיעָה לִהְיוֹת נִבְזֶה בְּעֵינָיו נִמְאָס וְלֵב נִשְׁבָּר וְרוּחַ נְמוּכָה — **there is nothing to stop you being "disgusting in your eyes, and repulsive"** (*Psalms* 15:4), brokenhearted and ego-deflated, בִּשְׁעַת הַשִּׂמְחָה מַמָּשׁ — *at the very same time* you are joyous.

מֵאַחַר כִּי הֱיוֹתוֹ נִבְזֶה בְּעֵינָיו וְכוּ' הוּא מִצַּד הַגּוּף וְנֶפֶשׁ הַבַּהֲמִית — **Because being "disgusting in your eyes etc.,"** is a re-

אֱלֹהוּת הַמְלוּבָּשׁ בָּהּ לְהַחֲיוֹתָהּ כַּנַּ"ל [בְּפֶ' ל"א] וְכָה"ג
אִיתָא בַּזֹהַר בְּכִיָּה תְּקִיעָא בְּלִבַּאי מִסְּטְרָא דָא וְחֶדְוָה
תְּקִיעָא בְּלִבַּאי מִסְּטְרָא דָא:

וַהֲיוֹתוֹ בְּשִׂמְחָה הוּא מִצַּד נֶפֶשׁ הָאֱלֹהִית וְנִיצוֹץ — flection of your body and Animal Soul,
אֱלֹהוּת הַמְלוּבָּשׁ בָּהּ לְהַחֲיוֹתָהּ — and being joyful is a reflection of your Divine Soul
and the spark of G-dliness enmeshed in it, energizing it, [בְּפֶרֶק ל"א] כַּנִּזְכָּר לְעֵיל
— as mentioned above in chapter 31.

Since you have two souls, it's possible for you to have two different feelings simultaneously. The *Tanya* now cites a precedent from the *Zohar* for this approach.

וּכְהַאי גַּוְנָא אִיתָא בַּזֹהַר — And it was in reference to such a case of experiencing opposite emotions simultaneously, that the *Zohar* states, that when Rabbi Shimon revealed wondrous secrets that explained the destruction of the Temple, his son Rabbi Elazar said that he felt, בְּכִיָּה תְּקִיעָא בְּלִבַּאי מִסְּטְרָא דָא — *"Tearfulness lodged into my heart on one side,"* as a result of the heightened awareness of the Temple's destruction, וְחֶדְוָה תְּקִיעָא בְּלִבַּאי מִסְּטְרָא דָא — *"and joy lodged into my heart on the other side,"* as a result of the revelation of wondrous new Torah insight (*Zohar* 3, 75a).

CHAPTER 35

YOUR STRUGGLE IS WORTH IT
SECTION ONE: THE PURPOSE OF ENDLESS STRUGGLE

16TH ADAR REGULAR | 4TH ADAR II LEAP

Throughout its pages, the *Tanya* has stressed that ordinary people, such as ourselves, should aim to master the external "garments" of thought, speech and action; we shouldn't be too concerned about shortcomings in our inner, emotional attachment to G-d. We're simply not capable of consistency in that area.

But all this might lead to the feeling that we've been given something of a "bad deal." Why *did* G-d create us with impaired abilities for a sustained emotional connection, and then ask us to worship Him with all our heart?

In the following chapters, the *Tanya* will address this issue, arguing that external mastery of the "garments" through practical *mitzvah* observance is of the utmost importance in G-d's eyes, perhaps even more so than inner feeling.

פרק לה והנה   לתוספת ביאור תיבת לעשותו
וגם להבין מעט מזעיר תכלית
בריאת הבינונים וירידת נשמותיהם לעו״הז להתלבש
44A בנפש הבהמית שמהקליפה וס״א מאחר שלא יוכלו
לשלחה כל ימיהם ולדחותה ממקומה מחלל השמאלי
שבלב שלא יעלו ממנה ההרהורים אל המוח כי מהותה

וְהִנֵּה לְתוֹסֶפֶת בֵּיאוּר תֵּיבַת לַעֲשׂוֹתוֹ — Let's clarify further the term **"so that you can do it"** in the verse, *"'For this (body of) commandment(s) which I am commanding you this day, is not concealed from you, nor is it far away…. Rather, the thing is very much within reach for you, in your mouth and in your heart, so that you can do it"* (*Deuteronomy* 30:14).

In chapter 17 we explained that the verse *"In your heart that you may do it,"* requires us to have a minimal level of love for G-d, sufficient only to bring about the practical observance of the *mitzvos*. The body of commandments are naturally "in your heart" but only sufficiently "that you can *do* it"; no more than that.

So we are left with the question: Why did G-d give (most of) us just enough love to do the *mitzvos,* and not more?

וְגַם לְהָבִין מְעַט מִזְעֵיר תַּכְלִית בְּרִיאַת הַבֵּינוֹנִים — And let's also try to get some minimal insight into the reason for which *beinonim* were created in this way?

As we learned above, a person does not really have free choice whether he will be able to surpass the level of *beinoni* (external mastery) and attain the level of *tzadik* (chapter 14, p. 172). Why has G-d created (most of) us in a way that we cannot rid ourselves of our evil?

וִירִידַת נִשְׁמוֹתֵיהֶם לְעוֹלָם הַזֶּה לְהִתְלַבֵּשׁ בְּנֶפֶשׁ הַבַּהֲמִית שֶׁמֵּהַקְּלִיפָּה וְסִטְרָא אַחֲרָא — And we need some insight into why the Divine **Souls** of *beinonim* came down into this world, to be enmeshed with an Animal Soul from *kelipah* and *sitra achra?*

G-d could have created us in a way that the Divine Soul and Animal Soul each had independent access to the body. But what He actually did was to enmesh the Divine Soul *in* the Animal Soul. The result is that if the Divine Soul wants to access the body, it must do so through the medium of the Animal Soul (see above p. 322).

But what's the point of that for a *beinoni*? The Divine Soul has to suffer enmeshment in the negative forces of *kelipah,* and for no apparent benefit since it will *never* influence the Animal Soul substantively. There seems nothing to be gained.

מֵאַחַר שֶׁלֹּא יוּכְלוּ לְשַׁלְּחָהּ כָּל יְמֵיהֶם — *Beinonim* seem doomed to an endless struggle since, **"they cannot send her (the Animal Soul) away all their days"** (see *Deuteronomy* 22:19), וְלִדְחוֹתָהּ מִמְּקוֹמָהּ מֵחָלָל הַשְּׂמָאלִי שֶׁבַּלֵּב — **and dislodge** the Animal Soul **from its place in the heart's left chamber,** שֶׁלֹּא יַעֲלוּ מִמֶּנָּה הַהִרְהוּרִים אֶל הַמּוֹחַ — **so that** the Animal Soul **shouldn't cause** inappropriate **thoughts to rise to the brain.**

וְעַצְמוּתָהּ שֶׁל נֶפֶשׁ הַבַּהֲמִית שֶׁמֵהַקְּלִיפָּה הִיא בְּתָקְפָּהּ
וּבִגְבוּרָתָהּ אֶצְלָם כְּתוֹלַדְתָּהּ רַק שֶׁלְּבוּשֶׁיהָ אֵינָם
מִתְלַבְּשִׁים בְּגוּפָם כַּנַּ"ל וְאִ"כּ לָמָּה זֶה יָרְדוּ נִשְׁמוֹתֵיהֶם
לְעוֹ"הַז לִיגַע לָרִיק חַ"ו לְהִלָּחֵם עִם הַיֵּצֶר כָּל יְמֵיהֶם וְלֹא
יֻכְלוּ לוֹ וּתְהִי זֹאת נֶחָמָתָם לְנַחֲמָם בְּכִפְלַיִם לְתוּשִׁיָּה
וְלִשְׂמֹחַ לִבָּם בַּה' הַשּׁוֹכֵן אִתָּם בְּתוֹךְ תּוֹרָתָם וַעֲבוֹדָתָם
וְהוּא בְּהַקְדִּים לְשׁוֹן הַיָּנוּקָא [בַּזֹּהַר פָּ' בָּלָק] עַל פָּסוּק
הֶחָכָם עֵינָיו בְּרֹאשׁוֹ וְכִי בְּאָן אֲתַר עֵינוֹי דְּבַר נָשׁ כוּ' אֶלָּא
קְרָא הֲכִי הוּא וַדַּאי דְּתָנָן לֹא יְהַךְ בַּר נָשׁ בְּגִלּוּיֵ' דְּרֵישָׁא

כִּי מַהוּתָהּ וְעַצְמוּתָהּ שֶׁל נֶפֶשׁ הַבַּהֲמִית שֶׁמֵּהַקְּלִיפָּה הִיא בְּתָקְפָּהּ וּבִגְבוּרָתָהּ אֶצְלָם — For, in the case of the *beinonim,* the deep core of the Animal Soul, from *kelipah,* remains as strong and as powerful as when they were born, כְּתוֹלַדְתָּהּ רַק שֶׁלְּבוּשֶׁיהָ אֵינָם מִתְלַבְּשִׁים בְּגוּפָם — and it is only that the Animal Soul's "garments" of impure thought, speech and action, **are unable to influence the body** due to the *beinoni's* self mastery, כַּנִּזְכָּר לְעֵיל — **as explained above,** in chapter 12, pp. 138*ff.*

וְאִם כֵּן — **And since this is the case,** we are left with a question, לָמָּה זֶה יָרְדוּ נִשְׁמוֹתֵיהֶם לָעוֹלָם הַזֶּה — **why do the souls** of *beinonim* **have to come down into this world** for a war which can't be won, לִיגַע לָרִיק חַס וְשָׁלוֹם לְהִלָּחֵם כָּל יְמֵיהֶם עִם הַיֵּצֶר וְלֹא יֻכְלוּ לוֹ — **for a futile struggle, G-d forbid, to battle in vain with the impulse to evil all their days, unable to prevail over it?**

SECTION TWO: THE ZOHAR ON THE POWER OF A MITZVAH

To address this concern, the *Tanya* will teach us a passage from the *Zohar.*

לְנַחֲמָם בְּכִפְלַיִם — *"Let this be their consolation,"* (see *Job* 21:2), וּתְהִי זֹאת נֶחָמָתָם לְתוּשִׁיָּה — **to offer them comfort with** *"a double measure of wisdom"* (*ibid.* 11:6), וְלִשְׂמֹחַ לִבָּם בַּה' הַשּׁוֹכֵן אִתָּם בְּתוֹךְ תּוֹרָתָם וַעֲבוֹדָתָם — **and to let their hearts rejoice with G-d, who is present with them in their Torah and worship.**

5TH ADAR II LEAP

וְהוּא בְּהַקְדִּים לְשׁוֹן הַיָּנוּקָא [בַּזֹּהַר פָּרָשַׁת בָּלָק] — **We first need to examine a teaching of the** inspired **child (yenukah) in the** *Zohar, Parshas Balak* (3, 187a), עַל פָּסוּק הֶחָכָם — **on the verse,** *"A wise man has* עֵינָיו בְּרֹאשׁוֹ *eyes in his head"* (*Ecclesiastes* 2:14).

וְכִי בְּאָן אֲתַר עֵינוֹי דְּבַר נָשׁ כוּ' — The *Zohar* asks, *"In what other place would a man's eyes be? Might they be in his body, or in his arm, such that (Shlomo) the 'wisest of all men' (who wrote this verse) is letting us know otherwise?"*

אֶלָּא קְרָא הֲכִי הוּא וַדַּאי — *"Rather,"* The *Zohar* answers, *"the verse definitely has the following implication."*

אַרְבַּע אַמּוֹת מַאי טַעְמָא דִּשְׁכִינְתָּא שַׁרְיָא עַל רֵישֵׁיהּ
וְכָל חָכָם עֵינוֹהִי וּמִילֵּי בְּרֵישֵׁיהּ אִינּוּן בְּהַהוּא דְּשַׁרְיָא
וְקַיְימָא עַל רֵישֵׁיהּ וְכַד עֵינוֹי תַּמָּן לִנְדַּע דְּהַהוּא נְהוֹרָא
דְּאַדְלִיק עַל רֵישֵׁיהּ אִצְטְרִיךְ לְמִשְׁחָא בְּגִין דְּגוּפָא דב"נ
אִיהוּ פְּתִילָה וּנְהוֹרָא אַדְלִיק לְעֵילָּא וּשְׁלֹמֹה מַלְכָּא צְוַח
וְאָמַר וְשֶׁמֶן עַל רֹאשְׁךָ אַל יֶחְסַר דְּהָא נְהוֹרָא דִּבְרֵאשׁוֹ
אִצְטְרִיךְ לְמִשְׁחָא וְאִינּוּן עוֹבָדָאן טָבָאן וע"ד הֶחָכָם עֵינָיו
בְּרֹאשׁוֹ עכ"ל. וְהִנֵּה בִּיאוּר מָשָׁל זֶה שֶׁהִמְשִׁיל אוֹר
הַשְּׁכִינָה לְאוֹר הַנֵּר שֶׁאֵינוֹ מֵאִיר וְנֶאֱחָז בִּפְתִילָה בְּלִי
שֶׁמֶן וְכָךְ אֵין הַשְּׁכִינָה שׁוֹרָה עַל גּוּף הָאָדָם שֶׁנִּמְשָׁל

אֲמֹות אַרְבַּע דְּרֵישָׁא בְּגִלּוּיָא נַשׁ בַּר יְהַךְ לֹא דִּתְנָן — *"We have learned that a person should not walk four cubits with his head uncovered"* (see *Talmud, Kidushin* 31a).

טַעְמָא מַאי — *"What's the reason?"*

רֵישֵׁיהּ עַל שַׁרְיָא שְׁכִינְתָּא דִּ — *"Because the Shechinah (Divine Presence) rests on his head,"* בְּרֵישֵׁיהּ וּמִילֵּי עֵינוֹהִי חָכָם וְכָל — *"and the eyes and words of every wise man are, 'on his head,'"* רֵישֵׁיהּ עַל וְקַיְימָא דְּשַׁרְיָא בְּהַהוּא אִינּוּן — *"meaning to say, (he is focused) on that which rests and remains on his head,"* i.e., upon the *Shechinah.*

תַּמָּן עֵינוֹי וְכַד — *"And when his eyes are there,"* and he's conscious of the *Shechinah's* presence, לְמִשְׁחָא אִצְטְרִיךְ רֵישֵׁיהּ עַל דְּאַדְלִיק דְּהַהוּא נְהוֹרָא לִנְדַּע — *"he will be aware that the flame lit above his head is in need of oil,"* פְּתִילָה אִיהוּ נַשׁ דְּבַר דְּגוּפָא בְּגִין — *that the flame lit above his head is in need of oil,"* לְעֵילָּא אַדְלִיק וּנְהוֹרָא — *"since a person's body is a wick, with a flame lit above it."*

יֶחְסַר אַל רֹאשְׁךָ עַל וְשֶׁמֶן וְאָמַר צְוַח מַלְכָּא וּשְׁלֹמֹה — *"And King Shlomo shouts out to us, 'Don't allow oil to be lacking from your head!"* (*Ecclesiastes* 9:8), נְהוֹרָא דְּהָא — דִּבְרֵאשׁוֹ לְמִשְׁחָא אִצְטְרִיךְ — *"because the flame on his head needs oil."*

טָבָאן עוֹבָדָאן וְאִינּוּן — And the *"oil" "refers to good deeds"* done by the person.

בְּרֹאשׁוֹ עֵינָיו הֶחָכָם דָּא וְעַל — *"And it was concerning this (concept that the verse says), 'A wise man has eyes in his head.'"*

לִשׁוֹנוֹ כָּאן עַד — **End of citation** from the *Zohar.*

17TH ADAR REGULAR | 6TH ADAR II LEAP

The *Tanya* now begins to unpackage the lesson here.

הַנֵּר לְאוֹר הַשְּׁכִינָה אוֹר שֶׁהִמְשִׁיל — Let's clarify this analogy, זֶה מָשָׁל בִּיאוּר וְהִנֵּה — **Let's clarify this analogy,** where the light of the *Shechinah* is compared to the light of a candle, מֵאִיר שֶׁאֵינוֹ — which won't shine and grasp its wick without oil, שֶׁמֶן בְּלִי בִּפְתִילָה וְנֶאֱחָז — **which won't shine and grasp its wick without oil.**

שֶׁנִּמְשָׁל הָאָדָם גּוּף עַל שׁוֹרָה הַשְּׁכִינָה אֵין — In the same way, the *Zohar* explains, לִפְתִילָה — the *Shechinah* won't rest on a person's body, which is compared to a

לפתילה אלא ע"י מעשים טובים דווקא ולא די לו
בנשמתו שהיא חלק אלוה ממעל להיות היא כשמן
לפתיל' מבואר ומובן לכל משכיל כי הנה נשמת האדם
אפי' הוא צדיק גמור עובד ה' ביראה ואהבה בתענוגי'
אעפ"כ אינה בטילה במציאות לגמרי ליבטל וליכלל
באור ה' ממש להיות לאחדים ומיוחדים ביחוד גמור רק
הוא דבר בפני עצמו ירא ה' ואוהבו. משא"כ המצות
ומעשים טובים שהן רצונו ית' ורצונו ית' הוא מקור

44B

"wick," אֶלָא עַל יְדֵי מַעֲשִׂים טוֹבִים דַּוְקָא — except through "good deeds" (mitzvos), exclusively.

וְלֹא דַי לוֹ בְּנִשְׁמָתוֹ שֶׁהִיא חֵלֶק אֱלוֹהַּ מִמַּעַל לִהְיוֹת הִיא כְּשֶׁמֶן לַפְּתִילָה — The implication here is that, **the soul alone,** despite the fact **that it is** *"a piece of G-d above"* (Job 31:2; above p. 44), **does not suffice to provide "oil" for the "wick,"** *i.e.,* to cause the *Shechinah* to rest on the body.

But if the soul is actually a "piece of G-d," shouldn't that be enough to cause the *Shechinah* to rest on the body?

SECTION THREE: WHY MITZVOS MAKE THE SHECHINAH SHINE

מְבוֹאָר וּמוּבָן לְכָל מַשְׂכִּיל — The answer will be **clarified and explained for any intelligent person,** in the following lines.

אֲפִילוּ הוּא צַדִּיק גָּמוּר עוֹבֵד ה' בְּיִרְאָה — כִּי הִנֵּה נִשְׁמַת הָאָדָם — **Now a person's soul,** וְאַהֲבָה בַּתַּעֲנוּגִים — **even if** that person **is a complete** *tzadik,* **worshiping G-d with reverence and** *"pleasurable love"* (Song 7:7; see above p. 174), אַף עַל פִּי כֵן אֵינָהּ — **nevertheless,** that soul **still does not lose its separate identity,** בְּטֵילָה בִּמְצִיאוּת לְגַמְרֵי — לִיבָּטֵל וְלִיכָּלֵל בְּאוֹר ה' מַמָּשׁ — which would enable it **to be extinguished and literally absorbed in G-d's light,** לִהְיוֹת לַאֲחָדִים וּמְיוּחָדִים בְּיִחוּד גָּמוּר — **and to merge completely** with G-d **in absolute unity.**

רַק הוּא דָבָר בִּפְנֵי עַצְמוֹ — יְרֵא ה' וְאוֹהֲבוֹ — **Rather,** the soul retains **its separate identity,** — **as one who is reverent** *of* **G-d, and a lover** *of* **Him,** but not one *with* Him.

Ultimately, the soul has a level of self-consciousness, which blocks it from becoming completely one with G-d.

To grasp the truth that nothing really exists outside G-d, you have to stop existing yourself. Otherwise your very being will contradict the truth you are trying to grasp.

מַה שֶּׁאֵין כֵּן הַמִּצְוֹת וּמַעֲשִׂים טוֹבִים — **But this is not the case with** *mitzvos* **and "good deeds"** שֶׁהֵן רְצוֹנוֹ יִתְבָּרֵךְ — **which are the will of G-d** *Himself, i.e.,* **totally merged** with Him.

החיים לכל העולמות והברואים שיורד אליהם על ידי
צמצומים רבים והסתר פנים של רצון העליון ב"ה
וירידת המדרגות עד שיוכלו להתהוות ולהבראות יש
מאין ודבר נפרד בפני עצמו ולא יבטלו במציאות כנ"ל
משא"כ המצות שהן פנימית רצונו ית' ואין שם הסתר
פנים כלל אין החיות שבהם דבר נפרד בפני עצמו כלל
אלא הוא מיוחד ונכלל ברצונו ית' והיו לאחדים ממש
ביחוד גמור. והנה ענין השראת השכינה הוא גילוי
אלהותו ית' ואור א"ס ב"ה באיזה דבר והיינו לומר
שאותו דבר נכלל באור ה' ובטל לו במציאות לגמרי

To clarify why any created entity (even a soul) can't receive the *Shechinah*, the *Tanya* will recap a lesson we learned earlier.

וּרְצוֹנוֹ יִתְבָּרֵךְ הוּא מְקוֹר הַחַיִּים לְכָל הָעוֹלָמוֹת וְהַבְּרוּאִים — **Now G-d's will is the source of life for all the worlds and creations,** שֶׁיּוֹרֵד אֲלֵיהֶם עַל יְדֵי צִמְצוּמִים רַבִּים — **and** this source energy only **passes down to** the worlds and creations **through many "diminishments" (tzimtzumim),** וְהֶסְתֵּר פָּנִים שֶׁל רָצוֹן הָעֶלְיוֹן בָּרוּךְ הוּא — **and the "Hiding of G-d's face"** (see *Deuteronomy* 31:17-18), so as to conceal **the supernal will of G-d,** וִירִידַת הַמַּדְרֵגוֹת עַד שֶׁיּוּכְלוּ לְהִתְהַוּוֹת וּלְהִבָּרְאוֹת יֵשׁ מֵאַיִן וְדָבָר נִפְרָד בִּפְנֵי עַצְמוֹ — **and this multiple downgrading of G-d's light was necessary to make possible the existence and creation of "something from nothing,"** the consciousness of **a separate entity,** וְלֹא יְבָטְלוּ בִּמְצִיאוּת — **that would not** be overwhelmed by G-d's light so much that it would **lose its separate sense of being,** כַּנִּזְכָּר לְעֵיל — **as described above,** (see chapter 21, p. 244).

מַה שֶּׁאֵין כֵּן הַמִּצְוֹת — **But this** diminishment of light **doesn't happen with the** *mitzvos,* שֶׁהֵן פְּנִימִית רְצוֹנוֹ יִתְבָּרֵךְ — **which are the inner,** undiluted **will of G-d,** וְאֵין שָׁם הֶסְתֵּר פָּנִים כְּלָל — **and which do not suffer in any way from the "Hiding of G-d's face,"** אֵין הַחַיּוּת שֶׁבָּהֶם דָּבָר נִפְרָד בִּפְנֵי עַצְמוֹ כְּלָל — **as a result, their energy is not separate** from G-d **at all,** אֶלָּא הוּא מְיוּחָד וְנִכְלָל בִּרְצוֹנוֹ יִתְבָּרֵךְ — **rather they are merged with, and absorbed in, the will of G-d,** וְהָיוּ לַאֲחָדִים מַמָּשׁ בְּיִחוּד גָּמוּר — **and they are totally united and seamlessly merged** with His will.

The loss of separate identity is a crucial point here, as the *Shechinah* cannot be present if another identity "blocks" the way.

וְהִנֵּה עִנְיַן הַשְׁרָאַת הַשְּׁכִינָה — **Now the meaning of the *Shechinah* "resting" on something,** הוּא גִּילּוּי אֱלֹהוּתוֹ יִתְבָּרֵךְ וְאוֹר אֵין סוֹף בָּרוּךְ הוּא בְּאֵיזֶה דָּבָר — **is that G-dliness and the Blessed Infinite Light is** openly **manifest in that thing,** וְהַיְינוּ לוֹמַר — **which means that** שֶׁאוֹתוֹ דָּבָר נִכְלָל בְּאוֹר ה' — **the thing is absorbed in G-d's light,**

שאז הוא ששורה ומתגלה בו ה' אחד אבל כל מה שלא
בטל אליו במציאות לגמרי אין אור ה' שורה ומתגלה
בו ואף צדיק גמור שמתדבק בו באהבה רבה הרי לית
מחשבה תפיסא ביה כלל באמת כי אמיתת ה' אלהים
אמת הוא יחודו ואחדותו שהוא לבדו הוא ואפס בלעדו
ממש. וא"כ זה האוהב שהוא יש ולא אפס לית מחשבה
דיליה תפיסא ביה כלל ואין אור ה' שורה ומתגלה בו
אלא ע"י קיום המצות שהן רצונו וחכמתו ית' ממש

וּבָטֵל לוֹ בִּמְצִיאוּת לְגַמְרֵי — **and has completely lost its separate identity in** the presence of that light, שֶׁאָז הוּא שֶׁשּׁוֹרָה וּמִתְגַּלֶּה בּוֹ ה' אֶחָד — **because it's** only **then that** we can say that the reality of **"One G-d," "rests"** and is manifest in that thing, since if the thing retains its identity, we have "two" and not "one."

אֲבָל כָּל מַה שֶּׁלֹּא בָּטֵל אֵלָיו בִּמְצִיאוּת לְגַמְרֵי — **But so long as the thing hasn't lost its identity completely in** G-d, אֵין אוֹר ה' שׁוֹרֶה וּמִתְגַּלֶּה בּוֹ — **the light of "One G-d," the** Shechinah, **won't rest and be revealed there.**

While at worship, the tzadik may not be self-aware, and he may become utterly immersed in thoughts of G-d. But the fact that he doesn't feel his identity, doesn't mean he's lost it, and this remains as a blockage for the Shechinah.

In fact, even the tzadik's thoughts about G-d are mortal conceptions which cannot grasp the truth of the Divine reality.

וְאַף צַדִּיק גָּמוּר שֶׁמִּתְדַּבֵּק בּוֹ בְּאַהֲבָה רַבָּה — **And even a complete tzadik who is bound to G-d with "great love"** (see p. 117) cannot be a vehicle for the light of "One G-d" to be revealed, הֲרֵי לֵית מַחֲשָׁבָה תְּפִיסָא בֵּיהּ כְּלָל בֶּאֱמֶת — **because in truth, "no thought can grasp Him at all"** (Tikunei Zohar 17a), כִּי אֲמִיתַּת ה' אֱלֹהִים אֱמֶת הוּא **— since** this thought exists in a separate being, and **the reality of "G-d, the true G-d"** (Jeremiah 10:10) **is** nondual oneness, that there are no separate beings, שֶׁהוּא לְבַדּוֹ הוּא — **that "He is the only one"** (Liturgy, High Holidays), וְאֶפֶס בִּלְעָדוֹ מַמָּשׁ — **and there's absolutely nothing other than Him.**

Separate consciousness is an ineffective tool to grasp the reality that there is no separate existence. It's rather like proving that you don't exist while looking in the mirror. The logic might make sense in your mind, but you know you're really here.

וְאִם כֵּן זֶה הָאוֹהֵב שֶׁהוּא יֵשׁ — **And if this is the case, then a person who loves** G-d, וְלֹא אֶפֶס — **since he's a separate entity, and not "nothing,"** לֵית מַחֲשָׁבָה דִּילֵיהּ תְּפִיסָא בֵּיהּ כְּלָל — amid such a consciousness of separateness, **"no thought (of his) can grasp Him at all,"** וְאֵין אוֹר ה' שׁוֹרֶה וּמִתְגַּלֶּה בּוֹ — **and the light of G-d won't rest and be revealed in him** through thinking or feeling about G-d.

אֶלָּא עַל יְדֵי קִיּוּם הַמִּצְוֹת — **Rather** G-d's presence will rest **through observing the** mitzvos, שֶׁהֵן רְצוֹנוֹ וְחָכְמָתוֹ יִתְבָּרֵךְ מַמָּשׁ — **which are the** undiluted **will and wisdom**

בְּלִי שׁוּם הֶסְתֵּר פָּנִים*
וְהִנֵּה כְּשֶׁהָאָדָם עוֹסֵק
בַּתּוֹרָה אֲזַי נִשְׁמָתוֹ שֶׁהִיא
נַפְשׁוֹ הָאֱלֹהִית עִם שְׁנֵי
לְבוּשֶׁיהָ הַפְּנִימִים לְבַדָּם
שֶׁהֵם כֹּחַ הַדִּבּוּר וּמַחֲשָׁבָה

הגהה

(וְכַאֲשֶׁר שָׁמַעְתִּי מִמּוֹרִי ע"ה פֵּי'
וְטַעַם לְמַ"ש בְּעֵ"ח שָׁאוֹר א"ס
ב"ה אֵינוֹ מִתְיַחֵד אֲפִי' בְּעוֹלָם
הָאֲצִילוּת אֶלָּא ע"י הִתְלַבְּשׁוּתוֹ
תְּחִלָּה בִּסְפִי' חָכְמָה וְהַיְנוּ מִשּׁוּם
שָׁא"ס ב"ה הוּא אֶחָד הָאֱמֶת

בְּלִי שׁוּם הֶסְתֵּר פָּנִים — **without any** *"Hiding of G-d's face,"* as we will discuss **of G-d,** further below.*

19TH ADAR REGULAR

Torah study is, of course a *mitzvah.* But the *Zohar* stressed that "good deeds" (i.e., practical *mitzvos*) are necessary in order for the *Shechinah* to rest on your body. The *Tanya* will clarify now why this is the case.

וְהִנֵּה כְּשֶׁהָאָדָם עוֹסֵק בַּתּוֹרָה — **Now, when a person is immersed in Torah study,** אֲזַי נִשְׁמָתוֹ שֶׁהִיא נַפְשׁוֹ הָאֱלֹהִית עִם שְׁנֵי לְבוּשֶׁיהָ — **then his soul, namely, his Divine Soul,** הַפְּנִימִים לְבַדָּם שֶׁהֵם כֹּחַ הַדִּבּוּר וּמַחֲשָׁבָה — **along with just its two inner "garments,"**

---

*הַגָּהָה — **NOTE.** The *Tanya* stated that in *"a separate entity,"* such as the soul, *"the light of G-d won't rest and be revealed."* In the note, we will explore the Kabbalistic sources for this teaching.

וְכַאֲשֶׁר שָׁמַעְתִּי מִמּוֹרִי עָלָיו הַשָּׁלוֹם — This follows **what I heard from my teacher of blessed memory,** the Maggid of Mezritch, פֵּירוּשׁ וְטַעַם לְמַה שֶׁכָּתוּב בְּעֵץ חַיִּים — who offered **an explanation and reasoning of what is written in *Etz Chaim*** (47:3), שָׁאוֹר אֵין סוֹף בָּרוּךְ הוּא אֵינוֹ מִתְיַחֵד אֲפִילוּ בְּעוֹלָם הָאֲצִילוּת — **that the Blessed Infinite Light will not merge even with the** highest, G-dly **World of *Atzilus,*** אֶלָּא עַל יְדֵי הִתְלַבְּשׁוּתוֹ תְּחִלָּה בִּסְפִירַת חָכְמָה — **except by first becoming enmeshed with the *sefirah* of chochmah,** and only afterwards will the Blessed Infinite Light spread to the other *sefiros* of *Atzilus.*

G-d's Infinite Light is incompatible even with the World of *Atzilus,* which contains only Divine attributes. But how could the Divine be incompatible with the Divine?

Because, ultimately, even though the attributes (*sefiros*) of *Atzilus* are G-dly, they do have a defined identity: G-d's kindness, G-d's discipline, *etc.* And that identity acts as a blockage for the Blessed Infinite Light, which is devoid of any limitation.

וְהַיְנוּ מִשּׁוּם שֶׁאֵין סוֹף בָּרוּךְ הוּא הוּא אֶחָד הָאֱמֶת — **This is because the Blessed Infinite One is the** only **true One,** שֶׁהוּא לְבַדּוֹ הוּא וְאֵין זוּלָתוֹ — and *"He is the only one"* (*Liturgy, High Holidays*), **and there is no other besides Him,** an energy which is incompatible with the "defined" G-dliness of *Atzilus.*

The exception to this is *chochmah*, since *chochmah's* identity is not centered around itself, and it is predominantly an inquisitiveness and openness to the "other"

45A נכללות באור ה' א"ס ב"ה
ומיוחדות בו ביחוד גמור
והיא השראת השכינה על
נפשו האלהית כמארז"ל שאפי' אחד שיושב ועוסק
בתורה שכינה עמו. אך כדי להמשיך אור והארת
השכינה גם על גופו ונפשו הבהמית שהיא החיונית
המלובשת בגופו ממש צריך לקיים מצות מעשיות
הנעשים ע"י הגוף ממש שאז כח הגוף ממש שבעשיה
זו נכלל באור ה' ורצונו ומיוחד בו ביחוד גמור והוא

שהוא לבדו הוא ואין זולתו וזו היא
מדרגת החכמה וכו'):

---

the powers of speech and thought, **נִכְלָלוֹת בְּאוֹר ה' אֵין סוֹף בָּרוּךְ הוּא** — are absorbed into the Infinite Light of G-d, **וּמְיוּחָדוֹת בּוֹ בְּיִחוּד גָּמוּר** — and merged with it seamlessly.

וְהִיא הַשְׁרָאַת הַשְׁכִינָה עַל נַפְשׁוֹ הָאֱלֹהִית — And this is the meaning of the term "resting of the *Shechinah*" on his Divine Soul.

שֶׁאֲפִילוּ — As our Sages of blessed memory taught, **כְּמַאֲמַר רַבּוֹתֵינוּ זִכְרוֹנָם לִבְרָכָה** — **אֶחָד שֶׁיּוֹשֵׁב וְעוֹסֵק בַּתּוֹרָה שְׁכִינָה עִמּוֹ** — that *"even if one person sits and is immersed in Torah, the Shechinah is with him"* (*Talmud, Brachos* 6a).

Torah study, however, only draws down the *Shechinah* upon the Divine Soul, and its two inner "garments" of thought and speech. It doesn't affect the "action" garment of the Divine Soul, or any of the Animal Soul's "garments," nor the body.

אַךְ כְּדֵי לְהַמְשִׁיךְ אוֹר וְהֶאָרַת הַשְׁכִינָה גַּם עַל גּוּפוֹ וְנַפְשׁוֹ הַבַּהֲמִית — But in order to pull the light and glimmer of the *Shechinah* upon your body and Animal Soul too, **שֶׁהִיא הַחִיּוּנִית הַמְלוּבֶּשֶׁת בְּגוּפוֹ מַמָּשׁ** — the "Animal Soul" being the energizing soul, which actually interacts with your body, **צָרִיךְ לְקַיֵּים מִצְוֹת מַעֲשִׂיּוֹת הַנַּעֲשׂוֹת עַל יְדֵי** — **הַגּוּף מַמָּשׁ** — to do this you need to observe practical *mitzvos*, which are actually carried out using the body, **שֶׁאָז כֹּחַ הַגּוּף מַמָּשׁ שֶׁבַּעֲשִׂיָּה זוֹ נִכְלָל בְּאוֹר ה' וּרְצוֹנוֹ** — because then your body's actual energy, invested in the *mitzvah* act, is absorbed

---

(see chapter 3, p. 58). Since it does not have a self-identity it is open to receive that which is above, and can act as a portal for the Blessed Infinite Light to enter.

וְזוֹ הִיא מַדְרֵגַת הַחָכְמָה וְכוּ' — And this consciousness represents the level of *chochmah, etc.*

This sheds some light on why the *tzadik's* soul, even though it is a "piece of G-d," can't receive the *Shechinah*. If even the Divine attributes themselves can't receive the undistilled light of G-d, (because, at some level, those attributes are entities to themselves), certainly, then, the soul, which really is a separate entity found in your body, can't act as a natural recipient for the *Shechinah*.

לְבוּשׁ הַשְּׁלִישִׁי שֶׁל נֶפֶשׁ הָאֱלֹהִית וַאֲזַי גַּם כֹּחַ נֶפֶשׁ
הַחִיּוּנִית שֶׁבְּגוּפוֹ מַמָּשׁ שֶׁמִּקְּלִיפַּת נוֹגַהּ נִתְהַפֵּךְ מֵרַע
לְטוֹב וְנִכְלָל מַמָּשׁ בִּקְדוּשָׁה כְּנֶפֶשׁ הָאֱלֹהִית מַמָּשׁ
מֵאַחַר שֶׁהוּא הַפּוֹעֵל וְעוֹשֶׂה מַעֲשֵׂה הַמִּצְוָה
שֶׁבִּלְעָדוֹ לֹא הָיְתָה נֶפֶשׁ הָאֱלֹהִית פּוֹעֶלֶת בַּגּוּף כְּלָל כִּי
הִיא רוּחָנִיִּית וְהַגּוּף גַּשְׁמִי וְחוּמְרִי וְהַמְּמֻצָּע בֵּינֵיהֶם
הִיא נֶפֶשׁ הַחִיּוּנִית הַבַּהֲמִית הַמְּלוּבֶּשֶׁת בְּדַם הָאָדָם

in G-d's light and His will, וּמְיוּחָד בּוֹ בְּיִחוּד גָּמוּר — and is merged with G-d's will seamlessly.

וְהוּא לְבוּשׁ הַשְּׁלִישִׁי שֶׁל נֶפֶשׁ הָאֱלֹהִית — And the soul power which motivates the observance of the practical mitzvos is the third "garment" of the Divine Soul, the garment of "action." So by observing a practical commandment you bring the Shechinah upon this third "garment," too.

וַאֲזַי גַּם כֹּחַ נֶפֶשׁ הַחִיּוּנִית שֶׁבְּגוּפוֹ מַמָּשׁ שֶׁמִּקְּלִיפַּת נוֹגַהּ — And then, when the Divine Soul's "garment" of action powers a practical mitzvah, the energizing Animal Soul from kelipas nogah, which interacts directly with the body, נִתְהַפֵּךְ מֵרַע לְטוֹב — is temporarily transformed from evil to good, וְנִכְלָל מַמָּשׁ בִּקְדוּשָׁה כְּנֶפֶשׁ הָאֱלֹהִית מַמָּשׁ — and is actually absorbed into holiness, like the Divine Soul itself.

This answers the questions posed earlier in the chapter: Why was it necessary to enmesh the Divine Soul into the Animal Soul? Why couldn't the Divine Soul have been given its own independent access to the body?

While the Animal Soul will never really change in its deep core, at the moment when a practical mitzvah is observed, the enmeshment relationship forces the Divine Soul to partner with the Animal Soul in order to access the body. And the result is: the Shechinah rests on the Animal Soul too.

מֵאַחַר שֶׁהוּא הַפּוֹעֵל וְעוֹשֶׂה מַעֲשֵׂה הַמִּצְוָה — The Shechinah rests on the Animal Soul because it is the one that caused the mitzvah deed, and performed it, שֶׁבִּלְעָדוֹ לֹא הָיְתָה נֶפֶשׁ הָאֱלֹהִית פּוֹעֶלֶת בַּגּוּף כְּלָל — and without the Animal soul, the Divine Soul would have had no influence on the body at all.

Since the Animal Soul was a crucial "player" in making the mitzvah take place, it acts as a medium through which the Shechinah's presence can shine.

כִּי הִיא רוּחָנִיִּית וְהַגּוּף גַּשְׁמִי וְחוּמְרִי — For the Divine Soul is purely spiritual, and the body, only physical and material, וְהַמְּמֻצָּע בֵּינֵיהֶם הִיא נֶפֶשׁ הַחִיּוּנִית הַבַּהֲמִית — and the intermediary between them is the energizing Animal Soul, הַמְּלוּבֶּשֶׁת בְּדַם — which interacts with the blood found in a person's heart הָאָדָם שֶׁבְּלִבּוֹ וְכָל הַגּוּף — and the rest of his body.

The Animal Soul provides a crucial function in enabling the Divine Soul to communicate with the body. That's why the Shechinah is able to rest on the Animal Soul.

שבלבו וכל הגוף ואף שמהותה ועצמותה של נפש
הבהמית שבלבו שהן מדותיה הרעים עדיין לא נכללו
בקדושה מ"מ מאחר דאתכפין לקדושה ובע"כ עונין
אמן ומסכימין ומתרצין לעשיית המצוה ע"י התגברות
נפשו האלהית שבמוח ששליט על הלב והן בשעה זו
בבחי' גלות ושינה כנ"ל ולכך אין זו מניעה מהשראת

SECTION FOUR: HOW CAN THE SHECHINAH REST ON KELIPAH?

20TH ADAR REGULAR

The conclusion we have come to here is striking. *Without a mitzvah,* even a *tzadik* can't cause the *Shechinah* to rest on his Divine Soul (even though that soul is a "piece of G-d"), because, ultimately, the Divine Soul has its own separate identity which blocks the *Shechinah.* Yet *with a mitzvah,* the *Shechinah* will even rest on the Animal Soul and the body, which are from *kelipah!*

This leaves us with an obvious question: Why does the *kelipah* of the Animal Soul, an energy which conceals and opposes G-d's unity, not cause the *Shechinah's* presence to be blocked?

וְאַף שֶׁמַּהוּתָהּ וְעַצְמוּתָהּ שֶׁל נֶפֶשׁ הַבַּהֲמִית שֶׁבְּלִבּוֹ שֶׁהֵן מִדּוֹתֶיהָ הָרָעוֹת עֲדַיִן לֹא נִכְלְלוּ בִּקְדֻשָּׁה — And even though the deep core of the Animal Soul found in your heart, (namely, its negative traits), still have not been absorbed into holiness and they remain a force of *kelipah,* מִכָּל מָקוֹם מֵאַחַר דְּאִתְכַּפְיָין לִקְדֻשָּׁה — nevertheless, it's still possible for the *Shechinah* to rest on the Animal Soul and its powers **since they have been *coerced* into a holy activity.**

וּבְעַל כָּרְחָן עוֹנִין אָמֵן — And, against their will, the powers of the Animal Soul voice their agreement, וּמַסְכִּימִין וּמִתְרַצִּין לַעֲשִׂיַּת הַמִּצְוָה — and they consent to, and approve of, *mitzvah* observance, עַל יְדֵי הִתְגַּבְּרוּת נַפְשׁוֹ הָאֱלֹהִית שֶׁבַּמּוֹחַ שֶׁשַּׁלִּיט עַל הַלֵּב — as a result of a strengthening of the Divine Soul in the brain, which *"rules over the heart"* (see chapter 12, p. 143).

Kelipah's will is to conceal G-d, which is why, under normal circumstances, it would block the *Shechinah.* But when the body observes a *mitzvah,* the Animal Soul is simply overpowered and forced to act against its will by the Divine Soul. And in that temporary state, even the Animal Soul can manifest the *Shechinah* (since, unwillingly, it participated in the *mitzvah*).

וְהֵן בְּשָׁעָה זוֹ בִּבְחִינַת גָּלוּת וְשֵׁינָה — And at that moment of the *mitzvah,* the deep core of the Animal Soul and its powers **are in a state of exile and dormancy,** כַּנִּזְכָּר לְעֵיל — as explained above in chapter 13 (p. 162).

וּלְכָךְ אֵין זוֹ מְנִיעָה מֵהַשְׁרָאַת הַשְּׁכִינָה עַל גּוּף הָאָדָם בְּשָׁעָה זוֹ — Therefore, the dormant deep core of the Animal Soul **doesn't hold back the *Shechinah* from resting on your body, at that moment** of the *mitzvah.*

השכינה על גוף האדם בשעה זו דהיינו שכח נפש
החיונית המלובש בעשיית המצוה הוא נכלל ממש
באור ה' ומיוחד בו ביחוד גמור וע"י זה ממשיך הארה
לכללות נפש החיונית שבכל הגוף וגם על הגוף הגשמי
בבחי' מקיף מלמעלה מראשו ועד רגליו וז"ש ושכינתא

It turns out that while the *powers* of your Animal Soul are *actively* coerced into performing a *mitzvah*, the *deep core* of your Animal Soul simply remains *passive*, and dormant during the act.

But why, then, is the deep core of the Animal Soul crucial and indispensable to the *mitzvah*? It appears that the deep core wasn't involved at all; it just didn't get in the way. And if it wasn't involved, why should the *Shechinah* shine through it?

The *Tanya* now addresses this point.

PRACTICAL LESSONS

Don't get discouraged by the fact that you can't seem to get rid of your Animal Soul, because every time you do a *mitzvah*, G-d's Infinite Light shines, even in your Animal Soul.

That's a remarkable feat; something that, without help from above, even the Divine Soul can't achieve.

דְּהַיְינוּ שֶׁכֹּחַ נֶפֶשׁ הַחִיּוּנִית הַמְלוּבָּשׁ בַּעֲשִׂיַּית הַמִּצְוָה — **What happens is: the** specific **power invested by the energizing** Animal **Soul in observing the *mitzvah*** with a specific part of your body, הוּא נִכְלָל מַמָּשׁ בְּאוֹר ה' וּמְיוּחָד בּוֹ בְּיחוּד גָּמוּר — **becomes literally absorbed in G-d's light, and seamlessly merged with it.**

It's only the specific "power" of the Animal Soul that is "literally absorbed" in G-d's light, *i.e.,* it enjoys a full revelation of the *Shechinah,* (as does the body part which carried out the *mitzvah*).

וְעַל יְדֵי זֶה מַמְשִׁיךְ הֶאָרָה לִכְלָלוּת נֶפֶשׁ הַחִיּוּנִית שֶׁבְּכָל הַגּוּף — **And, as a result, it draws a glimmer of light upon the** rest of the **energizing** Animal **Soul as a whole, found throughout the body,** וְגַם עַל הַגּוּף הַגַּשְׁמִי — **and also upon the physical body.**

The rest of the the Animal Soul, including its deep core, is not "literally absorbed" in the *Shechinah,* since it was not directly involved in the *mitzvah* act. But since the Animal Soul and its powers are ultimately one entity, "a glimmer" of the *Shechinah* does spread to it (and to the whole body).

בִּבְחִינַת מַקִּיף — But this "glimmer" only reaches the rest of the Animal Soul (and the body) in a secondary, **disengaged fashion (*makif*),** מִלְמַעְלָה מֵרֹאשׁוֹ וְעַד רַגְלָיו — hovering **outside** the body, **from head to foot.**

וְזֶהוּ שֶׁכָּתוּב דִּשְׁכִינְתָּא שַׁרְיָא עַל רֵישֵׁיהּ עַל דַּיְיקָא — **And this explains why** the above citation from the *Zohar* **is careful to say, "The *Shechinah* rests *upon the head*,"** suggesting that it hovers from *outside* the person.

שָׁרֵי עַל רֵישֵׁיהּ עַל דַּיְקָא וְכֵן אַכָּל בֵּי עֲשָׂרָה שְׁכִינְתָּא 45B
שַׁרְיָא. וְהִנֵּה כָּל בְּחִי' הַמְשָׁכַת אוֹר הַשְּׁכִינָה שֶׁהִיא
בְּחִי' גִּלּוּי אוֹר א"ס ב"ה אֵינוּ נִקְרָא שִׁנּוּי ח"ו בּוֹ ית'
וְלֹא רִבּוּי כִּדְאִיתָא בַּסַנְהֶדְרִין דְּאָמַר לֵיהּ הַהוּא מִינָא
לְרַבָּן גַּמְלִיאֵל אָמְרִיתוּ כָּל בֵּי עֲשָׂרָה שְׁכִינְתָּא שַׁרְיָא
כַּמָּה שְׁכִינְתָּא אִית לְכוּ וְהֵשִׁיב לוֹ מִמָּשָׁל מְאוֹר הַשֶּׁמֶשׁ
הַנִּכְנָס בַּחֲלוֹנוֹת רַבִּים כו' וְהַמַּשְׂכִּיל יָבִין:

וְכֵן אַכָּל בֵּי עֲשָׂרָה שְׁכִינְתָּא שַׁרְיָא — And similarly, *"Over every ten, the Shechinah rests"* (Talmud, Sanhedrin 39a), the emphasis is also that the Shechinah rests "over" them.

SECTION FIVE: LEVELS OF THE SHECHINAH

Chapter 35 concludes by addressing a philosophical issue. If the Shechinah was not manifest initially, and is only disclosed through Torah observance, does that not represent some sort of change? How is this to be squared with the principle of G-d's nondual oneness which we have learned, that G-d's presence never changes?

וְהִנֵּה כָּל בְּחִינַת הַמְשָׁכַת אוֹר הַשְּׁכִינָה — Now, every manifestation and expression of the Shechinah's light, שֶׁהִיא בְּחִינַת גִּלּוּי אוֹר אֵין סוֹף בָּרוּךְ הוּא — which is a revelation of the Blessed Infinite Light, אֵינוֹ נִקְרָא שִׁנּוּי חַס וְשָׁלוֹם בּוֹ יִתְבָּרֵךְ — could not be termed a "change" in G-d, Heaven forfend, וְלֹא רִבּוּי — nor an expression of multiplicity.

כִּדְאִיתָא בְּסַנְהֶדְרִין — The reason why this is the case can be gleaned from what is stated in the Talmud, Tractate *Sanhedrin* (ibid.), דְּאָמַר לֵיהּ הַהוּא מִינָא לְרַבָּן גַּמְלִיאֵל — that, *"A certain heretic said to Raban Gamliel,"* אָמְרִיתוּ כָּל בֵּי עֲשָׂרָה שְׁכִינְתָּא שַׁרְיָא — *"'You say that, 'Over every ten, the Shechinah rests,'* כַּמָּה שְׁכִינְתָּא אִית לְכוּ — *so how many Shechinahs do you have?"*

וְהֵשִׁיב לוֹ מִמָּשָׁל מְאוֹר הַשֶּׁמֶשׁ הַנִּכְנָס בַּחֲלוֹנוֹת רַבִּים כו' — And Raban Gamliel answered him with the example of sunlight from a single sun which can enter through many windows, *etc.*

The multiple "manifestations" and "expressions" of the Shechinah only exist when viewed through the "many windows" of the *recipients' perspective*. But from the true reality of G-d's perspective, His unity does not change through manifestation, just as the sun does not change when you open a window to let its light in.

וְהַמַּשְׂכִּיל יָבִין — And the wise will understand.

פרק לו והנה מודעת זאת מארז"ל שתכלית
בריאת עולם הזה הוא שנתאוה
הקב"ה להיות לו דירה בתחתונים. והנה לא שייך
לפניו ית' בחי' מעלה ומטה כי הוא ית' ממלא כל עלמין

CHAPTER 36

YOUR STRUGGLE IS WORTH IT (II)

SECTION ONE: G-D'S DISINTEREST IN THE SPIRITUAL WORDS

21ST ADAR REGULAR | 7TH ADAR II LEAP

In chapter 35 we began a discussion which the *Tanya* promised would be a great source of "consolation" and "comfort." Why, we asked, do most of us struggle *"to battle in vain with the impulse to evil… unable to prevail"* (pp. 387-8)?

The answer we learned was that when ordinary individuals such as ourselves perform a *mitzvah*, we engage the Animal Soul, bringing Divine revelation to even the lowest depth of *kelipah*. We bring G-d's light to the darkest of places.

In this chapter and the next, the *Tanya* will demonstrate that bringing illumination to a spiritually dark place is actually the most important thing anyone in the universe can do. It's nothing less than the purpose of creation.

וְהִנֵּה מוֹדַעַת זֹאת — Now, *"this thing is known"* (Isaiah 12:5), מַאֲמַר רַבּוֹתֵינוּ זִכְרוֹנָם לִבְרָכָה — the teaching of our Sages, of blessed memory, שֶׁתַּכְלִית בְּרִיאַת עוֹלָם הַזֶּה — that the ultimate purpose for which this world was created, הוּא שֶׁנִּתְאַוָּה הַקָּדוֹשׁ בָּרוּךְ הוּא לִהְיוֹת לוֹ דִירָה בַּתַּחְתּוֹנִים — was that *"the Blessed Holy One desired to have a home for Himself in the lowest realms (Dirah Ba-Tachtonim)"* (*Midrash Tanchuma, Naso* section 16).

Various Rabbinic texts have attempted to fathom G-d's purpose in creating the universe. The author of the *Tanya* was, of course, familiar with all these texts, but he pointed to this one particular *Midrash* as the *overwhelming motivating factor* for creation. (For a discussion of the various Rabbinic sources and the centrality of this *Midrash* see Rabbi Chaim Miller, *Rambam: Thirteen Principles of Faith, Principles 8-9* (Brooklyn: *Kol Menachem* 2007), pp. 188-193).

וְהִנֵּה לֹא שַׁיָּיךְ לְפָנָיו יִתְבָּרֵךְ בְּחִינַת מַעְלָה וּמַטָּה — Now obviously this *Midrash* is metaphorical, **since the notion of** being present in the **"upper"** or **"lower"** worlds **is not applicable to G-d**, כִּי הוּא יִתְבָּרֵךְ מְמַלֵּא כָּל עָלְמִין בְּשָׁוֶה — since *"He fills all worlds"* (see *Zohar* 3, 225a), **equally.**

בשוה. אלא ביאור הענין כי קודם שנברא העולם
היה הוא לבדו ית' יחיד ומיוחד וממלא כל המקום הזה
שברא בו העולם וגם עתה כן הוא לפניו ית' רק
שהשינוי הוא אל המקבלים חיותו ואורו ית' שמקבלים
ע"י לבושים רבים המכסים ומסתירים אורו ית' כדכתיב
כי לא יראני האדם וחי וכדפי' רז"ל שאפי' מלאכים הנק'
חיות אין רואין כו' וזהו ענין השתלשלות העולמות
וירידתם ממדרגה למדרג' ע"י ריבוי הלבושי' המסתירים
האור והחיות שממנו ית' עד שנברא עו"הז הגשמי

אֶלָּא בֵּיאוּר הָעִנְיָן — **Rather, this is how we should understand the matter.**

To explain this *Midrash*, the *Tanya* will draw on the Kabbalistic concept of Divine "diminishment" (*tzimtzum*) that we explored in chapter 21.

הָיָה הוּא לְבַדּוֹ יִתְבָּרֵךְ — **For, before the world was created,** כִּי קוֹדֶם שֶׁנִּבְרָא הָעוֹלָם וּמְמַלֵּא — יָחִיד וּמְיוּחָד — G-d was **"the One and only One"** (*Deuteronomy Rabah,* 2:31), כָּל הַמָּקוֹם הַזֶּה שֶׁבָּרָא בּוֹ הָעוֹלָם — **and He filled this entire space in which the world was created,** leaving no room for any other existence.

וְגַם עַתָּה כֵּן הוּא — **And the same is true now,** לְפָנָיו יִתְבָּרֵךְ — **from G-d's perspective.**

רַק שֶׁהַשִּׁינוּי הוּא אֶל הַמְקַבְּלִים חַיּוּתוֹ וְאוֹרוֹ יִתְבָּרֵךְ — **There is only a change** from the recipient's perspective, **for those who receive His energy and light.**

The process of creation didn't introduce a separate *existence* from G-d, but another *perspective*. To our eyes, it appears that G-d has made a separate world and endowed us with a separate consciousness. But from a higher perspective, from G-d's eyes, everything is just part of Him. As the *Tanya* will now explain, this feat was achieved by a "diminishment" (*tzimtzum*) of G-d's light (when perceived from the lower perspective) through many "filters."

שֶׁמְּקַבְּלִים עַל יְדֵי לְבוּשִׁים רַבִּים — **For** G-d's energy and light must be **received through many filters which** diminish the light, הַמְכַסִּים וּמַסְתִּירִים אוֹרוֹ יִתְבָּרֵךְ — **covering and hiding** G-d's **blessed light,** כְּדִכְתִיב כִּי לֹא יִרְאַנִי הָאָדָם וָחָי — **as the verse states, "For no man can see Me** (directly) **and live"** (*Exodus* 33:20).

וְכִדְפֵּירְשׁוּ רַבּוֹתֵינוּ זִכְרוֹנָם לִבְרָכָה — **And, as the Sages of blessed memory explained** this verse, שֶׁאֲפִילוּ מַלְאָכִים הַנִּקְרָאִים חַיּוֹת אֵין רוֹאִין כו' — **"Even the (angels called) Chayos** that carry the heavenly throne, **don't see** the glory (of G-d)" (*Numbers Rabah* 14:22).

וְזֶהוּ עִנְיָן הִשְׁתַּלְשְׁלוּת הָעוֹלָמוֹת — **This** veiling of G-d **is caused by the chain of spiritual worlds,** וִירִידָתָם מִמַּדְרֵגָה לְמַדְרֵגָה — **which are downgraded, rung by rung,** עַל יְדֵי רִיבּוּי הַלְּבוּשִׁים הַמַּסְתִּירִים הָאוֹר וְהַחַיּוּת שֶׁמִּמֶּנּוּ יִתְבָּרֵךְ — **through many filters which hide G-d's energy and light,** עַד שֶׁנִּבְרָא עוֹלָם הַזֶּה הַגַּשְׁמִי וְהַחוּמְרִי מַמָּשׁ — **until** so much veiling has taken place **that this very physical, material world is created.**

וְהַחוּמְרִי מַמָּשׁ וְהוּא הַתַּחְתּוֹן בְּמַדְרֵגָה שֶׁאֵין תַּחְתּוֹן
לְמַטָּה מִמֶּנּוּ בְּעִנְיַן הֶסְתֵּר אוֹרוֹ ית' וְחֹשֶׁךְ כָּפוּל וּמְכוּפָּל
עַד שֶׁהוּא מָלֵא קְלִיפּוֹת וְסִטְ"א שֶׁהֵן נֶגֶד ה' מַמָּשׁ לוֹמַ' אֲנִי
וְאַפְסִי עוֹד. וְהִנֵּה תַּכְלִית הִשְׁתַּלְשְׁלוּ' הָעוֹלְמוֹ' וִירִידָתָם
מִמַּדְרֵגָה לְמַדְרֵגָה אֵינוּ בִּשְׁבִיל עוֹלָמוֹת הָעֶלְיוֹנִי' הוֹאִיל
וְלָהֶם יְרִידָה מֵאוֹר פָּנָיו ית' אֶלָּא הַתַּכְלִית הוּא עֵו"הֹז

וְהוּא הַתַּחְתּוֹן בַּמַּדְרֵגָה — **And** this physical world is **the lowest rung** in the chain of spiritual worlds, שֶׁאֵין תַּחְתּוֹן לְמַטָּה מִמֶּנּוּ — **since there is nothing lower than it,** בְּעִנְיַן הֶסְתֵּר אוֹרוֹ יִתְבָּרֵךְ — **in the extent to which G-d's light is hidden,** וְחֹשֶׁךְ כָּפוּל וּמְכוּפָּל — **"a darkness doubled and redoubled"** (Exodus Rabah 14:3).

עַד שֶׁהוּא מָלֵא קְלִיפּוֹת וְסִטְרָא אָחֳרָא — The absence of Divine light results in kelipos filling this world **to the point that it is** filled **with** kelipos **and** sitra achra (p. 378), שֶׁהֵן נֶגֶד ה' מַמָּשׁ לוֹמַר אֲנִי וְאַפְסִי עוֹד — **which are entirely opposed to G-d,** saying, **"There's me, and there's no one else beside me"** (Isaiah 47:8; see chapter 22, p. 253).

SECTION TWO: WHAT GIVES G-D PLEASURE

8TH ADAR II LEAP

The above represents a summary of what we learned in chapter 21. Now the Tanya turns to why G-d should be so concerned about what transpires in the lower worlds.

וְהִנֵּה תַּכְלִית הִשְׁתַּלְשְׁלוּת הָעוֹלָמוֹת וִירִידָתָם מִמַּדְרֵגָה לְמַדְרֵגָה אֵינוּ בִּשְׁבִיל עוֹלָמוֹת הָעֶלְיוֹנִים — **Now,** the Dirah Ba-Tachtonim ("home for G-d in the lowest realm") idea teaches that **the ultimate purpose of the chain of spiritual worlds, and their progressive downgrade from rung to rung, is not for the sake of the upper worlds.**

This seems counterintuitive. Shouldn't G-d be more impressed by the worship of the angels and celestial beings in the upper worlds, who sing to Him in harmony and purity?

To debunk this myth, the Tanya will first explain why the purpose of creation can't be in the upper worlds (and after that we will address why it is, in fact, in the lower worlds).

הוֹאִיל וְלָהֶם יְרִידָה מֵאוֹר פָּנָיו יִתְבָּרֵךְ — **Because** even these upper worlds **represent a downgrade from the actual light of G-d's "face,"** and G-d would not have made the entire creation merely to achieve the downgrading of His light.

Let's forget about the lower worlds for a minute. Imagine that G-d would have only created the upper worlds, with all the angels singing to Him. What would be the point in that? Even the angels don't actually see G-d; they perceive a highly diminished version of His light. So there's no gain here, no "profit" to be had, just diminishment.

הַתַּחְתּוֹן שֶׁכָּךְ עָלָה בִּרְצוֹנוֹ יִת' לִהְיוֹת נַחַת רוּחַ לְפָנָיו
יִת' כַּד אִתְכַּפְיָא ס"א וְאִתְהַפֵּךְ חֲשׁוֹכָא לִנְהוֹרָא שֶׁיָּאִיר 46A
אוֹר ה' אֵין סוֹף ב"ה בִּמְקוֹם הַחֹשֶׁךְ וְהַס"א שֶׁל כָּל

אֶלָּא הַתַּכְלִית הוּא עוֹלָם הַזֶּה הַתַּחְתּוֹן — **Rather,** we are forced to conclude that, counterintuitively, **the purpose** of all the creation must be for the sake of **this lowest** physical **world.**

Obviously, this world represents an even greater "downgrade" of G-d's light than the upper worlds. So, clearly, if the purpose of creation rests here, there must be another property of the physical world that makes its creation "worthwhile" — an "upgrade," so to speak.

שֶׁכָּךְ עָלָה בִּרְצוֹנוֹ יִתְבָּרֵךְ — **Since** before any of the worlds were created, **it arose in G-d's will,** לִהְיוֹת נַחַת רוּחַ לְפָנָיו יִתְבָּרֵךְ — that He would have "a feeling of satisfaction" (*nachas ruach*), when His will would be obeyed down in the physical world.

It's hard to pin a rational reason as to *why* G-d chose what He chose. Ultimately, it's something we can't fully fathom, a Divine "desire" or "whim," so to speak. But in the following lines, the *Tanya* will offer some insight as to why a *mitzvah* performed in the lowest realms is so appealing to G-d.

כַּד אִתְכַּפְיָא סִטְרָא אָחֳרָא — For when G-d's will is obeyed in this world it causes the *sitra achra* to be subdued (*iskafya*), וְאִתְהַפֵּךְ חֲשׁוֹכָא לִנְהוֹרָא — and "darkness" is transformed (*is'hapcha*) to "light," שֶׁיָּאִיר אוֹר ה' אֵין סוֹף בָּרוּךְ הוּא בִּמְקוֹם הַחֹשֶׁךְ — so that the Infinite Light of G-d can shine in the place of prior "darkness" and *sitra achra,* וְהַסִּטְרָא אָחֳרָא שֶׁל כָּל עוֹלָם הַזֶּה כֻּלּוֹ — which previously filled **this** entire world, completely.

Practically speaking, if you were G-d and the worlds didn't yet exist, how would you demonstrate the truth that "nothing exists outside G-d"? One approach would be to do nothing, and just leave Yourself existing and everything else not-existing.

But another approach would be to create a force which *tried* to conceal your existence, but *ultimately failed* to do so. And while you would never be fooled by that

---

A CHASIDIC THOUGHT

When we say that a *mitzvah* is the Divine will, people usually imagine that we are playing an authority game: You have to do this because it is the Divine will. Mystics, however, mean something else when they invoke the idea of a higher will. They are trying to convey that this act represents the fulfillment of a very deep urge on the part of G-d, a yearning which transcends reason.

עו"הז כולו ביתר שאת ויתר עז ויתרון אור מן החשך
מהארתו בעולמות עליונים שמאיר שם ע"י לבושים
והסתר פנים המסתירים ומעלימים אור א"ס ב"ה שלא
יבטלו במציאות. ולזה נתן הקב"ה לישראל את

force, you could make creatures that were influenced by it. You would give them the choice whether to be drawn in by its illusion, or to reject it. And while it would be a very convincing force and exert power for a long time, eventually the force would be eliminated completely by creatures choosing good over evil. Then you would have demonstrated that "nothing exists outside G-d," *because anything that did oppose G-d was shown to be unsustainable.*

Every time a *mitzvah* is performed, we achieve part of that goal. And this gives us some insight into why it brings G-d pleasure and makes His creation "worthwhile."

בְּיֶתֶר שְׂאֵת וְיֶתֶר עֹז — And when G-d's light does shine in this physical world, which was previously dominated by the *sitra achra*, it shines with **"more dignity and more power"** (*Genesis* 49:3), וְיִתְרוֹן אוֹר מִן הַחֹשֶׁךְ — and with **"the advantage of light (which comes) from darkness"** (*Ecclesiastes* 2:13), מֵהֶאָרָתוֹ בְּעוֹלָמוֹת עֶלְיוֹנִים — which is superior **to the way it illuminates the upper worlds,** שֶׁמֵּאִיר שָׁם עַל יְדֵי לְבוּשִׁים וְהֶסְתֵּר פָּנִים — where it must shine through many filters, and the **"Hiding of G-d's face"** (see *Deuteronomy* 31:17-18), הַמַּסְתִּירִים וּמַעֲלִימִים אוֹר אֵין סוֹף בָּרוּךְ הוּא — **which hides,** or at least **conceals, the Blessed Infinite Light,** שֶׁלֹּא יִבָּטְלוּ בְּמְצִיאוּת — **in order that the individual identity** of the Upper Worlds **should not be eradicated,** which would be the case if G-d's light shined unfiltered.

When you do a *mitzvah* in this world, the truth shines. The lie of *kelipah* is eradicated. The truth can't shine fully in the upper worlds because they never completely eradicate the "hiding" of G-d; they always maintain the status quo (of "many filters"). The fullness of G-d's majesty is *always* hidden up there; and while it's usually hidden down here (and more so), we can break through that obscuring force and bring His true will to light, if we choose to do so.

SECTION THREE: HOW TO SEE G-D AND STILL SURVIVE

9TH ADAR II LEAP

It turns out that there *can* be a greater revelation of G-d in this world than in the upper worlds. Because, unlike the upper worlds, we are able to reverse, and eventually eliminate, the "diminishment" of G-d's light.

But this leaves us with a question: If G-d's light had to be dimmed so that the upper worlds could withstand it, how would the lower worlds cope with an even greater revelation of G-d's light, and still continue to exist?

וְלָזֶה נָתַן הַקָּדוֹשׁ בָּרוּךְ הוּא לְיִשְׂרָאֵל אֶת הַתּוֹרָה שֶׁנִּקְרֵאת עֹז וְכֹחַ — **And this is why**

התורה שנקר' עוז וכח וכמארז"ל שהקב"ה נותן כח
בצדיקים לקבל שכרם לעתיד לבא שלא יתבטלו
במציאות ממש באור ה' הנגלה לעתיד בלי שום לבוש
כדכתיב ולא יכנף עוד מוריך [פי' שלא יתכסה ממך
בכנף ולבוש] והיו עיניך רואות את מוריך וכתיב כי
עין בעין יראו וגו' וכתיב לא יהיה לך עוד השמש לאור
יומם וגו' כי ה' יהיה לך לאור עולם וגו'. ונודע שימות

the Blessed Holy One gave Israel the Torah, which is referred to by Scripture as *"strength"* (*Leviticus Rabah* 31:5, from *Proverbs* 21:22), **and** by the Sages as *"power"* (*Talmud, Brachos* 63a), since it gives us the power to withstand G-d's unfiltered revelation.

Torah is the unique "vessel" or "technology" that enables us to absorb this revelation, and not be wiped out of existence. The *Tanya* now cites a *Talmudic* teaching to illustrate this idea of Torah giving us the "power" to withstand revelation.

וּכְמַאֲמַר רַבּוֹתֵינוּ זִכְרוֹנָם לִבְרָכָה — **As in the teaching of our Sages, of blessed memory,** שֶׁהַקָּדוֹשׁ בָּרוּךְ הוּא נוֹתֵן כֹּחַ בַּצַּדִּיקִים לְקַבֵּל שְׂכָרָם לֶעָתִיד לָבֹא — **that G-d grants "power" to** *tzadikim* **enabling them to receive their reward in the future** (*Talmud, Sanhedrin* 100b), שֶׁלֹּא יִתְבַּטְּלוּ בִּמְצִיאוּת מַמָּשׁ — **in order that they will not be completely obliterated,** בְּאוֹר ה' הַנִּגְלֶה לֶעָתִיד בְּלִי שׁוּם לְבוּשׁ — **by G-d's light, which will be disclosed in the future without any filter.**

The *Tanya* now cites three scriptural verses that depict an undiluted revelation in the future that we will nevertheless be able to withstand.

כְּדִכְתִיב וְלֹא יִכָּנֵף עוֹד מוֹרֶיךָ [פֵּירוּשׁ שֶׁלֹּא יִתְכַּסֶּה מִמְּךָ בְּכָנָף וּלְבוּשׁ] וְהָיוּ עֵינֶיךָ רוֹאוֹת אֶת מוֹרֶיךָ — **As the verse states,** *"Your (Divine) Teacher will be enrobed no more,"* i.e., he will no longer hide Himself from you with a "robe" or filter, *"and your eyes will see your Teacher"* (*Isaiah* 30:20), וּכְתִיב כִּי עַיִן בְּעַיִן יִרְאוּ וְגוֹ' — **and another verse states,** *"For they shall see (G-d) eye to eye, etc."* (*ibid.* 52:8), וּכְתִיב לֹא יִהְיֶה לָךְ עוֹד הַשֶּׁמֶשׁ לְאוֹר יוֹמָם וְגוֹ' כִּי ה' יִהְיֶה לָךְ לְאוֹר עוֹלָם וְגוֹ — **and another verse states,** *"The sun will be no more your light by day... for G-d will be an everlasting light for you etc.,"* (*ibid.* 60:19-20).

PRACTICAL LESSONS

G-d created the worlds to demonstrate that nothing exists outside Him.

This is achieved by first allowing a force of duality to temporarily exist (*kelipah*), and then showing that the force is unsustainable.

When you do a *mitzvah*, it neutralizes the forces of *kelipah* and therefore fulfills the purpose of creation. The upper worlds can't do this.

Torah is the power and "technology" that makes it possible to receive Divine revelation without our identity being erased.

המשיח ובפרט כשיחיו המתים הם תכלית ושלימות
בריאות עולם הזה שלכך נברא מתחילתו*
וגם כבר היה לעולמים

הגהה
(וקבלת שכר עיקרו באלף
השביעי כמ"ש בלקוטי תורה
מהאר"י ז"ל):

מעין זה בשעת מתן תורה
כדכתי' אתה הראת לדעת
כי ה' הוא האלהים אין

SECTION FOUR: THE PURPOSE OF CREATION COMPLETED

וְנוֹדָע שֶׁיְמוֹת הַמָּשִׁיחַ וּבִפְרָט כְּשֶׁיִּחְיוּ הַמֵּתִים הֵם תַּכְלִית וּשְׁלֵימוּת בְּרִיאַת עוֹלָם הַזֶּה שֶׁלָּכָךְ נִבְרָא מִתְּחִילָּתוֹ — **And it's known** from the *Talmud* (*Sanhedrin* 98b), **that the ulti-mate and complete purpose of the world's creation, the reason why it was cre-ated to begin with, is the Messianic Era (especially the time when the dead will be revived).***

The *Talmud's* assertion that "the world was only created for Mashiach (the Messi-ah)" fits well with the central insight of this chapter. While each good deed *partially* fulfills the Divine intent for which the world was created (*"the sitra achra is subdued and darkness is transformed to light"*), the truth that "nothing exists outside G-d" will only be *fully* demonstrated when *kelipah* is eliminated completely. (And that will be, generally speaking, in the Messianic Era, although the absolute eradication of *kelipah* will take place later on, at *"the time when the dead will be revived"*).

22ND ADAR REGULAR | 10TH ADAR II LEAP

וְגַם כְּבָר הָיָה לְעוֹלָמִים מֵעֵין זֶה בִּשְׁעַת מַתַּן תּוֹרָה — **And also, a glimmer of this** rev-elation *"already has been"* (*Ecclesiastes* 1:10), **at the giving of the Torah,** at Mount Sinai, כְּדִכְתִיב אַתָּה הָרְאֵתָ לָדַעַת כִּי ה' הוּא הָאֱלֹהִים אֵין עוֹד מִלְּבַדּוֹ — **as the verse states, "You were shown** *(a vision through the heavens)* **to know that G-d is the**

---

*הַגָּהָה — *NOTE.* Normally it's understood that our work, the purpose for which we are here, takes place during the current era; and in the Messianic Era we will simply receive our reward.

But the *Tanya's* assertion here that our purpose "is the Messianic Era" seems to blur the boundary between the time of work and the time of reward. In this note, the *Tanya* clarifies that there will definitely be a clearly defined period of reward, and that will take place *after* the Messianic Era and the revival of the dead.

וְקַבָּלַת שָׂכָר — **And the** era **of receiving reward,** עִיקָרוֹ בָּאֶלֶף הַשְּׁבִיעִי — **is *primarily*** **during the "Seventh Millennium"** after the Messianic Era and revival of the dead, כְּמוֹ שֶׁכָּתוּב בְּלִקוּטֵי תּוֹרָה מֵהָאֲרִ"י זִכְרוֹנוֹ לִבְרָכָה — **as stated in *Likutei Torah* of Rabbi Isaac Luria, of blessed memory** (*Parshas Bereishis*).

עוֹד מִלְבַדּוֹ הַרְאַת מַמָּשׁ בְּרָאִיָה חוּשִׁיִּית כְּדִכְתִּיב וְכָל
הָעָם רוֹאִים אֶת הַקּוֹלוֹת רוֹאִים אֶת הַנִּשְׁמָע וּפִי' רַזַ"ל
מִסְתַּכְּלִים לְמִזְרָח וְשׁוֹמְעִין אֶת הַדִּבּוּר יוֹצֵא אָנֹכִי כוּ'.
וְכֵן לְאַרְבַּע רוּחוֹת וּלְמַעְלָה וּלְמַטָּה וְכִדְפֵי' בְּתִיקוּנִים
דְּלֵית אֲתַר דְּלָא מַלִּיל מִינֵיהּ עִמְּהוֹן כו' וְהַיְינוּ מִפְּנֵי גִּילּוּי
רְצוֹנוֹ יִת' בַּעֲשֶׂרֶת הַדִּבְּרוֹת שֶׁהֵן כְּלָלוֹת הַתּוֹרָה שֶׁהִיא
פְּנִימִית רְצוֹנוֹ יִת' וְחָכְמָתוֹ וְאֵין שָׁם הֶסְתֵּר פָּנִים כְּלָל
כְּמַ"שׁ כִּי בְאוֹר פָּנֶיךָ נָתַתָּ לָנוּ תּוֹרַת חַיִּים וְלָכֵן הָיוּ

(only) **G-d, there is none besides Him,"** (*Deuteronomy* 4:35), הַרְאֵתָ מַמָּשׁ בְּרָאִיָה
חוּשִׁיִּית — implying that **you were actually "shown"** G-d, in a way that could be
perceived **with sensory vision,** כְּדִכְתִּיב וְכָל הָעָם רוֹאִים אֶת הַקּוֹלוֹת — as the verse
states, *"And all the people could see the sounds* (which G-d spoke)," (*Exodus* 20:15),
רוֹאִים אֶת הַנִּשְׁמָע — *"They saw that which was audible, which is impossible to see
under any other circumstances"* (*Rashi* ibid. from *Mechilta*), וּפֵירְשׁוּ רַבּוֹתֵינוּ זִכְרוֹנָם
לִבְרָכָה מִסְתַּכְּלִים לַמִּזְרָח וְשׁוֹמְעִין אֶת הַדִּבּוּר יוֹצֵא אָנֹכִי כו' — and our **Sages of blessed
memory explained, that they would look eastward, and hear the First Command-
ment, *'I am'* etc.,** (see *Exodus Rabah* 5:9), וְכֵן לְאַרְבַּע רוּחוֹת וּלְמַעְלָה וּלְמַטָּה — **and
then** they would hear subsequent Commandments from all different directions, **the
four compass points, from above and below,** וְכִדְפֵּירְשׁוּ בַּתִּיקוּנִים דְּלֵית אֲתַר דְּלָא
מַלִּיל מִינֵיהּ עִמְּהוֹן כו' — as the *Tikunei Zohar* explains, *"There was no place to be
found, above or below, from which He did not speak"* to them (*Tikunei Zohar* 64b).

וְהַיְינוּ מִפְּנֵי גִּילּוּי רְצוֹנוֹ יִתְבָּרֵךְ בַּעֲשֶׂרֶת הַדִּבְּרוֹת — **This** unique experiencing of Divine
revelation with the senses took place **because G-d's will was disclosed in the Ten
Commandments,** שֶׁהֵן כְּלָלוּת הַתּוֹרָה — **which are the principles underlying the
whole Torah,** שֶׁהִיא פְּנִימִית רְצוֹנוֹ יִתְבָּרֵךְ וְחָכְמָתוֹ — the Torah being **the inner will
of G-d, and His wisdom,** וְאֵין שׁוּם הֶסְתֵּר פָּנִים כְּלָל — "inner" will meaning that it is
devoid of any *"Hiding of G-d's face"* **whatsoever,** כְּמוֹ שֶׁאוֹמְרִים כִּי בְאוֹר פָּנֶיךָ נָתַתָּ
לָנוּ תּוֹרַת חַיִּים — and we know that the Torah is a disclosure of G-d's "face" **as we
say** in the prayers, *"For with the light of Your face You gave us... the Torah of life"*
(*Liturgy, Amidah Prayer*).

The experience at Sinai was, essentially, the Torah's "mission statement." And
since the purpose of the Torah is to eliminate the *kelipos* so as to bring Divine revelation to this lowest world, a taste of this was experienced at Sinai.

The important difference being that in the future era the world will be *ready* for
that revelation, as a result of thousands of years of our eliminating *kelipah* through
mitzvah observance. But at Sinai, the world wasn't ready for such revelation, so it
wasn't yet sustainable.

וְלָכֵן הָיוּ בְּטֵלִים בִּמְצִיאוּת מַמָּשׁ — **That's why,** at the giving of the Torah, the people's **identity was voided** by the Divine revelation, which was too powerful for them

46B

בטלים במציאות ממש כמארז"ל שעל כל דיבור
פרחה נשמתן כו' אלא שהחזירה הקב"ה להן בטל
שעתיד להחיות בו את המתים והוא טל תורה שנקרא
עוז כמארז"ל כל העוסק בתורה טל תורה מחייהו כו'
רק שאח"כ גרם החטא ונתגשמו הם והעולם עד עת
קץ הימין שאז יזדכך גשמיות הגוף והעולם ויוכלו לקבל
גילוי אור ה' שיאיר לישראל ע"י התורה שנקר' עוז

כְּמַאֲמַר רַבּוֹתֵינוּ זִכְרוֹנָם לִבְרָכָה שֶׁעַל כָּל דִּיבּוּר פָּרְחָה נִשְׁמָתָן כו' — **as** to withstand, **our Sages taught, "At every Divine utterance their souls flew off etc.,"** (*Talmud, Shabbos* 88b).

Since the people couldn't handle the revelation, they expired, so Divine intervention was required.

אֶלָּא שֶׁהֶחֱזִירָה הַקָּדוֹשׁ בָּרוּךְ הוּא לָהֶן בְּטַל שֶׁעָתִיד לְהַחֲיוֹת בּוֹ אֶת הַמֵּתִים — **Only, G-d** **returned** their souls **to them using "the dew with which He will, in the future, revive the dead"** (*ibid.*; following *Isaiah* 26:19).

שֶׁנִּקְרָא עוֹז — וְהוּא טַל תּוֹרָה — **This is the "dew of Torah,"** — the property of Torah which, as stated above, **is referred to** by Scripture **as "strength"** because it empowers you to withstand intense revelation, כְּמַאֲמַר רַבּוֹתֵינוּ זִכְרוֹנָם לִבְרָכָה כָּל הָעוֹסֵק בַּתּוֹרָה טַל תּוֹרָה מְחַיֵּיהוּ כו' — **as in the teaching of our Sages, of blessed memory, "Whoever immerses himself in Torah** (in this world), **the dew of Torah will revive him** (in the future)" (*Tikunei Zohar,* 38b; see *Yalkut Shimoni, Isaiah,* section 431; *Talmud, Kesubos* 111b).

11TH ADAR II LEAP

At that point, after the Jews had been revived by the "dew" of Torah, the world was already primed and ready for Divine revelation.

רַק שֶׁאַחַר כָּךְ גָּרַם הַחֵטְא — **Only,** this idyllic state was not sustained **since, afterwards, the sin** of the Golden Calf **caused** its suspension, וְנִתְגַּשְׁמוּ הֵם וְהָעוֹלָם — since, as a result of the sin, the people **and the world, became more sensual,** and less capable of receiving Divine light.

Now that the idyllic state at Sinai has been lost, we will have to refine ourselves through hard work. When we have completed that task, this physical world will once again be ready for Divine revelation, enabling the purpose of creation to be fulfilled, a "home for G-d below."

שֶׁאָז יִזְדַּכֵּךְ — עַד עֵת קֵץ הַיָּמִין — **Until the time of the "End of Days"** (*Daniel* 12:13), גַּשְׁמִיּוּת הַגּוּף וְהָעוֹלָם — **for then the sensuality of the body, and the world, will have been** spiritually **refined,** וְיוּכְלוּ לְקַבֵּל גִּילּוּי אוֹר ה' שֶׁיָּאִיר לְיִשְׂרָאֵל — **making it possible to receive the disclosure of G-d's light which will shine to Israel,** עַל יְדֵי הַתּוֹרָה

ומיתרון ההארה לישראל יגיה חשך האומות גם כן
כדכתיב והלכו גוים לאורך וגו' וכתיב בית יעקב לכו
ונלכה באור ה' וכתיב ונגלה כבוד ה' וראו כל בשר
יחדיו וגו' וכתיב לבוא בנקרת הצורים ובסעיפי הסלעי'
מפני פחד ה' והדר גאונו וגו' וכמ"ש והופע בהדר גאון
עוזך על כל יושבי תבל ארצך וגו':

שֶׁנִּקְרֵאת עוֹז — and this will be made possible **through the Torah, which is referred to** by Scripture **as "strength,"** since it gives us the power to withstand unfiltered revelation.

In a final comment, the *Tanya* stresses that the revelations of the future will be enjoyed by all nations.

וּמִיּתְרוֹן הַהֶאָרָה לְיִשְׂרָאֵל — **And from the abundant revelation to Israel,** יַגִּיהַּ חֹשֶׁךְ הָאוּמוֹת גַּם כֵּן — light **will reach the "darkness" of the** other **nations, too.**

The *Tanya* offers five citations to demonstrate this point.

כְּדִכְתִיב וְהָלְכוּ גוֹיִם לְאוֹרֵךְ וְגוֹ' — **As the verse states,** *"Nations will come to your light etc.,"* (*Isaiah* 60:3), וּכְתִיב בֵּית יַעֲקֹב לְכוּ וְנֵלְכָה בְּאוֹר ה' — **and the verse states** that the nations will say to Israel, *"Come, house of Ya'akov, let's walk in the light of G-d"* (*ibid.* 2:5), וּכְתִיב וְנִגְלָה כְּבוֹד ה' וְרָאוּ כָל בָּשָׂר יַחְדָּיו וְגוֹ' — **and the verse states,** *"the glory of G-d will be revealed and all flesh will see together* that G-d is speaking" (*ibid.* 40:5), וּכְתִיב לָבוֹא בְּנִקְרֹת הַצּוּרִים וּבִסְעִיפֵי הַסְּלָעִים מִפְּנֵי פַּחַד ה' וַהֲדַר גְּאוֹנוֹ וְגוֹ' — **and the verse states,** *"they will go into the clefts of the rocks, and into the tops of the ragged rocks, for fear of G-d, and for the glory of His majesty,* when He arises *to shake mightily the earth"* (*ibid.* 2:21), וּכְמוֹ שֶׁאוֹמְרִים וְהוֹפַע בַּהֲדַר גְּאוֹן עוּזֶּךָ עַל כָּל — **and as we say** in the prayers, *"Shine forth in the majesty of Your triumphant strength over all the inhabitants of Your world"* (*Liturgy, High Holiday Amidah*).

CHAPTER 37

YOUR STRUGGLE IS WORTH IT (III)
SECTION ONE: A MITZVAH AND ITS REWARD

23RD ADAR REGULAR | 12TH ADAR II LEAP

Throughout chapters 35 and 36, the *Tanya* has attempted to offer us some "comfort" over our spiritual predicament. While we may not be able to worship G-d with the emotional intensity and consistency of the *tzadik*, we can achieve external mas-

פרק לז והנה תכלית השלימות הזה של ימות המשיח ותחיית המתים שהוא גילוי אור א"ס ב"ה בעו"הז הגשמי תלוי במעשינו ועבודתנו כל זמן משך הגלות כי הגורם שכר המצוה

tery over our actions, and that, the *Tanya* has argued, is actually more important in the scheme of things. It is sacred action, in the form of *mitzvah* observance, which fulfills G-d's purpose in creation, making a "home for G-d in the lowest realms." In this chapter, the *Tanya* continues to explore this theme in further depth.

וְהִנֵּה תַּכְלִית הַשְּׁלֵימוּת הַזֶּה — **Now the fullest expression of this** reality of a "home for G-d in the lowest realms" (*Dirah Ba-Tachtonim*), שֶׁל יְמוֹת הַמָּשִׁיחַ וּתְחִיַּת הַמֵּתִים — is, as we have learned in chapter 36, in the time **of the Messianic Era and the revival of the dead,** שֶׁהוּא גִּילוּי אוֹר אֵין סוֹף בָּרוּךְ הוּא בָּעוֹלָם הַזֶּה הַגַּשְׁמִי — since at that time **there will be a disclosure of the Blessed Infinite Light within this physical world.**

In chapter 36 we learned that G-d's purpose in creating the world will only be completely fulfilled in the future, during the Messianic Era. Yet, we also learned that the future "home for G-d in the lowest realms" is not a phenomenon disconnected with our activity in the current era. Rather,

תָּלוּי בְּמַעֲשֵׂינוּ וַעֲבוֹדָתֵנוּ — all this **is dependent on our** *mitzvah* **actions and our worship** in prayer, כָּל זְמַן מֶשֶׁךְ הַגָּלוּת — **throughout the whole period of exile,** which gradually and cumulatively neutralizes the forces of *kelipah*.

Of course, all the *mitzvos* performed since Sinai (14th century B.C.E.) contribute to this effect, but the *Tanya* points specifically to the worship of "*the whole period of exile*" (beginning 1st century C.E.). For it is during this last exile that *kelipah* forces are at their strongest and, as a result, the neutralizing power of each *mitzvah* is also at its strongest.

As we noted in the previous chapter, the Messianic Era is classically perceived as a time of reward, *i.e.,* a period of *human benefit* rather than *Divine satisfaction*. Yet here, the Messianic Era is framed as a time when G-d's desires for creation are finally fulfilled, when He finally enters His "home." To help reconcile these two approaches, the *Tanya* now offers a novel insight into the Sages' teaching, "*the reward for a mitzvah is a mitzvah*" (*Mishnah, Avos* 4:2).

כִּי הַגּוֹרֵם שְׂכַר הַמִּצְוָה הִיא הַמִּצְוָה בְּעַצְמָהּ — **Because, "***(That which causes) the re-ward for a mitzvah is* (that same) *mitzvah (itself)."*

The plain meaning of "*The reward for a mitzvah is a mitzvah*" is: "*A person that has done one mitzvah is orchestrated and assisted by Heaven to do another one, in order that he should be rewarded for both*" (Rabbi Ovadiah of Bartenura, *ibid.*).

However, the *Tanya* offers here a deeper explanation, that we are not speaking of one *mitzvah* leading to another, but one single *mitzvah*. The reward for a *mitzvah* is nothing other than *the spiritual result of performing it.*

היא המצוה בעצמה כי בעשייתה ממשיך האדם גילוי
אור א״ס ב״ה מלמעלה למטה להתלבש בגשמיות
עוה״ז בדבר שהיה תחלה תחת ממשלת קליפת
נוגה ומקבל חיותה ממנה שהם כל דברים הטהורים
ומותרי׳ שנעשית בהם המצוה מעשיית כגון קלף
התפילין ומזוזה וספר תורה וכמאמר רז״ל לא הוכשר
למלאכת שמים אלא טהורים ומותרים בפיך. וכן

מַמְשִׁיךְ הָאָדָם גִּילּוּי אוֹר אֵין — **Because through performing** the *mitzvah,* כִּי בַּעֲשִׂיָּיתָה
מִלְּמַעְלָה — **you "pull down" a disclosure of the Blessed Infinite Light,** סוֹף בָּרוּךְ הוּא
לְמַטָּה — **from "above" to "below,"** לְהִתְלַבֵּשׁ בְּגַשְׁמִיּוּת עוֹלָם הַזֶּה — **so that** the Blessed Infinite Light **becomes enmeshed in the physical fabric of this world.**

This reward is not something else given *in exchange* for performing the *mitzvah,*
like being paid money for doing a job. Rather, the reward is: you fulfilled the purpose
of creation by causing the Blessed Infinite Light to be
disclosed in this physical world (through your *mitzvah*).

Now we turn to the precise spiritual dynamics of the
mitzvah. As we learned previously, a *mitzvah* brings
about a "home for G-d below," because it causes G-d's
light to be disclosed in a physical object. And, in doing
so, the *mitzvah* elevates the forces of *kelipas nogah*
which had previously ruled that object, bringing pleasure to G-d on High.

בְּדָבָר שֶׁהָיָה תְּחִלָּה תַּחַת מֶמְשֶׁלֶת קְלִיפַת נוֹגַהּ — **And that**
disclosure of the Blessed Infinite Light comes into **an
object which had initially been under the control of** *kelipas nogah,* וּמְקַבֵּל חַיּוּתָה מִמֶּנָּה — **and** the object had
been **receiving its energy from** *kelipas nogah.*

PRACTICAL LESSONS

**The reward for a
mitzvah (in the
Messianic Era) is
to experience the
greatness of the
mitzvah itself, that it
brought G-d's Infinite
Light into the world.**

A *mitzvah* may only be performed with an object
which receives its energy from *kelipas nogah,* the least
potent form of *kelipah* which is capable of acting as a medium for G-d's presence
to be disclosed.

The *Tanya* now briefly reviews some examples of suitable *kelipas nogah* objects,
from the Animal and Plant Kingdoms, as well as from non-living matter.

שֶׁהֵם כָּל דְּבָרִים הַטְּהוֹרִים וּמוּתָּרִים שֶׁנַּעֲשִׂית בָּהֶם הַמִּצְוָה מַעֲשִׂיּית — *Kelipas nogah*
controls **all ritually pure and kosher items with which the practical *mitzvos* may be
observed,** כְּגוֹן קְלַף הַתְּפִילִין וּמְזוּזָה וְסֵפֶר תּוֹרָה — **such as,** in the Animal Kingdom,
the parchment on which *tefilin,* a *mezuzah* or Torah scroll may be written.

וּכְמַאֲמַר רַבּוֹתֵינוּ זִכְרוֹנָם לִבְרָכָה — **As our Sages, of blessed memory, taught,**
לֹא הוּכְשַׁר לִמְלֶאכֶת שָׁמַיִם אֶלָּא טְהוֹרִים — *"Only ritually pure species are fit for the*

אֶתְרוֹג שֶׁאֵינוֹ עָרְלָה*
וּמָעוֹת הַצְּדָקָה שֶׁאֵינָן גֶּזֶל
וְכַיּוֹצֵא בָּהֶם וְעַכְשָׁיו
שֶׁמְּקַיְּים בָּהֶם מִצְוֹת ה'
וּרְצוֹנוֹ הֲרֵי הַחַיּוּת שֶׁבָּהֶם
עוֹלֶה וּמִתְבַּטֵּל וְנִכְלָל בָּאוֹר
אֵ"ס ב"ה שֶׁהוּא רְצוֹנוֹ ית' הַמְּלוּבָּשׁ בָּהֶם מֵאַחַר שֶׁאֵין
שָׁם בְּחִי' הֶסְתֵּר פָּנִים כְּלָל לְהַסְתִּיר אוֹרוֹ ית' וְכֵן כֹּחַ

הגהה

(שֶׁהָעָרְלָה הִיא מִשְּׁלֹשׁ קְלִיפּוֹת
הַטְּמֵאוֹת לְגַמְרֵי שֶׁאֵין לָהֶם עֲלִיָּה
לְעוֹלָם כמ"ש בע"ח וכן כל מצוה
הַבָּאָה בַּעֲבֵירָה ח"ו):

47A

---

work of Heaven" (*Talmud, Shabbos* 28a), וּמוּתָּרִים בְּפִיךָ — and *"that which is per-missible for your mouth"* (*ibid.* 108a).

וְכֵן אֶתְרוֹג שֶׁאֵינוֹ עָרְלָה — **The same is true** in the Plant Kingdom; for example, you may use **an esrog (citron)** for a *mitzvah* (see *Leviticus* 23:40) provided **that it is not** prohibited by the Biblical injunction against *orlah** (which prohibits the first three years of fruit from a tree; *ibid.* 19:23-25), in which case it would come from the completely impure *kelipos*.

13TH ADAR II LEAP

וּמָעוֹת הַצְּדָקָה שֶׁאֵינָן גֶּזֶל וְכַיּוֹצֵא בָּהֶם — **Or,** an example from non-living matter would be **money to be given to charity that was not stolen,** *etc.*, because if it was stolen it would come from the completely impure *kelipos* and be unfit for use as a *mitzvah*.

The *Tanya* now describes what happens spiritually when a *mitzvah* is performed with a *kelipas nogah* object.

וְעַכְשָׁיו שֶׁמְּקַיֵּים בָּהֶם מִצְוֹת ה' וּרְצוֹנוֹ — **And now, when** you take one of these *kelipas nogah* objects **and use them to carry out G-d's mitzvah, which is His will,** הֲרֵי הַחַיּוּת שֶׁבָּהֶם עוֹלֶה וּמִתְבַּטֵּל — **what happens is, the** object's **energy is elevated,** its sense of separateness **is voided,** וְנִכְלָל בָּאוֹר אֵין סוֹף בָּרוּךְ הוּא — **and it's absorbed into the Blessed Infinite Light.**

שֶׁהוּא רְצוֹנוֹ יִתְבָּרֵךְ הַמְּלוּבָּשׁ בָּהֶם — And the disclosure of the Blessed Infinite Light here is nothing other than **G-d's will, as it is expressed in** the *mitzvos*, מֵאַחַר שֶׁאֵין — **since,** as we have learned, in the שָׁם בְּחִינַת הֶסְתֵּר פָּנִים כְּלָל לְהַסְתִּיר אוֹרוֹ יִתְבָּרֵךְ — Divine will expressed within the *mitzvos*, **there is no** *"Hiding of G-d's face"* at all **that would conceal His light** (see p. 262).

---

*הַגָּהָה — ***NOTE.*** שֶׁהָעָרְלָה הִיא מִשְּׁלֹשׁ קְלִיפּוֹת הַטְּמֵאוֹת לְגַמְרֵי שֶׁאֵין לָהֶם עֲלִיָּה לְעוֹלָם — **Since *orlah* is from the three completely impure *kelipos* that can never be elevated to G-d,** כְּמוֹ שֶׁכָּתוּב בְּעֵץ חַיִּים — **as stated in *Etz Chaim* (49:6).**

וְכֵן כָּל מִצְוָה הַבָּאָה בַּעֲבֵירָה — **And the same is true with a *mitzvah* brought about through a sin,** חַס וְשָׁלוֹם — **G-d forbid,** such as giving charity from stolen funds.

נפש החיונית הבהמית שבאברי גוף האדם המקיים
המצוה הוא מתלבש ג"כ בעשיה זו ועולה מהקליפה
ונכלל בקדושת המצוה שהיא רצונו ית' ובטל באור
א"ס ב"ה וגם במצות תלמוד תורה וק"ש ותפלה וכיוצא
בהן אף שאינן בעשיה גשמית ממש שתחת ממשלת
קליפת נוגה מ"מ הא קיימא לן דהרהור לאו כדבור דמי
ואינו יוצא ידי חובתו עד שיוציא בשפתיו וקיימא לן

וְכֵן כֹּחַ נָפֶשׁ הַחִיּוֹנִית הַבַּהֲמִית שֶׁבְּאֵבְרֵי גוּף הָאָדָם הַמְקַיֵּים הַמְצְוָה — **And** not only is the object's energy elevated when a *mitzvah* is observed, **the energizing Animal Soul found in the limbs of the person observing the *mitzvah*, is also** elevated, הוּא מִתְלַבֵּשׁ גַּם כֵּן בַּעֲשִׂיָּה זוֹ — **since** the Animal Soul, **too, was immersed in the act,** as we learned in chapter 35 (p. 394), וְעוֹלֶה מֵהַקְּלִיפָּה — **and it's elevated from** *kelipas nogah,* וְנִכְלָל בִּקְדוּשַׁת הַמְצְוָה שֶׁהִיא רְצוֹנוֹ יִתְבָּרֵךְ — **and becomes absorbed in the holiness of the *mitzvah*, which is G-d's will,** וּבָטֵל בְּאוֹר אֵין סוֹף בָּרוּךְ הוּא — **and** the Animal Soul's sense of separateness **is dissolved in the Blessed Infinite Light.**

SECTION TWO: TORAH STUDY ENGAGES THE PHYSICAL WORLD

So far we have been discussing "practical *mitzvos*" that involve the use of a physical object. But do *mitzvos* that are performed verbally, such as prayer and Torah study, come under the umbrella of "practical *mitzvos*"? Do they also make a "home for G-d below," even though they don't directly involve a physical object?

The *Tanya* will now argue that even prayer and Torah study do cause the Blessed Infinite Light to be disclosed in physical matter.

וְגַם בְּמִצְוֹת תַּלְמוּד תּוֹרָה וּקְרִיאַת שְׁמַע וּתְפִלָּה וְכַיּוֹצֵא בָּהֶן — **And even the *mitzvos* of reading the *Shema*, Torah study, and prayer etc.,** אַף שֶׁאֵינָן בַּעֲשִׂיָּה גַּשְׁמִית מַמָּשׁ — **while they do not involve a *substantive*, physical action** with an object which was previously **under the control of *kelipas nogah*,** שֶׁתַּחַת מֶמְשֶׁלֶת קְלִיפַּת נוֹגַהּ מִכָּל מָקוֹם — **nevertheless,** there is at least some minimal level of physical activity in the moving of the lips as you recite the words.

The *Tanya* now proves the significance of moving the lips, from the point of view of Jewish Law.

הָא קַיְימָא לָן דְּהִרְהוּר לָאו כְּדִבּוּר דָּמֵי — **For we maintain that** with *mitzvos* performed verbally, **"meditation does not count as recitation"** (*Talmud, Brachos* 20b), וְאֵינוֹ יוֹצֵא יְדֵי חוֹבָתוֹ עַד שֶׁיּוֹצִיא בִּשְׂפָתָיו — **and you do not fulfill your obligation** with these *mitzvos,* **until you make** the words **come out of your mouth** (*Tur* and *Shulchan Aruch, Orach Chaim* chapter 62), וְקַיְימָא לָן דַּעֲקִימַת שְׂפָתָיו הָוֵי מַעֲשֶׂה — **and we** maintain that, **"moving the lips constitutes a concrete action"** (*Talmud, Kerisos* 4a).

דְּעָקִימַת שְׂפָתָיו הָוֵי מַעֲשֶׂה כִּי אִי אֶפְשָׁר לַנֶּפֶשׁ הָאֱלֹהִית
לִבַטֵּא בִּשְׂפָתַיִם וּפֶה וְלָשׁוֹן וְשִׁינַּיִם הַגַּשְׁמִיִּים כִּי אִם
עַ"יְ נֶפֶשׁ הַחִיּוּנִית הַבַּהֲמִית הַמְלוּבֶּשֶׁת בְּאֶבְרֵי הַגּוּף
מַמָּשׁ וְכָל מַה שֶּׁמְּדַבֵּר בְּכֹחַ גָּדוֹל יוֹתֵר הוּא מַכְנִיס
וּמַלְבִּישׁ יוֹתֵר כֹּחוֹת מִנֶּפֶשׁ הַחִיּוּנִית בְּדִיבּוּרִים אֵלּוּ וְזֶ"שׁ
הַכָּתוּב כָּל עַצְמוֹתַי תֹּאמַרְנָה וְגוֹ' וְזֶ"שׁ רַזַ"ל אִם עֲרוּכָה

While Torah and prayer may not involve any "substantive" action, the *halachic* requirement to verbally articulate the words does constitute a type of action which engages the Animal Soul. So they are, at some level, "practical *mitzvos*."

כִּי אִי אֶפְשָׁר לַנֶּפֶשׁ הָאֱלֹהִית לִבַטֵּא בִּשְׂפָתַיִם וּפֶה וְלָשׁוֹן וְשִׁינַּיִם הַגַּשְׁמִיִּים — **For it's impossible for the Divine Soul to express itself through** verbal articulation via the **physical lips, mouth, tongue and teeth,** כִּי אִם עַל יְדֵי נֶפֶשׁ הַחִיּוּנִית הַבַּהֲמִית — **unless** the Divine Soul **acts through the medium of the energizing Animal Soul,** הַמְלוּבֶּשֶׁת בְּאֶבְרֵי הַגּוּף מַמָּשׁ — **because,** unlike the Divine Soul which cannot interact directly with the body, the Animal Soul **interacts with the body's limbs tangibly.**

PRACTICAL LESSONS

Even when you study Torah and pray, you make your body a Temple for the Divine by saying the words out loud and involving your body energetically.

The idea is not purely theoretical. It also has the following practical ramification.

וְכָל מַה שֶּׁמְּדַבֵּר בְּכֹחַ גָּדוֹל יוֹתֵר הוּא מַכְנִיס וּמַלְבִּישׁ יוֹתֵר כֹּחוֹת מִנֶּפֶשׁ הַחִיּוּנִית בְּדִיבּוּרִים אֵלּוּ — **And the louder you speak, the more you enter and immerse your energizing** Animal **Soul into those words.**

Practically speaking, when you study Torah and pray more energetically, saying the words with more gusto, your Animal Soul absorbs the Blessed Infinite Light to a greater extent, because it is more involved in the *mitzvah*.

The *Tanya* now cites Scriptural and Talmudic support for the idea of energetic involvement of the body in prayer and study.

וְזֶהוּ שֶׁאָמַר הַכָּתוּב כָּל עַצְמוֹתַי תֹּאמַרְנָה וְגוֹ' — **And the** need to involve the body in prayer **is implied by the verse, "*All my bones will exclaim: Who is like You, G-d?*"** (*Psalms* 35:10).

In Jewish Legal texts, this verse is cited as a source for involving the body in swaying movements during prayer (*Rema, Shulchan Aruch, Orach Chaim* 48:1).

וְזֶהוּ שֶׁאָמְרוּ רַבּוֹתֵינוּ זִכְרוֹנָם לִבְרָכָה — **And this is also stressed by the teaching of our Sages, of blessed memory,** which refers to the importance of studying Torah aloud, אִם עֲרוּכָה בְּכָל רַמַ"ח אֵיבָרִים מִשְׁתַּמֶּרֶת וְאִם לָאו אֵינָהּ מִשְׁתַּמֶּרֶת — "*Beruriah came across a disciple who was learning his traditions in a whisper. She rebuked*

בכל רמ"ח איברים משתמרת ואם לאו אינה משתמרת
כי השכחה היא מקליפת הגוף ונפש החיונית הבהמית
שהן מקליפת נוגה הנכללת לפעמים בקדושה והיינו
כשמשתיש כחן ומכניס כל כחן בקדושת התורה או
התפלה:

זאת ועוד אחרת שכח נפש החיונית המתלבשת
באותיות הדבור בת"ת או תפלה וכיוצא בהן
או מצות מעשיות הרי כל גידולו וחיותו מהדם שהוא
מקליפת נוגה ממש שהן כל אוכלין ומשקין שאכל

him, saying to him, "Isn't this written, 'Ordered in all things and retained' (2 Samuel 23:5)? **If it is ordered in those two hundred and forty-eight limbs** of yours, **it will be retained, and if not, it won't be retained"** (Talmud, Eruvin 54a).

The message here is that your Torah will be "retained" and remembered if your body is engaged when studying it.

כִּי הַשִּׁכְחָה הִיא מִקְּלִיפַת הַגּוּף וְנֶפֶשׁ הַחִיּוּנִית הַבַּהֲמִית — **For** the tendency of **forgetfulness is rooted in the** *kelipah* **of the body and energizing Animal Soul.**

If the cause of the forgetfulness (*kelipah*) can be eliminated (through energetic involvement), Torah is more likely to be retained and remembered.

שֶׁהֵן מִקְּלִיפַת נוֹגַהּ הַנִּכְלֶלֶת לִפְעָמִים בִּקְדוּשָׁה — And **since** the body and Animal Soul **are from** *kelipas nogah,* **which are capable of being** elevated and **absorbed into holiness,** the tendency to forgetfulness can be averted, וְהַיְינוּ כְּשֶׁמַּתִּישׁ כֹּחָן וּמַכְנִיס כָּל כֹּחָן בִּקְדוּשַׁת הַתּוֹרָה אוֹ הַתְּפִלָּה — **and that is when their powers are withdrawn** from non-sacred pursuits, **and fully immersed, into the sacred practice of Torah study or prayer,** *i.e.,* through involving the body and Animal Soul as much as possible, through verbalization and bodily involvement.

SECTION THREE: ELEVATING YOUR FOOD TO G-D

24TH ADAR REGULAR | 14TH ADAR II LEAP

In addition to the primary involvement of a.) the body and b.) Animal Soul in a *mitzvah* act, we will now turn to the secondary involvement of c.) the physical energy that powers them.

זֹאת וְעוֹד אַחֶרֶת שֶׁכֹּחַ נֶפֶשׁ הַחִיּוּנִית הַמִּתְלַבֶּשֶׁת בָּאוֹתִיּוֹת — And yet another point, — is that the energizing הַדִּבּוּר בְּתַלְמוּד תּוֹרָה אוֹ תְּפִלָּה וְכַיּוֹצֵא בָּהֶן אוֹ מִצְוֹת מַעֲשִׂיּוֹת Animal Soul's power invested in the spoken words of Torah study or prayer, *etc.,* or in practical commandments, הֲרֵי כָּל גִּידוּלוֹ וְחִיּוּתוֹ מֵהַדָּם — has been completely nourished and sustained by the blood, שֶׁהוּא מִקְּלִיפַת נוֹגַהּ מַמָּשׁ — which is from

47B ושתה ונעשו דם שהיו תחת ממשלתה וינקו חיותם
ממנה ועתה היא מתהפכת מרע לטוב ונכללת בקדוש'
ע"י כח נפש החיונית הגדל ממנה שנתלבש באותיות
אלו או בעשיה זו אשר הן הן פנימיות רצונו ית' בלי
שום הסתר פנים וחיותן נכלל ג"כ באור א"ס ב"ה שהוא
רצונו ית' ובחיותן נכלל ועולה ג"כ כח נפש החיונית

PRACTICAL LESSONS

A *mitzvah* elevates:
a.) your body; b.) your
Animal Soul and c.)
the food in your blood
which powers the act.

kelipas nogah itself, שֶׁהֵן כָּל אוֹכָלִין וּמַשְׁקִין שֶׁאָכַל וְשָׁתָה
— this nourishment of the blood being from **all the food
and drink that you ate and drank,** וְנַעֲשׂוּ דָם שֶׁהָיוּ תַּחַת
מֶמְשַׁלְתָּה — **which entered your blood, and came under
its ruling** spiritual **force** of *kelipas nogah,* וְיָנְקוּ חַיּוּתָם
מִמֶּנָּה — and **became its source of nourishment.**

The food and drink that gave you energy are an important participant in the *mitzvah.* Since that energy was from
the powers of *kelipas nogah* (through the blood), it follows
that when you do a *mitzvah,* you elevate that food/*kelipas
nogah* energy too — as the *Tanya* will now explain.

וְעַתָּה הִיא מִתְהַפֶּכֶת מֵרָע לְטוֹב וְנִכְלֶלֶת בִּקְדוּשָׁה — And now that you use this food energy in your blood to do a *mitzvah,* **it's transformed from negative** (*kelipas nogah*),
to good, and is absorbed into the powers of **holiness,** עַל יְדֵי כֹּחַ נֶפֶשׁ הַחִיּוּנִית,
through the power of the energizing Animal **Soul,** that made your body move to do
the *mitzvah,* הַגָּדֵל מִמֶּנָּה — since that power of your Animal Soul **was nourished by**
the food in your blood, זוֹ שֶׁנִּתְלַבֵּשׁ בָּאוֹתִיּוֹת אֵלּוּ אוֹ בַּעֲשִׂיָּה — and then that power of
your Animal Soul, nourished by the food in your blood, **immersed itself into those
words** of Torah study or prayer, **or into that** *mitzvah* **act,** אֲשֶׁר הֵן הֵן פְּנִימִיּוּת רְצוֹנוֹ
יִתְבָּרֵךְ בְּלִי שׁוּם הֶסְתֵּר פָּנִים — that *mitzvah* **being the actual inner will of G-d, devoid
of any** *"Hiding of G-d's face,"* וְחַיּוּתָן נִכְלָל גַּם כֵּן בְּאוֹר אֵין סוֹף בָּרוּךְ הוּא שֶׁהוּא רְצוֹנוֹ
יִתְבָּרֵךְ — and as a result, **the energy** from the food in your blood which powered
the Animal Soul to do the *mitzvah,* **becomes absorbed in the Blessed Infinite Light,
which is** in the *mitzvah,* since the *mitzvah* is **the will of G-d.**

וּבְחַיּוּתָן נִכְלָל וְעוֹלֶה גַּם כֵּן כֹּחַ נֶפֶשׁ הַחִיּוּנִית — And along with the energy from the
food in the blood, which is elevated through the *mitzvah,* **the power of the energizing** Animal **Soul** which was used to carry out the *mitzvah,* **is also elevated and
absorbed** in the Blessed Infinite Light.

SECTION FOUR: THE EFFECTS OF KELIPAS NOGAH ELEVATION

The effects of all this *kelipas nogah* elevation (through the body, Animal Soul and
the food energy that powered them) are cumulative, and will eventually result in the
entire global force of *kelipas nogah* being elevated to G-d.

וע"י זה תעלה ג"כ כללות קליפת נוגה שהיא כללות
החיות של עו"הז הגשמי והחומרי כאשר כל הנשמה
ונפש האלהית שבכל ישראל המתחלקת בפרטות
לששים רבוא תקיים כל נפש פרטית כל תרי"ג מצות
התורה שס"ה ל"ת להפריד שס"ה גידים של דם נפש
החיונית שבגוף שלא יינקו ויקבלו חיות בעבירה זו
מאחת משלש קליפות הטמאות לגמרי שמהן נשפעים

וְעַל יְדֵי זֶה תַּעֲלֶה גַם כֵּן כְּלָלוּת קְלִיפַּת נוֹגַה — **And through this the entire** global force
of *kelipas nogah* **will** eventually **be elevated, too,** שֶׁהִיא כְּלָלוּת הַחַיּוּת שֶׁל עוֹלָם הַזֶּה
הַגַּשְׁמִי וְהַחוּמְרִי — **which is the foundational energy of this physical, material world.**

15TH ADAR II LEAP

כַּאֲשֶׁר כָּל הַנְּשָׁמָה וְנֶפֶשׁ הָאֱלֹהִית שֶׁבְּכָל יִשְׂרָאֵל — **And** this global elevation will be
complete **when every** *neshamah* **and Divine Soul in all Israel,** globally, will cause
every Animal Soul to observe all the *mitzvos,* thereby elevating the entire structure
of *kelipas nogah* (as we shall see later in the chapter).

The *Tanya* now clarifies how many souls we are speaking of:

הַמִּתְחַלֶּקֶת בִּפְרָטוּת לְשִׁשִּׁים רִבּוֹא — "Israel" refers to a group of souls **which is divided into six hundred thousand core units** (which are then further subdivided into
millions of Jewish souls, which have been spread throughout history).

The census of Israelites in the desert after Sinai totaled approximately six hundred thousand individuals (*Numbers* 1:46). According to the Kabbalah, this hints
to a mystical reality that G-d created six hundred thousand basic soul units within
the Jewish people, and each of our souls is a "spark" from one of these core six
hundred thousand souls (see Rabbi Chaim Vital, *Sha'ar Ha-Gilgulim* chapter 17).
All of these soul units need to observe the Torah in order for *kelipas nogah* to be
elevated on a global level.

The discussion up to this point has centered around making a "home for G-d"
by observing the 248 positive commands, with the body and Animal Soul actively
engaging and elevating the world. But how do the 365 negative prohibitions fit into
this picture? How do we make a "home for G-d" through the prohibitions if they do
not demand any action, but rather, the cessation of action (*"Don't…"*)?

תְּקַיֵּם כָּל נֶפֶשׁ פְּרָטִית כָּל תַּרְיַ"ג מִצְוֹת הַתּוֹרָה — **Each, individual soul must observe all
six hundred and thirteen** *mitzvos* **of the Torah,** שַׁ"סַה לֹא תַעֲשֶׂה — including **the 365
prohibitions,** לְהַפְרִיד שַׁ"סַה גִּידִים שֶׁל דַּם נֶפֶשׁ הַחִיּוֹנִית שֶׁבַּגּוּף שֶׁלֹּא יִינְקוּ וִיקַבְּלוּ חִיּוּת
בַּעֲבֵירָה זוֹ מֵאַחַת מִשְּׁלֹשׁ קְלִיפוֹת הַטְּמֵאוֹת לְגַמְרֵי — **in order to keep the body's 365**
major **blood vessels, where the energizing Animal Soul is found, from being nourished by one** of these **sins,** which would cause them to **receive energy from one**

שס"ה לא תעשה דאורייתֹ' ועַנפיהן שהן מדרבנן ושוב
לא תוכל נפש החיונית לעלות אל ה' אם נטמאה
בטומאת השלש קליפות הטמאות שאין להן עליה
לעולם כ"א ביטול והעברה לגמרי כמ"ש ואת רוח
הטומאה אעביר מן הארץ ורמ"ח מצות עשה להמשיך
אור א"ס ב"ה למטה להעלות לו ולקשר ולייחד בו
כללות הנפש החיונית שברמ"ח אברי הגוף ביחוד גמור

שֶׁמֵּהֶן נִשְׁפָּעִים שס"ה לֹא תַעֲשֶׂה דְּאוֹרַיְיתָא — **of the three completely impure *kelipos*,** וְעַנְפֵיהֶן שֶׁהֵן מִדְּרַבָּנָן — **since it is** from the three completely impure *kelipos* that energy **flows to the 365 Biblical prohibitions and their Rabbinic derivatives.**

Keeping the body free from the completely impure *kelipos* (by refraining from the 365 prohibitions and their Rabbinic derivatives) is crucial because:

וְשׁוּב לֹא תוּכַל נֶפֶשׁ הַחִיּוֹנִית לַעֲלוֹת אֶל ה' אִם נִטְמְאָה בְּטוּמְאַת הַשָּׁלֹשׁ קְלִיפוֹת הַטְּמֵאוֹת — **Once the energizing** Animal **Soul** in the blood **is contaminated by one of the three impure *kelipos*, it can no longer be elevated to G-d,** שֶׁאֵין לָהֶן עֲלִיָּה לְעוֹלָם — **since,** unlike the permitted pleasures of *kelipas nogah*, the three completely impure *kelipos* **can never be elevated,** כִּי אִם בִּיטוּל וְהַעֲבָרָה לְגַמְרֵי — **rather they must be eradicated and removed completely,** כְּמוֹ שֶׁכָּתוּב וְאֶת רוּחַ הַטּוּמְאָה אַעֲבִיר מִן הָאָרֶץ — **as the verse states, *"I will remove the spirit of impurity from the earth"* (Zechariah 13:2),** indicating that the "spirit of (complete) impurity" must be "removed"; it cannot be elevated (see *A Chasidic Thought*).

וְרַמַ"ח מִצְוֹת עֲשֵׂה — **And,** in addition to refraining from the prohibitions, every soul must also observe **the 248 positive *mitzvos,*** לְהַמְשִׁיךְ אוֹר אֵין סוֹף בָּרוּךְ הוּא לְמַטָּה — which have the spiritual effect of **"pulling" the Blessed Infinite Light downwards** into this world, לְהַעֲלוֹת לוֹ — **and they also have the effect of elevating the person,** וּלְקַשֵּׁר וּלְיַיחֵד בּוֹ כְּלָלוּת הַנֶּפֶשׁ הַחִיּוֹנִית שֶׁבְּרַמַ"ח אֶבְרֵי הַגוּף בְּיִחוּד גָּמוּר — **connecting and merging the whole structure of the energizing** Animal **Soul, found in the 248 limbs of the body, to merge completely** with the Blessed Infinite Light.

A CHASIDIC THOUGHT

Refraining from the 365 prohibitions is crucial to keep the body clean from the impure kelipos which would contaminate the system, preventing the body's energy from being elevated to G-d. So the prohibitions don't actually *make* a "home for G-d"; it's just that violating any one of them impedes the process.

להיות לאחדים ממש כמו שעלה ברצונו ית' להיות לו
דירה בתחתונים והם לו למרכבה כמו האבות. ומאחר
שכללות נפש החיונית שבכללות ישראל תהיה מרכבה
קדושה לה' אזי גם כללות החיות של עו"הז שהיא
קליפת נוגה עכשיו תצא אז מטומאת' וחלאתה ותעלה
לקדושה להיות מרכבה לה' בהתגלות כבודו וראו כל
בשר יחדיו ויופיע עליהם בהדר גאון עוזו וימלא כבוד

By preventing the completely impure *kelipos* from entering the body (through refraining from the 365 prohibitions) there is then no obstacle to elevating the body to G-d, by means of the 248 positive *mitzvos*. And when this is achieved:

לִהְיוֹת לַאֲחָדִים מַמָּשׁ — Even the Animal Soul **becomes literally one with G-d,** כְּמוֹ שֶׁעָלָה בִּרְצוֹנוֹ יִתְבָּרֵךְ לִהְיוֹת לוֹ דִּירָה בַּתַּחְתּוֹנִים — thereby fulfilling **the will which arose in G-d's** mind before creation, **that He should have a "home in the lowest realms,"** וְהֵם לוֹ לְמֶרְכָּבָה כְּמוֹ הָאָבוֹת — **which have now become a "chariot," like the Patriarchs** (see pp. 259, 378).

25TH ADAR REGULAR | 16TH ADAR II LEAP

Now we can understand the *Tanya's* statement above, that *kelipas nogah* will be elevated to G-d globally when every individual soul will observe the 613 *mitzvos*.

וּמֵאַחַר שֶׁכְּלָלוּת נֶפֶשׁ הַחִיּוּנִית שֶׁבְּכְלָלוּת יִשְׂרָאֵל תִּהְיֶה מֶרְכָּבָה קְדוֹשָׁה לַה' — **And when the whole structure of the energizing Animal Soul in all of Israel will become a "chariot" to G-d,** אֲזַי גַּם כְּלָלוּת הַחַיּוּת שֶׁל עוֹלָם הַזֶּה שֶׁהִיא קְלִיפַת נוֹגַהּ עַכְשָׁיו תֵּצֵא אָז מְטוּמְאָתָהּ וְחֶלְאָתָהּ — **then the whole energy structure of this world, which is currently from** *kelipas nogah,* **will leave its "impurity and filth"** (see *Ezekiel* 24:11), וְתַעֲלֶה לִקְדוּשָׁה לִהְיוֹת מֶרְכָּבָה לַה' — **and be elevated to holiness, becoming a "chariot" to G-d.** בְּהִתְגַּלּוֹת כְּבוֹדוֹ וְרָאוּ כָל בָּשָׂר יַחְדָּיו — **And this will be in the Messianic Era when His "glory will be revealed and all flesh will see together** that G-d is speaking" (*Isaiah*

A CHASIDIC THOUGHT

The readers of the *Tanya* have now been "comforted" further for their predicament of constantly struggling "*to battle in vain with the impulse to evil... unable to prevail over it*" (p. 388). Ultimately, we are taught here, it is the practical commandments, performed in speech and action, that elevate the world and directly cause all the revelations of the Messianic Era. These activities are within the full control of all of us.

48A

ה' את כל הארץ וישראל יראו עין בעין כבמתן תורה
דכתיב אתה הראת לדעת כי ה' הוא האלהים אין עוד
מלבדו ועל ידי זה יתבלעו ויתבטלו לגמרי כל השלש
קליפות הטמאות כי יניקתן וחיותן מהקדושה עכשיו
היא ע"י קליפת נוגה הממוצעת ביניהן ונמצא כי כל
תכלית של ימות המשיח ותחיית המתים שהוא גילוי
כבודו ואלהותו ית' ולהעביר רוח הטומאה מן הארץ
תלוי בהמשכת אלהותו אור א"ס ב"ה לנפש החיונית
שבכללות ישראל בכל רמ"ח אבריה ע"י קיומה כל

וְיוֹפִיעַ עֲלֵיהֶם בַּהֲדַר גְּאוֹן עוּזּוֹ ,(40:5) — and He will **"Shine forth (over them) with the majesty of His triumphant strength"** (Liturgy, High Holiday Amidah), וְיִמְּלֵא כְבוֹד ה' — **"And the glory of G-d will fill all the earth,"** (Numbers 14:21), אֶת כָּל הָאָרֶץ — and Israel **"shall see (G-d) eye to eye"** (ibid. 52:8), יִרְאוּ עַיִן בְּעַיִן — like at the giving of the Torah, of which the verse states, **"You were shown to know that the G-d is G-d, there is none besides Him,"** (Deuteronomy 4:35), with the emphasis here on being "shown" G-d's presence (see above chapter 36, p. 405).

Kelipas nogah, then, is destined to be elevated in its entirety to G-d. But what will become of the three impure kelipos that cannot be elevated?

וְעַל יְדֵי זֶה — **And as a** direct **result of this** global elevation of the fundamental structure of kelipas nogah, יִתְבַּלְעוּ וְיִתְבַּטְּלוּ לְגַמְרֵי כָּל הַשָּׁלֹשׁ קְלִיפּוֹת הַטְּמֵאוֹת — **the three** completely impure kelipos **will be entirely consumed and eradicated,** כִּי יְנִיקָתָן וְחִיּוּתָן מֵהַקְּדוּשָׁה עַכְשִׁיו הִיא עַל יְדֵי קְלִיפַּת נוֹגַה הַמְמוּצַּעַת בֵּינֵיהֶן — **because, currently, their nourishment and sustenance comes from** the realm of **holiness via kelipas nogah,** which acts as an intermediary between them.

Therefore, when kelipas nogah will be eradicated, the three completely impure kelipos will automatically lose their source of sustenance and be eradicated too.

SECTION FIVE: WHY YOUR BODY IS SO IMPORTANT

17TH ADAR II LEAP

וְנִמְצָא כִּי כָּל תַּכְלִית שֶׁל יְמוֹת הַמָּשִׁיחַ וּתְחִיַּית הַמֵּתִים — It follows, then, that the ultimate goal of the Messianic Era and the revival of the dead, שֶׁהוּא גִּילּוּי כְּבוֹדוֹ — namely, the disclosure of Divine glory and G-dliness, and to "remove the spirit of impurity from the earth," תָּלוּי — וֶאֱלֹהוּתוֹ יִתְבָּרֵךְ וּלְהַעֲבִיר רוּחַ הַטּוּמְאָה מִן הָאָרֶץ **depends on:** a.) **"pulling" G-dliness** בְּהַמְשָׁכַת אֱלֹהוּתוֹ וְאוֹר אֵין סוֹף בָּרוּךְ הוּא לְנֶפֶשׁ הַחִיּוֹנִית שֶׁבְּכְלָלוּת יִשְׂרָאֵל בְּכָל רַמַ"ח אֲבָרֶיהָ עַל יְדֵי קִיוּמָהּ כָּל רַמַ"ח מִצְוֹת עֲשֵׂה — **and the Blessed Infinite Light into the energizing** Animal **Souls of all Israel, in all**

רמ"ח מצות עשה ולהעביר רוח הטומאה ממנה
בשמירת' כל שס"ה מצות ל"ת שלא יינקו ממנה שס"ה
גידיה כי כללות ישראל שהם ששים רבוא נשמות
פרטיות הם כללות החיות של כללות העולם כי
בשבילם נברא וכל פרט מהם הוא כולל ושייך לו
החיות של חלק אחד מששים רבוא מכללות העולם
התלוי בנפשו החיונית להעלותו לה' בעלייתה דהיינו
במה שמשתמש מעו"הז לצורך גופו ונפשו החיונית
לעבודת ה' כגון אכילה ושתיה ודומיהם ודירה וכל כלי
תשמישיו אלא ששים רבוא נשמות פרטיות אלו הן
שרשי' וכל שרש מתחלק לששים רבוא ניצוצות שכל

וּלְהַעֲבִיר רוּחַ **their 248 limbs, through the observance of all 248 positive** *mitzvos,*
הַטּוּמְאָה מִמֶּנָּה בִּשְׁמִירָתָהּ כָּל שַׁס"ה מִצְוֹת לֹא תַעֲשֶׂה שֶׁלֹּא יִינְקוּ מִמֶּנָּה שַׁס"ה גִּידֶיהָ
and b.) to remove the *"spirit of impurity"* **from** the energizing Animal Souls of all
Israel, **through refraining from all the 365 prohibitions, so that the 365** major **blood
vessels are not nourished** from the completely impure *kelipos.*

שֶׁהֵם שִׁשִּׁים — כִּי כְּלָלוּת יִשְׂרָאֵל — **Because the overall structure of** the souls of Israel,
רִבּוֹא נְשָׁמוֹת פְּרָטִיּוֹת — **which consists of six hundred thousand core soul units,**
הֵם כְּלָלוּת הַחַיּוּת שֶׁל כְּלָלוּת הָעוֹלָם — **represents the foundational** spiritual **energy
of the whole world,** כִּי בִּשְׁבִילָם נִבְרָא — **which was created for their sake** (*Rashi* to
Genesis 1:1).

וְכָל פְּרָט מֵהֶם הוּא כּוֹלֵל וְשַׁיָּיךְ לוֹ הַחַיּוּת שֶׁל חֵלֶק אֶחָד מִשִּׁשִּׁים רִבּוֹא מִכְּלָלוּת הָעוֹלָם
— **And each individual** core soul **is designated (and contains) the energy of one
six-hundred thousandth part of the whole** physical **world,** הַתָּלוּי בְּנַפְשׁוֹ הַחִיוֹנִית
לְהַעֲלוֹתוֹ לַה' בַּעֲלִיָּיתָהּ — and **the elevation of** that portion of the world to which a
soul has been designated, **is dependent on that energizing soul's elevation to G-d.**

דְּהַיְינוּ בְּמַה שֶׁמִּשְׁתַּמֵּשׁ מֵעוֹלָם הַזֶּה לְצוֹרֶךְ גּוּפוֹ וְנַפְשׁוֹ הַחִיוֹנִית לַעֲבוֹדַת ה' — **And this**
elevation of your specific portion of the world **takes place when you use this phys-
ical world to help your body and energizing** Animal Soul **worship G-d,** כְּגוֹן אֲכִילָה
וּשְׁתִיָּה וְדוֹמֵיהֶם וְדִירָה וְכָל כְּלֵי תַשְׁמִישָׁיו — **such as eating and drinking,** *etc.,* **as well
as** using your **home and all its equipment.**

The *Tanya* now clarifies how the millions of actual souls arise from the basic six
hundred thousand basic soul-roots.

אֶלָּא שֶׁשִּׁשִּׁים רִבּוֹא נְשָׁמוֹת פְּרָטִיּוֹת אֵלוּ הֵן שָׁרָשִׁים — **Only** there are, of course, more
that six hundred thousand souls, **since the six hundred thousand soul-units are
basic soul-roots,** וְכָל שֹׁרֶשׁ מִתְחַלֵּק לְשִׁשִּׁים רִבּוֹא נִיצוֹצוֹת — **and each** soul-root is

ניצוץ הוא נשמה אחת וכן בנפש ורוח בכל עולם
מארבע עולמות אצילו' בריאה יצירה עשיה וכל ניצוץ
לא ירד לעו"הז אף שהיא ירידה גדולה ובחי' גלות
ממש כי גם שיהיה צדיק גמור עובד ה' ביראה ואהבה
רבה בתענוגים לא יגיע למעלות דביקותו בה' בדחילו
ורחימו בטרם ירידתו לעו"הז החומרי לא מינה ולא
מקצתה ואין ערך ודמיון ביניהם כלל כנודע לכל משכיל
שהגוף אינו יכול לסבול כו' אלא ירידתו לעולם הזה

48B

subdivided into a further **six hundred thousand** soul-sparks, שֶׁכָּל נִיצוֹץ הוּא נְשָׁמָה אַחַת — **each spark being a single soul** (neshamah).

וְכֵן בְּנֶפֶשׁ וְרוּחַ — **And the same is true with** the other parts of the soul, nefesh and ruach which are also subdivided into a further six hundred thousand soul-sparks, בְּכָל עוֹלָם מֵאַרְבָּעָה עוֹלָמוֹת אֲצִילוּת בְּרִיאָה יְצִירָה עֲשִׂיָה — **and the same subdivision exists in each world, throughout each of the four worlds,** Atzilus, Briah, Yetzirah and Asiyah.

26TH ADAR REGULAR | 19TH ADAR II LEAP

We now return to the theme of "comfort" for our life-long task of struggling to observe the practical mitzvos.

וְכָל נִיצוֹץ לֹא יָרַד לְעוֹלָם הַזֶּה — **And each** soul-spark came down to this world, not for its own sake, but to influence the Animal Soul and body, as we shall see.

Before elaborating on this point, the Tanya notes parenthetically that for the soul to come into this world represented a very great "downgrade."

אַף שֶׁהִיא יְרִידָה גְדוֹלָה וּבְחִינַת גָּלוּת מַמָּשׁ — **And** coming into this world **is a very great "downgrade,"** for the soul, **a real experience of exile,** כִּי גַם שֶׁיִּהְיֶה צַדִּיק גָּמוּר עוֹבֵד ה' בְּיִרְאָה וְאַהֲבָה רַבָּה בַּתַעֲנוּגִים — **for even if** that soul/body combination were **to become a complete** tzadik, **worshiping G-d with reverence and "great" and "pleasurable" love** (see p. 117), לֹא יַגִּיע לְמַעֲלוֹת דְּבֵיקוּתוֹ בָּהּ' בְּדְחִילוּ וּרְחִימוּ בְּטֶרֶם יְרִידָתוֹ לָעוֹלָם הַזֶּה הַחוּמְרִי — **that soul wouldn't reach the same level of emotive connection to G-d, the love and fear that it experienced before coming down to this material world,** לֹא מִינָּה וְלֹא מִקְצָתָה — **"neither a part of it, nor a fraction of it"** (Talmud, Sotah 5a), וְאֵין עֵרֶךְ וְדִמְיוֹן בֵּינֵיהֶם כְּלָל — **there is simply no similarity or comparison at all** between these two states, כַּנוֹדָע לְכָל מַשְׂכִּיל שֶׁהַגוּף אֵינוֹ יָכוֹל לִסְבּוֹל כו' — **as every intelligent person realizes, that the body can't contain** the same level of emotive connection to G-d as a soul in heaven.

So if the soul has nothing to gain from the "exile" of coming down into a body, then what is the point of this "downgrade"?

אֶלָּא יְרִידָתוֹ לָעוֹלָם הַזֶּה לְהִתְלַבֵּשׁ בַּגוּף וְנֶפֶשׁ הַחִיּוֹנִית הוּא כְּדֵי לְתַקְנָם בִּלְבַד — **Rather**

לְהִתְלַבֵּשׁ בַּגּוּף וְנֶפֶשׁ הַחִיּוּנִית הוּא כְּדֵי לְתַקְּנָם בִּלְבַד
וּלְהַפְרִידָם מֵהָרַע שֶׁל שָׁלֹשׁ קְלִיפּוֹת הַטְּמֵאוֹת עַל יְדֵי
שְׁמִירַת שס"ה לֹא תַעֲשֶׂה וְעַנְפֵיהֶן וּלְהַעֲלוֹת נַפְשׁוּ
הַחִיּוּנִית עִם חֶלְקָה הַשַּׁיָּךְ לָהּ מִכְּלָלוּת עוֹ"הַז וּלְקַשְּׁרָם
וּלְיַחֲדָם בְּאוֹר א"ס ב"ה אֲשֶׁר יַמְשִׁיךְ בָּהֶם עַל יְדֵי קִיּוּמוֹ
כָּל רְמַ"ח מִצְוֹת עָשָׂה בְּנַפְשׁוֹ הַחִיּוּנִי' שֶׁהִיא הִיא הַמְקַיֵּים'
כָּל מִצְוֹת מַעֲשִׂיּוֹת כַּנַּ"ל וּכְמַ"שׁ [בע"ח שַׁעַר כ"ו] כִּי
הַנְשָׁמָה עַצְמָה אֵינָהּ צְרִיכָה תִיקּוּן כְּלָל כּוּ' וְלֹא הוּצְרְכָה
לְהִתְלַבֵּשׁ בָּעוֹ"הַז וְכוּ' רַק לְהַמְשִׁיךְ אוֹר לְתַקְּנָם כוּ' וְהוּא
מַמָּשׁ דּוּגְמַת סוֹד גָּלוּת הַשְּׁכִינָה לְבָרֵר נִיצוֹצִין וְכוּ'.

the soul's **"downgrade" as it is invested into a body and** energizing **Animal Soul, is only for the purpose of fixing** the body and Animal Soul, and not for the soul's own sake.

וּלְהַפְרִידָם מֵהָרַע שֶׁל שָׁלֹשׁ קְלִיפוֹת הַטְּמֵאוֹת — Namely: a.) **to keep** the body and Animal Soul **away from the negative powers of the three completely impure** *kelipos*, עַל יְדֵי שְׁמִירַת שַׁס"ה לֹא תַעֲשֶׂה וְעַנְפֵיהֶן — **through observing the 365** Torah **prohibitions and their** Rabbinic **derivatives.**

וּלְהַעֲלוֹת נַפְשׁוֹ הַחִיּוּנִית עִם חֶלְקָה הַשַּׁיָּךְ לָהּ מִכְּלָלוּת עוֹלָם הַזֶּה — **And: b.) to elevate the energizing** Animal **Soul, along with the** unique **portion of the world-at-large which has been designated to** that soul, וּלְקַשְּׁרָם — to connect and merge the Animal Soul/world **with the Blessed Infinite Light,** וּלְיַחֲדָם בְּאוֹר אֵין סוֹף בָּרוּךְ הוּא — אֲשֶׁר יַמְשִׁיךְ בָּהֶם עַל יְדֵי קִיּוּמוֹ כָּל רְמַ"ח מִצְוֹת עֲשֵׂה — **which is "pulled" upon** the Animal Soul/world **through observing all the 248 positive** *mitzvos*, בְּנַפְשׁוֹ הַחִיּוּנִית — שֶׁהִיא הִיא הַמְקַיֶּימֶת כָּל מִצְוֹת מַעֲשִׂיּוֹת כַּנִּזְכָּר לְעֵיל — **with the energizing** Animal **Soul, which, as mentioned above, is the active force that** powers the observance **of the practical commandments.**

The *Tanya* now cites a source in the teachings of *Arizal* for this conclusion, that the soul only comes down to elevate the body, and not for its own sake.

PRACTICAL LESSONS

Your soul "does not require fixing at all." It came down from heaven only to help your Animal Soul and body fulfill their purpose.

וּכְמוֹ שֶׁכָּתוּב [בְּעֵץ חַיִּים שַׁעַר כ"ו] כִּי הַנְשָׁמָה עַצְמָה אֵינָה צְרִיכָה תִיקּוּן כְּלָל כוּ' — As stated [in *Etz Chaim*, section 26, chapter 1], **that the soul itself** *"does not require fixing at all etc,"* וְלֹא הוּצְרְכָה לְהִתְלַבֵּשׁ בָּעוֹלָם הַזֶּה וְכוּ' רַק לְהַמְשִׁיךְ אוֹר לְתַקְּנָם כוּ' — and **was forced into this world,** into the body and Animal Soul, *"only to pull light upon them to fix them, etc.,"* וְהוּא מַמָּשׁ דּוּגְמַת סוֹד גָּלוּת הַשְּׁכִינָה לְבָרֵר נִיצוֹצִין וְכוּ' — **in a**

וּבָזֶה יוּבָן מַה שֶׁהִפְלִיגוּ רז"ל בִּמְאֹד מְאֹד בְּמַעֲלַת
הַצְּדָקָה וְאָמְרוּ שֶׁשְּׁקוּלָה כְּנֶגֶד כָּל הַמִּצְוֹת וּבְכָל תַּלְמוּד
יְרוּשַׁלְמִי הִיא נִק' בְּשֵׁם מִצְוָה סְתָם כִּי כָךְ הָיָה הֶרְגֵּל
הַלָּשׁוֹן לִקְרוֹא צְדָקָה בְּשֵׁם מִצְוָה סְתָם מִפְּנֵי שֶׁהִיא
עִיקַר הַמִּצְוֹת מַעֲשִׂיּוֹת וְעוֹלָה עַל כּוּלָנָה שֶׁכּוּלָן הֵן רַק
לְהַעֲלוֹת נֶפֶשׁ הַחִיּוּנִית לַה' שֶׁהִיא הִיא הַמְקַיֶּימֶת אוֹתָן
וּמִתְלַבֶּשֶׁת בָּהֶן לִיכָּלֵל בְּאוֹר א"ס ב"ה הַמְּלוּבָּשׁ בָּהֶן
וְאֵין לְךָ מִצְוָה שֶׁנֶּפֶשׁ הַחִיּוּנִית מִתְלַבֶּשֶׁת בָּהּ כָּל כָּךְ
כְּבְמִצְוַת הַצְּדָקָה שֶׁבְּכָל הַמִּצְוֹת אֵין מִתְלַבֵּשׁ בָּהֶן רַק

way that is *"directly comparable to (the secret of) the Shechinah's exile, which is for the sake of elevating sparks that have fallen."*

The soul resembles the *Shechinah* (Divine Presence) in that: a.) It did not come down into the world for its own sake; but rather, b.) for the sake of elevating the physical world with which it becomes enmeshed.

SECTION FIVE: THE IMPORTANCE OF CHARITY

27TH ADAR REGULAR | 20TH ADAR II LEAP

Based on וּבָזֶה יוּבָן מַה שֶׁהִפְלִיגוּ רַבּוֹתֵינוּ זִכְרוֹנָם לִבְרָכָה בִּמְאֹד מְאֹד בְּמַעֲלַת הַצְּדָקָה — **the above, we can appreciate why the Sages praised the virtue of charity to a very, very great extent,** וְאָמְרוּ שֶׁשְּׁקוּלָה כְּנֶגֶד כָּל הַמִּצְוֹת — **saying that it's** *"equivalent to all the other mitzvos put together"* (Talmud, Bava Basra 9a), וּבְכָל תַּלְמוּד יְרוּשַׁלְמִי הִיא נִקְרֵאת בְּשֵׁם מִצְוָה סְתָם — **and across the** *Jerusalem Talmud* **it's simply called, "the** *mitzvah***,"** without any further clarification (see *Jerusalem Talmud, Peah* 8:8; *Horayos* 3:4), כִּי כָךְ הָיָה הֶרְגֵּל הַלָּשׁוֹן לִקְרוֹא צְדָקָה בְּשֵׁם מִצְוָה סְתָם מִפְּנֵי שֶׁהִיא עִיקַר הַמִּצְוֹת מַעֲשִׂיּוֹת — **since it was normal to refer to charity simply as "the** *mitzvah***," because it's the most significant of all the practical commandments,** וְעוֹלָה עַל כּוּלָנָה — **and it surpasses them all.**

שֶׁכּוּלָן הֵן רַק לְהַעֲלוֹת נֶפֶשׁ הַחִיּוּנִית לַה' — **For, as we have seen, the purpose of all the** *mitzvos* **is only to elevate the energizing** Animal **Soul to G-d,** שֶׁהִיא הִיא הַמְקַיֶּימֶת אוֹתָן — **being that** the Animal Soul **is the active force that powers their observance,** וּמִתְלַבֶּשֶׁת בָּהֶן — **and it's the Animal Soul that becomes immersed in their** observance, לִיכָּלֵל בְּאוֹר אֵין סוֹף בָּרוּךְ הוּא הַמְּלוּבָּשׁ בָּהֶן — **resulting in** the Animal Soul **being absorbed in the Blessed Infinite Light which is "dressed" in** the *mitzvos.*

וְאֵין לְךָ מִצְוָה שֶׁנֶּפֶשׁ הַחִיּוּנִית מִתְלַבֶּשֶׁת בָּהּ כָּל כָּךְ כְּבְמִצְוַת הַצְּדָקָה — **And you have no** *mitzvah* **through which the energizing** Animal **Soul is immersed to a greater extent, than the** *mitzvah* **of charity,** שֶׁבְּכָל הַמִּצְוֹת אֵין מִתְלַבֵּשׁ בָּהֶן רַק כֹּחַ אֶחָד מִנֶּפֶשׁ הַחִיּוּנִית — **because, with the other** *mitzvos,* which momentarily engage just one

כח א' מנפש החיונית בשעת מעשה המצוה לבד אבל
בצדקה שאדם נותן מיגיע כפיו הרי כל כח נפשו
החיונית מלובש בעשיית מלאכתו או עסק אחר שנשתכר
בו מעות אלו וכשנותנן לצדקה הרי כל נפשו החיונית
עולה לה' וגם מי שאינו נהנה מיגיעו מ"מ הואיל
ובמעות אלו היה יכול לקנות חיי נפשו החיונית הרי
נותן חיי נפשו לה'. ולכן אמרו רז"ל שמקרבת את
הגאולה לפי שבצדק' אחת מעלה הרבה מנפש החיונית
מה שלא היה יכול להעלות ממנה כל כך כחות ובחי'

49A

part of the body, **only one component of the energizing** Animal **Soul is immersed in them,** בִּשְׁעַת מַעֲשֵׂה הַמִּצְוָה לְבָד — and this is only **at the moment when** each *mitzvah* **is observed,** אֲבָל בִּצְדָקָה שֶׁאָדָם נוֹתֵן מִיגִּיעַ כַּפָּיו — **but with charity, which a person gives from** money earned **through his hard work** over an extended period of time, הֲרֵי כָּל כֹּחַ נַפְשׁוֹ הַחִיּוּנִית מְלוּבָּשׁ בַּעֲשִׂיַּית מְלַאכְתּוֹ אוֹ עֵסֶק אַחֵר שֶׁנִּשְׂתַּכֵּר בּוֹ מָעוֹת אֵלּוּ וּכְשֶׁנּוֹתְנָן לִצְדָקָה — **the result is that all the powers of his energizing** Animal **Soul that were immersed in the manual labor, or other activity by which he accrued these funds,** are elevated through the charitable donation, הֲרֵי כָּל נַפְשׁוֹ הַחִיּוּנִית עוֹלָה לַה' — **so all of his energizing** Animal **Soul is elevated to G-d,** and not just one component of the soul, as is the case with the other *mitzvos*.

However, this argument seems to make sense only if a person earned his money by working hard. What if he inherited it? Or he won the lottery?

וְגַם מִי שֶׁאֵינוֹ נֶהֱנֶה מִיגִּיעוֹ — **And even a person who doesn't work to earn** money, which means that he didn't immerse his Animal Soul into the activity, מִכָּל מָקוֹם — **הוֹאִיל וּבְמָעוֹת אֵלּוּ הָיָה יָכוֹל לִקְנוֹת חַיֵּי נַפְשׁוֹ הַחִיּוּנִית** **nevertheless, since this money could have been used to purchase** food and drink **that would keep his energizing** Animal **Soul alive in his body,** הֲרֵי נוֹתֵן חַיֵּי נַפְשׁוֹ **לַה'** — **it follows that** by giving away some of that money, he's giving his soul's life to G-d.

וְלָכֵן אָמְרוּ רַבּוֹתֵינוּ זִכְרוֹנָם לִבְרָכָה שֶׁמְּקָרֶבֶת אֶת הַגְּאוּלָה — **And that's why our Sages of blessed memory taught that** charity, *"brings close the final Messianic Redemption"* (*Talmud, Bava Basra* 10a), לְפִי שֶׁבִּצְדָקָה אַחַת מַעֲלֶה הַרְבֵּה מִנֶּפֶשׁ הַחִיּוּנִית — **because through one act of charity you elevate a lot of the energizing** Animal **Soul,** מַה שֶּׁלֹּא הָיָה יָכוֹל לְהַעֲלוֹת מִמֶּנָּה כָּל כָּךְ כֹּחוֹת וּבְחִינוֹת בְּכַמָּה מִצְוֹת מַעֲשִׂיּוֹת אֲחֵרוֹת — **many "powers" and "components" of the Animal Soul, which you wouldn't have been able to elevate, even with several other practical commandments.**

PRACTICAL LESSONS

Charity is "equivalent to all the other mitzvos put together" because it elevates more of your body and Animal Soul to G-d than any other *mitzvah*.

בכמה מצות מעשיות אחרות. ומ"ש רז"ל שת"ת כנגד
כולם היינו מפני שת"ת היא בדבור ומחשבה שהם
לבושים הפנימי' של נפש החיונית וגם מהותן ועצמותן
של בחי' חב"ד מקליפת נוגה שבנפש החיונית נכללות
בקדושה ממש כשעוסק בתורה בעיון ושכל ואף
שמהותן ועצמותן של המדות חג"ת כו' לא יכלו להם

SECTION SIX: THREE SPIRITUAL VIRTUES OF TORAH STUDY

28TH ADAR REGULAR

Torah study was also praised by the Sages as being equal to all the other *mitzvos*. How does this square with the argument in our chapter that *mitzvos* of action further the purpose of creation to the greatest extent?

וּמַה שֶּׁאָמְרוּ רַבּוֹתֵינוּ זִכְרוֹנָם לִבְרָכָה שֶׁתַּלְמוּד תּוֹרָה כְּנֶגֶד כּוֹלָם — **And while our Sages,** of blessed memory, said that, *"the study of Torah is equal to them all,"* (Mishnah, Pe'ah 1:1) *i.e.,* to all the other *mitzvos* put together—this poses no contradiction to all the above.

הַיְינוּ מִפְּנֵי שֶׁתַּלְמוּד תּוֹרָה הִיא בְּדִבּוּר וּמַחֲשָׁבָה — **Because** the Sages taught this about Torah study to point to a particular virtue, **that Torah study is carried out with thought and speech,** שֶׁהֵם לְבוּשִׁים הַפְּנִימִים שֶׁל נֶפֶשׁ הַחִיּוּנִית — **which are the inner "garments" of the energizing** Animal **Soul.**

The Sages were suggesting: The study of Torah "is equal to them all" *in terms of its ability to influence the inner garments.* (Practical *mitzvos*, on the other hand, are the most powerful at elevating the outer "garment" of action.)

The *Tanya* now suggests a second unique advantage to Torah study, which led the Sages to declare it as *"equal to them all."*

וְגַם מַהוּתָן וְעַצְמוּתָן שֶׁל בְּחִינוֹת חָכְמָה בִּינָה וְדַעַת מִקְּלִיפַּת נוֹגַהּ שֶׁבְּנֶפֶשׁ הַחִיּוּנִית — **And** another advantage of the *mitzvah* of Torah study is that, not only the inner "garments," but **even the *kelipas nogah* powers of *chochmah*, *binah* and *da'as,*** in the **"deep core" of the energizing** Animal **Soul,** נִכְלָלוֹת בִּקְדוּשָׁה מַמָּשׁ — **are actually absorbed into** the realm of **holiness,** כְּשֶׁעוֹסֵק בַּתּוֹרָה בְּעִיּוּן וְשֵׂכֶל — **when Torah study is carried out in depth, engaging the mind.**

This notion that the "deep core" can be elevated to G-d seems to be a departure from the *Tanya's* general emphasis that the *beinoni can't* transform the deep core of his Animal Soul.

וְאַף שֶׁמַּהוּתָן וְעַצְמוּתָן שֶׁל הַמִּדּוֹת חֶסֶד גְּבוּרָה וְתִפְאֶרֶת כו' לֹא יָכְלוּ לָהֶם הַבֵּינוֹנִים לְהַפְּכָם לִקְדוּשָׁה — **And while,** we have argued above **that in the case of *beinonim,* their deep core emotional powers of *chesed*, *gevurah* and *tiferes* can't be transformed by them to be holy,** that doesn't mean to say that they can't transform

הבינונים להפכם לקדושה היינו משום שהרע חזק
יותר במדות מבחב"ד מפני יניקתן שם מהקדושה יותר
כידוע לי"ח: זאת ועוד אחרת והיא העולה על כולנה
במעלת עסק ת"ת על כל המצו' ע"פ מ"ש לעיל בשם
התיקוני' דרמ"ח פיקודין הן רמ"ח אברי' דמלכא וכמו
באדם התחתון ד"מ אין ערוך ודמיון כלל בין החיות
שברמ"ח אבריו לגבי החיות שבמוחין שהוא השכל
המתחלק לג' בחי' חב"ד ככה ממש ד"מ להבדיל
ברבבות הבדלות לאין קץ בהארת אור א"ס ב"ה
המתלבשות במצות מעשיות לגבי הארת אור א"ס

their *chochmah, binah* and *da'as* through Torah study, הַיְינוּ מִשּׁוּם שֶׁהָרַע חָזָק יוֹתֵר
בַּמִּדּוֹת מִבְּחָכְמָה בִּינָה וָדַעַת — **because the negative energy is stronger in the emotional powers** of *chesed, gevurah* and *tiferes* **than in** the intellectual powers of
chochmah, binah **and** *da'as,* which prevents the emotional powers from being elevated, מִפְּנֵי יְנִיקָתָן שָׁם מֵהַקְּדוּשָּׁה יוֹתֵר כַּיָּדוּעַ לְיוֹדְעֵי חָכְמָה נִסְתָּרָה — **because, as
is known to Kabbalists,** the emotional powers of *kelipah* are **more** successful in
"sucking" energy from the realm of holiness (see pp. 110-11; *Torah Ohr* 110d, 118c).

When we stated above that the deep core of the *beinoni's* Animal Soul can't be
elevated to G-d, that was largely true of the emotional faculties. But the intellectual
faculties of the deep core can be transformed, and that happens during Torah study.
That's another reason why Torah study is "equal to them all," because it affects the
deep core in a way that no other *mitzvah* does.

The *Tanya* now suggests a third unique advantage to Torah study, which led the
Sages to declare it as *"equal to them all."*

זֹאת וְעוֹד אַחֶרֶת וְהִיא הָעוֹלָה עַל כּוּלָּנָה בְּמַעֲלַת עֵסֶק תַּלְמוּד תּוֹרָה עַל כָּל הַמִּצְוֹת — **And
a further quality, most important of all, by which Torah study is superior to all the
other** *mitzvos,* עַל פִּי מַה שֶׁנִּזְכָּר לְעֵיל בְּשֵׁם הַתִּיקּוּנִים דְּרַמַ"ח פִּיקוּדִין הֵן רַמַ"ח אֵבְרִין
דְּמַלְכָּא — **can be gleaned from our earlier citation from the** *Tikunei Zohar,* **that
"the 248 positive mitzvos are the 248 organs of the King"** (*Tikunei Zohar* 74a; cited
above, chapter 23, p. 256).

אֵין — **For just as with mortal man, by way of example,** וּכְמוֹ בָאָדָם הַתַּחְתּוֹן דֶּרֶךְ מָשָׁל
עֵרוֹךְ וְדִמְיוֹן כְּלָל בֵּין הַחַיּוּת שֶׁבְּרַמַ"ח אֵיבָרָיו לְגַבֵּי הַחַיּוּת שֶׁבַּמּוֹחִין — **there's absolutely
no comparison or similarity between the life-energy in his 248 limbs and the life-
energy in the brain,** שֶׁהוּא הַשֵּׂכֶל הַמִּתְחַלֵּק לְשָׁלֹשׁ בְּחִינוֹת חָכְמָה בִּינָה וָדַעַת — **(namely the intellect, which is divided into the three components of** *chochmah, binah*
and *da'as),* כָּכָה מַמָּשׁ דֶּרֶךְ מָשָׁל — **so too, figuratively speaking** can we say of G-d,
לְהַבְדִּיל בְּרִבְבוֹת הַבְדָּלוֹת לְאֵין קֵץ — **(although the comparison** is obviously an utterly
inadequate one, since the physical world is **infinitely removed** from G-d), בְּהָאֲרַת

שבבחי' חב"ד שבחכמת התורה איש איש כפי שכלו
והשגתו. ואף שאינו משיג אלא בגשמיות הרי התורה
נמשלה למים שיורדים ממקום גבוה כו' כמ"ש לעיל
ואעפ"כ ארז"ל לא המדרש עיקר אלא המעשה והיום
לעשותם כתיב ומבטלין ת"ת לקיום מצוה מעשיית

אוֹר אֵין סוֹף בָּרוּךְ הוּא הַמִּתְלַבְּשׁוֹת בְּמִצְוֹת מַעֲשִׂיּוֹת לְגַבֵּי הֶאָרַת אוֹר אֵין סוֹף שֶׁבִּבְחִינַת חָכְמָה בִּינָה וְדַעַת שֶׁבְּחָכְמַת הַתּוֹרָה — that the light of the Blessed Infinite Light which is "dressed" in the practical commandments, is much less than the *chochmah, binah* and *da'as* of Torah wisdom.

Torah study, then, surpasses all the other commandments in terms of the *spiritual quality* of the Divine light invested in it.

אִישׁ אִישׁ כְּפִי שִׂכְלוֹ וְהַשָּׂגָתוֹ — Obviously the extent to which this light penetrates a person, depends on each individual's mental capacity and grasp of the Torah material.

וְאַף שֶׁאֵינוֹ מַשִּׂיג אֶלָּא בְּגַשְׁמִיּוּת — And even though when he studies a point of Jewish law, which speaks of this-worldly phenomena, a person only understands the physical "garb" in which the Blessed Infinite Light is "dressed," הֲרֵי הַתּוֹרָה נִמְשְׁלָה — nevertheless, Torah has been compared to water that *"flows (undiluted) from a higher level* to a lower one" (*Talmud, Ta'anis* 7a), *i.e.,* the Torah descended from its sublime setting within G-d's blessed will and wisdom, and has journeyed downwards one step after the other, down the spiral of spiritual worlds without suffering any dilution or diminishment at all, כְּמוֹ שֶׁנִּתְבָּאֵר לְעֵיל — as was explained above (chapter 4, p. 70).

So, to summarize, we have three qualities in which Torah study is superior to all the other *mitzvos*: a.) It elevates the inner "garments" of your Animal Soul to a greater extent; b.) It can even elevate the "deep core" of your Animal Soul (in its intellectual faculties only). c.) The quality of Divine light in this *mitzvah* is superior.

SECTION SEVEN: TORAH STUDY VERSUS MITZVAH OBSERVANCE

29TH ADAR REGULAR

Despite these three unique virtues of Torah study, the *Talmud* concluded that the practical commandments generally ought to take priority.

וְאַף עַל פִּי כֵן אָמְרוּ רַבּוֹתֵינוּ זִכְרוֹנָם לִבְרָכָה — Neverthe-less, our Sages said, *"The most important thing is not study, but practical observance"* (*Mishnah, Avos* 1:17), לֹא הַמִּדְרָשׁ עִיקָר אֶלָּא הַמַּעֲשֶׂה וְהַיּוֹם לַעֲשׂוֹתָם כְּתִיב — and Scripture stresses regarding the *mitzvos, "Do them today"* (*Deuteronomy* 7:11) meaning that "today," in this lifetime, in the physical world of action, the specific emphasis is on practical *mitzvos* (see chapter 17, p. 204).

כשא"א לעשותה ע"י אחרים משום כי זה כל האדם
ותכלית בריאתו וירידתו לעו"הז להיות לו ית' דירה
בתחתונים דוקא לאהפכא חשוכא לנהורא וימלא
כבוד ה' את כל הארץ הגשמית דייקא וראו כל בשר
יחדיו כנ"ל משא"כ כשאאפשר לעשותה ע"י אחרים אין   49B
מבטלין ת"ת אף שכל התורה אינה אלא פירוש המצות
מעשיות והיינו משום שהיא בחי' חב"ד של א"ס ב"ה

And — וּמְבַטְּלִין תַּלְמוּד תּוֹרָה לְקִיּוּם מִצְוָה מַעֲשִׂיִּת כְּשֶׁאִי אֶפְשָׁר לַעֲשׂוֹתָהּ עַל יְדֵי אֲחֵרִים
a further proof for the priority of action is the law that **Torah study must be stopped
to carry out a practical *mitzvah*,** in an instance when nobody else can do it (see
Talmud, Mo'ed Katan 9b).

מִשּׁוּם כִּי זֶה כָּל הָאָדָם — The reason for this emphasis on the practical *mitzvos* is
because, *"the conclusion of the matter is... observe His commandments, **for this is
the whole purpose of man"** (Ecclesiastes* 12:13), וְתַכְלִית בְּרִיאָתוֹ וִירִידָתוֹ לְעוֹלָם הַזֶּה
— **and the reason why you were created and** why your soul **came down into this
world,** לִהְיוֹת לוֹ יִתְבָּרֵךְ דִּירָה בַּתַּחְתּוֹנִים דַּוְקָא **— is specifically to make a** *"home for G-d in the lowest realms"*
(*Midrash Tanchuma, Naso,* section 16; see chapter 36, p.
399), לְאַהֲפָכָא חֲשׁוֹכָא לִנְהוֹרָא — **to** *"transform darkness
to light"* (*Zohar* 1, 4a), וְיִמָּלֵא כְבוֹד ה' אֶת כָּל הָאָרֶץ הַגַּשְׁמִית
דַּיְקָא — **so that** *"the glory of G-d will fill all the (material)
earth,"* **specifically,** וְרָאוּ כָל בָּשָׂר יַחְדָּיו — "And glory of
G-d will be revealed **and all flesh will see together** that
G-d is speaking" כַּנִּזְכָּר לְעֵיל — **as mentioned above.**

The practical *mitzvos* take priority, since they further
the purpose of creation to the greatest extent.

Nevertheless, if Torah study must be stopped to carry
out a practical *mitzvah* only in an instance when nobody
else is available to perform that *mitzvah*, it follows that
the reverse is also true:

מַה שֶּׁאֵין כֵּן כְּשֶׁאֶפְשָׁר לַעֲשׂוֹתָהּ עַל יְדֵי אֲחֵרִים — **This is
not so when there *is* somebody else to do** the practical
mitzvah, אֵין מְבַטְּלִין תַּלְמוּד תּוֹרָה — in such a case, **Torah
study must not be stopped** (*Mo'ed Katan* ibid).

But if it is practical *mitzvos* that further the purpose of creation, why wouldn't you
stop learning Torah to do a practical *mitzvah*?

אַף שֶׁכָּל הַתּוֹרָה אֵינָה אֶלָּא פֵּירוּשׁ הַמִּצְוֹת מַעֲשִׂיּוֹת — **Even though the Torah is nothing
other than a clarification of the practical *mitzvos*,** which makes it hard to understand why you wouldn't stop studying to do a *mitzvah,* וְהַיְינוּ מִשּׁוּם שֶׁהִיא בְּחִינַת

PRACTICAL LESSONS

**Torah lifts your soul
higher than any
other *mitzvah*. It just
doesn't further the
purpose of creation
as much as a practical
mitzvah. (So if the
practical *mitzvah* is
going to be carried
out by someone else
in any case, don't
stop studying!)**

ובעסקו בה ממשיך עליו אור א״ס ב״ה ביתר שאת
והארה גדולה לאין קץ מהארה והמשכה ע״י פקודין
שהן אברי' דמלכא וז״ש רב ששת חדאי נפשאי לך
קראי לך תנאי כמ״א באריכות: והנה המשכה
והארה זו שהאדם ממשיך ומאיר מהארת אור א״ס ב״ה
על נפשו ועל נפשות כל ישראל היא השכינ' כנסת ישראל
מקור כל נשמות ישראל כמ״ש לקמן ע״י עסק התורה

חָכְמָה בִּינָה וְדַעַת שֶׁל אֵין סוֹף בָּרוּךְ הוּא — nevertheless, the Sages taught that you shouldn't stop studying in this instance **because Torah is an expression of the** *chochmah, binah* and *da'as* of the Blessed Infinite Light, וּבְעָסְקוֹ בָּהּ מַמְשִׁיךְ עָלָיו אוֹר אֵין סוֹף בָּרוּךְ הוּא בְּיֶתֶר שְׂאֵת וְהָאָרָה גְּדוֹלָה לְאֵין קֵץ — **and by studying it you "pull" upon yourself the Blessed Infinite Light** *"with more dignity"* (Genesis 49:3), **and with incomparably more illumination,** מֵהָאָרָה וְהַמְשָׁכָה עַל יְדֵי פִּקּוּדִין שֶׁהֵן אֵבְרִין דְּמַלְכָּא — **than the illumination which is "pulled" through the** *mitzvos,* **which are** *"the (mere) limbs of the King."*

In an instance where a practical *mitzvah* won't be carried out by someone else, you need to stop studying and do the *mitzvah*, because the purpose of creation is at stake. But if someone else is going to do that practical *mitzvah* in any case, and the purpose of creation is going to be fulfilled, then you shouldn't stop studying. That's because through studying Torah, your soul will receive a higher level of Blessed Infinite Light than if you would have observed a practical *mitzvah*.

וְזֶהוּ שֶׁאָמַר רַב שֵׁשֶׁת חֲדָאִי נַפְשַׁאי לָךְ קְרָאי לָךְ תְּנָאי — **And this** disclosure of the Blessed Infinite Light through Torah **is why Rav Sheishes said,** *"Rejoice, O my soul! For you I have recited Scripture, for you I have studied Mishnah!"* (Talmud, Pesachim 68b), כְּמוֹ שֶׁנִּתְבָּאֵר בְּמָקוֹם אַחֵר בַּאֲרִיכוּת — **as is explained at length elsewhere** (see *Torah Ohr*, 75c).

Torah lifts the soul higher, whereas a *mitzvah* elevates the body more. That is why Rav Sheishes said "Rejoice, O my soul" specifically in reference to Torah study.

SECTION EIGHT: ANOTHER VIRTUE OF TORAH STUDY

1ST NISAN REGULAR

Above we learned that Torah study brings an unparalleled spiritual illumination to the soul. The *Tanya* now develops this idea further.

וְהִנֵּה הַמְשָׁכָה וְהָאָרָה זוֹ שֶׁהָאָדָם מַמְשִׁיךְ וּמֵאִיר מֵהֶאָרַת אוֹר אֵין סוֹף בָּרוּךְ הוּא עַל נַפְשׁוֹ — **Now this illumination of the Blessed Infinite Light which a person "pulls" and shines into his soul** through Torah study, וְעַל נַפְשׁוֹת כָּל יִשְׂרָאֵל — **(and** since all souls are connected he "pulls" it also upon the source of **the souls of all Israel,** הִיא הַשְּׁכִינָה כְּנֶסֶת יִשְׂרָאֵל מְקוֹר כָּל נִשְׁמוֹת יִשְׂרָאֵל — **namely, the** *Shechinah, Kneses*

נקראת בלשון קריאה קורא בתורה פי' שע"י עסק
התורה קורא להקב"ה לבוא אליו כביכול כאדם הקורא
לחבירו שיבא אליו וכבן קטן הקורא לאביו לבא אליו
להיות עמו בצוות' חדא ולא ליפרד ממנו ולישאר יחידי
ח"ו וז"ש קרוב ה' לכל קוראיו לכל אשר יקראוהו
באמת ואין אמת אלא תורה דהיינו שקורא להקב"ה
ע"י התורה דוקא לאפוקי מי שקורא אותו שלא על ידי
עסק התורה אלא צועק כך אבא אבא וכמו שקובל עליו

Yisrael, **source of all Jewish souls,** כְּמוֹ שֶׁיִּתְבָּאֵר לְקַמָּן — **as will be explained below in chapter 41, pp. 511***ff.***),** עַל יְדֵי עֵסֶק הַתּוֹרָה — **this illumination which comes as a result of Torah study,** נִקְרֵאת בִּלְשׁוֹן קְרִיאָה קוֹרֵא בַּתּוֹרָה — **is called** in Hebrew *keriah,* **as in the phrase** *korei ba-Torah* **("he reads the Torah").**

פֵּירוּשׁ — *Keriah* literally means "calling," so *korei ba-Torah* **means,** שֶׁעַל יְדֵי עֵסֶק הַתּוֹרָה קוֹרֵא לְהַקָּדוֹשׁ בָּרוּךְ הוּא לָבוֹא אֵלָיו כִּבְיָכוֹל — **that through studying Torah you "call" G-d, so to speak, to come to you,** כְּאָדָם הַקּוֹרֵא לַחֲבֵירוֹ שֶׁיָּבֹא אֵלָיו — **like a man calling to his friend to come to him,** וּכְבֵן קָטָן הַקּוֹרֵא לְאָבִיו לָבֹא אֵלָיו — **or like a small boy calling to his father to come to him,** לִהְיוֹת עִמּוֹ בְּצַוְותָא חֲדָא וְלֹא לִיפָּרֵד — **to be united with him,** מִמֶּנּוּ וְלִישָׁאֵר יְחִידִי חַס וְשָׁלוֹם — **and not to separate from him and remain alone, G-d forbid** (see Rabbi Dov Ber of Mezritch, *Imrei Tzadikim* (Zhitomir, 1901), p. 45a).

Only Torah study—not practical *mitzvah* observance—is referred to as "calling" G-d *directly.* This is an outstanding quality that places Torah study in a league of its own.

וְזֶהוּ שֶׁכָּתוּב קָרוֹב ה' לְכָל קוֹרְאָיו לְכֹל אֲשֶׁר יִקְרָאוּהוּ בֶאֱמֶת — **And this is the meaning of the verse,** *"G-d is close to all those who call to Him (kore'av), to all those who call him (yikrau'hu) in truth"* (*Psalms* 145:18), וְאֵין אֱמֶת אֶלָּא תּוֹרָה — **and** *"'Truth' refers to nothing other than Torah"* (*Talmud, Brachos* 5b).

דְּהַיְינוּ — **In other words,** the second half of the verse (*"to all those who call Him in truth"*) clarifies what is meant by the first half (*"all those who call to Him"*), שֶׁקּוֹרֵא לְהַקָּדוֹשׁ בָּרוּךְ הוּא עַל יְדֵי הַתּוֹרָה דַּוְקָא — **that the "calling" to G-d,** mentioned in the first half of the verse, **is specifically via the Torah,** the "truth" mentioned in the second half of the verse, לְאַפּוֹקֵי מִי שֶׁקּוֹרֵא אוֹתוֹ שֶׁלֹּא עַל יְדֵי עֵסֶק הַתּוֹרָה — **which excludes someone who "calls" to Him not via the Torah,** אֶלָּא צוֹעֵק כָּךְ אַבָּא אַבָּא — **and he merely cries out** in prayer **"Father! Father!"**

PRACTICAL LESSONS

Only through Torah do you "call" G-d directly and intimately, like a child calling out to his father to be united with him.

הנביא ואין קורא בשמך כו' וכמ"ש במ"א. ומזה יתבונן
המשכיל להמשיך עליו יראה גדולה בשעת עסק
התורה כמש"ל [פ' כ"ג]:

וּכְמוֹ שֶׁכּוֹבֵל עָלָיו הַנָּבִיא וְאֵין קוֹרֵא בְשִׁמְךָ כו' — **And, it is in reference to one** who "calls" to G-d in prayer (and not via the Torah) that **the prophet bemoans, *"there is no one who calls by Your name"*** (Isaiah 64:6), *i.e.,* G-d is being called (in prayer), but not by "His Name," the Torah, וּכְמוֹ שֶׁנִּתְבָּאֵר בְּמָקוֹם אַחֵר — **as is explained elsewhere** (see chapter 40, p. 491).

In other words, while prayer is also a type of "calling" directly to G-d, only Torah study possesses this quality in a truly authentic fashion.

וּמִזֶּה יִתְבּוֹנֵן הַמַּשְׂכִּיל — **With these ideas, an intelligent person can meditate,** לְהַמְשִׁיךְ עָלָיו יִרְאָה גְדוֹלָה בִּשְׁעַת עֵסֶק הַתּוֹרָה — **to generate a feeling of immense reverence when studying Torah,** [פֶּרֶק כ"ג] כְּמוֹ שֶׁנִּתְבָּאֵר לְעֵיל — the importance of which **was explained above, in chapter 23,** (pp. 259*ff*).

In summary: Through Torah study we connect with G-d more intimately; whereas through practical *mitzvos*, G-d's presence is drawn into the world to a greater extent. With the combined effect of Torah study and practical *mitzvos*, we make *"a home for G-d below"* in the fullest possible fashion.

CHAPTER 38

THE POWER OF KAVANAH (I)
SECTION ONE: PROOF THAT "THE SOUL DOESN'T NEED FIXING"

2ND NISAN REGULAR | 21ST ADAR II LEAP

In chapters 35-37, the *Tanya* has been offering us some "comfort" over our spiritual predicament. Most of us will struggle *"to battle in vain with the impulse to evil... unable to prevail over it"* (p. 388), because we are destined to carry out the most important of tasks: to bring Divine revelation (*Shechinah*), to the Animal Soul, body and physical world—the spiritually "darkest" of places. For this goal (which is nothing less than the purpose of creation!) the practical *mitzvos* are most effective, since they engage the body and Animal Soul to the greatest extent.

In chapter 37 we learned that even *mitzvos* performed through speech, such as Torah study and prayer, could be considered "practical *mitzvos*" which engage the body and Animal Soul, because *"moving the lips constitutes a concrete action"* (*Talmud, Kerisos* 4a).

פֶּרֶק לח וְהִנֵּה עִם כָּל הַנַּ"ל יוּבַן הֵיטֵב פְּסַק הַהֲלָכָה
הָעֲרוּכָה בַּתַּלְמוּד וּפּוֹסְקִי' דְּהִרְהוּר
לָאו כְּדִבּוּר דָּמֵי וְאִם קָרָא ק"ש בְּמַחֲשַׁבְתּוֹ וּבְלִבּוֹ לְבַד
בְּכָל כֹּחַ כַּוָּנָתוֹ לֹא יָצָא יְדֵי חוֹבָתוֹ וְצָרִיךְ לַחֲזוֹר וְלִקְרוֹת
וְכֵן בְּבִרְכַּת הַמָּזוֹן דְּאוֹרַיְיתָא וּבִשְׁאָר בִּרְכוֹת דְּרַבָּנָן
וּבִתְפִלָּ' וְאִם הוֹצִיא בִּשְׂפָתָיו וְלֹא כִּיוַּן לִבּוֹ יָצָא יְדֵי חוֹבָתוֹ

But, according to this logic, the *mitzvos* performed through speech appear to have something of a confused identity. Their practical component (moving the lips), elevates the Animal Soul and body, fulfilling the purpose of creation; whereas their mental and emotional component (understanding the Torah; connecting to G-d in prayer), does not.

In the following passage, the *Tanya* suggests that this somewhat bizarre conclusion is clearly supported by a point of Jewish Law.

וְהִנֵּה עִם כָּל הַנִּזְכָּר לְעֵיל — **Now following everything that has been written above** in chapter 37, יוּבַן הֵיטֵב פְּסַק הַהֲלָכָה הָעֲרוּכָה בַּתַּלְמוּד וּפּוֹסְקִים — **we can further appreciate the ruling of Jewish Law, as prescribed in the** *Talmud* **and** halachic **codes** (*Brachos* 20b; *Shulchan Aruch, Orach Chaim* 62:3, 101:2), דְּהִרְהוּר לָאו כְּדִבּוּר דָּמֵי — that *"meditation does not count as recitation"* (see p. 412).

וְאִם קָרָא קְרִיאַת שְׁמַע בְּמַחֲשַׁבְתּוֹ וּבְלִבּוֹ לְבַד — Which means that **if you read the** *Shema* **only in your thoughts,** and didn't articulate the words with your mouth, בְּכָל כֹּחַ כַּוָּנָתוֹ — even though you did so **with all your powers of concentration,** לֹא יָצָא יְדֵי חוֹבָתוֹ — nevertheless, **you did not fulfill the basic requirement** of the commandment to read the *Shema*, וְצָרִיךְ לַחֲזוֹר וְלִקְרוֹת — **and you have to go back and read it again,** enunciating the words.

וְכֵן בְּבִרְכַּת הַמָּזוֹן דְּאוֹרַיְיתָא — **The same law applies to** *Birkas Ha-Mazon* **(Grace After Meals), which is a Biblical requirement** (*Talmud, Brachos* 21a), וּבִשְׁאָר בִּרְכוֹת דְּרַבָּנָן — **and with the other blessings, that are Rabbinic Law** (*ibid.* 33a), which similarly, must be verbalized in order to fulfill the *mitzvah*.

וּבִתְפִלָּה — **And** the same is the case **with prayer,** which must be verbalized, even though prayer is primarily the "service of the heart" (*Shulchan Aruch ibid.*).

Evidently, thought alone without speech is not an acceptable form of worship in Jewish Law.

Now we turn to the reverse case, where the words were recited, but the thought was lacking.

וְאִם הוֹצִיא בִּשְׂפָתָיו וְלֹא כִּיוַּן לִבּוֹ — **But if you articulated the words** of the *Shema*, or prayer *etc.*, **though you were not attentive** to what you were saying, יָצָא יְדֵי חוֹבָתוֹ — **you** *did* **fulfill the basic requirements** of the *mitzvah*, בְּדִיעֲבַד — **"after the fact"** (*bedi'avad*), וְאֵין צָרִיךְ לַחֲזוֹר — **and you don't need to go back and repeat** the text.

50A בדיעבד ואין צריך לחזור לבד מפסוק ראשון של ק"ש
וברכה ראשונה של תפלת שמונה עשרה וכדאי'
[ברפ"ב דברכות] ע"כ מצות כוונה מכאן ואילך מצות
קריאה וכו'. והיינו משום שהנשמה אינה צריכה
תיקון לעצמה במצות רק להמשיך אור לתקן נפש
החיונית והגוף ע"י אותיות הדבור שהנפש מדברת בה'

Jewish Law will often express a *preferable* standard of observance (*lechatchila*), and a *minimally acceptable* (*bedi'avad*) standard, which should not be aimed for, but is legally acceptable once you have already done it. In this case, mindless words of *Shema* and prayer, though obviously not ideal, are considered acceptable "after the fact."

Obviously, G-d can stipulate how He wishes to be worshiped, and He could require worship through thought, speech or action. That, in itself, does not pose a problem. What is confusing here is why in the *mitzvos* of prayer, *Shema* and Torah study, the two components of thought and speech are bound by diametrically opposed laws (the speech is crucial and the thought is dispensable). The *Tanya's* concern here is: Why *in the context of a single mitzvah,* does speech become prioritized and thought marginalized? (*Notes on Tanya*).

Before answering the question, the *Tanya* first notes an exception to the rule.

Except — לְבַד מִפָּסוּק רִאשׁוֹן שֶׁל קְרִיאַת שְׁמַע וּבְרָכָה רִאשׁוֹנָה שֶׁל תְּפִלַּת שְׁמוֹנָה עֶשְׂרֵה **for the first verse of** *Shema* **and the first blessing of the** *Amidah* **prayer, which,** according to Talmudic law, *do* need to be repeated if you were not attentive to what you were saying, [בְּרֵישׁ פֶּרֶק ב' דִּבְרָכוֹת] וּכְדְאִיתָא — **as the** *Talmud* **states in the second chapter of** Tractate *Brachos* **(13b) about reading the** *Shema*, עַד כָּאן מִצְוַת "**Up to this point, the mitzvah involves correct** כַּוָּונָה מִכָּאן וְאֵילָךְ מִצְוַת קְרִיאָה וְכוּ' **intention; from this point onward, the mitzvah is simply one of reading the words aloud."*

Having noted this exception, the *Tanya* now proceeds to explain this legal status of speech/thought *mitzvos*, based on what we learned in the previous chapter.

The reason for the legal וְהַיְינוּ מִשּׁוּם שֶׁהַנְּשָׁמָה אֵינָה צְרִיכָה תִּיקּוּן לְעַצְמָה בַּמִּצְוֹת **emphasis on speech and de-emphasis on thought is because the soul itself "does not require fixing at all"** (see previous chapter, p. 422) **through** *mitzvos,* רַק לְהַמְשִׁיךְ **rather,** the purpose of *mitzvah* observance is to "**pull** אוֹר לְתַקֵּן נֶפֶשׁ הַחִיּוּנִית וְהַגּוּף **down"** G-d's **light in order to fix the energizing** Animal **Soul and the body,** עַל יְדֵי

---

*While this law is still in force today regarding the *Shema* (*Shulchan Aruch, Orach Chaim* 65:5), later authorities in Jewish Law have ruled that in the *Amidah* prayer, you *shouldn't* repeat the first blessing if you weren't attentive, because in all likelihood you will probably not be attentive the second time around either (*Rema, ibid.* 101:1).

מוצאות הפה וכן במצות מעשיות שהנפש עושה
בשאר אברי הגוף: אך אעפ"כ אמרו תפלה או שאר
ברכה בלא כוונה הן כגוף בלא נשמה פי' כי כמו שכל

מוֹצָאוֹת הַפֶּה — אוֹתִיּוֹת הַדִּבּוּר שֶׁהַנֶּפֶשׁ מְדַבֶּרֶת בְּה' — and therefore it's crucial that the *mitzvah* involves the Animal Soul and body, **through actual words spoken by the soul, using the "five organs of speech,"** which are the throat, lips, palate, tongue and teeth (*Sefer Yetzirah* 2:3).

וְכֵן בְּמִצְוֹת מַעֲשִׂיּוֹת שֶׁהַנֶּפֶשׁ עוֹשָׂה בִּשְׁאָר אֶבְרֵי הַגּוּף — **And the same is true with the practical commandments, which the** Animal **Soul performs through the body's other limbs.**

As we learned in chapter 37, even the *mitzvos* of saying the *Shema*, praying and studying Torah are primarily aimed at elevating your body, and that's why Jewish law stipulates bodily involvement ("moving the lips") as an indispensable component. On the other hand, the more spiritual mental/emotional components of the *mitzvah* are not (legally) crucial, since the soul "does not require fixing at all." They are not the reason why you are here, as a soul *in a body*.

SECTION TWO: MITZVAH AND KAVANAH — BODY AND SOUL

22ND ADAR II LEAP

This concludes our lengthy discussion, beginning back in chapter 35, about the virtue of practical *mitzvos* and their power to elevate the body and Animal Soul. In the following sections (until chapter 40), the *Tanya* will address "the other side of the coin," and highlight the great virtue of attuning the mind and heart to a *mitzvah*.

As we shall see, the emphasis on the practical component of the *mitzvos* ought not to undermine in any way the value we attach to a *miztvah's* mental/emotional components, which are also a *requirement* of Jewish Law. (And it's only that, *after the fact*, a lack of attentiveness doesn't legally disqualify a *mitzvah*).

אַךְ אַף עַל פִּי כֵן — **Nevertheless** all the above emphasis on the practical component of a *mitzvah* doesn't mean that attentiveness is unimportant, אָמְרוּ תְּפִלָּה אוֹ שְׁאָר בְּרָכָה בְּלֹא כַוָּונָה הֵן כְּגוּף בְּלֹא נְשָׁמָה — for **it has been said,** *"prayer (or other blessings) without attentiveness (kavanah) are like a body without a soul"* (see Rabbi Yitzchak Arama, *Akeidas Yitzchak, Sha'ar* 58).

The phrase "a body without a soul" seems, at first glance, to suggest lifelessness and death. But to say that a *mitzvah* without *kavanah* is "dead" and meaningless would contradict our entire discussion above that, even in the absence of attentiveness, there *is* great validity and significance to a *mitzvah*.

The *Tanya* therefore offers a different interpretation:

פֵּירוּשׁ כִּי כְּמוֹ שֶׁכָּל הַבְּרוּאִים שֶׁבָּעוֹלָם הַזֶּה שֶׁיֵּשׁ לָהֶם גּוּף וּנְשָׁמָה — **Which means that, just as all the created beings in this world have a body and a soul,** each having

הברואים שבעו"הז שיש להם גוף ונשמה שהם נפש
כל חי ורוח כל בשר איש ונשמת כל אשר רוח חיים
באפיו מכל בעלי חיים וה' מחיה את כולם ומהוה אותם
מאין ליש תמיד באור וחיות שמשפיע בהם שגם
הגוף החומרי ואפי' אבנים ועפר הדומם ממש יש בו
אור וחיות ממנו ית' שלא יחזור להיות אין ואפס כשהיה

their own separate sources of life-energy from G-d, so too, the practical deed of a *mitzvah* and its *kavanah,* each have their own life-energy. However, the life-energy of the "body" (practical deed) is far less than the life-energy of the "soul" (*kavanah*).

The phrase *"like a body without a soul"* doesn't mean to say that the "body" (deed) is dead and lifeless. It means that only the body's own minimal life-energy is present, as opposed to the abundance of life-energy found in the soul.

PRACTICAL LESSONS

"A *mitzvah* without attentiveness (*kavanah*) is like a body without a soul." Such a *mitzvah* is low in life-energy (like the body) and not high in life-energy (like the soul).

To clarify this point the *Tanya* will first illustrate how both the soul and body have their own separate source of life in G-d. First, we will demonstrate that the soul (at all three levels, *nefesh, ruach* and *neshamah*) is alive, with scriptural citations.

שֶׁהֵם נֶפֶשׁ כָּל חַי וְרוּחַ כָּל בְּשַׂר אִישׁ — For the soul is, *"the 'nefesh' of every living thing, and the 'ruach' of every individual being"* (*Job* 12:10), וְנִשְׁמַת כָּל אֲשֶׁר רוּחַ חַיִּים בְּאַפָּיו מִכָּל בַּעֲלֵי חַיִּים — and *"the 'neshama' of everything that has the spirit of life in its nostrils"* (see *Genesis* 7:22), which includes **all the animals.**

But this doesn't mean to say that the body is devoid of its own life-force from G-d, separate from the soul's. As we will discuss at length in the Second Book of *Tanya,* G-d brings all physical matter into existence *continually,* which means that there is a constant energetic life-force being pumped by G-d into all physical matter, regardless of the presence of any soul. In fact, even a rock must have its own Divine energy, otherwise it wouldn't continue to exist.

וַה' מְחַיֶּה אֶת כּוּלָם — And G-d *"gives them all life"* (*Nehemia* 9:6), both body and soul, matter and spirit, וּמְהַוֶּה אוֹתָם מֵאַיִן לְיֵשׁ תָּמִיד — and He brings them into being continually, something-from-nothing, בְּאוֹר וְחַיּוּת שֶׁמַּשְׁפִּיעַ בָּהֶם — through His light and energy which He pours into them, שֶׁגַּם הַגּוּף הַחוּמְרִי וַאֲפִילוּ אֲבָנִים וְעָפָר הַדּוֹמֵם — since even the physical body, and even completely motionless stones and dirt, contain "light" and "energy" from G-d, שֶׁלֹּא מַמָּשׁ יֵשׁ בּוֹ אוֹר וְחַיּוּת מִמֶּנּוּ יִתְבָּרֵךְ — otherwise they would return to be "null and void" יַחֲזוֹר לִהְיוֹת אַיִן וָאֶפֶס כְּשֶׁהָיָה (see *Isaiah* 40:17), **as they once were.**

ואעפ"כ אין ערך ודמיון כלל בין בחי' אור וחיו' המאיר
בגוף לגבי בחי' אור וחיות המאיר בנשמה שהיא נפש
כל חי ואף שבשניהם אור אחד שוה בבחי' הסתר
פנים ולבושי' שוים שהאור מסתתר ומתעלם ומתלבש
בו כי שניהם הם מעו"הז שבכללותו מסתתר בשוה
האור והחיות שמרוח פיו ית' בבחי' הסתר פנים וירידת

Even stones and dirt are "alive" in the sense that G-d's life-energy must constantly be pumped into them to maintain their existence. And, if stones and dirt have their own life-force, then certainly the physical body does too (independent of the soul).

וְאַף עַל פִּי כֵן אֵין עֵרֶךְ וְדִמְיוֹן כְּלָל בֵּין בְּחִינַת אוֹר וְחַיּוּת הַמֵּאִיר בַּגּוּף — **Nevertheless, there is simply no similarity or comparison at all, between the Divine light and energy which shines in the body,** לְגַבֵּי בְּחִינַת אוֹר וְחַיּוּת הַמֵּאִיר בַּנְּשָׁמָה — **to the light and energy which shines in the soul,** שֶׁהִיא נֶפֶשׁ כָּל חַי — **since** the soul is *overtly* alive, it's ***"the life of every living thing."***

So the statement that a *mitzvah* *"without attentiveness (kavanah) is like a body without a soul,"* means, not that the *mitzvah* is "dead" or invalid, but that it's low in life-energy (like the body) and not high in life-energy (like the soul).

SECTION THREE: THE HOLE AND THE CURTAIN

3RD NISAN REGULAR | 23RD ADAR II LEAP

When we speak here of the "soul," the reference is obviously to an Animal Soul (*"the 'nefesh' of every living thing... which includes all the animals"*). And, as we have learned, our Animal Soul is from *kelipas nogah*, a force which *hides* G-d's presence on earth (see p. 92).

So, if the soul we are speaking of here is from *kelipas nogah* and the body is also from *kelipas nogah*, could there really be a huge difference in their level of Divine "light and energy"? Both of them, after all, emanate from a force which *hides* G-d.

To clarify this point, the *Tanya* will first explain how G-d's light is hidden and diminished as it enters *kelipas nogah*, and thereby, the world.

וְאַף שֶׁבִּשְׁנֵיהֶם אוֹר אֶחָד שָׁוֶה — **And even though** the body and soul's **light is one and the same,** בִּבְחִינַת הֶסְתֵּר פָּנִים וּלְבוּשִׁים שָׁוִים — **in the sense that both** the body and soul's light suffers **equally from the** *"Hiding of G-d's face"* **and "filters,"** שֶׁהָאוֹר מִסְתַּתֵּר וּמִתְעַלֵּם וּמִתְלַבֵּשׁ בָּהֶם — **since** G-d's **light is** first **hidden and dimmed, and** only then **is it received by them,** כִּי שְׁנֵיהֶם הֵם מֵעוֹלָם הַזֶּה — **since both** the body and soul **are** entities found **in this world,** שֶׁבִּכְלָלוּתוֹ מִסְתַּתֵּר בְּשָׁוֶה הָאוֹר וְהַחַיּוּת שֶׁמֵּרוּחַ פִּיו יִתְבָּרֵךְ — **and as a whole,** this world conceals *equally* the light and energy from *"the breath of His mouth"* (see *Psalms* 33:6), בִּבְחִינַת הֶסְתֵּר פָּנִים וִירִידַת הַמַּדְרֵגוֹת

המדרגות בהשתלשלות העולמות ממדרגה למדרגה
בצמצומים רבים ועצומים עד שנתלבש בקליפת
נוגה להחיות כללות עו"הז החומרי דהיינו כל דברים
המותרים והטהורים שבעולם הזה וממנה ועל ידה
מושפעים דברים הטמאים כי היא בחי' ממוצעת כנ"ל

בְּהִשְׁתַּלְשְׁלוּת הָעוֹלָמוֹת מִמַּדְרֵגָה לְמַדְרֵגָה — through the *"Hiding of* G-d's *face"* (*hes-ter panim*) and the rung-by-rung downgrade of the chain of worlds, בְּצִמְצוּמִים רַבִּים וַעֲצוּמִים — through numerous, profound diminishments (*tzimtzumim*) of the Divine light.

If *kelipas nogah* is a force that hides G-d, making our autonomous existence possible, how could it be powered by G-d?

For this to happen, the Divine light in *kelipas nogah* must be hidden and dimmed numerous times. It must be "downgraded" so that its energy can be "compatible" with *kelipah.*

עַד שֶׁנִּתְלַבֵּשׁ בִּקְלִיפַּת נוֹגַהּ לְהַחֲיוֹת כְּלָלוּת עוֹלָם הַזֶּה הַחוּמְרִי — This process of hiding and diminishment continues progressively **until the** Divine **light** has been dimmed so much that it **can be received by** *kelipas nogah,* **to energize the overall infrastructure of this material world.**

▮▮▮▮▮▮▮▮▮

PRACTICAL LESSONS

The extent to which G-d's light shines into your *mitzvah*, is immeasurably greater when that *mitzvah* is accompanied with attentiveness (*kavanah*).

As we learned earlier, all objects and living creatures in this world derive their energy either from *kelipas nogah,* if they are permissible, or from the "completely impure *kelipos*," if they are forbidden. How, then, can the *Tanya* state here that *kelipas nogah alone* represents "the overall infrastructure of this material world" when there are so many forbidden things too, which are not powered by *kelipas nogah*?

דְּהַיְינוּ כָּל דְּבָרִים הַמּוּתָּרִים וְהַטְּהוֹרִים שֶׁבָּעוֹלָם הַזֶּה — Be-cause *kelipas nogah* is the energy of **all the permissible and ritually pure things in this world,** וּמִמֶּנָּה וְעַל יָדָהּ מוּשְׁפָּעִים דְּבָרִים הַטְּמֵאִים — **and it is from this** *kelipas nogah* energy, **and through its agency,** that energy then **flows to impure things,** the impure *kelipos,* כִּי הִיא בְּחִינָה מְמוּצַעַת כַּנִּזְכָּר לְעֵיל — since, **as was stated above,** *kelipas nogah* **is an intermedi-ary** between the holy powers and the impure *kelipos*. (chapter 37, p. 419).

Kelipas nogah represents "the overall infrastructure of this material world" be-cause *all* the Divine light and energy destined for this world first passes through it. Whatever energy the completely impure *kelipos* need, must be "sucked" from *kelipas nogah.*

אעפ"כ ההארה שהיא המשכת החיות אשר ה' מאיר

ומחיה דרך לבוש זה אינה שוה בכולן בבחי' צמצום   50B

So, returning to our question: If everything in the physical world is derived from *kelipas nogah,* which suffers from a *"Hiding of G-d's face,"* is there really such a difference between the Divine light and energy in the body (of *kelipah*) and the Animal Soul (of *kelipah*)? Why do we say that "a body without a soul" is severely lacking in Divine energy, if both body and soul suffer from *the same* formidable eclipse of G-d's light?

To answer the question, the *Tanya* will draw on a subtle but highly important distinction between *hester panim* ("hiding of G-d's face") and *tzimtzum* ("diminishment" of His light). We have encountered these terms before in the *Tanya,* but until this point they have been used relatively interchangeably. Now, however, the *Tanya* points to a significant difference between these two processes, in a discussion that will become central to the theme of this chapter.

The principle difference is this: *Hester panim* downgrades the *quality* of the Divine light, whereas *tzimtzum* diminishes the *quantity* of the light.

For example, if you obscured your view of someone's face with a piece of opaque black paper that had a tiny hole in it, you would have achieved *tzimtzum.* The image of the person would be the same quality as before, but there would be much less of the image's light coming through the aperture.

On the other hand, if instead of the paper you used a partially opaque filter or veil (without any hole), you would have achieved *hester panim:* concealment through a "garment." *Hester panim* alters the *quality* of the light, because the image is blurred or distorted.

All the Divine light and energy entering this world suffer from both *hester panim* and *tzimtzum.* But while the degree of *hester panim* remains constant (as we just learned), the level of *tzimtzum* is subject to significant fluctuation.

Hester panim, remains constant because everything in this world comes through the same filter of *kelipas nogah,* a "garment" which downgrades the *quality* of the light radically, and through which G-d's presence is only weakly discernible. But while the degree of *hester panim* remains the same, the level of *tzimtzum* (the *quantity* of that "low-quality" light) differs significantly in different objects and species. And that results in the Animal Soul having a much greater amount of Divine light and energy than the body.

אַף עַל פִּי כֵן — **Nevertheless,** despite the fact that everything in this world suffers from the same *hester panim* of *kelipas nogah,* הֶהָאָרָה שֶׁהִיא הַמְשָׁכַת הַחַיּוּת אֲשֶׁר ה', מֵאִיר וּמְחַיֶּה דֶּרֶךְ לְבוּשׁ זֶה — **the light (which is the flow of energy) that G-d shines through the filter** of this world **to provide it with energy,** אֵינָה שָׁוָה בְּכוּלָּן — **is** *not* **the same in all** recipients, בִּבְחִינַת צִמְצוּם וְהִתְפַּשְּׁטוּת — because it differs **in the**

והתפשטות כי בגוף הגשמי והדומם ממש כאבנים
ועפר ההארה היא בבחי' צמצום גדול אשר אין כמוהו
והחיות שבו מועטת כל כך עד שאין בו אפי' כח הצומח
ובצומח ההארה אינה בצמצום גדול כל כך. ודרך
כלל נחלקות לארבע מדרגות דומם צומח חי מדבר
כנגד ד' אותיות שם הוי"ה ב"ה שממנו מושפעים

extent of more **diminishment (tzimtzum)** in some cases, **and** more **manifestation,** in others.

4TH NISAN REGULAR | 24TH ADAR II LEAP

כִּי בַּגּוּף הַגַּשְׁמִי וְהַדּוֹמֵם מַמָּשׁ כַּאֲבָנִים וְעָפָר הָהָאָרָה הִיא בִּבְחִינַת צִמְצוּם גָּדוֹל אֲשֶׁר אֵין כָּמוֹהוּ — **For in the** soul-less **physical body, as well as completely motionless objects such as rocks and dust, there is a very diminished light; unparalleled, in fact,** in the level of *tzimtzum,* וְהַחִיּוּת שֶׁבּוֹ מוּעֶטֶת כָּל כָּךְ עַד שֶׁאֵין בּוֹ אֲפִילוּ כֹּחַ הַצוֹמֵחַ — **and the energy there is so minuscule that** these objects **do not even have the power of vegetative growth** present in the Plant Kingdom, וּבְצוֹמֵחַ הָהָאָרָה אֵינָה בְּצִמְצוּם גָּדוֹל כָּל כָּךְ — **while, in the Plant Kingdom, the** Divine **light is not as greatly diminished** as it is with motionless objects.

The hierarchy of non-living and living organisms — motionless objects, plants, animals and humans — represents a progressively weaker *tzimtzum*. The higher the life form, the more Divine "light and energy" is present and the weaker the *tzimtzum.*

וְדֶרֶךְ כְּלָל נֶחְלָקוֹת לְאַרְבַּע מַדְרֵגוֹת דוֹמֵם צוֹמֵחַ חַי מְדַבֵּר — **And, generally speaking,** the presence of Divine light and energy in the physical world **is divided into four levels: motionless objects, plants, animals and humans,** כְּנֶגֶד ד' אוֹתִיּוֹת שֵׁם הֲוָיָ"ה בָּרוּךְ הוּא — **corresponding to the four letters of G-d's blessed name, the** Tetragrammaton, שֶׁמְּמֶנּוּ מוּשְׁפָּעִים — **from where** the light and energy which **flows to them** is originally sourced (see *Etz Chaim* 40:1; 50:10).*

So, in the final analysis, is the Divine light equally eclipsed in the Animal Soul and the body? Yes and no. In terms of *hester panim,* it's the same; but in terms of *tzimtzum*, it's different.

And with this distinction in mind, the *Tanya* will now lead us, in the following section, to an innovative explanation why a *mitzvah "without attentiveness is like a body without a soul."*

---

*The inner reason why the Divine light and energy in this world differs radically across the range of objects and species, is (not only a function of an entity's ability to *receive* the light but, more significantly) because the light emanates *in its source* at different levels. The four letters of G-d's name, the Tetragrammaton, symbolically represent four categories of emanation (in the Divine World of *Atzilus*), which ultimately give rise to different tiers of existence here in this world. (For details see *Torah Ohr* 3d; *Likutei Sichos* vol. 6, p. 108*ff*).

וכמו שאין ערך ודמיון ההארה והמשכת החיו' שבדומם

וצומח להההארה והמשכת החיות המלובש בחי ומדבר

אף שבכולן אור אחד שוה בבחי' הסתר פנים ומלובש

בלבוש אחד בכולן שהוא לבוש נוגה כך אין ערך

ודמיון כלל בין הארת והמשכת אור א"ס ב"ה שהוא

פנימיות רצונו ית' בלי הסתר פנים ולבוש כלל המאירה

SECTION FOUR: KAVANAH BRINGS YOUR MITZVAH TO LIFE

The four tiers of existence (objects, plants, animals and humans) could broadly be divided into two groups:

a.) *Non-movers:* objects and plants—neither of which show *overt* signs of energetic life, and are *"like a body without a soul."*

b.) *Movers:* animals and humans—which are clearly alive and "soulful."

On this basis, the statement that a *mitzvah "without attentiveness (kavanah) is like a body without a soul"* will now be translated to mean: a *mitzvah* without attentiveness, lacks a perceptible Divine light, just like "non-movers" which have no overt soul quality. Yes, G-d is present in a *mitzvah* devoid of *kavanah*, but G-d is present in a rock too, and that doesn't mean that He is felt there.*

וּכְמוֹ שֶׁאֵין עֵרֶךְ וְדִמְיוֹן הַהָאָרָה וְהַמְשָׁכַת הַחַיּוּת שֶׁבַּדּוֹמֵם וְצוֹמֵחַ — **And just as there is no similarity or comparison between the light/energy flow into** a.) **motionless objects and plants,** which, like "a body without a soul" *don't* show overt signs of energetic life, לְהַהָאָרָה וְהַמְשָׁכַת הַחַיּוּת הַמְלוּבֶּשֶׁת בְּחַי וּמְדַבֵּר — **when contrasted to the light/energy flow received by** b.) **animals and humans** which, like "a body with a soul" *do* show overt signs of energetic life, אַף שֶׁבְּכוּלָּן אוֹר אֶחָד שָׁוֶה בִּבְחִינַת הֶסְתֵּר פָּנִים — **(even though** as we learned above, all four **of them have the same light in terms of** *"Hiding of G-d's face,"* וּמְלוּבָּשׁ בִּלְבוּשׁ אֶחָד שֶׁהוּא לְבוּשׁ נוֹגַהּ — **and they all share the same "filter," which is the "filter" of** *kelipas nogah*), כָּךְ אֵין עֵרֶךְ וְדִמְיוֹן כְּלָל בֵּין הָאָרַת וְהַמְשָׁכַת אוֹר אֵין סוֹף בָּרוּךְ הוּא — **so just as the overt energy of** objects/plants compared to humans/animals differs radically, **likewise, there is no similarity or comparison at all between:** a.) **the light/flow of the Blessed Infinite Light,** שֶׁהוּא פְּנִימִיּוּת רְצוֹנוֹ יִתְבָּרֵךְ בְּלִי הֶסְתֵּר פָּנִים וּלְבוּשׁ כְּלָל — **(which is G-d's inner will, without any** *"Hiding of G-d's face"* **or filter at all),** הַמְּאִירָה וּמְלוּבֶּשֶׁת בְּמִצְוֹת

---

*In parenthetical comments, the *Tanya* will be careful to stress that when comparing the light in objects and plants to the light in *mitzvos*, we are, of course, speaking of two different types of Divine light. In objects and plants, the light is a *kelipas nogah* energy which suffers from *hester panim* (Hiding of G-d's face). In a *mitzvah*, which is the undiluted will of G-d, the light doesn't have this drawback. So when we say that a *mitzvah* performed without attentiveness is lacking in light like a motionless object, it's only an illustration; we're actually speaking about *two completely different types of light*.

ומלובשת במצות מעשיות ממש. וכן במצות התלויות
בדבור וביטוי שפתים בלי כוונה שהוא נחשב כמעשה
ממש כנ"ל לגבי ההארה והמשכת אור א"ס ב"ה
המאירה ומלובשת בכוונת המצות מעשיות שהאדם
מתכוין בעשייתן כדי לדבקה בו ית' ע"י קיום רצונו

מַעֲשִׂיּוֹת מַמָּשׁ — that shines into and enters the purely physical component of the practical *mitzvos,* the physical deed itself, devoid of attentiveness, וְכֵן בְּמִצְוֹת הַתְּלוּיוֹת בְּדִבּוּר וּבִיטוּי שְׂפָתַיִם בְּלִי כַוָּונָה — (as well as the physical component of the verbally observed *mitzvos* and other verbal expressions, devoid of attentiveness, שֶׁהוּא נֶחְשָׁב כְּמַעֲשֶׂה מַמָּשׁ כַּנִּזְכָּר לְעֵיל — which, as mentioned above, are counted as an actual deed), לְגַבֵּי הַהֶאָרָה וְהַמְשָׁכַת אוֹר אֵין סוֹף בָּרוּךְ הוּא הַמְּאִירָה וּמְלוּבֶּשֶׁת — the level of Blessed Infinite Light in these mindless deeds is minuscule בְּכַוָּונַת הַמִּצְוֹת מַעֲשִׂיּוֹת — when contrasted to b.) the superior light/flow of the Blessed Infinite Light which shines and flows into the *kavanah* (attentiveness) accompanying the practical *mitzvos.*

For the sake of clarity, let's repeat this very long sentence again, without its parenthetical insertions: *"And just as there is no comparison between: a.) the light/energy flow into motionless objects and plants, when contrasted to: b.) the light/energy flow received by animals and humans—so too, there is no comparison between a.) the light/flow of the Blessed Infinite Light that shines into the physical component of the mitzvos, when contrasted to b.) the light/flow of the Blessed Infinite Light which shines into the kavanah accompanying the mitzvos."*

Framed slightly differently, the *Tanya's* argument here could be summed up as follows: You might think that, with a *mitzvah,* since there's no *hester panim,* there can't be *tzimtzum* either; so there can't be different levels of illumination between the *mitzvah* act and its *kavanah.* The *Tanya* tells us: No! We see from the spiritual dynamics of this world that *hester panim* and *tzimtzum* work independently. Even when you have G-d's undiluted light in a *mitzvah,* without *hester panim,* there can still be radically different levels of illumination, depending on *tzimtzum.* And that all depends on your *kavanah!*

SECTION FIVE: WHAT IS KAVANAH?

Kavanah, of course, is a broad term that can mean many different things. The *Tanya* now clarifies what type of *kavanah* our discussion refers to. (For more on this topic see "note" in the next section).

שֶׁהָאָדָם מִתְכַּוֵּין בַּעֲשִׂיָּיתָן כְּדֵי לְדָבְקָה בּוֹ יִתְבָּרֵךְ עַל יְדֵי קִיּוּם רְצוֹנוֹ — *Kavanah* here meaning **that the person is** generally **attentive that these** *mitzvah* **acts are being carried out to attach himself to G-d, through fulfilling** G-d's **will,** שֶׁהוּא וּרְצוֹנוֹ אֶחָד — since G-d **and His will are one.**

שֶׁהוּא וּרְצוֹנוֹ אֶחָד וְכֵן בְּכַוָּנַת הַתְּפִלָּה וק"ש וּבִרְכוֹתֶיהָ
וּשְׁאָר בְּרָכוֹת שֶׁבְּכַוָּנָתוֹ בָּהֶן מְדַבֵּק מַחֲשַׁבְתּוֹ וְשִׂכְלוֹ
בּוֹ ית' וְלֹא שֶׁדְּבֵיקוּת הַמַּחֲשָׁבָה וְשֵׂכֶל הָאָדָם בּוֹ ית'
הִיא מִצַּד עַצְמָהּ לְמַעְלָה מִדְּבֵיקוּ' קִיּוּם הַמִּצְוֹת מַעֲשִׂיו'
בְּפוֹעַל מַמָּשׁ כמ"ש לְקַמָּן אֶלָּא מִפְּנֵי שֶׁזֶּהוּ ג"כ רְצוֹנוֹ ית'

In addition to the practical *mitzvos* where an act is involved, this *kavanah* is also effective for *mitzvos* performed verbally, where there is no substantive act (other than moving the lips) — as the *Tanya* will now clarify.

וְכֵן בְּכַוָּנַת הַתְּפִלָּה וּקְרִיאַת שְׁמַע וּבִרְכוֹתֶיהָ וּשְׁאָר בְּרָכוֹת — **And, so too, with the** *kavanah* **accompanying prayer, the recital of the** *Shema* **with its blessings** before and after, **as well as other blessings,** שֶׁבְּכַוָּנָתוֹ בָּהֶן מְדַבֵּק מַחֲשַׁבְתּוֹ וְשִׂכְלוֹ בּוֹ יִתְבָּרֵךְ — **for** *kavanah* **during these** activities **connects your thoughts and mind with G-d.**

Understanding the Torah text you are studying, or the words of prayer you are saying, is not *kavanah*; it's part of the *mitzvah* itself. The *kavanah* is your intent that through understanding these sacred words, you connect your thoughts and mind with G-d.

SECTION SIX: THE MITZVAH/KAVANAH RELATIONSHIP

5TH NISAN REGULAR | 25TH ADAR II LEAP

Now we have established that a *mitzvah* performed with *kavanah* will channel an *immeasurably greater* amount of Divine light than a *mitzvah* performed without *kavanah,* the question is: Why? We can appreciate why *kavanah* would enhance a *mitzvah*, but why is it so transformative—its absence leaving the *mitzvah* "like a body without a soul"?

At first glance, the answer seems to be intuitive from our own experience. Watch one person fulfill a *mitzvah* without *kavanah*, and then watch a second person do the same act with joy, focus and spiritual intensity. Can't you fathom for yourself that G-d is so much closer to the second individual?

The *Tanya* dismisses this notion.

וְלֹא שֶׁדְּבֵיקוּת הַמַּחֲשָׁבָה וְשֵׂכֶל הָאָדָם בּוֹ יִתְבָּרֵךְ בְּפוֹעַל מַמָּשׁ — **But it's not that the ac- tual attachment of thought and the human mind to** G-d through *kavanah*, הִיא מִצַּד עַצְמָהּ לְמַעְלָה מִדְּבֵיקוּת קִיּוּם הַמִּצְוֹת מַעֲשִׂיּוֹת — **is, in its own right, higher than the connection through the practical** *mitzvos*, כְּמוֹ שֶׁיִּתְבָּאֵר לְקַמָּן — **as will be explained** immediately **below.**

No human embellishment can "enhance" G-d's will. The Divine will has its own stated parameters in the Torah: If you meet them, you will channel an Infinite Light that you wouldn't be able to reach on your own.

לדבקה בשכל ומחשבה וכוונת המצות מעשיו' ובכוונ'
ק"ש ותפלה ושאר ברכות והארת רצון העליון הזה
המאירה ומלובשת בכוונה זו היא גדולה לאין קץ
למעלה מעלה מהארת רצון העליון המאירה ומלובשת
בקיום המצות עצמן במעשה ובדבור בלי כוונה כגודל
מעלת אור הנשמה על הגוף שהוא כלי ומלבוש

51A

So it's not that your accompanying meditation (*kavanah*) adds depth and spiritual intensity "on top of" the *mitzvah*. That can't be the case because a *mitzvah* is the undiluted will of G-d, and no human power can add to that.

Rather, as the *Tanya* will now stress, *the kavanah is part of the mitzvah too*. And that's the *only* reason that *kavanah* acts as a vehicle for the pure Divine light of G-d's will.

— אֶלָּא מִפְּנֵי שֶׁזֶּהוּ גַם כֵּן רְצוֹנוֹ יִתְבָּרֵךְ לְדָבְקָה בְּשֵׂכֶל וּמַחֲשָׁבָה וְכַוָּנַת הַמִּצְוֹת מַעֲשִׂיּוֹת **Rather it's because connecting your mind and thoughts through** *kavanah* **in the practical commandments is** *also* **the will of G-d,** וּבְכַוָּנַת קְרִיאַת שְׁמַע וּתְפִלָּה וּשְׁאָר בְּרָכוֹת — **(as is** *kavanah* **during the recital of** *Shema***, prayer and all the other blessings).**

PRACTICAL LESSONS

Kavanah here refers to the general awareness that your *mitzvah* connects you with G-d, by fulfilling His will.

To have *kavanah* when performing a *mitzvah* act is the Divine will, just as the *mitzvah* act itself is the Divine will.

To have *kavanah* when performing a *mitzvah* act *is* the Divine will, just as the *mitzvah* act itself is the Divine will (see Rabbi Chaim Hezekiah Medini, *Sdei Chemed*, vol. 14, p. 129). And that's the *only* reason why the *kavanah* is able to help channel such a light in the first place.

(To draw upon our earlier discussion: All the Divine light which is naturally found in this world is plagued by *hester panim*. Only a *mitzvah* can bypass that. So if *kavanah* itself were not part of the *mitzvah*, but a human (worldly) enhancement, it wouldn't have the power to channel infinite *mitzvah* light, *i.e.*, the Divine will).

וְהָאָרַת רָצוֹן הָעֶלְיוֹן הַזֶּה הַמְּאִירָה וּמְלוּבֶּשֶׁת בְּכַוָּנָה זוֹ — **And the extent to which this Divine will shines into and enters this** *kavanah* **when the** *mitzvah* **act is performed,** הִיא גְדוֹלָה לְאֵין קֵץ לְמַעֲלָה מַעֲלָה מֵהֶאָרַת רְצוֹן הָעֶלְיוֹן הַמְּאִירָה וּמְלוּבֶּשֶׁת בְּקִיּוּם הַמִּצְוֹת עַצְמָן בְּמַעֲשֶׂה וּבְדִבּוּר בְּלִי כַוָּנָה — **is far, far greater, infinitely so, than the extent to which the Divine will shines into and enters the** *mitzvah* **acts themselves, or spoken words done without** *kavanah*, כְּגוֹדֶל מַעֲלַת אוֹר הַנְּשָׁמָה עַל הַגּוּף — **the difference being as much as the soul's light surpasses the body's.**

הנשמה כמו גוף המצוה שהוא כלי ומלבוש
לכוונתה ואף שבשתיהן במצוה ובכוונתה מלובש
רצון אחד פשוט בתכלית הפשיטות בלי שום שינוי
וריבוי ח"ו ומיוחד במהותו ועצמותו ית' בתכלית
היחוד אף על פי כן ההארה אינה שוה בבחינת

Up to this point our focus has been on how Divine light shines into the *mitzvah* and its *kavanah* separately. But is there any interaction between them? Does the *mitzvah* act itself become more illuminated when there is *kavanah;* or does the Divine light just shine into the *kavanah,* barely illuminating the *mitzvah* act?

The *Tanya* now clarifies:

שֶׁהוּא כְּלִי וּמַלְבּוּשׁ הַנְּשָׁמָה — The body being a "vessel" and "garment" for the soul, כְּמוֹ גוּף הַמִצְוָה עַצְמָהּ שֶׁהוּא כְּלִי וּמַלְבּוּשׁ לְכַוָּנָתָהּ — just as the "body" of the *mitzvah,* its physical component, is a "vessel" and "garment" for its *kavanah.*

The *Tanya* implies here that when *kavanah* accompanies a *mitzvah* act, the two interact symbiotically, like a soul in a body. Just as when a soul joins with a body in one living entity, the body shines overtly with the soul's light, likewise, when a *mitzvah* deed is performed with *kavanah,* the *mitzvah* deed also becomes a vehicle of expression for the superior Divine light shining through the *kavanah.*

The body/soul analogy in this chapter therefore teaches us two separate points. 1.) That when *kavanah* is lacking, there is only a minuscule illumination of Divine light in the *mitzvah* act, like a "body without a soul." 2.) But when *kavanah* does accompany a *mitzvah* act, then, like a body *with* a soul, a great deal of the superior light that shines into the *kavanah* also shines into the act. (See below, chapter 40, for further clarification of this idea.)

וְאַף שֶׁבִּשְׁתֵּיהֶן בַּמִצְוָה וּבְכַוָּנָתָהּ מְלוּבָּשׁ רָצוֹן אֶחָד פָּשׁוּט בְּתַכְלִית הַפְּשִׁיטוּת — And even though both of them, the *mitzvah* and its *kavanah*, are expressions of the same, utterly abstract and non-composite Divine will, בְּלִי שׁוּם שִׁינוּי וְרִיבּוּי חַס וְשָׁלוֹם — a single will that is devoid of change or multiplicity, G-d forbid, וּמְיוּחָד בְּמַהוּתוֹ — and יִתְבָּרֵךְ בְּתַכְלִית הַיִּחוּד a will that is merged with the very essence and being of G-d, seamlessly so, אַף עַל פִּי כֵן — nevertheless, despite the oneness and indivisibility of this will, הַהֶאָרָה אֵינָהּ שָׁוָה — the *illumination* of this will is not equal in

A CHASIDIC THOUGHT

Of the two *mitzvah* components, deed and *kavanah*, *kavanah* acts as a superior matrix through which Divine light can be revealed in this world. And that is why a *mitzvah* without *kavanah* lacks illumination "like a body without a soul."

צִמְצוּם וְהִתְפַּשְּׁטוּת* וְנֶחְלְקֶת גַּם כֵּן לְאַרְבַּע מַדְרֵגוֹת כִּי גּוּף הַמִּצְוֹת עַצְמָן מַמָּשׁ הֵן ב' מַדְרֵגוֹת

הגה"ה

(וכמ"ש בע"ח שכוונת המצות ותלמוד תורה היא במדרגת אור וגוף המצות הן מדרגות ובחי'

a *mitzvah* deed done with and without *kavanah*, בְּבְחִינַת צִמְצוּם וְהִתְפַּשְּׁטוּת — since this "illumination" is greatly **diminished** in a *mitzvah* act, **and** overtly **manifest** in its *kavanah*.*

While the light of G-d's will tends to shine more in the *kavanah* than the *mitzvah* act, that doesn't mean G-d wants the *kavanah* more. G-d wants the *kavanah* and the *mitzvah* equally. It's just that when G-d's light enters this world, it tends to shine more in the *kavanah* than in the *mitzvah* (for reasons explained in the "note").

How do we know that G-d wants the *kavanah* and the *mitzvah* equally? Because if G-d's will is a reflection of Him, a single G-d won't have more than a single will. The fact that there are 613 expressions of that will in the *mitzvos*, doesn't make it 613 different wills. It's one will which has 613 different modes of expression in this world; 613 facets of the same diamond, so to speak.

While the extent to which G-d's will is expressed in *mitzvah* and *kavanah* are equal (because there is no *hester panim*), that doesn't mean that the levels of illumination of that will can't be different (due to different degrees of *tzimtzum*).

SECTION SEVEN: LEVELS OF ACTION AND INTENT

Above, we suggested that, of the four categories (inactive objects, plants, animals and humans), the lower two "non-movers" (inactive objects and plants), correspond to the body, since they show no overt signs of life; and the upper two "movers" (animals and humans) correspond to the soul.

Based on this distinction, the *Tanya* will now discern two levels in the physical act of the *mitzvos* (the "body"), corresponding to inactive objects and plants; and two levels in *kavanah* (the "soul") of *mitzvos*, corresponding to animals and humans.

וְנֶחְלֶקֶת גַּם כֵּן לְאַרְבַּע מַדְרֵגוֹת — And the degree of illumination in the *mitzvos* **is also divided into four levels,** two in the *mitzvah* act and two in the *kavanah*.

כִּי גּוּף הַמִּצְוֹת עַצְמָן מַמָּשׁ הֵן ב' מַדְרֵגוֹת — **For in the "body" of the *mitzvos*** them-

---

*הַגָּהָ"ה — **NOTE.** Why is *kavanah* a much more effective vehicle for G-d's light than the *mitzvah* act? In this note, the *Tanya* explains this point from a source in the Kabbalah.

שֶׁכַּוָּנַת הַמִּצְוֹת וְתַלְמוּד — וּכְמוֹ שֶׁכָּתוּב בְּעֵץ חַיִּים — **And as stated in *Etz Chaim*** (40:2), תּוֹרָה הִיא בְּמַדְרֵגַת אוֹר — **that the *kavanos* of the *mitzvos* and Torah study** both of which take place in the mind **are on the level of "light,"** וְגוּף הַמִּצְוֹת הֵן מַדְרֵגוֹת

שֶׁהֵן מצות מעשיות ממש
ומצות התלויות בדבור
ומחשבה כמו תלמוד תורה

כלים שהם בחי' צמצום שע"י
צמצום האור נתהוו הכלים כידוע
לי"ח):

selves there are two levels, שֶׁהֵן מִצְוֹת מַעֲשִׂיּוֹת מַמָּשׁ — which are 1.) corresponding to the category of inactive objects, **the purely practical** *mitzvos* which involve actual, physical objects.

וּמִצְוֹת הַתְּלוּיוֹת בְּדִבּוּר וּמַחֲשָׁבָה — And 2.) corresponding to the Plant Kingdom, the *mitzvos* **observed through** the combination of **speech and thought,** כְּמוֹ תַּלְמוּד

וּבְחִינוֹת כֵּלִים — and the *mitzvah* acts are on the level and character of "vessels," שֶׁהֵם בְּחִינַת צִמְצוּם — which is a property of *tzimtzum* (diminishment).

As the Divine will passes through the highest spiritual World of *Atzilus*, it becomes "dressed" in the properties of that world. *Atzilus* consists of "lights" contained in "vessels," which is a physical analogy for different types of Divine energy. "Lights," as their name suggests, give forth raw, uncontained energy, which is a close reflection of their infinite, undefined source. The "lights" are then projected through ten, specific "vessels" which give character traits to the lights, and color them with clearly defined properties.

This, *Etz Chaim* notes, mirrors the *mitzvah* dynamic down here in the World of Action. The boundless "lights" represent your *kavanah* to connect with the unlimited G-d through the *mitzvah*; and the "vessels," your connection to G-d through precisely defined, physical acts.

This explains: 1.) Why the Divine will is more revealed in your *kavanah* than your *mitzvah* act—because the *kavanah* is rooted in "light" and revelation, whereas the act is rooted in "vessels," a power of diminishment.

And: 2.) Why the *Tanya* stresses here the *general kavanah* of attachment to G-d (see above, section five), and not the *specific kavanah* unique to each *mitzvah*—because *kavanah* is rooted in "lights" *before* they have entered "vessels," and, at that point, there are no specifics. There's just undefined, amorphous light (Rabbi Shmuel Grunem Esterman, *Biur Tanya*).

שֶׁעַל יְדֵי צִמְצוּם הָאוֹר נִתְהַוּוּ הַכֵּלִים — For it was through a diminishment of the light that the vessels were formed, כַּיָּדוּעַ לְיוֹדְעֵי חָכְמָה נִסְתָּרָה — as is known to the masters of hidden Kabbalistic wisdom (see *Etz Chaim* 47:1).

The Kabbalah stresses the deep *integration* of lights and vessels. While they are in many ways opposite energies, they are able to work together because the vessels are, in fact, light in a diminished form.

This integration is reflected in the *mitzvah* where 1.) the *kavanah* must be accompanied by a *mitzvah* act, otherwise it's not a *mitzvah;* and 2.) when a *mitzvah* is performed with *kavanah,* the *kavanah's* more powerful light will shine into the *mitzvah* act too.

וק"ש ותפלה וברכת המזון ושאר ברכות. וכוונת המצות
לדבקה בו ית' שהיא כנשמה לגוף נחלקת ג"כ לשתי
מדרגות כמו שתי מדרגות הנשמה שהן בגוף החומרי
שהן חי ומדבר. כי מי שדעתו יפה לדעת את ה'
ולהתבונן בגדולתו ית' ולהוליד מבינתו יראה עילאה
במוחו ואהבת ה' בחלל הימני שבלבו להיות נפשו
צמאה לה' לדבקה בו ע"י קיום התורה והמצות שהן
המשכת והארת אור א"ס ב"ה על נפשו לדבקה בו
ובכוונה זו הוא לומד ומקיים המצות וכן בכוונה זו
מתפלל ומברך הרי כוונה זו על ד"מ כמו נשמת

תּוֹרָה וּקְרִיאַת שְׁמַע וּתְפִלָּה וּבִרְכַּת הַמָּזוֹן וּשְׁאָר בְּרָכוֹת — **such as Torah study, recital of the *Shema*, prayer, grace after meals, and other blessings,** which, while having a physical component (speech), also have a more spiritual component (thought), like plants which, while generally motionless (physical), do show signs of life (spiritual).

וְכַוָּונַת הַמִּצְוֹת לְדָבְקָה בּוֹ יִתְבָּרֵךְ — **And the *kavanah* of the *mitzvos*, to connect to G-d,** שֶׁהִיא כְּנְשָׁמָה לַגּוּף — **which is like the "soul"** of a *mitzvah* when compared to the *mitzvah* act, **its "body,"** נֶחְלֶקֶת גַּם כֵּן לִשְׁתֵּי מַדְרֵגוֹת — this *kavanah* **is also sub-divided into two levels,** כְּמוֹ שְׁתֵּי מַדְרֵגוֹת הַנְּשָׁמָה שֶׁהֵן בַּגּוּף הַחוּמְרִי — **corresponding to the two types of soul found in physical bodies,** שֶׁהֵן חַי וּמְדַבֵּר — **namely,** the souls found in 3.) **animals and,** 4.) **humans.**

6TH NISAN REGULAR | 26TH ADAR II LEAP

The *Tanya* will now describe levels 3 and 4 in more detail, beginning with the ideal "human" level of *kavanah* (4).

כִּי מִי שֶׁדַּעְתּוֹ יָפָה לְדַעַת אֶת ה' וּלְהִתְבּוֹנֵן בִּגְדוּלָתוֹ יִתְבָּרֵךְ — **For if your "mental disposition is good"** (*Tanna de-be Eliyahu Zuta,* chapter 8), **to think about G-d, to contemplate His greatness,** וּלְהוֹלִיד מִבִּינָתוֹ יִרְאָה עִילָאָה בְּמוֹחוֹ — so **that your** powers of *binah* (cognition) give rise to **"higher reverence"** (*Zohar Chadash, Ki Sisa* 45d; see below chapter 43, p. 550) **in your mind,** וְאַהֲבַת ה' בְּחָלָל הַיְמָנִי — **and a love of G-d in your heart's right chamber,** שֶׁבְּלִבּוֹ — so that your soul thirsts for G-d, to connect to לִהְיוֹת נַפְשׁוֹ צְמֵאָה לַה' לְדָבְקָה בּוֹ — **so that your soul thirsts for G-d, to connect to Him,** עַל יְדֵי קִיּוּם הַתּוֹרָה וְהַמִּצְוֹת שֶׁהֵן הַמְשָׁכַת וְהָאָרַת אוֹר אֵין סוֹף בָּרוּךְ הוּא עַל נַפְשׁוֹ לְדָבְקָה בּוֹ — **through observing Torah and *mitzvos*, which "pull" the Blessed Infinite Light down to illuminate your soul, so as to connect with G-d,** וּבְכַוָּונָה זוֹ הוּא לוֹמֵד וּמְקַיֵּים הַמִּצְוֹת — **and it's with this intention that you study** Torah and you **observe *mitzvos*,** וְכֵן בְּכַוָּונָה זוֹ מִתְפַּלֵּל וּמְבָרֵךְ — **and it is with this intention that**

המדבר שהוא בעל שכל ובחירה ובדעת ידבר ומי
שדעתו קצרה לידע ולהתבונן בגדולת א״ס ב״ה
להוליד האהבה מבינתו בהתגלות לבו וכן היראה
במוחו ופחד ה' בלבו רק שזוכר ומעורר את האהבה 51B
הטבעית המסותרת בלבו ומוציאה מההעלם והסתר
הלב אל הגילוי במוח עכ״פ שיהיה רצונו שבמוחו
ותעלומות לבו מסכים ומתרצה ברצוי גמור באמת
לאמיתו למסו' נפשו בפועל ממש על יחוד ה' כדי לדבק
בו נפשו האלהית ולבושיה ולכללן ביחודו ואחדותו

you pray and recite blessings, הֲרֵי כַּוָּנָה זוֹ עַל דֶּרֶךְ מָשָׁל כְּמוֹ נִשְׁמַת הַמְדַבֵּר — **then this level of** *kavanah* **could be compared to** the highest of the four categories, **"human,"** שֶׁהוּא בַּעַל שֵׂכֶל וּבְחִירָה וּבְדַעַת יְדַבֵּר — **since a human has intellect, free choice, and speaks intelligently,** and you have engaged these higher, uniquely human faculties in your *kavanah*.

That is the ideal of level 4. But now we will turn to level 3, a lower level of *kavanah* (based on the discussions in *Tanya* chapters 16-25), corresponding to the instinctual properties of an "animal."

וּמִי שֶׁדַּעְתּוֹ קְצָרָה לֵידַע וּלְהִתְבּוֹנֵן בִּגְדוּלַת אֵין סוֹף בָּרוּךְ הוּא — **As for someone who is weak in his ability to think about G-d and contemplate the greatness of the Blessed Infinite One,** לְהוֹלִיד הָאַהֲבָה מִבִּינָתוֹ בְּהִתְגַּלּוּת לִבּוֹ — **and his** powers of *binah* (cognition) **won't give rise to a palpable love of G-d in his heart,** וְכֵן הַיִּרְאָה בְּמוֹחוֹ וּפַחַד ה' בְּלִבּוֹ — **nor a reverence of G-d in his mind, nor a fear of G-d in his heart,** רַק שֶׁזּוֹכֵר וּמְעוֹרֵר אֶת הָאַהֲבָה הַטִּבְעִית הַמְסוּתֶּרֶת בְּלִבּוֹ — **and all he can do is recall and awaken the natural, latent love in his heart,** וּמוֹצִיאָהּ מֵהֶעְלֵם — **and bring that** וְהֶסְתֵּר הַלֵּב אֶל הַגִּלּוּי בַּמּוֹחַ עַל כָּל פָּנִים love **out of its hidden, latent state so that** even if it can't inspire his heart to palpable emotion, **it's at least conscious in his mind,** שֶׁיִּהְיֶה רְצוֹנוֹ שֶׁבְּמוֹחוֹ וְתַעֲלוּמוֹת לִבּוֹ מַסְכִּים וּמִתְרַצֶּה בְּרִצּוּי גָּמוּר בֶּאֱמֶת לַאֲמִיתּוֹ לִמְסוֹר נַפְשׁוֹ **so that the will of his mind and the "hidden places" of his heart are in full and absolute agreement, with complete authenticity, to actually give** בְּפוֹעַל מַמָּשׁ עַל יְחוּד ה' **up his life to affirm G-d's unity,** if put to the test,

כְּדֵי לְדַבְּקָה בּוֹ נַפְשׁוֹ הָאֱלֹהִית וּלְבוּשֶׁיהָ **to attach to G-d his Divine Soul and** וּלְכָלְלָן בְּיִחוּדוֹ וְאַחְדּוּתוֹ — **and this** *theoretical* **willingness to give up his life is seriously contemplated so as to have enthusiasm**

שֶׁהוּא רָצוֹן הָעֶלְיוֹן הַמְלוּבָּשׁ בְּת״ת וּבְקִיּוּם הַמִּצְוֹת
כנ״ל וְגַם הַיִּרְאָה כְּלוּלָה בָּהּ לְקַבֵּל מַלְכוּתוֹ שֶׁלֹא לִמְרוֹד
בּוֹ ח״ו וּבְכַוָּונָה זוֹ הוּא סוּר מֵרַע וְעוֹשֶׂה טוֹב וְלוֹמֵד
וּמִתְפַּלֵּל וּמְבָרֵךְ בְּפֵירוּשׁ הַמִּלּוֹת לְבַדּוֹ בְּלֹא דְּחִילוּ
וּרְחִימוּ בְּהִתְגַּלּוּת לִבּוֹ וּמוֹחוֹ הֲרֵי כַּוָּונָה זוֹ עַד״מ כְּמוֹ
נִשְׁמַת הַחַי שֶׁאֵינוֹ בַּעַל שֵׂכֶל וּבְחִירָה וְכָל מִדּוֹתָיו
שֶׁהֵן יִרְאָתוֹ מִדְּבָרִים הַמַּזִּיקִים אוֹתוֹ וְאַהֲבָתוֹ לִדְבָרִים
הַנֶּאֱהָבִים אֶצְלוֹ הֵן רַק טִבְעִיִּים אֶצְלוֹ וְלֹא מִבִּינָתוֹ וְדַעְתּוֹ
וְכָךְ הֵן עַל ד״מ הַיִּרְאָה וְהָאַהֲבָה הַטִּבְעִיּוֹת הַמְסוּתָּרוֹת
בְּלֵב כָּל יִשְׂרָאֵל כִּי הֵן יְרוּשָׁה לָנוּ מֵאֲבוֹתֵינוּ וּכְמוֹ טֶבַע
בְּנַפְשׁוֹתֵינוּ כַּנִּזְכָּר לְעֵיל:

שֶׁהוּא רָצוֹן its garments, so that they can be absorbed in G-d's **unity and oneness,** הָעֶלְיוֹן הַמְלוּבָּשׁ בְּתַלְמוּד תּוֹרָה וּבְקִיּוּם הַמִּצְוֹת — which is the Divine will expressed through Torah study and *mitzvah* observance, כַּנִּזְכָּר לְעֵיל — as explained above (chapters 23, 35), וְגַם הַיִּרְאָה כְּלוּלָה בָּהּ — and as we have learned, **within** this "latent love" is also included fear (see above, chapter 19, p. 230), לְקַבֵּל מַלְכוּתוֹ שֶׁלֹא לִמְרוֹד בּוֹ חַס וְשָׁלוֹם — to accept G-d's **authority, not to rebel against Him, G-d forbid.**

וּבְכַוָּונָה זוֹ הוּא סוּר מֵרַע וְעוֹשֶׂה טוֹב — **And with** all this above *kavanah* he *"turns away from evil and does good,"* (see *Psalms* 34:15), וְלוֹמֵד וּמִתְפַּלֵּל וּמְבָרֵךְ — to study, pray and recite blessings, בְּפֵירוּשׁ הַמִּלּוֹת לְבַדּוֹ בְּלֹא דְּחִילוּ וּרְחִימוּ בְּהִתְגַּלּוּת לִבּוֹ וּמוֹחוֹ — but since he is unable to arouse emotion for G-d he contemplates **only** the translation of the words, without any palpable fear or love in his heart or mind.

הֲרֵי כַּוָּונָה זוֹ עַל דֶּרֶךְ מָשָׁל כְּמוֹ נִשְׁמַת הַחַי — This level of intent could be compared to the soul of an animal, שֶׁאֵינוֹ בַּעַל שֵׂכֶל וּבְחִירָה — that has no substantive intellect or free choice, וְכָל מִדּוֹתָיו שֶׁהֵן יִרְאָתוֹ מִדְּבָרִים הַמַּזִּיקִים אוֹתוֹ וְאַהֲבָתוֹ לִדְבָרִים הַנֶּאֱהָבִים אֶצְלוֹ — and all its emotions, which are the fear of things it deems harmful and the love of things it deems enjoyable, הֵן רַק טִבְעִיִּים אֶצְלוֹ וְלֹא מִבִּינָתוֹ וְדַעְתּוֹ — are merely innate to it, and not the result of its cognition or thought.

וְכָךְ הֵן עַל דֶּרֶךְ מָשָׁל הַיִּרְאָה וְהָאַהֲבָה הַטִּבְעִיּוֹת הַמְסוּתָּרוֹת בְּלֵב כָּל יִשְׂרָאֵל — This is analogous to the natural latent love and fear in the heart of all Israel, כִּי הֵן יְרוּשָׁה לָנוּ מֵאֲבוֹתֵינוּ — which are an "inheritance" from our Patriarchs, וּכְמוֹ טֶבַע בְּנַפְשׁוֹתֵינוּ — similar to a natural instinct of our souls, כַּנִּזְכָּר לְעֵיל — as mentioned above in chapters 18-19.

פרק לט וּמִפְּנֵי זה ג"כ נקראים המלאכים בשם
חיות ובהמות כדכתי' ופני אריה
אל הימין וגו' ופני שור מהשמאל וגו' לפי שאינם
בעלי בחירה ויראתם ואהבתם היא טבעית להם

THE POWER OF KAVANAH (II)

SECTION ONE: WHY THE ANGELS' WORSHIP IS LACKING

7TH NISAN REGULAR | 27TH ADAR II LEAP

Chapter 39 continues our discussion in chapter 38 about the spiritual power of attentiveness (*kavanah*) when performing a *mitzvah*. We have already learned how *kavanah* is the "soul" of a *mitzvah*, which floods it with Divine light. In this chapter we will discover the spiritual "address" which a *mitzvah* performed with *kavanah* is capable of reaching; and, conversely, where the *mitzvah* "ends up" when *kavanah* is lacking.

Our opening discussion continues exactly where we left off at the end of chapter 38, with the *Tanya*'s distinction between two general categories of *kavanah*. Preferably, we learned, your *kavanah* should arise from an awareness of G-d that you've *personally acquired* through real, contemplative work. But a lower level of *kavanah* can still be attained merely by stirring up *innate* feelings for G-d that you already have in your soul.

The higher level, the *Tanya* taught, is comparable to a "human," in that it is acquired through application of higher mental faculties. The lower level, is like an "animal," since it is based on an instinctual awareness that is already present in the psyche.

וּמִפְּנֵי זֶה גַּם כֵּן נִקְרָאִים הַמַּלְאָכִים בְּשֵׁם חַיּוֹת וּבְהֵמוֹת — **And this** description of lower, instinctual *kavanah* as "animal" in character **is also the reason why angels are called *chayos* ("wild beasts") and *behemos* ("animals"),** כְּדִכְתִיב וּפְנֵי אַרְיֵה אֶל הַיָּמִין, וּפְנֵי שׁוֹר מֵהַשְּׂמֹאל וְגוֹ' — **as the verse states** of Ezekiel's vision of a heavenly "chariot," that the angels appeared with *"a lion's face to the right... and an ox's face from the left etc.,"* (*Ezekiel* 1:10).

לְפִי שֶׁאֵינָם בַּעֲלֵי בְחִירָה — **The angels are compared to animals because they do not possess free choice** to acquire a personal, intellect-based, appreciation of G-d, וְיִרְאָתָם וְאַהֲבָתָם הִיא טִבְעִית לָהֶם — **and their** worship, through either **reverence or**

כמ"ש בר"מ פ' פנחס ולכן מעלת הצדיקים גדולה מהם
כי מדור נשמות הצדיקים הוא בעולם הבריאה ומדור
המלאכי' בעולם היצירה*
וההבדל שביניהם הוא כי
בעולם היצירה מאירות
שם מדותיו של א"ס ב"ה
לבדן שהן אהבתו ופחדו

הגה"ה
(והיינו בסתם מלאכים אבל יש
מלאכים עליונים בעולם הבריאה
שעבודתם בדחילו ורחימו שכליים
כמ"ש בר"מ שם שיש שני מיני

52A

love of G-d, is merely **instinctual for them,** כְּמוֹ שֶׁכָּתוּב בְּרַעְיָא מְהֵימָנָא פָּרְשַׁת פִּינְחָס — **as stated in** the *Zohar, Raya Mehemna, Parshas Pinchas* (3, 225a).

At first glance, the angels, who are purely spiritual, seem to bear no resemblance to animals, whose consciousness is focused exclusively on the physical world. But Scripture chose to describe the angels as "wild beasts" and "animals," to indicate that the angels' emotional enrapture with G-d, however impressive it may be, is ultimately instinctual for them, and not earned.

וְלָכֵן מַעֲלַת הַצַּדִּיקִים גְּדוֹלָה מֵהֶם — **And that's why the** *tzadikim* **are** considered to be **higher than** the angels (*Talmud, Sanhedrin* 93a; *Etz Chaim* 28:4), even though their awareness of G-d is much lower than that of angels, because what *tzadikim* achieve is earned and not instinctual.

As the *Tanya* will now explain, the inner reason why *tzadikim* are able to achieve more than angels is because their souls come from a higher place.

כִּי מְדוֹר נִשְׁמוֹת הַצַּדִּיקִים הוּא בְּעוֹלָם הַבְּרִיאָה — **For the** heavenly **soul "department"** **of** most *tzadikim* **is in the** higher, intellectual **world of** *Beriah* (see *Eimek Ha-Melech* 5:72), וּמְדוֹר הַמַּלְאָכִים בְּעוֹלָם הַיְצִירָה — whereas **the "department" of** most **angels** **is in the** lower, emotional **world of** *Yetzirah* (Rabbi Yitzchak Luria, *Sefer Ha-Likutim, Parshas Ki Seitzei; Etz Chaim* 47:3).*

The reason why *tzadikim* have more impressive achievements than the angels is because their souls are rooted in a higher world.

וְהַהֶבְדֵּל שֶׁבֵּינֵיהֶם הוּא כִּי בְּעוֹלָם הַיְצִירָה מְאִירוֹת שָׁם מִדּוֹתָיו שֶׁל אֵין סוֹף בָּרוּךְ הוּא לְבַדָּן — **The distinction between** these two worlds **being, that the** lower **World of**

---

*הַגָהָ"ה — **NOTE.** וְהַיְינוּ בְּסְתָם מַלְאָכִים — This "location" in the lower, emotional world of *Yetzirah* **is generally the case with angels,** אֲבָל יֵשׁ מַלְאָכִים עֶלְיוֹנִים בְּעוֹלָם **however, there are higher angels in the** higher, intellectual **world of** *Beriah,* שֶׁעֲבוֹדָתָם בְּדְחִילוּ וּרְחִימוּ שִׂכְלִיִּים — **that do worship G-d with an intellectu-** ally generated reverence and love.**

שֶׁיֵּשׁ שְׁנֵי מִינֵי — **As stated in** *Raya Mehemna* (**ibid.**), כְּמוֹ שֶׁכָּתוּב בְּרַעְיָא מְהֵימָנָא שָׁם

וְיִרְאָתוֹ כו'. וְכמ"ש חַיּוֹת הַקֹּדֶשׁ טִבְעִיִּים וְשִׂכְלִיִּים
וְכמ"ש בע"ח):

[בְּתִקּוּנִים וְע"ח] דְּשִׁית

סְפִירִין מְקַנְּנִין בִּיצִירָה וְלָכֵן זֹאת הִיא עֲבוֹדַת הַמַּלְאָכִים
תָּמִיד יוֹמָם וְלַיְלָה לֹא יִשְׁקוֹטוּ לַעֲמוֹד בְּיִרְאָה וָפַחַד וְכו'
וְהַיְנוּ כָּל מַחֲנֶה גַּבְרִיאֵל שֶׁמֵּהַשְּׂמֹאל וַעֲבוֹדַת מַחֲנֶה
מִיכָאֵל הִיא הָאַהֲבָה כו'. אֲבָל בְּעוֹלַם הַבְּרִיאָה מְאִירוֹת
שָׁם חָכְמָתוֹ וּבִינָתוֹ וְדַעְתּוֹ שֶׁל א"ס ב"ה שֶׁהֵן מְקוֹר

Yetzirah, where the angels are located, **is illuminated only by the emotional pow-ers of the Blessed Infinite One, '**שֶׁהֵן אַהֲבָתוֹ וּפַחְדּוֹ וְיִרְאָתוֹ כו **— namely, to love Him, to feel trepidation before Him and to revere Him *etc.,*** but the intellectual powers do not predominate.

The *Tanya* now cites various Kabbalistic sources that indicate this point.

וּכְמוֹ שֶׁכָּתוּב [בְּתִקּוּנִים וְעֵץ חַיִּים] דְּשִׁית סְפִירִין מְקַנְּנִין בִּיצִירָה **— As stated in the *Tikunei Zohar* (23a) and *Etz Chaim* (29:3; 47:2), that *"the six* emotional *sefiros of Atzilus* have their 'nest' in *Yetzirah,"*** i.e., it is in the World of *Yetzirah* that the Divine emotions predominate.

וְלָכֵן זֹאת הִיא עֲבוֹדַת הַמַּלְאָכִים תָּמִיד יוֹמָם וְלַיְלָה לֹא יִשְׁקוֹטוּ **— And that's why the worship of the angels** is **constant, day and night without rest.**

The fact that the angels' worship is constant (*"day and night without rest"*) shows that it is devoid of effort, because anything that takes effort is liable to fluctuate (Rabbi Yosef Yitzchak Schneersohn, *Sefer Ha-Ma'amarim* 5703, p. 84).

Another point demonstrating the angels' lack of autonomy and free choice is the fact that each angel is limited to one particular type of emotion.

לַעֲמוֹד בְּיִרְאָה וָפַחַד וְכו' **— And their task is either to stand in reverence and trepida-tion *etc.,*** וְהַיְנוּ כָּל מַחֲנֶה גַּבְרִיאֵל שֶׁמֵּהַשְּׂמֹאל **— as we find that each group of angels,** is "locked" into a specific mode of reverence, **the entire Camp of** Angel **Gavriel, to the left,** וַעֲבוֹדַת מַחֲנֶה מִיכָאֵל הִיא הָאַהֲבָה כו', **— whereas the worship of the Camp of** Angel **Michael, to the right, is** "locked" into a mode of **love, *etc.,*** (see *Zohar* 3, 118b).

Emotions, however, are only fixed when they are not grounded in intellect. And that is why the souls of *tzadikim,* from the higher intellectual world of *Beriah,* are superior.

אֲבָל בְּעוֹלַם הַבְּרִיאָה מְאִירוֹת שָׁם חָכְמָתוֹ וּבִינָתוֹ וְדַעְתּוֹ שֶׁל אֵין סוֹף בָּרוּךְ הוּא **— But the world of *Beriah* is illuminated by the Blessed Infinite One's** intellectual powers

---

חַיּוֹת הַקֹּדֶשׁ **— that there are two categories of** angels called holy *Chayos,* טִבְעִיִּים **— those** whose emotions are **innate, and those** whose emotions arise from **intellect,** וּכְמוֹ שֶׁכָּתוּב בְּעֵץ חַיִּים **— as is also stated in *Etz Chaim*** (50:7).

הַמִּדּוֹת וְאִם וְשֹׁרֶשׁ לָהֶן וּכְדְאִיתָא בְּתִקּוּנִים דְּאִימָּא
עִילָּאָה מְקַנְּנָא בִּתְלַת סְפִירָן בְּכֻרְסַיָּא שֶׁהוּא עוֹלָם
הַבְּרִיאָה וְלָכֵן הוּא מָדוֹר נִשְׁמוֹת הַצַּדִּיקִים עוֹבְדֵי ה'
בִּדְחִילוּ וּרְחִימוּ הַנִּמְשָׁכוֹת מִן הַבִּינָה וְדַעַת דְּגַדְלַת א"ס
ב"ה שֶׁאַהֲבָה זוֹ נִקְרָא רְעוּתָא דְּלִבָּא כַּנַּ"ל וּמֵרְעוּתָא

of *chochmah*, *binah* and *da'as*, שֶׁהֶן מְקוֹר הַמִּדּוֹת וְאִם וְשֹׁרֶשׁ לָהֶן — the intellectual powers **being the *source* of the emotions, their "mother" and root** (see p. 57).

Tzadikim don't just worship with the intellect, they worship G-d with the emotions of love and reverence, too. The distinction is that the angels' emotions are instinctual and fixed because they are not the product of intellectual work; whereas the emotions of *tzadikim* are fluid since they are a product of the mind.

The *Tanya* now cites proof from the *Tikunei Zohar* that *Beriah* is a world of the intellect.

וּכְדְאִיתָא בַּתִּקּוּנִים דְּאִימָּא עִילָּאָה מְקַנְּנָא בִּתְלַת סְפִירָן בְּכֻרְסַיָּא — **And as stated in the *Tikunei Zohar* (ibid.), "the supernal 'mother' has her 'nest' in the three** intellectual **sefiros of the 'throne,'"** שֶׁהוּא עוֹלָם הַבְּרִיאָה — the **"throne" referring to the world of *Beriah*** (Rabbi Moshe Cordovero, *Pardes Rimonim* 16:3; *Etz Chaim* 46:1).

In Ezekiel's vision, cited above, the angels (appearing as animals) were seen below *"the likeness of a throne"* (Ezekiel 1:26). For here we learn that the world above the angels (who inhabit *Yetzirah*) is called the "throne."

(*Beriah* is compared to a throne, on which you sit down, to indicate how the spiritual illumination in that world has been downgraded from the highest world of *Atzilus*, above it).

וְלָכֵן הוּא מָדוֹר נִשְׁמוֹת הַצַּדִּיקִים — **And that's why** the "intellectual" world of *Beriah* **is the soul-repository of *tzadikim*,** עוֹבְדֵי ה' בִּדְחִילוּ וּרְחִימוּ הַנִּמְשָׁכוֹת מִן הַבִּינָה וְדַעַת דְּגַדְלַת אֵין סוֹף בָּרוּךְ הוּא — **since *tzadikim* worship G-d with a reverence and love that result from cognition and recognition of the Blessed Infinite One's greatness.**

The *Tanya* now offers a further proof that intellect-based worship is associated with the world of *Beriah*. The proof has three elements: 1.) As we shall see later on, another term for the World of *Beriah* is "Upper Garden of Eden" 2.) The *Zohar* states that in order to enter the "Upper Garden of Eden," a soul must have carried out worship at the level called "desire of the heart." 3.) Above, in chapter 17, we learned that "desire of the heart" is intellect based.

Combining these three elements together we have proof that intellect-based worship ("desire of the heart") is connected with the world of *Beriah* (the "Upper Garden of Eden").

שֶׁאַהֲבָה זוֹ נִקְרָא רְעוּתָא דְּלִבָּא כַּנִּזְכָּר לְעֵיל — And, **as we mentioned above** (chapter 17, p. 203), **this love** experienced by *tzadikim*, when generated by the intel-

דלבא נעשה לבוש לנשמה בעולם הבריאה שהוא
גן עדן העליון כדלקמן וכמ"ש בזהר ויקהל אך
היינו דווקא נשמות ממש שהן בחי' מוחין דגדלות
א"ס ב"ה אבל בחי' הרוח של הצדיקים וכן שאר כל
נשמות ישראל שעבדו את ה' בדחילו ורחימו המסותרות
בלב כללו' ישראל אין עולות לשם רק בשבת ור"ח לבד

lect, is called *"desire of the heart"* (*Zohar* 3, 289b), וּמֵרְעוּתָא דְלִבָּא נַעֲשֶׂה לְבוּש
לְנְשָׁמָה בְּעוֹלָם הַבְּרִיאָה — and from *"desire of the heart"* a *"garment"* is formed
for the soul enabling it to inhabit the world of *Beriah,* שֶׁהוּא גַּן עֵדֶן הָעֶלְיוֹן כְּדִלְקַמָּן
— which, as will be explained later in this chapter, is the "Upper Garden of Eden,"
וּכְמוֹ שֶׁכָּתוּב בַּזֹהַר וַיַקְהֵל — as the *Zohar* states in its commentary on the Torah portion of *Vayakhel* (2, 210b).

8TH NISAN REGULAR

אַךְ הַיְינוּ דַוְוקָא נְשָׁמוֹת מַמָּשׁ — However, this association with the World of *Beriah* is
not applicable to all the levels of a *tzadik's* soul but only to its intellectual component, *i.e.,* not the *nefesh* or *ruach*, but the *neshamah,* exclusively.

Since *Beriah* is a world of intellect, only the part of a *tzadik's* soul which powers
its intellectual faculties can ascend there.

שֶׁהֵן בְּחִינַת מוֹחִין דְגַדְלוּת אֵין סוֹף בָּרוּךְ הוּא — Because the *neshamah* portion of the
soul powers **an expanded consciousness (*mochin de-gadlus*) of the Blessed Infinite One** (see chapter 12, p. 140).

אֲבָל בְּחִינַת הָרוּחַ שֶׁל הַצַדִיקִים — But the emotional powers in the souls of *tzadikim,* the *ruach,* וְכֵן שְׁאָר כָּל נִשְׁמוֹת יִשְׂרָאֵל שֶׁעָבְדוּ אֶת ה' בְּדְחִילוּ וּרְחִימוּ הַמְסוּתָּרוֹת
בְּלֵב כְּלָלוּת יִשְׂרָאֵל — (and, so too, all the other souls of Israel which worship G-d
through natural emotions, from a reverence and love which is naturally dormant
within the heart of all Israel), אֵין עוֹלוֹת לְשָׁם — these souls do not ascend there, to
the intellectual World of *Beriah.*

As we conclude this discussion of the unique qualities of the souls of *tzadikim*,
we cannot help but wonder how the topic is relevant to us, the readers of the *Tanya*,
who, in all likelihood, will never reach the level of *tzadik*.

However there are two highly relevant lessons each of us can take from this
discussion:

1.) If contemplative work renders *tzadikim* superior even to the angels, it must be
extremely powerful. (So, even if I won't reach the level of *tzadik*, I should still apply
myself to this important type of work).

2.) Even if I fail at contemplative work, and I rely on my natural, innate love for
G-d, I shouldn't feel that my worship lacks potency. After all, the angels rely on their
innate emotions and their love is certainly not lacking in intensity! (*Notes on Tanya*).

דרך העמוד שמג"ע התחתון לג"ע העליון שהוא עולם
הבריאה הנקרא ג"ע העליון להתענג על ה' וליהנות
מזיו השכינה כי אין הנאה ותענוג לשכל נברא אלא
במה שמשכיל ומבין ויודע ומשיג בשכלו ובינתו מה
שאפשר לו להבין ולהשיג מאור א"ס ב"ה ע"י חכמתו
ובינתו ית' המאירות שם בעולם הבריאה ומה שזוכות
נשמות אלו לעלות למעלה מהמלאכים אף שעבדו
בדחילו ורחימו טבעיים לבד היינו מפני שע"י דחילו
ורחימו שלהם אתכפיא ס"א המלובשת בגופם בין

52B

SECTION TWO: YOUR SOUL ON THE SABBATH

While we have learned that ordinary souls cannot enter the World of *Beriah*, the *Tanya* now notes an exception to this rule.

רַק בְּשַׁבָּת וְרֹאש חֹדֶשׁ לְבַד — Ordinary souls can't enter the World of *Beriah* **except for on the Sabbath and New Moon (***Rosh Chodesh***) when all the worlds are elevated up a rung (see *Zohar* 2, 156b),** דֶּרֶךְ הָעַמּוּד שֶׁמִּגַּן עֵדֶן הַתַּחְתּוֹן לְגַן עֵדֶן הָעֶלְיוֹן — and even ordinary souls are able to ascend **through the channel which passes from the "Lower Garden of Eden" to the "Higher Garden of Eden"** (see *Eimek Ha-Melech* 17:8), שֶׁהוּא עוֹלָם הַבְּרִיאָה הַנִּקְרָא גַן עֵדֶן הָעֶלְיוֹן — the "Higher Garden of Eden" being **the World of *Beriah*,** לְהִתְעַנֵּג עַל ה' וְלֵיהָנוֹת מִזִּיו הַשְּׁכִינָה — and when these souls pass to the "Higher Garden of Eden," **they are able to take pleasure in G-d, and "enjoy a ray of the Divine Presence"** (*Talmud, Brachos* 17a).

כִּי אֵין הֲנָאָה וְתַעֲנוּג לְשֵׂכֶל נִבְרָא — The reason why the "Upper Garden of Eden" (*i.e.,* the highest pleasure of heaven), is to be found in the world of intellect, the World of *Beriah* is **because there is no** real **enjoyment or pleasure for a created intellect,** אֶלָּא בְּמַה שֶׁמַּשְׂכִּיל וּמֵבִין וְיוֹדֵעַ וּמַשִּׂיג בְּשִׂכְלוֹ וּבִינָתוֹ — **other than grasping with the intellect, understanding with logic, and recognizing with the mind,** מַה שֶׁאֶפְשָׁר לוֹ **whatever could be understood or grasped** לְהָבִין וּלְהַשִּׂיג מֵאוֹר אֵין סוֹף בָּרוּךְ הוּא **of the Blessed Infinite Light,** עַל יְדֵי חָכְמָתוֹ וּבִינָתוֹ יִתְבָּרֵךְ הַמְּאִירוֹת שָׁם בְּעוֹלָם הַבְּרִיאָה — **which, of course, can't be known directly, but only through G-d's *chochmah* and *binah*, which shine there in the World of *Beriah*.**

But if *all* the worlds are elevated on the Sabbath and New Moon, why don't the angels also rise to the World of *Beriah* on these days?

וּמַה שֶׁזּוֹכוֹת נְשָׁמוֹת אֵלּוּ לַעֲלוֹת לְמַעְלָה מֵהַמַּלְאָכִים — **And the reason why these souls are permitted to rise** to the World of *Beriah*, **above the angels** which remain in *Yetzirah,* אַף שֶׁעָבְדוּ בִּדְחִילוּ וּרְחִימוּ טִבְעִיִּים לְבַד — **even though,** seemingly, these souls are no better than the angels, **as their worship is based only on an innate reverence and love,** and not something generated using their minds, הַיְינוּ מִפְּנֵי שֶׁעַל יְדֵי דְּחִילוּ וּרְחִימוּ שֶׁלָּהֶם אִתְכַּפְיָא סִטְרָא אַחֲרָא הַמְלוּבֶּשֶׁת בְּגוּפָם — **but the reason**

בבחי' סור מרע לכבוש התאוות ולשברן ובין בבחי'
ועשה טוב כנ"ל והם היו בעלי בחירה לבחור ברע ח"ו
ובחרו בטוב לאכפיא לס"א לאסתלקא יקרא דקב"ה
כו' כיתרון האור כו' כנ"ל והנה כל זה הוא במדור
הנשמות ומקום עמידתן אך תורתן ועבודתן נכללות

why these souls are allowed to rise to *Beriah* is **because** they have an advantage over the angels **in that their reverence and love causes the *sitra achra* within their bodies to be subdued,** unlike the angels which do not have a coarse, physical body.

בֵּין בִּבְחִינַת סוּר מֵרַע לִכְבּוּשׁ הַתַּאֲווֹת וּלְשַׁבְּרָן — The *sitra achra* is subdued **both when they *"turn away from evil"* (***Psalms* 34:15), overcoming and breaking free from their desires,** וּבֵין בִּבְחִינַת וַעֲשֵׂה טוֹב — as well as when they *"do good"* (ibid.), כַּנִּזְכָּר לְעֵיל — as mentioned above, (chapters 16, 25, 38).

Why should this quality, of suppressing the *sitra achra,* give souls the merit of entering the World of *Beriah,* a world of intellect where they do not really belong?

וְהֵם הָיוּ בַּעֲלֵי בְחִירָה לִבְחוֹר בְּרַע חַס וְשָׁלוֹם וּבָחֲרוּ בַּטּוֹב — **For** these souls **possessed free choice to choose evil, G-d forbid, and** instead **they chose good,** לְאַכְפְּיָא לְאַסְתַּלְקָא יְקָרָא דְקוּדְשָׁא בְּרִיךְ הוּא כו' — **to subdue the *sitra achra,*** לְסִטְרָא אָחֲרָא — *"to exalt the glory of the Blessed Holy One etc.,"* (***Zohar* 2, 128a), כִּיתְרוֹן הָאוֹר — *"like the advantage of light"* that comes from darkness" (***Ecclesiastes* 2:13), כו' — כַּנִּזְכָּר לְעֵיל — as mentioned above (chapters 12, 27, 33).

In choosing good over evil, these souls exercised their free choice. In that sense, they do share at least some resemblance to the souls of *tzadikim,* since *tzadikim* develop an intellectual appreciation of G-d through exercising their free choice..

Choosing good over evil isn't enough for a soul to earn a *permanent* place in the World of *Beriah,* but it is enough to help the soul enter there on Sabbath and New Moon, when the worlds are naturally shifting in that direction.

SECTION THREE: HOW YOUR MITZVOS ASCEND THE HEAVENS

Our discussion so far has focused on the different spiritual heights achieved *by the soul* through its worship; but we haven't discussed what happens *to the worship itself.* Where in the spiritual stratosphere do your *mitzvos* end up?

וְהִנֵּה כָּל זֶה הוּא בִּמְדוֹר הַנְּשָׁמוֹת — **Now the above discussion concerned the spiritual address of the souls,** וּמְקוֹם עֲמִידָתָן — **as well as the location where** the souls **were** temporarily **stationed** on the Sabbath and New Moon, אַךְ תּוֹרָתָן וַעֲבוֹדָתָן — **but** we didn't discuss what happens to **the Torah and worship** of those souls.

The Kabbalah teaches that each spiritual world contains both: a.) an "infrastructure"; and, b.) G-dly light that fills that infrastructure. The technical names for these are: a.) the infrastructure of "chambers" (*heichalos*), and b.) the lights of *sefiros.*

מַמָּשׁ בי"ס שֶׁהֵן בְּחִי' אֱלֹהוּת וְאוֹר א"ס מִתְיַחֵד בָּהֶן
בְּתַכְלִית הַיִּחוּד וְהַיְינוּ בי"ס דִּבְרִיאָה ע"י דְּחִילוּ וּרְחִימוּ
שִׂכְלִיִּים וּבי"ס דִּיצִירָה ע"י דְּחִילוּ וּרְחִימוּ טִבְעִיִי' וּבְתוֹכָן

Your soul, the *Tanya* will now explain, can only reach the "chamber" of any given world; but your *mitzvah*, which is actually G-d's will, merges with the *sefiros* in that world.

נִכְלָלוֹת מַמָּשׁ בי' סְפִירוֹת שֶׁהֵן בְּחִינַת אֱלֹהוּת — Your Torah and worship rise higher than any "chamber" **and are literally absorbed in the ten *sefiros*** of the appropriate world, which **are actual G-dliness,** וְאוֹר אֵין סוֹף מִתְיַחֵד בָּהֶן בְּתַכְלִית הַיִּחוּד — since **the Blessed Infinite Light is merged with** the *sefiros* **as perfectly as could be.**

PRACTICAL LESSONS

It's really important that you try to develop feelings for G-d through contemplative work in your mind.

That's because when you worship G-d based on ideas that you have acquired externally with your mind, you begin to transcend your self.

The difference between "chambers" and *sefiros*, is that G-d's Infinite Light is totally merged with the *sefiros*, whereas the "chambers" retain a separate identity. Your *mitzvah*, which is G-d's undiluted will, merges perfectly with the *sefiros*, but your soul, which is a separate entity from G-d, must remain in the "chambers."

וְהַיְינוּ — **To be precise,** the world which your worship reaches depends on whether it was inspired by contemplative work, or innate soul feelings, בי' סְפִירוֹת דִּבְרִיאָה — **through** worship motivated by **intellectually generated reverence and love,** the worship rises **to the ten *sefiros* of *Beriah*,** וּבי' סְפִירוֹת דִּיצִירָה עַל יְדֵי דְּחִילוּ וּרְחִימוּ טִבְעִיִּים — **whereas through** worship motivated by **natural reverence and love,** the worship rises **to the ten *sefiros* of *Yetzirah*.**

When you conjure the innate feelings of your soul for G-d it *seems* like you've transcended yourself, because you're focusing on G-d and not on your own concerns. The problem is, since these feelings are innate, they're really coming *from* your self-concept, and not *despite* it. You're feeling that it's all about G-d and not about you, but that's because it's natural for someone with your kind of soul to feel that way.

Worship from that level of consciousness reaches the World of *Yetzirah*. On one hand, it's worship—you're thinking about G-d—so it's far beyond this physical World of *Asiyah* where concern is focused on the self. But since your vision of "beyond the self" is actually *coming from yourself*, it's only one world up from the overtly self-centered consciousness of *Asiyah*.

But when your worship is rooted in an intellectual appreciation of G-d, it rises to a higher world. The intellect is capable of *objectivity*: it allows you to explore ideas and phenomena outside yourself. So when your mind contemplates G-d, leading you to worship, it's the *G-d concept* you've grasped (outside yourself), that has com-

מלובשות י"ס דאצי' ומיוחדות בהן בתכלית וי"ס דאצי'
מיוחדות בתכלית במאצילן א"ס ב"ה משא"כ הנשמו'
אינן נכללות באלהות די"ס אלא עומדות בהיכלות
ומדורין דבריאה או יצירה ונהנין מזיו השכינה הוא
אור א"ס ב"ה המיוחד בי"ס דבריאה או דיצי' והוא זיו

pelled you. Your worship wasn't motivated by your natural disposition or self-concept; it's a new, externally acquired, idea that has moved you.

So unlike the Worlds of *Asiyah* and *Yetzirah*, which both share an energy of "self," in *Beriah,* there is a paradigm shift as we begin to transcend the self (see *Sefer Ha-Ma'amarim Melukat,* vol. 5 (Brooklyn, 1992) pp. 236-7).

Above, the *Tanya* stated that your worship rises to the *sefiros* of either *Yetzirah* or *Beriah* (in contrast to the soul, which rises to the "chambers," but not the *sefiros*). We now continue that theme.

וּבְתוֹכָן מְלוּבָּשׁוֹת י' סְפִירוֹת דַּאֲצִילוּת — **And** within the ten *sefiros* of *Yetzirah* are enmeshed the ten *sefiros* of *Beriah,* and **within** the ten *sefiros* of *Beriah* are en-**meshed the ten *sefiros* of *Atzilus*,** וּמְיוּחָדוֹת בָּהֶן בְּתַכְלִית — **and the** ten *sefiros* of *Beriah* **are merged there** in *Atzilus* **perfectly,** וְי' סְפִירוֹת דַּאֲצִילוּת מְיוּחָדוֹת בְּתַכְלִית בְּמַאֲצִילָן אֵין סוֹף בָּרוּךְ הוּא — **and the ten *sefiros* of *Atzilus* are perfectly merged with their emanating source, the Blessed Infinite One.**

Once an entity merges with the *sefiros* in any world, it has a straight path to the Blessed Infinite One, because a.) the *sefiros* in every world are deeply enmeshed with each other; and b.) the highest of the worlds, *Atzilus*, is totally merged with the Blessed Infinite One. The Divine lights (*sefiros*) are capable of total enmeshment with each other, because they don't have a sense of separateness that would block such a merging.

מַה שָּׁאֵין כֵּן הַנְּשָׁמוֹת אֵינָן נִכְלָלוֹת בֵּאלֹהוּת דִּי' סְפִירוֹת — **But** while the *worship* rises to G-d, **that's not so with the *souls*, which are not absorbed into the ten Divine *sefiros,*** אֶלָּא עוֹמְדוֹת בְּהֵיכָלוֹת וּמְדוֹרִין דִּבְרִיאָה אוֹ יְצִירָה — **but rather, they remain in the "chambers" and "repositories" of** either *Beriah* or *Yetzirah*.

Being "stuck" in the "chambers" doesn't mean that the souls can't enjoy any Divine radiance. They are just limited to the diminished radiance shining in that world.

וְנֶהֱנִין מִזִּיו הַשְּׁכִינָה — **And** rather than actually merging with G-d, they merely **"enjoy the radiance of the Divine Presence"** from a distance, הוּא אוֹר אֵין סוֹף בָּרוּךְ הוּא הַמְיוּחָד בִּי' סְפִירוֹת דִּבְרִיאָה אוֹ דִיצִירָה — **the *"radiance of the Divine Presence"* re-ferring to the Blessed Infinite Light as it is merged with the ten *sefiros* of *Beriah* or *Yetzirah,*** shining through their filter in a diminished fashion.

Unlike the *sefiros*, whose energy flows *directly* from the Blessed Infinite One, the soul can only perceive a *diminished* G-dliness that shines to its vantage point (either the World of *Yetzirah* or *Beriah*).

תּוֹרָתָן וַעֲבוֹדָתָן מַמָּשׁ [עַ' זֹהַר וַיַקְהֵל דַּף ר"י] כִּי שְׂכַר מִצְוָה
הִיא מִצְוָה עַצְמָהּ: וְעוֹלַם הָאֲצִילוּת שֶׁהוּא לְמַעְלָה
מֵהַשֵּׂכֶל וְהַהַשָּׂגָה וְהַהֲבָנָה לְשֵׂכֶל נִבְרָא כִּי חָכְמָתוֹ
וּבִינָתוֹ וְדַעְתּוֹ שֶׁל אֵין סוֹף בָּרוּךְ הוּא מְיוּחָדוֹת שָׁם בּוֹ בְּתַכְלִית
הַיִּחוּד בְּיִחוּד עָצוּם וְנִפְלָא בְּיֶתֶר שְׂאֵת וְיֶתֶר עֹז לְאֵין קֵץ

וְהוּא זִיו תּוֹרָתָן וַעֲבוֹדָתָן מַמָּשׁ — **And this** "radiance" is, in fact, nothing other than the "radiance" of that person's **actual Torah and worship**, the Divine light of the *mitzvah* as it shines in that world (either *Yetzirah* or *Beriah*), [עַיֵּין זֹהַר וַיַקְהֵל דַּף ר"י] — **see Zohar, Vayakhel** (2, **210**b), כִּי שְׂכַר מִצְוָה הִיא מִצְוָה עַצְמָהּ — **since,** as we learned in chapter 37 (p. 409), *"the reward for a mitzvah is* the *mitzvah (itself)"* (see *Mishnah, Avos* 4:2).

The *Zohar* (ibid.) speaks of *"'garments,' made from the good deeds which a person did, following the commandments of the Torah. Through them, the soul stands in the Lower Garden of Eden clothed in these precious 'garments.' And if that soul ascends through the opening into the Higher Heaven (the Upper Garden of Eden), other precious and lofty garments are presented before her, made from the desire and attentiveness of the heart during Torah study and prayer."*

SECTION FOUR: HOW THE TRULY ENLIGHTENED WORSHIP G-D

9TH NISAN REGULAR | 28TH ADAR II LEAP

We have now established that: a.) A *mitzvah* rises to the *sefiros* of either *Yetzirah* or *Beriah* and from there it will pass upwards to the *sefiros* of *Atzilus*, and then merge with the Blessed Infinite Light. b.) Souls rise, through their worship, to the "chambers" of either *Yetzirah* or *Beriah*.

But could a soul rise to the highest of the four Worlds, *Atzilus*? The *Tanya* will now address this question.

וְעוֹלַם הָאֲצִילוּת שֶׁהוּא לְמַעְלָה מֵהַשֵּׂכֶל וְהַהַשָּׂגָה — **And as for the world of Atzilus,** וְהַהֲבָנָה לְשֵׂכֶל נִבְרָא — **which is beyond the mental capacity, grasp and understanding of a created intellect,** כִּי חָכְמָתוֹ וּבִינָתוֹ וְדַעְתּוֹ שֶׁל אֵין סוֹף בָּרוּךְ הוּא מְיוּחָדוֹת — **because the Blessed Infinite One's** *chochmah, binah* and *da'as* is utterly and perfectly merged with the light there in *Atzilus,* שָׁם בּוֹ בְּתַכְלִית הַיִּחוּד בְּיִחוּד עָצוּם — **with a merging which is more awesome and wondrous, with infinitely** וְנִפְלָא בְּיֶתֶר שְׂאֵת וְיֶתֶר עֹז לְאֵין קֵץ מִבְּעוֹלַם הַבְּרִיאָה *"more dignity and more power"* (Genesis 49:3), **than in the world of Beriah.**

Atzilus is not a "world" in the same sense as the other three worlds of *Beriah, Yetzirah* and *Asiyah,* which demonstrate some degree of separateness from G-d. The word *Atzilus* is derived from the word *etzel* which means "next to" or "close." Therefore *Atzilus* is *"utterly and seamlessly merged"* with G-d's Infinite Light.

מֵעוֹלָם הַבְּרִיאָה כִּי שָׁם יָרְדוּ לְהָאִיר בִּבְחִי' צִמְצוּם
כְּדֵי שֶׁיּוּכְלוּ שְׂכָלִים נִבְרָאִי' לְקַבֵּל מֵהֶן חַבַּ"ד לֵידַע אֶת
ה' וּלְהָבִין וּלְהַשִּׂיג אֵיזוֹ הַשָּׂגָה בְּאוֹר אֵ"ס בָּ"ה כְּפִי כֹּחַ
שְׂכָלִים הַנִּבְרָאִים שֶׁהֵם בַּעֲלֵי גְּבוּל וְתַכְלִית שֶׁלֹּא
יִתְבַּטְּלוּ בִּמְצִיאוּתָם וְלֹא יִהְיוּ בִּגְדַר נִבְרָאִים כְּלָל רַק
יַחְזְרוּ לַמְּקוֹרָם וְשָׁרְשָׁם שֶׁהוּא בְּחִי' אֱלֹהוּת מַמָּשׁ.
וְהִנֵּה צִמְצוּם זֶה הִיא סִבַּת הַהֶאָרָה שֶׁמְּאִירוֹת שָׁם
חַבַּ"ד שֶׁל אֵ"ס בָּ"ה לַנְּשָׁמוֹת אֵלּוּ בְּעוֹלָם הַבְּרִיאָה.
מַשָּׁא"כ בָּאֲצִילוּת שֶׁאֵינָם בִּבְחִי' צִמְצוּם כַּ"כ אַ"א   53A

And that's why *Atzilus* is *"beyond the mental capacity, grasp and understanding of a created intellect."* For a thing to be comprehensible to the human mind, it has to have defining properties and finite boundaries. Since *Atzilus* is "next to" the Infinite Light, it's also infinite, so the created intellect has no tools to grasp it.

כִּי שָׁם — **But there,** in the World of *Beriah,* יָרְדוּ לְהָאִיר בִּבְחִינַת צִמְצוּם — **the light has been downgraded, so that it shines in a diminished,** limited **fashion,** כְּדֵי שֶׁיּוּכְלוּ שְׂכָלִים נִבְרָאִים לְקַבֵּל מֵהֶן חָכְמָה בִּינָה וָדַעַת — **in order that created intellects can receive** G-d's *chochmah, binah and da'as,* לֵידַע אֶת ה' וּלְהָבִין וּלְהַשִּׂיג אֵיזוֹ הַשָּׂגָה בְּאוֹר **— to know G-d, and to understand and grasp something of the Blessed Infinite Light, within the intellectual capacity of their created** minds, שֶׁהֵם בַּעֲלֵי גְּבוּל וְתַכְלִית — **which are confined** in capacity **and limited** in scope.

שֶׁלֹּא יִתְבַּטְּלוּ בִּמְצִיאוּתָם — **So the diminishment of G-d's light in the World of *Beriah*** was necessary **in order that the existence** of separate, created intellects **should not become obliterated,** וְלֹא יִהְיוּ בִּגְדַר נִבְרָאִים כְּלָל — **and if,** instead of being obliterated, they would simply lose their separate identity through being reabsorbed back to their source, then **they wouldn't be "creations" at all any longer,** רַק יַחְזְרוּ לַמְּקוֹרָם וְשָׁרְשָׁם שֶׁהוּא בְּחִינַת אֱלֹהוּת מַמָּשׁ — **rather, they would simply be reabsorbed in their source and root, in G-dliness itself.**

29TH ADAR II LEAP

וְהִנֵּה צִמְצוּם זֶה הִיא סִבַּת הַהֶאָרָה שֶׁמְּאִירוֹת שָׁם חָכְמָה בִּינָה וָדַעַת שֶׁל אֵין סוֹף בָּרוּךְ הוּא לַנְּשָׁמוֹת אֵלּוּ בְּעוֹלָם הַבְּרִיאָה — **So, in the World of *Beriah,* it's this diminishment which enables the Blessed Infinite One's *chochmah, binah and da'as* to reach and illuminate these** created, separate **souls,** מַה שֶּׁאֵין כֵּן בָּאֲצִילוּת שֶׁאֵינָם בִּבְחִינַת צִמְצוּם כָּל כָּךְ — **but that wouldn't happen in *Atzilus* which has relatively little diminishment,** אִי אֶפְשָׁר לִשְׂכָלִים נִבְרָאִים לְקַבֵּל מֵהֶן — and **it's impossible for created intellects to receive** the light of G-d's undiminished intellect, וְלָכֵן לֵית מַחֲשָׁבְתָּא דִּילְהוֹן — **and that is why** we say that *"no thought (of theirs) can grasp Him at all"* (*Tikunei Zohar* 17a).

לשכלים נבראים לקבל מהן ולכן לית מחשבתא
דילהון תפיסא שם כלל לכן הוא מדור לצדיקי' הגדולים
שעבודתם היא למעלה מעלה אפי' מבחי' דחילו ורחימו
הנמשכות מן הבינה ודעת בגדולתו ית' כמו שעולם
האצילות הוא למעלה מעלה מבחי' בינה ודעת לשכל

Even though *Atzilus* is *"beyond the mental capacity, grasp and understanding of a created intellect,"* that doesn't mean that no soul can reach that level. You just can't use ordinary intellect to get there.

לָכֵן הוּא מָדוֹר לַצַּדִּיקִים הַגְּדוֹלִים — **That's why** for most souls, even *tzadikim*, the world of *Atzilus* cannot be their "home," and, consequently, *Atzilus* is only **the repository of** a few especially **great *tzadikim*.**

How do "great *tzadikim*" reach a consciousness of *Atzilus,* if, as we have explained, it's impossible for a created intellect to grasp?

שֶׁעֲבוֹדָתָם הִיא לְמַעְלָה מַעְלָה אֲפִילוּ מִבְּחִינַת דְּחִילוּ וּרְחִימוּ הַנִּמְשָׁכוֹת מִן הַבִּינָה וְדַעַת בִּגְדוּלָתוֹ יִתְבָּרֵךְ — **Because the worship** of "great *tzadikim*" is on a level that **vastly transcends even the** intellectually generated **reverence and love, which comes from** *binah* **and** *da'as* **of G-d's greatness,** כְּמוֹ שֶׁעוֹלָם הָאֲצִילוּת הוּא לְמַעְלָה מַעְלָה מִבְּחִינַת בִּינָה וְדַעַת לְשֵׂכֶל נִבְרָא — **just as the world of** *Atzilus* **vastly transcends the** *binah* **and** *da'as* **of any created intellect.**

The implication here is that "great *tzadikim*" do not worship through *"binah and da'as"* (cognition and recognition); but rather, they worship G-d through the highest intellectual power of *chochmah* (inquiry).

In fact, just as we learned that *"the six (emotional) sefiros have their 'nest' in Yetzirah,"* and, *"the supernal 'mother' (binah) has her 'nest' in the 'throne' (Beriah),"* we are also taught that *"the supernal 'father' (chochmah) 'nests' in Atzilus"* (Rabbi Shalom Buzaglo, *Mikdash Melech* to *Zohar* 2,220b).

Atzilus is not unreachable by the mind. It's just beyond the grasp of our cognitive apparatus, and can only be appreciated with *chochmah.* Why is this the case?

Above we explained that rational intellect (i.e., *binah* and *da'as*) can bring you to *Beriah,* because the intellect is objective and gets you "out of yourself." Emotions, we learned, are personal and biased, whereas the intellect can be transpersonal and objective (p. 457).

That is true to an extent. It's true that the subject which you are studying is transpersonal, it's something beyond and external to you. But the *tools* of intellectual processing with which you grasp the subject are very much personal. Those tools determine how *you* digest an idea which has come your way.

So it turns out that the experience of *Beriah* (rational intellect) is a *partial* transcendence of self, and not a full one. The external subject material gets you out of your self; but the tools of analysis draw you back into your ego.

נברא אלא עבודתם היתה בבחי' מרכבה ממש לא"ס
ב"ה וליבטל אליו במציאות ולהכלל באורו ית' הם

To completely transcend yourself, you need to access your power of *chochmah*.

Normally, your *chochmah* and *binah* work together in your mind, doing opposite jobs. *Chochmah* collects information from the outside, and *binah* processes it on the inside. To do that, *chochmah* needs to be in a state of wonderment, openness and humility; it needs to be detached from your self. (If you were constantly preoccupied with what ideas and events meant *to you*, you'd be a bad listener. You would never hear what another person is really saying, because one hundred percent of your attention would be on noting your own reaction.) So, for *chochmah* to do its job and receive wisdom from the outside it must be totally detached from self, and focused entirely on the "other."

Chochmah then feeds the tools of *binah* and *da'as* which process the raw information, analyzing it precisely, to work out what the idea means *to you*.

But imagine what would happen if you could get "stuck," so to speak, in *chochmah*, never progressing to the question: "What does this mean to me?" You'd be in a state of amazement and wonder at the universe. You'd lose your rigid sense of self, and see your role as a force put here for a greater cause. Most of your fears would drop away, because "loss" and "misfortune" are all bound up with your fragmented self-concept. Your thought about G-d wouldn't be, "What can G-d do for me?" but rather, "I am nothing but the power of G-d within me."

While you can't really know what *Atzilus* is like until you get there, the *Tanya* gives us one simple guidepost here: It's about transcending *binah* and *da'as* and reaching a consciousness of *chochmah* (See Rabbi Yosef Yitzchak Schneersohn, *Sefer Ha-Ma'amarim* 5700, p 33-34; 5703, pp. 164-5; Rabbi Menachem Mendel Schneerson, *Sefer Ha-Ma'amarim Melukat ibid.*; Rabbi Alexander Yudasin, *Ha-Lekach Ve-Ha-Libuv*).

PRACTICAL LESSONS

You only transcend yourself completely when you rise above the tendency to process everything cognitively, and can remain in a state of wonder and mental openness.

אֶלָּא עֲבוֹדָתָם הִיא בִּבְחִינַת מֶרְכָּבָה מַמָּשׁ לְאֵין סוֹף בָּרוּךְ הוּא — **Rather, the worship of** these souls of *Atzilus*, **is on the level of an actual "chariot" to the Blessed Infinite One,** וְלִיבָּטֵל אֵלָיו בִּמְצִיאוּת וּלְהִכָּלֵל בְּאוֹרוֹ יִתְבָּרֵךְ — **so that their** separate **identity is lost** in His, **and they are absorbed in G-d's light.**

As we have learned above (p. 378), the Sages compared the totally transpersonal state to a chariot, which doesn't follow its own personal concerns and is driven by something outside it (in this case, the awareness of G-d through *chochmah*).

The mind-state of "chariot" is the *result* of reaching the consciousness of *Atzilus* (*Sefer Ha-Ma'amarim* 5700, *ibid.*; *Igros Kodesh*, vol. 2, p. 142).

וכל אשר להם ע"י קיום התורה והמצוות ע"ד שאמרו
האבות הן הן המרכבה והיינו לפי שכל ימיהם היתה
זאת עבודתם. אך מי ששרש נשמתו קטן מהכיל
עבודה תמה זו ליבטל וליכלל באורו ית' בעבודתו
בקביעות רק לפרקים ועתים שהם עת רצון למעלה
וכמו בתפלת שמונה עשרה שהיא באצילות ובפרט
בהשתחוואו שבה שכל השתחוואה היא בבחי' אצילות
[כמ"ש בפרע"ח בקבל' שבת] כי היא ענין ביטול באורו
ית' להיות חשיב קמיה כלא ממש אזי ג"כ עיקר קביעות

הֵם וְכָל אֲשֶׁר לָהֶם — And this energy of *Atzilus* will influence, **"Both them and everything that is theirs"** (*Numbers* 16:33), *i.e.,* it will touch all of the "great *tzadik's*" relationships and possessions, עַל יְדֵי קִיּוּם הַתּוֹרָה וְהַמִּצְוֹת — **through the observance of Torah and *mitzvos*.**

עַל דֶּרֶךְ שֶׁאָמְרוּ הָאָבוֹת הֵן הֵן הַמֶּרְכָּבָה — Such *tzadikim* **resemble what** the Sages **said, "the Patriarchs were genuinely a 'chariot' to G-d"** (*Genesis Rabah* 47:6), וְהַיְינוּ לְפִי שֶׁכָּל יְמֵיהֶם הָיְתָה זֹאת עֲבוֹדָתָם — **because all their days,** the Patriarchs **worshiped on such a level** (see above, pp. 212, 259).

1ST NISAN LEAP

While this may seem beyond the reach of ordinary people, the *Tanya* now suggests that such a consciousness is attainable by us, at certain auspicious times.

אַךְ מִי שֶׁשֹּׁרֶשׁ נִשְׁמָתוֹ קָטָן מֵהָכִיל עֲבוֹדָה תַמָּה זוֹ — **But if your soul-root is underpowered for such a perfect level of worship** of *Atzilus,* לִיבָּטֵל וְלִיכָּלֵל בְּאוֹרוֹ יִתְבָּרֵךְ בַּעֲבוֹדָתוֹ בִּקְבִיעוּת — **to consistently shed your self-identity and become absorbed in G-d's light through worship,** רַק לִפְרָקִים — **you might only** achieve it **occasionally,** וְעִתִּים שֶׁהֵם עֵת רָצוֹן לְמַעְלָה — **at certain times which are "an auspicious moment"** (*Psalms* 69:14), **above.**

The *Tanya* gives an example of an "auspicious moment" when the energy of *Atzilus* is more accessible to us than usual.

וּכְמוֹ בִּתְפִלַּת שְׁמוֹנֶה עֶשְׂרֵה שֶׁהִיא בָּאֲצִילוּת — **Such as during the *Amidah* prayer, which has** the consciousness **of *Atzilus*** (*Pri Etz Chaim, Sha'ar Kerias Ha-Torah,* chapter 3), וּבְפְרָט בְּהִשְׁתַּחֲוָאוֹת שֶׁבָּהּ — **especially during the bows** during the *Amidah,* שֶׁכָּל הַשְׁתַּחֲוָאָה הִיא בִּבְחִינַת אֲצִילוּת — **since all bowing is an expression of** the transpersonal energy **of *Atzilus*,** [כְּמוֹ שֶׁכָּתוּב בְּפְרִי עֵץ חַיִּים בְּקַבָּלַת שַׁבָּת] — **as stated in *Pri Etz Chaim*** in its commentary on **welcoming Shabbos, *Sha'ar Shabbos*** chapter 5, כִּי הִיא עִנְיַן בִּיטוּל בְּאוֹרוֹ יִתְבָּרֵךְ — **because the theme** of bowing **is the dissolving of your identity in G-d's light,** לִהְיוֹת חָשִׁיב קַמֵּיהּ כְּלָא מַמָּשׁ — **to be "considered zero in His presence"** (*Zohar* 1, 11b), **literally.**

נשמתו הוא בעולם הבריאה [רק לפרקים בעת רצון
תעלה נשמתו לאצילות בבחי' מ"ן כידוע לי"ח]:
והנה שכר מצוה מצוה פי' שממשכרה נדע מהותה
ומדרגתה ואין לנו עסק בנסתרות שהם צדיקי' הגדולים
שהם בבחי' מרכבה רק הנגלו' לנו שאחריהם כל אדם
ימשוך לידע נאמנה מהות ומדרגת עבודת ה' בדחילו

קְבִיעוּת נִשְׁמָתוֹ הוּא בְּעוֹלָם הַבְּרִיאָה — But, ultimately, since **such a soul only** reaches the level of *Atzilus* occasionally, **its primary soul-location is in the World of** *Beriah,* [רַק לִפְרָקִים בְּעֵת רָצוֹן תַּעֲלֶה נִשְׁמָתוֹ לַאֲצִילוּת] — for only occasional-ly, at *"an auspicious moment"* will this soul rise to *Atzilus,* בִּבְחִינַת מַיִּין נוּקְבִין — at special moments of personal inspiration known as **"feminine waters"** (see above, chapter 10, p. 130), כַּיָּדוּעַ לְיוֹדְעֵי חָכְמָה נִסְתָּרָה] — as is known to those well versed in Kabbalistic **esoteric wisdom.**

A soul of *Beriah,* which worships G-d with intellectually generated love and rev-erence (the ideal advised in the *Tanya*), can still reach *Atzilus* consciousness *from time to time,* a level experienced consistently only by "great *tzadikim*."

SECTION FIVE: WHEN KAVANAH IS LACKING

10TH NISAN REGULAR | 2ND NISAN LEAP

So far we have discussed different levels of *kavanah* which propel your soul and your *mitzvah* to the worlds of *Yetzirah, Beriah* or *Atzilus.* Now we will turn to lower levels of attentiveness.

וְהִנֵּה שְׂכַר מִצְוָה מִצְוָה — **Now** as we stated above, *"the reward for a mitzvah is a mitzvah"* (*Mishnah, Avos* 4:2), פֵּירוּשׁ שֶׁמִּשְּׂכָרָהּ נֵדַע מַהוּתָהּ וּמַדְרֵגָתָהּ — **meaning that from its reward you can know the** *mitzvah's* **quality and level.**

In other words, from the spiritual "destination" where your *mitzvah* ends up, we can discern the *kavanah* you had when you performed it.

וְאֵין לָנוּ עֵסֶק בַּנִּסְתָּרוֹת — And *"we shall not concern ourselves with things esoteric"* (see *Talmud, Chagigah* 13a), שֶׁהֵם צַדִּיקִים הַגְּדוֹלִים שֶׁהֵם בִּבְחִינַת מֶרְכָּבָה — **namely, the great** *tzadikim* **who are on the level of a "chariot,"** which is unattainable for most of us, רַק הַנִּגְלוֹת לָנוּ — we shall **only** discuss *"those things revealed to us"* (*Deuteronomy* 29:28), שֶׁאַחֲרֵיהֶם כָּל אָדָם יִמְשׁוֹךְ — *i.e,* **things towards which every person ought to aim.**

לֵידַע נֶאֱמָנָה — You need **to have a profound recognition** of the following.

First the *Tanya* will summarize briefly what we have learned so far about *kavanah.*

מַהוּת וּמַדְרֵגַת עֲבוֹדַת ה' — **The spiritual quality and level of** your **Divine worship,** בִּדְחִילוּ וּרְחִימוּ בְּהִתְגַּלּוּת לִבּוֹ — **if it's done with palpable reverence and love in your**

וְרחִימוּ בהתגלות לבו הנמשכות מן הבינה ודעת
בגדולת א"ס ב"ה מקומה בי"ס דבריאה ועבודה
בדחילו ורחימו הטבעיים שבמוחו בי"ס דיצירה אבל
עבודה בלי התעוררות דחילו ורחימו אפי' במוחו בבחי'
גילוי דהיינו לעורר האהבה הטבעית המסותרת בלב
להוציאה מההעלם והסתר הלב אל הגילוי אפי' במוחו
ותעלומות לבו עכ"פ רק היא נשארת מסותרת בלב
כתולדתה כמו שהיתה קודם העבודה הרי עבודה זו
נשארת למטה בעולם הפירוד הנק' חיצוניות העולמות
ואין בה כח לעלות וליכלל ביחודו ית' שהן עשר ספי'

53B

heart, — הַנִּמְשָׁכוֹת מִן הַבִּינָה וָדַעַת בְּגַדוּלַת אֵין סוֹף בָּרוּךְ הוּא **that results from cognition and recognition of the Blessed Infinite One's greatness,** מְקוֹמָהּ בִּי' סְפִירוֹת דִּבְרִיאָה — **then the** spiritual **"address" of such worship is in the ten** *sefiros* **of** *Beriah.*

וַעֲבוֹדָה בְּדְחִילוּ וּרְחִימוּ הַטִּבְעַיִים שֶׁבְּמוֹחוֹ — **And worship** motivated by **the inherent reverence and love** which doesn't excite the heart, but remains as a "consent" **in the mind,** בְּי' סְפִירוֹת דִּיצִירָה — its spiritual "address" is **in the ten** *sefiros* **of** *Yetzirah.*

Now we will turn to the main topic of this section, a *mitzvah* which is lacking in *kavanah*. Again, this will have various levels.

אֲבָל עֲבוֹדָה בְּלִי הִתְעוֹרְרוּת דְּחִילוּ וּרְחִימוּ — **But worship that is not** motivated by **reverence and love,** אֲפִילוּ בְּמוֹחוֹ בִּבְחִינַת גִּילוּי — not even **consciously** as a "consent" in the mind, דְּהַיְינוּ לְעוֹרֵר הָאַהֲבָה הַטִּבְעִית הַמְסוּתֶּרֶת בַּלֵּב — **in other words,** you didn't even **awaken the love** already **dormant in your heart,** לְהוֹצִיאָהּ מֵהֶהְעְלֵם — **to bring it to light from its** prior state of **concealment, hidden in your heart,** וְהֶסְתֵּר הַלֵּב אֶל הַגִּילוּי אֲפִילוּ בְּמוֹחוֹ וְתַעֲלוּמוֹת לִבּוֹ עַל כָּל פָּנִים — you didn't **even** make it conscious as a "consent" **in your mind, or in your** *"hidden places in the heart"* (*Psalms* 44:22), **at the very least,** רַק הִיא נִשְׁאֶרֶת מְסוּתֶּרֶת בַּלֵּב כְּתוֹלַדְתָּהּ כְּמוֹ שֶׁהָיְתָה קוֹדֶם הָעֲבוֹדָה — **rather** that love **remains hidden in your heart, as it was at birth, in the same state as before your worship.**

הֲרֵי עֲבוֹדָה זוֹ נִשְׁאֶרֶת לְמַטָּה בְּעוֹלָם הַפֵּירוּד — **In that case, your worship will remain below, in the "world of separateness,"** הַנִּקְרָא חִיצוֹנִיּוּת הָעוֹלָמוֹת — also **known as the "superficial dimension" of the worlds,** וְאֵין בָּהּ כֹּחַ לַעֲלוֹת וְלִיכָּלֵל בְּיִחוּדוֹ יִתְבָּרֵךְ — as such worship **has not been empowered** by you **to rise and be absorbed in G-d's unity,** שֶׁהֵן עֶשֶׂר סְפִירוֹת הַקְּדוֹשׁוֹת — even in **the ten holy** *sefiros* of *Asiyah,* the lowest of the worlds.

The sharp distinction between a world's *sefiros*, which are Divine, and its "superficial dimension," which is not, is explained by Rabbi Shneur Zalman in one of his discourses.

הקדושות וכמ"ש בתיקונים דבלא דחילו ורחימו לא
פרחא לעילא ולא יכלא לסלקא ולמיקם קדם ה'. והיינו
אפי' אם אינו עוסק שלא לשמה ממש לשום איזו פניה
ח"ו אלא כמ"ש ותהי יראתם אותי מצות אנשי' מלומדה
פי' מחמת הרגל שהורגל מקטנותו שהרגילו ולימדו
אביו ורבו לירא את ה' ולעבדו ואינו עוסק לשמה

In the "superficial dimension" of the worlds, *"since the time when they were cre-ated, something-from nothing, the Blessed Infinite Light has never shone there, for they were created to be separate. If you learn without kavanah, the breath of your speech and all the powers of your (Animal) Soul from (kelipas) nogah only escape the (physical world of) four elements, but they remain in the 'chambers' and 'repos-itories' of, the 'superficial dimension,' very far from the light of G-d's face, as far as can be, may G-d have mercy"* (Rabbi Shneur Zalman, *Ma'amarei Admor Ha-Zakein, Liozna,* (Brooklyn: Kehos, 1957) p. 28).

וּכְמוֹ שֶׁכָּתוּב בַּתִּיקוּנִים דְּבְלָא דְחִילוּ וּרְחִימוּ לָא פָּרְחָא לְעֵילָא
וְלָא יָכְלָא לְסָלְקָא וּלְמֵיקָם קְדָם ה' — As the *Tikunei Zohar*
teaches, *"without reverence and love (a mitzvah) will not fly upwards... it can't rise up and stand before G-d"* (*Tikunei Zohar* 25b; see also *Talmud, Pesachim* 50b); i.e., it won't merge with the ten *sefiros* ("stand before G-d") in *any* world.

11TH NISAN REGULAR | 3RD NISAN LEAP

The *Tikunei Zohar* did not state that the *mitzvah* was done with an inappropriate or selfish intention. It was simply lacking the emotions of love and reverence of G-d. The *Tanya* gives us a practical illustration of such an intent.

וְהַיְינוּ אֲפִילוּ אִם אֵינוֹ עוֹסֵק שֶׁלֹא לִשְׁמָה מַמָּשׁ — This means that even if your worship was not completely inauthentic (*shelo lishmah*), לְשׁוּם אֵיזוֹ פְּנִיָה חַס וְשָׁלוֹם — carried out for some ulterior motive, G-d forbid, other than worshiping G-d, אֶלָּא כְּמוֹ שֶׁכָּתוּב וַתְּהִי יִרְאָתָם אוֹתִי מִצְוַת אֲנָשִׁים מְלוּמָּדָה — rather it was in the spirit of the verse, *"their reverence of Me is mitzvos of men performed by rote"* (Isaiah 29:13), פֵּירוּשׁ מֵחֲמַת הֶרְגֵּל שֶׁהוּרְגַּל מִקַּטְנוּתוֹ — meaning that the worship was done out of habit you've grown accustomed to from childhood, שֶׁהִרְגִּילוֹ וְלִימְּדוֹ אָבִיו וְרַבּוֹ לִירֹא — that your father and teacher trained you and taught you to behave אֶת ה' וּלְעָבְדוֹ — as one who reveres G-d and worships Him.

וְאֵינוֹ עוֹסֵק לִשְׁמָה מַמָּשׁ — But, on the other hand, your worship wasn't genuinely

PRACTICAL LESSONS

When you worship G-d, your soul can only ascend to one of the spiritual worlds, but your worship can ascend to G-d.

But "without reverence and love (a mitzvah) will not fly upwards... it can't rise up and stand before G-d," rather it will get stuck down here.

מַמָּשׁ כִּי לִשְׁמָהּ מַמָּשׁ אִי אֶפְשַׁר בְּלֹא הַתְעוֹרְרוּת דְּחִילוּ
וּרְחִימוּ הַטְּבָעִיִּים עכ"פ לְהוֹצִיאָן מֵהֶסְתֵּר הַלֵּב אֶל
הַגִּילּוּי בְּמוֹחַ וּתְעַלוּמוֹת לִבּוֹ עכ"פ כִּי כְּמוֹ שֶׁאֵין אָדָם
עוֹשֶׂה דָבָר בִּשְׁבִיל חֲבֵירוֹ לְמַלֹּאת רְצוֹנוֹ אא"כ אוֹהֲבוֹ
אוֹ יָרֵא מִמֶּנּוּ כָּךְ אִי אֶפְשַׁר לַעֲשׂוֹת לִשְׁמוֹ ית' בֶּאֱמֶת
לְמַלֹּאת רְצוֹנוֹ לְבַד בְּלִי זִכָּרוֹן וְהִתְעוֹרְרוּת אַהֲבָתוֹ
וְיִרְאָתוֹ כְּלָל בְּמוֹחוֹ וּמַחֲשַׁבְתּוֹ וּתְעַלוּמוֹת לִבּוֹ עכ"פ
וְגַם אַהֲבָה לְבַדָּהּ אֵינָהּ נק' בְּשֵׁם עֲבוֹדָה בְּלִי יִרְאָה
תַּתָּאָה לְפָחוֹת שֶׁהִיא מְסוּתֶּרֶת בְּלֵב כָּל יִשְׂרָאֵל כמ"ש
לְקַמָּן וּכְשֶׁעוֹסֵק שֶׁלֹּא לִשְׁמָהּ מַמָּשׁ לְשׁוּם אֵיזוֹ פְּנִיָּה

authentic (*lishmah*) either, כִּי לִשְׁמָהּ מַמָּשׁ אִי אֶפְשַׁר בְּלֹא הַתְעוֹרְרוּת דְּחִילוּ וּרְחִימוּ — הַטְּבָעִיִּים עַל כָּל פָּנִים — because it's impossible for worship to be genuinely authentic unless there's a stirring of innate reverence and love, at the very least, לְהוֹצִיאָן מֵהֶסְתֵּר הַלֵּב אֶל הַגִּילּוּי — to bring these emotions to light from their prior state of concealment in the heart, בְּמוֹחַ וּתְעַלוּמוֹת לִבּוֹ עַל כָּל פָּנִים — if not palpably in the heart, then at the very least in the brain and your *"hidden places in the heart"* (*Psalms* 44:22).

כִּי כְּמוֹ שֶׁאֵין אָדָם עוֹשֶׂה דָבָר בִּשְׁבִיל חֲבֵירוֹ לְמַלֹּאת רְצוֹנוֹ אֶלָּא אִם כֵּן אוֹהֲבוֹ אוֹ יָרֵא מִמֶּנּוּ — Because just as you wouldn't do something for your friend, to fulfill his will, unless you loved or revered him, כָּךְ אִי אֶפְשַׁר לַעֲשׂוֹת לִשְׁמוֹ יִתְבָּרֵךְ בֶּאֱמֶת לְמַלֹּאת רְצוֹנוֹ לְבַד בְּלִי זִכָּרוֹן וְהִתְעוֹרְרוּת אַהֲבָתוֹ וְיִרְאָתוֹ כְּלָל — likewise, it's impossible to do something authentically for G-d, to genuinely fulfill His will, without recalling or stirring your love and reverence of Him at all, בְּמוֹחוֹ וּמַחֲשַׁבְתּוֹ וּתְעַלוּמוֹת לִבּוֹ עַל כָּל פָּנִים — at the very least, in your brain and your *"hidden places of the heart"*

וְגַם אַהֲבָה לְבַדָּהּ אֵינָהּ נִקְרֵאת בְּשֵׁם עֲבוֹדָה בְּלִי יִרְאָה תַּתָּאָה לְפָחוֹת — And love alone, without at least a basic or "lower reverence" is not called real worship (see chapter 41, p. 492), שֶׁהִיא מְסוּתֶּרֶת בְּלֵב כָּל יִשְׂרָאֵל — and this "lower reverence" is latent in the heart of all Israel, כְּמוֹ שֶׁיִּתְבָּאֵר לְקַמָּן — as will be explained below (p. 502).

So worship which is devoid of any basic love and reverence, even if no ulterior motive is present, *"can't rise up and stand before G-d."*

SECTION SIX: WHEN AN ULTERIOR MOTIVE IS PRESENT

12TH NISAN REGULAR | 4TH NISAN LEAP

וּכְשֶׁעוֹסֵק שֶׁלֹּא לִשְׁמָהּ מַמָּשׁ — And if your observance is completely inauthentic (*shelo lishmah*), לְשׁוּם אֵיזוֹ פְּנִיָּה לִכְבוֹד עַצְמוֹ — for some self-serving, ulterior motive, כְּגוֹן לִהְיוֹת תַּלְמִיד חָכָם וּכְהַאי גַּוְונָא — such as studying Torah, not to worship

לכבוד עצמו כגון להיות ת"ח וכהאי גוונא אזי אותה
פניה שמצד הקליפה דנוגה מתלבשת בתורתו והתורה
היא בבחי' גלות בתוך הקליפה לפי שעה עד אשר
יעשה תשובה שמביאה רפואה לעולם שבשובו אל ה'
גם תורתו שבה עמו ולכן אמרו רז"ל לעולם יעסוק
אדם וכו' שמתוך שלא לשמה בא לשמה בודאי   **54A**
שבודאי סופי לעשות תשובה בגלגול זה או בגלגול

אֲזַי אוֹתָהּ פְּנִיָּה שֶׁמִּצַּד הַקְּלִיפָּה G-d, but **to become** celebrated as **a Torah scholar, etc.,** דְּנוֹגַהּ מִתְלַבֶּשֶׁת בְּתוֹרָתוֹ — **then the ulterior motive, which is from** *kelipas nogah,* **becomes enmeshed with your Torah,** וְהַתּוֹרָה הִיא בִּבְחִינַת גָּלוּת בְּתוֹךְ הַקְּלִיפּוֹת לְפִי שָׁעָה — **and the Torah becomes temporarily exiled in the** *kelipah.*

The failure to "*rise up and stand before G-d*" (in section five), is not the worst case scenario for your *mitzvah.* At that level, the *mitzvah* didn't go up to G-d, but it didn't go down to *kelipah* either.

But if you have a self-serving motive, then—temporarily—your *mitzvah* will be trapped by *kelipah.* That doesn't mean that *kelipah* has control over your *mitzvah.* It just means that the *kelipah* hides the *mitzvah's* energy (*Notes on Tanya*).

עַד אֲשֶׁר יַעֲשֶׂה תְּשׁוּבָה — **That is, until you do teshuvah,** שֶׁמְּבִיאָה רְפוּאָה לָעוֹלָם which **"brings healing to the world,"** (*Talmud, Yoma* 86a), שֶׁבְּשׁוּבוֹ אֶל ה' גַּם תּוֹרָתוֹ שָׁבָה עִמּוֹ — **since when you return to G-d, your Torah returns with you** from *kelipah.*

An interesting question here is: When you do *teshuvah* for prior worship conducted with an ulterior motive, thereby freeing that worship from the *kelipah* in which it had become enmeshed, to what world does your prior worship now ascend?

The answer is: It depends what motivated your *teshuvah.* If your *teshuvah* was motivated by intellectually generated love and reverence, the Torah will ascend to the World of *Beriah.* But if the *teshuvah* was motivated by innate love and reverence, the Torah will ascend to the World of *Yetzirah* (Rabbi Shmuel Grunem Esterman, *Biur Tanya*).

וְלָכֵן אָמְרוּ רַבּוֹתֵינוּ זִכְרוֹנָם לִבְרָכָה — **Therefore our Sages, of blessed memory, taught,** לְעוֹלָם יַעֲסוֹק אָדָם וְכוּ' שֶׁמִּתּוֹךְ שֶׁלֹּא לִשְׁמָהּ בָּא לִשְׁמָהּ — "*A person should always engage* in Torah study and performance of mitzvos, even inauthentically, for out of doing it inauthentically, he will come to do it authentically*" (*Talmud, Pesachim* 50b).

If inauthentic worship becomes enmeshed in *kelipah,* why does the *Talmud* encourage it? Apparently, the *Talmud* based its statement on the above point, that "*when you return to G-d, your Torah returns with you from kelipah.*"

בְּוַדַּאי שֶׁבְּוַדַּאי סוֹפוֹ לַעֲשׂוֹת תְּשׁוּבָה — **And** the *Talmud* reasoned that **it's an absolute certainty that you will eventually do teshuvah,** בְּגִלְגּוּל זֶה אוֹ בְּגִלְגּוּל אַחֵר — **either in**

אַחַר כִּי לֹא יִדַּח מִמֶּנּוּ נִדָּח אַךְ כְּשֶׁעוֹשֶׂה סְתָם לֹא לִשְׁמָהּ
וְלֹא שֶׁלֹּא לִשְׁמָהּ אֵין הַדָּבָר תָּלוּי בִּתְשׁוּבָה אֶלָּא מִיָּד
שֶׁחוֹזֵר וְלוֹמֵד דָּבָר זֶה לִשְׁמָהּ הֲרֵי גַם מַה שֶּׁלָּמַד בִּסְתָם
מִתְחַבֵּר וּמִצְטָרֵף לְלִימוּד זֶה וּפוֹרְחָא לְעֵילָא מֵאַחַר שֶׁלֹּא
נִתְלַבֵּשׁ בּוֹ עֲדַיִין שׁוּם קְלִיפָּה דְּנוֹגַהּ וְלָכֵן לְעוֹלָם יַעֲסוֹק

PRACTICAL LESSONS

A lack of kavanah can be rectified in one of two ways:

1. If you had no kavanah at all, then simply do the same mitzvah again with kavanah, and they will both "rise up and stand before G-d" together.

2. But if you had a self-serving intent, then teshuvah is required to free the mitzvah from the negative forces in which you have enmeshed it.

Ultimately, you should always be busy with Torah and mitzvos, regardless of your kavanah. The kavanah can always be corrected later on, but you won't have this opportunity to do this mitzvah again.

since — כִּי לֹא יִדַּח מִמֶּנּוּ נִדָּח **this incarnation or another,** even *"a banished person will not remain banished from Him"* (2 *Samuel* 14:14).

It's not that the inauthentic worship "rises to G-d." Actually, it gets trapped in *kelipah*. But inauthentic worship is still worthwhile *in the long run*, because you will definitely redeem it at some point later on.

(*"In this incarnation or another"* doesn't necessarily mean another lifetime. It could also refer to a period when there are major changes in your life — *Notes on Tanya*).

We now return to the "lower" level of inauthenticity mentioned above, where there is no *kavanah*, but no ulterior motive either (such as observance by rote).

But if your — אַךְ כְּשֶׁעוֹשֶׂה סְתָם לֹא לִשְׁמָהּ וְלֹא שֶׁלֹּא לִשְׁמָה **worship is neutral, neither inauthentic nor authentic,** אֵין הַדָּבָר תָּלוּי בִּתְשׁוּבָה — **then the criterion** for your worship to be elevated to G-d is far easier, and it **doesn't depend on teshuvah,** אֶלָּא מִיָּד שֶׁחוֹזֵר וְלוֹמֵד דָּבָר זֶה לִשְׁמָהּ — **rather, as soon as you go back and learn this** Torah with an **authentic** intent, הֲרֵי גַם מַה שֶּׁלָּמַד בִּסְתָם מִתְחַבֵּר וּמִצְטָרֵף לְלִימוּד זֶה וּפוֹרְחָא לְעֵילָא — **then the thing that you learned with "neutral" intent will "join" with the current** authentic **study, and "it will fly upwards"** together.

Teshuvah — מֵאַחַר שֶׁלֹּא נִתְלַבֵּשׁ בּוֹ עֲדַיִין שׁוּם קְלִיפָּה דְּנוֹגַהּ is not necessary in this case, **because** your "neutral" study **had not yet become enmeshed with any kelipas nogah,** so it doesn't require *teshuvah* to release it.

And therefore, when speak- — וְלָכֵן לְעוֹלָם יַעֲסוֹק אָדָם כו' ing of the "lower" level of inauthenticity, the mere absence of *kavanah*, we can clearly say that, *"A person should always engage* in Torah study and performance of mitzvos etc.,*"* because in such a case the "damage" is less. There is no enmeshment in *kelipah*, and no *teshuvah* is required, just another Torah session later on with the correct intent.

אָדָם כו' וכן הענין בתפלה שלא בכוונה כמ״ש בזהר:

פרק מ אך

כל זמן שלא חזר ולמד דבר זה
לשמה אין לימודו עולה אפי' בי״ס
המאירות בעולם היצירה והעשיה כי הספירות הן בחי'

וְכֵן הָעִנְיָן בִּתְפִלָּה שֶׁלֹּא בְכַוָּונָה — **And the same is true of prayer without concentration,** you simply have to pray again with concentration, and all your earlier prayers (devoid of concentration) will be elevated too.

כְּמוֹ שֶׁכָּתוּב בַּזֹּהַר — **As stated in the *Zohar*** (2, 245b).

The *Zohar* teaches: *"If a prayer... is not worthy, (a chief-angel) pushes it out, and it goes down and hovers about the world, standing at the lowest of the firmaments below, which conduct the world. And in charge of that firmament, there is a chief-angel by the name of Sahadi'el. He takes all the rejected prayers, called 'invalid prayers', and stores them until that person repents. And if he properly repents before his Master, and offers another, good prayer, then when the good one rises, the chief-angel Sahadi'el takes the (invalid) prayer and lifts it up, until it meets the good prayer. Then they both rise and intermingle together, and go up before the Holy King."*

CHAPTER 40

THE POWER OF KAVANAH (III)
SECTION ONE: HOW YOU CAN CREATE ANGELS

13TH NISAN REGULAR | 5TH NISAN LEAP

This chapter continues — and concludes — our discussion from chapters 38-39 about the importance of *kavanah* (attentiveness) during worship.

At the end of chapter 39 we learned that when Torah study is carried out without *kavanah*, it won't ascend to the spiritual worlds (and from there, to the Blessed Infinite One), until you study the text again with *kavanah*.

אַךְ כָּל זְמַן שֶׁלֹּא חָזַר וְלָמַד דָּבָר זֶה לִשְׁמָה — **But so long as you haven't gone back and studied this** Torah text with an **authentic** intent, אֵין לִימוּדוֹ עוֹלֶה אֲפִילוּ בִּי' סְפִירוֹת הַמְּאִירוֹת בְּעוֹלָם הַיְצִירָה וְהָעֲשִׂיָּה — **your study won't rise up even to the ten *sefiros* that illuminate the worlds of *Yetzirah* or *Asiyah*.**

As we learned in chapter 39, each spiritual world consists of *sefiros* (G-d's light, diminished to be compatible with that world), and an infrastructure of non-Divine

אלהות ובהן מתלבש ומתייחד אור א"ס ב"ה ממש ובלא
דחילו ורחימו לא יכלא לסלקא ולמיקם קדם ה' כמ"ש
בתיקונים רק לימודו עולה להיכלות ומדורין שהן
חיצוניות העולמות שבהן עומדים המלאכים וכמ"ש
הרח"ו ז"ל בשער הנבוא' פ"ב שמהתורה שלא בכוונה

"chambers." When you study Torah with authentic intent, it rises to the *sefiros* of one of the higher worlds, which contain (a glimmer of) the Blessed Infinite Light.

כִּי הַסְּפִירוֹת הֵן בְּחִינַת אֱלֹהוּת וּבָהֶן מִתְלַבֵּשׁ וּמִתְיַחֵד אוֹר אֵין סוֹף בָּרוּךְ הוּא מַמָּשׁ — Be-cause the *sefiros* are Divine, and the Blessed Infinite Light is literally merged and enmeshed with them.

If your intent is not for the sake of the Divine, your Torah can't merge with the Divine energy of the *sefiros*, even in the lowest world.

As we learned previously, the requirement for this "authentic," Divine intent is stated in the *Tikunei Zohar.*

וּבְלָא דְּחִילוּ וּרְחִימוּ לָא יָכְלָא לְסַלְקָא וּלְמֵיקַם קֳדָם ה' כְּמוֹ שֶׁכָּתוּב בַּתִּיקוּנִים — And, as the *Tikunei Zohar* states, without reverence and love for G-d your Torah *"can't rise up and stand before G-d"* (25b; see chapter 39, p. 466).

But when your Torah study "can't rise up and stand before G-d," where exactly does its energy go? (We're not talking here about the case mentioned in the previous chapter where the Torah becomes bound by *kelipah* due to selfish intentions. We're talking about when the intention was "neutral" — not for G-d, but not for yourself either, such as study performed out of rote).

רַק לִימוּדוֹ עוֹלֶה לְהֵיכָלוֹת וּמְדוֹרִין — Rather with "neutral" intent your study will as-cend not to the Divine *sefiros*, but to the "chambers" and "repositories" in those worlds, שֶׁהֵן חִיצוֹנִיּוּת הָעוֹלָמוֹת — which are the "superficial dimension" of the worlds, (see previous chapter, p. 465; *Etz Chaim* 40:14).

The "superficial dimension" of a world is its "infrastructure," those elements which are there to support the main content of the world, which is the Divine light.

שֶׁבָּהֶן עוֹמְדִים הַמַּלְאָכִים — And it's there, in the "superficial dimension" of the worlds that the angels are stationed.

Even though the angels are holy, since they are not the *purpose* of the world which contains them, they are considered "superficial" (see *Etz Chaim* 40:14).

The *Tanya* now cites a source for the idea, that Torah devoid of *kavanah* rises to the "superficial dimension" of the worlds, where the angels are stationed.

וּכְמוֹ שֶׁכָּתַב הָרַב חַיִּים וִיטַאל זִכְרוֹנוֹ לִבְרָכָה בְּשַׁעַר הַנְּבוּאָה פֶּרֶק ב' — As stated by Rabbi Chaim Vital, of blessed memory, in chapter 2 of *Sha'ar Ha-Yichudim,* in the section entitled *Sha'ar Ha-Nevu'ah,* שֶׁמֵּהַתּוֹרָה שֶׁלֹּא בְּכַוָּונָה נִבְרָאִים מַלְאָכִים בְּעוֹלַם הַיְצִירָה — that from Torah studied without authentic intent, angels are created in the world

נבראים מלאכים בעולם היצירה ומהמצות בלי כוונה
נבראים מלאכים בעולם העשייה וכל המלאכים
הם בעלי חומר וצורה אבל תורה שלא לשמה

of *Yetzirah*, וּמֵהַמִּצְוֹת בְּלִי כַוָּונָה נִבְרָאִים מַלְאָכִים בְּעוֹלַם הָעֲשִׂיָּיה — **and from** practical *mitzvos* observed **without** authentic **intent, angels are created in the** lower **world of *Asiyah*,** (the *mitzvos* involving action, when devoid of *kavanah*, have little light and energy of their own, so they cannot rise to *Yetzirah*).

As we noted above, angels inhabit the "superficial dimension" of each world. So Rabbi Chaim Vital's statement (that Torah studied without authentic intent creates angels), indicates that the Torah rises to the "superficial dimension" of the worlds, and not to the *sefiros.*

But we see that Torah study or a *mitzvah* devoid of *kavanah* does at least enjoy some level of spiritual ascent, and it rises to the level of the angels!

It turns out, then, that the *Tikunei Zohar's* teaching that worship devoid of *kavanah* "can't rise up and stand before G-d," doesn't mean that the worship can't rise *at all.* It just can't rise to the *sefiros* (and, thereby, to the Blessed Infinite One); but it can rise to at least the superficial dimension of *Asiyah* (in the case of a *mitzvah*), or *Yetzirah* (in the case of Torah study).

וְכָל הַמַּלְאָכִים הֵם בַּעֲלֵי חוֹמֶר וְצוּרָה — **And all the angels consist of both "matter" and "form"** (*Ramban*, end of *Sha'ar Ha-Gemul*), and therefore they are incompatible with the *sefiros* which are Divine.

Angels are, of course, *entirely spiritual* and they don't possess physical bodies; but they are a complex amalgam of different energies, not all of which are equally devoted to G-d. That's why the angels constantly sing and bow to G-d, in an effort to subdue that part of them which is less inclined to worship. Their "less inclined" component is what the mystics referred to as the angels' "matter" (*Toras Menachem, Hisva'aduyos* 5710, pp. 29-30).

The *Tanya* refers here to this concept of angelic "matter" and "form" to add clarity to the idea of a "neutral" intent. Lacking *kavanah* doesn't mean that your act was totally mindless. It means, for example, that you studied Torah or prayed, *and understood the meaning of the words you were saying,* but your intention wasn't to connect to G-d. That's why even the angel created by such worship has "matter" and "form" — "matter" corresponding to the physical enunciation of the words; and "form" corresponding to the basic understanding of what you were doing (Rabbi Levi Yitzchak Schneerson, cited in Rabbi Yehoshua Korf, *Likutei Biurim*).

Up to this point we have been discussing what happens to Torah study *devoid* of *kavanah.* Now we turn to the "spiritual address" of Torah studied with a *negative* intention, when the study was motivated by selfish reasons.

אֲבָל תּוֹרָה שֶׁלֹּא לִשְׁמָהּ מַמָּשׁ — **But Torah** which is studied with a **completely inau-**

מַמָּשׁ כְּגוֹן לִהְיוֹת ת"ח וכה"ג אֵינָהּ עוֹלָה כְּלָל לְמַעְלָה
אֲפִי' לְהֵיכָלוֹ' וּמְדוֹר הַמַּלְאָכִים דִּקְדוּשָׁה אֶלָּא נִשְׁאֶרֶת
לְמַטָּה בָּעוֹ"הֵז הַגַּשְׁמִי

שֶׁהוּא מְדוֹר הַקְּלִיפּוֹת*
וכמ"ש בזהר על פסוק מה
יתרון לאדם בכל עמלו
שֶׁיַּעֲמוֹל תַּחַת הַשֶּׁמֶשׁ

הַגָּה"ה

(כמ"ש בזהר ח"ג דף ל"א ע"ב
ודף קכ"א עמוד ב' עי' שם
ההיא מלה סלקא ובקעא רקיעין
כו' ואתער מה דאתער אי טב טב
כו' ע"ש ודף ק"ה ע"א מלה

thentic intent, כְּגוֹן לִהְיוֹת תַּלְמִיד חָכָם וּכְהַאי גַּוְונָא — such as to be celebrated as a Torah scholar, etc., אֵינָהּ עוֹלָה כְּלָל לְמַעְלָה — simply doesn't ascend heavenward at all, אֲפִילוּ לְהֵיכְלוֹת וּמְדוֹר הַמַּלְאָכִים דִּקְדוּשָׁה — even to the "chambers" and "re-positories" of the sacred angels, אֶלָּא נִשְׁאֶרֶת לְמַטָּה בָּעוֹלָם הַזֶּה הַגַּשְׁמִי שֶׁהוּא מְדוֹר הַקְּלִיפּוֹת — rather, that Torah remains below (temporarily—see p. 468), in this physical world, which is the "repository" of kelipos (Etz Chaim 41:1).*

The Tikunei Zohar's statement that Torah study without kavanah "can't rise up and stand before G-d," can mean two different things in different circumstances. If there is a "neutral" kavanah, then the Torah will rise; it just won't rise "before G-d" (and instead will get stuck in the "superficial dimension" of the spiritual worlds). But if there is selfish intent, then the Torah won't rise at all, and will become stuck in this world of kelipah.

The Tanya now brings two sources that support the idea that Torah performed with selfish intent doesn't rise from this world.

וּכְמוֹ שֶׁכָּתוּב בַּזֹּהַר עַל פָּסוּק מַה יִּתְרוֹן לָאָדָם בְּכָל עֲמָלוֹ שֶׁיַּעֲמוֹל תַּחַת הַשֶּׁמֶשׁ — As the Zohar (1, 223b) states, commenting on the verse, "What gain is there for man in

---

*הַגָּהָה — NOTE. In this "note" the Tanya offers four citations from the Zohar to support the idea that Torah study with "neutral" intent rises to the "superficial" chambers of the upper worlds. Multiple proofs are necessary since the notion is counterintuitive: Why should this Torah study rise to the spiritual realm when there is no kavanah to propel it?

וְדַף קכ"א, כְּמוֹ שֶׁכָּתוּב בַּזֹּהַר חֵלֶק ג' דַּף ל"א עַמּוּד ב' — As stated in Zohar 3, page 31b, עַמּוּד ב' עַיֵּין שָׁם — (and see also a similar comment on page 121b).

הַהִיא מִלָּה סָלְקָא וּבָקְעָא רְקִיעִין כו' — Zohar 3, 31b states: "That word (which a person speaks) rises up and pierces (the chambers of) the heavens etc.," וְאִתְעַר מַה דְּאִתְעַר — "and it arouses whatever it arouses (depending on what was said)," אִי טַב טַב כו' — "if (what was said was) good, (it will arouse) good; and if (what was said was) bad, (it will arouse) bad" (Zohar 3, 31b), עַיֵּין שָׁם — look there in the Zohar.

מִלָּה דְּאוֹרַיְיתָא אִתְעֲבִיד מִינֵּיהּ — And in the Zohar on page 105a, וְדַף ק"ה עַמּוּד א' קָלָא וְסָלִיק כו' — that when a person utters "a word of Torah, a voice is formed which rises etc."

דאוריתא אתעביד מיניה קלא   דַאֲפִילוּ עַמְלָא דְאוֹרַיְיתָא

וסליק כו' וד' קס"ח ע"ב קלין   אִי עָבִיד בְּגִין יְקָרֵיהּ כו'   54B

דאוריתא וצלותא בקעין רקיעין   וז"ש אשרי מי שבא לכאן

כו'):   ותלמודו בידו פי' שלא

נשאר למטה בעו"הז. ואף דאוריתא וקב"ה כולא חד

שהוא ורצונו אחד הרי קב"ה איהו ממלא כל עלמין

בשוה ואעפ"כ אין העולמות שוים במעלתם והשינוי

all his toil that he toils under the sun?" (Ecclesiastes 1:3), אִי — דַאֲפִילוּ עַמְלָא דְאוֹרַיְיתָא **that** "toil" without gain includes עָבִיד בְּגִין יְקָרֵיהּ כו' — **even *"toiling in Torah, if he does it for the sake of bringing honor to himself,*** then it will remain 'under the sun,' and it will not ascend heavenward" (Zohar 1, 223b).

וְזֶהוּ שֶׁאָמְרוּ מִי שֶׁבָּא לְכָאן וְתַלְמוּדוֹ בְּיָדוֹ — **And this explains the saying** of our Sages, *"Happy is he who comes here (to heaven) with his learning all in hand'* (Talmud, Pesachim 50a), פֵּירוּשׁ שֶׁלֹּא נִשְׁאַר לְמַטָּה בָּעוֹלָם הַזֶּה — **meaning** he should be happy that his Torah rose heavenward **and did not remain down in this world.**

SECTION TWO: WHY TORAH CAN'T RISE WITHOUT KAVANAH

14TH NISAN REGULAR

The *Tanya* now questions the fundamental assertion of *Tikunei Zohar,* that Torah study without *kavanah* "can't rise up and stand before G-d."

וְאַף דְּאוֹרַיְיתָא וְקוּדְשָׁא בְּרִיךְ הוּא כּוּלָא חַד — **For even though *"the Torah and G-d are totally one"*** (see Zohar 1, 24a; 2, 60a; see pp. 255ff.), שֶׁהוּא וּרְצוֹנוֹ אֶחָד — **since** G-d **is one with His will,** so how could any act of Torah *not* be able to ascend heavenward?

If Torah is the *undiluted* will of G-d even after its descent into this world, shouldn't it "rise up and stand before G-d," even without your *kavanah?*

הֲרֵי קוּדְשָׁא בְּרִיךְ הוּא אִיהוּ מְמַלֵּא כָּל עָלְמִין בְּשָׁוֶה — **But** the matter is not so simple since **the Blessed Holy One** also **pervades all worlds equally,** וְאַף עַל פִּי כֵן אֵין הָעוֹלָמוֹת שָׁוִים בְּמַעֲלָתָם — **and nevertheless, the worlds are *not* equal in level,** וְהַשִּׁינוּי הוּא מֵהַמְקַבְּלִים — **the differences arising as a result of the recipients.**

קָלִין דְּאוֹרַיְיתָא וּצְלוֹתָא בָּקְעִין — **And in the** *Zohar* **on page 168b,** וְדַף קס"ח עַמוּד ב' רְקִיעִין כו' — *"the voice of Torah and prayer* ascend upwards and **pierce** (the chambers of) **the heavens etc."**

In all of these citations, the *Zohar* does not stipulate that there must be a good intent with the spoken word of Torah in order for it to reach the "chambers" of the heavens. This provides proof for the *Tanya's* assertion that even with "neutral" intent, Torah study will ascend the "chambers" of the upper worlds.

הוא מהמקבלים בב' בחי' הא' שהעליונים מקבלים
הארה יותר גדולה לאין קץ מהתחתונים והשנית
שמקבלים בלי לבושים ומסכים רבים כ"כ כבתחתונים
ועו"הז הוא עולם השפל בב' בחי' כי ההארה שבו
מצומצמת מאד עד קצה האחרון ולכן הוא חומרי וגשמי

Your Torah study or *mitzvah* takes place *in this world, i.e.,* in a place where the Torah's identity as the undiluted will of G-d is *not* manifest. So, in order to break free from that reality and ascend to higher worlds where G-d's presence is evident, it needs the "boost" of your *kavanah.*

Your *kavanah* has that power because it takes place in the setting of this physical world where you and your mind are stationed. Despite the lie which the physical world wants to tell us—that G-d is not present and Torah is not His undiluted will—*kavanah* pierces through that illusion, and neutralizes it.

From G-d's perspective that illusion never existed, and the Torah you study is always one with Him. But from our perspective, unless there is *kavanah,* then your Torah can't rise to G-d because it's still "trapped" by the illusion of this world.

בְּב' בְּחִינוֹת — As we discussed in chapter 38, the Divine light that shines in the various worlds differs **in two respects.**

הָאֶחָד שֶׁהָעֶלְיוֹנִים מְקַבְּלִים הָאָרָה יוֹתֵר גְּדוֹלָה לְאֵין קֵץ מֵהַתַּחְתּוֹנִים — **The first is that the upper worlds are capable of receiving infinitely greater illumination than the lower worlds,** *i.e.,* there is less *tzimtzum* (diminishment in the *quantity*) of the light in the upper worlds.

וְהַשֵּׁנִית שֶׁמְּקַבְּלִים בְּלִי לְבוּשִׁים וּמָסַכִּים רַבִּים כָּל כָּךְ כְּהַתַּחְתּוֹנִים — **And the second is that the** upper worlds **receive** G-d's light **without as many filters and veils as the lower worlds,** *i.e.,* there is less *hester panim* (reduction in the *quality*) of the light.

As we discussed in chapter 38, *tzimtzum* is like looking at someone's illuminated face through a small aperture: it's the same image, but it doesn't shine as brightly. *Hester panim* is like looking at someone's face through a partially opaque filter which alters and distorts the image itself.

The Divine light and energy entering all the worlds suffers from both *hester panim* and *tzimtzum,* but in each world these forces operate to different extents.

וְעוֹלָם הַזֶּה הוּא עוֹלָם הַשָּׁפָל בְּב' בְּחִינוֹת — **And this world is the most inferior world of** all **in both these two respects,** *hester panim* and *tzimtzum,* כִּי הֶהָאָרָה שֶׁבּוֹ מְצוּמְצֶמֶת מְאֹד עַד קֵצֶה הָאַחֲרוֹן — firstly, **because the light found in it suffers from** *tzimtzum* **to the absolute extreme,** וְלָכֵן הוּא חוּמְרִי וְגַשְׁמִי — **which is why** this world is **material and physical.**

In this world, the Divine light and energy have been diminished so much that you can't even see it. That's why *"this world is material and physical."*

וְגַם זֹאת הִיא בִּלְבוּשִׁים וּמָסַכִּים רַבִּים עַד שֶׁנִּתְלַבְּשָׁה
בִּקְלִיפַּת נוֹגַהּ לְהַחֲיוֹת כָּל דְּבָרִים הַטְּהוֹרִים שֶׁבָּעוֹ"הז
וּבִכְלָלָם הוּא נֶפֶשׁ הַחִיּוּנִית הַמְדַבֶּרֶת שֶׁבָּאָדָם וְלָכֵן
כְּשֶׁמְדַבֶּרֶת דִּבְרֵי תּוֹרָה וּתְפִלָּה בְּלֹא כַוָּנָה אַף שֶׁהֵן
אוֹתִיּוֹת קְדוּשׁוֹת וְאֵין קְלִיפַּת נוֹגַהּ שֶׁבַּנֶּפֶשׁ הַחִיּוּנִית
מָסָךְ מַבְדִּיל כְּלָל לְהַסְתִּיר וְלָכַסּוֹת עַל קְדוּשָׁתוֹ ית'
הַמְלוּבֶּשֶׁת בָּהֶן כְּמוֹ שֶׁהִיא מַסְתֶּרֶת וּמְכַסָּה עַל קְדוּשָׁתוֹ
ית' שֶׁבַּנֶּפֶשׁ הַחִיּוּנִית כְּשֶׁמְדַבֶּרֶת דְּבָרִים בְּטֵלִי' וְשֶׁבַּנֶּפֶשׁ

וְגַם זֹאת הִיא בִּלְבוּשִׁים וּמָסַכִּים רַבִּים — **And** secondly, **even this** diminished light is additionally obscured by **many filters and veils,** עַד שֶׁנִּתְלַבְּשָׁה בִּקְלִיפַּת נוֹגַהּ — **to the extent that** the light is able to become **enmeshed in** the force of *kelipas nogah,* לְהַחֲיוֹת כָּל דְּבָרִים הַטְּהוֹרִים שֶׁבָּעוֹלָם הַזֶּה — **providing energy for all the ritually pure things in this world,** וּבִכְלָלָם הוּא נֶפֶשׁ הַחִיּוּנִית הַמְדַבֶּרֶת שֶׁבָּאָדָם — **including the en-ergizing** Animal **Soul, which powers speaking** in man.

For Divine light (truth) to power *kelipah* (falsehood), a diminishment of the *quantity* of the light (*tzimtzum*) is not enough. There also has to be a powerful *hester panim,* a downgrade in the *quality* of the light.

וְלָכֵן כְּשֶׁמְדַבֶּרֶת דִּבְרֵי תּוֹרָה וּתְפִלָּה בְּלֹא כַוָּנָה — **And therefore, when you speak words of Torah or prayer without intent,** אַף שֶׁהֵן אוֹתִיּוֹת קְדוּשׁוֹת — **even though the letters are sacred,** וְאֵין קְלִיפַּת נוֹגַהּ שֶׁבַּנֶּפֶשׁ הַחִיּוּנִית מָסָךְ מַבְדִּיל כְּלָל — **and the energizing** Animal **Soul's** *kelipas nogah* cannot, in any way, place a "veil of separa-tion," לְהַסְתִּיר וְלָכַסּוֹת עַל קְדוּשָׁתוֹ יִתְבָּרֵךְ הַמְלוּבֶּשֶׁת בָּהֶן — **to impose** *hester* **and hide the sanctity found in those** letters, nevertheless, the amount of G-d's light which shines *in this world* through these words of Torah or prayer spoken without intent is extremely diminished (due to the *tzimtzum* affecting this world).

In chapter 38, we were first introduced to the fundamental principle that *hester panim* and *tzimtzum* work independently of each other. In our case, the fact that *"the Torah and G-d are totally one"* means that Torah suffers from no *hester panim* at all, even in this physical world. His will, as expressed in the Torah, is undiluted, suffering no blurring or distortion.

But when it is expressed in this world, that will *does* suffer from *tzimtzum*. So (without *kavanah*) you have an act which is totally G-d's will, but that fact is barely evident and manifest.

That is, in essence, the *Tanya's* answer to our question (why it cannot rise and "stand before G-d"). But before clarifying the answer in detail, the *Tanya* will first digress slightly to compare Torah without *kavanah*, to the case of non-sacred talk.

כְּמוֹ שֶׁהִיא מַסְתֶּרֶת וּמְכַסָּה עַל קְדוּשָׁתוֹ יִתְבָּרֵךְ שֶׁבַּנֶּפֶשׁ הַחִיּוּנִית כְּשֶׁמְדַבֶּרֶת דְּבָרִים בְּטֵלִים — **Speaking words of Torah without *kavanah* is in no way comparable to speak-**

החיונית שבשאר בעלי חיים הטהורים דאף דלית אתר
פנוי מיני' מ"מ איהו סתימו דכל סתימין ונק' אל מסתתר
וגם ההארה והתפשטות החיות ממנו ית' מסתתרת
בלבושים ומסכים רבים ועצומים עד שנתלבשה
ונסתתרה בלבוש נוגה משא"כ באותיות הקדושות
של דברי תורה ותפלה דאדרבה קליפת נוגה מתהפכת

ing non-sacred words (devoid of Torah content or purpose), **where the energizing** Animal **Soul** *does* impose *hester* and hide G-d's holiness.

You can't compare Torah without *kavanah* (where there's no *hester panim* but there is *tzimtzum*), to non-sacred talk (where there is both *hester panim* and *tzimtzum*).

Non-sacred talk suffers from *hester panim* because it's powered by *kelipas nogah* (in your Animal Soul), which acts as a thick veil, downgrading the quality of the Divine light in this physical world.

וְשֶׁבַּנֶּפֶשׁ הַחִיּוּנִית שֶׁבִּשְׁאָר בַּעֲלֵי חַיִּים הַטְּהוֹרִים — **And** your Animal soul suffers from *hester panim* **in the same way as the energizing** Animal **Soul of all other living creatures, from a kosher species** which are from *kelipas nogah*.

This leads us to the difficult question of how G-d is found in *kelipas nogah* and evil. In Judaism's monotheistic belief, everything is from G-d. There cannot be a "demonic" force opposing Him which He Himself does not power.

וְאַף דְּלֵית אֲתַר פְּנוּי מִינֵּיהּ — **And even though, "There is no place devoid of Him"** (*Tikunei Zohar* 91b), and G-d is definitely *present* even in *kelipah* energy, מִכָּל מָקוֹם — **nevertheless, He is "the most hidden of all hidden (STimin)"** (ibid. 17a), and is called, **"a G-d that hides (miSTateR)"** (*Isaiah* 45:15), both terms share the same Hebrew root as "heSTeR").

That doesn't mean that G-d is totally hidden, and can't be found at all in the world. It means that,

וְגַם הַהֶאָרָה וְהִתְפַּשְּׁטוּת הַחַיּוּת מִמֶּנּוּ יִתְבָּרֵךְ — **even the light and energy that flows from Him** into this physical world, מִסְתַּתֶּרֶת בִּלְבוּשִׁים וּמָסְכִים רַבִּים וַעֲצוּמִים — **is hidden by numerous, powerful filters and veils,** עַד שֶׁנִּתְלַבְּשָׁה וְנִסְתַּתְּרָה בִּלְבוּשׁ נוֹגַהּ — **until** that energy **becomes enmeshed and hidden in the "filter" of** *kelipas nogah*.

While non-sacred words suffer from *hester panim* (being powered by *kelipas nogah*), sacred words of Torah do not.

מַה שֶּׁאֵין כֵּן בָּאוֹתִיּוֹת הַקְּדוֹשׁוֹת שֶׁל דִּבְרֵי תוֹרָה וּתְפִלָּה — **This is not the case with the sacred letters of Torah words and prayer** that you speak, דְּאַדְּרַבָּה קְלִיפַּת נוֹגַהּ — **where** not only is *kelipas nogah* absent from מִתְהַפֶּכֶת לְטוֹב וְנִכְלֶלֶת בִּקְדוּשָּׁה זוֹ — these acts (which are powered by the G-dly Soul), but, **on the contrary, the** *kelipas*

לטוב ונכללת בקדושה זו כנ"ל מ"מ ההארה שבהן
מקדושתו ית' היא בבחי' צמצום עד קצה האחרון
מאחר שהקול והדבור הוא גשמי אבל בתפלה בכוונה **55A**
ותורה בכוונה לשמה הרי הכוונה מתלבשת באותיות
הדבור הואיל והיא מקור ושרש להן שמחמתה

nogah is actually *transformed to good* and absorbed into holiness through this activity, כַּנִּזְכָּר לְעֵיל — **as mentioned above** (chapter 37, p. 412).

The sacred words of Torah do not suffer from *hester panim*, but in the absence of *kavanah*, they do suffer from *tzimtzum*.

מִכָּל מָקוֹם הַהֶאָרָה שֶׁבָּהֶן מִקְּדֻשָּׁתוֹ יִתְבָּרֵךְ — **Nevertheless, the glimmer of G-d's holy light which does shine in** these words of Torah or prayer spoken without intent, הִיא בִּבְחִינַת צִמְצוּם עַד קָצֶה הָאַחֲרוֹן — **suffers from** *tzimtzum* **to the absolute extreme.**

What is the cause of this "extreme" *tzimtzum*?

מֵאַחַר שֶׁהַקּוֹל וְהַדִּבּוּר הוּא גַשְׁמִי — **Since,** in this case, the light of the Torah or prayer is not expressed in the heart and mind (through *kavanah*), but only in the organs of speech, and **the voice and its speech are physical.**

The *tzimtzum* is particularly strong here because the *mitzvah* (devoid of *kavanah*) is taking place exclusively in the physical realm of speech, which is not conducive to Divine light. For, as we learned earlier in this chapter, the light found in the purely physical realm *"suffers from tzimtzum to the absolute extreme"* (p. 475).

15TH NISAN REGULAR

אֲבָל בִּתְפִלָּה בְּכַוָּנָה וְתוֹרָה בְּכַוָּנָה לִשְׁמָהּ — **But when prayer is carried out with con-centration, or Torah is studied with authentic intent,** הֲרֵי הַכַּוָּנָה מִתְלַבֶּשֶׁת בְּאוֹתִיּוֹת הַדִּבּוּר — **then the** *kavanah* **becomes enmeshed in the spoken letters.**

As we learned in chapter 38, *kavanah* is not an "enhancement" to the Divine will; rather, "connecting your mind and thoughts through *kavanah... is also* the will of G-d" (p. 443). The difference between the words of prayer (which are physical), and *kavanah*, (which is emotional/mental), is that *kavanah* is more suited to be a vehicle of expression for Divine light because there's less *tzimtzum* there.

So while the physical words of prayer suffer from too much *tzimtzum* and will not shine with more than a minuscule degree of Divine light, nevertheless, when they are "enmeshed" with *kavanah*, it's like a body receiving its soul, and even the phys-ical words can shine with G-d's light.

הוֹאִיל וְהִיא מָקוֹר וְשֹׁרֶשׁ לָהֶן — **And this merging of (the Divine light in the)** *kavanah* and the physical act of speaking Torah or prayer is possible **since the** *kavanah* **is the source and "root" of** this prayer or Torah study, שֶׁמֵּחֲמָתָהּ וּבְסִיבָּתָהּ הוּא מְדַבֵּר אוֹתִיּוֹת אֵלּוּ — **because it's the** direct **cause and reason which led to the speaking of these letters** of prayer or Torah.

ובסיבתה הוא מדבר אותיות אלו לכן היא מעלה אותן
עד מקומה בי"ס דיצירה או דבריאה לפי מה שהיא
הכוונה בדחילו ורחימו שכליים או טבעיים כו' כנ"ל
ושם מאיר ומתגלה אור א"ס ב"ה שהוא רצון העליון

Your reverence and love of G-d doesn't just energize Torah and prayer with *kavanah* during the act; it's also the cause that inspires you to do the act in the first place. And due to this extremely close relationship, of direct cause and effect, the Divine light in the *kavanah* is able to become enmeshed in the act itself.

PRACTICAL LESSONS

There are three categories of *kavanah* (intent). A *positive intent,* that your *mitzvah* is for G-d, will propel that *mitzvah* to the *sefiros* (Divine light in the heavens), and thereby to G-d.

A *neutral intent* — where you are focusing on what you are doing but it's not devotional worship — will send your *mitzvah* to the "superficial dimension" of the spiritual worlds, and create angels.

A *selfish intent*, will cause your mitzvah to get stuck in this physical world, and entangled in the negative forces of *kelipah*.

לָכֵן הִיא מַעֲלָה אוֹתָן עַד מְקוֹמָה — **Therefore,** since the holy intent merges with the speech and becomes enmeshed in it, the intent **raises** the physical spoken words, **to its own** higher **plane.**

As we learned above in this chapter, Torah or prayer devoid of *kavanah*, can only rise to the "superficial dimension" (the "chambers") of *Yetzirah*. But when *kavanah* accompanies the physical words, those words are raised to the Divine *sefiros* (of *Yetzirah* or *Beriah*) and thereby to the Blessed Infinite One.

בְּי' סְפִירוֹת דִּיצִירָה אוֹ דִּבְרִיאָה לְפִי מַה שֶׁהִיא הַכַּוָּונָה — **And** whether the words reach **the ten *sefiros* of *Yetzirah*** or the ten *sefiros* **of *Beriah* depends on the type of intent,** בְּדַחִילוּ וּרְחִימוּ שִׂכְלִיִּים — if accompanied **by intellectually generated reverence and love,** the words are propelled to the *sefiros* in the world of *Beriah*, אוֹ טִבְעָיִים כוּ' — **or** if accompanied by innate, **naturally** generated fear and love, the words are propelled to the *sefiros* in the world of *Yetzirah, etc.,* כַּנִּזְכָּר לְעֵיל — **as mentioned above** (chapter 39, p. 457).

(With the word "etc." the *Tanya* alludes to the further possibility of an elevation to the highest world of *Atzilus* (chapter 39, p. 459*ff.*). But since this is not generally available to the readers of *Tanya*, the author merely hinted to it—*Notes on Tanya*).

וְשָׁם מֵאִיר וּמִתְגַּלֶּה אוֹר אֵין סוֹף בָּרוּךְ הוּא — But regardless of which specific destination words with *kavanah* reach, the fact that they merge with the *sefiros* means they reach a place **where the Blessed Infinite Light shines and is disclosed** abundantly, unlike in this physical world where G-d's light is greatly diminished through *tzimtzum*.

ב"ה המלובש באותיות התורה שלומד ובכוונתן או
בתפלה ובכוונתה או במצוה ובכוונתה בהארה גדולה
לאין קץ מה שלא יכול להאיר ולהתגלות כלל
בעוד האותיות והמצוה בעו"הז הגשמי לא מינה
ולא מקצתה עד עת קץ הימין שיתעלה העולם
מגשמיותו ונגלה כבוד ה'

הגהה

וגו' כנ"ל באריכות* ‏(ושם מאיר ומתגלה ג"כ היחוד)

This new setting greatly reduces the problem of *tzimtzum*, from which the words of Torah or prayer suffered in this physical world. And since we are speaking here of a *mitzvah*, there is, of course, no *hester panim*.

שֶׁהוּא רָצוֹן הָעֶלְיוֹן בָּרוּךְ הוּא הַמְלוּבָּשׁ בְּאוֹתִיּוֹת הַתּוֹרָה שֶׁלוֹמֵד וּבְכַוָּנָתָן — And the Blessed Infinite Light **is** totally one with **the Divine will, which is expressed in the letters of Torah studied with intent,** אוֹ בִּתְפִלָּה וּבְכַוָּנָתָהּ אוֹ בְּמִצְוָה וּבְכַוָּנָתָהּ — **or the prayer** carried out with **concentration, or the *mitzvah*** performed with **holy intent.**

בְּהָאֶרֶה גְדוֹלָה לְאֵין קֵץ מַה שֶׁלֹּא יָכוֹל לְהָאִיר וּלְהִתְגַלוֹת כְּלָל בְּעוֹד הָאוֹתִיּוֹת וְהַמִּצְוָה בָּעוֹלָם הַזֶּה הַגַּשְׁמִי — And in the G-dly setting of the *sefiros* (in *Beriah* or *Yetzirah*), the Divine will is able **to shine infinitely more powerfully than when the *mitzvah*** act **or** spoken **letters** of Torah or prayer **remains** stuck **in this physical world** due to lack of proper intent, since the physical world suffers from a formidable *tzimtzum* which **does not allow** that light **to shine or be disclosed at all,** לֹא מִינָהּ וְלֹא מִקְצָתָהּ — **"neither a part of it, nor a fraction of it"** (Talmud, *Sotah* 5a).

The *Tanya* concludes this discussion by noting that, in the future, the *tzimtzum* of the physical world will be transmuted, allowing Divine light to shine even down here.

עַד עֵת קֵץ הַיָּמִין — **The** physical world will continue to obscure G-d's light, **until, the time of "End of Days"** (Daniel 12:13), שֶׁיִּתְעַלֶּה הָעוֹלָם מִגַּשְׁמִיּוּתוֹ — **when the world will be lifted from its material** limitations, וְנִגְלָה כְּבוֹד ה' וְגוֹ' — **"and the glory of G-d will be revealed** and all flesh will see together that G-d is speaking" (Isaiah 40:5), כַּנִּזְכָּר לְעֵיל בַּאֲרִיכוּת — **as was mentioned above at length*** (in chapters 36-37). See also *Likutei Sichos,* vol. 19, pp. 93ff., adapted in: Rabbi Chaim Miller, *Rambam: Thirteen Principles of Faith, Principles 6-7,* pp. 193-8).

6TH NISAN LEAP [UNTIL THE END OF THIS NOTE, ON P. 484]

הַגָּהָה* — **NOTE.** (In the earliest editions of the *Tanya*, the following "note" was included in the main body of the text. In fact, later on in the main text (pp. 485-7), the *Tanya* draws on ideas discussed here).

Up to this point we have focused on the power of *kavanah* to cause the Divine will to illuminate your *mitzvos* (after they have risen to *Yetzirah* or *Beriah*). In this note, the *Tanya* stresses another light that your *mitzvos* will receive, (once they

וּבְזֶה יוּבַן הֵיטֵב הָא העליון הנעשה בכל מצוה ות״ת
דְּדְחִילוּ וּרְחִימוּ נִקְרָאֵי' שהוא יחוד מדותיו ית' שנכללות
גַּדְפִין דְּ"מ כְּדִכְתִי' וּבִשְׁתַּיִם זו בזו ונמתקות הגבורות בחסדים

SECTION THREE: CONCLUDING THOUGHTS ON KAVANAH

7TH NISAN LEAP [UNTIL END OF NOTE ON P. 487]

וּבְזֶה — **Based on** all **this** discussion in chapters 35-37 about the importance of the *mitzvah* act, and the discussion from chapter 38 up to this point about the value of *kavanah,* יוּבַן הֵיטֵב הָא דְּדְחִילוּ וּרְחִימוּ נִקְרָאִים גַּדְפִין דֶּרֶךְ מָשָׁל — **we can explain well the metaphorical depiction of reverence and love as "wings"** of a bird, כְּדִכְתִיב, וּבִשְׁתַּיִם יְעוֹפֵף — **as the verse states,** *"they were flying with two"* (Isaiah 6:2), *i.e.,* that just as a bird needs two wings to fly, so too a *mitzvah* needs both love and

---

have risen to either of these worlds through *kavanah*). This additional light, discussed extensively in the Kabbalah, is: *Yichud Ha-Elyon* (the integration of Divine attributes).

According to the Kabbalah, a *mitzvah* actually has the power to *affect* the Divine attributes, the channels through which G-d's influence flows down into the worlds. Each of the ten Divine attributes express a different power of G-d, but while these powers were one and harmonious in their emanating source, after their light crystallized into distinct powers (in the world of *Atzilus*), "conflicts" can arise between them. For example, G-d's power of *chesed* (benevolence) can sometimes be at odds with His power of *gevurah* (restraint): *chesed* says "Give!" and *gevurah* says "Don't give!"

The solution to these "conflicts" is to *re-energize the attributes with unified light from the Source,* a light which preceded the separation into attributes. This higher light enables the opposing attributes to integrate with each other more effectively.

And that's what happens when you perform a *mitzvah*. You cause the Divine will (light from the Source) to shine down into the attributes, bringing about a greater degree of integration, referred to as *Yichud Ha-Elyon.*

וְשָׁם — **And there** in the *sefiros* of *Yetzirah* or *Beriah*, where your Torah and *mitzvos* ascend if performed with reverence and love, מֵאִיר וּמִתְגַּלֶּה גַּם כֵּן הַיִּחוּד הָעֶלְיוֹן הַנַּעֲשֶׂה בְּכָל מִצְוָה וְתַלְמוּד תּוֹרָה — **the** *Yichud Ha-Elyon* (merging of attributes) achieved through every *mitzvah* and act of **Torah study also shines and is disclosed.**

Since your *mitzvah* has been propelled to the spiritual worlds, through *kavanah*, it's now capable of receiving some of this "integrated light" (which shines down from the realm of Divine attributes, the World of *Atzilus,* which is above the Worlds of *Beriah* and *Yetzirah*).

שֶׁהוּא יִחוּד מִדּוֹתָיו יִתְבָּרֵךְ — **This "integrated light,"** *Yichud Ha-Elyon,* **is the merging of G-d's attributes** in the world of *Atzilus,* שֶׁנִּכְלָלוֹת זוֹ בָּזוֹ — **which became integrated with each other,** וְנִמְתָּקוֹת הַגְּבוּרוֹת בַּחֲסָדִים — **so that the** harsh **judgments are "sweetened" with kindness.**

ע"י עת רצון העליון א"ס ב"ה
המאיר ומתגלה בבחי' גילוי רב
ועצום באתערותא דלתתא היא
עשיית המצוה או עסק התורה
שבהן מלובש רצון העליון א"ס

יעופף [וכמ"ש הרח"ו ז"ל
בשער היחודים פי"א]
שהכנפים בעוף הן זרועות

reverence to propel it heavenward (as we will see below more clearly, from the *Tikunei Zohar*).

From the discussion in chapters 35-40 we now have a nuanced understanding of the relationship between a *mitzvah* act and its *kavanah*, which could be summed up in a number of points: 1.) Both the *mitzvah* act and its *kavanah* are the Divine will. 2.) Nevertheless, without the act being performed precisely, the entire *mitzvah* is disqualified, and *kavanah* will not help. 3.) A *mitzvah* act without *kavanah* is valid, but it only has a minuscule amount of Divine light and energy, like "a body without a soul," so it can't rise to G-d. 4.) Only a *mitzvah* with *kavanah* can escape the trappings of this world and rise to a place where it can be united with G-d.

This complex relationship is compared here to a bird (the *mitzvah* act) and it's two wings (the *kavanah,* resulting from love and reverence of G-d). The important point here is that the wings, while not crucial for its existence, are *part of the bird*. This brings to light that *kavanah* is not an "added feature" which propels a *mitzvah* act to its desired destination; it's part of the *mitzvah* itself.

[וּכְמוֹ שֶׁכָּתַב הָרַב חַיִּים וִיטַאל זִכְרוֹנוֹ לִבְרָכָה בְּשַׁעַר הַיִּחוּדִים פֶּרֶק י"א] — **And as Rabbi Chaim Vital of blessed memory wrote in Sha'ar Ha-Yichudim, chapter 11,** שֶׁהַכְּנָפַיִם בְּעוֹף הֵן זְרוֹעוֹת הָאָדָם כו' — **that a bird's wings are equivalent to a man's arms,** the

CONTINUE ON P. 484

A result of this integration is that many of the "restraint" orders issued by *gevurah* will be softened, allowing more light to flow down into the worlds from *chesed*. Without integration, the attributes will often be at odds with each other; but when the higher light of the Divine will shines, it enables them to find common ground and "agree" on more goodness to flow down into this world.

עַל יְדֵי עֵת רָצוֹן הָעֶלְיוֹן אֵין סוֹף בָּרוּךְ הוּא — **The integration of attributes can only occur when an even higher light is disclosed, through a moment of** disclosure of **the Divine will, the Blessed Infinite One,** הַמֵּאִיר וּמִתְגַּלֶּה בִּבְחִינַת גִּילּוּי רַב וְעָצוּם — **which shines and is disclosed profusely and intensely,** בְּאִתְעָרוּתָא דִלְתַתָּא הִיא עֲשִׂיַּית — **through "an awakening from below"** (*Zohar* 2, 135b), הַמִּצְוָה אוֹ עֵסֶק הַתּוֹרָה — **namely, the observance of a** *mitzvah* **or** act of **Torah study,** שֶׁבָּהֶן מְלוּבָּשׁ רָצוֹן הָעֶלְיוֹן אֵין סוֹף בָּרוּךְ הוּא — **and your** *mitzvah* **causes this great disclosure from above, because within** the *mitzvos* **the Divine will of the Blessed Infinite One is expressed.**

The Divine attributes don't solve their "conflicts" by themselves and require a higher light. You have the ability to "pull down" that higher light of the Divine will into the attributes, through observing a *mitzvah*.

That happens regardless of whether you have *kavanah* or not. But when you have *kavanah,* your *mitzvah* rises to *Yetzirah* or *Beriah* and acts as a channel

ב"ה אך עיקר היחוד הוא למעלה

מעלה בעולם האצילות ששם הוא מהות ועצמות מדותיו ית' מיוחדו'
במאצילן א"ס ב"ה ושם הוא מהות ועצמות רצון העליון א"ס
ב"ה והארתן לבד היא מאירה בבי"ע בכל עולם מהן לפי מעלתו
ואף שנפש האדם העוסק בתורה ומצוה זו אינה מאצילות מ"מ
הרי רצון העליון המלובש במצוה זו והוא הוא עצמו הדבר הלכה
והתורה שעוסק בה הוא אלהות ואור א"ס המאציל ב"ה שהוא
ורצונו אחד וברצונו ית' האציל מדותיו המיוחדות בו ית' וע"י

through which the "sweetened judgments" can flow down into this world. Put simply, *kavanah* can cause blessings of great abundance to flow into your life!

אַךְ עִיקַּר הַיִחוּד הוּא לְמַעְלָה מַעְלָה בְּעוֹלָם הָאֲצִילוּת — **However,** while the *sefiros* of the worlds of *Beriah* and *Yetzirah* do receive much of this light, **the main integration** of attributes **occurs much higher up in** the *sefiros* of **the world of *Atzilus*.**

The integration of Divine attributes (*Yichud Ha-Elyon*) actually occurs in the highest world of *Atzilus*, and only its effects shine below where your *mitzvah* is stationed (in *Yetzirah* or *Beriah*). The *Tanya* now explains why this is the case.

שֶׁשָּׁם הוּא מַהוּת וְעַצְמוּת מִדּוֹתָיו יִתְבָּרֵךְ — **Because** unlike in the worlds of *Beriah* and *Yetzirah* where the *sefiros* represent a mere *projection* of the Divine attributes, up **there,** in *Atzilus*, the *sefiros* are **the actual Divine attributes** *themselves*, **in their core,** מְיוּחָדוֹת בְּמַאֲצִילָן אֵין סוֹף בָּרוּךְ הוּא — **which are merged with their emanating source, the Blessed Infinite One.**

וְשָׁם הוּא מַהוּת וְעַצְמוּת רְצוֹן הָעֶלְיוֹן אֵין סוֹף בָּרוּךְ הוּא — **And** another reason why the main disclosure occurs in *Atzilus*, is because **that's where the Divine will of the Blessed Infinite One is actually found in its essential core.**

וְהָאָרָתָן לְבַד הִיא מְאִירָה בְּבְרִיאָה יְצִירָה וַעֲשִׂיָּה — **But only a glimmer of this shines in** the lower, created worlds of **Beriah, Yetzirah** and **Asiyah,** בְּכָל עוֹלָם מֵהֶן לְפִי מַעֲלָתוֹ — shining **in each world according to its** spiritual **qualities.**

One further point which needs to be clarified is: How are you able to influence *Atzilus* through your *mitzvah*?

וְאַף שֶׁנֶּפֶשׁ הָאָדָם הָעוֹסֵק בַּתּוֹרָה וּמִצְוָה זוֹ אֵינָהּ מֵאֲצִילוּת — **And even though the soul of the worshiper, who studied the Torah or observed the *mitzvah*, isn't in *Atzilus*,** מִכָּל מָקוֹם הֲרֵי רְצוֹן הָעֶלְיוֹן הַמְלוּבָּשׁ בְּמִצְוָה זוֹ — **nevertheless,** the worshiper is still able to influence attributes of *Atzilus* **because of the Divine will that is found in the *mitzvah*,** which is higher than those attributes.

וְהוּא הוּא עַצְמוֹ הַדָּבָר הֲלָכָה וְהַתּוֹרָה שֶׁעוֹסֵק בָּהּ — **And this is especially true of Torah** study, which, unlike the practical *mitzvos* that merely *express* the Divine will, **the point of *halacha* or Torah which you study *is* the Divine will** (see p. 260), הוּא אֱלֹהוּת — *i.e.,* **it is G-dliness, the Blessed Infinite Light, the emanating source,** וְאוֹר אֵין סוֹף הַמַּאֲצִיל בָּרוּךְ הוּא — **since He is one with His will.** שֶׁהוּא וּרְצוֹנוֹ אֶחָד

וּבְרְצוֹנוֹ יִתְבָּרֵךְ הָאֱצִיל מִדּוֹתָיו הַמְיוּחָדוֹת בּוֹ יִתְבָּרֵךְ — **And it is with that** same **Divine will that He emanated the attributes** of *Atzilus*, and brought them into being.

האדם כו' ובתיקונים פי' 55B | גילוי רצונו המתגלה ע"י עסק
שהעוסקים בתורה ומצות | תורה ומצוה זו הן נכללות זו בזו
בדחילו ורחימו נקראים | ונמתקות הגבורות בחסדים בעת
בנים ואם לאו נק' אפרוחים | רצון זו):
דלא יכלין לפרחא*
כי כמו שכנפי העוף

הגהה

(ובתיקון מ"ה דעופא הוא מט"ט

right and left arms corresponding to love and reverence, (*"chesed is the right arm, gevurah the left arm"—Tikunei Zohar* 17a).

The *Tanya* now cites another source for the idea that love and reverence are like the wings of a bird that make it fly.

וּבַתֵּיקוּנִים פֵּירְשׁוּ — **And the *Tikunei Zohar* comments** on the verse *"If you encounter a bird's nest... containing chicks or eggs, and the mother is sitting upon the chicks or upon the eggs, do not take the mother from upon the children"* (*Deuteronomy* 22:6).

שֶׁהָעוֹסְקִים בְּתוֹרָה וּמִצְוָה בִּדְחִילוּ וּרְחִימוּ נִקְרָאִים בָּנִים — Noting the dual expression, that the young birds are initially referred to as "chicks" and later as "children," the *Tikunei Zohar* comments **that if Torah and *mitzvos* are carried out with reverence and love they are called** mature **"children,"** וְאִם לָאו נִקְרָאִים אֶפְרוֹחִים דְּלָא יָכְלִין — **but if not, they are called** *"chicks that are unable to fly"* (see *Tikunei Zohar* 21a).*

In His essence, G-d is totally abstract and devoid of any attributes. The attributes came into being at some particular time because G-d *willed it so*.

G-d's will is the source of the attributes, which explains why Torah study and *mitzvah* observance (which express His undiluted will), are able to influence the attributes, shining a higher light on them.

וְעַל יְדֵי גִילוּי רְצוֹנוֹ הַמִּתְגַּלֶה עַל יְדֵי עֵסֶק תּוֹרָה וּמִצְוָה זוֹ — **And** that explains why, even though the worshiper remains down below, nevertheless, **by means of the disclosure of G-d's will that comes to light through this act of Torah study or *mitzvah* observance,** הֵן נִכְלָלוֹת זוֹ בָּזוֹ — **the attributes of *Atzilus* are integrated with one another,** וְנִמְתָּקוֹת הַגְּבוּרוֹת בַּחֲסָדִים — **causing the harsh judgments to be "sweetened" with kindness,** בְּעֵת רָצוֹן זוֹ — **at this moment** of disclosure of the Divine **will,** when the *mitzvah* is observed.

---

*הַגָּהָה — **NOTE.** In this note, the *Tanya* cites another passage from the *Tikunei Zohar,* clarifying more precisely how love and reverence are compared to "wings."

וּבְתִקּוּן מ"ה — **And in *Tikunei Zohar* section 45** (82b), it's clarified further, דְעוֹפָא הוּא מְטַ"ט — that **the "bird"** referred to in Genesis 1:20 (*"let a bird fly over the earth"*), **is**

רֵישָׁא דִּילֵיהּ י' וְגוּפָא וָא"ו וּתְרֵין
גַּדְפִּין ה' ה' כו' וְהַיְינוּ עוֹלָם
הַיְצִירָה שֶׁנִּקְרָא מט"ט וּבוֹ הֵן
גּוּפֵי הַלְכוֹת שֶׁבַּמִּשְׁנָה וְרֵישָׁא
דִּילֵיהּ הֵן הַמּוֹחִין וּבְחִי' חב"ד
שֶׁהֵן פְּנִימִיּוּת הַהַלְכוֹת וְסוֹדָן
וְטַעֲמֵיהֶן וּתְרֵין גַּדְפִּין דְּחִילוּ

אֵינָם עִיקַר הָעוֹף
וְאֵין חִיּוּתוֹ תָּלוּי בָּהֶם
כְּלָל כְּדַתְנָן נִיטְּלוּ אַגְפֵּיהָ
כְּשֵׁרָה וְהָעִיקָר הוּא רֹאשׁוֹ
וְכָל גּוּפוֹ וְהַכְּנָפַיִים אֵינָם
רַק מְשַׁמְּשִׁים לְרֹאשׁוֹ וְגוּפוֹ

8TH NISAN LEAP [UNTIL END OF NOTE ON P. 490]

The *Tanya* now clarifies the precise meaning of the bird/wings analogy. (This passage draws heavily on the ideas discussed in the "note" on pp. 480-84).

כִּי כְּמוֹ שֶׁכַּנְפֵי הָעוֹף אֵינָם עִיקַר הָעוֹף וְאֵין חִיּוּתוֹ תָּלוּי בָּהֶם כְּלָל — **For just as a bird's wings are not a crucial, life-sustaining part of their body,** כְּדַתְנָן נִיטְּלוּ אַגְפֵּיהָ כְּשֵׁרָה — **as the** *Mishnah* **indicates that if a bird's wings are removed, it is** not considered to have suffered a life-threatening injury and **is** *kosher* (see *Mishnah, Chullin* 3:4), וְהָעִיקָר הוּא רֹאשׁוֹ וְכָל גּוּפוֹ — **the main part** of the bird **being its head and the rest of its body** apart from the wings, וְהַכְּנָפַיִים אֵינָם רַק מְשַׁמְּשִׁים לְרֹאשׁוֹ וְגוּפוֹ לְפָרְחָא בְּהוֹן

---

the archangel **Metatron,** רֵישָׁא דִּילֵיהּ יוּ"ד וְגוּפָא וָא"ו וּתְרֵין גַּדְפִּין הֵ"א הֵ"א כו' — **whose "body"** is formed by the Tetragrammaton (*yud-hei-vav-hei*), **"his head a yud, body a vav, and his two wings, hei and hei."**

The *Tanya* now explains the detailed allusions of this passage in *Tikunei Zohar* to eventually clarify how the "wings" refer to reverence and love.

וְהַיְינוּ עוֹלָם הַיְצִירָה שֶׁנִּקְרָא מט"ט — **This** insight of *Tikunei Zohar* **is speaking of the World of** *Yetzirah*, **which is called** the domain of **Metatron** (see *ibid.* 79a; Rabbi Chaim Vital, *Sha'ar Ha-Mitzvos, Parshas Eikev*), וּבוֹ הֵן גּוּפֵי הַלְכוֹת שֶׁבַּמִּשְׁנָה — **in which** Metatron's "body" represents **the body of laws found in the** *Mishnah*.

As we learned in chapter 39, *"the six (emotional) sefiros have their 'nest' in Yetzirah."* Since these six emotions are the main energy of *Yetzirah*, they are alluded to by Metatron's central "body," formed by the *vav*, (since the *vav* in the Tetragrammaton, whose numerical value is six, alludes to the six emotional *sefiros*).

Your emotional reaction to something is essentially "yes" or "no," "like" or "dislike." That's why Metatron's "body" (the emotions) alludes to the *Mishnah*, which is a text that contains final legal rulings, which are basically either a "yes" (kosher/pure/permissible) or "no" (invalid/impure/forbidden).

וְרֵישָׁא דִּילֵיהּ הֵן הַמּוֹחִין וּבְחִינוֹת חָכְמָה בִּינָה וָדַעַת — **And** Metatron's **head** represents **the intellectual dimensions of** *chochmah, binah* and *da'as* of the *Mishnah*, שֶׁהֵן פְּנִימִיּוּת הַהַלְכוֹת וְסוֹדָן וְטַעֲמֵיהֶן — **which are the inner meaning of the laws, their secrets and rationales.**

לפרחא בהון וכך ד"מ
התורה ומצות הן עיקר
היחוד העליון ע"י גילוי
רצון העליון המתגלה על
ידיהן והדחילו ורחימו הם
מעלים אותן למקום
שיתגלה בו הרצון אור אין

ורחימו הן ה' עילאה שהיא רחימו
וה' תתאה היא יראה תתאה עול
מלכות שמים ופחד ה' כפחד
המלך ד"מ שהיא יראה חיצונית
ונגלית משא"כ יראה עילאה ירא
בושת היא מהנסתרות לה' אלהינו
והיא בחכמה עילאה יו"ד של שם
הוי"ה ב"ה כמ"ש בר"מ:

— וְכָךְ דֶּרֶךְ מָשָׁל — **the wings merely serving the head and body, to let them fly,** likewise, metaphorically speaking, we see a similar relationship between the act of a *mitzvah* (the "body") and its *kavanah* (the "wings").

הַתּוֹרָה וּמִצְוֹת הֵן עִיקַר הַיִחוּד הָעֶלְיוֹן — The act of speaking **Torah and** performing *mitzvos* constitutes the "head" and "body" of the *Yichud Ha-Elyon* (merging of Divine attributes), as we discussed at length in the "note" on pp. 480-84, עַל יְדֵי גִּילוּי רָצוֹן הָעֶלְיוֹן הַמִתְגַּלֶה עַל יְדֵיהֶן — and, as was also discussed in the "note," the power to bring about that *Yichud Ha-Elyon* **comes from the Divine will which is disclosed through** the acts of Torah and *mitzvos,* regardless of *kavanah.*

וְהַדְּחִילוּ וּרְחִימוּ הֵם מַעֲלִים אוֹתָן לְמָקוֹם — **And the reverence and love** are like the "wings" of the Torah and *mitzvos,* **which lift them to** a higher **place,** which is free from the limitations of this world, a world in which Divine light can't shine due to the many diminishments (*tzimtzumim*), שֶׁיִתְגַּלֶה בּוֹ הָרָצוֹן אוֹר אֵין סוֹף בָּרוּךְ הוּא וְהַיִחוּד —

The *Mishnah* does not give the inner reasons for its rulings, and these are clarified in other Jewish texts.

וּתְרֵין גַּדְפִין דְּחִילוּ וּרְחִימוּ — **And** Metatron's **two wings** which elevate the *Mishnah* and its inner reasons, are **reverence and love,** הֵן הֵ"א עִילָאָה שֶׁהִיא רְחִימוּ — **the first "upper"** *hei* of the Tetragrammaton **is love,** וְהֵ"א תַּתָּאָה הִיא יִרְאָה תַּתָּאָה — **and the second "lower"** *hei* of the Tetragrammaton **is "lower reverence."**

Below, in chapters 41-43, we will explore the difference between the two levels of lower and higher reverence. Here we touch upon the topic briefly.

עוֹל מַלְכוּת שָׁמַיִם — **"Lower reverence"** is **accepting the sovereign authority of G-d,** וּפַחַד ה' כְּפַחַד הַמֶּלֶךְ דֶּרֶךְ מָשָׁל — **and having trepidation before G-d, in a similar way you would have trepidation before a** human **king,** שֶׁהִיא יִרְאָה חִיצוֹנִית וְנִגְלֵית — **which is a superficial, palpable reverence.**

מַה שֶׁאֵין כֵּן יִרְאָה עִילָאָה — **Unlike "higher reverence"** (which is not referred to here in the *Tikunei Zohar*), יְרֵא בּוֹשֶׁת הִיא — **which is a reverence** arising **from a sense of shame** in G-d's presence, מֵהַנִּסְתָּרוֹת לַה' אֱלֹהֵינוּ — **from** *"the hidden things that are for G-d, our G-d"* (see *Deuteronomy* 29:28; chapter 43, pp. 550*ff.*).

וְהִיא בְּחָכְמָה עִילָאָה יוֹ"ד שֶׁל שֵׁם הֲוָיָ"ה בָּרוּךְ הוּא — **"Higher reverence"** is not con-

סוֹף בָּרוּךְ הוּא וְהַיִחוּד   הגהה

שֶׁהֵן יְצִירָה וּבְרִיאָה*   (אוֹ אֲפִילוּ בַּעֲשִׂיָּה בִּי"ס דִּקְדוּשָׁה

and in that higher place, it's possible for **the will of the Blessed Infinite Light and the** *Yichud Ha-Elyon* **to be manifest,** שֶׁהֵן יְצִירָה וּבְרִיאָה — **that** higher place **being** the *sefiros* of either the world of **Yetzirah or Beriah.***

---

nected with Metatron's second "wing," the second *hei,* but **with "Upper** *chochmah*" **represented by the** *Yud* **of the blessed Tetragrammaton,** כְּמוֹ שֶׁכָּתוּב בְּרַעְיָא מְהֵימְנָא — **as stated in the** *Zohar* (3, 122b), in the section **Raya Mehemna.** (For the connection between "higher reverence" and *chochmah* see chapter 43, p. 552).

*הַגָּהָה — **NOTE.** As we discussed in the second "note" in this chapter (pp. 480-84), a *mitzvah* is the Divine will (of the Blessed Infinite Light) which transcends *Atzilus,* the highest of the four spiritual words. So when any *mitzvah* is performed, it results in that will (and the Blessed Infinite Light) being "pulled down" into the highest world of *Atzilus.*

Once the Blessed Infinite Light has reached *Atzilus*, it can then shine down into the *sefiros* of the lower worlds, since the *sefiros* in all the worlds are a "fluid" energy that makes the transmission of light possible. However, as we learned above, "*only a glimmer of this shines in the lower, created worlds of Beriah, Yetzirah and Asiyah*" (p. 483).

In the current note, the *Tanya* elaborates on this idea further. The extent to which "a glimmer" of the Blessed Infinite Light shines down in the lower worlds depends not only on "each world according to its spiritual qualities," as we learned earlier, but also on *what type of worship you are performing*. Torah has a different power than practical *mitzvos* to "pull" the light down; and, as we shall see, different parts of the Torah also have different potencies.

(The ability of worship to "pull down" the Blessed Infinite Light into the lower worlds shouldn't be confused with our earlier discussion about Torah and *mitzvos* *ascending* to one of the spiritual worlds through *kavanah*. These are two different phenomena: 1.) An act of worship, since it is the Divine will, causes the Blessed Infinite Light to shine *downwards* into *Atzilus*, and a glimmer of that light then extends to the *sefiros* of the other worlds. 2.) *Kavanah* causes your worship to *ascend* from this physical world, (where the Blessed Infinite Light can't shine), to one of the spiritual worlds, (where it can). Your Torah or *mitzvah* becomes illuminated when, on its way up the worlds, it "meets" a glimmer of the Blessed Infinite Light which is shining downwards).

אוֹ אֲפִילוּ בַּעֲשִׂיָּה בִּי' סְפִירוֹת דִּקְדוּשָׁה — Your worship can cause a glimmer of the Blessed Infinite Light to shine down into the *sefiros* of *Beriah or Yetzirah,* **or even into** the world of **Asiyah, into its ten holy *sefiros.***

והנה אף דדחילו ורחימו   מקום מצות מעשיות וכן מקרא

הם ג"כ מתרי"ג מצות   אבל במשנה מתגלה היחוד ואור

16TH NISAN REGULAR | 9TH NISAN LEAP

The *Tanya* now questions the appropriateness of the "bird" analogy.

וְהִנֵּה אַף דְּדְחִילוּ וּרְחִימוּ הֵם גַּם כֵּן מִתַּרְיַ"ג מִצְוֹת — **Now even though reverence and love themselves count** as two of **the 613** *mitzvos* (*Rambam, Sefer Ha-Mitzvos,* Pos-

---

Up to this point, we haven't been focused too much on the *sefiros* of *Asiyah*, because they are of little practical relevance to your *mitzvah*: Without *kavanah*, your *mitzvah* won't even reach as high as the *sefiros* of *Asiyah* (only to *Asiyah's* superficial "chambers"; and with *kavanah,* your *mitzvah* will rise past *Asiyah* to the *sefiros* of *Yetzirah* or *Beriah*.

But here we are not addressing the question of how far up your *mitzvah* rises from this world, but how far downwards the Blessed Infinite Light will project (as a result of your *mitzvah*). And the answer to that question is: It depends what *mitzvah* you performed.

מְקוֹם מִצְוֹת מַעֲשִׂיּוֹת — The world of *Asiyah* being **the domain of the practical commandments.**

The world of *Asiyah* has two components: this physical world, and its spiritual counterpart. And, as we learned above, the spiritual component of *Asiyah* is also divided into a.) its (non-Divine) "superficial dimension" of "chambers" *etc.,* and b.) the *sefiros*, which are Divine lights.

The *Tanya* teaches us here that when you observe a practical commandment, it causes the Blessed Infinite Light to shine down through the *sefiros* of all the four worlds, including the *sefiros* of *Asiyah*.

(Still, even that won't help your *mitzvah* if it was devoid of *kavanah*, since, at the very best, a *mitzvah* without *kavanah* could rise to the "superficial dimensions" of *Asiyah*, but not to the *sefiros*, as we learned above, p. 465).

Now the *Tanya* turns to the *mitzvah* of Torah study, and its power to "pull down" a glimmer of the Blessed Infinite Light into the lower worlds.

וְכֵן מִקְרָא — **And, like** the practical *mitzvos,* the study of **Scripture** also causes a glimmer of the Blessed Infinite Light to shine in the *sefiros* of *Asiyah* (see *Zohar* 3, 254b; *Pri Etz Chaim Sha'ar Hanhagas Ha-Limud,* chapter 1).

Scripture, the "Written Torah," must be inscribed on parchment according to precise rules. The correct shape of the letters, along with their scribal "crowns" (*tagim*), are what render a Torah scroll valid. This enmeshment with the physical world indicates that the study of Scripture can "pull down" the Blessed Infinite Light to *sefiros* of *Asiyah* (*Ma'amarei Admor Ha-Zaken, Kesuvim,* vol. 1, pp. 26-7).

אעפ"כ נקראין גדפין להיות
כי תכלית האהבה היא
העבודה מאהבה ואהבה
בלי עבודה היא אהבה
בתענוגים להתענג על ה'

אין סוף ברוך הוא ביצירה
ובתלמוד בבריא' דהיינו שבלימוד
מקרא מתפשט היחוד ואור א"ס
ב"ה מאצילו' עד העשיה ובמשנה
עד היצירה לבדה ובתלמוד עד
הבריאה לבדה כי כולן באצילות

56A

itive Commands 3-4), implying that they are not mere "wings" to another *mitzvah,* but *mitzvos* in their own right, אַף עַל פִּי כֵן נִקְרָאִין גַּדְפִּין — **nevertheless,** even though they are enumerated as separate *mitzvos,* **it's appropriate to call them "wings,"** לִהְיוֹת כִּי תַּכְלִית הָאַהֲבָה הִיא הָעֲבוֹדָה מֵאַהֲבָה — **because the point of "love"** is not the love *per se,* but **worship coming from love.**

Generally speaking, love of G-d is always aimed at worship. However, there does exist a rare, very high level of love, experienced by *tzadikim,* known as "pleasurable love" (see p. 174). This level, the *Tanya* will now observe, is a pure love, not aimed at worship.

וְאַהֲבָה בְּלִי עֲבוֹדָה — **But** a rare type of **love** of G-d which *is* an end in itself, **without** leading to **worship,** הִיא אַהֲבָה בַּתַּעֲנוּגִים — **is** *"pleasurable love"* (*Song* 7:7; see chapter 9, pp. 117-8) לְהִתְעַנֵּג עַל ה' מֵעֵין עוֹלָם הַבָּא — **which is to take pleasure in**

אֲבָל בְּמִשְׁנָה מִתְגַּלֶּה הַיִּחוּד וְאוֹר אֵין סוֹף בָּרוּךְ הוּא בִּיצִירָה — **But** *Mishnah* study **dis-closes** a glimmer of **the** *Yichud Ha-Elyon* **and the Blessed Infinite Light** only down **into** the *sefiros* of *Yetzirah.*

Mishnah, the "Oral Torah," has less enmeshment with this world, and is only "physical" in the sense that its sacred words must be verbalized. Its light, there-fore, doesn't come all the way down from *Atzilus* to *Asiyah,* and only reaches to the World of *Yetzirah* (ibid. See above, "note" on p. 485 for a further connection between the *Mishnah* and *Yetzirah*).

וּבְתַלְמוּד בִּבְרִיאָה — **And** *Talmud* only draws the Blessed Infinite Light down **into** the *sefiros* of *Beriah.*

The *Talmud* is essentially the intellectual rationale *behind* the rulings of the *Mishnah.* In this sense it is purely spiritual, and can only reach the World of *Beriah* (*Ma'amarei Admor Ha-Zaken* ibid.).

In case we are confused about why the most holy part of Torah (Scripture) is as-sociated with the lowest world, the *Tanya* clarifies:

דְּהַיְינוּ שֶׁבְּלִימוּד מִקְרָא מִתְפַּשֵּׁט הַיִּחוּד וְאוֹר אֵין סוֹף בָּרוּךְ הוּא מֵאֲצִילוּת עַד הָעֲשִׂיָּה — **Namely, the study of Scripture causes the** *Yichud Ha-Elyon* **and the Blessed In-finite Light in** *Atzilus* **to extend** *all the way down* **to** *Asiyah,* וּבְמִשְׁנָה עַד הַיְצִירָה לְבַדָּה — **but with** *Mishnah* study **it only reaches** *Yetzirah,* וּבְתַלְמוּד עַד הַבְּרִיאָה לְבַדָּה — **and with** *Talmud* study **it only reaches** *Beriah.*

מעין עוה"ב וקבלת שכר   אבל קבלה אינה מתפשטת כלל

והיום לעשות' כתי' ולמחר   מאצילות לבי"ע כמ"ש בפרע"ח):

לקבל שכרם ומי שלא הגיע למדה זו לטעום מעין

עוה"ב אלא עדיין נפשו שוקקה וצמאה לה' וכלתה אליו

כל היום ואינו מרוה צמאונו במי התורה שלפניו הרי זה

G-d in a way that is a foretaste of the world-that-is-coming, וְקַבָּלַת שָׂכָר — so it's not really "worship" but **the reward received** for worship, performed already in this world.

וְהַיּוֹם לַעֲשׂוֹתָם כְּתִיב — **As the verse states** regarding the *mitzvos*, **"Do them today"** (*Deuteronomy* 7:11), וּלְמָחָר לְקַבֵּל שָׂכָר — **and it is only "tomorrow (in the afterlife) you will receive the reward"** (*Talmud, Eruvin* 22a; see chapter 17, p. 204).

But for most people who don't experience "pleasurable love," and don't experience a taste of the next world in this lifetime, love of G-d ought to motivate the worship of G-d.

וּמִי שֶׁלֹּא הִגִּיעַ לְמִדָּה זוֹ לִטְעוֹם מֵעֵין עוֹלָם הַבָּא — **But any person who has not reached this level, to taste something of the world-that-is-coming,** אֶלָּא עֲדַיִין נַפְשׁוֹ שׁוֹקֵקָה וּצְמֵאָה לַה' וְכָלְתָה אֵלָיו כָּל הַיּוֹם — **and instead** of actually experiencing the "taste"

Scripture is the most sacred part of the Torah and therefore it is the most spiritually powerful. This is expressed by the fact that it can project the Blessed Infinite Light to the furthest distance away from *Atzilus*, all the way down to (the *sefiros* of) *Asiyah*.

כִּי כוּלָּן בָּאֲצִילוּת — **For all** worship brings about the merging of the Blessed Infinite Light **with *Atzilus,*** and the only difference between the different types of worship is how far down the scheme of worlds that illumination will extend.

In a final comment, the *Tanya* clarifies the spiritual illumination that occurs through the study of Kabbalah.

אֲבָל קַבָּלָה אֵינָה מִתְפַּשֶּׁטֶת כְּלָל מֵאֲצִילוּת — **But *Kabbalah*** study **doesn't cause** the Blessed Infinite Light **to be projected beyond *Atzilus* at all,** לִבְרִיאָה יְצִירָה וַעֲשִׂיָּה — not to *Beriah, Yetzirah* or *Asiyah,* כְּמוֹ שֶׁכָּתוּב בִּפְרִי עֵץ חַיִּים — as stated in *Pri Etz Chaim* (ibid.).

While *Talmud* is purely intellectual (and not physical), it is only two "steps" away from the physical realm: 1.) It offers the reasons behind the rulings of the *Mishnah*; 2.) which dictates how *mitzvos* are to be observed in this world. So it has a worldly connection. Kabbalah, on the other hand, speaks of completely other-worldly phenomena, and it uses imagery which the mortal intellect cannot fully grasp. So when you study it, the light you generate in *Atzilus* doesn't flow down into the worlds, because it has nothing in common with them (*Ma'amarei Admor Ha-Zaken* ibid.).

כְּמִי שֶׁעוֹמֵד בַּנָּהָר וְצוֹעֵק מַיִם מַיִם לִשְׁתּוֹת כְּמוֹ שֶׁקּוֹבֵל עָלָיו הַנָּבִיא הוֹי כָּל צָמֵא לְכוּ לַמָּיִם. כִּי לְפִי פְּשׁוּטוֹ אֵינוֹ מוּבָן דְּמִי שֶׁהוּא צָמֵא וּמִתְאַוֶּה לִלְמוֹד פְּשִׁיטָא שֶׁיִּלְמוֹד מֵעַצְמוֹ וְלָמָּה לוֹ לַנָּבִיא לִצְעוֹק עָלָיו הוֹי וְכמ"ש במ"א בַּאֲרִיכוּת:

of G-d with "pleasurable love," **his soul longs and thirsts for G-d** from a distance, **"languishing for Him all day"** (see *Deuteronomy* 28:32), וְאֵינוֹ מַרְוֶה צְמָאוֹנוֹ בְּמֵי הַתּוֹרָה שֶׁלְּפָנָיו — **and** instead of the love motivating him to worship G-d and study Torah, this person **doesn't quench his thirst with the waters of Torah available to him,** הֲרֵי זֶה כְּמִי שֶׁעוֹמֵד בַּנָּהָר וְצוֹעֵק מַיִם מַיִם לִשְׁתּוֹת — **then he's like someone who stands next to a river and cries out,** *"Water! Where is* **water to drink?"**

If you love G-d, and thirst to connect to Him, then go and worship Him. If your love doesn't lead to worship then it's as if you were standing next to water, saying, "I need to drink!"

The *Tanya* offers a source for this idea.

כְּמוֹ שֶׁקּוֹבֵל עָלָיו הַנָּבִיא — **As the prophet bemoans over such a person,** הוֹי כָּל צָמֵא לְכוּ לַמָּיִם — *"Alas! Everyone who is thirsty go to the water"* (*Isaiah* 55:1).

כִּי לְפִי פְּשׁוּטוֹ — **For if we follow the simple interpretation** of this verse, which is *"every one that's willing to learn, let him come and learn"* (*Targum Yonasan*), אֵינוֹ מוּבָן — **it's not clear** what the verse is saying, דְּמִי שֶׁהוּא צָמֵא וּמִתְאַוֶּה לִלְמוֹד פְּשִׁיטָא שֶׁיִּלְמוֹד מֵעַצְמוֹ — **because obviously** a person who is thirsty for study and desires it, will come and study of his own accord, וְלָמָּה לוֹ לַנָּבִיא לִצְעוֹק עָלָיו הוֹי — **and why would the prophet bemoan and say** of him, "Alas"?

Rather, the verse appears to be speaking of a person who is thirsty for G-d, but doesn't realize that this emotional thirsting needs to be quenched practically through Torah and worship.

וּכְמוֹ שֶׁנִּתְבָּאֵר בְּמָקוֹם אַחֵר בַּאֲרִיכוּת — **As is explained elsewhere, at length** (see *Ma'amarei Admor Ha-Zakein al Parshios Ha-Torah*, vol. 1, pp. 172-3).

PRACTICAL LESSONS

"Love" and "reverence" are like the wings of a bird which enable your *mitzvah* to fly to the heavens.

Feelings for G-d need to be expressed in worship. Otherwise it's like standing in front of water and saying "I'm thirsty!"

Performing *mitzvos* with *kavanah* can help to "sweeten" harsh judgments in heaven.

פרק מא ברם   צריך להיות תמיד לזכרון ראשית
העבודה ועיקרה ושרשה. והוא
כי אף שהיראה היא שרש לסור מרע והאהבה לועשה

CHAPTER 41

A CRASH COURSE IN REVERENCE AND LOVE

SECTION ONE: HOW TO START WORSHIPING G-D

17TH NISAN REGULAR | 10TH NISAN LEAP

Now that we have discussed the *theoretical importance* of "reverence" and "love" when observing the Torah (the "wings of a bird" which enable a *mitzvah* to "fly" heavenward), the *Tanya* will now spend the next nine chapters exploring *practical methods* to generate these emotions. We will be taught meditations that are designed to produce a variety of feelings, and we will also be guided in how to recognize different stages of emotional maturity.

First, we will turn our attention to the basic feeling of reverence for G-d which, the *Tanya* will argue, must be the foundation of all worship.

רֵאשִׁית הָעֲבוֹדָה — **But you need to remember always,** בְּרַם צָרִיךְ לִהְיוֹת לְזִכָּרוֹן תָּמִיד וְעִיקָרָהּ וְשָׁרְשָׁהּ — **the beginning of worship, as well as its** ongoing **foundation and** nourishing **"root,"** וְהוּא — **which** is reverence, not love.

Reverence is the basic feeling upon which your relationship with G-d should be founded. You will never "graduate" from the need for reverence; even as your worship matures, it will always remain with you, just as a root nourishes a tree.

Love, as we shall see later, is of extreme importance in worship. But it is, so to speak, the "building" and not the "foundation."

כִּי אַף שֶׁהַיִּרְאָה הִיא שֹׁרֶשׁ לְסוּר מֵרַע — **Because, even though** we learned above (chapter 4, p. 65), **that reverence is the "root"** which motivates a person not to transgress any prohibitions, to *"turn away from evil"* (*Psalms* 34:14), וְהָאַהֲבָה לְוַעֲשֵׂה טוֹב — **and love** motivates the observance of positive commands, to *"do good"* (*ibid.*), which implies that neither reverence nor love is the "root" of *all* the mitzvos, אַף עַל פִּי כֵן — **nevertheless,** as we shall see, it's actually reverence that forms the basis of all worship (and love merely *energizes* the positive commands, but it's not their foundation—*Sefer Ha-Ma'amarim Melukat* vol. 4, p. 95, note 58).

טוב. אעפ"כ לא די לעורר האהבה לבדה לועשה טוב
ולפחות צריך לעורר תחלה היראה הטבעית המסותרת
בלב כל ישראל שלא למרוד בממ"ה הקב"ה כנ"ל
שתהא בהתגלות לבו או מוחו עכ"פ דהיינו להתבונן
במחשבתו עכ"פ גדולת א"ס ב"ה ומלכותו אשר היא

לֹא דַי לְעוֹרֵר הָאַהֲבָה לְבַדָּהּ לַעֲשֶׂה טוֹב — It's not sufficient to awaken love alone, וְלִפְחוֹת צָרִיךְ לְעוֹרֵר תְּחִלָּה הַיִּרְאָה הַטִּבְעִית הַמְסוּתֶּרֶת בְּלֵב כָּל יִשְׂרָאֵל, to *"do good,"* — and before awakening love, you first need to awaken, if not a profound reverence resulting from inner meditative work, then at least the innate reverence found dormant in the heart of all Israel, שֶׁלֹּא לִמְרוֹד בְּמֶלֶךְ מַלְכֵי הַמְּלָכִים הַקָּדוֹשׁ בָּרוּךְ הוּא — this basic reverence being not to act insubordinately towards *"the King, King of kings, the Blessed Holy One"* (*Liturgy, Alenu* prayer), כַּנִּזְכָּר לְעֵיל — as mentioned above, see (chapters 19, 25, 38 and 39).

Reverence will motivate you to worship G-d when *He* desires it, and not just when you feel like it. *"If you're attached to your own self-importance, you reveal that all your worship is really self-service. It's just another type of pleasure that you do to gratify yourself"* (Rabbi Shalom Dov Ber Schneersohn, *Kuntres Umayon* p. 104).

שֶׁתְּהֵא בְּהִתְגַּלּוֹת לִבּוֹ — You need to awaken this innate reverence so that it should be manifest openly in your heart, אוֹ מוֹחוֹ עַל כָּל פָּנִים — or if you can't do that, at least awaken some reverence through focusing your mind which is under your control, to think as you will.

Feelings for the invisible G-d should ideally be palpable in the heart, just as you would feel for something that you see with your eyes. But if you can't manage that, it's okay. As long as you can muster some sense of reverence in your mind, you can worship G-d.

דְּהַיְינוּ לְהִתְבּוֹנֵן בְּמַחֲשַׁבְתּוֹ עַל כָּל פָּנִים גְּדוּלַת אֵין סוֹף בָּרוּךְ הוּא — And the way to do this is by reflecting on the greatness of the Blessed Infinite One, even if not with intense focus of your mind, then in your general thoughts, at least.

SECTION TWO: A BASIC MEDITATION BEFORE ANY MITZVAH

Reverence of G-d is acquired in two phases. First you simply *accept* G-d's authority, even though you don't yet feel drawn to worship Him in your heart (and, if it was up to you, you'd rather do something else). You're a bit like a waiter in a restaurant, who obediently and carefully offers service, but only because he has to, not because he wants to. This initial phase is referred to as *Kabolas Ol*, "accepting G-d's sovereign authority." It's the beginning of worship because, *"it's something that you strongly resist and must force yourself to do out of necessity. In other words, if your spiritual flame is very weak and you can't get excited about anything G-dly,*

מלכות כל עולמים עליונים ותחתונים ואיהו ממלא כל
עלמין וסובב כל עלמין וכמ"ש הלא את השמים ואת

the solution is to force yourself to accept G-d's authority." (Rabbi Shalom Dov Ber Schneersohn, *Yom Tov Shel Rosh Ha-Shanah* 5666, p. 31).

In the second phase, you begin (not merely to accept but) to internalize and "own" your feelings of reverence for G-d, so that they manifest in your mind, your heart and your personality.

As we shall see, both phases (accepting and internalizing) are necessary for proper worship, but the *Tanya* will start with "basic meditation" aimed at helping you to *accept* G-d's authority at the beginning of worship. This is an extremely important and accessible meditation, which ought to be used daily in your struggle against selfish and negative inclinations.

"The Yetzer Hara is never lazy, and is very busy and industrious in his efforts to distract a Jew from his service to G-d. Therefore, you must have a ready weapon with which to combat him. For this reason, I suggest that you should study well, and learn by heart, the beginning of chapter 41... until those sacred words are engraved upon your mind and memory, so that you will always be able to recall them and think about them whenever the need arises to overcome a temptation, etc..." (Letter from the Lubavitcher Rebbe, 13th *Teves,* 5726).

On other occasions, this meditation has been recommended to help with anxiety (*Igros Kodesh* vol. 18, p. 356), depression (*ibid.* vol. 17, p. 227), laziness (*ibid.* vol. 11, p. 280), negative thinking (*ibid.* vol. 16, p. 263), anger and pride (*ibid.* vol. 14, p. 459), and bad character traits in general (*ibid.* vol. 18, p. 206).

The meditation explores four ideas: 1.) The awesomeness of G-d's power; 2.) His energizing presence in the world; 3) His personal relationship with you; 4.) His un-wavering interest in you.

וּמַלְכוּתוֹ אֲשֶׁר הִיא מַלְכוּת כָּל עוֹלָמִים עֶלְיוֹנִים וְתַחְתּוֹנִים — First, think of 1.) **His su-preme power which** *"rules over all worlds"* (*Psalms* 145:13), **upper and lower.**

Your reverence of any authority will be proportionate to that authority's power. G-d's power is supreme, ruling over the entire universe.

But thinking how G-d has power *over* the worlds is not enough. You also need to meditate upon G-d's presence *in* the world.

וְאִיהוּ מְמַלֵּא כָּל עָלְמִין — **And** contemplate how: 2.) All existence is saturated with G-d, *"who fills all worlds"* (see *Zohar* 3, 225a), וְסוֹבֵב כָּל עָלְמִין — **and how all ex-istence is engulfed in G-d who** *"transcends all worlds"* (*ibid.*), וּכְמוֹ שֶׁכָּתוּב הֲלֹא אֶת הַשָּׁמַיִם וְאֶת הָאָרֶץ אֲנִי מָלֵא — **as the verse states,** *"Do I not fill heaven and earth?"* (*Jeremiah* 23:24).

The next stage of the meditation is to contemplate how you are in a personal relationship with this all-powerful, all-present G-d.

הָאָרֶץ אֲנִי מָלֵא וּמַנִיחַ הָעֶלְיוֹנִים וְתַחְתּוֹנִים וּמְיַחֵד
מַלְכוּתוֹ עַל עַמּוֹ יִשְׂרָאֵל בִּכְלָל וְעָלָיו בִּפְרָט כִּי חַיָּב
אָדָם לוֹמַר בִּשְׁבִילִי נִבְרָא הָעוֹלָם וְהוּא גַם הוּא מְקַבֵּל
עָלָיו מַלְכוּתוֹ לִהְיוֹת מֶלֶךְ עָלָיו וּלְעָבְדוֹ וְלַעֲשׂוֹת רְצוֹנוֹ

וּמַנִּיחַ הָעֶלְיוֹנִים וְתַחְתּוֹנִים — **And** think how: 3). **He has disregarded the** worship of the **upper and lower** spiritual **worlds,** וּמְיַחֵד מַלְכוּתוֹ עַל עַמּוֹ יִשְׂרָאֵל — **and** in giving the Torah to us **He has specified His** desire to be worshipped **as King by His people, Israel.**

In giving the Torah to Israel, G-d entered into a unique relationship with one particular people. This ought to make you feel honored to be chosen by G-d to worship Him through this covenant.

But you might still think to yourself: There are many members of the covenant who worship G-d. Why is my contribution so important? Therefore the *Tanya* adds:

בִּכְלָל — That is, **generally speaking,** you have a unique relationship with G-d, due to His covenant with Israel, וְעָלָיו בִּפְרָט — but your relationship is even more personal than that, since G-d has indicated His desire to be worshipped **by you, in particular,** כִּי חַיָּב אָדָם לוֹמַר בִּשְׁבִילִי נִבְרָא הָעוֹלָם — since *"a person must say, 'The world was created for my sake'"* (*Mishnah, Sanhedrin* 37a).

The *Mishnah* (ibid.) derives this lesson from the narrative at the beginning of *Genesis*. G-d created the world initially with just one person, Adam, to teach us that, just like Adam, we all have a *personal* relationship with G-d, as if no one else existed.

וְהוּא גַם הוּא מְקַבֵּל עָלָיו מַלְכוּתוֹ — **And you, in turn, accept upon yourself G-d's sovereign authority,** לִהְיוֹת מֶלֶךְ עָלָיו — **that He is to be King over you.**

The awareness of G-d's special interest in you ought to be *reciprocated*. He thinks you're special. He's chosen you as an instrument of His deepest will, and that will make you want to mirror that energy.

And don't think that your response to Him is insignificant. Don't say to yourself, "What could my finite worship mean to an infinite G-d?" Because G-d is described here as a "King" to indicate that your worship *matters* to Him. In contrast to a dictator, who imposes his will on others whether they like it or not, the appointment of a king depends on public acceptance — *"there's no king without a people"* (see

A CHASIDIC THOUGHT

Love alone is self-serving. When you say "I love French fries," what you mean is, "I love myself, and French fries give me pleasure." To have a relationship with G-d, the foundation has to be reverence, the awareness that, "It's not about you."

בכל מיני עבודת עבד. והנה ה' נצב עליו ומלא כל
האלץ כבודו ומביט עליו ובוחן כליות ולב אם עובדו
כראוי. ועל כן צריך לעבוד לפניו באימה ובידאה 56B
כעומד לפני המלך ויעמיק במחשבה זו ויאריך בה כפי

Bachaye to *Genesis* 38:30). For the people to be in a relationship with the king, and be bound by his rulings, they must first crown Him and accept Him as their leader.

So, as strange as it may sound, *G-d wouldn't be a "king" without you*. He would be a dictator, but not a king, something which requires your acceptance.

And since, as we learned above, "He has disregarded" the rest of the universe, "and has specified His desire to be worshiped as King... by you, in particular," it follows that *the entire universe only exists for the sake of your worship.*

So when you, "accept upon yourself G-d's sovereign authority, that He is to be your King over you," you make the whole universe worthwhile.

וּלְעָבְדוֹ וְלַעֲשׂוֹת רְצוֹנוֹ בְּכָל מִינֵי עֲבוֹדַת עֶבֶד — Accepting G-d's authority means **to worship Him and to carry out His will, with all the different types of service required from a servant** (see *Ramban* to *Deuteronomy* 6:13).

You come to realize that the reason why you're here is for something much bigger than your own personal fulfillment and happiness. It's even bigger than your relationships, your career, your hopes and your wishes. Why were you put on this earth? You were born because G-d wanted you to fulfill His intent.

So you choose to express your relationship with G-d not only in your heart, but in *every aspect of your life,* through worshiping Him and carrying out His will.

11TH NISAN LEAP

The final section of this meditation encourages you to contemplate: 4) G-d's vigilance over all your actions, and His intimate awareness and concern with what you are doing.

וְהִנֵּה ה' נִצָּב עָלָיו — And, *"Look! G-d is standing over you!"* (see *Genesis* 28:13), וּמָלֹא וּמַבִּיט עָלָיו — and, *"all the earth is filled with His glory"* (*Isaiah* 6:3), כָל הָאָרֶץ כְּבוֹדוֹ — and He's watching you, *"He's checking (your)* וּבוֹחֵן כְּלָיוֹת וָלֵב אִם עוֹבְדוֹ כָּרָאוּי *inclinations and heart"* (*Jeremiah* 11:20), **to see if you're worshiping Him properly.**

The conclusion of these four points of meditation is:

וְעַל כֵּן צָרִיךְ לַעֲבוֹד לְפָנָיו בְּאֵימָה וּבְיִרְאָה — **And therefore you ought to worship Him with awe and reverence,** כְּעוֹמֵד לִפְנֵי הַמֶּלֶךְ — and your awareness of His presence should be palpable and tangible, **as if you were standing right in front of a king.**

You might imagine that by "letting go" and accepting G-d's authority you will be unhealthily denying your needs, urges and individuality. In reality, the opposite is true: Your sacred inner core, which subconsciously influences all of your thoughts and interactions with others, desperately needs to surrender itself, like a burning

יכולת השגת מוחו ומחשבתו וכפי הפנאי שלו לפני
עסק התורה או המצוה כמו לפני לבישת טלית ותפילין

flame needs oxygen. Self-centeredness starves that flame; surrender fuels it. So by
"letting go," you don't deny yourself, you discover yourself. *This isn't something
that erodes your identity... to the contrary, this is your identity"* (*Likutei Sichos* vol.
5, p. 246).

וְיַעֲמִיק בְּמַחֲשָׁבָה זוֹ וְיַאֲרִיךְ בָּה — **And you should think deeply about** all of **this, at
length,** כְּפִי יְכוֹלֶת הַשָּׂגַת מוֹחוֹ וּמַחֲשַׁבְתּוֹ — **however much your mind and thoughts
can grasp,** וּכְפִי הַפְּנַאי שֶׁלוֹ — **and according to your time
constraints,** לִפְנֵי עֵסֶק הַתּוֹרָה אוֹ הַמִּצְוָה — **especially before studying Torah or** performing a *mitzvah,* כְּמוֹ לִפְנֵי
לְבִישַׁת טַלִּית וּתְפִילִין — **such as** the daily worship of **don-
ning a *tallis* and** then ***tefillin.***

**Accepting G-d's
authority (*kabolas ol*)
must be the beginning
of all worship.**

**To acquire *kabolas ol*
contemplate how: 1.)
G-d is all powerful;
2.) He fills heaven
and earth; 3.) He
wants to have a
personal relationship
with you; and 4.)
Everything you do
matters to Him.**

**Think about all this
especially before
performing a *mitzvah*.**

As we learned above in chapter 4 (p. 66), the Torah was
not merely given *from* heaven, it's a taste of heaven *itself*.
The *mitzvos* and Torah texts provide Divine "clothing"
into which every part of your consciousness and behavior
can "dress" itself, to access G-d's Infinite Light. So when
you're about to observe a *mitzvah* or study Torah, it's important that you focus on what's inside the "clothing" (the
Divine will), and not let it be obscured by the "clothing"
itself (the reason for the *mitzvah* and the details of its observance).

And that's why the above meditation is extremely important *"before studying Torah or performing a mitzvah."*
Preparing yourself *"to worship Him and to carry out His
will, in any fashion that might be required of a servant,"*
means that you are focusing on the *mitzvah* as an instrument of Divine will, which is its core identity and inner
energy.

Even if the *mitzvah* has an obvious reason (such as
"don't kill" or "give charity"), it's important that you "accept G-d's sovereign authority" and be conscious of the
mitzvah as the Divine will, *before* you focus on the *mitzvah's* reason or utility. Because, in that way, you will access the inner light of the *mitzvah*, which is its most
powerful, transcendent energy.

But remember, accepting G-d's authority (*Kabolas Ol*), doesn't *in and of itself*
connect you to G-d. It's the *mitzvah* that is the Divine will, and that is what forms
your connection with G-d. *Kabolas Ol* opens you up and sensitizes you to the Divine
light within the *mitzvah*. It helps you focus on what the *mitzvah* is really about, And
that's why you should do the above meditation before studying Torah or performing
a *mitzvah* (see *Sefer Ha-Ma'amarim Melukat,* vol. 2, p. 20; vol. 5, p. 96).

וגם יתבונן איך שאור אין סוף ב"ה הסובב כל עלמין
וממלא כל עלמין הוא רצון העליון הוא מלובש באותיו'
וחכמת התורה או בציצית ותפילין אלו ובקריאתו או
בלבישתו הוא ממשיך אורו ית' עליו דהיינו על חלק
אלוה ממעל שבתוך גופו ליכלל וליבטל באורו יתברך

SECTION THREE: A REVERENCE MEDITATION

18TH NISAN REGULAR | 12TH NISAN LEAP

The first meditation above, was a basic preparedness and willingness to let G-d into your life, to "*accept* G-d's sovereign authority." A second phase, which you will aim for in the following three meditations, is a feeling of genuine reverence; a deeper connection where you progressively *absorb* and *internalize* the reality of G-d, (and "'pull' upon yourself G-d's Blessed Infinite Light").

אֵיךְ שֶׁאוֹר אֵין סוֹף בָּרוּךְ הוּא הַסּוֹבֵב כָּל — **You should also contemplate,** וְגַם יִתְבּוֹנֵן עָלְמִין וּמְמַלֵּא כָּל עָלְמִין — **how the Blessed Infinite Light, which** *"fills all worlds"* and *"transcends all worlds,"* הוּא רָצוֹן הָעֶלְיוֹן הוּא מְלוּבָּשׁ בְּאוֹתִיּוֹת וְחָכְמַת הַתּוֹרָה — *is* **the Divine will expressed** in an undiluted fashion **in the Torah** you are reading, **in its texts and ideas,** אוֹ בְּצִיצִית וּתְפִילִין אֵלוּ — **or in these** *tzitzis* **or** *tefillin* you are putting on, וּבִקְרִיאָתוֹ אוֹ בִּלְבִישָׁתוֹ — **and by reading** this Torah text, **or putting on** these *tzitzis* or *tefilin,* הוּא מַמְשִׁיךְ אוֹרוֹ יִתְבָּרֵךְ עָלָיו — **you "pull" upon yourself G-d's Blessed Light.**

דְּהַיְינוּ עַל חֵלֶק אֱלוֹהַּ מִמַּעַל — **The way this works is that** this light is "pulled" **upon** your Divine Soul, *"a piece of G-d above"* (*Job* 31:2; see chapter 2, p. 44), שֶׁבְּתוֹךְ גּוּפוֹ — **which is inside your body** and engages your body in the *mitzvah* act, לִיכָּלֵל וְלִיבָּטֵל בְּאוֹרוֹ יִתְבָּרֵךְ — **causing you to be "absorbed" and lose your** separate **identity within G-d's Blessed light.**

As your ego weakens and more of your inner being is receptive to G-d's light, you will begin to lose a sense of separateness from G-d. With each *mitzvah*, you open yourself up to the light which is shining on you at that moment, rendering yourself translucent to the Divine.

Obviously, this takes a lot more spiritual work than our first meditation. It's a kind of "phase 2" in your relationship with G-d, where the ego shifts from merely *recognizing* there is a higher power, and now aims to *vacate* its perception of separate self. You begin to shed the urge to do anything other than act as an instrument for the Divine will, becoming *"absorbed and losing your separate identity within G-d's Blessed light"* (see *Sichos Kodesh* 5732, vol. 2, pp. 254-5; *ibid.* 5733, vol. 2, p. 164).

PRACTICAL LESSONS

After you accept G-d's authority, you can then deepen the relationship by *absorbing and internalizing* your reverence for G-d's light — the light that you "pull" onto yourself when observing a *mitzvah*.

ודרך פרט בתפילין ליבטל וליכלל בחי' חכמתו ובינתו
שבנפשו האלהית בבחי' חכמתו ובינתו של א"ס ב"ה
המלובשות דרך פרט בפ' קדש והיה כי יביאך דהיינו
שלא להשתמש בחכמתו ובינתו שבנפשו בלתי לה'

SECTION FOUR: A REVERENCE MEDITATION FOR TEFILLIN

לִיבָּטֵל וְלִיכָּלֵל בְּחִינַת חָכְמָתוֹ — In the particular case of tefillin, וְדֶרֶךְ פְּרָט בִּתְפִילִין
— contemplate, וּבִינָתוֹ שֶׁבְּנַפְשׁוֹ הָאֱלֹהִית בִּבְחִינַת חָכְמָתוֹ וּבִינָתוֹ שֶׁל אֵין סוֹף בָּרוּךְ הוּא
that the chochmah (inquiry) and binah (cognition) powers of your Divine Soul
should lose their identity and be absorbed in the chochmah and binah powers of
the Blessed Infinite One.

A mitzvah, as we have just seen, "dissolves" your body and soul into G-d's light.
Tefillin, targets the mind in particular, allowing your mental powers to be raised up
and absorbed in G-d's mental powers.

הַמְלוּבָּשׁוֹת דֶּרֶךְ פְּרָט בִּפְרָשִׁיּוֹת — Since, as the Zohar (3, 262a-b) teaches, G-d's
chochmah and binah powers take expression, in particular, in two of the four sacred passages written on parchment inside the tefillin:

קֹדֶשׁ — The passage, "Sanctify to Me every firstborn, the first of each womb" (Exodus 13:1-10), has the energy of G-d's chochmah, the first stage of Divine emanation
towards the creations, which, like a womb, "opens the
whole flow of mercy and supernal light" (Zohar ibid.).

וְהָיָה כִּי יְבִיאֲךָ — And the passage inside the tefillin, beginning, "There will come a time when you will be brought,
by G-d, into the land of the Canaanites " (ibid. 11-16), has
the energy of G-d's binah, (hinted to by the fact that the
Torah mentions the Exodus from Egypt fifty times, corresponding to the "fifty gates" of binah—Zohar ibid).

דְּהַיְינוּ שֶׁלֹּא לְהִשְׁתַּמֵּשׁ בְּחָכְמָתוֹ וּבִינָתוֹ שֶׁבְּנַפְשׁוֹ בִּלְתִּי לַה'
לְבַדּוֹ — And so the result of your meditation on the first
two passages of tefillin should be the feeling that you're
not going to use your soul's chochmah and binah for
anything other than G-d alone.

Worshiping G-d doesn't mean that you lose all sense of rationality and intuition.
G-d doesn't want you to become a robot; He gave you mental powers so that you
dedicate them to His worship. And putting on tefillin helps you do that, because it
floods your powers of inquiry and cognition with Divine light.

In the second half of this meditation, we turn to the power of tefillin to refine your
emotions. As we learned above, (see p. 62), the transition from thinking to feeling takes place via the agency of da'as, (recognition; discernment), through which

לבדו וכן ליבטל ולכלול בחי' הדעת שבנפשו הכולל
חו"ג שהן יראה ואהבה שבלבו בבחי' דעת העליון
הכולל חו"ג המלובש בפ' שמע והיה אם שמוע והיינו
כמ"ש בש"ע לשעבד הלב והמוח כו' ובעטיפת ציצית

ideas become personally relevant. And this leads to the entire range of human emotions, which, broadly speaking, fall into the two categories of *chesed* (love; giving), and *gevurah* (discipline; fear).

וְכֵן — **And similarly** you should contemplate when putting on *tefillin,* לִיבָּטֵל וְלִיכָּלֵל בְּחִינַת הַדַּעַת שֶׁבְּנַפְשׁוֹ — **that your soul's power of *da'as* should lose its** separate **identity and be absorbed in G-d's *da'as*.**

הַכּוֹלֵל חֶסֶד וּגְבוּרָה שֶׁהֵן יִרְאָה וְאַהֲבָה שֶׁבְּלִבּוֹ — And since it is *da'as* that gives rise to all emotions, beginning with *chesed* and *gevurah,* when your *da'as* become absorbed in G-d's, **it** automatically **incorporates your *chesed* and *gevurah,* which are the reverence and love in your heart,** בִּבְחִינַת דַּעַת הָעֶלְיוֹן הַכּוֹלֵל חֶסֶד וּגְבוּרָה — when you put on *tefillin,* all of this becomes absorbed in G-d's **supernal *da'as,*** **which incorporates His *chesed* and *gevurah*.**

הַמְלוּבָּשׁ בְּפָרְשִׁיּוֹת — The two other **passages** in the *tefillin* **express** G-d's *chesed* and *gevurah,* שְׁמַע — the passage beginning, *"Hear O Israel... you should love..."* (Deuteronomy 6:4-9), corresponds to *chesed,* וְהָיָה אִם שָׁמוֹעַ — and the passage beginning, *"And if you will listen..."* (ibid. 11:13-21), corresponds to *gevurah,* since it speaks of Divine anger, *"beware not to let your heart be lured away... then the anger of G-d will be kindled against you"* (ibid. 16-17).

וְהַיְינוּ כְּמוֹ שֶׁכָּתוּב בְּשֻׁלְחָן עָרוּךְ — **And this** entire meditation is really an elaboration of the basic requirement **stated in the *Code of Jewish Law,*** לְשַׁעְבֵּד הַלֵּב וְהַמּוֹחַ כוּ' — that when putting on *tefillin,* you ought to contemplate that **you are placing your heart and mind** exclusively in G-d's **service** (Orach Chaim 25:5).

SECTION FIVE: A MEDITATION WHEN WEARING THE TALLIS

13TH NISAN LEAP

וּבַעֲטִיפַת צִיצִית — **And, when** you're **wrapped in** a *tallis,* adorned with **tzitzis,** carry out the following meditation.

It's somewhat perplexing that the *Tanya* offers this meditation for the *tallis, after* the meditation for *tefillin,* when practically speaking we put on the *tallis before* the *tefillin.* So it seems that we're speaking here of a *tallis* meditation *after tefillin have been put on.* In other words, this is a more advanced "phase 2" meditation, where G-d's light is absorbed not only into your heart and mind (with *tefillin*), but into your entire being, through the *tallis,* as we shall see (Sichos Kodesh, ibid.).

יכוין כמ"ש בזהר להמשיך עליו מלכותו ית' אשר היא
מלכות כל עולמים וכו' לייחדה עלינו מצוה זו והוא
כענין שום תשים עליך מלך ואזי אף אם בכל זאת לא

לְהַמְשִׁיךְ עָלָיו — **Contemplate what is written in the** *Zohar*, יְכַוֵּין כְּמוֹ שֶׁכָּתוּב בַּזֹהַר
מַלְכוּתוֹ יִתְבָּרֵךְ — that when doing this *mitzvah* you ought **to draw upon yourself G-d's sovereign authority.**

The difference between phases 1 and 2, is that in phase 1 you merely, "*accept* upon yourself G-d's sovereign authority," whereas in phase 2 your soul powers "lose their separate identity and are absorbed" in G-d's light, as you become one with G-d. This final meditation completes this process, to "draw upon yourself" G-d's light upon your *whole being* so that "you lose your separate identity (completely) and are absorbed within G-d's Blessed light."

PRACTICAL LESSONS

When you are wearing the *tallis*, contemplate how your whole being is absorbed in G-d's light.

אֲשֶׁר הִיא מַלְכוּת כָּל עוֹלָמִים וְכוּ' — **Contemplate that** even though G-d's authority **"*rules over all worlds etc.,*"** (*Psalms* 145:13), לְיַחֲדָה עָלֵינוּ — nevertheless, He has **specified** His desire to be worshiped **by us,** through the Torah, זוֹ — עַל יְדֵי מִצְוָה — **and through** observing **this** *mitzvah,* your whole being will internalize this reality.

Most *mitzvos* have a specific theme, relating to a particular element of worship. But, even though it's just one *mitzvah*, the *tallis* has the theme of accepting G-d's authority and worshiping Him *in general,* That's because the *tallis* engulfs your whole body, representing the alignment of your whole being with G-d.

וְהוּא כְּעִנְיַן שׁוּם תָּשִׂים עָלֶיךָ מֶלֶךְ — So putting on the *tallis* **is similar to the idea,** *"you shall surely place a king over yourself"* (*Deuteronomy* 17:15).

The verse, "you shall surely place a king over yourself," implies that until this point you were merely *willing* to have G-d as your king, but it is now, when wearing a *tallis,* that you are *entering fully* into that relationship.

SECTION SIX: WHY REVERENCE IS NEEDED FOR "FULL SERVICE"

We have now learned a series of meditations to a.) evoke the *acceptance* of G-d's authority (*Kabolas Ol*), and b.) foster a sense of mental or emotional *reverence*. The *Tanya* will now stress that both 'a' and 'b' are necessary for your *mitzvos* to be considered "full service" of G-d, ("*with a full heart*"—1 Chronicles 29:9; see Rabbi Shmuel Schneersohn, *Toras Shmuel, Mayim Rabim* 5636, p. 220).

וַאֲזַי אַף אִם בְּכָל זֹאת לֹא תִפּוֹל עָלָיו אֵימָה וָפַחַד בְּהִתְגַּלּוּת לִבּוֹ — **And then, even if** after contemplating **all of this doesn't result in a feeling of awe and trepidation**

תפול עליו אימה ופחד בהתגלות לבו מ"מ מאחר
שמקבל עליו מלכות שמים וממשיך עליו יראתו ית'
בהתגלות מחשבתו ורצונו שבמוחו וקבלה זו היא
אמיתית בלי שום ספק שהרי היא טבע נפשות כל
ישראל שלא למרוד במלך הקדוש ית' הרי התורה
שלומד או המצוה שעושה מחמת קבלה זו ומחמת
המשכת היראה שבמוחו נקראות בשם עבודה שלימה
ככל עבודת העבד לאדונו ומלכו מש"כ אם לומד   57A

מִכָּל מָקוֹם מֵאַחַר שֶׁמְּקַבֵּל עָלֶיךָ מַלְכוּת שָׁמַיִם, **actually coming upon your heart,** **nevertheless, since you've:** a.) **accepted G-d's sovereign authority,** וּמַמְשִׁיךְ עָלֶיךָ יְרָאתוֹ יִתְבָּרֵךְ בְּהִתְגַּלּוּת מַחֲשַׁבְתּוֹ וּרְצוֹנוֹ שֶׁבְּמוֹחוֹ — **and** b.) **you've drawn upon yourself a conscious reverence of G-d** at least **in your thoughts and in the will-power of your brain,** your acceptance of G-d's authority and mental reverence *together* are enough for your worship to be authentic; what the *Tanya* will soon refer to as "full service."

But if you don't feel like a servant of G-d in your heart, only in your mind, couldn't that signify that you don't really mean it authentically?

וְקַבָּלָה זוֹ הִיא אֲמִתִּית בְּלִי שׁוּם סָפֵק — **And** even though you don't feel it palpably in your heart, **this** mental **acceptance** of G-d's authority **is, without doubt, authentic,** שֶׁהֲרֵי הִיא טֶבַע נַפְשׁוֹת כָּל יִשְׂרָאֵל שֶׁלֹּא לִמְרוֹד בַּמֶּלֶךְ הַקָּדוֹשׁ יִתְבָּרֵךְ — **because all of Israel have it in their inherent soul disposition not to be insubordinate to the Blessed Holy King.**

הֲרֵי הַתּוֹרָה שֶׁלּוֹמֵד אוֹ הַמִּצְוָה שֶׁעוֹשֶׂה — **So the Torah that you study or the mitzvah that you perform,** מֵחֲמַת קַבָּלָה זוֹ — a.) **as a result of this acceptance** of G-d's authority, וּמֵחֲמַת הַמְשָׁכַת הַיִּרְאָה שֶׁבְּמוֹחוֹ — **and** b.) **as a result the conscious reverence felt** at least **in your brain,** נִקְרָאוֹת בְּשֵׁם עֲבוֹדָה שְׁלֵימָה — **is called "full service"** of G-d, כְּכָל עֲבוֹדַת הָעֶבֶד לַאֲדוֹנוֹ וּמַלְכוֹ — **like any service offered by a** loyal **servant to his master or king,** which is considered "full" so long as the work is done conscientiously and eagerly.

The *Tanya* requires both acceptance of G-d's authority *and* reverence for your worship to be considered "full service" (*Sefer Ha-Ma'amarim Melukat,* vol. 3, p. 264).

A CHASIDIC THOUGHT

Deep down, you do want to worship G-d. So whenever that sentiment surfaces consciously, even if it's only in your mind and not in your heart, you can be assured that it's genuine.

וּמְקַיֵּם הַמִּצְוָה בְּאַהֲבָה לְבַדָּהּ כְּדֵי לְדָבְקָה בּוֹ עַל יְדֵי
תּוֹרָתוֹ וּמִצְוֹתָיו אֵינָהּ נִקְרֵאת בְּשֵׁם עֲבוֹדַת הָעֶבֶד
וְהַתּוֹרָה אָמְרָה וַעֲבַדְתֶּם אֵת ה' אֱלֹהֵיכֶם וְגו' וְאוֹתוֹ

14TH NISAN LEAP

Later in this chapter we will discuss the status of worship carried out with acceptance of G-d's authority *alone*, without any mental or emotional reverence, and we will argue that it still represents a level of "service," albeit not a "full" one (see pp. 505-7). But, as the *Tanya* will now demonstrate, worship that is not motivated by any acceptance of G-d's authority *at all* is not considered "service," even if it is motivated by love.

מַה שֶּׁאֵין כֵּן לוֹמֵד וּמְקַיֵּים הַמִּצְוָה בְּאַהֲבָה לְבַדָּה — **This is not the case, however, if you study** Torah **or observe a** *mitzvah* **out of love alone,** without any basic obedience or reverence *at that moment,* it's not considered "service" of G-d at all.

It could be the case that *generally speaking* you do accept G-d's authority and you do revere Him. But for your act of Torah study or *mitzvah* to be considered genuine "service" of G-d (and not self-service) it needs to be *directly associated* with an acceptance of G-d's authority. And that's true even if you're observing a positive command, which is typically considered to be more of an expression of love than reverence (*Notes on Tanya*).

כְּדֵי לְדָבְקָה בּוֹ עַל יְדֵי תּוֹרָתוֹ וּמִצְוֹתָיו — **If you performed a** *mitzvah* exclusively with a feeling of love, that you want **to connect to Him though His Torah and His** *mitzvos* but you lacked an acceptance of G-d's authority at that moment, אֵינָהּ נִקְרֵאת בְּשֵׁם עֲבוֹדַת הָעֶבֶד — **it wouldn't be termed "service" of a** loyal **servant.**

Why is it so important that your worship (is motivated by acceptance of G-d's authority and as a result) falls under the category of "service"? What's lacking if you just perform a *mitzvah* because you love G-d, and you don't act like an obedient servant?

The *Tanya* now brings clarification of this point from both Scripture and the *Zohar*.

PRACTICAL LESSONS

Kabolas ol / reverence must be the foundation of all worship, even the observance of positive commands, because it gets you out of your ego and makes sure you're really doing the *mitzvah* for G-d, and not for yourself.

וְהַתּוֹרָה אָמְרָה וַעֲבַדְתֶּם אֵת ה' אֱלֹהֵיכֶם וְגו' — "Service" of G-d is necessary **since the Torah has said, "You shall serve G-d, your G-d etc.,"** (*Exodus* 23:25), וְאוֹתוֹ תַעֲבֹדוּ וְגו' — **and, "It is Him that you shall serve etc.,"** (*Deuteronomy* 13:5).

The fact that the Torah describes *all* worship of G-d as "service," indicates that accepting His authority and reverence should underlie each and every act of worship.

תעבודו וגו' וכמ"ש בזהר [פ' בהר] כהאי תורא
דיהבין עליה עול בקדמיתא בגין לאפקא מיניה טב
לעלמא כו' הכי נמי אצטריך לב"נ לקבלא עליה עול
מלכות שמים בקדמיתא כו' ואי האי לא אשתכח גביה
לא שריא ביה קדוש' כו' [ובר"מ שם ד' קי"א ע"ב] שכל
אדם צ"ל בשתי בחי' ומדרגות והן בחי' עבד ובחי' בן

[פָּרָשַׁת בְּהַר] וּכְמוֹ שֶׁכָּתוּב בַּזֹהַר — **And as the *Zohar* states, in *Parshas Behar* —** כְּהַאי תּוֹרָא דְּיָהֲבִין עֲלֵיהּ עוֹל בְּקַדְמֵיתָא בְּגִין לְאַפְּקָא מִינֵּיהּ טַב לְעָלְמָא כוּ' (3,108a), ***"like an ox that must first have a yoke placed upon it, so that it can become useful to the world...,"*** הָכֵי נַמֵי אִצְטְרִיךְ לְבַר נַשׁ לְקַבְּלָא עֲלֵיהּ עוֹל מַלְכוּת שָׁמַיִם בְּקַדְמֵיתָא כוּ' — ***"likewise, a person must first accept the 'yoke' (of G-d's sovereign authority)..."*** וְאִי הַאי לָא אִשְׁתְּכַח גַּבֵּיהּ לָא שַׁרְיָא בֵּיהּ קְדוּשָׁה כוּ' — ***"and if this doesn't happen to him, holiness won't rest on him...."***

This citation from the *Zohar* stresses two points:

1.) In the traditional paradigm, you are told to accept G-d's authority and obey Him because He's more powerful than you, and you do so because you're afraid of punishment. That's because you look at yourself as a tiny, separate fragment in the universe that could easily be crushed, so you obey the Master of the Universe to ensure the continuation of your (separate) survival.

But in the Chasidic/Mystical paradigm you see yourself as fundamentally inter-connected with G-d's light and everything in the universe. You seek a growing openness and a gradual dissolution of the separation between yourself, your environment and G-d. You know that your narcissistic shell and ego need to be loosened, rather like unclenching a fist, in order for you to become more open to the infinite. So you look at acceptance of G-d's authority (*kabolas ol*) as your key to transcending the ego and accessing sacred light — *"If this (kabolas ol) doesn't happen to him, then holiness won't rest on him."*

2.) The *Zohar* emphasizes that *kabolas ol* is necessary for *positive* activity, "like an ox that must first have a yoke placed upon it, *so that it can become useful to the world.*" This supports the *Tanya's* assertion throughout this chapter that *kabolas ol* should motivate even the observance of positive commands (*Notes on Tanya*).

[וּבְרַעְיָא מְהֵימְנָא שָׁם דַּף קי"א עַמּוּד ב'] — **And in** the section of the *Zohar* **ibid.** entitled ***Raya Mehemna* page 111b,** שֶׁכָּל אָדָם צָרִיךְ לִהְיוֹת בִּשְׁתֵּי בְּחִינוֹת וּמַדְרֵגוֹת — it's taught **that every person ought to function in two ways,** *i.e.,* **two levels** in his or her relationship with G-d, וְהֵן בְּחִינַת עֶבֶד וּבְחִינַת בֵּן — **both as a "servant"** who acts out of reverence and trepidation, **and as a "child,"** who acts out of love.

The *Zohar* (ibid.) teaches: *"Israel are referred to with two names by the Blessed Holy One. They are called 'servants,' as the verse states, "They are My servants"* (*Leviticus* 25:55); *and they are called 'children,' as the verse states, "You are chil-*

ואף דיש בן שהוא ג״כ עבד הרי אי אפשר לבא
למדרגה זו בלי קדימת היראה עילאה כידוע ליודעים:

dren to G-d your G-d" (*Deuteronomy* 14:1)..... *But though you are called a 'child'...
you must not exclude yourself from being a 'servant' who serves his Father in everything that glorifies His Father."*

This adds further support to the *Tanya's* assertion in this chapter, that *kabolas ol*
and reverence (the approach of the "servant") applies to all worship, "*everything
that glorifies His Father,*" even positive commands.

וְאַף דְּיֵשׁ בֵּן שֶׁהוּא גַם כֵּן עֶבֶד — **And while there is such a thing as a "child" who also**
has the virtues of **a "servant,"** this doesn't invalidate the above point.

A child may love his or her parent so much that he or she is totally devoted to the
parent and wants nothing other than to fulfill the wishes of the parent (see *Zohar*
cited in chapter 10, p. 129). Couldn't you, in a similar fashion, just love G-d so much,
and so selflessly, that you'd be willing to do anything that He wants? There does
seem to be a scenario where love alone *could* motivate a person to the level of
"service" without the need for *kabolas ol* and reverence, a conclusion which is at
odds with the theme of this chapter.

The *Tanya* answers:

הֲרֵי אִי אֶפְשָׁר לָבֹא לְמַדְרֵגָה זוֹ בְּלִי קְדִימַת הַיִּרְאָה עִילָאָה — **But** while there is such a
thing as a "child" who is motivated only by love and not reverence, **it's impossible
to reach such a level without *first* acquiring "higher reverence,"** כַּיָּדוּעַ לַיּוֹדְעִים —
as intelligent people realize.

As we shall see in the coming chapters, love and reverence are experiences
which follow a *developmental line*. "Selfless love" ("the 'child' who is also a 'servant'") is, in all but the most mature cases, a contradiction in terms, because love is
usually an expression of self. "Selfless love" does exist, but it is an advanced state
which must be preceded by a series of emotional growth phases. Most notably,
the *Tanya* stresses here, "selfless love" must follow a deeply transpersonal phase
which the *Zohar* refers to as "higher reverence." We will discuss below exactly what
this means, but it's clear that there is no path to worship that does not begin with,
and is not built on, reverence.

SECTION SEVEN: WHEN REVERENCE IS LACKING

19TH NISAN REGULAR | 15TH NISAN LEAP

In the previous section the *Tanya* stressed that "full service" of G-d requires both
acceptance of G-d's authority and reverence. But what if you manage one without
the other (phase 1 without phase 2)? Your meditations bring you to a basic acceptance of G-d authority, but you can't manage to feel any reverence, even in your
mind.

וְהִנֵּה אַף מִי שֶׁגַּם בְּמוֹחוֹ וּבְמַחֲשַׁבְתּוֹ אֵינוֹ מַרְגִּישׁ שׁוּם
יִרְאָה וּבוּשָׁה מִפְּנֵי פְּחִיתוּת עֵרֶךְ נַפְשׁוֹ מִמְּקוֹר חוּצְבָה
מִמַּדְרֵגוֹת תַּחְתּוֹנוֹ' דִּי"ס דַעֲשִׂיָּה אעפ"כ מֵאַחַר שֶׁמִּתְכַּוֵּין
בַּעֲבוֹדָתוֹ כְּדֵי לַעֲבוֹד אֶת הַמֶּלֶךְ הֲרֵי זוֹ עֲבוֹדָה גְּמוּרָה
כִּי הַיִּרְאָה וְהָעֲבוֹדָה נֶחְשָׁבוֹת לִשְׁתֵּי מִצְוֹת בְּמִנְיָן תרי"ג
וְאֵינָן מְעַכְּבוֹת זוֹ אֶת זוֹ. וְעוֹד שֶׁבֶּאֱמֶת מְקַיֵּם גַּם מִצְוַת

וְהִנֵּה אַף מִי שֶׁגַּם בְּמוֹחוֹ וּבְמַחֲשַׁבְתּוֹ אֵינוֹ מַרְגִּישׁ שׁוּם יִרְאָה וּבוּשָׁה — **Now even if** after following the above meditative practice, **you can't feel *any* sense of reverence or shame** to be in the presence of G-d, **even in your mind and thoughts,** מִפְּנֵי פְּחִיתוּת עֵרֶךְ נַפְשׁוֹ — **due to the poor quality of your soul,** מִמְּקוֹר חוּצְבָה מִמַּדְרֵגוֹת תַּחְתּוֹנוֹת דִּי' סְפִירוֹת דַעֲשִׂיָּה — **which was carved from its source in the lowest levels of the ten *sefiros* of the lowest world, *Asiyah*.**

Even if we attribute your failure to generate any feelings of reverence to weak soul powers, that still doesn't absolve you from the problem. If reverence is required for "full service," and you can't muster any reverence at all, where does that leave your worship?

אַף עַל פִּי כֵן מֵאַחַר שֶׁמִּתְכַּוֵּין בַּעֲבוֹדָתוֹ כְּדֵי לַעֲבוֹד אֶת הַמֶּלֶךְ הֲרֵי זוֹ עֲבוֹדָה גְּמוּרָה — **Nevertheless,** even in the absence of any sense of emotional/mental reverence (phase 2), **since your worship is done with the intention to serve the King** of the universe, and not for your own self-gratification, **it's an "intact worship."**

With *kabolas ol* and reverence (phases 1 and 2), your worship is "full"; but with *kabolas ol* alone, it's merely "intact," i.e., it's not lacking any disqualifying quality.

This seems to be at odds with our thinking throughout the chapter, which has stressed the extreme importance of reverence. So the *Tanya* now clarifies:

כִּי הַיִּרְאָה וְהָעֲבוֹדָה נֶחְשָׁבוֹת לִשְׁתֵּי מִצְוֹת בְּמִנְיָן תרי"ג — **Because in the enumeration of 613 *mitzvos*, "reverence" and "service" are counted as separate *mitzvos*** (*Bahag*; *Ramban*, notes to *Sefer Ha-Mitzvos*, positive command 5), וְאֵינָן מְעַכְּבוֹת זוֹ אֶת זוֹ — **and** therefore failure in **one doesn't invalidate the other.**

Jewish legal texts indicate that "service" (which is based on *kabolas ol*) and reverence (phase 2) are two separate requirements. And that's why your service remains "intact," even in the absence of reverence.

Now the *Tanya* will argue that even in the absence of an emotional or mental reverence of G-d, there is likely to be some sort of respect for G-d, at the very least, which could qualify as a very minimal level of "reverence."

וְעוֹד — **And what's more,** even if you just have *kabolas ol* and fail to feel any reverence in your heart or mind, שֶׁבֶּאֱמֶת מְקַיֵּם גַּם מִצְוַת יִרְאָה — **you will in fact fulfill the** minimal **biblical requirement of "reverence"** so long as you have a basic feeling of respect towards G-d.

יראה במה שממשיך היראה במחשבתו כי בשעה ורגע
זו עכ"פ מורא שמים עליו עכ"פ כמורא בשר ודם הדיוט
לפחות שאינו מלך המביט עליו שנמנע בעבורו מלעשות
דבר שאינו הגון בעיניו שזו נק' יראה כמו שאמר
רבן יוחנן בן זכאי לתלמידיו יהי רצון שיהא מורא
שמים עליכם כמורא בשר ודם כו' תדעו כשאדם עובר
עבירה אומר שלא יראני אדם כו' רק שיראה זו נקראת

בְּמַה שֶׁמַּמְשִׁיךְ הַיִּרְאָה בְּמַחֲשַׁבְתּוֹ — This minimal "reverence" consists of your conscious awareness, כִּי בְּשָׁעָה וְרֶגַע זוֹ עַל כָּל פָּנִים — that, at least during this specific moment when you are observing the mitzvah, מוֹרָא שָׁמַיִם עָלָיו עַל כָּל פָּנִים כְּמוֹרָא — you're respectful of G-d at least as much as you would be respectful of an ordinary human being (not a king) who's watching you, בָּשָׂר וָדָם הֶדְיוֹט לְפָחוֹת שֶׁאֵינוֹ מֶלֶךְ הַמַּבִּיט עָלָיו שֶׁנִּמְנָע בַּעֲבוּרוֹ מִלַעֲשׂוֹת דָּבָר שֶׁאֵינוֹ הָגוּן בְּעֵינָיו — since even when being watched by a human being that you respect, **you'd refrain from doing something that he found inappropriate.**

שֶׁזּוֹ נִקְרֵאת יִרְאָה — **This,** basic respect, **is considered** fulfillment of the basic biblical requirement of **"reverence."**

PRACTICAL LESSONS

If you have kabolas ol, even if you don't feel reverence for G-d (even in your mind), then your worship is "intact." If you feel reverence too, your worship is "full."

But without any kabolas ol you're not really serving G-d at all.

If you don't feel reverence for G-d (even in your mind), but you observe the mitzvos simply because you feel He's watching you, that counts as "reverence."

We're speaking here about an inappropriate act which, if nobody was watching, you would have done; or a good deed which, if nobody was watching, you wouldn't have bothered to do. The mere presence of a respectable onlooker is enough to motivate you to behave appropriately. If you can respect G-d at least as much as that, then, in a very minimal way, you've fulfilled the mitzvah to "revere G-d, your G-d" (Deuteronomy 10:20).

The Tanya now cites a proof from the Talmud that such a basic feeling that "someone is watching so I need to behave" could be considered actual reverence of G-d.

כְּמוֹ שֶׁאָמַר רַבָּן יוֹחָנָן בֶּן זַכַּאי לְתַלְמִידָיו — As Rabbi Yochanan ben Zakai said to his students as a blessing on his deathbed, יְהִי רָצוֹן שֶׁיְּהֵא מוֹרָא שָׁמַיִם עֲלֵיכֶם כְּמוֹרָא בָּשָׂר וָדָם כו' — "May it be G-d's will that you revere Heaven as much as you revere humans," תֵּדְעוּ כְּשֶׁאָדָם עוֹבֵר — and when his students complained, "Is that all?" he replied, "If only it would be so much! **You should know that when a person commits a transgression, he says, 'I hope no man sees me'"** (Talmud, Brachos 28b).

יראה תתאה ויראת חטא שקודמת לחכמתו ויראה
עילאה הוא ירא בושת כו' דאית יראה ואית יראה כו'
אבל בלי יראה כלל לא פרחא לעילא באהבה לבדה 57B
כמו שהעוף אינו יכול לפרוח בכנף אחד דדחילו ורחימו

SECTION EIGHT: WHY LOVE IS ALSO NECESSARY

So far in this chapter we have learned: 1.) That *kabolas ol* (acceptance of G-d's authority) is necessary for your worship to be considered some sort of "service."

2.) For your worship to be considered "full service," it requires also a feeling of reverence.

3.) This reverence should ideally be felt in the heart, though if it is felt in the mind, that's acceptable. In fact, even the basic awareness that someone is watching you from above, is considered reverence.

רַק שֶׁיִּרְאָה זוֹ נִקְרֵאת יִרְאָה תַּתָּאָה — **Only, this reverence,** *i.e.,* all the different levels we have been discussing in this chapter, would all **fall under the category of "lower reverence."**

As we will discuss at length in chapter 43, there are two very different experiences of reverence which can be reached at different stages in your spiritual maturity. Everything we have discussed in this chapter would fall under the category of "lower reverence," the general awareness of G-d's presence, that prompts you to observe His Torah and *mitzvos.*

וְיִרְאַת חֵטְא שֶׁקוֹדֶמֶת לְחָכְמָתוֹ — **And** "lower reverence" falls under the category of **"the reverence *necessary* not to sin, which precedes wisdom, *(i.e. Torah)*"** (see *Mishnah, Avos* 3:9), וְיִרְאָה עִילָאָה הוּא יְרֵא בּוֹשֶׁת כו' — **but "higher reverence" is a reverence** arising from a sense of **shame** in G-d's presence (see *Tikunei Zohar* 5b).

At "lower reverence" you feel the presence of G-d to the extent that you are eager to fulfill His will. At "higher reverence" your sense of His presence is more arresting, you are simply overwhelmed by Him. In other words, at "lower reverence" you revere His will; at "higher reverence" you revere G-d *Himself.* (We will discuss this in detail in chapter 43).

The *Tanya* brings proof from the *Zohar* that there are two categories of reverence.

דְּאִית יִרְאָה וְאִית יִרְאָה כו' — **For *"there's reverence, and then, there's reverence"*** of a different kind (*ibid.* 6a).

We now return to the idea, mentioned at the end of chapter 40, that a *mitzvah* is like a bird that can only fly heavenward if it has two "wings" of reverence and love.

אֲבָל בְּלִי יִרְאָה כְּלָל לָא פָּרְחָא לְעֵילָא בְּאַהֲבָה לְבַדָּה — **But in the absence of any reverence at all,** your *mitzvah* **will not "soar heavenward" with love alone,** כְּמוֹ שֶׁהָעוֹף

הן תרין גדפין [כמ"ש בתיקונים] וכן היראה לבדה היא
כנף אחד ולא פרחא בה לעילא אף שנק' עבודת עבד
וצריך להיות ג"כ בחי' בן לעורר האהבה הטבעית עכ"פ
המסותרת בלבו שתהא בהתגלות מוחו עכ"פ לזכור
אהבתו לה' אחד במחשבתו וברצונו לדבקה בו ית'
וזאת תהיה כוונתו בעסק התורה או המצוה הזו לדבקה

דִּדְחִילוּ וּרְחִימוּ הֵן — just as a bird can't fly with one wing, אֵינוּ יָכוֹל לִפְרוֹחַ בְּכָנָף אֶחָד — as [כְּמוֹ שֶׁכָּתוּב בַּתִּיקוּנִים] — reverence and love being the two wings, תְּרֵין גַּדְפִין — the *Tikunei Zohar* states (25b, see above p. 466).

But the reverse is also true: Despite the very fundamental need for reverence that we have explored in this chapter, if there is no love accompanying your *mitzvah*, it will be "grounded."

PRACTICAL LESSONS

Even if you feel reverence for G-d, your *mitzvah* won't rise to the heavens unless it's also observed out of love for G-d too.

Consider any conscious feelings of love for G-d as authentic, since deep in your soul you really do love G-d.

Practically, "love" means a desire for connection; you observe each *mitzvah* to attach yourself to G-d.

וְכֵן הַיִּרְאָה לְבַדָּה הִיא כָּנָף אֶחָד וְלָא פָּרְחָא בָהּ לְעֵילָא — **And** the same is true if your *mitzvah* is performed **with reverence alone, it will not soar heavenward with just one wing,** אַף שֶׁנִּקְרֵאת עֲבוֹדַת עֶבֶד — for **even though** reverence alone is sufficient for your worship **to be called the work of a** loyal **"servant,"** וְצָרִיךְ לִהְיוֹת גַּם כֵּן בְּחִינַת בֵּן — **you must also** worship G-d **at the level of** a loving **"child"** (see above, pp. 504-5).

As with reverence, if meditation doesn't produce any love in the heart, a feeling in the mind is acceptable.

לְעוֹרֵר הָאַהֲבָה הַטִּבְעִית עַל כָּל פָּנִים הַמְּסוּתֶּרֶת בְּלִבּוֹ — **You** need **to at least awaken the inherent love which is dormant in your heart,** שֶׁתְּהֵא בְּהִתְגַּלּוּת מוֹחוֹ עַל כָּל פָּנִים — and even if you don't feel it in your heart, **it should be at least conscious in your mind,** לִזְכּוֹר אַהֲבָתוֹ לַה' אֶחָד — בְּמַחֲשַׁבְתּוֹ וּבִרְצוֹנוֹ לְדַבְקָה בּוֹ יִתְבָּרֵךְ — **that you call to** mind your love for the One G-d, and your desire to connect with Him.

While the *Tikunei Zohar* stipulates that a *mitzvah* can't rise heavenward without two "wings" of reverence and love, the *Tanya* considers a feeling of reverence and love *in your mind* to be sufficient.

וְזֹאת תִּהְיֶה כַּוָּונָתוֹ בְּעֵסֶק הַתּוֹרָה אוֹ הַמִּצְוָה הַזּוֹ — **And** practically speaking, your feeling of love should be that with **each act of Torah study or *mitzvah* observance, you have the following *kavanah*,** לְדָבְקָה בּוֹ נַפְשׁוֹ הָאֱלֹהִית וְהַחִיּוּנִית

בו נפשו האלהית והחיונית ולבושיהן כנ"ל. אך אמנם
אמרו רז"ל לעולם אל יוציא אדם עצמו מן הכלל לכן
יתכוין ליחד ולדבקה בו ית' מקור נפשו האלהית ומקור
נפשות כל ישראל שהוא רוח פיו ית' הנק' בשם

וְלִבוּשֵׁיהֶן — that you desire **to connect your Divine and energizing** Animal **Souls, together with their "garments"** (of thought, speech and action) **to G-d,** כַּנִּזְכָּר לְעֵיל — **as stated above,** (chapters 23, 35, 37).

Love is the feeling of wanting to come close. In the case of a *mitzvah* it means that your whole being (both your souls and their "garments") embrace and become absorbed in G-d.

SECTION NINE: YOUR MITZVAH CONNECTS ALL SOULS WITH G-D

20TH NISAN REGULAR | 16TH NISAN LEAP

Up to this point we have discussed love of G-d as a *personal* longing for connection. The *Tanya* will now expand the discussion to include how your soul root, which is intrinsically bound with all the souls of Israel, connects to G-d on a *communal* level.

אַךְ אָמְנָם אָמְרוּ רַבּוֹתֵינוּ זִכְרוֹנָם לִבְרָכָה — **However, our Sages of blessed memory have taught,** לְעוֹלָם אַל יוֹצִיא אָדָם עַצְמוֹ מִן הַכְּלָל — *"A person should never exclude himself from the community"* (*Talmud, Brachos* 49b).

Your soul is not an isolated fragment. It's deeply connected with other souls. This awareness ought to be part of your *kavanah* when observing Torah and *mitzvos*.

לָכֵן יִתְכַּוֵּין — **Therefore** when worshiping G-d, **your intent should be,** in addition to everything stated above in this chapter (about love), you ought to have a further, more esoteric intent, לְיַחֵד וּלְדָבְקָה בּוֹ יִתְבָּרֵךְ מְקוֹר נַפְשׁוֹ הָאֱלֹהִית וּמְקוֹר נַפְשׁוֹת כָּל יִשְׂרָאֵל — **to merge with and attach to G-d** not only your own particular soul but also **your Divine Soul's source** which is one and the same as **the source of the souls of all Israel.**

Your soul has different layers and identities. Sometimes we stress its direct connection to G-d, saying that it *"is a piece of G-d, above"* (chapter 2, p. 44). But in this chapter we're going to discuss another element of your soul, its *worldly compatibility*.

The fact that your soul fits in your body and "speaks its language," shows that it has a worldly side. The worldly side of your soul is rooted in a Divine energy that has been diminished and veiled so as to be compatible with the world.

שֶׁהוּא רוּחַ פִּיו יִתְבָּרֵךְ — **The source of the "worldly" side of all souls is *"the breath of His mouth"*** (see *Psalms* 33:6).

When speaking of the inner identity of your soul, how it is "a piece of G-d," the *Tanya* stressed how G-d *"'blew into His nostrils the breath of life'* (Genesis 2:7), i.e.,*

שְׁכִינָה עַל שֵׁם שֶׁשּׁוֹכֶנֶת וּמִתְלַבֶּשֶׁת תּוֹךְ כָּל עָלְמִין
לְהַחֲיוֹתָן וּלְקַיְּימָן וְהִיא הִיא הַמַּשְׁפַּעַת בּוֹ כֹּחַ הַדִּבּוּר
הַזֶּה שֶׁמְּדַבֵּר בְּדִבְרֵי תוֹרָה אוֹ כֹּחַ הַמַּעֲשֶׂה הַזֶּה לַעֲשׂוֹת
מִצְוָה זוֹ וְיִחוּד זֶה הוּא עַל יְדֵי הַמְשָׁכַת אוֹר אֵין סוֹף בָּרוּךְ הוּא לְמַטָּה
עַל יְדֵי עֵסֶק הַתּוֹרָה וְהַמִּצְוֹת שֶׁהוּא מְלוּבָּשׁ בָּהֶן וְיִתְכַּוֵּין

from the innermost depths of his being... a deep rooted, inner energy" (chapter 2, p. 45). But since we're speaking in this chapter about the worldly layer of the soul, the *Tanya* quotes a different verse, *"with the breath of His mouth, all of their hosts (were made)"* a verse which speaks of the more superficial elements of creation (the "hosts").

הַנִּקְרָא בְּשֵׁם שְׁכִינָה עַל שֵׁם שֶׁשּׁוֹכֶנֶת וּמִתְלַבֶּשֶׁת תּוֹךְ כָּל עָלְמִין לְהַחֲיוֹתָן וּלְקַיְּימָן — The source of the "worldly" layer of the souls of Israel is from a diminished, "worldly" Divine light **which is called SHeCHiNah, due to the fact that it "inhabits" (SHoCHeNes) and is enmeshed in all the worlds, to give them life and to sustain them.**

All the energy in the world (and in the "worldly" dimension of your soul), emanates from *Shechinah*, a diminished energy. The only way to access an energy which is not veiled or diminished is through a *mitzvah*.

A *mitzvah* represents the "marriage," so to speak, of two types of energy. On the one hand it occurs in this world, so it's powered by the "worldly" energy of *Shechinah*. But on the other hand, that *mitzvah* is the undiluted Divine will, which expresses G-d's otherworldly, undiminished light.

וְהִיא הִיא הַמַּשְׁפַּעַת בּוֹ כֹּחַ הַדִּבּוּר הַזֶּה שֶׁמְּדַבֵּר בְּדִבְרֵי תוֹרָה — **And it is precisely this** *Shechinah* (worldly) energy **from which the power flows to you to** physically **speak the words, when you speak words of Torah,** אוֹ כֹּחַ הַמַּעֲשֶׂה הַזֶּה לַעֲשׂוֹת מִצְוָה זוֹ — **or the power to perform the act, when you do a particular** *mitzvah*.

From one perspective, the physical act of a *mitzvah* is a worldly act which, like everything in this world, is powered by the diminished energy of *Shechinah*.

PRACTICAL LESSONS

On a deeper level, be conscious of the *mitzvah's* power to connect the root of all souls to G-d.

וְיִחוּד זֶה — **But** since the Torah or *mitzvah* (which is taking place in this *Shechinah* powered world) *also* expresses the undiminished, other-worldly light of G-d's will, **there's a merging here** of the worldly power you used to perform the *mitzvah* (*Shechinah*) with its otherworldly light, the Divine will, הוּא עַל יְדֵי הַמְשָׁכַת אוֹר אֵין סוֹף בָּרוּךְ הוּא לְמַטָּה עַל יְדֵי עֵסֶק הַתּוֹרָה וְהַמִּצְוֹת — **and that's because the ob-servance of Torah and *mitzvos* "pulls" the** undiminished **Blessed Infinite Light downwards** into all the worlds, including this physical world, שֶׁהוּא מְלוּבָּשׁ בָּהֶן — **since the Blessed Infinite Light is present within** Torah and *mitzvos*.

לְהַמְשִׁיךְ אוֹרוֹ ית' עַל מְקוֹר נַפְשׁוֹ וְנַפְשׁוֹת כָּל יִשְׂרָאֵל
לְיַיחֲדָן וּכמ"ש לְקַמָּן פֵּי' יִחוּד זֶה בַּאֲרִיכוּת ע"ש. וְזֶהוּ
פֵּי' לְשֵׁם יִחוּד קב"ה וּשְׁכִינְתֵּיהּ בְּשֵׁם כָּל יִשְׂרָאֵל*

At the level of *personal kavanah*, you would focus on how your being has become absorbed in G-d's undiluted will through the *mitzvah*. But at the level of *communal kavanah*, your concern would be: How does the Blessed Infinite Light which I have "pulled" down with this *mitzvah* affect the source of all the souls of Israel?

וְיִתְכַּוֵּין לְהַמְשִׁיךְ אוֹרוֹ יִתְבָּרֵךְ עַל מְקוֹר נַפְשׁוֹ וְנַפְשׁוֹת כָּל יִשְׂרָאֵל לְיַיחֲדָן — **And** when you observe Torah and *mitzvos* **your *kavanah* should be that** G-d's Infinite **Light be "pulled" down into the** "worldly" **source of your soul, and into the** "worldly" **source of all souls of Israel, to merge them together.**

Since the source of all souls is *Shechinah* (a veiled, diminished energy), it benefits greatly from the illumination of the Blessed Infinite Light caused by your *mitzvah*. So in addition to invigorating yourself through a *mitzvah*, you also bring light to the root of all souls. And, in order not to "exclude yourself from the community," the *Tanya* suggests you ought to have this in mind when you do a *mitzvah*.

וּכְמוֹ שֶׁיִּתְבָּאֵר לְקַמָּן פֵּירוּשׁ יִחוּד זֶה בַּאֲרִיכוּת — As will be explained later at length the meaning of this "merging," עַיֵּין שָׁם — look there. (This idea doesn't seem to be elaborated "at length" anywhere in the *Tanya,* but see below chapter 46, and at length in Rabbi Shneur Zalman, *Likutei Torah, Shir Ha-Shirim* 40d-41a; Rabbi Shalom Dov Ber Schneersohn, *Sefer Ha-Ma'amarim* 5669, pp. 205-7; *Toras Menachem, Hisva'aduyos* vol. 26, pp. 62-4).

וְזֶהוּ פֵּירוּשׁ לְשֵׁם יִחוּד קוּדְשָׁא בְּרִיךְ הוּא וּשְׁכִינְתֵּיהּ בְּשֵׁם כָּל יִשְׂרָאֵל — **And this is the meaning of** the Kabbalistic *kavanah* said before the observance of *mitzvos* that the worship is being done ***For the sake of the merging of the Blessed Holy One with His Shechinah... in the name of all Israel**** (*Pri Etz Chaim Sha'ar Ha-Zemiros* chapter 5; according to *Siddur Ha-Rav* this is recited once daily — see *Likutei Sichos* volume 39, pp. 46-7).

This brief Kabbalistic *kavanah* sums up our whole discussion in one succinct phrase: You are conscious that through this *mitzvah* you are going to "pull" down the Infinite Light of the Blessed (Infinite) Holy One, into the *Shechinah*, thereby invigorating the souls of all Israel by connecting them with an other-worldly light.

And this *kavanah* forms part of the second "wing" of every *mitzvah*, (in our bird analogy), the love of G-d. Love is the feeling that you want to come close to G-d, and on the level of communal consciousness, it's the feeling that you want to draw the root of all souls close to G-d.

21ST NISAN REGULAR

Now it's easy to say the words, but could we ask the average worshiper to really care about such esoteric matters? The *Tanya* will answer that, due to its central im-

הגהה

(וגם על ידי זה יתמתקו גם כן
הגבורות בחסדים ממילא
בהתכללות המדות ויחודם על ידי
גילוי רצון העליון ב"ה המתגלה
למעלה באתערותא דלתתא הוא
גילויו למטה בעסק התורה
והמצוה שהן רצונו ית' וכמ"ש
באדרא רבא ובמשנת חסידים)

ואף שלהיות כוונה זו
אמיתית בלבו שיהיה לבו
חפץ באמת יחוד העליון
הזה צריך להיות בלבו
אהבה רבה לה' לבדו
לעשות נחת רוח לפניו
לבד ולא לרוות נפשו

portance, you should at least try. And, as we have often stressed, if you can't feel it in your heart, it's still an achievement to have it in your conscious mind.

וְאַף שֶׁלִּהְיוֹת כַּוָּונָה זוֹ אֲמִיתִּית בְּלִבּוֹ — **And though for this** *kavanah* **to be genuine in your heart,** שֶׁיִּהְיֶה לִבּוֹ חָפֵץ בֶּאֱמֶת יִחוּד הָעֶלְיוֹן הַזֶּה צָרִיךְ לִהְיוֹת בְּלִבּוֹ אַהֲבָה רַבָּה לַה' לְבַדּוֹ — **for your heart to genuinely desire this "merging," you would need to have** *ahavah rabah* **("great love") in your heart,** which is devoted **to G-d alone,** devoid of ego or self-interest (see p. 117), לַעֲשׂוֹת נַחַת רוּחַ לְפָנָיו לְבַד — **and for your worship to be genuine it would need to be carried out with the** *kavanah* **purely to give G-d** *"a feeling of satisfaction that I spoke and My will was carried out" (Rashi to Leviticus 1:9),* וְלֹא לִרְווֹת נַפְשׁוֹ הַצְּמֵאָה לַה' — **and not because** *you* **want to satisfy your soul's**

---

*הַגָּהָה — **NOTE.** In addition to the *altruistic* intent which we have described in the main text, there is also some *personal benefit* to be acquired from this esoteric *kavanah.* For, as we have already discussed in the previous chapter (in the second "note," pp. 480-84), the integration of spiritual energies can result in the "sweetening" of harsh judgments.

וְגַם עַל יְדֵי זֶה — **And also through this** integration of Divine lights in *Atzilus,* יִתְמַתְּקוּ גַּם כֵּן הַגְּבוּרוֹת בַּחֲסָדִים מִמֵּילָא — **harsh judgments will also be automatically "sweetened" by kindness,** בְּהִתְכַּלְלוּת הַמִּדּוֹת וְיִחוּדָם — **as the attributes** of judgment and kindness **are absorbed in, and integrated with, each other,** עַל יְדֵי גִּילוּי רָצוֹן הָעֶלְיוֹן — **due to the disclosure of the Blessed Divine will** in *Atzilus,* הַמִּתְגַּלֶּה — **revealed "above"** in *Atzilus* **as a result of** your *mitzvah* observance which is *"an awakening from below" (Zohar 2, 135b).*

הוּא גִּילוּיוֹ לְמַטָּה בְּעֵסֶק הַתּוֹרָה וְהַמִּצְוָה שֶׁהֵן רְצוֹנוֹ יִתְבָּרֵךְ — **And the reason why the** Divine will is revealed "above," is because **it is revealed "below" through your Torah study and** observance of *mitzvos,* **which** *are* **the Divine will** (as we have explained above, pp. 483, 498).

The "note" concludes with further sources from the *Kabbalah* that *mitzvos* have the effect of "sweetening" harsh judgments.

וּכְמוֹ שֶׁכָּתוּב בְּאִדְרָא רַבָּא — **As stated in** the *Zohar,* in the section entitled *Idra Raba* (*Zohar* 3, 128a-b), פֶּרֶק ד' אַנְפִּין אָרִיךְ מַסֶּכֶת חֲסִידִים וּבְמִשְׁנַת — **and in** Rabbi Im-

מסכת א"א פ"ד שתרי"ג מצות
התורה נמשכות מחיוורתא דא"א
שהוא רצון העליון מקור
החסדים):

הַצְמָאָה לַה' אֶלָּא כְּבָרָא 58A
דְּאִשְׁתַּדֵּל בָּתַר אֲבוּי וְאִמֵּיה
דְּרָחִים לוֹן יַתִּיר מִגַּרְמֵיה

thirst for G-d, אֶלָּא כְּבָרָא דְּאִשְׁתַּדֵּל בָּתַר אֲבוּי וְאִמֵּיה דְּרָחִים לוֹן יַתִּיר מִגַּרְמֵיה וְנַפְשֵׁיה כוּ'
— **rather** a non-selfish intention would be, *"Like a son who exerts himself for his father and mother, whom he loves more than himself, more than his own soul, and everything of his own he considers as worthless, existing only to carry out the will*

---

manuel Ricchi, ***Mishnas Chasidim, Maseches Arich Anpin*, chapter 4,** *Mishnah* 3, שֶׁתַּרְיַ"ג מִצְוֹת הַתּוֹרָה נִמְשָׁכוֹת מֵחִיוּוֹרְתָּא דַּאֲרִיךְ אַנְפִּין — **that the 613** *mitzvos* emanate from *Arich Anpin* (the "Long Face"), a term used in the Kabbalah to refer to the Divine will, **from its "whiteness,"** white being symbolic of mercy, שֶׁהוּא רָצוֹן הָעֶלְיוֹן מְקוֹר הַחֲסָדִים — indicating that **the Divine will** (*Arich Anpin*) is also **the source of kindness.**

This passage from *Zohar* expounds on the verse, *"The Ancient of Days sat, His garment like white snow"* (*Daniel* 7:9). "Ancient of Days" (*Atik Yomin*), says the *Zohar,* alludes to G-d as He preceded the Torah and the world. The *"white garment"* alludes to the *"impulse which arose in His will to create the Torah"* (*Zohar,* ibid.). This primordial Divine will is depicted as "white," alluding to an energy of compassion and mercy that has the power to neutralize negative forces and judgments (*"Master of white, his garment and light, seated on a throne of flames (i.e. negative forces) to subdue them,"* ibid.).

This "white garment" (the Divine will, source of compassion), is referred to by the *Zohar* (ibid.) as *Arich Anpin,* "Long Face," in contrast to more "exterior" Divine energies, which are termed *Ze'ir Anpin,* "Small Face," (following the *Talmud's* description of Ezekiel's heavenly chariot as displaying *"one large face and another small"* — *Sukkah* 5b; *Ezekiel* 10:4). But the two terms have a broader connotation than simply that of size. *Arich Anpin* is related to the term *Erech Apayim* ("slow to anger" — *Exodus* 34:6), suggesting a compassionate energy; whereas *Ze'ir Anpin* is suggestive of short-temperedness and quick judgment.

But, *"when Ze'ir Anpin gazes at this one (Arich Anpin), all below is restored and His face expands and lengthens"* (*Zohar* ibid.), growing more compassionate. In the *Tanya's* terminology, this would be equivalent to the Divine will (*Arich Anpin*) shining into the emotional attributes of *Atzilus* (*Ze'ir Anpin*), to sweeten their judgments. (The *Tanya* also cites *Mishnas Chasidim* where it is explicit that the "whiteness" of *Arich Anpin* illuminates all 613 *mitzvos*).

The conclusion, then, is that when we perform a *mitzvah,* we cause the Divine will to integrate the attributes of *Atzilus,* which is the Divine will, and that should be our main *kavanah.* But this will also have the effect of sweetening harsh judgments, bringing revealed blessings into our lives.

ונפשיה כו' [כמ"ש לעיל
בשם רעיא מהימנא]. מ"מ
יש לכל אדם להרגיל עצמו בכוונה זו כי אף שאינה
באמת לאמיתו לגמרי בלבו שיחפוץ בזה בכל לבו
מ"מ מעט מזער חפץ לבו בזה באמת מפני אהבה
הטבעית שבלב כל ישראל לעשות כל מה שהוא
רצון העליון ב"ה ויחוד זה הוא רצונו האמיתי והיינו יחוד

as was taught — [כְּמוֹ שֶׁנִּתְבָּאֵר לְעֵיל בְּשֵׁם רַעְיָא מְהֵימְנָא] *of his mother and father,"* **above** (chapter 10, p. 129), **from** *Ra'aya Mehemna* (*Zohar* 3, 281a; see also below, chapter 44, pp. 568*ff.*).

Unlike *kabolas ol* and reverence which are inherently devoid of self-interest, the emotion of love, even the love of G-d, is nearly always tinged with self-centeredness. Only those who have reached a very high degree of emotional maturity (*ahavah rabah*), can have a love which is *exclusively* for G-d (at the level of *"a child who is also a servant,"* above, Section Six).

מִכָּל מָקוֹם — **Nevertheless,** even though to have genuine intent when saying this Kabbalistic *kavanah* would seem beyond the reach of most people, יֵשׁ לְכָל אָדָם לְהַרְגִּיל עַצְמוֹ בְּכַוָּונָה זוֹ — **everyone should practice this** *kavanah* **regularly,** and at least *try* to mean it genuinely, כִּי אַף שֶׁאֵינָה בֶּאֱמֶת לַאֲמִיתוֹ לְגַמְרֵי בְּלִבּוֹ — **because even if you don't mean it with absolute, genuine conviction of your heart,** שֶׁיַּחְפּוֹץ — and you don't **desire it with all your heart,** בָּזֶה בְּכָל לִבּוֹ מִכָּל מָקוֹם מְעַט מִזְעֵר חָפֵץ לִבּוֹ — **nevertheless, to a very small extent** at least, **your heart** *does* **desire it genuinely,** בָּזֶה בֶּאֱמֶת — **as a result of the innate** מִפְּנֵי אַהֲבָה הַטִּבְעִית שֶׁבְּלֵב כָּל יִשְׂרָאֵל — **love found in the heart of all Israel,** לַעֲשׂוֹת כָּל מַה שֶׁהוּא רָצוֹן הָעֶלְיוֹן בָּרוּךְ הוּא — which represents an innate, embodied desire **to carry out whatever the Divine will may be** (see below chapter 44), וְיִחוּד זֶה הוּא רְצוֹנוֹ הָאֲמִיתִי — **and this merging** of G-d's Infinite Light with the *Shechinah*, the source of the souls of Israel, **is, in fact, the real** Divine **will.**

As we discussed at length in chapters 36-37, the Divine will is for a "home for G-d below"—for G-d's other-worldly light to penetrate and "inhabit" our ordinary, worldly context. But other-worldly light can't just come into this physical world without major changes happening in the chain of spiritual worlds above. There's a reason why that light didn't come down here in the first place!

That change is, essentially, a modification in the way that the highest spiritual world of *Atzilus* works. *Shechinah* (which is the lowest attribute of *Atzilus* (*malchus*), the last letter of the Tetragrammaton), is a light which is inherently compatible with the lower, created worlds. All the other lights above it are incompatible, and inherently other-worldly. So for that other-worldly light to come down into *Shechinah* and thereby to the world, something major has to happen: *the incompatible has to*

הָעֶלְיוֹן שֶׁבַּאֲצִילוּת הַנַּעֲשָׂה בְּאִתְעָרוּתָא דִלְתַתָּא עַ״יְ
יִחוּד נֶפֶשׁ הָאֱלֹהִית וְהִתְכַּלְּלוּתָהּ בְּאוֹר ה' הַמְלֻבָּשׁ
בַּתּוֹרָה וּמִצְוֹת שֶׁעוֹסֶקֶת בָּהֶן וְהָיוּ לַאֲחָדִי מַמָּשׁ כמש״ל
כִּי עַ״יְז מִתְיַחֲדִים ג״כ מְקוֹר הַתּוֹרָה וְהַמִּצְוֹת שֶׁהוּא
הַקְבָּ״ה עִם מְקוֹר נַפְשׁוֹ הָאֱלֹהִית הַנִּקְרָא בְּשֵׁם שְׁכִינָה
שֶׁהֵן בְּחִי' מְמַלֵּא כָּל עָלְמִין וּבְחִי' סוֹבֵב כָּל עָלְמִין כמ״ש

become compatible. And that's the essential point of the *kavanah*: "For the sake of the merging of the Blessed Holy One (incompatible, other-worldly light) with His *Shechinah*."

So when we speak of a "home for G-d below," there's both an effect and its cause. The effect is that otherworldly light inhabits and merges with this world; but the cause is *"the merging of the Blessed Holy One with His Shechinah"* that makes the merging down here possible.

That's why the *Tanya* stresses here, *"this merging is, in fact, the real Divine will,"* because it's the *cause* of "G-d's home below" (*Sefer Ha-Ma'amarim* 5669 ibid.).

וְהַיְינוּ יְחוּד הָעֶלְיוֹן שֶׁבַּאֲצִילוּת — This merging of the Blessed Infinite Light and the *Shechinah* which we are speaking of here **is the same phenomenon as the integration** of Divine attributes **above in** the world of *Atzilus* (that we discussed above in chapter 40, second note).

The *Shechinah* is, in fact, the lowest attribute of the world of *Atzilus*. So when we spoke earlier about a *mitzvah* pulling down the Blessed Infinite Light into *Atzilus* and integrating the attributes there, it's exactly the same phenomenon which is being discussed in this chapter.

הַנַּעֲשָׂה בְּאִתְעָרוּתָא דִלְתַתָּא — As we explained there, the integration of attributes **brought about by** a *mitzvah* done on earth, *"an awakening from below"* (*Zohar* 2, 135b), עַל יְדֵי יְחוּד נֶפֶשׁ הָאֱלֹהִית וְהִתְכַּלְּלוּתָהּ בְּאוֹר ה' הַמְלוּבָּשׁ בַּתּוֹרָה וּמִצְוֹת, שֶׁעוֹסֶקֶת בָּהֶן — which happens **when** a *mitzvah* is observed, and results in **your Divine Soul merging with, and becoming absorbed in,** G-d's light found in the Torah or *mitzvos* you are observing, וְהָיוּ לַאֲחָדִים מַמָּשׁ כְּמוֹ שֶׁנִּתְבָּאֵר לְעֵיל — **and they become utterly one, as explained above** (chapters 5, 23 and 40, second note).

This "awakening from below" also results in an "awakening from above," namely, the Blessed Infinite Light shining in *Atzilus* and integrating its attributes,

כִּי עַל יְדֵי זֶה מִתְיַחֲדִים גַּם כֵּן מְקוֹר הַתּוֹרָה וְהַמִּצְוֹת שֶׁהוּא הַקָּדוֹשׁ בָּרוּךְ הוּא עִם מְקוֹר נַפְשׁוֹ הָאֱלֹהִית הַנִּקְרָא בְּשֵׁם שְׁכִינָה — **because through this you also cause the** *source* **of Torah and** *mitzvos,* which is the otherworldly Divine energy referred to as "**the Blessed Holy One,**" to merge in *Atzilus* **with the source of** the worldly component of **your Divine Soul, which is called "***Shechinah***."**

In a final note, the *Tanya* indicates other terms used for these same concepts.

במ"א באריכות. אבל יחוד נפשו והתכללותה באור
ה' להיות לאחדים בזה חפץ כל אדם מישראל באמת
לאמיתו לגמרי בכל לב ובכל נפש מאהבה הטבעית
המסותרת בלב כל ישראל לדבקה בה' ולא ליפרד
ולהיות נכרת ונבדל ח"ו מיחודו ואחדותו ית' בשום אופן
אפי' במסירת נפש ממש ועסק התורה ומצות והתפלה
הוא ג"כ ענין מסירת נפש ממש כמו בצאתה מן הגוף

שֶׁהֵן בְּחִינַת מְמַלֵּא כָּל עָלְמִין וּבְחִינַת סוֹבֵב כָּל עָלְמִין — The worldly (*Shechinah*) and otherworldly ("Blessed Holy One") energies **are also referred to as** the light which **"fills all worlds"** and **"transcends all worlds,"** respectively (see *Zohar* 3, 225a), כְּמוֹ שֶׁנִּתְבָּאֵר בְּמָקוֹם אַחֵר בַּאֲרִיכוּת — **as is explained elsewhere at length** (see chapters 48 and 49).

Whatever terms you use, the theme behind the purpose of creation (Divine will) is the same: the merging of the compatible with the incompatible, the transcendent with the immanent, the infinite with the finite.

SECTION TEN: AN INNER DEVOTION WITH EVERY MITZVAH

22ND NISAN REGULAR

The *Tanya* now returns to our earlier discussion, about awakening the natural love in your heart to foster a *personal* relationship with G-d.

אֲבָל יְחוּד נַפְשׁוֹ וְהִתְכַּלְלוּתָהּ בְּאוֹר ה' לִהְיוֹת לַאֲחָדִים בָּזֶה חָפֵץ כָּל אָדָם מִיִּשְׂרָאֵל בֶּאֱמֶת לַאֲמִיתּוֹ — **But** while you may find it hard to genuinely desire the merging of these Divine energies on behalf of the whole community, **every person in Israel does have the genuinely authentic desire** at least **for his *own* soul to merge with, and be absorbed in, G-d's light, as one,** לְגַמְרֵי בְּכָל לֵב וּבְכָל נָפֶשׁ — **with all his heart and soul,** מֵאַהֲבָה הַטִּבְעִית הַמְסוּתֶּרֶת בְּלֵב כָּל יִשְׂרָאֵל לְדָבְקָה בַּה' — **arising from the innate love which is dormant in the heart of all Israel,** a desire **to connect to G-d,** וְלֹא לִיפָּרֵד וְלִהְיוֹת נִכְרַת וְנִבְדָּל חַס וְשָׁלוֹם מִיִּחוּדוֹ וְאַחְדוּתוֹ יִתְבָּרֵךְ בְּשׁוּם אוֹפֶן — **and not to be separated or cut off in any way, G-d forbid, from His absolute oneness,** אֲפִילוּ בִּמְסִירַת נָפֶשׁ מַמָּשׁ — **even** if this requires **actually giving up one's life (*mesiras nefesh*).**

Above we discussed how the innate love of your Divine Soul would be powerful enough to bring you to *mesiras nefesh* to give up your life for G-d, if it would ever come to that (p. 227). The *Tanya* re-visits this idea here, not in the literal sense of giving up your life, but in the sense of every *mitzvah* being a kind of devotional *mesiras nefesh,* giving over your soul to be "absorbed" in G-d.

וְעֵסֶק הַתּוֹרָה וּמִצְוֹת וְהַתְּפִלָּה הוּא גַּם כֵּן עִנְיַן מְסִירַת נֶפֶשׁ מַמָּשׁ — **But, in reality, studying Torah and** observing *mitzvos* **are also real *mesiras nefesh*,** כְּמוֹ בְּצֵאתָהּ מִן הַגּוּף

במלאת שבעים שנה שאינה מהרהרת בצרכי הגוף
אלא מחשבתה מיוחדת ומלובשת באותיות התורה
והתפלה שהן דבר ה' ומחשבתו ית' והיו לאחדים ממש
שזהו כל עסק הנשמות בג"ע כדאיתא בגמרא ובזהר
אלא ששם מתענגים בהשגתם והתכללותם באור ה'   58B
וזהו שתקנו בתחלת ברכות השחר קודם התפלה אלהי
נשמה וכו' ואתה נפחתה כו' ואתה עתיד ליטלה ממני

בִּמְלֹאת שִׁבְעִים שָׁנָה — since they demand your single-minded devotion, **similar to when** your soul will **leave your body** at the end of your life, **having fulfilled** the Biblical lifespan of **"seventy years"** (*Psalms* 90:10), שֶׁאֵינָהּ מְהַרְהֶרֶת בְּצָרְכֵי הַגּוּף — at which point your soul's devotion to G-d will be a total one, since it will **no longer be concerned with the body's needs.**

So when you study Torah or observe a *mitzvah* on earth with complete devotion, it's considered an act of *mesiras nefesh,* because it resembles the single-minded devotion of your soul to G-d, when it will leave your body.

As we discussed in chapter 19, the willingness to be a martyr for G-d rather than transgress His will even for a moment, is actually rooted in your love for Him. Only there, it's expressed in a negative way, when we referred to it as "reverence that is contained in love" (see p. 230). In the everyday setting, when your life isn't threatened, you can draw on this same *mesiras nefesh* energy from your soul to intensify the devotional quality of your worship.

Having mentioned that the soul is free from the concerns of the body in heaven, the *Tanya* now discusses briefly what the soul *will* be doing.

אֶלָּא מַחֲשַׁבְתָּהּ מְיֻחֶדֶת וּמְלוּבֶּשֶׁת בְּאוֹתִיוֹת הַתּוֹרָה וְהַתְּפִלָּה — **Rather,** in heaven, your soul's **thoughts will be** completely **devoted to, and immersed in,** the heavenly **words of the Torah and prayer,** שֶׁהֵן דְּבַר ה' וּמַחֲשַׁבְתּוֹ יִתְבָּרֵךְ — which are G-d's word and His thoughts, וְהָיוּ לַאֲחָדִים מַמָּשׁ — with which the soul **will be totally one.**

שֶׁזֶּהוּ כָּל עֵסֶק הַנְּשָׁמוֹת בְּגַן עֵדֶן — **For,** as we know, **this** immersion in Torah and prayer **is the singular occupation of the souls in** *Gan Eden* **(heaven),** כְּדְאִיתָא בַּגְּמָרָא וּבַזֹּהַר — **as stated in the** *Talmud* (*Brachos* 18b) **and** *Zohar* (1, 92b; 3, 173a).

אֶלָּא שֶׁשָּׁם מִתְעַנְגִּים בְּהַשָּׂגָתָם וְהִתְכַּלְלוּתָם בְּאוֹר ה' — **Only there,** in heaven, **it's** extremely **pleasurable** for the souls to **engage with G-d's light and be absorbed in it,** whereas in the earthly Torah experience, this dimension is lacking.

The *Tanya* will now show that the *kavanah* of devotional *mesiras nefesh* is conveyed by a passage in the morning prayers.

וְזֶהוּ שֶׁתִּקְּנוּ בִּתְחִלַּת בִּרְכוֹת הַשַּׁחַר קוֹדֶם הַתְּפִלָּה — **And this explains why the Sages composed** the following to be said **at the beginning of the morning blessings before the prayers,** אֱלֹהַי נְשָׁמָה וְכוּ' אַתָּה נְפַחְתָּ כוּ' וְאַתָּה עָתִיד לִיטְּלָהּ מִמֶּנִּי כוּ' — *"My*

כו' כלומ' מאחר שאתה נפחתה בי ואתה עתיד ליטלה
ממני לכן מעתה אני מוסרה ומחזירה לך לייחדה
באחדותך וכמ"ש אליך ה' נפשי אשא והיינו על ידי
התקשרות מחשבתי במחשבתך ודיבורי בדיבורך
באותיות התורה והתפלה ובפרט באמירה לה' לנכח
כמו ברוך אתה וכה"ג והנה בהכנה זו של מסירת נפשו
לה' יתחיל ברכות השחר ברוך אתה כו' וכן בהכנה

God! The soul which You gave me is pure... ***You breathed it into me... and You will eventually take it from me."***

It makes sense that we thank G-d for placing our souls in our bodies, that "*You breathed it into me,*" but what's the point in adding, "*and You will eventually take it from me*"?

This, the *Tanya* suggests, hints to our above idea of having single-minded devotion while the soul is in the body, comparable to its devotion in heaven after parting from the body.

כְּלוֹמַר — **In other words,** מֵאַחַר שֶׁאַתָּה נְפַחְתָּה בִּי וְאַתָּה עָתִיד לִיטְלָה מִמֶּנִּי — **since,** "*You breathed it into me... and You will eventually take it from me,*" לָכֵן מֵעַתָּה אֲנִי מוֹסְרָה וּמַחֲזִירָה לְךָ לְיַיחֲדָה בְּאַחְדּוּתְךָ — **therefore right now** I will try to approach the level when "You will eventually take it from me," and **I give** my soul **over and return it to you, to merge with your oneness,** וּכְמוֹ שֶׁכָּתוּב אֵלֶיךָ ה' נַפְשִׁי אֶשָּׂא — **as the verse states, "*To You, G-d, I lift up my soul,*"** (*Psalms* 25:1), וְהַיְינוּ עַל יְדֵי הִתְקַשְּׁרוּת מַחֲשַׁבְתִּי בְּמַחֲשַׁבְתְּךָ וְדִיבּוּרִי בְּדִיבּוּרְךָ בְּאוֹתִיוֹת הַתּוֹרָה וְהַתְּפִלָּה — **and the way I do this is by** devotionally **tying my thoughts to Your thoughts, and my words to Your words, through the Torah and prayer texts** which I study and recite, with the devotion of a disembodied soul in heaven.

וּבִפְרָט בַּאֲמִירָה לַה' לְנִכַח — And my feeling of handing my soul to You is **especially** pronounced, **when addressing G-d** directly **in the second person,** when the sense of His presence is particularly acute, כְּמוֹ בָּרוּךְ אַתָּה וּכְהַאי גַּוְונָא — **such as, "*Blessed are You etc.,*"** (a text which implies that "He is standing in front of you" — *Avudraham, Morning Blessings*).

23RD NISAN REGULAR | 17TH NISAN LEAP

וְהִנֵּה בַּהֲכָנָה זוֹ שֶׁל מְסִירַת נַפְשׁוֹ לַה' — **And it is with this** morning **preparation of** *mesiras nefesh* to G-d, יַתְחִיל בִּרְכוֹת הַשַּׁחַר בָּרוּךְ אַתָּה כו' — **you should begin to say the morning prayers, "*Blessed are You, etc.*"**

The *Tanya* now advises how this *kavanah* should influence Torah study.

וְכֵן בַּהֲכָנָה זוֹ יַתְחִיל לִלְמוֹד שִׁיעוּר קָבוּעַ מִיָּד אַחַר הַתְּפִלָּה — **And, with this preparation, you should begin a regular study session straight after prayer** (see *Shulchan Aruch, Orach Chaim* chapter 155).

זו יתחיל ללמוד שיעור קבוע מיד אחר התפלה וכן
באמצע היום קודם שיתחיל ללמוד צריכה הכנה זו
לפחות כנודע שעיקר ההכנה לשמה לעכב הוא בתחל׳
הלימוד בבינונים וכמו בגט וס״ת שצריכים לשמה
לעכב ודיו שיאמר בתחלת הכתיבה הריני כותב לשם
קדושת ס״ת או לשמו ולשמה כו׳ וכשלומד שעות
הרבה רצופות יש לו להתבונן בהכנה זו הנ״ל בכל

וְכֵן בְּאֶמְצַע הַיּוֹם קוֹדֶם שֶׁיַּתְחִיל לִלְמוֹד צְרִיכָה הַכָנָה זוֹ לְפָחוֹת — **And so too in the course of the day, you need to make this preparation at least before you begin to study,** even though you will not be able to maintain it during study, when you will be focusing on the content of the text, כַּנוֹדָע שֶׁעִיקַר הַהֲכָנָה לִשְׁמָה לְעַכֵּב הוּא בְּתְחִלַּת הַלִּימוּד בַּבֵּינוֹנִים — **since, as we know, in the case of** *beinonim,* who don't remain in a state of enraptured consciousness of the Divine at all times, **the crucial, key preparation to ensure that study is "for** the *mitzvah's* **sake," is at the** *outset* **of study,** since when they are actually studying, their minds will be focused on understanding the text, and not on the presence of G-d.

The *Tanya* offers an illustration from Jewish Law from which we see that having *kavanah* at the outset of study is sufficient.

וּכְמוֹ בְּגֵט וְסֵפֶר תּוֹרָה שֶׁצְּרִיכִים לִשְׁמָה לְעַכֵּב — **And this is similar to the case of a** *get* (divorce document) or Torah scroll, where** writing the text with the correct intention is a crucial condition in the document's validity (see *Talmud, Gittin* 54a), וְדַיוֹ שֶׁיֹּאמַר בְּתְחִלַּת הַכְּתִיבָה — but that doesn't mean that the scribe must have this intent the whole time he's writing, **rather it's sufficient** for the scribe **to say at the outset of the writing,** הֲרֵינִי כּוֹתֵב לְשֵׁם קְדוּשַׁת סֵפֶר תּוֹרָה — **"I'm writing this as a holy Torah scroll,"** אוֹ לִשְׁמוֹ וְלִשְׁמָה כוּ׳ — **or,** in the case of a *get,* **"I'm writing this for him and for her,** as a bill of divorce."

However, if you study for a very long period, it's not sufficient merely to have this intent at the outset, and your *kavanah* needs to be periodically refreshed.

וּכְשֶׁלּוֹמֵד שָׁעוֹת הַרְבֵּה רְצוּפוֹת — **But if you study for several hours in a row,** יֵשׁ לוֹ לְהִתְבּוֹנֵן בַּהֲכָנָה זוֹ הַנִּזְכֶּרֶת לְעֵיל — בְּכָל שָׁעָה וְשָׁעָה עַל כָּל פָּנִים — **you ought to contemplate the content of the above "preparation," at least once per hour.**

PRACTICAL LESSONS

Also, tap into your soul's ability for single-minded devotion (*mesiras nefesh*), the feeling that your soul belongs to G-d and you are "returning" it to Him through worship.

Do this before prayer and before study. And during study, stop and "refresh" this intent every hour, because all the worship in the universe returns to G-d each hour.

שעה ושעה עכ"פ כי בכל שעה ושעה היא המשכה
אחרת מעולמות עליונים להחיות התחתונים והמשכת
החיות שבשעה שלפניה חוזרת למקורה [בסוד רצוא
ושוב שבס' יצירה] עם כל התורה ומעשים טובים של
התחתונים כי בכל שעה שולט צירוף אחד מי"ב צירופי
שם הוי"ה ב"ה בי"ב שעות היום וצירופי שם אדנ"י
בלילה כנודע. והנה כל כוונתו במסירת נפשו לה'
ע"י התורה והתפלה להעלות ניצוץ אלהות שבתוכה

This advice is based on the command, *"Be careful not to forget G-d"* (Deuter-
onomy 8:11) which means, *"We are warned to remember G-d at all times… and the
Kabbalists have written that G-d's sacred name has twelve anagrams with which
He conducts the world during the twelve hours of the day and twelve hours of the
night, and He has commanded us not to forget Him during any one of those hours"*
(Rabbi Elazar Azkiri, *Sefer Charedim,* chapter 21).

The *Tanya* now elaborates on this idea:

כִּי בְּכָל שָׁעָה וְשָׁעָה הִיא הַמְשָׁכָה אַחֶרֶת מֵעוֹלָמוֹת עֶלְיוֹנִים לְהַחֲיוֹת הַתַּחְתּוֹנִים — **Because**
every hour there is a different flow of energy from the upper worlds to the lower
worlds, וְהַמְשָׁכַת הַחַיּוּת שֶׁבְּשָׁעָה שֶׁלְּפָנֶיהָ חוֹזֶרֶת לִמְקוֹרָהּ — **as the** unit of **energy-flow**
from the previous hour returns to its source, [בְּסוֹד רָצוֹא וָשׁוֹב שֶׁבְּסֵפֶר יְצִירָה] —
according to the secret of the world's oscillating energy which is constantly *"run-*
ning and returning" (Ezekiel 1:14), to and fro from its source, as **mentioned in Sefer**
Yetzirah (1:8), עִם כָּל הַתּוֹרָה וּמַעֲשִׂים טוֹבִים שֶׁל הַתַּחְתּוֹנִים — and when the energy of
the previous hour returns, it goes back **along with all the Torah and good deeds**
from the lower worlds, performed during that time, כִּי בְּכָל שָׁעָה שׁוֹלֵט צֵירוּף אֶחָד
— **for each hour is "ruled" by a different anagram** of one of G-d's sacred names.

The *Tanya* now specifies which sacred names function at different times.

מִי"ב צֵירוּפֵי שֵׁם הֲוָיָ"ה בָּרוּךְ הוּא בִּי"ב שְׁעוֹת הַיּוֹם — Namely, **during** each one of **the**
twelve hours of the day, the world is "ruled" by **one of twelve** different **anagrams**
of the blessed Tetragrammaton (HaVaYaH), וְצֵירוּפֵי שֵׁם אֲדֹנָ"י בַּלַּיְלָה — **and during**
the night, each hour is ruled by one of twelve different **anagrams of** G-d's **name**
A-D-N-Y, כַּנּוֹדָע — **as is known** from Rabbi Meir Poppers, *Me'oros Nasan (Me'orei*
Ohr), "mem," paragraph 21.

18TH NISAN LEAP

Finally, the *Tanya* stresses that the above *mesiras nefesh kavanah* ought to be carried out, not out of personal fulfillment, but to bring "satisfaction" to G-d.

וְהִנֵּה כָּל כַּוָּנָתוֹ בִּמְסִירַת נַפְשׁוֹ לַה' עַל יְדֵי הַתּוֹרָה וְהַתְּפִלָּה — **Now your whole intent in**
having *mesiras nefesh* for G-d in Torah and prayer, לְהַעֲלוֹת נִיצוֹץ אֱלֹהוּת שֶׁבְּתוֹכָהּ

לִמְקוֹרוֹ תְּהֵא רַק כְּדֵי לַעֲשׂוֹת נַחַת רוּחַ לְפָנָיו ית' כְּמָשָׁל
שִׂמְחַת הַמֶּלֶךְ בְּבוֹא אֵלָיו בְּנוֹ יְחִידוֹ בְּצֵאתוֹ מִן הַשִּׁבְיָה
וּבֵית הָאֲסוּרִים כנ"ל. וְהִנֵּה כַּוָּונָה זוֹ הִיא אֲמִיתִּית בֶּאֱמֶת 59A
לַאֲמִיתּוֹ לְגַמְרֵי בְּכָל נֶפֶשׁ מִיִּשְׂרָאֵל בְּכָל עֵת וּבְכָל שָׁעָה
מֵאַהֲבָה הַטִּבְעִית שֶׁהִיא יְרוּשָׁה לָנוּ מֵאֲבוֹתֵינוּ. רַק
שֶׁצָּרִיךְ לִקְבּוֹעַ עִתִּים לְהִתְבּוֹנֵן בִּגְדוּלַת ה' לְהַשִּׂיג דְּחִילוּ
וּרְחִימוּ שִׂכְלִיִּים וְכוּלֵי הַאי וְאוּלַי וְכוּ' כנ"ל:

לִמְקוֹרוֹ — **to lift the spark of G-dliness within you up to its source,** תְּהֵא רַק כְּדֵי
לַעֲשׂוֹת נַחַת רוּחַ לְפָנָיו יִתְבָּרֵךְ — **should be** with one purpose, **solely to give G-d** *"a*
feeling of satisfaction" and not for your own gratification, כְּמָשָׁל שִׂמְחַת הַמֶּלֶךְ בְּבוֹא
אֵלָיו בְּנוֹ יְחִידוֹ בְּצֵאתוֹ מִן הַשִּׁבְיָה וּבֵית הָאֲסוּרִים כַּנִּזְכָּר לְעֵיל — **as in the above men-**
tioned analogy of the *king's* **joy when his only son comes to him from prison,**
released from captivity (chapter 31, p. 356).

Again the *Tanya* will emphasize that even if this altruistic intent seems beyond
you, it is your innermost desire, stemming from the innate love of G-d in your soul.

וְהִנֵּה כַּוָּונָה זוֹ הִיא אֲמִיתִּית בֶּאֱמֶת לַאֲמִיתּוֹ לְגַמְרֵי בְּכָל נֶפֶשׁ מִיִּשְׂרָאֵל — **Now for every**
soul in Israel, this *kavanah* **is completely genuine and absolutely authentic,** בְּכָל
עֵת וּבְכָל שָׁעָה — **at every time and any moment,** even if you're not sure that you're
intentions are genuinely selfless,, מֵאַהֲבָה הַטִּבְעִית שֶׁהִיא יְרוּשָׁה לָנוּ מֵאֲבוֹתֵינוּ —
since **it comes from the innate love** of the soul which was **"inherited" by us from**
our fathers (see chapter 18, p. 212*ff.*).

רַק שֶׁצָּרִיךְ לִקְבּוֹעַ עִתִּים לְהִתְבּוֹנֵן בִּגְדוּלַת ה' — **Only** you shouldn't be satisfied with
"inherited" love, **and you must also schedule sessions to contemplate G-d's great-**
ness, לְהַשִּׂיג דְּחִילוּ וּרְחִימוּ שִׂכְלִיִּים — **so as to attain a reverence and love of** G-d,
generated **from the mind.**

וְכוּלֵי הַאי וְאוּלַי וְכוּ' — **And then perhaps with all this** effort, you will succeed, כַּנִּזְכָּר
לְעֵיל — **as has been explained above** in the previous chapters, the path to this goal.*

---

*In many of the earliest manuscripts of *Likutei Amarim*, which were circulated before the first
printed edition, the book ends here. Based on the available manuscripts, one writer has conjectured that the pre-print versions of the *Tanya* that were distributed saw four phases of development: 1.) Chapters 1-41. 2.) Chapters 42-43 were added. 3.) Chapters 44-50 were added.
4.) Chapters 51-53 were added. See *Kovetz Oholei Torah,* issue 1092 (Brooklyn, 2004), pp.
59-64.

פרק מב והנה במ"ש לעיל בענין יראה תתאה
יובן היטב מ"ש בגמ' על פסוק
ועתה ישראל מה ה' אלהיך שואל מעמך כי אם ליראה
את ה' אלהיך אטו יראה מילתא זוטרתי היא אין לגבי
משה מילתא זוטרתי היא וכו' דלכאורה אינו מובן
התירוץ דהא שואל מעמך כתיב. אלא הענין הוא כי

CHAPTER 42

ON THE PATH TO REVERENCE
SECTION ONE: HOW MOSHE'S SOUL INFLUENCES YOURS

24TH NISAN REGULAR | 19TH NISAN LEAP

In chapter 41 we touched briefly upon the *Zohar's* distinction between "lower reverence" and "higher reverence." At "lower reverence" you feel the awesome presence of G-d and you are eager to fulfill His will. At "higher reverence" your sense of His presence is more arresting and you are simply overwhelmed by G-d.

We didn't talk too much about "higher reverence" in the previous chapter, and we're not going to discuss it here either. First we need to discuss "lower reverence" more thoroughly, and explore some additional techniques for acquiring it.

וְהִנֵּה בְּמַה שֶׁנִּתְבָּאֵר לְעֵיל בְּעָנְיַן יְרָאָה תַּתָּאָה — **Now, based on what we have explained above** in the previous chapter **about "lower reverence"** which is a basic requirement for all *mitzvah* observance, positive or negative, יוּבַן הֵיטֵב מַה שֶּׁכָּתוּב בַּגְּמָרָא — **we'll be able to properly understand what's written in the *Talmud*,** עַל פָּסוּק וְעַתָּה יִשְׂרָאֵל מָה ה' אֱלֹהֶיךָ שׁוֹאֵל מֵעִמָּךְ כִּי אִם לְיִרְאָה אֶת ה' אֱלֹהֶיךָ — in its commentary **on the verse, "Now O Israel, what does G-d, your G-d, ask from you? Only that you revere G-d, your G-d"** (Deuteronomy 10:12), אַטוּ יְרָאָה מִילְתָא זוּטַרְתִּי הִיא — upon which the *Talmud* asks, **"Is reverence such a small thing?"**

To "revere G-d" seems to be a *considerable* demand. How can the verse state that this is "*only*" what G-d wants, implying that it is something minimal?

אֵין לְגַבֵּי מֹשֶׁה מִילְתָא זוּטַרְתִּי הִיא וְכוּ' — **And the *Talmud* answers, "Yes, for Moshe our Teacher, it's a small thing etc.,"** (Brachos 33b).

דְּלִכְאוֹרָה אֵינוֹ מוּבָן הַתֵּירוּץ — **But the answer doesn't seem to make sense,** דְּהָא שׁוֹאֵל מֵעִמָּךְ כְּתִיב — **since the verse stresses,** "what does G-d, your G-d, ask *from you*" and not "what does G-d ask *from Moshe*"?

כל נפש ונפש מבית ישראל יש בה מבחי' משרע"ה
כי הוא משבעה רועים הממשיכים חיות ואלהות לכללו'
נשמות ישראל שלכן נקראים בשם רועים ומשרע"ה

To answer this question, the *Tanya* draws on a Jewish mystical teaching, that some of the energy of Moses' soul can be accessed by all the souls of Israel.

אֶלָּא הָעִנְיָן הוּא כִּי כָּל נֶפֶשׁ וְנֶפֶשׁ מִבֵּית יִשְׂרָאֵל יֵשׁ בָּה מִבְּחִינַת מֹשֶׁה רַבֵּינוּ עָלָיו הַשָּׁלוֹם — **Rather, the explanation is that every single soul in Israel has** available to it **an element of** the soul of **Moshe our Teacher, of blessed memory.**

Tikunei Zohar (112a) states that Moshe's soul, *"extends into every single generation, into every tzadik and scholar who immerses himself in the Torah, even to (the entire generation), six hundred thousand (of them)."* This refers to *"a spark of Moshe's soul which extends into the tzadik or scholar when he is studying Torah, to help him understand its correct intent'"* (Rabbi Shalom Buzaglo, *Kisei Melech* ibid.).

Rabbi Chaim Vital expands this idea beyond the context of Torah scholars to all souls which, *"are included in Moshe, since it is from his (soul) they all are derived... they are all sparks from him"* (*Etz Chaim* 32:1).

The *Tanya* will argue in this chapter that the *Talmud's* statement that reverence was *"a small thing... for Moshe our teacher,"* was referring to the "spark" of Moshe's soul *within your soul.*

First, the *Tanya* cites a further source for the connection between Moshe's soul and the souls of Israel, based on the *Talmud* and Zohar.

כִּי הוּא מִשִּׁבְעָה רוֹעִים — **For,** according to the *Talmud* (*Sukkah* 52b) Moses **is one of the** *"seven shepherds"* (*Micah* 5:4) of the Jewish people.

Who are the "seven shepherds" and what is their function?

The *Zohar* teaches that, corresponding to the seven Divine (emotional) attributes, G-d *"created on earth, truly worthy men to sustain (the attributes), and to illuminate them (on earth)... and they are the fathers of the world, Avraham, Yitzchak, Ya'akov, Yosef, Moshe, Aharon and David"* (addendum to *Zohar* 3, 216b. For differing views over the identity of the "seven shepherds, see *Talmud* ibid., *Zohar Chadash* 104a, and discussion in *Igros Kodesh*, vol. 18, p 553).

In the *Tanya's* words:

הַמַּמְשִׁיכִים חִיוּת וֶאֱלֹהוּת לִכְלָלוּת נִשְׁמוֹת יִשְׂרָאֵל — The seven "shepherds" cause energy and G-dliness to flow to the souls of all Israel, שֶׁלָּכֵן נִקְרָאִים בְּשֵׁם רוֹעִים — which is why they are called "shepherds" who tend to their flock and "feed" them with spiritual powers.

According to the Kabbalah, these seven "shepherds" are responsible for "shepherding and nourishing" the light of G-d's emotional attributes into *Malchus* (see Rabbi Ya'akov Tzvi Yalish, *Kehillas Ya'akov*, entry *"rosh davar"*). And since *Malchus*

הוא כללו' כולם ונקרא רעיא מהימנא דהיינו שממשיך
בחי' הדעת לכללות ישראל לידע את ה' כל אחד כפי
השגת נשמתו ושרשה למעלה ויניקתה משרש נשמת

/Shechinah is the source of Jewish souls, (as we learned in chapter 41, pp. 510-1), the "seven "shepherds" nourish us directly, strengthening our ability to have love and reverence of G-d.

But why, then, do we only need a spark from Moshe's soul in order to worship G-d properly? Wouldn't we need a spark from all seven shepherds? The *Tanya* explains:

וּמֹשֶׁה רַבֵּינוּ עָלָיו הַשָּׁלוֹם הוּא כְּלָלוּת כּוּלָּם — **And** while each of the "shepherds" can nourish a particular attribute in our souls, **Moshe, our teacher, of blessed memory, combines them all,** nourishing all the attributes (including reverence of G-d), וְנִקְרָא רַעְיָא מְהֵימְנָא — **and** that is why throughout the *Zohar* **he is called the "faithful shepherd,"** being the archetypal "shepherd" who fulfills the function of them all (see Jerusalem *Talmud*, *Sanhedrin* 10:1).

Why is Moshe able to nourish our souls with all the emotional attributes, in contrast to the other "shepherds" who are limited to a particular attribute? The *Tanya* explains:

דְּהַיְינוּ שֶׁמַּמְשִׁיךְ בְּחִינַת הַדַּעַת לִכְלָלוּת יִשְׂרָאֵל — **And that's because** Moshe **causes** *da'as* **to flow to all** the souls of **Israel** (see *Etz Chaim* ibid.).

As we have learned, (p. 62) the transition from thinking to feeling takes place via the agency of *da'as*, (recognition), a process through which ideas become personally relevant. By nourishing our *da'as*, Moshe's soul influences the entire range of our emotions, enabling us to worship G-d.

לֵידַע אֶת ה' כָּל אֶחָד — This enables **each individual to have *da'as* of G-d.**

But the extent to which you succeed in acquiring *da'as* depends on three factors:

כְּפִי הַשָּׂגַת נִשְׁמָתוֹ — a.) It will be **according to** your **soul's own cognitive abilities,** וְשָׁרְשָׁהּ לְמַעְלָה — **and** b.) it depends on your soul's **root above** (see p. 420), וִינִיקָתָהּ מִשֹּׁרֶשׁ נִשְׁמַת מֹשֶׁה רַבֵּינוּ עָלָיו הַשָּׁלוֹם — and c.) it also depends on the level from which your soul **can draw** energy **from the root of Moshe's soul.**

Obviously, the *da'as* of Moshe's soul doesn't *replace* the *da'as* in your soul. It merely enhances whatever is there already. So even with this assistance, you're still limited by your soul's powers—both in terms of "nurture" (how well your soul has matured intellectually), and "nature," (your soul's spiritual root and its level of "access" to Moshe's soul).

But what gives Moshe's soul the ability to nourish your *da'as*? What is his special power?

הַמּוּשְׁרֶשֶׁת בְּדַעַת הָעֶלְיוֹן — Moshe's soul **being rooted in "Supernal *da'as*"** (*da'as Ha-Elyon*)**,** (Rabbi Chaim Vital, *Likutei Torah*, *Parshas Balak*).

משרע"ה המושרשת בדעת העליון שבי"ס דאצילות המיוחדות במאצילן ב"ה שהוא ודעתו אחד והוא המדע

So far in *Tanya* we have learned that *da'as* acts as an intermediary between the intellect and the emotions: *da'as* internalizes your thoughts so they become personally relevant, and that generates feelings. The process follows a strict hierarchy: Your innermost will and desire (*keser*) informs your intuition (*chochmah*), which is then analyzed by cognition (*binah*) and made personally relevant by *da'as,* leading to emotions.

There is however, a second pathway (indicated by *Zohar* 3, 292a), through which *da'as* can receive from *keser directly,* enabling you to feel the supra-rational desires of your soul without any substantive intellectual pondering first. This direct pathway from *keser* to *da'as* is referred to as accessing "supernal *da'as*" (see *Ma'amarei Admor Ha-Zaken* 5569, pp. 15-24; ibid. pp. 167-8).

Accessing "supernal *da'as*" doesn't mean you completely bypass your intellect; it's just that your *chochmah* and *binah* quickly align with the pre-conceived conclusion of your *da'as* (which it received from *keser*). It's as if your emotions are flowing directly from *keser,* and they just "pass through" *chochmah* and *binah* on the journey to your heart (ibid. pp. 16-17).

"Supernal *da'as,*" then, has the power to *bypass hierarchies* in the metaphysical realm. In this case, it "short-circuits" *keser* to *da'as,* effectively bypassing *chochmah* and *binah*.

As we shall see, since Moshe's soul is "rooted" in "supernal *da'as,*" Moshe has the power to "short circuit" connections between higher states of mind and the souls of Israel.

שֶׁבְּי' סְפִירוֹת דַּאֲצִילוּת — Moshe's soul, rooted in "supernal *da'as,*" is able to "short cut" the consciousness **of the ten *sefiros* of *Atzilus*** down into the souls of Israel, below in this world.

The reason why the physical world distracts us from an awareness of G-d, is because we have lost the consciousness of *Atzilus*. In *Atzilus,* G-d is real and "tangible," while the physical world is a distant dream. In this world, the opposite is true: physical reality is obvious and real, whereas to find G-d we need to enter the imaginative space of the mind.

Since Moshe's soul is rooted in "supernal *da'as,*" it can provide a "short-cut" for our souls to access a glimmer of the consciousness of *Atzilus,* making G-d's presence more real and tangible to us. While the vision may not be a clear one, it will definitely gives us a boost in the daily challenge of trying to worship an invisible G-d, in a world full of physical distractions and temptations (see Rabbi Menachem Mendel of Lubavitch (*Tzemach Tzedek*), *Derech Mitzvosecha,* 80a-82a).

הַמְיוּחָדוֹת בְּמַאֲצִילָן בָּרוּךְ הוּא — In *Atzilus,* all G-d's attributes **are merged with their emanating source,** שֶׁהוּא וְדַעְתּוֹ אֶחָד — and it is a place **where He and His *da'as***

כו'. וְעוֹד זאת יתר על כן בכל דור ודור יורדין ניצוצין
מנשמת משרע"ה ומתלבשין בגוף ונפש של חכמי
הדור עיני העדה ללמד דעת את העם ולידע גדולת ה'

are one, 'וְהוּא הַמַּדָּע כו — and He is simultaneously the power to know, the knower, and the knowledge (*Rambam, Laws of Foundations of the Torah* 2:10; see above, chapter 2, p. 46).

G-d Himself is absolutely one, devoid of any multiplicity. The created worlds (*Beriah, Yetzirah* and *Asiyah*), on the other hand, have the consciousness of multiplicity and separateness from G-d.

The highest world of *Atzilus* represents an intermediate phase between absolute oneness (G-d's essence) and multiplicity (the created worlds). On one hand, *Atzilus* does exhibit some multiplicity: it has *ten* different attributes of *chochmah, binah, da'as etc.* But, on the other hand, *Atzilus* has a profound unity, since the attributes are *"merged with their emanating source."*

So in *Atzilus*, there is multiplicity, *but without separateness*.

That is why the Kabbalists refer to *Atzilus*, not as G-d, but *G-dliness* (*Elokus*). A realm of *ten* attributes cannot be G-d, because G-d is one. But since the attributes are merged with G-d, without any separation, they could be called *G-dly*.

Rambam's statement that G-d *"and his da'as are one"* captures the character of *Atzilus*. There is the phenomenon of a distinct attribute (in this case, *da'as*), but it is nevertheless totally merged with G-d.

וְעוֹד זֹאת יָתֵר עַל כֵּן — And furthermore, we receive additional influence from Moshe's soul, through another pathway.

Up to this point the *Tanya* has been discussing how Moshe's soul influences your soul directly. But the connection has been a relatively weak one: you have only been able to draw energy from Moshe's soul; his soul did not actually *enter* you.

Now we will discuss another type of influence, where a "spark" from Moshe's soul actually enters a human being here on earth. This won't happen to you directly, as it's something experienced only by the sages of each generation; but by learning from contemporary sages, you will be able to receive an additional influence from Moshe's soul, in a more tangible way.

בְּכָל דּוֹר וָדוֹר יוֹרְדִין נִיצוֹצִין מִנִּשְׁמַת מֹשֶׁה רַבֵּינוּ עָלָיו הַשָּׁלוֹם — Because in every single generation, there is not only the (distant) influence of Moshe's soul, but actual "sparks" from Moshe's soul come down, וּמִתְלַבְּשִׁין בְּגוּף וְנֶפֶשׁ שֶׁל חַכְמֵי הַדּוֹר — and become enmeshed in both the body and soul of the sages of that generation (*Tikunei Zohar* 112a, cited above), עֵינֵי הָעֵדָה — the sages of each generation being the *"eyes of the congregation"* (*Numbers* 15:24), לְלַמֵּד דַּעַת אֶת הָעָם — and these sparks of Moshe's soul empower the sages *"to teach da'as to the people"* (*Ecclesiastes* 12:9), וְלֵידַע גְּדוּלַּת ה' — enabling the people to have *da'as* of the

ולעבדו בלב ונפש כי העבודה שבלב היא לפי הדעת
כמ"ש דע את אלהי אביך ועבדהו בלב שלם ונפש

greatness of G-d, וּלְעָבְדוֹ בְּלֵב וָנֶפֶשׁ — and through this *da'as* they will be empowered **to worship Him with heart and soul.**

The influence you receive from Moshe's soul via the contemporary sages is more powerful and tangible than the direct influence you receive from Moshe's soul, since: a.) In the contemporary sages, an *actual spark* of Moshe's soul is present; and, b.) that "spark" is embodied even in the *physical presence* of the contemporary sage, *"the body and soul of the sages."*

This additional power of the contemporary sages to nourish your *da'as* is stressed by the text of the *Tanya* here. Above, when discussing the direct influence of Moshe's soul, you were empowered simply *"to have da'as of G-d."* But here, when speaking of the influence of Moshe's soul through the contemporary sages, the *Tanya* stresses that you will be empowered, not only *"to have da'as of the greatness of G-d,"* but also, *"to worship Him with heart and soul."* The sages will empower you, not only to acquire *da'as*, but also to translate it practically into devotional worship.

The *Tanya* reminds us why *da'as* is so crucial:

כִּי הָעֲבוֹדָה שֶׁבַּלֵּב הִיא לְפִי הַדַּעַת **— For** the quality of **your heart's worship is proportionate to your** *da'as*, כְּמוֹ שֶׁכָּתוּב דַּע אֶת אֱלֹהֵי אָבִיךָ וְעָבְדֵהוּ בְּלֵב שָׁלֵם וְנֶפֶשׁ חֲפֵיצָה **— as the verse states,** *"Know (Da) the G-d of your father, and (then you will be able to) worship Him with a perfect heart and a yearning soul"* (*1 Chronicles* 28:9).

Faith alone, without *da'as*, doesn't compel you to worship G-d. The *Talmud* illustrates this with the example of *"the burglar who, as he enters his tunnel (to commit a burglary), prays to G-d (that he won't be caught)"* (*Talmud, Brachos* 63a, according to text of *Ein Ya'akov*). The burglar believes in G-d, but that doesn't stop him violating G-d's commandment, "Don't steal." He even prays to G-d for success in his burglary, asking G-d to help him violate G-d's will! Without *da'as* you can easily slip into a state of cognitive dissonance, where you're willing to perform an action that is contradictory to your belief.

That's why we find that, in Egypt, even after *"the people believed"* (*Exodus* 4:31), it was then necessary for the people *"to have da'as that I am G-d"* (ibid. 6:7; *Derech Mitzvosecha* ibid.).

PRACTICAL LESSONS

If you want your feelings for G-d to have stability and consistency, you need to nurture your *da'as*, the part of your soul that makes ideas personally relevant.

In this task your soul will be assisted by the soul powers of the Biblical figure Moshe.

The embodied energy of Moshe's soul is particularly strong in the sages of each generation, so by connecting with and learning from them, your *da'as* will grow.

חפיצה ולעתיד הוא אומר ולא ילמדו איש את רעהו
לאמר דעו את ה' כי כולם ידעו אותי וגו' אך עיקר
הדעת אינה הידיעה לבדה שידעו גדולת ה' מפי
סופרים ומפי ספרים אלא העיקר הוא להעמיק דעתו
בגדולת ה' ולתקוע מחשבתו בה' בחוזק ואומץ הלב
והמוח עד שתהא מחשבתו מקושרת בה' בקשר

59B

Da'as enhances your emotions for G-d with consistency and integrity. Without *da'as*, you might love G-d one minute, and then love something inappropriate a minute later (*Ma'amarei Admor Ha-Zakein* 5569, pp. 18-19).

וְלֶעָתִיד הוּא אוֹמֵר — **But** only **in the future era** will we have sufficient *da'as* of our own that we will no longer require the influence of the sages, as **the verse states,** וְלֹא יְלַמְּדוּ אִישׁ אֶת רֵעֵהוּ לֵאמֹר דְּעוּ אֶת ה' כִּי כוּלָּם יֵדְעוּ אוֹתִי וְגוֹ' — *"No longer will they* **need to teach one another, saying, 'know (da) G-d,' for all of them will know Me"** (*Jeremiah* 31:34).

Until that time, however, we are all dependent on the sages of our generation to nourish our powers of *da'as* in order to worship G-d properly.

SECTION TWO: HOW TO MEDITATE YOUR WAY TO DA'AS

Merely learning from the sages of the generation will not be enough. You will have to make a sustained effort in your meditative work if you want to acquire real *da'as*.

אַךְ עִיקַּר הַדַּעַת אֵינָה הַיְדִיעָה לְבַדָּה — **But the principle quality of** *da'as* **isn't mere** factual **knowledge,** as the term *da'as* superficially implies (*da'as* is often translated simply as "knowledge"), שֶׁיֵּדְעוּ גְּדוּלַת ה' מִפִּי סוֹפְרִים וּמִפִּי סְפָרִים — it isn't just that people **should have** factual **knowledge of G-d's greatness, from teachers and from books.**

אֶלָּא הָעִיקָר הוּא — **Rather the main point is** to *feel* the truth of these teachings by personally *connecting* with the ideas.

Your feeling for something depends on the depth with which your mind recognizes it and connects with it. The key to a successful *da'as* meditation doesn't depend on which particular thoughts you have about G-d; what matters is the *intensity* of those thoughts.

לְהַעֲמִיק דַּעְתּוֹ בִּגְדוּלַת ה' — The key to *da'as* is **through pondering deeply with your** *da'as* **on G-d's greatness,** וְלִתְקוֹעַ מַחֲשַׁבְתּוֹ בָּהּ בְּחוֹזֶק וְאוֹמֶץ הַלֵּב וְהַמּוֹחַ — **and fixating your thoughts on G-d, with an intensity of mind and determination of heart,** עַד שֶׁתְּהֵא מַחֲשַׁבְתּוֹ מְקוּשֶׁרֶת בָּהּ בְּקֶשֶׁר אַמִּיץ וְחָזָק — **until a firm and strong attachment is achieved between your thoughts and G-d.**

Da'as is achieved through an intense "fixation" and "attachment" of the mind on thoughts about G-d, to the point where you are drawn to Him and His worship. In

אַמִּיץ וְחָזָק כְּמוֹ שֶׁהִיא מְקוּשֶׁרֶת בְּדָבָר גַּשְׁמִי שֶׁרוֹאֶה
בְּעֵינֵי בָשָׂר וּמַעֲמִיק בּוֹ מַחֲשַׁבְתּוֹ כַּנּוֹדַע שֶׁדַּעַת הוּא
לְשׁוֹן הִתְקַשְּׁרוּת כְּמוֹ וְהָאָדָם יָדַע וְגוֹ' וְכֹחַ זֶה וּמִדָּה זוֹ
לְקַשֵּׁר דַּעְתּוֹ בַּה' יֵשׁ בְּכָל נֶפֶשׁ מִבֵּית יִשְׂרָאֵל בִּינִיקָתָהּ
מִנִּשְׁמַת מֹשֶׁרַע"ה רַק מֵאַחַר שֶׁנִּתְלַבְּשָׁה הַנֶּפֶשׁ בַּגּוּף

fact, this is suggested by the Biblical use of the term *da'as,* which can sometimes refer to "desire" or "will," as in *"From all the families of the earth I have desired (ya-dati) you alone"* (Amos 3:2). The implication here is that when you deeply recognize something's value, you will come to desire it (Rabbi Shneur Zalman, *Torah Ohr,* 88a).

But how do you calibrate *da'as?* How do you know when you've achieved it?

כְּמוֹ שֶׁהִיא מְקוּשֶׁרֶת בְּדָבָר גַּשְׁמִי שֶׁרוֹאֶה בְּעֵינֵי בָשָׂר — *Da'as* will "connect" you with an idea, **just like you're "connected" with a physical object that you see with your physical eyes,** וּמַעֲמִיק בּוֹ מַחֲשַׁבְתּוֹ — **and which you're thinking about deeply.**

If you meditate effectively, *da'as* has the potential to make spiritual ideas real to you, as if you had seen them with your physical eyes. It won't be that you've heard about G-d, or that someone told you He exists; through *da'as* you'll come to appreciate G-d as a living reality.

כַּנּוֹדַע שֶׁדַּעַת הוּא לְשׁוֹן הִתְקַשְּׁרוּת כְּמוֹ וְהָאָדָם יָדַע וְגוֹ' — **And we know that** the term ***"da'as"* suggests intimate connection as in,** *"Adam knew (yada) Eve"* (Genesis 4:1; see chapter 3, p. 62).

In addition to "knowledge" and "desire," *da'as* also implies "intimate connection." And this is acquired in three phases: 1.) *hiskashrus*—personally *connecting* to an idea, so that you feel its relevance to your life; 2.) *hakarah*—deeply *recognizing* the real impact of the idea on your life; and, 3.) *hargashah*—the shift from an intellectual recognition of an idea to an actual *feeling* of it (*Toras Menachem, Hisva'aduyos,* 5711, vol. 1, p. 232).

25TH NISAN REGULAR | 20TH NISAN LEAP

וְכֹחַ זֶה וּמִדָּה זוֹ — **And the potential** to acquire **this attribute** of *da'as* through meditative work, לְקַשֵּׁר דַּעְתּוֹ בַּה', — **to connect your *da'as* with G-d,** יֵשׁ בְּכָל נֶפֶשׁ מִבֵּית יִשְׂרָאֵל — **is within the ability of every soul in the House of Israel,** בִּינִיקָתָהּ מִנִּשְׁמַת מֹשֶׁה רַבֵּינוּ עָלָיו הַשָּׁלוֹם — **by virtue of the energy which is drawn from the soul of Moshe, our teacher, of blessed memory.**

Being connected to Moshe's soul doesn't mean that you will have *da'as* of G-d automatically or effortlessly. It just means that if you put your mind to it, and meditate with focus, you have the potential to succeed.

רַק מֵאַחַר שֶׁנִּתְלַבְּשָׁה הַנֶּפֶשׁ בַּגּוּף — **Only,** despite this inherent potential of your soul-connection with Moshe's soul, **since your soul is placed into your body,**

צְרִיכָה לִיגִיעָה רַבָּה וַעֲצוּמָה כְּפוּלָה וּמְכֻפֶּלֶת.
הָאַחַת הִיא יְגִיעַת בָּשָׂר לְבַטֵּשׁ אֶת הַגּוּף וּלְהַכְנִיעוֹ שֶׁלֹּא
יַחֲשִׁיךְ עַל אוֹר הַנֶּפֶשׁ כמש"ל בְּשֵׁם הַזֹּהַר דְּגוּפָא דְּלָא
סְלִיק בֵּיהּ נְהוֹרָא דְּנִשְׁמָתָא מְבַטְּשִׁין לֵיהּ וְהַיְנוּ עַל יְדֵי
הִרְהוּרֵי תְּשׁוּבָה מֵעוֹמֶק הַלֵּב כמ"ש שָׁם. וְהַשֵּׁנִית
הִיא יְגִיעַת הַנֶּפֶשׁ שֶׁלֹּא תִכְבַּד עָלֶיהָ הָעֲבוֹדָה לִיגַע

צְרִיכָה לִיגִיעָה רַבָּה וַעֲצוּמָה כְּפוּלָה וּמְכֻפֶּלֶת — **an enormously great and intense effort is required, doubled and redoubled,** to tap into that potential.

"(1) An enormously great and (2) intense effort... (3) doubled and (4) redoubled" suggests four distinct elements in your efforts to achieve *da'as.*

1.) *"Enormously great... effort"* indicates that a large *quantity* of time needs to be dedicated to this meditative work.

PRACTICAL LESSONS

You can't just rely on the Sages or on your soul energies to acquire *da'as.* You need to do some serious meditative work.

Da'as is acquired through intense focus on an idea about G-d, so that your mind becomes fixated and "attached" to it.

2.) *"Intense effort"* suggests that the meditation must be of a high *quality*, in great depth.

3.) The work is *"doubled"* in that it involves both the body and the soul.

4.) It is *"redoubled"* since in both areas (body and soul), two types of effort are required, as the *Tanya* will now clarify (Rabbi Alexander Yudasin, *Ha-Lekach Ve-Ha-Libuv*).

הָאַחַת הִיא יְגִיעַת בָּשָׂר — **Firstly, there is the effort with your body** in two ways, לְבַטֵּשׁ אֶת הַגּוּף — a.) **to "crush" the body** by reducing your enjoyment of the pleasures of this world, וּלְהַכְנִיעוֹ שֶׁלֹּא יַחֲשִׁיךְ עַל אוֹר הַנֶּפֶשׁ — **and** b.) **to subdue it,** with humbling thoughts, **so that** the body **won't eclipse the soul's light.**

כְּמוֹ שֶׁנִּתְבָּאֵר לְעֵיל בְּשֵׁם הַזֹּהַר — **As explained above** (chapter 29, p. 325), **citing the** *Zohar,* the need for "crushing" the body, דְּגוּפָא דְּלָא סְלִיק בֵּיהּ נְהוֹרָא דְּנִשְׁמָתָא מְבַטְּשִׁין לֵיהּ — **that** *"if a body won't give out the light of its soul, crush it,* **and the soul's light will come out"** וְהַיְנוּ עַל יְדֵי הִרְהוּרֵי תְּשׁוּבָה מֵעוֹמֶק הַלֵּב (Zohar 3, 168a), — and work of both "crushing" and "subduing" of the body **is carried out through thoughts of repentance from the depths of your heart,** כְּמוֹ שֶׁנִּתְבָּאֵר שָׁם — **as was explained there.**

21ST NISAN LEAP

וְהַשֵּׁנִית הִיא יְגִיעַת הַנֶּפֶשׁ שֶׁלֹּא תִכְבַּד עָלֶיהָ הָעֲבוֹדָה — **And secondly, there is the effort with the** will-power of your **soul,** to train your will to follow G-d **so that wor-**

מחשבתה להעמיק ולהתבונן בגדולת ה' שעה גדולה
רצופה כי שיעור שעה זו אינו שוה בכל נפש יש נפש
זכה בטבעה שמיד שמתבוננת בגדולת ה' יגיע אליה
היראה ופחד ה' כמ"ש בש"ע א"ח סימן א' כשיתבונן
האדם שהמלך הגדול ממ"ה הקב"ה אשר מלא כל
הארץ כבודו עומד עליו ורואה במעשיו מיד יגיע אליו
היראה וכו' ויש נפש שפלה בטבעה ותולדתה ממקור
חוצבה ממדרגות תחתונות די"ס דעשיה ולא תוכל
למצוא במחשבתה האלהות כ"א בקושי ובחזקה
ובפרט אם הוטמאה בחטאת נעורי' שהעוונות מבדילים

— **לִיגַּע מַחֲשַׁבְתָּה לְהַעֲמִיק וּלְהִתְבּוֹנֵן בִּגְדוּלַת ה',** ship shouldn't be a bother for you, and, practically speaking, this also has two elements, a.) **that you should put a lot of effort into deep, mindful meditation of G-d's greatness,** שָׁעָה גְדוֹלָה רְצוּפָה, — and b.) this meditation should be **for a long, uninterrupted period** (*Ha-Lekach Ve-Ha-Libuv* ibid.).

Exactly how long should this meditation be?

כִּי שִׁיעוּר שָׁעָה זוֹ אֵינוֹ שָׁוֶה בְּכָל נֶפֶשׁ — No fixed time can be given **because the period of time** necessary for this **isn't the same for everybody.**

יֵשׁ נֶפֶשׁ זַכָּה בְּטִבְעָהּ — Because, on the one hand, **there's the soul which is rarefied by nature,** שָׁמִיד שֶׁמִּתְבּוֹנֶנֶת בִּגְדוּלַת ה' יַגִּיעַ אֵלֶיהָ הַיִּרְאָה וּפַחַד ה' — **and when it meditates on the greatness of G-d, reverence and trepidation of G-d come upon it immediately,** כְּמוֹ שֶׁכָּתוּב בְּשֻׁלְחָן עָרוּךְ אוֹרַח חַיִּים סִימָן א' — **as written in the *Code of Jewish Law, Orach Chaim,* chapter 1,** כְּשֶׁיִּתְבּוֹנֵן הָאָדָם שֶׁהַמֶּלֶךְ הַגָּדוֹל מֶלֶךְ מַלְכֵי הַמְּלָכִים הַקָּדוֹשׁ בָּרוּךְ הוּא — **that when a person will meditate on the fact that, *"the great King (the "King, King of kings"), the Blessed Holy One,"*** אֲשֶׁר מְלֹא כָל הָאָרֶץ — ***"whose 'glory fills the earth,'"*** (Isaiah 6:3), *stands* כְּבוֹדוֹ עוֹמֵד עָלָיו וְרוֹאֶה בְּמַעֲשָׂיו — ***"whose 'glory fills the earth,' (Isaiah 6:3), stands before him, and is watching his actions..."*** מִיָּד יַגִּיעַ אֵלָיו הַיִּרְאָה וְכוּ' — ***"reverence will come upon him immediately."***

וְיֵשׁ נֶפֶשׁ שְׁפָלָה בְּטִבְעָהּ — **And then there is the soul which, by nature, is feeble,** וְתוֹלַדְתָּהּ מִמְּקוֹר חוּצָבָהּ מִמַּדְרֵגוֹת תַּחְתּוֹנוֹת דִי' סְפִירוֹת דַּעֲשִׂיָּה — **coming from a source carved from the lowest levels of the ten *sefiros* of the lowest world, *Asiyah*,** וְלֹא תוּכַל לִמְצוֹא בְּמַחֲשַׁבְתָּה הָאֱלֹהוּת כִּי אִם בְּקוֹשִׁי וּבְחֶזְקָה — **such a soul won't be able to harbor thoughts of G-dliness, without difficulty and persistence,** וּבִפְרַט אִם **— especially if** this "feeble" soul **has been** further impeded through becoming spiritually **contaminated by "sins of youth"** (see chapter 7, p. 100), שֶׁהָעֲוֹונוֹת מַבְדִּילִים כּוּ' **— since** sins make it harder to connect with G-d, as the verse states ***"your sins have separated you* from your G-d"** (Isaiah 59:2), [כְּמוֹ שֶׁכָּתוּב בְּסֵפֶר חֲסִידִים סִימָן ל"ה **— as stated** by Rabbi Yehudah *Ha-Chasid,* **in *Sefer***

כו' [כמ"ש בס"ח סי' ל"ה] ומ"מ בקושי ובחזק' שתתחזק
מאד מחשבתו באומץ ויגיעה רבה ועומק גדול להעמיק
בגדולת ה' שעה גדולה בודאי תגיע אליו עכ"פ היראה
תתאה הנ"ל וכמשארז"ל יגעתי ומצאתי תאמין וכדכתי'
אם תבקשנה ככסף וכמטמונים תחפשנה אז תבין
יראת ה' פי' כדרך שמחפש אדם מטמון ואוצר הטמון
בתחתיות הארץ שחופר אחריו ביגיעה עצומה כך צריך
לחפור ביגיעה עצומה לגלות אוצר של יראת שמים

60A

Chasidim, **chapter 35,** that *"you can't learn to connect your heart constantly to G-d unless you abandon sin, because sin separates you (from G-d) and causes you to forget your reverence (of Him)."*

The *Tanya* now encourages us that, even if we find meditation difficult, everyone has the potential to reach at least "lower reverence" for G-d.

וּמִכָּל מָקוֹם בְּקוֹשִׁי וּבְחָזְקָה — **But nevertheless,** even a "feeble" soul can sustain focused thoughts about G-d, *"with difficulty and through persistence"* (ibid.), שֶׁתִּתְחַזֵּק מְאֹד מַחֲשַׁבְתּוֹ בְּאוֹמֶץ וִיגִיעָה רַבָּה וְעוֹמֶק גָּדוֹל — **through a determined effort to focus the mind intently with profound concentration,** לְהַעֲמִיק בִּגְדוּלַת ה' שָׁעָה גְדוֹלָה — **thinking deeply about the greatness of G-d for a prolonged period,** בְּוַדַּאי תַּגִּיעַ אֵלָיו עַל כָּל פָּנִים הַיִּרְאָה תַּתָּאָה הַנִּזְכֶּרֶת לְעֵיל — **then this will definitely result in him at least acquiring the "lower reverence" mentioned above** (throughout chapter 41).

וּכְמוֹ שֶׁאָמְרוּ רַבּוֹתֵינוּ זִכְרוֹנָם לִבְרָכָה — **And, as the Sages, of blessed memory, said** of the fruitfulness of effort, יָגַעְתִּי וּמָצָאתִי תַּאֲמִין — *"If a person says, 'I have put in a lot of effort and I haven't succeeded,' don't believe him; but if he says, 'I have put in a lot of effort and I have succeeded,' believe him"* (Talmud, Megillah 6b).

(The *Tanya's* assurance that your persistent meditations will *definitely* result in a feeling of reverence, takes for granted that you have first repented for your sins. For, as cited above from *Sefer Chasidim,* the presence of any unrepented sins may act as an obstacle to the meditative process — *Notes on Tanya*).

וּכְדִכְתִיב אִם תְּבַקְשֶׁנָּה כַכֶּסֶף וְכַמַּטְמוֹנִים תַּחְפְּשֶׂנָה אָז תָּבִין יִרְאַת ה' — **And** inspiration for sustained meditative efforts can be found in the verse, *"If you seek it like silver, and search for it like buried treasure, then will you understand the reverence of G-d"* (Proverbs 2:4-5), פֵּירוּשׁ כְּדֶרֶךְ שֶׁמְחַפֵּשׂ אָדָם מַטְמוֹן וְאוֹצָר הַטָּמוּן בְּתַחְתִּיּוֹת הָאָרֶץ — שֶׁחוֹפֵר אַחֲרָיו בִּיגִיעָה עֲצוּמָה — **meaning that just like a person searching for a buried treasure hidden in the depths of the earth, will make a huge effort digging for it,** since he knows that it's definitely there, כָּךְ צָרִיךְ לַחְפֹּר בִּיגִיעָה עֲצוּמָה לְגַלּוֹת אוֹצָר — שֶׁל יִרְאַת שָׁמַיִם הַצָּפוּן וּמוּסְתָּר — **in the same way, you must make a huge effort to reveal the** *"fear of Heaven which is treasured"* (Talmud, Brachos 33b) **and hidden**

הצפון ומוסתר בבינת הלב של כל אדם מישראל שהיא
בחי' ומדרגה שלמעלה מהזמן והיא היראה הטבעית
המסותרת הנ"ל רק שכדי שתבא לידי מעשה בבחי'
יראת חטא להיות סור מרע במעשה דבור ומחשבה

well away, בְּבִינַת הַלֵּב שֶׁל כָּל אָדָם מִיִּשְׂרָאֵל — **in the** depths of the *"understanding heart"* (*Mishnah, Avos* 6:6), **of every person in Israel,** since you know that it's there.

The verse in Proverbs (*"If you seek it like silver, and search for it like buried treasure..."*), suggests that reverence of G-d is not something that really needs to be acquired, but discovered. It's hidden inside you like a buried treasure, and you will find it if you "dig" and search hard enough, by means of the appropriate meditations.

The verse promises that if you "dig" effectively, "then you will *understand* the reverence of G-d," which the *Tanya* interprets to mean an unearthing of "the '*understanding* heart' of every person in Israel."

שֶׁהִיא בְּחִינָה וּמַדְרֵגָה שֶׁלְּמַעְלָה מֵהַזְּמַן — **This** "understanding heart" **is an** innate **quality and level which transcends time,** which means that you can definitely access it at any time.

Your heart will inevitably feel a variety of different emotions at different times. But the "understanding" of your heart refers, not to actual feelings, but to the heart's innate capacity for emotional intelligence, a power which is not limited to a particular circumstance or time. Your capacity to revere G-d is not dependent on any temporal, external factors; rather it is a "treasure" which you can unearth at any time.

וְהִיא הַיִּרְאָה הַטִּבְעִית הַמְסוּתֶּרֶת הַנִּזְכֶּרֶת לְעֵיל — **And this** "treasure" is **the inherent, dormant reverence referred to above** (at the beginning of chapter 41), which is always present, at least in a dormant state, in every soul of Israel.

However, as we have consistently stressed in this chapter, if your inherent reverence remains dormant and "hidden," it isn't of any use to you. It may already be a "treasure" in your possession; but in order to cash it into usable "currency," you need to do some serious meditative work. Only by nourishing your *da'as* will you be able to access your dormant reverence, and begin to actually feel it.

רַק שֶׁכְּדֵי שֶׁתָּבֹא לִידֵי מַעֲשֶׂה — **Only, in order for** the dormant feelings **to motivate action,** בִּבְחִינַת יִרְאַת חֵטְא — at *"the* minimal level of *reverence* necessary not to sin,"* לִהְיוֹת סוּר מֵרַע בְּמַעֲשֶׂה דִּבּוּר וּמַחֲשָׁבָה — so that you *"turn away from evil"* (*Psalms* 34:14), **in action, speech and thought,** צָרִיךְ לְגַלּוֹתָהּ מִמַּצְפּוּנֵי בִּינַת הַלֵּב שֶׁלְּמַעְלָה

PRACTICAL LESSONS

Even if you don't find it easy to focus your thoughts, with a determined effort you will succeed. Imagine you were looking for a hidden treasure that you knew was there.

צריך לגלותה ממצפוני בינת הלב שלמעלה מהזמן
להביאה לבחי' מחשבה ממש שבמוח להעמיק בה
מחשבתו משך זמן מה ממש עד שתצא פעולתה
מהכח אל הפועל ממש דהיינו להיות סור מרע ועשה
טוב במחשבה דבור ומעשה מפני ה' הצופה ומביט
ומאזין ומקשיב ומבין אל כל מעשהו ובוחן כליותיו
ולבו וכמאמר רז"ל הסתכל בשלשה דברים כו' עין

מֵהַזְּמַן — **you need to bring out manifestly** those latent, intangible feelings **from the depths of your "understanding heart," which transcends time,** לַהֲבִיאָהּ לִבְחִינַת מַחֲשָׁבָה מַמָּשׁ שֶׁבַּמּוֹחַ — **and make them conscious,** if not as palpable feelings in the heart, then at least **as tangible thought in your brain,** לְהַעֲמִיק בָּהּ מַחֲשַׁבְתּוֹ מֶשֶׁךְ זְמַן מָה מַמָּשׁ — and then you need **to ponder** these ideas **deeply in** conscious **thought, for a substantive period of time,** עַד שֶׁתֵּצֵא פְּעוּלָתָהּ מֵהַכֹּחַ אֶל הַפּוֹעַל מַמָּשׁ — **until** this potential produces actual results, דְּהַיְינוּ לִהְיוֹת סוּר מֵרַע וַעֲשֵׂה טוֹב בְּמַחֲשָׁבָה — namely to **"turn away from evil and do good,"** in thought, speech דִּבּוּר וּמַעֲשֶׂה — **and action.**

מִפְּנֵי ה' הַצּוֹפֶה וּמַבִּיט וּמַאֲזִין וּמַקְשִׁיב וּמֵבִין אֶל כָּל מַעֲשֵׂהוּ — **At** this very basic level you're motivated, not out of a profound reverence of, and feeling for, G-d, but merely **because of the G-d who watches** *"and sees, hears and is attentive to, and understands,"* (*Liturgy, High Holidays*), **all of your deeds,** וּבוֹחֵן כְּלִיוֹתָיו וְלִבּוֹ — **and** *"He's checking (your) inclinations and heart"* (*Jeremiah* 11:20), וּכְמַאֲמַר רַבּוֹתֵינוּ — **as in the teach**ing of our Sages of blessed memory, זִכְרוֹנָם לִבְרָכָה הִסְתַּכֵּל בִּשְׁלֹשָׁה דְּבָרִים כו' עַיִן רוֹאָה וְאוֹזֶן שׁוֹמַעַת כו' **"Consider three things** and you will not come to sin. Know what is above you: *a seeing eye, a hearing ear,* and all your deeds are recorded in a book" (*Mishnah, Avos* 2:1).

A CHASIDIC THOUGHT

I was born with an innate capacity to revere G-d, which is always present in the depths of my soul. But to access that capacity, so that I can actually worship G-d with some real feeling, I need to make use of my *da'as*, my ability to take something abstract and make it tangible. In this task, I will be assisted by the energy of Moshe's soul, which I can access both directly and through the sages of my generation. When I apply my *da'as* effectively, through rigorous meditation, I can be assured that, at the very least, I will acquire a basic feeling of reverence (necessary for proper worship) that G-d is watching me and I don't want to disobey Him while He's watching.

רואה ואוזן שומעת כו' וגם כי אין לו דמות הגוף הרי
אדרבה הכל גלוי וידוע לפניו ביתר שאת לאין קץ
מראיית העין ושמיעת האזן עד"מ רק הוא עד"מ כמו

SECTION THREE: HOW G-D KNOWS HIS WORLD

26TH NISAN REGULAR | 22ND NISAN LEAP

The above quote describes G-d in physical terms, as having *"a seeing eye, a hearing ear."* Obviously this is a metaphor, since G-d does not have actual eyes and ears. But if G-d's eyes and ears are not literal, is the idea that "He's watching over us" also non-literal? The *Tanya* now assures us that this is not the case.

וְגַם כִּי אֵין לוֹ דְּמוּת הַגּוּף — **And while** G-d's "seeing eye" and "hearing ear" are metaphorical since G-d **"has no semblance of a body"** (Liturgy, Yigdal, following *Rambam, Third Principle of Faith*), הֲרֵי אַדְרַבָּה — **that doesn't mean** that G-d isn't really watching you, **but to the contrary,** the fact that He doesn't use actual eyes or ears means that His awareness of you is *greater.*

הַכֹּל גָּלוּי וְיָדוּעַ לְפָנָיו — Our Sages hinted to this idea by stating, **everything is *"revealed and known before Him"*** (*Talmud*, Shabbos 55a).

The Sages could have phrased this more simply, and said, "G-d knows." Why did they employ this somewhat cumbersome phrase, that everything is "revealed and known before Him"?

As the *Tanya* will explain, the Sages chose this phrase to teach us that G-d doesn't acquire knowledge in the same way that we do. For us mortals there is a *process:* initially we lack knowledge about a certain thing, then we gain access to some information, and after analyzing the information with our minds, we end up with knowl-

> ## PRACTICAL LESSONS
>
> The fact that G-d doesn't have eyes and ears doesn't mean He's not watching you. He really is!

edge. But this sharp dualism between *subject* (you) and *object* (the knowledge), couldn't be true of G-d, who is utterly one. G-d must know everything without having to go through the process of actually coming to know it.

That is why the Sages implied that everything is *already* "revealed and known before Him" (in the past tense), without Him having to actively acquire that knowledge.

בְּיֶתֶר שְׂאֵת לְאֵין קֵץ מֵרְאִיַּת הָעַיִן וּשְׁמִיעַת הָאֹזֶן עַל דֶּרֶךְ מָשָׁל — And through knowing in this way, G-d's awareness of you is **infinitely greater than, for example, through seeing with eyes or hearing with ears.**

The fact that G-d doesn't need eyes or ears to acquire knowledge doesn't make His awareness of your actions any less. Since He doesn't suffer from any dualism, G-d's knowledge is actually more powerful, because there is no schism between Him and what He knows.

אָדָם הַיּוֹדֵעַ וּמַרְגִּישׁ בְּעַצְמוֹ כָּל מַה שֶּׁנַּעֲשָׂה וְנִפְעַל
בְּאֶחָד מִכָּל רְמַ"ח אֵיבָרָיו כְּמוֹ קוֹר אוֹ חוֹם וַאֲפִי' חוֹם
שֶׁבְּצִפָּרְנֵי רַגְלָיו עַד"מ אִם נִכְוָה בָּאוֹר וְכֵן מַהוּתָם
וְעַצְמוּתָם וְכָל מַה שֶּׁמִּתְפָּעֵל בָּהֶם יוֹדֵעַ וּמַרְגִּישׁ בְּמוֹחוֹ
וּכְעֵין יְדִיעָה זוֹ עַד"מ יוֹדֵעַ הקב"ה כָּל הַנִּפְעָל בְּכָל
הַנִּבְרָאִים עֶלְיוֹנִים וְתַחְתּוֹנִים לִהְיוֹת כֻּלָּם מוּשְׁפָּעִי' מִמֶּנּוּ
ית' כמ"ש כִּי מִמְּךָ הַכֹּל וז"ש וְגַם כָּל הַיְצוּר לֹא נִכְחַד
מִמְּךָ וכמ"ש הרמב"ם [וְהִסְכִּימוּ לָזֶה חַכְמֵי הַקַּבָּלָה

And even though *"this concept defies coherent mortal comprehension"* (chapter 2, p. 47, from *Rambam*), the *Tanya* now teaches us an analogy to offer some insight into the way G-d knows things automatically.

רַק הוּא עַל דֶּרֶךְ מָשָׁל — **Rather, by way of illustration,** G-d knows everything, not through an active process of acquiring knowledge, כְּמוֹ אָדָם הַיּוֹדֵעַ וּמַרְגִּישׁ בְּעַצְמוֹ כָּל מַה שֶּׁנַּעֲשָׂה וְנִפְעַל מִכָּל רְמַ"ח אֵיבָרָיו — but **like a person knows and feels everything that's happening and occurring in each of the 248 limbs of his** body, כְּמוֹ וַאֲפִילוּ חוֹם שֶׁבְּצִפָּרְנֵי רַגְלָיו עַל דֶּרֶךְ מָשָׁל אִם נִכְוָה בָּאוֹר — **like cold or heat,** קוֹר אוֹ חוֹם — **or even, to give** an extreme **example, heat in his toenail when it's scorched by fire,** וְכֵן מַהוּתָם וְעַצְמוּתָם — **and** a person **also** intuitively knows the status of the **actual** limbs **themselves, in their core,** וְכָל מַה שֶּׁמִּתְפָּעֵל מֵהֶם יוֹדֵעַ וּמַרְגִּישׁ בְּמוֹחוֹ — **and all that is affected in them, he knows and feels** automatically **in his brain,** without having to consciously "collect" the information.

וּכְעֵין יְדִיעָה זוֹ עַל דֶּרֶךְ מָשָׁל — **In a vaguely comparable fashion to this example of** "automatic" **knowing** from within, יוֹדֵעַ הַקָּדוֹשׁ בָּרוּךְ הוּא אֶת כָּל הַנִּפְעָל בְּכָל הַנִּבְרָאִים — **G-d knows everything that's happening to all the creations,** עֶלְיוֹנִים וְתַחְתּוֹנִים — **upper and lower,** לִהְיוֹת כֻּלָּם מוּשְׁפָּעִים מִמֶּנּוּ יִתְבָּרֵךְ — **since** the life energy of **all** creations **flows from Him,** כְּמוֹ שֶׁכָּתוּב כִּי מִמְּךָ הַכֹּל — **as the verse states, *"for from You, all things come"*** (1 *Chronicles* 29:14), וְזֶהוּ שֶׁאוֹמְרִים וְגַם כָּל הַיְצוּר לֹא נִכְחַד מִמֶּךָּ — **and we say, *"and no creature is hidden from You"*** (*Liturgy, High Holidays*).

The world's existence flows directly from G-d and is intimately connected with Him. That's why He simply has knowledge of everything automatically, without having to acquire that knowledge. It's not dissimilar to the way you feel pain in your toe: You don't have to think, "I wonder if my toe hurts," and then go and find out. When it hurts, you simply know.

The *Tanya* now cites sources, from the Jewish philosophical and mystical traditions for the above point.

וּכְמוֹ שֶׁכָּתַב הָרַמְבַּ"ם — **And, as *Rambam* writes** (*Laws of Foundations of the Torah* 2:9-10), [וְהִסְכִּימוּ לָזֶה חַכְמֵי הַקַּבָּלָה כְּמוֹ שֶׁכָּתַב הָרְמַ"ק בַּפַּרְדֵּס] — **and the Kabbalists have concurred, as stated by Rabbi Moshe Cordovero (*Ramak*) in *Pardes Rimo-***

60B כמ"ש הרמ"ק בפרד"ס] שבידיעת עצמו כביכול יודע
כל הנבראים הנמצאים מאמיתת המצאו וכו' רק
שמשל זה אינו אלא לשכך את האזן אבל באמת אין
המשל דומה לנמשל כלל כי נפש האדם אפי' השכלית
והאלהית היא מתפעלת ממאורעי הגוף וצערו מחמת

nim (8:13), שֶׁבִּידִיעַת עַצְמוֹ כִּבְיָכוֹל יוֹדֵעַ כָּל הַנִּבְרָאִים — **that from knowing Himself, so to speak, G-d knows all of the creations,** הַנִּמְצָאִים מֵאֲמִיתַּת הִמָּצְאוֹ וְכוּ' — since *"everything that exists, in the heavens, the earth and everything in between, only exists from the truth of His existence"* (*Rambam ibid.* 1:1), so all existence is, in a sense, "part" of Him.

Rambam (*ibid.* 2:9-10) writes: *"Since He knows Himself... He knows everything; there is nothing hidden from Him... He doesn't know by means of an external knowledge that is separate from Him, the way we know things, because we and our knowledge are not identical. But for the Creator, may He be blessed, He, His knowledge and existence are absolutely one... He is the knower, and He is the known and He is the power to know itself, all as one."*

Ramak (*ibid.*) explains *Rambam's* statement according to Kabbalah. "The power to know," he writes, corresponds to *keser*, an energy that is aloof from the created universe and therefore precedes any knowledge of it. "The knower," refers to the inquisitive mind of G-d, so to speak, His *chochmah*; and "the known," is *binah*, the power through which G-d acquires real cognitive knowledge. And while all ten *sefiros* (Divine energies) are united with G-d, *Ramak* reminds us that there are different gradations in this unity. In contrast to the lower seven *sefiros*, whose connectedness to G-d's essence will fluctuate, *"the first three (keser, chochmah and binah) are united with Him in absolute oneness, to the extent that even after they have been emanated (and "left" G-d's essence so to speak) wondrous things are said about their unity, that 'the first three are considered as one.'"*

Of course, all our efforts to explain G-d's knowledge with an example from human experience, is fundamentally flawed, as the *Tanya* will now point out.

רַק שֶׁמָּשָׁל זֶה — **But this illustration** of G-d acquiring knowledge effortlessly, like a person feels his limbs, אֵינוֹ אֶלָּא לְשַׁכֵּךְ אֶת הָאֹזֶן — **serves only to** *"calm the ear"* (*Mechilta* to Exodus 19:18), in an attempt to render the incomprehensible, comprehensible, אֲבָל בֶּאֱמֶת אֵין הַמָּשָׁל דּוֹמֶה לַנִּמְשָׁל כְּלָל — **but in truth, the illustration** from man **bears no resemblance to the reality** in G-d whatsoever.

As the *Tanya* will now explain:

כִּי נֶפֶשׁ הָאָדָם אֲפִילוּ הַשִּׂכְלִית וְהָאֱלֹהִית — **For** G-d doesn't know the world as a result of being influenced by it, but that's not true of **a person's soul,** since **even** the more aloof **intellectual/Divine** souls, הִיא מִתְפַּעֶלֶת מִמְּאוֹרְעֵי הַגּוּף וְצַעֲרוֹ — *are* **influenced by what's happening to the body and by its pain,** מֵחֲמַת הִתְלַבְּשׁוּתָהּ מַמָּשׁ בַּנֶּפֶשׁ

התלבשותה ממש בנפש החיונית המלובשת בגוף
ממש אבל הקב"ה אינו מתפעל ח"ו ממאורעי העולם
ושינוייו ולא מהעול' עצמו שכולם אינן פועלים בו שום
שינוי ח"ו והנה כדי להשכיל זה היטב בשכלנו כבר
האריכו חכמי האמת בספריהם אך כל ישראל מאמינים
בני מאמיני' בלי שום חקירת שכל אנושי ואומרי' אתה

הַחִיּוּנִית — **because** the intellectual/Divine Souls **are actually enmeshed in the energizing** Animal **Soul,** הַמְלוּבֶּשֶׁת בַּגּוּף מַמָּשׁ — **which is actually enmeshed in the body,** and that is how they know what is happening in the body.

אֲבָל הַקָּדוֹשׁ בָּרוּךְ הוּא אֵינוֹ מִתְפָּעֵל חַס וְשָׁלוֹם מִמְּאוֹרְעֵי הָעוֹלָם וְשִׁינּוּיָיו — **But the Blessed Holy One is not in any way influenced (G-d forbid) by the happenings of the world and its fluctuations,** וְלֹא מֵהָעוֹלָם עַצְמוֹ — **nor by the world itself,** שֶׁכּוּלָם אֵינָן פּוֹעֲלִים בּוֹ שׁוּם שִׁינּוּי חַס וְשָׁלוֹם — **none of this brings about any change in Him, G-d forbid.**

Comparing G-d's knowledge to the way you know there's pain in your toe is both helpful and unhelpful. It's helpful in the sense that it enables you to get some idea how G-d's knowledge is not actively acquired but intuitively known. But it's unhelpful because it implies, incorrectly, that G-d's knowledge is influenced by the world (like your toe, which hurts you). The *Tanya* has offered us the illustration to provide some insight, provided that we are aware of its limitations.

וְהִנֵּה כְּדֵי לְהַשְׂכִּיל זֶה הֵיטֵב בְּשִׂכְלֵנוּ — **And in order for us to understand all this** as much as possible **with our** mortal **minds,** כְּבָר הֶאֱרִיכוּ חַכְמֵי הָאֱמֶת בְּסִפְרֵיהֶם — **the Kabbalists have already discussed it at length in their works.**

אַךְ כָּל יִשְׂרָאֵל מַאֲמִינִים בְּנֵי מַאֲמִינִים — **But** all of this is essentially unnecessary since **all of Israel are** *"believers, the children of believers"* (*Talmud, Shabbos* 97a), בְּלִי שׁוּם חֲקִירַת שֵׂכֶל אֱנוֹשִׁי — **without any** prior **investigation via human intellect,** וְאוֹמְרִים אַתָּה הוּא עַד שֶׁלֹּא נִבְרָא הָעוֹלָם וְכוּ' — **and we say,** *"You were alone before the world was created; You are alone since the world has been created etc.,"* (*Morning Liturgy*), כַּנִּזְכָּר לְעֵיל פֶּרֶק כ' — **as mentioned above, chapter 20** (p. 233).

Here the *Tanya* has touched upon a delicate and nuanced question: When given the choice between simple *faith* and *reason* ("investigation by human intellect"), which approach will lead us to the closest and most genuine appreciation of G-d?

Of the two approaches, reason appears, at first glance, to be the most seriously flawed, for it is obvious that human intellect is incapable of grasping G-d's true self. However sophisticated one's understanding of the Creator may become, it is but a finite conception which bears little resemblance to the infinite Creator.

When we believe in G-d, on the other hand, we have faith in *how He truly exists*, how He defies any mortal conception or imagination. So faith seems to be superior.

הוא עד שלא נברא העולם וכו' כנ"ל פ"כ: והנה
כל אדם מישראל יהיה מי שיהיה כשיתבונן בזה שעה
גדולה בכל יום איך שהקב"ה מלא ממש את העליונים
ואת התחתונים ואת השמים ואת הארץ ממש מלא
כל הארץ כבודו ממש וצופה ומביט ובוחן כליותיו ולבו

But faith, too, is limited. It tends to *reject* the empirical, sensory reality that we know, so it is not easily internalized into normal, everyday life.

In this respect, the superior quality of intellect becomes apparent. While the mind may not grasp G-d *as He is,* nevertheless, that which the intellect does succeed in understanding about G-d becomes real and tangible. Once grasped, intellectual concepts sit comfortably in the mind and become thoroughly internalized.

Since faith and reason each have their own advantages, the *Tanya* stresses the need for both. There is the virtue in the arguments that *"the Kabbalists have dis-cussed at length in their works";* and then there is the virtue of all Israel being *"be-lievers, the children of believers"* (see *Sefer Ha-Sichos* 5703, p. 117).

SECTION FOUR: KEEPING A REVERENCE MEDITATION "HANDY"

27TH NISAN REGULAR | 23RD NISAN LEAP

Now that we have clarified that G-d is really aware of everything that we do, we can now return to our meditation for reaching at least the lowest level of reverence "the minimal reverence necessary not to sin."

וְהִנֵּה כָּל אָדָם מִיִשְׂרָאֵל יִהְיֶה מִי שֶׁיִּהְיֶה — Now every person in Israel, whoever he may be, כְּשֶׁיִּתְבּוֹנֵן בָּזֶה שָׁעָה גְדוֹלָה בְּכָל יוֹם — if he will meditate on this each day for an extended period of time, אֵיךְ שֶׁהַקָּדוֹשׁ בָּרוּךְ הוּא מָלֵא מַמָּשׁ אֶת הָעֶלְיוֹנִים וְאֶת הַתַּחְתּוֹנִים — how the Blessed Holy one literally fills the upper and lower worlds, וְאֶת הַשָּׁמַיִם וְאֶת הָאָרֶץ מַמָּשׁ — *"the heavens and the earth"* (Jeremiah 23:24), מָלֵא, כָּל הָאָרֶץ כְּבוֹדוֹ מַמָּשׁ — and *"all the earth is filled with His glory"* (Isaiah 6:3), literally, וְצוֹפֶה וּמַבִּיט וּבוֹחֵן כְּלִיוֹתָיו וְלִבּוֹ — and that G-d watches and sees, and *"He's check-ing (your) inclinations and heart,"* וְכָל מַעֲשָׂיו וְדִיבּוּרָיו — as well as all your actions and words, וְכָל צְעָדָיו יִסְפּוֹר — and *"He counts your every step"* (see Job 31:4).

As we learned in chapter 41, "the minimal reverence necessary not to sin," doesn't require a deep recognition of the awesomeness of G-d. You simply must have the awareness that He is watching you all the time.

The *Tanya* now suggests that you keep the above meditation "up your sleeve," so that when you are confronted with a challenge to your Torah observance during the day, you can revisit the meditation for a moment, to avoid doing something you will later regret.

וכל מעשיו ודבוריו וכל צעדיו יספור אזי תקבע בלבו
היראה לכל היום כולו כשיחזור ויתבונן בזה אפילו
בהתבוננות קלה בכל עת ובכל שעה יהיה סור מרע
ועשה טוב במחשבה דבור ומעשה שלא למרות ח"ו
עיני כבודו אשר מלא כל הארץ וכמאמר רבן יוחנן בן
זכאי לתלמידיו כנ"ל וז"ש הכתוב כי אם ליראה את
ה' אלהיך ללכת בכל דרכיו שהיא יראה המביאה

אֲזַי תִּקָּבַע בְּלִבּוֹ הַיִּרְאָה לְכָל הַיּוֹם כֻּלּוֹ — And having carried out this meditation once in the morning, then **throughout the entire day, reverence will be "fixed" in your heart,** כְּשֶׁיַּחֲזוֹר וְיִתְבּוֹנֵן בָּזֶה אֲפִילּוּ בְּהִתְבּוֹנְנוּת קַלָּה — **so that if you will revisit the meditation even for a brief moment** when necessary to avoid temptation, בְּכָל עֵת וּבְכָל שָׁעָה יִהְיֶה סוּר מֵרַע וַעֲשֵׂה — then **at any time or moment,** טוֹב בְּמַחֲשָׁבָה דִבּוּר וּמַעֲשֶׂה — you'll be able to **"turn away from evil and do good,"** in **thought, speech and action,** שֶׁלֹּא לַמְרוֹת חַס וְשָׁלוֹם עֵינֵי — **so as not "to rebel against** כְּבוֹדוֹ אֲשֶׁר מָלֵא כָל הָאָרֶץ — **His honor"** (*Isaiah* 3:8), G-d forbid, while you are in G-d's presence which **"fills all the earth,"** וּכְמַאֲמַר רַבָּן יוֹחָנָן בֶּן — **as in the above-mentioned** זַכַּאי לְתַלְמִידָיו כַּנִּזְכָּר לְעֵיל — **saying of Rabbi Yochanan ben Zakai to his students,** *"May G-d help that you fear Heaven as much as you fear flesh and blood"* (chapter 41, p. 507).

PRACTICAL LESSONS

Meditating on the fact that G-d is watching you will help you to have the most basic level of reverence necessary to observe the Torah.

If you do this meditation in the morning, you can refresh it quickly later in the day, when temptation comes your way.

This concludes our meditation aimed at reaching a minimal level of "lower reverence," the basic awareness that "someone is watching me so I need to behave."

But how can we be sure that a minimal reverence is sufficient to fulfill the verse, *"What does G-d, your G-d, ask from you? Only that you revere G-d, your G-d"* (*Deuteronomy* 10:12; see above, p. 523)?

The *Tanya* will now show this from the verse itself.

וְזֶהוּ שֶׁאָמַר הַכָּתוּב — **And** the fact that **the verse** requires only a minimal level of reverence can be discerned from **what is stated** at the end of the verse, כִּי אִם לְיִרְאָה אֶת ה' אֱלֹהֶיךָ לָלֶכֶת בְּכָל דְּרָכָיו — G-d asks you *"only that you revere G-d, your G-d, **to go in all His ways."***

The second half of the verse (*"to go in all his ways"*) clarifies the level of reverence required by the first half (*"only that you revere G-d, your G-d"*):

שֶׁהִיא יִרְאָה הַמְּבִיאָה לְקִיּוּם מִצְוֹתָיו יִתְבָּרֵךְ — This implies that you need to have at least **a reverence sufficient to motivate the observance of G-d's** *mitzvos* (enough

לקיום מצותיו ית׳ בסור מרע ועשה טוב. והיא יראה
תתאה הנ״ל ולגבי משה דהיינו לגבי בחי׳ הדעת שבכל
נפש מישראל האלהית מילתא זוטרתי היא כנ״ל
[שהדעת הוא המקשר מצפוני בינת הלב אל בחי׳ גילוי
במחשבה ממש כידוע לי״ח] ועוד זאת יזכור כי כמו

61A

---

reverence *"to go in all His ways"*), בְּסוּר מֵרַע וַעֲשֵׂה טוֹב
— enough to *"turn away from evil and do good."*

וְהִיא יְרְאָה תַּתָּאָה הַנִּזְכֶּרֶת לְעֵיל — **And this** reverence
refers to all the levels of **"lower reverence" mentioned
above,** in chapter 41 (including the awareness that
"someone is watching me so I need to behave").

The verse is content with *any* level of reverence which
will lead to practical observance. This would include all
the levels of "lower reverence" which we discussed in
chapter 41, including the most basic level described by
Rabbi Yochanan ben Zakai that "someone is watching
me so I need to behave."

וּלְגַבֵּי מֹשֶׁה — **And** as the *Talmud* explained, **"for Moshe,"**
— דְּהַיְינוּ לְגַבֵּי בְּחִינַת הַדַּעַת שֶׁבְּכָל נֶפֶשׁ מִישְׂרָאֵל הָאֱלֹהִית
i.e., for the quality of *da'as* found in the **Divine Soul
of all Israel** which is nurtured by Moshe's soul, מִילְתָא

זוּטַרְתִּי הִיא כַּנִּזְכָּר לְעֵיל — *"it's a small thing,"* i.e., it's definitely possible for everyone
to nurture that reverence, **as explained above,** [שֶׁהַדַּעַת הוּא הַמְקַשֵּׁר מַצְפּוּנֵי בִּינַת
הַלֵּב אֶל בְּחִינַת גִּילּוּי בְּמַחֲשָׁבָה מַמָּשׁ כַּיָּדוּעַ לְיוֹדְעֵי חָכְמָה נִסְתָּרָה] — **since, as those**
familiar with hidden Kabbalistic **wisdom know,** *da'as* is what connects the hidden
"understanding of the heart" with substantive, conscious thought.

As we learned above, even if *da'as* doesn't bring you to have palpable feelings
for G-d in your heart, it will at the very least bring those feelings to *"substantive,
conscious thought." Da'as* is the bridge between your soul's natural, latent feelings
for G-d ("the understanding of the heart"), and your consciousness.

SECTION FIVE: EXERCISING YOUR DEDUCTIVE "MUSCLE"

28TH NISAN REGULAR | 24TH NISAN LEAP

Even with all the above insights and meditations, it's still a challenge to be constantly aware of an invisible G-d. In order to have a feeling for G-d's presence in a very
basic way, the *Tanya* offers us a further analogy.

כִּי כְּמוֹ שֶׁבְּמֶלֶךְ בָּשָׂר וְעוֹד זֹאת יִזְכּוֹר — **And you should also recall this further point,**
וְדָם עִיקַּר הַיִּרְאָה הִיא מִפְּנִימִיּוּתוֹ וְחַיּוּתוֹ וְלֹא מִגּוּפוֹ — **that just as a king of flesh and**

שבמלך בשר ודם עיקר היראה היא מפנימיותו וחיותו
ולא מגופו שהרי כשישן אין שום יראה ממנו. והנה
פנימיותו וחיותו אין נראה לעיני בשר רק בעיני
השכל על ידי ראיית עיני בשר בגופו ולבושיו שיודע
שחיותו מלובש בתוכם וא"כ ככה ממש יש לו לירא
את ה' ע"י ראיית עיני בשר בשמים וארץ וכל
צבאם אשר אור א"ס ב"ה

הגה"ה

(וגם נראה בראיית העין שהם

מלובש בהם להחיותם*

ואף שהוא ע"י התלבשות

בטלים לאורו ית' בהשתחוואתם כל

blood is primarily feared because of his inner identity **and his energy, and not because of his body,** שֶׁהֲרֵי כְּשִׁישֵׁן אֵין שׁוּם יִרְאָה מִמֶּנּוּ — the proof of this being that **when he is asleep,** and his identity and energy are not apparent, only his body, **he's no longer feared,** and, וְהִנֵּה פְּנִימִיּוּתוֹ וְחִיּוּתוֹ אֵין נִרְאָה לְעֵינֵי בָשָׂר רַק בְּעֵינֵי הַשֵּׂכֶל — **obviously, his inner** identity **and energy are not something visible to your physical eyes, but** are discerned effortlessly **through your mind's eye,** עַל יְדֵי רְאִיַּת עֵינֵי בָשָׂר בְּגוּפוֹ וּלְבוּשָׁיו שֶׁיּוֹדֵעַ שֶׁחִיּוּתוֹ מְלוּבָּשׁ בְּתוֹכָם — since **when your physical eyes see his body and clothes, you know** through deduction that the king's **energy is within them.**

While it might seem difficult to discern the truth of things beyond their outward, physical appearance, the *Tanya* reminds us that we do it all the time. When we recognize a person through the outward appearance of his or her body and clothing, we nevertheless infer the identity and character of that person through deduction. How is that so different from inferring G-d's energetic presence through the "garments" of this physical world?

וְאִם כֵּן כָּכָה מַמָּשׁ יֵשׁ לוֹ לִירָא אֶת ה' — **If so, then you ought to fear G-d through the very same** deduction, עַל יְדֵי רְאִיַּת עֵינֵי בָשָׂר בַּשָּׁמַיִם וָאָרֶץ וְכָל צְבָאָם — **through observing, with your physical eyes,** *"the skies, the earth and all their contents"* (*Genesis* 2:1), the King's **"clothes,"** so to speak, אֲשֶׁר אוֹר אֵין סוֹף בָּרוּךְ הוּא מְלוּבָּשׁ — בָּהֶם לְהַחֲיוֹתָם — and then deducing **that the Blessed Infinite Light is found within them, to give them life.***

Just as you effortlessly infer a person's identity and energy after seeing his or her external body and clothes, so too, you can easily deduce G-d's presence from see-

---

***הַגָהַ"ה — NOTE.** Through the example of "the king's clothing," the *Tanya* suggested how we might discern G-d's presence beneath the veneer of the physical world (G-d's "clothing," so to speak). In this note, the *Tanya* takes the argument further.

שֶׁהֵם בְּטֵלִים לְאוֹרוֹ יִתְבָּרֵךְ — **And it's also apparent to the eye,** וְגַם נִרְאָה בִּרְאִיַּת הָעַיִן בְּהִשְׁתַּחֲוָואָתָם כָּל יוֹם — that the heavenly bodies' **devotedly follow G-d's "light,"**

בלבושים רבים הרי אין
הבדל והפרש כלל ביראת
מלך בשר ודם בין שהוא
ערום ובין שהוא לבוש
לבוש אחד ובין שהוא

יום כלפי מערב בשקיעתם כמארז"ל
ע"פ וצבא השמים לך משתחוים
שהשכינה במערב ונמצא הילוכם
כל היום כלפי מערב הוא דרך
השתחואה וביטול והנה גם מי
שלא ראה את המלך מעולם ואינו
מכירו כלל אעפ"כ כשנכנס לחצר

ing His "clothes" (the contents of this physical world), and realizing that their inner identity and energy is the Blessed Infinite Light, to which they owe their ongoing existence.

This meditation is particularly powerful as it's not purely in your imagination; it's based on something that you are actually seeing with your physical eyes.

וְאַף שֶׁהוּא עַל יְדֵי הִתְלַבְּשׁוּת בִּלְבוּשִׁים רַבִּים — **And even though** the Blessed Infinite Light **is found** within all the different objects and creatures that fill this world **dressed in many "garments,"** and there is a huge metaphysical "distance" between the physical world and the Blessed Infinite Light, הֲרֵי אֵין הֶבְדֵּל וְהֶפְרֵשׁ כְּלָל בִּירְאַת מֶלֶךְ בָּשָׂר וָדָם — **nevertheless,** this is irrelevant, because as we see from our analogy **it makes absolutely no difference at all to the way you would fear a king of flesh and blood,** בֵּין שֶׁהוּא עָרוֹם וּבֵין שֶׁהוּא לָבוּשׁ לְבוּשׁ אֶחָד וּבֵין שֶׁהוּא לָבוּשׁ בִּלְבוּשִׁים רַבִּים — **if he is naked, wearing one garment, or if he is garbed in many robes.**

The amount of garments makes no difference. Once you realize they are *the king's garments,* then you will immediately discern the presence of the king.

Similarly, the fact that the Blessed Infinite Light is "garbed" by many worlds before it is manifested in the power to create physical matter, doesn't make your de-

---

כְּלַפֵּי מַעֲרָב בִּשְׁקִיעָתָם — **as they "bow" all day,** moving **towards the west, where** the sun **sets.**

כְּמַאֲמַר רַבּוֹתֵינוּ זִכְרוֹנָם לִבְרָכָה עַל פָּסוּק וּצְבָא הַשָּׁמַיִם לְךָ מִשְׁתַּחֲוִים — **As our Sages taught on the verse,** *"And the contents of the skies bow to You"* (*Nehemia* 9:6), שֶׁהַשְּׁכִינָה בַּמַּעֲרָב — **that the Divine Presence rests in the west** (*Talmud, Bava Basra* 25a), וְנִמְצָא הִילוּכָם כָּל הַיּוֹם כְּלַפֵּי מַעֲרָב הוּא דֶּרֶךְ הִשְׁתַּחֲוָואָה וּבִיטּוּל — **from which it follows that the** heavenly bodies' **movement the entire day towards the west is a form of "bowing" and devotion** towards the Divine Presence.

Even if you can't sense G-d's presence behind the physical veneer of this world, *you can see with your eyes* how the heavenly bodies "worship" G-d, shifting towards the west, where the Divine Presence is found.

The *Tanya* now puts this into the context of our example of "a king garbed in clothes":

וְהִנֵּה גַּם מִי שֶׁלֹא רָאָה אֶת הַמֶּלֶךְ מֵעוֹלָם וְאֵינוֹ מַכִּירוֹ כְּלָל — **Now even a person who never saw the king and wouldn't recognize him at all** personally, אַף עַל פִּי כֵן

לְבוּשׁ בִּלְבוּשִׁים רַבִּים אֶלָּא
הָעִיקָר הוּא הַהֶרְגֵּל לְהַרְגִּיל
דַּעְתּוֹ וּמַחְשַׁבְתּוֹ תָּמִיד
לִהְיוֹת קָבוּעַ בְּלִבּוֹ וּמוֹחוֹ תָּמִיד אֲשֶׁר כָּל מַה שֶּׁרוֹאֶה
בְּעֵינָיו הַשָּׁמַיִם וְהָאָרֶץ וּמְלוֹאָה הַכֹּל הֵם לְבוּשִׁים
הַחִיצוֹנִים שֶׁל הַמֶּלֶךְ הַקָּבָּ"ה וְעַל יְדֵי זֶה יִזְכּוֹר תָּמִיד עַל

הַמֶּלֶךְ וְרוֹאֶה שָׂרִים רַבִּים וְנִכְבָּדִים
מִשְׁתַּחֲוִים לְאִישׁ א' תִּפּוֹל עָלָיו
אֵימָה וָפַחַד):

duction any harder. As soon as you realize that the inner identity and energy of this physical world is G-d's light, you will be radically aware of His presence.

This deduction is not actually something very difficult, the *Tanya* now assures us; it's just something that requires practice, to train yourself to look beyond the surface appearance of things.

לְהַרְגִּיל דַּעְתּוֹ — אֶלָּא הָעִיקָר הוּא הַהֶרְגֵּל — **Rather, the main thing is practice,** לִהְיוֹת קָבוּעַ וּמַחְשַׁבְתּוֹ תָּמִיד — **to accustom your mind and conscious thoughts,** בְּלִבּוֹ וּמוֹחוֹ תָּמִיד — **so that your mind and heart are focused always,** אֲשֶׁר כָּל מַה שֶּׁרוֹאֶה בְּעֵינָיו הַשָּׁמַיִם וְהָאָרֶץ וּמְלוֹאָה הַכֹּל הֵם לְבוּשִׁים הַחִיצוֹנִים שֶׁל הַמֶּלֶךְ הַקָּדוֹשׁ בָּרוּךְ הוּא — on the fact **that everything your eyes see in "the skies, the earth and all their numerous components" are all the external "garments" of the King, the Blessed Holy One,** וְעַל יְדֵי זֶה יִזְכּוֹר תָּמִיד עַל פְּנִימִיוּתָם וְחַיּוּתָם — **and through this you will constantly recall their inner identity and energy,** which is G-d's light.

This meditation, of G-d's presence in the world, resembles the meditation we learned in chapter 33, *"to probe deeply in your mind picturing mentally and cognitively... how 'He fills all worlds" upper and lower and even how this lowly, physical world is filled with His glory"* (p. 370). There, however, the meditation was described

---

כְּשֶׁנִּכְנָס לַחֲצַר הַמֶּלֶךְ וְרוֹאֶה שָׂרִים רַבִּים וְנִכְבָּדִים מִשְׁתַּחֲוִים לְאִישׁ אֶחָד תִּפּוֹל עָלָיו אֵימָה וָפַחַד — **would nevertheless be gripped with awe and trepidation if he entered the king's courtyard and saw numerous high-ranking officials bowing to one particular person,** realizing that this must be the king.

The person who has never seen the king, and doesn't even recognize Him, represents the failure to discern G-d within the physical matter of this world. But even when this fails, you can still notice that other entities (the sun and planets) *do* discern; you see "numerous high-ranking officials bowing to one particular person." And that ought to lead you to reverence.

(While this is also a powerful meditation, the author of the *Tanya* placed it in a note because, according to this chapter's central argument, an additional meditation shouldn't be necessary. The chapter has stressed how, with sufficient effort, *anyone* can come to recognize G-d personally, so there needn't be a situation where you fail to discern G-d's presence in the world. But, as a plan 'b,' the *Tanya* offers us another meditation in the "note" — *Notes on Tanya*).

פְּנִימִיּוּתָם וחיותם וזה נכלל ג"כ בלשון אמונה שהוא
לשון רגילות שמרגיל האדם את עצמו כמו אומן
המאמן ידיו וכו'. וגם להיות לזכרון תמיד לשון חז"ל
קבלת עול מלכות שמים שהוא כענין שום תשים
עליך מלך כמ"ש במ"א וכו' כי הקב"ה מניח את

as leading to "faith" (*emunah*), whereas here the meditation is described as one of *intellectual* discernment and deduction, "to accustom *your mind*." To reconcile these two approaches, the *Tanya* suggests the following (*Notes on Tanya*).

וְזֶה נִכְלָל גַּם כֵּן בִּלְשׁוֹן אֱמוּנָה — **And this** cognitive meditative **practice could also be called** *emunah* (usually translated as "faith"), שֶׁהוּא לְשׁוֹן רְגִילוּת — **a term which also implies "practice,"** שֶׁמַּרְגִּיל הָאָדָם אֶת עַצְמוֹ כְּמוֹ אוּמָן הַמְאַמֵּן יָדָיו וְכוּ' — **that a person accustoms himself, like a skilled worker (***uman***), who trains (***me'amen***) his hands,** *etc.,* (see *A Chasidic Thought*).

SECTION SIX: REFRESHING YOUR KABOLAS OL

25TH NISAN LEAP

In the final analysis, the *Tanya* remains aware that meditative work has its ups and downs, and we won't always discern G-d's presence in the physical world to achieve feelings of reverence. So, as we conclude our discussion, the *Tanya* reminds us that while meditative results may fluctuate, we can always draw on our innate ability to *accept* G-d's authority, even when we can't muster any sense of reverence.

This represents the flip side of the faith/reason conflict. When reason (meditative work) fails, you can always rely on your faith in G-d, to accept His authority (*Notes on Tanya*).

וְגַם לִהְיוֹת לְזִכָּרוֹן תָּמִיד לְשׁוֹן חֲכָמֵינוּ זִכְרוֹנָם לִבְרָכָה קַבָּלַת עוֹל מַלְכוּת שָׁמַיִם — **And you should also call to mind constantly the phrase used by our Sages "accepting the yoke (***kabolas ol***) of G-d's sovereign authority"** (*Talmud, Brachos* 13a), שֶׁהוּא כְּעִנְיַן שׂוּם תָּשִׂים עָלֶיךָ מֶלֶךְ כְּמוֹ — שֶׁנִּתְבָּאֵר בְּמָקוֹם אַחֵר וְכוּ' — **which as is explained elsewhere** (in chapter 41) **is similar** to the *mitzvah,* **"you shall surely place a king over yourself"** (*Deuteronomy* 17:15),

PRACTICAL LESSONS

When meditation fails, you can always rely on *kabolas ol*, your willingness to accept G-d's authority even when you can't discern His presence.

Focus on *kabolas ol* especially when you recite the *Shema* and when you bow during *Shemoneh Esrei*.

הָעֶלְיוֹנִים וְהַתַּחְתּוֹנִים וּמְיַיחֵד מַלְכוּתוֹ עָלֵינוּ וְכוּ' וַאֲנַחְנוּ

61B מְקַבְּלִים וְכוּ' וְזֶהוּ עִנְיַן הַהִשְׁתַּחֲוָואוֹת שֶׁבִּתְפִלַּת י"ח

אַחַר קַבָּלַת עוֹל מַלְכוּת שָׁמַיִם בְּדִבּוּר בִּקְ"שׁ לַחֲזוֹר

וּלְקַבֵּל בְּפוֹעַל מַמָּשׁ בְּמַעֲשֶׂה וְכוּ' כְּמוֹ"שׁ בְּמָ"א:

כִּי הַקָּדוֹשׁ בָּרוּךְ הוּא מַנִּיחַ אֶת הָעֶלְיוֹנִים וְהַתַּחְתּוֹנִים — since the Blessed Holy One has disregarded the worship of the **upper and lower** spiritual **worlds,** וּמְיַיחֵד מַלְכוּתוֹ **— and** in giving the Torah to the Jewish people **He has specified His** de-sire to be worshiped **as king over us etc.,** עָלֵינוּ וְכוּ' וַאֲנַחְנוּ מְקַבְּלִים וְכוּ' **— and,** reciprocating the gesture, **we accept, etc.** (see p. 495).

In a final comment, the *Tanya* gives an illustration from our daily worship how *kabolas ol* is not something you do just once, but needs to be "refreshed" later on.

וְזֶהוּ עִנְיַן הַהִשְׁתַּחֲוָואוֹת שֶׁבִּתְפִלַּת י"ח **— And this is also the idea behind the** four times that we **bow during the** *Shemoneh Esrei* **prayer,** אַחַר קַבָּלַת עוֹל מַלְכוּת שָׁמַיִם בְּדִבּוּר בִּקְרִיאַת שְׁמַע **— after "accepting the yoke of G-d's sovereign authority" verbally when reciting the** *Shema,* לַחֲזוֹר וּלְקַבֵּל בְּפוֹעַל מַמָּשׁ בְּמַעֲשֶׂה וְכוּ' **— the bowing is in order to accept** "the yoke" **again tangibly, in an actual deed,** כְּמוֹ שֶׁנִּתְבָּאֵר בְּמָקוֹם אַחֵר **— as is explained elsewhere** (see Rabbi Shneur Zalman, *Likutei Torah,* *Deuteronomy* 98b).

A CHASIDIC THOUGHT

Having *emunah* doesn't just mean that you *believe* in G-d's presence in the world; it can also refer to the process of *training* your mind's eye to constantly penetrate the superficial appearance of things, to discern G-d.

Just as when a physicist handles a piece of metal he "sees" atoms, because his mind is so used to looking at the universe through the conceptual lens of science, you, too, can accustom yourself to "see" G-d in every worldly thing.

You can train yourself in this discipline to the extent you are aware of G-d's presence even in the most mundane, practical tasks, "like a skilled worker *who trains his hands.*"

פרק מג והנה על יראה תתאה זו שהיא לקיום
מצוותיו ית' בבחי' סור מרע ועשה
טוב אמרו אם אין יראה אין חכמה ויש בה בחי' קטנות

THE FULL SPECTRUM OF REVERENCE & LOVE

SECTION ONE: "EXPANDED" AND "CONTRACTED" MIND

29TH NISAN REGULAR | 26TH NISAN LEAP

Chapter 43 continues the *Tanya's* practical guide to generate emotions for G-d, which began in chapter 41 and will continue to the end of chapter 50.

In chapter 41 we were given an introduction to the importance of reverence and love, and how to achieve them at a basic level. Chapter 42 elaborated further on ideas and techniques to generate reverence.

Obviously, reverence and love can occur at different levels. But what is our "register" to calibrate these different levels? Our previous discussions have guided us mainly to recognize basic and "lower" forms of reverence and love. In this chapter we will explore the "higher" forms of these emotions, and clarify exactly what distinguishes them from their "lower" counterparts.

First, we will turn our attention to reverence. (In the second half of the chapter we will address love).

וְהִנֵּה עַל יִרְאָה תַּתָּאָה זוֹ — **Now regarding this "lower reverence"** which we have been discussing in chapters 41-42 שֶׁהִיא לְקִיּוּם מִצְוֹתָיו יִתְבָּרֵךְ — which we have defined as any reverence that directly inspires **the observance of G-d's mitzvos**, בִּבְחִינַת סוּר מֵרַע וַעֲשֵׂה טוֹב — both prohibitions and positive commands, **to** *"turn away from evil and do good"* (*Psalms* 34:14), אָמְרוּ אִם אֵין יִרְאָה אֵין חָכְמָה — regarding this "lower reverence" our Sages **said,** *"If there's no reverence, there's no wisdom"* (*Avos* 3:17).

As we learned in chapter 23, the notion of both a "lower reverence" (which *leads to* the observance of the Torah) and a "higher reverence (which *results from* Torah observance), is suggested by the *Mishnah's* teaching, *"If there's no reverence, there's no wisdom; if there's no wisdom, there's no reverence."*

ובחי' גדלות דהיינו כשנמשכת בחי' יראה זו
מההתבוננות בגדולת ה' דאיהו ממלא כל עלמין
ומהארץ לרקיע מהלך ת"ק שנה וכו' ובין רקיע לרקיע

The *Mishnah's* first statement, *"If there's no reverence, there's no wisdom"* points to a lower level of reverence that inspires you to observe the Torah (wisdom). The *Mishnah's* second statement, *"If there's no wisdom (Torah), there's no reverence,"* suggests a higher level of reverence which comes after Torah observance.

וְיֵשׁ בָּהּ בְּחִינַת קַטְנוּת וּבְחִינַת גַּדְלוּת — **And within** the category of "lower reverence" **there is a "contracted"** (*katnus*) frame of mind, **and an "expanded"** (*gadlus*) one.

"Lower reverence" from a "contracted" frame of mind is what we have been discussing throughout chapters 41-42: 1.) the basic awareness that G-d is watching you, 2.) deducing His presence by looking at the contents of the physical world as His "garments," and 3.) the meditations before *tallis* and *tefilin etc.*

Now the *Tanya* will briefly describe "lower reverence" from an "expanded" frame of mind.

דְּהַיְינוּ כְּשֶׁנִּמְשֶׁכֶת בְּחִינַת יִרְאָה זוֹ מֵהַהִתְבּוֹנְנוּת בִּגְדוּלַּת ה' — **Meaning to say that when this reverence is produced by meditating on G-d's greatness,** it's considered to be from an "expanded" frame of mind.

The meditations in chapters 41-42, were from a "contracted" frame of mind, because they didn't focus primarily on the greatness and awesomeness *of G-d.* They made you conscious that G-d is *watching you* and that the physical world veils His presence, but there wasn't a lot of detail about the wondrous power of G-d Himself. That focus on "G-d's greatness" is the hallmark of an "expanded" mind meditation.

דְּאִיהוּ מְמַלֵּא כָּל עָלְמִין — In an "expanded" mind meditation you contemplate **how "He fills all worlds"** (see *Zohar* 3, 225a), you ponder the awesomeness of G-d as expressed through the myriads of spiritual worlds He has created.

In a "contracted" frame of mind the emphasis is *on you*—how G-d is watching you and how you feel His presence. But in an "expanded" state of mind, the emphasis is *on G-d*—how He manifests His greatness in all the spiritual worlds.

The *Tanya* now cites a metaphorical description of the spiritual worlds, found in the *Talmud,* which might form the basis of an "expanded" mind meditation.

וּמֵהָאָרֶץ לָרָקִיעַ מַהֲלַךְ ת"ק שָׁנָה וְכוּ' וּבֵין רָקִיעַ לְרָקִיעַ כוּ' רַגְלֵי הַחַיּוֹת כְּנֶגֶד כּוּלָּן וְכוּ' — You contemplate **that *"a journey from earth to heaven takes five hundred years; and the thickness of the heaven is a journey of five hundred years; And so too, between each heaven and the one above it; and above them are the holy angels, and the feet of the angels are equal to all of them together etc.,"*** (*Talmud, Chagigah* 13a).

The *Talmud,* however, contains relatively little discussion of the spiritual worlds; but *seder hishtalshelus* (the chain of spiritual worlds) is discussed in great detail in the works of *Kabbalah* and *Chasidus.*

כו' רגלי החיות כנגד כולן וכו' וכן השתלשלות כל
העולמות למעלה מעלה עד רום המעלות אעפ"כ נקרא
יראה זו יראה חיצונית ותתאה מאחר שנמשכת
מהעולמות שהם לבושים של המלך הקב"ה אשר
מסתתר ומתעלם ומתלבש בהם להחיותם ולקיימם
להיות יש מאין וכו' רק שהיא השער והפתח לקיום
התורה והמצות. אך היראה עילאה ירא בשת ויראה

וְכֵן הַשְׁתַּלְשְׁלוּת כָּל הָעוֹלָמוֹת לְמַעְלָה מַעְלָה עַד רוּם הַמַּעֲלוֹת — **And** an "expanded" mind meditation will **also** include meditating **on the chain (***hishtalshelus***) of spiritual worlds, extending up and beyond, to the greatest heights.**

But, as the *Tanya* will now explain, even this "expanded mind" meditation will still only produce "lower reverence."

אַף עַל פִּי כֵן נִקְרֵאת יִרְאָה זוֹ יִרְאָה חִיצוֹנִית וְתַתָּאָה — **Nevertheless, the reverence** produced from **this** above mentioned meditation is still a "superficial" and "lower" reverence, (even though it is from an "expanded" state of mind).

מֵאַחַר שֶׁנִּמְשֶׁכֶת מֵהָעוֹלָמוֹת — It's "superficial" **because it's inspired by the** greatness of G-d as manifested *through the* created *worlds,* שֶׁהֵם לְבוּשִׁים שֶׁל הַמֶּלֶךְ הַקָּדוֹשׁ בָּרוּךְ הוּא — **which are the** mere "garments" of the King, the Blessed Holy One, אֲשֶׁר מִסְתַּתֵּר וּמִתְעַלֵּם וּמִתְלַבֵּשׁ בָּהֶם לְהַחֲיוֹתָם וּלְקַיְּמָם — **who is found in them** only in a **hidden, concealed and garbed way, so as to energize them and sustain them,** לִהְיוֹת יֵשׁ מֵאַיִן וְכוּ' — **so that there should be something-from-nothing.**

However much your emotions might be stirred by these meditations, you're not actually getting excited about G-d Himself, but rather, G-d's *influence*: the wondrous worlds that He has made. That's why it's termed a "superficial" reverence.

Why do we even bother ourselves with "lower reverence," if it is inferior and "superficial"?

רַק שֶׁהִיא הַשַּׁעַר וְהַפֶּתַח לְקִיּוּם הַתּוֹרָה וְהַמִּצְוֹת — **Only** "lower reverence" is important **since it is the gateway and passage to the observance of Torah and** *mitzvos.*

Emotional maturity follows a process. First there must be "lower reverence," which will inspire Torah observance; and that opens up the further possibility of reaching "higher reverence." You can't skip levels, because one builds on the other.

SECTION TWO: HOW TO ATTAIN "HIGHER REVERENCE"

אַךְ הַיִּרְאָה עִילָאָה יְרֵא בֹּשֶׁת — **But "higher reverence"** is a reverence arising **from** a sense of **shame** in G-d's presence (see *Tikunei Zohar* 5b), וְיִרְאָה פְּנִימִית — **and it is** a **"deep reverence"** (Rabbi Chaim Vital, *Otzaros Chaim,* introduction), שֶׁהִיא נִמְשֶׁכֶת

פְּנִימִית שֶׁהִיא נִמְשֶׁכֶת מִפְּנִימִית הָאֱלֹהוּת שֶׁבְּתוֹךְ
הָעוֹלָמוֹת עָלֶיהָ אָמְרוּ אִם אֵין חָכְמָה אֵין יִרְאָה דְּחָכְמָה

מִפְּנִימִית הָאֱלֹהוּת שֶׁבְּתוֹךְ הָעוֹלָמוֹת — **which results from an awareness,** not of the awesomeness of the spiritual worlds themselves, but **of the core G-dliness** *within* **the worlds.**

Think of the difference between the way you're impressed by a powerful man and the way you're impressed by a holy man. There are two major distinctions: 1.) A powerful man impresses you because of *what he can do*, his influence; a holy man impresses you because of *who he is*, a higher caliber of human being. 2.) Being in the presence of a powerful man doesn't really change you, but being in the presence of a holy man might deeply impact your life.

PRACTICAL LESSONS

If your reverence is inspired by the fact that G-d is watching you, or by the fact that the physical world veils His presence, then you have achieved *"lower reverence"* **from a "constricted" stated of mind.**

If your reverence is inspired by the awesomeness of G-d as expressed in the spiritual worlds, then you have achieved *"lower reverence"* **from an "expanded" state of mind.**

"Higher reverence" comes from an awareness (not of the awesomeness of the spiritual worlds themselves, but) of the core G-dliness *within* **the worlds.**

When you're impressed with a powerful man, you're not really revering him, but his influence. The thought of all that power may overwhelm you, but it doesn't change you inside. You're the same person as before; you've just encountered someone else who is much more powerful than you. That's like being impressed with the awesomeness of the spiritual worlds ("lower reverence"): you're impressed by what G-d can do, but not by G-d Himself.

At "higher reverence," you start to feel the actual presence of *G-d Himself, "the core G-dliness within the worlds."* You are revering G-d for who He is, and not what He can do.

To describe how the experience changes you, "Higher reverence" is also referred to here as *"reverence from (a deep sense of) shame."* When you are in the presence of a holy man, you begin to question your own inner worth. If another person can be that holy, that refined, what does it say about you? You begin to feel that, by this standard, you're life's achievements are embarrassing; that if this is what a human being can rise to, then you haven't even begun yet. Similarly, the experience of "higher reverence" is one of losing your identity in the presence of G-d. You begin to vacate and transcend yourself. You connect with the reality of G-d which leaves no room for any other separate existence (see Rabbi Shneur Zalman, *Siddur Tefilos Mi-Kol Ha-Shanah,* p. 151c).

עָלֶיהָ אָמְרוּ אִם אֵין חָכְמָה אֵין יִרְאָה — **It is of this** "higher reverence" that the Sages **said,** *"If there's no wisdom (chochmah), there's no reverence"* (*Mishnah, Avos ibid.*).

היא כ"ח מ"ה והחכמה מאין תמצא ואיזהו חכם הרואה
את הנולד פי' שרואה כל דבר איך נולד ונתהוה מאין

How do you reach a state of "higher reverence"?

The *Mishnah* indicates that it's through accessing your *chochmah* — as the *Tanya* will now explain. (The discussion draws from what we have already learned about *chochmah* in chapter 3, p. 58; chapter 18, pp. 215-8; and chapter 19, p. 223-9).

דְּחָכְמָה הִיא כ"חַ מָ"ה — **Since,** as we learned above (p. 58), the term **"chochmah"** is the fusion of two Hebrew words, *ko'ach* **("power")** and *mah* **("what?")** (*Zohar* 3, 34a), the "power (ability) to say 'What's this?'"

Your *chochmah's* identity is not centered around itself; it's predominantly an energy of inquisitiveness and openness to the "other." Since it doesn't have a sharply defined self-identity, it's sufficiently open to recognize the true reality of G-d (*"the core G-dliness within the worlds"*), which leaves no room for any separate existence.

The *Tanya* now cites two sources, one from Scripture and one from the *Talmud*, which hint to this quality of *chochmah*.

וְהַחָכְמָה מֵאַיִן תִּמָּצֵא — And Scripture states, **"But chochmah, from where (me'ayin) is it found?"** (*Job* 28:12).

The word *me'ayin* literally means, "from where," but it can also be translated "from nothing." Your natural tendency is to feel yourself as solid and taking up space ("something"); but when you access your *chochmah,* you sense that your existence is fluid and intangible ("nothing"), because it's really part of G-d (see Rabbi Dovber of Mezritch, *Ohr Torah,* section 95).

וְאֵיזֶהוּ חָכָם הָרוֹאֶה אֶת הַנּוֹלָד — **And** the *Talmud* also hints to the transpersonal energy of *chochmah* with the teaching: **"Who is a wise person (chacham)? One who sees the future outcome (lit. 'that which is born')"** (*Talmud, Tamid* 32a).

פֵּירוּשׁ שֶׁרוֹאֶה כָּל דָּבָר אֵיךְ נוֹלָד וְנִתְהַוֶּה מֵאַיִן לְיֵשׁ — **Meaning that** when you use your *chochmah,* **you "see"** (perceive) **how everything** in the universe **is "born" and comes into being** continually, **something-from-nothing.**

Normally, a meditation is carried out using *binah*, your cognitive powers of understanding. But *binah* can't get you to "higher reverence," because it's too bound up with your ego and self-concept. It's not capable of appreciating the fluidity of your (non)existence.

Binah has too much of your "self" involved because it works through *tools of analysis* that you've taken years to develop, and have become bound up with your world-view.

Chochmah, on the other hand, doesn't analyze a situation, it simply *sees* things the way they are, using the mind's "eye" (see Rabbi Shneur Zalman, *Likutei Torah, Deuteronomy* 91b).

ליש בדבר ה' ורוח פיו ית' כמ"ש וברוח פיו כל צבאם
ואי לזאת הרי השמים והארץ וכל צבאם בטלים
במציאות ממש בדבר ה' ורוח פיו וכלא ממש חשיבי
ואין ואפס ממש כביטול אור וזיו השמש בגוף השמש

בִּדְבַר ה' וְרוּחַ פִּיו יִתְבָּרֵךְ — Your *chochmah* will enable you to "see" how the world is utterly dependent on G-d's creative power, *"G-d's word... and the breath of His mouth"* (see *Psalms* 33:6), כְּמוֹ שֶׁכָּתוּב וּבְרוּחַ פִּיו כָּל צְבָאָם — as the verse states, *"and (from) the breath of His mouth, all (the world's) contents (come to be)"* (ibid.), וְאֵי לְזֹאת — and if so, the universe and its contents have no independent existence of their own, הֲרֵי הַשָּׁמַיִם וְהָאָרֶץ וְכָל צְבָאָם בְּטֵלִים בִּמְצִיאוּת מַמָּשׁ — which means that the apparently separate identities of *"the skies, the earth and all their contents"* (*Genesis* 2:1), are, in reality, voided by the power which creates them continually, to which they owe their existence, בִּדְבַר ה' וְרוּחַ פִּיו — that power being *"G-d's word... and the breath of His mouth."*

As we discussed at length in chapters 20-21, the creation of something-from-nothing is an *ongoing process.* Unlike a human creator, who produces a piece of art which then enjoys its own autonomous existence, G-d continually wills all of existence into being, otherwise it would revert to a state of primordial nothingness. Borrowing the Biblical metaphor of creation through Divine speech, "G-d's word" must continually be "spoken" into every detail of the universe to facilitate its ongoing existence.

PRACTICAL LESSONS

At "Higher reverence" you lose your sense of self in the presence of G-d; you connect with the reality of G-d which leaves no room for any other separate existence.

To do that, you need to use your *chochmah* which "sees" the reality of G-d the way it is, using the mind's "eye."

Ongoing creation teaches us that even when the world does enjoy existence, *that existence is an acquired property and not an inherent one.* All non-Divine existence always tends to self-annihilation and "re-absorption" back into its Divine source. The apparently static phenomenon of the world's independent existence is, in reality, dynamically sustained by a constant creative drive (see above, p. 235).

In order to "see" this truth, how the world is constantly created ("born") every moment, you must use your *chochmah.* Only *chochmah* is sufficiently "open-minded" to sense how everything in the universe is absorbed within the greater existence of G-d. All the other parts of your soul are too invested in your own self-concept to be open to an idea which challenges your separate, autonomous existence.

וּכְלָא מַמָּשׁ חֲשִׁיבֵי — And your *chochmah* enables you to perceive how all separateness *"is considered zero"* (*Zohar* 1, 11b), literally, וְאֵין וָאֶפֶס מַמָּשׁ — really, *"null and*

עצמה ואל יוציא אדם עצמו מהכלל שגם גופו ונפשו
ורוחו ונשמתו בטלים במציאות בדבר ה' ודבורו ית'

void" (see *Isaiah* 40:17), כְּבִיטוּל אוֹר וְזִיו הַשֶּׁמֶשׁ בְּגוּף הַשֶּׁמֶשׁ עַצְמָהּ — **just as the rays and light of the sun are voided** of their individual identity **within the globe of the sun itself** (see chapter 33, p. 370-1; *Sha'ar Ha-Yichud Ve-Ha-Emunah* chapter 3).

Inside the sun, light is present, but not as individual rays. Similarly, when viewed through the lens of *chochmah*, everything in the universe is seen to exist, but not as separate entities. All is subsumed in the One.

וְאַל יוֹצִיא אָדָם עַצְמוֹ מֵהַכְּלָל — **And *"a person should never remove himself from the group"*** (*Talmud, Brachos* 49b), which means that when we say everything in the universe is absorbed within G-d's existence, that includes you and your soul!

שֶׁגַּם גּוּפוֹ וְנַפְשׁוֹ וְרוּחוֹ וְנִשְׁמָתוֹ — Meaning **that** all the components of your soul, **your *nefesh, ruach* and *neshamah,*** בְּטֵלִים בִּמְצִיאוּת בִּדְבַר ה' — **are** also **voided of their** separate **identity by *"G-d's word,"*** the power which creates them.

Your soul is no different from anything else in the universe and it requires G-d's creative power every second in order to exist. You might feel that your existence is stable and given, but your *chochmah* will lend you a deeper insight, of being dissolved in the presence of G-d.

The above was a brief summary of what we learned in chapter 20 about the non-dual reality of G-d. In chapter 21, the idea was deepened with a further illustration, which the *Tanya* touches upon briefly here.

וְדִבּוּרוֹ יִתְבָּרֵךְ מְיוּחָד בְּמַחֲשַׁבְתּוֹ כו' — **And** as we learned in chapter 21, G-d's "speech" is not like human speech which leaves a person after it is spoken; rather, **G-d's "speech" is one with** Him, just like **His "thought."**

This subtle point greatly enhances our understanding of how deeply the world's separate identity is voided by G-d's creative power (His "word"). While we have seen that the world's continued dependence on G-d's speech voids any independent existence on the world's part, there seems to be a weak point in this argument. For the fact that G-d said, for example, "let there be light," means that G-d is involved with the existence of light. And, surely, if G-d is involving Himself with something, its existence can't be completely void?

To clarify this point, the *Tanya* taught us in chapter 21 (and repeats here), that G-d's "speech is one with His thought." G-d's thought, which *preceded* his speech, points to a level before any creative act took place through Divine speech. Obviously, at that pre-creation level the universe had no existence at all and it certainly didn't matter to Him.

So when we say that G-d's "speech is one with His thought" it means that G-d's pre-creation and post-creation "mindset" are really the same. Just as the universe was of no significance to Him before, at a deeper level, the same is true now.

מיוחד במחשבתו כו' וכנ"ל [פ' כ' וכ"א] באריכות בד"מ
מנפש האדם שדבור אחד מדבורו ומחשבתו כלא
ממש כו' וזש"ה הן יראת ה' היא חכמה. אך אי
אפשר להשיג ליראה וחכמה זו אלא בקיום התורה
והמצות ע"י יראה תתאה החיצונית וז"ש אם אין יראה
אין חכמה. והנה באהבה יש ג"כ שתי מדרגות אהבה

62A

וְכַנִּזְכָּר לְעֵיל [פֶּרֶק כ' וכ"א] בַּאֲרִיכוּת — **As we explained** these points **above at length** [chapters 20-21], בְּדֶרֶךְ מָשָׁל מִנֶּפֶשׁ הָאָדָם — **with an example from the human psyche,** שֶׁדִּבּוּר אֶחָד מִדְּבוּרוֹ וּמַחֲשַׁבְתּוֹ כְּלָא מַמָּשׁ כוּ' — where we concluded that if, even in the case of human beings, **one spoken word or thought is utterly insignificant** compared to the soul, (which has an *unlimited* power to speak and think), then certainly G-d's "speech" is insignificant compared to His thought, too.

Maintaining this consciousness represents the level of "higher reverence."

וְזֶהוּ שֶׁאָמַר הַכָּתוּב הֵן יִרְאַת ה' הִיא חָכְמָה — **And that is why the verse states, "***Look, reverence of G-d, that's wisdom (chochmah)***"** (*Job* 28:28), because the path to "higher reverence" is through using your *chochmah*.

אַךְ אִי אֶפְשָׁר לְהַשִּׂיג לְיִרְאָה וְחָכְמָה זוֹ אֶלָּא בְּקִיּוּם הַתּוֹרָה וְהַמִּצְוֹת — **However, it's impossible to attain this** "higher reverence" **and** *chochmah* **consciousness without** first observing Torah and *mitzvos.*

PRACTICAL LESSONS

It's impossible to attain "higher reverence" and *chochmah* consciousness without first elevating your mind through the observance of Torah and *mitzvos*.

While "lower reverence" is inspired by the greatness of G-d as manifested *through* the created worlds, "higher reverence" is an awareness of G-d as He *transcends* the worlds and voids their existence. Since you are a worldly creature, you can't fully tune into a light which transcends (and voids!) your existence.

That's why to reach "higher reverence" you need to first observe the *mitzvos*, which are "packets" of other-worldy Divine light, "*the 248 organs of the King*" (*Tikunei Zohar* 74a), which "*cause the light and life-energy from G-d's (transcendent) will to be 'dressed' in the worlds*" (chapter 23, p. 256). The *mitzvos* will help lift your mind to a perspective where you can see beyond the limitations of this world, which is necessary for "higher reverence" (*Toras Menachem, Sefer Ha-Ma'amarim Melukat,* vol. 3, p. 265).

עַל יְדֵי יִרְאָה תַּתָּאָה הַחִיצוֹנִית — **And, as we learned in chapter 41 (pp. 492-3), the** observance of Torah and *mitzvos* (which is the key to "higher reverence") **requires "superficial," "lower reverence."**

רבה ואהבת עולם. אהבה רבה היא אהבה בתענוגי'
והיא שלהבת העולה מאליה ובאה מלמעלה בבחי'
מתנה למי שהוא שלם ביראה כנודע על מאמר רז"ל

"Lower reverence," is an *indirect* requirement for "higher reverence," because "lower reverence" is a prerequisite for proper *mitzvah* observance, and *mitzvah* observance is a prerequisite for "higher reverence."

וְזֶהוּ שֶׁאָמְרוּ אִם אֵין יִרְאָה אֵין חָכְמָה — **And that's why** the Sages **said, "*If there's no reverence, there's no chochmah.*"** If you don't first have "lower reverence" and observe the commandments, you won't be able to reach the consciousness of *chochmah* and attain "higher reverence."

SECTION THREE: "GREAT LOVE" (AHAVAH RABAH)

30TH NISAN REGULAR

This concludes our discussion of reverence, which began in chapter 41. Now we turn to discuss the love for G-d, which is the second crucial component (the second "wing of the bird") that will propel your *mitzvos* heavenward.

וְהִנֵּה בְּאַהֲבָה יֵשׁ גַּם כֵּן שְׁתֵּי מַדְרֵגוֹת — **Now with love** of G-d, **there are also two levels,** אַהֲבָה רַבָּה וְאַהֲבַת עוֹלָם — a.) the higher level of **ahavah rabah, "great love,"** and b.) a lower level of **ahavas olam, "worldly love"** (*Jeremiah* 33:2).

The two terms "great love" and "worldly love" are taken from the daily liturgy (following *Talmud Brachos* 11b), and are often used in Kabbalistic works to describe different experiences of love we have for G-d (see, for example, Rabbi Isaiah Horowitz, *Shnei Luchos Ha-Bris, Be-Asarah Ma'amaros,* chapter 3).

אַהֲבָה רַבָּה הִיא אַהֲבָה בַּתַּעֲנוּגִים — *Ahavah rabah* **is** also described as *"pleasurable love"* (*Song* 7:7; see Rabbi Dov Ber of Mezritch, *Likutei Amarim,* section 70).

Normally you love something you don't already have; you're drawn to it and you desire it. But, as we learned in chapter 9 (pp. 117-8), a "pleasurable love," represents the joy of *already* being connected to G-d. In this sense, it resembles the love you have for yourself: there's no passionate yearning to be drawn to something. You just quietly take pleasure in yourself.

וְהִיא שַׁלְהֶבֶת הָעוֹלָה מֵאֵלֶיהָ — And "great love" is *"a flame that rises by itself"* (*Talmud, Shabbos* 21a), וּבָאָה מִלְמַעְלָה בִּבְחִינַת מַתָּנָה — meaning that it's impossible to acquire through your own efforts **and it comes** only as a kind of "gift from above,"** לְמִי שֶׁהוּא שָׁלֵם בְּיִרְאָה — **to a person who is** already **complete in** his or her **reverence of** G-d (see Rabbi Me'ir ibn Gabbai, *Avodas Ha-Kodesh* 1:28).

As we learned in chapter 14 (p. 172), "pleasurable love" is not a direct achievement of human worship, but a kind of reward received from G-d when everything else has been perfected — *"to take pleasure in G-d in a way that is a foretaste of the world-that-is-coming"* (chapter 40, p. 489).

דרכו של איש לחזר אחר אשה שאהבה נקראת איש
וזכר כמ"ש זכר חסדו ואשה יראת ה' כנודע ובלי
קדימת היראה אי אפשר להגיע לאהבה רבה זו כי
אהבה זו היא מבחי' אצילות דלית תמן קיצוץ ופירוד ח"ו

כַּנּוֹדָע עַל מַאֲמָר רַבּוֹתֵינוּ זִכְרוֹנָם לִבְרָכָה — As in the famous Chasidic **insight on the teaching of our Sages of blessed memory,** דַּרְכּוֹ שֶׁל אִישׁ לְחַזֵּר אַחַר אִשָּׁה — *"The way of a man is to seek a woman"* (*Talmud, Kidushin* 2b), שֶׁאֲהֲבָה נִקְרֵאת אִישׁ וְזָכָר — where, in this insight, **"love" is indicated Scripturally as "male" and "masculine"** (*zachar*).

PRACTICAL LESSONS

Love of G-d also has two levels. The higher *ahavah rabah* ("great love") is a "pleasurable love," the joy of already being connected to G-d.

Ahavah rabah can't be earned and will come only as a gift from above, to a person who is already complete in his or her reverence of G-d.

The way of love (the "masculine") is to "seek," and follow after reverence ("the feminine").

כְּמוֹ שֶׁכָּתוּב זָכַר חַסְדוֹ — **Scripture** hints to a connection between "masculine" (*zachar*) and "love" when it **states,** *"He remembers (zachar) His kindness"* (*Psalms* 98:3), "kindness" and "love" being related; וְאִשָּׁה יִרְאַת ה' — **and** Scripture hints to a connection between "feminine" and "reverence" with the words *"a woman, G-d revering"* (*Proverbs* 31:30) .

כַּנּוֹדָע — This insight **being known** from Rabbi Dov Ber of Mezritch (*Likutei Amarim,* section 110).

"The way of a 'man' (love) is to seek a 'woman' (reverence)," suggests that love ("man") comes to (*"seeks"*) a person who is complete in reverence of G-d.

וּבְלִי קְדִימַת הַיִּרְאָה אִי אֶפְשָׁר לְהַגִּיעַ לְאַהֲבָה רַבָּה זוֹ — **And** the explanation why **without first having** complete **reverence, it's impossible to reach this level of "great love,"** כִּי אֲהֲבָה זוֹ הִיא מִבְּחִינַת אֲצִילוּת — **is because this** "great love" is at the transpersonal **consciousness of Atzilus** (*Pri Etz Chaim, Sha'ar Ha-Krias Shema,* chapter 3), דְּלֵית תַּמָּן קִיצוּץ וּפֵירוּד — a realm *"where there is no slicing or separation"* (*Tikunei Zohar* 120a), חַס וְשָׁלוֹם — **G-d forbid,** so to receive "great love," your consciousness needs to be at the level of *Atzilus,* through attaining "higher reverence."

Unlike ordinary love, which fluctuates according to the circumstances, "great love" is a steady connection to G-d, which cannot be compromised by any worldly thing. To reach that level, your consciousness needs to be at the consciousness of *Atzilus,* at which point the physical veneer of this world is no longer able to hide G-d from you. The consciousness of *Atzilus* must be acquired through reaching "upper reverence."

אַךְ אהבת עולם היא הבאה מהתבונה ודעת בגדולת
ה' א"ס ב"ה הממלא כל עלמין וסובב כל עלמין וכולא

SECTION FOUR: "WORLDLY LOVE" (AHAVAS OLAM)

אַךְ אַהֲבַת עוֹלָם — **However** the lower level of **"worldly love,"** *can* be acquired through your efforts (it's not a gift from G-d), and it doesn't require you to reach "higher reverence" (the consciousness of *Atzilus*) first.

"Worldly love," as its name suggests, is a longing for G-d that you can acquire through your knowledge of the world. It's also called "worldly love" because *"anyone in the world can merit it, if he chooses"* (*Shnei Luchos Ha-Bris* ibid.).

הִיא הַבָּאָה מֵהִתְבּוֹנְנָה וְדַעַת בִּגְדוּלַת ה' אֵין סוֹף בָּרוּךְ הוּא — **"Worldly love" results from** meditating on **the greatness of the Blessed Infinite Light,** as it can be known *through the world,* using your *binah* and *da'as.*

Unlike the above "higher reverence" meditation, where you used your *chochmah* to directly "see" and perceive an other-worldly truth, here you use your *binah* and *da'as,* beginning with reality as they know it and continuing from there. *Binah* gradually discerns one thing from another in logical steps (the physical world exists through G-d, which means that G-d's creative energy must be everywhere, *etc.,*) and *da'as* then decides whether *binah's* conclusions are true and "real" for you.

PRACTICAL LESSONS

The lower level of *ahavas olam* ("worldly love") can be acquired through meditating on how G-d is the source of all pleasures and He transcends them.

The two approaches, *chochmah* and *binah/da'as,* each have their own strengths. *Chochmah* enables you to perceive a truth which is completely beyond (and incompatible with) your existence, leading to the identity-dissolving experience of "higher reverence." *Binah* and *da'as,* on the other hand, connect more with your ego and Animal Soul, so they bring you to "love G-d" (since love is an emotion which expresses ego and self), and you feel it more passionately and "physically." That's why the result of *binah/da'as* meditation is called "worldly love," because a.) it uses a "worldly" (egoic) part of your psyche (*binah* and *da'as*); and b.) the meditation begins with, and is anchored in, worldly phenomena.

הַמְמַלֵּא כָּל עָלְמִין — **To acquire** "worldly love" first you contemplate (with *binah* and *da'as*) how G-d *"fills all worlds"* (see *Zohar* 3, 225a), that G-d is the inner energy of every single thing in the universe, which He creates continually, וְסוֹבֵב כָּל עָלְמִין — **and** that will eventually lead you to the realization that G-d *"transcends all worlds"* (*ibid.*), that G-d's creative energies within the world are vastly surpassed by His energies beyond the world.

וְכוּלָּא קַמֵּיה כְּלָא מַמָּשׁ חֲשִׁיב — **And** this will lead you to the realization that *"in His presence, everything is considered zero,"* (*ibid.* 1:11b), **literally.**

קמיה כלא ממש חשיב וכביטול דבור אחד בנפש
המשכל׳ בעודו במחשבתה או בחמדת הלב כנ״ל אשר
ע״י התבוננו׳ זו ממילא תתפשט מדת האהבה שבנפש
מלבושיה דהיינו שלא תתלבש בשום דבר הנאה
ותענוג גשמי או רוחני לאהבה אותו ולא לחפוץ כלל

Even the awareness that G-d "fills all worlds" and "transcends all worlds" is ulti-mately based on a dualism of G-d-versus-world. But in the nondual consciousness that the *Tanya* has taught us (in chapters 20-21), there is only one reality—G-d. Everything else is "considered zero" in His presence.

The *Tanya* reminds us briefly of the illustration of this idea, taught in chapter 21.

וּכְבִיטוּל דִּבּוּר אֶחָד בַּנֶּפֶשׁ הַמַּשְׂכֶּלֶת — The world is "considered zero" in G-d's pres-ence **just as one** linguistic **phrase** produced by **the intellectual soul doesn't have its own identity** in the pre-linguistic part of the soul's consciousness, בְּעוֹדוֹ בְּמַחֲשַׁבְתָּה, אוֹ בְּחֶמְדַּת הַלֵּב — **while it still remains in the soul's** unarticulated **thought, or in a yearning of the heart,** כַּנִּזְכָּר לְעֵיל — **as mentioned above** in chapter 21 (p. 241-2).

Language only "kicks in" at a certain point in your psyche. What you later express as a verbalized thought, emerges from a pre-linguistic "whim" of the soul or of the heart. In it's pre-linguistic state, the "whim" exists, but has no tangible words. It's to-tally absorbed in the soul. That's similar to how, in reality, the world exists absorbed "within" G-d, devoid of any independent existence or identity.

אֲשֶׁר עַל יְדֵי הִתְבּוֹנְנוּת זוֹ מִמֵּילָא תִתְפַּשֵּׁט מִדַּת הָאַהֲבָה שֶׁבַּנֶּפֶשׁ מִלְּבוּשֶׁיהָ — **And this** above **meditation will instinctively cause the love in your soul to "strip off" her** prior **"garments,"** to detach herself from the things she loved before, דְּהַיְינוּ שֶׁלֹּא תִתְלַבֵּשׁ בְּשׁוּם דְּבַר הֲנָאָה וְתַעֲנוּג גַּשְׁמִי אוֹ רוּחָנִי לְאַהֲבָה אוֹתוֹ — **meaning that** your soul **will not attach its love to any pleasure or delight, be it physical or** even **spiritual,** וְלֹא לַחְפּוֹץ כְּלָל שׁוּם דָּבָר בָּעוֹלָם — **and it won't desire any worldly thing at all.**

You're drawn to love something based on your evaluation that it's good. Physi-cal pleasure makes you feel good, so you desire it; knowledge helps you to make sense of the world, so you want it.

That rule never changes: You will always love what you deem to be good. But you can challenge your assumptions of what constitutes "good," and transfer your love to something more valuable.

For example, you might love eating ice cream and cake every day, but when you ponder the fact that it will probably make you sick and shorten your life, you can "re-program" yourself to genuinely desire a more healthy diet. You supplant the desire for immediate sensual pleasure with the greater desire for a healthy and long life.

In a similar way, the *Tanya* promises, you can come to love G-d through a medita-tive practice which "devalues" the world and its pleasures, through the awareness of G-d's will as something even more desirable.

שום דבר בעולם בלתי ה' לבדו מקור החיים של כל
התענוגים שכולם בטילים במציאות וכלא ממש קמיה
חשיבי ואין ערוך ודמיון כלל ביניהם ח"ו כמו שאין
ערוך לאין ואפס המוחלט לגבי חיים נצחיים וכמ"ש
מי לי בשמים ועמך לא חפצתי בארץ כלה שארי
ולבבי צור לבבי וגו' וכמ"ש לקמן וגם מי שאין מדת
אהבה שבנפשו מלובשת כלל בשום תענוג גשמי או
רוחני יכול להלהיב נפשו כרשפי אש ושלהבת עזה

בִּלְתִּי לַה' לְבַדּוֹ מְקוֹר הַחַיִּים שֶׁל כָּל הַתַּעֲנוּגִים — Through the above meditation you can come to love **G-d alone, the living source of all pleasures,** שֶׁכּוּלָם בְּטֵלִים בְּמְצִיאוּת — **since all** the pleasures of this world **have no separate existence,** וּכְלָא מַמָּשׁ קַמֵּיהּ חֲשִׁיבֵי — **"and they are considered zero in His presence,"** literally, וְאֵין עֲרוֹךְ וְדִמְיוֹן כְּלָל בֵּינֵיהֶם חַס וְשָׁלוֹם — **and there is no comparison to be made in any way, between** them and Him, **G-d forbid,** כְּמוֹ שֶׁאֵין עֲרוֹךְ לְאַיִן וְאֶפֶס הַמּוּחְלָט לְגַבֵּי חַיִּים נִצְחִיִּים — **in the same way that you can't compare absolute** *"null and void"* **with eternal life.**

If we compare physical pleasures with the "pleasure" of G-d, it's easy to see that one is worthless compared to the other. While the physical world might seem alluring, your metaphysical intuition can easily see that this world has no power of its own and is utterly dependent on G-d. The world has nothing in its "bank account," nothing of its own supporting it. Its very existence is really "null and void."

G-d, on the other hand, is real, eternal, and powers all existence. *Do you want something that is worthless, or something of infinite value?*

וּכְמוֹ שֶׁכָּתוּב — **As the verse indicates** that all spiritual and physical pleasures are worthless compared to G-d, מִי לִי בַּשָּׁמַיִם וְעִמְּךָ לֹא חָפַצְתִּי בָאָרֶץ — *"Whom else do I have (to love) in heaven? And beside You, I want no one on earth,"* כָּלָה שְׁאֵרִי וּלְבָבִי צוּר לְבָבִי וְגוֹ' — *"my body and heart expire (out of love for You); G-d is forever the base of my heart and portion"* (Psalms 73:25-26).

וּכְמוֹ שֶׁיִּתְבָּאֵר לְקַמָּן — **And** the insignificance of this physical world and its pleasures **will be explained further below** (in chapter 48).

One problem with the above approach, of "switching" your worldly desires with something more lofty, is that it presumes you already enjoy physical pleasures immensely. But what if a person is not particularly drawn to physical indulgence? Does that mean the above meditation won't work for him and he won't be able to love G-d? The *Tanya* assures us this is not the case.

וְגַם מִי שֶׁאֵין מִדַּת אַהֲבָה שֶׁבְּנַפְשׁוֹ מְלוּבֶּשֶׁת כְּלָל בְּשׁוּם תַּעֲנוּג גַּשְׁמִי אוֹ רוּחָנִי — **And even if the love in a person's soul is not** strongly **attached to the desire of any pleasure,**

62B וְלַהַב הָעוֹלֶה הַשָּׁמַיְמָה ע"י הִתְבּוֹנְנוּ' הַנַּ"ל כמ"ש לקמן
וְהִנֵּה בְּחִ' אַהֲבָה זוֹ פְּעָמִים שֶׁקּוֹדֶמֶת לְיִרְאָה כְּפִי בְּחִ'
הַדַּעַת הַמּוֹלִידָהּ כַּנּוֹדָע [שֶׁהַדַּעַת כּוֹלֵל חֲסָדִים וּגְבוּרוֹת
שֶׁהֵם אַהֲבָה וְיִרְאָה וּפְעָמִים שֶׁהַחֲסָדִים קוֹדְמִים לְיִרד

physical or spiritual, יָכוֹל לְהַלְהִיב נַפְשׁוֹ כְּרִשְׁפֵּי אֵשׁ וְשַׁלְהֶבֶת עַזָּה — **he can still ignite his soul with** a love like **"flaming fire"** (*Song* 8:6) **and intense flames,** וְלַהַב הָעוֹלֶה הַשָּׁמַיְמָה — **a flame soaring heavenward** with love for G-d, עַל יְדֵי הַהִתְבּוֹנְנוּת הַנִּזְכֶּרֶת לְעֵיל — all this can be achieved **by means of the meditation mentioned above** in this chapter.

Even if a person is generally devoid of love and passion, as soon as He will meditate seriously on the above themes, he will begin to have strong feelings for G-d. The *Tanya* believes that everyone is capable of love, when they will find something or someone worth loving.

כְּמוֹ שֶׁיִּתְבָּאֵר לְקַמָּן — **As will be clarified later on** (in chapters 44 and 50).

SECTION FIVE: WHY OBSERVANCE MUST COME BEFORE LOVE

1ST IYAR REGULAR | 27TH NISAN LEAP

We have now established that the higher level of "great love" will always be preceded by "higher reverence." But does the lower level of "worldly love" come before or after "lower reverence"?

In chapter 3 we learned a general principle about meditation: *"When the cognitive powers of your rational soul focus deeply on the greatness of G-d... a sensation of awesome reverence will be born in your mind... and **after that,** your heart will be ignited with a rapturous love."* Reverence of G-d, it would seem, must always precede love of G-d.

However, as the *Tanya* will now note, there are "occasional" exceptions to this rule.

וְהִנֵּה בְּחִינַת אַהֲבָה זוֹ פְּעָמִים שֶׁקּוֹדֶמֶת לְיִרְאָה — **Now this** "worldly **love" can occasionally precede** "lower **reverence."**

Usually, reverence must precede love because your soul needs to weaken its attachments to worldly pleasures (through reverence), before it can come to love G-d (Rabbi Shlomo Chaim Kesselman, *Biurei Reb Shlomo Chaim*).

But, technically speaking, either emotion (reverence or love), could come first, as the *Tanya* will now explain.

כְּפִי בְּחִינַת הַדַּעַת הַמּוֹלִידָהּ — **It depends on the type of** *da'as* **which gives rise to it,** כַּנּוֹדָע — **as is known** (*Tanya, Igeres Ha-Kodesh,* sec. 15), [שֶׁהַדַּעַת כּוֹלֵל חֲסָדִים וּגְבוּרוֹת — **for** *da'as* **contains** the potential for both *chesed* and *gevurah* powers (see Rabbi Chaim Vital, *Etz Chaim*, 21:2), שֶׁהֵם אַהֲבָה וְיִרְאָה — **which** correspond to

ולהתגלות] ולכן אפשר לרשע ובעל עבירות שיעשה
תשובה מאהבה הנולדה בלבו בזכרו את ה' אלהיו ומ"מ
היראה ג"כ כלולה בה ממילא רק שהיא בבחי' קטנות
והעלם דהיינו יראת חטא למרוד בו ח"ו והאהבה היא

love and reverence, respectively, [וּפְעָמִים שֶׁהַחֲסָדִים קוֹדְמִים לֵירֵד וּלְהִתְגַּלּוֹת] — **and, sometimes, the** *chesed* **powers will come down and be disclosed first.**

Usually we have to work our way up the hierarchy of the *sefiros*. We begin with accepting G-d's authority (*malchus*), then work up to reverence (*gevurah*), which is followed by love (*chesed*). But *da'as* can bypass that strict linear pathway, since it has "parallel circuits" to both *chesed* and *gevurah* (*Biurei Reb Shlomo Chaim*).

Now we have learned the theoretical reasoning why "worldly love" can precede "lower reverence," the *Tanya* offers a practical illustration.

וְלָכֵן אֶפְשָׁר לְרָשָׁע וּבַעַל עֲבֵירוֹת שֶׁיַּעֲשֶׂה תְּשׁוּבָה מֵאַהֲבָה הַנּוֹלְדָה בְּלִבּוֹ — **And that's why it's possible for a** *rasha* **and sinful person** who lacks reverence **to repent out of love born in his heart** even without an initial feeling of reverence, בְּזָכְרוֹ אֶת ה' אֱלֹהָיו — as soon as ***"he remembers G-d, his G-d"*** (see *Judges* 8:34).

But could a person really repent and worship G-d with love alone? In chapter 41 we learned, *"It's not sufficient to awaken love alone... you first need to awaken at least the innate reverence found dormant in the heart of all Israel not to act insubordinately towards 'the King, King of kings'"* (p. 493).

The *Tanya* will answer that, even in the case of a "sinful person who repents out of love," there must be some reverence present.

וּמִכָּל מָקוֹם הַיִּרְאָה גַּם כֵּן כְּלוּלָה בָּה מִמֵּילָא — **However,** even a "sinful person who repents out of love" isn't completely devoid of reverence, since **reverence is automatically "included" in the love too.**

In chapter 19 we learned the idea of "reverence that is contained in love": You love G-d so much, that you cannot bear to do anything that would compromise your connection with Him (see p. 230). Even the "sinful person who repents out of love" must have some residual reverence "contained" in his love. But why, then, does he feel only love and not reverence?

רַק שֶׁהִיא בִּבְחִינַת קַטְנוּת וְהֶעְלֵם — **Only,** his reverence **is in a state of "contraction" and concealment.**

The person's reverence is dull, and undeveloped, while his love is powerful and overwhelming. His love eclipses his reverence; but the reverence is still there.

דְּהַיְינוּ יִרְאַת חֵטָא לִמְרוֹד בּוֹ — **Namely** his reverence is on the very basic level of ***"the minimal reverence necessary not to sin,"*** not **to act insubordinately towards** G-d, חַס וְשָׁלוֹם — **G-d forbid,** וְהָאַהֲבָה הִיא בְּהִתְגַּלּוּת לִבּוֹ וּמוֹחוֹ — **whereas his love is** strongly **palpable in his heart and mind.**

בהתגלות לבו ומוחו אך זהו דרך מקרה והוראת שעה
בהשגחה פרטית מאת ה' לצורך שעה כמעשה דר"א
בן דורדייא. אבל סדר העבודה הקבועה ותלויה
בבחירת האדם צריך להקדים תחלה קיום התורה
והמצות ע"י יראה תתאה בבחי' קטנות עכ"פ בסור
מרע ועשה טוב להאיר נפשו האלהית באור התורה
ומצותיה ואח"כ יאיר עליה אור האהבה [כי ואהבת
בגימטריא ב"פ אור כידוע לי"ח]:

The *Tanya* now notes that, while we have seen that it's possible for love to precede reverence, such a case is unusual and exceptional.

אַךְ זֶהוּ דֶּרֶךְ מִקְרֶה — **However this** phenomenon of love preceding reverence **is unusual,** וְהוֹרָאַת שָׁעָה בְּהַשְׁגָּחָה פְּרָטִית מֵאֵת ה' לְצוֹרֶךְ שָׁעָה — **and it's an "emergency measure" of Divine providence, due to the need of the hour,** כְּמַעֲשֵׂה דְּרַבִּי אֶלְעָזָר בֶּן

דּוּרְדָּיָּא — **as in the story of Rabbi Elazar ben Durdaya,** who was extremely sinful, but eventually had an awakening and repented (see *Talmud, Avodah Zarah* 17a).

PRACTICAL LESSONS

In most cases, to feel any real love for G-d you first need to observe Torah and *mitzvos* (which, as we have seen, requires "lower reverence").

אֲבָל סֵדֶר הָעֲבוֹדָה הַקְּבוּעָה וּתְלוּיָה בִּבְחִירַת הָאָדָם — **But in the normal sequence of worship, which is fixed and determined by man's free choice,** love will only come after Torah observance, צָרִיךְ לְהַקְדִּים תְּחִלָּה קִיּוּם הַתּוֹרָה וְהַמִּצְוֹת עַל יְדֵי יִרְאָה תַּתָּאָה — **you must first observe Torah and** *mitzvos* **through "lower reverence,"** בִּבְחִינַת קַטְנוּת עַל כָּל פָּנִים — **at least with its** minimal, **"contracted" state,** בְּסוּר מֵרַע וַעֲשֵׂה טוֹב — **and** *"turn away from evil and do good,"* לְהָאִיר נַפְשׁוֹ הָאֱלֹהִית בְּאוֹר הַתּוֹרָה וּמִצְוֹתֶיהָ — **so as to shine the "light" of Torah and** *mitzvos* **into your Divine Soul,** וְאַחַר כָּךְ יָאִיר עָלֶיהָ אוֹר הָאַהֲבָה — **and only after that can the "light" of love** for G-d **shine on you.**

In order to love G-d, you first need to internalize some of the "light of Torah and *mitzvos*." "Lower reverence" therefore leads to love *indirectly*. "Lower reverence" is necessary for Torah observance which is necessary for love of G-d.

[כִּי וְאָהַבְתָּ בְּגִימַטְרִיָּא ב' פְּעָמִים אוֹר כַּיָּדוּעַ לְיוֹדְעֵי חָכְמָה נִסְתָּרָה] — **For** *ve-ahavta* (**"And you shall love") has twice the numerical value of** *ohr* **("light"), as is known to the masters of hidden** Kabbalistic **wisdom** (Rabbi Meir Poppers, *Pri Etz Chaim, Sha'ar Krias Shema,* chapters 23, 25).

The fact that *ve-ahavta* has twice the numerical value of "light" hints to the above point that the path to loving G-d requires two components (two "lights"). You can't just have love (one single "light"). You first need to attain the "light" of Torah and *mitzvos*, and that will lead you to the "light" of love for G-d.

פרק מד והנה   כל מדרגת אהבה מב' מדרגות
אלו אהבה רבה ואהבת עולם
נחלקת לכמה בחי' ומדרגות לאין קץ כל חד לפום
שיעורא דיליה כמ"ש בז"הק ע"פ נודע בשערים בעלה
דא קב"ה דאיהו אתידע ואתדבק לכל חד לפום מה

CHAPTER 44

MORE LOVE MEDITATIONS
SECTION ONE: THE MANY LEVELS OF REVERENCE AND LOVE

2ND IYAR REGULAR | 28TH NISAN LEAP

Chapter 44 continues our discussion of emotions for G-d, which began in chapter 41 and will continue to the end of chapter 50.

The majority of this chapter will focus on two new love meditations. But first, in this section, we will conclude the discussion of the two types of love discussed in the previous chapter.

וְהִנֵּה כָּל מַדְרֵגַת אַהֲבָה מִב' מַדְרֵגוֹת אֵלוּ אַהֲבָה רַבָּה וְאַהֲבַת עוֹלָם — **Now each one of these two levels of love, "great love" and "worldly love,"** discussed in chapter 43, נֶחֱלֶקֶת לְכַמָּה בְּחִינוֹת וּמַדְרֵגוֹת לְאֵין קֵץ — **are subdivided into many types and infinite levels,** כָּל חַד לְפוּם שִׁיעוּרָא דִילֵיה — **"each individual according to his own capabilities"** (Zohar 1, 103a).

"Worldly love," as we have learned in chapter 43, is the direct product of meditative work. "Great love," is granted from G-d as a "gift from above," but will only come to a person who has first reached an impressive degree of emotional mastery. So both experiences depend, directly or indirectly, on meditative work, "each individual according to his own capabilities."

The *Tanya* now cites a source in the *Zohar* for the idea that there are many levels of emotional mastery, which depend on the success of your meditative work.

כְּמוֹ שֶׁכָּתוּב בַּזֹהַר הַקָּדוֹשׁ עַל פָּסוּק נוֹדָע בַּשְׁעָרִים בַּעְלָהּ — **As the *Zohar* teaches on the verse, "Her husband is known in the gates (she'arim)"** (Proverbs 31:23), דָּא קוּדְשָׁא בְּרִיךְ הוּא — **according to the *Zohar*, "this ('husband') is the Blessed Holy One."**

The *Zohar's* reading of "Her husband (i.e., G-d) is known in the gates," suggests that G-d can, in fact, be known. But doesn't He actually defy comprehension?

The answer to this question is in the second half of the verse, "in the gates (she'arim)." The term *she'arim* hints to the way that we can know G-d.

דמשער בלביה וכו' ולכן נקראי' דחילו ורחימו הנסתרות
לה' אלהינו ותורה ומצות הן הנגלות לנו ולבנינו לעשות
כו'. כי תורה אחת ומשפט אחד לכולנו בקיום כל
התורה ומצות בבחי' מעשה משא"כ בדחילו ורחימו
שהם לפי הדעת את ה' שבמוח ולב כנ"ל. אך אחת

דְּאִיהוּ אִתְיְדַע וְאִתְדַּבֵּק לְכָל חַד לְפוּם מַה דִּמְשַׁעֵר בְּלִבֵּיהּ וְכוּ' — *"For He makes Himself known and attaches Himself with each individual according to the conjectures of (di-mesha'er) his heart,* each individual according to his ability to connect to the spirit of wisdom" (Zohar 1, 103b).

"Her husband is known in the gates," is a metaphor for the emotional connection between us and G-d. We are "the wife" and G-d, "the husband." The city's gates are the "gates" of the heart, which are opened through contemplation. (The term for gate, *sha'ar,* is similar to the term *mesha'er,* "conjecture.") The verse is translated metaphorically by the *Zohar:* "G-d will become known to us, and experienced by us in the heart, according to the level at which we contemplate His greatness."

So if feelings for G-d depend on each individual's meditative abilities, then love for Him will be *"subdivided into many types and infinite levels,"* as the *Tanya* stated above.

But this also means nobody should see reverence and love as something unreachable. Every person can acquire these feelings for G-d in their own way (see Rabbi Shalom Dov Ber Schneersohn, *Kuntres Etz Chaim,* chapter 16).

וְלָכֵן נִקְרָאִים דְּחִילוּ וּרְחִימוּ הַנִּסְתָּרוֹת לַה' אֱלֹהֵינוּ — **And that's why reverence and love are referred to as, *"the hidden things that are for G-d, our G-d"*** (Deuteronomy 29:28), since *"if a person reveres the Blessed Holy One, or loves Him, no other person knows; it's something which is not revealed, except to him and his Creator,"* (Zohar 3, 123b), וְתוֹרָה וּמִצְוֹת הֵן הַנִּגְלוֹת לָנוּ וּלְבָנֵינוּ לַעֲשׂוֹת כוּ' — **whereas Torah and mitzvos are, *"the revealed things, for us and our children to do etc.,'"*** (Deuteronomy ibid.), since *"when a person studies Torah and observes positive commandments, it's revealed to everyone"* (Zohar ibid.).

Torah observance is external and objective ("revealed"). Love and reverence of G-d, on the other hand, are internal and subjective ("hidden"). That's because your love and reverence are a product of your own understanding and appreciation of G-d, which varies from person to person, *"each individual according to the conjectures of his heart."*

כִּי תּוֹרָה אַחַת וּמִשְׁפָּט אֶחָד לְכוּלָּנוּ בְּקִיּוּם כָּל הַתּוֹרָה וּמִצְוֹת בִּבְחִינַת מַעֲשֶׂה — **For when it comes to practically observing all of the Torah and *mitzvos,* we all have** one objective standard, *"one Torah and one law"* (Numbers 15:16), מַה שֶּׁאֵין כֵּן בְּדְחִילוּ וּרְחִימוּ — **but that's not the case with reverence and love,** שֶׁהֵם לְפִי הַדַּעַת אֶת ה' שֶׁבְּמוֹחַ וָלֵב — **which vary according to the knowledge of G-d found in the mind and heart,** כַּנִּזְכָּר לְעֵיל — **as explained above.**

הִיא אַהֲבָה הַכְּלוּלָה מִכָּל בְּחִי' וּמַדְרֵגוֹת אַהֲבָה רַבָּה
וְאַהֲבַת עוֹלָם וְהִיא שָׁוָה לְכָל נֶפֶשׁ מִיִּשְׂרָאֵל וִירוּשָׁה
לָנוּ מֵאֲבוֹתֵינוּ. וְהַיְינוּ מַ"שׁ הַזֹּהַר עַ"פ נַפְשִׁי אִוִּיתִיךָ
בַּלַּיְלָה וְגוּ' דִּירְחִים לְקַבְּ"ה רְחִימוּתָא דְּנַפְשָׁא וְרוּחָא כְּמָה
דְּאִתְדַּבְּקוּ אִילֵין בְּגוּפָא וְגוּפָא רָחִים לוֹן וְכוּ'. וְז"שׁ נַפְשִׁי

63A

SECTION TWO: UNLOCKING YOUR SOUL'S DEEP LOVE FOR G-D

As we have discussed earlier in the *Tanya*, feelings of reverence and love for G-d can come to you through two different methods. a.) Ideally you should *acquire* feelings for G-d through serious meditation (see chapters 3, pp. 57-63; chapter 9, pp. 115-6; chapter 16, pp. 188*ff.*); b.) but you could also use more simple meditative techniques to merely *awaken* the feelings for G-d which are *present already* in your soul (see chapters 18-19; chapter 25, pp. 284*ff.*).

Either of these two methods can produce acceptable results. From chapter 41 until this point, our love meditations have largely been exploring techniques of the first method, to acquire feelings for G-d through meditation. Now we will learn some advanced techniques of the second method, to awaken the love for G-d which is present already in your soul. (This is in addition to the basic techniques of the second method we have already learned in chapters 18-19 and 25).

הַכְּלוּלָה מִכָּל בְּחִינוֹת — אַךְ אַחַת הִיא אַהֲבָה — **But there is one** different **type of love,** וּמַדְרֵגוֹת אַהֲבָה רַבָּה וְאַהֲבַת עוֹלָם — **which contains all** the mutually exclusive qualities of **"great love" and "worldly love," in all its types and levels.**

This type of love which we will now discuss will be a "gift" from G-d, like "great love," but it will also be awakened through meditation like "worldly love." It will have the transcendent power of "great love," and the this-worldly immediacy of "worldly love." (In Section Seven below, this point will be discussed further).

וְהִיא שָׁוָה לְכָל נֶפֶשׁ מִיִּשְׂרָאֵל וִירוּשָׁה לָנוּ מֵאֲבוֹתֵינוּ — This type of love is a "gift" from G-d (like "great love") because **it's found equally in every soul of Israel, as an "inheritance" from our Patriarchs.**

The *Tanya* uses the term "inheritance from our Patriarchs" to describe an emotion which is inherent in your soul and merely needs to be awakened (see pp. 212*ff.*).

וְהַיְינוּ מַה שֶּׁכָּתַב הַזֹּהַר עַל פָּסוּק נַפְשִׁי אִוִּיתִיךָ בַּלַּיְלָה וְגוּ' — This type love is **what the** *Zohar* refers to in its commentary on the verse, *"My soul (nefesh), I have desired you at night, in the morning my spirit (ruach) longs for you"* (Isaiah 26:9), דִּירְחִים לְקוּדְשָׁא בְּרִיךְ הוּא רְחִימוּתָא דְּנַפְשָׁא וְרוּחָא — *"that you should love the Blessed Holy One* with a true love of the soul, which is a complete love, *a love of the nefesh and ruach,"* כְּמָה דְּאִתְדַּבְּקוּ אִילֵין בְּגוּפָא וְגוּפָא רָחִים לוֹן וְכוּ' — *"just as they* (the nefesh and ruach) **cling to the body and the body loves them,** so must a person love the Blessed Holy One and cling to Him" (Zohar 3, 68a).

אויתיך כלומר מפני שאתה ה' נפשי וחיי האמיתים
לכך אויתיך פי' שאני מתאוה ותאב לך כאדם המתאוה
לחיי נפשו וכשהוא חלש ומעונה מתאוה ותאב
שתשוב נפשו אליו וכן כשהוא הולך לישן מתאוה
וחפץ שתשוב נפשו אליו כשיעור משנתו כך אני
מתאוה ותאב לאור א"ס ב"ה חיי החיים האמיתיים
להמשיכו בקרבי ע"י עסק התורה בהקיצי משנתי

You ought to love G-d as much as your body loves your soul, meaning to say, as much as you love to be alive. Obviously, this is an inherent love because you don't have to learn to love being alive; you love it naturally.

The *Tanya* now suggests a simple meditation to awaken this type of love from its dormant state in your soul.

וְזֶהוּ שֶׁכָּתוּב נַפְשִׁי אִוִּיתִיךָ — **And this is** the meditation we learn from **the verse, "My soul, I have desired you,"** כְּלוֹמַר מִפְּנֵי שֶׁאַתָּה ה' נַפְשִׁי וְחַיַּי הָאֲמִיתִּים — **meaning to say: "Since you are G-d, my soul and my true life,"** לְכָךְ אִוִּיתִיךָ — **"therefore, 'I have desired you,'"** פֵּירוּשׁ שֶׁאֲנִי מִתְאַוֶּה וְתָאֵב לְךָ כְּאָדָם הַמִּתְאַוֶּה לְחַיֵּי נַפְשׁוֹ — **"meaning that I desire and crave for you like a person desires his own life and soul,"** וּכְשֶׁהוּא חַלָּשׁ וּמְעוּנֶּה — **"and just like a person becomes aware of how much he loves his life when he is weak and exhausted,"** מִתְאַוֶּה וְתָאֵב שֶׁתָּשׁוּב נַפְשׁוֹ אֵלָיו — **"and he desires and craves that his energy should return,"** וְכֵן כְּשֶׁהוּא הוֹלֵךְ לִישָׁן מִתְאַוֶּה וְחָפֵץ שֶׁתָּשׁוּב נַפְשׁוֹ אֵלָיו כְּשִׁיעוּר מִשְּׁנָתוֹ — **"and similarly, when he goes to bed, he desires and yearns that his soul will be returned to him when he wakes up from his sleep,"** כָּךְ אֲנִי מִתְאַוֶּה וְתָאֵב לְאוֹר אֵין סוֹף בָּרוּךְ הוּא חַיֵּי הַחַיִּים הָאֲמִיתִּים לְהַמְשִׁיכוֹ בְּקִרְבִּי — **"in the same way, I desire to draw inside me the Blessed Infinite Light, the true source of life."**

PRACTICAL LESSONS

Contemplate how G-d is the source of all your life and energy. Crave for Him like a hungry man craves food. Crave for him like a dying person craves life.

Life is the greatest pleasure of all, but you don't feel the pleasure because it's a constant one. Only when your life comes into question (for example due to illness, G-d forbid), do you realize how much it means to you. If you can call to mind how much you love life, then with the same intensity you can come to love G-d, "the true source of life."

The *Tanya* now explains the end of the verse, "My soul, I have desired you *at night.*"

עַל יְדֵי עֵסֶק הַתּוֹרָה בַּהֲקִיצִי מִשְּׁנָתִי בַּלַּיְלָה — **"In particular, I will express this love of G-d through studying Torah when I wake up from my sleep in the night,**

בלילה דאורייתא וקב"ה כולא חד. כמ"ש הזהר שם
דבעי בר נש מרחימותא דקב"ה למיקם בכל ליא
לאשתדלא בפולחניה עד צפרא כו'. ואהבה רבה
וגדולה מזו והיא מסותרת ג"כ בכל נפש מישראל
בירושה מאבותינו היא מ"ש בר"מ כברא דאשתדל
בתר אבוי ואימיה דרחים לון יתיר מגרמיה ונפשיה

דְאוֹרַיְיתָא וְקוּדְשָׁא בְּרִיךְ הוּא כּוּלָא חַד — and this will attach me to G-d since 'the Torah and G-d are totally one'" (see *Zohar* 1, 24a; 2, 60a).

דְּבָעֵי בַּר נַשׁ מֵרְחִימוּתָא — As is stated in the *Zohar* (ibid.), כְּמוֹ שֶׁכָּתַב הַזֹהַר שָׁם דְּקוּדְשָׁא בְּרִיךְ הוּא לְמֵיקִם בְּכָל לֵילָא לְאִשְׁתַּדְּלָא בְּפוּלְחָנֵיהּ עַד צַפְרָא כו' — "that out of love for the Blessed Holy One, a person ought to get up every night and exert himself in worship, until the morning."

During the day you feel connected to G-d because you're often involved in prayer, study and *mitzvah* observance. But when you meditate on the fact that your connection to G-d is your "life," the absence of a strong connection during the night hours, when you're asleep, might inspire you to wake up in the night and study Torah. (Of course, Jewish law doesn't *require* you to get up in the night and study; but it's something you might do out of love.)

SECTION THREE: FINDING YOUR SELFLESS LOVE

3RD IYAR REGULAR | 29TH NISAN LEAP

Now we will learn a second meditative technique to awaken the feelings for G-d which are present already in your soul. This technique is aimed at producing an even higher level of love than the meditation in Section Two.

וְאַהֲבָה רַבָּה וּגְדוֹלָה מִזוֹ — And a love greater and more expansive than this, וְהִיא מְסוּתֶּרֶת גַם כֵּן בְּכָל נֶפֶשׁ מִיִּשְׂרָאֵל בִּירוּשָׁה מֵאֲבוֹתֵינוּ — which is also latent in every soul of Israel, as an "inheritance" from our Patriarchs, but still requires meditation to awaken it, הִיא מַה שֶׁכָּתוּב בְּרַעְיָא מְהֵימְנָא — is what the *Zohar* in "*Raya Mehemna*" refers to as, כְּבְרָא דְּאִשְׁתַּדַּל בָּתַר אֲבוֹי וְאִמֵּיהּ דְּרָחִים לוֹן יַתִּיר מִגַּרְמֵיהּ וְנַפְשֵׁיהּ וְרוּחֵיהּ כו' — love "*like a son who exerts himself for his father and mother, whom he loves more than himself,* more than his own *nefesh, ruach* and *neshamah,*" (*Zohar* 3, 281a; see above chapter 10, p. 129; chapter 41, p. 505).

This passage in the *Zohar* was cited by Rabbi Dov Ber, the "Maggid" of Mezritch and earlier thinkers as depicting a completely selfless love (see Rabbi Eliyahu de-Vidas, *Reishis Chochmah, Sha'ar Ha-Ahavah,* chapter 8; Rabbi Chaim Tyrer of Czernowitz, *Be'er Mayim Chaim,* p. 59a).

Generally speaking, love is an emotion connected with your self-concept: It's the

ורוחיה כו' כי הלא אב אחד לכולנו. ואף כי מי הוא
זה ואיזהו אשר ערב לבו לגשת להשיג אפי' חלק אחד
מני אלף ממדרגת אהבת רעיא מהימנא. מ"מ הרי
אפס קצהו ושמץ מנהו מרב טובו ואורו מאיר לכללות
ישראל בכל דור ודור כמ"ש בתיקונים דאתפשטותיה

feeling that *you* would like to be closer to G-d. As we learned in chapter 41, *"the inherent love which is dormant in your heart is... your desire to connect with Him"* (p. 509).

Even the powerful love we just discussed in Section Two is still linked to your self-concept: It's *because* you love yourself and your life, that you love the source of your life — G-d. But the love depicted here by the *Zohar* is a devotion to G-d, *"whom he loves more than himself, more than his own nefesh, ruach and neshamah,"* i.e., more than your own life.

This love isn't about what *you* want, but what *G-d* wants. You manage to transcend your own desires, *even your desire to be close to G-d.* You yearn to fulfill the Divine will, not because *you want* to fulfill the Divine will, but because the Divine will *needs to be done* (Rabbi Shneur Zalman, *Short Discourses*, p. 435).

PRACTICAL LESSONS

For an utterly selfless love, contemplate G-d as your Father, whom you love so much that you would do anything for Him, even if it cost you your life.

כִּי הֲלֹא אָב אֶחָד לְכוּלָּנוּ — Since this love is a meditation about G-d as our father, it should be attainable by us all, **for *"don't we all have one Father"*** (*Malachi* 2:10), G-d Himself?

The love *"like a son who exerts himself etc.,"* is depicted by the *Zohar* as the unique level of Moshe, the "faithful shepherd": *"The faithful shepherd rose and bowed before the Blessed Holy One. He wept and said, 'May it please you to regard me as a son, that my actions towards the Blessed Holy One and His Shechinah be considered like a son who exerts himself etc.,'"* (*Zohar ibid.*).

How can the *Tanya* suggest that this unique level of Moshe is achievable by us?

וְאַף כִּי מִי הוּא זֶה וְאֵיזֶהוּ אֲשֶׁר עָרַב לִבּוֹ לָגֶשֶׁת לְהַשִּׂיג — **And, although, who could possibly say that he** *"has prepared his heart to come close to"* (*Jeremiah* 30:21), **and attain,** אֲפִילוּ חֵלֶק אֶחָד מִנִּי אֶלֶף מִמַּדְרֵגַת אַהֲבַת רַעְיָא מְהֵימְנָא — **the level of love of** Moshe, the *Raya Mehemna* (**"faithful shepherd"**), **even a thousandth of it?**

מִכָּל מָקוֹם הֲרֵי אֶפֶס קָצֵהוּ וְשֶׁמֶץ מֶנְהוּ מֵרַב טוּבוֹ וְאוֹרוֹ מֵאִיר לִכְלָלוּת יִשְׂרָאֵל בְּכָל דּוֹר וָדוֹר — **Nevertheless,** while this is a level of love indeed unique to Moshe, *"the very edge of"* (*Numbers* 23:13), **and** *"a tag end of"* (*Job* 4:12) this love **shines to all Israel** from Moshe's **abundant good and light,** כְּמוֹ שֶׁכָּתוּב בַּתִּיקוּנִים דְּאִתְפַּשְּׁטוּתֵיהּ בְּכָל

בכל דרא ודרא לאנהרא לון וכו' רק שהארה זו היא
בבחי' הסתר והעלם גדול בנפשות כל בית ישראל
ולהוציא אהבה זו המסותרת מההעלם וההסתר אל
הגילוי להיות בהתגלות לבו ומוחו לא נפלאת ולא
רחוקה היא אלא קרוב הדבר מאד בפיך ובלבבך
דהיינו להיות רגיל על לשונו וקולו לעורר כוונת לבו
ומוחו להעמיק מחשבתו בחיי החיים א"ס ב"ה כי הוא

63B

דְּרָא וְדָרָא לְאַנְהָרָא לוֹן וְכוּ' — as the *Tikunei Zohar* (112a) states that, *"an extension of him (Moshe) reaches into every single generation,"* to give our souls light (see chapter 42, p. 524).

It's true that this level of selfless love is unique to Moshe; but some of Moshe's light shines to all of us, empowering us to attain "the very edge of" selfless worship.

רַק שֶׁהֶאָרָה זוֹ הִיא בִּבְחִינַת הֶסְתֵּר וְהֶעְלֵם גָּדוֹל בְּנַפְשׁוֹת כָּל בֵּית יִשְׂרָאֵל — Only, this light of Moshe's soul is extremely hidden and concealed within the souls of all the House of Israel, so you might find it difficult to believe that you can actually attain it.

וּלְהוֹצִיא אַהֲבָה זוֹ הַמְסוּתֶרֶת מֵהֶעְלֵם וְהֶסְתֵּר — But, in reality, for this love to come out from its latent state, from being hidden and concealed, אֶל הַגִּילוּי לִהְיוֹת to be revealed, palpably in your בְּהִתְגַּלוֹת לִבּוֹ וּמוֹחוֹ heart and mind, is relatively simple if you apply the right meditative technique, לֹא נִפְלֵאת וְלֹא רְחוֹקָה הִיא — *"it's not beyond you, nor is it far away"* (Deuteronomy 30:11), אֶלָּא קָרוֹב הַדָּבָר מְאֹד בְּפִיךְ וּבִלְבָבְךָ — rather *"the thing is very much within reach for you, in your mouth and in your heart"* (ibid. 14).

If selfless love would be a level you had to reach unaided, it would indeed be a formidable task. But since you already have it in the deep recesses of your soul, all you need to do is find it. And that's "within reach" if you follow the correct meditative path.

דְּהַיְינוּ לִהְיוֹת רָגִיל עַל לְשׁוֹנוֹ — Namely, by accustoming your mouth, וְקוֹלוֹ לְעוֹרֵר כַּוָּנַת לִבּוֹ וּמוֹחוֹ — with *"audible vocalization, that stimulates concentration"* (Shnei Luchos Ha-Bris, Maseches Sukkah), of the mind and the heart, לְהַעֲמִיק מַחֲשַׁבְתּוֹ בְּחַיֵּי הַחַיִּים אֵין סוֹף בָּרוּךְ הוּא — to think deeply about the Giver of life, the Blessed Infinite One, כִּי הוּא אָבִינוּ מַמָּשׁ

PRACTICAL LESSONS

Observe Torah and *mitzvos* out of selfless love, purely to give G-d a "feeling of satisfaction."

These meditations should be practiced repeatedly so that "habit will become second nature." They should be done verbally and audibly, since "audible vocalization stimulates concentration."

If you think that selfless love is beyond you, don't worry, the light of Moshe's soul will help you reach this level. It's actually a power you already have in your soul.

אבינו ממש האמיתי ומקור חיינו ולעורר אליו האהבה
כאהבת הבן אל האב. וכשירגיל עצמו כן תמיד הרי
ההרגל נעשה טבע. ואף אם נדמה לו לכאורה שהוא
כח דמיוני לא יחוש מאחר שהוא אמת לאמיתו מצד

הָאֲמִיתִּי וּמְקוֹר חַיֵּינוּ — that He, quite literally, is our true Father, and the source of our life, וּלְעוֹרֵר אֵלָיו הָאַהֲבָה כְּאַהֲבַת הַבֵּן אֶל הָאָב — to stir up love for Him, like the love which a child has for a father.

וּכְשֶׁיַּרְגִּיל עַצְמוֹ כֵּן תָּמִיד הֲרֵי הַהֶרְגֵּל נַעֲשֶׂה טֶבַע — If you'll train yourself to do this consistently, then *"habit will become second nature"* (Rabbi Meir Aldabi, *Shevilei Emunah* 4:2), and you'll actually begin to *feel* a selfless love for G-d, like a child to his or her parent.

The key to success here is persistence. Since you already have a selfless love latently in your soul, you need to develop channels for that love to surface by training yourself to meditate on it consistently.

SECTION FOUR: HOW TO COMPENSATE FOR INAUTHENTIC LOVE

4TH IYAR REGULAR | 30TH NISAN LEAP

In Section Three the *Tanya* has taught:

1.) Everyone is capable of attaining an utterly selfless level of love for G-d, "like a son who exerts himself for his father and mother, whom he loves *more than himself."*

2.) We are all capable of this because selfless love is already present latently in our souls and we just need to "find" it and help it to surface.

3.) The key to doing this is meditating on the idea that, as a child of G-d, you love G-d more than you love yourself.

4.) This meditation should be done repeatedly so that "habit will become second nature"; and it should be done verbally and audibly, since "audible vocalization stimulates concentration."

Let's presume you are following the *Tanya's* advice and trying to develop ("uncover") the feeling that you love G-d more than yourself. You've recited the meditation verbally so many times that you're beginning to become convinced.

But are you really? Have you begun to love G-d more than yourself, or are you just being delusional?

וְאַף אִם נִדְמֶה לוֹ לִכְאוֹרָה שֶׁהוּא כֹּחַ דְּמְיוֹנִי — **And even if it seems at first** that merely by training yourself to think and feel this way, **you're deluding** yourself, לֹא יָחוּשׁ — **don't worry,** that's not true, מֵאַחַר שֶׁהוּא אֱמֶת לַאֲמִיתּוֹ מִצַּד עַצְמוֹ בִּבְחִינַת אַהֲבָה — **because the** selfless love **itself, as it's exists latently** in your heart, **is** מְסוּתֶּרֶת — **absolutely authentic.**

עַצְמוֹ בבחי' אהבה מסותרת רק שתועלת יציאתה אל
הגילוי כדי להביאה לידי מעשה שהוא עסק התורה
והמצות שלומד ומקיים ע"י זה כדי לעשות נחת רוח
לפניו ית' כבן העובד את אביו. ועל זה אמרו מחשבה
טובה הקב"ה מצרפה למעשה להיות גדפין לפרחא

Even if the conscious expression of your selfless love lacks a certain level of authenticity, that shouldn't discourage your efforts. Whatever you are feeling is anchored in, and flows from, something authentic.

But you might still ask: Your subconscious, "inherited" love is *already* authentic without any meditation, and so if your conscious love is inauthentic, then why bother to produce it at all? Just leave your authentic love intact in the recesses of your soul.

רַק שֶׁתּוֹעֶלֶת יְצִיאָתָהּ אֶל הַגִּילוּי — **Only, there is value in bringing** the love **out of its latent state, to be palpable,** even if the results are of dubious authenticity, כְּדֵי לַהֲבִיאָהּ לִידֵי מַעֲשֶׂה — **so that** the palpable love **can have a practical application,** שֶׁהוּא עֵסֶק הַתּוֹרָה וְהַמִּצְוֹת — **which is the observance of Torah and** *mitzvos.*

As we have learned, your Torah and *mitzvos* can't "fly heavenward" unless they have two "wings" of reverence and love of G-d (p. 466). Even if the love you generate using the above meditation is lacking in authenticity, it's still a very worthwhile exercise because that palpable love will elevate the *mitzvos* you perform to heaven.

But, again, we might ask: How could an *inauthentic* love be an effective "wing" to lift your *mitzvah* heavenward?

To answer this question, the *Tanya* will now draw on an idea we learned earlier, in chapter 16. Since G-d is aware of the limitations holding you back from producing authentic emotions through meditation, He will assist your *mitzvos* to develop the necessary "wings" from the imperfect results of your meditation, (so long as you have made some effort and you have the appropriate intention).

שֶׁלּוֹמֵד וּמְקַיֵּים עַל יְדֵי זֶה כְּדֵי לַעֲשׂוֹת נַחַת רוּחַ לְפָנָיו יִתְבָּרֵךְ — Practically speaking, **you study and practice** *mitzvos* with the selfless intention **to give G-d "a feeling of satisfaction"** (*Rashi* to *Leviticus* 1:9), and not for any personal gain, physical or spiritual, כְּבֵן הָעוֹבֵד אֶת אָבִיו — **like a son serving his father,** וְעַל זֶה אָמְרוּ מַחֲשָׁבָה טוֹבָה הַקָּדוֹשׁ בָּרוּךְ הוּא מְצָרְפָהּ לְמַעֲשֶׂה — **and** even if that's just your

PRACTICAL LESSONS

Even if the conscious expression of your selfless love lacks a certain level of authenticity, that shouldn't discourage your efforts. Whatever you're feeling is anchored in, and flows from, the selfless love of your soul, which *is* authentic. G-d will do the rest and "attach a good thought to the deed."

כנ"ל. והנחת רוח הוא כמשל שמחת המלך מבנו
שבא אליו בצאתו מבית האסורים כנ"ל או להיות לו

intention, and you don't really feel it authentically, our Sages **taught that, in such a case, the Blessed Holy One** *"attaches a good thought to the deed"* (*Talmud, Kiddushin* 40a), accepting your intention in the place of real feeling, לִהְיוֹת גַּדְפִין לְפָרְחָא — and your *mitzvos* performed with this intention will have **"wings to fly,"** heavenward, כַּנִּזְכָּר לְעֵיל — **as mentioned above,** in chapter 16, (pp. 196*ff*).

Through Divine grace, your selfless *intention* is considered by G-d as if you had selfless *love*. That's because, in your soul, you really do have selfless love, and your difficulty has been in expressing it consciously. Since you did make an effort to do so, G-d *"attaches a good thought to the deed"* and attributes your "deed" (*mitzvah*) as if it was performed with the selfless love you intended in your "thought."

This act of Divine grace makes your meditative efforts worthwhile, even if the results are somewhat inauthentic.

What, exactly, constitutes a selfless intention when observing a *mitzvah*? Above, the *Tanya* stated, it's "to give G-d a feeling of satisfaction." We will now clarify this idea further.

וְהַנַּחַת רוּחַ הוּא — **And the "feeling of satisfaction"** G-d receives, can be understood in two ways:

a.) כְּמָשָׁל שִׂמְחַת הַמֶּלֶךְ מִבְּנוֹ שֶׁבָּא אֵלָיו בְּצֵאתוֹ מִבֵּית הָאֲסוּרִים כַּנִּזְכָּר לְעֵיל — **It's like the earlier example of the king's joy from his son returning after being released from prison** (chapter 31, p. 356).

אוֹ לִהְיוֹת לוֹ דִּירָה בַּתַּחְתּוֹנִים כַּנִּזְכָּר לְעֵיל — **Or b.)** it may be Divine "satisfaction" **from** the idea **mentioned earlier** that *"The Blessed Holy One desired* **to have a home for Himself in the lowest realms (Dirah ba-Tachtonim),** *just as He has in the higher realms"* (*Midrash Tanchuma, Naso,* section 16; see chapters 36-37).

The Divine will is fulfilled by both these two dynamics together: a.) lifting the world *up* to G-d, and b.) drawing the Divine *down* into the world.

Therefore the *Tanya* mentions both "intentions" here: a.) When you observe a *mitzvah*, a Divine spark trapped down here in this world is released *back up* to G-d, giving Him great pleasure (like the return of a child from captivity). b.) But the *mitzvah* also has another effect, of *drawing down* the Divine here, in this lowly world, through sanctifying the physical and making a "home" for G-d "in the lowest realms" (Rabbi Nisan Nemenov, *Biurei Ha-Rav Nisan*).

SECTION FIVE: FROM YOUR LIPS TO YOUR HEART

So far in this chapter we have learned meditations to attain two types of love. In Section Two we learned to long for G-d just as we long for our own lives (the love hinted by the verse, *"My soul, I have desired you at night"*). In Section Three we

דירה בתחתונים כנ"ל והנה גם לבחי' נפשי אויתיך
הנ"ל קרוב הדבר מאד להוציאה מההעלם אל הגילוי
ע"י ההרגל תמיד בפיו ולבו שוין. אך אם אינו יכול

encountered *"a greater and more expansive,"* selfless love, *"like a son who exerts himself for his father and mother, whom he loves more than himself."*

Section Four continued to clarify difficulties we might have with the meditations of Section Three, aimed at producing selfless love. Even if the result is of dubious authenticity, the *Tanya* assured us, we ought to persist because G-d will compensate for our shortcomings and *"attach a good thought to the deed."*

Here in Section Five, we revisit the lower love of Section Two (the self-oriented love, *"My soul, I have desired you at night"*).

The *Tanya* will first address a practical question. In Section Three we learned that, in addition to mindful meditation, we should employ the practical technique, of "accustoming your mouth" with "audible vocalization, that stimulates concentration" until "habit will become second nature." This was taught in reference to the higher level of selfless love. But could it be used also for the lower level of self-oriented love (taught in Section Two)?

וְהִנֵּה גַּם לִבְחִינַת נַפְשִׁי אֲוִיתִיךָ הַנִּזְכָּר לְעֵיל — **Now even the** lower **level** of more self-oriented love **mentioned above** in Section Two of *"I have desired you at night etc.,"* (*Isaiah* 26:9), where you long for G-d because He is the source of your life, קָרוֹב הַדָּבָר מְאֹד לְהוֹצִיאָהּ מֵהַהֶעְלֵם אֶל הַגִּילּוּי — is *"very much within reach for you,"* meaning it's practically possible **to bring** this love **out from its latent state, to be palpable,** עַל יְדֵי הַהֶרְגֵּל

PRACTICAL LESSONS

If your meditation fails to generate any feelings in your heart then, at the very least, picture the love of G-d in your mind, and G-d will consider your *mitzvah* **to have been observed with love.**

תָּמִיד בְּפִיו וְלִבּוֹ שָׁוִין — through training yourself constantly, with *"your mouth and heart consistent"* (*Talmud, Pesachim* 63a), since, as we have explained, the love is already latent in your soul.

You *can* use the practical method of Section Three (habitual verbalization), even for the lower, self-oriented love (taught in Section Two). You simply have to be *"training yourself constantly, with your mouth and heart consistent."*

At first glance, this would seem to be no surprise. If habitual verbalization is effective at bringing even a *higher,* selfless love to consciousness, shouldn't it obviously be effective for a lower, self-orientated love?

Surprisingly, that's not the case. Generally speaking, the lower love is easier to achieve, because it's more relatable: *"I desire and crave for you like a person desires his own life and soul when he is weak and exhausted."* You know what it feels like to desire energy when you're weak and exhausted, so you try to feel the same "hunger" for G-d.

להוציאה אל הגילוי בלבו אעפ"כ יכול לעסוק בתורה
ומצות לשמן ע"י ציור ענין אהבה זו במחשבה שבמוחו

But it's *because* the power of this meditation lies in its relatability that habitual verbalization is less effective. Either you're going to relate to this idea, or you won't. Repeating it to yourself a thousand times won't seem to help that much.

The higher, selfless love, on the other hand, is more of an "acquired taste," a subtle, initially counterintuitive idea with which you will begin to resonate deeply only through repeated exposure. And that's why habitual verbalization is an excellent practical method for the higher, selfless type of love (*Notes on Tanya*).

Nevertheless, the *Tanya* suggests here that "*training yourself constantly, with 'your mouth and heart consistent*" (i.e., habitual verbalization), *can* be effective even for the lower level of more self-oriented love. Because, ultimately, we are speaking of a feeling that you have already in your soul, and since you only have to "*bring it out from its latent state, to be palpable,*" habitual verbalization can be effective, even if it takes a little more persistence.

אַךְ אִם אֵינוֹ יָכוֹל לְהוֹצִיאָהּ אֶל הַגִּלּוּי בְּלִבּוֹ — **But if you're not able to bring** even the lower level of self-oriented love **to palpable expression in your heart,** through persistent meditation and habitual verbalization, at least do the following.

The failure of meditation here is more severe than the failure (in Section Four) to reach higher, selfless love. In Section Four your meditations did produce some strong feelings for G-d, but your concern was that those feelings lacked authenticity. Here, however, "*you're not able to bring it to palpable expression in your heart.*" You've failed to generate *any* feeling of love for G-d.

אַף עַל פִּי כֵן יָכוֹל לַעֲסוֹק בַּתּוֹרָה וּמִצְוֹת לִשְׁמָן — **Nevertheless, you can still observe Torah and *mitzvos* with** sufficient **authenticity** to enable your worship to "fly" heavenward, עַל יְדֵי צִיּוּר עִנְיַן אַהֲבָה זוֹ בַּמַּחֲשָׁבָה שֶׁבְּמוֹחוֹ — **through,** at the very least, **picturing this love mentally, in your mind,** causing your *mitzvah* to be propelled heavenward with (the equivalent of) a "wing" of love, וּמַחֲשָׁבָה טוֹבָה הַקָּדוֹשׁ בָּרוּךְ הוּא — מְצָרְפָהּ כוּ' — **since the Blessed Holy One "*attaches a good thought* to the deed."**

If your meditation fails to generate any feelings in your heart then, at the very least, picture the love of G-d in your mind, and G-d will "attach a good thought to the deed," considering your *mitzvah* to have been observed with love (see also chapter 16, pp. 196*ff*.).

SECTION SIX: HOW HIGH CAN THIS LOVE LIFT YOUR MITZVOS?

5TH IYAR REGULAR | 1ST IYAR LEAP

We learned in chapter 39, that when a *mitzvah* is propelled heavenward, through your feelings of love (and reverence), it might end up at one of two spiritual locations: either the lower, emotional World of *Yetzirah* or the higher, intellectual World of *Beriah*. The final destination will depend on *how you generated* your feelings

ומחשבה טובה הקב"ה מצרפה כו': והנה ב' בחי'
אהבות אלו אף שהן ירושה לנו מאבותינו וכמו טבע
בנפשותינו וכן היראה הכלולה בהן שהיא לירא
מליפרד ח"ו ממקור חיינו ואבינו האמיתי ב"ה אעפ"כ
אינן נקראות בשם דחילו ורחימו טבעיים אלא כשהן

of love and reverence. If you merely stir up *innate* feelings for G-d that you already have in your soul, your *mitzvah* will only reach the lower World of *Yetzirah;* but if you do the more challenging spiritual work of *acquiring* feelings for G-d through sustained meditation, your *mitzvah* will reach the higher World of *Beriah*.

Are the meditations of this chapter aimed at *acquiring* love for G-d, or revealing an *innate* love? The *Tanya* will now argue that they're a kind of hybrid: In essence we're speaking of an innate love; but since some real contemplative work is needed to surface these emotions palpably, they have the advantage of acquired feelings, too. Practically speaking, the emotions of this chapter are sufficiently "acquired" to be capable of propelling your *mitzvah* to the higher World of *Beriah*.

וְהִנֵּה ב' בְּחִינוֹת אַהֲבוֹת אֵלּוּ — **Now both these types of love** we have discussed in this chapter: a.) the lower, self-oriented level of *"My soul, I have desired you at night etc.,"* (Section Two) and b.) the higher, selfless level of love, *"like a son who exerts himself for his father and mother, etc."* (Section Three), אַף שֶׁהֵן יְרוּשָׁה לָנוּ מֵאֲבוֹתֵינוּ וּכְמוֹ טֶבַע בְּנַפְשׁוֹתֵינוּ — **even though they are "inherited" from our Patriarchs and are instinctive for our souls,** which means that, in principle, they should only propel a *mitzvah* to the lower World of *Yetzirah;* nevertheless, in actual fact, they have the power to reach the higher World of *Beriah,* as we shall see.

Of course, for a *mitzvah* to ascend heavenward it requires *two* "wings," love and reverence (see p. 466). Where is the reverence, in this case? The *Tanya* now draws on a principle we have learned earlier, that if you uncover the innate love of your soul, it will "include" reverence within it (see p. 230).

וְכֵן הַיִּרְאָה הַכְּלוּלָה בָּהֶן — **And there is reverence also "included" in** these two types of love, שֶׁהִיא לִירָא מִלִּיפָּרֵד חַס וְשָׁלוֹם מִמְּקוֹר חַיֵּינוּ וְאָבִינוּ הָאֲמִיתִי בָּרוּךְ הוּא — namely, the basic **fear of being separated** G-d forbid, **from the source of our life, our true Blessed Father,** and that's sufficient to form the second "wing" for your *mitzvah,* along with the first "wing" of love.

How far will such a *mitzvah* ascend, if it is motivated by one of the two types of love described in this chapter, (along with the reverence "included" in it)? אַף עַל פִּי כֵן אֵינָן נִקְרָאוֹת בְּשֵׁם דְּחִילוּ וּרְחִימוּ טִבְעִיִּים — Despite the fact that we are speaking of "innate" forms of love which the soul has merely "inherited," **nevertheless,** in terms of how far heavenward they can propel your *mitzvah,* **these** emotions of love and reverence produced by the meditations of this chapter **aren't considered "innate" reverence and love,** which means that they can propel your *mitzvah* to the higher World of *Beriah*.

במוחו ומחשבתו לבד ותעלומות לבו ואז מקומן בי"ס
דיצירה ולשם הן מעלות עמהן התורה והמצות הבאות
מחמתן ובסיבתן. אבל כשהן בהתגלות לבו נק' רעותא
דלבא בזוהר ומקומן בי"ס דבריאה ולשם הן מעלות

But there is one proviso: Your *mitzvah* will be propelled to the higher World of *Beriah* only if you succeed in generating *palpable emotion* through the meditations in this chapter.

אֶלָּא כְּשֶׁהֵן בְּמוֹחוֹ וּמַחֲשַׁבְתּוֹ לְבַד — **But** if those emotions **remain purely cerebral, in your thoughts,** וְתַעֲלוּמוֹת לִבּוֹ — **or** just in your *"hidden places in the heart"* (*Psalms* 44:22), and not felt palpably in the heart as emotion, וְאָז מְקוֹמָן בִּ' סְפִירוֹת דִּיצִירָה — **then their** spiritual **address is in the ten *sefiros* of** the lower World of *Yetzirah*, וּלְשָׁם הֵן מַעֲלוֹת עִמָּהֶן הַתּוֹרָה וְהַמִּצְוֹת הַבָּאוֹת מֵחֲמָתָן וּבְסִיבָּתָן — **and it is to there that they** have the power to **elevate the Torah and *mitzvos* which they bring about and cause.**

(The *Tanya* doesn't mean that the "final destination" of your Torah and *mitzvos* must be in the World of *Yetzirah*. For as we have learned in chapter 16, when intellectually generated emotions are not palpable in the heart, G-d nevertheless "attaches a good thought to the deed," and lifts them up to the World of *Beriah*. What the *Tanya* means to say is that, if the meditations of this chapter don't generate palpable emotions, then they don't *intrinsically have the power* to lift your *mitzvah* higher than the World of *Yetzirah* — *Notes on Tanya*).

PRACTICAL LESSONS

If you manage to generate palpable emotions with the meditations of this chapter, it will have the power to elevate your mitzvos to the World of *Beriah*, (or even the World of *Atzilus*).

אֲבָל כְּשֶׁהֵן בְּהִתְגַּלּוּת לִבּוֹ — **But when** the emotions produced by any of the meditations of this chapter **are palpable in the heart,** נִקְרָאוֹת רְעוּתָא דְּלִבָּא בַּזֹּהַר — **they are** no longer defined as "innate" forms of love, but rather **what the *Zohar*** (3, 289b) **calls,** *"desire of the heart"* (*re'ussa de-liba*).

The *Tanya* can't term these emotions "intellectually generated," because they're not. They're innate emotions which have surfaced through intellectual work. But since these emotions come through intellectual work *and are palpable in the heart,* they come under the category of what the *Zohar* calls, "desire of the heart" (*Notes on Tanya*).

וּמְקוֹמָן בִּ' סְפִירוֹת דִּבְרִיאָה — **And** since these emotions fall under the category of "desire of the heart," **their** spiritual **address is in the ten *sefiros* of *Beriah*,** as we learned in chapter 39, p. 454, *"from 'desire of the heart' a 'garment' is formed for the soul enabling it to inhabit the World of Beriah."*

עמהן התורה והמצות הבאות מחמתן. מפני שיציאתן 64A
מההעלם והסתר הלב אל בחי' גילוי היא ע"י הדעת
ותקיעת המחשבה בחוזק והתבוננות עצומה מעומקא
דלבא יתיר ותדיר בא"ס ב"ה איך הוא חיינו ממש
ואבינו האמיתי ב"ה ומודעת זאת מ"ש בתיקונים כי
בעולם הבריאה מקננא תמן אימא עילאה שהיא
ההתבוננות באור א"ס חיי החיים ב"ה וכמאמר אליהו

וּלְשָׁם הֵן מַעֲלוֹת עִמְּהֶן הַתּוֹרָה וְהַמִּצְוֹת הַבָּאוֹת מֵחֲמָתָן — **And it is to there,** the World of *Beriah* **that** these palpable emotions, produced by the meditations of this chapter, **elevate the Torah and *mitzvos* which they bring about and cause.**

Before this chapter, we had learned that if you merely awaken "innate" love, it doesn't have the power (in and of itself) to lift a *mitzvah* higher than the World of *Yetzirah*. The *Tanya* has now introduced an exception to this rule. This limitation of "innate love" applies only in a case where *no serious meditative effort* is required to awaken it. But that's not true here. What is in essence an "innate" love, gains the spiritual potency of "acquired" love, when it is produced through intense meditative work.

מִפְּנֵי שֶׁיְצִיאָתָן מֵהַהָעֵלֵם וְהָסְתֵּר הַלֵּב אֶל בְּחִינַת גִּילוּי הִיא עַל יְדֵי הַדַּעַת — **Because the** force which **brings** these emotions **to be palpable, from concealment and latency in the heart, is *da'as,*** וּתְקִיעַת הַמַּחֲשָׁבָה בְּחוֹזֶק וְהִתְבּוֹנְנוּת עֲצוּמָה — and *da'as* involves **intense fixation of thought, through focused meditation,** מֵעוּמְקָא דְלִבָּא — יָתִיר וְתָדִיר בְּאֵין סוֹף בָּרוּךְ הוּא — *"from the depths of the heart,"* (*Zohar* 3, 70b), *"abundantly and frequently"* (*ibid.,* 1, 119a), **on the Blessed Infinite Light,** אֵיךְ הוּא חַיֵּינוּ מַמָּשׁ וְאָבִינוּ הָאֲמִיתִי בָּרוּךְ הוּא — **how He is literally our life and our true Blessed Father.**

Since you have toiled with your *da'as*, with *"intense fixation of thought through focused meditation,"* the result doesn't have the limitation of an innate love (which only reaches the World of *Yetzirah*). It's largely something you've earned for yourself, with your own intense efforts.

The *Tanya* now brings a proof for this point.

וּמוֹדַעַת זֹאת — **And** *"this thing is known"* (Isaiah 12:5), מַה שֶּׁכָּתוּב בַּתִּיקוּנִים — **what is written in the** *Tikunei Zohar,* כִּי בְּעוֹלָם הַבְּרִיאָה מְקַנְּנָא תַמָּן אִימָּא עִילָּאָה — **that in the World of *Beriah*, "the supernal 'mother' (binah) has her 'nest' there"** (see chapter 39, p. 453).

The World of *Beriah* is associated with *binah*. What practical experience does *binah* refer to?

שֶׁהִיא הַהִתְבּוֹנְנוּת בְּאוֹר אֵין סוֹף חַיֵּי הַחַיִּים בָּרוּךְ הוּא — **Which refers to the meditation on the Blessed Infinite Light, the source of life,** וּכְמַאֲמָר אֵלִיָּהוּ בִּינָה לִבָּא

בִּינָה לִבָּא וּבָהּ הַלֵּב מֵבִין. וְלֹא עוֹד אֶלָּא שֶׁבְּ' בְּחִי'
אַהֲבוֹת אֵלּוּ הַנַּ"ל הֵן כְּלוּלוֹת מִן בְּחִי' אַהֲבָה רַבָּה וּגְדוֹלָה
וּמְעוּלָה מִדְּחִילוּ וּרְחִימוּ שִׂכְלִיִּים אֲשֶׁר הָאַהֲבָה נק' לְעֵיל

וּבָהּ הַלֵּב מֵבִין — **as in the teaching of Elijah** in the *Tikunei Zohar* (17a)**, "Binah is the heart, through which the heart understands."**

While *binah* is a cognitive power, and not an emotional one, it's the *source* of all emotion. It's the mental "womb" in which ideas can "gestate" to the point where they might become relevant to you (through *da'as*).

The *Zohar* teaches us that if you make use of your *binah*, and do meditative work, your worship will "belong" in the World of *Beriah* (whose energy is *binah*). And that's true even when you're drawing on what is in essence an innate love.

SECTION SEVEN: HOW TO ACQUIRE "GREAT LOVE" FOR G-D

In this section, the *Tanya* will expand upon a statement made earlier (Section Two), that the love described in this chapter, *"contains 'great love' and 'worldly love,' in all its types and levels"* (discussed in chapter 43).

Let's recap briefly what these terms mean:

1.) The higher, "great love" (*ahavah rabah*), is a "pleasurable love," the joy of *already* being connected to G-d. It can't be earned and will come only as a "gift from above." *Ahavah rabah* is the consciousness of the World of *Atzilus,* which transcends intellect.

2.) The lower, "worldly love" (*ahavas olam*), is acquired through mindful meditation on how G-d transcends all worldly pleasures. *Ahavas olam* is the consciousness of the World of *Beriah,* the world of the intellect.

An even lower level (which we learned in chapters 18-19) is:

3.) "Dormant love" (*ahavah mesuteres*), a love inherent to the soul which is "inherited" at birth and needs only a brief meditation to awaken. Since it represents an innate emotion, its consciousness is the World of *Yetzirah,* the World of emotion.

שֶׁבְּ' בְּחִינוֹת אַהֲבוֹת אֵלּוּ הַנִּזְכָּרוֹת לְעֵיל — **these two** וְלֹא עוֹד אֶלָּא — **And what is more,** **types of love mentioned above** in this chapter can bring your consciousness, not only to the World of *Beriah*, (as mentioned in Section Five), but even to the World of *Atzilus,* הֵן כְּלוּלוֹת מִן בְּחִינַת אַהֲבָה רַבָּה — **and that's because the two types of love in** this chapter **contain** something **of the quality of "great love" (*ahavah rabah*),** which has the consciousness of *Atzilus.*

וּגְדוֹלָה וּמְעוּלָה מִדְּחִילוּ וּרְחִימוּ שִׂכְלִיִּים — **"Great love"** **being greater than, and superior to, intellectually generated reverence and love,** which has the consciousness of the World of *Beriah.* אֲשֶׁר הָאַהֲבָה נִקְרֵאת לְעֵיל בְּשֵׁם אַהֲבַת עוֹלָם — **which is the love referred to above** in chapter 43 as **"worldly love" (*ahavas olam*).**

בשם אהבת עולם רק שאעפ"כ צריך לטרוח בשכלו
להשיג ולהגיע גם לבחי' אהבת עולם הנ"ל הבאה
מהתבוננה ודעת בגדולת ה' כדי להגדיל מדורת אש
האהבה ברשפי אש ושלהבת עזה ולהב העולה

Here we see again the "hybrid" quality of the two types of love described in this chapter. On one hand, like intellectually generated love, they are able to lift you to the consciousness of the World of *Beriah.* Yet they also have the consciousness of *Atzilus,* the level of *ahavah rabah,* which is a more direct soul-appreciation of G-d, beyond the cognitive mind.

The *Tanya* doesn't clarify why an *ahavah rabah* experience can be reached through the meditations of this chapter. Perhaps it's because the two types of love described here are essentially an "inherited" form of love *awakened* by meditation, and since they are not, at their core, cognitive, they offer a more or less direct connection to G-d (the hallmark of *ahavah rabah*). And like *ahavah rabah,* these forms of love are a "gift from G-d," in the sense that their capacity is an "inherited" one and not earned.

SECTION EIGHT: WHY YOU STILL NEED "WORLDLY LOVE"

6TH IYAR REGULAR | 2ND IYAR LEAP

As we have seen, the two types of love discussed in this chapter are superior to "worldly love" (*ahavas olam*) since they incorporate an experience of the higher "great love" (*ahavah rabah*). So you might think: Why should I bother with "worldly love" at all? I'll just work on the meditations described in this chapter.

The *Tanya* warns us now that such a conclusion would be inadvisable. Even though it's lower, you still need to seek "worldly love."

רַק שֶׁאַף עַל פִּי כֵן צָרִיךְ לִטְרוֹחַ בְּשִׂכְלוֹ לְהַשִּׂיג וּלְהַגִּיעַ גַּם לִבְחִינַת אַהֲבַת עוֹלָם — Nevertheless, alongside your efforts with the meditations of this chapter, **you must invest the mental effort to also attain and reach the** lower **level of "worldly love,"** הַבָּאָה מֵהַתְבּוֹנְנָה וְדַעַת בִּגְדוּלַּת ה', הַנִּזְכֶּרֶת לְעֵיל — **mentioned above** in chapter 43, **— which results from** *understanding* **and** *knowing* **the greatness of G-d.**

But, why? Why should you aim for a lower level of "worldly love," when the meditations of this chapter can produce a love which has the advantages of both "worldly love" and "great love"?

כְּדֵי לְהַגְדִּיל מְדוּרַת אֵשׁ הָאַהֲבָה בְּרִשְׁפֵּי אֵשׁ וְשַׁלְהֶבֶת עַזָּה וְלַהַב הָעוֹלֶה הַשָּׁמַיְמָה — **"Worldly love" is necessary in order** to be passionate about G-d, **to engorge your "torch" of fiery love, like** *"flaming fire"* (*Song* 8:6) **and roaring flames, burning up to the heavens.**

The love produced by the meditations of this chapter stress your *closeness* to G-d. In the first meditation (Section Two), you ponder how G-d is the source of your

השמימה עד שמים רבים לא יוכלו לכבות וכו' ונהרות
לא ישטפוה וכו' כי יש יתרון ומעלה לבחי' אהבה
כרשפי אש ושלהבת עזה וכו' הבאה מהתבונה ודעת
בגדולת א"ס ב"ה על שתי בחי' אהבה הנ"ל כאשר
אינן כרשפי אש ושלהבת כו' כיתרון ומעלת הזהב

life and energy. In the second meditation (Section Three), you reflect on how G-d is your father. Both meditations imply a close connection: you're already in a relationship together.

As a result, it's likely that the love produced by these meditations will lack passion and "fire." Passion results from *distance*: you feel something is far away, perhaps unattainable, but you still crave it desperately. To generate a passionate love, the meditations of chapter 43 are more effective. You contemplate how, *"all the pleasures of this world have no separate existence, and they are considered zero in His presence, literally; and there is no comparison to be made in any way, between them and Him, G-d forbid, in the same way that you can't compare absolute null and void with eternal life."*

PRACTICAL LESSONS

Don't neglect the "worldly love" meditations of chapter 43, because: a.) they produce a more passionate love; and, b.) they make you focus on G-d's greatness — and that's the reason for your existence.

In the "worldly love" meditation, the pleasures of this world are of *no value*, and the connection to G-d is of *infinite value*. This stark contrast, between nothing and infinity, creates passion: You long to leave a place of no value and connect with the Infinite.

עַד שָׁמַיִם רַבִּים לֹא יוּכְלוּ לְכַבּוֹת וְגוֹ' וּנְהָרוֹת לֹא יִשְׁטְפוּהָ וְגוֹ' — "Worldly love" can generate passion **to the extent that** *"vast floods cannot extinguish love, nor rivers drown it away etc.,"* (*Song* 8:7).

The "floods" in this verse represent physical pleasures and pursuits which have the tendency to "extinguish" your love for G-d. The verse teaches us that you need to be passionate about G-d to withstand all the temptations of this world. And that passion is best attained through the meditations of chapter 43.

כִּי יֵשׁ יִתְרוֹן וּמַעֲלָה לִבְחִינַת אַהֲבָה כְּרִשְׁפֵּי אֵשׁ וְשַׁלְהֶבֶת עַזָּה וְכוּ' — **Because,** despite the fact that it is, generally speaking, a lower level of love, **there's an advantage and superiority to the type of** "worldly **love" which is like** *"flaming fire"* (*Song* 8:6) **and roaring flames etc.,** הַבָּאָה מֵהִתְבּוֹנְנָה וְדַעַת בִּגְדוּלַת אֵין סוֹף בָּרוּךְ הוּא — **which results from understanding and knowledge of the greatness of the Blessed Infinite One,** עַל שְׁתֵּי בְּחִינוֹת אַהֲבָה הַנִּזְכָּרוֹת לְעֵיל — **over the two types of love mentioned above** in this chapter, כַּאֲשֶׁר אֵינָן כְּרִשְׁפֵּי אֵשׁ וְשַׁלְהֶבֶת כוּ' — **(which,** generally speaking, **aren't like** *"flaming fire"* **and flames etc.).**

על הכסף וכו' כמ"ש לקמן וגם כי זה כל האדם
ותכליתו למען דעת את כבוד ה' ויקר תפארת גדולתו
איש איש כפי אשר יוכל שאת כמ"ש בר"מ פ' בא בגין
דישתמודעון ליה וכו' וכנודע:

כְּיִתְרוֹן וּמַעֲלַת הַזָּהָב עַל הַכֶּסֶף וְכו' — It's **like the** naturally apparent **advantage and superiority of gold over silver etc.,** כְּמוֹ שֶׁיִּתְבָּאֵר לְקַמָּן — **as we will explain later on** (chapter 50, p. 642).

Even if gold wasn't worth more than silver, you would still be struck by the special appearance of gold. Similarly, the passionate nature of "worldly love" has a *self-evident* advantage over the higher level of "great love" and the types of love described in this chapter.

וְגַם — **And also,** a second reason why you must also invest the mental effort to attain "worldly love," (even though the meditations of this chapter, generally speaking, produce a higher love), כִּי זֶה כָּל הָאָדָם וְתַכְלִיתוֹ — is *"because this is the whole purpose of man"* (*Ecclesiastes* 12:13), **and the reason for his existence,** לְמַעַן דַּעַת אֶת כְּבוֹד ה' וִיקַר תִּפְאֶרֶת גְּדוּלָתוֹ — man exists in order *"to know (da'as) the glory of G-d"* (*Habakuk* 2:14), **and "the splendor of His glorious kingdom"** (*Esther* 1:4), אִישׁ אִישׁ כְּפִי אֲשֶׁר יוּכַל שְׂאֵת — and while G-d intrinsically defies comprehension **each individual** must try to grasp *"as much as he can withstand"* (see *Genesis* 44:1).

A second reason why "worldly love" is indispensable, is because it *"results from understanding and knowledge of the greatness of the Blessed Infinite One."* And through this, you come to fulfill the purpose of your very existence, which is to know G-d.

The two types of love described in this chapter focus more on your *connection with G-d,* than your *knowledge of Him.* You contemplate how G-d is the source of your life, and how He is your father. But such a meditation is not necessarily going to dwell upon, *"the splendor of His glorious kingdom,"* etc. That's why the "worldly love" meditation of chapter 43 is so important, because it forces you to focus on "understanding and knowledge" of G-d, which is the purpose of your existence.

(It is, however, *possible* to follow the meditations of this chapter and generate a fiery passionate love. But to do that you need to focus not only on the closeness of G-d as your father *etc.,* but also on His distant greatness. The "worldly love" meditation in chapter 43, on the other hand, *by its very nature* generates a passionate love — *Notes on Tanya*).

The *Tanya* concludes with a source for its assertion that "the whole purpose of man" is "to know the glory of G-d":

כְּמוֹ שֶׁכָּתוּב בְּרַעְיָא מְהֵימְנָא פָּרָשַׁת בֹּא — **As is written in the** Zohar, **Raya Mehemna,** **Parshas Bo,** בְּגִין דְּיִשְׁתְּמוֹדְעוּן לֵיהּ וְכו' — that G-d emanated His different attributes, *"so that people should know Him etc.,"* (*Zohar* 2, 42b), וְכַנּוֹדָע — **and as is known** from *Etz Chaim* 1:1 (see above chapter 33, sections 1-2).

פרק מה עוד   יֵשׁ דֶּרֶךְ יָשָׁר לִפְנֵי אִישׁ לַעֲסוֹק
בְּתוֹרָה וּמִצְוֹת לִשְׁמָן עַ"י מדתו
שֶׁל יַעֲקֹב אע"ה שֶׁהִיא מִדַּת הָרַחֲמִ' לְעוֹרֵר בְּמַחֲשַׁבְתּוֹ
תְּחִלָּה רַחֲמִים רַבִּים לִפְנֵי ה' עַל נִיצוֹץ אֱלֹהוּת הַמְחַיֶּה

64B

נַפְשׁוֹ אֲשֶׁר יָרַד מִמְּקוֹרוֹ חַיֵּי הַחַיִּים א"ס ב"ה הַמְמַלֵּא
כָּל עָלְמִין וְסוֹבֵב כָּל עָלְמִין וְכוּלָא קַמֵּיהּ כְּלָא חֲשִׁיב
וְנִתְלַבֵּשׁ בְּמַשְׁכָא דְחִוְיָא הָרָחוֹק מְאוֹר פְּנֵי הַמֶּלֶךְ
בְּתַכְלִית הַהִרְחֵק כִּי הָעוֹ"הז הוּא תַּכְלִית הַקְּלִיפוֹ' הַגַּסוֹת

CHAPTER 45

WORSHIP THROUGH COMPASSION

SECTION ONE: WHY YOUR SOUL DESERVES COMPASSION

7TH IYAR REGULAR | 3RD IYAR LEAP

From chapter 41 until this point, the *Tanya* has taught us various meditations aimed at achieving reverence and love of G-d. In this chapter, we will focus on a third emotion: compassion.

עוֹד יֵשׁ דֶּרֶךְ יָשָׁר לִפְנֵי אִישׁ — **Also, *"there's a straightforward way for a person"*** (*Proverbs* 14:12), לַעֲסוֹק בַּתּוֹרָה וּמִצְוֹת לִשְׁמָן — **to observe Torah and *mitzvos* authentically,** with real emotions for G-d, a method which has reached us from the *Ba'al Shem Tov* (see *Ma'amarei Admor Ha-Zaken, Nevi'im,* p. 109).

עַל יְדֵי מִדָּתוֹ שֶׁל יַעֲקֹב אָבִינוּ עָלָיו הַשָּׁלוֹם שֶׁהִיא מִדַּת הָרַחֲמִים — **And this is through** awakening **the** emotional **attribute** associated with **our father Ya'akov, of blessed memory, which is the quality of compassion** (*Genesis Rabah* 78:8; *Zohar* 3, 37b).

לְעוֹרֵר בְּמַחֲשַׁבְתּוֹ תְּחִלָּה רַחֲמִים רַבִּים לִפְנֵי ה' — **You can do this by first,** before the observance of a *mitzvah,* **stirring in your mind a great deal of compassion before G-d,** עַל נִיצוֹץ אֱלֹהוּת הַמְחַיֶּה נַפְשׁוֹ — **over the spark of G-dliness that gives life to your soul,** אֲשֶׁר יָרַד מִמְּקוֹרוֹ חַיֵּי הַחַיִּים אֵין סוֹף בָּרוּךְ הוּא — **which has descended from its origin in the source of all life, the Blessed Infinite One,** הַמְמַלֵּא כָּל עָלְמִין וְסוֹבֵב כָּל עָלְמִין — **who *"fills all worlds,"* and *"transcends all worlds"*** (see *Zohar* 3,225a), וְכוּלָא קַמֵּיהּ כְּלָא חֲשִׁיב — **and *"in His presence, everything is considered zero"*** (*ibid.* 1:11b), וְנִתְלַבֵּשׁ בְּמַשְׁכָא דְחִוְיָא — **and that spark of G-dliness became enmeshed with** the body, which is compared to *"the (primordial) serpent's skin"* (*Tikunei Zohar* 10b; 48b), הָרָחוֹק מֵאוֹר פְּנֵי הַמֶּלֶךְ בְּתַכְלִית הַהִרְחֵק — **which is far from *"the light of the King's face"*** (*Proverbs* 16:15), **as far as can be,** כִּי הָעוֹלָם הַזֶּה הוּא תַּכְלִית הַקְּלִיפוֹת הַגַּסוֹת כוּ' — **for this world is an extreme expression of the most vulgar *kelipos, etc.***

כו' ובפרט כשיזכור על כל מעשיו ודבוריו ומחשבותיו
מיום היותו אשר לא טובים המה ומלך אסור ברהטים
ברהיטי מוחא כי יעקב חבל נחלתו. וכמשל המושך

וּבִפְרָט כְּשֶׁיִּזְכֹּר עַל כָּל מַעֲשָׂיו וְדִבּוּרָיו וּמַחְשְׁבוֹתָיו מִיּוֹם הֱיוֹתוֹ אֲשֶׁר לֹא טוֹבִים הֵמָּה — And your compassion will be **especially** profound, *"When you recall your own bad ways, and your doings,"* **all your actions, spoken words and thoughts** you have carried out **since the day you were born, "which were not good"** (*Ezekiel* 36:31).

The fact that your soul is trapped in your body would be pitiful even if you had never sinned. The thought of, *"all your actions, spoken words and thoughts you have carried out since the day you were born, 'which were not good,'"* makes that compassion all the more intense.

SECTION TWO: THE "EXILE" OF THE SHECHINAH IN YOUR SOUL

Since your soul (which is one with G-d) is trapped in your body, it is as if G-d is "trapped" too, so to speak.

וּמֶלֶךְ אָסוּר בָּרְהָטִים — And *"(even) a king is captivated by (your) flowing hair"* (*Song* 7:6).

In the Song of Songs, the bridegroom describes his bride as being so striking in beauty that even a king would be *"captivated by (your) flowing hair (rehatim)."*

בְּרְהִטֵי מוֹחָא — *Tikunei Zohar* (144b) interprets *rehatim* as *"flow of the mind."*

The *Tanya* combines the literal and *Zoharic* interpretations together to suggest that "the King" (G-d) is "captivated" (*i.e.*, trapped, so to speak), by *the inappropriate thoughts* of your mind, in which your holy soul is enmeshed. Contemplating how you have "trapped" G-d in such a way, causing the "exile of the *Shechinah* (Divine Presence)," ought to evoke more compassion.

The *Tanya* now offers another illustration of how you cause the *Shechinah* to be exiled through inappropriate use of your soul.

כִּי יַעֲקֹב חֶבֶל נַחֲלָתוֹ — *"For G-d's portion is His people, Ya'akov His allotted (chevel) inheritance"* (*Deuteronomy* 32:9).

The unusual use of the term *chevel* here, which usually refers to a "rope," invites interpretation. *Rashi* writes that Ya'akov *"is the third of the Patriarchs. He is endowed with a threefold merit: The merit of his grandfather, the merit of his father, and his own merit, totaling three, like a rope (chevel) composed of three strands."*

The *Tanya* offers another idea behind the "rope," as referring to the connection of the soul ("G-d's portion") with G-d.

וְכַמְשַׁל הַמּוֹשֵׁךְ בְּחֶבֶל וְכוּ' — **Just as when you pull a rope (chevel)** the other end follows, so too, when you sin, you drag holy energy to an impure place. (This idea is elaborated upon in *Tanya, Igeres Ha-Teshuvah*, chapter 5-6).

בחבל וכו' והוא סוד גלות השכינה. וע"ז נאמר וישוב
אל ה' וירחמהו לעורר רחמים רבים על שם ה' השוכן
אתנו כדכתיב השוכן אתם בתוך טומאתם. וזש"ה
וישק יעקב לרחל וישא את קולו ויבך. כי רחל היא

וְהוּא סוֹד גָּלוּת הַשְּׁכִינָה — **And this** enmeshment of the holy soul in inappropriate activity **is the secret of the** *Shechinah's* **exile** (see chapter 17, p. 208).

The *Tanya* discerns this idea through creatively reinterpreting a verse in Scripture.

וְעַל זֶה נֶאֱמַר וְיָשׁוֹב אֶל ה' וִירַחֲמֵהוּ — **And this is the idea behind the verse,** *"And let him return to G-d, and He will have compassion for him"* (Isaiah 55:7).

Literally, this means that if you return to G-d through repentance, "He" (G-d) will have mercy on "him" (the person). But, as is typical in Chasidic exegesis, the *Tanya* inverts the meaning of the verse, to read: "He (the person) will have compassion for Him (G-d)." It's because you "feel sorry" for G-d, whose holy spark in your soul has become dragged into sin, that you decide to "return to G-d."

לְעוֹרֵר רַחֲמִים רַבִּים עַל שֵׁם ה' הַשּׁוֹכֵן אִתָּנוּ — **You have great compassion for G-d's name which rests with us** even when we act inappropriately, כְּדִכְתִיב הַשּׁוֹכֵן אִתָּם בְּתוֹךְ טוּמְאָתָם — **as the verse states,** *"He rests with them amid their impurity"* (Leviticus 16:16).

SECTION THREE: HOW TO ACHIEVE INTIMACY WITH G-D

8TH IYAR REGULAR

Above, the *Tanya* mentioned that compassion is *"the emotional attribute associated with our father Ya'akov."* In Chasidic thought, the Patriarchs were the embodiment of spiritual energies, and their life events caused fundamental shifts in the way these energies are available to us. The *Tanya* now unveils the biblical secret of "compassion energy," as expressed through one of the actions of Ya'akov.

וְזֶהוּ שֶׁאָמַר הַכָּתוּב וַיִּשַּׁק יַעֲקֹב לְרָחֵל וַיִּשָּׂא אֶת קוֹלוֹ וַיֵּבְךְּ — **And this is the** mystical meaning of the verse, *"And Ya'akov kissed Rachel, he lifted his voice and he cried"* (Genesis 29:11).

A CHASIDIC THOUGHT

Your soul is sacred and pure; before it was placed in your body, it was one with G-d. Now that sacred, precious soul is trapped in a physical body. Thoughts such as these ought to arouse compassion for your soul.

כנסת ישראל מקור כל הנשמות. ויעקב במדתו
העליונה שהיא מדת הרחמים שבאצילות הוא המעורר
רחמים רבים עליה. וישא את קולו למעלה למקור
הרחמים העליונים הנק' אב הרחמים ומקורם. ויבך
לעורר ולהמשיך משם רחמים רבים על כל הנשמות
ועל מקור כנסת ישראל להעלותן מגלותן ולייחדן
ביחוד העליון אור א"ס ב"ה בבחי' נשיקין שהיא

First the *Tanya* will identify the spiritual energies represented by Rachel and
Ya'akov respectively.

כִּי רָחֵל הִיא כְּנֶסֶת יִשְׂרָאֵל מְקוֹר כָּל הַנְּשָׁמוֹת — **Since Rachel represents** the spiritual energy referred to by the *Zohar* as **Kneses Yisra'el** (*Zohar* 2, 29b), **the source
of all the souls** (see chapter 32, p. 363), וְיַעֲקֹב בְּמִדָּתוֹ הָעֶלְיוֹנָה שֶׁהִיא מִדַּת הָרַחֲמִים
שֶׁבַּאֲצִילוּת — **and Ya'akov, in his supernal paradigm, is** a reflection of **the** Divine
energy of compassion in the World of **Atzilus**, the world of Divine attributes.

Ya'akov "lifted his voice and he cried." What does this mean in the spiritual model
where Ya'akov represents Divine compassion and Rachel, our souls?

וַיִּשָּׂא אֶת — Ya'akov stirs **"great compassion" for her,** הוּא הַמְעוֹרֵר רַחֲמִים רַבִּים עָלֶיהָ
קוֹלוֹ לְמַעֲלָה לִמְקוֹר הָרַחֲמִים הָעֶלְיוֹנִים הַנִּקְרָא אַב הָרַחֲמִים וּמְקוֹרָם — **"and he lifted
his voice,"** upwards, to the source of supernal compassion, which is called **"the
father of all compassion"** i.e., its source.

The somewhat limited compassion of the World of *Atzilus* is insufficient to redeem the souls from their exile. Ya'akov must arouse *"great* compassion" for our
souls, from the "source of compassion," which is truly unlimited. In order to do this,
he must "lift up his voice," and reach to a higher source.

But merely *reaching* the higher source is not enough. He must then "pull down"
that energy onto the souls.

וַיֵּבְךְּ לְעוֹרֵר וּלְהַמְשִׁיךְ מִשָּׁם רַחֲמִים רַבִּים עַל כָּל הַנְּשָׁמוֹת וְעַל מְקוֹר כְּנֶסֶת יִשְׂרָאֵל — *"And
he cried,"* to stir up and subsequently **"pull" down from there "great compassion"
on all the souls, and on their source,** *Kneses Yisra'el.*

Finally, we learn the specific purpose of this compassion:

וּלְיַיחֲדָן בְּיִחוּד הָעֶלְיוֹן אוֹר אֵין — **To lift** the souls **up from their exile,** לְהַעֲלוֹתָן מִגָּלוּתָן
סוֹף בָּרוּךְ הוּא — **and to merge and unite them above with the Blessed Infinite Light.**

The souls have been exiled, due to bodily incarnation in general, as well as sin.
When Ya'akov (the compassion of *Atzilus*) "lifts his voice" and arouses a limitless
Divine compassion, from the "source of compassion," the souls are reconnected
with the Blessed Infinite Light from which they had been "exiled."

This is the mystical meaning of *"And Ya'akov kissed Rachel."*

אתדבקות רוחא ברוחא כמ"ש ישקני מנשיקות פיהו
דהיינו התקשרות דבור האדם בדבר ה' זו הלכה וכן
מחשבה במחשבה ומעשה במעשה שהוא מעשה
המצות. ובפרט מעשה הצדקה וחסד. דחסד דרועא
ימינא והוא בחי' חיבוק ממש כמ"ש וימינו תחבקני.
ועסק התורה בדבור ומחשבת העיון הן בחי' נשיקין

בְּבְחִינַת נְשִׁיקִין — The souls will be deeply connected with Blessed Infinite Light **in a manner of "kissing"** mouth to mouth, שֶׁהִיא אִתְדַּבְּקוּת רוּחָא בְּרוּחָא — **which is a "merging of spirit with spirit"** (Zohar 1, 184a), כְּמוֹ שֶׁכָּתוּב יִשָּׁקֵנִי מִנְּשִׁיקוֹת פִּיהוּ — **as the verse states, "let him kiss me with kisses of the mouth"** (Song 1:2).

The Torah depicts the deep union of the souls with the Blessed Infinite Light as "kissing," just as a physical kiss represents a profound bond of spirit between one individual and another.

Practically speaking, how is this bond achieved?

דְּהַיְינוּ הִתְקַשְּׁרוּת דִּבּוּר הָאָדָם בִּדְבַר ה' זוֹ הֲלָכָה — **This** "kissing" **refers to the connection of a person's spoken word with, "the word of G-d, which is Halacha (Jewish Law)"** (Talmud, Shabbos 138b), וְכֵן מַחֲשָׁבָה בְּמַחֲשָׁבָה — **and so too,** his **thoughts** with G-d's **thoughts,** וּמַעֲשֶׂה בְּמַעֲשֶׂה שֶׁהוּא מַעֲשֵׂה הַמִּצְוֹת — **and** his **actions with** G-d's **actions, namely the practical mitzvos.***

Now the Tanya briefly addresses the question: Are all mitzvos equal? Of course they equally represent the Divine will, but do some offer a more intimate connection with G-d than others?

וּבִפְרָט מַעֲשֵׂה הַצְּדָקָה וָחֶסֶד — **All the mitzvos provide an intimate connection with** G-d, but this is **especially so with acts of charity and kindness,** דְּחֶסֶד דְּרוֹעָא יְמִינָא — since **"kindness is G-d's right arm"** (Tikunei Zohar 17a), וְהוּא בְּחִינַת חִיבּוּק מַמָּשׁ — **and that is literally at the level of "hugging,"** כְּמוֹ שֶׁכָּתוּב וִימִינוֹ תְּחַבְּקֵנִי — **as the verse states, "and his right arm hugs me"** (Song 2:6).

---

*According to the Tanya's mystical interpretation, Scripture appears to offer the events in reverse sequence. In reality, Ya'akov *first* stirs great compassion for her ("he lifted his voice") and *only then* bonds with her ("and Ya'akov kissed Rachel"). The verse, however, puts it the other way around: "And Ya'akov kissed Rachel, he lifted his voice and he cried."

Scripture reverses the order to explain to us: How was Ya'akov *able* to connect with Rachel? How did he have the spiritual power necessary? And the verse answers: In order to achieve the connection of spirit to spirit ("And Ya'akov kissed Rachel"), he *first* had to arouse great compassion for her, ("he lifted his voice and he cried").

And that is the Tanya's lesson to us here: If we want to achieve a deep connection with G-d (like "kissing") through the observance of Torah and mitzvos, we first need to carry out the above compassion meditation for our souls.

ממש. והנה ע"י זה יכול לבוא לבחי' אהבה רבה
בהתגלות לבו כדכתיב ליעקב אשר פדה את אברהם
כמ"ש במ"א:

Charity is metaphorically associated with "G-d's right arm," to illustrate the particularly intimate connection it brings, analogous to a hug. This is a unique quality of "acts of charity and kindness" not shared with any other *mitzvah*.

(While above in chapter 4, p. 74, all *mitzvos* were depicted as a hug with G-d, the *Tanya* emphasizes here that charity is "*literally* (*mamash*) at the level of hugging," meaning that it expresses the intimate bond of hugging to a far greater extent — *Notes on Tanya*).

וְעֵסֶק הַתּוֹרָה בְּדִבּוּר וּמַחֲשָׁבָת הָעִיּוּן הֵן בְּחִינַת נְשִׁיקִין מַמָּשׁ — **And Torah study which is verbalized and studied with intense concentration is literally on the level of "kissing" G-d.**

As we have just learned, all *mitzvos* are on the level of "kissing" G-d, but Torah study is "*literally* (*mamash*) on the level of "kissing" G-d" (*Notes on Tanya*). Presumably, this is because Torah study is both "verbalized and studied," so there is an intimate bond to G-d through the body and the mind.

וְהִנֵּה עַל יְדֵי זֶה — **And through this process** of meditation described in this chapter, of arousing compassion on your soul, יָכוֹל לָבוֹא לִבְחִינַת אַהֲבָה רַבָּה בְּהִתְגַּלּוּת לִבּוֹ — **you can come to the experience of "great love," palpably in your heart.**

When you arouse "great compassion" from the "source of all compassion," you are accessing an extremely powerful energy. It can even propel you to the level of "great love."

As we have learned, "great love" always comes as a "gift from above" and not as the *direct* result of your spiritual work (p. 556). Here the "gift" is prompted by your compassion meditations and your charitable acts (Rabbi Alexander Yudasin, *Ha-Lekach Ve-Ha-Libuv*).

PRACTICAL LESSONS

Contemplate how far your soul has fallen, from its origin in G-d, to your lowly body. Compassion for your soul will infuse your *mitzvos* with authentic emotion for G-d.

This meditation will empower you to connect to G-d with every *mitzvah* as an intimate bond (a "kiss").

It is also a path that can bring you to *ahavah rabah* ("great love").

כְּדִכְתִיב לְיַעֲקֹב אֲשֶׁר פָּדָה אֶת אַבְרָהָם — We know that compassion (the trait of Ya'akov) can lead to love (the trait of Avraham), **as the verse states, "*to Ya'akov, who redeemed Avraham*"** (Isaiah 29:22), כְּמוֹ שֶׁנִּתְבָּאֵר בְּמָקוֹם אַחֵר — **as is explained elsewhere** (see chapter 32, p. 368; *Torah Ohr*, 51b).

Compassion has the power to "redeem love," to save you from a state where love eludes you. If your soul's flame is weak, and you're finding it difficult to arouse any love for G-d, try compassion.

65A פרק מו ויש דרך ישר לפני איש שוה לכל נפש
וקרוב הדבר מאד מאד לעורר
ולהאיר אור האהבה התקועה ומסותרת בלבו להיות
מאירה בתוקף אורה כאש בוערה בהתגלות לבו ומוחו
למסור נפשו לה' וגופו ומאודו בכל לב ובכל נפש ומאד

CHAPTER 46

HOW TO MIRROR G-D'S LOVE
SECTION ONE: AN EASIER METHOD TO AWAKEN YOUR SOUL

9TH IYAR REGULAR | 4TH IYAR LEAP

In chapters 41 to 45 we have discussed various meditative paths to attain reverence and love of G-d. While the techniques varied, they all required some serious contemplative work.

But what if you're not ready for that? Or you've tried it, and it's not working?

In chapters 46-49 the *Tanya* will share with us another method, which is more of a "reflection" than a full-blown meditation. So even if you can't manage a sustained focus on a single idea, you should be able to manage this method.

וְיֵשׁ דֶּרֶךְ יָשָׁר לִפְנֵי אִישׁ שָׁוֶה לְכָל נֶפֶשׁ — And *"there's a straightforward way for a person"* (Proverbs 14:12), **which is applicable to everybody,** וְקָרוֹב הַדָּבָר מְאֹד מְאֹד — **which is very, very much** *"within reach* for you" (Deuteronomy 30:14), it's easily and effectively implemented, **to** — לְעוֹרֵר וּלְהָאִיר אוֹר הָאַהֲבָה הַתְּקוּעָה וּמְסוּתֶּרֶת בְּלִבּוֹ **cause the glowing love which is wedged in your heart, and latent** there, **to awaken and shine.**

The *Tanya* stresses that the method in this chapter is *very, very* much "within reach," in contrast with the more challenging meditations we have learned earlier. In chapters 41-45, if you were feeling alienated from G-d, that was a problem, (not insurmountable, but a problem). But, as we shall see, the method of this chapter actually works *better*, the lower you are feeling spiritually. So it's very, very much "within reach", and "applicable to everybody" (*Notes on Tanya*).

לִהְיוֹת מְאִירָה בְּתוֹקֶף אוֹרָהּ כְּאֵשׁ בּוֹעֲרָה בְּהִתְגַּלּוּת לִבּוֹ וּמוֹחוֹ — This method will awaken the love in your heart **so that its light shines powerfully, as if it were a fire burning palpably in your heart and mind,** לִמְסוֹר נַפְשׁוֹ לַה' וְגוּפוֹ וּמְאוֹדוֹ — **to devote your soul, your body and your possessions to G-d,** בְּכָל לֵב וּבְכָל נֶפֶשׁ וּמְאֹד — with *"all*

מֵעוֹמְקָא דְלִבָּא בֶּאֱמֶת לַאֲמִיתּוֹ וּבִפְרָט בִּשְׁעַת ק"ש
וּבְרְכוֹתֶיהָ כְּמוֹ שֶׁיִּתְבָּאֵר. וְהוּא כַּאֲשֶׁר יָשִׂים אֶל לִבּוֹ
מַ"שׁ הַכָּתוּ' כַּמַּיִם הַפָּנִים לְפָנִים כֵּן לֵב הָאָדָם אֶל הָאָדָם
פֵּי' כְּמוֹ שֶׁכִּדְמוּת וְצוּרַת הַפָּנִים שֶׁהָאָדָם מַרְאֶה בַּמַּיִם כֵּן
נִרְאָה לוֹ שָׁם בַּמַּיִם אוֹתָהּ צוּרָה עַצְמָהּ כָּכָה מַמָּשׁ לֵב
הָאָדָם הַנֶּאֱמָן בְּאַהֲבָתוֹ לְאִישׁ אַחֵר הֲרֵי הָאַהֲבָה זוֹ
מְעוֹרֶרֶת אַהֲבָה בְּלֵב חֲבֵירוֹ אֵלָיו ג"כ לִהְיוֹת אוֹהֲבִים

*your **heart**, all your **soul** and all your **might**"* (ibid. 6:5), מֵעוֹמְקָא דְּלִבָּא בֶּאֱמֶת לַאֲמִיתּוֹ — **from the most genuine depths of your heart.**

You might imagine that since this method is straightforward, and can be used when your spiritual flame is very weak, the results will be poor. The *Tanya* assures us that, on the contrary, this method will awaken the most passionate and devotional love in your soul.

וּבִפְרָט בִּשְׁעַת קְרִיאַת שְׁמַע וּבִרְכוֹתֶיהָ — **And** this method **is particularly** effective **at the time when you recite the *Shema* and its blessings,** when you devote yourself to G-d with *"all your heart, all your soul and all your might,"* כְּמוֹ שֶׁיִּתְבָּאֵר — **as will be explained,** in chapter 49, at the conclusion of this discussion.

וְהוּא — **And this** *"straightforward way... to cause the light of love which is implanted in your heart, and latent there, to awaken and shine,"* כַּאֲשֶׁר יָשִׂים אֶל לִבּוֹ מַה שֶׁאָמַר הַכָּתוּב כַּמַּיִם הַפָּנִים לְפָנִים כֵּן לֵב הָאָדָם אֶל הָאָדָם — requires you **to take to heart the verse, "As face reflects face in water, so the heart of man to man"** (Proverbs 27:19).

This means, *"Just as water reflects back a face similar to the one gazing into it — a happy face reflects a happy one, a sad face reflects a sad one — the same is true with a person's heart. If a person's heart is good to his friend, his friend's heart will be good to him too. If it's nasty, he'll be nasty too"* (Metzudas David ibid.).

PRACTICAL LESSONS

Emotions are always mirrored. If you love someone, they will instinctively love you back.

The same is true with feelings for G-d. When you contemplate how G-d has shown love for you, your heart will automatically mirror back that love.

פֵּירוּשׁ — This verse **should be interpreted** as describing an *instinctual, automatic* phenomenon, כְּמוֹ שֶׁכִּדְמוּת וְצוּרַת הַפָּנִים שֶׁהָאָדָם מַרְאֶה בַּמַּיִם כֵּן נִרְאָה לוֹ שָׁם בַּמַּיִם אוֹתָהּ צוּרָה עַצְמָהּ — that **just as when a person shows the image and form of his face into water, that same form is visible there in the water,** כָּכָה מַמָּשׁ לֵב הָאָדָם — in exactly the same way, when one person's heart הַנֶּאֱמָן בְּאַהֲבָתוֹ לְאִישׁ אַחֵר **loves another person devotedly,** הֲרֵי הָאַהֲבָה זוֹ מְעוֹרֶרֶת אַהֲבָה בְּלֵב חֲבֵירוֹ אֵלָיו גַּם כֵּן — then the first person's love automatically **causes the love in his friend's heart to**

נאמנים זה לזה בפרט כשרואה אהבת חבירו אליו.
והנה זהו טבע הנהוג במדת כל אדם אף אם שניהם
שוים במעלה ועל אחת כמה וכמה אם מלך גדול ורב
מראה אהבתו הגדולה והעצומה לאיש הדיוט ונבזה

be stirred up towards him, too, לִהְיוֹת אוֹהֲבִים זֶה לָזֶה — so that the result is that **they both love** each other **and are devoted to each other.**

בְּפְרָט כְּשֶׁרוֹאֶה אַהֲבַת חֲבֵירוֹ אֵלָיו — This is true even if a person merely *knows* of his friend's love, or he *senses* it, and **it's especially the case when he** *sees* **his friend's love** overtly expressed **towards him.**

5TH IYAR LEAP

וְהִנֵּה זֶהוּ טֶבַע הַנָהוּג בְּמִדַּת כָּל אָדָם — **This is the natural,** instinctive and automatic **behavior pattern of all people.**

It's possible to interpret the verse in Proverbs as an *ethical lesson*: If someone is nice to you, *make the effort* to be nice back. However, the *Tanya* interprets the verse, not as an ethical lesson, but as a *psychological reality* ("*this is the natural behavior pattern of all people*"). If someone is nice to you, *naturally and inevitably* you will want to be nice back.

This principle will provide the foundation for a very straightforward method to arouse love for G-d. When you will contemplate how G-d has shown love towards you, your heart will naturally and automatically reciprocate feelings of love for G-d.

SECTION TWO: WHEN A GREAT PERSON LOVES YOU — A PARABLE

To depict precisely how G-d has shown His love to you, the *Tanya* will now present an intricate parable. In this section we will study the parable, and in the following sections we will decipher its message.

אַף אִם שְׁנֵיהֶם שָׁוִים בְּמַעֲלָה — An automatic mirroring of emotion will occur **even if the two individuals are of equal status,** וְעַל אַחַת כַּמָּה וְכַמָּה אִם מֶלֶךְ גָּדוֹל וְרַב מַרְאֶה — but all the more so will love evoke love if אַהֲבָתוֹ הַגְּדוֹלָה וְהָעֲצוּמָה לְאִישׁ הֶדְיוֹט — **a great and influential king demonstrates his abundant and intense love to an ordinary citizen.**

וְנִבְזֶה וּשְׁפַל אֲנָשִׁים וּמְנֻוָּול הַמּוּטָל בָּאַשְׁפָּה — And all the more so will love evoke love if that citizen is **disgusting and** *"the most lowly of men"* (*Daniel* 4:14), **disheveled and** *"cast in the garbage"* (*Talmud Chullin* 76b).

The first point which the parable wishes to make clear is that, while love will automatically evoke love even among equal men, the results will be much more powerful if a great individual shows his love for someone shameful and seemingly unlovable.

ושפל אנשים ומנוול המוטל באשפה ויורד אליו ממקו׳
כבודו עם כל שריו יחדיו ומקימו ומרימו מאשפתו
ומכניסו להיכלו היכל המלך חדר לפנים מחדר מקום
שאין כל עבד ושר נכנס לשם ומתייחד עמו שם ביחוד
וקירוב אמיתי וחיבוק ונישוק ואתדבקות רוחא ברוחא
בכל לב ונפש עאכ״ו שתתעורר ממילא האהבה כפולה
ומכופלת בלב ההדיוט ושפל אנשים הזה אל נפש המלך
בהתקשרות הנפש ממש מלב ונפש מעומקא דלבא
לאין קץ. ואף אם לבו כלב האבן המס ימס והיה למים

Having contrasted the status of the "king" and the "lowly man," the parable continues with a discussion of how the king demonstrates his love.

וְיוֹרֵד אֵלָיו מִמְּקוֹם כְּבוֹדוֹ עִם כָּל שָׂרָיו יַחְדָּיו — **And** to express his love, the king **travels down, along with all his ministers, from his glamorous location, to** meet **this** lowly citizen, וּמְקִימוֹ וּמְרִימוֹ מֵאַשְׁפָּתוֹ — **and** the king not only greets him, but **lifts him out of the dirt, dignifying him.**

וּמַכְנִיסוֹ לְהֵיכָלוֹ הֵיכַל הַמֶּלֶךְ — **And** to express his love further, the king does not leave the citizen, but **brings** the citizen **to his palace, the royal palace,** where ordinary people cannot usually enter, חֶדֶר לִפְנִים מֵחֶדֶר מָקוֹם שֶׁאֵין כָּל עֶבֶד וְשַׂר נִכְנָס לְשָׁם — and the king doesn't just bring him anywhere in the palace, but brings the "lowly man," **room by room,** to the most exclusive location, **to a place where no servant or minister may enter.**

וּמִתְיַיחֵד עִמּוֹ שָׁם בְּיִחוּד וְקֵירוּב אֲמִיתִי — **And** as if that were not enough, the king **interacts with him there, with a close and genuine interaction,** וְחִיבּוּק וְנִישּׁוּק וְאִתְדַּבְּקוּת רוּחָא בְּרוּחָא — **with hugs and kisses, and** a *"merging of spirit with spirit"* (Zohar 1, 184a), בְּכָל לֵב וָנֶפֶשׁ — **with all his heart and soul.**

PRACTICAL LESSONS

When G-d brought you into the Sinaitic covenant of Torah, it was like "a great king personally showing his love for a lowly person."

עַל אַחַת כַּמָּה וְכַמָּה שֶׁתִּתְעוֹרֵר מִמֵּילָא הָאַהֲבָה כְּפוּלָה וּמְכוּפֶּלֶת בְּלֵב הַהֶדְיוֹט וּשְׁפַל אֲנָשִׁים הַזֶּה אֶל נֶפֶשׁ הַמֶּלֶךְ — Now, if love evokes love in even ordinary circumstances, between equals, then in this most extreme case **there will definitely awaken spontaneously a doubled and redoubled feeling of love in the heart of this ordinary citizen and** *"most lowly of men,"* **towards the king's soul,** בְּהִתְקַשְּׁרוּת הַנֶּפֶשׁ מַמָּשׁ מִלֵּב וָנֶפֶשׁ — **a real soul-connection, from the heart and the soul,** מֵעוּמְקָא דְּלִבָּא לְאֵין קֵץ — **from the infinite depths of the** "lowly man's" **heart,** וְאַף אִם לִבּוֹ כְּלֵב הָאֶבֶן הַמֵּס יִמַּס — **and even if** the "lowly man's" **heart is** usually insensitive, **like a heart of stone,** *"it will surely melt"* (2 Samuel 17:10), **becoming** responsive and fluid like

וְתִשְׁתַּפֵּךְ נַפְשׁוֹ כַּמַּיִם כִּכְלוֹת הַנֶּפֶשׁ מַמָּשׁ לְאַהֲבַת הַמֶּלֶךְ: וְהִנֵּה כְּכָל הַדְּבָרִים הָאֵלֶּה וּכְכָל הַחִזָּיוֹן הַזֶּה
65B וְגָדוֹל יֶתֶר מְאֹד בְּכִפְלֵי כִפְלַיִים לְאֵין קֵץ עָשָׂה לָנוּ אֱלֹהֵינוּ כִּי לִגְדוּלָתוֹ אֵין חֵקֶר וְאִיהוּ מְמַלֵּא כָּל עָלְמִין וְסוֹבֵב כָּל עָלְמִין וְנוֹדַע מִזֹּהַ"ק וְהָאֲרִ"י ז"ל רִיבּוּי הַהֵיכָלוֹת

water, כַּמַּיִם — וְתִשְׁתַּפֵּךְ נַפְשׁוֹ כַּמַּיִם — *"and his soul will pour out"* (see *Job* 30:16), like water, בִּכְלוֹת הַנֶּפֶשׁ מַמָּשׁ לְאַהֲבַת הַמֶּלֶךְ — and it will really pine with love for the king.

Our new method to attain love for G-d, which is based on the above parable, is simple and effective (very, very much "within reach"). It will move even a person who is insensitive "like a heart of stone."

SECTION THREE: HOW G-D HAS SHOWN HIS LOVE FOR YOU

10TH IYAR REGULAR | 6TH IYAR LEAP

The *Tanya* will now decipher the parable and demonstrate its meaning to us.

וְהִנֵּה כְּכָל הַדְּבָרִים הָאֵלֶּה וּכְכָל הַחִזָּיוֹן הַזֶּה — Now, *"in accordance with all these words and in accordance with all of this insight"* (2 *Samuel* 7:17), וְגָדוֹל יֶתֶר מְאֹד בְּכִפְלֵי כִפְלַיִים לְאֵין קֵץ — but very much more so, doubled and redoubled, without end, עָשָׂה לָנוּ אֱלֹהֵינוּ — *"has our G-d done to us"* (see *Jeremiah* 5:19).

This parable is a precise description of the relationship which G-d has forged with every one of us.

The "ordinary citizen" who is "disgusting... the most lowly of men, disheveled and cast in the garbage" — is *you*. You're "ordinary," because your mind is too weak to meditate properly. You're "disgusting... the most lowly of men," because your character is unrefined. You're "disheveled and cast in the garbage," because you think, say and do inappropriate things (see Rabbi Alexander Yudasin, *Ha-Lekach Ve-Ha-Libuv*).

G-d is the "great and influential king" who has come to you, lifted you out of your pitiful state, dignified you and expressed His deep love for you!

כִּי לִגְדוּלָתוֹ אֵין חֵקֶר — G-d is "great" since *"His greatness can never be fathomed"* (*Psalms* 145:3), וְאִיהוּ מְמַלֵּא כָּל עָלְמִין וְסוֹבֵב כָּל עָלְמִין — and *"He fills all worlds"* and *"transcends all worlds"* (see *Zohar* 3, 225a).

וְנוֹדַע מִזֹּהַר הַקָּדוֹשׁ וְהָאֲרִ"י זִכְרוֹנוֹ לִבְרָכָה — And G-d is "influential" because, as the *Zohar* and *Arizal,* have made known, רִיבּוּי הַהֵיכָלוֹת וְהָעוֹלָמוֹת עַד אֵין מִסְפָּר — there are so many "chambers" and "worlds" over which G-d's influence spreads, that they are countless (see, for example, *Zohar* 3, 128; *Etz Chaim,* 2:2).

While the content of the spiritual worlds is described in detail by the *Zohar* and *Arizal,* it is also a topic which the *Talmud* touches upon, as the *Tanya* now mentions.

וְהָעוֹלָמוֹת עַד אֵין מִסְפָּר וּבְכָל עוֹלָם וְהֵיכָל רִיבּוֹא
רִבְבוֹת מַלְאָכִים לְאֵין קֵץ וְתַכְלִית. וּכְמ"שׁ בַּגְּמ' כְּתִיב
הֲיֵשׁ מִסְפָּר לִגְדוּדָיו וּכְתִיב אֶלֶף אַלְפִין יְשַׁמְּשׁוּנֵיהּ וְרִיבּוֹ
רִבְבָן קָדְמוֹהִי כוּ' וּמְשַׁנֵּי אֶלֶף אַלְפִין וְכוּ' מִסְפַּר גְּדוּד
אֶחָד אֲבָל לִגְדוּדָיו אֵין מִסְפָּר וְכוּלָּם קַמֵּיהּ כְּלָא מַמָּשׁ
חֲשִׁיבֵי וּבְטֵלִים בִּמְצִיאוּת מַמָּשׁ כְּבִיטּוּל דִּבּוּר א' מַמָּשׁ
לְגַבֵּי מַהוּת הַנֶּפֶשׁ הַמְדַבֶּרֶת וְעַצְמוּתָהּ בְּעוֹד שֶׁהָיָה
דִּיבּוּרוֹ עֲדַיִן בְּמַחְשַׁבְתָּהּ אוֹ בִּרְצוֹן וְחֶמְדַּת הַלֵּב כנ"ל
בַּאֲרִיכוּת: וְכוּלָּם שׁוֹאֲלִים אַיֵּה מְקוֹם כְּבוֹדוֹ וְעוֹנִים

וּבְכָל עוֹלָם וְהֵיכָל רִיבּוֹא רִבְבוֹת מַלְאָכִים — **And in each** spiritual **world and "chamber" there are hundreds of millions of angels** per brigade, לְאֵין קֵץ וְתַכְלִית — **and an unlimited number** of brigades.

וּכְמוֹ שֶׁכָּתוּב בַּגְּמָרָא הֲיֵשׁ מִסְפָּר לִגְדוּדָיו — **As the** *Talmud* **notes,** clarifying a contradiction between two verses, **"One verse states, 'Is there a number to His brigades?'"** (*Job* 25:3), implying an *unlimited* number of angels, וּכְתִיב אֶלֶף אַלְפִין — וִישַׁמְּשׁוּנֵיהּ וְרִיבּוֹ רִבְבָן קָדְמוֹהִי גוֹ' **"But another verse states, 'thousand upon thousands ministered unto Him, and a hundred million stood before Him'"** (*Daniel* 7:10), implying a large, but *limited* number of angels.

וּמְשַׁנֵּי אֶלֶף אַלְפִין וְכוּ' מִסְפַּר גְּדוּד אֶחָד אֲבָל לִגְדוּדָיו אֵין מִסְפָּר — **The** *Talmud* **answers** to resolve the contradiction, **"'Thousand upon thousands etc.,' is the size of one brigade, but there is no limit to the number of brigades"** (*Talmud, Chagigah* 13b).

The *Talmud* indicates that G-d rules over spiritual entities that are "beyond number," showing the great extent of G-d's influence. But in reality, of course, G-d is *more* than "great" and "influential"; as we have learned earlier in the *Tanya*, His presence is so powerful that it makes any other independent existence *impossible*.

וְכוּלָּם קַמֵּיהּ כְּלָא מַמָּשׁ חֲשִׁיבֵי — **And "In His presence, everything is considered zero"** (*Zohar* 1, 11b), וּבְטֵלִים בִּמְצִיאוּת מַמָּשׁ — **and the individual identities** of all the brigades of angels **are voided, literally,** כְּבִיטּוּל דִּבּוּר אֶחָד מַמָּשׁ לְגַבֵּי מַהוּת הַנֶּפֶשׁ — **like the way one spoken word is literally voided of its identity in the deep core of the soul, which powers speech,** הַמְדַבֶּרֶת וְעַצְמוּתָהּ בְּעוֹד שֶׁהָיָה דִּיבּוּרָהּ עֲדַיִן — **while that** soon-to-be-**spoken word was still in the soul's powers of** thought, or the pre-linguistic **will and desire of the heart,** בְּמַחְשַׁבְתָּהּ אוֹ בִּרְצוֹן וְחֶמְדַּת הַלֵּב כַּנִּזְכָּר לְעֵיל בַּאֲרִיכוּת — **as was discussed above, at length** (chapters 20-21).

7TH IYAR LEAP

We have demonstrated how G-d is the *"great and influential king"* of our parable. As we continue to decipher the parable, the *Tanya* will now explain how G-d, *"shows an abundant and intense love to an ordinary citizen."*

מלא כל הארץ כבודו הם ישראל עמו. כי הניח הקב"ה
את העליונים ואת התחתונים ולא בחר בכולם כי אם
בישראל עמו והוציאם ממצרים ערות הארץ מקום
הזוהמא והטומאה לא ע"י מלאך ולא ע"י כו' אלא הקב"ה
בכבודו ובעצמו ירד לשם כמ"ש וארד להצילו וגו' כדי

וְכוּלָם שׁוֹאֲלִים אַיֵּה מְקוֹם כְּבוֹדוֹ — And all the angels ask, "Where is the place of His glory?" (Liturgy, Kedushah), וְעוֹנִים מְלֹא כָל הָאָרֶץ כְּבוֹדוֹ — and they answer, that G-d's glory is not to be found in the heavens, but rather, "All the earth is filled with His glory" (ibid. from Isaiah 6:3), הֵם יִשְׂרָאֵל עַמּוֹ — G-d's "glory" on earth, referring to His people, Israel.

As the Zohar teaches: "'The earth and its fullness' (Psalms 24:1), refers to the Congregation of Israel… as it is written, 'All earth is filled with His glory'" (Zohar 2, 50a).

כִּי הִנִּיחַ הַקָּדוֹשׁ בָּרוּךְ הוּא אֶת הָעֶלְיוֹנִים וְאֶת הַתַּחְתּוֹנִים וְלֹא בָּחַר בְּכוּלָם — For the Blessed Holy One has disregarded the worship of the upper and lower worlds and He chose none of them, כִּי אִם בְּיִשְׂרָאֵל עַמּוֹ — except Israel, His people (see above chapter 41 p. 495; chapter 42, p. 547).

PRACTICAL LESSONS

Just think: G-d could have desired the worship of any creatures in the upper or lower worlds, *but* He chose yours.

G-d's choice of Israel over all the other inhabitants of the upper (and lower) worlds represents *"an abundant and intense love to an ordinary citizen."*

Now we turn to the detail that, even though the "ordinary citizen" is *"disgusting and the most lowly of men disheveled and cast in the garbage,"* nevertheless, *"to express his love, the king travels down, along with all his ministers, from his glamorous location to meet this lowly man and lifts him out of the dirt, dignifying him."*

וְהוֹצִיאָם מִמִּצְרַיִם עֶרְוַת הָאָרֶץ מְקוֹם הַזּוּהֲמָא וְהַטּוּמְאָה — And He took the Israelites out from Egypt, *"the land's depravity"* (Genesis 42:9), a place of spiritual pollution and impurity, i.e., from their state of being *"disheveled and cast in the garbage."*

לֹא עַל יְדֵי מַלְאָךְ וְלֹא עַל יְדֵי כו' אֶלָּא הַקָּדוֹשׁ בָּרוּךְ הוּא בִּכְבוֹדוֹ וּבְעַצְמוֹ יָרַד לְשָׁם — And "the king traveled down" Himself, *"not through an angel, nor through a fiery angel, nor through a messenger; rather it was the Blessed Holy One, Himself in His glory"* (Passover Hagadah), who went down there, כְּמוֹ שֶׁכָּתוּב וָאֵרֵד לְהַצִּילוֹ וְגוֹ' — as the verse states, *"I shall descend to rescue them etc.,"* (Exodus 3:8).

And the purpose of this special treatment is for the king to interact with the lowly man, *"with a close and genuine interaction, with hugs and kisses, and a 'merging of spirit with spirit,' with all his heart and soul."*

לקרבם אליו בקירוב ויחוד אמיתי בהתקשרות הנפש
ממש בבחי' נשיקין פה לפה לדבר דבר ה' זו הלכה
ואתדבקות רוחא ברוחא היא השגת התורה וידיעת
רצונו וחכמתו דכולא חד ממש. וגם בבחי' חיבוק הוא
קיום המצות מעשיות ברמ"ח אברים דרמ"ח פיקודין הן
רמ"ח אברין דמלכא כנז"ל. ודרך כלל נחלקין לשלש
בחי' ימין ושמאל ואמצע שהן חסד דין רחמים תרין

כְּדֵי לְקָרְבָם אֵלָיו בְּקֵירוּב וְיָחוּד אֲמִיתִּי — G-d took the Israelites out of Egypt **to bring them close to Him, in an intimate and genuine union,** בְּהִתְקַשְּׁרוּת הַנֶּפֶשׁ מַמָּשׁ בִּבְחִינַת נְשִׁיקִין פֶּה לְפֶה — a union which **connects profoundly with the soul, like** *Song of Songs* depicts this union as **a mouth-to-mouth kiss,** *"Let him kiss me with the kisses of his mouth"* (Song 1:2).

The *Tanya* deciphers the meaning of the "kiss" analogy.

לְדַבֵּר דְּבַר ה' זוֹ הֲלָכָה — This "kiss" referring to the intimate union with G-d **when a person speaks,** *"the word of G-d, which is Halacha"* (Talmud, Shabbos 138b), וְאִתְדַּבְּקוּת רוּחָא בְּרוּחָא הִיא הַשָּׂגַת הַתּוֹרָה וִידִיעַת רְצוֹנוֹ וְחָכְמָתוֹ דְּכוּלָא חַד מַמָּשׁ — **and** a *"merging of spirit with spirit"* (Zohar 1, 184a), **through understanding the Torah and knowing His wisdom and will, which are** *"totally one"* **with Him** (ibid. 24a).

וְגַם בִּבְחִינַת חִיבּוּק הוּא קִיּוּם הַמִּצְוֹת מַעֲשִׂיּוֹת בְּרַמַ"ח אֵבָרִים — **And also** we have the intimate union with G-d, depicted as **"hugging," through observing the practical** *mitzvos,* **with the 248 bodily parts** דְּרַמַ"ח פִּיקוּדִין הֵן רַמַ"ח אֵבָרִין דְּמַלְכָּא — **since** *"the 248 commands are the 248 limbs of the king"* (Tikunei Zohar 74a), כַּנִּזְכָּר לְעֵיל — **as mentioned above.**

We already discussed the analogy of "kissing" and "hugging" G-d through Torah and *mitzvos* in chapter 4, (p. 74) and chapter 45, (p. 587). "Hugging" is symbolic of the soul's deep and pleasurable devotion to a *mitzvah,* an inner embrace of the Blessed Infinite Light which is "dressed" in every *mitzvah* act (*Ma'amarei Admor Ha-Zaken,* 5563, vol. 2, p. 485). Here the *Tanya* adds a further detail.

וְדֶרֶךְ כְּלָל נֶחְלָקִין לְשָׁלֹשׁ בְּחִינוֹת יָמִין וּשְׂמֹאל וְאֶמְצַע — **And, generally speaking,** the 248 positive *mitzvos* are **divided into three "lines": right, left and center,** שֶׁהֵן חֶסֶד דִּין רַחֲמִים — **which are generosity (chesed), discipline (din) and compassion (rachamim),** respectively.

The core spiritual energies of the universe (*sefiros*), are divided into three "lines" or categories. The polar opposites of *chesed* ("give!") and *din* ("withhold!") represent the right and left "lines." *Rachamim* (compassion) is placed in the center, since it mediates between the two positions.

Chesed says, "Give to everyone, regardless of whether they are deserving." *Din* says, "Only give to the deserving." *Rachamim* agrees with *din* that *in principle* we

דרועין וגופא וכו'. וז"ש אשר קדשנו במצותיו כאדם
המקדש אשה להיות מיוחדת עמו ביחוד גמור כמ"ש
ודבק באשתו והיו לבשר אחד. ככה ממש ויתר על כן

should withhold benefits to the undeserving, but pleads for compassion, siding with *chesed.*

Since the *mitzvos* are the Divine will as expressed *in the world,* they inevitably take expression through the matrix of the *sefiros,* which are the world's core energies. That's why the *mitzvos* can, like the *sefiros,* be divided into three "lines" of *chesed, din* and *rachamim.*

These three "lines" correlate neatly with the *Mishnah's* statement, *"the world stands on three things: Torah, worship and acts of kindness"* (*Avos* 1:2). "Acts of kindness," such as charity, represent the right "line" of *chesed.* "Worship" through prayer, a process of disciplined self-examination, corresponds to the left line of *din.* And Torah, which guides us how to integrate *chesed* and *din* — when to act generously and when to exercise restraint — is the middle, mediating line of *rachamim* (Rabbi Shneur Zalman, *Likutei Torah, Deuteronomy* 4b).

תְּרֵין דְּרוֹעִין וְגוּפָא וְכו' — The Kabbalah refers to the three "lines" as *"the two arms and the body etc.,"* of G-d, so to speak (*Tikunei Zohar* 17a).

According to the *Tikunei Zohar,* the three "lines" of the *sefiros* are symbolically depicted as G-d's two "arms" and "body." Following this imagery, we might say that through observing the 613 *mitzvos* of the Torah, in all their three "lines," we hug, so to speak, the two "arms" and "body" of G-d.

SECTION FOUR: HOW YOU'RE MARRIED TO G-D

11TH IYAR REGULAR

Having deciphered the basic meaning of the parable, the *Tanya* will continue from here until chapter 49 to expand upon some of its key themes.

First we will explore further the idea of a *mitzvah* as an intimate union with G-d.

וְזֶהוּ שֶׁאוֹמְרִים אֲשֶׁר קִדְּשָׁנוּ בְּמִצְוֹתָיו — And to stress further the intimate union of a *mitzvah* we say, in the blessing recited before observing a *mitzvah,* "Blessed are you G-d... who has sanctified us (KiDiSHanu) with His mitzvos," כְּאָדָם הַמְקַדֵּשׁ אִשָּׁה — where the term *kidishanu* can also be translated as "married," like a man that marries (meKaDeSH) a woman (Avudraham, Morning Blessings).

Following this interpretation, the close connection with G-d through a *mitzvah* is symbolized as the intimate union of a husband and wife.

לִהְיוֹת מְיוּחֶדֶת עִמּוֹ בְּיִחוּד גָּמוּר — A man marries a woman to be one with her, in a complete union, כְּמוֹ שֶׁכָּתוּב וְדָבַק בְּאִשְׁתּוֹ וְהָיוּ לְבָשָׂר אֶחָד — as the verse states, "a man... clings to his wife and they become one flesh" (Genesis 2:24), כָּכָה מַמָּשׁ

66A לְאֵין קֵץ הוּא יִחוּד נֶפֶשׁ הָאֱלֹהִית הָעוֹסֶקֶת בַּתּוֹרָה וּמִצְוֹת
וְנֶפֶשׁ הַחִיּוֹנִית וּלְבוּשֵׁיהֶן הַנַּ״ל בְּאוֹר אֵין סוֹף ב״ה. וְלָכֵן
הִמְשִׁיל שְׁלֹמֹה ע״ה בְּשִׁיר הַשִּׁירִים יִחוּד זֶה לְיִחוּד
חָתָן וְכַלָּה בִּדְבִיקָה חֲשִׁיקָה וַחֲפִיצָה בְּחִיבּוּק וְנִישׁוּק.
וְזֶהוּ אֲשֶׁר קִדְּשָׁנוּ בְּמִצְוֹתָיו שֶׁהֶעֱלָנוּ לְמַעֲלַת קוֹדֶשׁ

וְיֶתֶר עַל כֵּן לְאֵין קֵץ — **and in exactly the same way, but with infinitely more** intensity,
הוּא יִחוּד נֶפֶשׁ הָאֱלֹהִית הָעוֹסֶקֶת בַּתּוֹרָה וּמִצְוֹת וְנֶפֶשׁ הַחִיּוֹנִית וּלְבוּשֵׁיהֶן הַנִּזְכָּרִים לְעֵיל
בְּאוֹר אֵין סוֹף בָּרוּךְ הוּא — **is the union of the G-dly soul with the Blessed Infinite
Light, when it observes Torah and** *mitzvos,* (which is united **along with the energizing Animal Soul and its "garments," mentioned above).**

8TH IYAR LEAP

וְלָכֵן הִמְשִׁיל שְׁלֹמֹה עָלָיו הַשָּׁלוֹם בְּשִׁיר הַשִּׁירִים יִחוּד זֶה לְיִחוּד חָתָן וְכַלָּה — **And that's
why, in his** *Song of Songs,* **Shlomo (Solomon) compared this union** of a person with
G-d **to the relationship of groom and bride,** in great detail.

בִּדְבִיקָה חֲשִׁיקָה וַחֲפִיצָה — And Scripture speaks of love
in terms of ***"attachment" "fervor,"*** and ***"desire"*** *(Genesis 34:3, 8, 19),* בְּחִיבּוּק וְנִישׁוּק — **with hugging and kissing,** to guide us in our relationship to G-d, through the
mitzvos.

Song of Songs speaks of the love of a groom and his
bride. While the *Song* does not state so explicitly, the
text has been understood as a metaphor for the love a
person ought to have for G-d (see *Rambam, Laws of Teshuvah* 10:3). In *Tanya* here, and in other mystical texts,
these metaphors are explained in detail.

In our parable, we were told how the "lowly man" is
brought by the king, "*to his palace, the royal palace,
room by room, to a place where no servant or minister
may enter.*" The implication here is that the lowly man is
elevated to the king's own level and standing, reaching
a place which the king alone inhabits.

The *Tanya* will now explain that *mitzvos* have this
power, to endow us with a glimmer of G-d's holiness.

PRACTICAL LESSONS

A *mitzvah* is an
intimate bond with
G-d, like a "hug."
Torah is like a "kiss."

Through Torah and
mitzvos, it is as if
you are married to
G-d, and share the
intimacy of husband
and wife. G-d lifts
you to the level of His
Supernal holiness.

וְזֶהוּ שֶׁאוֹמְרִים אֲשֶׁר קִדְּשָׁנוּ בְּמִצְוֹתָיו — **And this is why we say** in the traditional
text of the blessing before a *mitzvah,* "*Blessed are you G-d... **who has sanctified
us (kidishanu) with His mitzvos,***" שֶׁהֶעֱלָנוּ לְמַעֲלַת קוֹדֶשׁ הָעֶלְיוֹן בָּרוּךְ הוּא — which
implies **that He has elevated us to the level of** His blessed, ***"supernal holiness"***

העליון ב"ה שהיא קדושתו של הקב"ה בכבודו ובעצמו
וקדושה היא לשון הבדלה מה שהקב"ה הוא מובדל
מהעולמות והיא בחי' סובב כל עלמין מה שאינו יכול
להתלבש בהן. כי ע"י יחוד הנפש והתכללותה באור
א"ס ב"ה הרי היא במעלת ומדרגת קדושת א"ס ב"ה
ממש מאחר שמתייחדת ומתכללת בו ית' והיו לאחדים

שֶׁהִיא קְדוּשָׁתוֹ שֶׁל הַקָּדוֹשׁ בָּרוּךְ הוּא בִּכְבוֹדוֹ (Zohar 3, 297a; see chapter 27, p. 316),
וּבְעַצְמוֹ — **which is the holiness of the Blessed Holy One, Himself in His glory.**

The literal translation of *kidishanu*, is that G-d has *sanctified* us through the *mitzvos*. If we combine this with the allegorical interpretation, that He has *married* us through the *mitzvos* (becoming one with Him), it follows that He has sanctified us with some of His own holiness.

But what exactly is "holiness"? And how does G-d's "Supernal holiness" differ from the holiness of other entities?

וּקְדוּשָׁה הִיא לְשׁוֹן הַבְדָּלָה — Generally speaking, **the term "holiness" (*kedushah*) is a term meaning "separation"** and "distinction" from others (*Rashi, Leviticus* 19:2).

מַה שֶׁהַקָּדוֹשׁ בָּרוּךְ הוּא הוּא מוּבְדָּל מֵהָעוֹלָמוֹת — In reference to G-d, *kedushah* refers to **how the Blessed Holy One is separate from the** spiritual and physical **worlds,** וְהִיא בְּחִינַת סוֹבֵב כָּל עָלְמִין — His "holiness," **referring to the level at which "He transcends all worlds"** (see *Zohar* 3, 225a), מַה שֶׁאֵינוֹ יָכוֹל לְהִתְלַבֵּשׁ בָּהֶן — an energy so transcendent **that it cannot become enmeshed** in the worlds, since it has nothing in common with them.

PRACTICAL LESSONS

To be holy means to be separate. G-d is holy because His Infinite Light doesn't "fit" into the worlds.

G-d's energy is found in the universe in two general forms: *immanent* and *transcendent*. The immanent energy is sufficiently diminished and filtered to be accessible to the creations. The transcendent energy is relatively undiminished and is inherently unavailable. The *Tanya* clarifies here that when we speak of G-d's unique holiness (separateness), it refers to His transcendent energy.

Nevertheless, G-d planted this inherently transcendent energy into the *mitzvos*, making it accessible to us. That is to say, He empowered us to attain some of His holiness.

כִּי עַל יְדֵי יִחוּד הַנֶּפֶשׁ וְהִתְכַּלְלוּתָהּ בְּאוֹר אֵין סוֹף בָּרוּךְ הוּא — **Since through uniting your soul with the Blessed Infinite Light and becoming absorbed in it** through *mitzvos*, הֲרֵי הִיא בְּמַעֲלַת וּמַדְרֵגַת קְדוּשַׁת אֵין סוֹף בָּרוּךְ הוּא מַמָּשׁ — **you actually attain the status and level of the Blessed Infinite One's holiness,** מֵאַחַר שֶׁמִּתְיַיחֶדֶת וּמִתְכַּלֶּלֶת בּוֹ יִתְבָּרֵךְ וְהָיוּ לַאֲחָדִים מַמָּשׁ — **since you are merged with, and absorbed in Him, and you are utterly one.**

ממש. וז"ש והייתם לי קדושים כי קדוש אני ה' ואבדיל
אתכם מן העמים להיות לי ואומר ועשיתם את כל
מצותי והייתם קדושים לאלהיכם אני ה' אלהיכם וגו'
פי' כי ע"י קיום המצות הריני אלוה שלכם כמו אלהי
אברהם אלהי יצחק וכו' שנקרא כן מפני שהאבות היו
בחי' מרכבה לו ית' ובטלים ונכללים באורו. וככה
הוא בכל נפש מישראל בשעת עסק התורה והמצות

The term *kidishanu*, then, has taught us two things about our relationship with G-d. 1.) We are "married" to (joined with) Him; and 2.) We have a separateness from the world ("holiness") like Him. The first quality (marriage; connection), is largely the result of *positive commands* that bind us to G-d. The second quality (separateness) is achieved through being careful not to transgress any *prohibitions* of the Torah, separating ourselves from the world (*Notes on Tanya*).

And — וְזֶהוּ שֶׁכָּתוּב וִהְיִיתֶם לִי קְדֹשִׁים כִּי קָדוֹשׁ אֲנִי ה' וָאַבְדִּיל אֶתְכֶם מִן הָעַמִּים לִהְיוֹת לִי **this** unique holiness (transcendent energy), made available though the *mitzvos*, **is expressed by the verse, "*You should be holy for Me, for I, G-d, am holy, and I have distinguished you from the nations, to be Mine*"** (*Leviticus* 20:26).

In our parable, the king took the lowly man "*to a place where no servant or minister may enter.*" We see now that this hints to the "supernal holiness" which comes exclusively through the *mitzvos* and distinguishes Israel from the nations.

The unique relationship between G-d and Israel is highlighted by another verse.

Another — וְאוֹמֵר וַעֲשִׂיתֶם אֶת כָּל מִצְוֹתַי וִהְיִיתֶם קְדֹשִׁים לֵאלֹהֵיכֶם אֲנִי ה' אֱלֹהֵיכֶם וְגוֹ' **verse states, "*You will perform all My commandments and you will be holy to your G-d; I am G-d, your G-d etc.,*"** (*Numbers* 15:40-41).

Here Scripture adds that through observing *mitzvos*, Israel will be "holy to *your* G-d." In other words G-d becomes "ours," so to speak.

This means that G-d is telling us: פֵּירוּשׁ כִּי עַל יְדֵי קִיּוּם הַמִּצְוֹת הֲרֵינִי אֱלוֹהַּ שֶׁלָּכֶם **"Through the observance of *mitzvos*, I will be *your* G-d,"** כְּמוֹ אֱלֹהֵי אַבְרָהָם אֱלֹהֵי **— as in, "*the G-d of Avraham, the G-d of Yitzchak etc.,*"** (*Liturgy, Amidah*). יִצְחָק וְכוּ'

The — שֶׁנִּקְרָא כֵּן מִפְּנֵי שֶׁהָאָבוֹת הָיוּ בְּחִינַת מֶרְכָּבָה לוֹ יִתְבָּרֵךְ וּבְטֵלִים וְנִכְלָלִים בְּאוֹרוֹ **Patriarchs are referred to** by G-d **in this** personal **way because they were a "chariot" to G-d** (see p. 463), **voided** (of ego) **and absorbed in His "light,"** וְכָכָה הוּא בְּכָל נֶפֶשׁ מִיִּשְׂרָאֵל בִּשְׁעַת עֵסֶק הַתּוֹרָה וְהַמִּצְוֹת **— but the same is true of every soul in Israel, at the time when it observes Torah and *mitzvos*,** because the light in each *mitzvah* lifts the soul to that level.

A *mitzvah* has an implanted light sufficient to lift us up (momentarily) to the level which the Patriarchs achieved through their spiritual work.

ולכן חייבו רז"ל לקום ולעמוד מפני כל עוסק במצוה
אף אם הוא בור ועם הארץ והיינו מפני ה' השוכן
ומתלבש בנפשו בשעה זו רק שאין נפשו מרגשת
מפני מסך החומר הגופני שלא נזדכך ומחשיך עיני

The Patriarchs were able to achieve this intimate union with G-d "all their days" and in "all their limbs" (see above, pp. 259, 379). We can only achieve it: a.) at the moment we observe a *mitzvah*, and b.) with the particular limb(s) which the *mitzvah* involves. But the *quality* of the connection is the same; it's a complete merging and union with the Blessed Infinite Light.

This principle, that a *mitzvah* will temporarily grant us some of G-d's "Supernal holiness," will help us appreciate a point of Jewish Law.

And that's — וְלָכֵן חִייְבוּ רַבּוֹתֵינוּ זִכְרוֹנָם לִבְרָכָה לָקוּם וְלַעֲמוֹד מִפְּנֵי כָּל עוֹסֵק בְּמִצְוָה — **why our Sages of blessed memory required us to rise and remain standing before anyone performing a *mitzvah*** (Jerusalem Talmud, *Bikurim* 3:3), אַף אִם הוּא בּוּר וְעַם הָאָרֶץ — **even if** the one observing the *mitzvah* is **a morally uncultivated person or ignorant** of Jewish law.

If this person has neither ethical nor intellectual achievements, why would the Sages insist that we stand in his presence?

וְהַיְינוּ מִפְּנֵי ה' הַשּׁוֹכֵן וּמִתְלַבֵּשׁ בְּנַפְשׁוֹ בְּשָׁעָה זוֹ — You must stand before such a person **because G-d rests and is present tangibly in his soul *at that moment*,** when he performs the *mitzvah*.

When a "morally uncultivated and ignorant" person performs a *mitzvah*, G-d's transcendent light is present momentarily in his soul. Out of respect for that, the Sages required you to rise. You're not standing for the person, but for the Divine "light" shining in His soul at that moment.

SECTION FIVE: WHY DON'T YOU FEEL G-D "HUGGING" YOU?

If you really do receive a direct revelation of G-d's Supernal holiness "present tangibly" in your soul when performing a *mitzvah*, why don't you feel it?

Only your soul doesn't feel it, רַק שֶׁאֵין נַפְשׁוֹ מַרְגֶּשֶׁת מִפְּנֵי מָסָךְ הַחוֹמֶר הַגּוּפָנִי שֶׁלֹּא נִזְדַּכֵּךְ וּמַחֲשִׁיךְ עֵינֵי הַנֶּפֶשׁ מֵרְאוֹת מַרְאוֹת אֱלֹהִים — **because of the unrefined "veil" of your body's physical matter, which obstructs the "eyes" of your soul from *"seeing visions of G-d"*** (Ezekiel 1:1).

This notion of physical matter posing a "veil" which obstructs the soul from "seeing" Divine revelation, was taught by *Rambam* in his *Guide for the Perplexed*.

"Matter is a strong 'veil,' preventing the apprehension of that which is separate from matter as it truly is. It does this even if it is the noblest and purest matter, I mean to say even if it is the matter of the heavenly spheres. All the more so is

הנפש מראות אלהים כמו האבות וכיוצא בהן
שראו עולמם בחייהם. וז"ש אסף ברוח הקדש בעד
כל כנסת ישראל שבגולה ואני בער ולא אדע בהמות
הייתי עמך ואני תמיד עמך. כלומר שאע"פ שאני
כבהמה בהיותי עמך ולא אדע ולא ארגיש בנפשי יחוד

this true for the dark and turbid matter that is ours. Hence, whenever our intellect aspires to apprehend G-d or one of the (separate) intellects, there will be this great veil interposed between the two" (Guide 3, 9).

כְּמוֹ הָאָבוֹת וְכַיּוֹצֵא בָּהֶן שֶׁרָאוּ עוֹלָמָם בְּחַיֵּיהֶם — Because of this, you do not see Divine revelation **like the Patriarchs and others, who** *"saw their (future)* **world in their life-** *time"* (Talmud, Brachos 17a).

A few exceptional figures, such as the Patriarchs, did succeed in refining their physical bodies enough to perceive lofty visions. But this is definitely the exception, not the rule.

12TH IYAR REGULAR | 9TH IYAR LEAP

This phenomenon, of being oblivious to the revelations of a *mitzvah*, is especially true in the generations of exile compared with Temple times.

וְזֶהוּ שֶׁאָמַר אָסָף — **And this** idea of Divine revelation being present in the soul (when a *mitzvah* is observed), but not felt, **is what Asaf spoke of** in the following verse, בְּרוּחַ הַקֹּדֶשׁ בְּעַד כָּל כְּנֶסֶת יִשְׂרָאֵל שֶׁבַּגּוֹלָה — and even though he said it in Temple times, when Israel were on a spiritual high, he was actually speaking of the future **by means of Divine Inspiration, on behalf of all the Jewish people** later on **in exile,** who would be in a spiritually desensitized state.

וַאֲנִי בַעַר וְלֹא אֵדַע בְּהֵמוֹת הָיִיתִי עִמָּךְ וַאֲנִי תָּמִיד עִמָּךְ — Asaf said, *"And I was a fool, without da'as, I behaved like animals towards You; yet I was always with You"* (Psalms 73:22-23).

As we have learned, the soul's power of *da'as* is the source of all feeling and emotion, because it renders ideas personally relevant (see chapter 3, pp. 62-3). Asaf bemoaned, on behalf of the Jewish people in exile whose spiritual sensitivities would be weak, that they wouldn't feel the Divine light in a *mitzvah* because they lacked *da'as* ("like an animal").

כְּלוֹמַר שֶׁאַף עַל פִּי שֶׁאֲנִי כַּבְּהֵמָה בִּהְיוֹתִי עִמָּךְ וְלֹא אֵדַע — The verse **means to say that even though I was like an animal when I was with You,** because I was **without** *da'as*, וְלֹא אַרְגִּישׁ בְּנַפְשִׁי זֶה — **and I didn't feel this union** with You **in my soul** which takes place when observing a *mitzvah*, I was nevertheless still connected to You through the *mitzvah*.

Before continuing to explain the second half of the verse, the *Tanya* recaps briefly what we have learned about the experience of *da'as* generating the feelings of reverence and love of G-d.

66B

זה שתפול עליה אימתה ופחד תחלה ואח"כ אהבה
רבה בתענוגים או כרשפי אש כמדת הצדיקי' שנזדכך
חומרם וכנודע שדעת הוא לשון הרגשה בנפש והוא
כולל חסד וגבורה. אעפ"כ אני תמיד עמך כי אין
החומר מונע יחוד הנפש באור א"ס ב"ה הממלא כל
עלמין וכמ"ש גם חושך לא יחשיך ממך. ובזה יובן
חומר עונש איסור מלאכה בשבתות וחמץ בפסח

שֶׁתְּפּוֹל עָלֶיהָ אֵימָתָה וָפַחַד תְּחִלָה — Engaging *da'as* would cause that, **firstly, *"fear and trepidation will fall upon her"*** (see *Exodus* 15:16), on my soul, וְאַחַר כָּךְ אַהֲבָה — **followed by great/pleasurable love,** or love like רַבָּה בַּתַּעֲנוּגִים אוֹ כְּרִשְׁפֵּי אֵשׁ *"flaming fire"* (*Song* 8:6), כְּמִדַּת הַצַּדִיקִים שֶׁנִּזְדַּכֵּךְ חוּמְרָם — **like the experience of** *tzadikim,* **who have refined their physical** bodies.

וְכַנּוֹדָע שֶׁדַּעַת הוּא לְשׁוֹן הַרְגָּשָׁה בַּנֶּפֶשׁ — **For, as is known, the term *da'as* implies a feeling of the soul** (see pp. 529-30), וְהוּא כּוֹלֵל חֶסֶד וּגְבוּרָה — **and it includes** the potential for both *chesed* (**love**) and *gevurah* (**reverence and trepidation**) of G-d, depending on the content of your meditation (see chapter 41).

Now we return to explain the second half of the verse said by Asaf "on behalf of all the Jewish people in exile."

אַף עַל פִּי כֵן אֲנִי תָמִיד עִמָּךְ — **Nevertheless,** even though I lacked *da'as,* that didn't prevent my *mitzvos* from forming an intimate connection with You, so, ***"I was always with You,"*** כִּי אֵין הַחוֹמֶר מוֹנֵעַ יְחוּד הַנֶּפֶשׁ בְּאוֹר אֵין סוֹף בָּרוּךְ הוּא — **because the physical matter** of my body **does not prevent my soul from becoming one with the Blessed Infinite Light,** הַמְמַלֵּא כָּל עָלְמִין — **and the "Infinite Light" has the power to** *"fill all worlds,"* and connect even with my physical body, regardless of how spiritually insensitive it may be, וּכְמוֹ שֶׁכָּתוּב גַּם חוֹשֶׁךְ לֹא יַחְשִׁיךְ מִמֶּךָ — **as the verse states,** ***"Even darkness would not obscure from You"*** (*Psalms* 139:12).

The "darkness" of the unrefined physical body might prevent you from *feeling* the Divine light in a *mitzvah;* but it *"would not obscure from You."* It won't prevent you from *connecting intimately* with G-d through the *mitzvah.* And that's because G-d's light is infinite, so it can connect with anything it chooses, (it *"fills all worlds"*). Even though G-d's light is, in essence, a transcendent and "supernal holiness," it has the power to "fill," and be tangibly present, even in your body (although, in a spiritually desensitized state, you may not feel it).

Based on the above discussion, we will be able to make some sense of a perplexing detail in Jewish Law.

וּבָזֶה יוּבַן — **And** the above discussion **will help us to understand,** חוֹמֶר עוֹנֶשׁ אִיסוּר מְלָאכָה בְּשַׁבָּתוֹת וְחָמֵץ בְּפֶסַח — **why the prohibitions of work on the Sabbath and** eating *chametz* (**leaven**) **on Passover, carry such severe** penalties in the Torah (see *Exodus* 12:15; *Numbers* 15:35), הַשָּׁוֶה לְכָל נֶפֶשׁ — **applicable to all** Jews **equally.**

השוה לכל נפש לפי שאף בנפש בור ועם הארץ גמור
מאיר אור קדושת שבת וי"ט ונידון בנפשו בכרת
וסקילה על חילול קדושה זו. וגם משהו חמץ או
טלטול מוקצה פוגם בקדושה שעל נפשו כמו בקדושת
נפש הצדיק כי תורה אחת לכולנו. [ומ"ש בהמות

Perhaps, we could understand why a person *who feels the presence of G-d* might be treated severely for desecrating the Sabbath or Passover. But why should a spiritually numb or religiously ignorant person be given the same treatment?

לְפִי שֶׁאַף בְּנֶפֶשׁ בּוּר וְעַם הָאָרֶץ גָּמוּר מֵאִיר אוֹר קְדוּשַׁת שַׁבָּת וְיוֹם טוֹב — **Because the light and holiness of the Sabbath and Festivals shines even in the soul of the morally uncultivated and the religiously ignorant,** וְנִידּוֹן בְּנַפְשׁוֹ בְּכָרֵת וּסְקִילָה עַל חִילוּל קְדוּשָׁה זוֹ — **and so** *"he's culpable with his soul"* (*Talmud, Bava Kama* 35a) **for profaning this holiness, with** *kares* **("cutting off" of the soul) for eating** *chametz* **on Passover, or stoning for violating the Sabbath.**

While "the morally uncultivated and the religiously ignorant" may not *feel* G-d's presence, they will nevertheless draw the Blessed Infinite Light into their souls through observing a *mitzvah*. Whether they feel it or not, *they are in G-d's presence,* literally, and an act of disrespect to the King is therefore judged with severity.

וְגַם מַשֶּׁהוּ חָמֵץ אוֹ טִלְטוּל מוּקְצֶה — **And even** consuming **a very minuscule amount of** *chametz* (*Shulchan Aruch, Orach Chaim* 447), **or moving a** forbidden *muktzeh* **item** (*Talmud, Shabbos* 123b), פּוֹגֵם בַּקְּדוּשָׁה שֶׁעַל נַפְשׁוֹ — **denigrates the holiness which is** drawn through *mitzvah* observance **upon the soul of** even the morally uncultivated and the religiously ignorant, כְּמוֹ בִּקְדוּשַׁת נֶפֶשׁ הַצַּדִּיק — **just as** it would compromise **the holiness of a** *tzadik's* **soul,** כִּי תּוֹרָה אַחַת לְכוּלָּנוּ — **because we all have** *"one Torah and one law"* (*Numbers* 15:16).

The *tzadik* and "the morally uncultivated" both draw *the same* Blessed Infinite Light into their souls through their *mitzvah* observance. They differ only in their *experience* of that Light, whether they feel it or not.

SECTION SIX: DON'T FEEL BAD ABOUT YOUR LACK OF FEELING

This notion, that G-d's light "rests and is present tangibly" (*shochein u-mislabeish*) in your soul and yet you can't feel it, is still difficult to fully understand. If you can't feel it, then how is it "present tangibly"?

To clarify this issue further, the *Tanya* will offer an esoteric commentary on the above verse, *"And I was a fool, without da'as, I behaved like animals towards You."*

[וּמַה שֶׁכָּתוּב בְּהֵמוֹת לְשׁוֹן רַבִּים לְרַמֵּז — **And the reason why the verse states "animals" in the plural,** which seems inconsistent, since the rest of the verse is phrased in the singular, **is to hint** that all types of *da'as,* even in their most sublime forms, are deficient like an animal.

לשון רבים לרמז כי לפניו ית׳ גם בחי׳ דעת העליון
הכולל חו״ג נדמה כבהמות ועשייה גופנית לגבי אור

Compared to the *da'as* of a *tzadik*, your *da'as* feels deficient. A *tzadik's da'as* generates a powerful feeling of love and reverence for G-d all the time; your *da'as* is challenged to generate even a moderate feeling.

But such deficiencies are *relative*. The *da'as* of an embodied *tzadik's* soul here on earth can't be compared to the *da'as* of that soul when it was disembodied in heaven, before the *tzadik* was born. And even the *da'as* of a disembodied *tzadik's* soul can't be compared to the *da'as* of the World of *Atzilus*, which is the *da'as* of the Creator.

And, as we learned in chapter 42, even in the Creator's *da'as* there are different levels. There is the "normative" *da'as* of the World of *Atzilus*, but we also know of a "Supernal *da'as*" (*da'as Ha-Elyon*), which can channel energies from *above* the World of *Atzilus*.

The *Tanya* will now make the striking assertion that, from a certain perspective, all forms of *da'as* are deficient, even "Supernal *da'as*"!

כִּי לְפָנָיו יִתְבָּרֵךְ גַּם בְּחִינַת דַּעַת הָעֶלְיוֹן — **Because, before G-d Himself, even the level of Supernal *da'as*,** is deficient.

G-d's energies (*sefiros*) of *da'as* did not always exist. They were *emanated* by Him as part of the creative process. So even "Supernal *da'as*" can be seen in two radically different ways, depending on the perspective. From our point of view, "Supernal *da'as*" is a profoundly holy energy, intimately bound with G-d Himself as a *Divine* attribute. But from the Infinite Light's perspective, it's just something He made, just as He made stones and potatoes.

הַכּוֹלֵל חֶסֶד וּגְבוּרָה — And this is despite the fact that "Supernal *da'as*" **contains** the potential for revealed, palpable energies of **chesed** and **gevurah.**

You feel that your *da'as* is deficient because it doesn't produce any palpable love (*chesed*) or reverence (*gevurah*) of G-d. But you should know that even "Supernal *da'as*" which *does* produce *chesed* and *gevurah,* is still deficient, from a certain perspective.

נִדְמֶה כִּבְהֵמוֹת וַעֲשִׂיָּיה גוּפָנִית לְגַבֵּי אוֹר אֵין סוֹף — **Compared to the Infinite Light,** "Supernal *da'as*" **appears** as low **as "animals" and bodily movement.**

From the Blessed Infinite Light's perspective, all material and spiritual things in the universe, even the Divine energies (attributes) that He emanated (such as "Supernal *da'as*"), are equally insignificant. He made them all, and none of them could exist without Him.

Our verse hints to this point by phrasing "animals," a term which alludes to the deficiency of *da'as,* in the plural. The suggestion is: Don't think just *your da'as* is

א״ס כמ״ש כולם בחכמה עשית ונק׳ בהמה רבה כמ״ש

a deficient "vessel" to express G-d's light; all forms of *da'as* have this problem, to some degree or another, even the most pristine, "Supernal *da'as*."

The *Tanya* now cites a verse which, in its Chasidic interpretation, points to the insignificance of all creations and emanations.

כְּמוֹ שֶׁכָּתוּב כּוּלָם בְּחָכְמָה עָשִׂיתָ — **As the verse states, "You made them all with wisdom (chochmah)"** (*Psalms* 104:24).

The verse seems to connect the most sublime entity in the universe, *chochmah* (of the highest world, *Atzilus*) with the lowest thing in the universe, physical action (*"You made them all"*). This hints to the fact that, from the Infinite Light's perspective, both *chochmah* and the physical world are of *equal insignificance* (see "note" in chapter 2, pp. 46-48).

We have explained that the term "animals" in the verse, *"I behaved like animals towards You"* hints to "Supernal *da'as*." The *Tanya* notes that this point is clarified by other texts.

וְנִקְרָא בְּהֵמָה רַבָּה — In Chabad thought, "Supernal *da'as*" is sometimes **referred to by the term "great animal"** (*Jonah* 4:11), כְּמוֹ שֶׁנִּתְבָּאֵר בְּמָקוֹם אַחֵר — **as is explained elsewhere** (see *Likutei Torah, Leviticus* 35d; *Deuteronomy* 13c-d).

As we discussed in chapter 42 (pp. 525-6), Supernal *da'as* can enable you to feel the supra-rational desires of your soul without any substantive intellectual pondering first. That's why it's sometimes referred to as an "animal," because animals act out of emotional impulse and not logic. But it's a *"great* animal" because this energy is leading you to more lofty and spiritual aspirations, away from the more physical concerns of an ordinary animal.

The *Tanya* cites a further teaching about the spiritual significance of the term "animal."

וְהוּא שֵׁם בַּ״ן בְּגִימַטְרִיָּא בְּהֵמָ״ה — **And** the term *behemah* ("animal") **is associated with G-d's Name,** when spelled in *plene* form, which has the *gematria* (numerical equivalent) **of 52 (Ba"N), the same** *gematria* **as the word** *BeHeMaH* (Rabbi Chaim Vital, *Etz Chaim,* 48:4).

Gematria is a system of Rabbinic interpretation, based on the numerical value assigned to each Hebrew letter-consonant. The word *BeHeMaH* (*beis–hei–mem–hei*), has the total numerical value of (2 plus 5, plus 40, plus 5, equals) 52.

Gematria is applied extensively in the Kabbalah to G-d's name, the Tetragrammaton (*yud–hei–vav–hei*), to demonstrate the presence of different Divine energies at work. When written in *plene* or "expanded" form (where each of the four letters is spelled out in full, as if it were a word), the Tetragrammaton can be spelled in many different ways. For example, the "word" *hei* could be spelled *hei-alef, hei-hei,* or *hei-yud. Vav* could be spelled *vav-alef-vav, vav-yud-vav,* or *vav-vav.* This creates the

בְּמ"א. וְהוּא שֵׁם בַּ"ן בְּגִימַ' בַּהמַ"ה שֶׁלִּפְנֵי הָאֲצִילוּת]:

possibility for spelling the Tetratgrammaton in 27 different ways, with 13 different numerical values!

Particular significance is attributed to the plene spellings with the values of 72 (A"B), 63 (Sa"G), 45 (Ma"H) and 52 (Ba"N), which are associated with the energies of *chochmah, binah,* Divine emotions, and *malchus,* respectively.

The *Tanya* (following *Etz Chaim*) notes that the word *behemah* ("animal") shares the same numerical value as the Divine Name Ba"N, which corresponds to *malchus.* This alludes to the fact that *malchus* is the *lowest* Divine energy of the World of *Atzilus,* hinted to by the *sub-human* status of "animal."

שֶׁלִּפְנֵי הָאֲצִילוּת] — But in this discussion we are speaking, not of *Atzilus,* but of the "Great Animal" **which precedes *Atzilus.***

In another configuration, Ma"H is symbolic of the World of *Atzilus* in general, and BaN suggestive of the more raw, primordial energies which are *above Atzilus* (in the realm of *tohu* or "chaos"). This closely resembles our discussion of the "Great Animal" type of emotions described above (see Rabbi Shneur Zalman, *Ma'amarei Admor Ha-Zaken,* 5569, p. 82).

CHAPTER 47

YOUR DAILY EXODUS FROM EGYPT
SECTION ONE: TO ESCAPE THE BODY'S "IMPRISONMENT"

13TH IYAR REGULAR | 10TH IYAR LEAP

After guiding us through various meditative paths to generate feelings for G-d, in chapters 41-45, the *Tanya* introduced a new method in chapter 46, of *mirroring* emotions for G-d. Since the human heart naturally mirrors any love it receives, the *Tanya* suggested we contemplate the great love G-d has shown for us, which would produce a reciprocal love for Him in our hearts.

G-d's love, we learned, was shown to us as a people at the Exodus from Egypt and the giving of the Torah at Sinai. When G-d took us out from Egypt, it was as if a great king came personally from his glorious palace to a "dirty place," to lift us out of the "trash." When He gave us the Torah, it was as if He took us into His personal chamber and gave us 613 ways to be intimate with Him.

Here in chapter 47, the *Tanya* addresses a problem we might have with this narrative. How could the story of the Exodus and Sinai, which happened *in the past to our ancestors,* generate a feeling that G-d loves *us now?*

פרק מז והנה בכל דור ודור וכל יום ויום חייב
אדם לראות עצמו כאילו הוא יצא
היום ממצרים. והיא יציאת נפש האלהית ממאסר
הגוף משכא דחויא ליכלל ביחוד אור א"ס ב"ה ע"י עסק
התורה והמצות בכלל ובפרט בקבלת מלכות שמים

The *Tanya* will answer that, in addition to the historical events, the Exodus and Sinai are, spiritually speaking, an *ongoing* reality. We will learn how to relive the Exodus each day in our personal lives, and experience G-d's love for us in the present (*Notes on Tanya*).

וְהִנֵּה בְּכָל דּוֹר וָדוֹר וְכָל יוֹם וָיוֹם חַיָּיב אָדָם לִרְאוֹת עַצְמוֹ כְּאִילוּ הוּא יָצָא הַיּוֹם מִמִּצְרַיִם — Now, *"In each and every generation, a person must see himself as if he had personally escaped from Egypt,"* (*Mishnah, Pesachim* 116b), **and,** not only in each and every generation, but, **each and every day** (*Deuteronomy* 16:3; *Mishnah, Brachos* 12b).

וְהִיא יְצִיאַת נֶפֶשׁ הָאֱלֹהִית מִמַּאֲסַר הַגּוּף מַשְׁכָא דְחִוְיָא — Our daily, personal "escape from Egypt" **refers to the "escape" of the G-dly soul from its "imprisonment" by the body, "the (Primordial) Serpent's skin"** (*Tikunei Zohar* 10b), לִיכָּלֵל בְּיִחוּד אוֹר אֵין סוֹף בָּרוּךְ הוּא — **to become absorbed in, and unified with, the Blessed Infinite Light.**

The Hebrew word for "Egypt," *Mitzrayim*, is a derivative of *metzar*, which means confinement through limitations. Your personal *Mitzrayim* represents how you are "imprisoned" by limiting energies that hold you back from spiritual growth and connection to G-d.

Most of the time, these "imprisoning" forces are imposed by the body, which has a self-centered energy of *kelipah*. That's why the *Tikunei Zohar* associates the body with the Primordial Serpent, because the body tends to lead you in the wrong direction, away from G-d.

Your daily task, then, is to "escape from *Mitzrayim*" and free yourself from the self-serving orientation of the body, and connect with G-d.

Practically speaking, how do you do that?

עַל יְדֵי עֵסֶק הַתּוֹרָה וְהַמִּצְוֹת בִּכְלָל — **Through Torah study and observance of mitzvos,** which you carry out throughout the day, since Torah and *mitzvos* cause the Infinite Light of G-d to rest in your soul (as we learned in chapter 46).

However, when G-d's light reaches you through a *mitzvah*, you might not be aware of it. Therefore, the *Tanya* now explains, your "escape from *Mitzrayim*" takes place most powerfully at a time when you're conscious of it.

וּבִפְרָט בְּקַבָּלַת מַלְכוּת שָׁמַיִם בִּקְרִיאַת שְׁמַע — **And, in particular** your "escape from *Mitzrayim*" **is when you** consciously *"accept G-d's sovereign authority upon yourself"* (*Talmud, Brachos* 13a), **at the time of reciting the *Shema*,** שֶׁבָּה מְקַבֵּל וּמַמְשִׁיךְ

בק"ש שבה מקבל וממשיך עליו יחודו ית' בפירוש
באמרו ה' אלהינו ה' אחד. וכמש"ל כי אלהינו הוא
כמו אלהי אברהם וכו' לפי שהיה בטל ונכלל ביחוד
אור א"ס ב"ה רק שאברהם זכה לזה במעשיו והילוכו
בקודש ממדרגה למדרגה. כמ"ש ויסע אברם הלוך

עָלָיו יִחוּדוֹ יִתְבָּרֵךְ בְּפֵירוּשׁ — in which you *overtly* accept G-d's unity and consciously "pull" down G-d's Infinite Light **upon yourself,** to become absorbed in, and unified with it, בְּאָמְרוֹ ה' אֱלֹהֵינוּ ה' אֶחָד — **when saying** the words, **"G-d is our G-d, G-d is one"** (Deuteronomy 6:4).

The verse in Deuteronomy seems to state a truth *about* G-d, that He is one. Where do we see our unification *with* G-d in this text?

וּכְמוֹ שֶׁנִּתְבָּאֵר לְעֵיל כִּי אֱלֹהֵינוּ הוּא כְּמוֹ אֱלֹהֵי אַבְרָהָם וְכוּ' — **And, as explained above** in the previous chapter (p. 600), **that** the phrase *"G-d is our G-d,"* is a personal association with the Almighty, **as in "the G-d of Abraham etc.,"** (Liturgy, Amidah), לְפִי שֶׁהָיָה בָּטֵל וְנִכְלָל בְּיִחוּד אוֹר אֵין סוֹף בָּרוּךְ הוּא — because when you "accept the sovereign authority of G-d upon yourself" your ego **is voided and you become absorbed in the oneness of the Blessed Infinite Light,** like Avraham was, all his days.

"G-d is our G-d" doesn't mean that we own G-d; that would be the ego speaking. On the contrary, it means that we are so utterly devoted to Him and devoid of ego, that we belong to Him. He's willing to call Himself, "Avraham's (and his children's) G-d," because when it comes to worshiping G-d, Avraham was utterly devoted.

רַק שֶׁאַבְרָהָם זָכָה לָזֶה בְּמַעֲשָׂיו וְהִילוּכוֹ בַּקּוֹדֶשׁ מִמַּדְרֵגָה לְמַדְרֵגָה — **Only,** unlike us, **Avraham merited this** personal association with G-d **through his own acts** of worship, **advancing in holiness, level upon level,** כְּמוֹ שֶׁכָּתוּב וַיִּסַּע אַבְרָם הָלוֹךְ וְנָסוֹעַ וְגוֹ' — as the verse hints, **"And Avram journeyed onward in stages etc.,"** (Genesis 12:9).

According to the *Zohar,* the Torah's description of Avraham's geographic advancement hints to his spiritual growth: *"He accepted the sovereign authority of G-d, with all its linked rungs, and then he knew that the Blessed Holy One rules over all... Then Avraham was crowned from rung to rung... as the verse states, 'And Avram journeyed onward in stages'"* (Zohar 1, 80a).

PRACTICAL LESSONS

You "escape from Egypt" every day when you release yourself from the self-centered energy of your body and become absorbed in G-d's Infinite Light.

This happens any time you do a *mitzvah,* but be aware of it especially when reciting the *Shema.*

When you say the words, *"G-d is our G-d, G-d is one,"* think how your ego is being voided as you are absorbed in the oneness of the Blessed Infinite Light.

ונסוע וגו': אבל אנחנו ירושה ומתנה היא לנו שנתן
לנו את תורתו והלביש בה רצונו וחכמתו ית' המיוחדים   67A
במהותו ועצמותו ית' בתכלית היחוד והרי זה כאלו נתן
לנו את עצמו כביכול. כמ"ש בז"הק ע"פ ויקחו לי
תרומה [דלי כלומר אותי והל"ל ותרומה אלא משום

But just because we're descended from Avraham, who worshiped G-d so admirably, doesn't mean that our worship is of the same caliber.

אֲבָל אֲנַחְנוּ יְרוּשָׁה וּמַתָּנָה הִיא לָנוּ — **But as far as we are concerned,** our personal unification with G-d's Infinite Light through the Torah **is,** not something we've earned through our own merits, but an "inheritance" (*Deuteronomy* 33:4), **and a "gift" (*matanah*) to us** (*Talmud Brachos* 5a; *Nedarim* 38a), שֶׁנָּתַן לָנוּ אֶת תּוֹרָתוֹ — that "He gave (natan) us His Torah" (*Liturgy, Blessings on the Torah*).

Our "inheritance" and "gift" is the opportunity to connect with the unveiled, Blessed Infinite Light of G-d, through studying and observing the Torah.

וְהִלְבִּישׁ בָּהּ רְצוֹנוֹ וְחָכְמָתוֹ יִתְבָּרֵךְ — **And He implanted His blessed will and wisdom** in the Torah, הַמְיוּחָדִים בְּמַהוּתוֹ וְעַצְמוּתוֹ יִתְבָּרֵךְ בְּתַכְלִית הַיִּחוּד — that will and wisdom **being one with His very essence and being, in total unity,** וַהֲרֵי זֶה כְּאִלּוּ נָתַן לָנוּ אֶת עַצְמוֹ כִּבְיָכוֹל — **and so it's as if He gave us His own very self, so to speak.**

The *Tanya's* emphasis that, in giving the Torah "it's as if He gave us His own very self" is echoed in the *Talmudic* teaching that *anochi* ("I"), the first word of the Ten Commandments, is an acronym for *ana nafshi kesavis yehavis*, *"with My soul I have written, have given"* (*Talmud, Shabbos* 105a, according to text of *Ein Ya'akov*). With this statement G-d declared that the Torah is a direct expression of His inner essence, G-d's very "soul," so to speak. There are no veils here, no layers of emanation, just a pure expression of G-d Himself.

The *Tanya* now cites a teaching of the *Zohar* which stresses this idea.

כְּמוֹ שֶׁכָּתוּב בַּזֹּהַר הַקָּדוֹשׁ עַל פָּסוּק וְיִקְחוּ לִי תְּרוּמָה — **As the holy *Zohar*** (2, 140b comments on the verse, *"They should take Me (ve-yikchu li) an offering"* (*Exodus* 25:2).

Read literally, the instruction "they should take" refers to the "offering" at the end of the verse — the offering is to be taken. ("Me" is the subject *to whom* the offering is "taken.") The verse is commanding us to take an offering for G-d.

But the *Zohar* offers an alternative interpretation, that "Me" is the *object* which is to be "taken." In this reading, the first part of the verse is a complete statement: "They should take Me." We are to "take G-d," so to speak, through observing the Torah, because G-d's light is invested in every *mitzvah*.

[דְּלִי כְּלוֹמַר אוֹתִי — The *Zohar* reads **"Me"** not in the context of "take an offering *for* Me" but as if the verse said, **"take Me, myself."**

But the *Zohar's* reading leaves the end of the verse ("an offering") as an isolated

דכולא חד ע"ש היטב]: וז"ש ותתן לנו ה' אלהינו באהבה כו' כי באור פניך נתת לנו ה' אלהינו כו' ולזה

phrase, devoid of any conjunction with the beginning of the verse. The verse is no longer coherent and effectively reads, "They should take Me; an offering"

וַהֲוָה לֵיה לְמֵימַר וּתְרוּמָה — The *Zohar* therefore asks: According to this reading, **the verse should have placed** a conjunction between the first and second halves of the verse, "They should take Me *and* (they should take) **an offering"?**

The *Zohar* answers that, in this case, the word "and" was *purposefully omitted* from the text, to hint to a deep truth. What can we learn from the missing "and"?

אֶלָּא מִשּׁוּם דְּכוּלָּא חַד — **Rather,** the text purposefully omitted the conjunction ("and") from the phrase *"They should take Me; an offering,"* **in order** to hint that "Me" (G-d) and "an offering" (a *mitzvah*) *"are entirely one* without any separation."

The conjunction "and" indicates that two entities are connected together, but they remain separate and are not merged as one.

If the verse would have used the correct grammar and stated, "Take Me (G-d) *and* an offering (a *mitzvah*)," it would have sent us the incorrect message that G-d is not completely one with a *mitzvah*. So the text introduced a grammatical crudity, omitting the necessary conjunction ("and"), to teach us that G-d/the *mitzvah*, "are entirely one without any separation."

עַיֵּין שָׁם הֵיטֵב] — **Look there carefully** in the *Zohar*.

This notion, that G-d is one with the *mitzvos*, and becomes "ours" so to speak through the "gift" of the Torah, can also be discerned through a creative re-reading of the liturgy.

וְזֶהוּ שֶׁאוֹמְרִים וַתִּתֶּן לָנוּ ה' אֱלֹהֵינוּ בְּאַהֲבָה כו' — **And this is why we say,** *"And You have given us, G-d our G-d, with love etc.,"* (*Liturgy, Festivals*).

Read literally, "G-d our G-d" is a clarification of the word "You," *i.e.*, the one doing the *giving*. It is as if the verse had said: *"G-d our G-d has given us…."*

But in the *Tanya's* reading here, "G-d our G-d" is the *object* being given. *"You have given us G-d our G-d,"* means that You (G-d) have given us the opportunity to have G-d as our own, the possibility of "G-d (becoming) our G-d." It is as if the text stated, *"And (through the intimate bond of a mitzvah) You have given us, (the opportunity to make) G-d our G-d."*

כִּי בְאוֹר פָּנֶיךָ נָתַתָּ לָנוּ ה' אֱלֹהֵינוּ כו' — And similarly *"For with the light of Your face, you gave us, G-d our G-d… the Torah of life"* (*Liturgy, Amidah Prayer*).

This could similarly be read, *"For with the light of Your face, you gave us (the opportunity to make) G-d our G-d."*

וְלָזֶה — **And as a result of this,** since this opportunity to be one with G-d has been given to us all as an "inheritance" and a "gift" that we don't have to earn,

אין מונע לנו מדביקות הנפש ביחודו ואורו ית' אלא הרצון
שאם אין האדם רוצה כלל ח"ו לדבקה בו כו'. אבל
מיד שרוצה ומקבל וממשיך עליו אלהותו ית' ואומר ה'
אלהינו ה' אחד הרי ממילא נכללת נפשו ביחודו ית' דרוח
אייתי רוח ואמשיך רוח והיא בחי' יציאת מצרים ולכן
תקנו פ' יציאת מצרים בשעת ק"ש דוקא. אף שהיא
מצוה בפני עצמה ולא ממצות ק"ש כדאיתא בגמרא
ופוסקים אלא מפני שהן דבר אחד ממש. וכן בסוף פ'

אֵין מוֹנֵעַ לָנוּ מִדְּבֵיקוּת הַנֶּפֶשׁ בְּיִחוּדוֹ וְאוֹרוֹ יִתְבָּרֵךְ אֶלָּא הָרָצוֹן — nothing other than our will is holding us back from connecting our souls with G-d's oneness and light, שֶׁאִם אֵין הָאָדָם רוֹצֶה כְּלָל חַס וְשָׁלוֹם לְדָבְקָה בּוֹ כוּ' — since if a person doesn't want to connect with Him at all, G-d forbid, he has the free will to do so.

אֲבָל מִיַּד שֶׁרוֹצֶה וּמְקַבֵּל וּמַמְשִׁיךְ עָלָיו אֱלֹהוּתוֹ יִתְבָּרֵךְ — But as soon as you desire G-dliness, accept it and "pull" it on yourself, וְאוֹמֵר ה' — and you say, "G-d is our G-d, G-d is one," אֱלֹהֵינוּ ה' אֶחָד הֲרֵי מִמֵּילָא נִכְלֶלֶת נַפְשׁוֹ בְּיִחוּדוֹ יִתְבָּרֵךְ — then without having to reach the level of Avraham, your soul is automatically absorbed in G-d's oneness, דְּרוּחַ אַייתֵי — since "spirit evokes spirit and 'pulls' down spirit" רוּחַ וְאַמְשִׁיךְ רוּחַ (Zohar 2, 162b; 1, 99b), when your "spirit" calls to G-d, He will "pull" His Infinite spirit upon you.

וְהִיא בְּחִינַת יְצִיאַת מִצְרַיִם — And this is a daily experience of "escaping from Egypt," to "desire G-dliness, accept it and 'pull' it on yourself," when reciting the Shema, thereby empowering your G-dly soul to "escape" from the "imprisonment" of your body.

וְלָכֵן תִּקְּנוּ פָּרָשַׁת יְצִיאַת מִצְרַיִם בִּשְׁעַת קְרִיאַת שְׁמַע דַּוְקָא — And that's why the Sages instituted that a third Biblical passage about the Exodus from Egypt (Numbers 15:37-41), is read along with the two paragraphs of Shema (Talmud, Brachos 12b), אַף שֶׁהִיא מִצְוָה בִּפְנֵי עַצְמָהּ וְלֹא מִמִּצְוַת קְרִיאַת שְׁמַע — even though recalling the Exodus from Egypt is a separate mitzvah, and is not part of the mitzvah of reciting the Shema, כְּדְאִיתָא בַּגְּמָרָא וּפוֹסְקִים — as stated in the Talmud and Codes (Brachos 21a; Shulchan Aruch, Orach Chaim 67:1), so why should we bring them together in one reading?

אֶלָּא מִפְּנֵי שֶׁהֵן דָּבָר אֶחָד מַמָּשׁ — Rather, the connection can be appreciated based on the above discussion, because, spiritually speaking, they're the same thing, since our daily "escape from Egypt" is through reciting the Shema.

Spiritually speaking, saying the Shema is the same thing as "escaping Egypt." (That's why we read the two ideas together every day).

This ability to "escape" your limitations and connect with the Infinite Light is G-d's "gift" and "inheritance" to you in the Torah. You don't have to earn it, you just need to do it.

יְצִיאַת מִצְרַיִם מְסַיֵּים ג"כ אֲנִי ה' אֱלֹהֵיכֶם וְהַיְינוּ גַם
כֵּן כְּמַשְׁ"ל:

פֶּרֶק מח וְהִנֵּה כַּאֲשֶׁר יִתְבּוֹנֵן הַמַּשְׂכִּיל בִּגְדוּלַת
אֵ"ס בָּ"ה כִּי כִּשְׁמוֹ כֵּן הוּא אֵ"ס

וְכֵן בְּסוֹף פָּרָשַׁת יְצִיאַת מִצְרַיִם מְסַיֵּים גַם כֵּן אֲנִי ה' אֱלֹהֵיכֶם — **And that's why the passage about the escape from Egypt concludes,** *"I am G-d, your G-d"* (*Numbers* 15:41),
וְהַיְינוּ גַם כֵּן כְּמוֹ שֶׁנִּתְבָּאֵר לְעֵיל — **which is the same concept mentioned above,** that
through the Exodus, G-d becomes "our G-d."

In conclusion: When you will contemplate how, every single day, G-d shows you
the love of a "great king" who comes to a *"lowly man, disheveled and "cast in the
garbage and lifts him out from the dirt"* (pp. 591-2), *i.e.,* from the "imprisonment" of
your body, you will naturally want to mirror a great love back to Him. We will continue to explore this theme in the following chapters.

THE PARADOX OF THE TZIMTZUM

SECTION ONE: WHY DIMINISHMENT OF G-D'S LIGHT IS CRUCIAL

14TH IYAR REGULAR | 11TH IYAR LEAP

Chapter 48 continues a series of discussions, extending from chapter 46 to chapter
49, related to the subject of *mirroring G-d's love.*

In chapter 46 we learned that the heart naturally and instinctively mirrors love, *"As
face reflects face in water, so the heart of man to man"* (*Proverbs* 27:19). The *Tanya*
has offered us various reflections on G-d's love for us, so that our hearts might
mirror back that love to Him. In chapter 46 we considered how G-d's love shown
to us at the Exodus from Egypt was like a "great king" lifting a "lowly man" from the
dirt, bringing him to the palace and showering him with hugs and kisses. In chapter
47, we learned how, spiritually speaking, the Exodus is relevant every day, since it
represents the ongoing opportunity, "gifted" to us from G-d, for personal liberation.

In this chapter we will discuss another dimension of G-d's love for us, how He
made the "effort," so to speak, to diminish His Infinite Light to enable us to exist.

וְהִנֵּה כַּאֲשֶׁר יִתְבּוֹנֵן הַמַּשְׂכִּיל בִּגְדוּלַת אֵין סוֹף בָּרוּךְ הוּא — **Now when an intelligent person will contemplate the greatness of the Blessed Infinite One,** כִּי כִּשְׁמוֹ כֵּן הוּא אֵין

וְאֵין קֵץ וְתַכְלִית כְּלָל לָאוֹר וְחַיּוּת הַמִּתְפַּשֵּׁט מִמֶּנּוּ ית'
בִּרְצוֹנוֹ הַפָּשׁוּט וּמְיוּחָד בְּמַהוּתוֹ וְעַצְמוּתוֹ ית' בְּתַכְלִית
הַיִּחוּד וְאִילּוּ הָיְתָה הַשְׁתַּלְשְׁלוּת הָעוֹלָמוֹת מֵאוֹר א"ס ב"ה
בְּלִי צִמְצוּמִי' רַק כְּסֵדֶר הַמַּדְרֵגוֹת מִמַּדְרֵגָה לְמַדְרֵגָה
בְּדֶרֶךְ עִלָּה וְעָלוּל לֹא הָיָה הָעוה"ז נִבְרָא כְּלָל כְּמוֹ שֶׁהוּא
עַתָּה בִּבְחִי' גָבוּל וְתַכְלִית מֵהָאָרֶץ לָרָקִיעַ מַהֲלַךְ ת"ק
שָׁנָה וְכֵן בֵּין כָּל רָקִיעַ לְרָקִיעַ וְכֵן עוֹבִי כָּל רָקִיעַ וְרָקִיעַ

סוֹף וְאֵין קֵץ וְתַכְלִית כְּלָל לָאוֹר וְחַיּוּת הַמִּתְפַּשֵּׁט מִמֶּנּוּ יִתְבָּרֵךְ — and, as this name sug-gests, **there is no end, finality or limit whatsoever to the light and energy emerging from Him,** the "intelligent person" will realize what a huge gap separates an infinite G-d from this finite world.

Before continuing our discussion, the *Tanya* briefly clarifies an important point re-garding this metaphor of G-d's "light," which is commonly used in Kabbalistic works.

בִּרְצוֹנוֹ הַפָּשׁוּט וּמְיוּחָד בְּמַהוּתוֹ וְעַצְמוּתוֹ יִתְבָּרֵךְ בְּתַכְלִית הַיִּחוּד — This light emerg-ing **through His non-composite will that is united with His essence and being, in complete unity.**

The Kabbalists preferred the metaphor of G-d's "light" (over other terms such as "flow," or "influence") because "light" stresses a *direct connection* and continuity with its source. The light is *"united with His essence and being, in complete unity,"* just as the light which emerges from a bulb is clearly connected with its source.

But, just as a light bulb doesn't *choose* to emit its light, the term "G-d's light" could also send the mistaken impression that G-d was somehow forced to emit this energy. To correct any such impression, the *Tanya* stresses that G-d's light emerged *intentionally, "through His non-composite will."*

Now we return to our main theme, the problem of a finite world emanating from G-d's Infinite Light.

וְאִילּוּ הָיְתָה הַשְׁתַּלְשְׁלוּת הָעוֹלָמוֹת מֵאוֹר אֵין סוֹף בָּרוּךְ הוּא בְּלִי צִמְצוּמִים — And if the **spiritual worlds had unfolded from the Blessed Infinite Light without any** radical **diminishments,** רַק כְּסֵדֶר הַמַּדְרֵגוֹת מִמַּדְרֵגָה לְמַדְרֵגָה בְּדֶרֶךְ עִלָּה וְעָלוּל — and the cre-ation of the spiritual and physical worlds **would have only followed a *sequential,* cause-and-effect process,** where each phase is *relative* to the next, לֹא הָיָה הָעוֹלָם הַזֶּה נִבְרָא כְּלָל כְּמוֹ שֶׁהוּא עַתָּה בִּבְחִינַת גָבוּל וְתַכְלִית — **this world couldn't have been created at all, in its current limited and finite form.**

If you start with an infinite light, and then diminish it by any percentage, you will still be left with infinity. However many *relative* changes you would make, you would never transform the infinite to the finite.

ואפי' עו"הב וג"ע העליון מדור נשמות הצדיקי' הגדולים
והנשמו' עצמן ואצ"ל המלאכי' הן בבחי' גבול ותכלית כי
יש גבול להשגתן באור א"ס ב"ה המאיר עליהן
בהתלבשות חב"ד כו'. ולכן יש גבול להנאתן שנהנין
מזיו השכינה ומתענגין באור ה' כי אין יכולין לקבל
הנאה ותענוג בבחי' א"ס ממש שלא יתבטלו ממציאותן
ויחזרו למקורן. והנה פרטיות הצמצומים איך ומה אין

67B

And — מֵהָאָרֶץ לָרָקִיעַ מַהֲלַךְ ת"ק שָׁנָה וְכֵן בֵּין כָּל רָקִיעַ לְרָקִיעַ וְכֵן עוֹבִי כָּל רָקִיעַ וְרָקִיעַ we see that the universe is finite since *"a journey from the earth to the firmament takes five hundred years, and so too, between each firmament and the one above it,"* and so too, *"the thickness of each firmament"* (*Talmud, Chagigiah* 13a).

While the *Talmud* stresses the immensity of the universe, it also defines and limits it. A journey of "five hundred years" is certainly a vast one, but it is finite.

And even the — וַאֲפִילוּ עוֹלָם הַבָּא וְגַן עֵדֶן הָעֶלְיוֹן מְדוֹר נִשְׁמוֹת הַצַּדִּיקִים הַגְּדוֹלִים world-that-is-coming and the upper chamber of *Gan Eden* (Heaven), where the souls of great *tzadikim* dwell, are limited and finite, וְהַנְּשָׁמוֹת עַצְמָן וְאֵין צָרִיךְ לוֹמַר הַמַּלְאָכִים הֵן בִּבְחִינַת גְּבוּל וְתַכְלִית — and the disembodied souls themselves (and it goes without saying, the angels) are limited and finite.

We know this because there is a limit to their comprehension of the — כִּי יֵשׁ גְּבוּל לְהַשָּׂגָתָן בְּאוֹר אֵין סוֹף בָּרוּךְ הוּא הַמֵּאִיר עֲלֵיהֶן בְּהִתְלַבְּשׁוּת חָכְמָה בִּינָה וָדַעַת כו' Blessed Infinite Light, which shines to them through the limiting filter of *chochmah, binah* and *da'as,* וְלָכֵן יֵשׁ גְּבוּל לַהֲנָאָתָן שֶׁנֶּהֱנִין מִזִּיו הַשְּׁכִינָה וּמִתְעַנְּגִין בְּאוֹר ה', and consequently there's a limit to the pleasure they get from *"basking in a ray of the Divine Presence"* (*Talmud, Brachos* 17a), and enjoying G-d's light (see chapter 39, p. 450*ff.*) כִּי אֵין יְכוֹלִין לְקַבֵּל הֲנָאָה וְתַעֲנוּג בִּבְחִינַת אֵין סוֹף מַמָּשׁ — because they can't actually receive pleasure and enjoyment directly from the Infinite One, שֶׁלֹּא יִתְבַּטְלוּ מִמְּצִיאוּתָן וְיַחְזְרוּ לִמְקוֹרָן — without their sense of independent existence being voided, which would cause them to return to their source in G-d.

The *Talmud* stresses that the souls receive only "a ray" (*ziv*) of the Divine Presence, indicating that their experience is highly limited and filtered. Two reasons are given for this: 1.) The souls access this light through comprehension, which is limited. 2.) If they were given more light, their individuality would be erased and they would simply "dissolve" in G-d.

There is nothing, then, in any of the spiritual or physical worlds that is truly infinite. So, in order for G-d's Infinite Light to be received by the worlds, a radical diminishment of the light was necessary, which we will discuss in the next section.

כאן מקום ביאורם. אך דרך כלל הן הם בחי' הסתר
והעלם המשכת האור והחיות שלא יאיר ויומשך
לתחתונים בבחי' גילוי להתלבש ולהשפיע בהן
ולהחיותם להיות יש מאין. כי אם מעט מזער אור
וחיות בכדי שיהיו בבחי' גבול ותכלית שהיא הארה
מועטת מאד וממש כלא חשיבי לגבי בחי' הארה בלי
גבול ותכלית ואין ביניהם ערך ויחס כלל כנודע פי'

SECTION TWO: THE UNDIMINISHED LIGHT

15TH IYAR REGULAR | 12TH IYAR LEAP

וְהִנֵּה פְּרָטִיּוּת הַצִּמְצוּמִים אֵיךְ וּמָה — **Now, as for the details of these diminishments, the "how's" and the "what's,"** אֵין כָּאן מְקוֹם בֵּיאוּרָם — **here is not the place to elaborate.**

Our discussion here is a practically oriented one. It's aimed at demonstrating how G-d's diminishments were an expression of His love for you, so that you can mirror that love. We won't be carrying out a thorough analysis of the complex and nuanced *tzimtzum* (diminishment) concept; we need just enough detail to help us fulfill our goal.

אַךְ דֶּרֶךְ כְּלָל הֵן הֵם בְּחִינַת הֶסְתֵּר וְהֶעְלֵם הַמְשָׁכַת הָאוֹר וְהַחַיּוּת — **But, generally speaking,** the diminishments **are a hiding and a concealment of G-d's light and energy flow,** שֶׁלֹּא יָאִיר וְיוּמְשַׁךְ לַתַּחְתּוֹנִים בִּבְחִינַת גִּילּוּי — **so that** an Infinite Light **shouldn't flow into, and palpably illuminate, the lower worlds.**

The purpose of the diminishments was to make your existence possible. It's a "restraint out of love" on G-d's part: He held back His light from you so that it wouldn't overwhelm and erase you.

לְהִתְלַבֵּשׁ וּלְהַשְׁפִּיעַ בָּהֶן וּלְהַחֲיוֹתָם לִהְיוֹת יֵשׁ מֵאַיִן — **G-d didn't diminish His light *completely*,** because some light must **flow into and become enmeshed in** the lower worlds **to power them to be something-from-nothing,** otherwise they wouldn't exist at all, כִּי אִם מְעַט מִזְעֵר אוֹר וְחַיּוּת — **but just a tiny, minuscule amount of light and energy** is necessary for this creative process, בִּכְדֵי שֶׁיִּהְיוּ בִּבְחִינַת גְּבוּל וְתַכְלִית — just enough light **so that** the lower worlds **can exist in a limited, finite form.**

We need to have *some* light/energy from G-d, otherwise the world wouldn't exist; but it must be a *radically diminished* light, to make finite existence possible.

The *Tanya* now elaborates upon how "minuscule" the diminished light really is.

שֶׁהִיא הֶאָרָה מוּעֶטֶת מְאֹד — **And this** radically diminished light **is a very small glimmer of light,** וּמַמָּשׁ כְּלָא חֲשִׁיבֵי לְגַבֵּי בְּחִינַת הֶאָרָה בְּלִי גְּבוּל וְתַכְלִית — and it's literally *"considered zero"* (Zohar 1, 11b) **in comparison to** its source, **the unlimited, Infinite**

מלת ערך במספרים שאחד במספר יש לו ערך לגבי
מספר אלף אלפים שהוא חלק אחד מני אלף אלפים
אבל לגבי דבר שהוא בבחי׳ בלי גבול ומספר כלל אין
כנגדו שום ערך במספרים שאפי׳ אלף אלפי אלפים
וריבוא רבבות אינן אפי׳ כערך מספר אחד לגבי אלף
אלפי אלפים וריבוא רבבות אלא כלא ממש חשיבי.
וככה ממש היא בחי׳ ההארה מועטת זו המתלבשת
בעולמות עליונים ותחתונים להשפיע בהם להחיותם
לגבי ערך אור הגנוז ונעלם שהוא בבחי׳ א״ס ואינו

וְאֵין בֵּינֵיהֶם עֵרֶךְ וְיַחַס כְּלָל — and there's no relative-value or comparison between them at all. Light,

כַּנּוֹדָע פֵּירוּשׁ מִלַּת עֵרֶךְ בְּמִסְפָּרִים — Because, mathematically, the term "relative-value" has a straightforward meaning, שֶׁאֶחָד בְּמִסְפָּר יֵשׁ לוֹ עֵרֶךְ לְגַבֵּי מִסְפָּר אֶלֶף אֲלָפִים — where, for example, the number "one" has a relative-value to the number "one million," שֶׁהוּא חֵלֶק אֶחָד מִנִּי אֶלֶף אֲלָפִים — it being a one-millionth part of it, אֲבָל לְגַבֵּי דָּבָר שֶׁהוּא בִּבְחִינַת בְּלִי גְבוּל וּמִסְפָּר כְּלָל אֵין כְּנֶגְדּוֹ שׁוּם עֵרֶךְ בְּמִסְפָּרִים — but compared to something that is infinite and beyond number, it has no relative-value at all, mathematically, שֶׁאֲפִילוּ אֶלֶף אַלְפֵי אֲלָפִים וְרִיבּוֹא רְבָבוֹת — so that even a million or one hundred million compared to infinity, אֵינָן אֲפִילוּ כְּעֵרֶךְ מִסְפָּר אֶחָד לְגַבֵּי — isn't even one millionth or one hundred millionth of infinity, אֶלֶף אַלְפֵי אֲלָפִים וְרִבּוֹא רְבָבוֹת — rather, it's literally "considered zero." אֶלָא כְּלָא מַמָּשׁ חֲשִׁיבֵי

13TH IYAR LEAP

וְכָכָה מַמָּשׁ הִיא בְּחִינַת הַהָאָרָה מוּעֶטֶת זוֹ הַמִּתְלַבֶּשֶׁת בְּעוֹלָמוֹת עֶלְיוֹנִים וְתַחְתּוֹנִים לְהַשְׁפִּיעַ בָּהֶם לְהַחֲיוֹתָם — And it's exactly the same with the minuscule glimmer of G-d's light enmeshed in the upper and lower worlds, through which their life energy flows to them, לְגַבֵּי עֵרֶךְ אוֹר הַגָּנוּז וְנֶעְלָם שֶׁהוּא בִּבְחִינַת אֵין סוֹף — which is "considered zero" in comparison to G-d's hidden and concealed light, which is infinite.

The term "hidden and concealed," used here in reference to the Infinite Light, could be confusing. After all, you can't actually see *any* of G-d's spiritual "light," neither the Infinite Light nor the minuscule and finite light which reaches the worlds. So why does the *Tanya* use the term "hidden and concealed," only in reference to the Infinite Light?

The issue here is not whether the light is visible, but rather, if it is *receivable* and *compatible* with your existence, because in order for your existence to continue every second, you must receive G-d's energizing light. So "hidden and concealed" here means that the light is *unavailable* to you and *incompatible* with your existence.

מתלבש ומשפיע בעולמות בבחי' גילוי להחיותם אלא
מקיף עליהם מלמעלה ונקרא סובב כל עלמין. ואין
הפי' סובב ומקיף מלמעלה בבחי' מקום ח"ו כי לא
שייך כלל בחי' מקום ברוחניות. אלא ר"ל סובב ומקיף
מלמעלה לענין בחי' גילוי השפעה כי ההשפעה שהוא
בבחי' גילוי בעולמו' נקראת בשם הלבשה שמתלבשת
בעולמות כי הם מלבישים ומשיגים ההשפעה שמקבלים
משא"כ ההשפעה שאינה בבחי' גילוי אלא בהסתר

68A

וְאֵינוֹ מִתְלַבֵּשׁ וּמַשְׁפִּיעַ בָּעוֹלָמוֹת בִּבְחִינַת גִּילוּי לְהַחֲיוֹתָם — The Infinite Light, which is "hidden and concealed," **doesn't become enmeshed in the worlds palpably, to provide them with energy.**

Obviously, G-d's Infinite Light is everywhere: right here, right now. It's in the room with you and it's inside your body. The problem is that it just passes right through you, like a radio wave, because you cannot receive it.

To depict this phenomenon, the *Zohar* describes this light as "circling" or "encompassing," not because it's really outside you, but to stress how it's inaccessible to you.

אֶלָּא מַקִּיף עֲלֵיהֶם מִלְמַעְלָה — **Rather** the Infinite Light is often described as **"encompassing"** the worlds in a disengaged fashion, as if it were **above** them (see p. 265), וְנִקְרָא סוֹבֵב כָּל עָלְמִין — **and it's called** by the *Zohar*, the light which *"transcends (lit. 'circles') all worlds"* (see *Zohar* 3, 225a).

וְאֵין הַפֵּירוּשׁ סוֹבֵב וּמַקִּיף מִלְמַעְלָה בִּבְחִינַת מָקוֹם — **But this isn't a** *spatial* reference **to something** physically **circling and encompassing from above,** חַס וְשָׁלוֹם — which would imply that G-d isn't present in the world, **G-d forbid,** כִּי לֹא שַׁיָּיךְ כְּלָל — בְּחִינַת מָקוֹם בְּרוּחָנִיּוּת — it was obviously not meant in the spatial sense **because, in spirituality, there is no notion of** physical **space.**

אֶלָּא רוֹצֶה לוֹמַר סוֹבֵב וּמַקִּיף מִלְמַעְלָה לְעִנְיַן בְּחִינַת גִּילוּי הַשְׁפָעָה — **Rather,** the spatial terminology is a metaphor **to imply that** *in terms of palpable flow* it's as if the light was **circling and encompassing from above** without extending below.

The Infinite Light, is, of course, found everywhere. But if we are to speak in terms of where that light/energy can be *received as an accessible flow,* we have to say that it's beyond us, "above" us, so to speak.

כִּי הַהַשְׁפָּעָה שֶׁהִיא בִּבְחִינַת גִּילוּי בָּעוֹלָמוֹת נִקְרֵאת בְּשֵׁם הַלְבָּשָׁה — **Because, a flow** which is palpable in the worlds is called "enmeshed," שֶׁמִּתְלַבֶּשֶׁת בָּעוֹלָמוֹת כִּי הֵם — **since it meshes with the worlds, which** מַלְבִּישִׁים וּמַשִּׂיגִים הַהַשְׁפָּעָה שֶׁמְּקַבְּלִים — integrate and grasp the flow that they receive, מַה שֶּׁאֵין כֵּן הַהַשְׁפָּעָה שֶׁאֵינָהּ בִּבְחִינַת — מַה שֶּׁאֵין כֵּן הַהַשְׁפָּעָה שֶׁאֵינָהּ בִּבְחִינַת **integrate and grasp the flow that they receive,** גִּילוּי אֶלָּא בְּהֶסְתֵּר וְהֶעְלֵם וְאֵין הָעוֹלָמוֹת מַשִּׂיגִים מַשִּׂיגִים אוֹתָהּ — **which isn't true with a flow**

והעלם ואין העולמות משיגים אותה אינה נקראת
מתלבשת אלא מקפת וסובבת הלכך מאחר שהעולמות
הם בבחי' גבול ותכלית נמצא שאין השפעת אור א"ס
מתלבש ומתגלה בהם בבחי' גילוי רק מעט מזער
הארה מועטת מצומצמת מאד מאד והיא רק כדי
להחיותם בבחי' גבול ותכלית. אבל עיקר האור בלי
צמצום כ"כ נק' מקיף וסובב מאחר שאין השפעתו
מתגלית בתוכם מאחר שהם בבחי' גבול ותכלית.
והמשל בזה הנה הארץ הלזו הגשמיות אף שמלא כל

that's not palpable to the recipients, **but remains hidden and concealed, unable to be grasped by the worlds,** אֵינָה נִקְרֵאת מִתְלַבֶּשֶׁת אֶלָּא מַקֶּפֶת וְסוֹבֶבֶת — such a flow is not called "enmeshed" but "encompassing" or "encircling."

Now we have clarified the term "encircling," the *Tanya* explains how it is applicable to the Blessed Infinite Light.

הִלְכָךְ מֵאַחַר שֶׁהָעוֹלָמוֹת הֵם בִּבְחִינַת גְּבוּל וְתַכְלִית — **Therefore, since the worlds are limited and *finite*,** נִמְצָא שֶׁאֵין הַשְׁפָּעַת אוֹר אֵין סוֹף מִתְלַבֶּשֶׁת וּמִתְגַּלֶּה בָּהֶם בִּבְחִינַת גִּלּוּי — **it follows that the Blessed *Infinite* Light can't be enmeshed, or palpably revealed, in them.**

רַק מְעַט מִזְעֵר הֶאָרָה מוּעֶטֶת מְצוּמְצֶמֶת מְאֹד מְאֹד — **That is, except for a tiny, minuscule, sliver of light, which is very, very slight and diminished,** וְהִיא רַק כְּדֵי לְהַחֲיוֹתָם — **and this is merely to energize them in a finite and limited** בִּבְחִינַת גְּבוּל וְתַכְלִית **way,** אֲבָל עִיקַר הָאוֹר בְּלִי צִמְצוּם כָּל כָּךְ נִקְרָא מַקִּיף וְסוֹבֵב — **but the primary component of the light, devoid of any significant diminishment, is called "encompassing" or "encircling,"** מֵאַחַר שֶׁאֵין הַשְׁפָּעָתוֹ מִתְגַּלִּית בְּתוֹכָם מֵאַחַר שֶׁהֵם בִּבְחִינַת גְּבוּל וְתַכְלִית — **because it doesn't flow palpably into** the worlds, **which are limited and finite.**

The presence of the Blessed Infinite Light is something of a paradox. The light is "present" and accessible only in a radically diminished form; but the real, undiminished light is "non-present" (and merely "encircles us"), in the sense that it's inaccessible to us. And that's despite the fact that it's really right here.

16TH IYAR REGULAR | 14TH IYAR LEAP

וְהַמָּשָׁל בָּזֶה — **An illustration of this** paradoxical concept of how G-d's Infinite Light is "present" and "non-present" at the same time, הִנֵּה הָאָרֶץ הַלְּזוּ הַגַּשְׁמִית — **can be gleaned from this physical earth.**

As we have discussed in chapter 38, the world's contents can be divided into two general categories: a.) *Non-movers:* objects and plants — neither of which show overt signs of energetic life; and b.) *Movers:* animals and humans — which are clearly alive and soulful, more clearly evidencing the spirit of G-d.

הארץ כבודו. והיינו אור א"ס ב"ה כמ"ש הלא את
השמים ואת הארץ אני מלא נאם ה'. אעפ"כ אין
מתלבש בתוכה בבחי' גילוי ההשפעה רק חיות מעט
מזער בחי' דומם וצומח לבד וכל אור א"ס ב"ה נק' סובב
עליה אף שהוא בתוכה ממש. מאחר שאין השפעתו
מתגלית בה יותר רק משפיע בה בבחי' הסתר והעלם
וכל השפעה שבבחי' הסתר נקרא מקיף מלמעלה כי

("This physical earth," refers to the actual planet itself, composed of inorganic matter and vegetation, *i.e.*, non-movers, which hide G-d's spirit significantly.)

The *Tanya* will now discuss how the Infinite Light is manifest in this most inanimate part of the universe. Again, we will see a paradox of presence/non-presence.

אַף שֶׁמְּלֹא כָל הָאָרֶץ כְּבוֹדוֹ — **While,** on one hand, ***"All the earth is filled with His glory"*** (*Isaiah* 6:3), וְהַיְינוּ אוֹר אֵין סוֹף בָּרוּךְ הוּא — *"His glory"* **referring to** G-d Himself, **the Blessed Infinite Light,** כְּמוֹ שֶׁכָּתוּב הֲלֹא אֶת הַשָּׁמַיִם וְאֶת הָאָרֶץ אֲנִי מָלֵא נְאָם ה' — **as the verse states, '*Do I (personally) not fill heaven and earth?' says G-d*** (*Jeremiah* 23:24), אַף עַל פִּי כֵן אֵין מִתְלַבֵּשׁ בְּתוֹכָה בִּבְחִינַת גִּילוּי הַהַשְׁפָּעָה — **nevertheless,** while the Blessed Infinite Light may fill the world, **its flow doesn't get palpably enmeshed with** the physical earth, רַק חַיּוּת מְעַט מִזְעָר בְּחִינוֹת דּוֹמֵם וְצוֹמֵחַ לְבַד — **except for the tiny, minuscule amount of energy evident in motionless matter and plants,** וְכָל אוֹר אֵין סוֹף בָּרוּךְ הוּא נִקְרָא סוֹבֵב עָלֶיהָ — **and all of the Blessed Infinite Light** in the world is totally inaccessible, so **it's described as "encircling"** the world, אַף שֶׁהוּא בְּתוֹכָה — even though it's actually in the world, מַמָּשׁ — **even though it's actually in** the world, מֵאַחַר שֶׁאֵין הַשְׁפָּעָתוֹ מִתְגַּלֵּית בָּהּ יוֹתֵר — **because its influence is not felt there more palpably,** רַק מַשְׁפִּיעַ בָּהּ בִּבְחִינַת — הֶסְתֵּר וְהֶעְלֵם — **only as a heavily veiled and concealed influence.**

But why should the inaccessible quality of the light be referred to as encompassing *from above*? What does this spatial analogy add?

וְכָל הַשְׁפָּעָה שֶׁבִּבְחִינַת הֶסְתֵּר נִקְרָא מַקִּיף מִלְמַעְלָה — **Any veiled influence is referred to as "encompassing from above,"** כִּי עָלְמָא דְּאִתְכַּסְיָא הוּא לְמַעְלָה בְּמַדְרֵגָה מֵעָלְמָא דְּאִתְגַּלְיָא — **because the "unmanifest world" is above the level of the "manifested world"** (see *Zohar* 1, 18a; 154b; chapter 26, p. 301).

The encircling light is intrinsically aloof from and incompatible with the world. It is from an energy which defies any worldly manifestation. This is the meaning of the term "above" in this context.

SECTION THREE: A PHYSICAL ILLUSTRATION OF "ENCIRCLING"

וּלְקָרֵב אֶל הַשֵּׂכֶל יוֹתֵר — **And to make this easier to understand,** let's offer a physical example.

עָלְמָא דְאִתְכַּסְיָא הוּא לְמַעְלָה בְּמַדְרֵגָה מֵעָלְמָא דְאִתְגַּלְיָא
וְלִקְרַב אֶל הַשֵּׂכֶל יוֹתֵר הוּא בְּדֶרֶךְ מָשָׁל. כְּמוֹ הָאָדָם
שֶׁמְּצַיֵּיר בְּדַעְתּוֹ אֵיזֶה דָבָר שֶׁרָאָה אוֹ שֶׁרוֹאֶה הִנֵּה אַף
שֶׁכָּל גּוּף עֶצֶם הַדָּבָר הַהוּא וְגַבּוֹ וְתוֹכוֹ וְתוֹךְ תּוֹכוֹ כּוּלּוֹ
מְצוּיָּיר בְּדַעְתּוֹ וּמַחֲשַׁבְתּוֹ מִפְּנֵי שֶׁרָאָהוּ כּוּלּוֹ אוֹ שֶׁרוֹאֵהוּ
הִנֵּה נִקְרֵאת דַּעְתּוֹ מַקֶּפֶת הַדָּבָר הַהוּא כּוּלּוֹ. וְהַדָּבָר
הַהוּא מוּקָּף בְּדַעְתּוֹ וּמַחֲשַׁבְתּוֹ רַק שֶׁאֵינוֹ מוּקָּף בְּפוֹעַל
מַמָּשׁ רַק בְּדִמְיוֹן מַחֲשֶׁבֶת הָאָדָם וְדַעְתּוֹ. אֲבָל הַקָּבָּ"ה
דִּכְתִיב בֵּיהּ כִּי לֹא מַחְשְׁבוֹתַי מַחְשְׁבוֹתֵיכֶם כוּ' הֲרֵי

הוּא בְּדֶרֶךְ מָשָׁל כְּמוֹ הָאָדָם שֶׁמְּצַיֵּיר בְּדַעְתּוֹ אֵיזֶה דָבָר שֶׁרָאָה אוֹ שֶׁרוֹאֶה — The simultaneous presence and non-presence of the Infinite Light, which we are depicting with the term "encompass," **is comparable to a person's mind** encompassing an object **when he pictures something that he saw, or is seeing.**

הִנֵּה אַף שֶׁכָּל גּוּף עֶצֶם הַדָּבָר הַהוּא — Now, **even though the entire actual object,** כּוּלּוֹ מְצוּיָּיר בְּדַעְתּוֹ וּמַחֲשַׁבְתּוֹ — **its outside, inside and core,** וְגַבּוֹ וְתוֹכוֹ וְתוֹךְ תּוֹכוֹ — **is pictured completely in his mind and thoughts,** מִפְּנֵי שֶׁרָאָהוּ כּוּלּוֹ אוֹ שֶׁרוֹאֵהוּ — **because he saw, or is seeing, all of it,** nevertheless, the person's knowledge has no *influence* on the actual object, in any way.

הִנֵּה נִקְרֵאת דַּעְתּוֹ מַקֶּפֶת הַדָּבָר הַהוּא כּוּלּוֹ — **So** even though **you could say that his mind "encompasses" every** detail of **that object,** וְהַדָּבָר הַהוּא מוּקָּף בְּדַעְתּוֹ וּמַחֲשַׁבְתּוֹ — **and** you also could say **the object** itself **is absorbed in and engulfed by his mindful thoughts,** because there is a complete picture of the object in his head, nevertheless the object doesn't feel it.

This provides us with a practical example how one thing could "encompass" or "engulf" another and yet have no overt influence on it. Your mind "engulfs" the object, but the object doesn't sense it at all.

רַק שֶׁאֵינוֹ מוּקָּף בְּפוֹעַל מַמָּשׁ — **Nevertheless,** obviously, the object **isn't *really* engulfed** in his mind, **in a physical sense,** רַק בְּדִמְיוֹן מַחֲשֶׁבֶת הָאָדָם וְדַעְתּוֹ — it's only engulfed **in the person's imaginative thoughts in his mind.**

To be precise, it is the *imaginative image* of an object which is engulfed by the mind, not the object itself.

15TH IYAR LEAP

However, this limitation doesn't apply to G-d. When He knows an object, that object is *literally* engulfed by Him (and His knowledge).

דִּכְתִיב בֵּיהּ כִּי לֹא מַחְשְׁבוֹתַי — But with the Blessed Holy One, אֲבָל הַקָּדוֹשׁ בָּרוּךְ הוּא — of whom it is written, *"For My thoughts are not your thoughts* מַחְשְׁבוֹתֵיכֶם גוֹ'

68B מחשבתו ודעתו שיודע כל הנבראים מקפת כל נברא
ונברא מראשו ועד תחתיתו ותוכו ותוך תוכו הכל
בפועל ממש. למשל כדור הארץ הלזו הרי ידיעתו ית'
מקפת כל עובי כדור הארץ וכל אשר בתוכו ותוך תוכו
עד תחתיתו הכל בפועל ממש שהרי ידיעה זו היא
חיות כל עובי כדור הארץ כולו והתהוותו מאין ליש
רק שלא היה מתהוה כמות שהוא עתה בעל גבול
ותכלית וחיות מועטת מאד כדי בחי' דומם וצומח. אם
לא ע"י צמצומים רבים ועצומים שצמצמו האור והחיות
שנתלבש בכדור הארץ להחיותו ולקיימו בבחי' גבול
ותכלית ובבחי' דומם וצומח בלבד אך ידיעתו ית'

— הֲרֵי מַחֲשַׁבְתּוֹ וְדַעְתּוֹ כָּל שֶׁיּוֹדֵעַ כָּל הַנִּבְרָאִים מַקֶּפֶת כָּל נִבְרָא וְנִבְרָא *etc.,"* (Isaiah 55:8), **His mindful thoughts, through which He knows all the creations,** *do* **engulf each individual creation,** מֵרֹאשׁוֹ וְעַד תַּחְתִּיתוֹ וְתוֹכוֹ וְתוֹךְ תּוֹכוֹ — **from top to bottom, its in- side and its core,** הַכֹּל בְּפוֹעַל מַמָּשׁ — **G-d's thoughts engulf them all in actual reality.**

Since G-d and his knowledge is everywhere, when He knows an object, He en- compasses it, literally.

17TH IYAR REGULAR

לְמָשָׁל — **To bring out** this point further, כַּדּוּר הָאָרֶץ הַלֵּזוֹ — consider **this earth's globe,** הֲרֵי יְדִיעָתוֹ יִתְבָּרֵךְ מַקֶּפֶת כָּל עוֹבִי כַּדּוּר הָאָרֶץ — **G-d's knowledge encompass- es the entire diameter of the earth's globe,** וְכָל אֲשֶׁר בְּתוֹכוֹ וְתוֹךְ תּוֹכוֹ עַד תַּחְתִּיתוֹ — **and everything inside it, to its core and extremity,** הַכֹּל בְּפוֹעַל מַמָּשׁ — **all in actual reality,** שֶׁהֲרֵי יְדִיעָה זוֹ הִיא חִיוּת כָּל עוֹבִי כַּדּוּר הָאָרֶץ כּוּלוֹ — **because this "knowledge"** is, in fact, **the sustaining energy of the whole earth in its entirety,** וְהִתְהַוּוּתוֹ מֵאַיִן לְיֵשׁ — **and** it's the power which continually **brings** the earth **into being, some- thing-from-nothing.**

רַק שֶׁלֹּא הָיָה מִתְהַוֶּה כְּמוֹת שֶׁהוּא עַתָּה בַּעַל גְּבוּל וְתַכְלִית — **Only** the earth **couldn't have been created in its present, limited and finite form,** וְחִיּוּת מוּעֶטֶת מְאֹד כְּדֵי — **with** only **a very minuscule energy that allows for mineral and vegetable forms,** בְּחִינוֹת דּוֹמֵם וְצוֹמֵחַ — **if it were not for numerous, profound diminishments,** אִם לֹא עַל יְדֵי צִמְצוּמִים רַבִּים וַעֲצוּמִים — **which diminished the light and energy that is enmeshed in the earth's globe (so as to power and sustain it),** שֶׁצִּמְצְמוּ הָאוֹר וְהַחִיּוּת שֶׁנִּתְלַבֵּשׁ בְּכַדּוּר הָאָרֶץ — **to be ex- tremely limited,** לְהַחֲיוֹתוֹ וּלְקַיְּימוֹ — **enough to power mere motionless objects and plants.** בִּבְחִינַת גְּבוּל וְתַכְלִית — וּבִבְחִינוֹת דּוֹמֵם וְצוֹמֵחַ בִּלְבָד —

On one hand, G-d's "knowledge" represents a diminished light which has been dimmed sufficiently to be compatible with the earth, to be *"enmeshed in the earth's globe, so as to power and sustain it."*

הַמְיוּחֶדֶת בְּמַהוּתוֹ וְעַצְמוּתוֹ. כִּי הוּא הַמַּדָּע וְהוּא הַיּוֹדֵעַ
וְהוּא הַיָּדוּעַ וּבִידִיעַת עַצְמוֹ כִּבְיָכוֹל יוֹדֵעַ כָּל הַנִּבְרָאִים
וְלֹא בִּידִיעָה שֶׁחוּץ מִמֶּנּוּ כִּידִיעַת הָאָדָם. כִּי כּוּלָם
נִמְצָאִים מֵאֲמִיתָתוֹ יִתְבָּרֵךְ. וְדָבָר זֶה אֵין בִּיכוֹלֶת הָאָדָם
לְהַשִּׂיגוֹ עַל בּוּרְיוֹ וְכוּ'*

הֲרֵי יְדִיעָה זוֹ מֵאַחַר שֶׁהִיא
בְּבחִי' אֵ"ס אֵינָה נִקְרָא' בְּשֵׁם

הַגָּהָה
(כמ"ש הרמב"ם ז"ל והסכימו
עמו חכמי הקבלה כמ"ש

16TH IYAR LEAP

אַךְ יְדִיעָתוֹ יִתְבָּרֵךְ הַמְיוּחֶדֶת בְּמַהוּתוֹ וְעַצְמוּתוֹ — **Nevertheless,** this illustration is inaccurate in the sense that **G-d's knowledge,** at its core, **is** not a diminished light, but **one with His essence and being.**

The "light" of G-d's knowledge as it is found in the world, is in an extremely diminished form. In its pre-diminished state, that light is totally one with G-d, and expresses His true infinitude.

The *Tanya* now cites proof that "G-d's knowledge is one with His essence and being," and does not share the same qualities as human knowledge.

כִּי הוּא הַמַּדָּע וְהוּא הַיּוֹדֵעַ וְהוּא הַיָּדוּעַ — **For,** as *Rambam* writes, G-d **is** simultaneously **the power to know, the knower and the known,** וּבִידִיעַת עַצְמוֹ כִּבְיָכוֹל יוֹדֵעַ כָּל הַנִּבְרָאִים — **and through knowing Himself, so to speak, He knows all the creations,** וְלֹא בִּידִיעָה שֶׁחוּץ מִמֶּנּוּ כִּידִיעַת הָאָדָם — **not by knowing something outside of Him, as is the case with human knowledge,** כִּי כּוּלָם נִמְצָאִים מֵאֲמִיתָתוֹ יִתְבָּרֵךְ — **because all existence is actually derived from His true** existence, וְדָבָר זֶה אֵין בִּיכוֹלֶת הָאָדָם לְהַשִּׂיגוֹ עַל בּוּרְיוֹ וְכוּ' — **though this concept defies coherent mortal comprehension, etc.,***(Rambam, Laws of Foundations of the Torah,* 2:9-10; see above chapter 2, pp. 46-7; chapter 42, pp. 536ff.).

On one hand, the light of G-d's knowledge is *compatible* with the earth, energizing it and sustaining it; but on the other hand, that same knowledge is *incompatible* with us, demonstrating uniquely Divine properties.

This paradox is depicted by the analogy of G-d's light "encircling" the world.

הֲרֵי יְדִיעָה זוֹ — **Now this knowledge,** מֵאַחַר שֶׁהִיא בְּבְחִינַת אֵין סוֹף — **since it is from the Infinite One,** אֵינָה נִקְרֵאת בְּשֵׁם מִתְלַבֶּשֶׁת בְּכַדּוּר הָאָרֶץ שֶׁהוּא בַּעַל גְּבוּל וְתַכְלִית

---

*הַגָּהָה — **NOTE.** The following echoes the *Tanya's* comments above in the author's note to chapter 2 (pp. 46-8). See there for further clarification.

כְּמוֹ שֶׁכָּתַב הָרַמְבָּ"ם זִכְרוֹנוֹ לִבְרָכָה — **As** *Rambam,* of blessed memory, wrote, וְהִסְכִּימוּ עִמּוֹ חַכְמֵי הַקַּבָּלָה — **and the sages of the Kabbalah agreed with** *Rambam,* on this point, כְּמוֹ שֶׁכָּתוּב בַּפַּרְדֵּ"ס מֵהָרמַ"ק זִכְרוֹנוֹ לִבְרָכָה — **as Rabbi Moshe Cordovero wrote in** *Pardes* (4:4; 8:13).

מתלבשת בכדור הארץ
שהוא בעל גבול ותכלית
אלא מקפת וסובבת. אף
שידיעה זו כוללת כל עביו
ותוכו בפועל ממש ומהווה אותו עי"ז מאין ליש וכמ"ש
במ"א:

בפרד"ס מהרמ"ק ז"ל וכ"ה לפי
קבלת האר"י ז"ל בסוד הצמצו'
והתלבשות אורות בכלים כמש"ל
פ"ב):

— can't be said to be enmeshed in the earth's globe, which is absolutely finite, אַף שֶׁיְּדִיעָה — rather it "encompasses" and "encircles" the earth, אֶלָּא מַקֶּפֶת וְסוֹבֶבֶת — זוֹ כּוֹלֶלֶת כָּל עָבְיוֹ וְתוֹכוֹ בְּפוֹעַל מַמָּשׁ — despite the fact that the whole diameter of the earth **and its contents are actually subsumed in that knowledge,** וּמְהַוֶּוה אוֹתוֹ עַל יְדֵי זֶה מֵאַיִן לְיֵשׁ — and the diminished "light" of that knowledge **creates the world, something-from-nothing,** וּכְמוֹ שֶׁנִּתְבָּאֵר בְּמָקוֹם אַחֵר — **as explained further elsewhere** (*Tanya, Sha'ar ha-Yichud ve-ha-Emunah,* chapter 7).

The *Tanya* cited *Rambam* to prove that G-d is totally one with his knowledge. This might seem problematic since *Rambam* followed the school of Philosophy which was often at odds with the Kabbalistic school of thought on which Chasidic thought is based. Nevertheless, in this case, *"the sages of the Kabbalah agreed."*

וְכֵן הוּא לְפִי קַבָּלַת הָאֲרִ"י זִכְרוֹנוֹ לִבְרָכָה — **And the same is true according to Lurianic** **Kabbalah,** בְּסוֹד הַצִּמְצוּמִים וְהִתְלַבְּשׁוּת אוֹרוֹת בַּכֵּלִים — *Rambam's* **view** can be con-textualized **through the secret doctrine of infinite "lights" being diminished to the** point that they could **enter** finite **"vessels,"** כְּמוֹ שֶׁנִּתְבָּאֵר לְעֵיל פֶּרֶק ב' — **as explained** **above, in chapter 2.**

פרק מט והנה אף כי פרטי בחי' ההסתר וההעלם
אור א"ס ב"ה בהשתלשלות
העולמות עד שנברא עו"הז הגשמי עצמו מספר ומינים
ממינים שונים כידוע לטועמים מעץ החיים: אך דרך
69A
כלל הם שלשה מיני צמצומים עצומים כלליים.

CHAPTER 49

LOVE, TRANSCENDENCE & RESPONSIBILITY

SECTION ONE: THE "DIMINISHMENTS" AND THEIR PURPOSE

18TH IYAR REGULAR | 17TH IYAR LEAP

Chapter 49 concludes the *Tanya's* guide to mirroring G-d's love, which began in chapter 46. This contemplative technique is based on the verse, *"As face reflects face in water, so the heart of man to man"* (*Proverbs* 27:19), when someone shows you love, your heart will instinctively want to mirror that love back.

In chapters 46-47 the *Tanya* reflected on a number of love gestures which G-d has shown to us, depicting them through a parable of *"a great and influential king who demonstrates his abundant and intense love to an ordinary citizen."*

Chapters 48-49 focus on one particular expression of G-d's love for us: the diminishment (*tzimtzum*) of His Infinite Light, which makes our finite existence possible. Since diminishment is an extremely subtle, abstract concept, the *Tanya* spent chapter 48 explaining some of its finer nuances to us.

Here in chapter 49, the diminishment will be "personalized" as an act of love, carried out by G-d for us.

וְהִנֵּה אַף כִּי פְּרָטֵי בְּחִינוֹת הַהֶסְתֵּר וְהֶעְלֵם אוֹר אֵין סוֹף בָּרוּךְ הוּא בְּהִשְׁתַּלְשְׁלוּת הָעוֹלָמוֹת עַד שֶׁנִּבְרָא עוֹלָם הַזֶּה הַגַּשְׁמִי — Now, while the precise steps by which the Blessed Infinite Light is concealed and hidden through the chain of spiritual **worlds, until the point where this physical world itself is created,** עַצְמוֹ מִסְפַּר — these steps are *"too numerous to recount"* (*Psalms* 40:6), in *quantity,* וּמִינִים מִמִּינִים שׁוֹנִים — **and,** in *quality,* they are **of very many different types,** כַּיָּדוּעַ לַטּוֹעֲמִים מֵעֵץ הַחַיִּים — **as is known to those who have tasted from,** the Kabbalah, **the "Tree of Life,"** אַךְ דֶּרֶךְ כְּלָל — **nevertheless, generally speaking, there** הֵם שְׁלֹשָׁה מִינֵי צִמְצוּמִים עֲצוּמִים כְּלָלִיִּים **are three major, profound diminishments.**

לשלשה מיני עולמות כלליים. ובכל כלל יש ריבוא
רבבות פרטיים. והם שלשה עולמות בי"ע. כי עולם
האצילו' הוא אלהות ממש. וכדי לברוא עולם הבריא'
שהן נשמות ומלאכים עליונים אשר עבודתם לה'
בבחי' חב"ד המתלבשים בהם והם משיגים ומקבלים
מהם היה תחלה צמצום עצום כנ"ל. וכן מבריאה
ליצירה. כי אור מזער המתלבש בעולם הבריא'
עדיין הוא בבחי' א"ס לגבי עולם היצירה. ואי אפשר

The *Tanya* explains its classification of three major diminishments.

לִשְׁלֹשָׁה מִינֵי עוֹלָמוֹת כְּלָלִיִּים — These three major diminishments make possible the three radical transitions that give rise **to the three major** spiritual **worlds,** וּבְכָל כְּלָל יֵשׁ רִבּוֹא רְבָבוֹת פְּרָטִים — **(although within each major category there are hundreds of millions of details),** וְהֵם שְׁלֹשָׁה עוֹלָמוֹת בְּרִיאָה יְצִירָה וַעֲשִׂיָּה — these three spiritual worlds being **the worlds of** *Beriah, Yetzirah* and *Asiyah.*

The emergence of the spiritual worlds is an extremely complex, multifaceted process, but if we are to generalize, three major diminishments of G-d's light were required to produce the three major spiritual worlds.

But what of the fourth and highest world, *Atzilus*?

כִּי עוֹלָם הָאֲצִילוּת הוּא אֱלֹהוּת מַמָּשׁ — No *profound* diminishment was necessary to bring about the highest world of *Atzilus,* **because the world of** *Atzilus* contains no separate entities from G-d and **is actual G-dliness.**

Atzilus is not a *created world,* but a place of direct *Divine emanation.* So while, *Atzilus* does experience some level of diminishment of G-d's light (as a limitless light takes the "form" of ten distinct energies, or *sefiros*), it doesn't require a *"major, profound"* diminishment.

וּכְדֵי לִבְרוֹא עוֹלָם הַבְּרִיאָה — But in order to create the world of *Beriah*, שֶׁהֵן נְשָׁמוֹת וּמַלְאָכִים עֶלְיוֹנִים — which does contains *separate* intelligences, **the souls and higher angels,** אֲשֶׁר עֲבוֹדָתָם לה' בִּבְחִינַת חָכְמָה בִּינָה וְדַעַת הַמִּתְלַבְּשִׁים בָּהֶם — who **worship G-d through the** powers of *chochmah, binah* and *da'as* from *Atzilus* invested in them, וְהֵם מַשִּׂיגִים וּמְקַבְּלִים מֵהֶם — and in order that these *finite* souls and angels should **grasp** these *infinite* powers of *Atzilus* and **receive from them,** הָיָה תְּחִלָּה צִמְצוּם עָצוּם — there had to be first a *profound* diminishment of the lights of *Atzilus,* כַּנִּזְכָּר לְעֵיל — **as mentioned above** (pp. 436, 622).

וְכֵן מִבְּרִיאָה לִיצִירָה — **And, so too, from** the intellectual World of *Beriah* to the emotional World of *Yetzirah* a profound diminishment was required, כִּי אוֹר מְעַט מְזָעֵר הַמִּתְלַבֵּשׁ בְּעוֹלָם הַבְּרִיאָה — **because the minuscule sliver of light which is found in the world of** *Beriah,* עֲדַיִן הוּא בִּבְחִינַת אֵין סוֹף לְגַבֵּי עוֹלָם הַיְצִירָה — is still uncontainable in the world of *Yetzirah,* וְאִי אֶפְשָׁר לְהִתְלַבֵּשׁ בּוֹ אֶלָּא עַל יְדֵי צִמְצוּם וְהֶעְלֵם — and

להתלבש בו אלא ע״י צמצום והעלם וכן מיצירה לעשיה
[וכמ״ש במ״א ביאור שלשה צמצומים אלו באריכות
לקרב אל שכלינו הדל] ותכלית כל הצמצומים הוא
כדי לברוא גוף האדם החומרי ולאכפייא לס״א ולהיות
יתרון האור מן החושך בהעלות האדם את נפשו האלהית
והחיונית ולבושיה וכל כחות הגוף כולן לה׳ לבדו כנ״ל
באריכות. כי זה תכלית השתלשלות העולמות. והנה
כמים הפנים לפנים כמו שהקב״ה כביכול הניח וסילק

it's impossible for that light to be received by and **enmeshed** in the world of *Beriah,* **except through** profound **diminishment and concealment.**

וְכֵן מִיצִירָה לַעֲשִׂיָּה — **And, so too, from** the emotional World of *Yetzirah* **to** the action-World of *Asiyah,* a profound diminishment is required, since the light of *Yetzirah* is uncontainable in *Asiyah.*

[וּכְמוֹ שֶׁנִּתְבָּאֵר בְּמָקוֹם אַחֵר בֵּיאוּר שְׁלֹשָׁה צִמְצוּמִים אֵלּוּ בַּאֲרִיכוּת — **And these three diminishments are explained elsewhere at length** (*Ma'amarei Admor Ha-Zaken* 5562, p. 154), לְקָרֵב אֶל שִׂכְלֵנוּ הַדַּל] — **to bring them closer to our impoverished** human **intellect.**

Having reviewed a basic outline of the diminishment process, the *Tanya* now reminds us of its purpose.

וְתַכְלִית כָּל הַצִּמְצוּמִים הוּא כְּדֵי לִבְרוֹא גּוּף הָאָדָם הַחוֹמְרִי — **The purpose of all these diminishments is to** eventually **create the sensuous human body,** וּלְאַכְפַּיְיא לְסִטְרָא אַחֲרָא — **so that** the body will resist its self-gratifying inclinations and thereby **subdue the** *sitra achra,* וְלִהְיוֹת יִתְרוֹן הָאוֹר מִן הַחוֹשֶׁךְ — **and,** since this struggle will take place in our spiritually "dark" world, **there will be** *"the advantage of light that comes from darkness"* (*Ecclesiastes* 2:13), בְּהַעֲלוֹת הָאָדָם אֶת נַפְשׁוֹ הָאֱלֹהִית וְהַחִיּוּנִית — **and the person will elevate** *"to G-d alone"* וּלְבוּשֵׁיהֶן וְכָל כֹּחוֹת הַגּוּף כּוּלָּן לַה׳ לְבַדּוֹ (*Exodus* 22:19), both **his Divine and energizing,** Animal **Souls, along with their "garments," as well as all of his body's powers,** כַּנִּזְכָּר לְעֵיל בַּאֲרִיכוּת — **as mentioned above, at length,** כִּי זֶה תַכְלִית הִשְׁתַּלְשְׁלוּת הָעוֹלָמוֹת — **since this is the purpose of the** entire **chain of worlds** (chapters 36-37).

SECTION TWO: HOW YOU CAN "DIMINISH" YOURSELF FOR G-D

In Section One, the *Tanya* connected two ideas. a.) The immense and complex diminishments of G-d's light necessary for the creation process. b.) All this was carried out *for our sake,* so we could elevate our soul(s) and body to G-d through worship.

וְהִנֵּה כַּמַּיִם הַפָּנִים לַפָּנִים — **Now,** as we learned in chapter 46, the human heart automatically mirrors emotion, *"As in water, face reflects face, so the heart of man to man"* (*Proverbs* 27:19).

לצד אחד דרך משל את אורו הגדול הבלתי תכלית
וגנזו והסתירו בג' מיני צמצומים שונים. והכל בשביל
אהבת האדם התחתון להעלותו לה'. כי אהבה דוחקת
הבשר. עאכ"ו בכפלי כפליים לאין קץ כי ראוי לאדם

If you will reflect on all these "diminishments" as an expression of G-d's love, your heart will automatically mirror that love back to G-d.

כְּמוֹ שֶׁהַקָּדוֹשׁ בָּרוּךְ הוּא כִּבְיָכוֹל הִנִּיחַ וְסִילֵּק לִצְדָדִין דֶּרֶךְ מָשָׁל אֶת אוֹרוֹ הַגָּדוֹל הַבִּלְתִּי תַּכְלִית — **Since the Blessed Holy One set aside, so to speak, His great, endless light, dispersing it away to the sides** (*Etz Chaim* 1:2), **figuratively speaking,** you should have a reciprocal response, (which we will describe below).

In works of Kabbalah, the "diminishment" of G-d's light is usually presented as an abstract, metaphysical idea, depicting how a finite world arose from an infinite G-d. But here in the *Tanya*, the "diminishment" is *personalized*. It's now a story of G-d's love for you, how He went to great lengths to restrain His infinitude which posed a fatal obstacle to having a relationship with you.

Since G-d is omnipotent, we usually don't perceive anything as being difficult for Him, or as demanding any effort. But in the imagery of the Kabbalah, the "diminishment" was, figuratively speaking, a painful experience for G-d. He was willing to strip Himself of any (manifest) infinitude *"dispersing it away to the sides"* so as to sustain a relationship with your finite self. It's as if G-d "reinvented" Himself, just so that He could become your G-d.

PRACTICAL LESSONS

Out of great love for you, G-d restrained any manifestation of His infinitude, which would have posed a fatal obstacle in having a relationship with you.

וּגְנָזוֹ וְהִסְתִּירוֹ בִּשְׁלֹשָׁה מִינֵי צִמְצוּמִים שׁוֹנִים — **And in** addition to "dispersing" His Infinite Light, **He hid and concealed** the (partially) finite light that remained **in the three different types of** major, profound **diminishment** mentioned above, thereby creating the three major worlds.

וְהַכֹּל בִּשְׁבִיל אַהֲבַת הָאָדָם הַתַּחְתּוֹן לְהַעֲלוֹתוֹ לַה' — **And all this was for the sake of** a reciprocal reaction **of lowly human love,** which would motivate you **to elevate** all the worlds back **to G-d,** through worship.

G-d did all this *for you.* He stripped Himself of infinitude (figuratively speaking), and He diminished the light that remained, again and again, until it would be dim enough to allow you to exist.

While the "diminishment," a Kabbalistic concept, is not mentioned in the *Talmud,* the *Tanya* now offers a Talmudic citation which illustrates the idea.

כִּי אַהֲבָה דּוֹחֶקֶת אֶת הַבָּשָׂר — **Since, "Love squeezes the flesh"** (*Talmud, Bava Metzia* 84a).

ג"כ להניח ולעזוב כל אשר לו מנפש ועד בשר
ולהפקיר הכל בשביל לדבקה בו ית' בדביקה חשיקה
וחפיצה ולא יהיה שום מונע מבית ומבחוץ לא גוף ולא

The *Talmud* (ibid.) relates: *"Rabbi Yishmael ben Rabbi Yose and Rabbi Eleazar ben Rabbi Shimon (were so fat that) when they bumped into each other, a couple of oxen could go (under their bellies) in-between and not touch them. A certain high-class lady said to them, 'Your children can't possibly be yours!'.... They said to her: 'Love squeezes the flesh.'"*

Following Rabbi Dov Ber, the "Maggid of Mezritch," the *Tanya* offers this *Talmudic* idea of loving self-diminishment (of "flesh"), to illustrate G-d's self-diminishment (of "light"), out of love for you (*Maggid Devarav Le-Ya'akov*, section 93).

עַל אַחַת כַּמָּה וְכַמָּה בְּכִפְלֵי כִפְלַיִם לְאֵין קֵץ — And, mirroring G-d's "diminishment" for you, **all the more so, *"doubled and redoubled"*** (*Midrash Sechel Tov, Exodus* chapter 12), **to no end,** should you mirror G-d's loving "diminishment."

The *Tanya* here echoes its statement in chapter 46. Love will mirror love, *"even if the two individuals are of equal status, but all the more so if a great and influential king demonstrates his abundant and intense love to an ordinary citizen."* Since it is not a human equal but the infinite G-d who has shown His love for you, your reaction should be *"doubled and redoubled to no end."*

But how, exactly, do you mirror G-d's "diminishment" out of love for you?

כִּי רָאוּי לְאָדָם גַּם כֵּן לְהַנִּיחַ וְלַעֲזוֹב כָּל אֲשֶׁר לוֹ — **For** in response to G-d's "diminishment," **a person ought to similarly disregard and *"relinquish everything that is his"*** (*Genesis* 39:6), that might act as an obstacle to worship.

The Infinite Light, which was an obstacle to G-d's relationship with you, was *completely dispersed* by G-d *"away to the sides."* This ought to inspire you to completely disregard anything that distracts you from worshiping G-d.

What type of influences are we talking about?

מִנֶּפֶשׁ וְעַד בָּשָׂר — This includes all types of distractions, *"from the soul to the flesh"* (*Isaiah* 10:18), whether they be intellectual, social or sensory.

וּלְהַפְקִיר הַכֹּל בִּשְׁבִיל לְדָבְקָה בּוֹ יִתְבָּרֵךְ בִּדְבִיקָה חֲשִׁיקָה וַחֲפִיצָה —You ought to **let go of it all to connect to G-d, with *"attachment, fervor and desire"*** (*Genesis Rabah* 80:7).

You can't be passionate about both worship and self-gratification at the same time. Worship is not about you; it's about being of service to something bigger than you. To worship G-d devotedly, you need to mentally disregard and devalue anything that might get in the way.

וְלֹא יְהְיֶה שׁוּם מוֹנֵעַ מִבַּיִת וּמִחוּץ — **And nothing should get in the way, personally or circumstantially,** לֹא גוּף וְלֹא נֶפֶשׁ — **neither** the temptations of **the body nor the** Animal **Soul,** וְלֹא מָמוֹן וְלֹא אִשָּׁה וּבָנִים — and circumstantially, an overstated concern with **finances or family.**

נפש ולא ממון ולא אשה ובנים. ובזה יובן טוב טעם
ודעת לתקנת חכמים שתקנו ברכות ק"ש שתים לפניה
כו' דלכאורה אין להם שייכות כלל עם קריאת שמע 69B
כמ"ש הרשב"א ושאר פוסקי'. ולמה קראו אותן ברכות

The *Tanya* is, of course, not suggesting that you neglect your finances or your family. The main point is that *when it's time for worship,* other concerns shouldn't be on your mind. Also, if worship is your passion, you will find a way to devote as much time and energy to it as you can.

SECTION THREE: MIRRORING G-D'S LOVE DURING THE SHEMA

19TH IYAR REGULAR

In chapter 46 the *Tanya* mentioned that the contemplative method of mirroring G-d's love *"is particularly (effective) at the time when you recite the Shema and its blessings."* In the following section, we will explain why this is the case.

וּבְזֶה יוּבַן טוֹב טַעַם וָדַעַת — **And this will help us explain,** *"with good reasoning and understanding"* (*Psalms* 119:66), לְתַקָּנַת חֲכָמִים שֶׁתִּקְנוּ בְּרְכוֹת שְׁמַע שְׁתַּיִם — **the Rabbinic enactment to recite** two **blessings before reading the Shema,** *"In the morning, two blessings before it... and in the evening, two before it"* (*Mishnah*, *Brachos* 11a). לְפָנֶיהָ כוּ'

The *Shema* is a twice-daily, Biblically ordained declaration of faith, performed by reading aloud certain scriptural passages. The Rabbis also introduced two benedictions (blessings) to be recited before the *Shema*.

דְּלְכְאוֹרָה אֵין לָהֶן שַׁיְּיכוּת כְּלָל עִם קְרִיאַת שְׁמַע — **We need** clarification on this matter **since, superficially, the content** of these two blessings before the *Shema,* **seems to have no relevance at all to reading the Shema,** כְּמוֹ שֶׁכָּתְבוּ הָרַשְׁבָּ"א — **as Rabbi Shlomo ben Aderes has commented,** (*Rashba, Responsa* 1:47), וּשְׁאָר פּוֹסְקִים — **as well as other authorities** (Rabbi Yosef Caro, *Beis Yosef, Orach Chaim,* chapter 46).

The point of reciting a blessing before a *mitzvah* is to focus awareness and concentration on the act which is about to be carried out. But in the case of the *Shema* neither of the two blessings seem to relate directly to the *mitzvah.* (The blessings seem to be general praises of G-d's wisdom and power, the wondrous activities of the angels, and G-d's love for us).

Due to this problem, many authorities have concluded that these blessings are not actually recited *on the Shema* but they are merely passages which happen to precede the *Shema* in the liturgy. But, if this is the case:

וְלָמָּה קָרְאוּ אוֹתָן בְּרְכוֹת קְרִיאַת שְׁמַע — **Why are they** commonly **referred to as "the blessings on the Shema,"** וְלָמָּה תִּקְנוּ אוֹתָן לְפָנֶיהָ דַּוְוקָא — **and why were they placed** in the liturgy **specifically before** the *Shema?*

ק"ש ולמה תקנו אותן לפניה דווקא. אלא משום שעיקר
ק"ש לקיים בכל לבבך כו' בשני יצריך כו' דהיינו לעמוד
נגד כל מונע מאהבת ה'. ולבבך הן האשה וילדיה.
שלבבו של אדם קשורה בהן בטבעו. כמשארז"ל ע"פ
הוא אמר ויהי זו אשה הוא צוה ויעמוד אלו בנים.
ונפשך ומאדך כמשמעו חיי ומזוני להפקיר הכל בשביל

To answer these questions we first need to clarify the main theme of the *Shema* reading.

אֶלָּא מִשׁוּם שֶׁעִיקָר קְרִיאַת שְׁמַע לְקַיֵּים בְּכָל לְבָבְךָ כוּ' — **Rather,** these blessings were placed before the *Shema* **because** they prepare you for **the main point of reading the *Shema*** which **is to inspire you** to love G-d, ***"with all your heart (levavcha) etc.,"*** (*Deuteronomy* 6:5), בְּשְׁנֵי יְצָרֶיךָ כוּ' — the use of the term *levav* (לבב) rather than the contracted form *lev* (לב), suggests the presence of two elements of the heart, which implies that you should love G-d, ***"with both your impulses, etc.,"*** (*Talmud*, *Brachos* 54a), both the "impulse to good" and the "impulse to evil" (See chapter 9, p. 117).

How, exactly, do you love G-d with the "impulse to evil"?

דְּהַיְינוּ לַעֲמוֹד נֶגֶד כָּל מוֹנֵעַ מֵאַהֲבַת ה' — Practically speaking **this means overcoming anything that holds you back from loving G-d.**

You love G-d with the "impulse to evil" by minimizing and disregarding any self-gratifying activities to which it draws you — *"overcoming anything that holds you back from loving G-d."*

Above we pointed to an undue concern with family and finances as the two main sources of distraction from worship. The *Tanya* will now demonstrate how these two concerns are alluded to in the text of the *Shema* itself.

וּלְבָבְךָ הֵן הָאִשָּׁה וִילָדֶיהָ — **Since** *"You shall love G-d with **your heart"*** (*Deuteronomy* 6:5) **means** a worship which is not unduly distracted by **your wife and children,** שֶׁלְבָבוֹ שֶׁל אָדָם קְשׁוּרָה בָּהֶן בְּטִבְעוֹ — **to whom a man's heart is naturally bound.**

כְּמוֹ שֶׁאָמְרוּ רַבּוֹתֵינוּ זִכְרוֹנָם לִבְרָכָה עַל פָּסוּק הוּא אָמַר וַיֶּהִי — **As our Sages of blessed memory commented on the verse, ***"'For He spoke, and it came to be'"*** (*Psalms* 33:9), זוֹ אִשָּׁה — **"this refers to a wife,"** הוּא צִוָּה וַיַּעֲמוֹד — ***"'He commanded, and it remained"*** (ibid.), אֵלוּ בָנִים — **"this refers to children"** (*Talmud*, *Shabbos* 152a).

The Sages understood that a man's love for his wife and children is not something rational. It is something decreed by G-d, *"He spoke, and it came to be etc."*

וְנַפְשְׁךָ וּמְאֹדֶךָ כְּמַשְׁמָעוֹ חַיֵּי וּמְזוֹנֵי — **And** the words *"you should love G-d... with all your soul and all your might"* (*Deuteronomy* ibid.), **follow their implied meaning of "health" and "finances"** (*Talmud*, *Brachos* ibid.), that should not be allowed to unduly interfere with worship.

אהבת ה'. ואיך יבא האדם החומרי למדה זו לכך
סידרו תחלה ברכות יוצר אור. ושם נאמר ונשנה
באריכות ענין וסדר המלאכים העומדים ברום עולם
להודיע גדולתו של הקב"ה איך שכולם בטלים לאורו
ית' ומשמיעים ביראה כו' ומקדישים כו' ואומרים ביראה
קדוש כו' כלומר שהוא מובדל מהן ואינו מתלבש בהן
בבחי' גילוי אלא מלא כל הארץ כבודו היא כנסת ישראל

לְהַפְקִיר הַכֹּל בִּשְׁבִיל אַהֲבַת ה' — The text of the *Shema* implies that, **for the sake of loving G-d, you ought to let go of** your tendency to be overly concerned with **all of them.**

18TH IYAR LEAP

Now we have clarified the "main point" of the *Shema,* we can return to our earlier question: How are the two blessings before it an appropriate preparation?

וְאֵיךְ יָבָא הָאָדָם הַחוֹמְרִי לְמִדָּה זוֹ — **And** the Sages were concerned: **How can man, who is sensuous, come to such a state** where he "lets go" of attachment to distractions that are naturally bound to his heart?

לְכָךְ סִידְּרוּ תְּחִלָּה בִּרְכַּת יוֹצֵר אוֹר — **To assist in this task,** the Sages **introduced** the two blessings **before** the *Shema*, the first **blessing** (in the morning) starting with the words, *"Blessed are you, G-d... who* **forms light."**

וְשָׁם נֶאֱמַר וְנִשְׁנָה בַּאֲרִיכוּת עִנְיָן וְסֵדֶר הַמַּלְאָכִים הָעוֹמְדִים בְּרוּם עוֹלָם — **For,** in the text of this blessing, **the phenomenon of the angels and their lineup,** *"standing at the heights of the universe"* is described and elaborated upon at length, לְהוֹדִיעַ גְדוּלָתוֹ שֶׁל הַקָּדוֹשׁ בָּרוּךְ הוּא — **to convey the greatness of the Blessed Holy One,** אֵיךְ שֶׁכּוּלָּם בְּטֵלִים לְאוֹרוֹ יִתְבָּרֵךְ — **how** the angels **are all overwhelmed by His light,** וּמַשְׁמִיעִים בְּיִרְאָה כו' — וּמַקְדִּישִׁים כו' וְאוֹמְרִים בְּיִרְאָה קָדוֹשׁ כו' — *"and proclaim aloud with awe... and sanctify... and exclaim with awe, 'Holy, Holy, Holy is G-d,'"* כְּלוֹמַר שֶׁהוּא מוּבְדָּל מֵהֶם וְאֵינוֹ מִתְלַבֵּשׁ בָּהֶם בִּבְחִינַת גִּילוּי — **"Holy"** meaning that He is **separate from them and does not become palpably enmeshed with them.**

אֶלָּא מְלֹא כָל הָאָרֶץ כְּבוֹדוֹ — **Nevertheless,** unlike the heavens, which are separate and removed from G-d, the angels recognize that, on the contrary, *"all the earth is*

PRACTICAL LESSONS

The main point of reading the *Shema* is to release yourself from attachment to worldly temptations that hold you back from loving G-d. You do this by awakening a devotional love for G-d.

The blessings before the *Shema* help you in this task. In the first blessing, contemplate how G-d loves you so much that He withheld His light from the angels, but made it accessible to you.

למעלה וישראל למטה כנ"ל. וכן האופנים וחיות
הקודש ברעש גדול וכו' ברוך כבוד ה' ממקומו לפי
שאין יודעים ומשיגים מקומו וכמ"ש כי הוא לבדו
מרום וקדוש. ואח"כ ברכה שניה אהבת עולם אהבתנו

filled with His glory," — הִיא כְּנֶסֶת יִשְׂרָאֵל לְמַעְלָה וְיִשְׂרָאֵל לְמַטָּה — *"the earth"* referring specifically **to the source of souls, *Kneses Yisrael,* and Israel, below,** — כַּנִּזְכָּר לְעֵיל — **as stated above** (chapter 46, p. 595).

The angels proclaim in wonder: G-d's Infinite Light is far beyond and removed from us, but it is to be found in the souls of Israel on earth!

וְכֵן הָאוֹפַנִּים וְחַיּוֹת הַקּוֹדֶשׁ בְּרַעַשׁ גָּדוֹל וְכוּ' בָּרוּךְ כְּבוֹד ה' מִמְּקוֹמוֹ — **And similarly** *"The (angels known as) 'ophanim' and the (angels known as) 'holy chayos' with a mighty noise... offer praise and say, 'Blessed be the glory of G-d from His place'* (Ezekiel 3:12),"* — לְפִי שֶׁאֵין יוֹדְעִים וּמַשִּׂיגִים מְקוֹמוֹ — which again expresses their distance from G-d, **in that they don't know** where He really is, so they just speak of **"His place,"** — וּכְמוֹ שֶׁאוֹמְרִים כִּי הוּא לְבַדּוֹ מָרוֹם וְקָדוֹשׁ — **as they** similarly say, *"For He alone is exalted and holy."*

To summarize: The message of the first blessing before the *Shema* is a very special love which G-d has shown for you. G-d's Infinite Light is inaccessible even to the angels, but He has made it available to you!

19TH IYAR LEAP

The *Tanya* highlights a similar theme in the second blessing before the *Shema*.

וְאַחַר כָּךְ בְּרָכָה שְׁנִיָּה אַהֲבַת עוֹלָם אֲהַבְתָּנוּ ה' — **And then in the second blessing, "** אֱלֹהֵינוּ — which begins with the words, **"With a 'worldly love'"*** (Jeremiah 33:2), *You*

---

*The text of the second blessing before the *Shema* is the subject of a Talmudic dispute which has never been fully resolved. *"Rabbi Yehudah said in the name of Shmuel, 'It begins with the words, "With great love (ahavah rabah)...."'" But the Rabbis say, 'With a worldly love' (ahavas olam)"* (Talmud, *Brachos* 11b).

The *Geonim* suggested a compromise, to say "with great love" in the morning blessings before the *Shema*, and "with a worldly love" in the evening blessings (*Tosfos ibid.*,) and this is the view followed by Ashkenazic communities (*Rema, Shulchan Aruch, Orach Chaim* 61:1). Sefardic communities rejected this compromise and followed *Rambam* (*Laws of Reading Shema* 1:6), and *Rif* (*Brachos* 12a), employing the text "with a worldly love," both in the morning and the evening (*Shulchan Aruch, ibid.*).

The Kabbalists adopted the latter approach: *"We do not say 'with great love" (in the morning) because 'great love' refers to Atzilus, and here in the blessings before the *Shema*, we are still in the chambers (of Beriah)"* (*Pri Etz Chaim, Gate of Reading Shema,* chapter 3). The *Tanya's* author followed the view of the Kabbalists.

ה' אלהינו. כלומר שהניח כל צבא מעלה הקדושים
והשרה שכינתו עלינו להיות נקרא אלהינו. כמו אלהי
אברהם כו' כנ"ל. והיינו כי אהבה דוחקת הבשר ולכן
נקרא אהבת עולם שהיא בחי' צמצום אורו הגדול
הבלתי תכלית להתלבש בבחי' גבול הנקרא עולם
בעבור אהבת עמו ישראל כדי לקרבם אליו ליכלל
ביחודו ואחדותו ית'. וז"ש חמלה גדולה ויתירה פי'

have loved us, G-d our G-d," — כְּלוֹמַר שֶׁהֵנִיחַ כָּל צְבָא מַעֲלָה הַקְּדוֹשִׁים — implying that
G-d **disregarded the entire brigade of supernal, holy** angels, וְהִשְׁרָה שְׁכִינָתוֹ עָלֵינוּ
— **and He caused His presence to rest on** *us,* **to be called** *our* לִהְיוֹת נִקְרָא אֱלֹהֵינוּ
G-d, — **as** in the phrase *"the G-d of Avraham,"* כְּמוֹ אֱלֹהֵי אַבְרָהָם כוּ' — **as** כַּנִּזְכָּר לְעֵיל
mentioned above (chapter 46, p. 600).

וְהַיְינוּ כִּי אַהֲבָה דּוֹחֶקֶת אֶת הַבָּשָׂר — **And this,** as we explained above, **is because** *"Love squeezes the flesh,"*
out of love for us He diminished His light, to be compatible with our existence.

The *Tanya* highlights more hints to this idea in the text
of the second blessing:

וְלָכֵן נִקְרֵאת אַהֲבַת עוֹלָם — **And that's why** the second
blessing before the *Shema* is **referred to as *"worldly***
love" (*ahavas olam*).

Kabbalistic works, such as the *Tanya*, follow the
Zohar's distinction of "great love" (*ahavah rabah*) and
"worldly love" (*ahavas olam*) as referring to two different
levels of love. *"Why is it called ahavah rabah? Because
a person who is in that state of love, is connected to the
higher world. Ahavas olam, is the secret of the lower
world"* (*Zohar* 3, 263b).

(The term *ahavas olam* is often translated in prayer
books as "everlasting love," but since the *Tanya's* dis-
cussion is based on the *Zohar*—that *ahavas olam* is a love associated with the
"lower world"—the term is translated here as "worldly love.")

שֶׁהִיא בְּחִינַת צִמְצוּם אוֹרוֹ הַגָּדוֹל הַבִּלְתִּי תַכְלִית לְהִתְלַבֵּשׁ בִּבְחִינַת גְּבוּל הַנִּקְרָא עוֹלָם —
The second blessing refers to "worldly love" **because** G-d's love for us **is expressed**
through **a diminishment of His great, boundless light into a limited form, the term**
"world" implying limitation, בַּעֲבוּר אַהֲבַת עַמּוֹ יִשְׂרָאֵל כְּדֵי לְקָרְבָם אֵלָיו — **and He did**
this **out of love for His people, Israel, to bring them close to Him,** לִיכָּלֵל בְּיִחוּדוֹ
וְאַחְדוּתוֹ יִתְבָּרֵךְ — **so they can be absorbed in His nondual oneness,** through observing the Torah.

PRACTICAL LESSONS

In the second
blessing, contemplate
how G-d "pushed
aside" His Infinite
Light so as to have a
relationship with you;
and He chose your
body to be a sacred
"temple," dedicated
to His worship.

70A

יתירה על קרבת אלהים שבכל צבא מעלה. ובנו בחרת מכל עם ולשון הוא הגוף החומרי הנדמה בחומריותו לגופי אומות העולם. וקרבתנו וכו' להודות וכו' ופי' הודאה יתבאר במ"א. וליחדך כו' ליכלל ביחודו ית' כנ"ל והנה כאשר ישים המשכיל אלה הדברים אל עומקא דלבא ומוחא אזי ממילא כמים הפנים לפנים תתלהט נפשו ותתלבש ברוח נדיבה להתנדב להניח ולעזוב

וְזֶהוּ שֶׁאוֹמְרִים חֶמְלָה גְדוֹלָה וִיתֵירָה — And that's also **why we say** in the second blessing before the *Shema*, **"with great and abundant compassion You had compassion toward us,"** פֵּירוּשׁ יְתֵירָה עַל קִרְבַת אֱלֹהִים שֶׁבְּכָל צָבָא מַעְלָה — **meaning** a compassion **greater than any closeness shown to the whole heavenly brigade** of angels.

וּבָנוּ בָחַרְתָּ מִכָּל עַם וְלָשׁוֹן — The second blessing later states, **"And you chose us from every people and tongue,"** הוּא הַגּוּף הַחוּמְרִי הַנִּדְמֶה בְּחוּמְרִיּוּתוֹ לְגוּפֵי אוּמּוֹת הָעוֹלָם — **referring to** His choice to be worshiped through **our physical body,** **whose sensuous inclinations seem identical to the bodies of other nations.**

וְקֵרַבְתָּנוּ וְכוּ' לְהוֹדוֹת וְכוּ' — And the second blessing continues, **"and You brought us close...** to Your great name in love, **to give thanks** to You," וּפֵירוּשׁ הוֹדָאָה יִתְבָּאֵר — **the meaning of "giving thanks" being explained elsewhere** (*Tanya, Igeres Ha-Kodesh*, section 15; *Torah Ohr* 45c), וּלְיַחֶדְךָ כוּ' לִיכָּלֵל בְּיִחוּדוֹ יִתְבָּרֵךְ — **"And proclaim Your unity, etc,"** meaning **to be absorbed in** G-d's **unity,** כַּנִּזְכָּר לְעֵיל — **as mentioned above** (pp. 600, 609, 612).

20TH IYAR REGULAR | 20TH IYAR LEAP

Having demonstrated the theme of G-d's love *for you* in the blessings before the *Shema*, the *Tanya* now discusses the corresponding feelings of love *for G-d* which you will experience when taking these words to heart. (And this is the final answer to our question: How are these blessings a preparation for saying the *Shema*?)

וְהִנֵּה כַּאֲשֶׁר יָשִׂים הַמַּשְׂכִּיל אֵלֶּה הַדְּבָרִים אֶל עוּמְקָא דְּלִבָּא וּמוֹחָא — **Now when any intelligent person will impress these words upon the depths of his heart and mind,** אֲזַי מִמֵּילָא כַּמַּיִם הַפָּנִים לְפָנִים תִּתְלַהֵט נַפְשׁוֹ — **then, instinctively, "as in water, face reflects face,"** his soul will be ignited, וְתִתְלַבֵּשׁ בְּרוּחַ נְדִיבָה לְהִתְנַדֵּב לְהָנִיחַ וְלַעֲזוֹב כָּל — **and he will be infused with "a generous spirit"** (*Psalms* 51:14), **to** אֲשֶׁר לוֹ מִנֶּגֶד — **willingly disregard and "relinquish everything that is his."**

G-d "pushed aside" His Infinite Light so as to have a relationship with you. He disregarded the sweet songs of millions of angels and chose to focus instead on your worship. He even chose your body to be a sacred "temple" dedicated to His worship. When you ponder these thoughts, your heart will want to mirror all that love back to G-d.

כל אשר לו מנגד ורק לדבקה בו ית' וליכלל באורו
בדביקה חשיקה וכו' בבחי' נשיקין ואתדבקות רוחא
ברוחא כנ"ל. אך איך היא בחי' אתדבקות רוחא ברוחא
לזה אמר והיו הדברים האלה כו' על לבבך ודברת בם

וְרַק לִדְבָקָה בּוֹ יִתְבָּרֵךְ וְלִיכָּלֵל בְּאוֹרוֹ בִּדְבִיקָה חֲשִׁיקָה וְכוּ' — **And** you will want to be devoted **only to connect to G-d, and be absorbed in His light, with attachment and fervor, *etc.,*** בִּבְחִינַת נְשִׁיקִין וְאִתְדַּבְּקוּת רוּחָא בְּרוּחָא — **with the intensity of "kissing" and *"merging of spirit with spirit,"*** כַּנִּזְכָּר לְעֵיל — **as mentioned above** (chapter 46, p. 596).

The goal of awakening love for G-d is to inspire your devotional attachment to Him. In its most intense form, this devotion is compared to "kissing" or a merging of spirit with G-d, as we have discussed previously.

SECTION FOUR: TO BE AS INTIMATE WITH G-D AS YOU CAN

From the above discussion, you could get the impression that all G-d requires from you is to have a feeling of love for Him, a desire to escape your existence and return your soul to Him. This, of course, is not true. Judaism requires worship through actions *in this world,* not the escape from it.

The *Tanya* suggests that the next verse of the *Shema* addresses this issue.

אַךְ אֵיךְ הִיא בְּחִינַת אִתְדַּבְּקוּת רוּחָא בְּרוּחָא — **But** since Judaism demands worldly activity, **how is this *"merging of spirit with spirit"* achieved**, practically speaking?

— לָזֶה אָמַר וְהָיוּ הַדְּבָרִים הָאֵלֶּה גוּ' עַל לְבָבֶךָ וְדִבַּרְתָּ בָּם גוּ' **To explain this,** the next verse of the *Shema* states, ***"And these words (of Torah)... shall be upon your heart, and you shall speak of them etc.,"*** (*Deuteronomy* 6:6-7).

The third verse of the *Shema* teaches us that devotional attachment to G-d ("merging spirit with spirit") is achieved, practically speaking, through Torah study.

An emotional longing for G-d alone won't connect you with Him — for how could a finite being such as yourself, bridge the chasm that separates you from an Infinite G-d? However, within the Torah, G-d has placed His very self, so when you take the Torah "upon your heart" and understand it deeply, you "merge spirit with spirit" and "kiss" G-d, so to speak.

As we learned above, in chapter 5, the mind-to-mind connection with G-d that takes place through Torah study is *"a phenomenal merging experience. There is*

PRACTICAL LESSONS

Devotional attachment to G-d ("kissing" and "merging spirit with spirit") is achieved, practically speaking, through Torah study, especially the study of Halachah (Jewish Law).

כו' וכמ"ש בע"ח שיחוד הנשיקין עיקרו הוא יחוד חב"ד
בחב"ד והוא עיון התורה והפה הוא מוצא הרוח וגילויו
בבחי' גילוי והיינו בחי' הדבור בד"ת. כי על מוצא פי

no other merging experience like it. Nothing remotely comparable exists in the physical world, where you become completely one (with another entity) from every conceivable perspective" (p. 78).

Still, the metaphor of "kissing" implies a raw connection of spirit, not a cognitive one. How could the *Tanya* equate "kissing" G-d with a connection *of the mind?*

וּכְמוֹ שֶׁכָּתוּב בְּעֵץ חַיִּים שֶׁיִּחוּד הַנְּשִׁיקִין עִיקָרוֹ הוּא יִחוּד חָכְמָה בִּינָה וְדַעַת בְּחָכְמָה בִּינָה וְדַעַת — **For, as stated in *Etz Chaim*** (30:2), **the union** with G-d described as **"kissing" is primarily** a union of your mental faculties of **chochmah, binah** and **da'as** with G-d's **chochmah, binah** and **da'as,** וְהוּא עִיּוּן הַתּוֹרָה — **which,** in our case of *"these words... upon your heart,"* **refers to the cognitive analysis of Torah.**

Etz Chaim defines "hugging" G-d as an emotional connection, and "kissing" G-d as a mental one. This is ample proof for the *Tanya's* assertion here that in-depth Torah study (with the mind) is an intimate experience of "kissing" G-d.

We've now established a source for the idea, but an explanation is still lacking. Why should a connection to G-d with the mind be compared to a kiss, performed with the mouth?

Generally speaking, Torah study can be divided into two categories: a.) the *process* of clarifying the law, through complex analysis and debate; which is then followed by, b.) the final *conclusion*, the law (*halachah*) itself.

Earlier in the *Tanya*, the intimate "kissing" of G-d was associated specifically with *halachah* (b), the study of legal conclusions: *"'let him kiss me with kisses of the mouth,' this refers to... halachah"* (chapter 45, p. 587). We will now clarify this point further.

וְהַפֶּה הוּא מוֹצָא הָרוּחַ וְגִילּוּיוֹ בִּבְחִינַת גִּילּוּי — **And** "kisses of the mouth" alludes specifically to the study of legal conclusions, *halachah,* **since the mouth expresses and discloses the deliberations** of the mind **overtly,** just as *halachah* provides an overt and practical conclusion to a legal discussion.

Your mouth expresses the final conclusions of your mental deliberations. And that's why the comprehension of *halachah* in particular is described as *"kisses of the mouth"* with G-d, because it is the conclusion of a Torah discussion/analysis (*Notes on Tanya*).

וְהַיְינוּ בְּחִינַת הַדִּבּוּר בְּדִבְרֵי תּוֹרָה — **So** the metaphor of a "kiss" with G-d highlights **the nature of speech** to bring thoughts to their conclusion, which is specifically **when** halachic **"words of Torah"** are studied, since *"the 'word of G-d' is halachah"* (*Talmud, Shabbos* 138b).

ה' יחיה האדם ומ"מ לא יצא ידי חובתו בהרהור ועיון
לבדו עד שיוציא בשפתיו כדי להמשיך אור א"ס ב"ה
למטה עד נפש החיונית השוכנת בדם האדם המתהוה

21ST IYAR LEAP

To further stress the importance of legal *conclusions* in the Torah (G-d's "mouth," so to speak), over theoretical Torah discussions, the *Tanya* cites Scripture.

כִּי עַל מוֹצָא פִי ה' יְחְיֶה הָאָדָם — *"Because on every utterance of G-d's mouth does man live"* (Deuteronomy 8:3).

Studying the *halachic* conclusions of the Torah has the exclusive quality of connecting you with G-d's "mouth," so to speak (the final conclusions of His "thought"), and this is important since Scripture points to G-d's "mouth" as life-giving — *"on every utterance of G-d's mouth does man live."*

Our conclusion, then, is that the most intimate connection with G-d, of "kissing" and "merging spirit with spirit," is through study of *halachah* with the mind. It is only with the mind that you can have *"a phenomenal merging experience, where you become completely one (with another entity) from every conceivable perspective"*; and it is only through studying *halachah* that you connect with G-d's life-giving "mouth," so to speak (*Notes on Tanya*).

SECTION FIVE: SPIRITUAL YEARNING/SACRED RESPONSIBILITY

וּמִכָּל מָקוֹם — **Nevertheless,** despite the fact that your "spirit with spirit" connection with G-d is primarily through the *mental* comprehension of Torah, לֹא יָצָא יְדֵי חוֹבָתוֹ בְּהִרְהוּר וְעִיּוּן לְבַדּוֹ — **you still don't fulfill your obligation** of Torah study with **thought and contemplation alone,** עַד שֶׁיּוֹצִיא בִּשְׂפָתָיו — **until** the words of Torah are **audibly vocalized** (see p. 412).

And, as we explained in chapter 37, Torah must be vocalized because:

כְּדֵי לְהַמְשִׁיךְ אוֹר אֵין סוֹף בָּרוּךְ הוּא לְמַטָּה — **In order to "pull" the Blessed Infinite Light down here,** עַד נֶפֶשׁ הַחִיּוּנִית הַשּׁוֹכֶנֶת בְּדַם הָאָדָם — **right down to your energizing** Animal **Soul, which rests in your blood,** הַמִּתְהַוֶּה מִדּוֹמֵם צוֹמֵחַ חַי — **and since** the blood **is sustained by** nourishment from **mineral, vegetable and animal matter,** you thereby "pull" the Blessed Infinite Light into those realms too (see p. 413).

We appear to have a conflict here between your *spiritual yearnings* and *sacred responsibility*. Having read the *Shema* (and its preceding blessings), you are burning with a desire to disregard all worldly concerns and connect intimately with G-d. You realize that the best way of doing that is through the mental comprehension of Torah, which is a spiritual yearning (since activities of the mind are detached and unworldly).

But how does your transcendent, spiritual yearning fit with the requirement to vocalize the text of the Torah with your mouth? Pronouncing words clearly and cor-

מדוממם צומח חי כדי להעלות כולן לה' עם כל העולם
כולו ולכללן ביחודו ואורו ית' אשר יאיר לארץ
ולדרים בבחי' גילוי ונגלה כבוד ה' וראו כל בשר וכו'
שזהו תכלית השתלשלות כל העולמות להיות כבוד ה'
מלא כל הארץ הלזו דוקא בבחי' גילוי לאהפכא חשוכא
לנהורא ומרירא למיתקא כנ"ל באריכות. וזהו תכלית

rectly is very much a practical, worldly activity and not something which feels transcendent or spiritual (*Notes on Tanya*).

The transcendent orientation of the *Shema* and its blessings doesn't seem to be
a source of inspiration for you to carry out the technical task of pronouncing words
precisely. Therefore the *Tanya* clarifies:

כְּדֵי לְהַעֲלוֹת כּוּלָן לַה' — The reason why you need to pronounce the words precisely, to "pull" down G-d's light into all the aspects of your physical being, is **in
order to elevate it all to G-d,** עם כָּל הָעוֹלָם כּוּלוֹ — **along with the rest of the world,**
וּלְכָלְלָן בְּיִחוּדוֹ וְאוֹרוֹ יִתְבָּרֵךְ — **to be absorbed in G-d's oneness and light.**

Your spiritual yearning to transcend the world and be intimate with G-d does
not deeply conflict with your sacred responsibility to remain in the world and bring
G-d's light into it. There is really one goal here: elevation and transcendence. The
question is: do you want to just elevate yourself to G-d, or do you want to elevate
the world with you?

By studying Torah with your mind, you elevate yourself to be intimate with G-d,
and by pronouncing the words of Torah precisely, you elevate the physical world.
While the methods might be different, the goal is the same: It's all about elevation
(*Notes on Tanya*).

אֲשֶׁר יָאִיר לָאָרֶץ וְלַדָּרִים עָלֶיהָ בִּבְחִינַת גִּילּוּי — And this elevation of the physical world
will one day *"shine upon the earth and its inhabitants"* (*Liturgy*), **in a palpable way,**
וְנִגְלָה כְּבוֹד ה' וְרָאוּ כָל בָּשָׂר וְגוֹ' — *"And the glory of G-d will be revealed and all flesh
will see together that G-d is speaking"* (*Isaiah* 40:5).

While the *goal* of your sacred responsibility might be the same as the goal of
your spiritual yearning, it doesn't always feel that way emotionally. Your love of
G-d awakened by reading the *Shema* will awaken in you the urge to transcend the
world, not be engaged with it. To address this concern, the *Tanya* continues:

שֶׁזֶּהוּ תַּכְלִית הִשְׁתַּלְשְׁלוּת כָּל הָעוֹלָמוֹת — **For this** elevation of the physical world **is
the purpose for which the entire chain of worlds** was created, לִהְיוֹת כְּבוֹד ה' מָלֵא
כָל הָאָרֶץ הַלָּזוּ דַּוְקָא בִּבְחִינַת גִּילּוּי — **so that G-d's glory should fill all of** *this* **earth,
in particular, in a palpable way,** לְאַהֲפָכָא חֲשׁוֹכָא לִנְהוֹרָא וּמְרִירָא לְמִיתְקָא כַּנִּזְכָּר לְעֵיל
בַּאֲרִיכוּת — **with darkness transformed to light, and bitterness to sweetness, as
mentioned above at length** (chapter 36-37).

כוונת האדם בעבודתו להמשיך אור אין סוף ברוך
הוא למטה רק שצריך תחלה העלאת מ"ן למסור לו
נפשו ומאודו כנ"ל:

וְזֶהוּ תַּכְלִית כַּוָּנַת הָאָדָם בַּעֲבוֹדָתוֹ — **For this is man's purpose and the goal of his worship,** לְהַמְשִׁיךְ אוֹר אֵין סוֹף בָּרוּךְ הוּא לְמַטָּה — **to "pull" the Blessed Infinite Light down here.**

Worship doesn't have two goals: to transcend the world and (paradoxically) to remain in it, to sanctify it. There's just one purpose: *"to 'pull' the Blessed Infinite Light down here."* When you are lifted to a mood of transcendence by reciting the *Shema,* remember that the arrows ultimately point down to this world. The purpose of your love and desire for transcendence is to motivate you to do your sacred work of illuminating the physical world with G-d's light (*Notes on Tanya*).

But why, then, do we bother with transcendence at all? Why should we read the *Shema*, and be inspired to transcend the world, only to then make a 180-degree turn, and focus our energies back down here?

רַק שֶׁצָּרִיךְ תְּחִלָּה הַעֲלָאַת מַיִּין נוּקְבִין — **Only** in order to be empowered to bring G-d's light down here, **you first need to "elevate feminine waters"** (see chapter 10, p. 130), through love of G-d and a desire for transcendence, לִמְסוֹר לוֹ נַפְשׁוֹ וּמְאוֹדוֹ — **to "hand over" to** G-d **your soul and your possessions,** כַּנִּזְכָּר לְעֵיל — **as mentioned above.**

In order to bring G-d's light into the world (which is your purpose) you need to be luminous yourself. By reading the *Shema* and its blessings intently, you will develop a desire to transcend the world and be intimate with G-d. Now that you are charged and energized, you can better fulfill your purpose of bringing G-d's light down here, into this world.

So, ultimately, while your *spiritual yearning* for transcendence and your *sacred responsibility* of engaging with this world do represent opposite modes, they are profoundly interconnected. In principle, they *share the same goal* of elevating yourself and the world to G-d. And practically, one depends on the other: You can only be effective in your sacred responsibility when you have first been energized by your spiritual yearnings (*Notes on Tanya*).

PRACTICAL LESSONS

The purpose of awakening transcendent, devotional love through saying the *Shema*, is ultimately to energize you to carry out your sacred Torah responsibility in this world.

פרק נ והנה   כל בחי' ומדרגות אהבה הנ"ל הן
מסטרא דימינא ובחי' כהן איש
חסד ונק' כסף הקדשים מלשון נכסוף נכספת לבית   70B

CHAPTER 50

LOVE FROM THE "LEFT SIDE"

SECTION ONE: WHEN YOUR SOUL IS ON FIRE

21ST IYAR REGULAR | 22ND IYAR LEAP

This chapter concludes an extensive discussion on meditative approaches to achieve love of G-d, spanning back to chapter 43. As we shall soon see, this final chapter touches upon a more intense form of love than we have yet encountered, which stems from a different spiritual energy.

וְהִנֵּה כָּל בְּחִינוֹת וּמַדְרֵגוֹת אַהֲבָה הַנִּזְכָּרוֹת לְעֵיל — **Now all the types and levels of love mentioned above** from chapter 43 onwards, הֵן מִסְטְרָא דְּיַמִּינָא — all have in common that they **are from the "right side"** (*Tikunei Zohar* 5a), of the "tree" of spiritual energies, the *sefiros*.

As we have learned, the core spiritual energies of the universe (*sefiros*), are divided into three "lines" or categories. The polar opposites of *chesed* (giving) and *gevurah* (restraint), represent the right and left "lines." *Rachamim* (compassion) is placed in the center, since it mediates between the two positions.

Love, which is an experience of closeness, is usually associated with the right side of giving and generosity. When such a feeling is mutual between two parties, their love draws them together.

וּבְחִינַת כֹּהֵן אִישׁ חֶסֶד — **And** the right side is associated with the **figure of the priest** (*kohen*) who, according to the Kabbalah, is *"a man (with the energy) of chesed"* (*Zohar* 3, 306b).

The priests were responsible for drawing G-d's presence (the *Shechinah*) to rest in the Holy Temple, an activity associated with the "right side" of bringing things closer together. This is because the priests themselves possessed a soul-energy of *chesed*.

וְנִקְרָאוֹת כֶּסֶף הַקְּדָשִׁים — **And** all these levels of love which we have discussed in the previous chapters, that stem from the right side, **are called** by the *Zohar* (2, 115a), *"silver (kesef) of sacred gifts"* (2 *Kings* 12:5).

אָבִיךְ. אַךְ יֵשׁ עוֹד בְּחִי' אַהֲבָה הָעוֹלָה עַל כּוּלָנה
כְּמַעֲלַת הַזָּהָב עַל הַכֶּסֶף וְהִיא אַהֲבָה כְּרִשְׁפֵּי אֵשׁ מִבְּחִי'
גְּבוּרוֹת עֶלְיוֹנוֹת דְּבִינָה עִילָאָה דְּהַיְינוּ שֶׁעַ"י הִתְבּוֹנְנוּת

It was the priests who received all the gifts of silver in the Holy Temple, *"All the silver of sacred gifts that is brought to the house of G-d... let the priests take it"* (ibid.). As the *Tanya* will now explain, this offers us a further hint between the role of the priests and the emotion of love.

מִלְּשׁוֹן נִכְסוֹף נִכְסַפְתָּה לְבֵית אָבִיךְ — **And** the word *KeSeF* (silver) **is related to the phrase, "you longed so much (niKhSoF niKhSaFtah) for your father's house"** (Genesis 31:30), suggesting a longing for closeness and love.

In our chapter, however, we will discuss a different type of love, which is associated with the "left side" of *gevurah*.

אַךְ יֵשׁ עוֹד בְּחִינַת אַהֲבָה הָעוֹלָה עַל כּוּלָנה — **But there is another type of love which surpasses all of these** levels, discussed in chapters 43-49, all of which are compared to silver (*kesef*), כְּמַעֲלַת הַזָּהָב עַל הַכֶּסֶף — this higher love from the "left side" is compared to gold, and it's superior to all the other levels we have discussed, **to the same extent that** the captivating luster of **gold surpasses silver** (see *Zohar* 2, 148a), וְהִיא אַהֲבָה כְּרִשְׁפֵּי אֵשׁ — **and this** higher, "golden" love **is a love like** *"flaming fire"* (Song 8:6), מִבְּחִינַת גְּבוּרוֹת עֶלְיוֹנוֹת — **which is from the energy of the heavenly *gevuros*,** on the left side.

This higher love, from the left side, is more powerful than the other types of love emanating from the right side. Right side love, which draws two individuals close together, is compared to water, which binds substances together. But love from the left side is destructive like fire (*"flaming fire"*); it's a force so strong that it can rip you apart. We see this also from the tendency of flames to flicker up, away from their wick, indicating that this type of love tears you away from your worldly existence.

First we must clarify why love from the left side is higher than its counterpart from the right side. This seems inconsistent with the hierarchy of *sefiros*, in which *gevurah* on the left, follows *after chesed,* on the right.

דְּבִינָה עִילָאָה — Love from the left side is higher since it emanates, not merely from *gevurah* (which is lower than *chesed*), but **from upper *binah*,** (see *Zohar* 1, 245a; 2, 216b).

It's true that *gevurah* is lower than *chesed*, but the love from the left side of *gevurah* is rooted in the higher energy of *binah* (which is the "left" in the upper triad of *chochmah-binah-da'as*).

The *Tanya* now explains briefly the meditative process which leads to the fiery love of the left side.

דְּהַיְינוּ שֶׁעַל יְדֵי הַהִתְבּוֹנְנוּת בִּגְדוּלַת אֵין סוֹף בָּרוּךְ הוּא — **And this** higher love comes **through contemplating the greatness of the Blessed Infinite Light,** דְּכוּלָּא קַמֵּיה

בגדולת א״ס ב״ה דכולא קמיה כלא ממש חשיב
תתלהט ותתלהב הנפש ליקר תפאר׳ גדולתו ולאסתכל׳
ביקרא דמלכא כרשפי אש שלהבת עזה העולה למעל׳
וליפרד מהפתילה והעצים שנאחזת בהן והיינו על ידי
תגבורת יסוד האש אלהי שבנפש האלהית ומזה באה
לידי צמאון וכמ״ש צמאה לך נפשי ואח״כ לבחי׳ חולת
אהבה ואח״כ באה לידי כלות הנפש ממש כמ״ש גם

כְּלָא מַמָּשׁ חֲשִׁיב — that *"in His presence, everything is considered zero"* (*Zohar* 1, 11b), literally, תִּתְלַהֵט וְתִתְלַהֵב הַנֶּפֶשׁ לִיקַר תִּפְאֶרֶת גְּדוּלָתוֹ — then your soul will ignite and become aflame for *"the glorious beauty of His greatness"* (*Esther* 1:4), וּלְאַסְתַּכְּלָא בִּיקָרָא דְמַלְכָּא — and *"to gaze at the glory of the King"* (*Zohar* 1, 38a-b, 199a; 2, 134a, 247b), כְּרִשְׁפֵּי אֵשׁ שַׁלְהֶבֶת עַזָּה — with a love like *"flaming fire"* and intense flames, הָעוֹלָה לְמַעְלָה וְלִיפָּרֵד מֵהַפְּתִילָה וְהָעֵצִים שֶׁנֶּאֱחֶזֶת בָּהֶן — that ascend upwards to detach themselves from the wick or the lumber on which they are grasped.

Flickering flames look as if they are trying to ascend upwards and leave their wick. While this would result in the flames being extinguished, they don't seem to care. They have a self-annihilating desire for transcendence.

Similarly, a fiery love is so powerful that it makes your soul want to "run away" to G-d and leave behind your bodily existence (your "wick"). Such an intense emotion comes from the realization that bodily existence makes real closeness to G-d impossible: you can only "gaze at the glory of the King" when detached from the body.

וְהַיְינוּ עַל יְדֵי תִגְבּוֹרֶת יְסוֹד הָאֵשׁ אֱלֹהִי שֶׁבַּנֶּפֶשׁ הָאֱלֹהִית — And this emotion comes through an intensification of elemental fire in the G-dly soul.

The comparison to fire here is not incidental. Your soul actually contains elemental fire, and when your fire is aroused through the above meditation, it produces this fiery (left side, *gevurah*) love.

וּמִזֶּה בָּאָה לִידֵי צִמָּאוֹן — And through this fiery love **you come to thirst** for G-d, not out of a feeling of distance from G-d, imposed by sins of the Animal Soul, but simply because G-d feels distant even to your Divine Soul, וּכְמוֹ שֶׁכָּתוּב צָמְאָה לְךָ נַפְשִׁי — **as the verse states,** *"My (Divine) soul (naturally) thirsts for You"* (*Psalms* 63:2).

וְאַחַר כָּךְ לִבְחִינַת חוֹלַת אַהֲבָה — **And then** you progress **to a state of** *"love-sickness"* (*Song of Songs* 2:5), where you can't get G-d off your mind, and your distance from Him makes you feel sick, וְאַחַר כָּךְ בָּאָה לִידֵי כְּלוֹת הַנֶּפֶשׁ מַמָּשׁ — **and then to a state of actual soul-languish** where your soul desires to depart from the body, כְּמוֹ שֶׁכָּתוּב וְגַם כָּלְתָה נַפְשִׁי — **as the verse states,** *"My soul longs, indeed, it languishes"* (*Psalms* 84:3).

כלתה נפשי והנה מכאן יצא שורש הלוים למטה
[ולעתיד שהעולם יתעלה יהיו הם הכהנים וכמ״ש
האר״י ז״ל ע״פ והכהנים הלוים שהלוים של עכשיו יהיו
כהנים לעתיד] ועבודת הלוים היתה להרים קול רינה
ותודה בשירה וזמרה בניגון ונעימה בבחי׳ רצוא ושוב

Above, the *Tanya* noted that love from the right side (*chesed*) is associated with the figure of the priest. Now we will see that love from the left side is associated with the levites.

וְהִנֵּה מִכָּאן יָצָא שׁוֹרֶשׁ הַלְוִיִם לְמַטָּה — **And it is from here,** the heavenly *gevuros* of upper *binah*, **that the** spiritual **root of earthly levites is derived,** a higher source than the souls of the priests, which are rooted in *chesed*.

Why are the levites, whose rank is lower than the priests, associated with a higher energy? The *Tanya* clarifies:

[וְלֶעָתִיד שֶׁהָעוֹלָם יִתְעַלֶּה — **And in the future, when the world will be elevated,** יִהְיוּ הֵם הַכֹּהֲנִים — **they,** the levites, **will** be elevated to their rightful place, to **become the priests.**

The status of the current "earthly levites" does not reflect their superior spiritual root in the heavenly *gevuros* of *binah*. This is because the world has not yet been elevated to the point where the physical world is an accurate reflection of its spiritual source.

וּכְמוֹ שֶׁאָמַר הָאַר״י זִכְרוֹנוֹ לִבְרָכָה עַל פָּסוּק וְהַכֹּהֲנִים הַלְוִיִם — As *Arizal* commented on the verse, *"and the priests, the levites"* (*Ezekiel* 44:15), שֶׁהַלְוִיִם שֶׁל עַכְשָׁיו יְהִיוּ **that those who are currently levites will, in the future, become the** כֹּהֲנִים לֶעָתִיד] **priests** (*Likutei Torah,* ibid.).

Arizal's teaching, that the role of levites and priests will be changed, seems to contradict the basic principle of faith that the laws of the Torah will never change (*Rambam, Ninth Principle*). To clarify that this is not the case, the *Tanya* stresses, "those who are *currently* levites will, in the future, become the priests." *I.e.,* the souls of the current levites will, in the future, be reincarnated into priestly families. No law will change; it is only that a person who will be *halachically* born as a priest will in his essence be a levite, and *vice versa*. Spiritually, the priests and levites will swap roles, but this transformation will not require any legal innovation (*Notes on Tanya*).

The role of the levites, of making music in the Temple, actually hints to their spiritual path of fiery love.

וַעֲבוֹדַת הַלְוִיִם הָיְתָה לְהָרִים קוֹל רִנָּה וְתוֹדָה — **And the worship of the levites was to raise their** *"voice in joy and gratitude"* (*Psalms* 42:5), בְּשִׁירָה וְזִמְרָה בְּנִיגוּן וּנְעִימָה — *"in song and melody"* (*Zohar* 3, 109b), **tunefully and pleasantly,** בִּבְחִינַת רָצוֹא וָשׁוֹב — music being so intense that it sometimes evokes the contradictory emotions, as in **the energetic cycling of** the angels which were first *"running and then returning"*

שֶׁהִיא בְּחִי' אַהֲבָה עַזָּה זוֹ כְּשַׁלְהֶבֶת הַיּוֹצֵא מִן הַבָּזָק כְּדְאִיתָא בַּגְּמ' [פ"ב דַּחֲגִיגָה] וְאִי אֶפְשָׁר לְבָאֵר עִנְיָן זֶה הֵיטֵב בְּמִכְתָּב רַק כָּל אִישׁ נִלְבָּב וְנָבוֹן הַמַּשְׂכִּיל עַל דָּבָר וּמַעֲמִיק לְקַשֵּׁר דַּעְתּוֹ וּתְבוּנָתוֹ בַּה' יִמְצָא טוֹב וְאוֹר הַגָּנוּז בְּנַפְשׁוֹ הַמַּשְׂכֶּלֶת כָּל חַד לְפוּם שִׁיעוּרָא דִּילֵיהּ [יֵשׁ מִתְפָּעֵל כוּ' וְיֵשׁ מִתְפָּעֵל כוּ'] אַחֲרֵי קְדִימַת יִרְאַת חֵטְא לִהְיוֹת סוּר מֵרָע בְּתַכְלִית שֶׁלֹּא לִהְיוֹת עֲווֹנוֹתֵיכֶם מַבְדִּילִים כוּ' ח"ו. וְהִנֵּה סֵדֶר הָעֲבוֹדָה בְּעֵסֶק הַתּוֹרָה

שֶׁהִיא בְּחִינַת אַהֲבָה עַזָּה זוֹ כְּשַׁלְהֶבֶת הַיּוֹצְאָה מִן הַבָּזָק — this is a type of love so strong that it's like the flame emerging from a crucible, כְּדְאִיתָא בַּגְּמָרָא [פֶּרֶק ב' דַּחֲגִיגָה] — as the *Talmud* states in chapter 2 of Tractate *Chagigah* (13b).

וְאִי אֶפְשָׁר לְבָאֵר עִנְיָן זֶה הֵיטֵב בְּמִכְתָּב — But this experience can't be explained properly in writing, רַק כָּל אִישׁ נִלְבָּב וְנָבוֹן — only every man with a wise and understanding heart, הַמַּשְׂכִּיל עַל דָּבָר וּמַעֲמִיק לְקַשֵּׁר דַּעְתּוֹ וּתְבוּנָתוֹ בַּה' — who thinks about the matter and delves deeply to connect his *da'as* and *binah* to G-d, יִמְצָא טוֹב וְאוֹר הַגָּנוּז בְּנַפְשׁוֹ הַמַּשְׂכֶּלֶת — will find goodness and light hidden in his intellectual soul, כָּל חַד לְפוּם שִׁיעוּרָא דִּילֵיהּ — "*each individual according to his own capabilities*" (*Zohar* 1, 103a), [יֵשׁ מִתְפָּעֵל כוּ' וְיֵשׁ מִתְפָּעֵל כוּ'] — because one person will be moved in one way, and someone else in another.

The *Tanya* again stresses that we are speaking here of an advanced meditation carried out by a pious worshiper, and not by someone who longs for closeness to G-d because of his sins.

אַחֲרֵי קְדִימַת יִרְאַת חֵטְא — Such a level can only be reached after first having "*the reverence necessary not to sin*" (*Mishnah Avos* 3:9), לִהְיוֹת סוּר מֵרָע בְּתַכְלִית — to utterly "*turn away from evil*" (*Psalms* 34:15), שֶׁלֹּא לִהְיוֹת עֲווֹנוֹתֵיכֶם מַבְדִּילִים כוּ' — so that there will not be a situation of, "*Your sins were a separation* between you and G-d etc.,*" (*Isaiah* 59:2), חַס וְשָׁלוֹם — G-d forbid.

SECTION TWO: "RUNNING" AND "RETURNING"

22ND IYAR REGULAR | 23RD IYAR LEAP

The fiery love described in this chapter won't actually inspire you to observe the Torah and its *mitzvos*. It will just make you want to leave your body and be one with G-d. How, then, is it compatible with Torah observance?

While fiery love won't directly inspire observance, it will prompt a *rebound emotion* (the "returning" following the "running" away to G-d), a concomitant desire to live in this world, in a body. It is this rebound "returning" that will propel you to observance, as the *Tanya* will now explain.

והמצות הנמשכת מבחי' אהבה עזה זו היא בבחי' שוב
לבד כמ"ש בספר יצירה ואם רץ לבך שוב לאחד פי'
ואם רץ לבך היא תשוקת הנפש שבלב בחלל הימני
כשמתגברת ומתלהבת ומתלהטת במאד מאד עד
כלות הנפש ממש להשתפך אל חיק אביה חיי החיים
ב"ה ולצאת ממאסרה בגוף הגופני וגשמי לדבקה בו ית'
אזי זאת ישיב אל לבו מארז"ל כי ע"כ אתה חי בגוף
הזה להחיותו כדי להמשיך חיים עליוני' מחיי החיים ב"ה
למטה ע"י תורת חיים להיות דירה בתחתוני' לאחדותו
ית' בבחי' גילוי כמש"ל וכמ"ש בז"הק למהוי אחד

71A

וְהִנֵּה סֵדֶר הָעֲבוֹדָה בְּעֵסֶק הַתּוֹרָה וְהַמִּצְוֹת הַנִּמְשֶׁכֶת מִבְּחִינַת אַהֲבָה זוֹ — Now the way in which this intense love inspires worship through Torah and *mitzvah* observance, is indirect, הִיא בִּבְחִינַת שׁוֹב לְבָד — it's only through the rebound experience of "returning," which takes place *after* the feeling of fiery love, כְּמוֹ שֶׁכָּתוּב בְּסֵפֶר יְצִירָה וְאִם רָץ לִבְּךָ שׁוּב לְאֶחָד — as stated in *Sefer Yetzirah* (1:8), "*If your heart runs, return to one*" (see *Tikunei Zohar* 7a).

The *Tanya* now works through the cycle of emotions, from a yearning to depart from the body ("running"), to the rebound emotion, when you "return to one."

פֵּירוּשׁ וְאִם רָץ לִבְּךָ הִיא — The meaning of "*if your heart runs*" is, תְּשׁוּקַת הַנֶּפֶשׁ שֶׁבַּלֵּב בְּחָלָל הַיְמָנִי — the yearning of your Divine Soul in the right chamber of your heart, כְּשֶׁמִּתְגַּבֶּרֶת וּמִתְלַהֶבֶת וּמִתְלַהֶטֶת בִּמְאֹד מְאֹד עַד כְּלוֹת הַנֶּפֶשׁ מַמָּשׁ — when it surges, flames and glows exceedingly, to the point where your soul actually languishes to be free from your body, לְהִשְׁתַּפֵּךְ אֶל חֵיק חַיֵּי הַחַיִּים בָּרוּךְ הוּא — to collapse into the embrace of your Divine Father, the Blessed source-of-life, וְלָצֵאת מִמַּאֲסָרָהּ בַּגּוּף הַגּוּפָנִי וְגַשְׁמִי לְדָבְקָה בּוֹ יִתְבָּרֵךְ — and to free yourself from the imprisonment of your sensuous, physical body, so as to attach yourself to G-d.

אֲזֵי זֹאת יָשִׁיב אֶל לִבּוֹ מַאֲמַר רַבּוֹתֵינוּ זִכְרוֹנָם לִבְרָכָה — Then, when you reach that state of "running," in order to inspire the rebound emotion, to "return to one," take to heart the following teaching of our Sages of blessed memory (*Mishnah Avos* 4:22), כִּי עַל כָּרְחֲךָ אַתָּה חַי בַּגּוּף הַזֶּה לְהַחֲיוֹתוֹ — that "*without your consent, you live*" in this body, to keep it alive, כְּדֵי לְהַמְשִׁיךְ חַיִּים עֶלְיוֹנִים מֵחַיֵּי הַחַיִּים בָּרוּךְ הוּא לְמַטָּה — in order to bring Supernal life energy down into it, from the Blessed source-of-life, עַל יְדֵי תּוֹרַת חַיִּים — through the Torah-of-life, לִהְיוֹת דִּירָה בַּתַּחְתּוֹנִים לְאַחְדוּתוֹ יִתְבָּרֵךְ — so that there should be a "*home (for G-d's oneness) in the lower worlds*" (*Midrash Tanchuma, Naso*, section 16), felt palpably, כְּמוֹ שֶׁנִתְבָּאֵר לְעֵיל — as stated above (chapter 36, p. 401ff.).

At the moment of your "running," call to mind that you were never given the choice whether or not to live this bodily life. G-d put you here for a reason, to carry

באחד פי' שהיחוד הנעלם יהיה בבחי' עלמא דאתגליא
וז"ש לכה דודי וכו' ובזה יובן מארז"ל ע"כ אתה חי וע"כ

out your sacred responsibility of observing the Torah down here on earth. You might desire to leave your body and unite with G-d, but *G-d's will is for you to remain in your body* and carry out the mission for which He placed you here. This is the emotion of "returning."

וּכְמוֹ שֶׁכָּתוּב בַּזֹּהַר הַקָּדוֹשׁ לְמֶהֱוֵי אֶחָד בְּאֶחָד — **And, as the** *Zohar* (2, 135a) similarly states, *"that there be One in the one,"* פֵּירוּשׁ שֶׁהַיִחוּד הַנֶּעְלָם יְהְיֶה בִּבְחִינַת עָלְמָא דְאִתְגַּלְיָא — **meaning that G-d's hidden oneness should be apparent as oneness in the "manifest world,"** through Torah activity down here, in this world.

וְזֶהוּ שֶׁאוֹמְרִים לְכָה דוֹדִי וְכוּ' — **And this is the meaning of what we say,** *"Come my beloved and greet the bride (kalah)"* (*Liturgy, Friday Night Prayers*).

The term *kalah* alludes to the languishing of the soul to leave the body (*kelos ha-nefesh*). Our reaction to this ought to be "come": to rebound into the world, thereby bringing G-d's presence ("my beloved") down here.

וּבָזֶה יוּבָן מַאֲמַר רַבּוֹתֵינוּ זִכְרוֹנָם לִבְרָכָה — **And this will help us to clarify the teaching of our Sages, of blessed memory,** עַל כָּרְחָךְ אַתָּה חַי וְעַל כָּרְחָךְ וְכוּ' — *"Without your consent, you live, and without your consent, you die"* (*Mishnah, Avos* 4:22), וְאֶלָּא אֵיךְ יְהְיֶה רְצוֹנוֹ — **and this is perplexing since these are two contradictory sentiments, so what, then, should your desire be?**

PRACTICAL LESSONS

The strongest love for G-d that you can have comes from the "fire" in your soul. It's a desire to leave your body and be one with your Maker.

This love won't actually inspire you to observe the Torah, but the rebound emotion—of recalling your Divinely allotted purpose in life—will.

The *Mishnah's* first statement ("*Without your consent, you live*") suggests that at a peak spiritual moment, when you want to transcend bodily existence, you must come to the realization that G-d's will is for you to worship G-d in a body and "return" (you must now *"live"* even though it is *"without your consent"*).

Nevertheless, if you stay in a state of "returning" for too long, you might find bodily existence so enjoyable that you lose interest in worshiping G-d. So another peak moment of "running" will be necessary to keep you in a state of spiritual "fitness." To reach the state of "running" you must follow the *Mishnah's* second statement: you yearn to transcend bodily life (to "die," so to speak), even though it is currently *"without your consent."*

But once you reach a state of "running," you will again need to shift into a mood of "returning" again, (to fulfill the Divine will, as above), and so on, in a constant cycle.

Since both emotions of "running" and "returning" are required for worship, the *Mishnah* mentions them both:

וכו' ואלא איך יהיה רצונו וכמ"ש במ"א באריכות על
משנה זו ע"כ אתה חי בעזרת חיי החיים ב"ה:

פרק נא והנה   לתוספת ביאור לשון הינוקא
דלעיל צריך לבאר תחלה להבין

"Without your consent, you live" ("returning"), and *"without your consent, you die"*
("running").

וּכְמוֹ שֶׁנִּתְבָּאֵר בְּמָקוֹם אַחֵר בַּאֲרִיכוּת עַל מִשְׁנָה זוֹ עַל כָּרְחֲךָ אַתָּה חַי — **As is explained
elsewhere a lengthy commentary on this** *Mishnah,* ***"without your consent, you
live"*** (see *Torah Ohr* 25b; 36a), בְּעֶזְרַת חַיֵּי הַחַיִּים בָּרוּךְ הוּא — **with the help of the
Blessed source-of-life.**

CHAPTER 51

WHAT IS THE "SHECHINAH"? (I)

SECTION ONE: WHERE IS YOUR SOUL LOCATED?

23RD IYAR REGULAR | 24TH IYAR LEAP

We have now concluded a long section of the *Tanya,* spanning chapters 41-50,
devoted to meditative techniques aimed at arousing reverence and love of G-d.

The final three chapters, 51-53, represent a sort of addendum to the *Tanya.* (In
all but one of the manuscripts of the *Tanya* circulated before the book was printed,
these chapters are absent — *Likutei Amarim First Versions, Based on Earliest Manuscripts* (Brooklyn: Kehos, 1981), p. 411). The material here is particularly complex
and philosophical in nature, which may explain why the author chose to include it
only at the end of the book.

These final chapters offer further clarification of a passage from the *Zohar* that
we learned in chapter 35: *"A person should not walk four cubits with his head uncovered. What's the reason? Because the Shechinah (Divine Presence) rests on his
head and the eyes and words of every wise man are, 'on his head,' meaning to say,
(his attention is focused) on that which rests and remains on his head (i.e., upon the
Shechinah)"* (*Zohar* 3, 187a).

Chapters 51-53 continue the analysis of this passage, seeking to clarify exactly
what the *Zohar* means by the *Shechinah* "resting" in a certain location.

וְהִנֵּה לְתוֹסֶפֶת בֵּיאוּר לְשׁוֹן הַיַּנּוּקָא דִּלְעֵיל — **Let's clarify further the citation from the
"child"** (*yenukah*) **in the** *Zohar,* **that we encountered in chapter 35 (p. 100).**

קְצָת עִנְיַן הַשְׁרָאַת הַשְּׁכִינָה שֶׁהָיְתָה שׁוֹרָה בְּבֵית
קָדְשֵׁי קָדָשִׁים וְכֵן כָּל מָקוֹם הַשְׁרָאַת הַשְּׁכִינָה מַה עִנְיָנוֹ הֲלֹא
מָלֵא כָּל הָאָרֶץ כְּבוֹדוֹ וְלֵית אֲתָר פָּנוּי מִנֵּיהּ. אַךְ הָעִנְיָן
כְּדִכְתִיב וּמִבְּשָׂרִי אֶחֱזֶה אֱלוֹהַּ שֶׁכְּמוֹ שֶׁנִּשְׁמַת הָאָדָם
הִיא מְמַלְּאָה כָּל רְמַ"ח אֵבְרֵי הַגּוּף מֵרֹאשׁוֹ וְעַד רַגְלוֹ
וְאַף עַל פִּי כֵן עִקַּר מִשְׁכָּנָהּ וְהַשְׁרָאָתָהּ הִיא בַּמּוֹחַ וּמֵהַמּוֹחַ
מִתְפַּשֶּׁטֶת לְכָל הָאֵבָרִים וְכָל אֵבָר מְקַבֵּל מִמֶּנָּה חַיּוּת
וְכֹחַ הָרָאוּי לוֹ לְפִי מֶזֶג וּתְכוּנָתוֹ הָעַיִן לִרְאוֹת וְהָאֹזֶן

צָרִיךְ לְבָאֵר תְּחִלָּה לְהָבִין קְצָת עִנְיַן הַשְׁרָאַת הַשְּׁכִינָה — **We first need to have a bit more understanding about the idea of the** *Shechinah* **"resting" on an object in this world,** שֶׁהָיְתָה שׁוֹרָה בְּבֵית קָדְשֵׁי קָדָשִׁים — **we say that it "rested" in the chamber of the Holy-of-Holies** in the Temple, וְכֵן כָּל מָקוֹם הַשְׁרָאַת הַשְּׁכִינָה — **and so too, in all other instances of the** *Shechinah* **"resting,"** מַה עִנְיָנוֹ — **what does that mean?**

הֲלֹא מָלֵא כָּל הָאָרֶץ כְּבוֹדוֹ — **How** can we say that G-d's presence "rests" in a particular place (implying that it doesn't rest in another), when **"all the earth is filled with His glory"** (*Isaiah* 6:3), וְלֵית אֲתָר פָּנוּי מִנֵּיהּ — **and "there is no place empty of Him"** (*Tikunei Zohar* 91b)?

אַךְ הָעִנְיָן כְּדִכְתִיב וּמִבְּשָׂרִי אֶחֱזֶה אֱלוֹהַּ — **However, the explanation is** as follows, based on the verse, **"From my flesh I shall perceive G-d,"** (*Job* 19:26), that spiritual phenomena can be discerned from the human body, which was created in the image of G-d.

שֶׁכְּמוֹ שֶׁנִּשְׁמַת הָאָדָם הִיא מְמַלְּאָה כָּל רְמַ"ח אֵבְרֵי הַגּוּף מֵרֹאשׁוֹ וְעַד רַגְלָיו — **It's similar** to the notion that **a person's soul fills all the 248 parts of his body, from head to toe,** וְאַף עַל פִּי כֵן עִקַּר מִשְׁכָּנָה וְהַשְׁרָאָתָה הִיא בַּמּוֹחַ — **and, nevertheless,** while the soul is found throughout the body, **the main location and "resting" of the soul is in the brain.**

G-d is, of course, to be found everywhere. But just as your soul expresses your humanity and higher functions in your brain to a greater extent than in the rest of the body, so too, G-d's presence could be said to "rest" primarily on the holy site of the Temple.

The *Tanya* continues to discuss how the soul's manifestation in the brain flows to the rest of the body.

וּמֵהַמּוֹחַ מִתְפַּשֶּׁטֶת לְכָל הָאֵבָרִים — **And from the brain,** the life-giving power of the soul **flows** equally **to all the body's parts,** וְכָל אֵבָר מְקַבֵּל מִמֶּנָּה חַיּוּת וְכֹחַ הָרָאוּי לוֹ לְפִי — **and each bodily part receives from** the soul **a specialized energy and power, depending on** that organ's **temperament and properties,** מֶזֶג וּתְכוּנָתוֹ הָעַיִן לִרְאוֹת — **for example, the eye** gets energy **to see;** וְהָאֹזֶן לִשְׁמוֹעַ וְהַפֶּה לְדַבֵּר וְהָרַגְלַיִם לַהֲלוֹךְ

לשמוע והפה לדבר והרגלים להלוך כנראה בחוש
שבמוח מרגיש כל הנפעל ברמ"ח אברים וכל הקורות
אותם. והנה אין שינוי קבלת הכחות והחיות שבאברי
הגוף מן הנשמה מצד עצמה ומהותה שיהיה מהותה
ועצמותה מתחלק לרמ"ח חלקי' שונים מתלבשי' ברמ"ח
מקומו' כפי ציור חלקי מקומו' אברי הגוף שלפי זה נמצא
עצמותה ומהותה מצוייר בציור גשמי ודמות ותבנית
כתבנית הגוף ח"ו אלא כולה עצם אחד רוחני פשוט
ומופשט מכל ציור גשמי ומבחי' וגדר מקום ומדה וגבול
גשמי מצד מהותה ועצמות' ולא שייך במהות' ועצמותה
לומר שהיא במוחין שבראש יותר מברגלים מאחר
שמהותה ועצמותה אינה בגדר ובחי' מקום וגבול גשמי

718

the ear to hear; the mouth to speak; and the feet to walk, כְּנִרְאֶה בְחוּשׁ שֶׁבַּמוֹחַ — מַרְגִּישׁ כָּל הַנִּפְעָל בְּרַמַ"ח אֵבָרִים וְכָל הַקּוֹרוֹת אוֹתָם — as we know from our own experience that the soul in the brain is connected with the organs since **the brain feels everything the 248 bodily parts do and everything that happens to them.**

The *Tanya* explains how the soul's energy passes to the various bodily parts.

וְהִנֵּה אֵין שִׁינּוּי קַבָּלַת הַכֹּחוֹת וְהַחַיּוּת שֶׁבְּאֵבְרֵי הַגּוּף מִן הַנְּשָׁמָה מִצַּד עַצְמָהּ וּמַהוּתָהּ — **Now, the different powers and energies which the body's parts receive are not a direct product of the soul's core itself,** שֶׁיִּהְיֶה מַהוּתָהּ וְעַצְמוּתָהּ מִתְחַלֵּק לְרַמַ"ח — in other words, it's not that the soul itself is divided *in its core* into חֲלָקִים שׁוֹנִים — **248 separate pieces,** מִתְלַבְּשִׁים בְּרַמַ"ח מְקוֹמוֹת כְּפִי צִיּוּר חֶלְקֵי מְקוֹמוֹת אֵבְרֵי הַגּוּף — **which then enter 248 different locations,** each power "fitting" into the precise form of the various parts of the body's anatomy, שֶׁלְּפִי זֶה נִמְצָא עַצְמוּתָהּ וּמַהוּתָהּ מְצוּיָּר — **because if this were true, it would mean** that the soul's Divine essence and core would be cast in a physical form, shape and image, like the body's image, בְּצִיּוּר גַּשְׁמִי וּדְמוּת וְתַבְנִית כְּתַבְנִית הַגּוּף — **G-d forbid.** חַס וְשָׁלוֹם

אֶלָּא כּוּלָהּ עֶצֶם אֶחָד רוּחָנִי פָּשׁוּט וּמוּפְשָׁט מִכָּל צִיּוּר גַּשְׁמִי — **Rather, in truth, the soul is just one single, non-composite spiritual essence, totally devoid of physical form,** וּמִבְּחִינַת וְגֶדֶר מָקוֹם וּמִדָּה וּגְבוּל גַּשְׁמִי מִצַּד מַהוּתָהּ וְעַצְמוּתָהּ — **and it's devoid of any notion or semblance of physical space, dimension, or boundary, in its essential core,** וְלֹא שַׁיָּיךְ בְּמַהוּתָהּ וְעַצְמוּתָהּ לוֹמַר שֶׁהוּא בַּמּוֹחִין שֶׁבָּרֹאשׁ יוֹתֵר מִבָּרַגְלַיִם — **so it makes no sense to say that the** soul's essential core is found more in the brain of the head than in the feet, מֵאַחַר שֶׁמַּהוּתָהּ וְעַצְמוּתָהּ אֵינוֹ בְּגֶדֶר וּבְחִינַת מָקוֹם וּגְבוּל גַּשְׁמִי — **since the essential core of the soul doesn't possess physical, spatial attributes or boundaries.**

רק שתרי"ג מיני כחות וחיות כלולים בה במהותה
ועצמותה לצאת אל הפועל והגילוי מההעלם להחיות
רמ"ח אברין ושס"ה גידין שבגוף ע"י התלבשותם בנפש
החיונית שיש לה ג"כ רמ"ח ושס"ה כחות וחיות הללו.
והנה על המשכת כל התרי"ג מיני כחות וחיות מהעלם
הנשמה אל הגוף להחיותו עליה אמרו שעיקר משכנה
והשראתה של המשכה זו וגילוי זה הוא כולו במוחין
שבראש ולכן הם מקבלים תחלה הכח והחיות הראוי
להם לפי מזגם ותכונתם שהן חב"ד וכח המחשבה וכל
השייך למוחין ולא זו בלבד אלא גם כללות כל המשכות

רַק שֶׁתַּרְיַ"ג מִינֵי כֹחוֹת וְחַיּוּת כְּלוּלִים בָּהּ בְּמַהוּתָהּ וְעַצְמוּתָהּ — Only, within that essential core is absorbed *in potential* 613 different types of power and energy, לָצֵאת אֶל הַפּוֹעֵל וְהַגִּלּוּי מֵהֶהְעֵלֶם — which can actually emerge and be revealed from their hidden potential state, לְהַחֲיוֹת רַמַ"ח אֵבְרִין וְשַׁסַּ"ה גִידִין שֶׁבַּגּוּף — to energize the 248 bodily parts and 365 major blood vessels of the body, עַל יְדֵי הִתְלַבְּשׁוּתָם — through engagement with the energizing, Animal Soul, בְּנֶפֶשׁ הַחִיּוּנִית — which also possesses this array of 248/365 גַּם כֵּן רַמַ"ח וְשַׁסַּ"ה כֹחוֹת וְחַיּוּת הַלָּלוּ — types of power and energy.

Like its Creator, the pure Divine soul cannot possibly be a composite entity of different powers. On the other hand, each of the body's parts require specific and diverse powers for their functioning. We must therefore say that, while the specific powers don't actually exist within the soul, the soul nevertheless produces them out of its innate potential.

24TH IYAR REGULAR

וְהִנֵּה עַל הַמְשָׁכַת כָּל הַתַּרְיַ"ג מִינֵי כֹחוֹת וְחַיּוּת מֵהֶעְלֵם הַנְּשָׁמָה אֶל הַגּוּף לְהַחֲיוֹתוֹ — Now it was regarding the flow into the body of all these 613 types of powers and energies, from a state of latency in the soul, עָלֶיהָ אָמְרוּ שֶׁעִיקַּר מִשְׁכָּנָהּ וְהַשְׁרָאָתָהּ שֶׁל — that it was said that the main location הַמְשָׁכָה זוֹ וְגִלּוּי זֶה הוּא כּוּלוֹ בַּמּוֹחִין שֶׁבָּרֹאשׁ — and "resting" of this flow and soul-expression is all in the brain within the head.

The idea of the soul "resting" in a particular location always refers to the *particular powers* of the soul, and not its core. We say that the soul "rests" primarily in the head, because the head receives the most important of the soul powers.

וְלָכֵן הֵם מְקַבְּלִים תְּחִלָּה הַכֹּחַ וְהַחַיּוּת הָרָאוּי לָהֶם לְפִי מִזְגָּם וּתְכוּנָתָם — Therefore the intellectual powers **receive first** from the soul, **the power and energy which is suitable for them, befitting their temperament and properties,** שֶׁהֵן חָכְמָה בִּינָה וָדַעַת — namely the powers of *chochmah, binah* and *da'as,* וְכֹחַ הַמַּחֲשָׁבָה וְכָל הַשַּׁיָּיךְ לַמּוֹחִין — the power of thought and everything relating to the brain.

החיות לשאר האברים ג"כ כלולה ומלובשת במוחין
שבראש ושם הוא עיקרה ושרשה של המשכ' זו בבחי'
גילוי האור והחיו' של כל הנשמ' כולה ומשם מתפשטת
הארה לשאר כל האברים ומקבל כל א' כח וחיו' הראוי
לו כפי מזגו ותכונתו כח הראיה מתגלה בעין וכח
השמיעה באוזן וכו'. וכל הכחות מתפשטים מהמוח
כנודע כי שם הוא עיקר משכן הנשמה כולה בבחי' גילוי
שנגלית שם כללו' החיות המתפשט ממנה. רק כחותיה
של כללות החיות מאירים ומתפשטים משם לכל אברי
הגוף כדמיון האור המתפשט ומאיר מהשמש לחדרי
חדרים [ואפילו הלב מקבל מהמוח ולכן המוח שליט
עליו בתולדתו כנ"ל]:

Another reason for the importance of the brain as the soul's main "location", is because it acts as a kind of "hub" for the other soul powers, before they pass to the rest of the body.

וְלֹא זוֹ בִּלְבָד — **And** the brain **doesn't only** receive power and energy from the soul for itself, אֶלָּא גַם כְּלָלוּת כָּל הַמְשָׁכוֹת הַחַיּוּת לִשְׁאָר הָאֵבָרִים גַּם כֵּן כְּלוּלָה וּמְלוּבֶּשֶׁת בְּמוֹחִין שֶׁבָּרֹאשׁ — **rather, all of the powers and energies destined for the other limbs also enter and are** initially **contained within the brain in the head.**

וְשָׁם הוּא עִיקָרָהּ וְשָׁרְשָׁהּ שֶׁל הַמְשָׁכָה זוֹ בִּבְחִינַת גִּילוּי הָאוֹר וְהַחַיּוּת שֶׁל כָּל הַנְּשָׁמָה כּוּלָּהּ — **And there, in the brain, is the nucleus and root of all** soul-flow, **the disclosure of all the soul's light and energy,** וּמִשָּׁם מִתְפַּשֶּׁטֶת הָאָרָה לִשְׁאָר כָּל הָאֵבָרִים — **and it is from there, in the brain, that illumination from the soul spreads to all the rest of the limbs,** וּמְקַבֵּל כָּל אֶחָד כֹּחַ וְחַיּוּת הָרָאוּי לוֹ כְּפִי מִזְגּוֹ וּתְכוּנָתוֹ — **each** limb receiving the power and energy appropriate for it, befitting its temperament and properties, כֹּחַ הָרְאִיָּה מִתְגַּלֶּה בָּעַיִן וְכֹחַ הַשְּׁמִיעָה בָּאוֹזֶן וְכוּ' — **the** soul's **power of sight is disclosed in the eye, and the** soul's **power of hearing in the ear,** *etc.,* וְכָל הַכֹּחוֹת מִתְפַּשְּׁטִים מֵהַמוֹחַ כַּנּוֹדָע — **for, as we know, all these** soul powers spread to the limbs from the brain.

כִּי שָׁם הוּא עִיקָר מִשְׁכַּן הַנְּשָׁמָה כּוּלָּהּ בִּבְחִינַת גִּילוּי — **For there, in the brain, is the entire soul's primary location, in its overtly expressed form,** שֶׁנִּגְלֵית שָׁם כְּלָלוּת הַחַיּוּת — **for there, all the energy that is going to emerge from it to the** body is already **disclosed,** הַמִּתְפַּשֵּׁט מִמֶּנָּה רַק כְּחוֹתֶיהָ שֶׁל כְּלָלוּת הַחַיּוּת מְאִירִים וּמִתְפַּשְּׁטִים מִשָּׁם לְכָל אֶבְרֵי הַגּוּף — **and only specific powers, drawing from all that energy, will shine from there and spread to all the body's** specific parts, כְּדִמְיוֹן הָאוֹר הַמִּתְפַּשֵּׁט וּמֵאִיר מֵהַשֶּׁמֶשׁ לְחַדְרֵי חֲדָרִים — **like light that spreads and shines from the sun into pri-**vate rooms.

וככה ממש עד"מ א"ס ב"ה ממלא כל עלמין
להחיותם ובכל עולם יש
ברואים לאין קץ ותכלית רבוא רבבות מיני מדרגות
מלאכים ונשמות כו' וכן ריבוי העולמות אין לו קץ וגבול
גבוה על גבוה כו'. והנה מהותו ועצמותו של א"ס ב"ה
שוה בעליונים ותחתונים כמשל הנשמה הנ"ל וכמ"ש

72A

[וַאֲפִילוּ הַלֵּב מְקַבֵּל מֵהַמּוֹחַ — **And even the heart receives** its energy **from the brain,** וְלָכֵן הַמּוֹחַ שַׁלִּיט עָלָיו בְּתוֹלַדְתוֹ כַּנִּזְכָּר לְעֵיל] — **which is why the brain inherently rules over it, as stated above** (chapter 12, p. 143).

In conclusion: 1.) The soul's core is non-composite and devoid of any specific powers. 2.) In the brain, many specific powers emerge from the latent potential of the soul, that will later enter all the limbs and organs to energize them. 3.) After the brain takes the powers it needs, the remaining powers spread from the brain into the rest of the body.

The idea of the soul "resting" primarily in the brain refers to "2" and "3." At level "1," the soul does not yet have a specific location.

SECTION TWO: HOW THE SHECHINAH "RESTS" IN ALL WORLDS

25TH IYAR REGULAR | 25TH IYAR LEAP

Following the parallel between the human and Divine image — *"from my flesh I shall perceive G-d"* — the *Tanya* will now compare the "resting" of the soul in a particular location to the "resting" of the *Shechinah.*

וְכָכָה מַמָּשׁ עַל דֶּרֶךְ מָשָׁל — **And, figuratively speaking,** the way in which the soul-powers energize the individual limbs **is identical,** אֵין סוֹף בָּרוּךְ הוּא מְמַלֵּא כָּל עָלְמִין לְהַחֲיוֹתָם — to the way that **the Blessed Infinite One fills** the individual components of **all the worlds and energizes them,** וּבְכָל עוֹלָם יֵשׁ בְּרוּאִים לְאֵין קֵץ וְתַכְלִית — and these components are very numerous since **in each world there are endless and limitless creatures,** רְבוֹא רְבָבוֹת מִינֵי מַדְרֵגוֹת מַלְאָכִים וּנְשָׁמוֹת כו' — **hundreds of millions of levels of angels and souls etc.,** וְכֵן רִיבּוּי הָעוֹלָמוֹת אֵין לוֹ קֵץ וּגְבוּל גָּבוֹהַּ עַל גָּבוֹהַּ כו' — **as well as a vast number of worlds, without end or limit, each higher than the other.**

וְהִנֵּה מַהוּתוֹ וְעַצְמוּתוֹ שֶׁל אֵין סוֹף בָּרוּךְ הוּא שָׁוֶה בָּעֶלְיוֹנִים וְתַחְתוֹנִים — **But,** unlike these numerous components, which all differ in the Divine illumination they receive, **the** *essential core* **of the Blessed Infinite Light is found** *equally* **in the upper and lower worlds,** כְּמָשָׁל הַנְּשָׁמָה הַנִּזְכָּר לְעֵיל — **as in the above example of** the essential core of **the soul** which has no specific location in the body.

The *Tanya* cites a source from the *Zohar* indicating that the essential core of G-d's light has no specific location.

בתיקונים דאיהו סתימו דכל סתימין פי' דאפי' בעלמין סתימין דלעילא הוא סתום ונעלם בתוכם כמו שהוא סתום ונעלם בתחתוני' כי לית מחשבה תפיסא ביה כלל אפי' בעולמות עליונים. ונמצא כמו שמצוי שם כך נמצא בתחתונים ממש. וההבדל שבין עולמו' עליונים ותחתונים הוא מצד המשכת החיות אשר א"ס ב"ה ממשיך ומאיר בבחי' גילוי מההעלם [שזה אחד מהטעמי' שההשפעה והמשכות החיות מכונה בשם אור עד"מ]

וּכְמוֹ שֶׁכָּתוּב בַּתִּיקּוּנִים דְּאִיהוּ סְתִימוּ דְּכָל סְתִימִין — And as *Tikunei Zohar* (17a) states that G-d is *"hidden from all the hidden,"* פֵּירוּשׁ דַּאֲפִילוּ בְּעָלְמִין סְתִימִין דִּלְעֵילָא הוּא — meaning that even within the hidden worlds above (*"all the hidden"*), He still remains *"hidden"* and concealed, סָתוּם וְנֶעְלָם בְּתוֹכָם כְּמוֹ שֶׁהוּא סָתוּם וְנֶעְלָם בַּתַּחְתּוֹנִים — just as He is hidden and concealed in the lower worlds, כִּי לֵית מַחֲשָׁבָה תְּפִיסָא בֵּיהּ כְּלָל אֲפִילוּ בְּעוֹלְמוֹת עֶלְיוֹנִים — since *"no thought can grasp Him at all"* (ibid.), even in the upper worlds, וְנִמְצָא כְּמוֹ שֶׁמָּצוּי שָׁם כָּךְ נִמְצָא בַּתַּחְתּוֹנִים מַמָּשׁ — so it follows that His essential core is found there, in exactly the same way that it's found here.

26TH IYAR LEAP

Having explained how the Blessed Infinite One's essential core is present equally everywhere, we can appreciate that only the *flow* and *disclosure* of the Light varies from world to world.

וְהַהֶבְדֵּל שֶׁבֵּין עוֹלָמוֹת עֶלְיוֹנִים וְתַחְתּוֹנִים הוּא מִצַּד הַמְשָׁכַת הַחַיּוּת — And the difference between the upper and lower worlds is not in the presence of the essential core-Light itself, but in the flow of energy from the Blessed Infinite One, אֲשֶׁר אֵין סוֹף בָּרוּךְ הוּא מַמְשִׁיךְ וּמֵאִיר בִּבְחִינַת גִּילוּי מֵהַהֶעְלֵם — the extent to which the Blessed Infinite One flows and shines light openly, from its prior concealment, and that flow is more in the upper worlds than the lower.

Just as your soul's presence in your various limbs only differs in terms of its powers and not its core, the same is true of the Blessed Infinite One's presence throughout the worlds.

[שֶׁזֶּה אֶחָד מֵהַטְּעָמִים שֶׁהַהַשְׁפָּעָה וְהַמְשָׁכַת הַחַיּוּת מְכוּנָה בְּשֵׁם אוֹר עַל דֶּרֶךְ מָשָׁל] — And this is one of the reasons why the flow and distribution of energy from G-d is referred to figuratively as "light."

If you block the flow of water in a pipe, pressure builds up in the water's source; but if you block the ray of light coming out from a light bulb, the bulb remains unaffected. That's why the Kabbalists chose to depict the emergence of G-d's energy as "light," to indicate that He remains unaffected by whatever happens to it. The message is: You simply can't influence G-d in any way.

לְהַחַיּוֹת הָעוֹלָמוֹת וְהַבְּרוּאִים שֶׁבָּהֶם שֶׁהָעוֹלְמוֹ' הָעֶלְיוֹנִי'
מְקַבְּלִים בִּבְחִי' גִּילוּי קְצָת יוֹתֵר מֵהַתַּחְתּוֹנִי' וְכָל הַבְּרוּאֵי'
שֶׁבָּהֶם מְקַבְּלִים כָּל אֶ' כְּפִי כֹחוֹ וְתְכוּנָתוֹ שֶׁהִיא תְּכוּנַת
וּבְחִי' הַמְשָׁכָה הַפְּרָטִית אֲשֶׁר א"ס ב"ה מַמְשִׁיךְ וּמֵאִיר
לוֹ. וְהַתַּחְתּוֹנִים אֲפִי' הָרוּחָנִיִּים אֵינָם מְקַבְּלִים בִּבְחִי'
גִּילּוּי כ"כ רַק בִּלְבוּשִׁים רַבִּים אֲשֶׁר א"ס ב"ה מַלְבִּישׁ
בָּהֶם הַחַיּוּת וְהָאוֹר אֲשֶׁר מַמְשִׁיךְ וּמֵאִיר לָהֶם לְהַחַיּוֹתָם
וְכָּ"כ עָצְמוּ וְגָבְרוּ הַלְּבוּשִׁים אֲשֶׁר א"ס ב"ה מַלְבִּישׁ
וּמַסְתִּיר בָּהֶם הָאוֹר וְהַחַיּוּת עַד אֲשֶׁר בָּרָא בּוֹ עוֹה"ז
הַחוֹמְרִי וְהַגַּשְׁמִי מַמָּשׁ וּמְהַוֵּוהוּ וּמְחַיֵּהוּ בְּחַיּוּת וְאוֹר
אֲשֶׁר מַמְשִׁיךְ וּמֵאִיר לוֹ אוֹר הַמְלוּבָּשׁ וּמְכוּסֶּה וּמוּסְתָּר
בְּתוֹךְ הַלְּבוּשִׁים הָרַבִּים וְהָעֲצוּמִים הַמַּעֲלִימִים וּמַסְתִּירֵי'

לְהַחַיּוֹת הָעוֹלָמוֹת וְהַבְּרוּאִים שֶׁבָּהֶם — And this flow of "light" from G-d **energizes the worlds and the creatures found there,** שֶׁהָעוֹלְמוֹת הָעֶלְיוֹנִים מְקַבְּלִים בִּבְחִינַת גִּילוּי — **the higher worlds receiving a little more disclosure than the ones below,** קְצָת יוֹתֵר מֵהַתַּחְתּוֹנִים — וְכָל הַבְּרוּאִים שֶׁבָּהֶם מְקַבְּלִים כָּל אֶחָד כְּפִי כֹחוֹ וּתְכוּנָתוֹ — **all the creatures in these** worlds **receiving** a different amount of "light," **according to their capabilities and disposition,** שֶׁהִיא תְּכוּנַת וּבְחִינַת הַמְשָׁכָה הַפְּרָטִית אֲשֶׁר אֵין סוֹף בָּרוּךְ הוּא מַמְשִׁיךְ וּמֵאִיר לוֹ — **so there is an individualized flow from the Blessed Infinite Light flowing and shining to each recipient, fitting the** recipient's **capabilities and disposition.**

While the upper worlds are suited to receive the flow of G-d's light, the lower worlds are not, as the *Tanya* continues to explain.

וְהַתַּחְתּוֹנִים אֲפִילוּ הָרוּחָנִיִּים אֵינָם מְקַבְּלִים בִּבְחִינַת גִּילוּי כָּל כָּךְ — **But the lowest worlds, even the spiritual ones, don't receive so much disclosure** of the light, רַק בִּלְבוּשִׁים רַבִּים אֲשֶׁר אֵין סוֹף בָּרוּךְ הוּא מַלְבִּישׁ בָּהֶם הַחַיּוּת וְהָאוֹר אֲשֶׁר מַמְשִׁיךְ וּמֵאִיר לָהֶם לְהַחַיּוֹתָם — **rather, when the Blessed Infinite Light provides them with compatible energy and light to sustain them, He does so through formidable filters.**

27TH IYAR LEAP

וְכָל כָּךְ עָצְמוּ וְגָבְרוּ הַלְּבוּשִׁים אֲשֶׁר אֵין סוֹף בָּרוּךְ הוּא מַלְבִּישׁ וּמַסְתִּיר בָּהֶם הָאוֹר וְהַחַיּוּת — **And the filters through which the Blessed Infinite One filters and hides His light and energy from** the lower worlds **become progressively so strong and powerful,** עַד אֲשֶׁר בָּרָא בּוֹ עוֹלָם הַזֶּה הַחוֹמְרִי וְהַגַּשְׁמִי מַמָּשׁ — **to the point where this physical world of** inanimate **matter is created,** in which G-d's light can't be discerned at all.

וּמְהַוֵּוהוּ וּמְחַיֵּהוּ בְּחַיּוּת וְאוֹר אֲשֶׁר מַמְשִׁיךְ וְאוֹר אֲשֶׁר מַמְשִׁיךְ וּמֵאִיר לוֹ — And while even inanimate matter **is created and sustained by the energy and light which flows and shines to it,** אוֹר הַמְלוּבָּשׁ וּמְכוּסֶּה וּמוּסְתָּר בְּתוֹךְ הַלְּבוּשִׁים הָרַבִּים וְהָעֲצוּמִים — it's **a light filtered,**

האוֹר וְהַחַיּוּת עַד שֶׁאֵין נִרְאֶה וְנִגְלֶה שׁוּם אוֹר וְחַיּוּת רַק
דְּבָרִים חוֹמְרִיִּים וְגַשְׁמִיִּים וְנִרְאִים מֵתִים אַךְ בְּתוֹכָם יֵשׁ **72B**
אוֹר וְחַיּוּת הַמְהַוֶּה אוֹתָם מֵאַיִן לְיֵשׁ תָּמִיד שֶׁלֹּא יַחְזְרוּ
לִהְיוֹת אַיִן וְאֶפֶס כְּשֶׁהָיוּ וְאוֹר זֶה הוּא מֵא"ס ב"ה רַק
שֶׁנִּתְלַבֵּשׁ בִּלְבוּשִׁים רַבִּים וּכְמ"שׁ בְּעֵ"חַ שֶׁאוֹר וְחַיּוּת
כַּדּוּר הָאָרֶץ הַחוֹמְרִי הַנִּרְאֶה לְעֵינֵי בָשָׂר הוּא מִמַּלְכוּת
דְּמַלְכוּת דַּעֲשִׂיָּה וּבְתוֹכָהּ מַלְכוּת דִּיצִירָה(*) וְכוּ' עַד
שֶׁבְּתוֹךְ כֻּלָּן י"ס דַאֲצִילוּת הַמְיֻחָדוֹת בְּמַאֲצִילָן א"ס ב"ה:

*)[בדפוסים הקודמים הי' כתוב "מלכות דמלכות דעשיה" ונ"ל דצ"ל "מלכות דיצירה" וכ"ה באגה"ק
סי' כ"ה המתחיל להבין אמרי בינה כו'. אשר נמצא לפנינו גוף כתי"ק].

hidden and concealed through numerous powerful filters, הַמַּעֲלִימִים וּמַסְתִּירִים
הָאוֹר וְהַחַיּוּת — **which hide and conceal the light and energy,** עַד שֶׁאֵין נִרְאֶה וְנִגְלֶה
— **to the point where,** in inanimate matter, **neither light nor energy is** שׁוּם אוֹר וְחַיּוּת
visible or apparent, רַק דְּבָרִים חוֹמְרִיִּים וְגַשְׁמִיִּים וְנִרְאִים מֵתִים — **only crude, physical
matter which appears inanimate.**

אַךְ בְּתוֹכָם יֵשׁ אוֹר וְחַיּוּת הַמְהַוֶּה אוֹתָם מֵאַיִן לְיֵשׁ תָּמִיד — **Nevertheless,** in reality, **within those** apparently inanimate things, **there's a light and energy which brings them
into being continually, something-from-nothing,** שֶׁלֹּא יַחְזְרוּ לִהְיוֹת אַיִן וְאֶפֶס כְּשֶׁהָיוּ
— **so that they shouldn't return to be** *"null and void"* (see *Isaiah* 40:17) **as they
were originally.**

In a concluding thought, the *Tanya* stresses that G-d's diminished light which
powers this world, and the Blessed Infinite Light, are not separate.

וְאוֹר זֶה הוּא מֵאֵין סוֹף בָּרוּךְ הוּא — **But this light** which sustains the physical world, **is**
ultimately **from the Blessed Infinite Light,** רַק שֶׁנִּתְלַבֵּשׁ בִּלְבוּשִׁים רַבִּים — **only it has
passed through numerous filters.**

שֶׁאוֹר וְחַיּוּת כַּדּוּר הָאָרֶץ — **As stated in** *Etz Chaim* (50:1), וּכְמוֹ שֶׁכָּתוּב בְּעֵץ חַיִּים
הַחוֹמְרִי הַנִּרְאֶה לְעֵינֵי בָשָׂר — **that the light and energy in the earth's physical globe,**
apparent to our eyes, הוּא מִמַּלְכוּת דְּמַלְכוּת דַּעֲשִׂיָּה — **is from** the lowest level of the
lowest *sefirah*-energy, *malchus* of *malchus,* from the lowest spiritual world, *Asiyah,*
וּבְתוֹכָהּ מַלְכוּת דִּיצִירָה וְכוּ' — **but** since all spiritual entities are interconnected, **within** *malchus* of *Asiyah* is *malchus* of the next world, *Yetzirah,* and so on up through
the worlds, עַד שֶׁבְּתוֹךְ כֻּלָּן י' סְפִירוֹת דַאֲצִילוּת — **so that within all** expressions of
malchus **are the ten** *sefiros* **of** *Atzilus,* הַמְיֻחָדוֹת בְּמַאֲצִילָן אֵין סוֹף בָּרוּךְ הוּא — **that
are united with their emanating source, the Blessed Infinite One** (see note to chap-
ter 6, p. 90-91).

Since the *sefiros* are interconnected, even the lowest *sefirah* in the lowest world
contains something of the highest *sefirah* of the highest world, which receives directly from the Blessed Infinite Light.

[Our discussion will continue directly in the following chapter.]

פרק נב וכמו שבנשמת האדם עיקר גילוי כללות
החיות הוא במוחין וכל האברים
מקבלים אור וכח לבד המאיר להם ממקור גילוי החיות
שבמוחין ככה ממש עד"מ עיקר גילוי כללות המשכת
החיות להחיות העולמות והברואים שבהם הוא מלובש

CHAPTER 52

WHAT IS THE "SHECHINAH"? (II)
SECTION ONE: A DEFINITION OF "SHECHINAH"

26TH IYAR REGULAR | 28TH IYAR LEAP

Chapter 51 compared the soul's presence in the human body to G-d's presence in the world. We learned that: 1.) The soul's *non-composite core*, which is devoid of any specific powers, transcends any direct interaction with the body. 2.) In the brain, many *specific powers* emerge from the soul's latent potential, that will later enter all the limbs and organs to energize them. 3.) After the brain takes whatever powers it needs, the remaining powers then spread from the brain to the rest of the body.

In chapter 51 we compared phases '1' and '3' of this process to G-d's manifestation in the world. Initially, we learned, G-d is *"hidden from all the hidden,"* totally transcending the universe, just as the soul's non-composite essence transcends the body (stage '1'). We then discussed the heavenly equivalent of stage '3,' how G-d's light is diminished and filtered to be compatible with each of the worlds, just as the soul's specific powers are delivered to individual limbs and organs.

What we didn't discuss in chapter 51 was the heavenly equivalent of phase '2,' how soul powers initially emerge in the brain before interacting with the body. What is the equivalent to phase '2' in the scheme of Divine emergence?

The *Tanya* will turn to that question now.

וּכְמוֹ שֶׁבְּנִשְׁמַת הָאָדָם עִיקַּר גִּילּוּי כְּלָלוּת הַחַיּוּת הוּא בַּמּוֹחִין — **And just as with a person's soul, the primary emergence of its total energy,** before that energy actually enters any limbs or organs **is in the brain,** וְכָל הָאֵבָרִים מְקַבְּלִים אוֹר וְכֹחַ לְבָד — **and all the bodily parts receive a mere** flow of **light and power** from that total energy, הַמֵּאִיר לָהֶם מִמְּקוֹר גִּילּוּי הַחַיּוּת שֶׁבַּמּוֹחִין — **which shines to them from the source of manifest** total soul **energy in the brain,** כָּכָה מַמָּשׁ עַל דֶּרֶךְ מָשָׁל — **the same is true precisely (figuratively speaking)** with G-d, עִיקַּר גִּילּוּי כְּלָלוּת הַמְשָׁכַת הַחַיּוּת לְהַחֲיוֹת — עָקַּר גִּילּוּי כְּלָלוּת הַמְשָׁכַת הַחַיּוּת לְהַחֲיוֹת, הָעוֹלָמוֹת וְהַבְּרוּאִים שֶׁבָּהֶם — namely, **the primary manifestation of the total energy**

וְנִכְלָל בִּרְצוֹנוֹ וְחָכְמָתוֹ וּבִינָתוֹ וְדַעְתּוֹ יִת' הֻנַּק' בְּשֵׁם
מוֹחִין וְהֵן הֵן הַמְלוּבָּשִׁים בַּתּוֹרָה וּמִצְווֹתֶיהָ וְגִילּוּי כְּלָלוּת
הַמְשָׁכָה זוֹ הוּא מְקוֹר הַחַיּוּת אֲשֶׁר הָעוֹלָמוֹת מְקַבְּלִי' כָּל
אֶ' בִּפְרָטוּת רַק הָאָרָה מִתְפַּשֶּׁטֶת וּמְאִירָה מִמְּקוֹר זֶה
כְּדִמְיוֹן אוֹר הַמִּתְפַּשֵּׁט מֵהַשֶּׁמֶשׁ עַד"מ וְכֹחוֹת אֶבְרֵי הַגּוּף
מֵהַמּוֹחַ הַנַּ"ל וּמְקוֹר זֶה הוּא הַנִּקְרָא עָלְמָא דְאִתְגַּלְיָא

הוּא מְלוּבָּשׁ וְנִכְלָל בִּרְצוֹנוֹ וְחָכְמָתוֹ **that flows to the worlds and their inhabitants,** וּבִינָתוֹ וְדַעְתּוֹ יִתְבָּרֵךְ — **is found,** before it reaches them, **absorbed and expressed within G-d's will and His *chochmah, binah* and *da'as*,** הַנִּקְרָאִים בְּשֵׁם מוֹחִין — **which are called,** in the Kabbalah, the Divine **"brain."**

As we learned in chapter 51, the soul's *essential core* transcends the body and has no specific "location" in it. It is the *manifest powers* of the soul, emerging from the soul's essential core, that directly energize the body. And these powers begin their emergence in the brain area, before they enter the body itself.

Since man is created in the image of G-d, the above precisely reflects the spiritual unfolding through which G-d energizes the world. The essence of G-d's Blessed Infinite Light transcends everything; it's only His "powers" that emerge from the Infinite Light, which energize the universe. The initial emergence of these powers occurs in G-d's mental energies of "will," *chochmah, binah* and *da'as.* So, figuratively speaking, G-d's powers also emerge first in His "brain," as is the case with human beings.

וְהֵן הֵן הַמְלוּבָּשִׁים בַּתּוֹרָה וּמִצְווֹתֶיהָ — **And these** Divine "brain" energies **take expression in the Torah,** G-d's *chochmah, binah* and *da'as,* **and its *mitzvos*,** G-d's will.

As the *Zohar* teaches, *"The Blessed Holy One looked into the Torah and created the world"* (*Zohar* 2, 161b). The Divine light and energy which initially emerged as the Torah's heavenly root (G-d's wisdom and will), is what powers the universe.

הוּא מְקוֹר וְגִילּוּי כְּלָלוּת הַמְשָׁכָה זוֹ — **And the disclosure of this total** energy flow, הַחַיּוּת אֲשֶׁר הָעוֹלָמוֹת מְקַבְּלִים — **is the source of energy which the worlds** eventually **receive,** כָּל אֶחָד בִּפְרָטוּת רַק הָאָרָה מִתְפַּשֶּׁטֶת וּמְאִירָה מִמְּקוֹר זֶה — **each** detail of each world eventually receiving **an individualized measure of light which spreads out and shines from this** energy source, the Divine "brain" as expressed in the Torah, כְּדִמְיוֹן אוֹר הַמִּתְפַּשֵּׁט מֵהַשֶּׁמֶשׁ עַל דֶּרֶךְ מָשָׁל — **in a similar way, for example, that light rays emerge from the sun,** וְכֹחוֹת אֶבְרֵי הַגּוּף מֵהַמּוֹחַ — **and** in the same way **that powers** emerge **from the brain for the body's parts,** הַנִּזְכָּר לְעֵיל — **as mentioned above** in chapter 51.

Again, we are speaking here of phase '2,' where individualized powers have emerged from the Blessed Infinite Light, but they haven't yet entered the universe.

וּמְקוֹר זֶה הוּא הַנִּקְרָא עָלְמָא דְאִתְגַּלְיָא — **And this** phase '2' **source** of powers that have emerged from the Blessed Infinite Light but haven't entered the universe, **is**

וּמַטְרוֹנִית' וְאִימָא תַתָּאָה וּשְׁכִינָה מִלְּשׁוֹן וְשָׁכַנְתִּי בְּתוֹכָם
עַל שֵׁם שֶׁמָּקוֹר זֶה הוּא רֵאשִׁית הִתְגַּלּוּת אוֹר א"ס אֲשֶׁר
מַמְשִׁיךְ וּמֵאִיר לְעוֹלָמוֹת בִּבְחִי' גִּילוּי וּמִמָּקוֹר זֶה נִמְשָׁךְ
לְכָל א' הָאוֹר וְחַיּוּת פְּרָטִי הָרָאוּי לוֹ וְשׁוֹכֵן וּמִתְלַבֵּשׁ
בְּתוֹכָם לְהַחֲיוֹתָם וְלָכֵן נִקְרָא אֵם הַבָּנִים עד"מ וּכְנֶסֶת
יִשְׂרָאֵל שֶׁמָּקוֹר זֶה נֶאֶצְלוּ נְשָׁמוֹת דַאֲצִי' וְנִבְרְאוּ
נְשָׁמוֹת דִּבְרִיאָה וְכוּ' וְכוּלָּן אֵינָן רַק מֵהִתְפַּשְׁטוּת הַחַיּוּת
וְהָאוֹר מֵהַמָּקוֹר הַזֶּה הַנִּק' שְׁכִינָה כְּהִתְפַּשְׁטוּת הָאוֹר

referred to by various names in the *Zohar*: **"the manifest world"** (*Zohar* 1, 18a; 154b), וְאִימָא תַתָּאָה — **and** the feminine imagery of **"matron"** (ibid. 3, 230a), וּמַטְרוֹנִיתָא — **and** — **"Mother to the lower world"** (ibid. 74a), וּשְׁכִינָה מִלְּשׁוֹן וְשָׁכַנְתִּי בְּתוֹכָם — and **Shechinah,** as in the phrase, **"I will rest (shochanti) among them"** (*Exodus* 25:8).

These various terms are used by the *Zohar* to describe phase '2' energy. The *Tanya* now clarifies the significance of each term (*Notes on Tanya*).

עַל שֵׁם שֶׁמָּקוֹר זֶה הוּא רֵאשִׁית הִתְגַּלּוּת אוֹר אֵין סוֹף — The term *"manifest"* world **indicates that this source is the initial *disclosure* of the Infinite Light** capable of being received by creations.

אֲשֶׁר מַמְשִׁיךְ וּמֵאִיר לְעוֹלָמוֹת בִּבְחִינַת גִּילוּי — The comparison to a "matron," who implements the affairs of the royal *household*, conveys the idea **that this source flows into and illuminates** *the worlds* **palpably.**

וּמִמָּקוֹר זֶה נִמְשָׁךְ לְכָל אֶחָד הָאוֹר וְחַיּוּת פְּרָטִי הָרָאוּי לוֹ — **And** the term "mother" is used to stress how **it's from this source that an appropriate,** *individualized* **flow of light and energy** later **reaches each** world or creature, like a mother who cares for each of her children's needs.

וְשׁוֹכֵן וּמִתְלַבֵּשׁ בְּתוֹכָם לְהַחֲיוֹתָם — **And** the term *"Shechinah"* is used to emphasize how this energy **rests (shochen) in them, and becomes enmeshed in them to give them life.**

Having explained how this phase '2' energy is the source of energy for all the worlds, the *Tanya* notes that it is also the source of our souls.

וְלָכֵן נִקְרָא אֵם הַבָּנִים עַל דֶּרֶךְ מָשָׁל — **And that's why** this phase '2' source **is** also referred to as **"mother of the children"** (*Psalms* 113:9), וּכְנֶסֶת יִשְׂרָאֵל — **and Kneses Yisrael, "Congregation of Israel"** (*Zohar* ibid.), שֶׁמָּקוֹר זֶה נֶאֶצְלוּ נְשָׁמוֹת דַאֲצִילוּת — **since it's from this source that the souls of** *Atzilus* **are emanated** וְנִבְרְאוּ נְשָׁמוֹת דִּבְרִיאָה וְכוּ' — **and the souls of** *Beriah* **are created,** as well as the other souls.

וְכוּלָּן — **And they,** the souls and the energies which power each detail of the universe, אֵינָן רַק מֵהִתְפַּשְׁטוּת הַחַיּוּת וְהָאוֹר מֵהַמָּקוֹר הַזֶּה הַנִּקְרָא שְׁכִינָה — **are all nothing** other than energy and light which have emerged from this source, which is called **"Shechinah,"** כְּהִתְפַּשְׁטוּת הָאוֹר מֵהַשֶּׁמֶשׁ — **just as light emerges from the sun.**

מהשמש אבל השכינה עצמה שהיא ראשית הגילוי   73A
ועיקרו מה שא"ס ב"ה מאיר לעולמות בבחי' גילוי והיא
מקור כל המשכות החיות שבכל העולמות [שכל החיו'
שבהם אינו רק אור המתפשט ממנה כאור המתפשט

SECTION TWO: THE SHECHINAH AND ITS ENERGY FLOW

27TH IYAR REGULAR | 29TH IYAR LEAP

Phase '2,' could be subdivided into two processes. a.) There is an initial disclosure of the *total energy* which will power everything in the universe. b.) This total energy is then spliced into various "powers," which are suitable for the various components of the universe.

As the *Tanya* will now clarify, process 'a' is what we refer to as "the *Shechinah* itself"; whereas process 'b' is the way in which *"an appropriate, individualized flow of light and energy"* emerges from the *Shechinah* to power the various components of the universe (before that energy actually reaches them in phase '3').

אֲבָל הַשְּׁכִינָה עַצְמָהּ שֶׁהִיא רֵאשִׁית הַגִּילּוּי וְעִיקָּרוֹ מַה שֶּׁאֵין סוֹף בָּרוּךְ הוּא מֵאִיר לָעוֹלָמוֹת בִּבְחִינַת גִּילּוּי — **But the** *Shechinah* **itself is the initial and primary manifestation of the Blessed Infinite One in a disclosable fashion,** that will eventually **shine to the worlds.**

The term "disclosable" here is somewhat confusing. As we shall soon see, "the *Shechinah* itself" is actually *incompatible* with the worlds. (It's just closer to the worlds than the Blessed Infinite One.)

The difference is that the Blessed Infinite One is *totally* "hidden" (or non-disclosable) in the sense that, being infinite, it is incompatible with the created worlds which are defined by limits and boundaries.

The *Shechinah*, on the other hand, is incompatible with the worlds only in practice, not in principle. Think of it as music that's so loud it would burst your eardrums, but if you would just turn down the volume a bit, then you would be able to hear it. That's why the *Tanya* refers to the *Shechinah's* light as "disclosable," not because the worlds are able to access it, but because it's sufficiently diminished to be a starting point for the universe.

וְהִיא מְקוֹר כָּל הַמְשָׁכוֹת הַחַיּוּת שֶׁבְּכָל הָעוֹלָמוֹת — **The** *Shechinah* **itself is the root of all the energy-flows that are found in all the worlds,** [שֶׁכָּל הַחַיּוּת שֶׁבָּהֶם אֵינוֹ רַק אוֹר הַמִּתְפַּשֵּׁט מִמֶּנָּה כְּאוֹר הַמִּתְפַּשֵּׁט מֵהַשֶּׁמֶשׁ — **since all the energy** in the worlds **is nothing other than "light" which has emerged from** the *Shechinah*, **like light emerges from the sun.**

"Light emerging from the sun," is the way the *Tanya* depicts process 'b' flowing from process 'a' (in phase '2'). The light coming out of the sun is compatible with the worlds, whereas the sun itself is too powerful for the worlds.

מהשמש] א"א לעולמות לסבול ולקבל אור שכינתה
שתשכון ותתלבש בתוכם ממש בלא לבוש המעלים
ומסתיר אורה מהם שלא יתבטלו במציאות לגמרי
במקורם כביטול אור השמש במקורו בגוף השמש
שאין נראה שם אור זה רק עצם גוף השמש בלבד.
ומהו הלבוש שיוכל להסתירה ולהלבישה ולא יתבטל
במציאות באורה הוא רצונו ית' וחכמתו וכו' המלובשים
בתורה ומצותיה הנגלית לנו ולבנינו דאורייתא מחכמה

אִי אֶפְשָׁר לָעוֹלָמוֹת לִסְבּוֹל וּלְקַבֵּל אוֹר שְׁכִינָתָה — It's impossible for the worlds to withstand and receive the light of the *Shechinah* itself, שֶׁתִּשְׁכּוֹן וְתִתְלַבֵּשׁ בְּתוֹכָם מַמָּשׁ — in a way that the *Shechinah's* light can rest and be really enmeshed in them, בְּלֹא לְבוּשׁ הַמַּעֲלִים וּמַסְתִּיר אוֹרָה מֵהֶם — without a filter to hide and conceal the light of the *Shechinah* from them, שֶׁלֹּא יִתְבַּטְּלוּ בִּמְצִיאוּת לְגַמְרֵי בִּמְקוֹרָם — so that they don't, in the presence of their unfiltered source, lose their individual identity completely.

כְּבִיטוּל אוֹר הַשֶּׁמֶשׁ בִּמְקוֹרוֹ בְּגוּף הַשֶּׁמֶשׁ — The identity-erasing intensity of the *Shechinah* could be compared to the way in which rays of sunlight lose their identity in their source, the globe of the sun, שֶׁאֵין נִרְאֶה שָׁם אוֹר זֶה — since there, in the globe of the sun, these rays are not apparent as individual rays, רַק עֶצֶם גּוּף הַשֶּׁמֶשׁ בִּלְבַד — and there's just one discernible entity, the actual globe of the sun itself.

SECTION THREE: SHECHINAH AND THE TORAH

1ST SIVAN LEAP

So how do we evolve from process 'a' to process 'b'? How can the *Shechinah*, which is too powerful to allow us to have any independent existence, be dimmed sufficiently that the worlds can emerge?

וּמַהוּ הַלְּבוּשׁ שֶׁיּוּכַל לְהַסְתִּירָהּ וּלְהַלְבִּישָׁהּ וְלֹא יִתְבַּטֵּל בִּמְצִיאוּת בְּאוֹרָהּ — And what is the filter capable of hiding and filtering the *Shechinah*, without losing its identity from her overwhelming light?

הוּא רְצוֹנוֹ יִתְבָּרֵךְ וְחָכְמָתוֹ וְכוּ' הַמְלוּבָּשִׁים בַּתּוֹרָה וּמִצְוֹתֶיהָ — The filter is G-d's will and wisdom *etc.*, as expressed in the earthly Torah and its *mitzvos*, הַנִּגְלֵית לָנוּ וּלְבָנֵינוּ — "*the revealed things, for us and our children*" (*Deuteronomy* 29:28).

The Torah is a Divine energy which is compatible with the created worlds; it constitutes "revealed things," an energy which is accessible to us. Therefore it can act as a means by which the *Shechinah's* light can become compatible with the worlds.

דְּאוֹרַיְיתָא מֵחָכְמָה נָפְקַת — The Torah has this power since it is rooted in an energy *higher* than the *Shechinah*, for "*the Torah emerged from chochmah*" (*Zohar*

נפקת היא חכמה עילאה דלעילא לעילא מעלמא
דאתגליא דאיהו חכים ולא בחכמה ידיעה וכו' וכמש"ל
שאור א"ס ב"ה מלובש ומיוחד בחכמה עילאה והוא
ית' וחכמתו אחד רק שירדה בסתר המדרגות ממדריגה
למדריגה בהשתלשלות העולמות עד שנתלבשה

הִיא חָכְמָה עִילָאָה דִּלְעֵילָא לְעֵילָא מֵעָלְמָא דְאִתְגַּלְיָא ,(121a ,2 — which refers to "Upper *chochmah*" that vastly transcends the "manifest world," the domain of the
Shechinah.

As we learned above, the *Shechinah* is a "disclosable" energy belonging to the
"manifest world" — it's still too intense for the worlds to receive, but it's on the same
"wavelength." *Chochmah*, on the other hand, is a higher energy which transcends the
"manifest world." That's why the "filter" of Torah (*chochmah*) doesn't become "voided" by the overwhelming light of the *Shechinah.* The *Tanya* now supports this point.

דְּאִיהוּ חַכִּים וְלָא בְּחָכְמָה יְדִיעָה וְכוּ' — For He is *"wise, but not with a known wisdom
(chochmah)"* (*Tikunei Zohar* 17b).

G-d's *chochmah* bears no resemblance to ours; it is not a "known *chochmah*"
as far as we are concerned. This indicates that "Upper *chochmah*" transcends the
"manifest world."

שָׁאוֹר אֵין סוֹף בָּרוּךְ הוּא מְלוּבָּשׁ וּכְמוֹ שֶׁנִּתְבָּאֵר לְעֵיל — And as was explained above,
וּמְיוּחָד בְּחָכְמָה עִילָאָה — that the Blessed Infinite Light is expressed in, and unified
with, Upper *chochmah*, וְהוּא יִתְבָּרֵךְ וְחָכְמָתוֹ אֶחָד — and *"He and His chochmah are
one"* (see chapters 18, 19, 35).

Chochmah, then, is a phase '1' energy, utterly incompatible with the worlds. But
how does that empower the Torah to make the *Shechinah more* compatible with
the worlds?

The Torah can do this because it integrates two paradoxical energies. Torah's
inner power stems from the fact that it is higher than the *Shechinah,* from the realm
of *"Upper chochmah."* But, on the other hand, the Torah's *overt energy* is that of
"revealed things, for us and our children," something which the lower worlds can
accommodate.

That's why Torah energy can provide the bridge between the utterly transcendent
phase '1' (the Blessed Infinite Light) and phase '3' (the "delivery" of the *Shechinah*
to the lower worlds), because the Torah has a dual identity: It is rooted in "Upper
chochmah" but "packaged" in a way of *"revealed things, for us and our children."*

רַק שֶׁיָּרְדָה בְּסֵתֶר הַמַּדְרֵגוֹת — Only, while the Torah's inner energy of *"Upper
chochmah"* remains transcendent and other-worldly, it has also journeyed downwards through *"the hidden places in the steps"* (*Song* 2:14), without losing its
inner energy, מִמַּדְרֵיגָה לְמַדְרֵיגָה בְּהִשְׁתַּלְשְׁלוּת הָעוֹלָמוֹת — passing down through
one step after the other, down the chain of spiritual worlds, עַד שֶׁנִּתְלַבְּשָׁה בִּדְבָרִים

בדברים גשמיים שהן תרי"ג מצות התורה. ובירידתה
בהשתלשלו' מעולם לעולם גם השכינה ירדה ונתלבשה
בה בכל עולם ועולם וזהו היכל ק"ק שבכל עולם
ועולם וכמ"ש בזהר וע"ח שהשכינה שהיא מלכות
דאצילות [שהיא בחי' גילוי אור א"ס ב"ה וחיות שמאיר
לעולמות ולכן היא נקראת דבר ה' ורוח פיו כביכול
עד"מ כמו שבאדם הדבור הוא מגלה מחשבתו

גַּשְׁמִיִּים — **to the point where it has expressed itself in physical things,** שֶׁהֵן תְּרַיַ"ג
הַתּוֹרָה מִצְוֹת — **namely, the 613** *mitzvos* **of the Torah.**

Since the Torah has bridged the gap between the otherworldly and the worldly, it can endow the *Shechinah* with that same ability, and make her energy accessible to the lower worlds.

28TH IYAR REGULAR | 2ND SIVAN LEAP

Ultimately, however, the earthly Torah, *"the revealed things, for us and our children,"* is an entity *in this physical world*. How would that help the *Shechinah* sustain all the *spiritual* worlds?

To answer this question, the *Tanya* now explains that a version of the "earthly" Torah actually exists in every world, and each world receives its energy from the *Shechinah* through the Torah of that world.

וּבִירִידָתָהּ בְּהִשְׁתַּלְשְׁלוּת מֵעוֹלָם לְעוֹלָם גַּם הַשְּׁכִינָה יָרְדָה וְנִתְלַבְּשָׁה בָּהּ בְּכָל עוֹלָם וְעוֹלָם
— **And as** the Torah **descended through the chain** of spiritual worlds, **from one world to the next, the** *Shechinah***, too, descended, and became enmeshed in each and every world,** through the Torah of that world, וְזֶהוּ הֵיכַל קָדְשֵׁי קָדָשִׁים שֶׁבְּכָל עוֹלָם
וְעוֹלָם — **and this** presence of the *Shechinah* in each world, mediated by the Torah, **is** what the Kabbalah refers to as the **"Most-Sacred-Chamber" in each and every world.**

The *Tanya* now cites sources from the Kabbalah to demonstrate this point.

וּכְמוֹ שֶׁכָּתוּב בַּזֹּהַר וְעֵץ חַיִּים — **And as stated in the** *Zohar* (3, 161b) and *Etz Chaim*
(46:2), שֶׁהַשְּׁכִינָה שֶׁהִיא מַלְכוּת דַּאֲצִילוּת — **that the** *Shechinah* **is,** in fact, the lowest *sefirah, malchus,* of the highest World, *Atzilus.*

שֶׁהִיא בְּחִינַת גִּילוּי אוֹר אֵין סוֹף בָּרוּךְ הוּא וְחִיּוּת שֶׁמֵּאִיר לְעוֹלָמוֹת] — And *malchus* of
Atzilus **is an** initial **disclosure of the Blessed Infinite Light and energy which** is suitable to be filtered so that it will **illuminate the worlds,** which is precisely how we have described the *Shechinah,* above, as a "disclosable" energy, וְלָכֵן הִיא נִקְרֵאת
דְּבַר ה' וְרוּחַ פִּיו כִּבְיָכוֹל עַל דֶּרֶךְ מָשָׁל — **which is why** *malchus* of *Atzilus* **is figuratively called, "G-d's word... and the breath of His mouth"** (see *Psalms* 33:6), **so to speak** (see *Etz Chaim* 22:5), כְּמוֹ שֶׁבָּאָדָם הַדִּבּוּר הוּא מְגַלֶּה מַחֲשַׁבְתּוֹ הַסְּתוּמָה וְנֶעְלָמָה

הסתומה ונעלמה להשומעים] היא מתלבשת בהיכל
ק"ק דבריאה שהיא חב"ד דבריאה ובהתלבשותן
במלכות דבריאה נבראו הנשמות והמלאכי' שבבריאה
וגם משם נמשך התלמוד שלפנינו וכמש"ל בשם   73B
התיקונים שבעולם הבריאה מאירות ומשפיעות שם
חכמתו ובינתו ודעתו של א"ס ב"ה בבחי' צמצום עצום

לְהַשּׁוֹמְעִים — just as human speech discloses hidden and concealed thoughts to an audience.]

Now that we have established that the *Shechinah* is synonymous with *malchus* of *Atzilus,* the *Tanya* will now trace the process through which this energy passes down through the spiritual worlds.

הִיא מִתְלַבֶּשֶׁת בְּהֵיכַל קָדְשֵׁי קָדָשִׁים דִּבְרִיאָה — And *malchus* of *Atzilus,* the *Shechinah,* is **then** filtered so that it can **become enmeshed in the Most-Sacred-Chamber of** the next world down, the World of *Beriah,* שֶׁהוּא חָכְמָה בִּינָה וְדַעַת דִּבְרִיאָה — the Most-Sacred-Chamber of *Beriah* being the **chochmah, binah and da'as of *Beriah*.**

Even after the *Shechinah* has reached the Most-Sacred-Chamber (the *chochmah, binah* and *da'as*) of the World of *Beriah,* it is still too transcendent to power the creation of separate entities. For that to occur, the energy must pass to the lowest *sefirah* of the World of *Beriah* — *malchus.*

וּבְהִתְלַבְּשׁוּתָן בְּמַלְכוּת דִּבְרִיאָה נִבְרְאוּ הַנְּשָׁמוֹת וְהַמַּלְאָכִים שֶׁבַּבְּרִיאָה — **And when** *chochmah, binah* and *da'as* of the World of *Beriah* (in which is enmeshed the *Shechinah, malchus* of *Atzilus*), **become enmeshed in *Malchus* of *Beriah*,** the souls **and angels of *Beriah* are created.**

Finally, we have actual creations, the separate intelligences of souls and angels!

As we learned above, it is the Torah in each world which integrates the *Shechinah* energy into that world, facilitating the creation of separate entities. What Torah energy is associated with *malchus* of *Beriah*?

וְגַם מִשָּׁם נִמְשָׁךְ הַתַּלְמוּד שֶׁלְּפָנֵינוּ — **And also from there,** *malchus* of *Beriah,* **is derived the *Talmud* that we possess.**

Why is the *Talmud* in particular associated with the World of *Beriah,* more than, say, the Scriptures or the legal rulings of the *Mishnah*? As the *Tanya* will now explain, the *Talmud* represents the complex legal analyses which require application of the intellect. Therefore *Talmud,* is associated with *Beriah,* the World of Intellect.

וּכְמוֹ שֶׁנִּתְבָּאֵר לְעֵיל בְּשֵׁם הַתִּיקוּנִים — **And has also been explained above** in chapter 39, **citing the *Tikunei Zohar*** (23a), שֶׁבְּעוֹלַם הַבְּרִיאָה מְאִירוֹת וּמַשְׁפִּיעוֹת שָׁם חָכְמָתוֹ — **that there in the World of *Beriah*, the chochmah, binah and da'as,** the intellectual powers **of the Blessed Infinite One shine**

בכדי שיוכלו הנשמות והמלאכים שהם בעלי גבול
ותכלית לקבל השפעה מבחי' חב"ד אלו ולכן נמשך
משם התלמוד שהוא ג"כ בחי' חב"ד שהתהלמוד הוא
טעמי ההלכות על בורײן והטעמים הם בחי' חב"ד
וההלכות עצמן הן ממדותיו של א"ס ב"ה שהן חסד דין
רחמים כו' שמהן נמשך ההיתר והאיסור והכשר והפסול
והחיוב והפטור כמ"ש בתיקוני'. ובהתלבשות מלכות
דאצי' במלכות דבריאה מתלבשת בהיכל ק"ק דיצי'
שהוא חב"ד דיצירה ובהתלבשותן במלכות דיצירה

בִּבְחִינַת צִמְצוּם עָצוּם בְּכְדֵי שֶׁיּוּכְלוּ הַנְּשָׁמוֹת וְהַמַּלְאָכִים שֶׁהֵם בַּעֲלֵי גְבוּל **and flow,** וְתַכְלִית לְקַבֵּל הַשֶּׁפָעָה מִבְּחִינַת חָכְמָה בִּינָה וְדַעַת אֵלוּ — albeit **through formidable diminishments, so that the limited, finite souls and angels can receive the flow from these** powers of *chochmah, binah* and *da'as.*

וְלָכֵן נִמְשָׁךְ מִשָּׁם הַתַּלְמוּד שֶׁהוּא גַם כֵּן בְּחִינַת חָכְמָה בִּינָה וְדַעַת — **And that's why the** *Talmud,* **which is also from** *chochmah, binah* **and** *da'as,* **is derived from** the World of *Beriah,* שֶׁהַתַּלְמוּד הוּא טַעֲמֵי הַהֲלָכוֹת עַל בּוּרְיָין — **because the** *Talmud* **is a rigorous clarification of the reasons for the laws,** וְהַטַעֲמִים הֵם בְּחִינַת חָכְמָה בִּינָה וְדַעַת — **and these reasons are an expression of** *chochmah, binah* **and** *da'as.*

Beriah is a world in which the intellect of G-d (His *chochmah, binah* and *da'as*) predominate. That's why the Torah of that world is a cognitive one, the *Talmud.*

וְהַהֲלָכוֹת עַצְמָן הֵן מִמְּדוֹתָיו שֶׁל אֵין סוֹף בָּרוּךְ הוּא — **But** in contrast to *Talmud,* the analysis of the laws, **the laws themselves are** an expression **of the** emotional attributes of the Blessed Infinite Light, שֶׁהֵן חֶסֶד דִּין רַחֲמִים כו' — **which are kindness, judgment and mercy** *etc.,* שֶׁמֵּהֶן נִמְשָׁךְ הַהֶיתֵּר וְהָאִיסוּר וְהַכְּשֵׁר וְהַפָּסוּל וְהַחִיוּב וְהַפְּטוּר — **and they are the spiritual source of the permitted and the forbidden; the kosher and the invalid; the obligated and the exempt,** כְּמוֹ שֶׁכָּתוּב בַּתִּיקוּנִים — **as stated in** the *Tikunei Zohar* (48a, 124a).

The laws of the Torah are binaries: something is either permitted or forbidden, obligated or exempt *etc*. This is an expression of a more emotional energy, since emotions are essentially binary: either you want to come closer to something, or distance yourself from it.

29TH IYAR REGULAR

וּבְהִתְלַבְּשׁוּת מַלְכוּת דַאֲצִילוּת בְּמַלְכוּת דִבְרִיאָה — **And after** *malchus* **of** *Atzilus* **has become enmeshed** down as far as *malchus* **of** *Beriah,* מִתְלַבֶּשֶׁת בְּהֵיכַל קָדְשֵׁי קָדָשִׁים דִיצִירָה — **it can then become enmeshed in the Most-Sacred-Chamber of** *Yetzirah,* שֶׁהוּא חָכְמָה בִּינָה וְדַעַת דִיצִירָה — **which is** *chochmah, binah* **and** *da'as* **of** *Yetzirah.*

נוצרו הרוחות והמלאכים שביצירה וגם משם היא
המשנה שלפנינו שהיא הלכות פסוקות הנמשכות ג"כ
מחב"ד של א"ס ב"ה רק שבחי' חב"ד שהם טעמי
ההלכות הם מלובשים וגנוזי' בגופי ההלכות ולא בבחי'
גילוי וגופי ההלכו' שהן בבחי' גילוי הן הן הארת מדותיו
של א"ס ב"ה בבחי' גילוי כמש"ל בשם התיקוני' דשית
ספירן מקננין ביצירה שהן דרך כל קוין ימין ושמאל
להקל מסטרא דחסד דהיינו להתיר שיוכל לעלות אל

וּבְהִתְלַבְּשׁוּתָן בְּמַלְכוּת דִּיצִירָה — And when it subsequently becomes enmeshed in *malchus of Yetzirah,* נוֹצְרוּ הָרוּחוֹת וְהַמַּלְאָכִים שֶׁבִּיצִירָה — the spirits and angels of *Yetzirah* are formed.

As we pass down through the worlds, the same pattern is followed. *Malchus* of a higher world first enters the Most-Sacred-Chamber of the next, lower world. From there it passes down to *malchus* of the lower world, at which point it can power the separate creations of that world.

The Torah of each world, which facilitates the creative process, is likewise found in the *malchus* of that world.

וְגַם מִשָּׁם הִיא הַמִּשְׁנָה שֶׁלְפָנֵינוּ — And from there, *malchus* of Yetzirah, is also derived the *Mishnah* that we possess, שֶׁהִיא הֲלָכוֹת פְּסוּקוֹת — which consists of legal rulings, הַנִּמְשָׁכוֹת גַּם כֵּן מֵחָכְמָה בִּינָה וְדַעַת שֶׁל אֵין סוֹף בָּרוּךְ הוּא — which while they are also derived initially from the *chochmah, binah* and *da'as* of the Blessed Infinite One which is the source of the entire Torah, רַק שֶׁבְּחִינוֹת חָכְמָה בִּינָה וְדַעַת שֶׁהֶם — nevertheless, טַעֲמֵי הַהֲלָכוֹת הֵם מְלוּבָּשִׁים וּגְנוּזִים בְּגוּפֵי הַהֲלָכוֹת וְלֹא בִּבְחִינַת גִּילוּי — in the *Mishnah,* the qualities of *chochmah, binah* and *da'as,* which are the reasons for the laws, are not manifest, but are discretely implied within the legal rulings themselves, וְגוּפֵי הַהֲלָכוֹת שֶׁהֵן בִּבְחִינַת גִּילוּי הֵן הֵן הֶאָרַת מִדוֹתָיו שֶׁל אֵין סוֹף בָּרוּךְ הוּא בְּבְחִינַת גִּילוּי — whereas the legal rulings themselves, which are overt in the *Mishnah,* are an illumination from the Blessed Infinite One's emotional attributes, shining manifestly.

And that's why the *Mishnah's* place is the World of *Yetzirah,* the world of emotion.

כְּמוֹ שֶׁנִתְבָּאֵר לְעֵיל בְּשֵׁם הַתִּיקוּנִים — As explained above in chapter 39, citing the *Tikunei Zohar* (23a), דְשִׁית סְפִירָן מְקַנְנִין בִּיצִירָה — that *"the six (emotional) sefiros (of Atzilus) have their 'nest' in Yetzirah,"* i.e., that is where the emotions predominate, שֶׁהֵן דֶרֶךְ כְּלָל שְׁנֵי קַוִין יָמִין וּשְׂמֹאל — these six generally boiling down to two lines of "right" and "left," לְהָקֵל מִסְטְרָא דְחֶסֶד דְהַיְינוּ לְהַתִּיר שֶׁיוּכַל לַעֲלוֹת אֶל ה' — the "right" side of *chesed* expressing itself as *halachic* leniency, to allow something to be elevated to G-d, אוֹ לְהַחֲמִיר כו' — or the "left" side expressing stringency, that something can't be elevated.

ה' או להחמיר כו' והכל ע"פ חכמה עילאה דאצי' ובינה
ודעת כלולות בה ומיוחדות בא"ס ב"ה כי בתוך כולן
מלובשות חב"ד דאצילות שאור א"ס ב"ה מיוחד בהן
בתכלית היחוד וכן בדרך זה ירדה השכינה ונתלבשה
בהיכל ק"ק דעשיה וכל עולם מג' עולמות אלו
מתחלק לרבבות מדריגות הנקראות גם כן עולמות
פרטים ומלכות דאצילו' מלובשת במלכות*
של כל עולם פרטי

74A

הגה"ה
(ובזה יובן לשון הכתוב מלכותך
מלכות כל עולמים):

יורדת ומתלבשת בהיכל
ק"ק שהוא חב"ד שבעולם

The *Tanya* now clarifies that just because the *Mishnah* expresses the emotional energy of G-d, that doesn't mean to say that it's disconnected from G-d's intellectual powers, which are the root of the entire Torah.

וְהַכֹּל עַל פִּי חָכְמָה עִילָּאָה דַּאֲצִילוּת — **But all these** rulings, like the *Talmud*, are dictated by the Upper *chochmah* of *Atzilus*, וּבִינָה וָדַעַת כְּלוּלוֹת בָּהּ — and *binah/da'as* are included in it, וּמְיוּחָדוֹת בְּאֵין סוֹף בָּרוּךְ הוּא — and all the rulings are united with the Blessed Infinite One, כִּי בְּתוֹךְ כּוּלָּן מְלוּבָּשׁוֹת חָכְמָה בִּינָה וָדַעַת דַּאֲצִילוּת — because all of them express *chochmah, binah* and *da'as* of *Atzilus*, שָׁאוֹר אֵין סוֹף בָּרוּךְ הוּא מְיוּחָד בָּהֶן בְּתַכְלִית הַיִּחוּד — which are merged and totally one with the Blessed Infinite Light.

We now continue to trace the *Shechinah's* descent into the lowest World of *Asiyah*.

וְכֵן בְּדֶרֶךְ זֶה יָרְדָה הַשְּׁכִינָה וְנִתְלַבְּשָׁה בְּהֵיכַל קָדְשֵׁי קָדָשִׁים דְּעֲשִׂיָּה — **And following a** similar path, the **Shechinah then descends** from *malchus* of *Yetzirah* and becomes **enmeshed in the Most-Sacred-Chamber of** *Asiyah*.

All of the above is, of course, a general overview. In reality there are thousands of levels through which the *Shechinah* descends, which are categorized generally into three worlds.

וְכָל עוֹלָם מִג' עוֹלָמוֹת אֵלּוּ מִתְחַלֵּק לְרִבְבוֹת מַדְרֵיגוֹת — **And each world, of these** three worlds, is subdivided into tens of thousands of levels, הַנִּקְרָאוֹת גַּם כֵּן עוֹלָמוֹת — which are also called mini-worlds in their own right, פְּרָטִים — which are also called mini-worlds in their own right, וּמַלְכוּת דַּאֲצִילוּת — but what they all have in common is that the מְלוּבֶּשֶׁת בַּמַּלְכוּת* שֶׁל כָּל עוֹלָם פְּרָטִי — *Shechinah, malchus* of *Atzilus*, is enmeshed in the *malchus* of every individual יוֹרֶדֶת וּמִתְלַבֶּשֶׁת בְּהֵיכַל קָדְשֵׁי קָדָשִׁים שֶׁהוּא חָכְמָה בִּינָה וָדַעַת שֶׁבָּעוֹלָם mini-**world,**

הַגָּהָ"ה* — *NOTE.* וּבָזֶה יוּבָן לְשׁוֹן הַכָּתוּב מַלְכוּתְךָ מַלְכוּת כָּל עוֹלָמִים — **And this ex**plains the verse, *"Your malchus is the malchus of all worlds"* (Psalms 145:13).

שלמטה ממנו במדרגה. והנה מהשכינה המלובשת
בהיכל ק"ק של כל עולם ועולם כללי או פרטי
נמשך ומתפשט ממנה אור וחיות לכל העולם והברואים
שבו נשמות ומלאכים וכו' כי כולם נבראו בעשרה
מאמרות שבמעשה בראשית שהם דבר ה' הנקרא
בשם שכינה:

שֶׁלְּמַטָּה מִמֶּנּוּ בְּמַדְרֵגָה — which then descends and becomes enmeshed in the
Most-Sacred-Chamber (which is the *chochmah, binah* and *da'as*) of the mini-world
a level below it.

The chapter concludes by stressing that ultimately, the creative power within each world (or mini-world) does not derive from the world itself, but from the
Shechinah energy enmeshed in that world.

וְהִנֵּה מֵהַשְּׁכִינָה הַמְלוּבֶּשֶׁת בְּהֵיכַל קָדְשֵׁי קָדָשִׁים שֶׁל כָּל עוֹלָם וְעוֹלָם כְּלָלִי אוֹ פְּרָטִי —
And, from the *Shechinah,* as it is enmeshed in the Most-Sacred-Chamber of each
general or mini-world, נִמְשָׁךְ וּמִתְפַּשֵּׁט מִמֶּנָּה אוֹר וְחִיּוּת לְכָל הָעוֹלָם וְהַבְּרוּאִים שֶׁבּוֹ
— light and energy flow to that entire world (or mini-world), נְשָׁמוֹת וּמַלְאָכִים וְכוּ'
and to the creatures in it, such as the souls and angels *etc.,* כִּי כּוּלָם נִבְרְאוּ בַּעֲשָׂרָה
מַאֲמָרוֹת שֶׁבְּמַעֲשֵׂה בְרֵאשִׁית — for they are all created, not by that world itself but
from the Ten Utterances of the creative act, שֶׁהֵם דְּבַר ה' הַנִּקְרָא בְּשֵׁם שְׁכִינָה — that
Biblically speaking is the "word" of G-d, which is called *Shechinah* in the Kabbalah.

One might think that *"Your malchus"* and *"the malchus of all the worlds"* are totally separate entities. The verse teaches us that this is not the case, and, in fact, *"Your
malchus **is** the malchus of all worlds."*

This supports the *Tanya's* statement that *"malchus* of *Atzilus* (i.e., *'Your malchus')*
is enmeshed in the *malchus* of every individual mini-world (i.e., *"the malchus of all
the worlds"*).

פרק נג וְהִנֵּה כשהיה בית ראשון קיים שבו היה
הארון והלוחות בבית ק"ק היתה
השכינה שהיא מלכות דאצילות שהיא בחי' גילוי אור
א"ס ב"ה שורה שם ומלובשת בעשרת הדברות ביתר
שאת ויתר עז בגילוי רב ועצום יותר מגילויה בהיכלות
ק"ק שלמעלה בעולמות עליונים כי עשרת הדברות הן
כללות התורה כולה דנפקא מגו חכמה עילאה דלעילא

WHAT IS THE "SHECHINAH"? (III)

SECTION ONE: THE SHECHINAH IN THE TEMPLE

1ST SIVAN REGULAR | 3RD SIVAN LEAP

Chapter 53 completes our discussion of the concept of the *Shechinah* (Divine Presence), with which we have been occupied throughout chapters 51-52.

שֶׁבּוֹ הָיָה הָאָרוֹן — וְהִנֵּה כְּשֶׁהָיָה בֵּית רִאשׁוֹן קַיָּם — **Now when the First Temple existed,** וְהַלּוּחוֹת בְּבֵית קָדְשֵׁי קָדָשִׁים — **containing the Ark and Tablets in the Most-Sacred Chamber ("Holy-of-Holies") Chamber,** הָיְתָה הַשְּׁכִינָה שֶׁהִיא מַלְכוּת דַּאֲצִילוּת שֶׁהִיא — בְּחִינַת גִּילוּי אוֹר אֵין סוֹף בָּרוּךְ הוּא שׁוֹרָה שָׁם — the *Shechinah* (which as we learned in chapter 52, is *malchus* of *Atzilus*, an overt disclosure of the Blessed Infinite Light) rested there, וּמְלוּבֶּשֶׁת בַּעֲשֶׂרֶת הַדִּבְּרוֹת — **and it manifested through the Ten Commandments** on the Tablets, בְּיֶתֶר שְׂאֵת וְיֶתֶר עָז בְּגִילוּי רַב וְעָצוּם יוֹתֵר מִגִּילוּיָה — בְּהֵיכְלוֹת קָדְשֵׁי קָדָשִׁים שֶׁלְּמַעְלָה בְּעוֹלָמוֹת עֶלְיוֹנִים — with *"more dignity and more power"* (Genesis 49:3), with a greater, more formidable degree of disclosure than in the Most-Sacred-Chambers of the spiritual Worlds, *Yetzirah* and *Beriah*.

In chapter 53 we learned how the *Shechinah's* light was gradually dimmed as it passed down through the chain of spiritual worlds. We would expect, then, that upon reaching this physical world, the *Shechinah's* light would be at its weakest. But, counterintuitively, the *Tanya* tells us here that the *Shechinah* shines down in this world *"with a greater, more formidable degree of disclosure than in the Most-Sacred-Chambers of the spiritual Worlds."*

כִּי עֲשֶׂרֶת הַדִּבְּרוֹת הֵן כְּלָלוּת הַתּוֹרָה כּוּלָּה — **Because** the *Shechinah* manifests in this physical world through the **Ten Commandments,** on the Tablets, **which incorporate the whole Torah,** דְּנָפְקָא מִגּוֹ חָכְמָה עִילָאָה — which *"emerged from Upper*

לעילא מעלמא דאתגליא וכדי לחקקן בלוחות אבנים
גשמיים לא ירדה ממדרגה למדרגה כדרך השתלשלות
העולמות עד עוה"ז הגשמי כי עוה"ז הגשמי מתנהג
בהתלבשות הטבע הגשמי והלוחות מעשה אלהים המה
והמכתב מכתב אלהים הוא למעלה מהטבע של עוה"ז
הגשמי הנשפע מהארת השכינה שבהיכל ק"ק דעשיה
שממנה נמשך אור וחיות לעולם העשיה שגם עוה"ז

chochmah" (*Zohar* 2, 121a), דִּלְעֵילָא לְעֵילָא מֵעָלְמָא דְּאִתְגַּלְיָא — that vastly tran-scends the "manifest world."

As we learned in chapter 52, the *Shechinah* is, in essence, a "disclosable" energy, fundamentally compatible with the created worlds. That's why *Shechinah* is associated with the "manifest world," *i.e.*, energies which are accessible to us.

Torah, on the other hand, is rooted in "Upper *chochmah*," which is an elusive, non-disclosable and "hidden" energy. But since the *Shechinah* shines in this world through the Torah (the Tablets), the disclosure is intensified.

But if the Torah is "non-disclosable," how is it available to us at all? How can it be manifest in this world, through the Tablets?

וּכְדֵי לְחָקְקָן בְּלוּחוֹת אֲבָנִים גַּשְׁמִיִּים — And when this Upper *chochmah* was engraved on the physical Tablets of stone, לֹא יָרְדָה מִמַּדְרֵגָה לְמַדְרֵגָה כְּדֶרֶךְ הִשְׁתַּלְשְׁלוּת הָעוֹלָמוֹת — it didn't journey down the chain of spiritual worlds, one step after the other, עַד עוֹלָם הַזֶּה הַגַּשְׁמִי — down to this physical world, כִּי עוֹלָם הַזֶּה הַגַּשְׁמִי מִתְנַהֵג בְּהִתְלַבְּשׁוּת הַטֶּבַע הַגַּשְׁמִי — because this world functions through the filter of nature, וְהַלֻּחוֹת מַעֲשֵׂה אֱלֹהִים הֵמָּה וְהַמִּכְתָּב מִכְתַּב אֱלֹהִים הוּא — whereas *"the Tablets were the work of G-d, and the writing was the writing of G-d"* (Exodus 32:16), לְמַעְלָה מֵהַטֶּבַע שֶׁל עוֹלָם הַזֶּה הַגַּשְׁמִי — transcending the nature of this physical world.

When G-d personally engraved the Tablets, He effectively "by-passed" the chain of spiritual worlds, and manifested "Upper chochmah" in the physical Tablets.

הַנִּשְׁפָּע מֵהֶאָרַת הַשְּׁכִינָה שֶׁבְּהֵיכַל קָדְשֵׁי קָדָשִׁים דַּעֲשִׂיָּה — The physical world, on the other hand, is under the influence of the *Shechinah* as it is enmeshed in the Most-Sacred-Chamber of *Asiyah*, שֶׁמִּמֶּנָּה נִמְשָׁךְ אוֹר וְחִיּוּת לְעוֹלָם הָעֲשִׂיָּה שֶׁגַּם עוֹלָם הַזֶּה, בִּכְלָלוֹ — from where light and energy flows to the world of *Asiyah*, which includes this physical world.

The final result of the chain-descent of worlds is what we call "nature." In this lowest of worlds, the World of *Asiyah*, nature is governed by the flow of Divine energy (*Shechinah*), which first enters the world through the Most-Sacred-Chamber of *Asiyah* (as we learned in chapter 52).

בכללו אלא בחי' חכמה עילאה דאצילות שהיא כללות
התורה שבי' הדברות נתלבשה במלכות דאצי' ודבריא'
לבדן והן לבדן המיוחדות באור א"ס שבתוכן הן
הנקראות בשם שכינה השורה בק"ק דבית ראשון ע"י
74B התלבשותה בי' הדברות החקוקות בלוחות שבארון
בנס ומעשה אלהים חיים [הוא עלמא דאתכסיא המקנן

The Torah's light "by-passed" nature (*Asiyah*). But as the *Tanya* will now clarify, it did not bypass *all* of the created worlds — just the lowest two (*Yetzirah* and *Asiyah*), but not the highest created world (*Beriah*).

אֶלָּא בְּחִינַת חָכְמָה עִילָּאָה דַאֲצִילוּת שֶׁהִיא כְּלָלוּת הַתּוֹרָה שֶׁבִּי' הַדִּבְּרוֹת — But "**Upper chochmah**" of the highest world of *Atzilus*, **which is** manifested directly in **the Ten Commandments, that contain the whole Torah,** נִתְלַבְּשָׁה בְּמַלְכוּת דַאֲצִילוּת וְדִבְרִיאָה לְבַדָּן — **became enmeshed** down the chain of spiritual worlds only as far as *malchus* of *Atzilus* and *malchus* of *Beriah,* but nothing lower, וְהֵן לְבַדָּן הַמְיוּחָדוֹת בְּאוֹר אֵין סוֹף — **and what we** שֶׁבְּתוֹכָן הֵן הַנִּקְרָאוֹת בְּשֵׁם שְׁכִינָה בְּקָדְשֵׁי קָדָשִׁים דְּבַיִת רִאשׁוֹן **call "the Shechinah that rested in the Holy-of-Holies in the First Temple" consisted of them alone** (*malchus* of *Atzilus* and *malchus* of *Beriah*) **united with the Blessed Infinite Light inside them.**

While our world is powered by *malchus* of *Asiyah,* (which is "nature"), the *Shechinah* in the First Temple was powered by the other-worldly energy of *malchus* of *Atzilus* and *malchus* of *Beriah*.

עַל יְדֵי הִתְלַבְּשׁוּתָה בִּי' הַדִּבְּרוֹת הַחֲקוּקוֹת בְּלוּחוֹת שֶׁבָּאָרוֹן בְּנֵס — **And this** light was **enmeshed in the Ten Commandments which were miraculously engraved on the Tablets, within the Ark.**

The other-worldly energy of the Tablets, which transcended nature, came to light through the miraculous way in which their engraved letters stayed in place. As the *Talmud* teaches, "*The (unconnected core of the hollow letters) final-mem (ם) and samech (ס) that appeared in the Tablets of the Ten Commandments stood there by a miracle*" (*Shabbos* 104a).

וּמַעֲשֵׂה אֱלֹהִים חַיִּים — The Tablets were able to express the energies of *Atzilus* and *Beriah* because they were **the work of the "Living G-d"** (*Deuteronomy* 5:22), [הוּא עָלְמָא דְאִתְכַּסְיָא — the term "Living G-d" **referring to** *binah* of *Atzilus* (*Zohar* 3, 245a), which is **the "unmanifest world"** (*Tikunei Zohar* 23a), הַמְקַנֵּן בְּעוֹלָם הַבְּרִיאָה — and, as we have learned, *binah* of *Atzilus* takes expression and **"nests" in the World of Beriah** (see chapter 39, p. 453), [כַּנּוֹדָע לְיוֹדְעֵי חָכְמָה נִסְתָּרָה] — **as is familiar to those knowledgeable in hidden,** Kabbalistic **wisdom.**

2ND SIVAN REGULAR | 4TH SIVAN LEAP

The above discussion related specifically to the First Temple. The *Tanya* will now address the spiritual properties of the Second Temple.

בעולם הבריאה כנודע לי"ח] ובבית שני שלא היה
בו הארון והלוחות אמרז"ל שלא היתה שכינה שורה
בו. פי' מדרגת שכינה שהיתה שורה בבית ראשון
שלא כדרך השתשלות העולמות אלא בבית שני
היתה שורה כדרך השתשלות והתלבשות מלכות
דאצי' במלכות דבריאה ודבריא' במלכו' דיצירה ודיצי'
בהיכל ק"ק דעשי' וק"ק דעשי' היה מתלבש בק"ק
שבבהמ"ק שלמטה ושרתה בו השכינה מלכות דיצירה
המלובשת בק"ק דעשיה. ולכן לא היה רשאי שום

וּבְבַיִת שֵׁנִי שֶׁלֹּא הָיָה בּוֹ הָאָרוֹן וְהַלּוּחוֹת — **And in the Second Temple, where the**
Ark and Tablets were absent, (*Talmud, Yoma* 21b), אָמְרוּ רַבּוֹתֵינוּ זִכְרוֹנָם לִבְרָכָה שֶׁלֹּא
הָיְתָה שְׁכִינָה שׁוֹרָה בּוֹ — **our Sages, of blessed memory, taught that the** *Shechinah*
did not rest there (*ibid*.).

However, the Sages didn't mean to say that the *Shechinah* wasn't present *at all*
in the Second Temple.

פֵּירוּשׁ מַדְרֵגַת שְׁכִינָה שֶׁהָיְתָה שׁוֹרָה בְּבַיִת רִאשׁוֹן — Rather, **this means that** *the level of*
Shechinah **which rested in the First Temple** wasn't present in the Second Temple.

שֶׁלֹּא כְּדֶרֶךְ הִשְׁתַּלְשְׁלוּת הָעוֹלָמוֹת — In other words, the *Shechinah's* presence in the
Second Temple didn't **bypass the chain of worlds,** like it did in the First Temple (as
we discussed above).

אֶלָּא בְּבַיִת שֵׁנִי הָיְתָה שׁוֹרָה כְּדֶרֶךְ הִשְׁתַּלְשְׁלוּת — **Rather, in the Second Temple, the**
Shechinah **did rest,** but it first **passed through the chain of worlds,** וְהִתְלַבְּשׁוּת
מַלְכוּת דַּאֲצִילוּת בְּמַלְכוּת דִּבְרִיאָה — **with** *malchus* **of** *Atzilus* **first expressing itself**
in *malchus* **of** *Beriah,* וְדִבְרִיאָה בְּמַלְכוּת דִּיצִירָה — **and then** *malchus* **of** *Beriah* **ex-**
pressing itself in *malchus* **of** *Yetzirah,* וְדִיצִירָה בְּהֵיכַל קָדְשֵׁי קָדָשִׁים דַּעֲשִׂיָּה — **and**
then *malchus* **of** *Yetzirah* **expressing itself in the Most-Sacred-Chamber of** *Asiyah,*
וְקָדְשֵׁי קָדָשִׁים דַּעֲשִׂיָּה הָיָה מִתְלַבֵּשׁ בְּקָדְשֵׁי קָדָשִׁים שֶׁבְּבֵית הַמִּקְדָּשׁ שֶׁלְּמַטָּה — **and the**
Most-Sacred-Chamber of *Asiyah* **then expressed itself in the "Holy of Holies" in the**
physical Temple, וְשָׁרְתָה בּוֹ הַשְּׁכִינָה מַלְכוּת דִּיצִירָה הַמְלוּבֶּשֶׁת בְּקָדְשֵׁי קָדָשִׁים דַּעֲשִׂיָּה
— **and there the** "*Shechinah*" **rested** which was not the same level of *Shechinah* as
in the First Temple but, *malchus* **of** *Yetzirah* **enmeshed in the Most-Sacred-Cham-**
ber of *Asiyah.*

Unlike the rest of the world, which only has a direct revelation of *malchus* of
Asiyah, the Second Temple was superior in that it manifested *"malchus of Yetzirah*
enmeshed in the Most-Sacred-Chamber of Asiyah."

וְלָכֵן לֹא הָיָה רַשַּׁאי שׁוּם אָדָם לִיכָּנֵס שָׁם — **And because** of this revelation, not found
anywhere else on earth, **no person was allowed to enter there,** לְבַד כֹּהֵן גָּדוֹל

אדם ליכנס שם לבד כהן גדול ביה"כ ומשחרב בית
המקדש אין לו להקב"ה בעולמו אלא ד"א של הלכה
בלבד ואפילו אחד שיושב ועוסק בתורה שכינה עמו
כדאית' בברכו' פ"ק פי' שכינה עמו כדרך השתלשלות
והתלבשות מלכות דאצילות במלכות דבריאה ויצירה
ועשיה כי תרי"ג מצות התורה רובן ככולן הן מצות

בְּיוֹם הַכִּפּוּרִים — except the High Priest on the Day of Atonement (Mishnah, Kelim 1:9).

SECTION TWO: THE SHECHINAH'S PRESENCE NOWADAYS

The *Tanya* continues to discuss the presence of the *Shechinah* on earth, after the destruction of the Second Temple.

וּמִשֶּׁחָרֵב בֵּית הַמִּקְדָּשׁ אֵין לוֹ לְהַקָּדוֹשׁ בָּרוּךְ הוּא בְּעוֹלָמוֹ אֶלָּא ד' אַמוֹת שֶׁל הֲלָכָה בִּלְבָד — **And after the** Second **Temple was destroyed** the presence of the *Shechinah* on earth has persisted, as the *Talmud* states, *"**the Blessed Holy One has no other place in His world other than the four cubits of Jewish law alone**"* (*Talmud, Brachos* 8a), וַאֲפִילוּ אֶחָד שֶׁיּוֹשֵׁב וְעוֹסֵק בַּתּוֹרָה שְׁכִינָה עִמּוֹ — and *"**even if one person sits and studies Torah, the Shechinah is with him,**"* כְּדאִיתָא בִּבְרָכוֹת פֶּרֶק קַמָּא — as **stated in the first chapter of** *Talmud,* Tractate *Brachos* (6a).

The *Tanya* now clarifies the meaning of these statements.

פֵּירוּשׁ שְׁכִינָה עִמּוֹ כְּדֶרֶךְ הִשְׁתַּלְשְׁלוּת — **Meaning that** through study of the law, the level of *Shechinah* present is even lower than in the Second Temple, a light **which has passed** *completely* **through the chain of worlds,** *"is with him,"* וְהִתְלַבְּשׁוּת מַלְכוּת דַּאֲצִילוּת בְּמַלְכוּת דִּבְרִיאָה וִיצִירָה וַעֲשִׂיָּה — *i.e., malchus* of *Atzilus* first **enmeshing itself in** *malchus* **of** *Beriah,* then *malchus* of *Yetzirah,* all the way down to *malchus* of *Asiyah.*

In the First Temple, the *Shechinah's* light significantly bypassed the worlds. In the Second Temple, the *Shechinah's* light (*"malchus* of *Yetzirah* enmeshed in the Most-Sacred-Chamber of *Asiyah"*), was still higher than the Divine light present in this world (*malchus* of *Asiyah*). But the "*Shechinah*" present when "the law" is studied (and observed) in the current era, is essentially the same level of Divine light as is present in the physical world.

(Only, as we have learned (p. 419), the world receives its Divine light through the "garment" of *kelipas nogah,* whereas when the *Shechinah* shines, it does so *directly*).

Why must the *Shechinah* manifest itself through *malchus* of *Asiyah?* The *Tanya* explains:

מעשיות וגם התלויות בדבור ומחשבה כמו ת״ת ובהמ״ז
וק״ש ותפלה הא קיימא האי לן דהרהור לאו כדבור דמי
ואינו יוצא ידי חובתו בהרהור וכוונה לבד עד שיוציא
בשפתיו וקי״ל דעקימת שפתיו הוי מעשה ותרי״ג
מצות התורה עם שבע מצות דרבנן בגימטריא כת״ר
שהוא רצון העליון ב״ה המלובש בחכמתו יתברך

כִּי תַּרְיַ״ג מִצְוֹת הַתּוֹרָה רוּבָּן כְּכוּלָּן הֵן מִצְוֹת מַעֲשִׂיּוֹת — **Because virtually all of the 613 commandments of the Torah are practical** *mitzvos.*

Since most Torah activity occurs in the sphere of action, for the *Shechinah* to be present in the "four cubits of the law," it must manifest through the spiritual energy which powers the World of Action, *malchus* of *Asiyah.*

וְגַם הַתְּלוּיוֹת בְּדִבּוּר וּמַחֲשָׁבָה — **And even** *mitzvos* **which** do not involve action, but rather, **require speech and thought,** כְּמוֹ תַּלְמוּד תּוֹרָה וּבִרְכַּת הַמָּזוֹן וּקְרִיאַת שְׁמַע וּתְפִלָּה — **such as Torah study, grace after meals, reading the** *Shema* **and prayer,** הָא קַיְימָא לָן דְּהִרְהוּר לָאו כְּדִבּוּר דָּמֵי — we nevertheless see the crucial role of action even there, since **we maintain that** *"meditation does not count as recitation"* (*Talmud, Brachos* 20b; see pp. 412, 432), וְאֵינוֹ יוֹצֵא יְדֵי חוֹבָתוֹ בְּהִרְהוּר וְכַוָּונָה לְבָד, **and you don't fulfill your obligation with thought and intention alone,** עַד שֶׁיּוֹצִיא **until the words come out of your lips,** בִּשְׂפָתָיו — וּקַיְימָא לָן דַּעֲקִימַת שְׂפָתָיו הָוֵי מַעֲשֶׂה — **and we maintain that,** *"moving the lips constitutes a concrete action"* (*Talmud, Kerisos* 4a).

The *Talmud* (cited above) refers to the *Shechinah* being present in *"the four cubits of Jewish Law."* The *Tanya* now clarifies the specific reference to Jewish *law,* (rather than "Torah" in general).

וְתַרְיַ״ג מִצְוֹת הַתּוֹרָה עִם שֶׁבַע מִצְוֹת דְּרַבָּנָן בְּגִימַטְרִיָּא כֶּתֶ״ר — **And** "Jewish Law" refers to the **613** *mitzvos* **of the Torah, together with the seven Rabbinic** *mitzvos,* **totaling 620, the numerical value of the word** *keser* **("crown"),** שֶׁהוּא רָצוֹן הָעֶלְיוֹן בָּרוּךְ הוּא — **and in Kabbalah,** *keser* **is the Blessed Divine will.**

"Jewish Law" represents the final, practical conclusions of the Torah, the actual Divine will, the way that Torah is to be expressed in this world. The *Talmud* therefore referred to "Jewish law" in particular, to point to the transcendent quality of *keser* expressed in Jewish Law.

Willpower is higher than wisdom: you can will yourself to do anything, regardless of whether it makes sense or not. And the same is true, figuratively speaking, of G-d's will and wisdom: the Divine will (*keser*), is higher than *chochmah* (Divine wisdom). Nevertheless, as the *Tanya* will now explain, "Jewish law" represents an expression of the Divine will (*keser*) through the lens of *chochmah.*

הַמְלוּבָּשׁ בְּחָכְמָתוֹ יִתְבָּרֵךְ — In the Torah, this Divine will, *keser,* **is enmeshed in Divine**

הַמְיוּחָדוֹת בְּאוֹר א״ס ב״ה בְּתַכְלִית הַיִחוּד וְה׳
בְּחָכְמָה יָסַד אֶרֶץ הִיא תּוֹרָה שֶׁבְּעַל פֶּה דְּנָפְקָא
מֵחָכְמָה עִילָאָה כְּמוֹ״שׁ בַּזֹהַר דְּאַבָּא יָסַד בְּרַתָּא.
וְז״שׁ הַיְנוּקָא דְּנְהוֹרָא עִילָאָה דְּאַדְלִיק עַל רֵישֵׁיהּ הִיא

הַמְיוּחָדוֹת בְּאוֹר אֵין סוֹף בָּרוּךְ הוּא בְּתַכְלִית הַיִחוּד — and both *keser* and *chochmah*, *chochmah* **are merged with the Blessed Infinite Light in perfect unity.**

But what of the "Oral Law"? Does this also share the spiritual intensity of *keser* and *chochmah?* The *Tanya* cites proof that it does.

וַה׳ בְּחָכְמָה יָסַד אֶרֶץ — **And, "G-d, through chochmah, founded the earth"** (*Proverbs* 3:19), הִיא תּוֹרָה שֶׁבְּעַל פֶּה — **"the earth" referring to the Oral Law** (*Zohar* 1, 247b), דְּנָפְקָא מֵחָכְמָה עִילָאָה — **which,** like the Written Law, **emerged from Upper chochmah,** כְּמוֹ שֶׁכָּתוּב בַּזֹהַר דְּאַבָּא יָסַד בְּרַתָּא — **as the Zohar** (3, 258a) **states, "the father (chochmah) who fathered the daughter (the Oral Law)."**

As manifest here in this world, the Oral Law is lower than the Written Law: it is the "daughter," not the "father"; the "earth" and not the "heavens." But in their root, both Written and Oral laws are manifestations of *chochmah* energy, which, as we have just learned, is *"merged with the Blessed Infinite Light in perfect unity."*

SECTION FOUR: WHY THE SHECHINAH NEEDS "OIL"

3RD SIVAN REGULAR | 5TH SIVAN LEAP

Having spent the last three chapters discussing the concept of *Shechinah,* the *Tanya* now returns to the issue that concerned us at the opening of chapter 51. There, we had sought further clarification of the teaching attributed to a "child" in the *Zohar* (3, 187a).

"A person should not walk four cubits with his head uncovered. What's the reason? Because the Shechinah (Divine Presence) rests on his head and the eyes and words of every wise man are, 'on his head,' meaning to say, (his attention is focused) on that which rests and remains on his head (i.e., upon the Shechinah). And when his eyes are there, he will be aware that the flame lit above his head (the Shechinah) is in need of oil, since a person's body is a wick, with a flame lit above it."

"And King Shlomo shouts out to us, 'Don't allow oil to be lacking from your head!'" (Ecc. 9:8), because the flame on his head needs oil, (oil) referring to good deeds."

Now that we have clarified the term "*Shechinah*" at length, we can return to the *Zohar's* words.

וְזֶהוּ שֶׁאָמַר הַיְנוּקָא — **And** all **this** discussion will help us clarify **the statement of the "child" (yenuka) in the Zohar,** דְּנְהוֹרָא עִילָאָה דְּאַדְלִיק עַל רֵישֵׁיהּ הִיא שְׁכִינְתָּא אִצְטְרִיךְ

75A

שכינתא אצטריך למשחא פי' להתלבש בחכמה הנק'
שמן משחת קדש כמ"ש בזהר ואינון עובדין טבין הן
תרי"ג מצות הנמשכות מחכמתו ית' כדי לאחוז אור
השכינה בפתילה היא נפש החיונית שבגוף הנקראת
פתילה עד"מ כי כמו שבנר הגשמי האור מאיר ע"י
כליון ושריפת הפתילה הנהפכת לאש כך אור השכינה
שורה על נפש האלהית על ידי כליון נפש הבהמית
והתהפכותה מחשוכא לנהורא וממרירו למתקא בצדיקים
או לפחות ע"י כליון לבושיה שהן מחשבה דבור ומעשה
והתהפכותן מחשך הקליפות לאור ה' א"ס ב"ה המלובש
ומיוחד במחשבה דבור ומעשה תרי"ג מצות התורה

לְמִשְׁחָא — that *"the (spiritual) flame lit above his head,"* which is the *Shechinah,* *"is in need of oil."*

פֵּירוּשׁ לְהִתְלַבֵּשׁ בְּחָכְמָה — Meaning that this "flame" of the *Shechinah* needs to be enmeshed with *chochmah,* הַנִקְרֵאת שֶׁמֶן מִשְׁחַת קֹדֶשׁ כְּמוֹ שֶׁכָּתוּב בַּזֹּהַר — since *chochmah,* as the *Zohar* (3, 7b) states, is called, *"holy anointing oil"* (Exodus 30:25).

וְאִינּוּן עוֹבְדִין טָבִין — And the *yenuka* interprets the oil as, *"these good deeds,"* הֵן תַּרְיַ"ג מִצְוֹת הַנִמְשָׁכוֹת מֵחָכְמָתוֹ יִתְבָּרֵךְ — which are the 613 *mitzvos* which flow from G-d's *chochmah* into this world, כְּדֵי לֶאֱחוֹז אוֹר הַשְּׁכִינָה בַּפְּתִילָה — so as to keep the "flame" of the *Shechinah* attached to the "wick."

הִיא נֶפֶשׁ הַחִיּוּנִית שֶׁבַּגּוּף — And the "wick" refers to the energizing Animal Soul in the body, הַנִקְרֵאת פְּתִילָה עַל דֶּרֶךְ מָשָׁל — which is called a "wick," figuratively speaking, כִּי כְּמוֹ שֶׁבַּנֵּר הַגַּשְׁמִי הָאוֹר מֵאִיר עַל יְדֵי כִּלְיוֹן וּשְׂרֵיפַת הַפְּתִילָה הַנֶהְפֶּכֶת לְאֵשׁ — for just as with a physical candle, light shines as a result of the destruction and burning of fuel in the wick, which is transformed into fire, כָּךְ אוֹר הַשְּׁכִינָה שׁוֹרֶה — so too, the light of the *Shechinah* rests on the Divine Soul through the "destruction" of negative urges of the Animal Soul and its transformation to a force for the good.

מֵחֲשׁוֹכָא לִנְהוֹרָא וּמִמְּרִירוּ לִמְתַקָּא בַּצַּדִּיקִים — This transformation might be a complete one, from darkness to light, from bitter to sweet, as is the case with *tzadikim* (chapter 10, p. 124), אוֹ לְפָחוֹת עַל יְדֵי כִּלְיוֹן לְבוּשֶׁיהָ שֶׁהֵן מַחֲשָׁבָה דִּבּוּר וּמַעֲשֶׂה וְהִתְהַפְּכוּתָן מֵחֹשֶׁךְ הַקְּלִיפוֹת לְאוֹר ה' אֵין סוֹף בָּרוּךְ הוּא הַמְלוּבָּשׁ וּמְיוּחָד בְּמַחֲשָׁבָה דִּבּוּר וּמַעֲשֶׂה שֶׁל תַּרְיַ"ג מִצְוֹת הַתּוֹרָה בֵּבֵּינוֹנִים — or at least, in the case of *beinonim,* through the "destruction" of the Animal Soul's "garments" of thought, speech and action, and their transformation from the darkness of *kelipos* to the light of G-d, the Blessed Infinite One, that's found in, and united with, the 613 *mitzvos* of the Torah.

בבינונים כי ע"י התהפכות נפש הבהמית הבאה מקליפ'
נוגה מחשוכא לנהורא וכו' נעשה בחי' העלאת מ"ן
להמשיך אור השכינה היא בחי' גילוי אור א"ס ב"ה על
נפשו האלהית שבמוחין שבראשו ובזה יובן היטב מ"ש
כי ה' אלהיך אש אוכלה הוא וכמ"ש במ"א:

נשלם חלק ראשון בעז"ה ית' וית'

The — כִּי עַל יְדֵי הִתְהַפְּכוּת נֶפֶשׁ הַבַּהֲמִית הַבָּאָה מִקְּלִיפַּת נוֹגַה מֵחֲשׁוֹכָא לִנְהוֹרָא וְכוּ' "destruction" of the Animal Soul is necessary **because through transforming the Animal Soul, which is derived from** *kelipas nogah,* **from darkness to light,** *etc.,* נַעֲשָׂה בְּחִינַת הַעֲלָאַת מַיִּין נוּקְבִין — **the elevation of "feminine waters" is achieved,** *i.e.,* human potential is awakened (see p. 130), לְהַמְשִׁיךְ אוֹר הַשְּׁכִינָה הִיא בְּחִינַת גִּילּוּי — אוֹר אֵין סוֹף בָּרוּךְ הוּא עַל נַפְשׁוֹ הָאֱלֹהִית שֶׁבַּמּוֹחִין שֶׁבְּרֹאשׁוֹ — **which,** in a reciprocal gesture from Above, **causes the light of the** *Shechinah,* **which is a disclosure of the Blessed Infinite Light, to be "pulled" on your G-dly soul,** which rests primarily in the brain of your head.

וּבָזֶה יוּבַן הֵיטֵב מַה שֶּׁכָּתוּב כִּי ה' אֱלֹהֶיךָ אֵשׁ אוֹכְלָה הוּא — **And this will clarify well the verse,** *"For G-d your G-d is a consuming fire"* (*Deuteronomy* 4:24), וּכְמוֹ שֶׁנִּתְבָּאֵר בְּמָקוֹם אַחֵר — **as is explained elsewhere,** that just as fire can only burn when there is fuel, so too, the light of G-d will only shine in you when it is "fueled" by Torah observance and the "destruction" of your Animal Soul (see Rabbi Dov Ber of Mezritch, *Ohr Torah,* section 44; Rabbi Shneur Zalman, *Torah Ohr* 97a; *Likutei Torah, Leviticus* 25c).

נִשְׁלַם חֵלֶק רִאשׁוֹן בְּעֶזְרַת ה' יִתְבָּרֵךְ וְיִתְעַלֶּה — **With G-d's help, may He be blessed and exalted, this concludes the first part** of the *Tanya, The Book of the Inbetweeners (Sefer Shel Beinonim).*

GLOSSARY

Achorayim. Negative "behind" energy which comes into existence only when G-d's "face" is hidden through powerful diminishments.

Ahavah Rabah. "Great love," an altruistic love of G-d, devoid of self-interest, which is bestowed as a "gift from above."

Ahavas Olam. "Worldly love," a love of G-d generated through contemplation of G-d's presence in the world.

Amidah. "Standing prayer," also known as *Shmoneh Esrei*, the climax of each prayer service which is recited in silent devotion while standing.

Animal Soul. One of two souls in the Jew, stemming from *kelipah,* which gives life to the physical body, and tends to a consciousness of separation and egocentricity.

Arizal. A Hebrew acronym for *Adonenu Rabbi Yitzchak Zichrono Livracha* "our master Rabbi Yitzchak of blessed memory," referring to Rabbi Yitzchak Luria (1534-1572), who founded the highly influential and authoritative school of Lurianic Kabbalah.

Asiyah. "Action," the lowest of the four supernal worlds, having both a spiritual and physical component.

Atzilus. "Emanation," the highest of the four supernal worlds, adjacent to the infinite source of creation.

Ba'al Shem Tov. "Master of the Good Name," an appellation given to Rabbi Yisrael ben Eliezer (1698-1760), the founder of Chasidism.

Ba'al Teshuvah (pl. *Ba'alei Teshuvah*). "Master of penitence," one who "returns" from a non-observant lifestyle to become a Torah observant Jew.

Beinoni (pl. *beinonim*). An "inbetweener" who is neither *rasha* nor *tzadik*. In the *Tanya's* definition a *beinoni* may be tempted to transgress, but will never actually do so.

Beriah. "Creation," the second highest of the four supernal worlds.

Besht. Hebrew acronym for the *Ba'al Shem Tov.*

Binah. "Cognition," in the human soul, it is the power of precise, rational thought which forms the second stage of the intellectual process, following from *chochmah.* In its heavenly source, *binah* is the second of the ten *sefiros.*

Bitul. "Surrender [of the ego]," an inner shift away from egoic behavior and thinking.

Chabad. A Hebrew acronym of *chochmah, binah* and *da'asn* the three intellectual *sefiros.* It also refers to the school of Chasidic thought founded by Rabbi Shneur Zalman of Liadi, which emphasizes the role of mindful contemplation in worship.

Chasid (pl. *chasidim*). A devotee of the Chasidic movement.

Chasidism. A spiritual revivalist movement beginning in the southern Kingdom of Poland (today western Ukraine) in the 18th century, based on teachings of the *Ba'al Shem Tov.*

Chasidus. Chasidic teachings.

Chayos Ha-Kodesh. "Holy beasts," angels in the World of *Yetzirah.*

Chesed. "Kindness," a *sefirah* representing love, abundance, generosity and revelation. It stands in opposition to the *sefirah* of *gevurah.*

Chochmah. "Inquiry," in the human soul, it is the precognitive power of inspiration and creativity, which feeds *binah,* the second stage of the intellectual process. In its heavenly source, *chochmah* is the first of the ten *sefiros* which acts as a "window" to the Blessed Infinite Light.

Da'as. "Recognition," the third intellectual *sefirah,* following from *chochmah* and *binah. Da'as* does not add any new information; rather, it fosters an attachment to the existing idea, to render it "real" and relevant.

Din. Judgment energy which is the source of negative spiritual forces.

Dirah Ba-Tachtonim. "A home [for G-d] below," a Midrashic statement depicting the purpose of the world's creation, to make G-d's presence palpable here.

Divine Soul. One of two souls in the Jew, which is a "piece of G-d." It stimulates a consciousness of unity and devotion to G-d.

En-Sof. "Without end," a term in the Kabbalah used to refer to G-d.

Garments. The faculties of thoughts, speech, and action in which the soul "dresses" itself.

Gevurah. "Severity," one of the ten *sefiros* signifying, fear, discipline, restraint and judgment. It stands in opposition to the *sefirah* of *chesed.*

Halachah. Jewish law.

Hishtalshelus. The unfolding "chain" of spiritual worlds through which G-d powers the universe.

Ibur. "Soul-impregnation," a kind of reincarnation that takes place during a person's lifetime, where, by Divine decree, a spark of a departed soul joins the soul of a living person.

Igeres Ha-Teshuvah. Third section of *Tanya*, discussing the concept of repentence.

Is'hapcha: The approach of "transforming" negative forces completely.

Iskafya. The approach of "subduing" negative forces, when they cannot be eliminated completely.

Kabbalah. Jewish esoteric wisdom which has been received from a reliable source.

Kabolas Ol. "Accepting G-d's sovereign authority," submission to the Divine Will, especially in reference to observance of the *mitzvos*.

Kavanah (pl. *Kavanos*): "Intention," thoughts and feelings that accompany prayer and the performance of *mitzvos*.

Kares. A "cutting off" of the soul from its Divine source, which results from certain, severe transgressions.

Kelipah (pl. *Kelipos*). "Peel," a Kabbalistic term referring to negative and evil forces. *Kelipah* conceals the presence of G-d just as peel hides a fruit.

Kelipas Nogah. "Bright *kelipah*," a negative energy that contains some good and has the possibility of being transformed to holiness.

Keser. "Crown," the highest of the *sefiros*, acting as a medium between the Blessed Infinite Light and the other sefiros.

Kelos Ha-Nefesh. "Languishing of the soul," an intense passionate state, where the soul desires the extinction of its own separate identity, so as to merge with G-d.

Makif. "Surrounding [light]," a Divine energy which cannot be confined within limited, defined vessels and is only present in a disengaged fashion.

Malchus. "Sovereignty," the tenth and lowest of the *sefiros*, identified in Kabbalah with the feminine, *Shechinah*, the palpable presence of G-d on earth.

Mesiras Nefesh. "Handing over of the soul," devotion to G-d to the point of self-sacrifice.

Midrash. Homilies and commentaries on the Torah by the Talmudic Rabbis.

Mishnah. Fundamental collection of the legal pronouncements and discussion of the *Tanna'im*, compiled by Rabbi Yehudah ha-Nassi early in the third century. The *Mishnah* is the basic text of the Oral Law.

Misnagdim. Hostile opponents to the Chasidic movement.

Mitzvah (pl. *mitzvos*). "Commandment," the Divine commandments articulated in the Torah.

Nefesh. Lowest of three levels of the soul, responsible for basic body intelligence.

Neshama. Highest of three levels of the soul, responsible for self-conscious intelligence.

Rasha (pl. *resha'im*). Literally, "a wicked person." In the *Tanya* the term refers to a person guilty of any transgression.

Rashi. Acronym for Rabbi Shlomo Yitzchaki (1040-1105), author of fundamental commentary to the Bible and Talmud.

Ratzon Ha-Elyon. "Higher will," the inner will of G-d.

Rebbe. Spiritual leader of a Chasidic group.

Ruach. Second of three levels of the soul, responsible for emotional intelligence.

Sefirah (pl. *Sefiros*). A network of ten "energies" or "potencies" in the human soul. These mirror the ten heavenly *sefiros*, the Divine forces through which G-d influences the universe.

Shaloh. Acronym for *Shnei Luchos Habris*, "The two tablets of the Covenant", an encyclopedic compilation of ritual, ethics, and mysticism by Rabbi Isaiah Horowitz (1560-1630).

Sheviras Ha-Kelim. "Shattering of the Vessels," a term in Lurianic Kabbalah referring to a primordial, spiritual event where finite "vessels" could not contain infinite "lights" and shattered. The fragments of these "vessels" fell into our world and are "redeemed" by Torah activity.

Shechinah. The "Divine presence" which is palpable and manifest on earth.

Shulchan Aruch. Universally accepted Code of Jewish Law encompassing all areas of practical *halachah*, by Rabbi Yosef Caro (1488-1575).

Sitra Achra. "Other side," that which does not belong to the side of holiness.

Sovev-Kol-Almin. "Encircles-all-worlds," a Divine light and energy that is incompatible with the created worlds because it is too intense to engage with the worlds and become enmeshed with them.

Talmud. Comprehensive term for the *Mishnah* and *Gemara* as joined in the two compilations known as *Babylonian Talmud* (6th century) and *Jerusalem Talmud* (5th century).

Tetragrammaton. Sacred Divine Name which is never pronounced, consisting of four letters, *yud-hei-vav-hei.*

Tikun Chatzos. A service mourning the destruction of the Temple, to be recited at midnight by individuals or small groups, sitting on the ground. It was instituted in the sixteenth century C.E. in the Kabbalistic circles of Safed. (Nowadays, it is barely practiced).

Tiferes. "Beauty," the sixth of the *sefiros* which harmonizes the influences of *chesed* and *gevurah.*

Tohu. "Chaos," an intense, disorderly Divine energy which precedes *tikun,* the "corrected" heavenly system of interconnected *sefiros.*

Tzadik (pl. *tzadikim*). Literally, "a righteous person." In the *Tanya* the term refers to a person who has transformed their Animal Soul to good.

Tzimtzum. "Diminishment," a process described in Lurianic Kabbalah through which the Infinite Light of G-d was diminished to enable the creation of a finite universe.

Yetzirah. "Formation," the third of four supernal worlds.

Yesod. "Foundation," the ninth *sefirah,* which connects the energies above it with the tenth *sefirah, malchus.*

Yichud Ha-Elyon. "Integration of Divine attributes," a harmonization of the channels through which G-d's influence flows down into the worlds.

Zohar. Primary text of Kabbalah, containing the teachings of Rabbi Shimon ben Yochai and his disciples in the form of a commentary on the Torah. First published in the late 13th century by Rabbi Moshe de Leon (c. 1250–1305), in Spain.